Cases and Materials on
Constitutional and Administrative Law

···

Seventh Edition

Michael J. Allen

LLB, LLM, Barrister

Brian Thompson

LLB, MLitt

OXFORD

UNIVERSITY PRESS

OXFORD
UNIVERSITY PRESS

Great Clarendon Street, Oxford OX2 6DP

Oxford University Press is a department of the University of Oxford.
It furthers the Universityís objective of excellence in research, scholarship,
and education by publishing worldwide in

Oxford New York

Auckland Bangkok Buenos Aires Cape Town Chennai
Dar es Salaam Delhi Hong Kong Istanbul Karachi Kolkata
Kuala Lumpur Madrid Melbourne Mexico City Mumbai Nairobi
S„o Paulo Shanghai Singapore Taipei Tokyo Toronto

Oxford is a registered trade mark of Oxford University Press
in the UK and in certain other countries

Published in the United States
by Oxford University Press Inc., New York

First published Blackstone Press 1990

© M. J. Allen, B. Thompson, 2002

The moral rights of the authors have been asserted
Database right Oxford University Press (maker)

Second Edition 1992
Reprinted 1993
Third Edition 1994
Reprinted 1995
Fourth Edition 1996
Fifth Edition 1998
Reprinted 2000
Sixth Edition 2000
Seventh Edition 2002, reprinted 2002, 2003

British Library Cataloguing in Publication Data

A CIP catalogue record for this book is available from the British Library

ISBN 0-19-925525-3

Typeset by Re neCatch Limited, Bungay, Suffolk
Printed in Great Britain by
Ashford Colour Press Limited,
Gosport, Hampshire

Cases and Materials on Constitutional and Administrative Law

OUTLINE CONTENTS

DETAILED CONTENTS

8 Judicial Review: The Grounds 568

9 The Availability of Judicial Review 651

10 Ombudsmen 693

PREFACE

This edition comes two years after the previous edition but despite the short space of time involved there has been a considerable amount of activity of constitutional significance, mainly as measures in the Labour Government's reform programme begin to take effect, but also the courts have handed down numerous decisions of constitutional import, particularly in the period since 2 October 2000 when the Human Rights Act 1998 came into effect. As a result most chapters have had new material added and several have been subjected to major revisions. New material includes discussion of the Sewel Convention relating to legislation by the Westminster Parliament in respect of matters devolved to the Scottish Parliament; extracts from major appellate decisions on the Human Rights Act 1998, such as *R v Lambert* [2001] UKHL 26, *R v A (No. 2)* [2001] UKHL 25, *R v Secretary of State for the Home Dept., ex parte Daly* [2001] UKHL 26, *Stott (Procurator Fiscal, Dunfermline) v Brown* [2001] 2 WLR 817, PC, *R (H) v London North and East Region Mental Health Review Tribunal* [2001] EWCA Civ 415, *Douglas v Hello! Ltd* [2001 2 WLR 992, and *Wilson v First County Trust Ltd* [2001] EWCA Civ 633. Material on judicial review includes the Civil Procedure Rules Part 54 and the associated Pre-action Protocol and *R (Cowl) v Plymouth City Council (Practice Note)* [2001] EWCA Civ 1935; and *In Re Medicaments and Related Classes of Goods (No 2)* [2000] EWCA Civ 350; on bias and *R (Bibi) v Newham London Borough Council* [2001] EWCA Civ 607, on substantive legitimate expectations. There are also extracts from the *Review of Tribunals* chaired by Sir Andrew Leggatt.

As this edition is being published by Oxford University Press, we wish to thank the team at OUP for all their assistance and for the way they ensured a smooth transition of the title from Blackstone Press Ltd who published the first six editions of this book to themselves.

Michael Allen
Brian Thompson
June 2002

ACKNOWLEDGEMENTS

The authors and publishers would like to thank and gratefully acknowledge the following for permission to reproduce copyright material:

T.R.S. Allan: 'The Limits of Parliamentary Sovereignty' [1985] *Public Law* 614.

R. Baldwin & J. Houghton: 'Circular Arguments: The Status and Legitimacy of Administrative Rules' [1986] *Public Law* 239.

E. Barendt: 'Dicey and Civil Liberties' [1985] *Public Law* 596.

Lord Bingham of Cornhill:
'The Courts and the Constitution' (1996/97) 7 *King's College Law Journal* 12;
'The European Convention on Human Rights: Time to Incorporate' (1993) 109 *Law Quarterly Review* 390.

Basil Blackwell Publisher Ltd:
(1975), P. Norton (ed.), *Parliament in the 1980s* (1985);
H. F. Rawlings, 'Judicial Review and the Control of Government' (1986) 64 *Public Administration*;
C. Scott, 'Accountability in the Regulatory State' (2000) 27 *Journal of Law and Society*.

V. Bogdanor: Introduction to *Constitutions in Democratic Politics* (1988, Ashgate Publishing Limited).

R. Brazier: 'How Near is a Written Constitution?' (2001) 52 *Northern Ireland Legal Quarterly* 1.

H. Calvert: *Constitutional Law in Northern Ireland* (1968, Stevens & Sons and Northern Ireland Legal Quarterly).

The *Cambridge Law Journal*, Professor Ian Leigh and Professor Laurence Lustgarten for permission to reproduce Leigh and Lustgarten, 'Making Rights Real: the Courts, Remedies and the Human Rights Act' (1999) 58 *Cambridge Law Journal* 509.

Cambridge University Press: Elster and Slagstad (eds.), *Constitutionalism and Democracy* (1988).

Canada Law Book Company, through the Canadian Copyright Licensing Agency (CANCOPY): *Reference Re Amendment of the Constitution of Canada* (1982) 125 *Dominion Law Reports* (3d) 1.

Centre for Public Law, University of Cambridge: *Constitutional Reform in the United Kingdom: Practice and Principles* (1998).

Charter 88:
'A Written Constitution', http://www.gn.apc.org/charter88/politics/written.html;
Anthony Lester QC, 'A Bill of Rights For Britain' (*Manchester Papers*, 1991), http://www.gn.apc.org/charter88/pubs/manpaps/lester.html

Commission for Local Administration in England for permission to reproduce extracts from annual reports and digest of cases.

The Constitution Unit, School of Public Policy, UCL: *Human Rights Legislation* (1996).

The Court of Justice of the European Communities, extracts from the *European Court Reports*.

P. Craig: 'Dicey: Unitary, Self-correcting Democracy and Public Law' (1990) 106 *Law Quarterly Review* 105.

K.C. Davis: *Discretionary Justice* (1969, Louisiana State University Press). Reprinted by permission of Louisiana State University Press. Copyright © 1969 Louisiana State University Press.

C. Dewing and S. Watson: Sir Ivor Jennings, *The Law and the Constitution* (5th edn., University of London Press Ltd).

Mrs V.J. Duffy: Peter Duffy, QC: 'The European Convention on Human Rights, Issues Relating to its Interpretation in the Light of the Human Rights Bill' in *Constitutional Reform in the United Kingdom: Practice and Principles* (1998, Centre for Public Law, University of Cambridge).

Mrs S.E. Finer: S.E. Finer, *Comparative Government* (1970, Allen Lane The Penguin Press).

C.J. Friedrich: *Limited Government: A Comparison* (1974, Prentice Hall Inc.).

W. Green: The Scottish Law Publisher: extracts from *Scots Law Times*.

J.A.G. Griffith & M. Ryle: *Parliament: Functions, Practice and Procedures* (1989, Sweet & Maxwell Ltd).

Lord Hailsham of St. Marylebone: *The Dilemma of Democracy* (1978, Collins).

The Hansard Society for Parliamentary Government: *Making the Law* (1993); *The Challenge for Parliament: Making Government Accountable* (2001).

K.H. Hendry: 'The Tasks of Tribunals: Some Thoughts' (1982) 1 *Civil Justice Quarterly* 253.

R.F.V. Heuston: *Essays in Constitutional Law* (2nd edn., 1964, Stevens & Sons Ltd).

M. Hunt: 'The "Horizontal Effect" of the Human Rights Act' [1998] *Public Law* 423.

The Incorporated Council for Law Reporting for England and Wales: extracts from the Law Reports and the Weekly Law Reports.

Lord Irvine of Lairg:
    The Tom Sargant Memorial Lecture, 'The Development of Human Rights in Britain under an Incorporated Convention on Human Rights' 16 December 1997;
    Address to the 3rd Clifford Chance Conference on the Impact of a Bill of Rights on English Law, 28 November 1997;
    'Activism and Restraint: Human Rights and the Interpretative Process' [1999] *European Human Rights Law Review* 350.

D. Judge: *The Parliamentary State* (1993, Sage Publications Ltd.) reprinted by permission of Sage Publications Ltd.

S. Kentridge, QC: 'The Incorporation of the European Convention on Human Rights' in *Constitutional Reform in the United Kingdom: Practice and Principles* (1998, Centre for Public Law, University of Cambridge).

F. Klug, R. Singh & M. Hunt: 'Rights Brought Home: a briefing on the Human Rights Bill with amendments' (1997, Human Rights Incorporation Project, King's College, London).

F. Klug, K. Starmer and S. Weir: *The Three Pillars of Liberty: Political Rights and Freedoms in the United Kingdom* (1996, Routledge).

Sir John Laws: 'Law and Democracy' [1995] *Public Law* 81.

Macmillan Press Ltd: *An Introduction to the Study of the Law of the Constitution* (10th edn.) by A.V. Dicey with an introduction by E.C.S. Wade. © Macmillan Press Ltd.

G. Marshall and G. Moodie: *Some Problems of the Constitution* (5th edn. 1971, Hutchinson & Co. (Publishers) Ltd).

P. McAuslan and J. McEldowney: *Law, Legitimacy and the Constitution* (1985, Sweet & Maxwell Ltd).

J. McEldowney: *Public Law* (2nd edn., 1998, Sweet & Maxwell Ltd).

C.H. McIlwain: *Constitutionalism Ancient and Modern*, (1947, Revised Edition, Cornell University Press).

R. Miliband: *The State in Capitalist Society* (1969, Weidenfeld & Nicolson Ltd).

C. Munro: *Studies in Constitutional Law* (2nd edn., 1999, Butterworths). © Reed Elsevier Ltd. Reproduced by permission of The Butterworths Division of Reed Elsevier (UK) Limited.

W.F. Murphy: 'Constitutions, Constitutionalism and Democracy' in D. Greenberg, S.N. Katz, M.B. Oliviero & S.C. Wheatley (eds.), *Constitutionalism and Democracy* (1993, Oxford University Press Inc., USA). Used by permission of Oxford University Press, Inc.

Oxford University Press for permission to reprint extracts from the following articles in *Parliamentary Affairs*:
F.F. Ridley, 'There is no British Constitution: A Dangerous Case of the Emperor's Clothes' vol. 41, No. 3 (1988);
R. Rose, 'Law as a Resource of Public Policy' vol. 39, No. 3 (1986);
L. Wolf-Phillips, 'A Long Look at the British Constitution' vol. 37, No. 4 (1984).

Oxford University Press for permission to reprint extracts from the following books:
R. Barker, *Political Legitimacy and the State* (1990);
P. Cane, *An Introduction to Administrative Law*, (3rd edn. 1996);
J. Jowell and D. Oliver (eds.), *The Changing Constitution* (2nd edn., 1989);
H.L.A. Hart, *The Concept of Law* (1961);
C.B. Macpherson, *The Real World of Democracy* (1966);
G. Marshall, *Constitutional Theory* (1971);
G. Richardson and H. Genn, *Administrative Law and Government Action* (1994);
M.J.C. Vile, *Constitutionalism and the Separation of Powers* (1967);
K.C. Wheare, *Modern Constitutions* (2nd edn., 1966).

A. Page: 'MPs and the Redress of Grievances' [1985] *Public Law* 1.

H. F. Rawlings: 'Judicial Review and the Control of Government' (1986) 64 *Public Administration*.

R. Rawlings: 'Parliamentary Redress of Grievance' in C. Harlow (ed.), *Public Law and Politics* (1986, Sweet & Maxwell).

J. Raz: 'The Rule of Law and its Virtue' (1977) 93 *Law Quarterly Review* 195.

C. Scott: 'Accountability in the Regulatory State' (2000) 27 *Journal of Law and Society*.

The Scottish Council of Law Reporting: extracts from Session Cases.

The Estate of C.F. Strong, M.G. Clarke and Sidgwick & Jackson Ltd: C.F. Strong, *Modern Political Constitutions* (8th edn., 1972).

A.T.H. Smith: 'Comment I on "Dicey and Civil Liberties"' [1985] *Public Law* 608.

Sweet & Maxwell Ltd: extracts from various articles in *Law Quarterly Review*, *Public Law* and *European Human Rights Law Review*, and extracts from *Common Market Reports*, *European Human Rights Reports* and *Criminal Appeal Reports*.

Vacher Dod Publishing Ltd for permission to reprint extracts from The Hansard Society, *The Challenge for Parliament: Making Government Accountable* (2001).

Sir William Wade, QC: 'The United Kingdom's Bill of Rights' in *Constitutional Reform in the United Kingdom: Practice and Principles* (1998, Centre for Public Law, University of Cambridge).

G. Wilson: 'Postscript: The Courts, Law and Convention' in Nolan and Sedley (eds.), *The Making and Remaking of the British Constitution* (1997, Legal Research Institute, School of Law, University of Warwick).

The Rt. Hon. Lord Woolf of Barnes: 'Droit Public – English Style' [1995] *Public Law* 57.

Crown and Parliamentary copyright material is reproduced with the permission of the Controller of Her Majesty's Stationery Office.

Every effort has been made to contact copyright holders to obtain their permission to use extracts.

TABLE OF CASES

Note: Cases reported in full are shown in **bold type**.

TABLE OF STATUTES

Note: Statutes, and sections thereof, which are set out in full are shown in **bold type**.

TABLE OF EUROPEAN LEGISLATION

1

Constitutional Law in the United Kingdom

SECTION 1: Introduction

NOTE: Constitutional law is the law relating to the constitution. While this statement may be true, it is not particularly helpful. To study constitutional law we need to discover what a constitution is. There are many competing definitions. While many clubs, organizations and other groupings have constitutions, our concern is with the constitutions of nation-states.

Thomas Paine, *Rights of Man* in *The Complete Works of Thomas Paine*
pp. 302–303

A constitution is not the act of a government, but of a people constituting a government, and a government without a constitution is power without right. . . . A constitution is a thing antecedent to a government; and a government is only the creature of a constitution.

It was Paine's belief that England lacked a constitution, as he stated at p. 370 that 'the continual use of the word "constitution" in the English parliament shows there is none and the whole is merely a form of government without a constitution, and constituting itself with what power it pleases'. Paine admired, by contrast, the recent American Constitution.

C. H. McIlwain, *Constitutionalism Ancient and Modern*
(1947), pp. 8–10

. . . [T]he analysis Paine made of the early American constitution was remarkably acute. The significant points in that analysis are these:

That there is a fundamental difference between a people's government and that people's constitution, whether the government happens to be entrusted to a king or to a representative assembly.

That this constitution is 'antecedent' to the government.

That it defines the authority which the people commits to its government, and in so doing thereby limits it.

That any exercise of authority beyond these limits by any government is an exercise of 'power without right.'

That in any state in which the distinction is not actually observed between the constitution and the government there is in reality no constitution, because the will of the government has no check upon it, and that state is in fact a despotism.

One thing alone Paine fails to make fully clear. If a government exercises some 'power without right,' it seems to be necessarily implied that the people have a corresponding right to resist. But is this a legal or is it only a political right? Is such resistance a legalized rebellion or merely an extralegal revolution? Or, further, is it possible to incorporate in the framework of the state itself some provision or institution by which a governmental act or command *ultra vires* may be declared to be such, and subjects therefore exempted from its operation and released from any legal obligation to observe or obey it? In short, can government be limited legally and effectively by any method short of force? To these questions Paine gives no clear answer. It might be assumed that forcible resistance to power without right must itself be legal and not revolutionary; but in every case there seems no recourse except to force of some kind.

The one conspicuous element lacking in Paine's construction therefore seems to be the element of judicial review. Writing when he did, and as he did, to justify an actual rebellion, it is perhaps not strange that he was thinking primarily of politics rather than of law, that the 'rights' he had in mind were the rights of man rather than the rights of the citizen, or that the sanction for these rights should be extralegal action rather than any constitutional check. Paine, like many idealists in a hurry, was probably impatient of the slowness of legal remedies for existing abuses. But others, who were more constitutionally minded than he, had begun to feel that any such remedies, to be truly effective, must ultimately have the sanction of law. Years before, Lord Camden had insisted that the principles of the law of nature must be incorporated in the British Constitution if they were to be observed, and that they actually were so incorporated. The necessary inference from such a principle as his is that the interpreters of law should be the ones to define the rights of individuals and to trace the bounds of legitimate government over them. The protection of rights became for him, and for all who thought as he did, the enforcement of 'constitutional limitations.'

QUESTION

What did Paine mean by 'antecedent'? Did he mean that the constitution must exist prior in time to the Government or that the principles of the constitution should be superior in character, and binding in authority, to the actions of government? If the former is correct, does the United Kingdom have a constitution? (See the discussion which follows.) If the latter is correct, could the United Kingdom ever have constitutional government? (See Chapter 2.)

NOTE: Paine expressed a concept of constitutions which involved 'the conscious formulation by a people of its fundamental law' (McIlwain, *op. cit.*, p. 3). This would find expression in a written document or documents. The alternative view sees constitutions not as a conscious creation but rather as an evolutionary consequence made up of 'substantive principles to be deduced from a nation's actual institutions and their development' (McIlwain, *ibid.*). This could include an unwritten or uncodified constitution. This view was expressed by Bolingbroke.

Bolingbroke, *A Dissertation upon Parties* (1733–34) in *The Works of Lord Bolingbroke*
(1841), II, p. 88

By constitution we mean, whenever we speak with propriety and exactness, that assemblage of laws, institutions and customs, derived from certain fixed principles of reason, directed to certain fixed objects of public good, that compose the general system according to which the community hath agreed to be governed. . . . We call this a good government, when . . . the whole administration of public affairs is wisely pursued, and with a strict conformity to the principles and objects of the constitution.

QUESTION

When Paine stated that a governmental act contrary to the constitution is an act of 'power without right', did he thereby imply that such an act would be unconstitutional? In Bolingbroke's terms such an act would warrant the conclusion that the government is not a good one; is this the same thing?

NOTE: It can be argued that, according to Bolingbroke's definition, the United Kingdom has a constitution, as there are laws, institutions, and customs which combine to create a system of government to which the community agrees, or at least, from which it does not appear to dissent. This is the traditional view of most constitutional lawyers. Constitutional theorists have further refined their analysis of constitutions, creating other points of comparison. For example, K. C. Wheare, *Modern Constitutions* (1966), Chapter 2, proposed six classifications of constitutions: (1) written and unwritten; (2) rigid and flexible; (3) supreme and subordinate; (4) federal and unitary; (5) separated powers and fused powers; (6) republican and monarchical. If Wheare's definitions are applied to the United Kingdom, it may be said that there is an unwritten constitution in the sense that it is uncodified. There is no supreme or fundamental constitutional law, and the processes for changing the constitution are flexible. The state is a unitary, monarchical one where powers are fused, there being a parliamentary Executive as opposed to a presidential Executive.

While most writers on the constitution are satisfied that, by comparison with the various definitions, the United Kingdom does have a constitution, some writers insist that there is no constitution.

F. F. Ridley, 'There is no British Constitution: A Dangerous Case of the Emperor's Clothes'

(1988) 41 *Parliamentary Affairs*, pp. 340–43, 359–60

Having a constitution seems to be a matter of self-respect: no state is properly dressed without. Every democracy except Britain, New Zealand and (with qualifications) Israel seems to have a written constitution, plainly labelled. Not to be left out of the world of constitutional democracies, British writers define constitution in a way which appears to give us one too, even though there is no document to prove it. The argument is that a constitution need not be embodied in a single document or, indeed, wholly written. We say instead that a country's constitution is a body of rules – some laws, some conventions – which regulate its system of government. Such a definition does not, however, bridge the gap between Britain and the rest of the world by providing us with a substitute for a documentary constitution: it simply shifts the ground, by using the word in an entirely different way.

We see this ambiguity in K C Wheare's now classic book on constitutions.

> The word constitution is commonly used in at least two senses in ordinary discussion of political affairs. First of all, it is used to describe the whole system of government, the collection of rules which establish and regulate it. These rules are partly legal and partly non-legal. When we speak of the British constitution that is the normal, if not the only possible meaning the word has. Everywhere else it is used in the sense of legal rules embodied in one document.

But that is not the real distinction. Foreign usage is not particularly concerned with the documentary character of a constitution. It appears in that form, but that is not its essential. Everywhere save Britain the constitution is defined as a special category of law. British usage dissolves the distinction between constitutional law and other laws because British courts recognise no such distinction. British political scientists, for their part, dissolve the distinction between law and other rules of behaviour because they are not much interested in law: for them, the constitution is practice.

Books of an old-fashioned sort with British Constitution in their title describe significant laws, conventions and institutions. This approach is now dismissed as formalistic by political scientists who regard such accounts as incomplete, if not misleading. They are right if their aim is to describe a system of government. In no country are all the important laws that shape the system of government embodied in a constitutional document. Nor can the operation of constitutional law be understood without reference to the practice of politics. Such arguments, however, miss the essential character of constitutions altogether. The wide focus of political scientists is right if their aim is to describe a system of government. Equating it with a study of the constitution, however, may owe less to a desire for realism than to a lack of concern about legal matters. This is often justified on the grounds that law is not a distinct and important element in understanding systems of government, but there are professional reasons too. Political studies did not originate in law faculties, as in continental Europe, and never subsequently developed any real interest in law. As a result, we get books called The British System of Government or, more fashionably, The British Political System, where politics is added to institutions. What such books include when they claim to describe the British 'constitution' depends on what their authors consider important to the framework of the system: what the 'constitution' consists of thus emerges from a survey of the system and is not determined by an independent, non-political definition that precedes it.

Much the same applies to books by lawyers. Works entitled Constitutional Law cover a selection of laws that appear important to the author, together with important conventions and often a reduced version of the topics treated by institutionally oriented political scientists. Since there appear to be no consequences in judicial practice if the label constitutional is applied to a particular law, it is in the end no more than a convenient way for textbook writers to organise their material, just as they produce books on industrial law or commercial law. That emerges clearly from one textbook definition of the study of constitutional law as 'that body of knowledge dealing with the law of the constitution in a broader sense . . . matters pertaining to the organisation of government and its relation to citizens'. That may cover almost anything, indeed F W Maitland said that 'there is hardly any department of law which does not, at one time or another, become of constitutional importance.'

Though there is broad agreement on the contents of such books on constitutional law, in the last resort it depends on what academic lawyers consider relevant – and a quick survey of standard textbooks will show that at the margins there are significant variations in what is brought into the orbit of the British 'constitution'. In the absence of legal criteria that distinguish constitutional law from other laws, the definition becomes so broad that it defines nothing at all. In the context of the British legal system, the term constitutional law is thus literally meaningless. Borrowing from political science for their definition of the British constitution, however, academic lawyers hardly even really address the question whether in legal, or indeed logical, terms Britain has a constitution at all.

Such accounts of the British 'constitution' are only superficially the result of the absence of a constitutional document. Because we feel uneasy about our difference from other democracies which do have labelled constitutions, we turn to what is now a peculiarly British usage of the word to prove that we are not really different at all. One purpose of this article is to show that Britain *is* different, and different in ways that are important politically as well as in law. It is to show that Britain does not really have a constitution at all, merely a system of government, even if some parts of it are more important to our democratic order than others or are treated (perhaps: were treated until Mrs Thatcher's time) with greater veneration. It may be embarrassing to explain that, as in the nursery tale, the Emperor has no clothes after all, that the constitutional attire his courtiers claim to see is empty words, but that is the essential of this article. Unless we face up to that fact, moreover, any discussion of how we can safeguard certain democratic arrangements that we regarded as part of the British 'constitution' in the past (e.g. the independence of local government) or entrench others (e.g. a Bill of Rights) against an 'elective dictatorship' will run into the sand.

Constitutions and their Characteristics
Use of the word constitution as the manner in which a polity is organised, the main characteristic of its governmental system, is undoubtedly the historic one. By the end of the eighteenth century,

however, the word came to have another meaning. The American War of Independence and the French Revolution marked a turning point after which the new meaning became universal, Britain excepted. It applied to a special form of law embodied as a matter of convenience in a single document. As used elsewhere, it is now a term of law not politics. Constitutions there have certain essential characteristics, none of them found in Britain. Without these characteristics, it is impossible to distinguish a constitution from a description of the system of government in a way that is analytically precise. Without them, it is impossible to say that a country has a constitution in the current international sense of the word. More important, lest this be thought a linguistic quibble, without them a system of government lacks the legitimacy a constitution gives and a political system the protection it offers.

The characteristics of a constitution are as follows.

(1) It establishes, or constitutes, the system of government. Thus it is prior to the system of government, not part of it, and its rules can not be derived from that system.

(2) It therefore involves an authority outside and above the order it establishes. This is the notion of the constituent power ('pouvoir constituant' – because we do not think along these lines, the English translation sounds strange). In democracies that power is attributed to the people, on whose ratification the legitimacy of a constitution depends and, with it, the legitimacy of the governmental system.

(3) It is a form of law superior to other laws – because (i) it originates in an authority higher than the legislature which makes ordinary law and (ii) the authority of the legislature derives from it and is thus bound by it. The principle of hierarchy of law generally (but not always) leads to the possibility of judicial review of ordinary legislation.

(4) It is entrenched – (i) because its purpose is generally to limit the powers of government, but also (ii) again because of its origins in a higher authority outside the system. It can thus only be changed by special procedures, generally (and certainly for major change) requiring reference back to the constituent power.

James Bryce made all these points at the turn of the century. Defining a constitution as a framework of political society organised through law, he distinguished between 'statutory' and 'common law' types of constitutions. Of the former, he wrote: 'The instrument in which a constitution is embodied proceeds from a source different from that whence spring other laws, is regulated in a different way, and exerts a sovereign force. It is enacted not by the ordinary legislative authority but by some higher and specially empowered body. When any of its provisions conflict with a provision of the ordinary law, it prevails and the ordinary law must give way.' Bryce's alternative, the idea of a common-law constitution, is perhaps another way of saying that the British 'constitution' just grew, as the common law itself. His definition of a statutory constitution does, however, allow us to distinguish constitutional law from other law by clear criteria, thus giving the term not just a specific meaning, but a meaning with consequences. Though he, too, declared the distinction between written and unwritten constitutions old-fashioned, it is a pity that his summary has not served as a starting point for subsequent commentaries on the British 'constitution'.

. . . [T]he term British constitution is near meaningless even as used by British writers. It is impossible to isolate parts of the system of government to which the label may authoritatively be attached. There is no test to discriminate between constitutional and less than constitutional elements since labelling has no defined consequence, unlike countries where constitutions are a higher form of law. If used descriptively, as Wheare and others suggest, it is simply a fancy-dress way of saying the British system of government and at best redundant. More dangerous, those who talk of a British constitution may mislead themselves into thinking that there are parts of the system to which a special sanctity attaches. But in that normative sense the term is equally meaningless. When significant parts of the system are reformed, we have no test to tell us whether the outcome is an improper breach of the constitutional order, a proper amendment, or whether the reformed institutions were not part of the 'constitution' at all. I may be told that this is an academic quibble since our democratic politicians know what is of constitutional significance in our way of government, approach such matters differently from other reforms, and are politically if not legally constrained. That, however, is not the case. Our system of government is being changed, with increasing disregard for tradition, the only unwritten rules to which one might appeal as 'constitutional' principles.

There is cause for concern about the muddled way we think about the British 'constitution'; there is even greater cause for concern about the political consequences of its nature. It is sometimes said that our 'constitution' is now under stress as major changes occur far more rapidly than before in its written and unwritten parts. Is this due to changing ideas about how the British system of government should be organised, widely held, or is it simply that the government of the day is using its power to change the system in the pursuit of its own political goals? Is the constitutional order evolving or is it under attack? We have moved from consensus to conflict in politics: have we moved in that direction, too, as regards our constitutional order, taking that to mean the broad principles underlying the way government is organised and power exercised? Many old principles no longer command universal agreement and there are well-supported demands for new principles. We have had debates on the entrenchment of rights; on federalism or regional devolution as against the unitary state; on the case for consensus rather than majority as a basis for government, on the relative weight of national versus local mandates and the independence of local government; on the duty of civil servants; on electoral reform with all its implications for the operations of government; on who should define the national interest; on open government and official secrecy; on complementing representative democracy by referenda and other forms of participation – and much else. Political disagreement and disagreement on the proper constitutional order are linked. An ideologically-committed government, determined to implement its policies, will support different constitutional principles from those who want consensus policy-making; those concerned primarily with individual freedom and the rights of the public will support different principles from those who want strong government – and so on. Since opinion is now deeply divided on so many issues, one can probably no longer talk of the constitutional order as if it were a reflection of public opinion.

There are no grounds for complacency about British democracy.

NOTE: In the extract which follows, Brazier makes the point that the British constitution is largely written but remains uncodified.

R. Brazier, 'How Near is a Written Constitution?'
(2001) 52 *Northern Ireland Legal Quarterly*, pp. 3–5

As every schoolchild is supposed to know, the United Kingdom does not have a written constitution. A British citizen has to seek the rules of the constitution in a daunting number of places – legislation, judicial decisions, statements about constitutional conventions, the law and practice of Parliament, European Community law, and so on. It is hardly surprising that the interested citizen will normally leave those sources to one side and rely instead on books written by authoritative writers, and those who aspire to be authoritative. But just listing the primary materials which form the constitution demonstrates the extent to which the British constitution is largely a written one. Indeed, all the sources exist as official statements made by organs of the state, except for conventions, most of which have been reduced to writing only by the unofficial efforts of constitutional commentators. The British constitution is written, but it is not codified into a single official document, or limited number of such documents, setting out those legal rules which prescribe how the state is to be governed.

In implementing its range of reforms the Labour Government has caused Parliament to enact an additional and substantial corpus of statute law of a constitutional character. While, therefore, the United Kingdom still lacks a codified constitution, it has been given rather more of a written constitution by the addition of sixteen Acts of Parliament which, in whole or in part, add to the British constitution.[13] Perhaps most importantly towards that end, the United Kingdom now has the kind of Bill of Rights which features prominently in so many national constitutions, supplied by the Human Rights Act 1998. The lacuna which had existed in the enforcement of civil rights has now been filled. The devolution statutes have answered – at least for the time being – many long-standing queries about the appropriate relationships between the various parts of Great Britain, and with luck of the United Kingdom, and have redefined the juridical balance between them; the composition of the national legislature has been radically altered by the House of Lords Act 1999; and so on. There has been an exponential growth in the body of constitutional statute law since 1997, and because statute overrides case law and convention in the constitutional order the new laws represent some of the ground work which would be required for the production of a codified constitution. When it was still in opposition the Labour Party recognized that its legislative programme would have that effect in the narrower sense of the phrase constitution-making. In what was then its main constitutional policy document, *A New Agenda for Democracy*, adopted four years before coming to power, the party claimed that its changes would be a significant step in the direction of a written constitution, and the paper stated that the party would leave open the question of whether at a later stage progress should be made towards formal codification. Now that statement needs to be put into context. On the one hand, it was the first move – however tentative – by either of the two big political parties towards the idea of constitutional codification. On the other hand the statement did not really take account of all the other areas of the constitution which Labour's proposed changes would not affect but which would have to be reassessed and considered for inclusion in any constitutional code. For even after Labour's current reform programme has been fully implemented it would leave vital matters untouched, such as the monarchy, prerogative powers enjoyed by Ministers, the powers of the House of Commons, and the judicial system. Clearly, too, that statement in the policy paper was over-terse, in that it ignored other important matters which would be crucial in any codification exercise, such as how and by whom it would be undertaken. Nor did the comments about codification find any place in Labour's 1997 General Election manifesto.

NOTE: The House of Lords Select Committee on the Constitution has the following terms of reference:

> To examine the constitutional implications of all public bills coming before the House; and to keep under review the operation of the constitution.

One of the first problems the Committee faced was to determine what the constitution was. It sought to address this question in its First Report.

Reviewing the Constitution: Terms of Reference and Method of Working
(2001–2002), HL 11

17. . . . [T]he Committee could, if we so wished, look at any of a wide range of topics within our terms of reference. A glance at the contents page of any book on constitutional matters reveals the wide range of possible headings:

[Footnotes 10–12 omitted]
[13] As in constitutional law generally, describing a statute as one of constitutional import can be a matter of choice. But the principal Acts are the Referendums (Scotland and Wales) Act 1997, the Data Protection Act 1997, the Scotland Act 1998, the Government of Wales Act 1998, the Northern Ireland Act 1998, the Greater London Authority (Referendum) Act 1998, the Human Rights Act 1998, the Regional Development Agencies Act 1998, the European Parliamentary Elections Act 1999, the Greater London Authority Act 1999, the House of Lords Act 1999, the Local Government Act 1999, the Regulation of Investigatory Powers Act 2000, the Political Parties, Elections and Referendums Act 2000, the Disqualifications Act 2000, and the Representation of the People Act 2000.
[Footnotes 14, 15 omitted]

- Government
- the Royal Prerogative
- Parliament
- the Judiciary and judicial review
- the constitutional position of the Civil Service
- citizenship
- personal freedoms, liberties and free speech
- the EU
- devolution
- referendums
- electoral reform.

18. Many books have been written on, and many attempts have been made to consider, these and other topics which are thought to form the constitution of the United Kingdom. The constitution is said to be in flux, and the sense of what it is constantly evolving. The constitution is uncodified and although it is in part written there is no single, accepted and agreed list of statutes which form that part of the constitution which is indeed written down. While we would not wish, nor would we have the time, to write another such book ourselves, we nevertheless agreed that there was need to set for ourselves some kind of definition of what issues might fall within our remit. We do not see this as a dry academic exercise: our primary motive in doing so is as the first stage in determining which constitutional issues are in fact significant. There are many issues that are politically important both to individuals in the House and outside, and there are many issues which are matters of public debate. We would not wish to become a parliamentary magnet to which issues were attracted merely because the label 'constitutional' was attached to them by those who thought them import-ant. A definitional exercise will, in our view, both help us to determine which issues are indeed of significance, and therefore form topics for our consideration, and assist us in working out the boundaries of our work in terms of overlap with that of other committees.

   19. We accordingly asked all our witnesses what their definition was of the constitution. We are very grateful to those who responded and also to those who gave good reasons for not supplying a definition as such. We are very conscious that, given everything said in the preceding paragraphs, this was indeed something of a trick question. Lord Alexander of Weedon told us 'it is of the essence of our constitution that it is constitutional issues as they evolve. That seems to me largely to defy any attempt at a rigid definition' (Q 23). The Leader of the House, Baroness Jay of Paddington, said that it was 'quite difficult to formulate a specific definition' but that the Government understood what was meant by the specifics of constitutional reform and that they did constitute a constitutional package (Q 175). Lord Strathclyde, Leader of the Conservative Peers offered us 'anything that affects the way we are governed, the balance between the different powers of Parliament and its associated repos-itories of powers. It is about the authorities under which we are governed' (Q 128). Lord Rodgers of Quarry Bank, Leader of the Liberal Democrat Peers, offered us 'the political and administrative structure, whether based on statute or convention, by which we are governed' (Q 63). Lord Craig of Radley, Convenor of the Cross Bench Peers, while not claiming to have any instant answer, referred to power, the exercise of power and the sharing of the exercising of power, a need for 'some form of checking balance' and 'a form of consensus or as near consensus as is reasonable to expect to be able to go ahead'. He referred to the balance between the various elements exercising authority and power (Q 154). Tony Wright MP, Chairman of the Commons Public Administration Committee, sug-gested that 'the constitution is . . . whatever it is at any one time and we make it up as we go along . . . it is something to do with the relationship between citizens and the state and between the different parts of the state' (QQ 89, 91).

   20. Against the background of these very helpful comments, which serve not least to illustrate the difficulties of any attempt to define a constitution we offer as our own working definition: 'the set of

laws, rules and practices that create the basic institutions of the state, and its component and related parts, and stipulate the powers of those institutions and the relationship between the different institutions and between those institutions and the individual.'

21. We offer the following as the five basic tenets of the United Kingdom Constitution (phrases in italics indicate subjects falling within the remit of other parliamentary committees . . .):

- Sovereignty of the Crown in Parliament
- The Rule of Law, encompassing *the rights of the individual*
- Union State
- Representative Government
- Membership of the Commonwealth, *the European Union*, and other international organisations.

QUESTIONS

1. Does the provision of a list of tenets of the constitution amount to a definition of the constitution?

2. Is there any truth in the following statement by Sidney Low, in *The Governance of England* (1904), p. 12: 'British government is based upon a system of tacit understandings. But the understandings are not always understood'?

3. Colin Munro, *Studies in Constitutional Law* (1999), p. 3, states:

> The true distinction . . . is between states where some of the more important constitutional rules have been put in a document, or a set of associated documents, given special recognition, and states where the constitution has many sources, none of which enjoys such recognition.

Is this an adequate explanation, or does the sanctity accorded to a constitution serve other important purposes such as helping to guarantee freedom and placing restraints on the exercise of power by government?

4. Is there some inherent virtue in a system of government derived from a constitution, which is lacking in a country which does not have such a codified constitution? Indeed, why are constitutions enacted? See Wheare, below.

K. C. Wheare, *Modern Constitutions*

(1966), pp. 4–8

[W]hat a Constitution says is one thing, and what actually happens in practice may be quite another. We must take account of this possible difference in considering the form and worth of Constitutions. What is more, we must be ready to admit that although almost all countries in the world have a Constitution, in many of them the Constitution is treated with neglect or contempt. Indeed in the middle of the twentieth century it can be said that the majority of the world's population lives under systems of government where the government itself and particularly the executive government are of more importance and are treated with more respect or fear than the Constitution. It is only in the states of Western Europe, in the countries of the British Commonwealth, in the United States of America, and in a few Latin-American states that government is carried on with due regard to the limitations imposed by a Constitution; it is only in these states that truly 'constitutional government' can be said to exist. . . .

Since the Constitution of a country is only a part of that country's whole system of government, does it make any difference whether a country has a Constitution or not? The short answer is that in many countries the fact that there is a Constitution does make a difference. This brings to light a characteristic which most Constitutions exhibit. They are usually endowed with a higher status, in some degree, as a matter of law, than other legal rules in the system of government. At the least it is usually laid down that the amendment of the Constitution can take place only through a special process different from that by which the ordinary law is altered. . . .

It is natural to ask . . . why it is that countries have Constitutions, why most of them make the Constitution superior to the ordinary law, and, further, why Britain, at any rate, has no Constitution, in this sense, at all.

If we investigate the origins of modern Constitutions, we find that, practically without exception, they were drawn up and adopted because people wished to make a fresh start, so far as the statement of their system of government was concerned. The desire or need for a fresh start arose either because, as in the United States, some neighbouring communities wished to unite together under a new government; or because, as in Austria or Hungary or Czechoslovakia after 1918, communities had been released from an Empire as the result of a war and were now free to govern themselves; or because, as in France in 1789 or the U.S.S.R. in 1917, a revolution had made a break with the past and a new form of government on new principles was desired; or because, as in Germany after 1918 or in France in 1875 or in 1946, defeat in war had broken the continuity of government and a fresh start was needed after the war. The circumstances in which a break with the past and the need for a fresh start come about vary from country to country, but in almost every case in modern times, countries have a Constitution for the very simple and elementary reason that they wanted, for some reason, to begin again and so they put down in writing the main outline, at least, of their proposed system of government. This has been the practice certainly since 1787 when the American Constitution was drafted, and as the years passed no doubt imitation and the force of example have led all countries to think it necessary to have a Constitution.

This does not explain, however, why many countries think it necessary to give the Constitution a higher status in law than other rules of law. The short explanation of this phenomenon is that in many countries a Constitution is thought of as an instrument by which government can be controlled. Constitutions spring from a belief in limited government. Countries differ however in the extent to which they wish to impose limitations. Sometimes the Constitution limits the executive or subordinate local bodies; sometimes it limits the legislature also, but only so far as amendment of the Constitution itself is concerned; and sometimes it imposes restrictions upon the legislature which go far beyond this point and forbid it to make laws upon certain subjects or in a certain way or with certain effects. Whatever the nature and extent of the restrictions, however, they are based upon a common belief in limited government and in the use of a Constitution to impose these limitations.

The nature of the limitations to be imposed on a government, and therefore the degree to which a Constitution will be supreme over a government, depends upon the objects which the framers of the Constitution wish to safeguard. In the first place they may want to do no more than ensure that the Constitution is not altered casually or carelessly or by subterfuge or implication; they may want to secure that this important document is not lightly tampered with, but solemnly, with due notice and deliberation, consciously amended. In that case it is legitimate to require some special process of constitutional amendment – say that the legislature may amend the Constitution only by a two-thirds majority or after a general election or perhaps upon three months' notice.

The framers of Constitutions often have more than this in mind. They may feel that a certain kind of relationship between the legislature and the executive is important; or that the judicature should have a certain guaranteed degree of independence of the legislature and executive. They may feel that there are certain rights which citizens have and which the legislature or the executive must not invade or remove. They may feel that certain laws should not be made at all. . . .

In some countries only one of the considerations mentioned above may operate, in others some, and in some, all. Thus, in the Irish Constitution, the framers were anxious that amendment should be a deliberate process, that the rights of citizens should be safeguarded, and that certain types of laws should not be passed at all, and therefore they made the Constitution supreme and imposed restrictions upon the legislature to achieve these ends. The framers of the American Constitution also had these objects in mind, but on top of that they had to provide for the desire of the thirteen colonies to be united for some purposes only and to remain independent for others. This was an additional reason for giving supremacy to the Constitution and for introducing certain extra safeguards into it.

NOTE: As Ridley recognizes the framers of a constitution may have particular aims in mind. Constitutions may serve different functions in different countries or even within the same country at different times.

W. F. Murphy, 'Constitutions, Constitutionalism and Democracy' in *Constitutionalism and Democracy*, D. Greenberg, S. N. Katz, M. B. Oliviero and S. C. Wheatley (eds)
(1993), pp. 8–10

What Are the Functions of a Constitution?
A Constitution as Sham, Cosmetic, or Reality. The principal function of a sham constitutional text is to deceive. Lest US citizens revel in righteousness, they might recall that Charles A. Beard charged the framers of the US text with hypocrisy, and the Conference of Critical Legal Studies still so accuses the entire American legal system. Whether Beard and the Critics have told the full story, they have reminded us that a constitutional document's representation of itself, its people, their values, and decisional processes is imperfect. Thus, even reasonably authoritative texts play a cosmetic role, allowing a nation to hide its failures behind idealistic rhetoric. But, insofar as a text is authoritative, its rhetoric also pushes a people to renew their better selves.

A Constitution as a Charter for Government. At minimum, an authoritative constitutional text must sketch the fundamental modes of legitimate governmental operations: who its officials are, how they are chosen, what their terms of office are, how authority is divided among them, what processes they must follow, and what rights, if any, are reserved to citizens. Such a text need not proclaim any substantive values, beyond obedience to itself; if it does proclaim values, they might be those of Naziism or Stalinism, anathema to constitutional democracy.

A Constitution as Guardian of Fundamental Rights. Thus the question immediately arises about the extent to which a constitutional text relies on or incorporates democratic and/or constitutional theories. Insofar as a text is authoritative and embodies democratic theory, it must protect rights to political participation. Insofar as it is authoritative and embodies constitutionalism, it must protect substantive rights by limiting the power of the people's freely chosen representatives.

The Constitution as Covenant, Symbol, and Aspiration. Insofar as a constitution is a covenant by which a group of people agree to (re)transform themselves into a nation, it may function for the founding generation like a marriage consummated through the pledging partners' positive, active consent to remain a nation for better or worse, through prosperity and poverty, in peace and war.

For later generations, a constitution may operate more as an arranged marriage in which consent is passive, for the degree of choice is then typically limited. Even where expatriation is a recognized right, exit from a society offers few citizens a viable alternative. Revolution becomes a legal right only if it succeeds and transforms revolutionaries into founders. And deeply reaching reform from within a constitutional framework tends to become progressively more difficult, for a system usually endures only by binding many groups to its terms.

The myth of a people's forming themselves into a nation presents a problem not unlike that between chicken and egg. To agree in their collective name to a political covenant, individuals must have already had some meaningful corporate identity *as a people*. Thus the notion of constitution as covenant must mean it formalizes or solidifies rather than invents an entity: it solemnizes a previous alliance into a more perfect union.

A constitution's formative force varies from country to country and time to time. The French, one can plausibly argue, have been the French under monarchies, military dictatorships, and assorted republics. It is also plausible, however, to contend that Germans have been a different people under the Kaiser, the Weimar Republic, the Third Reich, and the Federal Republic. In polyglotted societies such as Canada, India, and the United States or those riven by religious divisions and bleeding memories of civil war such as Ireland, 'there may be no other basis for uniting a nation of so many disparate groups.' A constitution may thus function as a uniting force, 'the only principle of order', for there may be 'no [other] shared moral or social vision that might bind together a nation.' [Sanford Levinson, *Constitutional Faith* (1988) p. 73.] It is difficult to imagine what has united the supposedly United States more than the political ideas of the Declaration of Independence and the text of 1787.

Reverence for the constitution may transform it into a holy symbol of the people themselves. The creature they created can become their own mythical creator. This symbolism might turn a constitutional text into a semisacred covenant, serving 'the unifying function of a civil religion.' [T. Grey, 'The Constitution as Scripture' (1984) 37 *Stanford Law Review* 1, 18.] In America, 'The Bible of verbal inspiration begat the constitution of unquestioned authority.'

Religious allusions remind us, however, that this symbolic role may also have a dark side. Long histories of bitter and often murderous struggles among Christians and among Muslims demonstrate that a sacred text may foster division rather than cohesion, conflict rather than harmony. The 'potential of a written constitution to serve as the source of fragmentation and disintegration' [Levinson] is nowhere more savagely illustrated than in the carnage of the US Civil War. For, ultimately, that fratricidal struggle was over two visions of one constitutional document. The result was a gory war that wiped out more than 600,000 lives. Complicating analysis is the fact that when the blood of battle dried, the document of 1787, duly amended, resumed its unifying role.

In a related fashion, a constitution may serve as a binding statement of a people's aspirations for themselves as a nation. A text may silhouette the sort of community its authors/subjects are or would like to become: not only their governmental structures, procedures, and basic rights, but also their goals, ideals, and the moral standards by which they want others, including their own posterity, to judge the community. In short, a constitutional text may guide as well as express a people's hopes for themselves as a society. The ideals the words enshrine, the processes they describe, and the actions they legitimize must either help to change the citizenry or at least reflect their current values. If a constitutional text is not 'congruent with' ideals that form or will reform its people and so express the political character they have or are willing to try to put on, it will quickly fade.

NOTE: While endless argument could be engaged upon on the question whether or not the United Kingdom has a constitution, perhaps a more profitable issue for consideration is whether the system of government in the United Kingdom displays congruence with certain values, principles, and concepts associated with constitutional government in a liberal democratic state. Wheare's remarks above should be noted, namely, that in many countries the constitution is 'treated with neglect or contempt'. Thus the existence of a (codified) constitution of itself may not be a guarantee against repressive or totalitarian governments which disregard individual liberty and abrogate human rights.

V. Bogdanor (ed.), Introduction to *Constitutions in Democratic Politics*
(1988), pp. 3–7

Constitutions are not, of course, confined to democratic states. Indeed, the vast majority of the 159 member states comprising the United Nations possess codified constitutions, although less than a third of these can fairly claim democratic credentials. The latter can, declares S E Finer with pardonable exaggeration, be counted on one's fingers and toes. Conversely, three countries which are indubitably democracies – Britain, Israel and New Zealand – lack . . . codified constitutions.

In the modern world, constitutions are almost ubiquitous and they are indeed part of the tribute which vice pays to virtue. For there *is* a conceptual connection, not so much between the constitution as a document and democracy, but between modern constitutionalism and the idea of a liberal democracy. Whether a country has a codified constitution is hardly something of great importance to the political scientist. Whether it achieves the aims which constitutions are intended to help achieve, is a matter of far greater moment. For codified constitutions are, after all, valued as a means to the end of limiting governmental power; and, in a democracy, limiting also the power of the people to whom government is responsible. The Founding Fathers in drawing up the American Constitution had, after all, two aims, not one. The first was to draw up a structure of government which could serve to protect the people from government, from the danger of a tyranny of the majority in the legislature; but the second aim was to protect the people from themselves.

Thus, the relationship between constitutionalism and liberalism . . . is by no means a simple or straightforward one. To live under an effectively working constitution is not the same as living under a regime of moral *laissez-faire*. Constitutional government presupposes a certain set of virtues amongst the ruled; and these virtues must include self-restraint, a willingness not to push the pursuit of one's aims beyond a certain point. In the 1930s, Mr Justice Stone declared that the United States Supreme Court ought not to see itself as the sole guardian of the constitution. While the other branches of the Constitution were limited by institutional restraints, by checks and balances, the only restraint which limited the Court was its sense of self-restraint. By analogy, one might argue that in a democracy in which the people are, in effect, sovereign, the only effective restraint in the last resort is likely to be that of the people over themselves. Constitutions thus both liberate and bind; they provide for a framework of ordered freedom within a set of rules which prevents both majorities and their elected representatives from doing what they might otherwise wish to do.

The term 'constitution', as S E Finer shows, is to be understood in positivistic terms as a code of rules which aspire to regulate the allocation of functions, powers and duties among the various agencies and officers of government, and defines the relationships between these and the public. Yet, even defined in these terms, the existence of a constitution, in so far as it is observed, serves to limit power. For, to allocate functions, powers and duties is also, *ipso facto*, to limit power. There must be some gain to the citizen, however minimal, in living under a constitution which regularises the way in which power is exercised; even where government is authoritarian, it matters that it is not arbitrary.

Yet, a number of democratic constitutions today contain more than a mere organisation chart of functions and powers; they contain Bills of Rights, which may also include a charter of social and economic rights, something characteristic of constitutions of the twentieth century, although generally honoured more in the breach than in the observance.

. . . [I]n the case of Britain and Israel, two countries without codified constitutions, such pressure as exists to adopt one is based less on the desire to possess a clear-cut organisational chart delimiting the institutions of government than on a feeling that rights would be better protected under a codified constitution than they are at present.

The concept of a constitution is closely bound up with the notion of the limitation of government by law, a source of authority higher than government and beyond its reach. An enacted constitution is a means – although, as the examples of Britain, Israel and New Zealand show, not an essential means – of securing this end. The law, it is suggested, is logically prior to government, and therefore constitutes a standard by which the actions of government are to be evaluated. It is . . . this 'appeal to a pre-existing law' which 'is the essence of constitutionalism'.

Yet analysis of constitutions cannot be restricted simply to the document called 'the Constitution', or to constitutional law. For a working constitution in a democracy implies reference to certain norms and standards which lie beyond and outside the document itself, and which cannot easily be inferred from it by someone who is not steeped in the history and culture of the country concerned. When conduct on the part of a government or some other public body is dubbed 'unconstitutional', what is often meant is not necessarily that the law has been broken, but rather that the action is out of keeping with the style or, more broadly, the 'way of life' of a country. . . .

This kind of appeal – to constitutional conventions – can, of course, also be raised in countries without codified constitutions. When, in Britain, it is suggested that the policies of the Conservative Government towards local authorities since 1979 raise constitutional questions, what is meant is not that these policies are in any sense illegal, but rather . . . that they breach hitherto accepted understandings, albeit tacit, as to how relationships between central government and local authorities should be ordered. These tacit understandings, which, in Sidney Low's graphic phrase, are so often misunderstood, may not be written down; yet they exert a normative influence upon those concerned with central/local relations comparable to, and perhaps greater than, the influence exerted by a constitutional document. What makes Britain together with Israel and New Zealand, constitutional democracies, despite the absence of codified constitutions, is this very fact that their governments in general feel under pressure to conform to such norms; when accused of unconstitutional action their defence is not that the term 'unconstitutional' is without meaning, but that their actions can, despite appearances, be defended in constitutional terms.

Thus, in addition to the basic meaning of 'constitution' – a document containing, at the very least, a code of rules setting out the allocation of functions, powers and duties among the various agencies and officers of government – there is a wider meaning of constitution, according to which every democratic state has a constitution. This wider meaning comprehends the normative attitudes held by the people towards government, their conception of how power ought to be regulated, of what it is proper to do and not to do. There are, as it were, pre-constitutional norms regulating government, and it is upon these that the health and viability of democratic systems will depend.

SECTION 2: Constitutionalism

Governments wield considerable power. Constitutions, while they may create the institutions of government and allocate power to these institutions, also generally seek to control or restrain the exercise of power. The principle of constitutionalism rests on this idea of restraining the government in its exercise of power. Constitutionalism, therefore, is to be set in contradistinction to arbitrary power.

M. J. C. Vile, *Constitutionalism and the Separation of Powers*
(1967), p. 1

Western institutional theorists have concerned themselves with the problem of ensuring that the exercise of governmental power, which is essential to the realization of the values of their societies, should be controlled in order that it should not itself be destructive of the values it was intended to promote. The great theme of the advocates of constitutionalism, in contrast either to the theorists of utopianism, or of absolutism, of the right or of the left, has been the frank acknowledgment of the role of government in society, linked with the determination to bring that government under control and to place limits on the exercise of its power.

C. J. Friedrich, *Limited Government: A Comparison*
(1974), pp. 13–14

Constitutionalism by dividing power provides a system of effective restraints upon governmental action. In studying it, one has to explore the methods and techniques by which such restraints are established and maintained. Putting it another, more familiar, but less exact way, it is a body of rules ensuring fair play, thus rendering the government 'responsible.' There exist a considerable number of such techniques or methods.

The question confronts us: how did the idea of restraints arise? And who provided the support that made the idea victorious in many countries? There are two important roots to the idea of restraints. One is the medieval heritage of natural-law doctrine. For while the royal bureaucrats gained the upper hand in fact, the other classes in the community who had upheld the medieval constitutionalism – the barons and the free towns, and above all the church – developed secularized versions of natural law. At the same time, they clung to residual institutions, such as the *parlements* in France. After the task of unification had been accomplished, and the despotic methods of absolutism could no longer be justified, these elements came foward with the idea of a separation of power. Both the English and the French revolutions served to dramatize these events.

The other root of the idea of restraints is shared by medieval and modern constitutionalism and is peculiar to some extent to Western culture. It is Christianity, and more specifically the Christian doctrine of personality. The insistence upon the individual as the final value, the emphasis upon the transcendental importance of each man's soul, creates an insoluble conflict with any sort of absolutism. Here lies the core of the objection to all political conceptions derived from Aristotelian and other Greek sources. Since there exists a vital need for government just the same, this faith in the worth of each human being is bound to seek a balance of the two needs in some system of restraints which protects the individual, or at least minorities, against any despotic exercise of political authority. It is quite in keeping with this conflict that the apologists of unrestrained power have, in all ages of Western civilization, felt the necessity of *justifying* the exercise of such power, a necessity which was not felt elsewhere.

Nor was it felt by all in the West. Bacon and Hobbes, Bodin and Spinoza, and even Machiavelli insisted that some sort of inanimate force, such as reason, natural law, or enlightened self-interest would bring about a self-restraint. But a deep-seated distrust of power was part of the tradition that taught that 'my Kingdom is not of this world,' and that states are usually just 'great robber bands,' since they lack justice. Hence self-restraint of the ruler must be reinforced by effective institutions: restraints upon the arbitrary exercise of governmental power.

Modern constitutionalism then has always been linked with the problem of power, in theory as well as in practice. Historically, it constitutes a reaction against the concentration of power that accompanied the consolidation of modern states, dynastic and national. Its theorists have insisted on the importance of limiting and defining the power acquired by monarchs. Whilst Hobbes described the rational structure of such a concentration of power and developed it into a veritable philosophy of power, Locke, taking up the challenge, demanded that the exercise of this power, although it was derived from the ultimate and unified source of all power – the people – remain divided by virtue of a fundamental decision.

QUESTIONS

1. Which of the ideas of self-restraint or institutional restraint is the dominant one in the British system of government?

2. In the United Kingdom there is no codified constitution expressly imposing limits on governmental power. Is governmental power limited in other ways?

NOTE: In the United Kingdom, where Parliament is supreme and may enact, amend, or repeal any law it chooses, there is no distinction between 'ordinary' laws and 'constitutional' laws. Laws of constitutional significance are not accredited 'fundamental' status – they have no special sanctity. No special procedures are required for amending or repealing such laws. Indeed, in the absence of a codified constitution, it is arguable that it is impossible to state what laws are of constitutional significance without reference to constitutions elsewhere to see what kinds of matters are dealt with therein. A further consequence is, as Bogdanor states in

'Britain: the Political Constitution' in Bogdanor, *Constitutions in Democratic Politics*, p. 56, that 'the term "unconstitutional" cannot in Britain mean contrary to law; instead it means contrary to convention, contrary to some understanding of what it is appropriate to do. But, unfortunately, there is by no means universal agreement on what the standards of appropriateness are or ought to be'. Should this be a matter of concern? Is it not sufficient to entrust Parliament with the task of ensuring that constitutionalism is respected in the United Kingdom?

J. Elster, 'Introduction' in *Constitutionalism and Democracy*, Elster and Slagstad (eds)
(1988), pp. 8–9

Why would a political assembly want to abdicate from the full sovereignty which in principle it possesses, and set limits on its own future actions? In an intergenerational perspective, the question is what right one generation has to limit the freedom of action of its successors, and why the latter should feel bound by constraints laid down by their ancestors. A natural (although possibly misleading) point of departure is to consider individual analogies. Why, for instance, would two individuals want to form a legal marriage instead of simply cohabiting? What possible advantages could they derive from limiting their future freedom of action and by making it more difficult to separate should they form the wish to do so? One obvious answer is that they want to protect themselves against their own tendency to act rashly, in the heat of passion. By raising the costs of separation and imposing legal delays, marriage makes it less likely that the spouses will give way to strong but temporary impulses to separate. By increasing the expected duration of the relationship, legal marriage also enhances the incentive to have children, to invest in housing and make other long-term decisions. These decisions, in turn create bonds between the spouses and reinforce the marriage.

These answers have partial analogues in the constitutional domain. It is a truism that constitutional constraints make it more difficult for the assembly or the society to change its mind on important questions. Groups no less than individuals (although not in quite the same sense as individuals) are subject to fits of passion, self-deception and hysteria which may create a temporary majority for decisions which will later be regretted. But then, one may ask, why could the members of the assembly not simply undo the decisions if and when they come to regret them? The presumption must be, after all, that the assembly knows what it is doing, not that it needs to be protected against itself.

Part of the answer to this question is suggested by the marriage analogy. The expected stability and duration of political institutions is an important value in itself, since they allow for long-term planning. Conversely, if all institutions are up for grabs all the time, individuals in power will be tempted to milk their positions for private purposes, and those outside power will hesitate to form projects which take time to bear fruit. Moreover, if nothing could ever be taken for granted, there would be large deadweight losses arising from bargaining and factionalism.

Another part of the answer is that not all unwise decisions can be undone. Imagine that a majority untrammelled by constitutional constraints decides that an external or internal threat justifies a suspension of civil liberties, or that retroactive legislation should be enacted against 'enemies of the people.' In the first place, such measures have victims whom one cannot always compensate at later times. Examples abound: the internment of the American Japanese during the Second World War, the excesses during the Chinese Cultural Revolution, the *Berufsverbot* against Communists in several countries. When society again comes to its senses, the victims may be dead or their lives destroyed. In the second place, the temporary suspension of rights easily leads to the permanent abolition of majority rule itself and to its replacement by dictatorship. It suffices to cite the years 1794 and 1933. This is possibly the central argument for constitutional constraints on democracy: without such constraints democracy itself becomes weaker, not stronger.

QUESTION

If Elster's analogy is not false, does it mean that the United Kingdom system of government lacks legitimacy?

SECTION 3: **Legitimacy**

Why, following a revolution, does a government which has effective power backed up with military force, seek to make a constitution? Friedrich, in *Limited Government: A Comparison*, p. 118, states that such a response is 'motivated by the belief that such a constitution, if popularly approved, would give them the right to rule, over and above the mere power to do so'. If a government has the right to rule it is regarded as legitimate, and this, in turn, provides it with authority. Legitimacy, therefore, is a quality which is valuable to government.

S. E. Finer, *Comparative Government*
(1970), pp. 30–31

The stable and effective exercise of a government's power is that which derives from its authority. By this I mean that the commands to do or to abstain proceed from persons who – no matter whether this is logical or reasonable or justifiable by any objective criterion – are *believed* to be persons who have the moral right to issue them: so that, correlatively, those to whom the commands are addressed feel a moral *duty* to obey them. Authority represents a two-way process: a claim to be obeyed, and a recognition that this claim is morally right. No public recognition of a claim means no authority.

Where a population recognizes a moral duty to obey, there is no need for the government to reason with it, persuade it, bribe it or threaten it, though all these exercises of power may be necessary for the marginal recalcitrants. The mere recognition of a duty to obey achieves for the government what an overwhelming application of violence would not satisfactorily achieve. As Rousseau said: 'The strongest is never strong enough unless he succeeds in turning might into right and obedience into duty.' As human nature goes, fear is certainly the father of power, but authority is its mother. To inculcate the population with the belief that their rulers have the right to demand obedience and they the corresponding duty to give it is the principal art of government.

QUESTION

What, then, is legitimacy, and how is it acquired?

D. Beetham, *The Legitimation of Power*
(1991), pp. 11–12, 15–20, 25–27 and 34–36

The different dimensions of legitimacy

The key to understanding the concept of legitimacy lies in the recognition that it is multi-dimensional in character. It embodies three distinct elements or levels, which are qualitatively different from one another. Power can be said to be legitimate to the extent that:

(i) it conforms to established rules
(ii) the rules can be justified by reference to beliefs shared by both dominant and subordinate, and
(iii) there is evidence of consent by the subordinate to the particular power relation. . . .

(i) The first and most basic level of legitimacy is that of rules . . . Power can be said to be legitimate in the first instance if it is acquired and exercised in accordance with established rules. For convenience I shall call the rules governing the acquisition and exercise of power the 'rules of power'. These rules may be unwritten, as informal conventions, or they may be formalised in legal codes or judgments. . . .

The opposite of legitimacy according to the rules is, simply, *illegitimacy*; power is illegitimate where it is either acquired in contravention of the rules (expropriation, usurpation, coup d'état), or exercised in a manner that contravenes or exceeds them. The illegal acquisition of power usually has more profound, because more all-pervasive, consequences for legitimacy than some breach or contravention in its exercise, though that depends upon the seriousness of the breach, and whether it is repeated. Where the rules of power are continually broken, we could speak of a condition of chronic illegitimacy.

(ii) On its own, legal validity is insufficient to secure legitimacy, since the rules through which power is acquired and exercised themselves stand in need of justification. This is the second level of legitimacy: power is legitimate to the extent that the rules of power can be justified in terms of beliefs shared by both dominant and subordinate. What kinds of justification and what kinds of belief are needed? To be justified, power has to be derived from a valid source of authority (this is particularly true of political power); the rules must provide that those who come to hold power have the qualities appropriate to its exercise; and the structure of power must be seen to serve a recognisably general interest, rather than simply the interests of the powerful. These justifications in turn depend upon beliefs current in a given society about what is the rightful source of authority; about what qualities are appropriate to the exercise of power and how individuals come to possess them; and some conception of a common interest, reciprocal benefit, or societal need that the system of power satisfies.

No society is characterised by a complete uniformity of beliefs. Indeed, one of the distinctive features of power relations is the difference of circumstances, opportunities and values between dominant and subordinate groups. Yet without a minimum of the appropriate beliefs defined above being shared between the dominant and the subordinate, and indeed among the subordinate themselves, there can be no basis on which justifications for the rules of power can find a purchase. Naturally what counts as an adequate or sufficient justification will be more open to dispute than what is legally valid, and there is no ultimate authority to settle such questions; nevertheless clear limits are set by logic and the beliefs of a given society to what justifications are plausible or credible within it.

This second level or dimension of legitimacy has its corresponding negative or opposite. Rules of power will lack legitimacy to the extent that they cannot be justified in terms of shared beliefs: either because no basis of shared belief exists in the first place (e.g. slavery, 'artificial' or divided communities); or because changes in belief have deprived the rules of their supporting basis (e.g. hereditary rule or male power, in face of a declining belief in the superior qualities supposedly ascribed by birth or sex); or because changing circumstances have made existing justifications for the rules implausible, despite beliefs remaining constant. [For example] it is argued that the British electoral system, with its first-past-the-post rules determining who shall be elected in each constituency, is losing its legitimacy, and to an extent therefore also weakening that of the governments elected under it. This is not because of any shift in people's beliefs, but because the rules have increasingly delivered results that diverge, both regionally and nationally, from the proportion of votes cast, and hence from accepted notions about the representative purpose of elections in a democracy. It is the increasingly unrepresentative character of the electoral system, and its consequent vulnerability to attack in a society that believes in representation, that is the basis for the weakening legitimacy of governments appointed under it. The vulnerability was there before it was exploited, and the weakening of legitimacy took place before people publicly acknowledged it. It may have taken the poll-tax legislation to bring the issue to the forefront of public attention. But the potential for doing so was already present in the growing discrepancy between the rules and the beliefs or values underpinning them. . . .

These different situations clearly have widely differing significance, but they can all be described as examples, not so much of illegitimacy, as of *legitimacy deficit* or weakness.

(iii) The third level of legitimacy involves the demonstrable expression of consent on the part of the subordinate to the particular power relation in which they are involved, through actions which provide evidence of consent. . . . [T]he importance of actions such as concluding agreements with a superior, swearing allegiance, or taking part in an election, is the contribution they make *to* legitimacy. They do this in two ways. The first is that they have a subjectively binding force for those who have taken part in them, regardless of the motives for which they have done so. Actions expressive of consent, even if undertaken purely out of self-interest, will introduce a moral component into a relationship, and create a normative commitment on the part of those engaging in them. Secondly, such actions have a publicly symbolic or declaratory force, in that they constitute an express acknowledgement on the part of the subordinate of the position of the powerful, which the latter are able to use as confirmation of their legitimacy to third parties not involved in the relationship, or those who have not taken part in any expressions of consent. They are thus often associated with impressive forms of ceremonial. . . .

What is common to legitimate power everywhere . . . is the need to 'bind in' . . . the subordinate, through actions or ceremonies publicly expressive of consent, so as to establish or reinforce their obligation to a superior authority, and to demonstrate to a wider audience the legitimacy of the powerful.

It is in the sense of the public actions of the subordinate, expressive of consent, that we can properly talk about the 'legitimation' of power, not the propaganda or public relations campaigns, the 'legitimations' generated by the powerful themselves. And if the public expression of consent contributes to the legitimacy of the powerful, then the withdrawal or refusal of consent will by the same token detract from it. Actions ranging from non-cooperation and passive resistance to open disobedience and militant opposition on the part of those qualified to give consent will in different measure erode legitimacy, and the larger the numbers involved, the greater this erosion will be. At this level, the opposite or negative of legitimacy can be called *delegitimation*.

For power to be fully legitimate, then, three conditions are required: its conformity to established rules; the justifiability of the rules by reference to shared beliefs; the express consent of the subordinate, or of the most significant among them, to the particular relations of power. All three components contribute to legitimacy, though the extent to which they are realised in a given context will be a matter of degree. Legitimacy is not an all-or-nothing affair. . . . Every power relation knows its breaches of the rules or conventions; in any society there will be some people who do not accept the norms underpinning the rules of power, and some who refuse to express their consent, or who do so only under manifest duress. What matters is how widespread these deviations are, and how substantial in relation to the underlying norms and conventions that determine the legitimacy of power in a given context. Legitimacy may be eroded, contested or incomplete; and judgements about it are usually judgements of degree, rather than all-or-nothing.

Above all, the analysis I have given above demonstrates that legitimacy is not a single quality that systems of power possess or not, but a set of distinct criteria, or multiple dimensions, operating at different levels, each of which provides moral grounds for compliance or cooperation on the part of those subordinate to a given power relation. By the same token, power can be non-legitimate in very different ways, which I have signalled by the different terms: illegitimacy, legitimacy deficit and delegitimation. The erosion of justificatory norms, slavery, conquest, dictatorship, coup d'état, separatist agitation, revolutionary mobilisation – all are examples where power lacks some element of legitimacy, but does so in very different ways. The accompanying diagram summarises in tabular

Table 1.1 The three dimensions of legitimacy

Criteria of Legitimacy	Form of Non-legitimate Power
i conformity to rules (legal validity)	illegitimacy (breach of rules)
ii justifiability of rules in terms of shared beliefs	legitimacy deficit (discrepancy between rules and supporting beliefs, absence of shared beliefs)
iii legitimation through expressed consent	delegitimation (withdrawal of consent)

form the different dimensions of legitimate and non-legitimate power that I have distinguished, to reinforce the argument of the text.

The significance of legitimacy

Legitimacy, as we have seen, comprises the moral or normative aspect of power relationships; or, more correctly, the sum of these aspects. . . .

To consider first the behaviour of those subordinate within a power relationship; its legitimacy provides them with moral grounds for cooperation and obedience. Legitimate power or authority has the right to expect obedience from subordinates, even where they may disagree with the content of a particular law or instruction; and subordinates have a corresponding obligation to obey. This obligation is not absolute – hence the dilemmas that occur when people are required by a legitimate superior to do things that are morally objectionable to them, as opposed to inconvenient or merely stupid. But it is the right that legitimacy gives those in authority to require obedience in principle, regardless of the content of any particular law or instruction, that makes it so important to the coordination of people's behaviour in all spheres of social life.

The legitimacy or rightfulness of power, then, provides an explanation for obedience through the obligation it imposes on people to obey, and through the *grounds or reasons* it gives for their obedience.

However, normative grounds or reasons are not the only reasons people have for obedience. . . .

[P]ower relations are almost always constituted by a framework of incentives and sanctions, implicit if not always explicit, which align the behaviour of the subordinate with the wishes of the powerful. They do so by giving people good reasons of a different kind, those of self-interest or prudence, for not stepping out of line. Obedience is therefore to be explained by a complex of reasons, moral as well as prudential, normative as well as self-interested, that legitimate power provides for those who are subject to it. This complexity may make it difficult to determine the precise balance of reasons in any one situation; but it is important to distinguish them analytically, since each makes a very different kind of contribution to obedience. . . .

[What are the consequences of legitimacy for the behaviour of the dominant within a power relationship?]

If legitimacy, as I have argued, enhances the order, stability and effectiveness of a system of power, then we should expect that the powerful will seek to secure and maintain the legitimacy of their power, in view of its advantages to them. Here again, however, we must be careful to avoid drawing the wrong conclusions from a mistaken definition of legitimacy. If we reduce it to people's 'belief in legitimacy', then we are likely to conclude that the way in which the powerful maintain their legitimacy is primarily by means of ideological work, and through the influence they have over the beliefs and ideas of the subordinate. . . .

I do not wish to discount altogether the role of ideological work, particularly in reinforcing the basic norms that underpin a given system of power, though I shall want to argue later that the processes involved are complex ones, and have been oversimplified in much of the relevant literature. What I would emphasise at this point, however, is that we need to look quite elsewhere for the effect of legitimacy on the behaviour of the powerful. If legitimate power is, as I have argued, power that is valid according to rules, and where the rules themselves are justifiable by and in conformity with underlying norms and beliefs, then the main way in which the powerful will maintain their legitimacy is by respecting the intrinsic limits set to their power by the rules and the underlying principles on which they are grounded. Legitimate power, that is to say, is limited power; and one of the ways in which it loses legitimacy is when the powerful fail to observe its inherent limits.

What are these limits? I would draw attention to two different kinds. One kind of limit is set by the rules which determine what the powers of the powerful are, and what they can rightly expect those subordinate to them to do – which specify, in other words, the respective duties and obligations of those involved in a power relationship. These rules may be largely conventional, or they may be legally defined. A feature of the modern world is the increasingly precise legal specification of the respective powers, or 'sphere of competence', of each powerholder. Even today, however, there is still considerable room left for 'custom and practice', for conventional understandings built up over time through processes of struggle and compromise, which govern the expectations of the powerful and the subordinate about what is, and is not, required of them; what can, and cannot, legitimately be demanded.

For the powerful to breach these rules in a substantial way, say by imposing some new or additional obligation on subordinates without warning or consultation, is either to invite action for legal redress, or, where the law is silent, to provoke informal protests which may develop into a more widespread crisis of legitimacy for the system of power. Unless they are arrogant or stupid, powerholders will only take such action when it is essential to some important purpose, or if they are driven to it by a serious predicament of their own. The fact that mostly they do not do so, and that they mostly respect the rules and conventions governing their relations with those subordinate to them, makes it easy to overlook an essential feature of legitimacy: that it sets limits to the behaviour of the powerful as well as imposing obligations on the subordinate. Because we more readily notice what the powerful do than what they refrain from doing, this essential feature of legitimacy tends to go unremarked.

The other kind of constraint which their need to maintain legitimacy imposes on the powerful is a more fundamental one: to respect the basic principles that underpin the rules or system of power, and to protect them from challenge. Rulers who derive their legitimacy from a divine source must respect religious traditions and defer to religious authorities; they will regard any threat to religion or religious belief as among the most serious they face. Those who derive their authority from the people will ignore at their peril any insistent and widespread popular current of opinion; to be seen to favour foreign interests at the expense of national ones will do more damage to their standing than almost anything else. Those who claim a monopoly of representation of the working class by virtue of a privileged knowledge of their interests cannot afford to allow independent sources of working-class opinion to find expression, or alternative institutions of representation to develop, which might challenge their monopoly. The legitimating ideas and justificatory principles that underpin the given institutions of power define which challenges the ruler has to take most seriously, because they strike at the basis of the system of rule itself.

QUESTION

If a government, using its majority in Parliament, passes appropriate laws empowering it to do specified acts, are its activities thereby rendered legitimate because they are done in accordance with the law, regardless of how oppressive or repugnant those laws might be? See Chapter 4 and also the extract which follows.

P. McAuslan and J. F. McEldowney, 'Legitimacy and the Constitution: the Dissonance between Theory and Practice' in *Law, Legitimacy and the Constitution*

(1985), pp. 11–14

Legitimacy . . . does not deal so much with whether activities of government are lawful as whether they accord with what are generally perceived to be or what have for long been held up to be, the fundamental principles of the constitution according to which government is or ought to be conducted. Lawfulness is clearly an issue in so far as one of the fundamental principles of the British, no less than most other constitutions, is that government action should take place under the authority of, and in accordance with law – the narrow literal meaning of the rule of law – so that repeated unlawful actions or a perceived casualness towards the duty to comply with the law would in itself begin to raise doubts about the legitimacy of governmental action. The rule of law is generally thought to have a broader 'political' meaning which covers the same ground as, if it is not quite synonymous with, the concept of limited government. This meaning embraces such matters as fair and equitable administrative practices; recognition of the rights of political opposition and dissent; complying with constitutional conventions; adequate means of redress of grievances about governmental action affecting one. Thus a government which while adhering to the rule of law narrowly defined, flouted all or most of the practices generally thought to be covered by the rule of law broadly defined would also give rise to doubts about its legitimacy. One of the clearest and best examples of a government on the whole scrupulous to comply with the rule of law narrowly defined yet consistently flouting it, as to the majority of its citizens, when broadly defined is the government of the Republic of South Africa, in relation to its non-white citizens.

What makes the issue of the legitimacy of our constitutional arrangements so problematic is the general open-endedness of those arrangements; that is, the difficulty of knowing whether a practice or non-practice is or is not constitutional.

Even where practices may not differ over time, or place, there may be an inconsistency about them or a lack of knowledge about them, or a long-standing dispute about them, which could make it equally difficult to argue that following or not following a practice was or was not constitutional or legitimate. Probably the best example of this is the use of the royal prerogative, and the extent to which the courts may pass judgment on any particular use. Notwithstanding that the royal prerogative as a source of power for the government antedates Acts of Parliament, has been at the root of a civil war and a revolution in England and has been litigated about on countless major occasions in respect of its use both at home and overseas, its scope is still unclear as is the role of the courts in relation thereto. The use by the Prime Minister of powers under the royal prerogative to ban trade unions at the Government Communication Headquarters at Cheltenham in 1983 was contested both for its lawfulness – that is whether such powers could be used and if so whether they were used correctly – and also for its legitimacy – that is whether, even if the constitutional power existed, this was a proper and fair use of the power. It can be seen that questions of lawfulness and legitimacy shade into one another here though the answers do not: the lawfulness of the action taken, confirmed by the House of Lords in 1984 (*Council of Civil Service Unions* v *Minister for the Civil Service* [1984] 3 All ER 935) did not and does not dispose of its legitimacy.

The G.C.H.Q. case is valuable for another point. We have pointed out that lawfulness is not to be confused with legitimacy. No more is constitutionality. What the Prime Minister did was not merely lawful; she exercised the constitutional powers of her office in the way in which those powers had always been exercised. That is, the use of the royal prerogative as the legal backing for the management of the public service, the principle that a civil servant is a servant of the Crown and holds office at the pleasure of the Crown is one of the best known principles of constitutional law, hallowed by usage and sanctioned by the courts. What is in issue from the perspective of legitimacy is whether the particular use made of that undoubted constitutional power, the manner of its use, and the justification both for the use and manner of use – that considerations of national security required both a banning of trade unions and no consultation with affected officers before the ban was announced – was a fair and reasonable use of power? Did it accord with legitimate expectations of fair and reasonable persons or was it a high-handed exercise of power of a kind more to be expected of an authoritarian government than one guided by and subscribing to principles of limited government?

In considering the issue of legitimacy in relation to our constitutional arrangements and the exercise of governmental power, what has to be done is to examine a range of practices, decisions, actions (and non-practices, -decisions and -actions) statements and policies which between them can amount to a portrait of power, so that we can form a judgment or an assessment of that power set against the principles of limited government outlined and discussed so far. It is not every failure to comply with law or every constitutional and non-constitutional short cut which adds up to an approach to powers which give rise to questions of legitimacy. If that were so, there would scarcely be a government in the last 100 years which could be regarded as legitimate, but it is those uses of power and law which seem to betray or which can only be reasonably explained by a contempt for or at least an impatience with the principles of limited government and a belief that the rightness of the policies to be executed excuse or justify the methods whereby they are executed. If, as we believe to be the case, powers are being so exercised, then the issue of constitutional legitimacy which arises is quite simple: what is the value or use of a constitution based on and designed to ensure the maintenance of a system of limited government if it can, quite lawfully and even constitutionally, be set on one side? Have we not in such circumstances arrived at that 'elective dictatorship' of which Lord Hailsham gave warning in 1977:

> It is only now that men and women are beginning to realize that representative institutions are not necessarily guardians of freedom but can themselves become engines of tyranny. They can be manipulated by minorities, taken over by extremists, motivated by the self-interest of organised millions.

Occasionally the people from whom legitimacy ultimately derives, pass judgment on government.

McAuslan and McEldowney, ibid. p. 1

> Mr Clive Ponting's acquittal by a jury in February 1985, after he had admitted to passing official Government papers to a person not authorised to receive them, the very essence of section 2 of the Official Secrets Act 1911, and despite the most explicit summing up by the trial judge that they should convict, raises the question of what motivated the jury. It would suggest that when faced with a choice between a case which rests on constitutional theories about limited government derived from a 'higher law' which controlled what government could legitimately do, and a case which rested on actual practices of government bolstered by actual law, the jury preferred the theory of what the constitution ought to be to the practice of what it is. Little wonder that, as one newspaper put it, Ministers were aghast at the verdict. The *Concise Oxford Dictionary* defines 'aghast' as meaning terrified. This essay will seek to show Ministers would indeed have good reason to be terrified if ordinary people began preferring constitutional theory to government practice and acted on their preferences in their judgment of politicians. More particularly the jury's verdict in the Ponting trial may be seen then as the response of ordinary people to trends in government practices which seem to them to be, in perhaps indefinable ways, wrong.

QUESTIONS

1. In this case it was a jury of twelve which, by its verdict, appeared to be commenting on the legitimacy of governmental action in attempting to mislead the Foreign Affairs Select Committee about the circumstances surrounding the sinking of the *General Belgrano*, an Argentinian warship, during the Falklands Campaign in 1982. These twelve jurors may, or may not, have been representative of the views of the public. Are there more representative ways in which public sentiments regarding governmental action may be expressed?

2. Is majority rule under a system of parliamentary democracy a sufficient guarantee of legitimacy? What does majority rule mean in the context of the United Kingdom?

SECTION 4: **Democracy**

In the opening sentences of *Le Contrat Social* (1762) Rousseau stated:

Man is born free and everywhere he is in chains. One thinks himself the master of others, and still remains the greater slave than they. How did this change come about? I do not know. What can make it legitimate? That question I think I can answer.

The answer he gave was that the only ground of legitimacy is to be found in the general will of the people, as only the people can say who has the right to rule them. Thus it is the people who give legitimacy to a constitution – sovereignty resides with the people and, in turn, where the constitution sets up a system of elected representative government, that government acquires its authority both from the constitution and the people who elect it.

Does the constitution in the United Kingdom (if there is one) have a democratic basis? Is the system of government democratic? A starting point is to examine what a liberal-democracy is.

C. B. Macpherson, *The Real World of Democracy*
(1966), pp. 4–11

[O]ur liberal-democracy, like any other system, is a system of power; that it is, indeed, again like any other, a double system of power. It is a system by which people can be *governed*, that is, made to do things they would not otherwise do, and made to refrain from doing things they otherwise might do. Democracy as a system of government is, then, a system by which power is exerted by the state over individuals and groups within it. But more than that, a democratic government, like any other, exists to uphold and enforce a certain kind of society, a certain set of relations between individuals, a certain set of rights and claims that people have on each other both directly, and indirectly through their rights to property. These relations themselves are relations of power – they give different people, in different capacities, power over others. . . .

[L]iberal-democracy and capitalism go together. Liberal-democracy is found only in countries whose economic system is wholly or predominantly that of capitalist enterprise. And, with few and mostly temporary exceptions, every capitalist country has a liberal-democratic political system. . . .

The claims of democracy would never have been admitted in the present liberal-democracies had those countries not got a solid basis of liberalism first. The liberal democracies that we know were liberal first and democratic later. To put this in another way, before democracy came in the Western world there came the society and the politics of choice, the society and politics of competition, the society and politics of the market. This was the liberal society and state. It will be obvious that I am using liberal here in a very broad sense. I use it in what I take to be its essential sense, to mean that both the society as a whole and the system of government were oganized on a principle of freedom of choice. . . .

To make this society work, or to allow it to operate, a non-arbitrary, or responsible, system of government was needed. And this was provided, by revolutionary action in England in the seventeenth century, in America in the eighteenth, in France in the eighteenth and nineteenth, and by a variety of methods in most other Western countries sometime within those centuries. What was established was a system whereby the government was put in a sort of market situation. The government was treated as the supplier of certain political goods – not just the political good of law and order in general, but the specific political goods demanded by those who had the upper hand in running that particular kind of society. What was needed was the kind of laws and regulations, and tax structure, that would make the market society work, or allow it to work, and the kind of state services – defence, and even military expansion, educa- tion, sanitation, and various sorts of assistance to industry, such as tariffs and grants for railway development – that were thought necessary to make the system run efficiently and profitably. These were the kinds of political goods that were wanted. But how was the demand to call forth the supply? How to make government responsive to the choices of those it was expected to cater to? The way was of course to put governmental power into the hands of men who were made subject to periodic elections at which there was a choice of candidates and parties. The electorate did not need to be a democratic one, and as a general rule was not; all that was needed was an electorate consisting of the men of substance, so that the government would be responsive to their choices.

To make this political choice an effective one, there had to be certain other liberties. There had to be freedom of association – that is, freedom to form political parties, and freedom to form the kind of associations we now know as pressure groups, whose purpose is to bring to bear on parties and on governments the combined pressure of the interests they represent. And there had to be freedom of speech and publication, for without these the freedom of association is of no use. These freedoms could not very well be limited to men of the directing classes. They had to be demanded in principle for everybody. The risk that the others would use them to get a political voice was a risk that had to be taken.

So came what I am calling the liberal state. Its essence was the system of alternate or multiple parties whereby governments could be held responsible to different sections of the class or classes that had a political voice. There was nothing necessarily democratic about the responsible party system. In the country of its origin, England, it was well established, and working well, half a century or a century before the franchise became at all democratic. This is not surprising, for the job of the liberal state was to maintain and promote the liberal society, which was not essentially a democratic or an equal society. The job of the competitive party system was to uphold the competitive market society, by keeping the government responsive to the shifting majority interests of those who were running the market society.

However, the market society did produce, after a time, a pressure for democracy which became irresistible. . . .

So finally the democratic franchise was introduced into the liberal state. It did not come easily or quickly. In most of the present liberal-democratic countries it required many decades of agitation and organization, and in few countries was anything like it achieved until late in the nineteenth century. The female half of the population had to wait even longer for an equal political voice: not until substantial numbers of women had moved out from the shelter of the home to take an independent place in the labour market was women's claim to a voice in the political market allowed.

So democracy came as a late addition to the competitive market society and the liberal state. The point of recalling this is, of course, to emphasize that democracy came as an adjunct to the competitive liberal society and state. It is not simply that democracy came later. It is also that democracy in these societies, was demanded, and was admitted, on competitive liberal grounds. Democracy was demanded, and admitted, on the ground that it was unfair not to have it in a competitive society. It was something the competitive society logically needed. . . .

What the addition of democracy to the liberal state did was simply to provide constitutional channels for popular pressures, pressures to which governments would have had to yield in about the same measure anyway, merely to maintain public order and avoid revolution. By admitting the mass of the people into the competitive party system, the liberal state did not abandon its fundamental nature; it simply opened the competitive political system to all the individuals who had been created by the competitive market society. The liberal state fulfilled its own logic. In so doing, it neither destroyed nor weakened itself; it strengthened both itself and the market society. It liberalized democracy while democratizing liberalism.

QUESTION

If this view is correct, did, or does, the 'constitution' in the United Kingdom have a democratic basis, i.e. was, or is, its legitimacy to be found in the general will of the people? See Ridley, below.

F. F. Ridley, 'There is no British Constitution: A Dangerous Case of the Emperor's Clothes'
(1988) 41 *Parliamentary Affairs*, pp. 340, 343–345

The first characteristic of a constitution . . . is that it constitutes – or reconstitutes – a system of government. . . . [I]n constitutional theory a governmental order derives its legitimacy from the constituent act which establishes it. . . .

Democratic constitutions universally state the principle of popular sovereignty and their legitimacy now rests on popular enactment. This follows the American tradition: 'We the people of the United States . . . do ordain and establish this constitution'. Similar words are found almost everywhere. Some may invoke a higher sanctity for parts of the constitution than the will of the people. Thus the American Bill of Rights is founded on the Declaration of Independence's self-evident truths that all men are endowed by their Creator with certain inalienable rights, but that does not alter the source of the constitution's authority. . . .

The people are generally called on to elect a special constituent assembly mandated to draft a constitution, though this may not always be the case – as in General de Gaulle's constitution for the Fifth Republic. Although the American constitution was ratified by state legislatures, in more recent times the people are almost universally called on to ratify it in a referendum. . . .

Britain never developed this idea of popular sovereignty in constitutional terms, even if we sometimes talk of the sovereignty of the electorate in political terms. Even if the latter were true, it would merely allow the people to choose their government: it does not base the governmental order, the British 'constitution', on their authority and thus only gives them only half their right. (Moreover, since a parliamentary majority can change that order, prolong its own life, alter the franchise or reform the electoral system, even the political rights of the electorate depend on Parliament.) What we have, instead, is the sovereignty of Parliament. Parliament determines – and alters – the country's system of government. If we ask where that power comes from, the answer is broadly that Parliament claimed it and the courts recognised it. The people never came into the picture. The liberal (middle-class) democracies established in Europe had, despite their generally limited franchise, to base their constitutions on the principle that ultimate authority was vested in the people. Britain seems to be the sole exception to this democratic path.

QUESTION

If, as it is argued, the 'constitution' of the United Kingdom had no democratic basis, is the system of government nevertheless democratic? See Finer, below.

S. E. Finer, *Comparative Government*
(1970), pp. 63–66

(1) The primary meaning of democracy is government which is derived from public opinion and is accountable to it. As to *accountability;* this implies that it is not sufficient for a government to justify its existence because at some time in the past it was representative of popular opinion; for the two may have diverged since then. 'Accountability' entails that a government must continuously test its representativeness, that is to say whether its claim that it is 'derived from public opinion' is still valid.

(2) This public opinion, it must therefore be presumed, is overtly and freely expressed. For if it is not, how can anybody *know* that the government is still 'derived from public opinion', i.e. is still representative? But 'overtly and freely to express opinion' implies some opportunity and machinery for making that opinion known, and therefore implies some kind of a suffrage, some kind of a voice or vote. . . .

(3) In matters of contention between sections of public opinion it is the majority opinion that prevails.

These three characteristics must, it seems, form part of any definition of democracy. . . .

Thus the first assumption of liberal-democracy is that it is a democracy in the sense expressed above. But liberal-democracy is a *qualified* democracy. In this type of government there are other presuppositions or assumptions beyond the one which we have already stated.

The first of these is that government is *limited.* This implies that the government is operating in a world of autonomous, spontaneously self-creating, voluntary associations. In such conditions the government operates only at the margin of social activity. That it ought to interfere and regulate or even suppress these autonomous, self-creating, voluntary associations is a matter for it to prove: it is not assumed. . . . The authority of government therefore is limited; and this can be expressed by saying that certain rights of the individual and of the private association are safeguarded. A kind of ring fence is drawn around them and the onus lies on the government to show whether, why and to what extent this ought to be breached.

The second qualification to democracy in this particular 'liberal' form is that society is recognized as being *pluralistic.* . . . To recognize society as being pluralistic, therefore, carries the additional assumption that the government sets out to rule, not in the interest of any one group or alliance of groups, but in the common interest of all. . . .

This highlights the third qualification: the liberal-democratic type of government is one in which *it is denied that there is any objective science of society or of morals*. On the contrary, it is assumed that in the last resort truth is a matter of individual consciences where all consciences are held, by an act of faith, to be equal either in the sight of God or in the sight of man. Two working conclusions follow from this, namely, toleration and the qualification of majority rule.

Why toleration? Because if there is no objective science of society and morals, then clearly no group, not even the government, has any moral justification for imposing any creed, philosophy, religion or ideology upon the rest of society. Again, since it is assumed by this act of faith that all individuals are equal in the sight of God, man or both, then dissent must be tolerated and each has the right to put his own point of view. Again, since truth is held to be individual and also fallible, rulership will be both conditional and also temporary; because clearly the views as to what is true and therefore proper for government to act upon will change from time to time as opinion fluctuates amongst the body of the people. So, this qualified form of democracy entails that the government is representative of and responsive to public opinion; and that where this opinion is not unanimous it is representative of and responsive to the majority. But these majorities will usually be constantly changing. . . .

But even majority rule is seriously qualified in the liberal-democracy. . . . But being a liberal-democracy also implies that the minorities must be given a chance to become a majority; and that means, therefore, that they must be given a chance status and a means to convert the majority. In order to make this possible, certain guarantees and machinery would have to be established.

NOTES:

1. The ideas in the last paragraph of the extract from Finer, above, are taken further by Sir Stephen Sedley, 'The Common Law and the Constitution' in Lord Nolan and Sir Stephen Sedley, *The Making and Remaking of the British Constitution* (London, 1997), p. 5 where he states:

   A democracy is more than a state in which power resides in the hands of a majority of elected representatives: it is a state in which individuals and minorities have an assurance of certain basic protections from the majoritarian interest, and in which independent courts of law hold the responsibility for interpreting, applying and – importantly – supplementing the law laid down by Parliament in the interests of every individual, not merely the represented majority.

   See further Chapter 7.

2. See further *United Communist Party of Turkey* v *Turkey* (1998) 26 EHRR 121, at p. 472 below.

3. Where there is a permanent majority, however, representative democracy may fail to provide legitimation either of a government or of the system of government. See Barker, below.

R. Barker, *Political Legitimacy and the State*
(1990), pp. 141–143

It is difficult to determine in any precise way the contribution of elections to the maintenance of legitimacy. By comparing the history of Northern Ireland with that of the rest of the United Kingdom it is clear that the mere fact of elections is not sufficient. If the result is never in any doubt, so that it is not 'the people' but always and only a section and that the same section of them which confers consent on government, then those who feel themselves permanently excluded will also feel no great obligations to the regime. No legitimacy without representation. . . .

On the other hand, so long as the electoral system appears to give due weight to most parties, the fact that individual votes may often have little effect does not deter them from being cast. Voters turn out in large numbers in safe seats where their individual support or opposition to the sitting candidate can make no difference whatsoever to the result. Voting has a ritual aspect, whereby citizens formally and publicly show their preferences for one party over others, and hence their willingness to accept the result of the contest, and their legitimation of that result. It enables people to identify with those who lead or govern them, to see politicians and rulers as both special and, at the same time, exemplifying the character of their followers. . . .

Thus two broad sanctioning functions can be identified in voting. First of the policies of particular governments, second of the governing system in general, of the state. These may of course in practice be confused or entangled with each other, as they are in Northern Ireland, or as they are in any state where the elections are largely or wholly a political ritual or a way of mobilizing mass support or approval for a regime in which party and state are indistinguishable, and electoral choice between contestants for office non-existent. Once this occurs the democratic process can have an important function in *failing* to legitimize the state, and in providing justification for a rejection by groups of subjects not only of particular governments, but of more general constitutional arrange-ments. The predictable ineffectiveness of the nationalist vote in Northern Ireland can be used to justify rejection not just of a particular government but of the whole constitutional structure which maintains the inclusion of Northern Ireland in the United Kingdom rather than in a new all-Ireland state. In a smaller way after 1987 the emergence of a Scottish electorate overwhelmingly hostile to a Conservative government in power on the basis of English electoral success can sustain nationalist arguments for the general illegitimacy of the constitutional arrangements of the United Kingdom.

NOTE: The theory of limited government appears to demand more than simple majority rule. It is important to examine whether the system of government in the United Kingdom has advanced beyond this idea of the 'rightness' of the majority. This involves an examination of how elections operate, how governments acquire power, and how they use that power. Do they claim authority simply on the basis of electoral victory to do as they please, including changing the constitutional framework, or do they find themselves restrained from so acting by certain fundamental principles?

Endeavouring to answer such questions has, in the past, involved largely value judgements. Political scientists are now attempting to develop indices to assist in informing such judgements. The extract which follows outlines some of the issues involved.

David Beetham, 'Key Principles and Indices for a Democratic Audit' in *Defining and Measuring Democracy*, Beetham, D. (ed.)
(1994), pp. 25–30

First, it is necessary to explain the idea of a 'democratic audit' itself. This is the simple but ambitious project of assessing the state of democracy in a single country. Like other Western countries, the UK calls itself a democracy, and claims to provide a model for others to follow. Yet how democratic is it actually? And how does it measure up to the standards that it uses to assess others, including the countries of the Third World? Such questions are not accidental, but are provoked by a widespread sense of disquiet within the UK at the state of its political institutions – a disquiet which runs deeper than the mere fact that a single party has been in power for so long . . .

The project of a democratic audit, then, not only requires a clear specification of what exactly is to be audited. It also requires a robust and defensible conception of democracy, from which can be derived specific criteria and standards of assessment. An account of this conception and these criteria is provided in the following section.

Principles and indices of democracy
. . . Democracy is a *political* concept, concerning the collectively binding decisions about the rules and policies of a group, association or society. It claims that such decision-making should be, and it is realized to the extent that such decision-making actually is, subject to the control of all members of the collectivity considered as equals. That is to say, democracy embraces the related principles of *popular control* and *political equality*. In small-scale and simple associations, people can control collective decision-making directly, through equal rights to vote on law and policy in person. In large and complex associations, they typically do so indirectly, for example through appointing representatives to act for them. Here popular control usually takes the form of control over decision-*makers*, rather than over decision-making itself; and typically it requires a complex set of institutions and practices to make the principle effective. Similarly political equality, rather than being realized in an equal say in decision-making directly, is realized to the extent that there exists an equality of votes between electors, an equal right to stand for public office, an equality in the conditions for making one's voice heard and in treatment at the hands of legislators, and so on.

These two principles, of popular control and political equality, form the guiding thread of a democratic audit. They are the principles which inform those institutions and practices of Western countries that are characteristically democratic; and they also provide a standard against which their level of democracy can be assessed. As they stand, however, they are too general. Like the indices developed by other political scientists, they need to be broken down into specific, and where possible, measurable, criteria for the purpose of assessment or audit.

To do this we have separated the process of popular control over government into four distinct, albeit overlapping, dimensions. First and most basic is the popular election of the parliament or legislature and the head of government. The degree or extent of popular control is here to be assessed by such criteria as: the *reach* of the electoral process (that is, which public offices are open to election, and what powers they have over non-elected officials); its *inclusiveness* (what exclusions apply, both formally and informally, to parties, candidates and voters, whether in respect of registration or voting itself); its *fairness* as between parties, candidates and voters, and the range of effective choice it offers the latter; its *independence* from the government of the day; and so on. These criteria can be summed up in the familiar phrase 'free and fair elections', though this phrase does not fully capture all the aspects needed for effective popular control.

The second dimension for analysis concerns what is known as 'open and accountable government'. Popular control requires, besides elections, the continuous accountability of government: directly, to the electorate, through the public justification for its policies; indirectly, to agents acting on the people's behalf. In respect of the latter, we can distinguish between the *political* accountability of government to the legislature or parliament for the content and execution of its policies; its *legal* accountability to the courts for ensuring that all state personnel, elected and non-elected, act within the laws and powers approved by the legislature; its *financial* accountability to both the legislature and the courts. Accountability in turn depends upon public knowledge of what government is up to, from sources that are independent of its own public relations machine. In all these aspects, a democratic audit will need to assess the respective powers and independence, both legal and actual, of different bodies: of the legislature and judiciary in relation to the executive; of the investigative capacity of the media; of an independent public statistical service; of the powers of individual citizens to seek redress in the event of maladministration or injustice.

Underpinning both the first two dimensions of popular control over government is a third: guaranteed civil and political rights or liberties. The freedoms of speech, association, assembly and movement, the right to due legal process, and so on, are not something specific to a particular *form* of democracy called 'liberal democracy'; they are essential to democracy as such, since without them no effective popular control over government is possible . . . These rights or liberties are necessary if citizens are to communicate and associate with one another independently of government; if they are to express dissent from government or to influence it on an ongoing basis; if electoral choice and accountability is to be at all meaningful. A democratic audit will need to assess not only the legally prescribed content of these citizens' rights, but also the effectiveness of the institutions and procedures whereby they are guaranteed in practice.

A fourth dimension of popular control concerns the arena of what is called 'civil society': the nexus of associations through which people organize independently to manage their own affairs, and which can also act as a channel of influence upon government and a check on its powers. This is a more contestable dimension of democracy, not only because the criteria for its assessment are much less well formed than for the other three areas, but also because there is room for disagreement as to whether it should be seen as a necessary *condition for* democracy, or as an essential *part of* it. Our view is that a democratic society is a part of democracy, and goes beyond the concept of 'civil society', with its stress on the *independence* of societal self-organization, to include such features as: the representativeness of the media and their accessibility to different social groups and points of view; the public accountability and internal democracy of powerful private corporations; the degree of political awareness of the citizen body and the extent of its public participation; the democratic character of the political culture and of the education system.

The criteria or indices of popular control can thus be divided into four interrelated segments, which go to make up the major dimensions of democracy for contemporary societies. . . . A complete democratic audit should examine each segment in turn, to assess not only the effectiveness of popular control in practice, but also the degree of political equality in each area: under free and fair elections, how far each vote is of equal value, and how far there is equality of opportunity to stand for public office, regardless of which section of society a person comes from; under open and accountable government, whether any individuals or groups are systematically excluded from access to, or influence upon, government, or redress from it; under civil and political rights or liberties, whether these are effectively guaranteed to all sections of society; under democratic society, the degree of equal opportunity for self-organization, access to the media, redress from powerful corporations, and so on.

SECTION 5: Limited Government

The concept of limited government comprises two ideals, that of accountability of government for the exercise of its powers, and that of limits placed on the exercise of those powers. What, then, are the conditions for accountable or, as it is often termed, responsible government?

Jack Lively, *Democracy*
(1975), pp. 43–44

What then are the conditions necessary for the existence of responsible government? What is needed to ensure that some popular control can be exerted over political leadership, some govern-mental accountability can be enforced? Two main conditions can be suggested, that governments should be removable by electoral decisions and that some alternative can be substituted by electoral decision. The alternative, it should be stressed, must be more than an alternative governing group. It must comprehend alternatives in policy, since it is only if an electoral decision can alter the actions of government that popular control can be said to be established. . . . To borrow the economic analogy, competition is meaningless, or at any rate cannot create consumer sovereignty, unless there is some product differentiation.

In detail there might be a great deal of discussion about the institutional arrangements necessary to responsible government, but in general some are obvious. There must be free elections, in which neither the incumbent government nor any other group can determine the electoral result by means other than indications of how they will act if returned to power. Fraud, intimidation and bribery are thus incompatible with responsible government. . . . Another part of the institutional frame neces-sary to responsible government is freedom of association. Unless groups wishing to compete for leadership have the freedom to organize and formulate alternative programmes, the presentation of alternatives would be impossible. Lastly, freedom of speech is necessary since silent alternatives can never be effective alternatives. In considering such arrangements, we cannot stick at simple legal considerations; we must move from questions of 'freedom from' to questions of 'ability to'. The absence of any legal bar to association will not, for example, create the ability to associate if there are heavy costs involved which only some groups can bear. Nor will the legal guarantee of freedom of speech be of much use if access to the mass media is severely restricted.

This could be summed up by saying that responsible government depends largely upon the existence of, and free competition between, political parties.

Whether the British system of government creates the conditions for responsible government is doubted in some quarters. Lord Hailsham spoke of 'elective dictatorship'.

Lord Hailsham, *The Dilemma of Democracy*
(1978), pp. 21–22

The old party structure, which for so long guaranteed the evolutionary character of our society, seems to me to have broken down. . . .

[I]t seems to me that we are moving more and more in the direction of an elective dictatorship, not the less objectionable in principle because it is inefficient in practice, and not the less tyrannical in its nature because the opposed parties, becoming more and more polarized in their attitudes, seek with some prospects of success to seize the new levers of power and use them alternately to reverse the direction taken by their immediate predecessors. All the more unfortunate does this become in the presence of narrow majorities, each representing a minority of the electorate, sometimes a small minority, and when at least one of the parties believes that the prerogatives and rights conferred by electoral victory, however narrow, not merely entitle but compel it to impose on the helpless but unorganized majority irreversible changes for which it never consciously voted and to which most of its members are opposed.

It seems to me that this is a situation the reverse of liberal and even the reverse of democratic, in the sense in which the word has hitherto been understood. Fundamental and irreversible changes ought only to be imposed, if at all, in the light of an unmistakable national consensus. It follows that, if I am right, the overriding need of the moment is to pursue policies and enact legislation to ensure that a like situation to the present is never allowed to recur. It is true that the present nature of the threat can be seen to come from the left. But this need not necessarily be so, and almost certainly it will not always be so. . . .

My thesis is that our institutions must be so structurally altered that, so far as regards permanent legislation, the will of the majority will always prevail against that of the party composing the executive for the time being, and that, whoever may form the government of the day will be compelled to follow procedures and policies compatible with the nature of Parliamentary democracy and the rule of freedom under law.

QUESTIONS

1. Lord Hailsham wrote in 1978; has anything changed since then to contradict his thesis, or have subsequent events confirmed his worst fears? See also Leslie Wolf-Phillips, below.

2. N. Johnson, 'Constitutional Reform: Some Dilemmas for a Conservative Philosophy' in *Conservative Party Politics* (Layton-Henry, ed., 1980), at p. 139, stated: 'A relative majority in the House of Commons may rest on a minority position in the country. Government on these terms is tolerable if the party in power recognises that there are limits to what it is entitled to do.' Is there any evidence that such limits have been recognized in the last 20 years?

Leslie Wolf-Phillips, 'A Long Look at the British Constitution'
(1984) 37 *Parliamentary Affairs*, pp. 385, 398–401

The idealised view of the British system is that, under a head of State insulated from politics, generally admired, and with long and varied experience, the government of the day is led by a Prime Minister whose party has been given a parliamentary majority by a mature electorate which has participated in free and open elections. Parliament debates the great issues of the day, controls national expenditure and taxation, criticises government policy as an aid to its improvement, scrutinises the work of the central administration, and ensures the redress of collective and individual grievances. The Prime Minister heads a government composed of a Cabinet of her senior ministers and about eighty non-Cabinet ministers all bound to a policy implicitly approved by the electorate; the Prime Minister and all her colleagues must justify their actions and their policies before parliament, and if parliament withdraws its confidence, they must resign and face the stern judgment of the electorate upon their stewardship. Each minister has departmental responsibility and can be called to account for the working of his department before parliament; if incompetence or maladministration be proved then the minister will be called upon to resign either by the Prime Minister or by the direct action of parliament. The Queen as Head of State gives overall stability to the political system and the Prime Minister as Head of Government is one who has served a long apprenticeship in parliament in high office of state and who is the elected leader of a party which has the confidence of the nation. The 'Unwritten Constitution' has the virtue of flexibility and permits the wide use of constitutional conventions, both permitting and facilitating evolutionary consensual change. Finally, the House of Lords provides a forum removed from party ties and considerations, where the experienced and distinguished perform functions of assistance, advice, continuity and, when needed, a measure of restraint on the popularly-elected transient majority in the House of Commons.

What is the reality? The extension of the franchise, the growth of national mass parties and the development of the mass media have changed the nature of general elections, which have become largely personalised into a contest between party leaders. The majority of the electorate are only marginally politically conscious, and the personalisation of political issues and allegiances reflect this marginality. The voting pattern for the parties is so uniform throughout the country that the influence on a constituency of a particular candidate is insignificant; candidates without the support of a major party can expect to fail and minor or ad hoc or single-interest parties can expect to be swept aside. . . . Elections cannot be, and should not be regarded as, a means for approving the details of comprehensive manifestoes and the electors often seem to vote against a party rather than for the winning party. . . .

The only mandate that most electors consider they have given to newly-elected Members of Parliament is to support the party and its leader; certainly, the Prime Minister expects, and usually gets, the support of the mass of the parliamentary majority party and the entire hundred or so members of the Government that is formed.

The supremacy of the Prime Minister is further enhanced by the authority to obtain (or threaten to obtain) a dissolution of parliament, the possibility of rebel Members being disowned and replaced by their constituency parties, the feelings of loyalty to one's party and the fear of giving aid and comfort to the opposition parties. Whatever the formal constitutional conventions and party rules, the Prime Minister is normally in effective control. Not only does he or she have the authority to appoint and dismiss or advance or relegate ministers, but there is also access to the patronage system for honours, awards and selection of candidates for high public office. The appointments and preferments policies of the present Prime Minister has shown the influence that can be borne in these matters. The former belief that the Prime Minister was primus inter pares (first among equals) has given way to the realisation that the office-holder is primum mobile (the first mover). The Prime Minister dominates the cabinet, its members wait upon a summons; there is control and prior approval of the agenda from the Prime Minister; the skilful exploitation of collective responsibility by the Prime Minister can neutralise and isolate a recalcitrant cabinet minority which has no choice but to 'shut up or get out'; the Prime Minister has wide access to a network of policy-making cabinet committees, and 'deals' can be made in inter-departmental committees, cabinet committees, or between the Prime Minister and individual ministers. Business laid before the full cabinet has often been the subject of previous informal agreement between the Prime Minister and certain colleagues in order that opposition may be outmanoeuvred. . . .

In brief, the actual Westminster model is that of authoritarian single-party governments in a House of Commons dominated by the Prime Minister and composed largely of disciplined parties with most votes in the House of Commons being highly predictable; every three or four years there is a general election held under a crude simple majority electoral system with minimal participation by the electorate in the choice of who shall be their candidate, though they do have the choice between the candidates who are selected by the party activists; between 20% and 30% of the electorate do not vote at all. Governments rarely fall as a result of a vote in the House of Commons and resignations under ministerial responsibility are almost as rare. The vast majority of legislation proposed by the government of the day is passed; it is rare, indeed it is well-nigh impossible, for legislation to be passed of which the government does not approve. Orthodox constitutional theory bestows on individual members the right of independent action and does not regard them as the representative of the party without which they would not have been elected; over-solicitude for the wishes of their constituents would probably lead them into conflict with the party in parliament. The parties at large are not seen as the formers of policy for the government; that is a task reserved for the parliamentary members of the governing party.

NOTE: In what other ways may the powers of government be limited? At the outset it must be recognized that there are three institutions of government, each with specific functions. The legislature has the function of making new law or amending or repealing existing law. The executive has the administrative function of conducting government in accordance with the law. The judiciary has the function of interpreting the law and applying it to specific cases. In 1690 John Locke identified a danger arising from the possession of more than one power. In his *Second Treatise of Civil Government*, Chapter XII, para. 143, Locke stated:

> It may be too great a temptation to human frailty, apt to grasp at power, for the same persons who have the power of making laws, to have also in their hands the power to execute them, whereby they may exempt themselves from obedience to the laws they make, and suit the law, both in its making and execution, to their own private advantage.

This idea was developed further by Montesquieu, the French philosopher, who expressed the view that it was the separation of powers of government which ensured the liberty of the English. He expressed the doctrine in *L'Esprit des Lois*, Book XI, Chapter VI (2nd edn, vol. 1, p. 220) as follows:

> When the Legislative Power is united with the Executive Power in the same person or body of magistrates, there is no liberty because it is to be feared that the same Monarch or the same Senate will make tyrannical laws in order to execute them tyrannically. There is no liberty if the Judicial Power is not separated from the Legislative Power and from the Executive Power. If it were joined with the Legislative Power, the power over the life and liberty of citizens would be arbitrary, because the Judge would be Legislator. If it were joined to the Executive Power, the Judge would have the strength of an oppressor. All would be lost if the same man, or the same body of chief citizens, or the nobility, or the people, exercised these three powers, that of making laws, that of executing public decisions, and that of judging the crimes or the disputes of private persons.

This was a somewhat idealized view which did not truly reflect the political reality in England at the time. Montesquieu's views, however, were particularly influential in the eighteenth century as a reading of the Constitution of the United States of America reveals.

C. F. Strong, *Modern Political Constitutions*
(1972), pp. 211–212

Now, in no constitutional state is it true that the legislative and executive functions are in precisely the same hands, for . . . the executive must always be a smaller body than the legislature. But it is not to this distinction that the theory of the separation of powers points. The application of the theory means not only that the executive shall not be the same body as the legislature but that these two bodies shall be isolated from each other, so that the one shall not control the other. Any state which has adopted and maintained this doctrine in practice in its full force has an executive beyond the control of the legislature. Such an executive we call non-parliamentary or fixed. This type of executive still exists in the United States, whose Constitution has not been altered in this particular since its inception. But France, which, as we have said, applied the doctrine in its first constitutions born of the Revolution, later adopted the British executive system, and this feature appeared in the Constitutions of the Third and Fourth Republics, and again, though greatly modified, in that of the Fifth Republic. The system is one in which a cabinet of ministers is dependent for its existence on the legislature of which it is a part, the members of the executive being also members of the legislature.

This system, generally known as the Cabinet system, has been, in its broad features, adopted by most European constitutional states, and it matters not at all whether they are called monarchies or republics. It is also characteristic of the governments of British Commonwealth countries, old and new. The non-parliamentary system, on the other hand, is peculiar to the United States and those Latin American Republics which have founded their constitutions upon that of their great neighbour.

Lord Bingham of Cornhill, 'The Courts and the Constitution'
(1996/97), 7 *King's College Law Journal*, 15–16

Every fourth-former knows that powers exercised on behalf of the state fall under three broad heads, the legislative, the executive and the judicial. The legislature makes the law, the executive carries it out and the judiciary, in case of doubt or dispute, interprets and applies it. Life in the fourth form is pleasantly simple.

But of course it is not quite as simple as that. True, Parliament does enact new laws – 3,233 pages of it in 1985 – but it also has important functions in debating policy, holding ministers to account and providing a forum for the redress of grievances. True, the executive does implement the laws made by Parliament, but it also plays a crucial role in initiating almost all new legislation; ministers exercise many powers which are not conferred by Parliament and ministers also, acting under legislative authority and usually subject to parliamentary control, make laws in the form of subordinate legislation – 6,518 pages of it in 1985. True again, the judges interpret and apply the laws made by Parliament. But the cases which reach the courts are not usually cases in which Parliament has made its intention clear. In such cases there is nothing to litigate about. It is when the intention of parliament is unclear, or where Parliament has failed to provide for a particular eventuality at all, that litigation ensues. The essential function of the court is then to declare the law which it infers that Parliament intended to make, or would have made if it had addressed the point at all. This is not a legislative role, but nor is it a purely interpretative role, since the court may have to do a good deal more than elicit the meaning of what Parliament has enacted. In the great expanses of English law which are largely untouched by statute, the function of the courts is, I would suggest, even less interpretative, since the legal issues which fall to be decided rarely fall squarely within the ratio of an earlier decision, unless it is sought to challenge that decision. More often cases arise on the border between one decision and another, or at the confluence of two or more competing principles or in an area where there is virtually no relevant authority. The courts have then to decide, in the light of legal principle and such authority as there is, and having regard to the apprehended practical consequences of one decision as opposed to another, what the law should be. The courts also have a role in providing a forum for the redress of grievances and in holding the executive to account, if in either case (but only if) a breach of the law is shown. So the functions of legislature, executive and judiciary are not quite as distinct as one might suppose.

Nor, in contrast with many constitutions, notably the American, does our constitution provide for any rigid separation of powers. The fact that the cabinet, as the engine of the executive, and all other ministers, are necessarily members of one or other House of the legislature is indeed the clearest possible negation of the doctrine. But between the legislature and the executive on the one hand and the judiciary on the other the separation is all but total. . . .

G. Marshall, *Constitutional Theory*

(1971), pp. 103–104

A separation between the judicial and the legislative and executive branches obviously exists in both Britain and the United States in the sense that in practice the judges are secure in their offices and have an independent status. But whether the separation of powers doctrine implies the existence of that degree of checking or controlling which has come to be known as judicial review in the American sense is not easy to decide. The right to invalidate legislation obviously in one sense invades the principle that each department has an independent sphere of action and a right to take its own view on matters of constitutionality. On the other hand, the controlling or checking functions of the judicial branch can only consist in impartial application of the law, and where constitutional law places restrictions on legislative power, a duty to declare the law seems to imply a duty to declare when such restrictions have been violated, whether by the legislature or by anyone else.

NOTE: In the United States the Supreme Court in *Marbury* v *Madison* (1803) 1 Cranch 137, decided that it had the power to declare both the acts of Congress and of the President to be unconstitutional. In the United Kingdom courts have refused to adjudicate upon the validity of Acts of Parliament, but they have developed the doctrine of judicial review by which the exercise of power by other authorities may be reviewed in the courts.

R v *London Transport Executive, ex parte Greater London Council*

[1983] QB 484, Court of Appeal

KERR LJ: . . . Authorities invested with discretionary powers by an Act of Parliament can only exercise such powers within the limits of the particular statute. So long as they do not transgress their statutory powers, their decisions are entirely a matter for them, and – in the case of local authorities – for the majority of the elected representatives; subject, however, to one important proviso. This is – again to put it broadly – that they must not exercise their powers arbitrarily or so unreasonably that the exercise of the discretion is clearly unjustifiable. This is an imperfect and generalised paraphrase of the well-known statement of Lord Greene MR in *Associated Provincial Picture Houses Ltd* v *Wednesbury Corporation* [1948] 1 KB 223, 229, which has come to be known as the *Wednesbury* principle and applied in countless cases.

If an authority misdirects itself in law, or acts arbitrarily on the basis of considerations which lie outside its statutory powers, or so unreasonably that its decisions cannot be justified by any objective standard of reasonableness, then it is the duty and function of the courts to pronounce that such decisions are invalid when these are challenged by anyone aggrieved by them and who has the necessary locus standi to do so.

The role of the courts in the constitution was further elucidated in the following cases.

Duport Steels Ltd v *Sirs*

[1980] 1 WLR 142, House of Lords

Private steel companies sought injunctions against the Iron and Steel Trades Confederation who were calling on workers in the private sector of the steel industry to come out on strike to support workers in the public sector who were striking over pay. The correct interpretation of s. 13(1) of the Trade Union and Labour Relations Act 1974 (as amended in 1976) was central to the case. Section 13(1) conferred immunity from liability in tort for an act done by a person 'in contemplation or furtherance of a trade dispute'. The Court of Appeal reversed the judge's decision to refuse the injunctions sought.

LORD DIPLOCK: . . . My Lords, at a time when more and more cases involve the application of legislation which gives effect to policies that are the subject of bitter public and parliamentary controversy, it cannot be too strongly emphasised that the British constitution, though largely unwritten, is firmly based upon the separation of powers; Parliament makes the laws, the judiciary interpret them. When Parliament legislates to remedy what the majority of its members at the time perceive to be a defect or a lacuna in the existing law (whether it be the written law enacted by existing statutes or the unwritten common law as it has been expounded by the judges in decided cases), the role of the judiciary is confined to ascertaining from the words that Parliament has approved as expressing its intention what that intention was, and to giving effect to it. Where the meaning of the statutory words is plain and unambiguous it is not for the judges to invent fancied ambiguities as an excuse for failing to give effect to its plain meaning because they themselves consider that the consequences of doing so would be inexpedient, or even unjust or immoral. In controversial matters such as are involved in industrial relations there is room for difference of opinion as to what is expedient, what is just and what is morally justifiable. Under our constitution it is Parliament's opinion on these matters that is paramount.

A statute passed to remedy what is perceived by Parliament to be a defect in the existing law may in actual operation turn out to have injurious consequences that Parliament did not anticipate at the time the statute was passed; if it had, it would have made some provision in the Act in order to prevent them. It is at least possible that Parliament when the Acts of 1974 and 1976 were passed did not anticipate that so widespread and crippling use as has in fact occurred would be made of sympathetic withdrawals of labour and of secondary blacking and picketing in support of sectional interests able to exercise 'industrial muscle.' But if this be the case it is for Parliament, not for the judiciary, to decide whether any changes should be made to the law as stated in the Acts, and, if so, what are the precise limits that ought to be imposed upon the immunity from liability for torts committed in the course of taking industrial action. These are matters on which there is a wide legislative choice the exercise of which is likely to be influenced by the political complexion of the government and the state of public opinion at the time amending legislation is under consideration.

It endangers continued public confidence in the political impartiality of the judiciary, which is essential to the continuance of the rule of law, if judges, under the guise of interpretation, provide their own preferred amendments to statutes which experience of their operation has shown to have had consequences that members of the court before whom the matter comes consider to be injurious to the public interest. The frequency with which controversial legislation is amended by Parliament itself (as witness the Act of 1974 which was amended in 1975 as well as in 1976) indicates that legislation, after it has come into operation, may fail to have the beneficial effects which Parliament expected or may produce injurious results that Parliament did not anticipate. But, except by private or hybrid Bills, Parliament does not legislate for individual cases. Public Acts of Parliament are general in their application; they govern all cases falling within categories of which the definitions are to be found in the wording of the statute. So in relation to section 13(1) of the Acts of 1974 and 1976, for a judge (who is always dealing with an individual case) to pose himself the question: 'Can Parliament really have intended that the acts that were done in this particular case should have the benefit of the immunity?' is to risk straying beyond his constitutional role as interpreter of the enacted law and assuming a power to decide at his own discretion whether or not to apply the general law to a particular case. The legitimate questions for a judge in his role as interpreter of the enacted law are: 'How has Parliament, by the words that it has used in the statute to express its intentions, defined the category of acts that are entitled to the immunity? Do the acts done in this particular case fall within that description?'

LORD SCARMAN: . . . My basic criticism of all three judgments in the Court of Appeal is that in their desire to do justice the court failed to do justice according to law. When one is considering law in the hands of the judges, law means the body of rules and guidelines within which society requires its judges to administer justice. Legal systems differ in the width of the discretionary power granted to judges: but in developed societies limits are invariably set, beyond which the judges may not go. Justice in such societies is not left to the unguided, even if experienced, sage sitting under the spreading oak tree.

In our society the judges have in some aspects of their work a discretionary power to do justice so wide that they may be regarded as law-makers. The common law and equity, both of them in essence systems of private law, are fields where, subject to the increasing intrusion of statute law, society has been content to allow the judges to formulate and develop the law. The judges, even in this, their very own field of creative endeavour, have accepted, in the interests of certainty, the self-denying ordinance of 'stare decisis,' the doctrine of binding precedent: and no doubt this judicially imposed limitation on judicial law-making has helped to maintain confidence in the certainty and evenhandedness of the law.

But in the field of statute law the judge must be obedient to the will of Parliament as expressed in its enactments. In this field Parliament makes, and un-makes, the law: the judge's duty is to interpret and to apply the law, not to change it to meet the judge's idea of what justice requires. Interpretation does, of course, imply in the interpreter a power of choice where differing constructions are possible. But our law requires the judge to choose the construction which in his judgment best meets the legislative purpose of the enactment. If the result be unjust but inevitable, the judge may say so and invite Parliament to reconsider its provision. But he must not deny the statute. Unpalatable statute law may not be disregarded or rejected, merely because it is unpalatable. Only if a just result can be achieved without violating the legislative purpose of the statute may the judge select the construction which best suits his idea of what justice requires. Further, in our system the rule 'stare decisis' applies as firmly to statute law as it does to the formulation of common law and equitable principles. And the keystone of 'stare decisis' is loyalty throughout the system to the decisions of the Court of Appeal and this House. The Court of Appeal may not overrule a House of Lords decision: and only in the exceptional circumstances set out in the Practice Statement of July 1, 1966 (*Practice Statement (Judicial Precedent)* [1966] 1 WLR 1234), will this House refuse to follow its own previous decisions.

Within these limits, which cannot be said in a free society possessing elective legislative institutions to be narrow or constrained, judges, as the remarkable judicial career of Lord Denning himself shows, have a genuine creative role. Great judges are in their different ways judicial activists. But the constitution's separation of powers, or more accurately functions, must be observed if judicial independence is not to be put at risk. For, if people and Parliament come to think that the judicial power is to be confined by nothing other than the judge's sense of what is right (or, as Selden put it, by the length of the Chancellor's foot), confidence in the judicial system will be replaced by fear of it becoming uncertain and arbitrary in its application. Society will then be ready for Parliament to cut the power of the judges. Their power to do justice will become more restricted by law than it need be, or is today.

Appeal allowed.

R v *Her Majesty's Treasury, ex parte Smedley*
[1985] 1 QB 657, Court of Appeal

SIR JOHN DONALDSON MR: . . . I think that I should say a word about the respective roles of Parliament and the courts. Although the United Kingdom has no written constitution, it is a constitutional convention of the highest importance that the legislature and the judicature are separate and independent of one another, subject to certain ultimate rights of Parliament over the judicature which are immaterial for present purposes. It therefore behoves the courts to be ever sensitive to the paramount need to refrain from trespassing upon the province of Parliament or, so far as this can be avoided, even appearing to do so. Although it is not a matter for me, I would hope and expect that Parliament would be similarly sensitive to the need to refrain from trespassing upon the province of the courts.

NOTE: In the long-running debate preceding the enactment of the Human Rights Act 1998 (see Chapter 7), the issue of separation of powers, particularly the relationship between Parliament and the courts, was a recurrent theme. The respective roles of Parliament and the courts following the Act coming into force in October 2000 have been articulated by Lord Irvine of Lairg, the Lord Chancellor, on a number of occasions.

Lord Irvine of Lairg LC, 'Constitutional Reform and a Bill of Rights'
[1997] *European Human Rights Law Review* 483

The British Constitution is firmly based on the separation of powers. It is essential that incorporation is achieved in a way which does nothing to disturb that balance. It is for Parliament to pass laws, not the judges. It is for the judges to interpret these laws and to develop the common law, not for Parliament or the executive. It is also for the courts to ensure that the powers conferred by Parliament on the executive and other bodies are neither exceeded nor abused but exercised lawfully. That will continue to be so after the European Convention becomes part of our domestic law.

Incorporation will enhance the judges' powers to protect the individual against the abuse of power by the State. We have a high quality of judicial review in this country. It has often rightly held the executive to account and improved the quality of administrative decision making. So the concept of judges protecting the citizen and holding the executive to account is nothing new. What is new is that the judges will be given a framework by Parliament within which to interpret the law.

Incorporating basic human rights into our domestic law will be a major new departure. It will offer new challenges. What is critical is that the form of incorporation sits comfortably with our United Kingdom institutions. It must not disturb the supremacy of Parliament. It should not put the judges in a position where they are seen as at odds with Parliament. That would be a recipe for conflict and mutual recrimination. It is vital that the courts should not become involved in a process of policy evaluation which goes far beyond its allotted constitutional role. In a democratic society, compromises between competing interests must be resolved by Parliament – or if Parliament so decides, by Ministers.

NOTE: The form of incorporation which has been adopted will not permit the courts to strike down or disapply legislation which is incompatible with the European Convention on Human Rights. This contrasts with the position arising from our membership of the European Community. As a result of s. 2(4) of the European Communities Act 1972, courts have acquired the power to disapply legislation which is inconsistent with EC law (see *R* v *Secretary of State for Transport, ex parte Factortame Ltd (No. 2)* [1991] 1 AC 603, at p. 90 below).

QUESTION

If separation of powers as expressed by Montesquieu does not exist, is there nevertheless sufficient separation of functions and a sufficient incidence of checks and balances to guarantee the maintenance of liberty?

SECTION 6: **The State**

The next idea to consider in this chapter is the state. Wade and Bradley in *Constitutional and Administrative Law* (1985), p. 3, state that 'constitutional law concerns the relationship between the individual and the state, seen from a particular viewpoint, namely the notion of law. . . . Law is not merely a matter of the rules which govern relations between private individuals. . . . Law concerns the structure and powers of the state'. If we are to examine the ambit of constitutional law in the United Kingdom, we need to have some notion of what the state is.

C. F. Strong, *Modern Political Constitutions*
(1972), pp. 4–5

[T]he state is something more than a mere collection of families, or an agglomeration of occupational organisation, or a referee holding the ring between the conflicting interests of the voluntary associations which it permits to exist. In a properly organized political community the state exists for society and not society for the state; yet, however socially advanced a people may be, the society which it constitutes – made up of families, clubs, churches, trade unions, etc. – is not to be trusted to maintain itself without the ultimate arbitrament of force.

All associations make rules and regulations for their conduct, and when men are associated politically these rules and regulations are called laws, the power to make these being the prerogative of the state and of no other association. Thus, in the words of R M MacIver, a 'state is the fundamental association for the maintenance and development of social order, and to this end its central institution is endowed with the united power of the community.' But this definition might conceivably cover a pastoral or nomadic society which, indeed, found a bond of union in the patriarch or head of the family who, in some sort, discharged the powers of government. Such a society, however, lacks territoriality, an indispensable condition of true political organization, a condition emphasized by H J W Hetherington when he says: 'The state is the institution or set of institutions which, in order to secure certain elementary common purposes and conditions of life, unites under a single authority the inhabitants of a clearly-marked territorial area.' But what is this 'united power of the community' in the first, this 'single authority' in the second definition? It is the power or authority to make law. So we come to the definition given by Woodrow Wilson: 'A state is a people organized for law within a definite territory.'

S. E. Finer, *Comparative Government*
(1970), p. 24

The defining characteristics of a state . . . are: (1) It is a territorially defined association. (2) It embraces, compulsorily, all the persons in that territory. (3) It possesses the monopoly of violence throughout this area, by virtue of which it has the capacity, even if not the moral authority, to guarantee the finality of its decision in political disputes arising from the conflict of individuals or groups within its territory. (4) As a necessary accompaniment of all this, it has a body of persons who exercise this monopoly of violence in its name, namely, the common government.

R. Miliband, *The State in Capitalist Society*
(1969), pp. 49–54

There is one preliminary problem about the state which is very seldom considered, yet which requires attention if the discussion of its nature and role is to be properly focused. This is the fact that 'the state' is not a thing, that it does not, as such, exist. What 'the state' stands for is a number of particular institutions which, together, constitute its reality, and which interact as parts of what may be called the state system.

The point is by no means academic. For the treatment of one part of the state – usually the government – as the state itself introduces a major element of confusion in the discussion of the nature and incidence of state *power*; and that confusion can have large political consequences. Thus, if it is believed that the government is in fact the state, it may also be believed that the assumption of governmental power is equivalent to the acquisition of state power. Such a belief, resting as it does on vast assumptions about the nature of state power, is fraught with great risks and disappointments. To understand the nature of state power, it is necessary first of all to distinguish, and then to relate, the various elements which make up the state system.

It is not very surprising that government and state should often appear as synonymous for it is the government which speaks on the state's behalf. It was the state to which Weber was referring when he said, in a famous phrase, that, in order to be, it must 'successfully claim the monopoly of the legitimate use of physical force within a given territory'. But 'the state' cannot claim anything: only the government of the day, or its duly empowered agents, can. Men, it is often said, give their allegiance not to the government of the day but to the state. But the state, from this point of view, is a nebulous entity; and while men may choose to give their allegiance to it, it is to the government that they are required to give their obedience. A defiance of its orders is a defiance of the state, in whose name the government alone may speak and for whose actions it must assume ultimate responsibility. . . .

A second element of the state system which requires investigation is the administrative one, which now extends far beyond the traditional bureaucracy of the state, and which encompasses a large variety of bodies, often related to particular ministerial departments, or enjoying a greater or lesser degree of autonomy – public corporations, central banks, regulatory commissions, etc. – and concerned with the management of the economic, social, cultural and other activities in which the state is now directly or indirectly involved. The extraordinary growth of this administrative and bureaucratic element in all societies, including advanced capitalist ones, is of course one of the most obvious features of contemporary life; and the relation of its leading members to the government and to society is also crucial to the determination of the role of the state.

Formally, officialdom is at the service of the political executive, its obedient instrument, the tool of its will. In actual fact it is nothing of the kind. Everywhere and inevitably the administrative process is also part of the political process; administration is always political as well as executive, at least at the levels where policy-making is relevant, that is to say in the upper layers of administrative life. . . . Officials and administrators cannot divest themselves of all ideological clothing in the advice which they tender to their political masters, or in the independent decisions which they are in a position to take. The power which top civil servants and other state administrators possess no doubt varies from country to country, from department to department, and from individual to individual. But nowhere do these men *not* contribute directly and appreciably to the exercise of state power. . . .

Some of these considerations apply to all other elements of the state system. They apply for instance to a third such element, namely the military, to which may, for present purposes, be added the para-military, security and police forces of the state, and which together form that branch of it mainly concerned with the 'management of violence'.

In most capitalist countries, this coercive apparatus constitutes a vast, sprawling and resourceful establishment, whose professional leaders are men of high status and great influence, inside the state system and in society. . . .

Whatever may be the case in practice, the formal constitutional position of the administrative and coercive elements is to serve the state by serving the government of the day. In contrast, it is not at all the formal constitutional duty of judges, at least in Western-type political systems, to serve the purposes of their governments. They are constitutionally independent of the political executive and protected from it by security of tenure and other guarantees. Indeed, the concept of judicial independence is deemed to entail not merely the freedom of judges from responsibility to the political executive, but their active duty to protect the citizen *against* the political executive or its agents, and to act, in the state's encounter with members of society, as the defenders of the latter's rights and liberties. . . . But in any case, the judiciary is an integral part of the state system, which affects, often profoundly, the exercise of state power.

So too, to a greater or lesser degree, does a fifth element of the state system, namely the various units of sub-central government. In one of its aspects, sub-central government constitutes an extension of central government and administration, the latter's antennae or tentacles. In some political systems it has indeed practically no other function. In the countries of advanced capitalism, on the other hand, sub-central government is rather more than an administrative device. In addition to being agents of the state these units of government have also traditionally performed another function. They have not only been the channels of communication and administration from the centre to the periphery, but also the voice of the periphery, or of particular interests at the periphery; they have been a means of overcoming local particularities, but also platforms for their expression, instruments of central control and obstacles to it. For all the centralisation of power, which is a major feature of government in these countries, sub-central organs of government . . . have remained power structures in their own right, and therefore able to affect very markedly the lives of the populations they have governed.

Much the same point may be made about the representative assemblies of advanced capitalism. Now more than ever their life revolves around the government; and even where, as in the United States, they are formally independent organs of constitutional and political power, their relationship with the political executive cannot be a purely critical or obstructive one. That relationship is one of conflict *and* cooperation.

Nor is this a matter of division between a pro-government side and an anti-government one. *Both* sides reflect this duality. For opposition parties cannot be wholly uncooperative. Merely by taking part in the work of the legislature, they help the government's business.

As for government parties, they are seldom if ever single-minded in their support of the political executive and altogether subservient to it. They include people who, by virtue of their position and influence must be persuaded, cajoled, threatened or bought off.

It is in the constitutionally-sanctioned performance of this cooperative and critical function that legislative assemblies have a share in the exercise of state power. That share is rather less extensive and exalted than is often claimed for these bodies. But . . . it is not, even in an epoch of executive dominance, an unimportant one.

QUESTION

Is the Government the State, or is it an institution or servant of the State? See the cases which follow.

D v *National Society for the Prevention of Cruelty to Children*
[1978] AC 171, House of Lords

The mother of a child (alleged by an informant to be the victim of ill-treatment) brought an action against the NSPCC for damages for nervous shock alleged to be the result of the society's investigation pursuant to the informant's complaint. The mother sought discovery of the identity of the informant. The NSPCC, an independent body incorporated by royal charter, claimed 'public interest immunity' as justifying its refusal to disclose the identity of its informants. The mother argued that the society could not rely on this defence as it was not part of the State.

LORD SIMON OF GLAISDALE: . . . '[T]he state' cannot on any sensible political theory be restricted to the Crown and the departments of central government (which are, indeed, part of the Crown in constitutional law). The state is the whole organisation of the body politic for supreme civil rule and government – the whole political organisation which is the basis of civil government. As such it certainly extends to local – and, as I think, also statutory – bodies in so far as they are exercising autonomous rule.

Chandler v *Director of Public Prosecutions*
[1964] AC 763, House of Lords

The appellants, in seeking to further the aims of the Campaign for Nuclear Disarmament, entered and sought to immobilize an airfield. The airfield was a 'prohibited place' under s. 3 of the Official Secrets Act 1911. The appellants were charged with conspiracy to commit a breach of s. 1 of the Act, whereby it is an offence to enter any prohibited place 'for any purpose prejudicial to the safety or interests of the State'. The appellants argued that their actions were not prejudicial to the safety or interests of the State, but rather it was their belief that their actions would be beneficial to the state. They further argued that 'State' means the numerical collection of inhabitants in the geographical area and not the Government or organs of government through which the State expresses its intentions.

LORD REID: . . . Next comes the question of what is meant by the safety or interests of the State. 'State' is not an easy word. It does not mean the Government or the Executive. 'L'Etat c'est moi' was a shrewd remark, but can hardly have been intended as a definition even in the France of the time. And I do not think that it means, as counsel argued, the individuals who inhabit these islands. The statute cannot be referring to the interests of all those individuals because they may differ and the interests of the majority are not necessarily the same as the interests of the State. Again we have seen only too clearly in some other countries what can happen if you personify and almost deify the State. Perhaps the country or the realm are as good synonyms as one can find and I would be prepared to accept the organised community as coming as near to a definition as one can get.

LORD DEVLIN: . . . What is meant by 'the State'? Is it the same thing as what I have just called 'the country'? Mr Foster, for the appellants, submits that it means the inhabitants of a particular geographical area. I doubt if it ever has as wide a meaning as that. I agree that in an appropriate context the safety and interests of the State might mean simply the public or national safety and interests. But the more precise use of the word 'State,' the use to be expected in a legal context, and the one which I am quite satisfied . . . was intended in this statute, is to denote the organs of government of a national community. In the United Kingdom, in relation at any rate to the armed forces and to the defence of the realm, that organ is the Crown. So long as the Crown maintains armed forces for the defence of the realm, it cannot be in its interest that any part of them should be immobilised.

LORD PEARCE: . . . I cannot accept the argument that the words 'the interests of the State' in this context mean the interests of the amorphous populace, without regard to the guiding policies of those in authority, and that proof of possible ultimate benefit to the populace may for the purposes of the Act justify an act of spying or sabotage. The protection covers certain specified places which are obviously vital to defence and other places to which the Secretary of State sees fit to extend the protection. . . . Parliament clearly intended to give stringent protection to such places. It is hard to believe that it intended to withhold that protection in all cases where a jury might think that the place in question was not necessary or desirable or where the authorities could not by evidence justify their policies to a jury's satisfaction. Questions of defence policy are vast, complicated, confidential, and wholly unsuited for ventilation before a jury. In such a context the interests of the State must in my judgment mean the interests of the State according to the policies laid down for it by its recognised organs of government and authority, the policies of the State as they are, not as they ought, in the opinion of a jury, to be. Anything which prejudices those policies is within the meaning of the Act 'prejudicial to the interests of the State.'

QUESTIONS

1. In the trial of Clive Ponting the judge directed the jury that the phrase 'in the interests of the State' in s. 2 of the Official Secrets Act 1911 means 'in the interests of the Government of the day'. This view was supported by the Attorney-General, Sir Michael Havers, in a speech in the House of Commons, but was contested by Lord Denning in a speech in the House of Lords. Who was correct? See Barker, below.

2. If the 'government' is synonymous with the 'State', does this have any consequences for ideas such as constitutionalism and limited government? See Barker, below.

3. If the government determines the interests of the State, does this harbour any threat to individual liberty?

R. Barker, *Political Legitimacy and the State*
(1990), pp. 183–184

The Ponting case also illustrates the ways in which the legitimacy of the state may be threatened if any of its various temporary governors act in a way which breaks down the distinction between state and government, and by wrapping the acts of particular governments in the flag of the state, make it impossible to attack one without assaulting the other. A distinction between the state, as the institution which carries on the function of government, and the government as the politicians currently in office, makes it possible to oppose policies without denying legitimacy, or even to challenge the legitimacy of particular ministerial procedures, without confronting the constitution as a whole. When that distinction is eroded, so is the possibility of loyal opposition. Thus a state whose institutions appear to be newly absorbed or influenced by the partisan considerations of government is likely to suffer erosion of legitimacy whenever it is challenged on a particular point. But so long as the distinction remains, disaffection in so far as it appeals to existing principles of legitimacy, can be both conservative and loyal. Vivienne Hart has pointed out how many actions, of which she takes populism as her example, which have been presented as subversive of government, are in fact defensive of the constitution in general against the constitutionally subversive, or supposed constitutionally subversive actions of particular governments and politicians.

The view that states imperil their own legitimacy when they offend their own subjects' conservative conceptions of constitutionality is found more amongst other academic students of politics than amongst political scientists themselves. Patrick McAuslan and John McEldowney write of the contribution to disaffection throughout western Europe of what they term the gap 'between on the one hand the rhetoric of democracy, of even-handed administration, and of equal opportunities for all, and on the other the increasing centralization and insensitivity of public administration'. Resistance to government can rest on support for the constitution. It is both 'the response of ordinary people to trends in government practices which seem to them to be, in perhaps indefinable ways, wrong' and a preference for 'the theory of what the constitution ought to be to the practice of what it is'. Much that appears as rejection of the legitimacy of the state is in fact quite the reverse. Moreover because the forms and principles of legitimacy present at any one time are likely to be varied, it is not simply a case of appealing to principles against practices, but can also be a matter of appealing against practices justified by one form of legitimacy to alternative practices justified by other principles.

SECTION 7: **Constitutional Reform**

The issue of constitutional reform was hotly debated for much of the last half of the twentieth century. Gradually a shift occurred as a realization dawned on many in positions of influence that all things British are not necessarily perfect and our constitutional arrangements are no exception. The two extracts which follow highlight the defects in our constitutional arrangements which resulted in the demand for reform. The first is an analysis from an academic public lawyer while the second is a call for reform from an independent campaigning organization which launched a public appeal for a new constitutional settlement in 1988.

John F. McEldowney, *Public Law*
(1998), pp. 768–773

Demands for a written constitution have come from the Liberal Democrats ['*We the people* . . .' – *Towards a Written Constitution* (1990)], the Institute of Public Policy Research [*The Constitution of the United Kingdom* (1991)] and from Charter 88. Prominent constitutional lawyers have called for a written constitution, most notably Lord Scarman ['Bill of Rights and Law Reform' in Holme and Elliott, *1688–1988: Time for a New Constitution* (1988), pp. 103–111] and Lord Hailsham, though the latter has been less enthusiastic in recent years. In recent years an increasing body of intellectual opinion has favoured constitutional reform from political thinkers on both the left and the right in politics. However, contemporary writing of the 1980s and 90s is reminiscent of writing in the 1970s and even past diagnosis of the post-war period. Oliver has identified [*Government in the United Kingdom* (1991), pp. 3–40] a number of factors which may have created pressure for reform and may be summarised as follows.

The post-war consensus over the range of activities carried out by the public sector has come under the strain. Polarisation of the two major political parties has contributed to marked differences in attitudes to the public sector. The election of Mrs Thatcher's Government in 1979 and four successive Conservative Party election victories thereafter have allowed many fundamental changes to be introduced into the delivery of public services. Privatisation is also relevant in the trend away from State ownership in favour of Public Company Act companies for the delivery of public services. Market forces and the consumer are perceived as satisfactory regulators of public services with the minimum of direct State intervention.

Changes in policy perceptions in the early 1980s about the role of local government have created tensions in the relationship between central and local government. The trend in favour of more centralised power has encouraged stronger central government as preferable to weak local authorities. . . . At the same time discontent over the United Kingdom's constitutional arrangements argue for reform and some go as far as to include a written constitution.

Supporters of constitutional reform highlight the weaknesses in parliamentary control over the Executive as evidenced by the accretion of centralised governmental power. In the aftermath of a period of strong government with large overall majorities, electoral reform is favoured, linked to the need for a fairer balance in the composition of the House of Commons.

There is also criticism on how the Cabinet form of government decision-making operates. This relates to the view that the Cabinet is not able to make longer term strategic plans. . . . It is argued that the Cabinet system of government needs reform. Oliver noted :

> Neither the Cabinet as a whole nor ministers individually have the support of staff that could enable them to take a strategic view of government policy, or indeed of the policy in their own departments.

During the life cycle of party politics the style and perception of government may differ, very often according to the personality of the Prime Minister. However, to some commentators, weaknesses in the institutions of the government such as the Cabinet system are apparent and suggest that reforms should be introduced.

The ethos of governmental secrecy is also perceived as a major weakness in the system of parliamentary accountability. This is said to limit the amount of information available on the administration of government and allows government too much flexibility in deciding on the ground rules which apply to its decisions. The temptation is to see secrecy, as supported by the law, as self-serving the interests of government in its political objectives rather than serving the interests of Parliament. The quality of government decision-making is said to suffer from the lack of transparency in government consultation and discussion. . . . Demanding greater openness in government may not necessarily increase Parliament's role in holding government to account for its actions.

Centralisation is said to cause pressure on the efficiency and effectiveness of government because the system of Cabinet decision-making suffers from 'overload.' This phenomenon is not confined to the government but may be found in the various parliamentary methods of accountability such as select committees, debates on the passage of Bills and the scrutiny of government legislation. The tendency is that back-bench MPs may become overworked and inefficient. . . . Doubts about the present institutional resources of Parliament to scrutinise the Executive have a long history of reluctance on the part of the government of the day to accept criticism or make amendments to Bills in response to back-bench concerns.

The case for reform of the House of Lords is also made out by the desire to improve accountability, effectiveness and improve the representative nature of the upper chamber. Reform of the House of Lords, while acceptable as a means of improving democratic accountability, is limited to the extent that it may not alter the historical political balance in favour of the Conservative Party and is in any event difficult to achieve. . . .

The case for the introduction of some form of devolution is also taken to justify a written constitution. Devolution, as a response to nationalism in Scotland and Wales in the late 1970s, may also be seen as a means to decentralise central government powers. . . .

The interest and attention given to a written constitution also arises through concern that a Bill of Rights might best be delivered through the mechanism of a Constitution setting out the allocation of functions between the legislature, the Executive and the judiciary. The diagnosis that existing arrangements for the protection of the citizen are weak and ineffectual are a reflection of factors that may contribute to weakness in our Constitution. Government is entitled to use its parliamentary majority to enact laws but those laws may infringe individual rights. There is little opportunity in such circumstances for the courts to do anything other than give effect to Parliament's authority.

The arguments against a Bill of Rights such as mistrust of judicial power, concern over the doctrine of parliamentary sovereignty, and the question of how adequately to entrench the enactment of a Bill of Rights against possible revocation, may be answered by the adoption of a written constitution.

The arguments against adopting a written constitution emphasise the flexibility inherent in existing arrangements. The tradition of an unwritten constitution has reinforced the supremacy of Parliament in both the narrow legal sense, and in the broader sense of political majoritarian government. Change may be accomplished without any general rethink of the constitutional arrangements. Adaptation may be seen as part of an organic growth unhindered by the restraint of a constitutional requirement to give the judiciary a final say in any change. The virtues of the present system must not be overlooked even if it is desirable to consider reforms. It is often conceded that many of the reforms mentioned above may be enacted without a written constitution. The strengths of a flexible unwritten constitution may be found in the primacy given to the political process. This may be weakened by entrenching in a written constitution those matters currently governed by convention or political choices. A written constitution might mark a shift from political decision-making to judicial scrutiny which may be too narrow and restrictive of the political choices on offer to the electorate.

Charter 88, 'A Written Constitution'

(http://www.charter88.org.uk)

A written Constitution

Where does it say what the government can and cannot do? Nowhere. There are no written rules. This is how Britain is governed.

Unwritten rules are dangerous

There are laws, rules and principles that define powers and rights in our society – and these, effectively, are our constitution. But these rules and principles are not written down in one place. They've evolved in a haphazard way through centuries of custom and practice, so they're buried in hundreds of years of legal judgments.

And this situation causes problems. Unwritten rules are too easy to change, particularly when power is concentrated in one place: the 'Crown in Parliament', or in practice, the government of the day.

Because we have no written constitution, governments can and do pass laws that restrict our rights. They can transfer power from elected bodies to unelected appointees. They can chip away at local democracy. They can act in secret and Parliament is powerless to call them to account. We've seen it happen.

A new contract

A constitution sets out the relationship between us, as individuals, and the state that governs in our name. It defines the powers of the state and its agencies: national, regional and local government, the judges and the lawmakers. It specifies who can do what, and what the limits of their powers are.

We need a new written constitution to modernise our democracy. To give citizens positive rights in law, to make government as open and accountable as possible, to share power between different political institutions, and to set out a new and fairer system of voting.

Limits on power

With a clear statement of what governments can and cannot do in law, we stand on firmer ground to challenge abuses of power.

A new written constitution will help to create a system of checks and balances. Power will no longer be concentrated in one place. Governments, when they pass legislation, will have to answer to an authority other than the parliament they may control. Minorities will have protection from the possible oppression of a parliamentary majority. Individuals will know when the state or its agencies have overstepped the limits of their authority.

Citizens not subjects

- Our constitution must be accessible. Every citizen should know what her or his rights are. Everyone should be able to find out who has the authority to do what. Everyone must be able to understand it, not just legal experts.
- Our constitution must belong to the people. When there are disputes about what is constitutional, a new court could arbitrate – one that includes lay members as well as judges.
- Our constitution must stand above party politics and above the laws that governments pass. Amendments could only be made in clearly defined circumstances and with overwhelming support – such as a two-thirds majority in a reformed Parliament, or after a citizens' referendum.

. . .

In a modern democracy, there need to be some hard and fast rules about what our governments can and cannot do. About the limits of state authority. About the rights of individuals, and about how citizens can participate in the government of our country. We need a written constitution to make these rules clear.

NOTE: Following its election in May 1997, the New Labour Government embarked on a programme of constitutional reform which included devolution for Scotland, Wales, and Northern Ireland (see Scotland Act 1998, Wales Act 1998, and Northern Ireland Act 1988), the incorporation of the European Convention on Human Rights into domestic law (see Human Rights Act 1998), the publication of a White Paper, *Your Right to Know*, on freedom of information, followed by a Freedom of Information Act 2000, the removal of the right of hereditary peers to sit in the House of Lords (House of Lords Act 1999), and a promise to address the issue of regional assemblies in England and to set up an Electoral Commission to consider electoral reform.

QUESTIONS

1. Will these reforms simply paper over the cracks in our constitutional arrangements, leaving a number of the systemic problems to resurface in the future; or do they represent a major root and branch reform equivalent to a new constitutional settlement?

2. On 5 March 1997, the Labour and Liberal Democrat Joint Consultative Committee on Constitutional Reform published its Report which specified the following objectives which the constitution should serve: 'to secure a government that is democratic and a society that is open and free . . . [in which] each individual citizen should have equal rights and responsibilities . . . [and] the aim is to guarantee civil liberty, social cohesion and economic opportunity'. Will the programme of reform on which New Labour embarked achieve these objectives?

3. In *This Time: Our Constitutional Revolution* (1997) Anthony Barnett, the founding Director of Charter 88, states (at p. 6):

   The need for a written constitution is more important now that Britain has a government that is altering the unwritten one so radically. The new Labour reforms . . . are partial measures. Will they democratise power in an impartial and principled way, or are they designed to gerrymander it, as the opposition claims? Might they prove to be concessions that uphold the existing system, rather than moves towards the 'new constitutional settlement' which Tony Blair called for when he campaigned to become Labour leader?'

   Compare your response to these questions now with that when you have completed your course on constitutional law.

4. At p. 8 (*op. cit.*) Barnett states:

   A written constitution cannot prevent abuses and corruption if that is what those in power wish. . . . But it can help to combat such abuses. . . . [T]he American judge Justice Learned Hand said, 'Liberty lives in the hearts and minds of men. When it dies then no constitution, no laws can save it.' This famous caution should be the starting point for every constitution. Such documents are not solutions or panaceas. . . . The justification for writing down a British constitution is, negatively, to limit if not eliminate the corruption and incompetence of the old system, and, positively, to renew and greatly expand the indigenous spirit of liberty and democracy.

Do you agree?

NOTE: The issues considered in this chapter have been, to a certain extent, theoretical. They are, however, issues of continuing relevance to any study of the constitution of the United Kingdom. Questions which it is worth keeping in mind when reading the remaining chapters in this book would be the following:

(a) To what extent is the doctrine of constitutionalism respected in the United Kingdom?

(b) To what extent does the principle of legitimacy inform constitutional debate?

(c) Is the principle of limited government respected? To what extent is government made accountable by (i) Parliament, (ii) the electorate, and (iii) the courts?

(d) Will the Labour Government's programme of constitutional reform provide sufficient protection for fundamental rights in face of the competing claims of the 'majoritarian principle'?

(e) Does the absence of a clear concept of the State, separate and distinguishable from government, prejudice individual rights?

2

The Legislative Supremacy of Parliament

NOTE: The doctrine of 'the legislative supremacy of Parliament' is often referred to as 'parliamentary sovereignty'. 'Sovereignty' is a word open to misunderstanding and one that is used in the sphere of international law (for example, the dispute with Argentina over the sovereignty of the Falkland Islands), and also in the political arena (for example, there is considerable rhetoric on sovereignty in the debates on the United Kingdom's membership of the European Community and on subsequent issues such as the Single European Act 1986 and European Monetary Union). To avoid confusion with these ideas, the terms 'legislative supremacy of Parliament' or 'parliamentary supremacy' will be used. These terms have the virtue that they express clearly the central legal concept of the doctrine – that is, that under our constitutional arrangements Parliament is legislatively supreme. In the extracts from cases and other materials which follow, where the term 'sovereignty' is used, the judges or writers are using it in the sense of 'supremacy'.

SECTION 1: **The Legislative Supremacy of Parliament as a 'Rule of Recognition'**

Part of the function of Parliament is to make laws, which it does by enacting statutes. These laws impose obligations on citizens, and obedience to these obligations is enforced by the courts. Why is a particular statute regarded as valid? Why do courts apply the law as declared in statutes and enforce their provisions? Whence does Parliament derive this power to make law?

H. L. A. Hart, *The Concept of Law*
(1961), pp. 89–107

The Elements of Law
It is, of course, possible to imagine a society without a legislature, courts or officials of any kind. Indeed, there are many studies of primitive communities which not only claim that this possibility is realized but depict in detail the life of a society where the only means of social control is that general attitude of the group towards its own standard modes of behaviour in terms of which we have characterized rules of obligation. . . . [W]e shall refer to such a social structure as one of primary rules of obligation. If a society is to live by such primary rules alone, there are certain conditions which, granted a few of the most obvious truisms about human nature and the world we live in, must clearly be satisfied. The first of these conditions is that the rules must contain in some form restrictions on the free use of violence, theft, and deception to which human beings are tempted but which

they must, in general, repress, if they are to coexist in close proximity to each other. . . . Secondly, though such a society may exhibit the tension, already described, between those who accept the rules and those who reject the rules except where fear of social pressure induces them to conform, it is plain that the latter cannot be more than a minority, if so loosely organized a society of persons, approximately equal in physical strength, is to endure: for otherwise those who reject the rules would have too little social pressure to fear. . . .

It is plain that only a small community closely knit by ties of kinship, common sentiment, and belief, and placed in a stable environment, could live successfully by such a régime of unofficial rules. In any other conditions such a simple form of social control must prove defective and will require supplementation in different ways. In the first place, the rules by which the group lives will not form a system, but will simply be a set of separate standards, without any identifying or common mark, except of course that they are the rules which a particular group of human beings accepts. They will in this respect resemble our own rules of etiquette. Hence if doubts arise as to what the rules are or as to the precise scope of some given rule, there will be no procedure for settling this doubt, either by reference to an authoritative text or to an official whose declarations on this point are authoritative. For, plainly, such a procedure and the acknowledgement of either authoritative text or persons involve the existence of rules of a type different from the rules of obligation or duty which *ex hypothesi* are all that the group has. This defect in the simple social structure of primary rules we may call its *uncertainty*.

A second defect is the *static* character of the rules. The only mode of change in the rules known to such a society will be the slow process of growth, whereby courses of conduct once thought optional become first habitual or usual, and then obligatory, and the converse process of decay, when deviations, once severely dealt with, are first tolerated and then pass unnoticed. There will be no means, in such a society, of deliberately adapting the rules to changing circumstances, either by eliminating old rules or introducing new ones: for, again, the possibility of doing this presupposes the existence of rules of a different type from the primary rules of obligation by which alone the society lives. . . .

The third defect of this simple form of social life is the *inefficiency* of the diffuse social pressure by which the rules are maintained. Disputes as to whether an admitted rule has or has not been violated will always occur and will, in any but the smallest societies, continue interminably, if there is no agency specially empowered to ascertain finally, and authoritatively, the fact of violation. . . .

The remedy for each of these three main defects in this simplest form of social structure consists in supplementing the *primary* rules of obligation with *secondary* rules which are rules of a different kind. The introduction of the remedy for each defect might, in itself, be considered a step from the pre-legal into the legal world; since each remedy brings with it many elements that permeate law: certainly all three remedies together are enough to convert the régime of primary rules into what is indisputably a legal system. . . .

The simplest form of remedy for the *uncertainty* of the régime of primary rules is the introduction of what we shall call a 'rule of recognition'. This will specify some feature or features possession of which by a suggested rule is taken as a conclusive affirmative indication that it is a rule of the group to be supported by the social pressure it exerts. The existence of such a rule of recognition may take any of a huge variety of forms, simple or complex. It may, as in the early law of many societies, be no more than that an authoritative list or text of the rules is to be found in a written document or carved on some public monument. . . .

In a developed legal system the rules of recognition are of course more complex; instead of identifying rules exclusively by reference to a text or list they do so by reference to some general characteristic possessed by the primary rules. This may be the fact of their having been enacted by a specific body, or their long customary practice, or their relation to judicial decisions. Moreover, where more than one of such general characteristics are treated as identifying criteria, provision may be made for their possible conflict by their arrangement in an order of superiority, as by the common subordination of custom or precedent to statute, the latter being a 'superior source' of law. . . . [E]ven in this simplest form, such a rule brings with it many elements distinctive of law. By providing an authoritative mark it introduces, although in embryonic form, the idea of a legal system: for the rules are now not just a discrete unconnected set but are, in a simple way, unified. Further, in the simple operation of identifying a given rule as possessing the required feature of being an item on an authoritative list of rules we have the germ of the idea of legal validity.

The remedy for the *static* quality of the régime of primary rules consists in the introduction of what we shall call 'rules of change'. The simplest form of such a rule is that which empowers an individual or body of persons to introduce new primary rules for the conduct of the life of the group, or of some class within it, and to eliminate old rules. . . . [I]t is in terms of such a rule, and not in terms of orders backed by threats, that the ideas of legislative enactment and repeal are to be understood. Such rules of change may be very simple or very complex: the powers conferred may be unrestricted or limited in various ways: and the rules may, besides specifying the persons who are to legislate, define in more or less rigid terms the procedure to be followed in legislation. Plainly, there will be a very close connexion between the rules of change and the rules of recognition: for where the former exists the latter will necessarily incorporate a reference to legislation as an identifying feature of the rules, though it need not refer to all the details of procedure involved in legislation. Usually some official certificate or official copy will, under the rules of recognition, be taken as a sufficient proof of due enactment. Of course if there is a social structure so simple that the only 'source of law' is legislation, the rule of recognition will simply specify enactment as the unique identifying mark or criterion of validity of the rules. . . .

The third supplement to the simple régime of primary rules, intended to remedy the *inefficiency* of its diffused social pressure, consists of secondary rules empowering individuals to make authoritative determinations of the question whether, on a particular occasion, a primary rule has been broken. The minimal form of adjudication consists in such determinations, and we shall call the secondary rules which confer the power to make them 'rules of adjudication'. Besides identifying the individuals who are to adjudicate, such rules will also define the procedure to be followed. Like the other secondary rules these are on a different level from the primary rules: though they may be reinforced by further rules imposing duties on judges to adjudicate, they do not impose duties but confer judicial powers and a special status on judicial declarations about the breach of obligations. Again these rules, like the other secondary rules, define a group of important legal concepts: in this case the concepts of judge or court, jurisdiction and judgment. Besides these resemblances to the other secondary rules, rules of adjudication have intimate connexions with them. Indeed, a system which has rules of adjudication is necessarily also committed to a rule of recognition of an elementary and imperfect sort. This is so because, if courts are empowered to make authoritative determinations of the fact that a rule has been broken, these cannot avoid being taken as authoritative determinations of what the rules are. So the rule which confers jurisdiction will also be a rule of recognition, identifying the primary rules through the judgments of the courts and these judgments will become a 'source' of law. . . .

If we stand back and consider the structure which has resulted from the combination of primary rules of obligation with the secondary rules of recognition, change and adjudication, it is plain that we have here not only the heart of a legal system, but a most powerful tool for the analysis of much that has puzzled both the jurist and the political theorist. . . .

Rule of Recognition and Legal Validity
In a modern legal system where there are a variety of 'sources' of law, the rule of recognition is . . . complex: the criteria for identifying the law are multiple and commonly include a written constitution, enactment by a lesiglature, and judicial precedents. In most cases, provision is made for possible conflict by ranking these criteria in an order of relative subordination and primacy. It is in this way that in our system 'common law' is subordinate to 'statute'. . . .

In the day-to-day life of a legal system its rule of recognition is very seldom expressly formulated as a rule; though occasionally, courts in England may announce in general terms the relative place of one criterion of law in relation to another, as when they assert the supremacy of Acts of Parliament over other sources or suggested sources of law. For the most part the rule of recognition is not stated, but its existence is *shown* in the way in which particular rules are identified, either by courts or other officials or private persons or their advisers. . . .

The use of unstated rules of recognition, by courts and others, in identifying particular rules of the system is characteristic of the internal point of view. Those who use them in this way thereby manifest their own acceptance of them as guiding rules and with this attitude there goes a characteristic vocabulary different from the natural expressions of the external point of view. Perhaps the simplest of these is the expression, 'It is the law that . . . ', which we may find on the lips not only of judges, but of ordinary men living under a legal system, when they identify a given rule of the system. . . . This attitude of shared acceptance of rules is to be contrasted with that of an observer who records *ab extra* the fact that a social group accepts such rules but does not himself accept them. The natural expression of this external point of view is not 'It is the law that . . . ' but 'In England they recognize as law . . . whatever the Queen in Parliament enacts . . . .' To say that a given rule is valid is to recognize it as passing all the tests provided by the rule of recognition and so as a rule of the system. We can indeed simply say that the statement that a particular rule is valid means that it satisfies all the criteria provided by the rule of recognition. . . .

The rule of recognition providing the criteria by which the validity of other rules of the system is assessed is in an important sense, which we shall try to clarify, an *ultimate* rule: and where, as is usual, there are several criteria ranked in order of relative subordination and primacy one of them is *supreme*. . . .

Of these two ideas, supreme criterion and ultimate rule, the first is the easiest to define. We may say that a criterion of legal validity or source of law is supreme if rules identified by reference to it are still recognized as rules of the system, even if they conflict with rules identified by reference to the other criteria, whereas rules identified by reference to the latter are not so recognized if they conflict with the rules identified by reference to the supreme criterion. A similar explanation in comparative terms can be given of the notions of 'superior' and 'subordinate' criteria which we have already used. It is plain that the notions of a superior and a supreme criterion merely refer to a *relative* place on a scale and do not import any notion of legally *unlimited* legislative power. Yet 'supreme' and 'unlimited' are easy to confuse – at least in legal theory. One reason for this is that in the simpler forms of legal system the ideas of ultimate rule of recognition, supreme criterion, and legally unlimited legislature seem to converge. For where there is a legislature subject to no constitutional limitations and competent by its enactment to deprive all other rules of law emanating from other sources of their status as law, it is part of the rule of recognition in such a system that enactment by that legislature is the supreme criterion of validity. This is, according to constitutional theory, the position in the United Kingdom. But even systems like that of the United States in which there is no such legally unlimited legislature may perfectly well contain an ultimate rule of recognition which provides a set of criteria of validity, one of which is supreme. This will be so, where the legislative competence of the ordinary legislature is limited by a constitution which contains no amending power, or places some classes outside the scope of that power. Here there is no legally unlimited legislature, even in the widest interpretation of 'legislature'; but the system of course contains an ultimate rule of recognition and, in the clauses of its constitution, a supreme criterion of validity. . . .

Some writers, who have emphasized the legal ultimacy of the rule of recognition, have expressed this by saying that, whereas the legal validity of other rules of the system can be demonstrated by reference to it, its own validity cannot be demonstrated but is 'assumed' or 'postulated' or is a 'hypothesis'. This may, however, be seriously misleading. Statements of legal validity made about particular rules in the day-to-day life of a legal system whether by judges, lawyers, or ordinary citizens do indeed carry with them certain presuppositions. They are internal statements of law expressing the point of view of those who accept the rule of recognition of the system and, as such, leave unstated much that could be stated in external statements of fact about the system. What is thus left unstated forms the normal background or context of statements of legal validity and is thus said to be 'presupposed' by them. But it is important to see precisely what these presupposed matters are, and not to obscure their character. They consist of two things. First, a person who seriously asserts the validity of some given rule of law, say a particular statute, himself makes use of a rule of recognition which he accepts as appropriate for identifying the law. Secondly, it is the case that this rule of recognition, in terms of which he assesses the validity of a particular statute, is not only accepted by him but is the rule of recognition actually accepted and employed in the general operation of the system. If the truth of this presupposition were doubted, it could be established by reference to actual practice: to the way in which courts identify what is to count as law, and to the general acceptance of or acquiescence in these identifications. . . .

Where . . . as in a mature legal system, we have a system of rules which includes a rule of recognition so that the status of a rule as a member of the system now depends on whether it satisfies certain criteria provided by the rule of recognition, this brings with it a new application of the word 'exist'. The statement that a rule exists may now no longer be what it was in the simple case of customary rules – an external statement of the *fact* that a certain mode of behaviour was generally accepted as a standard in practice. It may now be an internal statement applying an accepted but unstated rule of recognition and meaning (roughly) no more than 'valid given the systems criteria of validity'. In this respect, however, as in others a rule of recognition is unlike other rules of the system. The assertion that it exists can only be an external statement of fact. For whereas a subordinate rule of a system may be valid and in that sense 'exist' even if it is generally disregarded, the rule of recognition exists only as a complex, but normally concordant, practice of the courts, officials, and private persons in identifying the law by reference to certain criteria. Its existence is a matter of fact.

QUESTION

What is the Rule of Recognition in the United Kingdom?

Dicey, *The Law of the Constitution*
(10th edn, 1965), pp. 39–40

The principle of Parliamentary sovereignty means neither more nor less than this, namely, that Parliament thus defined has, under the English constitution, the right to make or unmake any law whatever; and, further, that no person or body is recognised by the law of England as having a right to override or set aside the legislation of Parliament.

A law may, for our present purpose, be defined as 'any rule which will be enforced by the courts.' The principle then of Parliamentary sovereignty may, looked at from its positive side, be thus described: Any Act of Parliament, or any part of an Act of Parliament, which makes a new law, or repeals or modifies an existing law, will be obeyed by the courts. The same principle, looked at from its negative side, may be thus stated: There is no person or body of persons who can, under the English constitution, make rules which override or derogate from an Act of Parliament, or which (to express the same thing in other words) will be enforced by the courts in contravention of an Act of Parliament.

NOTE: Parliament is the supreme law-maker, but what is Parliament? The words of enactment at the beginning of every statute are as follows:

> Be it enacted by the Queen's most Excellent Majesty, by and with the advice and consent of the Lords Spiritual and Temporal, and Commons, in this present Parliament assembled, and by the authority of the same, as follows:—

Thus it is the Queen in Parliament which enacts legislation. A measure having received the approval of a majority in both Houses and the Royal Assent is recognized by the common law as an Act of Parliament. This position has been modified, however, by the Parliament Acts 1911 and 1949, under which a Bill may be presented for the Royal Assent provided it has been passed by the House of Commons and other procedural requirements complied with, although it has not been passed by the House of Lords. If a Bill does not obtain the approval of a majority in each House, or if the Parliament Acts are not complied with, or if the Royal Assent is withheld, the product should not be regarded as an authentic Act of Parliament.

The courts, therefore, recognize as law and accord primacy to those measures which Parliament passes as Acts.

Why is Parliament legislatively supreme, and why are its enactments accorded primacy?

SECTION 2: The Political Context

A common view is that the legal concept of the legislative supremacy of Parliament can, and indeed must, be distinguished from the political concept of sovereignty. This view, however, has been challenged. T. R. S. Allan suggests that political concepts should inform judicial decisions about the precise meaning of supremacy.

T. R. S. Allan, 'The Limits of Parliamentary Sovereignty'
[1985] *Public Law* 614

No greater testimony exists to the power and resilience of positivism in modern legal thought than the debate between constitutional lawyers about the nature of parliamentary sovereignty. At the root of almost all analyses of the nature and scope of the doctrine lies an unquestioned separation of legal from political principle. The political notion of the ultimate sovereignty of the electorate must be distinguished from the legal doctrine of legislative supremacy: the courts owe their allegiance to the latter and recognise no 'trust' between Parliament and people. Dicey was clear on the point, observing that

> 'the courts will take no notice of the will of the electors. The judges know nothing about any will of the people except in so far as that will is expressed by an Act of Parliament, and would never suffer the validity of a statute to be questioned on the ground of its having been passed or kept alive in opposition to the wishes of the electors.'

The extent of judicial loyalty to statute enjoined by the doctrine of parliamentary sovereignty therefore depends on the correct interpretation of the legal principle alone. It is a matter of accurately formulating the fundamental rule of the legal order. Its *existence* may be conceded to be a matter of political fact, but its normative content is a matter of law: the courts are required to enforce the terms of the most recent statement of Parliament's will, expressed in the usual form. . . .

In short, the fundamental rule that accords legal validity to Acts of Parliament is not itself the foundation of the legal order, beyond which the lawyer is forbidden to look. The fundamental rule, however it should properly be characterised, derives its legal authority from the underlying moral or political theory of which it forms a part. The sterility and inconclusiveness of modern debate about the nature of sovereignty stems from Dicey's attempt to divorce legal doctrine from political principle. Legal questions which challenge the nature of our constitutional order can only be answered in terms of the political morality on which that order is based. . . .

The legal doctrine of legislative supremacy articulates the courts' commitment to the current British scheme of parliamentary democracy. It ensures the effective expression of the political will of the electorate through the medium of its parliamentary representatives. If some conception of the nature and dimensions of the relevant political community provides the framework for the operation of the doctrine, equally some conception of democracy must provide its substantive political content. In other words, the courts' continuing adherence to the legal doctrine of sovereignty must entail commitment to some irreducible, minimum concept of the democratic principle. That political commitment will naturally demand respect for the legislative measures adopted by Parliament as the representative assembly, a respect for which the legal doctrine is in almost all likely circumstances a suitable expression. That respect cannot, however, be a limitless one. A parliamentary enactment whose effect would be the destruction of any recognisable form of democracy (for example, a measure purporting to deprive a substantial section of the population of the vote on the grounds of their hostility to Government policies) could not consistently be applied by the courts as law. Judicial obedience to the statute in such (extreme and unlikely) circumstances could not coherently be justified in terms of the doctrine of parliamentary sovereignty since the statute would plainly undermine the fundamental political principle which the doctrine serves to protect. The practice of judicial obedience to statute cannot itself be based on the authority of statute: it can only reflect a judicial choice based on an understanding of what (in contemporary conditions) political morality demands. The limits of that practice of obedience must therefore be constituted by the boundaries of that political morality. An enactment which threatened the essential elements of any plausible conception of democratic government would lie beyond those boundaries. It would forfeit, by the same token, any claim to be recognised as law.

Although, therefore, Dicey's sharp distinction between the application and interpretation of statute suffices for most practical purposes, it ultimately breaks down in the face of changing views of the contours of the political community or of serious threats to the central tenets of liberal democracy. Presumptions of legislative intent, which draw their strength from judicial perceptions of widely held notions of justice and fairness, cannot in normal circumstances override the explicit terms of an Act of Parliament. This is because a commitment to representative government and loyalty to democratic institutions are themselves fundamental constituents of our collective political morality. Judicial notions of justice must generally give way to those expressed by Parliament where they are inconsistent. The legal authority of statute depends in the final analysis, however, on its compatibility with the central core of that shared political morality. If Parliament ceased to be a representative assembly, in any plausible sense of the idea, or if it proceeded to enact legislation undermining the democratic basis of our institutions, political morality might direct judicial resistance rather than obedience. No neat distinction between legal doctrine and political principle can be sustained at this level of adjudication. Questions about the scope and limits of the doctrine of sovereignty are necessarily questions about the proper relations between the courts and Parliament. Such questions cannot be settled by resort to competing formulations of some supposed pre-existing legal rule: it is the scope and content of that rule which is itself in issue. Answers can only be supplied as a matter of political morality – and in terms of the values which the judges accept as fundamental to our constitutional order.

Dicey's insistence on distinguishing legal from political sovereignty entails an equivalent separation of law and convention. Neither distinction can be sustained when the courts are required to determine the limits of parliamentary sovereignty. The nature and limits of parliamentary sovereignty are constituted, in the same way that conventions are constituted, by the political morality which underlies the legal order. In this sense, the legal doctrine of sovereignty is the most fundamental of our constitutional conventions. I have argued that the limits of sovereignty are contained in the courts' central commitment to representative democracy: a purported statute which attempted to subvert democracy could derive no legal authority from the doctrine. Paradoxically, Dicey gives implicit support for this view when he considers the distinction between legal and political sovereignty in the context of conventions. He observes that, 'if Parliament be in the eye of the law a supreme legislature, the essence of representative government is, that the legislature should represent or give effect to the will of the political sovereign, *i.e.* of the electoral body, or of the nation.' His examination of a number of important constitutional conventions leads him to the conclusion that they are united in character by the possession of a single purpose – to secure that Parliament and government are ultimately subject to the wishes of the electorate. The right to demand a dissolution is the most striking example, since it represents an appeal from the legal to the political sovereign. 'The conventions of the constitution now consist of customs which (whatever their historical origin) are at the present day maintained for the sake of ensuring the supremacy of the House of Commons, and ultimately, through the elective House of Commons, of the nation. Our modern code of constitutional morality secures, though in a roundabout way, what is called abroad the 'sovereignty of the people'. Dicey presents conventions as a means of harmonising legal and political sovereignty, which remain conceptually distinct. A view of legal sovereignty as a component of political morality, however, locates its authority in the source from which the 'validity of constitutional maxims' is derived: it is equally 'subordinate and subservient to the fundamental principle of popular sovereignty.'

A residual judicial commitment to preserving the essentials of democracy does not provide the only constraint on parliamentary supremacy. The political morality which underlies the legal order is not exhausted by our attachment to democratic government. It consists also in attitudes about what justice and fairness require in the relations between government and governed, and some of these must be fundamental. If these attitudes authorise a restrictive approach to the interpretation of statutes which, more broadly construed, would threaten fundamental values, they might equally justify rejection of statutes whose infringement of such values was sufficiently grave. If an ambiguous penal provision should, as a matter of principle, be narrowly construed in the interests of liberty and fairness, a criminal statute which lacked all precision – authorising the punishment of whatever conduct officials deemed it expedient to punish – should, on the same principle, be denied any application at all. It would be sufficient for the court to deny its application to the particular circumstances of the case before it: there would in practice be no need to make a declaration of invalidity. The result, however, would be the same: the strength of the principle of interpretation, in effect denying the statute any application at all, would reflect the scale of the affront to the moral and political values we accept as fundamental. . . .

The limits of sovereignty clearly cannot be stated with any precision. The scope of the legal doctrine, and its implications for constitutional change, cannot be settled except by analysis of the political morality which gives it its authority. The boundaries of sovereignty must be determined in the light of the prevailing moral and political climate when difficult questions of constitutional authority arise. No single characterisation or particular formulation of the rule enjoining judicial obedience to statute can supply answers in advance. . . .

QUESTIONS

1. Allan states that a 'parliamentary enactment whose effect would be destruction of any recognisable form of democracy . . . could not consistently be applied by the courts as law'. This begs a question as to what is democracy? For example, what would the courts do if Party A obtaining 40 per cent of the vote gained 60 per cent of the seats in the legislature because the remaining 60 per cent of the vote was split between three other parties, and then it embarked on a legislative programme which was discriminatory, anti-libertarian and anti-democratic? What would political morality demand? How would the judges discover this political morality? Would it make any difference if Party A fought the election campaign on a manifesto which openly outlined its policies, as opposed to the adoption of these policies after winning the election? If the judges refused to enforce the offensive legislation and an election was held with the same result followed by a reintroduction of the legislation, what would judges then do?

2. Is the 'shared political morality' of majoritarianism an adequate substitute for constitutionalism? Does Allan suggest that it is? What do you think he means when he states:

> The political morality which underlies the legal order is not exhausted by our attachment to democratic government. It consists also in attitudes about what justice and fairness require in the relations between government and the governed, and some of these must be fundamental.

Who decides what justice and fairness require?

NOTE: What Allan is perhaps attempting to identify is a higher order of law which places a limit on the supremacy of Parliament. But this is, perhaps, to misstate the issue; the problem is not so much the supremacy of Parliament but the appropriation of that supremacy by the Executive which to all intents and purposes exercises a stranglehold over Parliament. Recent judicial appointees are showing a greater preparedness to challenge the Diceyan orthodoxy and to recognize the imperative of democracy – to recognize values more fundamental than a majority in Parliament.

The Rt. Hon. Lord Woolf of Barnes, 'Droit Public – English Style'
[1995] *Public Law* 57

. . . But what happens if a party with a large majority in Parliament uses that majority to abolish the courts' entire power of judicial review in express terms? It is administratively expensive, absorbs far too large a proportion of the legal aid fund and results in the judiciary having misconceived notions of grandeur. Do the courts then accept that the legislation means what it says? I am sure this is in practice unthinkable. It will never happen. But if it did, for reasons I will now summarise, my own personal view is that they do not. . . . Our parliamentary democracy is based on the rule of law.

One of the twin principles upon which the rule of law depends is the supremacy of the Parliament in its legislative capacity. The other principle is that the courts are the final arbiters as to the interpretation and application of the law. As both Parliament and the courts derive their authority from the rule of law so both are subject to it and can not act in manner which involves its repudiation. The respective roles do not give rise to conflict because the courts and Parliament each respects the role of the other. For example, Parliament is meticulous in upholding the *sub judice* rule so as to avoid interfering with the role of the courts. Equally the courts always respect the privileges of Parliament and will not become involved with the internal workings of Parliament. In addition the courts will seek to give effect wherever possible to both primary and subordinate legislation. The courts will for example where there is a conflict between Community and domestic legislation uphold the domestic legislation as far as possible. The courts will also readily accept legislation which controls how it exercises its jurisdiction or which confers or modifies its existing statutory jurisdiction. I however, see a distinction between such legislative action and that which seeks to undermine in a fundamental way the rule of law on which our unwritten constitution depends by removing or substantially impairing the entire reviewing role of the High Court on judicial review, a role which in its origin is as ancient as the common law, predates our present form of parliamentary democracy and the Bill of Rights.

My approach . . . does involve dispensing with fairy tales once and for all, but I would suggest this is healthy. It involves a proper recognition of both the pillars of the rule of law and the equal responsibility that Parliament and the courts are under to respect the other's burdens and to play their proper part in upholding the rule of law. I see the courts and Parliament as being partners both engaged in a common enterprise involving the upholding of the rule of law. It is reflected in the way that frequently the House of Lords in its judicial capacity will stress the desirability of legislation when faced with the new problems that contemporary society can create rather than creating a solution itself.

There are however situations where already, in upholding the rule of law, the courts have had to take a stand. The example that springs to mind is the *Anisminic* case [1969] 2 AC 147. In that case even the statement in an Act of Parliament that the Commission's decision 'shall not be called in question in any court of law' did not succeed in excluding the jurisdiction of the court. Since that case Parliament has not again mounted such a challenge to the reviewing power of the High Court. There has been, and I am confident there will continue to be, mutual respect for each other's roles.

However, if Parliament did the unthinkable, then I would say that the courts would also be required to act in a manner which would be without precedent. Some judges might chose to do so by saying that it was an unrebuttable presumption that Parliament could never intend such a result. I myself would consider there were advantages in making it clear that ultimately there are even limits on the supremacy of Parliament which it is the courts' inalienable responsibility to identify and uphold. They are limits of the most modest dimensions which I believe any democrat would accept. They are no more than are necessary to enable the rule of law to be preserved.

The Hon. Sir John Laws, 'Law and Democracy'
[1995] *Public Law* 74

. . .

Democracy and fundamental rights
As a matter of fundamental principle, it is my opinion that the survival and flourishing of a democracy in which basic rights (of which freedom of expression may be taken as a paradigm) are not only respected but enshrined requires that those who exercise democratic, political power must have limits set to what they may do: limits which they are not allowed to overstep. If this is right, it is a function of democratic power itself that it be not absolute. . . .

The government's constituency is the whole body of such citizens; and a democratic government can have no remit but to act in what it perceives to be their best interests. It may get it wrong, and let the people down. But it cannot *knowingly* do so, for that would be to act in bad faith; and no government can justify its own bad faith by pointing to the fact that it was elected by the people. That would be to assert that the electorate endorsed in advance the government's right deliberately to act against its interests, which is an impossible proposition.

Thus the free will of every citizen is a premise of all the government's dealings with the people, and so conditions its duty to act in good faith towards them. It cannot fulfil its duty without recognising this; but such a recognition entails the need to accord fundamental rights, high among them the right of freedom of expression . . .

Any but the crudest society will be ordered, will have, in whatever form, a government. Its citizens will make judgments about the government. The government can no more deny their right to do so, without also denying their nature as free and rational beings, than it can deny their right to make judgments upon each other. But more than this, the government cannot be *neutral* about free speech. If it is not to be denied, it must be permitted; there is no room for what the logicians would call an undisturbed middle; and if it must be permitted, it must be entrenched and protected, since its vindication is not a matter of legitimate political choice but an axiom of any community of free human beings. In the end the government's duty to good faith requires it to accord this fundamental freedom to the people.

The imperative of higher-order law
Now it is only by means of compulsory law that effective rights can be accorded, so that the medium of rights is not persuasion, but the power of rule: the very power which, if misused, could be deployed to subvert rights. We therefore arrive at this position: the constitution must guarantee by

positive law such rights as that of freedom of expression, since otherwise its credentials as a medium of honest rule are fatally undermined. But this requires for its achievement what I may call a higher-order law: a law which cannot be abrogated as other laws can, by the passage of a statute promoted by a government with the necessary majority in Parliament. Otherwise the right is not in the keeping of the constitution at all; it is not a guaranteed right; it exists, in point of law at least, only because the government chooses to let it exist, whereas in truth no such choice should be open to any government.

The democratic credentials of an elected government cannot justify its enjoyment of a right to abolish fundamental freedoms. If its power in the state is in the last resort absolute, such fundamental rights as free expression are only privileges; no less so if the absolute power rests in an elected body. The byword of every tyrant is 'My word is law'; a democratic assembly having sovereign power beyond the reach of curtailment or review may make just such an assertion, and its elective base cannot immunise it from playing the tyrant's role. . . .

Since in the last resort the government rules by consent, the source of public power is not the strong arm of the ruler, but the people themselves.

Even so, the fundamental sinews of the constitution, the cornerstones of democracy and of inalienable rights, ought not by law to be in the keeping of the government, because the only means by which these principles may be enshrined in the state is by their possessing a status which no government has the right to destroy. I have already argued this position in relation to fundamental individual rights; now I assert it also as regards democracy itself. It is a condition of democracy's preservation that the power of a democratically elected government – or Parliament – be not absolute. The institution of free and regular elections, like fundamental individual rights, has to be vindicated by a higher-order law: very obviously, no government can tamper with it, if it is to avoid the mantle of tyranny; no government, therefore, must be allowed to do so. . . .

The thrust of this reasoning is that the doctrine of Parliamentary sovereignty cannot be vouched by Parliamentary legislation; a higher-order law confers it, and must of necessity limit it. Thus it is not, and cannot be, established by the measures which set in place the constitutional reforms of the late seventeenth century; nor by any legislation. Indeed Lord Browne-Wilkinson's construction of Article 9 of the Bill of Rights 1688, to which I have already referred, means only that no impediment may be placed on Parliamentary processes, such as, for instance, by a claim against an MP for defamation; it is no more nor less than a rule of absolute legal privilege. It has nothing to do with the question whether statutes in proper form are by law beyond challenge. Its effect is that no constraint of any kind is to be imposed on the freedom of Parliament to debate whatever it likes. That is of course a vital principle, and the courts have been at pains to respect what they regard as Parliament's rights. But it says nothing about the legal supremacy of legislation; the existence of a power in the courts to strike down a statute as inconsistent with a fundamental right or, were it to happen, with democracy itself, does not in any sense touch the freedom of members of either House, uninhibited by any law, to say whatever they choose during a Bill's passage.

So the rules which establish and vindicate a government's power are in a different category from laws which assume the existence of the framework, and are made under it, because they prescribe the framework itself. In states with written constitutions the rules are of course to be found in the text of the constitution, which, typically, will also contain provisions as to how they may be changed. Generally the mechanisms under which the framework may be changed are different from those by which ordinary laws, not part of the framework, may be repealed or amended; and the mechanisms will be stricter than those in place for the alteration of ordinary law.

But in Britain the rules establishing the framework possess, on the face of it, no different character from any other statute law. The requirement of elections at least every five years may in theory be altered by amending legislation almost as readily – though the 'almost' is important – as a provision defining dangerous dogs. The conventions under which cabinet government is carried on could in theory be changed with no special rules at all, as could any of the norms by which the government possesses the authority to govern. The rules by which the power of a government is conferred are in effect the same as the rules by which the government may legislate upon other matters after it has gained power. In the end the sanction for the maintenance of democracy is in point of law no greater than the sanction for the maintenance of the dangerous dogs definition. . . .

Conclusion

We may now come full circle, and after this long discussion I can identify what seems to me to be the essence of the difference between judicial and elective power. The latter consists in the authority to make decisions of policy within the remit given by the electorate; this is a great power, with which neither the judges nor anyone else have any business to interfere. This is the place held by democracy in our constitution. It is the place of government. Within it, Parliament, even given its present unsatisfactory relationship with the Executive, is truly and totally supreme. It possesses what we may indeed call a political sovereignty. It is a sovereignty which cannot be objected to, save at the price of assaulting democracy itself. But it is not a constitutional sovereignty; it does not have the status of what earlier I called a sovereign text, of the kind found in states with written constitutions. Ultimate sovereignty rests, in every civilised constitution, not with those who wield governmental power, but in the conditions under which they are permitted to do so. The constitution, not the Parliament, is in this sense sovereign. In Britain these conditions should now be recognised as consisting in a framework of fundamental principles which include the imperative of democracy itself and those other rights, prime among them freedom of thought and expression, which cannot be denied save by a plea of guilty to totalitarianism.

For its part judicial power in the last resort rests in the guarantee that this framework will be vindicated. It consists in the assurance that, however great the democratic margin of appreciation (to use Strasbourg's language) that must be accorded to the elected arm of the state, the bedrock of pluralism will be maintained. We have no other choice. The dynamic settlement between the powers of the state requires, in the absence of a constitutional scripture, just such a distribution of authority. The judges are rightly and necessarily constrained not only by a prohibition against intrusion into what is Parliament's proper sphere, but by the requirement, and the truth, that they have in their duty no party political bias. Their interest and obligation in the context of this discussion is to protect values which no democratic politician could honestly contest: values which, therefore, may be described as apolitical, since they stand together above the rancorous but vital dissensions of party politicians. The judges are constrained also, and rightly, by the fact that their role is reactive; they cannot initiate; all they can do is to apply principle to what is brought before them by others. Nothing could be more distinct from the duty of political creativity owed to us by Members of Parliament.

Though our constitution is unwritten, it can and must be articulated. Though it changes, the principles by which it goes can and must be elaborated. They are not silent; they represent the aspirations of a free people. They must be spoken and explained and, indeed, argued over. Politicians, lawyers, scholars, and many others have to do this. Constitutional theory has, perhaps, occupied too modest a place here in Britain, so that the colour and reach of public power has not been exposed to a glare that is fierce enough. But the importance of these matters is so great that, whatever the merits or demerits of what I have had to say, we cannot turn our backs on the arguments. We cannot risk the future growth without challenge of new, perhaps darker, philosophies. We cannot fail to give principled answers to those who ask of the nature of state power by what legal alchemy, in any situation critical to the protection of our freedoms, the constitution measures the claims of the ruler and the ruled. The imperatives of democracy and fundamental rights do not only demand acceptance; they demand a vindication that survives any test of intellectual rigour.

QUESTIONS

1. Has Sir John Laws successfully identified fundamental values arising from the notion of democracy which will be adequate to deal effectively with the worst excesses of naked majoritarianism? Is it the role of a judge to identify such values and exalt them to a position superior to an Act of Parliament?

2. Does the form in which the Human Rights Act 1998 incorporates the European Convention on Human Rights into the domestic law of the United Kingdom result in the creation of a higher order of law guaranteeing fundamental rights to UK citizens? Has the position of Parliament, as the ultimate arbiter determining whether and to what extent rights are protected in the United Kingdom, been weakened by the Human Rights Act 1998? (See further Chapter 7.)

NOTE: What would happen if there was a revolution and the monarchy was overthrown, Parliament dissolved and all its members imprisoned, and new elections held to a Constitutional Convention which draws up a new constitution with a presidential system of government and a single chamber assembly? If this new order is accepted by the people and the courts, the currently accepted doctrine of the legislative supremacy of Parliament would become redundant (cf. *Madzimbamuto* v *Lardner-Burke* [1969] 1 AC 645, *post* p. XX). It is power and politics which operate in such a situation, not legal theory. Under the old order the new regime would be regarded as illegal, but it will acquire its own legitimacy from the obedience shown to it. Sovereignty, as a political concept, ultimately resides in the people; if the people accept the new legal order they will thereby give to it validity and legitimacy. For example, while the Declaration of Independence in 1776 and the enactment of the United States Constitution in 1787 were illegal under the old legal order, they were validated by, and received their legitimacy and authority from, the People of the United States, who accepted them and agreed to abide by the new constitution.

Our constitutional order has evolved from the position where an absolute monarch was supreme, to the current position where Parliament is legislatively supreme. The biggest jump in this evolutionary process occurred in the seventeenth century with the Glorious Revolution of 1688, which led to the establishment of the doctrine of the legislative supremacy of Parliament. The ultimate authority for the doctrine stems from the acceptance by the people of William III as the new monarch, and the acceptance by the courts of the new legal order founded on this doctrine as expressed legally in the common law.

SECTION 3: **The Nature of the Legislative Supremacy of Parliament**

What are the implications of the legislative supremacy of Parliament? Dicey's statement of the doctrine (*ante* p. 54) may be converted into three propositions which will be examined in more detail. They are:

A: Parliament is the supreme law-making authority.

B: The legislative powers of Parliament are unlimited.

C: No other body has authority to rule on the validity of its enactments.

Each of these propositions will be examined separately.

A: Parliament – the supreme law-making authority

In the fourteenth century Parliament emerged as an effective, if not supreme, law-making body. In the seventeenth century James I, by insisting on his right to rule by prerogative, created the conditions in which the battle between the Monarch and Parliament for supremacy was fought in the courts.

The Case of Proclamations
(1611) 12 Co Rep 74; 77 ER 1352

> The King sought to check the overgrowth of the capital by issuing a proclamation to prohibit the building of new homes in London. He also sought to preserve wheat for human consumption and issued a proclamation prohibiting the manufacture of starch from wheat. The Commons complained that this was an abuse of proclamations, and the King sought the opinion of Chief Justice Coke who consulted with his fellow judges.

In the same term it was resolved by the two Chief Justices, Chief Baron, and Baron Altham, upon conference betwixt the Lords of the Privy Council and them, that the King by his proclamation cannot create any offence which was not an offence before, for then he may alter the law of the land by his proclamation in a high point; for if he may create an offence where none is, upon that ensues fine and imprisonment: also the law of England is divided into three parts, common law, statute law, and custom; but the King's proclamation is none of them: also *malum aut est malum in se, aut prohibitum*, that which is against common law is *malum in se, malum prohibitum* is such an offence as is prohibited by Act of Parliament, and not by proclamation.

Also, it was resolved, that the King hath no prerogative, but that which the law of the land allows him.

But the King for prevention of offences may by proclamation admonish his subjects that they keep the laws, and do not offend them; upon punishment to be inflicted by the law, &c.

Lastly, if the offence be not punishable in the Star-Chamber, the prohibition of it by proclamation cannot make it punishable there: and after this resolution, no proclamation imposing fine and imprisonment was afterwards made, &c.

NOTE: The Stuart kings also claimed to have other prerogative powers of considerable importance, namely a *suspending* power, which could be used to postpone the operation of a statute for an indefinite period, and a *dispensing* power, which could be used to relieve offenders from the statutory penalties they had incurred. It was James II's use of the suspending power in respect of penal laws relating to religion in the Declarations of Indulgence 1687 and 1688 which led to the revolution of 1688.

In the area of taxation it had been established by the time of Edward I that direct taxes could only be levied with the consent of Parliament. However, the Stuarts claimed they could raise money by means of the prerogative. First, the prerogative relating to foreign affairs was used to regulate trade by the imposition of duties (see *The Case of Impositions (Bate's Case)* (1606) 2 St Tr 371). Secondly, the prerogative power to defend the realm in face of an emergency was used to raise money for the navy. The King was found to be the sole judge of whether an emergency existed (see *The Case of Shipmoney (R v Hampden)* (1637) 3 St Tr 825).

The claims by the Stuart kings to rule by prerogative were resolved by the Bill of Rights 1689.

The Bill of Rights 1689
I Will & Mary Sess 2 ch 2

Whereas the late King James the second, by the Assistance of divers Evil Counsellors, Judges, and Ministers, imployed by him did endeavour to Subvert and extirpate the Protestant Religion, and the Lawes and Liberties of this Kingdome. . . .

And whereas the said late King James the second having abdicated the Government and the throne being thereby vacant.

His Highnesse the Prince of Orange (whom it hath pleased Almighty God to make the glorious Instrument of delivering this Kingdom from Popery and Arbitrary Power) Did (by the advice of the Lords Spirituall and Temporall and divers principall persons of the Commons) Cause Letters to be written to the Lords Spirituall and Temporall being Protestants and other Letters to the several Countyes Cities Universities Burroughs and Cinqe Ports for the chuseing of such persons to represent them as were of right to be sent to Parliament to meet and sitt at Westminster upon the two and twentieth day of January in this Year 1688 in order to such an establishment as that their Religion Lawes and Libertyes might not againe be in danger of being subverted.

Upon which Letters Elections haveing been accordingly made.

And thereupon the said Lords Spirituall and Temporall and Commons pursuant to their respective letters and Elections being now assembled in a full and free representative of this nation taking into their most serious consideration the best meanes for atteyneing the ends aforesaid Doe in the first place (as their Ancestors in like Case have usually done) for the vindicating and asserting their antient rights and Liberties, Declare.

[1.] That the pretended power of suspending of Lawes or the execution of Lawes by Regall Authority without Consent of Parliament is illegall.

[2.] That the pretended power of dispensing with lawes or the Execution of lawes by regall authority as it has been assumed and exercised of late is illegall.

[3.] That the Commission for erecting the late Courte of Commissioners for Ecclesiasticall Causes and all other Commissions and Courts of like nature are illegall and pernicious.

[4.] That levying of money for or to the use of the Crowne by pretence of Prerogative without Grant of Parliament for longer time or in other manner, than the same is or shall be granted is illegall.

[5.] That it is the right of the Subjects to petition the King and all Committments and prosecutions for such petitioning are illegall.

[6.] That the raiseing or keeping a Standing Army within the Kingdom in time of Peace unlesse it be with consent of Parliament is against Law.

[7.] That the Subjects which are Protestants may have Armes for their defence Suitable to their Condition and as allowed by Law.

[8.] That Elections of Members of Parliament ought to be free.

[9.] That the freedome of Speech and debates or proceedings in Parliament ought not to be impeached or questioned in any Courte or place out of Parliament.

[10.] That excessive Bayle ought not to be required nor excessive fynes imposed nor cruel and unusuall Punishments inflicted.

[11.] That Jurors ought to be duely impannelled and returned and Jurors which passe upon men in tryalls for high Treason ought to be freeholders.

[12.] That all Grants and promises of fynes and forfeitures of particular persons before conviction are illegall and void.

[13.] And that for redress of all greivances and for the amending, strengthening and preserving of the Lawes, Parliaments ought to be held frequently.

And they do claime demand and insist upon all and singular the premises as their undoubted Rights and Liberties and that noe Declarations Judgements Doeings or proceedings to the prejudice of the People in any of the said premisses ought in any wise to bee drawne hereafter into Consequence or Example.

To which demand of their rights they are particularly Encouraged by the declaration of his Highnesse the Prince of Orange as being the only Meanes for obteyning a full redress and remedy therein.

Haveing therefore an intire Confidence that his said Highnesse the Prince of Orange will perfect the deliverance soe farr advanced by him and will still preserve them from the violation of their rights which they have here asserted and from all other attempts upon their Religion Rights and Liberties.

The said Lords Spirituall and Temporall and Commons Assembled at Westminster doe Resolve.

That William and Mary Prince and Princesse of Orange bee and bee declared, King and Queen of England France and Ireland and the Dominions thereunto belonging to hold the Crowne and Royall Dignity of the said Kingdom's and Dominions to them the said Prince and Princesss during their lives and the life of the Survivor of them and that the Sole and full exercise of the Regall Power be only in and executed by the said Prince of Orange in the Names of the said Prince and Princesse during their Joynt lives And after their deceases the said Crowne and Royall Dignity of the said Kingdoms and Dominions to be to the heires of the body of the said Princesse: And for default of such Issue to the Princesse Anne of Denmarke and the heires of her body. And for default of such Issue to the heires of the body of the said Prince of Orange.

And the said Lords Spirituall and Temporall and Commons doe pray the said Prince and Princesse of Orange to accept the same accordingly. . . .

Upon which their said Majestyes did accept the crowne and royall dignitie of the kingdoms of England France and Ireland and the dominions thereunto belonging. . . . And thereupon their Majestyes were pleased that the said lords spirituall and temporall and commons being the two Houses of Parlyament should continue to sitt and with their Majesty's royall concurrence make effectuall provision for the settlement of the religion lawes and liberties of this kingdome soe that the same for the future might not be in danger againe of being subverted, to which the said lords spirituall and temporall and commons did agree and proceede to act accordingly. Now in pursuance of the premisses the said lords spirituall and temporall and commons in Parlyament assembled for the ratifying confirming and establishing the said declaration and the articles clauses matters and things therein contained by the force of a law made in due forme by authority of Parlyament doe pray that it may be declared and enacted that all and singular the rights and liberties asserted and claimed in the said declaration are the true auntient and indubitable rights and liberties of the people of this kingdome and soe shall be esteemed allowed adjudged deemed and taken to be and that all and every the particulars aforesaid shall be firmly and strictly holden and observed as they are expressed in the said declaration. And all officers and ministers whatsoever shall serve their Majestyes and their successors according to the same in all times to come. . . .

D. Judge, *The Parliamentary State*
(1993), p. 20

The Constitutional Settlement of 1689 and the Rise of the Liberal State
The potency of the Constitutional Settlement of 1689 stems from its implicit principle of the supremacy of parliament in law. The acceptance by William and Mary of the gift of the crown was conditional upon the terms set by parliament. Henceforth, monarchical power was dependent upon parliament rather than *vice versa*. After 1689, as Munro points out:

Parliament was to be its own master and free from interference . . . Parliaments were to be held frequently, and the election of their members was to be free. The Crown's power to levy taxes was made subject to parliamentary consent, its power to keep a standing army made subject to statute, and powers of suspending or dispensing with laws . . . were declared illegal. (1987: 80)

In other words, what was asserted and accepted in 1689 was the principle of *parliamentary sovereignty*, whereby parliament secured legal supremacy amongst the institutions of the state. Thus, not only was the monarchy subordinated to parliament, but, also, the last vestiges of the claim of the courts that parliament could not legislate in derogation of the principles of the common law were removed. Constitutional theory was at last reconciled to the legal practice that had been developing for nearly a century.

Above all, therefore, the Bill of Rights was a restraint upon arbitrary behaviour. Its passage confirmed the distinctiveness of English state development from its continental European counterparts. The concentration of power in the hands of the monarch and the exclusion of parliament from policy making – the political hallmarks of absolutism – were outlawed in England in 1689. The authority of statute was conferred upon the pre-existing principles – of consent and representation – so confirming the differences between the state-form in England and those in the absolutist regimes in France and Prussia for example. . . .

B: The unlimited legislative powers of Parliament

Several cases have arisen where this idea has been tested.

There is a presumption used by the courts when construing statutes that Parliament does not intend to legislate contrary to the principles of international law, and, as far as possible, a statute will be interpreted in a way which avoids conflict. What do the courts do, however, when there is a clear conflict between a statute of the United Kingdom Parliament and the principles of international law? The answer is given in the following case.

Mortensen v *Peters*
(1906) 14 SLT 227, High Court of Justiciary

Mortensen was the captain of a Norwegian trawler charged with illegal trawl fishing in waters within the Moray Firth contrary to a bye-law made by the Fishery Board for Scotland under s. 7 of the Herring Fishery (Scotland) Act 1889. The Act defined the area for which bye-laws could be made, that is, all of the Moray Firth, although much of it comprised international waters. The trawler had been fishing five miles off the coast in international waters but within the prohibited area. Mortensen was convicted by the Sheriff's Court and appealed.

THE LORD JUSTICE GENERAL: My Lords, I apprehend that the question is one of construction and of construction only. In this Court we have nothing to do with the question of whether the legislature has or has not done what foreign powers may consider a usurpation in a question with them. Neither are we a tribunal sitting to decide whether an act of the legislature is *ultra vires* as in contravention of generally acknowledged principles of international law. For us an Act of Parliament duly passed by Lords and Commons and assented to by the King, is supreme, and we are bound to give effect to its terms. . . .

It is said by the appellant . . . that International Law has firmly fixed that a locus such as this is beyond the limits of territorial sovereignty; and that consequently it is not to be thought that in such a place the legislature could seek to affect any but the King's subjects.

It is a trite observation that there is no such thing as a standard of International Law, extraneous to the domestic law of a kingdom, to which appeal may be made. International Law, so far as this Court is concerned, is the body of doctrine regarding the international rights and duties of States which has been adopted and made part of the Law of Scotland. Now can it be said to be clear by the law of Scotland that the locus here is beyond what the legislature may assert right to affect by legislation against all whomsoever for the purpose of regulating methods of fishing?

I do not think I need say anything about what is known as the three-mile limit. It may be assumed that within the three miles the territorial sovereignty would be sufficient to cover any such legislation as the present. It is enough to say that that is not a proof of the counter proposition that outside the three miles no such result could be looked for. The locus, although outside the three-mile limit, is within the bay known as the Moray Firth, and the Moray Firth, says the respondent, is *intra fauces terrae*. Now, I cannot say that there is any definition of what *fauces terrae* exactly are. But there are at least three points which go far to shew that this spot might be considered as lying therein.

1st. The dicta of the Scottish Institutional Writers seem to show that it would be no usurpation, according to the law of Scotland, so to consider it.

Thus, Stair, II i. 5: 'The vast ocean is common to all mankind as to navigation and fishing, which are the only uses thereof, because it is not capable of bounds; but when the sea is inclosed in bays, creeks, *or otherwise is capable of any bounds or meiths as within the points of such lands*, or within the view of such shores, then it may become proper, but with the reservation of passage for commerce as in the land.' And Bell, Pr. S 639: 'The Sovereign . . . is proprietor of the narrow seas within cannon shot of the land, and the *firths*, gulfs, and bays around the Kingdom.'

2nd. The same statute puts forward claims to what are at least analogous places. If attention is paid to the Schedule appended to section 6, many places will be found far beyond the three-mile limit – *e.g.*, the Firth of Clyde near its mouth. I am not ignoring that it may be said that this in one sense is proving *idem per idem*, but none the less I do not think the fact can be ignored.

3rd. There are many instances to be found in decided cases where the right of a nation to legislate for waters more or less landlocked or landembraced, although beyond the three-mile limit, has been admitted.

They will be found collected in the case of the *Direct United States Cable Company* v *Anglo-American Telegraph Company*, LR 2 App Cas 394, the bay there in question being Conception Bay, which has a width at the mouth of rather more than 20 miles.

It seems to me therefore, without laying down the proposition that the Moray Firth is for every purpose within the territorial sovereignty, it can at least be clearly said that the appellant cannot make out his proposition that it is inconceivable that the British legislature should attempt for fishery regulation to legislate against all and sundry in such a place. And if that is so, then I revert to the considerations already stated which as a matter of construction make me think that it did so legislate.

LORD KYLLACHY: . . . A legislature may quite conceivably, by oversight or even design, exceed what an international tribunal (if such existed) might hold to be its international rights. Still, there is always a presumption against its intending to do so. I think that is acknowledged. But then it is only a presumption; and, as such, it must always give way to the language used if it is clear, and also to all counter presumptions which may legitimately be had in view in determining, on ordinary principles, the true meaning and intent of the legislation. Express words will, of course, be conclusive; and so also will plain implication.

Now it must, I think, be conceded that the language of the enactment here in question is fairly express – express, that is to say, to the effect of making an unlimited and unqualified prohibition, applying to the whole area specified, and affecting everybody – whether British subjects or foreigners.

LORD JOHNSTON: [delivered a concurring judgment]

Appeal dismissed.

NOTE: In *Cheney* v *Conn* [1968] 1 All ER 779, a taxpayer challenged an assessment of income tax made under the Finance Act 1964 on the ground that part of the money raised would be used for the manufacture of nuclear weapons contrary to a treaty, the Geneva Convention, to which the United Kingdom was party. Ungoed-Thomas J stated:

> What the statute itself enacts cannot be unlawful, because what the statute says and provides is itself the law, and the highest form of law that is known to this country. It is the law which prevails over every other form of law, and it is not for the court to say that a parliamentary enactment, the highest law in this country, is illegal.

See also *R* v *Secretary for the Home Department, ex parte Thakrar* [1974] QB 684.

If international law can place no limitation on Parliament's powers, can time do so?

In *Burmah Oil Co.* v *Lord Advocate* [1965] AC 75, HL, the company was successful in its claim for compensation against the Crown for the destruction of its installations in Burma during the Second World War, the destruction having been ordered by the commander of British forces to prevent the installations falling into the hands of the advancing Japanese forces. In response to this decision Parliament hastily passed the War Damage Act 1965 with retrospective effect to deny entitlement to compensation for damage for acts lawfully done by the Crown during a war in which the Sovereign was engaged.

C: Ruling on the validity of Parliament's enactments

The statement of Dicey above also suggests that no person or body has authority to rule on the validity of Parliament's enactments. Is it possible to challenge the validity of an Act of Parliament in the courts? In countries with a written constitution the ordinary courts or a constitutional court will have jurisdiction to determine whether the acts of the legislature are constitutional. In the United States the Supreme Court, in *Marbury* v *Madison* (1803) 1 Cranch 137, declared that it had power to decide whether or not the Acts of Congress conformed with the Constitution. In the United Kingdom the doctrine of legislative supremacy dictates that Parliament has power to legislate on constitutional matters. Thus Parliament may change the constitution by Act of Parliament. This being so, is it possible to challenge an Act on the ground that it is unconstitutional? Chief Justice Coke was of opinion that the courts could intervene if Parliament enacted outrageous legislation. He stated in *Dr Bonham's Case* (1610) 8 Co Rep 114, at p. 118:

In many cases, the common law will control Acts of Parliament, and sometimes adjudge them to be utterly void: for when an Act of Parliament is against common right and reason, or repugnant, or impossible to be performed, the common law will control it, and adjudge such an Act to be void.

However, this statement precedes the Glorious Revolution of 1688, since when the doctrine of the supremacy of Parliament has developed its modern meaning. In *Ex p. Canon Selwyn* (1872) 36 JP 54 a question arose regarding the validity of the Irish Church Act 1869. Cockburn CJ stated:

[T]here is no judicial body in the country by which the validity of an act of parliament could be questioned. An act of the legislature is superior in authority to any court of law. We have only to administer the law as we find it, and no court could pronounce a judgment as to the validity of an act of Parliament.

In *Pickin* v *British Railways Board* [1974] AC 765, Lord Reid stated:

In earlier times many learned lawyers seem to have believed that an Act of Parliament could be disregarded in so far as it was contrary to the law of God or the law of nature or natural justice, but since the supremacy of Parliament was finally demonstrated by the Revolution of 1688 any such idea has become obsolete.

In *Manuel* v *Attorney-General* [1983] Ch 77, Sir Robert Megarry VC stated, at p. 86:

[T]he duty of the court is to obey and apply every Act of Parliament, and . . . the court cannot hold any such Act to be ultra vires. Of course there may be questions about what the Act means, and of course there is power to hold statutory instruments and other subordinate legislation ultra vires. But once an instrument is recognised as being an Act of Parliament, no English court can refuse to obey it or question its validity.

But what happens if there are two Acts on the statute books which conflict with one another? See the case which follows.

Ellen Street Estates Limited v *Minister of Health*
[1934] 1 KB 590, Court of Appeal

The Acquisition of Land (Assessment of Compensation) Act 1919 provided by s. 2 for the assessment of compensation in respect of land acquired compulsorily for public purposes according to certain rules. Section 7(1) stated 'The provisions of the Act or order by which the land is authorised to be acquired, or of any Act incorporated therewith, shall in relation to the matters dealt with in this Act, have effect subject to this Act, and so far as inconsistent with this Act those provisions shall cease to have or shall not have effect . . .'. The Housing Act 1925, s. 46 provided for the assessment of compensation for land acquired compulsorily under an improvement or reconstruction scheme made under that Act in a manner differing in certain respects from that prescribed by the Act of 1919. Section 7(1) could be construed as applying to previous enactments, but it was argued that it applied also to subsequent enactments. If this was so, inconsistent provisions in the 1925 Act would be of no effect.

SCRUTTON LJ: . . . Such a contention involves this proposition, that no subsequent Parliament by enacting a provision inconsistent with the Act of 1919 can give any effect to the words it uses. Sect. 46, sub-s. 1, of the Housing Act, 1925, says this: 'Where land included in any improvement or reconstruction scheme . . . is acquired compulsorily,' certain provisions as to compensation shall apply. These are inconsistent with those contained in the Acquisition of Land (Assessment of Compensation) Act, 1919, and then s. 46, sub-s. 2, of the Act of 1925 provides: 'Subject as aforesaid, the compensation to be paid for such land shall be assessed in accordance with the Acquisition of Land (Assessment of Compensation) Act, 1919.' I asked Mr Hill [for the appellants] what these last quoted words mean, and he replied they mean nothing. That is absolutely contrary to the constitutional position that Parliament can alter an Act previously passed, and it can do so by repealing in terms the previous Act – Mr Hill agrees that it may do so – and it can do it also in another way – namely, by enacting a provision which is clearly inconsistent with the previous Act.

MAUGHAM LJ: . . . The Legislature cannot, according to our constitution, bind itself as to the form of subsequent legislation, and it is impossible for Parliament to enact that in a subsequent statute dealing with the same subject-matter there can be no implied repeal. If in a subsequent Act Parliament chooses to make it plain that the earlier statute is being to some extent repealed, effect must be given to that intention just because it is the will of the Legislature.

Appeal dismissed.

QUESTIONS

1. Was this case concerned with the *content* of the legislation or the *form* of the legislation?
2. When Maugham LJ stated that Parliament cannot bind itself as to the form of subsequent legislation, was this *obiter* or *ratio*?

NOTES AND QUESTIONS

1. The doctrine of implied repeal is a consequence of the traditional Diceyan view of supremacy: if Parliament cannot bind future Parliaments as to the content of legislation, subsequent legislation which is incompatible with a prior Act necessarily must be taken to have repealed the incompatible earlier provision. In New Zealand a Bill of Rights Act was passed in 1990 which sought to eliminate the possibility of judges declaring statutory provisions void for incompatibility with the Act. The Act expressly provided:

   4. No courts shall, in relation to any enactment (whether passed or made before or after the commencement of this Bill of Rights):—
   (a) hold any provision of the enactment to be impliedly repealed or revoked, or to be in any way invalid or ineffective; or
   (b) decline to apply any provision of the enactment

   by reason only that the provision is inconsistent with any provision of this Bill of Rights.

   Emmerson, 'Opinion: This Year's Model – The Options for Incorporation' [1997] EHRLR 313, at 325 states:

   It is important to scotch the notion that there is some sort of constitutional imperative for adopting a model with such obvious shortcomings. The New Zealand Act is not a faithful reflection of even the most orthodox view of parliamentary sovereignty. By expressly excluding the doctrine of implied repeal in relation to Acts passed before the Bill of Rights Act, it institutionalises a principle of legislative supremacy which is quite out of step with British constitutional theory, and which fails to acknowledge the constitutional character of human rights legislation.

   The Human Rights Act 1998 provides:

   3.—(1) So far as it is possible to do so, primary legislation and subordinate legislation must be read and given effect in a way which is compatible with the Convention rights.
   (2) This section—
   (a) applies to primary legislation and subordinate legislation whenever enacted;
   (b) does not affect the validity, continuing operation or enforcement of any incompatible primary legislation; and
   (c) does not affect the validity, continuing operation or enforcement of any incompatible subordinate legislation if (disregarding any possibility of revocation) primary legislation prevents removal of the incompatibility.

   Where it is not possible to construe a statute consistently with the Human Rights Act, the inconsistent statute takes precedence regardless of whether it was enacted before or after the Human Rights Act. In the White Paper, *Rights Brought Home: The Human Rights Bill*, Cm 3782, the Government stated:

> 2.13 The Government has reached the conclusion that courts should not have the power to set aside primary legislation, past or future, on the ground of incompatibility with the Convention. This conclusion arises from the importance which the Government attaches to Parliamentary sovereignty. In this context, Parliamentary sovereignty means that Parliament is competent to make any law on any matter of its choosing and no court may question the validity of any Act that it passes. . . . To make provision in the Bill for courts to set aside Acts of Parliament would confer on the judiciary a general power over the decisions of Parliament which under our present constitutional arrangements they do not possess, and would be likely on occasions to draw the judiciary into serious conflict with Parliament.

Does this passage misstate the traditional doctrine of supremacy? When a court applies the doctrine of implied repeal in respect of an earlier statutory provision which is incompatible with a later Act of Parliament, is it respecting the will of Parliament or is it setting itself above Parliament and adjudicating on the validity of legislation?

2. Has the Government in the White Paper confused implied repeal of earlier legislation with setting aside incompatible subsequent legislation?

3. While there may be a reluctance on the part of the courts to rule on the validity of Acts of Parliament, a related issue which has arisen is whether they may adjudicate upon the question whether something purporting to be an Act of Parliament actually is such. It is the Queen in Parliament which enacts legislation. Under the common law, for a Bill to become law it must be approved by the Lords and Commons and receive the Royal Assent. If an Act is challenged on the basis that there have been procedural defects during its passage through Parliament, will the courts look behind the formal words of enactment and inquire whether the requirements of the common law have been satisfied?

Pickin v *British Railways Board*
[1974] AC 765, House of Lords

Pickin was a railway enthusiast who, in 1969, purchased from the owner of a piece of land adjoining a disused railway line, all his estate and interest in the railway land and track. By s. 259 of a private Act of Parliament of 1836 setting up the railway line, it was provided that, if a line should be abandoned, the lands acquired for the track should vest in the owners for the time being of the adjoining lands. Pickin brought an action against the Board, claiming that by virtue of s. 259 he was the owner of that land to mid-track. The Board claimed that it owned the land by virtue of a private Act of Parliament, the British Railways Act 1968. Pickin claimed that the relevant provision (s. 18) of the 1968 Act was invalid and ineffective to deprive him of his title, as Parliament had been misled by the Board to obtain the passage of the Act. In particular the Bill was presented as being unopposed, but notice had not been given to affected landowners as required by Standing Orders. In addition, the preamble to the Bill contained a false recital that plans of the lands and a book of reference to such plans containing the names of the owners, lessees, and occupiers of the said land were duly deposited with the clerk of the county council. The Board sought to have these claims struck out as frivolous, vexatious, and an abuse of the process of the court.

LORD REID: . . . The idea that a court is entitled to disregard a provision in an Act of Parliament on any ground must seem strange and startling to anyone with any knowledge of the history and law of our constitution, but a detailed argument has been submitted to your Lordships and I must deal with it.

I must make it plain that there has been no attempt to question the general supremacy of Parliament. In earlier times many learned lawyers seem to have believed that an Act of Parliament could be disregarded in so far as it was contrary to the law of God or the law of nature or natural justice, but since the supremacy of Parliament was finally demonstrated by the Revolution of 1688 any such idea has become obsolete.

The respondent's contention is that there is a difference between a public and a private Act. There are of course great differences between the methods and procedures followed in dealing with public and private Bills, and there may be some differences in the methods of construing their provisions. But the respondent argues for a much more fundamental difference. There is little in modern authority that he can rely on. The mainstay of his argument is a decision of this House, *Mackenzie* v *Stewart* in 1754.

[In the Court of Appeal Pickin successfully argued that this case was authority for the House of Lords refusing to give effect to a private Act obtained by fraud.]

. . . It appears to me that far the most probable explanation of the decision is that it was a decision as to the true construction of the Act. . . . [I]t seems to me much more likely that Lord Hardwicke LC adopted [the construction argued for by Mackenzie] than that he laid down some new constitutional principle that the court had the power to give relief against the provision of a statute.

If the decision was only as to the construction of a statutory provision that would explain why the case has received little attention in later cases. . . .

In my judgment the law is correctly stated by Lord Campbell in *Edinburgh and Dalkeith Railway Co.* v *Wauchope* (1842) 8 Cl & F 710; 1 Bell 252. Mr Wauchope claimed certain wayleaves. The matter was dealt with in a private Act. He appears to have maintained in the Court of Session that the provisions of that Act should not be applied because it had been passed without his having had notice as required by Standing Orders. . . . Lord Campbell [stated]:

> I must express some surprise that such a notion should have prevailed. It seems to me there is no foundation for it whatever; all that a court of justice can look to is the parliamentary roll; they see that an Act has passed both Houses of Parliament, and that it has received the royal assent, and no court of justice can inquire into the manner in which it was introduced into Parliament, what was done previously to its being introduced, or what passed in Parliament during the various stages of its progress through both Houses of Parliament. I therefore trust that no such inquiry will hereafter be entered into in Scotland, and that due effect will be given to every Act of Parliament, both private as well as public, upon the just construction which appears to arise upon it.

No doubt this was obiter but, so far as I am aware, no one since 1842 has doubted that it is a correct statement of the constitutional position.

The function of the court is to construe and apply the enactments of Parliament. The court has no concern with the manner in which Parliament or its officers carrying out its Standing Orders perform these functions. Any attempt to prove that they were misled by fraud or otherwise would necessarily involve an inquiry into the manner in which they had performed their functions in dealing with the Bill which became the British Railways Act 1968.

In whatever form the respondent's case is pleaded he must prove not only that the appellants acted fraudulently but also that their fraud caused damage to him by causing the enactment of section 18. He could not prove that without an examination of the manner in which the officers of Parliament dealt with the matter. So the court would, or at least might, have to adjudicate upon that.

For a century or more both Parliament and the courts have been careful not to act so as to cause conflict between them. Any such investigations as the respondent seeks could easily lead to such a conflict, and I would only support it if compelled to do so by clear authority. But it appears to me that the whole trend of authority for over a century is clearly against permitting any such investigation.

The respondent is entitled to argue that section 18 should be construed in a way favourable to him and for that reason I have refrained from pronouncing on that matter. But he is not entitled to go behind the Act to show that section 18 should not be enforced. Nor is he entitled to examine proceedings in Parliament in order to show that the appellants by fraudulently misleading Parliament caused him loss. I am therefore clearly of opinion that this appeal should be allowed. . . .

LORD MORRIS OF BORTH-Y-GEST: . . . The question of fundamental importance which arises is whether the court should entertain the proposition that an Act of Parliament can so be assailed in the courts that matters should proceed as though the Act or some part of it had never been passed. I consider that such doctrine would be dangerous and impermissible. It is the function of the courts to administer the laws which Parliament has enacted. In the processes of Parliament there will be much consideration whether a Bill should or should not in one form or another become an enactment. When an enactment is passed there is finality unless and until it is amended or repealed by Parliament. In the courts there may be argument as to the correct interpretation of the enactment: there must be none as to whether it should be on the Statute Book at all.

  . . . The conclusion which I have reached results, in my view, not only from a settled and sustained line of authority which I see no reason to question and which I think should be endorsed but also from the view that any other conclusion would be constitutionally undesirable and impracticable. It must surely be for Parliament to lay down the procedures which are to be followed before a Bill can become an Act. It must be for Parliament to decide whether its decreed procedures have in fact been followed. It must be for Parliament to lay down and to construe its Standing Orders and further to decide whether they have been obeyed: it must be for Parliament to decide whether in any particular case to dispense with compliance with such orders. It must be for Parliament to decide whether it is satisfied that an Act should be passed in the form and with the wording set out in the Act. It must be for Parliament to decide what documentary material or testimony it requires and the extent to which Parliamentary privilege should attach. It would be impracticable and undesirable for the High Court of Justice to embark upon an inquiry concerning the effect or the effectiveness of the internal procedures in the High Court of Parliament or an inquiry whether in any particular case those procedures were effectively followed.

  [His Lordship referred to *Edinburgh and Dalkeith Railway Co.* v *Wauchope* and several other cases and continued.]

  Of equal clarity was the passage in the judgment of Willes J in 1871 when in *Lee* v *Bude and Torrington Junction Railway Co.* (1871) LR 6 CP 576 (in which case it was alleged that Parliament had been induced to pass an Act by fraudulent recitals) he said, at p. 582:

  'Are we to act as regents over what is done by Parliament with the consent of the Queen, Lords, and Commons? I deny that any such authority exists. If an Act of Parliament has been obtained improperly, it is for the legislature to correct it by repealing it: but, so long as it exists as law, the courts are bound to obey it. The proceedings here are judicial, not autocratic, which they would be if we could make laws instead of administering them.'

  . . . In the result I have not been persuaded that any doubt has been cast upon principles which are soundly directed as being both desirable and reasonable and which furthermore have for long been firmly established by authority.

  I would allow the appeal. . . .

Appeal allowed.

QUESTIONS

1. Are Standing Orders of the House of Commons the equivalent of statute law?

2. Does this case overrule the authority of *The Prince's Case* (1606) 8 Co Rep 1a,

where it was stated that an enactment, even though entered on the parliamentary roll, would not be an Act of Parliament if assented to by the King and the Lords, or the King and the Commons, as the assent of all three is necessary?

3. When Lord Morris stated 'It must surely be for Parliament to lay down the procedures which are to be followed before a Bill can become an Act. It must be for Parliament to decide whether its decreed procedures have in fact been followed', was he referring to procedures laid down in Standing Orders or in Acts of Parliament?

NOTE: In the extract which follows, Professor Geoffrey Wilson challenges the traditional Diceyan view that courts will not question the validity of a statute on the grounds of its contents (*cf.* Laws, *ante* p. 59), and Woolf, *ante* p. 58).

G. Wilson, 'Postscript: The Courts, Law and Convention' in Nolan and Sedley (eds), *The Making and Remaking of the British Constitution* (1997), pp. 114–116

It should be said straight away that even the hard-core notion of the unlimited powers of statute is not as unassailable and self-evident as is usually suggested. Quite apart from the fact that, as a doctrine which is rooted in convention as well as law, its continuation in any form depends on its acceptance by the courts, its legal credentials also merit a closer look. . . . But it is a strange feature of writing on this subject that the strongest statements of the principle in all its glory, cited without comment in all the books, are from three cases on private railway Acts, in two of which the House of Lords said it was not prepared to listen to challenges to the validity of a statute on the grounds that the procedures of Parliament had not been observed in their enactment, something for which it did not need to rely on constitutional principle as this is something it had been told not to do by the Bill of Rights, together with a case in the Court of Queen's Bench in which the plaintiffs were told that they could not argue that a statute was invalid on the ground that it had been obtained from Parliament by fraud on the part of the promoters. Somewhat surprisingly these three cases, all of which, besides being relatively trivial, centred on alleged failures of procedure and not the contents of the legislation, are constantly cited for the much wider proposition that the courts will not listen to any challenge to the validity of an Act of Parliament on any ground whatever. They are set alongside statements like that of Leslie Stephen [*Science of Ethics* (1882), p. 143], cited by Dicey, that if an Act of Parliament provided that all blue-eyed babies should be murdered that would be the law of the land which the judges would be under a constitutional duty to enforce.

It is clear that none of these cases raised any real issue as to what the courts would and should do were they faced with legislation which clearly violated a basic constitutional or moral principle. A better test would be if the government and Parliament ever enacted a statute which was so abhorrent that the courts were forced to face up to this problem – imprisoning members of the opposition for example, or authorising the execution of a minority group. Everyone recognises that it is easier to have an absolute negative to intervention rather than run the risk of allowing a line to be drawn somewhere, which could vary with individual judges. At the same time there seems to be a real difficulty in saying on the one hand that to imagine such a statute being enacted is unthinkable without also saying that were such a statute enacted it is not unthinkable that the courts should be expected as a matter of law to enforce it. It may even be that the experience of Nazi Germany has modified views as to what is appropriate and that today's judges, and if not today's then tomorrow's, ought to accept that experience of this kind can lead them to take a different view from that of judges dealing with cases involving private railway Acts in the nineteenth century and that it is not too late at the end of the twentieth to rethink the position.

Just as it can still be argued that the Queen has a reserve power to save the constitution by refusing to agree to legislation or by dismissing a government, even though in practice it might not prove effective, so too one can argue that the judges have a power of last resort to defend the constitution, and not simply by resigning. Nobody should be surprised if in a real case of legislative enormity the courts did not discover a higher principle of law by which they felt free or even obliged to ignore the current version of the doctrine not only in the name of constitutional convention but also in the name of law.

This suggests that even as a matter of strict law the doctrine is not as absolute and inviolable as it is usually presented. The fact that it is the courts which have the last word and may not yet have pronounced it, has been recently confirmed by their recent action in accepting the supremacy of Community law even over statute, something which shows that the doctrine is not as durable as was once thought and also that it ultimately depends on its continued acceptance by the courts.

SECTION 4: Can Parliament Limit the Powers of its Successors?

The answer to this question depends upon the nature of parliamentary supremacy. There are differing theories. Hart recognized that there could be uncertainty regarding the nature of the rule of recognition.

H. L. A. Hart, *The Concept of Law*
(1961), pp. 145–146

In the overwhelming majority of cases the formula 'Whatever the Queen in Parliament enacts is law' is an adequate expression of the rule as to the legal competence of Parliament, and is accepted as an ultimate criterion for the identification of law, however open the rules thus identified may be at their periphery. But doubts can arise as to its meaning or scope; we can ask what is meant by 'enacted by Parliament' and when doubts arise they may be settled by the courts. What inference is to be drawn as to the place of courts within a legal system from the fact that the ultimate rule of a legal system may thus be in doubt and that courts may resolve the doubt. Does it require some qualification of the thesis that the foundation of a legal system is an accepted rule of recognition specifying the criteria of legal validity?

To answer these questions we shall consider here some aspects of the English doctrine of the sovereignty of Parliament, though, of course, similar doubts can arise in relation to ultimate criteria of legal validity in any system. Under the influence of the Austinian doctrine that law is essentially the product of a legally untrammelled will, older constitutional theorists wrote as if it was a logical necessity that there should be a legislature which was sovereign, in the sense that it is free, at every moment of its existence as a continuing body, not only from legal limitations imposed *ab extra*, but also from its own prior legislation. That Parliament is sovereign in this sense may now be regarded as established, and the principle that no earlier Parliament can preclude its 'successors' from repealing its legislation constitutes part of the ultimate rule of recognition used by the courts in identifying valid rules of law. It is, however, important to see that no necessity of logic, still less of nature, dictates that there should be such a Parliament; it is only one arrangement among others, equally conceivable, which has come to be accepted with us as the criterion of legal validity. Among these others is another principle which might equally well, perhaps better, deserve the name of 'sovereignty'. This is the principle that Parliament should *not* be incapable of limiting irrevocably the legislative competence of its successors but, on the contrary, should have this wider self-limiting power. Parliament would then at least once in its history be capable of exercising an even larger sphere of legislative competence than the accepted established doctrine allows to it. The requirement that at every moment of its existence Parliament should be free from legal limitations including even those imposed by itself is, after all, only one interpretation of the ambiguous idea of legal omnipotence. It in effect makes a choice between a *continuing* omnipotence in all matters not affecting the legislative competence of successive parliaments, and an unrestricted *self-embracing* omnipotence the exercise of which can only be enjoyed once. These two conceptions of omnipotence have their parallel in two conceptions of an omnipotent God: on the one hand, a God who at every moment of His existence enjoys the same powers and so is incapable of cutting down those powers, and, on the other, a God whose powers include the power to destroy for the future his omnipotence. Which form of omnipotence – continuing or self-embracing – our Parliament enjoys is an empirical question concerning the form of rule which is accepted as the ultimate criterion in identifying the law. Though it is a question about a rule lying at the base of a legal system, it is still a question of fact to which at any given moment of time, on some points at least, there may be a quite determinate answer. Thus it is clear that the presently accepted rule is one of continuing sovereignty, so that Parliament cannot protect its statutes from repeal.

NOTE: Dicey was a proponent of the 'continuing' theory of parliamentary supremacy, usually referred to as the 'traditional' theory. Others have tended towards the 'self-embracing' theory, or a variant of it. Proponents of this 'new' view would argue that Parliament may change the procedures governing law-making. The two extracts which follow summarize this view and point to its consequences.

R. F. V. Heuston, *Essays in Constitutional Law*
(2nd edn, 1964), Ch. 1, pp. 6–8

Summary of New View
It is suggested that the new view can be summarised thus:

(1) Sovereignty is a legal concept: the rules which identify the sovereign and prescribe its composition and functions are logically prior to it.

(2) There is a distinction between rules which govern, on the one hand, (a) the composition, and (b) the procedure, and, on the other hand, (c) the area of power, of a sovereign legislature.

(3) The courts have jurisdiction to question the validity of an alleged Act of Parliament on grounds 2 (a) and 2 (b), but not on ground 2 (c).

(4) This jurisdiction is exercisable either before or after the Royal Assent has been signified – in the former case by way of injunction, in the latter by way of declaratory judgment.

G. Marshall, *Constitutional Theory*
(1971), pp. 42–43

Dicey simply implied, without examining, the proposition that authority in a 'sovereign' Parliament must be exercised at all times by a simple majority of legislators, who, since they are unrestricted in their powers, can always repeal any constitutional protections or restrictions on power enacted into law by their predecessors. To do Dicey justice, the Sovereign described in the *Law of the Constitution* is the British Parliament (though he did sometimes speak in terms of sovereigns in general). But even in relation to the British Parliament he did not fully examine the possibility that Parliament as at present constituted might conceivably bind the future or circumscribe the freedom of future legislators, not by laying down blanket prohibitions or attempting to enact a fundamental Bill of Rights, but by using their authority to provide different forms and procedures for legislation. A referendum or a joint sitting, for example, might be prescribed before certain things could be done. Or a two-thirds majority. Or a seventy-five per cent or eighty per cent majority. If it is also provided that any repeal of such provisions should not be by simple majority, the courts may be able to protect the arrangements laid down by declaring in suitable proceedings that any purported repeal by simple majority of a protected provision is *ultra vires* as being not, in the sense required by law, an 'Act of

Parliament'. In this finding they would not be in any way derogating from parliamentary sovereignty but protecting Parliament's authority from usurpation by those not entitled for the purpose in hand to exercise it. Thus, for the English lawyer or political theorist, sovereignty may be purged of its dangerous absolutism. He can believe both in an ultimate Sovereign and in the possibility of restraint imposed by law upon the way in which legal power is used. He can believe in the possibility even of a modified Bill of Fundamental Rights grafted into the British constitution – or, to be more accurate, in a relatively fundamental set of provisions in which selected civil liberties are protected from attack in the future by, so to speak, taking out legislative insurance in the present, in the shape of requirements of special procedures or majorities. This would be to do rather more than is done in Canada's Bill of Rights, which declares certain rights and freedoms to be fundamental, but leaves them open to attack by any future legislation which specifically declares itself to apply, notwithstanding the Bill of Rights.

For the views of a proponent of the continuing theory of supremacy, see H.W. R. Wade, 'The Basis of Legal Sovereignty' [1955] CLJ 172.

A: The problem of entrenchment

The Parliament Acts 1911–49 provide that in certain circumstances a Bill may become an Act in the absence of approval by the Lords. The 1911 Act, which removed the power of the House of Lords to veto legislation, replacing it with a two-year delaying power, was enacted in accordance with the then existing law which required majorities in both Houses approving the Bill before it received the Royal Assent. The 1949 Act, which reduced the delaying power to one year, was likewise enacted in accordance with the then existing law as laid down in the 1911 Act. These Acts made alterations in the procedures for enacting legislation by dispensing, in certain circumstances, with the requirement that the Lords assent to legislation. If Parliament can make the passage of legislation easier in certain circumstances, could it impose procedural requirements to make the passage of legislation more difficult, for example, a requirement that a majority of voters vote in a referendum in favour of the proposed legislation, or a requirement of an enhanced majority in the Commons such as two-thirds instead of a simple majority? This issue has arisen in several Commonwealth cases.

Attorney-General for New South Wales v *Trethowan and Others*
[1932] AC 526, Privy Council

> Under s. 5 of the Colonial Laws Validity Act 1865, the legislature of New South Wales had full power to legislate for its own constitution, powers, and procedure, provided that these laws were passed in 'the manner and form' required by the law in force at the time, whether it be imperial or colonial. In 1929 the Constitution (Legislative Council) Amendment Act was passed, which inserted a new s. 7A in the Constitution Act 1902, providing that no Bill for abolishing the Legislative Council should be presented to the Governor for His Majesty's assent until it had been approved by a majority of electors voting in a referendum and, further, that any Bill to repeal this referendum requirement must also be approved at a referendum. In 1930, following a change in government, both houses of the

legislature passed two Bills, one to repeal s. 7A and the other to abolish the Legislative Council, both of which the government intended to present for the Royal Assent without referenda being held. The plaintiffs were members of the Legislative Council and sought a declaration that the two Bills could not be presented for Royal Assent until approved by the electors in accordance with s. 7A, and injunctions restraining the presentation of the Bills.

LORD SANKEY LC: . . . [T]he point involved in the case, . . . is really a short one – namely, whether the legislature of the State of New South Wales has power to abolish the Legislative Council of the said State, or to repeal s. 7A of the Constitution Act, 1902, except in the manner provided by the said s. 7A. It will be sufficient for this Board to decide any other question if, and when, it arises.

[Section 5 of the Colonial Laws Validity Act 1865 provides:

> Section 5. – Every colonial legislature shall have and be deemed at all times to have had full power within its jurisdiction to establish Courts of Judicature, and to abolish and reconstitute the same, and to alter the constitution thereof, and to make provision for the administration of justice therein; and every representative legislature shall, in respect to the colony under its jurisdiction, have, and be deemed at all times to have had, full power to make laws respecting the constitution, power, and procedure of such legislature; provided that such laws shall have been passed in such manner and form as may from time to time be required by any Act of parliament, letters patent, Order in Council, or colonial law, for the time being in force in the said colony.]

. . . In their Lordships' opinion the legislature of New South Wales had power under s. 5 of the Act of 1865 to enact the Constitution (Legislative Council) Amendment Act, 1929, and thereby to introduce s. 7A into the Constitution Act, 1902. In other words, the legislature had power to alter the constitution of New South Wales by enacting that Bills relating to specified kind or kinds of legislation (e.g., abolishing the Legislative Council or altering its constitution or powers, or repealing or amending that enactment) should not be presented for the Royal assent until approved by the electors in a prescribed manner. There is here no question of repugnancy. The enactment of the Act of 1929 was simply an exercise by the legislature of New South Wales of its power (adopting the words of s. 5 of the Act of 1865) to make laws respecting the constitution, powers and procedure of the authority competent to make the laws for New South Wales.

The whole of s. 7A was competently enacted. It was intra vires s. 5 of the Act of 1865, and was (again adopting the words of s. 5) a colonial law for the time being in force when the Bill to repeal s. 7A was introduced in the Legislative Council.

The question then arises, could *that* Bill, a repealing Bill, after its passage through both chambers, be lawfully presented for the Royal assent without having first received the approval of the electors in the prescribed manner? In their Lordships' opinion, the Bill could not lawfully be so presented. The proviso in the second sentence of s. 5 of the Act of 1865 states a condition which must be fulfilled before the legislature can validly exercise its power to make the kind of laws which are referred to in that sentence. In order that s. 7A may be repealed (in other words, in order that *that* particular law 'respecting the constitution, powers and procedure' of the legislature may be validly made) the law for that purpose must have been passed in the manner required by s. 7A, a colonial law for the time being in force in New South Wales. An attempt was made to draw some distinction between a Bill to repeal a statute and a Bill for other purposes and between 'making' laws and the word in the proviso, 'passed.' Their Lordships feel unable to draw any such distinctions. As to the proviso they agree with the views expressed by Rich J [in the High Court of Australia] in the following words: 'I take the word "passed" to be equivalent to "enacted." The proviso is not dealing with narrow questions of parliamentary procedure'; and later in his judgment: 'In my opinion the proviso to s. 5 relates to the entire process of turning a proposed law into a legislative enactment, and was intended to enjoin fulfilment of every condition and compliance with every requirement which existing legislation imposed upon the process of law making.'

Again, no question of repugnancy here arises. It is only a question whether the proposed enactment is intra vires or ultra vires s. 5. A Bill, within the scope of sub – s. 6 of s. 7A, which received the Royal assent without having been approved by the electors in accordance with that section, would not be a valid Act of the legislature. It would be ultra vires s. 5 of the Act of 1865. Indeed, the presentation of the Bill to the Governor without such approval would be the commission of an unlawful act.

In the result, their Lordships are of opinion that s. 7A of the Constitution Act, 1902, was valid and was in force when the two Bills under consideration were passed through the Legislative Council and the Legislative Assembly. Therefore these Bills could not be presented to the Governor for His Majesty's assent unless and until a majority of the electors voting had approved them.

For these reasons, their Lordships are of opinion that the judgment of the High Court dismissing the appeal from the decree of the Supreme Court of New South Wales was right. . . .

Appeal dismissed.

QUESTION

If the United Kingdom Parliament enacted a provision to the same effect as s. 7A, designed to protect the position of the House of Lords, would a subsequent Bill abolishing this provision and the House of Lords become an Act on receiving the Royal Assent, or would the referenda requirements be regarded by the courts as necessary prerequisites to the Bill becoming an Act?

NOTE: There is a division of view among constitutional theorists as to the relevance of the *Trethowan* case to the United Kingdom. Those who adhere to the traditional theory of supremacy argue that the decision is of no relevance as the New South Wales legislature was a subordinate legislature (see, e.g. Wade, 'The Basis of Legal Sovereignty' [1955] CLJ 172; Munro, *Studies in Constitutional Law*, 2nd edn, Chapter 5). The proponents of this view rely on *Ellen St Estates Ltd* v *Minister of Health* (*supra*). Opponents of this view argue that the decision is applicable on the basis that at common law there is a rule that legislation may be enacted only in such manner and form as is prescribed by the law (see, e.g. Heuston, *Essays in Constitutional Law*, Chapter 1; Fazal, 'Entrenched Rights and Parliamentary Sovereignty' (1974) PL 295). If an Act lays down a specific procedure to be followed before it may be repealed, this is the law, and a measure passed in the normal way ignoring this procedure has not been passed in the manner and form prescribed by the law and therefore is not an Act of Parliament. Support for this view is found in *Harris* v *Minister of the Interior* 1952 (2) SA 428, and *Bribery Commissioner* v *Ranasinghe* [1965] AC 172. In the latter case the Privy Council held that the procedural requirement of the constitution of Ceylon regarding judicial appointments of a two-thirds majority of the legislature, was binding on the sovereign Parliament of Ceylon, which could not, therefore, set up the Bribery Commission by an ordinary Act of Parliament. The Privy Council held that the official copy of the statute was not conclusive of its validity if it appeared that the correct procedures had not been followed. Lord Pearce stated, at p. 197:

> [A] legislature has no power to ignore the conditions of law-making that are imposed by the instrument which itself regulates its power to make law. This restriction exists independently of the question whether the legislature is sovereign. . . .

This statement would appear to lend support to Heuston and Fazal. However, the traditional theorists argue that *Harris* and *Ranasinghe* are not relevant to the United Kingdom because the legislatures of South Africa and Ceylon were subject to constitutent instruments, whereas the

United Kingdom has no written constitution. Latham in *The Law and the Commonwealth* (1949), p. 523, states:

> When the purported sovereign is anyone but a single actual person, the designation of him must include the statement of the rules for ascertainment of his will, and these rules, since their observance is a condition of the validity of his legislation are Rules of Law logically prior to him.

Is it crucial that these rules should be contained in a formal written constitution? Heuston believes not; he states (*supra*, at p. 26):

> It cannot make any difference whether the rules which identify the sovereign come entirely from the common law (as they did before 1911 in the United Kingdom) or entirely from statute (as they do in Ireland, New South Wales and South Africa) or partly from the common law and partly from statute (as they do in the United Kingdom since 1911). It is hard to see why those who argue thus should attach so much importance to the formal source of the complex set of rules identifying the location and composition of the sovereign. . . . The point here is the simple one that until these rules (whatever their source) have been changed in accordance with the manner which they themselves prescribe they must be obeyed.

QUESTIONS

1. Is it a necessary concomitant of supremacy that Parliament's powers to legislate be not subject to any procedural restraint? Marshall, 'Parliamentary sovereignty: the new horizons' [1997] *Public Law* 1, at p. 4 states:

> . . . May a sovereign legislative body that acts by simple majority protect particularly important statutes of its own making . . . by providing for its repeal or amendment to require a specific majority, or possibly the backing of a referendum? . . . No UK enactment has ever attempted such a thing and in 1978 the House of Lords Select Committee on a Bill of Rights was advised that it was not possible. But of course it is possible if the courts believe that the power to change the law extends to a power to change the law about the way law is made. There is nothing in Dicey's concept of parliamentary sovereignty that is incompatible with this possibility. Procedurally and tactically it would be prudent for a special majority requirement to be applied not to an enacted Bill at the stage of a royal assent, but so as to prevent the further progress of any Bill of the prescribed kind that has not been carried by the required special majority at its second reading. Caution would suggest that an entrenching Act should also provide a judicial remedy to secure its enforcement, expressed to operate notwithstanding any existing rules as to standing or parliamentary privilege. If the remedy is effective, there would not then, on any view, be a later alleged Act of Parliament to rival the authority of the entrenchment statute or to threaten it with implicit repeal.

2. Is Dixon misguided in stating, in 'The Law and the Constitution' (1935) 51 LQR 590, at p. 604, that the *Trethowan* case was:

> a modern reconciliation of the supremacy of the law and the supremacy of Parliament. For it is a demarcation of the limits of the operation of the two principles. The law existing for the time being is supreme when it prescribes the conditions which must be fulfilled to make a law. But on the question what may be done by a law so made, Parliament is supreme over the law?

3. Imagine that in response to an outbreak of terrorism the government introduced the Anti-Terrorism (Emergency Provisions) Bill which was rushed through all its parliamentary stages in a day receiving the Royal Assent the following day. The Home Secretary, who introduced the Bill, did not make a 'statement of compatibility' as required by s. 19(1)(a) of the Human Rights Act 1998 (see p. 495, *post*), nor did he make a statement that the government wished the House to proceed with the Bill although he was unable to make a statement of compatibility. T is arrested by the police exercising new powers accorded them by the Anti-Terrorism (Emergency Provisions) Act. T applies to the Divisional Court for a writ of *habeas corpus* arguing that his arrest is unlawful as the Anti-Terrorism (Emergency Provisions) Act is not a duly enacted Act of Parliament. How might the court determine his application?

B: The Acts of Union

So far it has been assumed that Parliament is not subject to any constituent instrument. However, in 1707 the Parliaments of England and Scotland passed Acts of Union ratifying the Treaty of Union and creating the new Parliament of Great Britain. In 1800 a similar union took place between Great Britain and Ireland, creating the United Kingdom of Great Britain and Ireland. As these Acts of Union were antecedent to the new Parliaments they created, it is arguable that they were constituent Acts bringing into being a new state and a new Parliament (see Mitchell, *Constitutional Law* (2nd edn, 1968), pp. 69–74; Calvert, *Constitutional Law in Northern Ireland* (1968), Chapter 1; for a contrary view see Munro, *Studies in Constitutional Law* (1999), Chapter 5).

Certain provisions of the Treaties were declared to be fundamental and unalterable. The subsequent history reveals, however, that such provisions have been amended or repealed (see, e.g. the Universities (Scotland) Act 1853 and the Irish Church Act 1869); indeed the Union with Ireland was dissolved in 1922 when most of Ireland was given independence, with only Northern Ireland remaining in the United Kingdom. The issue of the nature of the Acts of Union has been argued in several Scottish cases but was not finally adjudicated upon.

MacCormick v *Lord Advocate*
[1953] SC 396, Court of Session, Inner House

Two members of the Scottish public petitioned the Court of Session for a declaration that a proclamation describing the Queen as 'Elizabeth the Second of the United Kingdom of Great Britain' was illegal, as being contrary to Article I of the Treaty and Acts of Union. The Lord Advocate argued that there was no conflict with Article I and that the number 'II' was authorized by the Royal Titles Act 1953. *Held*: The petition was dismissed, and the petitioners' appeal to the First Division of the Inner House was likewise dismissed on the grounds that there was nothing in Article I which forbade the use of the numeral, the petitioners had no title to sue, and the Royal Titles Act 1953 was irrelevant as it was enacted after the designation 'Elizabeth the Second' had been adopted and used. The President then went on to express his opinion on the Union legislation.

THE LORD PRESIDENT (COOPER): . . . The principle of the unlimited sovereignty of Parliament is a distinctively English principle which has no counterpart in Scottish constitutional law. . . . Considering that the Union legislation extinguished the Parliaments of Scotland and England and replaced them by a new Parliament, I have difficulty in seeing why it should have been supposed that the new Parliament of Great Britain must inherit all the peculiar characteristics of the English Parliament but none of the Scottish Parliament, as if all that happened in 1707 was that Scottish representatives were admitted to the Parliament of England. That is not what was done. Further, the Treaty and the associated legislation, by which the Parliament of Great Britain was brought into being as the successor of the separate Parliaments of Scotland and England, contain some clauses which expressly reserve to the Parliament of Great Britain powers of subsequent modification, and other clauses which either contain no such power or emphatically exclude subsequent alteration by declarations that the provision shall be fundamental and unalterable in all time coming, or declarations of a like effect. I have never been able to understand how it is possible to reconcile with elementary canons of construction the adoption by the English constitutional theorists of the same attitude to these markedly different types of provisions.

The Lord Advocate conceded this point by admitting that the Parliament of Great Britain 'could not' repeal or alter such 'fundamental and essential' conditions. . . . I have not found in the Union legislation any provision that the Parliament of Great Britain should be 'absolutely sovereign' in the sense that that Parliament should be free to alter the Treaty at will. . . .

But the petitioners have still a grave difficulty to overcome on this branch of their argument. Accepting it that there are provisions in the Treaty of Union and associated legislation which are 'fundamental law,' and assuming for the moment that something is alleged to have been done – it matters not whether with legislative authority or not – in breach of that fundamental law, the question remains whether such a question is determinable as a justiciable issue in the Courts of either Scotland or England, in the same fashion as an issue of constitutional *vires* would be cognisable by the Supreme Courts of the United States, or of South Africa or Australia. I reserve my opinion with regard to the provisions relating expressly to this Court and to the laws 'which concern private right' which are administered here. This is not such a question, but a matter of 'public right' (articles 18 and 19). To put the matter in another way, it is of little avail to ask whether the Parliament of Great Britain 'can' do this thing or that, without going on to inquire who can stop them if they do. Any person 'can' repudiate his solemn engagement but he cannot normally do so with impunity. Only two answers have been suggested to this corollary to the main question. The first is the exceedingly cynical answer implied by Dicey (Law of the Constitution, (9th ed.) p. 82) in the statement that 'it would be rash of the Imperial Parliament to abolish the Scotch law courts, and assimilate the Law of Scotland to that of England. But no one can feel sure at what point Scottish resistance to such a change would become serious.' The other answer was that nowadays there may be room for the invocation of an 'advisory opinion' from the International Court of Justice. On these matters I express no view. This at least is plain, that there is neither precedent nor authority of any kind for the view that the domestic Courts of either Scotland or England have jurisdiction to determine whether a governmental act of the type here in controversy is or is not conform to the provisions of a Treaty, least of all when that Treaty is one under which both Scotland and England ceased to be independent states and merged their identity in an incorporating union. From the standpoint both of constitutional law and of international law the position appears to me to be unique, and I am constrained to hold that the action as laid is incompetent in respect that it has not been shown that the Court of Session has authority to entertain the issue sought to be raised. . . .

NOTE: In *Gibson v Lord Advocate* 1975 SLT 134, a Scottish fisherman challenged an EEC Regulation which had become law by virtue of the European Communities Act 1972. The Regulation gave member states equal access to fishing grounds. Gibson argued that this was invalid, being in breach of Article XVIII which forbade 'alteration . . . in the laws which concern private right except for the evident utility of the subjects within Scotland'. Lord Keith held that the control of fishing in territorial waters was not a matter of private right but of public law, and thus was not protected by Article XVIII. However, he went on to state *obiter*:

> Like Lord President Cooper, I prefer to reserve my opinion on what the question would be if the United Kingdom Parliament passed an Act purporting to abolish the Court of Session or the Church of Scotland or to substitute English law for the whole body of Scots private law. I am, however, of opinion that the question whether a particular Act of the United Kingdom Parliament altering a particular aspect of Scots private law is or is not 'for the evident utility' of the subjects within Scotland is not a justiciable issue in this court. The making of decisions upon what must essentially be a political matter is no part of the function of the court, and it is highly undesirable that it should be.

By contrast, in *Stewart* v *Henry* 1989 SLT (SH Ct) 34, Sheriff Stewart went so far as to say that he saw 'no absolute bar to a court's considering the question whether a particular change in the law is for the evident utility of the subjects in Scotland'. In the most recent case of *Pringle* 1991 SLT 330, which, like *Stewart* v *Henry*, concerned the legislation which introduced the community charge in Scotland one year earlier than in England and Wales, it was argued that this contravened Art. IV of the Scots Act of Union which it was claimed required that there should be no difference in the rights, privileges and advantages enjoyed by citizens in Great Britain unless expressly provided for in the treaty. The petitioner did not seek to have the relevant statute (the Abolition of Domestic Rates Etc. (Scotland) Act 1987) declared invalid but rather sought relief from his own liability under the Act to pay the charge because of its alleged contravention of Art. IV. The First Division of the Inner House dismissed the petition on the basis that it did not have jurisdiction to grant the exceptional remedy sought. While this was sufficient to decide the case Lord Hope, the Lord President, declined to accept the respondent registration officer's submission that the petitioner's arguments that the 1987 Act breached Art. IV raised a non-justiciable issue. Lord Hope stated (at p. 333):

> The fact that the methods of raising finance for local government in the two parts of the United Kingdom were different for the year in question would not be sufficient to persuade me, without a much more detailed inquiry into the overall effects of these differences, that there was a failure to do what this part of Art. IV intended should be done.

The inference to be drawn is that Lord Hope believed there might be circumstances in which a court could consider whether legislation was inconsistent with union legislation. The question of the constitutional effect of the Scots Articles of Union continues to remain unresolved.

In *Ex p. Canon Selwyn*, (1872) 36 JP 54, the issue of the validity of the Irish Church Act 1869 was raised. This Act disestablished and disendowed the Episcopal Church in Ireland which Article 5 of the Treaty of Union had established for ever. Mandamus was sought against the Lord President of the Council, commanding him to present to the Queen a petition asking her to refer for adjudication the question whether her assent to the Irish Church Act 1869 was contrary to the Coronation Oath and the Act of Settlement 1700. The application was refused by Cockburn CJ on the ground that 'there is no judicial body in the country by which the validity of an act of parliament could be questioned. An act of the legislature is superior in authority to any court of law'. Calvert takes issue with Cockburn CJ.

H. Calvert, *Constitutional Law in Northern Ireland*
(1968), p. 21

These are strong words. But whilst the Coronation Oath did contain a solemn pledge to maintain the unified and established Church of England and Ireland, it is not here suggested that an Act can be challenged on this ground, or on grounds of contravention of the Act of Settlement. What it is suggested could have been, and what, surprisingly, was not argued in *Ex parte Canon Selwyn*, is that the severance and disestablishment of the Church of Ireland was a legal act power to effect which was withheld from the Parliament of the United Kingdom by its constituent Acts. It is all very well to speak of applying 'the law as we find it.' That begs the question of what we find. A judge appointed before 1800 and continuing in office after 1800 would find himself in a considerable dilemma. Sworn to uphold the laws of parliament, he would find two conflicting laws of two different parliaments, one purporting to disestablish the Irish Church and the other, which constituted the parliament enacting the first, having imposed upon it a statutory prohibition from disestablishing. It is, again, all very well to speak of 'an act of the legislature' being 'superior in authority to any court of law.' No doubt it is – but that is not the question. The question may be viewed as being whether 'an act of the legislature' is 'superior in authority' to a prior constituent Act of a predecessor parliament. There is a difference, which has been overlooked but which may well be crucial, between a parliament repealing its own Acts, and a parliament purporting to repeal the Acts of its constituent predecessor. English courts have never been faced, four square, with this question and English law has therefore never finally made up its mind – *a fortiori* Irish law.

QUESTIONS

1. Is Cockburn CJ's dictum reconcilable with the *obiter dicta* in *MacCormick* and *Gibson*?

2. Middleton, 'New Thoughts on the Union' 1954 JR 37, at p. 49, states that 'the fact that Parliament has done something cannot prove that it was entitled to do it'. Do the amendments to, and breaches and repeals of, provisions of the Acts of Union reveal that Parliament is supreme and unconstrained in its powers, or is it the case that Parliament is limited but there is no authority competent to rule on the validity of its Acts, that is, the amendments and repeals are invalid in legal theory but in political reality they exist and are acted upon?

3. Jennings, in *The Law and the Constitution* (5th edn, 1959), p. 170, argues that as the Acts of Union were passed to ratify two treaties, the amendments to these treaties were carried out in accordance with the maxim *nebus sic stantibus*, that is, it is a tacit condition attaching to all treaties that they shall cease to be obligatory so soon as the state of facts and conditions upon which they were founded has substantially changed. Is this a satisfactory explanation for the subsequent amendments to these treaties? If the conditions have not substantially changed in respect of a particular provision, would legislation in respect of it be illegal? If so, could or would any court declare it invalid?

C: Independence

One of the problems which constitutional lawyers have had to deal with this century is the granting of independence to many Commonwealth countries. This usually followed a two-stage process, with the colony being granted first Dominion status and subsequently being granted full independence. Section 4 of the Statute of Westminster provides:

No Act of Parliament of the United Kingdom passed after the commencement of this Act shall extend, or be deemed to extend, to a Dominion as part of the law of that Dominion unless it is expressly declared in that Act that that Dominion has requested and consented to, the enactment thereof.

This gives rise to the question whether Parliament could ignore this provision and legislate directly for a Dominion without its request or consent? In *British Coal Corporation* v *The King* [1935] AC 500, at p. 520, Lord Sankey stated, regarding the application of s. 4 to Canada:

It is doubtless true that the power of the Imperial Parliament to pass on its own initiative any legislation that it thought fit extending to Canada remains in theory unimpaired: indeed, the Imperial Parliament could, as a matter of abstract law, repeal or disregard s. 4 of the Statute. . . . But that is theory and has no relation to realities.

In *Blackburn* v *Attorney-General* [1971] 1 WLR 1037, at p. 1040, Lord Denning stated:

We have all been brought up to believe that, in legal theory, one Parliament cannot bind another and that no Act is irreversible. But legal theory does not always march alongside political reality. Take the Statute of Westminster 1931, which takes away the power of Parliament to legislate for the Dominions. Can anyone imagine that Parliament could or would reverse that Statute? Take the Acts which have granted independence to the Dominions and territories overseas. Can anyone imagine that Parliament could or would reverse those laws and take away their independence? Most clearly not. Freedom once given cannot be taken away. Legal theory must give way to practical politics.

However, legal theory still dominates judicial reasoning. In 1965 when Rhodesia declared UDI, the Southern Rhodesia Act 1965 was rushed through Parliament. In terms of practical politics the Act had no effect in Rhodesia, where it was ignored. However, in *Madzimbamuto* v *Lardner-Burke* [1969] 1 AC 645, Lord Reid recited legal theory:

It is often said that it would be unconstitutional for the United Kingdom Parliament to do certain things, meaning that the moral, political and other reasons against doing them are so strong that most people would regard it as highly improper if Parliament did these things. But that does not mean that it is beyond the power of Parliament to do these things. If Parliament chose to do any of them, the courts could not hold the Act of Parliament invalid.

Is it therefore impossible for Parliament to divest itself of the power to legislate for independent territories? Dicey's solution to the problem was the idea of abdication. He stated (p. 54 *supra*, at p. 68):

The impossibility of placing a limit on the exercise of sovereignty does not in any way prohibit either logically, or in matter of fact, the abdication of sovereignty. This is worth observation, because a strange dogma is sometimes put forward that a sovereign power, such as the Parliament of the United Kingdom, can never by its own act divest itself of sovereignty. This position is, however, clearly untenable.

QUESTION

In 1982 the United Kingdom Parliament enacted a new constitution for Canada by the Canada Act, and terminated its own legislative competence for Canada. Section 2 provides:

No Act of the Parliament of the United Kingdom passed after the Constitution Act 1982 comes into force shall extend to Canada as part of its law.

If Parliament subsequently legislated for Canada would this legislation be *ultra vires*? Would a United Kingdom court be acting unconstitutionally in light of Dicey's doctrine of abdication, if it did not declare the offending statute invalid?

NOTE: The confusion which reigns in this area is evident in the following case.

Manuel v *Attorney-General*
[1983] Ch 77, Chancery Division

The Canada Act 1982 was enacted following the request of the Senate and House of Commons of Canada, and with the agreement of nine of the ten provincial governments. The claimants (previously called 'plaintiffs' were Aboriginal (Indian) Chiefs and sought declarations to the effect that the United Kingdom parliament had no power to amend the constitution of Canada so as to prejudice the Aboriginal nations without their consent, and that the Canada Act 1982 was *ultra vires*. The basis of their claim was that the enactment of the Canada Act 1982 was inconsistent with and a derogation from the constitutional safeguards provided for the Aboriginal peoples by the Statute of Westminster 1931 and the British North America Acts. The claimants' contention was that the consent of all the provincial legislatures, the Aboriginal nations of Canada and the federal Parliament were necessary before amendments to the Canadian Constitution (contained in the British North America Acts) could be enacted. The Attorney-General moved that the statement of claim be struck out as showing no reasonable cause of action.

MEGARRY VC: . . . On the face of it, a contention that an Act of Parliament is ultra vires is bold in the extreme. It is contrary to one of the fundamentals of the British Constitution. . . .

As was said by Lord Morris of Borth-y-Gest, at p. 789, it is not for the courts to proceed 'as though the Act or some part of it had never been passed'; there may be argument on the interpretation of the Act, but 'there must be none as to whether it should be on the Statute Book at all.' Any complaint on such matters is for Parliament to deal with and not the courts. . . .

Mr Macdonald [counsel for the claimants] was, of course, concerned to restrict the ambit of the decision in *Pickin* v *British Railways Board*. He accepted that it was a binding decision for domestic legislation, but he said that it did not apply in relation to the Statute of Westminster 1931 or to the other countries of the Commonwealth. He also contended that it decided no more than that the courts would not inquire into what occurred in the course of the passage of a bill through Parliament, relying on what Lord Reid said at p. 787. This latter point is, I think, plainly wrong, since it ignores the words 'what was done previously to its being introduced' which Lord Reid cited with approval on that page. The wider point, however, is founded upon the theory that Parliament may surrender its sovereign power over some territory or area of land to another person or body. . . . After such a surrender, any legislation which Parliament purports to enact for that territory is not merely ineffective there, but is totally void, in this country as elsewhere, since Parliament has surrendered the power to legislate; and the English courts have jurisdiction to declare such legislation ultra vires and void. . . .

[The claimants argued that the United Kingdom Parliament had, by the Statute of Westminster 1931, transferred sovereignty to Canada and had deprived itself of all power to legislate for Canada subject only to s. 7 of that Act. Section 7 reserved to Parliament the power to repeal, amend or alter the British North America Acts. The claimants further argued that the true meaning of s. 4 of the 1931 Act dictated that these residuary legislative powers could only be exercised pursuant to the actual request and consent of the Dominion. For these purposes 'Dominion' meant not merely the Parliament of Canada but all the constituent constitutional factions of the Dominion, namely, Parliament, the provincial legislatures and the Aboriginal nations. As no such general consent had been given it was argued that the United Kingdom Parliament could not legislate for Canada. Megarry VC continued.] I am bound to say that from first to last I have heard nothing in this case to make me doubt the simple rule that the duty of the court is to obey and apply every Act of Parliament, and that the court cannot hold any such Act to be ultra vires. Of course there may be questions about what the Act means, and of course there is power to hold statutory instruments and other subordinate legislation ultra vires. But once an instrument is recognised as being an Act of Parliament, no English court can refuse to obey it or question its validity.

In the present case I have before me a copy of the Canada Act 1982 purporting to be published by Her Majesty's Stationery Office. After reciting the request and consent of Canada and the submission of an address to Her Majesty by the Senate and House of Commons of Canada, there are the words of enactment:

> 'Be it therefore enacted by the Queen's Most Excellent Majesty, by and with the advice and consent of the Lords Spiritual and Temporal, and Commons, in this present Parliament assembled, and by the authority of the same, as follows: . . .'

There has been no suggestion that the copy before me is not a true copy of the Act itself, or that it was not passed by the House of Commons and the House of Lords, or did not receive the Royal Assent. . . . The Canada Act 1982 is an Act of Parliament, and sitting as a judge in an English court I owe full and dutiful obedience to that Act.

I do not think that, as a matter of law, it makes any difference if the Act in question purports to apply outside the United Kingdom. I speak not merely of statutes such as the Continental Shelf Act 1964 but also of statutes purporting to apply to other countries. If that other country is a colony, the English courts will apply the Act even if the colony is in a state of revolt against the Crown and direct enforcement of the decision may be impossible: see *Madzimbamuto* v *Lardner-Burke* [1969] 1 AC 645. It matters not if a convention had grown up that the United Kingdom Parliament would not legislate for that colony without the consent of the colony. Such a convention would not limit the powers of Parliament, and if Parliament legislated in breach of the convention, 'the courts could not hold the Act of Parliament invalid': see p. 723. Similarly if the other country is a foreign state which has never been British, I do not think that any English court would or could declare the Act ultra vires and void. No doubt the Act would normally be ignored by the foreign state and would not be enforced by it, but that would not invalidate the Act in this country. Those who infringed it could not claim that it was void if proceedings within the jurisdiction were taken against them. Legal validity is one thing, enforceability is another. Thus a marriage in Nevada may constitute statutory bigamy punishable in England (*Trial of Earl Russell* [1901] AC 446), just as acts in Germany may be punishable here as statutory treason: *Joyce* v *Director of Public Prosecutions* [1946] AC 347. Parliament in fact legislates only for British subjects in this way; but if it also legislated for others, I do not see how the English courts could hold the statute void, however impossible it was to enforce it, and no matter how strong the diplomatic protests.

I do not think that countries which were once colonies but have since been granted independence are in any different position. Plainly once statute has granted independence to a country, the repeal of the statute will not make the country dependent once more; what is done is done, and is not undone by revoking the authority do to it. Heligoland did not in 1953 again become British. But if Parliament then passes an Act applying to such a country, I cannot see why that Act should not be in the same position as an Act applying to what has always been a foreign country, namely, an Act which the English courts will recognise and apply but one which the other country will in all probability ignore. . . .

For the reasons that I have given, I have come to the conclusion that the statement of claim in the Manuel action discloses no reasonable cause of action, and that, despite the persuasions of Mr Macdonald, this is plain and obvious enough to justify striking out the statement of claim. . . .

Perhaps I may add this. I have grave doubts about the theory of the transfer of sovereignty as affecting the competence of Parliament. In my view, it is a fundamental of the English constitution that Parliament is supreme. As a matter of law the courts of England recognise Parliament as being omnipotent in all save the power to destroy its own omnipotence. Under the authority of Parliament the courts of a territory may be released from their legal duty to obey Parliament, but that does not trench on the acceptance by the English courts of all that Parliament does. Nor must validity in law be confused with practical enforceability.

The claimants appealed.

Court of Appeal

SLADE LJ: Mr Macdonald's argument will be seen to depend on a number of propositions, each one of which would be essential to its success at the trial of the action. Included among these essential propositions, though they are by no means the only ones, are the following three, each one of which must be established as arguable, if the plaintiffs are to succeed on this appeal: (1) that Parliament can effectively tie the hands of its successors, if it passes a statute which provides that any future legislation on a specified subject shall be enacted only with certain specified consents; (2) that section 7 (1) of the Statute of 1931 did not absolve the United Kingdom Parliament from the need to comply with the conditions of section 4 of the Statute of 1931 in enacting the Canada Act 1982, if the latter Act was to extend to Canada as an effective Act; (3) that the conditions of section 4 of the Statute of 1931 have not in fact been complied with in relation to the Canada Act 1982.

At least at first sight, the first of these propositions conflicts with the general statement of the law made by Maugham LJ in *Ellen Street Estates Ltd* v *Minister of Health* [1934] 1 KB 590, 597 [*supra* p. 69]. . . . For the purposes of this judgment we are content to assume in favour of the plaintiffs that the first of the three propositions to which we have referred is correct, though we would emphasise that we are not purporting to decide it. . . .

As regards the second of them, Mr Macdonald submitted that the Canada Act 1982 does not fall within the exempting provisions of section 7 (1) of the Statute of 1931, on the grounds that its provisions go beyond a mere 'repeal, amendment or alteration of the British North America Acts.' We do not think it has been or could be disputed that at least a substantial part of the contents of the Constitution Act 1982, if regarded in isolation, would amount to no more than a mere 'repeal, amendment or alteration of the British North America Acts,' within those exempting provisions. Mr Macdonald, however, has submitted that at least some others of its contents (for example, the Charter of Rights and Freedoms) fall outside such exemption and accordingly make it necessary that the conditions of section 4 of the Statute of 1931 should be complied with in relation to the whole of the Canada Act 1982.

By far the greater part of the plaintiffs' argument on this appeal has been devoted to an attempt to show that the conditions of section 4 have not been complied with in this context.

In the circumstances we will proceed to consider the third of the propositions referred to above which relates to section 4 of the Statute of 1931. We will revert briefly to the second of them and to section 7 at the end of this judgment.

For the time being, therefore, let it be supposed that Parliament, in enacting the Canada Act 1982, had precisely to comply with the conditions of section 4 of the Statute of 1931, if that new Act was to be valid and effective. What then are the conditions which section 4 imposes? It is significant that, while the Preamble to the Statute of 1931 recites that

> it is in accord with the established constitutional position that no law hereafter made by the Parliament of the United Kingdom shall extend to any of the said Dominions as part of the law of that Dominion otherwise than at the request and with the consent of that Dominion: . . .

Section 4 itself does *not* provide that no Act of the United Kingdom Parliament shall extend to a

Dominion as part of the law of that Dominion unless the Dominion has *in fact* requested and consented to the enactment thereof. The condition that must be satisfied is a quite different one, namely, that it must be 'expressly declared in that Act that that Dominion has requested, and consented to, the enactment thereof.' Though Mr Macdonald, as we have said, submitted that section 4 requires not only a declaration but a true declaration of a real request and consent, we are unable to read the section in that way. There is no ambiguity in the relevant words and the court would not in our opinion be justified in supplying additional words by a process of implication; it must construe and apply the words as they stand: see *Maxwell on Interpretation of Statutes*, 12th ed. (1969), p. 33 and the cases there cited. If an Act of Parliament contains an express declaration in the precise form required by section 4, such declaration is in our opinion conclusive so far as section 4 is concerned.

There was, we think, nothing unreasonable or illogical in this simple approach to the matter on the part of the legislature, in reserving to itself the sole function of deciding whether the requisite request and consent have been made and given. The present case itself provides a good illustration of the practical consequences that would have ensued, if section 4 had made an actual request and consent on the part of a Dominion a condition precedent to the validity of the relevant legislation, in such manner that the courts or anyone else would have had to look behind the relevant declaration in order to ascertain whether a statute of the United Kingdom Parliament, expressed to extend to that Dominion, was valid. There is obviously room for argument as to the identity of the representatives of the Dominion of Canada appropriate to express the relevant request and consent. Mr Macdonald, while firm in his submission that all legislatures of the Provinces of Canada had to join the Federal Parliament in expressing them, seemed less firm in his submission that all the Indian Nations had likewise to join. This is a point which might well involve difficult questions of Canadian constitutional law. Moreover, if all the Indian Nations did have to join, further questions might arise as to the manner in which the consents of these numerous persons and bodies had to be expressed and as to whether all of them had in fact been given. As we read the wording of section 4, it was designed to obviate the need for any further inquiries of this nature, once a statute, containing the requisite declaration, had been duly enacted by the United Kingdom Parliament. Parliament, having satisfied itself as to the request and consent, would make the declaration and that would be that.

Mr Macdonald submitted in the alternative that, even if section 4 on its proper construction does not itself bear the construction which he attributed to it, nevertheless, in view of the convention referred to in the third paragraph of the preamble, the actual request and consent of the Dominion is necessary before a law made by the United Kingdom Parliament can extend to that Dominion as part of its law. Whether or not an argument on these lines might find favour in the courts of a Dominion, it is in our opinion quite unsustainable in the courts of this country. The sole condition precedent which has to be satisfied if a law made by the United Kingdom Parliament is to extend to a Dominion as part of its law is to be found stated in the body of the Statute of 1931 itself (section 4). This court would run counter to all principles of statutory interpretation if it were to purport to vary or supplement the terms of this stated condition precedent by reference to some supposed convention, which, though referred to in the preamble, is not incorporated in the body of the Statute.

In the present instance, therefore, the only remaining question is whether it is arguable that the condition precedent specified in section 4 of the Statute of 1931 has not been complied with in relation to the Canada Act 1982. Is it arguable that it has not been 'expressly declared in that Act that that Dominion has requested, and consented to, the enactment thereof'? In our judgment this proposition is not arguable, inasmuch as the preamble to the Canada Act 1982 begins with the words 'Whereas Canada has requested and consented to the enactment of an Act of the Parliament of the United Kingdom to give effect to the provisions hereinafter set forth . . .'.

. . . [W]e conclude that, if and so far as the conditions of section 4 of the Statute of 1931 had to be complied with in relation to the Canada Act 1982, they were duly complied with by the declaration contained in the preamble to that Act.

Consequently, it is unnecessary to consider further the second of the three propositions referred to earlier in this judgment. It is unnecessary to consider whether the Constitution Act 1982 contains provisions which go beyond 'the repeal, amendment or alteration of the British North America Acts' so as to fall outside the exempting provisions of section 7(1) of the Statute of 1931 and thus within section 4 of that Act. If it does contain such provisions, the express declaration of a request and consent required by section 4 is duly contained in the Canada Act 1982. If it contains no such provisions (as we understood Mr Mummery would have sought to submit on behalf of the Attorney-General, though we did not think it necessary to call on him), no declaration of request and consent was necessary.

QUESTIONS

1. Did the Court of Appeal decide whether Parliament can give up its sovereignty over a particular territory?

2. Did the Court of Appeal decide whether the validity of an Act of Parliament could be dependent upon the presence or absence of the consent of some other body?

3. How would Megarry VC answer the two questions above?

4. One of the fears of the proponents of the traditional theory of supremacy is that if Parliament could bind itself it could create a legislative vacuum. In cases of granting independence, a power to legislate is given to another body so there is no risk of a vacuum being created. The problem with the fully self-embracing theory of supremacy is that it does give rise to the possibility of Parliament binding its successors not to legislate on certain matters without transferring power to another body. In light of this and the above analysis, is it possible to argue that supremacy is a divisible concept: continuing with regard to the subject-matter of legislation; self-embracing with regard to territorial competence; and partly self-embracing with regard to the procedures to be followed and the manner and form in which legislation must be enacted?

NOTE: In Chapter 3 the impact of the United Kingdom's membership of the European Community on the traditional view of the legislative supremacy of Parliament is explored. In *R v Secretary of State for Transport, ex parte Factortame (No. 2)* [1991] 1 AC 603, at 659, Lord Bridge stated that 'it was the duty of a United Kingdom court, when delivering final judgment, to override any rule of national law found to be in conflict with any directly enforceable rule of Community law'. In the context of EC law the effect of this decision is to abandon the traditional Diceyan view and to accept that Parliament has accorded priority to EC law over national law so long as the UK remains a member of the EC. The model for incorporation of EC law into domestic law in s. 2 of the European Communities Act 1972 (particularly s. 2(4)) has not been adopted in the Human Rights Act 1998 for incorporating the European Convention on Human Rights into United Kingdom law. This Act is premised on the traditional Diceyan view of the legislative supremacy of Parliament. (See further Chapter 7.)

SECTION 5: Devolution and the Legislative Supremacy of Parliament

The United Kingdom is made up of four countries – England, Scotland, Wales, and Northern Ireland. The Parliament of the United Kingdom at Westminster may legislate for all parts of the kingdom, but some public Acts do not extend to Scotland or to Northern Ireland. In turn, some Acts apply only to Scotland or Northern Ireland. Wales never had its own Parliament and Scotland's Parliament was abolished in 1707 when the Act of Union created a single Parliament for Great Britain to legislate for England, Wales and Scotland. In 1800 the Act of Union with Ireland abolished the Irish Parliament and established the Parliament of Great Britain and Ireland to legislate for all four countries. The Government of Ireland Act 1920 divided Ireland into the six counties of Northern Ireland and the remaining 26 counties of Southern Ireland. In 1922 the southern counties were given Dominion status and in 1937 the Irish Government unilaterally adopted an independent constitution finally accepted by the United Kingdom in the Ireland Act 1949. Between 1921 and 1972 Northern Ireland had its own Parliament at Stormont which enacted many laws dealing with domestic affairs such as crime, policing agriculture, health, and education. In 1972 the Stormont Parliament was suspended and subsequently abolished by the Northern Ireland Act 1974.

In the 1960s the growth of Scottish and Welsh nationalism was recognized by the Labour Government which, in 1969, appointed a Royal Commission on the Constitution under the chairmanship of Lord Kilbrandon which considered the case for devolving governmental functions to new institutions in Scotland and Wales and regions of England. In 1974 the Labour Government announced proposals for elected assemblies for Wales (to have administrative powers) and Scotland (to have legislative powers). The devolution project faced opposition in Parliament and Bills for devolving powers to Scotland and Wales were not finally passed until 1978. In the referenda which followed, the requisite 40 per cent threshold in favour of devolution was not achieved in either country and the Acts were repealed.

When Labour returned to power in 1997 devolution was once again on the agenda and two White Papers were published, *Scotland's Parliament* (Cm 3658) and *A Voice for Wales* (Cm 3718). The proposals again were for a Parliament for Scotland with general legislative powers limited through a list of reserved matters upon which only Westminster could legislate, and an Assembly for Wales which would have subordinate legislative powers. The proposals in the White Papers were submitted to referenda in the two countries. In Scotland 74.3 per cent (on a turnout of 60.4 per cent) voted in favour of a Scottish Parliament and 63.5 per cent also voted in favour of that Parliament having tax-varying powers. In Wales 50.3 per cent (on a turnout of 50 per cent) voted in favour of the Assembly. The Scotland Act 1998 and the Government of Wales Act 1998 made devolution a reality. As the Welsh Assembly does not have primary legislative powers, it will not be considered further in this chapter.

In Northern Ireland during the 1990s there were discussions with the main political parties to seek to develop new political institutions which would provide a basis for a peaceful resolution of the conflict. In talks promoted by the Labour Government the main political parties which were committed to democracy and non-violence participated alongside representatives from the British and Irish Governments. The outcome of the talks was the Belfast Agreement signed on 10 April 1998 (Good Friday) which set out the arrangements for devolution of legislative and executive powers to a new Northern Ireland Assembly. In a referendum held on 22 May 1998, 71 per cent (on a turnout of 81 per cent) expressed their support for the Belfast Agreement. On 25 June 1999, elections were held to the new Northern Ireland Assembly under the Northern Ireland (Elections) Act 1998. The Northern Ireland Act 1998 provided for devolution of executive and legislative powers to the Assembly which took place on 2 December 1999. On 11 February 2000, the Assembly was suspended following disagreement over the question of decommissioning paramilitary arsenals. The Secretary of State for Northern Ireland, Peter Mandelson, lifted the suspension on 28 May 2000 and the Assembly had its first meeting on 5 June 2000. Problems over decommissioning continued to bedevil the Assembly and Executive resulting in two further suspensions of devolved government in August and September 2001. Further examination of the powers of the Assembly will not be attempted in this edition due to the fluidity of the devolution project in Northern Ireland.

The Scottish Parliament is a subordinate legislature with its competence limited by ss. 29 and 30 of the Scotland Act 1998, which delimit its legislative powers by stating what is outside the Parliament's legislative competence, with the implication that everything else is within its competence. Special provisions are included to provide for questions of *vires* to be resolved both during the passage of a Bill (see s. 31, *post*) and subsequent to its passage prior to receipt of the Royal Assent (see ss. 32–35, *post*). A question whether an Act of the Scottish Parliament or any provision of such an Act is within the legislative competence of the Parliament (a 'devolution issue') may arise in legal proceedings in Scotland or elsewhere in the United Kingdom. In addition there is machinery in Sch. 6 for proceedings for the determination of a devolution issue to be instituted by the Advocate General or the Lord Advocate. If the Scottish legislation transgresses into reserved areas, it will, to that extent, be void. If there is a conflict between a Scottish Act and an earlier United Kingdom Act, the former will prevail in respect of devolved matters but the latter will prevail in respect of reserved matters. If subsequent UK legislation conflicts with an earlier Act of the Scottish Parliament on a devolved matter this would raise the question whether the UK Act impliedly repeals the Scottish Act.

White Paper, *Scotland's Parliament* Cm 3658

CHAPTER 2   WHAT THE SCOTTISH PARLIAMENT CAN DO

2.1 The Government are committed to creating a Scottish Parliament which will extend democratic control over the widespread responsibilities currently exercised by The Scottish Office and other Scottish Departments. These have nearly 12,000 civil servants serving Scotland's needs. What is required is a more effective democratic framework. This Chapter sets out what will be devolved, and the roles of the Scottish Parliament and the new Scottish Executive.

2.2 The proposed settlement reflects the changes in The Scottish Office's responsibilities over the past 20 years and the Government's commitment to establish a Scottish Parliament with wide-ranging powers including some matters not currently discharged by The Scottish Office. Among the areas to be devolved, not included in the devolution proposals of the Scotland Act 1978, are economic development, financial and other assistance to industry, universities, training, forestry, certain transport matters, the police and the prosecution system.

The Scottish Parliament

2.3 The role of the Scottish Parliament will be to make laws in relation to devolved matters in Scotland. In these devolved areas, it will be able, by virtue of the devolution legislation, to amend or repeal existing Acts of the UK Parliament and to pass new legislation of its own in relation to devolved matters. It will also be able to consider and pass private legislation, promoted by individuals or bodies (for example local authorities) in relation to devolved matters.

2.4 All matters that are not specifically reserved . . . will be devolved. Devolved matters over which the Scottish Parliament will have legislative power include:

Health . . .
Education and training . . .
Local government, social work and housing . . .
Economic development and transport . . .
Law and home affairs . . .
Environment . . .
Agriculture forestry and fishing . . .
Sport and the arts . . .

The Scottish Executive

2.6 The Scottish Executive, which will be accountable to the Scottish Parliament, will exercise executive responsibility in relation to devolved matters. The relationship between the Scottish Executive and the Scottish Parliament will be similar to the relationship between the UK Government and the UK Parliament. The Executive will consist of the First Minister plus a team of Scottish Ministers including Law Officers. The statutory powers and duties exercised by Ministers of the Crown in Scotland in relation to devolved matters will be transferred to Ministers of the Scottish Executive.

CHAPTER 3   SCOTLAND WITHIN THE UNITED KINGDOM

3.1 The Government want a United Kingdom which everyone feels part of, can contribute to, and in whose future all have a stake. The Union will be strengthened by recognising the claims of Scotland, Wales and the regions with strong identities of their own. The Government's devolution proposals, by meeting these aspirations, will not only safeguard but also enhance the Union.

3.2 There are many matters which can be more effectively and beneficially handled on a United Kingdom basis. By preserving the integrity of the UK, the Union secures for its people participation in an economic unit which benefits business and provides access to wider markets and investment and increases prosperity for all. Scotland also benefits from strong and effective defence and foreign policies and a sense of belonging to a United Kingdom.

Reserved matters
3.3 The matters which the Government propose to reserve in the light of these considerations are listed below in general terms:

- The constitution of the United Kingdom . . .;
- UK foreign policy . . .;
- UK defence and national security . . .;
- The protection of borders and certain matters subject to border controls . . .;
- The stability of the UK's fiscal, economic and monetary system . . .;
- Common markets for UK goods and services . . .;
- Employment legislation . . .;
- Social security policy and administration . . .;
- Regulation of certain professions . . .;
- Transport safety and regulation . . .;
- Certain other matters presently subject to UK or GB regulation or operation including the UK Research Councils, nuclear safety, the control and safety of medicines, reciprocal health agreements, the designation of assisted areas, the Ordnance Survey, the regulatory framework for broadcasting and film classification including the regulation of the distribution of video recordings, the licensing of theatres and cinemas, cultural property matters dealt with at UK level, gambling and the National Lottery and data protection. In addition a number of matters in the health sector, including abortion, human fertilisation and embryology, genetics, xenotransplantation and vivisection will be reserved in view of the need for a common approach. Equality legislation (covering racial, gender and disability discrimination) will be reserved.

3.4 The Government believe that reserving powers in these areas will safeguard the integrity of the UK and the benefits of a consistent and integrated approach.

CHAPTER 4   THE NEW CONSTITUTIONAL ARRANGEMENTS

. . .

Nature of the new constitutional arrangements
4.2 Under the Government's proposals, the UK Parliament will devolve wide ranging legislative powers to the Scottish Parliament. Scotland will of course remain an integral part of the United Kingdom. The Queen will continue to be Head of State of the United Kingdom. The UK Parliament is and will remain sovereign in all matters: but as part of the Government's resolve to modernise the British constitution Westminster will be choosing to exercise that sovereignty by devolving legislative responsibilities to a Scottish Parliament without in any way diminishing its own powers. The Government recognise that no UK Parliament can bind its successors. The Government however believe that the popular support for the Scottish Parliament, once established, will make sure that its future in the UK constitution will be secure.

. . .

The structure of government in Scotland

4.7 As outlined in Chapter 2, executive power in devolved areas will be exercised by the Scottish Executive. The Scottish Parliament will hold the Executive to account for its actions. Ministers of the Scottish Executive will be answerable to the Scottish Parliament, and that Parliament's committees will be able to scrutinise and report on the effectiveness of the Executive's administrative action and its use of public monies voted to it by the Parliament.

. . .

Liaison machinery

4.12 The role of the Secretary of State for Scotland will be to secure the passage and implementation of the legislation to establish the Scottish Parliament; and then to support its initial development. Once the Scottish Parliament is in being, and the Scottish Executive established, the responsibilities of the Secretary of State for Scotland will change. The focus will be on promoting communication between the Scottish Parliament and Executive and between the UK Parliament and Government on matters of mutual interest; and on representing Scottish interests in reserved areas.

4.13 The Scottish Executive will need to keep in close touch with Departments of the UK Government. Good communication systems will be vital. Departments in both administrations will develop mutual understandings covering the appropriate exchange of information, advance notification and joint working. The principles will be as follows:

- the vast majority of matters should be capable of being handled routinely among officials of the Departments in question;
- if further discussion is needed on any issue, the Cabinet Office and its Scottish Executive counterpart will mediate, again at official level;
- on some issues there will need to be discussions between the Scottish Executive and Ministers in the UK Government.

4.14 Representatives of the UK Government (usually the Secretary of State for Scotland) and the Scottish Executive will meet from time to time, to discuss particular issues or simply to take stock of relations. These arrangements will be updated regularly to reflect the evolution of administrative conventions of co-operation and joint working.

Reaching agreement

4.15 The Scottish Executive and the UK Government may from time to time take different views of the Scottish Parliament's legislative powers. There will therefore be procedures for identifying and resolving any such difficulties. The Government believe that, given an open and constructive relationship between the UK Government and the Scottish Executive, problems will usually be resolved quickly and amicably.

4.16 In drafting legislation for consideration by the Scottish Parliament, the Scottish Executive will take legal advice to ensure that the provisions brought forward are within the Scottish Parliament's powers. In any cases of uncertainty, there will be consultation with the Scottish Executive Law Officers and as necessary more widely. It will be for the Presiding Officer of the Scottish Parliament to satisfy himself or herself that legislation, whether brought forward by the Executive or by others, is intra vires before giving approval to introduction. These pre-legislative checks will ensure that any potential difficulties are identified at the earliest possible point. During the Parliamentary passage of legislation, it will fall to the Presiding Officer to certify that all amendments selected for debate are within the remit of the Scottish Parliament. UK Government Departments will be able to discuss any concerns which they might have with the Scottish Executive at that stage.

4.17 Prior to a Scottish Bill being passed forward from the Presiding Officer to receive Royal Assent, there will be a short delay period to ensure that the UK Government is content as to vires.

In the event of a dispute between the Scottish Executive and the UK Government about vires remaining unresolved, there will be provision for it to be referred to the Judicial Committee of the Privy Council. For this purpose the Judicial Committee will consist of the Lords of Appeal in Ordinary. At least five Law Lords will sit in any case. The size and composition of the Committee will be decided by the Senior Law Lord (or, in his absence, the next senior Law Lord who is available) who will also decide where the Committee is to sit in any particular case. As appropriate, this might be in Edinburgh. The Judicial Committee will also be able to hear any subsequent disputes about devolution issues in relation to secondary legislation and Acts of the Scottish Parliament after Royal Assent.

International relations

4.18 Special arrangements will be needed for the handling of questions of international relations, and for the exercise of domestic powers which are capable of affecting the UK's international relations. The guiding principle is that the UK should be able to speak with one voice in the international arena and to advance policies (for example in international negotiations) which take proper account of the interests of all parts of the UK. It will also be essential that the UK Government is in a position to implement obligations it has undertaken in good faith internationally or which are imposed on the United Kingdom by international law.

4.19 For these principles to be implemented effectively where devolved areas of responsibility are involved, arrangements will be made for the Scottish Executive to play a part in the conduct of international negotiations through close liaison with the Whitehall Departments concerned; or in appropriate cases through direct representation on the UK delegation. The Scottish Executive and Parliament will also, where necessary, implement the international obligations which fall on the UK Government and Parliament.

Scotland Act 1998

. . .

28. Acts of the Scottish Parliament

(1) Subject to section 29, the Parliament may make laws, to be known as Acts of the Scottish Parliament.

. . .

(5) The validity of an Act of the Scottish Parliament is not affected by any invalidity in the proceedings of the Parliament leading to its enactment.

. . .

(7) This section does not affect the power of the Parliament of the United Kingdom to make laws for Scotland.

29. Legislative competence

(1) An Act of the Scottish Parliament is not law so far as any provision of the Act is outside the legislative competence of the Parliament.

(2) A provision is outside that competence so far as any of the following paragraphs apply—
  (a) it would form part of the law of a country or territory other than Scotland, or confer or remove functions exercisable otherwise than in or as regards Scotland,
  (b) it relates to reserved matters,
  (c) it is in breach of the restrictions in Schedule 4,
  (d) it is incompatible with any of the Convention rights or with Community law,
  (e) it would remove the Lord Advocate from his position as head of the systems of criminal prosecution and investigation of deaths in Scotland.

(3) For the purposes of this section, the question whether a provision of an Act of the

Scottish Parliament relates to a reserved matter is to be determined, subject to subsection (4), by reference to the purpose of the provision, having regard (among other things) to its effect in all the circumstances.

(4) A provision which—

(a) would otherwise not relate to reserved matters, but

(b) makes modifications of Scots private law, or Scots criminal law, as it applies to reserved matters,

is to be treated as relating to reserved matters unless the purpose of the provision is to make the law in question apply consistently to reserved matters and otherwise.

30. Legislative competence: supplementary

(1) Schedule 5 (which defines reserved matters) shall have effect.

(2) Her Majesty may by Order in Council make any modifications of Schedule 4 or 5 which She considers necessary or expedient.

. . .

31. Scrutiny of Bills before introduction

(1) A member of the Scottish Executive in charge of a Bill shall, on or before introduction of the Bill in the Parliament, state that in his view the provisions of the Bill would be within the legislative competence of the Parliament.

(2) The Presiding Officer shall, on or before the introduction of a Bill in the Parliament, decide whether or not in his view the provisions of the Bill would be within the legislative competence of the Parliament and state his decision.

. . .

32. Submission of Bills for Royal Assent

(1) It is for the Presiding Officer to submit Bills for Royal Assent.

(2) The Presiding Officer shall not submit a Bill for Royal Assent at any time when—

(a) the Advocate General, the Lord Advocate or the Attorney General is entitled to make a reference in relation to the Bill under section 33,

(b) any such reference has been made but has not been decided or otherwise disposed of by the Judicial Committee, or

(c) an order may be made in relation to the Bill under section 35.

(3) The Presiding Officer shall not submit a Bill in its unamended form for Royal Assent if—

(a) the Judicial Committee have decided that the Bill or any provision of it would not be within the legislative competence of the Parliament, or

(b) a reference made in relation to the Bill under section 33 has been withdrawn following a request for withdrawal of the reference under section 34(2)(b).

. . .

33. Scrutiny of Bills by the Judicial Committee

(1) The Advocate General, the Lord Advocate or the Attorney General may refer the question of whether a Bill or any provision of a Bill would be within the legislative competence of the Parliament to the Judicial Committee for decision.

(2) Subject to subsection (3), he may make a reference in relation to a Bill at any time during—

(a) the period of four weeks beginning with the passing of the Bill, and

(b) any period of four weeks beginning with any subsequent approval of the Bill in accordance with standing orders made by virtue of section 36(5).

(3) He shall not make a reference in relation to a Bill if he has notified the Presiding Officer that he does not intend to make a reference in relation to the Bill, unless the Bill has been approved as mentioned in subsection (2)(b) since the notification.

34. ECJ references

(1) This section applies where—
  (a) a reference has been made in relation to a Bill under section 33,
  (b) a reference for a preliminary ruling has been made by the Judicial Committee in connection with that reference, and
  (c) neither of those references has been decided or otherwise disposed of.

(2) If the Parliament resolves that it wishes to reconsider the Bill—
  (a) the Presiding Officer shall notify the Advocate General, the Lord Advocate and the Attorney General of that fact, and
  (b) the person who made the reference in relation to the Bill under section 33 shall request the withdrawal of the reference.

(3) In this section 'a reference for a preliminary ruling' means a reference of a question to the European Court under Article 177 of the Treaty establishing the European Community, Article 41 of the Treaty establishing the European Coal and Steel Community or Article 150 of the Treaty establishing the European Atomic Energy Community.

35. Power to intervene in certain cases

(1) If a Bill contains provisions—
  (a) which the Secretary of State has reasonable grounds to believe would be incompatible with any international obligations or the interests of defence or national security, or
  (b) which make modifications of the law as it applies to reserved matters and which the Secretary of State has reasonable grounds to believe would have an adverse effect on the operation of the law as it applies to reserved matters,
  he may make an order prohibiting the Presiding Officer from submitting the Bill for Royal Assent.

(2) The order must identify the Bill and the provisions in question and state the reasons for making the order.

(3) The order may be made at any time during—
  (a) the period of four weeks beginning with the passing of the Bill,
  (b) any period of four weeks beginning with any subsequent approval of the Bill in accordance with standing orders made by virtue of section 36(5),
  (c) if a reference is made in relation to the Bill under section 33, the period of four weeks beginning with the reference being decided or otherwise disposed of by the Judicial Committee.

(4) The Secretary of State shall not make an order in relation to a Bill if he has notified the Presiding Officer that he does not intend to do so, unless the Bill has been approved as mentioned in subsection (3)(b) since the notification.

(5) An order in force under this section at a time when such approval is given shall cease to have effect.
  . . .

37. Acts of Union

The Union with Scotland Act 1706 and the Union with England Act 1707 have effect subject to this Act.
  . . .

101. Interpretation of Acts of the Scottish Parliament etc.

(1) This section applies to—
  (a) any provision of an Act of the Scottish Parliament, or of a Bill for such an Act, and
  (b) any provision of subordinate legislation made, confirmed or approved, or purporting

to be made, confirmed or approved, by a member of the Scottish Executive, which could be read in such a way as to be outside competence.

(2) Such a provision is to be read as narrowly as is required for it to be within competence, if such a reading is possible, and is to have effect accordingly.

(3) In this section 'competence'—

(a) in relation to an Act of the Scottish Parliament, or a Bill for such an Act, means the legislative competence of the Parliament, and

(b) in relation to subordinate legislation, means the powers conferred by virtue of this Act.

102. Powers of courts or tribunals to vary retrospective decisions

(1) This section applies where any court or tribunal decides that—

(a) an Act of the Scottish Parliament or any provision of such an Act is not within the legislative competence of the Parliament, or

(b) a member of the Scottish Executive does not have the power to make, confirm or approve a provision of subordinate legislation that he has purported to make, confirm or approve.

(2) The court or tribunal may make an order—

(a) removing or limiting any retrospective effect of the decision, or

(b) suspending the effect of the decision for any period and on any conditions to allow the defect to be corrected.

(3) In deciding whether to make an order under this section, the court or tribunal shall (among other things) have regard to the extent to which persons who are not parties to the proceedings would otherwise be adversely affected.

(4) Where a court or tribunal is considering whether to make an order under this section, it shall order intimation of that fact to be given to—

(a) the Lord Advocate, and

(b) the appropriate law officer, where the decision mentioned in subsection (1) relates to a devolution issue (within the meaning of Schedule 6),

unless the person to whom the intimation would be given is a party to the proceedings.

(5) A person to whom intimation is given under subsection (4) may take part as a party in the proceedings so far as they relate to the making of the order.

3

The European Union

NOTES:

1. The Treaty on European Union (TEU) was signed at Maastricht on 7 February 1992 but the European Union it established only came into existence on 1 November 1993.

2. The structure of the European Union has been likened to the facade of a Greek temple and, in particular, to its pillars. There are three separate pillars in the Union. The most important of these is the one based upon the European Communities. The other two pillars deal with arrangements for (a) a Common Foreign and Security Policy; and (b) inter-governmental cooperation in justice and home affairs.

   The European Communities are comprised of the European Coal and Steel Community (ECSC), the European Community (EC), which was originally named as the European Economic Community (EEC), and the European Atomic Energy Community (EURATOM). The three Communities together create a new legal order which has a constitution provided by treaties. The ECSC was established in 1952 by Belgium, France, Germany, Italy, Luxembourg, and The Netherlands. In 1957 they established the EEC and EURATOM. Subsequently other countries joined these Communities – Denmark, Ireland, and the UK in 1973, Greece in 1982, Portugal and Spain in 1986, Austria, Finland, and Sweden in 1995. Norway has on two occasions rejected joining in referendums, however, along with Iceland and Liechtenstein, it is linked to the 15 Member States in the European Economic Area.

3. The EC is the most important of the three Communities. It seeks to establish a single market in which there are (a) no barriers to trade amongst the Member States, and (b) freedom of movement of capital and of people, both as workers and as providers of services. This project is more than one of economic cooperation as it involves a degree of economic and political integration. This is demonstrated by the framework and practice of the EC by which member states have agreed policies, the implementation of which is shared between Community institutions and themselves; and (b) the increasing scope of their partnership. Economic integration has been advanced by the Single European Act 1986 (SEA) and the TEU. Both of these treaties amended the founding treaties of the Communities. The SEA not only set a time-table for the completion of the single market, but also amended the decision-making process in respect of matters relating to the single market, while the TEU set out a timetable and process for a common currency and further revised the Community's decision-making processes. Integration in political matters is not as advanced as in the economic sphere. The SEA introduced European Political Cooperation and the TEU elaborated upon this second pillar by replacing it with the Common Foreign and Security Policy, and adding a third pillar dealing with cooperation in home affairs and justice. These two pillars are outside the special legal order of the European Communities' pillar.

4. The Treaty of Amsterdam (1997) has amended the TEU and the Treaty of Rome. In the UK the European Communities (Amendment) Act 1998 incorporated the Treaty of Amsterdam into domestic law. The amendments to the Treaty of Rome include the creation of a new

Title IIIa – Visas, asylum, immigration, and other policies related to the freedom of movement of persons. The Treaty of Amsterdam also provides a Protocol under which the UK and Ireland have 'opted out' of measures related to Title IIIa, thus allowing them to maintain their border controls and to have their own common travel area.

5. The Treaty of Nice (2001) will make changes to the institutional arrangements to enable the 15 member Union to cope with enlargement following the accession of the candidate countries. This treaty has not yet been ratified.

The Treaty of Amsterdam has renumbered the Articles of the TEU and Treaty of Rome, and in extracts from these Treaties the new number is given first, with the previous one in square brackets.

SECTION 1: **The Framework of the Union and the EC**

In these extracts from the TEU and the Treaty of Rome, the framework for the Union and EC is laid out with more detail given for the EC. The treaties list objectives and create institutions which are to carry out specified tasks.

Treaty on European Union

His Majesty the King of the Belgians,
Her Majesty the Queen of Denmark,
The President of the Federal Republic of Germany,
The President of the Hellenic Republic,
His Majesty the King of Spain,
The President of the French Republic,
The President of Ireland,
The President of the Italian Republic,
His Royal Highness the Grand Duke of Luxembourg,
Her Majesty the Queen of the Netherlands,
The President of the Portuguese Republic,
Her Majesty the Queen of the United Kingdom of Great Britain and Northern Ireland,

RESOLVED to mark a new stage in the process of European integration undertaken with the establishment of the European Communities,

RECALLING the historic importance of the ending of the division of the European Continent and the need to create firm bases for the construction of the future Europe,

CONFIRMING their attachment to the principles of liberty, democracy and respect for human rights and fundamental freedoms and of the rule of law,

DESIRING to deepen the solidarity between their peoples while respecting their history, their culture and their traditions,

DESIRING to enhance further the democratic and efficient functioning of the institutions so as to enable them better to carry out, within a single institutional framework, the tasks entrusted to them,

RESOLVED to achieve the strengthening and the convergence of their economies and to establish an economic and monetary union including, in accordance with the provisions of this Treaty, a single and stable currency,

DETERMINED to promote economic and social progress for their peoples, within the context of the accomplishment of the internal market and of reinforced cohesion and environmental protection, and to implement policies ensuring that advances in economic integration are accompanied by parallel progress in other fields,

RESOLVED to establish a citizenship common to nationals of the countries,

RESOLVED to implement a common foreign and security policy including the eventual framing of a common defence policy, which might in time lead to a common defence, thereby reinforcing the European identity and its independence in order to promote peace, security and progress in Europe and in the world,

REAFFIRMING their objective to facilitate the free movement of persons, while ensuring the safety and security of their peoples, by including provisions on justice and home affairs in this Treaty,

RESOLVED to continue the process of creating an ever closer union among the peoples of Europe, in which decisions are taken as closely as possible to the citizen in accordance with the principle of subsidiarity,

IN VIEW of further steps to be taken in order to advance European integration,

HAVE DECIDED to establish a European Union. . . .

TITLE I   COMMON PROVISIONS

Article 1 [ex Article A]

By this Treaty, the High Contracting Parties establish among themselves a European Union, hereinafter called 'the Union'.

This Treaty marks a new stage in the process of creating an ever closer union among the peoples of Europe, in which decisions are taken as openly as possible and as closely as possible to the citizen.

The Union shall be founded on the European Communities, supplemented by the policies and forms of cooperation established by this Treaty. Its task shall be to organise, in a manner demonstrating consistency and solidarity, relations between the Member States and between their peoples.

Article 2 [ex Article B]

The Union shall set itself the following objectives:

— to promote economic and social progress and a high level of employment and to achieve balanced and sustainable development, in particular through the creation of an area without internal frontiers, through the strengthening of economic and social cohesion and through the establishment of economic and monetary union, ultimately including a single currency in accordance with the provisions of this Treaty;

— to assert its identity on the international scene, in particular through the implementation of a common foreign and security policy including the progressive framing of a common defence policy, which might lead to a common defence, in accordance with the provisions of Article 17;

— to strengthen the protection of the rights and interests of the nationals of its Member States through the introduction of a citizenship of the Union;

— to maintain and develop the Union as an area of freedom, security and justice, in which the free movement of persons is assured in conjunction with appropriate measures with respect to external border controls, immigration, asylum and the prevention and combating of crime;

— to maintain in full the acquis communautaire and build on it with a view to considering to what extent the policies and forms of cooperation introduced by this Treaty may need to be revised with the aim of ensuring the effectiveness of the mechanisms and the institutions of the Community.

The objectives of the Union shall be achieved as provided in this Treaty and in accordance with the conditions and the timetable set out therein while respecting the principle of subsidiarity as defined in Article 5 of the Treaty establishing the European Community.

Article 3 [ex Article C]

The Union shall be served by a single institutional framework which shall ensure the consistency and the continuity of the activities carried out in order to attain its objectives while respecting and building upon the acquis communautaire.

The Union shall in particular ensure the consistency of its external activities as a whole in the context of its external relations, security, economic and development policies. The Council and the Commission shall be responsible for ensuring such consistency and shall cooperate to this end. They shall ensure the implementation of these policies, each in accordance with its respective powers.

Article 4 [ex Article D]

The European Council shall provide the Union with the necessary impetus for its development and shall define the general political guidelines thereof.

The European Council shall bring together the Heads of State or of Government of the Member States and the President of the Commission. They shall be assisted by the Ministers for Foreign Affairs of the Member States and by a Member of the Commission. The European Council shall meet at least twice a year, under the chairmanship of the Head of State or of Government of the Member State which holds the Presidency of the Council.

The European Council shall submit to the European Parliament a report after each of its meetings and a yearly written report on the progress achieved by the Union.

Article 5 [ex Article E]

The European Parliament, the Council, the Commission, the Court of Justice and the Court of Auditors shall exercise their powers under the conditions and for the purposes provided for, on the one hand, by the provisions of the Treaties establishing the European Communities and of the subsequent Treaties and Acts modifying and supplementing them and, on the other hand, by the other provisions of this Treaty.

Article 6 [ex Article F]

1. The Union is founded on the principles of liberty, democracy, respect for human rights and fundamental freedoms, and the rule of law, principles which are common to the Member States.

2. The Union shall respect fundamental rights, as guaranteed by the European Convention for the Protection of Human Rights and Fundamental Freedom signed in Rome on 4 November 1950 and as they result from the constitutional traditions common to the Member States, as general principles of Community law.

3. The Union shall respect the national identities of its Member States.

4. The Union shall provide itself with the means necessary to attain its objectives and carry though its policies.

Article 7 [ex Article F.1]

1. The Council, meeting in the composition of the Heads of State or Government and acting by unanimity on a proposal by one third of the Member States or by the Commission and after obtaining the assent of the European Parliament, may determine the existence of a serious and

persistent breach by a Member State of principles mentioned in Article 6(1), after inviting the government of the Member State in question to submit its observations.

2. Where such a determination has been made, the Council, acting by a qualified majority, may decide to suspend certain of the rights deriving from the application of this Treaty to the Member State in question, including the voting rights of the representative of the government of that Member State in the Council. In doing so, the Council shall take into account the possible consequences of such a suspension on the rights and obligations of natural and legal persons.

The obligations of the Member State in question under this Treaty shall in any case continue to be binding on that State.

3. The Council, acting by a qualified majority, may decide subsequently to vary or revoke measures taken under paragraph 2 in response to changes in the situation which led to their being imposed.

4. For the purposes of this Article, the Council shall act without taking into account the vote of the representative of the government of the Member State in question. Abstentions by members present in person or represented shall not prevent the adoption of decisions referred to in paragraph 1. A qualified majority shall be defined as the same proportion of the weighted votes of the members of the Council concerned as laid down in Article 205(2) of the Treaty establishing the European Community.

This paragraph shall also apply in the event of voting rights being suspended pursuant to paragraph 2.

5. For the purposes of this Article, the European Parliament shall act by a two-thirds majority of the votes cast, representing a majority of its members. . . .

NOTE: When the Treaty of Nice is ratified under the amended Article 7 of the Treaty on European Union, the European Council can declare the existence of a serious and persistent breach of fundamental rights. If this occurs, the Council may suspend certain of the rights of the country concerned. This will also be supplemented with a preventive instrument which, following a proposal of one-third of the Member States, the Parliament, or the Commission, the Council, acting by a four-fifths majority of its members and with the assent of the European Parliament, can declare that a clear danger exists of a Member State committing a serious breach of fundamental rights and address to that Member State appropriate recommendations. The Court of Justice will be competent (Article 46 of the Treaty on European Union) only for disputes concerning procedural provisions under Article 7, and not for the appreciation of the justification or the appropriateness of the decisions taken pursuant to this provision.

Treaty Establishing The European Community

His Majesty the King of the Belgians,
The President of the Federal Republic of Germany,
The President of the French Republic,
The President of the Italian Republic,
His Royal Highness the Grand Duke of Luxembourg,
Her Majesty the Queen of the Netherlands,

DETERMINED to lay the foundations of an ever closer union among the peoples of Europe,

RESOLVED to ensure the economic and social progress of their countries by common action to eliminate the barriers which divide Europe,

AFFIRMING as the essential objective of their efforts the constant improvement of the living and working conditions of their peoples,

RECOGNISING that the removal of existing obstacles calls for concerted action in order to guarantee steady expansion, balanced trade and fair competition,

ANXIOUS to strengthen the unity of their economies and to ensure their harmonious development by reducing the differences existing between the various regions and the backwardness of the less favoured regions,

DESIRING to contribute, by means of a common commercial policy, to the progressive abolition of restrictions on international trade,

INTENDING to confirm the solidarity which binds Europe and the overseas countries and desiring to ensure the development of their prosperity, in accordance with the principles of the Charter of the United Nations,

RESOLVED by thus pooling their resources to preserve and strengthen peace and liberty, and calling upon the other peoples of Europe who share their ideal to join in their efforts,

HAVE DECIDED to create a European Community . . .

PART ONE   PRINCIPLES

Article 1
By this Treaty, the High Contracting Parties establish among themselves a European Community.

Article 2
The Community shall have as its task, by establishing a common market and an economic and monetary union and by implementing the common policies of activities referred to in Articles 3 and 4, to promote throughout the Community a harmonious and balanced development of economic activities, sustainable and non-inflationary growth respecting the environment, a high degree of convergence of economic performance, a high level of employment and of social protection, the raising of the standard of living and quality of life, and economic and social cohesion and solidarity among Member States.

Article 3
1. For the purposes set out in Article 2, the activities of the Community shall include, as provided in this Treaty and in accordance with the timetable set out therein:
    (a) the elimination, as between Member States, of customs duties and quantitative restrictions on the import and export of goods, and of all other measures having equivalent effect;
    (b) a common commercial policy;
    (c) an internal market characterised by the abolition, as between Member States, of obstacles to the free movement of goods, persons, services and capital;
    (d) measures concerning the entry and movement of persons in the internal market as provided for in Title IV;
    (e) a common policy in the sphere of agriculture and fisheries;
    (f) a common policy in the sphere of transport;
    (g) a system ensuring that competition in the internal market is not distorted;
    (h) the approximation of the laws of Member States to the extent required for the functioning of the common market;
    (i) the promotion of co-ordination between employment policies of the Member States with a view to enhancing their effectiveness by developing a co-ordinated strategy for employment;
    (j) a policy in the social sphere comprising a European Social Fund;
    (k) the strengthening of economic and social cohesion;

    (l)   a policy in the sphere of the environment;

    (m) the strengthening of the competitiveness of Community industry;

    (n) the promotion of research and technological development;

    (o) encouragement for the establishment and development of trans-European networks;

    (p) a contribution to the attainment of a high level of health protection;

    (q) a contribution to education and training of quality and to the flowering of the cultures of the Member States;

    (r) a policy in the sphere of development cooperation;

    (s) the association of the overseas countries and territories in order to increase trade and promote jointly economic and social development;

    (t) a contribution to the strengthening of consumer protection;

    (u) measures in the spheres of energy, civil protection and tourism.

    2. In all the activities referred to in this Article, the Community shall aim to eliminate inequalities, and to promote equalities, between men and women.

Article 4 [ex Article 3a]

    1. For the purposes set out in Article 2, the activities of the Member States and the Community shall include, as provided in this Treaty and in accordance with the timetable set out therein, the adoption of an economic policy which is based on the close coordination of Member States' economic policies, on the internal market and on the definition of common objectives, and conducted in accordance with the principle of an open market economy with free competition.

    2. Concurrently with the foregoing, and as provided in this Treaty and in accordance with the timetable and the procedures set out therein, these activities shall include the irrevocable fixing of exchange rates leading to the introduction of a single currency, the ECU, and the definition and conduct of a single monetary policy and exchange rate policy the primary objective of both of which shall be to maintain price stability and, without prejudice to this objective, to support the general economic policies in the Community, in accordance with the principle of an open market economy with free competition.

    3. These activities of the Member States and the Community shall entail compliance with the following guiding principles; stable prices, sound public finances and monetary conditions and a sustainable balance of payments.

Article 5 [ex Article 3b]

The Community shall act within the limits of the powers conferred upon it by this Treaty and of the objectives assigned to it therein.

    In areas which do not fall within its exclusive competence, the Community shall take action, in accordance with the principle of subsidiarity, only if and in so far as the objectives of the proposed action cannot be sufficiently achieved by the Member States and can therefore, by reason of the scale of effects of the proposed action, be better achieved by the Community.

    Any action by the Community shall not go beyond what is necessary to achieve the objectives of this Treaty.

Article 6 [ex Article 3c]

Environmental protection requirements must be integrated into the definition and implementation of the Community policies and activities referred to in Article 3, in particular with a view to promoting sustainable development.

Article 7 [ex Article 4]

    1. The tasks entrusted to the Community shall be carried out by the following institutions:

    — a European Parliament,

— a Council,

— a Commission,

— a Court of Justice,

— a Court of Auditors.

Each institution shall act within the limits of the powers conferred upon it by this Treaty.

2. The Council and the Commission shall be assisted by an Economic and Social Committee and a Committee of the Regions acting in an advisory capacity.

Article 8 [ex Article 4a]

A European System of Central Banks (hereinafter referred to as 'ESCB') and a European Central Bank (hereinafter referred to as 'ECB') shall be established in accordance with the procedures laid down in this Treaty; they shall act within the limits of the powers conferred upon them by this Treaty and by the Statute of the ESCB and of the ECB (hereinafter referred to as 'Statute of the ESCB') annexed thereto.

Article 9 [ex Article 4b]

A European Investment Bank is hereby established, which shall act within the limits of the powers conferred upon it by this Treaty and the Statute annexed thereto.

Article 10 [ex Article 5]

Member States shall take all appropriate measures, whether general or particular, to ensure fulfilment of the obligations arising out of this Treaty or resulting from action taken by the institutions of the Community. They shall facilitate the achievement of the Community's tasks.

They shall abstain from any measure which could jeopardise the attainment of the objectives of this Treaty.

Article 11 [ex Article 5a]

1. Member States which intend to establish closer cooperation between themselves may be authorised, subject to Articles 43 and 44 of the Treaty on European Union, to make use of the institutions, procedures and mechanisms laid down by this Treaty, provided that the cooperation proposed:

(a) does not concern areas which fall within the exclusive competence of the Community;

(b) does not affect Community policies, actions or programmes;

(c) does not concern the citizenship of the Union or discriminate between nationals of Member States;

(d) remains within the limits of the powers conferred upon the Community by this Treaty; and

(e) does not constitute a discrimination or a restriction of trade between Member States and does not distort the conditions of competition between the latter.

2. The authorisation referred to in paragraph 1 shall be granted by the Council, acting by a qualified majority on a proposal from the Commission and after consulting the European Parliament.

If a member of the Council declares that, for important and stated reasons of national policy, it intends to oppose the granting of an authorisation by qualified majority, a vote shall not be taken. The Council may, acting by a qualified majority, request that the matter be referred to the Council, meeting in the composition of the Heads of State or Government, for decision by unanimity.

Member States which intend to establish closer cooperation as referred to in paragraph 1 may address a request to the Commission, which may submit a proposal to the Council to that effect.

In the event of the Commission not submitting a proposal, it shall inform the Member States concerned of the reasons for not doing so.

3. Any Member State which wishes to become a party to cooperation set up in accordance with this Article shall notify its intention to the Council and to the Commission, which shall give an opinion to the Council within three months of receipt of that notification. Within four months of the date of that notification, the Commission shall decide on it and on such specific arrangements as it may deem necessary.

4. The acts and decisions necessary for the implementation of cooperation activities shall be subject to all the relevant provisions of this Treaty, save as otherwise provided for in this Article and in Articles 43 and 44 of the Treaty on European Union.

5. This Article is without prejudice to the provisions of the Protocol integrating the Schengen acquis into the framework of the European Union.

Article 12 [ex Article 6]
Within the scope of application of this Treaty, and without prejudice to any special provisions contained therein, any discrimination on grounds of nationality shall be prohibited.

The Council, acting in accordance with the procedure referred to in Article 252, may adopt rules designed to prohibit such discrimination.

Article 13 [ex Article 6a]
Without prejudice to the other provisions of this Treaty and within the limits of the powers conferred by it upon the Community, the Council, acting unanimously on a proposal from the Commission and after consulting the European Parliament, may take appropriate action to combat discrimination based on sex, racial or ethnic origin, religion or belief, disability, age or sexual orientation.

Article 14 [ex Article 7a]
1. The Community shall adopt measures with the aim of progressively establishing the internal market over a period expiring on 31 December 1992, in accordance with the provisions of this Article and of Articles 15, 26, 47(2), 49, 80, 93 and 95 and without prejudice to the other provisions of this Treaty.

2. The internal market shall comprise an area without internal frontiers in which the free movement of goods, persons, services and capital is ensured in accordance with the provisions of this Treaty.

3. The Council, acting by a qualified majority on a proposal from the Commission, shall determine the guidelines and condition necessary to ensure balanced progress in all the sectors concerned.

Article 15 [ex Article 7c]
When drawing up its proposals with a view to achieving the objectives set out in Article 14, the Commission shall take into account the extent of the effort that certain economies showing differences in development will have to sustain during the period of establishment of the internal market and it may propose appropriate provisions.

If these provisions take the form of derogations, they must be of a temporary nature and must cause the least possible disturbance to the functioning of the common market.

Article 16 [ex Article 7d]
Without prejudice to Articles 73, 86 and 87, and given the place occupied by services of general economic interest in the shared values of the Union as well as their role in promoting social and territorial cohesion, the Community and the Member States, each within their respective powers

and within the scope of application of this Treaty, shall take care that such services operate on the basis of principles and conditions which enable them to fulfil their missions.

PART TWO   CITIZENSHIP OF THE UNION

Article 17 [ex Article 8]

1. Citizenship of the Union is hereby established.

Every person holding the nationality of a Member State shall be a citizen of the Union.

2. Citizens of the Union shall enjoy the rights conferred by this Treaty and shall be subject to the duties imposed thereby.

Article 18 [ex Article 8a]

1. Every citizen of the Union shall have the right to move and reside freely within the territory of the Member States, subject to the limitations and conditions laid down in this Treaty and by the measures adopted to give it effect.

2. The Council may adopt provisions with a view to facilitating the exercise of the rights referred to in paragraph 1 in accordance with the procedure referred to in Article 251. The Council shall act unanimously throughout this procedure.

Article 19 [ex Article 8b]

1. Every citizen of the Union residing in a Member State of which he is not a national shall have the right to vote and to stand as a candidate at municipal elections in the Member State in which he resides, under the same conditions as nationals of that State. This right shall be exercised subject to detailed arrangements to be adopted by the Council, acting unanimously on a proposal from the Commission and after consulting the European Parliament; these arrangements may provide for derogations where warranted by problems specific to a Member State.

2. Without prejudice to Article 190(4) and to the provisions adopted for its implementation, every citizen of the Union residing in a Member State of which he is not a national shall have the right to vote and to stand as a candidate in elections to the European Parliament in the Member State in which he resides, under the same conditions as nationals of that State. This right shall be exercised subject to detailed arrangements adopted by the Council, acting unanimously on a proposal from the Commission and after consulting the European Parliament; these arrangements may provide for derogations where warranted by problems specific to a Member State.

Article 20 [ex Article 8c]

Every citizen of the Union shall, in the territory of a third country in which the Member State of which he is a national is not represented, be entitled to protection by the diplomatic or consular authorities of any Member State, on the same conditions as the nationals of that State. Member States shall establish the necessary rules among themselves and start the international negotiations required to secure this protection.

Article 21 [ex Article 8d]

Every citizen of the Union shall have the right to petition the European Parliament in accordance with Article 194.

Every citizen of the Union may apply to the Ombudsman established in accordance with Article 195.

Every citizen of the Union may write to any of the institutions or bodies referred to in this Article or in Article 7 in one of the languages in Article 314 and have an answer in the same language.

Article 22 [ex Article 8e]

The Commission shall report to the European Parliament, to the Council and to the Economic and Social Committee every three years on the application of the provisions of this Part. This report shall take account of the development of the Union.

On this basis, and without prejudice to the other provisions of this Treaty, the Council, acting unanimously on a proposal from the Commission and after consulting the European Parliament, may adopt provisions to strengthen or to add to the rights laid down in this Part, which it shall recommend to the Member States for adoption in accordance with their respective constitutional requirements.

PART THREE   COMMUNITY POLICIES
TITLE I   FREE MOVEMENT OF GOODS

Article 23 [ex Article 9]

1. The Community shall be based upon a customs union which shall cover all trade in goods and which shall involve the prohibition between Member States of customs duties on imports and exports and of all charges having equivalent effect, and the adoption of a common customs tariff in their relations with third countries.

2. The provisions of Article 25 and of Chapter 2 of this Title shall apply to products originating in Member States and to products coming from third countries which are in free circulation in Member States.

Article 24 [ex Article 10]

Products coming from a third country shall be considered to be in free circulation in a Member State if the import formalities have been complied with and any customs duties or charges having equivalent effect which are payable have been levied in that Member State, and if they have not benefited from a total or partial drawback of such duties or charges.

CHAPTER 1   THE CUSTOMS UNION

Article 25 [ex Article 12]

Member States shall refrain from introducing between themselves any new customs duties on imports or exports or any charges having equivalent effect, and from increasing those which they already apply in their trade with each other.

Charges having equivalent effect shall be prohibited between Member States. This prohibition shall also apply to customs duties of a fiscal nature.

. . .

CHAPTER 2   ELIMINATION OF QUANTITATIVE RESTRICTIONS BETWEEN MEMBER STATES

Article 28 [ex Article 30]

Quantitative restrictions on imports and all measures having equivalent effect shall, without prejudice to the following provisions, be prohibited between Member States.

Article 29 [ex Article 34]

Quantitative restrictions on exports, and all measures having equivalent effect, shall be prohibited between Member States.

. . .

CHAPTER 3 APPROXIMATION OF LAWS

Article 94 [ex Article 100]

The Council shall, acting unanimously on a proposal from the Commission and after consulting the European Parliament and the Economic and Social Committee, issue directives for the approximation of such laws, regulations or administrative provisions of the Member States as directly affect the establishment or functioning of the common market.

Article 95 [ex Article 100a]

1. By way of derogation from Article 94 and save where otherwise provided in this Treaty, the following provisons shall apply for the achievement of the objectives set out in Article 14. The Council shall, acting in accordance with the procedure referred to in Article 251 and after consulting the Economic and Social Committee adopt the measures for the approximation of the provisions laid down by law, regulation or administrative action in Member States which have as their object the establishment and functioning of the internal market.

2. Paragraph 1 shall not apply to fiscal provisions, to those relating to the free movement of persons nor to those relating to the rights and interests of employed persons.

3. The Commission, in its proposals envisaged in paragraph 1 concerning health, safety, environmental protection and consumer protection, will take as a base a high level of protection, taking account in particular of any new development based on scientific facts. Within their respective powers, the European Parliament and the Council will also seek to achieve this objective.

4. If, after the adoption by the Council or by the Commission of a harmonisation measure, a Member State deems it necessary to maintain national provisions on grounds of major needs referred to in Article 36, or relating to the protection of the environment or the working environment, it shall notify the Commission of these provisions as well as the grounds for maintaining them.

5. Moreover, without prejudice to paragraph 4, if, after the adoption by the Council or by the Commission of a harmonisation measure, a Member State deems it necessary to introduce national provisions based on new scientific evidence relating to the protection of the environment or the working environment on grounds of a problem specific to that Member State arising after the adoption of the harmonisation measure, it shall notify the Commission of the envisaged provisions as well as the grounds for introducing them.

6. The Commission shall, within six months of the notifications as referred to in paragraphs 4 and 5, approve or reject the national provisions involved after having verified that they are not a means of arbitrary discrimination or a disguised restriction on trade between Member States and that they shall not constitute an obstacle to the functioning of the internal market.

In the absence of a decision by the Commission within this period the national provisions referred to in paragraphs 4 and 5 shall be deemed to have been approved.

When justified by the complexity of the matter and in the absence of danger for human health, the Commission may notify the Member State concerned that the period referred to in this paragraph may be extended for a further period of up to six months.

7. When, pursuant to paragraph 6, a Member State is authorised to maintain or introduce national provisions derogating from a harmonisation measure, the Commission shall immediately examine whether to propose an adaptation to that measure.

8. When a Member State raises a specific problem on public health in a field which has been the subject of prior harmonisation measures, it shall bring it to the attention of the Commission which shall immediately examine whether to propose appropriate measures to the Council.

9. By way of derogation from the procedure laid down in Articles 226 and 227, the Commission and any Member State may bring the matter directly before the Court of Justice if it

considers that another Member State is making improper use of the powers provided for in this Article.

10. The harmonisation measures referred to above shall, in appropriate cases, include a safeguard clause authorising the Member States to take, for one or more of the non-economic reasons referred to in Article 30, provisional measures subject to a Community control procedure.

. . .

PART FIVE   INSTITUTIONS OF THE COMMUNITY
TITLE I   PROVISIONS GOVERNING THE INSTITUTIONS
CHAPTER 1   THE INSTITUTIONS
SECTION 1   THE EUROPEAN PARLIAMENT

Article 189 [ex Article 137]

The European Parliament, which shall consist of representatives of the peoples of the States brought together in the Community, shall exercise the powers conferred upon it by this Treaty.

The number of Members of the European Parliament shall not exceed seven hundred.

Article 190 [ex Article 138]

1. The representatives in the European Parliament of the peoples of the States brought together in the Community shall be elcted by direct universal suffrage.

2. The number of representatives elected in each Member State shall be as follows:

Belgium	25
Denmark	16
Germany	99
Greece	25
Spain	64
France	87
Ireland	15
Italy	87
Luxembourg	6
Netherlands	31
Austria	21
Portugal	25
Finland	16
Sweden	22
United Kingdom	87

In the event of amendments to this paragraph, the number of representatives elected in each Member State must ensure appropriate representation of the peoples of the States brought together in the Community

3. Representatives shall be elected for a term of five years.

4. The European Parliament shall draw up a proposal for elections by direct universal suffrage in accordance with a uniform procedure in all Member States.

The Council shall, acting unanimously after obtaining the assent of the European Parliament, which shall act by a majority of its component members, lay down the appropriate provisions, which it shall recommend to Member States for adoption in accordance with their respective constitutional requirements.

5. The European Parliament shall, after seeking an opinion from the Commission and with the approval of the Council acting unanimously, lay down the regulations and general conditions governing the performance of the duties of its Members.

Article 191 [ex Article 138a]

Political parties at European level are important as a factor for integration within the Union. They contribute to forming a European awareness and to expressing the political will of the citizens of the Union.

Article 192 [ex Article 138b]

Insofar as provided in this Treaty, the European Parliament shall participate in the process leading up to the adoption of Community acts by exercising its powers under the procedures laid down in Articles 251 and 252 and by giving its assent or delivering advisory opinions.

The European Parliament may, acting by a majority of its members, request the Commission to submit any appropriate proposal on matters on which it considers that a Community act is required for the purpose of implementing this Treaty.

Article 193 [ex Article 138c]

In the course of its duties, the European Parliament may, at the request of a quarter of its members, set up a temporary Committee of Inquiry to investigate, without prejudice to the powers conferred by this Treaty on other institutions or bodies, alleged contraventions or maladministration in the implementation of Community law, except where the alleged facts are being examined before a court and while the case is still subject to legal proceedings.

The temporary Committee of Inquiry shall cease to exist on the submission of its report.

The detailed provisions governing the exercise of the right of inquiry shall be determined by common accord of the European Parliament, the Council and the Commission.

Article 194 [ex Article 138d]

Any citizen of the Union, and any natural or legal person residing or having its registered office in a Member State, shall have the right to address, individually or in association with other citizens or persons, a petition to the European Parliament on a matter which comes within the Community's fields of activity and which affect him, her or it directly.

Article 195 [ex Article 138e]

1. The European Parliament shall appoint an Ombudsman empowered to receive complaints from any citizen of the Union or any natural or legal person residing or having its registered office in a Member State concerning instances of maladministration in the activities of the Community institutions or bodies, with the exception of the Court of Justice and the Court of First Instance acting in their judicial role.

In accordance with his duties, the Ombudsman shall conduct inquiries for which he finds grounds, either on his own initiative or on the basis of complaints submitted to him direct or through a member of the European Parliament, except where the alleged facts are or have been the subject of legal proceedings. Where the Ombudsman establishes an instance of maladministration, he shall refer the matter to the institution concerned, which shall have a period of three months in which to inform him of its views. The Ombudsman shall then forward a report to the European Parliament and the institution concerned. The person lodging the complaint shall be informed of the outcome of such inquiries.

The Ombudsman shall submit an annual report to the European Parliament on the outcome of his inquiries.

2. The Ombudsman shall be appointed after each election of the European Parliament for the duration of its term of office. The Ombudsman shall be eligible for reappointment.

The Ombudsman may be dismissed by the Court of Justice at the request of the European Parliament if he no longer fulfils the conditions required for the performance of his duties or if he is guilty of serious misconduct.

3. The Ombudsman shall be completely independent in the performance of his duties. In the performance of those duties he shall neither seek nor take instructions from any body. The Ombudsman may not, during his term of office, engage in any other occupation, whether gainful or not.

4. The European Parliament shall, after seeking an opinion from the Commission and with the approval of the Council acting by a qualified majority, lay down the regulations and general conditions governing the performance of the Ombudsman's duties.

Article 196 [ex Article 139]
The European Parliament shall hold an annual session. It shall meet, without requiring to be convened, on the second Tuesday in March.

The European Parliament may meet in extraordinary session at the request of a majority of its members or at the request of the Council or of the Commission.

Article 197 [ex Article 140]
The European Parliament shall elect its President and its officers from among its members.

Members of the Commission may attend all meetings and shall, at their request, be heard on behalf of the Commission.

The Commission shall reply orally or in writing to questions put to it by the European Parliament or by its members.

The Council shall be heard by the European Parliament in accordance with the conditions laid down by the Council in its rules of procedure.

Article 198 [ex Article 141]
Save as otherwise provided in this Treaty, the European Parliament shall act by an absolute majority of the votes cast.

The rules of procedure shall determine the quorum.

Article 199 [ex Article 142]
The European Parliament shall adopt its rules of procedure, acting by a majority of its members.

The proceedings of the European Parliament shall be published in the manner laid down in its rules of procedure.

Article 200 [ex Article 143]
The European Parliament shall discuss in open session the annual general report submitted to it by the Commission.

Article 201 [ex Article 144]
If a motion of censure on the activities of the Commission is tabled before it, the European Parliament shall not vote thereon until at least three days after the motion has been tabled and only by open vote.

If the motion of censure is carried by a two-thirds majority of the votes cast, representing a majority of the members of the European Parliament, the members of the Commission shall resign as a body. They shall continue to deal with current business until they are replaced in accordance with Article 214. In this case, the term of office of the members of the Commission appointed to replace them shall expire on the date on which the term of office of the members of the Commission obliged to resign as a body would have expired.

NOTE: The Treaty of Nice when ratified would change the allocation of MEPs for Member States. Given that it is unclear when the various candidates for membership would actually join the allocation given here will not be implemented for the Parliament to be elected in 2004.

Member States	Candidate countries
Belgium **22**	Bulgaria **17**
Denmark **13**	Cyprus **6**
Germany **99**	Czech Republic **20**
Greece **22**	Estonia **6**
Spain **50**	Hungary **20**
France **72**	Latvia **8**
Ireland **12**	Lithuania **12**
Italy **72**	Malta **5**
Luxembourg **6**	Poland **50**
Netherlands **25**	Romania **33**
Austria **17**	Slovakia **13**
Portugal **22**	Slovenia **7**
Finland **13**	
Sweden **18**	
United Kingdom **72**	

SECTION 2   THE COUNCIL

Article 202 [ex Article 145]
To ensure that the objectives set out in this Treaty are attained, the Council shall, in accordance with the provisions of this Treaty:
— ensure coordination of the general economic policies of the Member States;
— have power to take decisions;
— confer on the Commission, in the acts which the Council adopts, powers for the implementation of the rules which the Council lays down. The Council may impose certain requirements in respect of the exercise of these powers. The Council may also reserve the right, in specific cases, to exercise directly implementing powers itself. The procedures referred to above must be consonant with principles and rules to be laid down in advance by the Council, acting unanimously on a proposal from the Commission and after obtaining the Opinion of the European Parliament.

Article 203 [ex Article 146]
The Council shall consist of a representative of each Member State at ministerial level, authorised to commit the government of that Member State.

The office of President shall be held in turn by each Member State in the Council for a term of six months in the order decided by the Council acting unanimously.

Article 204 [ex Article 147]
The Council shall meet when convened by its President on his own initiative or at the request of one of its members or of the Commission.

Article 205 [ex Article 148]
1. Save as otherwise provided in this Treaty, the Council shall act by a majority of its members.

2. Where the Council is required to act by a qualified majority, the votes of its members shall be weighted as follows:

```
Belgium  . . . . . . . . . . . . . . . . . . . . . .   5
Denmark . . . . . . . . . . . . . . . . . . . . . .   3
Germany . . . . . . . . . . . . . . . . . . . . . .  10
Greece . . . . . . . . . . . . . . . . . . . . . . .   5
Spain . . . . . . . . . . . . . . . . . . . . . . . .   8
France . . . . . . . . . . . . . . . . . . . . . . .  10
Ireland . . . . . . . . . . . . . . . . . . . . . . .   3
Italy . . . . . . . . . . . . . . . . . . . . . . . .  10
Luxembourg  . . . . . . . . . . . . . . . . . . . .   2
Netherlands  . . . . . . . . . . . . . . . . . . . .   5
Austria . . . . . . . . . . . . . . . . . . . . . . .   4
Portugal  . . . . . . . . . . . . . . . . . . . . . .   5
Finland . . . . . . . . . . . . . . . . . . . . . . .   3
Sweden . . . . . . . . . . . . . . . . . . . . . . .   4
United Kingdom . . . . . . . . . . . . . . . . . .  10
```

For their adoption, acts of the Council shall require at least:

— 62 votes in favour where this Treaty requires them to be adopted on a proposal from the Commission,

— 62 votes in favour, cast by at least 10 members, in other cases.

3. Abstentions by members present in person or represented shall not prevent the adoption by the Council of acts which required unanimity.

Article 206 [ex Article 150]

Where a vote is taken, any member of the Council may also act on behalf of not more than one other member.

Article 207 [ex Article 151]

1. A committee consisting of the Permanent Representatives of the Member States shall be responsible for preparing the work of the Council and for carrying out the tasks assigned to it by the Council.

The Committee may adopt procedural decisions in cases provided for in the Council's Rules of Procedure.

2. The Council shall be assisted by a General Secretariat, under the responsibility of a Secretary-General, High Representative for the common foreign and security policy, who shall be assisted by a Deputy Secretary General responsible for the running of the General Secretariat. The Secretary-General and the Deputy Secretary General shall be appointed by the Council acting unanimously.

The Council shall decide on the organisation of the General Secretariat.

3. The Council shall adopt its Rules of Procedure. For the purpose of applying Article 255(3), the Council shall elaborate in these Rules the conditions under which the public shall have access to Council documents. For the purpose of this paragraph, the Council shall define the cases in which it is to be regarded as acting in its legislative capacity, with a view to allowing greater access to documents in those cases, while at the same time preserving the effectiveness of its decision making process. In any event, when the Council acts in its legislative capacity, the results of votes and explanations of vote as well as statements in the minutes shall be made public.

Article 208 [ex Article 152]

The Council may request the Commission to undertake any studies the Council considers desirable for the attainment of the common objectives, and to submit to it any appropriate proposals.

Article 209 [ex Article 153]

The Council shall, after receiving an opinion from the Commission, determine the rules governing the committees provided for in this Treaty.

Article 210 [ex Article 154]

The Council shall, acting by a qualified majority, determine the salaries, allowances and pensions of the President and members of the Commission, and of the President, Judges, Advocates-General and Registrar of the Court of Justice. It shall also, again by a qualified majority, determine any payment to be made instead of remuneration.

NOTE: When ratified the Treaty of Nice will, from 2005, change the weighting of Member States for voting purposes for current Member States and allocate votes for the candidate countries when they accede to the Union. The criteria for qualified majority voting will be if a decision receives a specified number of votes (this threshold will be reviewed in the light of successive accessions); and if a decision is approved by a majority of Member States. In addition, a Member State may ask for confirmation that the qualified majority represents at least 62 per cent of the total population of the Union. If this is found not to be the case, the decision will not be adopted.

Member States	Candidate countries
Belgium **12**	Bulgaria **10**
Denmark **7**	Cyprus **4**
Germany **29**	Czech Republic **12**
Greece **12**	Estonia **4**
Spain **27**	Hungary **12**
France **29**	Latvia **4**
Ireland **7**	Lithuania **7**
Italy **29**	Malta **3**
Luxembourg **4**	Poland **27**
Netherlands **13**	Romania **14**
Austria **10**	Slovakia **7**
Portugal **12**	Slovenia **4**
Finland **7**	
Sweden **10**	
United Kingdom **29**	

SECTION 3   THE COMMISSION

Article 211 [ex Article 155]

In order to ensure the proper functioning and development of the common market, the Commission shall:

— ensure that the provisions of this Treaty and the measures taken by the institutions pursuant thereto are applied;

— formulate recommendations or deliver opinions on matters dealt with in this Treaty, if it expressly so provides or if the Commission considers it necessary;

— have its own power of decision and participate in the shaping of measures taken by the Council and by the European Parliament in the manner provided for in this Treaty;

— exercise the powers conferred on it by the Council for the implementation of the rules laid down by the latter.

Article 212 [ex Article 156]

The Commission shall publish annually, not later than one month before the opening of the session of the European Parliament, a general report on the activities of the Community.

Article 213 [ex Article 157]

1. The Commission shall consist of twenty members, who shall be chosen on the grounds of their general competence and whose independence is beyond doubt.

The number of members of the Commission may be altered by the Council, acting unanimously.

Only nationals of Member States may be members of the Commission. The Commission must include at least one national of each of the Member States, but may not include more than two members having the nationality of the same State.

2. The members of the Commission shall, in the general interest of the Community, be completely independent in the performance of their duties.

In the performance of these duties, they shall neither seek nor take instructions from any government or from any other body. They shall refrain from any action incompatible with their duties. Each Member State undertakes to respect this principle and not to seek to influence the members of the Commission in the performance of their tasks.

The members of the Commission may not, during their term of office, engage in any other occupation, whether gainful or not. When entering upon their duties they shall give a solemn undertaking that, both during and after their term of office, they will respect the obligations arising therefrom and in particular their duty to behave with integrity and discretion as regards the acceptance, after they have ceased to hold office, of certain appointments or benefits. In the event of any breach of these obligations, the Court of Justice may, on application by the Council or the Commission, rule that the member concerned be, according to the circumstances, either compulsorily retired in accordance with Article 216 or deprived of his right to a pension or other benefits in its stead.

Article 214 [ex Article 158]

1. The members of the Commission shall be appointed, in accordance with the procedure referred to in paragraph 2, for a period of five years, subject, if need be, to Article 201.

Their term of office shall be renewable.

2. The governments of the Member States shall nominate by common accord the person they intend to appoint as President of the Commission; the nomination shall be approved by the European Parliament.

The governments of the Member States shall, by common accord with the nominee for President, nominate the other persons whom they intend to appoint as Members of the Commission.

The President and the other members of the Commission thus nominated shall be subject as a body to a vote of approval by the European Parliament. After approval by the European Parliament, the President and the other members of the Commission shall be appointed by common accord of the governments of the Member States.

Article 215 [ex Article 159]

Apart from normal replacement, or death, the duties of a member of the Commission shall end when he resigns or is compulsorily retired.

The vacancy thus caused shall be filled for the remainder of the member's term of office by a new member appointed by common accord of the governments of the Member States. The Council may, acting unanimously, decide that such a vacancy need not be filled.

In the event of resignation, compulsory retirement or death, the President shall be replaced for the remainder of his term of office. The procedure laid down in Article 214(2) shall be applicable for the replacement of the President.

Save in the case of compulsory retirement under Article 216, members of the Commission shall remain in office until they have been replaced.

Article 216 [ex Article 160]
If any member of the Commission no longer fulfils the conditions required for the performance of his duties or if he has been guilty of serious misconduct, the Court of Justice may, on application by the Council or the Commission, compulsorily retire him.

Article 217 [ex Article 161]
The Commission may appoint a Vice-President or two Vice-Presidents from among its members.

Article 218 [ex Article 162]
1. The Council and the Commission shall consult each other and shall settle by common accord their methods of cooperation.
2. The Commission shall adopt its Rules of Procedure so as to ensure that both it and its departments operate in accordance with the provisions of this Treaty. It shall ensure that these rules are published.

Article 219 [ex Article 163]
The Commission shall act by a majority of the number of members provided for in Article 213.

A meeting of the Commission shall be valid only if the number of members laid down in its Rules of Procedure is present.

NOTE: When the Treaty of Nice is ratified then, from 2005, there will be one commissioner from each Member State. Once there are 27 Member States the Council will decide unanimously on the exact number of commissioners but there will be fewer commissioners than Member States and a system of rotation will have to be agreed.

SECTION 4   THE COURT OF JUSTICE

Article 220 [ex Article 164]
The Court of Justice shall ensure that in the interpretation and application of this Treaty the law is observed.

Article 221 [ex Article 165]
The Court of Justice shall consist of 15 Judges.

The Court of Justice shall sit in plenary session. It may, however, form chambers, each consisting of three, five or seven judges, either to undertake certain preparatory inquiries or to adjudicate on particular categories of cases in accordance with rules laid down for these purposes.

The Court of Justice shall sit in plenary session when a Member State or a Community institution that is a party to the proceedings so requests.

Should the Court of Justice so request, the Council may, acting unanimously, increase the number of judges and make the necessary adjustments to the second and third paragraphs of this Article and to the second paragraph of Article 223.

Article 222 [ex Article 166]
The Court of Justice shall be assisted by eight Advocates-General. However, a ninth Advocate-General shall be appointed as from 1 January 1995 until 6 October 2000.

It shall be the duty of the Advocate-General, acting with complete impartiality and independence, to make, in open court, reasoned submissions on cases brought before the Court of Justice, in order to assist the Court in the performance of the task assigned to it in Article 220.

Should the Court of Justice so request, the Council may, acting unanimously, increase the number of Advocates-General and make the necessary adjustments to the third paragraph of Article 223.

Article 223 [ex Article 167]
The Judges and Advocates-General shall be chosen from persons whose independence is beyond doubt and who possess the qualifications required for appointment to the highest judicial offices in their respective countries or who are jurisconsults of recognised competence; they shall be appointed by common accord of the Governments of the Member States for a term of six years.

Every three years there shall be a partial replacement of the Judges. Eight and seven Judges shall be replaced alternately.

Every three years there shall be a partial replacement of the Advocates-General. Four Advocates-General shall be replaced on each occasion. Retiring Judges and Advocates-General shall be eligible for reappointment.

The Judges shall elect the President of the Court of Justice from among their number for a term of three years. He may be re-elected.

Article 224 [ex Article 168]
The Court of Justice shall appoint its Registrar and lay down the rules governing his service.

Article 225 [ex Article 168a]
1. A Court of First Instance shall be attached to the Court of Justice with jurisdiction to hear and determine at first instance, subject to a right of appeal to the Court of Justice on points of law only and in accordance with the conditions laid down by the Statute, certain classes of action or proceeding defined in accordance with the conditions laid down in paragraph 2. The Court of First Instance shall not be competent to hear and determine questions referred for a preliminary ruling under Article 234.

2. At the request of the Court of Justice and after consulting the European Parliament and the Commission, the Council, acting unanimously, shall determine the classes of action or proceeding referred to in paragraph 1 and the composition of the Court of First Instance and shall adopt the necessary adjustments and additional provisions to the Statute of the Court of Justice. Unless the Council decides otherwise, the provisions of this Treaty relating to the Court of Justice, in particular the provisions of the Protocol on the Statute of the Court of Justice, shall apply to the Court of First Instance.

3. The members of the Court of First Instance shall be chosen from persons whose independence is beyond doubt and who possess the ability required for appointment to judicial office; they shall be appointed by common accord of the governments of the Member States for a term of six years. The membership shall be partially renewed every three years. Retiring members shall be eligible for reappointment.

4. The Court of First Instance shall establish its Rules of Procedure in agreement with the Court of Justice. Those rules shall require the unanimous approval of the Council.

Article 226 [ex Article 169]
If the Commission considers that a Member State has failed to fulfil an obligation under this Treaty, it shall deliver a reasoned opinion on the matter after giving the State concerned the opportunity to submit its observations.

If the State concerned does not comply with the opinion within the period laid down by the Commission, the latter may bring the matter before the Court of Justice.

Article 227 [ex Article 170]
A Member State which considers that another Member State has failed to fulfil an obligation under this Treaty may bring the matter before the Court of Justice.

Before a Member State brings an action against another Member State for an alleged infringement of an obligation under this Treaty, it shall bring the matter before the Commission.

The Commission shall deliver a reasoned opinion after each of the States concerned has been given the opportunity to submit its own case and its observations on the other party's case both orally and in writing.

If the Commission has not delivered an opinion within three months of the date on which the matter was brought before it, the absence of such opinion shall not prevent the matter from being brought before the Court of Justice.

Article 228 [ex Article 171]

1. If the Court of Justice finds that a Member State has failed to fulfil an obligation under this Treaty, the State shall be required to take the necessary measures to comply with the judgment of the Court of Justice.

2. If the Commission considers that the Member State concerned has not taken such measures it shall, after giving that State the opportunity to submit its observations, issue a reasoned opinion specifying the points on which the Member State concerned has not complied with the judgment of the Court of Justice.

If the Member State concerned fails to take the necessary measures to comply with the Court's judgment within the time-limit laid down by the Commission, the latter may bring the case before the Court of Justice. In so doing it shall specify the amount of the lump sum or penalty payment to be paid by the Member State concerned which it considers appropriate in the circumstances.

If the Court of Justice finds that the Member State concerned has not complied with its judgment it may impose a lump sum or penalty payment on it.

This procedure shall be without prejudice to Article 227.

Article 229 [ex Article 172]

Regulations adopted jointly by the European Parliament and the Council, and by the Council, pursuant to the provisions of this Treaty, may give the Court of Justice unlimited jurisdiction with regard to the penalties provided for in such regulations.

Article 230 [ex Article 173]

The Court of Justice shall review the legality of acts adopted jointly by the European Parliament and the Council, of acts of the Council, of the Commission and of the ECB, other than recommendations and opinions, and of acts of the European Parliament intended to produce legal effects vis-à-vis third parties.

It shall for this purpose have jurisdiction in actions brought by a Member State, the Council or the Commission on grounds of lack of competence, infringement of an essential procedural requirement, infringement of this Treaty or of any rule of law relating to its application, or misuse of powers.

The Court shall have jurisdiction under the same conditions in actions brought by the European Parliament and by the ECB for the purpose of protecting their prerogatives.

Any natural or legal person may, under the same conditions, institute proceedings against a decision addressed to that person or against a decision which, although in the form of a regulation or a decision addressed to another person, is of direct and individual concern to the former.

The proceedings provided for in this Article shall be instituted within two months of the publication of the measure, or of its notification to the plaintiff, or, in the absence thereof, of the day on which it came to the knowledge of the latter, as the case may be.

Article 231 [ex Article 174]

If the action is well founded, the Court of Justice shall declare the act concerned to be void.

In the case of a regulation, however, the Court of Justice shall, if it considers this necessary, state which of the effects of the regulation which it has declared void shall be considered as definitive.

Article 232 [ex Article 175]
Should the European Parliament, the Council or the Commission, in infringement of this Treaty, fail to act, the Member States and the other institutions of the Community may bring an action before the Court of Justice to have the infringement established.

The action shall be admissible only if the institution concerned has first been called upon to act. If, within two months of being so called upon, the institution concerned has not defined its position, the action may be brought within a further period of two months.

Any natural or legal person may, under the conditions laid down in the preceding paragraphs, complain to the Court of Justice that an institution of the Community has failed to address to that person any act other than a recommendation or an opinion.

The Court of Justice shall have jurisdiction, under the same conditions, in actions or proceedings brought by the ECB in the areas falling within the latter's field of competence and in actions or proceedings brought against the latter.

Article 233 [ex Article 176]
The institution or institutions whose act has been declared void or whose failure to act has been declared contrary to this Treaty shall be required to take the necessary measures to comply with the judgment of the Court of Justice.

The obligation shall not affect any obligation which may result from the application of the second paragraph of Article 288.

This Article shall also apply to the ECB.

Article 234 [ex Article 177]
The Court of Justice shall have jurisdiction to give preliminary rulings concerning:
   (a) the interpretation of this Treaty;
   (b) the validity and interpretation of acts of the institutions of the Community and of the ECB;
   (c) the interpretation of the statutes of bodies established by an act of the Council, where those statutes so provide.

Where such a question is raised before any court or tribunal of a Member State, that court or tribunal may, if it considers that a decision on the question is necessary to enable it to give judgment, request the Court of Justice to give a ruling thereon.

Where any such question is raised in a case pending before a court or tribunal of a Member State against whose decisions there is no judicial remedy under national law, that court or tribunal shall bring the matter before the Court of Justice.

Article 235 [ex Article 178]
The Court of Justice shall have jurisdiction in disputes relating to compensation for damage provided for in the second paragraph of Article 288.

Article 236 [ex Article 179]
The Court of Justice shall have jurisdiction in any dispute between the Community and its servants within the limits and under the conditions laid down in the Staff Regulations or the Conditions of Employment.

Article 237 [ex Article 180]
The Court of Justice shall, within the limits hereinafter laid down, have jurisdiction in disputes concerning:

(a) the fulfilment by Member States of obligations under the Statute of the European Investment Bank. In this connection, the Board of Directors of the Bank shall enjoy the powers conferred upon the Commission by Article 266;

(b) measures adopted by the Board of Governors of the European Investment Bank. In this connection, any Member State, the Commission or the Board of Directors of the Bank may institute proceedings under the conditions laid down in Article 230;

(c) measures adopted by the Board of Directors of the European Investment Bank. Proceedings against such measures may be instituted only by Member States or by the Commission, under the conditions laid down in Article 230, and solely on the grounds of non-compliance with the procedure provided for in Article 21(2), (5), (6) and (7) of the Statute of the Bank;

(d) the fulfilment by national central banks of obligations under this Treaty and the Statute of the ESCB. In this connection the powers of the Council of the ECB in respect of national central banks shall be the same as those conferred upon the Commission in respect of Member States by Article 226. If the Court of Justice finds that a national central bank has failed to fulfil an obligation under this Treaty, that bank shall be required to take the necessary measures to comply with the judgment of the Court of Justice.

Article 238 [ex Article 181]
The Court of Justice shall have jurisdiction to give judgment pursuant to any arbitration clause contained in a contract concluded by or on behalf of the Community, whether that contract be governed by public or private law.

Article 239 [ex Article 182]
The Court of Justice shall have jurisdiction in any dispute between Member States which relates to the subject matter of this Treaty if the dispute is submitted to it under a special agreement between the parties.

Article 240 [ex Article 183]
Save where jurisdiction is conferred on the Court of Justice by this Treaty, disputes to which the Community is a party shall not on that ground be excluded from the Jurisdiction of the courts or tribunals of the Member States.

Article 241 [ex Article 184]
Notwithstanding the expiry of the period laid down in the fifth paragraph of Article 230, any party may, in proceedings in which a regulation adopted jointly by the European Parliament and the Council, or a regulation of the Council, of the Commission, or of the ECB is at issue, plead the grounds specified in the second paragraph of Article 230 in order to invoke before the Court of Justice the inapplicability of that regulation.

Article 242 [ex Article 185]
Actions brought before the Court of Justice shall not have suspensory effect. The Court of Justice may, however, if it considers that circumstances so require, order that application of the contested act be suspended.

Article 243 [ex Article 186]
The Court of Justice may in any cases before it prescribe any necessary interim measures.

Article 244 [ex Article 187]
The judgments of the Court of Justice shall be enforceable under the conditions laid down in Article 256.

Article 245 [ex Article 188]

The Statute of the Court of Justice is laid down in a separate Protocol.

The Council may, acting unanimously at the request of the Court of Justice and after consulting the Commission and the European Parliament, amend the provisions of Title III of the Statute.

The Court of Justice shall adopt its Rules of Procedure. These shall require the unanimous approval of the Council.

NOTE: As the Court (ECJ) is already overloaded with cases, which can only increase with the accession of new Member States, the Treaty of Nice seeks to relieve the workload of the ECJ, share tasks between the ECJ and the Court of First Instance (CFI) more effectively, and allow for the creation of specialized chambers for particular areas (such as disputes involving European officials). An appeal in cassation can be made before the CFI against a decision by the specialized chambers. The Treaty also stipulates that the ECJ, which in an enlarged Union will continue to consist of one judge for each Member State, may sit in a Grand Chamber of 13 judges instead of always meeting in a plenary session attended by all judges.

The CFI becomes the common law judge for all direct actions (particularly proceedings against a decision (Article 230 of the EC Treaty), action for failure to act (Article 232 of the EC Treaty), and action for damages (Article 235 of the EC Treaty), with the exception of those which will be attributed to a specialized chamber and those the statute reserves for the ECJ itself.

The ECJ retains responsibility for other proceedings (particularly action for failure to fulfil obligations, Article 226 of the EC Treaty), but the statute can entrust to the CFI categories of proceedings other than those listed in Article 225 of the EC Treaty. The ECJ retains competence for investigating questions referred for a preliminary ruling; however, pursuant to Article 225 of the EC Treaty, the statute may entrust to the CFI the responsibility for preliminary rulings in certain specific matters.

SECTION 5   THE COURT OF AUDITORS

Article 246 [ex Article 188a]

The Court of Auditors shall carry out the audit.

Article 247 [ex Article 188b]

1. The Court of Auditors shall consist of 15 members.

2. The members of the Court of Auditors shall be chosen from among persons who belong or have belonged in their respective countries to external audit bodies or who are especially qualified for this office. Their independence must be beyond doubt.

3. The members of the Court of Auditors shall be appointed for a term of six years by the Council, acting unanimously after consulting the European Parliament.

However, when the first appointments are made, four members of the Court of Auditors, chosen by lot, shall be appointed for a term of office of four years only.

The members of the Court of Auditors shall be eligible for reappointment. They shall elect the President of the Court of Auditors from among their number for a term of three years. The President may be re-elected.

4. The members of the Court of Auditors shall, in the general interest of the Community, be completely independent in the performance of their duties.

In the performance of these duties, they shall neither seek nor take instructions from any government or from any other body. They shall refrain from any action incompatible with their duties.

5. The members of the Court of Auditors may not, during their term of office, engage in any other occupation, whether gainful or not. When entering upon their duties they shall give a

solemn undertaking that, both during and after their term of office, they will respect the obligations arising therefrom and in particular their duty to behave with integrity and discretion as regards the acceptance, after they have ceased to hold office, of certain appointments or benefits.

6. Apart from normal replacement, or death, the duties of a member of the Court of Auditors shall end when he resigns, or is compulsorily retired by a ruling of the Court of Justice pursuant to paragraph 7.

The vacancy thus caused shall be filled for the remainder of the member's term of office.

Save in the case of compulsory retirement, members of the Court of Auditors shall remain in office until they have been replaced.

7. A member of the Court of Auditors may be deprived of his office or of his right to a pension or other benefits in its stead only if the Court of Justice, at the request of the Court of Auditors, finds that he no longer fulfils the requisite conditions or meets the obligations arising from his office.

8. The Council, acting by a qualified majority, shall determine the conditions of employment of the President and the members of the Court of Auditors and in particular their salaries, allowances and pensions. It shall also, by the same majority, determine any payment to be made instead of remuneration.

9. The provisions of the Protocol on the Privileges and Immunities of the European Communities applicable to the Judges of the Court of Justice shall also apply to the members of the Court of Auditors.

Article 248 [ex Article 188c]

1. The Court of Auditors shall examine the accounts of all revenue and expenditure of the Community. It shall also examine the accounts of all revenue and expenditure of all bodies set up by the Community is so far as the relvant constituent instrument does not preclude such examination.

The Court of Auditors shall provide the European Parliament and the Council with a statement of assurance as to the reliability of the accounts and the legality and regularity of the underlying transactions which shall be published in the *Official Journal of the European Communities*.

2. The Court of Auditors shall examine whether all revenue has been received and all expenditure incurred in a lawful and regular manner and whether the financial management has been sound. In doing so, it shall report in particular on any cases of irregularity.

The audit of revenue shall be carried out on the basis both of the amounts established as due and the amounts actually paid to the Community.

The audit of expenditure shall be carried out on the basis both of commitments undertaken and payments made.

These audits may be carried out before the closure of accounts for the financial year in question.

3. The audit shall be based on records and, if necessary, performed on the spot in the other institutions of the Community, on the premises of any body which manages revenue or expenditure on behalf of the Community and in the Member States, including on the premises of any natural or legal person in receipt of payments from the budget. In the Member States the audit shall be carried out in liaison with the national audit bodies or, if these do not have the necessary powers, with the competent national departments. The Court of Auditors and the national audit bodies of the Member States shall cooperate in a spirit of trust while maintaining their independence. These bodies or departments shall inform the Court of Auditors whether they intend to take part in the audit.

The other institutions of the Community, any bodies managing revenue or expenditure on behalf of the Community, any natural or legal person in receipt of payments from the budget and the national audit bodies or, if these do not have the necessary powers, the competent national departments, shall forward to the Court of Auditors, at its request, any document or information necessary to carry out its task.

In respect of the European Investment Bank's activity in managing Community expenditure and revenue, the Court's rights of access to information held by the Bank shall be governed by an agreement between the Court, the Bank and the Commission. In the absence of an agreement, the Court shall never the less have access to information necessary for the audit of Community expenditure and revenue managed by the Bank.

4. The Court of Auditors shall draw up an annual report after the close of each financial year. It shall be forwarded to the other institutions of the Community and shall be published, together with the replies of these institutions to the observations of the Court of Auditors, in the *Official Journal of the European Communities*.

The Court of Auditors may also, at any time, submit observations, particularly in the form of special reports, on specific questions and deliver opinions at the request of one of the other institutions of the Community.

It shall adopt its annual reports, special reports or opinions by a majority of its members.

It shall assist the European Parliament and the Council in exercising their powers of control over the implementation of the budget.

NOTE: Upon ratification of the Treaty of Nice there would be one national from each Member State in the Court of Auditors and they would be appointed by the Council by a qualified majority and could organize themselves into chambers to adopt certain reports and opinions.

CHAPTER 2   PROVISIONS COMMON TO SEVERAL INSTITUTIONS

Article 249 [ex Article 189]
In order to carry out their task and in accordance with the provisions of this Treaty, the European Parliament acting jointly with the Council, the Council and the Commission shall make regulations and issue directives, take decisions, make recommendations or deliver opinions.

A regulation shall have general application. It shall be binding in its entirety and directly applicable in all Member States.

A directive shall be binding, as to the result to be achieved, upon each Member State to which it is addressed, but shall leave to the national authorities the choice of form and methods.

A decision shall be binding in its entirety upon those to whom it is addressed. Recommendations and opinions shall have no binding force.

Article 250 [ex Article 189a]
1. Where, in pursuance of this Treaty, the Council acts on a proposal from the Commission, unanimity shall be required for an act constituting an amendment to that proposal, subject to Article 251(4) and (5).

2. As long as the Council has not acted, the Commission may alter its proposal at any time during the procedures leading to the adoption of a Community act.

Article 251 [ex Article 189b]
1. Where reference is made in this Treaty to this Article for the adoption of an act, the following procedure shall apply.

2. The Commission shall submit a proposal to the European Parliament and the Council.

The Council, acting by a qualified majority after obtaining the opinion of the European Parliament,
 — if it approves all the amendments contained in the European Parliament's opinion, may adopt the proposed act thus amended;

— if the European Parliament does not propose any amendments, may adopt the proposed act;

— shall otherwise adopt a common position and communicate it to the European Parliament. The Council shall inform the European Parliament fully of the reasons which led it to adopt its common position. The Commission shall inform the European Parliament fully of its position.

If, within three months of such communication, the European Parliament:

(a) approves the common position or has not taken a decision, the act in question shall be deemed to have been adopted in accordance with that common position;

(b) rejects, by an absolute majority of its component members, the common position, the proposed act shall be deemed not to have been adopted;

(c) proposes amendments to the common position by an absolute majority of its component members, the amended text shall be forwarded to the Council and to the Commission, which shall deliver an opinion on those amendments.

3. If, within three months of the matter being referred to it, the Council, acting by a qualified majority, approves all the amendments of the European Parliament, the act in question shall be deemed to have been adopted in the form of the common position thus amended; however, the Council shall act unanimously on the amendments on which the Commission has delivered a negative opinion. If the Council does not approve all the amendments, the President of the Council, in agreement with the President of the European Parliament, shall within six weeks convene a meeting of the Conciliation Committee.

4. The Conciliation Committee, which shall be composed of the members of the Council or their representatives and an equal number of representatives of the European Parliament, shall have the task of reaching agreement on a joint text, by a qualified majority of the members of the Council or their representatives and by a majority of the representatives of the European Parliament. The Commission shall take part in the Conciliation Committee's proceedings and shall take all the necessary initiatives with a view to reconciling the positions of the European Parliament and the Council. In fulfilling this task, the Conciliation Committee shall address the common position on the basis of the amendments proposed by the European Parliament.

5. If, within six weeks of its being convened, the Conciliation Committee approves a joint text, the European Parliament, acting by an absolute majority of the votes cast, and the Council, acting by a qualified majority, shall each have a period of six weeks from that approval in which to adopt the act in question in accordance with the joint text. If either of the two institutions fails to approve the proposed act within that period, it shall be deemed not to have been adopted.

6. Where the Conciliation Committee does not approve a joint text, the proposed act shall be deemed not to have been adopted.

7. The periods of three months and six weeks referred to in this Article shall be extended by a maximum of one month and two weeks respectively at the initiative of the European Parliament or the Council.

Article 252 [ex Article 189c]

Where reference is made in this Treaty to this Article for the adoption of an act, the following procedure shall apply:

(a) The Council, acting by a qualified majority on a proposal from the Commission and after obtaining the opinion of the European Parliament, shall adopt a common position.

(b) The Council's common position shall be communicated to the European Parliament. The Council and the Commission shall inform the European Parliament fully of the reasons which led the Council to adopt its common position and also of the Commission's position.

If, within three months of such communication, the European Parliament approves this common position or has not taken a decision within that period, the Council shall definitively adopt the act in question in accordance with the common position.

(c) The European Parliament may, within the period of three months, referred to in point (b), by an absolute majority of its component members, propose amendments to the Council's common position. The European Parliament may also, by the same majority, reject the Council's common position. The result of the proceedings shall be transmitted to the Council and the Commission.

If the European Parliament has rejected the Council's common position, unanimity shall be required for the Council to act on a second reading.

(d) The Commission shall, within a period of one month, re-examine the proposal on the basis of which the Council adopted its common position, by taking into account the amendments proposed by the European Parliament.

The Commission shall forward to the Council, at the same time as its re-examined proposal, the amendments of the European Parliament which it has not accepted, and shall express its opinion on them. The Council may adopt these amendments unanimously.

(e) The Council, acting by a qualified majority, shall adopt the proposal as re-examined by the Commission.

Unanimity shall be required for the Council to amend the proposal as re-examined by the Commission.

(f) In the cases referred to in points (c), (d) and (e), the Council shall be required to act within a period of three months. If no decision is taken within this period, the Commission proposal shall be deemed not to have been adopted.

(g) The periods referred to in points (b) and (f) may be extended by a maximum of one month by common accord between the Council and the European Parliament.

Article 253 [ex Article 190]

Regulations, directives and decisions adopted jointly by the European Parliament and the Council, and such acts adopted by the Council or the Commission, shall state the reasons on which they are based and shall refer to any proposals or opinions which were required to be obtained pursuant to this Treaty.

Article 254 [ex Article 191]

1. Regulations, directives and decisions adopted in accordance with the procedure referred to in Article 251 shall be signed by the President of the European Parliament and by the President of the Council and published in the *Official Journal of the European Communities*. They shall enter into force on the date specified in them or, in the absence thereof, on the twentieth day following that of their publication.

2. Regulations of the Council and of the Commission, as well as directives of those institutions which are addressed to all Member States, shall be published in the *Official Journal of the European Communities*. They shall enter into force on the date specified in them or, in the absence thereof, on the twentieth day following that of their publication.

3. Other directives, and decisions, shall be notified to those to whom they are addressed and shall take effect upon such notification.

Article 255 [ex Article 191a]

1. Any citizen of the Union, and any natural or legal person residing or having its registered office in a Member State, shall have a right of access to European Parliament, Council and

Commission documents, subject to the principles and the conditions to be defined in accordance with paragraphs 2 and 3.

2. General principles and limits on grounds of public or private interest governing this right of access to documents shall be determined by the Council, acting in accordance with the procedure referred to in Article 189b within two years of the entry into force of the Treaty of Amsterdam.

3. Each institution referred to above shall elaborate in its own Rules of Procedure specific provisions regarding access to its documents.

Article 256 [ex Article 192]
Decisions of the Council or of the Commission which impose a pecuniary obligation on persons other than States, shall be enforceable.

Enforcement shall be governed by the rules of civil procedure in force in the State in the territory of which it is carried out. The order for its enforcement shall be appended to the decision, without other formality than verification of the authenticity of the decision, by the national authority which the government of each Member State shall designate for this purpose and shall make known to the Commission and to the Court of Justice.

When these formalities have been completed on application by the party concerned, the latter may proceed to enforcement in accordance with the national law, by bringing the matter directly before the competent authority.

Enforcement may be suspended only by a decision of the Court of Justice. However, the courts of the country concerned shall have jurisdiction over complaints that enforcement is being carried out in an irregular manner.

NOTE: When the Treaty of Nice is ratified then the co-decision procedure in Article 251 will be extended to cover some areas in which unanimity is required. This procedure will thus be the predominant one where the treaties stipulate qualified majority voting.

CHAPTER 3   THE ECONOMIC AND SOCIAL COMMITTEE

Article 257 [ex Article 193]
An Economic and Social Committee is hereby established. It shall have advisory status.

The Committee shall consist of representatives of the various categories of economic and social activity, in particular, representatives of producers, farmers, carriers, workers, dealers, craftsmen, professional occupations and representatives of the general public.

Article 258 [ex Article 194]
The number of members of the Economic and Social Committee shall be as follows:

Belgium	12
Denmark	9
Germany	24
Greece	12
Spain	21
Finland	9
France	24
Ireland	9
Italy	24
Luxembourg	6
Netherlands	12
Austria	12

Portugal 12
Finland. 9
Sweden. 12
United Kingdom 24

The members of the committee shall be appointed by the Council, acting unanimously, for four years. Their appointments shall be renewable.

The members of the Committee may not be bound by any mandatory instructions. They shall be completely independent in the performance of their duties, in the general interest of the Community.

The Council acting by a qualified majority, shall determine the allowances of members of the Committee.

Article 259 [ex Article 195]

1. For the appointment of the members of the Committee, each Member State shall provide the Council with a list containing twice as many candidates as there are seats allotted to its nationals.

The composition of the Committee shall take account of the need to ensure adequate representation of the various categories of economic and social activity.

2. The Council shall consult the Commission. It may obtain the opinion of European bodies which are representative of the various economic and social sectors to which the activities of the Community are of concern.

Article 260 [ex Article 196]

The Committee shall elect its chairman and officers from among its members for a term of two years.

It shall adopt its Rules of Procedure. The Committee shall be convened by its chairman at the request of the Council or of the Commission. It may also meet on its own initiative.

Article 261 [ex Article 197]

The Committee shall include specialised sections for the principal fields covered by this Treaty.

These specialised sections shall operate within the general terms of reference of the Committee. They may not be consulted independently of the Committee.

Sub-committees may also be established within the Committee to prepare on specific questions or in specific fields, draft opinions to be submitted to the Committee for its consideration.

The Rules of Procedure shall lay down the methods of composition and the terms of reference of the specialised sections and of the sub-committees.

Article 262 [ex Article 198]

The Committee must be consulted by the Council or by the Commission where this Treaty so provides. The Committee may be consulted by these institutions in all cases in which they consider it appropriate. It may issue an opinion on its own initiative in cases in which it considers such action appropriate.

The Council or the Commission shall, if it considers it necessary, set the Committee, for the submission of its opinion, a time-limit which may not be less than one month from the date on which the chairman receives notification to this effect. Upon expiry of the time-limit, the absence of an opinion shall not prevent further action.

The opinion of the Committee and that of the specialised section, together with a record of the proceedings, shall be forwarded to the Council and to the Commission.

The Committee may be consulted by the European Parliament.

NOTE: Upon ratification of the Treaty of Nice the maximum limit of the members of both the Economic and Social Committee and the Committee of the Regions will have been set at 350 with the allocations to the current Member States being unchanged and those for the candidate Member States as follows:

Country	Members
Poland	21
Romania	15
Bulgaria	12
Czech Republic	12
Hungary	12
Lithuania	9
Slovakia	9
Estonia	7
Latvia	7
Slovenia	7
Cyprus	6
Malta	5

CHAPTER 4   THE COMMITTEE OF THE REGIONS

Article 263 [ex Article 198a]
A Committee consisting of representatives of regional and local bodies, hereinafter referred to as 'the Committee of the Regions', is hereby established with advisory status.
The number of members of the Committee of the Regions shall be as follows:

Belgium	12
Denmark	9
Germany	24
Greece	12
Spain	21
France	24
Ireland	9
Italy	24
Luxembourg	6
Netherlands	12
Austria	12
Portugal	12
Finland	9
Sweden	12
United Kingdom	24

The members of the Committee and an equal number of alternate members shall be appointed for four years by the Council acting unanimously on proposals from the respective Member States. Their term of office shall be renewable.

The member of the Committee may not be bound by any mandatory instructions. They shall be completely independent in the performance of their duties, in the general interests of the Community.

Article 264 [ex Article 198b]
The Committee of the Regions shall elect its chairman and officers from among its members for a term of two years. It shall adopt its Rules of Procedure.

The Committee shall be convened by its chairman at the request of the Council or of the Commission. It may also meet on its own initiative.

Article 265 [ex Article 198c]
The Committee of the Regions shall be consulted by the Council or by the Commission where this Treaty so provides and in all other cases in which one of these two institutions considers it appropriate.

The Council or the Commission shall, if it considers it necessary, set the Committee, for the submission of its opinion, a time-limit which may not be less than one month from the date on which the chairman receives notification to this effect. Upon expiry of the time-limit, the absence of an opinion shall not prevent further action.

Where the Economic and Social Committee is consulted pursuant to Article 262, the Committee of the Regions shall be informed by the Council or the Commission of the request for an opinion. Where it considers that specific regional interests are involved, the Committee of the Regions may issue an opinion on the matter.

The Committee of the Regions may be consulted by the European Parliament. It may issue an opinion on its own initiative in cases in which it considers such action appropriate.

The opinion of the Committee, together with a record of the proceedings, shall be forwarded to the Council and to the Commission.

NOTES:
1. Subsidiarity is a principle which seeks to devolve powers. Its application to the EC is set out in Article 5 (ex 3b). Some Member States are concerned about the powers which may be exercised at the Community level rather than at national level. For academic discussion of Article 5, see Emiliou 'Subsidiarity: An Effective Barrier against "the Enterprises of Ambition"?' (1992) 17 EL Rev 383; Toth 'The Principle of Subsidiarity in the Maastricht Treaty' (1992) CML Rev 1079; Cass 'The Word That Saves Maastricht? The Principle of Subsidiarity and the Division of Powers within the European Community' (1992) CML Rev 1107; Hartley 'Constitutional and Institutional Aspects of the Maastricht Agreement' (1993) 42 ICLQ 213, at 214–18; Gonzalez 'The Principle of Subsidiarity' (1995) 20 EL Rev 355, and Weatherill and Beaumont *EU Law* (1999) at 27–32, 159–61. Opinion is divided on the justiciability of the principle of subsidiarity, but it may be that the political effect of the provision is such to ensure that there will be agreement between the Community institutions and the Member States, thereby obviating a challenge mounted on this principle before the European Court of Justice (ECJ).
2. The balance amongst the Community's institutions is quite different from that of organs of government in European states. The Commission is a permanent body and has important powers of proposal and supervision. It is required to act in the interests of the Community.

    The Council will usually have the determinative say in the legislative processes and it represents the views of the Member States. Within the Council legislation can be made acting by qualified majority voting (QMV) and by unanimity. Before the SEA, despite provision for QMV, unanimity was the rule. It was agreed that the completion of the single market was both important and unlikely to be achieved through unanimity, so it was agreed that QMV was to apply to single market measures. The range of measures to which QMV can be applied has been increased by the TEU (and will be increased further upon ratification of the Treaty of Nice).

The European Parliament (EP) has limited powers. It is mainly a consultative body and its ability to hold the Commission to account by censure (Article 201 (ex 144)) is too blunt to be useful. The EP did help to force the resignation of the Commission in March 1999, even though a motion of censure had not been passed. The issue was financial mismanagement, highlighted in a report by the Court of Auditors. The Commission resigned *en bloc* following the damning conclusions in a report of a committee of experts which had been appointed after the censure motion. (See A. Tomkins, 'Responsibility and Resignation in the European Commission' (1999) 62 MLR 744.)

The EP tends to take a Community view. The EP has been given greater powers under Article 251 (ex 189b) which has had its remit expanded. If it is minded to, the EP could veto an act, whereas under Article 252 (ex 189c) the Council can override the EP's views if it acts unanimously.

The ECJ is of great importance and not just to lawyers. The ECJ as the final interpreter of the treaties and Community legislation has played a significant role in the development of the Communities and shaped a new legal order with distinctive legal doctrines. Two of these are explored in Section B.

3. The TEU amended Article 228 (ex 171) so that there is now provision for the imposition of a financial sanction where a Member State has not taken the necessary measures to comply with a judgment by the ECJ that the Member State has failed to fulfil a Community obligation. See Article 7 of the TEU for the sanctions which a member state could be subjected to if it were in breach of the founding principles of the Union.

4. The TEU set out the timetable for the single currency, the Euro, and the economic convergence criteria which those member states which wished to join would have to meet. In May 1998 it was agreed that the first wave of Member States participating in the single currency would number 11 out of the 15. Finland, Sweden, and the UK, despite meeting the convergence criteria, chose not to participate; while Greece did not meet the criteria. From 1999 the Euro can be used in banking, and in 2002 the Euro notes and coins will be issued and the national currencies of the participating Member States will be phased out.

A decision by the UK government and Parliament to join the single currency would have to be approved in a referendum.

SECTION 2: **The Relationship between Community Law and UK Law**

The treaties have created a new legal order in which measures made by the Community institutions become part of the law of the Member States. Some measures, regulations, are directly applicable, i.e. they become part of the domestic law of the Member States without any implementing action being taken, whereas the Member States implement directives. In these circumstances it is possible that there could be confusion over, or conflict between, Community law and the domestic law of the Member States. Accordingly, the European Court of Justice (ECJ), has been given the jurisdiction of the final interpreter of Community law. Under Article 234 (ex 177), national courts may seek preliminary rulings by asking questions on matters of Community law which are relevant points in cases before them. The decisions of the ECJ under this procedure have played an important part in the development of Community law.

A: Supremacy of Community law

One of the most important doctrines of Community law developed by the ECJ is that of supremacy.

(a) *The European Court of Justice's view*

Van Gend en Loos v *Nederlandse Administratie der Belastingen* Case 26/62
[1963] ECR 1, European Court of Justice

> Article 12 of the European Economic Community (EEC) Treaty (now Article 25) required Member States not to introduce new customs duties or charges having equivalent effect, nor to increase existing duties on trade between Member States. The plaintiff imported aminoplasts from West Germany into the Netherlands. Before the EEC Treaty came into force the duty was 3 per cent. Subsequently it was increased to 8 per cent under an international agreement. The claimant (formerly 'plaintiff') challenged this increase in the Dutch revenue courts. The Amsterdam *Tariefcommissie* sought a preliminary ruling on the interpretation of Article 12 from the ECJ.

II – The first question

A – *Jurisdiction of the Court*

The Government of the Netherlands and the Belgian Government challenge the jurisdiction of the Court on the ground that the reference relates not to the interpretation but to the application of the Treaty in the context of the constitutional law of the Netherlands, and that in particular the Court has no jurisdiction to decide, should the occasion arise, whether the provisions of the EEC Treaty prevail over Netherlands legislation or over other agreements entered into by the Netherlands and incorporated into Dutch national law. The solution of such a problem, it is claimed, falls within the exclusive jurisdiction of the national courts, subject to an application in accordance with the provisions laid down by Articles 169 [now 226] and 170 [now 227] of the Treaty.

However in this case the Court is not asked to adjudicate upon the application of the Treaty according to the principles of the national law of the Netherlands, which remains the concern of the national courts, but is asked, in conformity with subparagraph (a) of the first paragraph of Article 177 [now 234] of the Treaty, only to interpret the scope of Article 12 [now 25] of the said Treaty within the context of Community law and with reference to its effect on individuals. This argument has therefore no legal foundation.

The Belgian Government further argues that the Court has no jurisdiction on the ground that no answer which the Court could give to the first question of the Tariefcommissie would have any bearing on the result of the proceedings brought in that court.

However, in order to confer jurisdiction on the Court in the present case it is necessary only that the question raised should clearly be concerned with the interpretation of the Treaty. The considerations which may have led a national court or tribunal to its choice of questions as well as the relevance which it attributes to such questions in the context of a case before it are excluded from review by the Court of Justice.

It appears from the wording of the questions referred that they relate to the interpretation of the Treaty. The Court therefore has the jurisdiction to answer them.

This argument, too, is therefore unfounded.

B – *On the substance of the Case*

The first question of the Tariefcommissie is whether Article 12 of the Treaty has direct application in national law in the sense that nationals of Member States may on the basis of this Article lay claim to rights which the national court must protect.

To ascertain whether the provisions of an international treaty extend so far in their effects it is necessary to consider the spirit, the general scheme and the wording of those provisions.

The objective of the EEC Treaty, which is to establish a Common Market, the functioning of which is of direct concern to interested parties in the Community, implies that this Treaty is more than an agreement which merely creates mutual obligations between the contracting states. This view is confirmed by the preamble to the Treaty which refers not only to governments but to peoples. It is also confirmed more specifically by the establishment of institutions endowed with sovereign rights, the exercise of which affects Member States and also their citizens. Furthermore, it must be noted that the nationals of the states brought together in the Community are called upon to cooperate in the functioning of this Community through the intermediary of the European Parliament and the Economic and Social Committee.

In addition the task assigned to the Court of Justice under Article 177 [now 234], the object of which is to secure uniform interpretation of the Treaty by national courts and tribunals, confirms that the states have acknowledged that Community law has an authority which can be invoked by their nationals before those courts and tribunals.

The conclusion to be drawn from this is that the Community constitutes a new legal order of international law for the benefit of which the states have limited their sovereign rights, albeit within limited fields, and the subjects of which comprise not only Member States but also their nationals. Independently of the legislation of Member States, Community law therefore not only imposes obligations on individuals but is also intended to confer upon them rights which become part of their legal heritage. These rights arise not only where they are expressly granted by the Treaty, but also by reason of obligations which the Treaty imposes in a clearly defined way upon individuals as well as upon the Member States and upon the institutions of the Community.

With regard to the general scheme of the Treaty as it relates to customs duties and charges having equivalent effect it must be emphasized that Article 9, which bases the Community upon a customs union, includes as an essential provision the prohibition of these customs duties and charges. This provision is found at the beginning of the part of the Treaty which defines the 'Foundations of the Community'. It is applied and explained by Article 12 [now 25].

The wording of Article 12 [now 25] contains a clear and unconditional prohibition which is not a positive but a negative obligation. This obligation, moreover, is not qualified by any reservation on the part of states which would make its implementation conditional upon a positive legislative measure enacted under national law. The very nature of this prohibition makes it ideally adapted to produce direct effects in the legal relationship between Member States and their subjects.

The implementation of Article 12 [now 25] does not require any legislative intervention on the part of the states. The fact that under this Article it is the Member States who are made the subject of the negative obligation does not imply that their nationals cannot benefit from this obligation.

In addition the argument based on Articles 169 [now 226] and 170 [now 227] of the Treaty put forward by the three Governments which have submitted observations to the Court in their statements of case is misconceived. The fact that these Articles of the Treaty enable the Commission and the Member States to bring before the Court a State which has not fulfilled its obligations does not mean that individuals cannot plead these obligations, should the occasion arise, before a national court, any more than the fact that the Treaty places at the disposal of the Commission ways of ensuring that obligations imposed upon those subject to the Treaty are observed, precludes the possibility, in actions between individuals before a national court, of pleading infringements of these obligations.

A restriction of the guarantees against an infringement of Article 12 [now 25] by Member States to the procedures under Articles 169 [now 226] and 170 [now 227] would remove all direct legal protection of the individual rights of their nationals. There is the risk that recourse to the procedure under these Articles would be ineffective if it were to occur after the implementation of a national decision taken contrary to the provisions of the Treaty.

The vigilance of individuals concerned to protect their rights amounts to an effective supervision in addition to the supervision entrusted by Articles 169 [now 226] and 170 [now 227] to the diligence of the Commission and of the Member States.

It follows from the foregoing considerations that, according to the spirit, the general scheme and the wording of the Treaty, Article 12 [now 25] must be interpreted as producing direct effects and creating individual rights which national courts must protect.

The ECJ ruled that Article 12 produced direct effects and created rights which national courts must protect and left it to the Tariefcommissie to determine if Article 12 had been breached by the Dutch revenue authorities.

NOTE: The style of judgment of the ECJ is somewhat different from a common law court. The ECJ uses consequentialist or purposive reasoning. The policy behind the creation of a Common Market is to remove trade barriers, and this will affect individuals. It would be counter to this policy to allow Member States to determine EC matters. The ECJ concludes that there is a new legal order created by the Treaties, and they provide that the ECJ is to be the final authority on the interpretation of the Treaties and EC law.

The case also makes clear that provisions of the Treaties which do not make explicit reference to individuals can, nevertheless, produce direct effects, that is create rights for individuals which national courts are to protect. The governments which filed briefs before the ECJ argued unsuccessfully that only the Commission and Member States could take legal action, under Articles 169–170 (now 226–227) of the EEC Treaty, against any Member State which was not honouring its EC obligations.

The nature of the new legal order was further developed in the following case.

Costa v *ENEL* Case 6/64
[1964] ECR 585, European Court of Justice

Mr Costa refused to pay an electricity bill. He was opposed to the nationalization of the Italian electricity industry which had occurred after the EEC Treaty had come into force. In defending his non-payment Mr Costa argued that the nationalization legislation breached Articles 102, 93, 53, and 37 (now 97, 88 and 31) of the EEC Treaty. The magistrate, the *Giudice Conciliatore*, sought a preliminary ruling from the ECJ.

The complaint is made that the Milan court has requested an interpretation of the Treaty which was not necessary for the solution of the dispute before it.

Since, however, Article 177 is based upon a clear separation of functions between national courts and the Court of Justice, it cannot empower the latter either to investigate the facts of the case or to criticize the grounds and purpose of the request for interpretation.

On the submission that the court was obliged to apply the national law
The Italian Government submits that the request of the Giudice Conciliatore is 'absolutely inadmissible', inasmuch as a national court which is obliged to apply a national law cannot avail itself of Article 177 [now 234].

By contrast with ordinary international treaties, the EEC Treaty has created its own legal system which, on the entry into force of the Treaty, became an integral part of the legal systems of the Member States and which their courts are bound to apply.

By creating a Community of unlimited duration, having its own institutions, its own personality, its own legal capacity and capacity of representation on the international plane and, more particularly, real powers stemming from a limitation of sovereignty or a transfer of powers from the States to the Community, the Member States have limited their sovereign rights, albeit within limited fields, and have thus created a body of law which binds both their nationals and themselves.

The integration into the laws of each Member State of provisions which derive from the Community, and more generally the terms and the spirit of the Treaty, make it impossible for the States, as a corollary, to accord precedence to a unilateral and subsequent measure over a legal system accepted by them on a basis of reciprocity. Such a measure cannot therefore be inconsistent with that legal system. The executive force of Community law cannot vary from one State to another in deference to subsequent domestic laws, without jeopardizing the attainment of the objectives of the Treaty set out in Article 5(2) [now 10(2)] and giving rise to the discrimination prohibited by Article 7 [now repealed].

The obligations undertaken under the Treaty establishing the Community would not be unconditional, but merely contingent, if they could be called in question by subsequent legislative acts of the signatories. Wherever the Treaty grants the States the right to act unilaterally, it does this by clear and precise provisions (for example Articles 15, 93(3), 223, 224 and 225 [now repealed, 88, 296, 297 and 298]). Applications, by Member States for authority to derogate from the Treaty are subject to a special authorization procedure (for example Articles 8(4), 17(4), 25, 26, 73 [now repealed], the third subparagraph of Article 93(2) [now 88(2)], and 226 [now repealed]) which would lose their purpose if the Member States could renounce their obligations by means of an ordinary law.

The precedence of Community law is confirmed by Article 189 [now 249], whereby a regulation 'shall be binding' and 'directly applicable in all Member States'. This provision, which is subject to no reservation, would be quite meaningless if a State could unilaterally nullify its effects by means of a legislative measure which could prevail over Community law.

It follows from all these observations that the law stemming from the Treaty, an independent source of law, could not, because of its special and original nature, be overridden by domestic legal provisions, however framed, without being deprived of its character as Community law and without the legal basis of the Community itself being called into question.

The transfer by the States from their domestic legal system to the Community legal system of the rights and obligations arising under the Treaty carries with it a permanent limitation of their sovereign rights, against which a subsequent unilateral act incompatible with the concept of the Community cannot prevail. Consequently Article 177 [now 234] is to be applied regardless of any domestic law, whenever questions relating to the interpretation of the Treaty arise.

The ECJ ruled that subsequent national measures cannot take precedence over EC law and that, whilst Articles 53 and 37(2) produced direct effects creating rights for individuals which national courts must protect, this was not so for Articles 102 and 93.

NOTE: The ECJ again showed that EC provisions which do not specifically mention individuals may still create rights for them. The ECJ also developed its views about the new legal order, and stated that the logic of EC law gives it supremacy over the municipal law of the Member States.

The full extent of this supremacy of EC law is revealed in the following case.

Internationale Handelsgesellschaft GmbH v *Einfuhr – und Vorratsstelle fur Getreide und Futtermittel* Case 11/70
[1970] ECR 1125, European Court of Justice

> The claimant (then called 'plaintiff'), a German company, had to obtain a licence to export cornflour. The EC provisions required a performance deposit, that is, if a licensee failed to export the full amount permitted in the licence then the deposit would be forfeit. The claimant failed to export the full amount specified in the licence and so forfeited the deposit. The claimant challenged this in the administrative court, the *verwaltungsgericht*. The German court sought a pre-liminary ruling on the EC provisions, as the court thought that they were in conflict with the basic rights guaranteed in the West German constitution.

[2] . . . It appears from the grounds of the order referring the matter that the Verwaltungsgericht has until now refused to accept the validity of the provisions in question and that for this reason it considers it to be essential to put an end to the existing legal uncertainty. According to the evaluation of the Verwaltungsgericht, the system of deposits is contrary to certain structural principles of national constitutional law which must be protected within the framework of Community law, with the result that the primacy of supranational law must yield before the principles of the German Basic Law. More particularly, the system of deposits runs counter to the principles of freedom of action and of disposition, of economic liberty and of proportionality arising in particular from Articles 2 (1) and 14 of the Basic Law. The obligation to import or export resulting from the issue of the licences, together with the deposit attaching thereto, constitutes an excessive intervention in the freedom of disposition in trade, as the objective of the regulations could have been attained by methods of intervention having less serious consequences.

The protection of fundamental rights in the Community legal system
[3] Recourse to the legal rules or concepts of national law in order to judge the validity of measures adopted by the institutions of the Community would have an adverse effect on the uniformity and efficacy of Community law. The validity of such measures can only be judged in the light of Community law. In fact, the law stemming from the Treaty, an independent source of law, cannot because of its very nature be overridden by rules of national law, however framed, without being deprived of its character as Community law and without the legal basis of the Community itself being called in question. Therefore the validity of a Community measure or its effect within a Member State cannot be affected by allegations that it runs counter to either fundamental rights as formulated by the constitution of the State or the principles of a national constitutional structure.

[4] However, an examination should be made as to whether or not any analogous guarantee inherent in Community law has been disregarded. In fact, respect for fundamental rights forms an integral part of the general principles of law protected by the Court of Justice. The protection of such rights, whilst inspired by the constitutional traditions common to the Member States, must be ensured within the framework of the structure and objectives of the Community. It must therefore be ascertained, in the light of the doubts expressed by the Verwaltungsgericht, whether the system of deposits has infringed rights of a fundamental nature, respect for which must be ensured in the Community legal system.

The ECJ upheld the provisions creating the system of performance deposits.

NOTES:
1. So far we have looked at conflicts between the municipal law of Member States and EC law where the ECJ, in its rulings, has affirmed the supremacy of the latter. The ECJ has taken

this view further by declaring that EC law prevails over any conflicting provisions of Bills of Rights in Member States' constitutions. Again, this followed on from the logic of the Treaties that EC law applies uniformly throughout the Member States. The ECJ stated that it will protect fundamental rights. In *Nold* v *Commission* (Case 4/73) [1974] ECR 491 the ECJ reaffirmed that fundamental rights form part of the general principles of law protected by the court. It was also stated that the court would draw inspiration from the constitutional traditions common to the Member States and from international treaties for the protection of human rights which Member States may have collaborated on or ratified.

2. The declaration of the supremacy of EC law by the ECJ creates a problem for national courts: they are supposed to protect the rights conferred by EC law even where they conflict with the law of Member States. How can this be done if a national court cannot strike down a municipal statute, as where, for example, only the Member State's Constitutional Court can carry out such action? Advice was offered in the following case.

Amministrazione delle Finanze dello Stato v *Simmenthal SpA* Case 106/77
[1978] ECR 629, European Court of Justice

Simmenthal imported beef into Italy. In an earlier case, *Simmenthal SpA* v *Italian Minister of Finance* (Case 35/76) [1976] ECR 1871, the ECJ had ruled that the Italian law requiring importers to pay for public health and veterinarian checks at the border was contrary to Articles 30 and 12 (now 28 and 25) of the EEC Treaty. The Italian court ordered the refund of these fees paid by Simmenthal, and the Ministry argued that until the Constitutional Court set aside the legislation they had a good defence. The Italian court sought a preliminary ruling.

[13] The main purpose of the first question is to ascertain what consequences flow from the direct applicability of a provision of Community law in the event of incompatibility with a subsequent legislative provision of a Member State.

[14] Direct applicability in such circumstances means that rules of Community law must be fully and uniformly applied in all the Member States from the date of their entry into force and for so long as they continue in force.

[15] These provisions are therefore a direct source of rights and duties for all those affected thereby, whether Member States or individuals, who are parties to legal relationships under Community law.

[16] This consequence also concerns any national court whose task it is as an organ of a Member State to protect, in a case within its jurisdiction, the rights conferred upon individuals by Community law.

[17] Furthermore, in accordance with the principle of the precedence of Community law, the relationship between provisions of the Treaty and directly applicable measures of the institutions on the one hand and the national law of the Member States on the other is such that those provisions and measures not only by their entry into force render automatically inapplicable any conflicting provision of current national law but – in so far as they are an integral part of, and take precedence in, the legal order applicable in the territory of each of the Member States – also preclude the valid adoption of new national legislative measures to the extent to which they would be incompatible with Community provisions.

[18] Indeed any recognition that national legislative measures which encroach upon the field within which the Community exercises its legislative power or which are otherwise incompatible with the provisions of Community law had any legal effect would amount to a corresponding denial of

the effectiveness of obligations undertaken unconditionally and irrevocably by Member States pursuant to the Treaty and would thus imperil the very foundations of the Community.

[19] The same conclusion emerges from the structure of Article 177 [now 234] of the Treaty which provides that any court or tribunal of a Member State is entitled to make a reference to the Court whenever it considers that a preliminary ruling on a question of interpretation or validity relating to Community law is necessary to enable it to give judgment.

[20] The effectiveness of that provision would be impaired if the national court were prevented from forthwith applying Community law in accordance with the decision or the case-law of the Court.

[21] It follows from the foregoing that every national court must, in a case within its jurisdiction, apply Community law in its entirety and protect rights which the latter confers on individuals and must accordingly set aside any provision of national law which may conflict with it, whether prior or subsequent to the Community rule.

[22] Accordingly any provision of a national legal system and any legislative, administrative, or judicial practice which might impair the effectiveness of Community law by withholding from the national court having jurisdiction to apply such law the power to do everything necessary at the moment of its application to set aside national legislative provisions which might prevent Community rules from having full force and effect are incompatible with those requirements which are the very essence of Community law.

[23] This would be the case in the event of a conflict between a provision of Community law and a subsequent national law if the solution of the conflict were to be reserved for an authority with a discretion of its own, other than the court called upon to apply Community law, even if such an impediment to the full effectiveness of Community law were only temporary.

[24] The first question should therefore be answered to the effect that a national court which is called upon, within the limits of its jurisdiction, to apply provisions of Community law is under a duty to give full effect to those provisions, if necessary refusing of its own motion to apply any conflicting provision of national legislation, even if adopted subsequently, and it is not necessary for the court to request or await the prior setting aside of such provision by legislation or other constitutional means.

The ECJ ruled:

A national court which is called upon, within the limits of its jurisdiction, to apply provisions of Community law is under a duty to give full effect to those provisions, if necessary refusing of its own motion to apply any conflicting provisions of national legislation, even if adopted subsequently, and it is not necessary for the court to request or await the prior setting aside of such provisions by legislation or other constitutional means.

NOTE: While the ECJ states that any national court may set aside municipal legislation, this does not mean that such legislation is entirely void. It is only of no effect where there is a conflict between it and EC law.

QUESTIONS

1. The ECJ has declared that the Treaties have created a new legal order. Within this new legal order, what is the hierarchy of ranking amongst EC law, constitutional law, and ordinary municipal law?

2. What is the relationship between the ECJ and the national courts in this legal order?

(b) *The United Kingdom courts' view*

The traditional view of legislative supremacy explored in Chapter 2 would appear to conflict with the ECJ's rulings on the supremacy of Community law.

In order for Community law to become part of the UK's domestic law, it had to be incorporated by legislation. This was done by the following provisions.

The European Communities Act 1972

2.—(1) All such rights, powers, liabilities, obligations and restrictions from time to time created or arising by or under the Treaties, and all such remedies and procedures from time to time provided for by or under the Treaties, as in accordance with the Treaties are without further enactment to be given legal effect or used in the United Kingdom shall be recognised and available in law, and be enforced, allowed and followed accordingly; and the expression 'enforceable Community right' and similar expressions shall be read as referring to one to which this subsection applies.

(2) Subject to Schedule 2 of this Act, at any time after its passing Her Majesty may by Order in Council, and any designated Minister or department may by regulations, make provision—

(a) for the purpose of implementing any Community obligation of the United Kingdom, or enabling any such obligation to be implemented, or of enabling any rights enjoyed or to be enjoyed by the United Kingdom under or by virtue of the Treaties to be exercised; or

(b) for the purpose of dealing with matters arising out of or related to any such obligation or rights or the coming into force, or the operation from time to time, of subsection (1) above;

and in the exercise of any statutory power or duty, including any power to give directions or to legislate by means of orders, rules, regulations or other subordinate instrument, the person entrusted with the power or duty may have regard to the objects of the Communities and to any such obligation or rights as aforesaid.

In this subsection 'designated Minister or department' means such Minister of the Crown or government department as may from time to time be designated by Order in Council in relation to any matter or for any purpose, but subject to such restrictions or conditions (if any) as may be specified by the Order in Council.

(4) The provision that may be made under subsection (2) above includes, subject to Schedule 2 to this Act, any such provision (of any such extent) as might be made by Act of Parliament, and any enactment passed or to be passed, other than one contained in this Part of this Act, shall be construed and have effect subject to the foregoing provisions of this section; but, except as may be provided by any Act passed after this Act, Schedule 2 shall have effect in connection with the powers conferred by this and the following sections of this Act to make Orders in Council and regulations.

3.—(1) For the purposes of all legal proceedings any question as to the meaning or effect of any of the Treaties, or as to the validity, meaning or effect of any Community instrument, shall be treated as a question of law (and, if not referred to the European Court, be for determination as such in accordance with the principles laid down by and any relevant decision of the European Court).

(2) Judicial notice shall be taken of the Treaties, of the Official Journal of the Communities and of any decision of, or expression of opinion by, the European Court on any such question as

aforesaid; and the Official Journal shall be admissible as evidence of any instrument or other act thereby communicated of any of the Communities or of any Community institution.

NOTE: Section 2(1) incorporates *some* EC law into UK law. This EC law is known as directly applicable EC law. Such law comes into effect in the UK without any further legislative action being taken by Parliament.

Section 2(2) provides for the making of delegated legislation in order to implement EC obligations. Schedule 2 specifies the limitations upon such legislative action, and some of these include the inability to increase taxation, or to introduce retrospective measures, or to create new criminal offences.

Section 2(4) provides that subsequent legislation is to be construed and to have effect subject to ss. 2(1) and (2). Does this resolve any problems of conflict between EC and UK law subsequent to the passage of the European Communities Act 1972?

The courts have taken time to accustom themselves to Community law. There has been a variety of approaches taken on the issue of the supremacy of Community law. One approach is that of implied repeal which is illustrated by a dictum from Lord Denning MR in *Felixstowe Dock and Railway Co* v *British Transport Docks Board* [1976] CMLR 655. In this case the British Transport Docks Board (the Board) wished to take over the Felixstowe Dock and Railway Company (the Company). Terms were agreed between the parties but the Board, as a statutory body with limited powers, needed parliamentary approval for this action. In an unsuccessful challenge to the agreement by the Company, the ownership of which had changed, it was argued, *inter alia*, that the agreement was contrary to EEC competition law and Article 86 (now 82) of the EEC Treaty in particular. Lord Denning MR said, at pp. 644–5:

> It seems to me that once the Bill is passed by Parliament and becomes a Statute that will dispose of all discussion about the Treaty. These courts will have to abide by the Statute without regard to the Treaty at all.

Another approach would give priority to Community law over inconsistent UK law, unless the domestic legislation expressly repudiates Community obligations. This approach can also be illustrated by dicta from Lord Denning MR, on this occasion from *Macarthys* v *Smith* [1979] ICR 785. This case involved a claim of unlawful discrimination on grounds of sex in relation to equal pay. Ms Smith's contract of employment contained some minor differences from the contract of her male predecessor in the post. She received a smaller weekly wage than her male predecessor. The company's defence was that provisions of the Equal Pay Act 1970, as amended by the Sex Discrimination Act 1975, meant that Ms Smith was only entitled to compare her pay with that of a male employee engaged in 'like work' at the same time as her. Ms Smith argued that Article 119 (now 141) of the EEC Treaty permitted her to base a claim on a comparison with her male predecessor. In the Court of Appeal Lord Denning MR said, at p. 789:

> In construing our statute, we are entitled to look to the Treaty as an aid to its construction, and even more, not only as an aid but as an overriding force. If on close investigation it should appear that our legislation is deficient – or is inconsistent with Community law – by some oversight of our draftsmen – then it is our bounden duty to give priority to Community law. Such is the result of section 2(1) and (4) of the European Communities Act 1972.
>
> I pause here, however, to make one observation on a constitutional point. Thus far I have assumed that our Parliament, whenever it passes legislation, intends to fulfil its obligations under the Treaty. If the time should come when our Parliament deliberately passes an Act – with the intention of repudiating the Treaty or any provision in it – or intentionally of acting inconsistently with it – and says so in express terms – then I should have thought that it would be the duty of our courts to follow the statute of our Parliament. I do not however envisage any such situation. As I said in *Blackburn* v *Attorney-General* [1971] WLR 1037, 1040: 'But, if Parliament should do so, then I say we will consider that event when it happens.' Unless there is such an intentional and express repudiation of the Treaty, it is our duty to give priority to the Treaty. In the present case I assume that the United Kingdom intended to fulfil its obligations under article 119.

The House of Lords appears to have accepted that membership of the Communities and the European Communities Act 1972 have altered the rules on legislative supremacy where there is inconsistency between Community law and domestic law.

R v *Secretary of State for Transport, ex parte Factortame Ltd and Others*
[1990] 2 AC 85, House of Lords

The applicants were companies which owned fishing vessels, the majority of which had first been registered as Spanish before being re-registered as British vessels. The UK government was concerned that the operation of quotas under the Common Fisheries Policy would adversely affect the British fishing industry by the inclusion in the UK quotas of vessels fishing for the Spanish market. Parliament passed the Merchant Shipping Act 1988 and the Merchant Shipping (Registration of Fishing Vessels) Regulations 1988 (SI 1988 No. 1926) which would have the effect of ending the applicants' registration under the Merchant Shipping Act 1894 and precluding them from registration under the new regulations. The applicants claimed that the legislation was contrary to those provisions of EC law which (i) prohibited discrimination on grounds of nationality between member states, (ii) prohibited restrictions on exports between Member States, (iii) created a common market in agricultural products, (iv) provided for the freedom of movement of workers and the freedom of establishment of companies, (v) required that nationals of member states are to be treated equally with respect to participation in the capital of companies established in the EC. The Divisional Court decided to seek a preliminary ruling from the ECJ and decided to order as interim relief that, pending the ECJ's preliminary ruling on the compatibility of the UK law with EC law, Part II of the 1988 Act and the 1988 regulations be disapplied, and that the Secretary of State be restrained from applying them in respect of the applicants so as to enable the applicants' vessels to continue to be registered as British. On appeal the Court of Appeal reversed the decision on the granting of interim relief which involved the overriding of the UK legislation. This was appealed to the House of Lords. The relationship between domestic law and Community law was explained in a preliminary passage before dealing with the point about interim relief.

LORD BRIDGE: . . . By virtue of section 2(4) of the Act of 1972 Part II of the Act of 1988 is to be construed and take effect subject to directly enforceable Community rights and those rights are, by section 2(1) of the Act of 1972, to be 'recognised and available in law, and . . . enforced, allowed and followed accordingly; . . .' This has precisely the same effect as if a section were incorporated in Part II of the Act of 1988 which in terms enacted that the provisions with respect to registration of British fishing vessels were to be without prejudice to the directly enforceable Community rights of nationals of any member state of the EEC. Thus it is common ground that, in so far as the applicants succeed before the ECJ in obtaining a ruling in support of the Community rights which they claim, those rights will prevail over the restrictions imposed on registration of British fishing vessels by Part II of the Act of 1988 and the Divisional Court will, in the final determination of the application for judicial review, be obliged to make appropriate declarations to give effect to those rights.

NOTES:
1. Both the Court of Appeal and the House of Lords were of the view that domestic law did not

allow, as interim relief, the disapplying of a statute where it had not been established that the statute was in breach of Community law. The House of Lords sought a preliminary ruling on this point from the ECJ which ruled that 'a national court which in a case before it concerning Community law considers itself that the sole obstacle which precludes it from granting interim relief is a rule of national law must set aside that rule' (*R* v *Secretary of State for Transport, ex parte Factortame Ltd* [1989] 3 CMLR 1). Subsequently the House of Lords considered the application for interim relief and decided to grant it (*R* v *Secretary of State for Transport, ex parte Factortame Ltd (No. 2)* [1991] 1 AC 603). The ECJ ruled on the Divisional Court's questions about the compatibility of the Merchant Shipping Act 1988 with Community law and ruled that Article 52 (now 43) had been infringed because of the local national and residence requirements for registration of owners of fishing vessels (*R* v *Secretary of State for Transport, ex parte Factortame Ltd (No. 3)* (Case C-221/89) [1991] 3 CMLR 589).

Before the ECJ gave its rulings on the questions referred to it by the High Court and House of Lords, the European Commission brought a successful action for interim relief in an action under Article 169 (now 226) against the UK, requiring that the nationality requirement of s. 14 of the Merchant Shipping Act 1988 be suspended (*Re Nationality of Fishermen: EC Commission* v *UK* (Case C-246/89R) [1989] 3 CMLR 601). This was implemented by the Merchant Shipping Act (Amendment) Order 1989 (SI 1989 No. 2006). Finally the ECJ upheld the Commission's challenge under Article 169 that the nationality requirements breached Articles 7, 52, and 221 (now repealed, 43 and 294) of the EEC Treaty (*Re Nationality of Fishermen: EC Commission* v *UK* (Case C-246/89) [1991] 3 CMLR 706).

2. See also *R* v *Secretary of State for Employment, ex parte Equal Opportunities Commission* [1994] 2 WLR 409, at p. 384 *post*.

3. In *Thoburn* v *Sunderland City Council*, *Hunt* v *Hackney London Borough Council*, *Harman and Another* v *Cornwall County Council*, and *Collins* v *Sutton London Borough Council*, *The Times*, 22 March 2002 the relationship between domestic and EU law was raised in appeals against conviction. It was argued unsuccessfully that the European Communities Act 1972, s. 2 had been impliedly repealed by Weights and Measures Act 1985, s. 1. Laws LJ outlined four propositions. First, the 1972 Act incorporated into domestic law all the specific rights and obligations which EU law created, and made them supreme. Secondly, the 1972 Act could not be impliedly repealed because it was a constitutional statute. Thirdly, English common law recognized a category of constitutional statutes. Fourthly, domestic law was the fundamental legal basis for the United Kingdom's relationship with the EU. The balance struck by those four propositions would give full weight both to the proper supremacy of Community law and to the proper supremacy of the United Kingdom.

QUESTIONS

1. Does the experience of UK membership of the EC support Bradley's suggestion in his essay 'The Sovereignty of Parliament – in Perpetuity?', in Jowell and Oliver *The Changing Constitution* (3rd edn, 1994), that the orthodox doctrine of the supremacy of Parliament is not an immutable part of British constitutional law?

2. If the doctrine of the supremacy of Parliament can no longer be regarded as an immutable part of British constitutional law, is it possible to argue that Parliament could find a method of entrenching a Bill of Rights against subsequent amendment? Do the cases discussed in this section suggest a method or methods which could be used for this purpose?

B: Direct effect and directives

(a) *Early development*

In *Van Gend en Loos* (*ante* p. 134), the ECJ ruled that Community law can confer rights upon individuals which national courts must protect. Thus Community law may have a direct effect in Member States' domestic law. In that case it was held that Article 12 (now 25) of the Treaty of Rome had direct effect. Could a directive do this? A directive sets an objective which Member States are to implement, and in doing this they have a certain degree of discretion. The test for direct effect in *Van Gend en Loos* focused upon the unconditional nature of the prohibition in Article 12.

Van Duyn v *Home Office* Case 41/74
[1974] ECR 1337, European Court of Justice

> Van Duyn, a Dutch woman, wished to take up employment with the Church of Scientology in the UK but was refused leave to enter by the Home Office. She sought to show that she could benefit from Community law on the freedom of movement of workers, particularly Article 48 (now 39) and Directive 64/221/ EEC. The Home Office contended that the public policy exemption to the freedom of movement of workers applied here as they claimed that the Church was socially undesirable. The High Court made an Article 177 reference (now 234), and one of the questions asked of the ECJ concerned the direct effect of directives.

[9] The second question asks the Court to say whether Council Directive No. 64/221 of 25 February 1984 on the coordination of special measures concerning the movement and residence of foreign nationals which are justified on grounds of public policy, public security or public health is directly applicable so as to confer on individuals rights enforceable by them in the courts of a Member State.

[10] It emerges from the order making the reference that the only provision of the Directive which is relevant is that contained in Article 3 (1) which provides that 'measures taken on grounds of public policy or public security shall be based exclusively on the personal conduct of the individual concerned.'

[11] The United Kingdom observes that, since Article 189 [now 249] of the Treaty distinguishes between the effect ascribed to regulations, directives and decisions, it must therefore be presumed that the Council, in issuing a directive rather than making a regulation, must have intended that the directive should have an effect other than that of a regulation and accordingly that the former should not be directly applicable.

[12] If, however, by virtue of the provisions of Article 189 [now 249] regulations are directly applicable and, consequently, may by their very nature have direct effects, it does not follow from this that other categories of acts mentioned in that Article can never have similar effects. It would be incompatible with the binding effect attributed to a directive by Article 189 [now 249] to exclude, in principle, the possibility that the obligation which it imposes may be invoked by those concerned. In particular, where the Community authorities have, by directive, imposed on Member States the obligation to pursue a particular course of conduct, the useful effect of such an act would be weakened if individuals were prevented from relying on it before their national courts and if the later were prevented from taking it into consideration as an element of Community law. Article 177 [now 234], which empowers national courts to refer to the Court questions concerning the validity and

interpretation of all acts of the Community institutions, without distinction, implies furthermore that these acts may be invoked by individuals in the national courts. It is necessary to examine, in every case, whether the nature, general scheme and wording of the provision in question are capable of having direct effects on the relations between Member States and individuals.

[13] By providing that measures taken on grounds of public policy shall be based exclusively on the personal conduct of the individual concerned, Article 3 (1) of Directive No. 64/221 is intended to limit the discretionary power which national laws generally confer on the authorities responsible for the entry and expulsion of foreign nationals. First, the provision lays down an obligation which is not subject to any exception or condition and which, by its very nature, does not require the intervention of any act on the part either of the institutions of the Community or of Member States. Secondly, because Member States are thereby obliged, in implementing a clause which derogates from one of the fundamental principles of the Treaty in favour of individuals, not to take account of factors extraneous to personal conduct, legal certainty for the persons concerned requires that they should be able to rely on this obligation even though it has been laid down in a legislative act which has no automatic direct effect in its entirety.

[14] If the meaning and exact scope of the provision raise questions of interpretation, these questions can be resolved by the courts, taking into account also the procedure under Article 177 [now 234] of the Treaty.

[15] Accordingly, in reply to the second question, Article 3 (1) of Council Directive No. 64/221 of 25 February 1964 confers on individuals rights which are enforceable by them in the courts of a Member State and which the national courts must protect.

NOTE: In para. 12 the ECJ partially bases the direct effect of a directive on the weakening of the useful effect of the measure if individuals could not rely upon it in their national courts.

Compare the requirement of unconditionality in *Van Gend en Loos* with the treatment of the Member State's discretion in implementing the directive in para. 13.

Pubblico Ministerio v *Ratti* Case 148/78
[1979] ECR 1629, European Court of Justice

Ratti was charged with breaching certain Italian provisions although he had acted in conformity with Community law measures. These measures were directives made by the Council on the approximation of laws relating to the classification, packaging, and labelling of (a) solvents (No. 73/173/EEC), and (b) paints, varnishes, printing inks, adhesives, and similar products (No. 77/728/EEC). The period within which Directive 73/173/EEC should have been implemented had expired. If it had been implemented then the relevant Italian provisions should have been repealed. The period for the implementation of Directive 77/728/EEC had not yet expired. When implemented it would also have the effect of repealing the relevant Italian provisions. The *Pretura Penale* made an Article 177 (now 234) reference.

[18] This question raises the general problem of the legal nature of the provisions of a directive adopted under Article 189 [now 249] of the Treaty.

[19] In this regard the settled case-law of the Court, last reaffirmed by the judgment of 1 February 1977 in Case 51/76 *Nederlandse Ondernemingen* [1977] 1 ECR 126, lays down that, whilst under Article 189 [now 249] regulations are directly applicable and consequently, by their nature capable of producing direct effects, that does not mean that other categories of acts covered by that article can never produce similar effects.

[20] It would be incompatible with the binding effect which Article 189 [now 249] ascribes to directives to exclude on principle the possibility of the obligations imposed by them being relied on by persons concerned.

[21] Particularly in cases in which the Community authorities have, by means of directive, placed Member States under a duty to adopt a certain course of action, the effectiveness of such an act would be weakened if persons were prevented from relying on it in legal proceedings and national courts prevented from taking it into consideration as an element of Community law.

[22] Consequently a Member State which has not adopted the implementing measures required by the directive in the prescribed periods may not rely, as against individuals, on its own failure to perform the obligation which the directive entails.

[23] It follows that a national court requested by a person who has complied with the provisions of a directive not to apply a national provision incompatible with the directive not incorporated into the internal legal order of a defaulting Member State, must uphold that request if the obligation in question is unconditional and sufficiently precise.

[24] Therefore the answer to the first question must be that after the expiration of the period fixed for the implementation of a directive a Member State may not apply its internal law – even if it is provided with penal sanctions – which has not yet been adapted in compliance with the directive, to a person who has complied with the requirements of the directive. . . .

[39] In a fifth question the national court asks whether Council Directive No. 77/728 of 7 November 1977, in particular Article 9 thereof, is immediately and directly applicable with regard to the obligations imposed on Member States to refrain from action as from the date of notification of that directive in a case where a person, acting upon a legitimate expectation, has complied with the provisions of that directive before the expiry of the period within which the Member State must comply with the said directive.

[40] The objective of that directive is analogous to that of Directive No. 73/173 in that it lays down similar rules for preparations intended to be used as paints, varnishes, printing inks, adhesives and similar products, and containing dangerous substances.

[41] Article 12 of that directive provides that Member States must implement it within 24 months of its notification, which took place on 9 November 1977.

[42] That period has not yet expired and the States to which the directive was addressed have until 9 November 1979 to incorporate the provisions of Directive No. 77/728 into their internal legal orders.

[43] It follows that, for the reasons expounded in the grounds of the answer to the national court's first question, it is only at the end of the prescribed period and in the event of the Member State's default that the directive – and in particular Article 9 thereof – will be able to have the effects described in the answer to the first question.

NOTE: If directives are to have direct effect they must be precise and unconditional and the period for their implementation must have expired.

QUESTION

How does the ECJ justify holding that directives may have direct effect given the wording of Article 249 (ex 189) (*ante* p. 126)?

(b) *Horizontal and vertical effect*

Marshall v *Southampton and South West Hampshire Area Health Authority (Teaching)* Case 152/84
[1986] ECR 723, European Court of Justice

> Marshall was dismissed by her employer when she reached the age of 62. She claimed that this was discrimination on grounds of sex as a male employee would not have been forced to retire at this age. Under the Sex Discrimination Act 1975 matters relating to retirement were excluded from the scope of sex discrimination. It was argued that the Equal Treatment Directive 76/207/EEC gave her a remedy for this situation; however, this directive had not been implemented in the UK although the period for implementation had expired. The Court of Appeal made an Article 177 (now 234) reference. The ECJ first found that this situation constituted sex discrimination.

[39] Since the first question has been answered in the affirmative, it is necessary to consider whether Article 5(1) of Directive No. 76/207 may be relied upon by an individual before national courts and tribunals.

[40] The appellant and the Commission consider that the question must be answered in the affirmative. They contend in particular, with regard to Articles 2(1) and 5(1) of Directive No. 76/207, that those provisions are sufficiently clear to enable national courts to apply them without legislative intervention by the Member States, at least so far as overt discrimination is concerned.

[41] In support of that view, the appellant points out that directives are capable of conferring rights on individuals which may be relied upon directly before the courts of the Member States; national courts are obliged by virtue of the binding nature of a directive, in conjunction with Article 5 [now 10] of the EEC Treaty, to give effect to the provisions of directives where possible, in particular when construing or applying relevant provisions of national law (judgment of 10 April 1984 in Case 14/83 *Von Colson and Kamann* v *Land Nordrhein-Westfalen* [1984] ECR 1891). Where there is any inconsistency between national law and Community law which cannot be removed by means of such a construction, the appellant submits that a national court is obliged to declare that the provision of national law which is inconsistent with the directive is inapplicable.

[42] The Commission is of the opinion that the provisions of Article 5(1) of Directive No. 76/207 are sufficiently clear and unconditional to be relied upon before a national court. They may therefore be set up against section 6(4) of the Sex Discrimination Act, which, according to the decisions of the Court of Appeal, has been extended to the question of compulsory retirement and has therefore become ineffective to prevent dismissals based upon the difference in retirement ages for men and for women.

[43] The respondent and the United Kingdom propose, conversely, that the second question should be answered in the negative. They admit that a directive may, in certain specific circumstances, have direct effect as against a Member State in so far as the latter may not rely on its failure to perform its obligations under the directive. However, they maintain that a directive can never impose obligations directly on individuals and that it can only have direct effect against a Member State *qua* public authority and not against a Member State *qua* employer. As an employer a State is no different from a private employer. It would not therefore be proper to put persons employed by the State in a better position than those who are employed by a private employer.

[44] With regard to the legal position of the respondent's employees the United Kingdom states that they are in the same position as the employees of a private employer. Although according to United

Kingdom constitutional law the health authorities, created by the National Health Service Act 1977, as amended by the Health Services Act 1980 and other legislation, are Crown bodies and their employees are Crown servants, nevertheless the administration of the National Health Service by the health authorities is regarded as being separate from the Government's central administration and its employees are not regarded as civil servants.

[45] Finally, both the respondent and the United Kingdom take the view that the provisions of Directive No. 76/207 are neither unconditional nor sufficiently clear and precise to give rise to direct effect. The directive provides for a number of possible exceptions, the details of which are to be laid down by the Member States. Furthermore, the wording of Article 5 is quite imprecise and requires the adoption of measures for its implementation.

[46] It is necessary to recall that, according to a long line of decisions of the Court (in particular its judgment of 19 January 1982 in Case 8/81 *Becker* v *Finanzamt Münster-Innenstadt* [1982] ECR 53), wherever the provisions of a directive appear, as far as their subject-matter is concerned, to be unconditional and sufficiently precise, those provisions may be relied upon by an individual against the State where that State fails to implement the directive in national law by the end of the period prescribed or where it fails to implement the directive correctly.

[47] That view is based on the consideration that it would be incompatible with the binding nature which Article 189 [now 249] confers on the directive to hold as a matter of principle that the obligation imposed thereby cannot be relied on by those concerned. From that the Court deduced that a Member State which has not adopted the implementing measures required by the directive within the prescribed period may not plead, as against individuals, its own failure to perform the obligations which the directive entails.

[48] With regard to the argument that a directive may not be relied upon against an individual, it must be emphasized that according to Article 189 [now 249] of the EEC Treaty the binding nature of a directive, which constitutes the basis for the possibility of relying on the directive before a national court, exists only in relation to 'each Member State to which it is addressed'. It follows that a directive may not of itself impose obligations on an individual and that a provision of a directive may not be relied upon as such against such a person. It must therefore be examined whether, in this case, the respondent must be regarded as having acted as an individual.

[49] In that respect it must be pointed out that where a person involved in legal proceedings is able to rely on a directive as against the State he may do so regardless of the capacity in which the latter is acting, whether employer or public authority. In either case it is necessary to prevent the State from taking advantage of its own failure to comply with Community law.

[50] It is for the national court to apply those considerations to the circumstances of each case; the Court of Appeal has, however, stated in the order for reference that the respondent, Southampton and South West Hampshire Area Health Authority (Teaching), is a public authority.

[51] The argument submitted by the United Kingdom that the possibility of relying on provisions of the directive against the respondent *qua* organ of the State would give rise to an arbitrary and unfair distinction between the rights of State employees and those of private employees does not justify any other conclusion. Such a distinction may easily be avoided if the Member State concerned has correctly implemented the directive in national law.

[52] Finally, with regard to the question whether the provision contained in Article 5 (1) of Directive No. 76/207, which implements the principle of equality of treatment set out in Article 2(1) of the directive, may be considered, as far as its contents are concerned, to be unconditional and sufficiently precise to be relied upon by an individual as against the State, it must be stated that the provision, taken by itself, prohibits any discrimination on grounds of sex with regard to working conditions, including the conditions governing dismissal, in a general manner and in unequivocal

terms. The provision is therefore sufficiently precise to be relied on by an individual and to be applied by the national courts.

[53] It is necessary to consider next whether the prohibition of discrimination laid down by the directive may be regarded as unconditional, in the light of the exceptions contained therein and of the fact that according to Article 5(2) thereof the Member States are to take the measures necessary to ensure the application of the principle of equality of treatment in the context of national law.

[54] With regard, in the first place, to the reservation contained in Article 1(2) of Directive No. 76/207 concerning the application of the principle of equality of treatment in matters of social security, it must be observed that, although the reservation limits the scope of the directive *ratione materiae*, it does not lay down any condition on the application of that principle in its field of operation and in particular in relation to Article 5 of the directive. Similarly, the exceptions to Directive No. 76/207 provided for in Article 2 thereof are not relevant to this case.

[55] It follows that Article 5 of Directive No. 76/207 does not confer on the Member States the right to limit the application of the principle of equality of treatment in its field of operation or to subject it to conditions and that that provision is sufficiently precise and unconditional to be capable of being relied upon by an individual before a national court in order to avoid the application of any national provision which does not conform to Article 5 (1).

[56] Consequently, the answer to the second question must be that Article 5(1) of Council Directive No. 76/207 of 9 February 1976, which prohibits any discrimination on grounds of sex with regard to working conditions, including the conditions governing dismissal, may be relied upon against a State authority acting in its capacity as employer, in order to avoid the application of any national provision which does not conform to Article 5(1).

NOTES:
1. The ECJ has limited the direct effect of directives to vertical effect, i.e. where an individual is seeking enforcement of rights against a State body. Enforcement of rights against another private individual, or horizontal effect, is not possible where a directive is the source of the rights.
2. It has been suggested that a reason for the ECJ changing the basis for giving direct effect to directives from 'useful effect' (*Van Gend en Loos*) to estoppel (*Ratti* and *Marshall*) was that it restricted the operation of direct effect, and this might lessen the opposition of national courts to the impact of Community law upon the legal systems of Member States.

(c) *The scope of vertical effect*

In order to benefit from vertical effect of directives an individual must be seeking enforcement against a state body. Guidance on what constitutes the state was given in the following case.

Foster v *British Gas* Case C–188/89
[1990] ECR I–3313, European Court of Justice

The applicant had been made to retire earlier than her male colleagues. She wished to rely upon the Equal Treatment Directive No. 76/207/EEC. The employer was the British Gas Corporation (BGC). The BGC was a statutory corporation and under the Gas Act 1972 it was responsible for developing and maintaining a system of gas supply in Great Britain and had a monopoly of the supply of gas. The Secretary of State appointed the members of the BGC and could issue directions on matters affecting the national interest. The BGC was required to submit reports to the Secretary of State and to run a balanced budget over two successive financial years. The House of Lords made an Article 177 (now 234) reference.

[13] Before considering the question referred by the House of Lords, it must first be observed as a preliminary point that the United Kingdom has submitted that it is not a matter for the Court of Justice but for the national courts to determine, in the context of the national legal system, whether the provisions of a directive may be relied upon against a body such as the BGC.

[14] The question what effects measures adopted by Community institutions have and in particular whether those measures may be relied on against certain categories of persons necessarily involves interpretation of the articles of the Treaty concerning measures adopted by the institutions and the Community measure in issue.

[15] It follows that the Court of Justice has jurisdiction in proceedings for a preliminary ruling to determine the categories of persons against whom the provisions of a directive may be relied on. It is for the national courts, on the other hand, to decide whether a party to proceeding before them falls within one of the categories so defined.

Reliance on the provisions of the directive against a body such as the BGC

[16] As the Court has consistently held (see the judgment in Case 8/81 *Becker* v *Finanzamt Münster-Innenstadt* [1982] ECR 53, paragraphs 23 to 25), where the Community authorities have, by means of a directive, placed Member States under a duty to adopt a certain course of action, the effectiveness of such a measure would be diminished if persons were prevented from relying upon it in proceedings before a court and national courts were prevented from taking it into consideration as an element of Community law. Consequently, a Member State which has not adopted the implementing measures required by the directive within the prescribed period may not plead, as against individuals, its own failure to perform the obligations which the directive entails. Thus, wherever the provisions of a directive appear, as far as their subject-matter is concerned, to be unconditional and sufficiently precise, those provisions may, in the absence of implementing measures adopted within the prescribed period, be relied upon as against any national provision which is incompatible with the directive or in so far as the provisions define rights which individuals are able to assert against the State.

[17] The Court further held in its judgment in Case 152/84 *Marshall*, paragraph 49, that where a person is able to rely on a directive as against the State he may do so regardless of the capacity in which the latter is acting, whether as employer or as public authority. In either case it is necessary to prevent the State from taking advantage of its own failure to comply with Community law.

[18] On the basis of those considerations, the Court has held in a series of cases that unconditional and sufficiently precise provisions of a directive could be relied on against organizations or bodies which were subject to the authority or control of the State or had special powers beyond those which result from the normal rules applicable to relations between individuals.

[19] The Court has accordingly held that provisions of a directive could be relied on against tax authorities (the judgments in Case 8/81 *Becker*, cited above, and in Case C–221/88 *ECSC* v *Acciaierie e Ferriere Busseni (in liquidation)* [1990] ECR I–495), local or regional authorities (judgment in Case 103/88 *Fratelli Constanzo* v *Comune di Milano* [1989] ECR 1839), constitutionally independent authorities responsible for the maintenance of public order and safety (judgment in Case 222/84 *Johnston* v *Chief Constable of the Royal Ulster Constabulary* [1986] ECR 1651), and public authorities providing public health services (judgment in Case 152/84 *Marshall*, cited above).

[20] It follows from the foregoing that a body, whatever its legal form, which has been made responsible, pursuant to a measure adopted by the State, for providing a public service under the control of the State and has for that purpose special powers beyond those which result from the

normal rules applicable in relations between individuals is included in any event among the bodies against which the provisions of a directive capable of having direct effect may be relied upon.

[21] With regard to Article 5 (1) of Directive 76/207 it should be observed that in the judgment in Case 152/84 *Marshall*, cited above, paragraph 52, the Court held that that provision was unconditional and sufficiently precise to be relied on by an individual and to be applied by the national courts.

[22] The answer to the question referred by the House of Lords must therefore be that Article 5 (1) of Council Directive 76/207 of 9 February 1976 may be relied upon in a claim for damages against a body, whatever its legal form, which has been made responsible, pursuant to a measure adopted by the State, for providing a public service under the control of the State and has for that purpose special powers beyond those which result from the normal rules applicable in relations between individuals.

NOTE: In *Fratelli Constanzo* v *Comune di Milano* (Case 103/88) [1989] ECR 1839 the ECJ held that the State included local authorities.

(d) *Indirect effect*

It does seem unfair that direct effect of directives depends upon whether one is in conflict with a state body. A possible method of circumventing the vertical/horizontal distinction has been claimed as a result of the reasoning in the next case.

Von Colson and Kamann v *Land Nordrhein-Westfalen* Case 14/83
[1984] ECR 1891, European Court of Justice

The applicants had been rejected for jobs on the grounds of sex. The Hamm *arbeitsgericht* held that there had been discrimination on grounds of sex but that the only remedy available under German law was the reimbursement of their travel expenses. Von Colson argued that this was contrary to Article 6 of the Equal Treatment Directive 76/207/EEC. Under this directive Member States are to introduce into their legal systems measures to enable victims of sex discrimination to pursue their claims by judicial process. Measures could include requiring employers to offer victims posts, or to receive adequate compensation. The directive left it to the discretion of Member States to choose the remedy which met the objectives of the directive. An Article 177 (now 234) reference was made.

[22] It is impossible to establish real equality of opportunity without an appropriate system of sanctions. That follows not only from the actual purpose of the directive but more specifically from Article 6 thereof which, by granting applicants for a post who have been discriminated against recourse to the courts, acknowledges that those candidates have rights of which they may avail themselves before the courts.

[23] Although, as has been stated in the reply to Question 1, full implementation of the directive does not require any specific form of sanction for unlawful discrimination, it does entail that that sanction be such as to guarantee real and effective judicial protection. Moreover it must also have a real deterrent effect on the employer. It follows that where a Member State chooses to penalize the breach of the prohibition of discrimination by the award of compensation, that compensation must in any event be adequate in relation to the damage sustained.

[24] In consequence it appears that national provisions limiting the right to compensation of persons who have been discriminated against as regards access to employment to a purely nominal amount,

such as, for example, the reimbursement of expenses incurred by them in submitting their application, would not satisfy the requirements of an effective transposition of the directive.

[25] The nature of the sanctions provided for in the Federal Republic of Germany in respect of discrimination regarding access to employment and in particular the question whether the rule in Paragraph 611a (2) of the Bürgerliches Gesetzbuch excludes the possibility of compensation on the basis of the general rules of law were the subject of lengthy discussion before the Court. The German Government maintained in the oral procedure that that provision did not necessarily exclude the application of the general rules of law regarding compensation. It is for the national court alone to rule on that question concerning the interpretation of its national law.

[26] However, the Member States' obligation arising from a directive to achieve the result envisaged by the directive and their duty under Article 5 [now 10] of the Treaty to take all appropriate measures, whether general or particular, to ensure the fulfilment of that obligation, is binding on all the authorities of Member States including, for matters within their jurisdiction, the courts. It follows that, in applying the national law and in particular the provisions of a national law specifically introduced in order to implement Directive No. 76/207, national courts are required to interpret their national law in the light of the wording and the purpose of the directive in order to achieve the result referred to in the third paragraph of Article 189 [now 249].

[27] On the other hand, as the above considerations show, the directive does not include any unconditional and sufficiently precise obligation as regards sanctions for discrimination which, in the absence of implementing measures adopted in good time may be relied on by individuals in order to obtain specific compensation under the directive, where that is not provided for or permitted under national law.

[28] It should, however, be pointed out to the national court that although Directive No. 76/207/EEC, for the purpose of imposing a sanction for the breach of the prohibition of discrimination, leaves the Member States free to choose between the different solutions suitable for achieving its objective, it nevertheless requires that if a Member States chooses to penalize breaches of that prohibition by the award of compensation, then in order to ensure that it is effective and that it has a deterrent effect, that compensation must in any event be adequate in relation to the damage sustained and must therefore amount to more than purely nominal compensation such as, for example, the reimbursement only of the expenses incurred in connection with the application. It is for the national court to interpret and apply the legislation adopted for the implementation of the directive in conformity with the requirements of Community law, in so far as it is given discretion to do so under national law.

The Court ruled, in answer to the questions referred:

(1) Directive No. 76/207/EEC does not require discrimination on grounds of sex regarding access to employment to be made the subject of a sanction by way of an obligation imposed on the employer who is the author of the discrimination to conclude a contract of employment with the candidate discriminated against.

(2) As regards sanctions for any discrimination which may occur, the directive does not include any unconditional and sufficiently precise obligation which, in the absence of implementing measures adopted within the prescribed time-limits, may be relied on by an individual in order to obtain specific compensation under the directive, where that is not provided for or permitted under national law.

(3) Although Directive No. 76/207/EEC, for the purpose of imposing a sanction for the breach of the prohibition of discrimination, leaves the Member States free to choose between the different solutions suitable for achieving its objective, it nevertheless requires that if a Member State chooses

to penalise breaches of that prohibition by the award of compensation, then in order to ensure that it is effective and that it has a deterrent effect, that compensation must in any event be adequate in relation to the damage sustained and must therefore amount to more than purely nominal compensation such as, for example, the reimbursement only of the expenses incurred in connection with the application. It is for the national court to interpret and apply the legislation adopted for the implementation of the directive in conformity with the requirements of Community law, in so far as it is given discretion to do so under national law.

NOTE: This approach is quite different from that used for direct effect. Using Article 10 (ex 5) (see *ante* p. 107), the ECJ states that national courts must fulfil Community law obligations.

The ECJ has not settled the boundaries of this doctrine of 'indirect effect'. Compare the following two cases.

Marleasing SA v *La Commercial Internacional de Alimentacion SA* Case C–106/89
[1990] ECR I–4135, European Court of Justice

Marleasing wished to have the company, La Commercial, declared a nullity on the basis of Spanish law. Article 11 of Directive 68/151/EEC lists the exclusive grounds on which nullity may be ordered, and this did not include the ground sought by Marleasing. This directive had not been implemented by Spain and the deadline had expired. The *Juzgado de Primera Instancia e Instrucción* made an Article 177 (now 234) reference on the status of the directive.

[6] With regard to the question whether an individual may rely on the directive against a national law, it should be observed that, as the Court has consistently held, a directive may not of itself impose obligations on an individual and, consequently, a provision of a directive may not be relied upon as such against such a person (judgment in Case 152/84 *Marshall* v *Southampton and South-West Hampshire Area Health Authority* [1986] ECR 723).

[7] However, it is apparent from the documents before the Court that the national court seeks in substance to ascertain whether a national court hearing a case which falls within the scope of Directive 68/151 is required to interpret it's national law in the light of the wording and the purpose of that directive in order to preclude a declaration of nullity of a public limited company on a ground other than those listed in Article 11 of the directive.

[8] In order to reply to that queseion, it should be observed that, as the Court pointed out in its judgment in Case 14/83 *Von Colson and Kamann* v *Land Nordrhein-Westfalen* [1984] ECR 1891, paragraph 26, the Member States' obligation arising from a directive to achieve the result envisaged by the directive and their duty under Article 5 [now 10] of the Treaty to take all appropriate measures, whether general or particular, to ensure the fulfilment of that obligation, is binding on all the authorities of Member States including, for matters within their jurisdiction, the courts. It follows that, in applying national law, whether the provisions in question were adopted before or after the directive, the national court called upon to interpret it is required to do so, as far as possible, in the light of the wording and the purpose of the directive in order to achieve the result pursued by the latter and thereby comply with the third paragraph of Article 189 [now 249] of the Treaty.

[9] It follows that the requirement that national law must be interpreted in conformity with Article 11 of Directive 68/151 precludes the interpretation of provisions of national law relating to public limited companies in such a manner that the nullity of a public limited company may be ordered on grounds other than those exhaustively listed in Article 11 of the directive in question.

[10] With regard to the interpretation to be given to Article 11 of the directive, in particular Article 11 (2) (b), it should be observed that that provision prohibits the laws of the Member States from providing for a judicial declaration of nullity on grounds other than those exhaustively listed in the directive, amongst which is the ground that the objects of the company are unlawful or contrary to public policy.

[11] According to the Commission, the expression 'objects of the company' must be interpreted as referring exclusively to the objects of the company as described in the instrument of incorporation or the articles of association. It follows, in the Commission's view, that a declaration of nullity of a company cannot be made on the basis of the activity actually pursued by it, for instance defrauding the founders' creditors.

[12] That argument must be upheld. As is clear from the preamble to Directive 69/151, its purpose was to limit the cases in which nullity can arise and the retroactive effect of a declaration of nullity in order to ensure 'certainty in the law as regards relations between the company and third parties, and also between Members' (sixth recital). Furthermore, the protection of third parties 'must be ensured by provisions which restrict to the greatest possible extent the grounds on which obligations entered into in the name of the company are not valid'. It follows, therefore, that each ground of nullity provided for in Article 11 of the directive must be interpreted strictly. In those circumstances the words 'objects of the company' must be understood as referring to the objects of the company as described in the instrument of incorporation or the articles of association.

[13] The answer to the question submitted must therefore be that a national court hearing a case which falls within the scope of Directive 68/151 is required to interpret its national law in the light of the wording and the purpose of that directive in order to preclude a declaration of nullity of a public limited company on a ground other than those listed in Article 11 of the directive.

Officier van Justitie v *Kolpinghuis Nijmegen* Case 80/86
[1987] ECR 3969, European Court of Justice

A café owner was prosecuted for stocking for sale and delivery mineral water which was, in fact, tap water with added carbon dioxide. As part of the prosecution's case reliance was placed on Directive 80/777/EEC, which, at the time of the alleged offence, had not been incorporated into Dutch law even though the implementation deadline had expired. The *Arrondismentsrechtbank* made an Article 177 (now 234) reference.

[6] The first two questions concern the possibility whether the provisions of a directive which has not yet been implemented in national law in the Member State in question may be applied as such.

[7] In this regard it should be recalled that, according to the established case-law of the Court (in particular its judgment of 19 January 1982 in Case 8/81 *Becker* v *Finanzamt Münster-Innenstadt* [1982] ECR 53), wherever the provisions of a directive appear, as far as their subject-matter is concerned, to be unconditional and sufficiently precise, those provisions may be relied upon by an individual against the State where that State fails to implement the directive in national law by the end of the period prescribed or where it fails to implement the directive correctly.

[8] That view is based on the consideration that it would be incompatible with the binding nature which Article 189 [now 249] confers on the directive to hold as a matter of principle that the obligaton imposed thereby cannot be relied on by those concerned. From that the Court deduced that a Member State which has not adopted the implementing measures required by the directive

within the prescribed period may not plead, as against individuals, its own failure to perform the obligations which the directive entails.

[9] In its judgment of 26 February 1986 in Case 152/84 *Marshall* v *Southampton and South-West Hampshire Area Health Authority* [1986] ECR 723, the Court emphasized, however, that according to Article 189 [now 249] of the EEC Treaty the binding nature of a directive, which constitutes the basis for the possibility of relying on the directive before a national court, exists only in relation to 'each Member State to which it is addressed'. It follows that a directive may not of itself impose obligations on an individual and that a provision of a directive may not be relied upon as such against such a person before a national court.

[10] The answer to the first two questions should therefore be that a national authority may not rely, as against an individual, upon a provision of a directive whose necessary implementation in national law has not yet taken place.

The third question

[11] The third question is designed to ascertain how far the national court may or must take account of a directive as an aid to the interpretation of a rule of national law.

[12] As the Court stated in its judgment of 10 April 1984 in Case 14/83 *Von Colson and Kamann* v *Land Nordrhein-Westfalen* [1984] ECR 1891, the Member States' obligation arising from a directive to achieve the result envisaged by the directive and their duty under Article 5 [now 10] of the Treaty to take all appropriate measures, whether general or particular, to ensure the fulfilment of that obligation, is binding on all the authorities of Member States including, for matters within their jurisdiction, the courts. It follows that, in applying the national law and in particular the provisions of a national law specifically introduced in order to implement the directive, national courts are required to interpret their national law in the light of the wording and the purpose of the directive in order to achieve the result referred to in the third paragraph of Article 189 [now 249] of the Treaty.

[13] However, that obligation on the national court to refer to the content of the directive when interpreting the relevant rules of its national law is limited by the general principles of law which form part of Community law and in particular the principles of legal certainty and non-retroactivity. Thus the Court rules in its judgment of 11 June 1987 in Case 14/86 *Pretore di Salò* v *X* [1987] ECR 2545 that a directive cannot, of itself and independently of a national law adopted by a Member State for its implementation, have the effect of determining or aggravating the liability in criminal law of persons who act in contravention of the provisions of that directive.

[14] The answer to the third question should therefore be that in applying its national legislation a court of a Member State is required to interpret that legislation in the light of the wording and the purpose of the directive in order to achieve the result referred to in the third paragraph of Article 189 [now 249] of the Treaty, but a directive cannot, of itself and independently of a law adopted for its implementation, have the effect of determining or aggravating the liability in criminal law of persons who act in contravention of the provisions of that directive.

The fourth question

[15] The question whether the provisions of a directive may be relied upon as such before a national court arises only if the Member State concerned has not implemented the directive in national law within the prescribed period or has implemented the directive incorrectly. The first two questions were answered in the negative. However, it makes no difference to those answers if on the material date the period which the Member State had in which to adopt national law had not yet expired. As regards the third question concerning the limits which Community law might impose on the obligation or power of the national court to interpret the rules of its national law in the light of the directive, it makes no difference whether or not the period prescribed for implementation has expired.

[16] The answer to the fourth question must therefore be that it makes no difference to the answers

set out above if on the material date the period which the Member State had in which to adapt national law had not yet expired.

NOTE: *Marleasing* seems to be very wide, covering national law made both before and after the directive (para. 8). Should it, like *Kolpinghuis Nijmegen*, be understood as subject to the general principles of Community law, including, for example, legal certainty and non-retroactivity?

(e) *Damages for failure to implement a directive*

Francovich v *Italian Republic* Joined Cases C–6/90 and C–9/90
[1991] ECR I–5357, European Court of Justice

Directive 80/987 was intended to guarantee employees a minimum level of protection under Community law in the event of the insolvency of their employer. Italy had not implemented the Directive before the period for doing so had expired. Employees who had not been paid by reason of their employers' insolvency sought the Directive's guarantee directly from the Italian state or, in the alternative, compensation. On Article 177 (now 234) references the ECJ was asked if an individual who had been adversely affected by a member state's failure to implement Directive 80/987 could directly invoke the legislation against that Member State to obtain the guarantees which the state should have provided. The ECJ held on the first part of the question that, even though the Directive's provisions relating to the content of the guarantee were sufficiently unconditional and precise, the Directive did not identify the person liable to provide the guarantee and the state could not be considered liable to pay those guarantees solely on the ground that it had failed to implement the directive. On the second part of the question:

Liability of the State for loss and damage resulting from breach of its obligations under Community law

[28] In the second part of the first question the national court seeks to determine whether a Member State is obliged to make good loss and damage suffered by individuals as a result of the failure to transpose Directive 80/987.

[29] The national court thus raises the issue of the existence and scope of a State's liability for loss and damage resulting from breach of its obligations under Community law.

[30] That issue must be considered in the light of the general system of the Treaty and its fundamental principles.

(a) The existence of State liability as a matter of principle

[31] It should be borne in mind at the outset that the EEC Treaty has created its own legal system, which is integrated into the legal systems of the Member States and which their courts are bound to apply. The subjects of that legal system are not only the Member States but also their nationals. Just as it imposes burdens on individuals, Community law is also intended to give rise to rights which become part of their legal patrimony. Those rights arise not only where they are expressly granted by the Treaty but also by virtue of obligations which the Treaty imposes in a clearly defined manner both on individuals and on the Member States and the Community institutions (see the judgments in Case 26/62 *Van Gend en Loos* [1963] ECR 1 and Case 6/64 *Costa* v *ENEL* [1964] ECR 585).

[32] Furthermore, it has been consistently held that the national courts whose task it is to apply the provisions of Community law in areas within their jurisdiction must ensure that those rules take full

effect and must protect the rights which they confer on individuals (see in particular the judgments in Case 106/77 *Amministrazione delle Finanze dello Stato* v *Simmenthal* [1978] ECR 629, paragraph 16, and Case C–213/89 *Factortame* [1990] ECR I–2433, paragraph 19.

[33]   The full effectiveness of Community rules would be impaired and the protection of the rights which they grant would be weakened if individuals were unable to obtain redress when their rights are infringed by a breach of Community law for which a Member State can be held responsible.

[34]   The possibility of obtaining redress from the Member State is particularly indispensable where, as in this case, the full effectiveness of Community rules is subject to prior action on the part of the State and where, consequently, in the absence of such action, individuals cannot enforce before the national courts the rights conferred upon them by Community law.

[35]   It follows that the principle whereby a State must be liable for loss and damage caused to individuals as a result of breaches of Community law for which the State can be held responsible is inherent in the system of the Treaty.

[36]   A further basis for the obligation of Member States to make good such loss and damage is to be found in Article 5 [now 10] of the Treaty, under which the Member States are required to take all appropriate measures, whether general or particular, to ensure fulfilment of their obligations under Community law. Among these is the obligation to nullify the unlawful consequences of a breach of Community law (see, in relation to the analogous provision of Article 86 of the ECSC Treaty, the judgment in Case 6/60 *Humblet* v *Belgium* [1960] ECR 559).

[37]   It follows from all the foregoing that it is a principle of Community law that the Member States are obliged to make good loss and damage caused to individuals by breaches of Community law for which they can be held responsible.

(b) The conditions for State liability

[38]   Although State liability is thus required by Community law, the conditions under which that liability gives rise to a right to reparation depend on the nature of the breach of Community law giving rise to the loss and damage.

[39]   Where, as in this case, a Member State fails to fulfil its obligation under the third paragraph of Article 189 [now 249] of the Treaty to take all the measures necessary to achieve the result prescribed by a directive, the full effectiveness of that rule of Community law requires that there should be a right to reparation provided that three conditions are fulfilled.

[40]   The first of those conditions is that the result prescribed by the directive should entail the grant of rights to individuals. The second condition is that it should be possible to identify the content of those rights on the basis of the provisions of the directive. Finally, the third condition is the existence of a causal link between the breach of the State's obligation and the loss and damage suffered by the injured parties.

[41]   Those conditions are sufficient to give rise to a right on the part of individuals to obtain reparation, a right founded directly on Community law.

[42]   Subject to that reservation, it is on the basis of the rules of national law on liability that the State must make reparation for the consequences of the loss and damage caused. In the absence of Community legislation, it is for the internal legal order of each Member State to designate the competent courts and lay down the detailed procedural rules for legal proceedings intended fully to safeguard the rights which individuals derive from Community law (see the judgments in Case 60/75 *Russo* v *AIMA* [1976] ECR 45, Case 33/76 *Rewe* v *Landwirtschaftskammer Saarland* [1976] ECR 1989 and Case 158/80 *Rewe* v *Hauptzollamt Kiel* [1981] ECR 1805).

[43]   Further, the substantive and procedural conditions for reparation of loss and damage laid down by the national law of the Member States must not be less favourable than those relating to similar domestic claims and must not be so framed as to make it virtually impossible or excessively difficult

to obtain reparation (see, in relation to the analogous issue of the repayment of taxes levied in breach of Community law, *inter alia* the judgment in Case 199/82 *Amministrazione delle Finanze dello Stato* v *San Giorgio* [1983] ECR 3595).

[44] In this case, the breach of Community law by a Member State by virtue of its failure to transpose Directive 80/987 within the prescribed period has been confirmed by a judgment of the Court. The result required by that directive entails the grant to employees of a right to a guarantee of payment of their unpaid wage claims. As is clear from the examination of the first part of the first question, the content of that right can be identified on the basis of the provisions of the directive.

[45] Consequently, the national court must, in accordance with the national rules on liability, uphold the right of employees to obtain reparation of loss and damage caused to them as a result of failure to transpose the directive.

[46] The answer to be given to the national court must therefore be that a Member State is required to make good loss and damage caused to individuals by failure to transpose Directive 80/987.

NOTES:

1. It seems that this liability on Member States includes failures to fulfil Community obligations other than a failure to implement a Directive within the specified period. See Ross 'Beyond *Francovich*' (1993) 56 MLR 55; Steiner 'From Direct Effect to *Francovich*: Shifting Means of Enforcement of Community Law' (1993) 18 EL Rev 3.

2. The principle in *Francovich* was developed in Joined Cases C-49/93 and C-48/93 *Brasserie du Pêcheur SA* v *Federal Republic of Germany, R* v *Secretary of State for Transport, ex parte Factortame* [1996] ECR-I 1029, in which the ECJ ruled that where damage to an individual had been caused by a breach of Community law attributable to a national legislature acting in a field in which it has wide discretion to make legislative choices:

   individuals suffering loss or injury thereby are entitled to reparation where the rule of Community law is intended to confer rights upon them, the breach is sufficiently serious and there is a direct causal link between the breach and the damage sustained by the individuals. Subject to that reservation, the state must make good the consequences of the loss or damage caused by the breach of Community law attributable to it, in accordance with its national law on liability. However the conditions laid down by the applicable national laws must not be less favourable than those relating to similar domestic claims or framed in such a way as in practice to make it impossible or excessively difficult to obtain compensation. Pursuant to the national legislation which it applies, reparation of loss or damage cannot be made conditional upon fault (intentional or negligent) on the part of the organ of the State responsible for the breach, going beyond that of a sufficiently serious breach of Community law.

   The Court was using the same basis for a Member State's liability as that under Article 288 (ex 215) for liability of the Community for damage caused to individuals by unlawful legislative measures adopted by its institutions.

   In Joined Cases C-178/94, C-179/94, C-188/94, C-189/94, and C-190/94 *Dillenkofer and others* v *Federal Republic of Germany* [1996] ECR I-4845, the ECJ held that failure to take any measures to implement a Directive to achieve its intended result within the prescribed period constitutes *per se* a serious breach of Community law for those individuals who can show a causal link between that failure and damage suffered.

(f) *The United Kingdom courts' views on directives*

The interpretation of directives by the House of Lords is somewhat confusing. Compare the following cases.

Duke v *GEC Reliance Ltd*
[1988] AC 618, House of Lords

The complainant had been dismissed in accordance with the employer's policy on different retirement ages for male and female employees. Whilst *Marshall* held that this constituted sex discrimination, it also held that directives did not have horizontal effect. The complainant argued that the Sex Discrimination Act 1975 ought to have been interpreted according to the guidance in *Von Colson* so that it conformed to Community law. An appeal was made to the House of Lords.

LORD TEMPLEMAN: . . . [I]t is now submitted that the appellant is entitled to damages from the respondent because Community law requires the Equal Pay Act enacted on 29 May 1970 and the Sex Discrimination Act enacted on 12 November 1975 to be construed in a manner which gives effect to the Equal Treatment Directive dated 9 February 1976 as construed by the European Court of Justice in *Marshall's* case published on 20 February 1986. Of course a British court will always be willing and anxious to conclude that United Kingdom law is consistent with Community law. Where an Act is passed for the purpose of giving effect to an obligation imposed by a directive or other instrument a British court will seldom encounter difficulty in concluding that the language of the Act is effective for the intended purpose. But the construction of a British Act of Parliament is a matter of judgment to be determined by British courts and to be derived from the language of the legislation considered in the light of the circumstances prevailing at the date of enactment. The circumstances in which the Equal Pay Act 1970 and the Sex Discrimination Act 1975 were enacted are set forth in the 1974 White Paper, in the judgment of Phillips J in *Roberts* v *Cleveland Area Health Authority* [1978] ICR 370, in the judgment of Browne-Wilkinson J in *Roberts* v *Tate & Lyle Food and Distribution Ltd* [1983] ICR 521 and in the submission of the United Kingdom Government in *Marshall's* case [1986] QB 401. The Acts were not passed to give effect to the Equal Treatment Directive and were intended to preserve discriminatory retirement ages. Proposals for the Equal Treatment Directive dated 9 February 1976 were in circulation when the Bill for the Sex Discrimination Act 1975 was under discussion but it does not appear that these proposals were understood by the British Government or the Parliament of the United Kingdom to involve the prohibition of differential retirement ages linked to differential pensionable ages.

The appellant relied on the speech of Lord Diplock in *Garland* v *British Rail Engineering Ltd* [1983] 2 AC 751, 770–771. Lord Diplock expressed the view that section 6(4) of the Sex Discrimination Act 1975 could and should be construed in the manner consistent with article 119 [now 141] of the EEC Treaty, the Equal Pay Directive and the Equal Treatment Directive. In *Garland's* case, following a reference to the European Court of Justice it was established that there had been discrimination contrary to article 119 [now 141] which has direct effect between individuals. It was thus unnecessary to consider the effect of the Equal Treatment Directive. Lord Diplock observed, at p. 771, that:

> even if the obligation to observe the provisions of article 119 were an obligation assumed by the United Kingdom under an ordinary international treaty or convention and there was no question of the Treaty obligation being directly applicable as part of the law to be applied by the courts in this country without need for any further enactment, it is a principle of construction of United Kingdom statutes, now too well established to call for citation of authority, that the words of a statute passed after the Treaty has been signed and dealing with the subject matter of the international obligation of the United Kingdom, are to be construed, if they are reasonably capable of bearing such a meaning, as intended to carry out the obligation, and not to be inconsistent with it. . . . The instant appeal does not present an appropriate occasion to consider whether, having regard to the express direction as to the construction of enactments 'to be passed' which is contained in section 2 (4) anything short of an express positive statement in an Act of Parliament passed after 1

January 1973, that a particular provision is intended to be made in breach of an obligation assumed by the United Kingdom under a Community treaty, would justify an English court in construing that provision in a manner inconsistent with a Community treaty obligation of the United Kingdom, however wide a departure from the prima facie meaning of the language of the provision might be needed in order to achieve consistency.

On the hearing of this appeal, your Lordships have had the advantage, not available to Lord Diplock, of full argument which has satisfied me that the Sex Discrimination Act 1975 was not intended to give effect to the Equal Treatment Directive as subsequently construed in the *Marshall* case [1986] QB 401 and that the words of section 6(4) are not reasonably capable of being limited to the meaning ascribed to them by the appellant. Section 2(4) of the European Communities Act 1972 does not in my opinion enable or constrain a British court to distort the meaning of a British statute in order to enforce against an individual a Community directive which has no direct effect between individuals. Section 2(4) applies and only applies where Community provisions are directly applicable.

The jurisdiction, composition and powers of the European Court of Justice are contained in articles 164 to 188 [now 220 and 245] of the EEC Treaty. Those sections include the following:

164. The Court of Justice shall ensure that in the interpretation and application of this Treaty the law is observed. . . .

177. The Court of Justice shall have jurisdiction to give preliminary rulings concerning: (a) the interpretation of this Treaty; (b) the validity and interpretation of Act of the institutions of the Community; (c) the interpretation of the statutes of bodies established by an act of the council, where those statutes so provide.

The submission that the Sex Discrimination Act 1975 must be construed in a manner which gives effect to the Equal Treatment Directive as construed by the European Court of Justice in *Marshall's* case is said to be derived from the decision of the European Court of Justice in *Von Colson and Kamann* v *Land Nordrhein-Westfalen* (Case 14/83) [1984] ECR 1891, delivered on 10 April 1984. In the *Von Colson* case the European Court of Justice ruled that the provisions of the Equal Treatment Directive which require equal treatment for men and women in access to employment do not require a member state to legislate so as to compel an employer to conclude a contract of employment with a woman who has been refused employment on the grounds of sex. The Directive does not specify the nature of the remedies which the member states must afford to a victim of discrimination. But the court also ruled, at p. 1910:

3. Although [the Equal Treatment Directive] 76/207/EEC for the purpose of imposing a sanction for the breach of discrimination, leaves the member states free to choose between the different solution suitable for achieving its object, it nevertheless requires that if a member state chooses to penalise breaches of that prohibition by the award of compensation, then in order to ensure that it is effective and that it has a deterrent effect, that compensation must in any event be adequate in relation to the damage sustained and must therefore amount to more than purely nominal compensation such as, for example, the reimbursement only of the expenses incurred in connection with the application. It is for the national court to interpret and apply the legislation adopted for the implementation of the Directive in conformity with the requirements of Community law, in so far as it is given discretion to do so under national law.

In the *Von Colson* case the German court which submitted the case for a ruling asked whether it was acceptable that a woman who applied for a job and was refused because she was a woman, contrary to the intent of the Equal Treatment Directive, was only entitled under the German domestic law prohibiting such discrimination to the recovery of her expenses (if any) of her application. The German Government in making representations to the European Court expressed the view that under German law compensation for discrimination could include general damages for the loss of the job or of the opportunity to take up the job. The ruling of the European Court of Justice did not constrain the national court to construe German law in accordance with Community law but ruled that if under German law the German court possessed the power to award damages which were adequate and which fulfilled the objective of the Equal Treatment Directive then it was the duty of the German court to act accordingly.

The *Von Colson* case is no authority for the proposition that the German court was bound to invent a German law of adequate compensation if no such law existed and no authority for the proposition that a court of a member state must distort the meaning of a domestic statute so as to conform with Community law which is not directly applicable. If, following the *Von Colson* case, the German court adhered to the view that under German law it possessed no discretion to award adequate compensation, it would have been the duty of the German Government in fulfilment of its obligations under the Treaty of Rome to introduce legislation or evolve some other method which would enable adequate compensation to be obtained, just as the United Kingdom Government became bound to introduce legislation to amend the Equal Pay Act 1970 and the Sex Discrimination Act 1975 in the light of *Marshall's* case. Mrs Advocate-General Rozès in her opinion, delivered on 31 January 1984 in the *von Colson* case, said, at p. 1919:

> In proceedings under article 177 it is not for me to express a view on questions which fall exclusively within the jurisdiction of the national courts inasmuch as they concern the application of national law.

The EEC Treaty does not interfere and the European Court of Justice in the *von Colson* case did not assert power to interfere with the method or result of the interpretation of national legislation by national courts.

It would be most unfair to the respondent to distort the construction of the 1975 Sex Discrimination Act in order to accommodate the 1976 Equal Treatment Directive as construed by the European Court of Justice in the 1986 *Marshall* case. As between the appellant and the respondent the Equal Treatment Directive did not have direct effect and the respondent could not reasonably be expected to reduce to precision the opaque language which constitutes both the strength and the difficulty of some Community legislation. The respondent could not reasonably be expected to appreciate the logic of Community legislators in permitting differential retirement pension ages but prohibiting differential retirement ages. The respondent is not liable to the appellant under Community law. I decline to hold that liability under British law attaches to the respondent or any other private employer to pay damages based on wages which women over 60 and under 65 did not earn before the amending Sex Discrimination Act 1986 for the first time and without retrospective effect introduced the statutory tort of operating differential retirement ages. I would dismiss this appeal.

Appeal dismissed.

Pickstone v *Freemans plc*
[1989] AC 66, House of Lords

The ECJ had ruled in *Commission of the European Communities* v *United Kingdom* (Case 61/81) [1982] ICR 578, that UK law did not meet Community law requirements on the principle that men and women should receive equal pay for work of equal value. Following this decision the Equal Pay Act 1970 was amended. Women who were employed as warehouse operatives were paid less than a man who was employed as a checker warehouse operative. The women contended that as the work of the two jobs was of equal value, then, under the amended Equal Pay Act 1970, s. 1(2)(c), they were entitled to the higher rate of pay. The Industrial Tribunal rejected the claim on the basis that their case came within s. 1(2)(a) of the 1970 Act as there was a man who was employed at the same rate as the women in the post of warehouse operative. The Court of Appeal allowed the women's appeal on the basis of conformity with Article 119 (now 141) of the EEC Treaty. The employers appealed to the House of Lords.

LORD TEMPLEMAN: . . . Section 1(2)(a) of the Act of 1970 as amended in 1975, was not further amended by the Regulations of 1983. Paragraph (a) enables any woman to claim equal pay with a man in the same employment engaged on like work. By section 1(4) like work is work of the same or a broadly similar nature where the differences in work are not of practical importance. The issue of 'like work' is decided by the industrial tribunal.

Section 1(2)(b) of the Act of 1970 as amended in 1975, was also not further amended by the Regulations of 1983. Paragraph (b) enables a woman to claim equal pay for work rated as equivalent to that of a man by a job evaluation study. By section 1(5) the issue of 'equivalent work' is decided by the job evaluation study. Such a study can only be carried out with the consent and cooperation of the employer.

In compliance with the ruling of the European Court of Justice in *Commission of the European Communities* v *United Kingdom of Great Britain and Northern Ireland* (Case 61/81) [1982] ICR 578, the Regulations of 1983 introduced into the Act of 1970 as amended in 1975, a provision which enables a woman to claim equal pay for work of equal value where the employer refuses to consent to a job evaluation study. The Regulations introduced into the Act section 1(2)(c) which modifies any term in a woman's contract which is less favourable than a term of a similar kind in the contract of a man

(c) where a woman is employed on work which, not being work in relation to which paragraph (a) or (b) above applies, is, in terms of the demands made on her (for instance under such headings as effort, skill and decision), of equal value to that of a man in the same employment.

. . .

According to the employers in the present appeal, the Regulations of 1983 had the additional effect of depriving some women of the right to pursue their claims by judicial process or otherwise although they considered themselves wronged by failure to apply the principle of equal pay. The respondents may have a valid complaint in that they are not receiving equal pay with Mr Phillips for work of equal value. But if the respondents seek to remedy that discrimination under section 1(2)(c) of the Act of 1970 as amended by the Regulations, they will be debarred because they are employed on 'work in relation to which paragraph (a) or (b) above applies.' It is said that paragraph (a) operates, not because the respondents are employed on like work with Mr Phillips but because the respondents are employed on like work with some other man. Since paragraph (c) is expressed to apply only when a woman is employed on work which is not 'work in relation to which paragraph (a) or (b) above applies,' it follows, so it is said, that where a woman is employed on like work with any man or where a woman is employed on work rated as equivalent with any man, no claim can be made under paragraph (c) in respect of some other man who is engaged on work of equal value. In my opinion paragraph (a) or (b) only debars a claim under paragraph (c) where paragraph (a) or (b) applies to the man who is the subject of the complaint made by the woman. If the tribunal decide that the respondents are engaged 'on like work' with Mr Phillips then paragraph (a) applies and the respondents are not entitled to proceed under paragraph (c) and to obtain the report of an Acas expert. If there is a job evaluation study which covers the work of the respondents and the work of Mr Phillips then the respondents are debarred from proceeding under paragraph (c) unless the job evaluation study itself was discriminatory.

Whenever there is a claim for equal pay, the complainant, or the complainant's trade union representative supporting the claimant, may wish to obtain a report from an Acas expert under paragraph (c) to use for the purpose of general pay bargaining and in the hope of finding ammunition which will lead to a general increase in wage levels irrespective of discrimination. For this purpose the more Acas reports there are the better. It may be significant that in the present case a claim is made under paragraph (c) and not under paragraph (a) as well, or, in the alternative, although it is obvious that work of equal value in terms of the demands made on a woman under such headings as effort, skill and decision which may amount to discrimination under paragraph (c) may also be work of a broadly similar nature with differences of no practical importance which found a complaint under paragraph (a). If there is discrimination in pay the industrial tribunal must be able to grant a remedy. But the remedy available under paragraph (c) is not to be applied if the complainant has a remedy in respect of the male employee with whom she demands parity under paragraph (a) or if paragraph (b) applies to the woman and to that male employee. To prevent exploitation of paragraph (c) the tribunal must decide in the first instance whether the complainant and the man with whom she seeks parity are engaged on 'like work' under paragraph (a). If paragraph (a) applies, no Acas report is required. If paragraph (a) does not apply, then the tribunal considers whether paragraph (b) applies to the complainant and the man with whom she seeks parity; if so, the tribunal can only proceed under paragraph (c) if the job evaluation study obtained for the purposes of paragraph (b) is itself discriminatory. If paragraph (b) applies then, again, no Acas report is necessary. If paragraphs (a) and (b) do not apply, the tribunal must next consider whether there are reasonable grounds for determining that the work of the complainant and the work of the man with whom she seeks parity is of equal value. If the tribunal are not so satisfied, then no Acas report is required. The words in paragraph (c) on which the employers rely were not intended to create a new form of permitted discrimination. Paragraph (c) enables a claim to equal pay as against a specified man to be made without injustice to an employer. When a woman claims equal pay for work of equal value, she specifies the man with whom she demands parity. If the work of the woman is work in relation to which paragraph (a) or (b) applies in relation to that man, then the woman cannot proceed under paragraph (c) and cannot obtain a report from an Acas expert. In my opinion there must be implied in paragraph (c) after the word 'applies' the words 'as between the woman and the man with whom she claims equality.' This construction is consistent with Community law. The employers' construction is inconsistent with Community law and creates a permitted form of discrimination without rhyme or reason.

Under Community law, a woman is entitled to equal pay for work of equal value to that of a man in the same employment. That right is not dependent on there being no man who is employed on the same work as the woman. Under British law, namely the Equal Pay Act 1970 as amended in 1975, a woman was entitled to equal pay for work rated as equivalent with that of a man in the same employment. That right was not dependent on there being no man who was employed on the same work as the woman. Under the ruling of the European Court of Justice in *Commission of the European Communities* v *United Kingdom of Great Britain and Northern Ireland* (Case 61/81) [1982] ICR 578, the Equal Pay Act 1970 as amended in 1975 was held to be defective because the Act did not entitle every woman to claim before a competent authority that her work had the same value as other work, but only allowed a claim by a woman who succeeded in persuading her employer to consent to a job evaluation scheme. The Regulations of 1983 were intended to give full effect to Community law and to the ruling of the European Court of Justice which directed the United Kingdom Government to introduce legislation entitling any woman to equal pay with any man for work of equal value if the difference in pay is due to the difference in sex and is therefore discriminatory. I am of the opinion that the Regulations of 1983, upon their true construction, achieve the required result of affording a remedy to any woman who is not in receipt of equal pay for work equal in value to the work of a man in the same employment.

In *Murphy* v *Bord Telecom Eireann* (Case 157/86) [1988] ICR 445, 29 women were employed as factory workers engaged in such tasks as dismantling, cleaning, oiling and reassembling telephones and other equipment; they claimed the right to be paid at the same rate as a specified male worker employed in the same factory as a stores labourer engaged in cleaning, collecting and delivering equipment and components and in lending general assistance as required. The European Court of

Justice in their judgment, at p. 449, paragraph 9, said that the principle of equal pay for men and women

> forbids workers of one sex engaged in work of equal value to that of workers of the opposite sex to be paid a lower wage than the latter on grounds of sex, it a fortiori prohibits such a difference in pay where the lower-paid category of workers is engaged in work of higher value.

I cannot think that in Community law or in British law the result would be any different if instead of there being 29 women working on telephone maintenance and one male stores labourer, there were 28 women and one man working on telephone maintenance and one male stores labourer.

The draft of the Regulations of 1983 was not subject to any process of amendment by Parliament. In these circumstances the explanations of the Government and the criticisms voiced by Members of Parliament in the debates which led to approval of the draft Regulations provide some indications of the intentions of Parliament. The debate on the draft Regulations in the House of Commons which led to their approval by Resolution was initiated by the Under Secretary of State for Employment who, in the reports of the House of Commons for 20 July 1983 *Hansard*, column 479 et seq. said:

> The Equal Pay Act allows a woman to claim equal pay with a man . . . if she is doing the same or broadly similar work, or if her job and his have been rated equal through job evaluation in effort, skill and decision. However, if a woman is doing different work from a comparable man, or if the jobs are not covered by a job evaluation study, the woman has at present no right to make a claim for equal pay. This is the gap identified by the European Court, which we are closing. . . .

In the course of his speech at column 485, the Minister outlined the procedure which will apply if a claim is made under paragraph (c) in the following words:

> Under the amending Regulations which are the subject of this debate, an employee will be able to bring a claim for equal pay with an employee of the opposite sex working in the same employment on the ground that the work is of equal value. When this happens, conciliation will first be attempted, as in all equal pay claims. If conciliation is unsuccessful, the industrial tribunal will take the following steps. First, it will check that the work is not in fact so similar that the case can be heard under the current Act. Secondly, it will consider whether the jobs have already been covered by a job evaluation scheme and judged not to be of equal value. If this is the case, the claim may proceed only if the original job evaluation scheme is shown to have been sexually discriminatory. Having decided that the case should proceed, the tribunal will first invite the parties to see if they can settle the claim voluntarily. If not, the tribunal will consider whether to commission an independent expert to report on the value of the jobs. It will not commission an expert's report if it feels that it is unreasonable to determine the question of value – for example, if the two jobs are quite obviously of unequal value. Nor . . . will it commission an expert's report if the employer shows at this stage that inequality in pay is due to material factors other than sex discrimination. . . .

Thus it is clear that the construction which I have placed upon the Regulations corresponds to the intentions of the Government in introducing the Regulations. In the course of the debate in the House of Commons, and in the corresponding debate in the House of Lords, no one suggested that a claim for equal pay for equal work might be defeated under the Regulations by an employer who proved that a man who was not the subject of the complaint was employed on the same or on similar work with the complainant. The Minister took the view, and Parliament accepted the view, that paragraph (c) will only apply if paragraphs (a) and (b) are first held by the tribunal not to apply in respect of the work of the woman and the work of the man with whom she seeks parity of pay. This is also the only view consistent with Community law.

In *von Colson and Kamann* v *Land Nordrhein-Westfalen* (Case 14/83) [1984] ECR 1891, 1910–1911, the European Court of Justice advised that in dealing with national legislation designed to give effect to a Directive:

> 3. . . . It is for the national court to interpret and apply the legislation adopted for the implementation of the Directive in conformity with the requirements of Community law, in so far as it is given discretion to do so under national law.

In *Duke* v *GEC Reliance Systems Ltd* [1988] AC 618 this House declined to distort the construction of an Act of Parliament which was not drafted to give effect to a Directive and which was not capable of complying with the Directive as subsequently construed by the European Court of Justice. In the present case I can see no difficulty in construing the Regulations of 1983 in a way which gives effect to the declared intention of the Government of the United Kingdom responsible for drafting the Regulations and is consistent with the objects of the EEC Treaty, the provisions of the Equal Pay Directive and the rulings of the European Court of Justice. I would dismiss the appeal.

Appeal dismissed.

NOTE: In *Pickstone* their Lordships referred to *Hansard* to determine the intention of Parliament in passing the amendments to the 1970 statute.

QUESTIONS

1. Why was it distortion in *Duke* to interpret the legislation as being in conformity with Community law but permissible in *Pickstone*?

2. If the interpretation of *Von Colson* in *Duke* is incompatible with *Marleasing*, is it in accordance with *Kolpinghuis Nijmegen*?

Litster v *Forth Dry Dock & Engineering Co. Ltd*
[1990] 1 AC 546, House of Lords

A company had become insolvent and gone into receivership. An hour before the receiver transferred the business assets to a new owner, the employees were made redundant. Directive 77/187/EEC provides safeguards for employees where a business is transferred from one owner to another. Article 4(1) of the directive stops a new owner from evading the safeguards by prohibiting dismissal of employees by the old owner. The directive was implemented by the Transfer of Undertakings (Protection of Employment) Regulations 1981. Regulation 5(1) allows employees of the old owner to pursue claims against the new owner, but according to reg. 5(3), the employee must have been in employment immediately before the transfer. The employees succeeded in claims before the Industrial Tribunal and the Employment Appeal Tribunal. The appeal to the Court of Session was allowed on the basis that the employees were not employed immediately before the transfer. On appeal to the House of Lords.

LORD KEITH: . . . In *Pickstone* v *Freemans Plc* [1989] AC 66 there had been laid before Parliament under paragraph 2 (2) of Schedule 2 to the European Communities Act 1972 the draft of certain Regulations designed, and presented by the responsible ministers as designed, to fill a lacuna in the equal pay legislation of the United Kingdom which had been identified by a decision of the European Court of Justice. On a literal reading the regulation particularly relevant did not succeed in completely filling the lacuna. Your Lordships' House, however, held that in order that the manifest purpose of the Regulations might be achieved and effect given to the clear but inadequately expressed intention of Parliament certain words must be read in by necessary implication.

In the present case the Transfer of Undertakings (Protection of Employment) Regulations 1981 were similarly laid before Parliament in draft and approved by resolutions of both Houses. They were so laid as designed to give effect to Council Directive (77/187/EEC) dated 14 February 1977. It is plain that if the words in regulation 5 (3) of the Regulations of 1981 'a person so employed immediately before the transfer' are read literally, as contended for by the second respondents, Forth Estuary Engineering Ltd, the provisions of regulation 5 (1) will be capable of ready evasion through the transferee arranging with the transferor for the latter to dismiss its employees a short time before the transfer becomes operative. In the event that the transferor is insolvent, a situation commonly forming the occasion for the transfer of an undertaking, the employees would be left with worthless claims for unfair dismissal against the transferor. In any event, whether or not the transferor is insolvent, the employees would be deprived of the remedy of reinstatement or re-engagement. The transferee would be under no liability towards the employees and a coach and four would have been driven through the provisions of regulation 5 (1).

A number of decisions of the European Court, in particular *P. Bork International A/S* v *Foreningen af Arbejdsledere i Danmark* (Case 101/87) [1989] IRLR 41 have had the result that where employees have been dismissed by the transferor for a reason connected with the transfer, at a time before the transfer takes effect, then for purposes of article 3 (1) of Council Directive (77/187/EEC) (which corresponds to regulation 5 (1)) the employees are to be treated as still employed by the undertaking at the time of the transfer.

In these circumstances it is the duty of the court to give to regulation 5 a construction which accords with the decisions of the European Court upon the corresponding provisions of the Directive to which the regulation was intended by Parliament to give effect. The precedent established by *Pickstone* v *Freemans Plc* indicates that this is to be done by implying the words necessary to achieve that result. So there must be implied in regulation 5 (3) words indicating that where a person has been unfairly dismissed in the circumstances described in regulation 8 (1) he is to be deemed to have been employed in the undertaking immediately before the transfer or any of a series of transactions whereby it was effected.

My Lords, I would allow the appeal.

LORD TEMPLEMAN: . . . Thus, it is said, since the workforce of Forth Dry Dock were dismissed at 3.30 p.m., they were not employed 'immediately before the transfer' at 4.30 p.m. and therefore regulation 5 (1) did not transfer any liability for the workforce from Forth Dry Dock to Forth Estuary. The argument is inconsistent with the Directive. In *P. Bork International A/S* v *Foreningen af Arbejdsledere i Danmark* (Case 101/87) [1989] IRLR 41, 44 the European Court of Justice ruled that:

> the only workers who may invoke Directive [(77/187/EEC)] are those who have current employment relations or a contract of employment at the date of the transfer. The question whether or not a contract of employment or employment relationship exists at that date must be assessed under national law, subject, however, to the observance of the mandatory rules of the Directive concerning the protection of workers against dismissal by reason of the transfer. It follows that the workers employed by the undertaking whose contract of employment or employment relationship has been terminated with effect on a date before that of the transfer, in breach of article 4 (1) of the Directive, must be considered as still employed by the undertaking on the date of the transfer with the consequence, in particular, that the obligations of an employer towards them are fully transferred from the transferor to the transferee in accordance with article 3 (1) of the Directive.

In *Von Colson and Kamann* v *Land Nordrhein-Westfalen* (Case 14/83) [1984] ECR 1891, 1909 the European Court of Justice dealing with Council Directive (76/207/EEC), forbidding discrimination on grounds of sex regarding access to employment, ruled that:

the member states' obligation arising from a Directive to achieve the result envisaged by the Directive and their duty under article 5 of the Treaty to take all appropriate measures, whether general or particular, to ensure the fulfilment of that obligation, is binding on all the authorities of member states including, for matters within their jurisdiction, the courts. It follows that, in applying the national law and in particular the provisions of a national law specifically introduced in order to implement Directive [(76/207/EEC)] national courts are required to interpret their national law in the light of the wording and the purpose of the Directive in order to achieve the result referred to in the third paragraph of article 189.

Thus the courts of the United Kingdom are under a duty to follow the practice of the European Court of Justice by giving a purposive construction to Directives and to Regulations issued for the purpose of complying with Directives. In *Pickstone* v *Freemans Plc* [1989] AC 66, this House implied words in a regulation designed to give effect to Council Directive (75/117/EEC) dealing with equal pay for women doing work of equal value. If this House had not been able to make the necessary implication, the Equal Pay (Amendment) Regulations 1983 (SI 1983 No. 1794) would have failed their object and the United Kingdom would have been in breach of its treaty obligations to give effect to Directives. In the present case, in the light of Council Directive (77/187/EEC) and in the light of the ruling of the European Court of Justice in *Bork's* case [1989] IRLR 41, it seems to me, following the suggestion of my noble and learned friend, Lord Keith of Kinkel, that paragraph 5 (3) of the Regulations of 1981 was not intended and ought not to be construed so as to limit the operation of regulation 5 to persons employed immediately before the transfer in point of time. Regulation 5 (3) must be construed on the footing that it applies to a person employed immediately before the transfer or who would have been so employed if he had not been unfairly dismissed before the transfer for a reason connected with the transfer. . . .

LORD OLIVER: . . . The critical question, it seems to me, is whether, even allowing for the greater latitude in construction permissible in the case of legislation introduced to give effect to this country's Community obligations, it is possible to attribute to regulation 8 (1) when read in conjunction with regulation 5, the same result as that attributed to article 4 in the *Bork* case [1989] IRLR 41. Purely as a matter of language, it clearly is not. Regulation 8(1) does not follow literally the wording of article 4 (1). It provides only that if the reason for the dismissal of the employee is the transfer of the business, he has to be treated 'for the purposes of Part V of the 1978 Act' as unfairly dismissed so as to confer on him the remedies provided by sections 69 to 79 of the Act (including, where it is considered appropriate, an order for reinstatement or re-engagement). If this provision fell to be construed by reference to the ordinary rules of construction applicable to a purely domestic statute and without reference to Treaty obligations, it would, I think, be quite impermissible to regard it as having the same prohibitory effect as that attributed by the European Court to article 4 of the Directive. But it has always to be borne in mind that the purpose of the Directive and of the Regulations was and is to 'safeguard' the rights of employees on a transfer and that there is a mandatory obligation to provide remedies which are effective and not merely symbolic to which the Regulations were intended to give effect. The remedies provided by the Act of 1978 in the case of an insolvent transferor are largely illusory unless they can be exerted against the transferee as the Directive contemplates and I do not find it conceivable that, in framing Regulations intending to give effect to the Directive, the Secretary of State could have envisaged that its purpose should be capable of being avoided by the transparent device to which resort was had in the instant case. *Pickstone* v *Freemans Plc* [1989] AC 66, has established that the greater flexibility available to the court in applying a purposive construction to legislation designed to give effect to the United Kingdom's Treaty obligations to the Community enables the court, where necessary, to supply by implication words appropriate to comply with those obligations: see particularly the speech of Lord Templeman, at pp. 120–121. Having regard to the manifest purpose of the Regulations, I do not, for my part, feel inhibited from making such an implication in the instant case. The provision in regulation 8(1) that a dismissal by reason of a transfer is to be treated as an unfair dismissal, is merely a different way of saying that the transfer is not to 'constitute a ground for dismissal' as contemplated by article 4 of the Directive and there is no good reason for denying to it the same effect as that attributed to that article. In effect this involves reading regulation 5(3) as if there were inserted after the words 'immediately before the transfer' the words 'or would have been so employed if he had not been unfairly dismissed in the circumstances described in regulation 8(1).' For my part, I would make such an implication which is entirely consistent with the general scheme of the Regulations and which is necessary if they are effectively to fulfil the purpose for which they were made of giving effect to the provisions of the Directive.

Appeal dismissed.

Finnegan v *Clowney Youth Training Program Ltd*
[1990] 2 AC 407, House of Lords

The facts of this case are similar to *Duke* (see p. 160) – the employer operated different retirement ages for male and female employees. The difference between the two cases lies in the fact that the parties to this case came from Northern Ireland where the relevant legislation was the Sex Discrimination (Northern Ireland) Order 1976 which had been made after the Equal Treatment Directive 76/207/EEC. The relevant provisions of the 1976 Order were the same as those in the Sex Discrimination Act 1975. The employee was successful in arguing sex discrimination before the Industrial Tribunal, but the Court of Appeal of Northern Ireland held that Parliament intended the 1976 Order to have the same effect in Northern Ireland as the 1975 Act did in England. On appeal to the House of Lords.

LORD BRIDGE: . . . [T]he relevant legislation by Order in Council applicable to Northern Ireland has been designed to reproduce precisely the substance of the legislation enacted by the Westminster Parliament. Thus, on turning to the Sex Discrimination (Northern Ireland) Order 1976, we find that article 8 reproduces precisely the provisions of section 6 of the English Act of 1975 and in the Equal Pay Act (Northern Ireland) 1970, set out in Schedule 1 to the Order of 1976 as amended by that Order, section 6 (1A) reproduces precisely the provisions of section 6 (1A) of the English Act of 1970. Similarly, following the *Marshall* case [1987] QB 401, appropriate amendments to the Order of 1976 were made by the Sex Discrimination (Northern Ireland) Order 1988 which precisely reproduced in article 4 the provisions of section 2 of the English Act of 1986.

On the face of it, therefore, the enactment applicable to the circumstances of the present employee's claim is indistinguishable from the enactment which fell to be applied in *Duke* v *GEC Reliance Systems Ltd* [1988] AC 618 and would appear, therefore, to dictate the inevitable result that the appeal must fail. This was the view of the Court of Appeal in Northern Ireland. Counsel for the employee submits, however, that a crucial distinction is to be derived from the chronology, in that the English Act of 1975 was passed before the Council of the European Communities adopted the Equal Treatment Directive, on 9 February 1976, whereas the Order of 1976 was not made until July of that year. He referred us to a familiar line of authority for the proposition that the national legislation of a member state of the European Community which is enacted for the purpose of implementing a European Council Directive must be construed in the light of the Directive and must, if at all possible, be applied in a sense which will effect the purpose of the Directive: see *Von Colson and Kamann* v *Land Nordrhein-Westfalen* (Case 14/83) [1984] ECR 1891; *Pickstone* v *Freemans Plc* [1989] AC 66; *Litster* v *Forth Dry Dock and Engineering Co. Ltd* [1990] 1 AC 546.

I entirely accept the validity of the proposition, but I do not accept that it has any application here.

Before the decision in the *Marshall* case [1986] QB, 401 it is apparent from the history I have recounted that neither the United Kingdom Parliament nor the United Kingdom Government perceived any conflict between the provisions of section 6 (4) of the Sex Discrimination Act 1975 and section 6 (1A) of the Equal Pay Act 1970 on the one hand and the provisions of the European Equal Treatment Directive on the other hand, such as to call for amendment of the English statutes after the adoption of the Directive. Accordingly, it would appear to me to be wholly artificial to treat the Order of 1976 enacting identical provisions for Northern Ireland, because it was made after the Directive, as having been made with the purpose of implementing Community law in the same sense as the Regulations which fell to be construed in the *Pickstone* and *Litster* cases. The reality is that article 8 (4) of the Order of 1976 being in identical terms and in an identical context to section 6 (4) of the English Act of 1975, must have been intended to have the identical effect. To hold otherwise would be, as in *Duke* v *GEC Reliance Systems Ltd* [1988] AC 618, most unfair to the employers in that it would be giving retrospective operation to the amending Order of 1988 and effectively eliminating the distinction between Community law which is of direct effect between citizens of member states and Community law which only affects citizens of member states when it is implemented by national legislation.

Alternatively counsel for the employee invited us to depart from *Duke* v *GEC Reliance Systems Ltd* in pursuance of *Practice Statement (Judicial Precedent)* [1966] 1 WLR 1234. I need only say that, so far from being persuaded that the decision in that case was wrong, I entertain no doubt that it was right for the reasons so clearly set out in the speech of Lord Templeman.

We were further invited to make a reference to the European Court of Justice under article 177 [now 234] of the EEC Treaty. In my opinion, however, the determination of the appeal does not depend on any question of Community law. The interpretation of the Order of 1976 is for the United Kingdom courts and it is not suggested that the Equal Treatment Directive is of direct effect between citizens.

I would dismiss the appeal.

Appeal dismissed.

QUESTIONS

1. Has the House of Lords in these four cases simply been consistent in seeking to ascertain if the domestic legislation was intended to implement Community law?

2. Lord Bridge is correct in *Finnegan*, in that there was no question of horizontal effect, but should their lordships not have asked the ECJ for advice on the application of *Von Colson*, given that the Northern Irish legislation was passed after the directive?

NOTE: See Szyszczak (1990) 15 EL Rev 480 for a critical review of these four cases.

Webb v *EMO Air Cargo (UK) Ltd (No. 2)*
[1995] 1 WLR 1454, House of Lords

The applicant was engaged by the employers initially with a view to her replacing, after a probationary period, a pregnant employee during the latter's maternity leave. Shortly after her appointment the applicant discovered that she too was pregnant and the employers dismissed her. Her claim that her dismissal was discrimination contrary to the Sex Discrimination Act 1975, s. 1, was rejected by an industrial tribunal, who held that the reason for her dismissal was her anticipated inability to carry out the primary task of covering for the absent employee. Appeals to the Employment Appeal Tribunal and the Court of Appeal were dismissed. On appeal to the House of Lords their Lordships sought a preliminary ruling from the ECJ on the implementation of the principle of the Equal Treatment Directive (76/207/EEC). The ECJ ruled that Article 2(1) when read with Article 5(1) of the directive precluded dismissal of an employee who had been recruited for an unlimited term with a view to replacing another employee during the latter's maternity leave and who could not do so because shortly after her recruitment, she had herself been found to be pregnant.

LORD KEITH OF KINKEL: ... The provisions of the Act of 1975 which your Lordships must endeavour to construe, so as to accord if at all possible with the ruling of the European Court, are section 1(1)(a) and section 5(3).

Section 1(1)(a) provides:

> A person discriminates against a woman in any circumstances relevant for the purposes of any provision of this act if – (a) on the ground of her sex he treats her less favourably than he treats or would treat a man . . .

Section 5(3) provides:

> A comparison of the cases of persons of different sex or marital status under section 1(1) or 3(1) must be such that the relevant circumstances in the one case are the same, or not materially different, in the other.

The reasoning in my speech in the earlier proceedings [1993] 1 WLR 49, 53–55 was to the effect that the relevant circumstances which existed in the present case and which should be taken to be present in the case of the hypothetical man was unavailability for work at the time when the worker was particularly required, and that the reason for the unavailability was not a relevant circumstance. So it was not relevant that the reason for the woman's unavailability was pregnancy, a condition which could not be present in a man.

The ruling of the European Court proceeds on an interpretation of the broad principles dealt with in articles 2(1) and 5(1) of Council Directive (76/207/EEC). Sections 1(1)(a) and 5(3) of the Act of 1975 set out a more precise test of unlawful discrimination, and the problem is how to fit the terms of that test into the ruling. It seems to me that the only way of doing so is to hold that, in a case where a woman is engaged for an indefinite period, the fact that the reason why she will be temporarily unavailable for work at a time when to her knowledge her services will be particularly required is pregnancy is a circumstance relevant to her case, being a circumstance which could not be present in the case of the hypothetical man. It does not necessarily follow that pregnancy would be a relevant circumstance in the situation where the woman is denied employment for a fixed period in the future during the whole of which her pregnancy would make her unavailable for work, nor in the situation where after engagement for a such a period the discovery of her pregnancy leads to cancellation of the engagement.

Appeal allowed.

QUESTION

Did their Lordships here distort the construction of the Sex Discrimination Act 1975 so as to make it conform to the Equal Treatment Directive as interpreted by the ECJ?

4

The Rule of Law

NOTE: The rule of law is considered to be one of the fundamental doctrines of the Constitution of the United Kingdom. The constitution is said to be founded on the idea of the rule of law, and this is a concept favoured by politicians and lawyers being imported into many debates. Despite its currency in political and constitutional discussion its meaning is far from precise, and it may mean different things to different people at different times.

Governments wield considerable power. Constitutions are concerned with the allocation of power and the control of its exercise. The doctrine of the rule of law is concerned with the latter. Aristotle stated that 'the rule of law is preferable to the rule of any individual'. This sentiment was echoed centuries later by English jurists.

Report of the Committee on Ministers' Powers
Cmd. 4060, 1932, pp. 71–72

The supremacy or rule of law – Its history and meaning

1. The supremacy or rule of the law of the Land is a recognised principle of the English Constitution. The origin of the principle must be sought in the theory, universally held in the Middle Ages, that law of some kind – the law either of God or man – ought to rule the world. Bracton, in his famous book on English law, which was written in the first half of the thirteenth century, held this theory, and deduced from it the proposition that the king and other rulers were subject to law. He laid it down that the law bound all members of the state, whether rulers or subjects; and that justice according to law was due both to ruler and subject. This view was accepted by the common lawyers of the fourteenth and fifteenth centuries and is stated in the Year Books. In 1441, in the Year Book 19 Henry VI Pasch. pl. 1, it is said: 'the law is the highest inheritance which the king has; for by the law he and all his subjects are ruled, and if there was no law there would be no king and no inheritance.'

The rise of the power of Parliament in the fourteenth and fifteenth centuries both emphasized and modified this theory of the supremacy of the law. That the rise of the power of Parliament emphasized the theory is shown by the practical application given to it by Chief Justice Fortescue in Henry VI's reign. He used it as the premise, by means of which he justified the control which Parliament had gained over legislation and taxation. That the rise of the power of Parliament modified the theory is shown by the manner in which the theory of the supremacy of the law was combined with the doctrine of the supremacy of Parliament. The law was supreme, but Parliament could change and modify it . . .

The only period when this conception of the rule of law was seriously questioned was in the Stuart period. The Stuart Kings considered that the Royal prerogative was the sovereign power in the State, and so could override the law whenever they saw fit. Chief Justice Coke was dismissed from the bench because he asserted the supremacy of the law. But his views as to the supremacy of the law were accepted by Parliament when it passed the Petition of Right in 1628, and when it abolished the Court of the Star Chamber and the jurisdiction of the Privy Council in England in 1641. Those views finally triumphed as the result of the Great Rebellion, and the Revolution of 1688. In this, as in other matters, Coke's writings passed on the views of the medieval English lawyers into modern English law. But these views were passed on with one important addition, which was the result of the rise, in the sixteenth century, of the modern territorial state. The law which was thus supreme was the law of England; and this included the law, written and unwritten, administered by the Courts of Common Law, by the Courts of Equity, by the Court of Admiralty, and by the Ecclesiastical Courts. Thus the modern doctrine of the rule of law has come, as the result of this long historical development, to mean the supremacy of all parts of the law of England, both enacted and unenacted.

NOTE: Chief Justice Coke's assertion of the supremacy of law was stated clearly in the case which follows.

Prohibitions del Roy
(1607) 12 Co Rep 63; 77 ER 1342

Note, upon Sunday the 10th of November in this same term, the King, upon complaint made to him by Bancroft, Archbishop of Canterbury, concerning prohibitions, the King was informed, that when the question was made of what matters the Ecclesiastical judges have cognizance, either upon the exposition of the statutes concerning tithes, or any other thing ecclesiastical, or upon the statute 1 El. concerning the high commission or in any other case in which there is not express authority in law, the King himself may decide it in his Royal person; and that the Judges are but the delegates of the King, and that the King may take what causes he shall please to determine, from the determination of the Judges, and may determine them himself. And the Archbishop said, that this was clear in divinity, that such authority belongs to the King by the word of God in the Scripture. To which it was answered by me, in the presence, and with the clear consent of all the Judges of England, and Barons of the Exchequer, that the King in his own person cannot adjudge any case, either criminal, as treason, felony, &c. or betwixt party and party, concerning his inheritance, chattels, or goods, &c. but this ought to be determined and adjudged in some Court of Justice. . . . And the Judges informed the King, that no King after the Conquest assumed to himself to give any judgment in any cause whatsoever, which concerned the administration of justice within this realm, but these were solely determined in the Courts of Justice.

[T]hen the King said, that he thought the law was founded upon reason, and that he and others had reason, as well as the Judges: to which it was answered by me, that true it was, that God had endowed His Majesty with excellent science, and great endowments of nature; but His Majesty was not learned in the laws of his realm of England, and causes which concern the life, or inheritance, or goods, or fortunes of his subjects, are not to be decided by natural reason but by the artificial reason and judgment of law, which law is an act which requires long study and experience, before that a man can attain to the cognizance of it: that the law was the golden met-wand and measure to try the causes of the subjects; and which protected His Majesty in safety and peace: with which the King was greatly offended, and said, that then he should be under the law, which was treason to affirm, as he said; to which I said, that Bracton saith, *quod Rex non debet esse sub homine, sed sub Deo et lege.*

NOTE: The law to which the Crown was subject was the common law as changed from time to time by Parliament. It is worth noting that at this time Parliament was not as active in legislating as it is now; the common law was the main source of law and legislation was very much a subsidiary source.

SECTION 1: **Government according to the Law**

Government according to the law means that the Executive or any civil authority or government official cannot exercise a power unless such exercise of it is authorized by some specific rule of law.

Entick v Carrington
(1765) 19 St Tr 1030, Court of Common Pleas

> Two King's messengers, under the authority of a warrant issued by the Secretary of State, broke and entered Entick's house and took away his papers. Entick was alleged to be the author of seditious writings. When the messengers were sued by Entick for trespass to his house and goods, it was argued that the warrant was legal as the power to issue such warrants was essential to government as 'the only means of quieting clamours and sedition'.

LORD CAMDEN CJ: . . . This power, so claimed by the Secretary of State, is not supported by one single citation from any law book extant. It is claimed by no other magistrate in this kingdom but himself. . . .

Before I state the question, it will be necessary to describe the power claimed by this warrant in its full extent. If honestly exerted, it is a power to seize that man's papers, who is charged upon oath to be the author or publisher of a seditious libel; if oppressively, it acts against every man, who is so described in the warrant, though he be innocent. . . .

Such is the power, and therefore one should naturally expect that the law to warrant it should be clear in proportion as the power is exorbitant.

If it is law, it will be found in our books. If it is not to be found there, it is not law.

The great end, for which men entered into society, was to secure their property. That right is preserved sacred and incommunicable in all instances, where it has not been taken away or abridged by some public law for the good of the whole. The cases where this right of property is set aside by positive law, are various. Distresses, executions, forfeitures, taxes, etc. are all of this description; wherein every man by common consent gives up that right, for the sake of justice and the general good.

By the laws of England, every invasion of private property, be it ever so minute, is a trespass. No man can set his foot upon my ground without my licence, but he is liable to an action, though the damage be nothing. . . . If he admits the fact, he is bound to shew by way of justification, that some positive law has empowered or excused him. The justification is submitted to the judges, who are to look into the books; and see if such a justification can be maintained by the text of the statute law, or by the principles of common law. If no such excuse can be found or produced, the silence of the books is an authority against the defendant, and the plaintiff must have judgment.

According to this reasoning, it is now incumbent upon the defendants to shew the law, by which this seizure is warranted. If that cannot be done, it is a trespass.

Papers are the owner's goods and chattels: they are his dearest property; and are so far from enduring a seizure that they will hardly bear an inspection; and though the eye cannot by the laws of England be guilty of a trespass, yet where private papers are removed and carried away, the secret nature of those goods will be an aggravation of the trespass, and demand more considerable damages in that respect. Where is the written law that gives any magistrate such a power? I can safely answer, there is none, and therefore it is too much for us without such authority to pronounce a practice legal, which would be subversive of all the comforts of society. . . .

I come now to the practice since the Revolution, which has been strongly urged, with this emphatical addition, that an usage tolerated from the area of liberty, and continued downwards to this time through the best ages of the constitution, must necessarily have a legal commencement. Now, though that pretence can have no place in the question made by this plea, because no such practice is there alleged; yet I will permit the defendant for the present to borrow a fact from the special verdict, for the sake of giving it an answer.

If the practice began then, it began too late to be law now. If it was more ancient, the Revolution is not to answer for it; and I could have wished, that upon this occasion the Revolution had not been considered as the only basis of our liberty. . . .

With respect to the practice itself, if it goes no higher, every lawyer will tell you, it is much too modern to be evidence of the common law. . . .

This is the first instance I have met with, where the ancient immemorable law of the land, in a public matter, was attempted to be proved by the practice of a private office. The names and rights of public magistrates, their power and forms of proceeding as they are settled by law, have been long since written, and are to be found in books and records. Private customs indeed are still to be sought from private tradition. But who ever conceived a notion, that any part of the public law could be buried in the obscure practice of a particular person?

To search, seize, and carry away all the papers of the subject upon the first warrant: that such a right should have existed from the time whereof the memory of man runneth not to the contrary, and never yet have found a place in any book of law; is incredible. But if so strange a thing could be supposed, I do not see, how we could declare the law upon such evidence.

But still it is insisted, that there has been a general submission, and no action brought to try the right.

I answer, there has been a submission of guilt and poverty to power and the terror of punishment. But it would be strange doctrine to assert that all the people of this land are bound to acknowledge that to be universal law, which a few criminal booksellers have been afraid to dispute. . . .

It is then said, that it is necessary for the ends of government to lodge such a power with a state officer; and that it is better to prevent the publication before than to punish the offender afterwards. . . . [W]ith respect to the argument of State necessity, or a distinction that has been aimed at between State offences and others, the common law does not understand that kind of reasoning, nor do our books take notice of any such distinctions. . . .

If the king himself has no power to declare when the law ought to be violated for reason of State, I am sure we his judges have no such prerogative.

Lastly, it is urged as an argument of utility, that such a search is a means of detecting offenders by discovering evidence. . . .

In the criminal law such a proceeding was never heard of; and yet there are some crimes, such for instance as murder, rape, robbery, and house-breaking, to say nothing of forgery and perjury, that are more atrocious than libelling. But our law has provided no paper-search in these cases to help forward the conviction. . . .

If, however, a right of search for the sake of discovering evidence ought in any case to be allowed, this crime above all others ought to be excepted, as wanting such a discovery less than any other. It is committed in open day-light, and in the face of the world; every act of publication makes new proof; and the solicitor of the treasury, if he pleases, may be the witness himself. . . .

I have now taken notice of everything that has been urged upon the present point; and upon the whole we are all of opinion, that the warrant to seize and carry away the party's papers in the case of a seditious libel, is illegal and void.

QUESTION

Lord Camden CJ stated that 'by the laws of England every invasion of private property, be it ever so minute, is a trespass'. Is this still true? See, for example, s. 8 of the Police and Criminal Evidence Act 1984; s. 26(1) of the Theft Act 1968, s. 6(1) of the Criminal Damage Act 1971; ss. 7 and 24 of the Forgery and Counterfeiting Act 1981; s. 46 of the Firearms Act 1968; s. 23(3) of the Misuse of Drugs Act 1971; s. 3 of the Obscene Publications Act 1959; s. 27 of the Drug Trafficking Act 1994; s. 2(4) of the Criminal Justice Act 1987; and Sched. 5 to the Terrorism Act 2000.

NOTE: Views on the legality of official action, however, may differ. Lord Camden revealed an enthusiasm for liberty in a sweeping declaration when he stated:

> The great end for which men entered into society, was to secure their property. That right is preserved sacred and incommunicable in all instances, where it has not been taken away or abridged by some public law for the good of the whole.

In the extracts from the case which follows, echoes of Lord Camden's approach may be discerned in the judgment of Lord Denning in the Court of Appeal; whereas a much more restrictive approach was adopted in the House of Lords, having important consequences for the rights of the citizen, the power of Government, and the effectiveness of the rule of law in controlling the official exercise of power.

R v *Inland Revenue Commissioners, ex parte Rossminster Ltd*
[1980] AC 952, Court of Appeal

Section 20C of the Taxes Management Act 1970, as amended, provides:

'(1) If the appropriate judicial authority' – and he is defined as the circuit judge – 'is satisfied on information on oath given by an officer of the board that – (a) there is reasonable ground for suspecting that an offence involving any form of fraud in connection with, or in relation to, tax has been committed and that evidence of it is to be found on premises specified in the information; and (b) in applying under this section, the officer acts with the approval of the board given in relation to the particular case, the authority may issue a warrant in writing authorising an officer of the board to enter the premises, if necessary by force, at any time within 14 days from the time of issue of the warrant, and search them. . . . (3) On entering the premises with a warrant under this section, the officer may seize and remove any things whatsoever found there which he has reasonable cause to believe may be required as evidence for the purposes of proceedings in respect of such an offence as is mentioned in subsection (1) above. . . .'

Suspecting that some unspecified tax fraud had been committed by Rossminster Ltd, officers of the Inland Revenue obtained warrants to search Rossminster's premises. The officers seized anything which they believed might be required as evidence of a tax fraud, but they did not inform Rossminster Ltd of the offences suspected or of the persons suspected of having committed them. The warrants simply followed the wording in s. 20C without specifying what particular offences were suspected. The Court of Appeal, reversing the decision of the Divisional Court, granted, *inter alia*, an order of certiorari to quash the warrants.

LORD DENNING: . . . Beyond all doubt this search and seizure was unlawful unless it was authorised by Parliament. . . . The trouble is that the legislation is drawn so widely that in some hands it might be an instrument of oppression. It may be said that 'honest people need not fear: that it will never be used against them: that tax inspectors can be trusted, only to use it in the case of the big, bad frauds.' This is an attractive argument, but I would reject it. Once great power is granted, there is a danger of it being abused. Rather than risk such abuse, it is, as I see it, the duty of the courts so to construe the statute as to see that it encroaches as little as possible upon the liberties of the people of England. . . .

The warrant is challenged on the ground that it does not specify any particular offence. . . . The justification is: 'We do not wish to tell more to those we suspect because we do not want them to know too much about what we intend to do. Otherwise they will be on their guard.'

Is this a just excuse? The words 'an offence involving any form of fraud in connection with, or in relation to, tax' are very wide words. We were taken by Mr Davenport through a number of offences which might be comprised in them. There is no specific section in the Act itself. But there are a number of other offences which involve fraud. . . . It seems to me that these words 'fraud . . . in relation to . . . tax' are so vague and so general that it must be exceedingly difficult for the officers of the Inland Revenue themselves to know what papers they can take or what they cannot take. . . . The vice of a general warrant of this kind – which does not specify any particular offence – is two-fold. It gives no help to the officers when they have to exercise it. It means also that they can roam wide and large, seizing and taking pretty well all a man's documents and papers.

There is some assistance to be found in the cases. I refer to the law about arrest – when a man is arrested under a warrant for an offence. It is then established by a decision of the House of Lords that the warrant has to specify the particular offence with which the man is charged: see *Christie* v *Leachinsky* [1947] AC 573. I will read what Viscount Simon said, at p. 585:

> If the arrest was authorised by magisterial warrant, or if proceedings were instituted by the issue of a summons, it is clear law that the warrant or summons must specify the offence . . . it is a principle involved in our ancient jurisprudence. Moreover, the warrant must be founded on information in writing and on oath and, except where a particular statute provides otherwise, the information and the warrant must particularise the offence charged.

Lord Simmonds put it more graphically when he said, at p. 592:

> Arrested with or without a warrant the subject is entitled to know why he is deprived of his freedom, if only in order that he may, without a moment's delay, take such steps as will enable him to regain it.

So here. When the officers of the Inland Revenue come armed with a warrant to search a man's home or his office, it seems to me that he is entitled to say: 'Of what offence do you suspect me? You are claiming to enter my house and to seize my papers.' And when they look at the papers and seize them, he should be able to say: 'Why are you seizing these papers? Of what offence do you suspect me? What have these to do with your case?' Unless he knows the particular offence charged, he cannot take steps to secure himself or his property. So it seems to me, as a matter of construction of the statute and therefore of the warrant – in pursuance of our traditional role to protect the liberty of the individual – it is our duty to say that the warrant must particularise the specific offence which is charged as being fraud on the revenue.

If this be right, it follows necessarily that this warrant is bad. It should have specified the particular offence of which the man is suspected. On this ground I would hold that certiorari should go to quash the warrant.

House of Lords

LORD WILBERFORCE: . . . The integrity and privacy of a man's home, and of his place of business, an important human right has, since the second world war, been eroded by a number of statutes passed by Parliament in the belief, presumably, that his right of privacy ought in some cases to be over-ridden by the interest which the public has in preventing evasions of the law. Some of these powers of search are reflections of dirigisme and of heavy taxation, others of changes in mores. . . . A formidable number of officials now have powers to enter people's premises, and to take property away, and these powers are frequently exercised, sometimes on a large scale. Many people, as well as the respondents, think that this process has gone too far; that is an issue to be debated in Parliament and in the press.

The courts have the duty to supervise, I would say critically, even jealously, the legality of any purported exercise of these powers. They are the guardians of the citizens' right to privacy. But they must do this in the context of the times, i.e. of increasing Parliamentary intervention, and of the modern power of judicial review. In my respectful opinion appeals to 18th century precedents of arbitrary action by Secretaries of State and references to general warrants do nothing to throw light on the issue. Furthermore, while the courts may look critically at legislation which impairs the rights of citizens and should resolve any doubt in interpretation in their favour, it is no part of their duty, or power, to restrict or impede the working of legislation, even of unpopular legislation; to do so would be to weaken rather than to advance the democratic process. . . .

[On the question of the validity of the warrants his Lordship went on to state] I can understand very well the perplexity, and indeed indignation, of those present on the premises, when they were searched. Beyond knowing, as appears in the warrant, that the search is in connection with a 'tax fraud,' they were not told what the precise nature of the fraud was, when it was committed, or by whom it was committed. In the case of a concern with numerous clients, for example, a bank, without this knowledge the occupier of the premises is totally unable to protect his customers' confidential information from investigation and seizure. I cannot believe that this does not call for a fresh look by Parliament. But, on the plain words of the enactment, the officers are entitled if they can persuade the board and the judge, to enter and search *premises* regardless of whom they belong to: a warrant which confers this power is strictly and exactly within the parliamentary authority, and the occupier has no answer to it. I accept that some information as regards the person(s) who are alleged to have committed an offence and possibly as to the approximate dates of the offences must almost certainly have been laid before the board and the judge. But the occupier has no right to be told of this at this stage, nor has he the right to be informed of the 'reasonable grounds' of which the judge was satisfied. . . .

The Court of Appeal took the view that the warrants were invalid because they did not sufficiently particularise the alleged offence(s). The court did not make clear exactly what particulars should have been given – and indeed I think that this cannot be done. The warrant followed the wording of the statute 'fraud in connection with or in relation to tax': a portmanteau description which covers a number of common law (cheating) and statutory offences (under the Theft Act 1968 et al.). To require specification at this investigatory stage would be impracticable given the complexity of 'tax frauds' and the different persons who may be involved (companies, officers of companies, accountants, tax consultants, taxpayers, wives of taxpayers etc.). Moreover, particularisation, if required, would no doubt take the form of a listing of one offence and/or another or others and so would be of little help to those concerned. Finally, there would clearly be power, on principles well accepted in the common law, after entry had been made in connection with one particular offence, to seize material bearing upon other offences within the portmanteau. So, particularisation, even if practicable, would not help the occupier.

I am unable, therefore, to escape the conclusion, that adherence to the statutory formula is sufficient.

LORD SCARMAN: . . . My Lords, I agree that these appeals should be allowed and add some observations only because of the importance of the issues raised, and because I share the anxieties felt by the Court of Appeal. If power exists for officers of the Board of Inland Revenue to enter premises, if necessary by force, at any time of the day or night and then seize and remove any things whatsoever found there which they have reasonable cause to believe may be required as evidence for the purposes of proceedings in respect of any offence or offences involving any form of fraud in connection with, or in relation to, tax, it is the duty of the courts to see that it is not abused: for it is a breath-taking inroad upon the individual's right of privacy and right of property. Important as is the public interest in the detection and punishment of tax frauds, it is not to be compared with the public interest in the right of men and women to be secure in the privacy of their homes, their offices, and their papers. Yet if the law is that no particulars of the offence or offences suspected, other than that they are offences of tax fraud, need be given, how can the householder, or occupier of premises, hope to obtain an effective judicial review of the entry, search and seizure at the time of the events or shortly thereafter? And telling the victim that long after the event he may go to law and recover damages if he can prove the revenue acted unlawfully is cold comfort – even if he can afford it.

It is therefore with regret that I have to accept that, if the requirements of section 20C of the Taxes Management Act 1970, a section which entered the law as an amendment introduced by section 57 of the Finance Act 1976, are met, the power exists to enter, and search premises, and seize and remove things there found and that the prospect of an immediate judicial review of the exercise of the power is dim. Nevertheless, what Lord Camden CJ said in *Entick* v *Carrington* (1765) 19 State Tr 1029, 1066, remains good law today:

> No man can set his foot upon my ground without my licence, but he is liable to an action, though the damage be nothing . . . If he admits the fact, he is bound to show by way of justification, that some positive law has empowered or excused him.

The positive law relied on in this case is the statute. If the requirements of the statute have been met, there is justification: but, if they have not, there is none . . ..

Appeals allowed.

NOTE: But where courts are asked to determine the legality of the exercise of a discretionary power conferred by a statute they have shown a readiness to impose limits derived from common law principles as the following case discloses. (See further, *R* v *Lord Chancellor, ex parte Witham* [1998] QB 575; *Chesterfield Properties plc* v *Secretary of State for the Environment* [1998] JPL 568; *R* v *Lord Saville, ex parte A* [1999] 4 All ER 860, *post* pp. 462–3.)

R v *Secretary of State for the Home Department, ex parte Pierson*
[1998] AC 539, House of Lords

In 1985, P was convicted of the murder of his parents and received two mandatory life sentences to be served concurrently. Under the system then in operation in 1988 (Criminal Justice Act 1961, s. 61, subsequently the Criminal Justice Act 1991, s. 35(2), and now the Crime (Sentences) Act 1997, s. 29) the Home Secretary, on the basis that P had committed a double premeditated murder, fixed the penal element of the sentence (or 'tariff' which represents the period to be served to satisfy the requirements of retribution and deterrence) at 20 years which represented the minimum period P should serve before he could be considered for release on licence. (The trial judge and Lord Chief Justice had recommended a tariff of 15 years.) In accordance with the then practice the judicial recommendations on tariff, and reasons for the Home Secretary's departure from them, were not communicated to P, neither was he asked to make representations thereon.

In June 1993 the House of Lords ruled in *R* v *Secretary of State for the Home Department, ex parte Doody and Others* [1994] 1 AC 531 (P being one of the 'others') that before fixing the 'tariff ' the Home Secretary was required to disclose to a prisoner the recommendations of the judiciary and provide an opportunity for the prisoner to make written representations. In July 1993 the then Home Secretary announced that the tariff period would be reviewed before any mandatory life sentence prisoner would be considered for release, and in exceptional cases it

might be increased. In August 1993, P was informed of the judicial recommendations in his case and the Home Secretary's reason for recommending 20 years,
namely that 15 years would have been appropriate for a single premeditated
murder but that this was a double murder. In response P's solicitors indicated that
the murders were part of a single incident and were unpremeditated. The Home
Secretary responded in May 1994, accepting that the murders were part of a
single incident and unpremeditated but indicating that he considered 20 years
the appropriate tariff. P applied by way of judicial review for an order of certiorari
to quash the Home Secretary's decision on the grounds that it was irrational
representing, in effect, an increase in the period.

The House of Lords (by a majority of three to two) quashed the Home Secretary's decision, as to confirm a tariff of 20 years originally fixed on the basis of
aggravating factors which did not exist amounted to an increase in the tariff.

LORD STEYN: . . . In public law the emphasis should be on substance rather than form. This case
should also not be decided on a semantic quibble about whether the Home Secretary's function is
strictly 'a sentencing exercise.' The undeniable fact is that in fixing a tariff in an individual case the
Home Secretary is making a decision about the punishment of the convicted man. . . .

That brings me to the question whether any legal consequences flow from the characterisation of
the Home Secretary's function as involving a decision on punishment. It is a general principle of the
common law that a lawful sentence pronounced by a judge may not retrospectively be increased. In
1971 that principle was put on a statutory basis. . . . The general principle of our law is therefore that
a convicted criminal is entitled to know where he stands so far as his punishment is concerned. He is
entitled to legal certainty about his punishment. His rights will be enforced by the courts. Under
English law a convicted prisoner, in spite of his imprisonment, retains all civil rights which are not
taken away expressly or by necessary implication: *Raymond* v *Honey* [1983] 1 AC 1, 10H. The
question must now be considered whether the Home Secretary, in making a decision on punishment, is free from the normal constraint applicable to a sentencing power. It is at this stage of the
examination of the problem that it becomes necessary to consider where in the structure of public
law it fits in. Parliament has not expressly authorised the Home Secretary to increase tariffs retrospectively. If Parliament had done so that would have been the end of the matter. Instead Parliament
has by section 35(2) of the Act of 1991 entrusted the power to take decisions about the release of
mandatory life sentence prisoners to the Home Secretary. The statutory power is wide enough to
authorise the fixing of a tariff. But it does not follow that it is wide enough to permit a power
retrospectively to increase the level of punishment.

The wording of section 35(2) of the Act of 1991 is wide and general. It provides that 'the Secretary
of State may . . . release on licence a life prisoner who is not a discretionary life prisoner.' There is no
ambiguity in the statutory language. The presumption that in the event of ambiguity legislation is
presumed not to invade common law rights is inapplicable. A broader principle applies. Parliament
does not legislate in a vacuum. Parliament legislates for a European liberal democracy founded on
the principles and traditions of the common law. And the courts may approach legislation on this
initial assumption. But this assumption only has prima facie force. It can be displaced by a clear and
specific provision to the contrary . . .

In his *Law of the Constitution*, 10th ed. (1959), Dicey explained the context in which Parliament
legislates, at p. 414:

By every path we come round to the same conclusion, that Parliamentary sovereignty has
favoured the rule of law, and that the supremacy of the law of the land both calls forth the
exertion of Parliamentary sovereignty, and leads to its being exercised in a spirit of legality.

. . .

The operation of the principle of legality can further be illustrated by reference to the decision of the House of Lords in *Reg.* v *Secretary of State for the Home Department, Ex parte Doody* [1994] 1 AC 531. In that case the House of Lords held that the common law principles of procedural fairness required disclosure to a prisoner of the advice to the Home Secretary of the trial judge and of the Lord Chief Justice in order to enable the prisoner to make effective representations before the Home Secretary fixed the tariff. The premise was that Parliament must be presumed to have intended that the Home Secretary would act in conformity with the common law principle of procedural fairness. And our public law is, of course, replete with other instances of the common law so supplementing statutes on the basis of the principle of legality. . . .

Turning back to the circumstances of the present case, it was easy to conclude that the legislation authorises the policy of fixing a tariff. The wide statutory discretion of the Home Secretary justified that conclusion. But a general power to increase tariffs lawfully fixed is qualitatively in a different category. It contemplates a power unheard of in our criminal justice system until the 1993 policy statement of the Home Secretary (Mr Michael Howard) (Hansard (HC Debates), 27 July 1993, cols. 861–864: written answer). Such a power is not essential to the efficient working of the system: without a power to increase tariffs the system worked satisfactorily between 1983 and 1993. But I do not rest my judgment on this point. The critical factor is that a general power to increase tariffs duly fixed is in disharmony with the deep rooted principle of not retrospectively increasing lawfully pronounced sentences. In the absence of contrary indications it must be presumed that Parliament entrusted the wide power to make decisions on the release of mandatory life sentence prisoners on the supposition that the Home Secretary would not act contrary to such a fundamental principle of our law. There are no contrary indications. Certainly, there is not a shred of evidence that Parliament would have been prepared to vest a general power in the Home Secretary to increase retrospectively tariffs duly fixed. The evidence is to the contrary. When Parliament enacted section 35(2) of the Act of 1991 – the foundation of the Home Secretary's present power – Parliament knew that since 1983 successive Home Secretaries had adopted a policy of fixing in each case a tariff period, following which risk is considered. Parliament also knew that it was the practice that a tariff, once fixed, would not be increased. That was clear from the assurance in the 1983 policy statement (Mr Leon Brittan (Hansard (HC Debates), 30 November 1983, cols. 505–507: written answer) that 'except where a prisoner has committed an offence for which he has received a further custodial sentence, the formal review date will not be put back.' What Parliament did not know in 1991 was that in 1993 a new Home Secretary would assert a general power to increase the punishment of prisoners convicted of murder whenever he considered it right to do so. It would be wrong to assume that Parliament would have been prepared to give to the Home Secretary such an unprecedented power, alien to the principles of our law. . . .

The correct analysis of this case is in terms of the rule of law. The rule of law in its wider sense has procedural and substantive effect. . . . Unless there is the clearest provision to the contrary, Parliament must be presumed not to legislate contrary to the rule of law. And the rule of law enforces minimum standards of fairness, both substantive and procedural. I therefore approach the problem in the present case on this basis.

It is true that the principle of legality only has prima facie force. But in enacting section 35(2) of the Act of 1991, with its very wide power to release prisoners, Parliament left untouched the fundamental principle that a sentence lawfully passed should not retrospectively be increased. Parliament must therefore be presumed to have enacted legislation wide enough to enable the Home Secretary to make decisions on punishment on the basis that he would observe the normal constraint governing that function. Instead the Home Secretary has asserted a general power to increase tariffs duly fixed. Parliament did not confer such a power on the Home Secretary.

It follows that the Home Secretary did not have the power to increase a tariff lawfully fixed. . . .

It was agreed before your Lordships' House that the Home Secretary's decision letter of 6 May

1994 did communicate a decision to Mr Pierson to increase the tariff in his case. That decision was in my judgment unlawful and ought to be quashed. My conclusion is based on the proposition that the Home Secretary has no general power to increase a tariff fixed and communicated.

NOTE: While the above case and *Entick* v *Carrington* display exemplary respect for the rule of law and the legality principle, there have been events in recent history which suggest that this doctrine is still not fully understood or accepted. In Northern Ireland in 1971, powers granted under the Civil Authorities (Special Powers) Act (N.I.) 1922 were exercised by the Northern Ireland government to intern persons suspected of having acted or being about to act in a manner prejudicial to the preservation of peace or the maintenance of order. Some of those interned were interrogated by the security forces. The Crompton Report (Cmnd. 4823, 1971) detailed the interrogation procedures as including keeping the detainees' heads covered with hoods; subjecting them to continuous monotonous noise; deprivation of sleep; deprivation of food and water, apart from meagre rations of bread and water at six-hourly intervals; and making the detainees stand facing a wall with legs apart and hands raised. Three Privy Counsellors (Lord Parker of Waddington, a former Lord Chief Justice, J. A. Carpenter, a former Cabinet Minister, and Lord Gardiner, a former Lord Chancellor) were given the task of examining these procedures. They failed to agree and produced two conflicting reports.

Report of the Committee of Privy Counsellors appointed to consider authorised procedures for the interrogation of persons suspected of terrorism
Chairman: Lord Parker of Waddington, Cmnd. 4901, 1972

The Majority in their Report noted that the information obtained from interrogating suspects was responsible for saving lives. While not accepting that the end justified the means, they considered that the measure of whether the means were morally acceptable had to take account of the prevailing conditions. Thus expressions such as 'humane', 'inhuman', 'humiliating', and 'degrading' would acquire different meanings under different conditions. In light of the conditions prevailing, the Majority considered that the interrogation techniques would be acceptable provided there were proper safeguards 'limiting the occasion on which and the degree to which they can be applied'. Thus the techniques should only be used 'in cases where it is considered vitally necessary to obtain information', and then they should be applied in conformity with the Directive on Military Interrogation. There should be guidelines to assist the interrogator 'as to the degree to which in any particular circumstances the techniques can be applied', breach of which should result in a report to his superior officer. The techniques should only be used under the express authority of a UK minister, who should lay down guidelines on their use which should remain secret. The Majority considered that the Minister should be advised by a small and experienced Committee appointed by the Prime Minister in consultation with the Leader of the Opposition. If the techniques used involved criminal assaults or gave rise to civil liability, the Majority recommended that the Minister should take legal advice and 'if need be steps to ensure protection for those taking part in the operation'. There should be a senior officer in overall control at the interrogation centre and a panel of skilled interrogators. Further, a doctor with some psychiatric training should be present to observe interrogations and to warn the controller if interrogation was being pressed too far. Finally there should be a procedure for the investigation of complaints.

LORD GARDINER'S REPORT: . . .

Were they authorised?

8. We have found this a point of some difficulty because our terms of reference appear to assume that the procedures were or are authorised. The only evidence before us on this point was that it could not be said that UK Ministers had ever approved them specifically, as opposed to agreeing the general principles set out in the Directive on Military Interrogation. If any document or Minister had purported to authorise them, it would have been invalid because the procedures were and are illegal by the domestic law and may also have been illegal by international law. I regard this point as so important that I must develop it.

9. I agree with my colleagues that the only relevant document is the Directive. This lays down two requirements:

  (a) Those concerned are to acquaint themselves with the laws of the country concerned, and are not to act unlawfully under any circumstances whatever.
  (b) They are to follow the principles laid down in Article 3 of The Geneva Convention Relative to the Treatment of Prisoners of War (1949) and these include the prohibition of 'outrages upon personal dignity, in particular, humiliating and degrading treatment'.

10. Domestic law

  (a) By our own domestic law the powers of police and prison officers are well known. Where a man is in lawful custody it is lawful to do anything which is reasonably necessary to keep him in custody but it does not further or otherwise make lawful an assault. Forcibly to hood a man's head and keep him hooded against his will and handcuff him if he tries to remove it, as in one of the cases in question, is an assault and both a tort and a crime. So is wall-standing of the kind referred to. Deprivation of diet is also illegal unless duly awarded as a punishment under prison rules. So is enforced deprivation of sleep.
  (b) In Northern Ireland in normal times the powers of the police and prison officers in relation to those in custody are substantially the same except for an immaterial difference in their Judges' Rules. Of the Regulations scheduled to the Civil Authorities (Special Powers) Act (Northern Ireland) 1922, Regulation 10 provides that 'Any officer of the Royal Ulster Constabulary, for the preservation of the peace and maintenance of order, may authorise the arrest without warrant and detention for a period of not more than 48 hours of any person for the purpose of interrogation'. This Regulation does not in any way extend the ordinary police powers as to the permissible methods or limits of interrogation. Regulation 11 provides a limited power of detention and a limited right to photograph and finger-print and Regulation 12 a limited right of internment. . . .
  (c) We have received both written and oral representations from many legal bodies and individual lawyers from both England and Northern Ireland. There has been no dissent from the view that the procedures are illegal alike by the law of England and the law of Northern Ireland. . . .
  (d) This being so, no Army Directive and no Minister could lawfully or validly have authorised the use of the procedures. Only Parliament can alter the law. The procedures were and are illegal. . . .

20. I am not in favour of making such a recommendation for each of the following five reasons:

(1) I do not believe that, whether in peace time for the purpose of obtaining information relating to men like the Richardson gang or the Kray gang, or in emergency terrorist conditions, or even in war against a ruthless enemy, such procedures are morally justifiable against those suspected of having information of importance to the police or army, even in the light of any marginal advantages which may thereby be obtained.

(2) If it is to be made legal to employ methods not now legal against a man whom the police believe to have, but who may not have, information which the police desire to obtain, I, like many of our witnesses, have searched for, but been unable to find, either in logic or in morals, any limit to the degree of ill-treatment to be legalised. The only logical limit to the degree of ill-treatment to be legalised would appear to be whatever degree of ill-treatment proves to be necessary to get the information out of him, which would include, if necessary, extreme torture. I cannot think that Parliament should, or would, so legislate.

(3) Our witnesses have felt great difficulty in even suggesting any fixed limits for noise threshold or any time limits for noise, wall-standing, hooding, or deprivation of diet or sleep.

All our medical witnesses agreed that the variations in what people can stand in relation to both physical exhaustion and mental disorientation are very great and believe that to fix any such limits is quite impracticable. . . .

(4) It appears to me that the recommendations made by my colleagues in the concluding part of their Report necessarily envisage one of two courses.

One is that Parliament should enact legislation enabling a Minister, in a time of civil emergency but not, as I understand it, in time of war, to fix the limits of permissible degrees of ill-treatment to be employed when interrogating suspects and that such limits should then be kept secret.

I should respectfully object to this, first, because the Minister would have just as much difficulty as Parliament would have in fixing the limits of ill-treatment and, secondly, because I view with abhorence any proposal that a Minister should in effect be empowered to make secret laws: it would mean that United Kingdom citizens would have no right to know what the law was about police powers of interrogation.

The other course is that a Minister should fix such secret limits without the authority of Parliament, that is to say illegally, and then, if found out, ask Parliament for an Act of Indemnity.

I should respectfully object even more to this because it would in my view be a flagrant breach of the whole basis of the Rule of Law and of the principles of democratic government.

(5) Lastly, I do not think that any decision ought to be arrived at without considering the effect on the reputation of our own country.

For many years men and women and a number of international organisations have been engaged in trying patiently to raise international moral standards, particularly in the field of human rights. The results are to be found in the Universal Declaration of Human Rights, the four Geneva Conventions, which 129 countries have signed and ratified, the International Covenant on Civil and Political Rights and The European Convention on Human Rights. . . . And this is not all. The World Conference on Religion and Peace, representative of all the world's religions, held in October 1970 declared

> The torture and ill-treatment of prisoners which is carried out with the authority of some Governments constitute not only a crime against humanity, but also a crime against the moral law

while the subsequent Consultation of all the Christian Churches declared

> There is today a growing concern at the frequency with which some authorities resort to the torture or inhuman treatment of political opponents or prisoners held by them. . . . There exists at the present time, in certain regions of the world, regimes using systematic methods of torture carried out in the most refined way. Torture itself becomes contagious. . . . The expediency of the moment should never silence the voice of the Church Authorities when condemnation of inhuman treatment is called for.

There have been, and no doubt will continue to be, some countries which act in this way whatever Conventions they have signed and ratified. We have not in general been one of these. If, by a new Act of Parliament, we now depart from world standards which we have helped to create, I believe that we should both gravely damage our own reputation and deal a severe blow to the whole world movement to improve Human Rights.

NOTE: Lord Gardiner's view was eventually adopted by the Government and the interrogation procedures were discontinued. The issue of the interrogation of internees eventually reached the European Court of Human Rights on a reference from the government of Ireland alleging that the interrogation procedures breached Art. 3 of the European Convention on Human Rights. In *Ireland* v *United Kingdom* (1978) 2 EHRR 25, the European Court of Human Rights held that the procedures amounted to inhuman and degrading treatment contrary to Art. 3 but did not amount to torture.

QUESTIONS

If the Government in response to the majority report had introduced legislation to authorize the interrogation procedures complained of, would the doctrine of the rule of law have provided any further protection to citizens interned and subjected to these procedures? Is the rule of law to be equated simply with the idea of legality, or does it impose some moral constraints on Government?

NOTES:
1. Now that the Human Rights Act 1998 is in force, if a similar situation arises, a UK court could hold such procedures to be in breach of the Convention (see Chapter 7). This begs the question, however, of what would happen if a government, faced with the problem of terrorism, used its majority in Parliament to enact primary legislation to authorize similar interrogation procedures?
2. If the rule of law is to have any meaning in a democratic society, it must mean at least that those who enforce the law abide by the law; there must be no room for an 'ends justifies the means' mentality. This is confirmed by the following case.

R v *Horseferry Road Magistrates' Court, ex parte Bennett*
[1994] AC 42, House of Lords

Bennett, a New Zealand citizen, was wanted by United Kingdom police for a series of offences allegedly committed by him. He was arrested in South Africa but there was no extradition treaty between South Africa and the United Kingdom. The South African police, however, placed him on an aircraft bound for London where he was arrested by English police officers. The magistrates committed Bennett to the Crown Court for trial. He applied for judicial review of their decision alleging that he had been returned to the jurisdiction against his will as a result of kidnapping or quasi-extradition. He further alleged that this had occurred at the request of the English police and that the South African police had placed him on the plane on the pretext of deporting him to New Zealand via London thereby enabling English police to arrest him. Bennett contended that in these circumstances it would be an abuse of the process of the court to permit the prosecution to proceed. The Divisional Court dismissed his application for judicial review of the magistrates' decision on the basis that even if he had been kidnapped and illegally removed from South Africa with the collusion of English police officers, the court had no jurisdiction to inquire into these matters and prevent a prosecution as these were not relevant to the issue of whether he would have a fair trial. The House of Lords (Lord Oliver dissenting) reversed the decision of the Divisional Court.

LORD GRIFFITHS: . . . Your Lordships have been urged by the respondents to uphold the decision of the Divisional Court and the nub of its submission is that the role of the judge is confined to the forensic process. The judge, it is said, is concerned to see that the accused has a fair trial and that the process of the court is not manipulated to his disadvantage so that the trial itself is unfair; but the wider issues of the rule of law and the behaviour of those charged with its enforcement, be they police or prosecuting authority, are not the concern of the judiciary unless they impinge directly on the trial process. In support of this submission your Lordships have been referred to *R v Sang* [1979] 2 All ER 1222 esp at 1230, 1245–1246, [1980] AC 402 esp at 436–437, 454–455 where Lord Diplock and Lord Scarman emphasise that the role of the judge is confined to the forensic process and that it is no part of the judge's function to exercise disciplinary powers over the police or the prosecution. . . .

[After examining the cases on abuse of process his Lordship continued:]

Your Lordships are now invited to extend the concept of abuse of process a stage further. In the present case there is no suggestion that the appellant cannot have a fair trial, nor could it be suggested that it would have been unfair to try him if he had been returned to this country through extradition procedures. If the court is to have the power to interfere with the prosecution in the present circumstances it must be because the judiciary accept a responsibility for the maintenance of the rule of law that embraces a willingness to oversee executive action and to refuse to countenance behaviour that threatens either basic human rights or the rule of law.

My Lords, I have no doubt that the judiciary should accept this responsibility in the field of criminal law. The great growth of administrative law during the latter half of this century has occurred because of the recognition by the judiciary and Parliament alike that it is the function of the High Court to ensure that executive action is exercised responsibly and as Parliament intended. So also should it be in the field of criminal law and if it comes to the attention of the court that there has been a serious abuse of power it should, in my view, express its disapproval by refusing to act upon it.

. . .

The courts, of course, have no power to apply direct discipline to the police or the prosecuting authorities, but they can refuse to allow them to take advantage of abuse of power by regarding their behaviour as an abuse of process and thus preventing a prosecution.

LORD BRIDGE OF HARWICH: . . . There is, I think, no principle more basic to any proper system of law than the maintenance of the rule of law itself. When it is shown that the law enforcement agency responsible for bringing a prosecution has only been enabled to do so by participating in violations of international law and of the laws of another state in order to secure the presence of the accused within the territorial jurisdiction of the court, I think that respect for the rule of law demands that the court take cognisance of that circumstance. To hold that the court may turn a blind eye to executive lawlessness beyond the frontiers of its own jurisdiction is, to my mind, an insular and unacceptable view. Having then taken cognisance of the lawlessness it would again appear to be a wholly inadequate response for the court to hold that the only remedy lies in civil proceedings at the suit of the defendant or in disciplinary or criminal proceedings against the individual officers of the law enforcement agency who were concerned in the illegal action taken. Since the prosecution could never have been brought if the defendant had not been illegally abducted, the whole proceeding is tainted. If a resident in another country is properly extradited here, the time when the prosecution commences is the time when the authorities here set the extradition process in motion. By parity of reasoning, if the authorities, instead of proceeding by way of extradition, have resorted to abduction, that is the effective commencement of the prosecution process and is the illegal foundation on which it rests. . . .

Appeal allowed. Case remitted to Divisional Court for further consideration.

NOTE: The idea of government according to law has been illustrated in a range of decisions by the courts developing the principles of *ultra vires* (*post*, Chapter 8) and natural justice (*post*, Chapter 8) which are the central doctrines in administrative law. By development of these doctrines the courts have sought to control the ways in which authorities exercise their powers and the procedures they adopt. Thus the exercise of a power by an authority will be struck down as *ultra vires* where the authority acts in excess of the power (see, e.g., *Laker Airways Ltd* v *Department of Trade* [1977] QB 643), or it abuses the power by exercising it ignoring relevant considerations or taking irrelevant considerations into account (see, e.g., *Associated Provincial Picture Houses Ltd* v *Wednesbury Corporation* [1948] 1 KB 223), or where it exercises the power for an improper purpose (see, e.g., *Roberts* v *Hopwood* [1925] AC 578), or it exercises the power unreasonably (*Wednesbury, ante*). Where powers are exercised courts may also impose procedural requirements upon the authority exercising the power to ensure that the decision to exercise the power was taken in accordance with the rules of natural justice or, more recently, that the decision respected the requirements of fairness. Thus the decision-maker should be unbiased and the subject of the decision should have had a fair hearing. What is fair may vary with the circumstances, but matters which will be taken into account are whether the subject received adequate notice of the hearing and the charges, was allowed to present his case in a written or oral form and call witnesses, and whether he was allowed legal representation.

While these developments may help protect the citizen from the arbitrary exercise of power, do they have any effect on the legislature in controlling the laws it may pass and, therefore, the powers it may bestow upon government and other official agencies?

SECTION 2: **The Rule of Law as a Broad Political Doctrine**

Bradley and Ewing, *Constitutional and Administrative Law* (12th edn, 1997), p. 108, state:

If the law is not to be merely a means of achieving whatever ends a particular government may favour, the rule of law must go beyond the principle of legality. The experience and values of the legal system are relevant not only to the question, 'What legal authority *does* the government have for its acts?' but also to the question, 'What legal powers *ought* the government to have?'

Several other writers have sought to specify certain minimum standards which laws should attain.

J. Raz, 'The Rule of Law and its Virtue'
(1977) 93 LQR, pp. 195–202

. . . The rule of law is a political ideal which a legal system may lack or may possess to a greater or lesser degree. That much is common ground. It is also to be insisted that the rule of law is just one of the virtues which a legal system may possess and by which it is to be judged. It is not to be confused with democracy, justice, equality (before the law or otherwise), human rights of any kind or respect for persons or for the dignity of man. A non-democratic legal system, based on the denial of human rights, on extensive poverty, on racial segregation, sexual inequalities and religious persecution may, in principle, conform to the requirements of the rule of law better than any of the legal systems of the more enlightened western democracies. This does not mean that it will be better than those western democracies. It will be an immeasurably worse legal system, but it will excel in one respect: in its conformity to the rule of law. . . .

1. The Basic Idea

'The rule of law' means literally what it says: The rule of the law. Taken in its broadest sense this means that people should obey the law and be ruled by it. But in political and legal theory it has come to be read in a narrower sense, that the government shall be ruled by the law and subject to it. The ideal of the rule of law in this sense is often expressed by the phrase 'government by law and not by men.' No sooner does one use these formulae than their obscurity becomes evident. Surely government must be both by law and by men. It is said that the rule of law means that all government action must have foundation in law, must be authorised by law. But is not that a tautology? Actions not authorised by law cannot be the actions of the government as a government. They would be without legal effect and often unlawful. . . . There is more to the rule of law than the law and order interpretation allows. It means more even than law and order applied to the government. I shall proceed on the assumption that we are concerned with government in the legal sense and with the conception of the rule of law which applies to government and to law and is no mere application of the law and order conception.

The problem is that now we are back with our initial puzzle. If the government is, by definition, government authorised by law the rule of law seems to amount to an empty tautology, not a political ideal.

The solution to this riddle is in the difference between the professional and the lay sense of law. For the lawyer anything is the law if it meets the conditions of validity laid down in the system's rules of recognition or in other rules of the system. This includes the constitution, parliamentary legislation, ministerial regulations, policeman's orders, the regulations of limited companies, conditions imposed in trading licences, etc. To the layman the law consists only of a subclass of these. To him the law is essentially a set of open, general and relatively stable laws. Government by law and not by men is not a tautology if 'law' means general, open and relatively stable law. In fact the danger of this interpretation is that the rule of law might set too strict a requirement, one which no legal system can meet and which embodies very little virtue. It is humanly inconceivable that law can consist only of general rules and it is very undesirable that it should. Just as we need government both by laws and by men, so we need both general and particular laws to carry out the jobs for which we need the law.

The doctrine of the rule of law does not deny that every legal system should consist of both general, open and stable rules (the popular conception of law) and particular laws (legal orders), an essential tool in the hands of the executive and the judiciary alike. As we shall see, what the doctrine requires is the subjection of particular laws to general, open and stable ones. It is one of the important principles of the doctrine that *the making of particular laws should be guided by open and relatively stable general rules*.

This principle shows how the slogan of the rule of law and not of men can be read as a meaningful political ideal. The principle does not, however, exhaust the meaning of the rule of law and does not by itself illuminate the reasons for its alleged importance. Let us, therefore, return to the literal sense of the 'rule of law.' It has two aspects: (1) that people should be ruled by the law and obey it, and (2) that the law should be such that people will be able to be guided by it. As was noted above, it is with the second aspect that we are concerned: the law must be capable of being obeyed. A person conforms with the law to the extent that he does not break the law. But he obeys the law only if part of his reason for conforming is his knowledge of the law. Therefore, if the law is to be obeyed *it must be capable of guiding the behaviour of its subjects*. It must be such that they can find out what it is and act on it.

This is the basic intuition from which the doctrine of the rule of law derives: the law must be capable of guiding the behaviour of its subjects. It is evident that this conception of the rule of law is a formal one. It says nothing about how the law is to be made: by tyrants, democratic majorities or any other way. It says nothing about fundamental rights, about equality or justice. It may even be thought that this version of the doctrine is formal to the extent that it is almost devoid of content. This is far from the truth. Most of the requirements which were associated with the rule of law before it came to signify all the virtues of the state can be derived from this one basic idea.

2. Some Principles

Many of the principles which can be derived from the basic idea of the rule of law depend for their validity or importance on the particular circumstances of different societies. There is little point in trying to enumerate them all, but some of the more important ones might be mentioned:

(1) *All laws should be prospective, open and clear*. One cannot be guided by a retroactive law. It does not exist at the time of action. Sometimes it is then known for certain that a retroactive law will be enacted. When this happens retroactivity does not conflict with the rule of law (though it may be objected to on other grounds). The law must be open and adequately publicised. If it is to guide people they must be able to find out what it is. For the same reason its meaning must be clear. An ambiguous, vague, obscure or imprecise law is likely to mislead or confuse at least some of those who desire to be guided by it.

(2) *Laws should be relatively stable*. They should not be changed too often. If they are frequently changed people will find it difficult to find out what the law is at any given moment and will be constantly in fear that the law has been changed since they last learnt what it is. But more important still is the fact that people need to know the law not only for short-term decisions (where to park one's car, how much alcohol is allowed in duty free, etc.) but also for long-term planning. Knowledge of at least the general outlines and sometimes even of details of tax law and company law are often important for business plans which will bear fruit only years later. Stability is essential if people are to be guided by law in their long-term decisions. . . .

(3) *The making of particular laws (particular legal orders) should be guided by open, stable, clear and general rules*. It is sometimes assumed that the requirement of generality is of the essence of the rule of law. This notion derives (as noted above) from the literal interpretation of 'the rule of law' when 'law' is read in its lay connotations as being restricted to general, stable and open law. It is also reinforced by a belief that the rule of law is particularly relevant to the protection of equality and that equality is related to the generality of law. The last belief is, as has been often noted before, mistaken. Racial, religious and all manner of discrimination is not only compatible but often institutionalised by general rules.

The formal conception of the rule of law which I am defending does not object to particular legal orders as long as they are stable, clear, etc. But of course particular legal orders are mostly used by government agencies to introduce flexibility into the law. A police constable regulating traffic, a licensing authority granting a licence under certain conditions, all these and their like are among the more ephemeral parts of the law. As such they run counter to the basic idea of the rule of law. They make it difficult for people to plan ahead on the basis of their knowledge of the law. This difficulty is overcome to a large extent if particular laws of an ephemeral status are enacted only within a framework set by general laws which are more durable and which impose limits on the unpredictability introduced by the particular orders.

Two kinds of general rules create the framework for the enactment of particular laws: Those which confer the necessary powers for making valid orders and those which impose duties instructing the power-holders how to exercise their powers. Both have equal importance in creating a stable framework for the creation of particular legal orders.

Clearly, similar considerations apply to general legal regulations which do not meet the requirement of stability. They too should be circumscribed to conform to a stable framework. Hence the requirement that much of the subordinate administrative law-making should be made to conform to detailed ground rules laid down in framework laws. It is essential, however, not to confuse this argument with democratic arguments for the close supervision of popularly-elected bodies over law-making by non-elected ones. These further arguments may be valid but have nothing to do with the rule of law, and though sometimes they reinforce rule of law type arguments, on other occasions they support different and even conflicting conclusions.

(4) *The independence of the judiciary must be guaranteed.* It is of the essence of municipal legal systems that they institute judicial bodies charged, among other things, with the duty of applying the law to cases brought before them and whose judgments and conclusions as to the legal merits of those cases are final. Since just about any matter arising under any law can be subject to a conclusive court judgment it is obvious that it is futile to guide one's action on the basis of the law if when the matter comes to adjudication the courts will not apply the law and will act for some other reasons. The point can be put even more strongly. Since the court's judgment establishes conclusively what is the law in the case before it, the litigants can be guided by law only if the judges apply the law correctly. Otherwise people will only be able to be guided by their guesses as to what the courts are likely to do – but these guesses will not be based on the law but on other considerations.

The rules concerning the independence of the judiciary – the method of appointing judges, their security of tenure, the way of fixing their salaries and other conditions of service – are designed to guarantee that they will be free from extraneous pressures and independent of all authority save that of the law. They are, therefore, essential for the preservation of the rule of law.

(5) *The principles of natural justice must be observed.* Open and fair hearing, absence of bias and the like are obviously essential for the correct application of the law and thus, through the very same considerations mentioned above, to its ability to guide action.

(6) *The courts should have review powers over the implementation of the other principles.* This includes review of both subordinate and parliamentary legislation and of administrative action, but in itself it is a very limited review – merely to ensure conformity to the rule of law.

(7) *The courts should be easily accessible.* Given the central position of the courts in ensuring the rule of law (see principles 4 and 6) it is obvious that their accessibility is of paramount importance. Long delays, excessive costs, etc., may effectively turn the most enlightened law to a dead letter and frustrate one's ability effectively to guide oneself by the law.

(8) *The discretion of the crime preventing agencies should not be allowed to pervert the law.* Not only the courts but also the actions of the police and the prosecuting authorities can subvert the law. The prosecution should not be allowed, e.g. to decide not to prosecute for commission of certain crimes, or for crimes committed by certain classes of offenders. The police should not be allowed to allocate its resources so as to avoid all effort to prevent and detect certain crimes or prosecute certain classes of criminals.

This list is very incomplete. Other principles could be mentioned and those which have been mentioned need further elaboration and further justification (why – as required by my sixth principle – should the courts and not some other body be in charge of reviewing conformity to the rule of law? etc.). My purpose in listing them was merely to illustrate the power and fruitfulness of the formal conception of the rule of law. It should, however, be remembered that in the final analysis the doctrine rests on its basic idea that the law should be capable of providing effective guidance. The principles do not stand on their own. They must be constantly interpreted in light of the basic idea.

The eight principles listed fall into two groups. Principles 1 to 3 require that the law should conform to standards designed to enable it effectively to guide action. Principles 4 to 8 are designed to ensure that the legal machinery of enforcing the law should not deprive it of its ability to guide through distorted enforcement and that it shall be capable of supervising conformity to the rule of law and provide effective remedies in cases of deviation from it. All the principles directly concern the system and method of government in matters directly relevant to the rule of law. Needlesss to say many other aspects in the life of a community may, in more indirect ways, either strengthen or weaken the rule of law. A free press run by people anxious to defend the rule of law is of great assistance in preserving it, just as a gagged press or one run by people wishing to undermine the rule of law is a threat to it. But we need not be concerned here with these more indirect influences.

NOTE: See also Lon. L. Fuller, *The Morality of Law* (2nd edn, 1969).

Some of the principles identified by Raz are given judicial expression in the cases which follow.

A: Laws should be clear

Merkur Island Shipping Corp. v *Laughton and Others*
[1983] 2 AC 570, Court of Appeal

In an action arising from a trade dispute between the owners and crew of a ship, members of the International Transport Workers' Federation were sued for damages for losses arising from secondary industrial action in which they had been involved. In deciding whether a trade union was immune from tortious liability, the court had to construe three statutes: The Trade Union and Labour Relations Act 1974, the Trade Union and Labour Relations (Amendment) Act 1976, and the Employment Act 1980.

LORD DONALDSON MR: . . . At the beginning of this judgment I said that whilst I had reached the conclusion that the law was tolerably clear, the same could not be said of the way in which it was expressed. The efficacy and maintenance of the rule of law, which is the foundation of any parliamentary democracy, has at least two pre-requisites. First, people must understand that it is in their interests, as well as in that of the community as a whole, that they should live their lives in accordance with the rules and all the rules. Second, they must know what those rules are. Both are equally important and it is the second aspect of the rule of law which has caused me concern in the present case, the ITF having disavowed any intention to break the law.

In industrial relations it is of vital importance that the worker on the shop floor, the shop steward, the local union official, the district officer and the equivalent levels in management should know what is and what is not 'offside.' And they must be able to find this out for themselves by reading plain and simple words of guidance. The judges of this court are all skilled lawyers of very considerable experience, yet it has taken us hours to ascertain what is and what is not 'offside,' even with the assistance of highly experienced counsel. This cannot be right.

We have had to look at three Acts of Parliament, none intelligible without the other. We have had to consider section 17 of the Act of 1980, which adopts the 'flow' method of Parliamentary draftsmanship, without the benefit of a flow diagram. We have furthermore been faced with the additional complication that subsection (6) of section 17 contains definitions which distort the natural meaning of the words in the operative subsections. It was not always like this. If you doubt me, look at the comparative simplicity and clarity of Sir Mackenzie Chalmers's Sale of Goods Act 1893, his Bills of Exchange Act 1882, and his Marine Insurance Act 1906. But I do not criticise the draftsman. His instructions may well have left him no option. My plea is that Parliament, when legislating in respect of circumstances which directly affect the 'man or woman in the street' or the 'man or woman on the shop floor' should give as high a priority to clarity and simplicity of expression as to refinements of policy. Where possible, statutes, or complete parts of statutes, should not be amended but re-enacted in an amended form so that those concerned can read the rules in a single document. When formulating policy, ministers, of whatever political persuasion, should at all times be asking themselves and asking parliamentary counsel: 'Is this concept too refined to be capable of expression in basic English? If so, is there some way in which we can modify the policy so that it can be so expressed?' Having to ask such questions would no doubt be frustrating for ministers and the legislature generally, but in my judgment this is part of the price which has to be paid if the rule of law is to be maintained.

These sentiments were echoed by Lord Diplock in the House of Lords, at p. 612:

LORD DIPLOCK: . . . I see no reason for doubting that those upon whom the responsibility for deciding whether and if so what industrial action shall be taken in any given circumstances wish to obey the law, even though it be a law which they themselves dislike and hope will be changed through the operation of this country's constitutional system of parliamentary democracy. But what the law is, particularly in the field of industrial relations, ought to be plain. It should be expressed in terms that can be easily understood by those who have to apply it even at shop floor level. I echo everything that the Master of the Rolls has said in the last three paragraphs of his judgment in this case. Absence of clarity is destructive of the rule of law; it is unfair to those who wish to preserve the rule of law; it encourages those who wish to undermine it. The statutory provisions which it became necessary to piece together into a coherent whole in order to decide the stage 3 point are drafted in a manner which, having regard to their subject matter and the persons who will be called upon to apply them, can, in my view, only be characterised as most regrettably lacking in the requisite degree of clarity.

B: Laws should be prospective

Phillips v *Eyre*
(1870) LR 6 QB 1, Exchequer Chamber

> The legislature of Jamaica had passed an Indemnity Act following the suppression of a rebellion in the colony. If the Act was valid it would prevent the claimant suing for assault and false imprisonment.

WILLES J: . . . Retrospective laws are, no doubt, prima facie of questionable policy, and contrary to the general principle that legislation by which the conduct of mankind is to be regulated ought, when introduced for the first time, to deal with future acts, and ought not to change the character of past transactions carried on upon the faith of the then existing law. . . . Accordingly, the Court will not ascribe retrospective force to new laws affecting rights, unless by express words or necessary implication it appears that such was the intention of the legislature. . . .

  In fine, allowing the general inexpediency of retrospective legislation, it cannot be pronounced naturally or necessarily unjust. There may be occasions and circumstances involving the safety of the state, or even the conduct of individual subjects, the justice of which, prospective laws made for ordinary occasions and the usual exigencies of society for want of prevision fails to meet, and in which the execution of the law as it stood at the time may involve practical public inconvenience and wrong, summum jus summa injuria. Whether the circumstances of the particular case are such as to call for special and exceptional remedy is a question which must in each case involve matter of policy and discretion fit for debate and decision in the parliament which would have had jurisdiction to deal with the subject-matter by preliminary legislation, and as to which a court of ordinary municipal law is not commissioned to inquire or adjudicate.

NOTE: See also *R* v *Secretary of State for the Home Department, ex parte Pierson* [1998] AC 539, *ante* p. 179.

QUESTIONS

1. Can the doctrine of the rule of law prevent Parliament enacting retrospective laws? (See War Damage Act 1965, enacted pursuant to *Burmah Oil Co* v *Lord Advocate* [1965] AC 75, *ante* p. 68.)

2. Is Lord Reid's confidence misplaced when he states in *Waddington* v *Miah* [1974] 2 All ER 377, at p. 379, that 'it is hardly credible that any government department would promote or that Parliament would pass retrospective criminal legislation'? See s. 1 of the War Crimes Act 1991, which provides:

1. Jurisdiction over certain war crimes

(1) Subject to the provisions of this section, proceedings for murder, manslaughter or culpable homicide may be brought against a person in the United Kingdom irrespective of his nationality at the time of the alleged offence if that offence—

(a) was committed during the period beginning with 1st September 1939 and ending with 5th June 1945 in a place which at the time was part of Germany or under German occupation; and

(b) constituted a violation of the laws and customs of war.

(2) No proceedings shall by virtue of this section be brought against any person unless he was on 8th March 1990, or has subsequently become, a British citizen or resident in the United Kingdom, the Isle of Man or any of the Channel Islands.

(Retrospective penal legislation contravenes Art. 7 of the European Convention on Human Rights.)

C: The independence of the judiciary must be guaranteed

The maintenance of the independence of the judiciary is essential if the rule of law is to be respected. In his presidential address to the Holdsworth Club in 1950, Lord Justice Denning, as he then was, stated:

No member of the Government, no Member of Parliament and no official of any government department has any right whatever to direct or influence or to interfere with the decisions of any of the judges. It is the sure knowledge of this that gives the people their confidence in judges. . . . The critical test which they must pass if they are to receive the confidence of the people is that they must be independent of the executive.

Independence requires that judges must be free to interpret and apply the law as they see fit subject only to correction on appeal to a higher court. A crucial role is played by the Lord Chancellor in protecting the independence of the judiciary. In the Twelfth Francis Mann Lecture delivered by Lord Hailsham (see 'The Office of Lord Chancellor and the Separation of Powers' (1989) 8 *Civil Justice Quarterly* 308), he described this duty as follows:

. . . the essential function of the Lord Chancellor in the working of the constitution remains the same. He is in the business of defending and preserving the independence and integrity of the judiciary. If he does it well, then he is a good Lord Chancellor whatever his other defects. If he does it ill, whatever his other qualities, he is not.

The then Lord Chancellor, Lord Mackay, expressed similar views in the House of Lords in the debate 'The Judiciary: Independence' (see HL Deb vol 554, cols 751–804, 27 April 1994) where he stated (at col 791):

I personally believe very strongly and fundamentally in the independence of the judiciary. I also believe that it is vitally important for the Lord Chancellor to do all he can to preserve the independence of the judiciary.

This debate, however, was initiated by the then Shadow Lord Chancellor, Lord Irvine of Lairg, following concerns that Lord Mackay had sought to interfere with the way in which the President of the Employment Appeal Tribunal, Mr Justice Wood, implemented procedures for dealing with notices of appeal to the Tribunal. The EAT may only deal with appeals from decisions of Industrial Tribunals which disclose a point of law. The procedure to be followed is laid down in the Employment Appeal Tribunal Rules 1980 (SI 1980 No. 2035) which were made by the Lord Chancellor under the Employment Protection (Consolidation) Act 1978, s. 35 and Schedule 11. Rule 3(2) provided:

Where it appears to the Registrar that the grounds of appeal stated in the notice of appeal do not give the Appeal Tribunal jurisdiction to entertain the appeal, he shall notify the appellant accordingly informing him of the reasons for the opinion and, subject to paragraph . . . (5) of this rule, no further action shall be taken on the appeal.

By 1990 there was a serious backlog of cases and the Lord Chancellor and Treasury made it clear that it was unlikely that additional High Court judges would be appointed. On 1 May 1992 following written proposals which were discussed at the AGM of the Tribunal in April, Mr Justice Wood introduced a new form of procedure which involved the possibility of a preliminary oral hearing before a judge if he considered that justice required it, to assist in determining whether the notice of appeal contained a point of law. The Lord Chancellor considered that this did not comply with the rules and that it was slowing down the processing of appeals. In December 1992 he commenced correspondence with Mr Justice Wood.

Letter dated December 18, 1992 from Lord Mackay to Mr Justice Wood

As you know, over the last year and more, I have been concerned at the growing backlog of cases at the EAT. . . . I wish to ensure that public money is not wasted on preliminary hearings in cases where there is no point of law shown in the Notice of Appeal. I am disappointed to note that you are still making little use of the power which Rule 3 gives you to reject notices which in your opinion show no point of law to give the tribunal jurisdiction to register the appeal.

I need hardly remind you that the backlog of cases in England and Wales started the year at an unacceptably high level and has continued to rise rapidly. I cannot sit by and watch the state of affairs get worse. Equally, I am unwilling to commit more expensive resources in the way of judges to sit extra courts while procedural rules which allow for cheap and efficient disposal of clearly unmeritorious cases might be used to much greater effect.

A meeting took place between Mr Justice Wood and Lord Mackay on 1 February 1993 followed by a further exchange of letters in which Lord Mackay encouraged Mr Justice Wood to use Rule 3 in full to dismiss 'unmeritorious' or 'hopeless' appeals. Mr Justice Wood responded on 5 March 1993, by indicating that preliminary hearings were not used in the case of 'unmeritorious' or 'hopeless' appeals but only in the case of ambiguous notices stating:

In these ambiguous cases my predecessors have clearly thought it expeditious, economical and conducive to justice to resolve the ambiguity by fixing an early oral hearing. I share their view, and cannot see any alternative way of fairly resolving the problem. . . .

Letter dated 19 March 1993 from Lord Mackay to Mr Justice Wood

I did not seek further discussion of Rule 3 but had sought to make it clear to you that I was not prepared to accept preliminary hearings being held where Rule 3 provides a cheap and expeditious procedure for final disposal of a purported appeal.

I ask you again for your immediate assurance that Rule 3 is henceforth to be applied in full and that preliminary hearings are not being used where no jurisdiction is shown in a notice of appeal.

If you do not feel you can give me that assurance, I must ask you to consider your position.

This letter was widely viewed as a demand for Mr Justice Wood to cease using preliminary hearings or resign although Lord Mackay denied this subsequently (see HL Deb vol 553, col 498, 21 March 1994).

Letter dated 23 April 1993 from Mr Justice Wood to Lord Mackay

In your letter of March 19 you express disappointment with my letter of the 5th and say that you do not wish further discussion of Rule 3. Both that letter and this are, of course, my own, but they have been written after consultation with many others on the Bench. The statement of the law in that letter is, in our view, correct.

Your letter also puts your criticisms in rather a different form. You refer specifically to Preliminary Hearing Procedures and demand, in effect, that they be phased out, save for use as the equivalent of a hearing for directions.

[Mr Justice Wood repeated the arguments he had made previously justifying the use of preliminary hearings and concluded the letter:]

I have, of course, given the most serious consideration to my position as you required of me. You have demanded that I exercise my judicial function in a way which you regard as best suited to your Executive purposes, but I have to say that in all the circumstances that present themselves to me and in the light of the existing law, I cannot regard compliance with your demand as conducive to justice.

You express disappointment. I express profound regret that it has ever been the uncomfortable duty of a judge in this country in compliance with his Judicial Oath, to write to a Lord Chancellor refusing a demand such as the one which you have made of me.

The Lord Chancellor's Private Secretary formally acknowledged receipt of this letter on 5 May 1993 stating that the Lord Chancellor would reply shortly; he never did. In March and April 1994 the *Observer* ran stories about this dispute between Mr Justice Wood and Lord Mackay. The issues were fully aired in the debate in the House of Lords on 27 April 1994.

The Judiciary: Independence
House of Lords, HL Deb vol. 554, cols. 751–804 April 27, 1994

Lord Irvine of Lairg rose to ask Her Majesty's Government whether, given the documents placed by the Lord Chancellor in the Library of the House concerning the differences arising during the period 1991 to 1993 between him and the then President of the Employment Appeal Tribunal, Mr Justice Wood, on the proper procedures for dealing with notices of appeal to that Tribunal, they are satisfied that the independence of the judiciary has been upheld.

The noble Lord said: My Lords, this debate is not of narrow interest to lawyers and judges alone. It is about the fundamental principle, vital for all, that the courts are wholly independent of the Executive. Our constitution, largely unwritten, is firmly based on the separation of powers. Parliament makes laws; the judiciary interprets and applies them. Thus, the fundamental principle is that the courts must be wholly independent of the Executive. I am confident that the noble and learned Lord would be the first to affirm that fundamental principal. . . . For myself, I would be disposed to accept – others may disagree – that a Lord Chancellor is entitled to satisfy himself that any court is having regard to all its powers and duties for the efficient disposal of its business and is applying and fulfilling them in accordance with its own judicial interpretation of them. However, what a Lord Chancellor is not entitled to do is to demand that a judge or court substitute for its own judicial view of the extent of its powers and duties the extra-judicial views of the Lord Chancellor. I invite the noble and learned Lord the Lord Chancellor to say whether he agrees with those propositions; and to make clear the powers he conceives that he has – and had, in relation to Sir John Wood – and how those powers arise.

LORD DONALDSON OF LYMINGTON: . . . The third issue concerns the perception of the noble and learned Lord the Lord Chancellor of his dual role as a judge and as a Minister. When in 1971 the NIRC [National Industrial Relations Court] was established, the noble Lord, Lord Carr of Hadley, was the Secretary of State for Employment. I well remember his asking me on a social occasion whether, as president, I was responsible to the Lord Chancellor or to the Lord Chief Justice. I replied that I was responsible to neither. I was responsible solely to the law and to my own conscience. I have no doubt that I was right. That is what the independence of the judiciary is all about. The judiciary as a whole is independent of the Executive. But it must never be forgotten that every judge is independent of every other judge.

The position was, in some ways to my regret, no different 11 years later when I was appointed Master of the Rolls. I could invite; I could advise; I could seek to persuade; I could, if you will, exercise leadership. But I could never require a Lord Justice to do or to refrain from doing anything, and I never sought to do so.

The Lord Chancellor in his capacity as head of the judiciary is in no different a position. He could and did seek to persuade Sir John Wood that Sir John was not making full and proper use of the Rule 3 procedure as required by the law. But if that failed – as it did – there was nothing further that he could do in his judicial capacity. No judge can ask another judge for an undertaking – still less an undertaking in writing which casts doubt upon the validity of an oral undertaking given by the judge – that he will act contrary to the law as that judge sees it. Still less can he be asked to 'consider his position' if he refuses.

In his capacity as a Minister, the Lord Chancellor is responsible to Parliament for the administration of justice. That responsibility is not, however, unlimited. It extends only to the extent that Parliament has given him authority to supply or withhold resources or give directions. If Sir John Wood's view of the true scope of the Rule 3 procedure was unacceptable to the Lord Chancellor in his capacity as a Minister, his only remedy was to secure an amendment of Rule 3 putting his interpretation beyond doubt. Had he done so, I am absolutely certain that Sir John would have given effect to the rule as amended.

This apparent lack of accountability on the part of the judiciary may well seem an odd situation, particularly in this day and age when we hear so much about accountability. Our freedom under the law depends upon it, and I have to say that it has stood the test of time. That it can produce what has been described as constructive friction between the judiciary on the one hand and the Lord Chancellor and his department on the other is not open to doubt. However, given the necessary degree of sensitivity on both sides, the emphasis is usually upon the word 'constructive' rather than upon the word 'friction'.

LORD OLIVER OF AYLMERTON: . . . We have no written constitution, but the concept of judicial independence, which goes back to the Act of Settlement, is one with which we have all grown up. It is a concept of no very certain content and there is concern both in the judiciary and in the legal profession now that in recent years, under pressure from government, from civil servants and particularly from the Treasury, it is being more and more narrowly construed with an eye more to what is boasted to be 'value for money' than to fairness and impartiality in our system of justice. . . .

His Lordship referred to Lord Denning's presidential address to the Holdsworth Club in 1950 (*ante* p. 193).

I would have hoped that what my noble and learned friend Lord Denning said was so well entrenched in our constitution that it could not be challenged. Recent pronouncements in this House have seemed to indicate that the noble and learned Lord the Lord Chancellor and his department interpret the principle of judicial independence in a very much more restricted sense and as meaning simply this: that judicial independence is infringed only if an attempt is made to indicate or influence the decision in a particular individual case. I hope very much that I am wrong about that because one has only to think about it to see where the logical train then leads. On that analysis, a direction in the 1930s by the German Ministry of Justice that judges were not to decide disputes in favour of members of the Jewish faith or against party members would have been no infringement of their judicial independence – and that, of course, is palpably absurd. . . .

Was the constitutional principle of judicial independence infringed by what occurred in this case? The noble and learned Lord the Lord Chancellor did not, I feel quite sure, have any intention whatever to overstep the bounds of his constitutional authority, but I am bound to say that it seems to me that on any analysis at all the pressure which was applied in this case, for whatever reason, constituted an attempt by the Executive – no doubt in the praiseworthy interests of economy and expedition – to overbear the conscience of a judge in the way in which he was to exercise his judicial duty and his judicial discretion – not, it is true, in an individual case but in the case generally of those individuals who are not sufficiently articulate to make it clear beyond any doubt that they are within the jurisdiction which they seek to invoke. And in the case of a court many of whose clientele are without legal aid, without legal assistance, some of them ill-educated perhaps and some perhaps belonging to ethnic minorities without a full command of the English language, that is a matter of very grave public concern.

I recognise that there are a lot of people – I dare say that there are perhaps some noble Lords among them – who regard Her Majesty's judges as unduly sensitive about their independence from Executive interference, equiparating that with a claim to be immune from control and from any criticism. I do not, for my part, think that that is true or fair – but then I would say that, wouldn't I? But we are not talking about criticism. We are talking about interference with the judicial function – about dictation. I would remind the House that whatever failings there may be perceived to be in the judiciary, it is the judge alone who stands between the power of the state and the freedom of the individual under the law.

I also recognise – indeed, we must all recognise – the very real difficulties which confront the noble and learned Lord the Lord Chancellor in fulfilling his responsibilities for overseeing the administration of justice and in steering a course dictated by the multiplicity of hats which his office compels him to wear. Judges are, after all, human beings and they are susceptible to ordinary human frailty. If the noble and learned Lord forms the opinion that a judge is not doing his job properly – if, for instance, he spends more time on the golf course than in court, or if he does *The Times* crossword on the Bench, or brings discredit on his office by his private life – then it is, of course, his duty to take him to task, even, if necessary, to the extent of urging him to resign his office.

So we must all recognise the noble and learned Lord's difficulties and accept that he is right to be concerned with the proper deployment of judicial resources. It is he who has to answer for the perceived shortcomings in the administration of the courts and it is his right and his duty to counsel, to persuade and, if necessary, to criticise. But the question, as always, is: Where do you draw the line?

Advice, counsel, persuasion, criticism and, if need be, yes, protest fall on one side of the line. But Parliament has established an appellate hierarchy to correct judicial errors of law; and direct Executive interference or attempted interference in the way in which a judge conscientiously seeks to comply with his judicial oath is a different matter altogether. I have to say – and I say it with regret and with the utmost deference to the noble and learned Lord – that it is, I think, very difficult for anyone who has read this correspondence to accept that it did not fall on the wrong side of the line. It cannot be construed otherwise – and I know that the learned judge did so construe it – than as an attempt to coerce a judge to carry out his judicial function and exercise his judicial discretion in a manner contrary to the reasoned dictates of his own conscience.

THE LORD CHANCELLOR (LORD MACKAY OF CLASHFERN): . . . I personally believe very strongly and fundamentally in the independence of the judiciary. I also believe that it is vitally important for the Lord Chancellor to do all that he can to preserve the independence of the judiciary.

Judicial independence does not mean that judges are above the law. The rule of law applies to them and to their work. When Parliament in a statute provides rules to which a tribunal is subject, the judges who are members of that tribunal are, in my view, bound to apply those rules. . . .

What I asked Mr Justice Wood, then president of the EAT, in my letter of 19th March 1993, to do was to assure me that he would apply one of these rules as laid down for the EAT. This rule had been made, as the noble Lord, Lord Mishcon, said, as long ago as 1976, was modified in 1980 and was still in force in the form then modified in 1991, 1992 and 1993 – that is, in the whole period to which the correspondence referred to in the question of the noble Lord, Lord Irvine of Lairg, relates. I did not ask Mr Justice Wood to adopt my reading of the rule. Contrary to what has been suggested, I had no quarrel with his reading of the rule, as given in his lengthy letter, which preceded the letter of 19th March. . . .

My situation is that all through this correspondence I was concerned to ensure that the rules laid down by Parliament were being operated by Mr Justice Wood and the Employment Appeal Tribunal as a whole. I was not substituting my reading of the rules for his reading or anything of that kind. I was anxious that he should apply the rules as he understood them.

EARL RUSSELL: My Lords, I am grateful to the noble and learned Lord for giving way, but could he say whether Mr Justice Wood ever failed to observe the rules as he, Mr Justice Wood, understood them?

THE LORD CHANCELLOR: My Lords, it is as clear as a pikestaff. I thought that I had made it clear; but obviously I have failed. I shall try to make it clear now. Mr Justice Wood was not applying the rule at all at the beginning of this correspondence. He made it perfectly plain, as I understand it, that he did not think that that rule was suitable for use in England and Wales. That is the passage that I read from the very first document. I do not know whether the noble Earl has the document. I regard this as extremely important because it is fundamental to my whole approach to the situation, and I should not like the noble Earl to be in any difficulty about it. On page 5 of the first document he states:

> 'There are remarkably few cases which are clearly frivolous on the face of the documentation. This is really a case of *de minimis*. In Scotland an HEO (unqualified) sends an appeal back to the appellant as disclosing no point of law if he so thinks. There is an appeal from him to the Judge. Having considered this rather different procedure I do not consider it desirable here in England and Wales nor do I like it particularly.'

The procedure to which he refers is Rule 3 of the employment appeal rules—

EARL RUSSELL: My Lords, I am sorry to intervene again, but can the noble and learned Lord show us that Mr Justice Wood was contravening Rule 3(2) as he understood it?

THE LORD CHANCELLOR: My Lords, he was not applying it at all. There is no question of a difficulty of interpretation: he was just not applying the rule at all. He thought it was unsuitable. He did not consider the procedure under the rule,

'desirable here in England and Wales nor do I like it particularly.'

He was declining to apply it altogether. It was not a question of the rule as he understood it; he was not applying it at all. That is a much more fundamental point. I hope that I have made it clear now.

That was the position that I encountered. It has been said more than once that I was seeking to rule out the use of the procedures of preliminary hearings in cases that were doubtful. That is not my position and never has been. What I asked from Mr Justice Wood in the ultimate letter was, as I said, an assurance that he was fully applying the rule. If he was not prepared to give me that assurance, he should consider his position. . . . I have never suggested that it is not appropriate to use preliminary hearings in a doubtful case. What I have suggested, and what I think Mr Justice Wood agreed, was that it was not appropriate for preliminary hearings to be used in a case in which it was clear that there was no jurisdiction in the tribunal. . . .

I was asking him to give me the assurance that he was applying the rule which Parliament had laid down to regulate the affairs of the Employment Appeal Tribunal. I see that my noble and learned friend wishes to intervene. I give way.

LORD ACKNER: My Lords, I am much obliged. Can my noble and learned friend tell the House exactly what are his criticisms of the letter from Mr Justice Wood of 5th March 1993?

THE LORD CHANCELLOR: My lords, I have no particular criticism of the letter. I am saying that the letter sets out Mr Justice Wood's understanding of the rule. I have no quarrel with that. However, what I did find absent from the letter was an undertaking by Mr Justice Wood that he would apply the rule. That is an important difference – that he would apply the rule. Your Lordships may think that the distinction is not important, but I believe that I will be able to show the House that it is.

LORD CALLAGHAN OF CARDIFF: My Lords, I am struggling to try to get to the truth of the matter. I just do not understand – and I apologise to all the other distinguished Members here who do – the status of such rules of Parliament. Is the Lord Chancellor the final arbiter of their meaning? Alternatively, is there some other body which is able to determine how the rules should be applied if there is a difference between a judge and the Lord Chancellor? For example, is there any appeal available?

THE LORD CHANCELLOR: My Lords, if there is a question of the meaning of the rule between myself and somebody else, I could have that determined in the court, if it were necessary. But this was not a question of the meaning of the rule. He was setting out the meaning of the rule at great length but I had not asked for that. What I had asked him for was an assurance that he was applying the rule, because your Lordships will remember that this correspondence started with an analysis by Mr Justice Wood in which he said this rule was not appropriate for England and Wales for reasons which he gave.

Parliament, or at least the Lord Chancellor under the authority of Parliament, had enacted the rule for England and Wales and had done so, in its form then in operation, in 1980. Therefore the opinion of Mr Justice Wood as to whether or not it was a good rule was of absolutely no consequence. So far as I was concerned, there was no dispute whatever between me and Mr Justice Wood about the meaning of the rule. What I wanted to know was whether he was applying the rule, and if he was applying the rule there was no problem about him saying so. He could give me that undertaking perfectly well. But he was not applying the rule, why not – not or else. Why not? 'What is your position? You are a statutory tribunal operating statutory rules. If you are not able to give me an assurance that you are applying the rules applicable to the tribunal, what is your explanation? What is your position? Consider it very carefully', because it must be quite wrong for a judge, subject to rules laid down by Parliament, not to apply them. That is the crux of this matter.

The response from Mr Justice Wood to my letter makes no reference whatever to terminating his position either as the President of the Employment Appeal Tribunal or as a judge. None whatever. I am not directing this correspondence to anyone except Mr Justice Wood; and he certainly did not in this letter of reply make any reference whatsoever to his entitlement to office as a judge, or as the President of Appeal Tribunal. What he says, in effect, is 'I am not giving this undertaking because it is contrary to my judicial oath'. I summarise as your Lordships have heard the whole letter. The point I make about that is that the judicial oath is that, 'I would write to all manner of persons according to the laws and usages of this realm'. So far as this is concerned, one of these laws was Rule 3 of the Employment Appeal Tribunal rules. I still do not understand why that undertaking was not given, but there was hope in his letter of 23rd April 1993 which states at the foot of page 1:

> 'In May 1992, in anticipation of the vast increase in the number of appeals, we introduced a new system under Rule 3'.

That is when he began to move from his original position as stated at the beginning of the document to the operation of Rule 3. The letter continues:

> 'We would not claim that it is perfect, and with experience it is being refined'.

So Mr Justice Wood was telling me that procedures in his EAT were moving, and I was delighted with that and anxious to see that that would happen. That is the reason I gave no further response to Mr Justice Wood, because I had seen before that he reacted quite strongly in his paper that went round the EAT to pressure being put on him to apply the rules as Parliament had enacted them. But then after a while, in May 1992, he did in fact make a move. I had hoped that the corresponding thing would happen after April 1993 and that he would fully apply the rule.

Many noble Lords have said that this has been a most unhappy debate. Your Lordships will understand that it has been a most unhappy matter for me ever since this matter arose. I certainly very greatly regret that this arose between me and Mr Justice Wood; and certainly looking back on it now with hindsight I wish that I had expressed myself more plainly. But I am absolutely satisfied that the basic matter that I was seeking is a matter to which I was well entitled under the law of this land and was in no way prejudicial to the proper judicial independence of the judge. I am a strong believer in the independence of the judiciary individually and as a whole; and so long as I have the privilege of holding the office which I do, I shall do everything in my power to uphold that. But it is part of the principle that that independence is exercised according to and under the rule of law and I have responsibility for that also.

Some wider matters have been raised in the debate, going beyond what was mentioned in the Question. The office of the Lord Chancellor is a difficult one: I can attest to that. However, I do not think that it is easy to work out, against the background of our system, a good alternative that would protect, as this office does, the independence of the judiciary. I believe that it is important that in this country the Supply for the Crown is voted by the House of Commons. Therefore, it is necessary that there be some person accountable to Parliament who has responsibility for the courts. I believe that the arrangement under which the Lord Chancellor, as head of the judiciary, is also responsible to Parliament for the administration of the courts is probably as good an arrangement as we can achieve. I am open to detailed suggestions as to how this might be done. I know that some of my noble and learned friends in previous incarnations have been asked to provide me with some detail of their thoughts on these matters. However, I know that it is so difficult that the thoughts in writing are still awaited.

As I said at the outset, I am extremely grateful to the noble Lord, Lord Irvine of Lairg, for raising the matter, and also for the manner in which he raised it. It was put forward in a fair manner, giving me an opportunity to explain the matter fully. I greatly regret that I have taken much longer in doing so then I should normally have liked to, but I regard the matter as of fundamental importance, as your Lordships have done. It is important that your Lordships should understand that I was not telling this judge how to do his work. All I was telling him was that I wished him to give me the assurance that he was applying the rules which had been enacted under the authority of Parliament by my predecessors as Lord Chancellor.

I utterly repudiate any suggestion that I have wrongfully interfered with the independence of the judiciary or that I have in any way misled your Lordships at any time in the answers that I have given. I thoroughly believe that my answer was as truthful and as full as I could possibly give in the circumstances of an oral Question.

I also take the view that these are matters of importance about which we need continually to be on our guard. I am extremely sorry if I have caused any offence whatever to Mr Justice Wood. If I could have thought of better language, with hindsight I would have used it. But I was thinking entirely of the position which he had as a judge in a statutory tribunal with statutory rules. That is what I had in mind, nothing else. The letter was directed to him and not to anyone else.

I am grateful to your Lordships for your patience in listening to this, I do not wish to trespass on that patience any longer. . . .

QUESTIONS

1. Was the Lord Chancellor guilty of unwarranted Executive interference in judicial affairs?

2. Should financial considerations take priority over the demands of justice? Is it for the judiciary or the Executive to determine what the 'demands of justice' are?

3. Is there a need to reconsider the office of Lord Chancellor as suggested by Lord Lester of Herne Hill in the above debate:

I recognise that the Lord Chancellor has a duty to ensure that the legal system is efficiently administered and that it is financially accountable. I share the view of the noble Lord, Lord Irvine of Lairg, about that. Judicial independence does not mean that judges should be immune from being disciplined when they fail to perform their duties properly; or that the budget for the legal system is to be determined by the judges rather than by Parliament. But what it does mean, I suggest, is that the old system has become, in the office of Lord Chancellor, too institutionally schizophrenic to be able to reconcile the divergent, and to some extent inconsistent, requirements of public accountability, judicial independence and efficiency in the administration of justice. We surely need some new institution, some kind of judicial and legal services commission to protect the independence of the judges and of the legal profession from the pressures which the Lord Chancellor, as a politically active and administratively vigorous Minister of Justice, and his officials are driven to exert.

NOTE: The issue of judicial independence has arisen in a different context recently in Scotland following devolution, which resulted in the Human Rights Act 1998 coming into force.

Starrs and Chalmers v *Procurator Fiscal, Linlithgow*
11 November 1999, High Court of Justiciary (Appeal)

The complainers were on trial for summary offences before a temporary sheriff in Linlithgow sheriff court. The complainers raised a 'devolution issue', namely that trial before a temporary sheriff was incompatible with an accused person's right to a fair hearing before an independent and impartial tribunal under Article 6 of the European Convention. The sheriff ruled against the complainers who appealed to the High Court by bills of advocation.

LORD REED: . . . Article 6 paragraph 1 of the European Convention on Human Rights provides *inter alia*:

> In the determination of his civil rights and obligations or of any criminal charge against him, everyone is entitled to a fair and public hearing within a reasonable time by an independent and impartial tribunal established by law.

The principal issue raised in these appeals is whether that right is violated by the trial of an accused person before a temporary sheriff. . . .

The issue arises in consequence of the enactment of the Scotland Act 1998. Section 57(2) of that Act provides:

> A member of the Scottish Executive has no power to make any subordinate legislation, or to do any other act, so far as the legislation or act is incompatible with any of the Convention rights or with community law.

The Lord Advocate is a member of the Scottish Executive: section 44(1)(c). It is conceded by the Solicitor General for Scotland, who represented the Lord Advocate in the proceedings before us, that the prosecution of a trial by a procurator fiscal or one of his or her deputes involves a number of steps which amount to 'acts' within the meaning of section 57(2), and that those acts are to be treated as the acts of the Scottish Executive for the purposes of that provision. The 'Convention rights' to which section 57(2) refers include the rights guaranteed by Article 6 of the European Convention on Human Rights: section 126(1) of the Scotland Act, read with section 1(1)(a) of the Human Rights Act 1998. Accordingly, subject to section 57(3) of the Scotland Act (which excludes the application of section 57(2) in certain specified circumstances), it is *ultra vires* for a procurator fiscal to prosecute a trial before a temporary sheriff if such a sheriff is not an independent and impartial tribunal within the meaning of Article 6.

Temporary sheriffs are a statutory creation. The relevant provisions are contained in section 11 of the Sheriff Courts (Scotland) Act 1971. Section 11(1) (which has subsequently been substituted by the Law Reform (Miscellaneous Provisions) (Scotland) Act 1980) deals with the appointment of temporary sheriffs principal. Section 11(2) is in the following terms:

> Where as regards any sheriffdom—
> (a) a sheriff is by reason of illness or otherwise unable to perform his duties as sheriff, or
> (b) a vacancy occurs in the office of sheriff, or
> (c) for any other reason it appears to the Secretary of State expedient so to do in order to avoid delay in the administration of justice in that the sheriffdom,
> the Secretary of State may appoint a person (to be known as a temporary sheriff) to act as a sheriff for the sheriffdom.

The Solicitor General explained to us that all appointments are made under section 11(2)(c). The words 'for any other reason', in subsection (2)(c), are not construed *eiusdem generis* with illness, inability or a vacancy in subsection (2)(a) and (b). They are not, in other words, construed as referring to some temporary exigency (other than illness, inability or a vacancy) which the Secretary of State has identified in a particular sheriffdom. They are construed as conferring a wide discretion on the Secretary of State which can be used, as it has been used, to create a large pool of persons, each appointed to act as a sheriff for every sheriffdom in Scotland, and available to supplement the permanent sheriffs as and when the need arises, to the extent of performing (at present) 25% of the total workload.

Section 11(3) stipulates the formal qualification for appointment as a temporary sheriff, namely qualification as an advocate or solicitor for at least five years. This is a lesser requirement than for appointment on a permanent basis, for which the minimum period is ten years: section 5(1).

Section 11(4) provides:

> The appointment of a temporary sheriff principal or of a temporary sheriff shall subsist until recalled by the Secretary of State.

The Solicitor General accepted that the effect of this provision is that a temporary sheriff holds office at pleasure. . . . Section 11(4) can be contrasted with the provisions of section 12, which provide security of tenure to permanent sheriffs. Under section 12, a permanent sheriff can be removed from office only by an order which is subject to annulment in pursuance of a resolution of either House of Parliament. Such an order can only be made on a report by the Lord President and the Lord Justice Clerk to the effect that the sheriff is unfit for office by reason of inability, neglect of duty or misbehaviour. Such a report can only be made following an investigation by the Lord President and the Lord Justice Clerk. These provisions, the history and effect of which are discussed in *Stewart* v *Secretary of State for Scotland*, 1998 SC (HL) 81, strengthened the protection previously given to sheriffs, in accordance with recommendations contained in the Report of the Grant Committee on the Sheriff Court (Cmnd. 3248, 1967). Temporary sheriffs are expressly excluded from the scope of these provisions: section 12(7).

. . .

The temporary sheriffs form a pool of persons who have been actually appointed to shrieval office, rather than a pool from whom appointments might be made when occasion arose. Far from the pool existing so as to avoid willingness to act being construed as a desire for a permanent appointment, membership of the pool of temporary sheriffs has increasingly come to be coveted as a step on the road towards a permanent appointment, and on the Lord Advocate's side it has equally come to be seen to some extent as, in effect, a probationary period during which potential candidates for a permanent appointment can be assessed.

. . .

In relation to section 11(4), the Solicitor General accepted that this impliedly conferred upon the Secretary of State a power to recall the appointment at will. . . . It was common ground that section 11(4) in particular provided no security of tenure whatsoever for temporary sheriffs. The issue in dispute, so far as security of tenure was concerned, was whether the degree of protection which in practice existed, as a consequence of the involvement of the Lord Advocate and his independence from the political process, was sufficient to satisfy the requirements of Article 6 of the Convention.

. . .

As I have mentioned, the Solicitor General's position was that section 11(4) implicitly conferred an unlimited power to recall, with the consequence that temporary sheriffs held office at pleasure, protected only by the integrity and good sense of the Lord Advocate. There was no duty to give reasons for the recall of an appointment. It was not suggested that there was scope for any close scrutiny of decisions to recall an appointment by way of judicial review. This was also the position of the appellants.

. . .

I turn next to consider whether the temporary sheriff is an 'independent and impartial tribunal' within the meaning of Article 6 paragraph 1 of the Convention. It should be noted at the outset that it is not sufficient for the purposes of Article 6 that an independent and impartial tribunal is available at the level of an appellate court, where the subject matter of the proceedings is a criminal charge. The accused person is entitled to be tried at first instance by a court which fully meets the requirements of Article 6 paragraph 1: see the *De Cubber* judgment of 26 October 1984, Series A no. 86, paras 31–32; and the *Findlay* judgment of 25 February 1997, Reports of Judgments and Decisions, 1997-I, para. 79.

In order to establish whether a body can be considered to be 'independent', regard must be had, *inter alia*, to the manner of appointment of its members and their term of office, to the existence of guarantees against outside pressures and to the question whether the body presents an appearance of independence: see, *inter alia*, the *Bryan* judgment of 22 November 1995, Series A no. 335-A, para. 37.

Considering first the manner of appointment of temporary sheriffs, the Solicitor General maintained that appointment by the Executive was not objectionable, and founded upon the *Campbell and Fell* judgment of 28 June 1984, Series A no. 80, para. 79. The Solicitor General founded in particular on the observation in *Campbell and Fell* that judges can be appointed by or on the advice of a Minister having responsibilities in the field of the administration of the courts, without losing their independence.

So far as the initial appointment (rather than the subsequent renewal of appointments) of temporary sheriffs is concerned, I agree that appointment by the Executive is not inherently objectionable.
. . .

Considering next the term of office of temporary sheriffs, the appointment is expressed so as to subsist for twelve months unless previously recalled.
. . .

A short term of office is not, in my opinion, necessarily objectionable . . . Temporary appointments are however apt to create particular problems from the point of view of independence, particularly where the duration of the appointment is not fixed so as to expire upon the completion of a particular task or upon the cessation of a particular state of affairs (such as some emergency or exigency), but is a fixed period of time of relatively short duration. In particular, such a term of office is liable to compromise the judge's independence where the appointment can be renewed, as the European Court of Human Rights recognised in the *Çiraklar* judgment [judgment of 28 October 1998, Reports of Judgments and Decisions 1998-VII, where the European Court of Human Rights indicated (at para. 39) that a term of office which lasted only four years, and could be renewed, was a factor pointing towards a lack of independence]. The possibility of renewal was also emphasised by the Commission in its Opinion in the same case (at para. 46). The same point has also been emphasised in other cases (e.g. the *Incal* judgment of 9 June 1998, Reports of Judgments and Decisions 1998-IV). As is stated in the European Charter on the statute for judges, adopted in Strasbourg in July 1998 under the auspices of the Council of Europe (DAJ/DOC (98) 23) (at para. 3.3.)

> Clearly, the existence of probationary periods or renewal requirements presents difficulties if not dangers from the angle of the independence and impartiality of the judge in question, who is hoping to be established in post or to have his or her contract renewed.

Other international instruments demonstrate an equal awareness of these dangers. For example, the Universal Declaration on the Independence of Justice, adopted in Montreal in June 1983 by the World Conference on the Independence of Justice (UN DOC.E/CN.4/Subs.2/1985/18/Add.6 Annex IV), provides (at para. 2.20):

> The appointment of temporary judges and the appointment of judges for probationary periods is inconsistent with judicial independence. Where such appointments exist, they should be phased out gradually.

The European Charter and the Universal Declaration are not legally binding instruments, but they indicate the way in which international opinion has developed, and the existence of a consensus as to the dangers posed to judicial independence by short renewable periods of appointment. . . . I also note that the United Kingdom practice of appointing temporary judges appears to be unusual within a European context (see S. Shetreet and J. Deschenes, *Judicial Independence: The Contemporary Debate* (1985), at pp. 35 . . .): it appears that in almost all the other systems surveyed the appointment of a temporary judge by the Executive for a period of one year, renewable at the discretion of the Executive, would be regarded as unconstitutional.

So far as temporary sheriffs are concerned, the period of one year is in itself much shorter than the periods considered in the *Campbell and Fell*, *Çiraklar* and *Incal* judgments. What to my mind is of critical importance, however, is that renewal is both possible and expected, but is at the discretion of the Executive. In effect, temporary sheriffs have their judicial careers broken up into segments of one year, so as to provide the Executive with the possibility of re-considering their appointment on an annual basis. This has obvious implications for security of tenure . . . It also appears to me to be important that temporary sheriffs may well be potential candidates for a permanent appointment in the event of a vacancy occurring, as is recognised in the notes issued to candidates for appointment as temporary sheriffs. The danger to judicial independence in such circumstances is subtle, but has been well described by Kirby J of the High Court of Australia, speaking extra-judicially, in a paper which was drawn to our attention:

> But what of the lawyer who would welcome a permanent appointment? What of the problem of such a lawyer faced with a decision which might be very upsetting to government, unpopular with the media or disturbing to some powerful body with influence? Anecdotal stories soon spread about the 'form' of acting judges which may harm their chances of permanent appointment in a way that is unjust. Such psychological pressures, however subtle, should not be imposed on decision-makers.

('Independence of the Judiciary – Basic Principles, New Challenges', delivered to a Human Rights Institute Conference organised by the International Bar Association on 12 June 1998.) The then Chief Justice of Australia, Sir Gerard Brennan, has also drawn attention to the threat to judicial independence posed by the appointment of acting judges, observing that 'judicial independence is at risk when future appointment or security of tenure is within the gift of the executive' ('The State of the Judicature', (1998) 72 ALJ 33, 34).

Given that temporary sheriffs are very often persons who are hoping for graduation to a permanent appointment, and at the least for the renewal of their temporary appointment, the system of short renewable appointments creates a situation in which the temporary sheriff is liable to have hopes and fears in respect of his treatment by the Executive when his appointment comes up for renewal: in short, a relationship of dependency. This is in my opinion a factor pointing strongly away from 'independence' within the meaning of Article 6.

. . .

The next matter to be considered is the existence of guarantees against outside pressures. In this regard, counsel for the appellants founded upon a number of factors. They submitted in the first place that the power to recall the appointment of a temporary sheriff, or to decline to renew the appointment, is vested in the Scottish Executive, and in practice is exercised by the Lord Advocate. The temporary sheriff can even be deprived of his appointment in substance by being informally 'sidelined', without any formal recall or non-renewal, if he incurs the displeasure of officials. The consequence is to make the temporary sheriff entirely dependent upon the Scottish Executive, and in particular upon the Lord Advocate, for the continuation and renewal of his appointment. This, it was submitted, is particularly objectionable when the Scottish Executive, and in practice the Lord Advocate, is also responsible for making the permanent appointments which many temporary sheriffs are hoping to obtain. The objection becomes even more serious when it is appreciated that the Lord Advocate is also responsible for the criminal prosecutions which take place before temporary sheriffs. For the temporary sheriff to occupy a role subordinate to one of the parties to proceedings before him is, it was submitted, inconsistent with judicial independence. Reference was made in that regard to the *Sramek* judgment of 22 October 1984, Series A No. 84, and to the *Piersack* judgment of 1 October 1982, Series A No. 53.

Secondly, counsel for the appellants founded upon the absence of any security of tenure by temporary sheriffs. The power to recall an appointment, or to decline to renew it, or to deprive it of substance by failing or refusing to provide work, was not subject to any formal control, either as to the criteria to be applied or as to the procedures to be followed. Counsel emphasised the contrast, in this regard, between the insecure position of temporary sheriffs and the security afforded to permanent sheriffs.

Thirdly, counsel for the appellants founded upon the lack of financial security enjoyed by temporary sheriffs, and the consequent pressure upon them to hope for a permanent appointment.
. . .

In my opinion, the most important of the three factors relied upon by the appellants is the absence of security of tenure. It was common ground before us that, as a matter of law, a temporary sheriff can be removed from office at any time for any reason. It was also common ground that a temporary sheriff can be appointed on an annual basis and that his allocation to courts, and the renewal of his appointment, are thereafter within the unfettered discretion of the Executive. . . . I am prepared to proceed on the basis that a temporary sheriff does not, as a matter of law, enjoy anything which constitutes security of tenure in the normally accepted sense of that term.

There can be no doubt as to the importance of security of tenure to judicial independence: it can reasonably be said to be one of the cornerstones of judicial independence. The critical importance of judicial security of tenure has been recognised in Scots law since at least the declaration in Article 13 of the Claim of Right 1689 (cap. 28, APS IX 38) that 'the changing the nature of the judges' gifts *ad vitam aut culpam* into commissions *durante beneplacito*' is 'contrary to law'. As Lord Blackburn said in *Mackay and Esslement* v *Lord Advocate*, 1937 SC 860, 865:

. . . if the office (being salaried) is judicial, then it is inconsistent with the common law nature of the office that its tenure should be precarious.

Security of tenure is similarly treated as fundamental in numerous international instruments. One example is the UN Basic Principles on the Independence of the Judiciary, adopted by General Assembly resolutions 40/32 (1985) and 40/146 (1985). Paragraphs 11 and 12 provide:

11. The term of office of judges, their independence, security, adequate remuneration, conditions of service, pensions and the age of retirement shall be adequately secured by law.

12. Judges, whether appointed or elected, shall have guaranteed tenure until a mandatory retirement age or the expiry of their term of office, where such exists.

The importance of security of tenure to temporary judges in particular is one of the principles stated in the Latimer House Guidelines, 'Parliamentary Supremacy and Judicial Independence' adopted by representatives of the Commonwealth Magistrates' and Judges' Association and other bodies in June 1998. They state (at para. 11.1):

Judicial appointments should normally be permanent; whilst in some jurisdictions, contract appointments may be inevitable, such appointments should be subject to appropriate security of tenure.

So far as the European Convention is concerned, the importance of security of tenure is equally well recognised. In *Application No. 7360/76, Zand* v *Austria* (1978) 15 DR 70, for example, the Commission stated (at para. 80):

. . . according to the principles of the rule of law in democratic states which is the common heritage of the European countries, the irremovability of judges during their term of office, whether it be for a limited period of time or for lifetime, is a necessary corollary of their independence from the Administration and thus included in the guarantees of Article 6(1) of the Convention.
. . .

It is apparent that the system as operated depends on an assessment by the Scottish Executive, or in practice an assessment by the Lord Advocate, of what should be regarded as grounds for removal from office (or as grounds for not renewing the appointment or for deciding not to allocate work to a particular temporary sheriff, which are in substance equivalent to removal from office), and of what general policies should be followed (e.g. as to retiral age). The practice may alter from time to time, as in fact happened when the age limit of 65 was introduced. I do not doubt that the system has been operated by successive Lords Advocate with integrity and sound judgment, free from political considerations, and with a careful regard to the need to respect judicial independence. That is no doubt why it has operated for so long without occasioning any widespread expression of public concern, although disquiet has on occasion been expressed by members of the judiciary and others in Parliament and in academic or professional contexts. There is however no objective guarantee of security of tenure, such as can be found in section 12 of the 1971 Act; and I regard the absence of such a guarantee as fatal to the compatibility of the present system with Article 6.

The Solicitor General emphasised that it is inconceivable that the Lord Advocate would interfere with the performance of judicial functions. I readily accept that; but that is not the point. Judicial independence can be threatened not only by interference by the Executive, but also by a judge's being influenced, consciously or unconsciously, by his hopes and fears as to his possible treatment by the Executive. It is for that reason that a judge must not be dependent on the Executive, however well the Executive may behave: 'independence' connotes the absence of dependence. It also has to be borne in mind that judicial independence exists to protect the integrity of the judiciary and confidence in the administration of justice, and thus society as a whole, in bad times as well as good. The adequacy of judicial independence cannot appropriately be tested on the assumption that the Executive will always behave with appropriate restraint: as the European Court of Human Rights has emphasised in its interpretation of Article 6, it is important that there be 'guarantees' against outside pressures. In short, for the judiciary to be dependent on the Executive flies in the face of the principle of the separation of powers which is central to the requirement of judicial independence in Article 6.

The same approach can be found in the judgment of the Supreme Court of Canada in *R v Valente* (1985) 34 DLR (4th) 161, delivered by Le Dain J, concerned with the question whether a court was an 'independent and impartial tribunal' within the meaning of section 11(d) of the Canadian Charter of Rights and Freedoms.

. . .

In *Valente*, Le Dain J said (at 169–170):

> Although there is obviously a close relationship between independence and impartiality, they are nevertheless separate and distinct values or requirements. Impartiality refers to a state of mind or attitude of the tribunal in relation to the issues and the parties in a particular case. The word 'impartial', as Howland CJO noted [in the lower court], connotes absence of bias actual or perceived. The word 'independent' in s. 11(d) reflects or embodies the traditional constitutional value of judicial independence. As such, it connotes not merely a state of mind or attitude in the actual exercise of judicial functions, but a status or relationship to others, particularly in the Executive Branch of government, that rests on objective conditions or guarantees.

In support of that approach, Le Dain J cited Article 6 of the European Convention. In a subsequent part of his judgment, Le Dain J disapproved the approach of the lower court, which had focused upon whether there could be any reasonable apprehension that the tribunal would not act in an independent manner in the particular adjudication, as confusing independence with impartiality.

I respectfully agree with the approach taken by Le Dain J, and in particular with his description of judicial independence as 'a status or relationship resting on objective conditions or guarantees', which I believe to be equally applicable to the concept of independence contained in Article 6. As the Supreme Court of Canada has subsequently explained, the requirement that there be objective guarantees follows from the fact that independence is a question of status: the objective guarantees define that status (*Reference re: Public Sector Pay Reduction Act (P.E.I.), s. 10* (1997) 150 DLR (4th) 577, 629, *per* Lamer CJC). Viewed in this way, the objective guarantees and the appearance of independence are not two entirely distinct concepts: rather, the objective guarantees must be such as to ensure an appearance of independence (*ibid*, at 630 *per* Lamer CJC). I also agree with the observation in *Valente* (at 176) that 'security of tenure, because of the importance that has tradition-ally been attached to it, must be regarded as the first of the essential conditions of judicial independence', and with the observation (at 180) that 'the essence of security of tenure . . . is a tenure, whether until an age of retirement, for a fixed term, or for a specific adjudicative task, that is secure against interference by the executive or other appointing authority in a discretionary or arbitrary manner.'

. . .

I would only add this. Conceptions of constitutional principles such as the independence of the judiciary, and of how those principles should be given effect in practice, change over time. Although the principle of judicial independence has found expression in similar language in Scotland and England since at least the late seventeenth century, conceptions of what it requires in substance – of what is necessary, or desirable, or feasible – have changed greatly since that time. What was regarded as acceptable even as recently as 1971 may no longer be regarded as acceptable. The effect given to the European Convention by the Scotland Act and the Human Rights Act in particular represents, to my mind, a very important shift in thinking about the constitution. It is fundamental to that shift that human rights are no longer dependent solely on conventions, by which I mean values, customs and practices of the constitution which are not legally enforceable. Although the Conven-tion protects rights which reflect democratic values and underpin democratic institutions, the Con-vention guarantees the protection of those rights through legal processes, rather than political processes. It is for that reason that Article 6 guarantees access to independent courts. It would be inconsistent with the whole approach of the Convention if the independence of those courts itself rested upon convention rather than law.

. . .

The remaining factors relied upon by the appellants do not appear to me to be in themselves fatal to judicial independence, but certain of them are relevant to my opinion that the one year renewable appointment, and the absence of security of tenure, are both objectionable. The fact that the power to recall or renew an appointment is vested in the Executive forms part of my reasoning in conclud-ing that temporary sheriffs lack independence. On the other hand, I am not persuaded that it is necessarily objectionable to have such powers vested in the Executive, provided adequate safe-guards exist (for example, safeguards of the same general nature as are found in section 12 of the 1971 Act or in section 95 of the Scotland Act). The fact that the Lord Advocate also has respons-ibilities as the head of the system of criminal prosecution in Scotland does not necessarily, in my opinion, create any additional problem, again provided that safeguards of the kind I have mentioned are in place. It is important to remember that the Lord Advocate's constitutional independence, now entrenched in the Scotland Act, has the consequence that his only ministerial interest in the conduct of a criminal trial should be to ensure that all the material evidence is placed before the court and that the charges against the accused are properly tried: he should have no ministerial interest in what the outcome of the trial may be (subject to his right to appeal against an unduly lenient sentence). The remaining matter referred to, namely the absence of financial security and the consequent aspiration by some temporary sheriffs for a permanent appointment, does not appear to me to raise an issue in itself under Article 6, but it is one of the factors landing me to conclude that a renewable annual appointment, without security of tenure, is inconsistent with judicial independence.

. . .

My conclusion is fortified by the requirement under Article 6 that the tribunal must present an appearance of independence. I understand this requirement to mean that the test of independence must include the question whether the tribunal should reasonably be perceived as independent. The importance of that question is that the tribunal must be one which commands public confidence:

otherwise, to adopt the words of Le Dain J in *Valente* (at 172), 'the system will not command the respect and acceptance that are essential to its effective operation'. Even if I were mistaken in my conclusion that the necessary objective guarantees of independence were lacking, it seems to me that the need for the temporary sheriff's appointment to be renewed annually at the discretion of the Executive, and his lack of security of tenure, are in any event factors which could give rise to a reasonable perception of dependence upon the Executive. The necessary appearance of independence is therefore in my opinion absent.

. . .

Appeals allowed. Bills of Advocation passed.

NOTE: Following the decision in *Starrs and Chalmers* v *P.F. Linlithgow*, no new business was allocated to temporary sheriffs. In the Bail, Judicial Appointments etc. (Scotland) Act 2000, s. 6 abolishes the position of temporary sheriff and s. 7 creates the new position of part-time sheriff to address the concerns about security of tenure raised in the High Court.

The Lord Chancellor carried out a review of the terms of service of part-time judicial office-holders in England and Wales, and Northern Ireland. On 12 April 2000 he announced that all Assistant Recorders would be appointed Recorders and that new arrangements to ensure independence would be brought in for part-time judicial appointments and certain part-time Tribunals appointments. The essential elements of the new arrangements are generally as follows:

(a) Part-time appointments will be for a period of not less than five years, subject to the relevant upper age limit.

(b) Where appointments are renewable this will normally be done automatically, except for limited and specified grounds.

(c) Removal from office will likewise be only on limited and specific grounds.

(d) Wherever it is administratively possible, the offer of a minimum number of sitting days will be guaranteed.

(e) Subject to statutory provision, the specified grounds for non-renewal will generally be:
   (i)   misbehaviour,
   (ii) incapacity,
   (iii) persistent failure to comply with sitting requirements (without good reason),
   (iv) failure to comply with training requirements,
   (v)   sustained failure to observe the standards reasonably expected from a holder of such office,
   (vi) part of a reduction in numbers because of changes in operational requirements,
   (vii) part of a structural change to enable recruitment of new appointees.

(f) The grounds for removal will generally be as at (i)–(v) above.

(g) Decisions not to renew or to remove on grounds (i)–(v) will be taken by the Lord Chancellor only with the concurrence of the Lord Chief Justice and following an investigation conducted by a judge nominated by him.

(h) Decisions not to renew on grounds (vi)–(vii) will be on a 'first in first out' principle and the decision to use such grounds and the extent to which they will be used will be decided by the Lord Chancellor with the concurrence of the Lord Chief Justice.

The Lord Chancellor's own position is open to question being, as he is, a member of the Legislature, Executive and Judiciary. This is particularly so following the decision of the European Court of Human Rights in *McGonnell* v *United Kingdom* (Application no. 28488/95), 8 February 2000. In Guernsey the Bailiff is President of the States of Election, President of the States of Deliberation, President of the Royal Court, President of the Court of Appeal and head of the Administration. As such he has legislative, executive, and judicial powers. The Bailiff had presided over the States of Deliberation, Guernsey's legislative body, when a development plan was adopted. This plan applied to McGonnell's land. McGonnell, having had planning permission to permit residential use of his land refused by Guernsey Island's Development Committee, appealed. His appeal was heard by the Guernsey Royal Court Bailiff and was rejected. McGonnell applied to the European Commission of Human Rights alleging a breach of Article 6(1). On a reference to the European Court of Human Rights, the Court found in his favour on the basis that even though it had not been suggested that the Bailiff had been subjectively biased, he had lacked the independence or objective impartiality required by the Convention due to his involvement in the legislative process relating to the development plan prior to his judicial involvement with McGonnell's appeal and, accordingly, McGonnell had legitimate reasons to assume his decision may have been influenced thereby.

The Lord Chancellor's position here may be subject to similar challenge. In particular, he played a key role in the legislative process resulting in the enactment of the Human Rights Act 1998 and has written and lectured widely on the subject (see Chapter 7 *post*). It would be difficult to envisage him being able to sit in a House of Lords case in his judicial capacity which involved any consideration of the Human Rights Act. It will be interesting to see whether one of the early casualties of the Human Rights Act is the very Minister who played such a central role in its passage through its parliamentary stages.

SECTION 3: Dicey and the Rule of Law

Dicey's views on the rule of law cannot be ignored because of the lasting influence he has had. His influence is all the more remarkable in light of the widespread criticisms which have been levelled against his views. Dicey's views derived from his understanding of the nature of representative democracy in the UK as 'unitary [and] self-correcting . . . in which the will of the electors was expressed through Parliament, and in which Parliament controlled the government' (P. Craig, *Public Law and Democracy in the United Kingdom and the United States of America* (1990)). In *An Introduction to the Study of the Law of the Constitution*, Dicey devoted a large part of the book to his exposition of the rule of law, to which he attributed three meanings. The views of Dicey's critics will be stated after each.

A: The rule of law and discretionary powers

A. V. Dicey, *An Introduction to the Study of the Law of the Constitution* (10th edn, 1965), pp. 188 and 202

We mean, in the first place, that no man is punishable or can be lawfully made to suffer in body or goods except for a distinct breach of law established in the ordinary legal manner before the ordinary courts of the land. In this sense the rule of law is contrasted with every system of government based on the exercise by persons in authority of wide, arbitrary, or discretionary powers of constraint. . . . It means . . . The absolute supremacy or predominance of regular law as opposed to the influence of arbitrary power, and excludes the existence of arbitrariness, of prerogative, or even of wide discretionary authority on the part of the government. Englishmen are ruled by the law, and by the law alone; a man may with us be punished for a breach of the law, but he can be punished for nothing else.

Sir Ivor Jennings, *The Law and the Constitution*
(5th edn, 1959), pp. 54–58

Dicey and the Rule of Law

The particular principle of the individualist or *laissez-faire* school was that any substantial discretionary power was a danger to liberty. The fact that he held such a principle was not explicitly avowed by Dicey, because he assumed that he was analysing not his own subjective notions (shared, of course, by many of his contemporaries), but the firm and unalterable principles of English constitutional law. . . . We need only contest the idea that the rule of law and discretionary powers are contradictory.

If we look around us we cannot fail to be aware that public authorities do in fact possess wide discretionary powers. Many of them formed part of the law even when Dicey wrote in 1885. Any court can punish me for contempt of court by imprisoning me for an indefinite period. If I am convicted of manslaughter, I may be released at once or imprisoned for life. If I am an alien, my naturalisation is entirely within the discretion of the Home Secretary. If the Queen declares war against the rest of the world, I am prohibited from having dealings abroad. If the country is in danger, my property can be taken, perhaps without compensation. If a public health authority wants to flood my land in order to build a reservoir, it can take it from me compulsorily. I can be compelled to leave my work for a month or more, in order to serve on a jury. All these powers, and many more, were possessed by public authorities in 1885, and can still be exercised.

Dicey did not mention all these, because nowhere in his book did he consider the *powers* of authorities. He seemed to think that the British Constitution was concerned almost entirely with the *rights of individuals*. He was imagining a constitution dominated by the doctrine of *laissez-faire*. The function of government, as he unconsciously assumed, was to protect the individual against internal and external aggression. Given such protection, each individual was allowed to live his life almost as he pleased, so long as he did not interfere with the similar liberty of others. He regarded this as desirable, and therefore tended to minimise the extent to which public authorities could interfere with private action. . . .

Nevertheless, the argument need not be placed entirely on this narrow ground. For the main discretionary power is placed in England not in the executive but in Parliament. Parliament, as has already been emphasised, can pass what legislation it pleases. It is not limited by any written constitution. Its powers are not only wide, but unlimited. In most countries, not only the administrative authorities but also the legislature have powers limited by the constitution. This, one would think, is the most effective rule of law. In England, the administration has powers limited by legislation, but the powers of the legislature are not limited at all. There is still, it may be argued, a rule of law, but the law is that the law may at any moment be changed.

Dicey attempts to meet this argument in two ways. 'The commands of Parliament,' he said, 'can be uttered only through the combined action of its three constituent parts, and must, therefore, always take the shape of formal and deliberate legislation.' Formal it may be; it may not be deliberate. We saw – Dicey saw before he died in 1922 – how the Defence of the Realm Act was passed in 1914. The Cabinet decided that it wanted drastic powers. The majority which it commanded in the House of Commons supported its motion to suspend the Standing Orders. The Bill was passed through at one sitting. The House of Lords did the same. Thus at one stroke, without any long deliberation, the Cabinet acquired the powers it needed. The 'gold standard' was similarly swept away in 1931. The Cabinet ordered the Bank of England not to exchange notes into gold. The next day Parliament met and the necessary legislation was passed through not only to make paper currency inconvertible, but also to ratify the illegal acts of the Cabinet and of the Bank before the Act was passed. Here was arbitrary power indeed, but it was by no means as arbitrary as the powers exercised by Parliament in 1939 and 1940.

R. F. V. Heuston, 'The Rule of Law' in *Essays in Constitutional Law*
(2nd edn, 1964), pp. 40–42

The Rule of Law and Discretionary Powers

Two criticisms have, however, been made of this aspect of Dicey's definition. First, it is said that it is difficult to distinguish between regular law and arbitrary power. If the law gives the power, how can it be arbitrary or irregular? It may be very undesirable for such a power to have been given, but if it has been given, and validly given according to the legislative forms of that particular society, how, it is said, can it be criticised as being contrary to the Rule of Law? . . . What is authorised by the law cannot indeed be illegal within the framework of that particular system, but it may very well be contrary to the Rule of Law as a principle of constitutional government. The difficulty no doubt arises from the fact that Dicey described his doctrine as 'the Rule of Law,' thereby giving the impression that it was in some way a legal principle, whereas it is in truth only a constitutional principle based upon the practice of liberal democracies of the Western world. In this sense, the doctrine is still perfectly true today. Everyone, high or low, must be prepared to justify his acts by a reference to some statutory or common law power which authorises him to act precisely in the way in which he claims he can act. Superior orders or state necessity are no defence to an action otherwise illegal.

Secondly, it has been said that Dicey erred in saying that the doctrine of the Rule of Law 'excludes the existence even of wide discretionary authority on the part of the government.' This is certainly not true today. Modern government, as is well known, cannot be carried on at all without a host of wide discretionary powers, which are granted to the executive by the large number of statutes annually passed by Parliament. But it must be remembered, first of all, the kind of man Dicey was, and secondly, the times in which he wrote. First, Dicey was in politics an old-fashioned Whig. He was also a very typical example of the common lawyer who does not seriously believe in the existence of the Statute Book. To the true common lawyer the law is to be found in the law reports and books of authority. There are indeed statutes, but they can always be looked up if the opportunity arises. The judges, as has been well said, have never entered into the spirit of the Benthamite game and have always treated the statute as an interloper upon the rounded majesty of the common law. Secondly, it must be recalled that Dicey's great work was written in the early 1880s, a period when the *laissez-faire* state of the Victorians was only just beginning to give way to the welfare state of the modern world. Dicey was an acute, a marvellously acute, judge of public opinion and of the impact upon public opinion of legislative power, but even he hardly foresaw the extent to which statutory powers of government would change the nature of English constitutional law. Today the fundamental problem is that of the control of discretionary powers, and it is indeed a serious criticism of Dicey's doctrine that he suggests that discretionary powers are in some way undesirable or unnecessary.

Kenneth Culp Davis, *Discretionary Justice*
(1971), pp. 17 and 42

Even when rules can be written, discretion is often better. Rules without discretion cannot fully take into account the need for tailoring results to unique facts and circumstances of particular cases. The justification for discretion is often the need for individualized justice. This is so in the judicial process as well as in the administrative process.

Every governmental and legal system in world history has involved both rules and discretion. No government has ever been a government of laws and not of men in the sense of eliminating all discretionary power. Every government has always been *a government of laws and of men*. A close look at the meaning of Aristotle, the first user of the phrase 'government of laws and not of men,' shows quite clearly that he did not mean that governments could exist without discretionary power. . . .

Elimination of all discretionary power is both impossible and undesirable. The sensible goal is development of a proper balance between rule and discretion. Some circumstances call for rules, some for discretion, some for mixtures of one proportion, and some for mixtures of another proportion. In today's American legal system, the special need is to eliminate *unnecessary* discretionary power, and to discover more successful ways to confine, to structure, and to check necessary discretionary power.

NOTE: Compare Heuston's first point with the contrasting views expressed in the Court of Appeal and the House of Lords in the *Rossminster* case above, p. 176. Heuston asserted that no one had sought to criticize Dicey's views as they related to the criminal law. Since Heuston wrote, these views have also been subjected to criticism.

A. T. H. Smith, 'Comment'
[1985] *Public Law* 608

. . . Whilst constitutional lawyers and jurists talk in terms of Diceyan rhetoric – that 'no man is punishable or can be made lawfully to suffer in body or goods except for a distinct breach of law established in the ordinary legal manner before the ordinary courts of the land. In this sense the rule of law is contrasted with every system of government based on the exercise by persons in authority of wide, arbitrary, or discretionary powers of constraint,' the reality within the criminal process is rather different. My thesis is that (1) English criminal law is inherently offensive to the principle of legality – being a common law system, it is in places highly uncertain, and one that is therefore necessarily retrospective in character when the law is judicially developed; (2) that the judges (by whom I mean principally the House of Lords) in administering it are not currently sufficiently concerned with the protection of civil liberties; and (3) that the enactment of a criminal code would provide a fixed and objective starting point for delineating the permissible restrictions on the right to personal freedom, even if it could not solve all the problems of certainty inherent in a government by laws and men.

The Diceyan model was that the judges constituted a bulwark between the citizen and the State in the protection of the citizen's civil liberties. He illustrated this by reference to freedoms of the person, speech, and assembly, and argued that the law had been developed by the judges to support and bolster these values. It is commonly supposed by constitutional theorists and jurists that this protective pattern repeats itself throughout the criminal process, and that the rule of law infiltrates and permeates the criminal justice system through the application of *nulla poena* principles, with concomitant rules enjoining the strict interpretation of criminal statutes and narrowing where possible the ambit of the criminal law. Criminal lawyers think otherwise. Glanville Williams, for example, observes: '. . . in criminal cases, the courts are anxious to facilitate the conviction of villains, and they interpret the law wherever possible to secure this.' There seems to be, then, a gap between rhetoric and practice in the application and moulding of the scope of the substantive criminal law, and one that should be recognised and if possible accommodated by constitutional theorists.

Dicey's principal concern was with encroachment by the Executive (including the police) on civil liberties. He would, I think, warmly applaud the activities of the judges in the area that we now call administrative law. When a man's property and livelihood or his reputation are at stake in civil proceedings, the judges exhibit an admirable concern to protect the citizen against an encroaching State; they have fashioned what Professor Wade says amounts to a constitution. Furthermore, when they are supervising the agency of the State at the sharp end of the criminal law, the police, they frequently act in the way that Dicey suggests that they do and should.

There are other times, however, when civil libertarians will see their supervision as less commendable, instancing perhaps *Sang* [1980] AC 402, *Wills* v *Bowley* [1983] 1 AC 57 and *Mohammed-Holgate* v *Duke* [1984] AC 437. My assertion is that the checks and balances system that obtains as between the police and the courts, even if it is sometimes out of kilter, is not available at all as a fetter in the administration by the judges of the substantive criminal law, and that when the courts behave as an integral part of an institution whose principal purpose is the prevention of crime through the use of the criminal law, civil liberties are at risk. Against this possibly unwitting combination of police and courts, there is very little protective covering for the individual who has, in all probability, been up to some socially distasteful activity. One does not wish to exaggerate the threat that this poses. After all, the process is for the most part highly visible, the defendant has counsel to argue his corner and there is rarely any public expression of concern about the judges' manipulation of the substantive criminal law in a country where such criticism is liberally permitted. But the aims of the criminal justice system should include provision for the best safeguards of civil liberties as are compatible with maximum social protection, and a starting point for this should be the enactment of a criminal code. Decisions as to the mental element of the law of murder or rape, for example, upon which the liberty of the subject vitally depends, should be treated as legislative ones, and not be left at large for determination by the judiciary as at present.

My criticism of the present system of criminal law adjudication is arguably less apt now than it was in Dicey's time. Since then, the judges have formally foresworn their claim to be able to create new crimes. But I find it strange that Dicey did not see that the state of the substantive criminal law, with the discretion that it accorded to the judges themselves, was at odds with the principles he espoused. Even as Dicey was handing in his manuscript to his publishers in 1884, that other great Victorian jurist, Sir James Stephen, was deciding in his judicial capacity in *Price* that it was not for the judges to create new crimes in such a way as to outlaw cremation. Stephen's view was that the criminal law could best reflect the principles of legality if reduced to a criminal code. But his efforts in that direction had only two years previously finally foundered on the hostility of his judicial brethren to the prospect of having their discretionary powers and authority reduced.

NOTE: Article 7 of the European Convention on Human Rights (*post* p. 466) prohibits the retrospective imposition of criminal liability. Thus the creation by statute of offences with retrospective effect or the recognition by the courts of new common law offences with retrospective effect is offensive to the Convention (see *X Ltd and Y* v *UK* Case No. 8710/79, 28 DR 77 (1982)). A more frequent problem, however, is that of courts increasing the ambit of a particular offence either through the medium of statutory interpretation or the development of the common law definition of the offence to meet a new situation. In such a situation there is no breach of the Convention if such an interpretation or development was reasonably foreseeable at the time the act was performed or the omission occurred and was consistent with the essence of the offence (see *X Ltd and Y* v *UK* Case No. 8710/79 28 DR 77 (1982) at p. 81 and *SW* v *UK* Case No. 47/1994/ 494/576 and *CR* v *UK* Case No. 48/1994/495/577 (1995) *The Times*, 5 December).

B: The rule of law and equality

A. V. Dicey, *An Introduction to the Study of the Law of the Constitution*
pp. 202–203

It means . . . equality before the law, or the equal subjection of all classes to the ordinary law of the land administered by the ordinary law courts; the 'rule of law' in this sense excludes the idea of any exemption of officials or others from the duty of obedience to the law which governs other citizens or from the jurisdiction of the ordinary tribunals; there can be with us nothing really corresponding to the 'administrative law' (*droit administratif*) or the 'administrative tribunals' (*tribunaux administratifs*) of France. The notion which lies at the bottom of the 'administrative law' known to foreign countries is, that affairs or disputes in which the government or its servants are concerned are beyond the sphere of the civil courts and must be dealt with by special and more or less official bodies. This idea is utterly unknown to the law of England, and indeed is fundamentally inconsistent with our traditions and customs.

R. F. V. Heuston, 'The Rule of Law' in *Essays in Constitutional Law*
(2nd edn, 1964), pp. 44–48

. . . This exposition is still perfectly true in the sense that the social or political or economic status of an individual is by itself no answer to legal proceedings, civil or criminal. Everyone, whatever his position, must be ready to justify his actions by reference to some specific legal rule and be ready so to justify them in the ordinary courts. . .

This aspect of Dicey's doctrine has been criticised by Sir Ivor Jennings on the ground that it seems to suggest that officials have the same rights and duties as citizens. If Dicey did indeed mean that, then he was obviously wrong, for modern statutes have conferred wide powers on officials which the ordinary citizen has not got. Gas Board officials may enter my premises to collect the money from the meter, but my neighbours cannot. Officials of the Ministry of Supply can enter my rooms to see if I am conducting researches into nuclear fission, but the college porter cannot. Conversely, the Oxford City Council, as the local education authority, is under a duty to educate my children free although my employers, the University of Oxford and Pembroke College, are not. Many other examples could be produced. There is something in this criticism. We have already seen that Dicey was perhaps a little reluctant to read the Statute Book, and that if he had done so more regularly he might perhaps have altered some of his phrases. Nevertheless, I do not think that Sir Ivor Jennings' criticism touches the heart of the matter. This has been very well put by Lord Wright: 'all are equally subject to the law, though the law as to which some are subject may be different from the law to which others are subject.' In other words, however great the powers or the duties conferred upon the executive, all are equally responsible before the ordinary courts for the exercise of their powers, rights and duties. As was said in *R* v *Brixton Prison Governor, ex parte Soblen* [1963] 2 QB 243 at p. 273, *per* Stephenson J:

> I have no doubt that one of the court's most important duties is to see so far as possible that the great officers of State and those who act under their orders, no less than public bodies and private individuals, act lawfully in the exercise of their powers; and the greater the power which is exercised, and the higher the authority exercising it, the more important is the discharge by the court of this duty, and the more difficult.

A second criticism is much more serious. It arises from Dicey's assertion that the Rule of Law precludes anything corresponding to the administrative law (*droit administratif*) of France. This belief dominated English thinking for so long that not many years ago a Lord Chief Justice could refer to the phrase 'administrative law' as 'Continental jargon.' It is only within the last decade that it has become a respectable phrase. It is clear to us today that Dicey misunderstood the nature and functions of French administrative law, and especially the function of the *conseil d'état*, the chief court in the administrative hierarchy. This is not the time to go into detail; it is enough to say here that although the *conseil d'état* is not composed of professional judges, there are no grounds for supposing that it is in any way biased in favour of the administration. Indeed, there seems to be good reason to think that the liberties of the citizen are in many ways better protected by the *conseil d'état* than by the High Court of Justice. The mere fact that French officials are exempt from process in the ordinary civil courts does not necessarily mean that they are legally irresponsible. To Dicey, however, who had to the full the common lawyer's belief that it is the duty of the Queen's courts to control and supervise the activities of all other tribunals and persons within the realm, the notion that officials might be subject to a special system of rules administered in a special system of courts, was necessarily a very curious one.

NOTE: While it is accepted that, if the rule of law is to be adhered to, it is necessary that citizens be given legal protection against unlawful conduct on the part of officials, Dicey regarded it as necessary that such protection be afforded by the ordinary courts. He did not consider it possible to maintain the rule of law if there was a separate system of public law administered by separate courts, as occurred in France and many other continental countries. Dicey believed that this system was biased in favour of officials and that English law provided better protection. Dicey's influence was such that this view affected the development of administrative law for many years. It is only within the last 30 to 40 years that administrative law has come to be recognized as a separate branch of law, although the United Kingdom still lacks a separate system of administrative courts. There are, however, many tribunals dealing with administrative matters. In whatever way it is to be administered, the essential issue, if the rule of law is to be respected, is simply whether officials are subject to, and controlled by, the law.

Equality before the law should mean that no one is above the law. As with all rules, however, there are exceptions: for example, foreign sovereigns and diplomats, their staffs and families are immune from criminal prosecution or civil action; members of Parliament enjoy certain privileges; and judges enjoy the privilege of being immune from civil liability for anything said or done in the course of their office. These exceptions are limited and, in the case of judges and MP's, are designed to further the rule of law by giving protection to the institutions upon which a liberal democracy is founded, namely, an independent judiciary and an elected legislature.

In explaining his second proposition, Dicey stated that 'every man, whatever be his rank or condition, is subject to the ordinary law of the realm and amenable to the jurisdiction of the ordinary tribunals' (at p. 193). The accuracy of this statement came under challenge in the following case.

In re M
[1993] 3 WLR 433, House of Lords

M, a citizen of Zaire, arrived in the UK seeking political asylum. The Home Office rejected his application and ordered his removal from the UK, which was to take place by 6.30 pm on 1 May 1991. At 5.20 pm (after the Court of Appeal had refused an application for leave to apply for judicial review of the decision) a fresh application for leave to move for judicial review, alleging new grounds, was made to Garland J in chambers. Garland J indicated at about 5.30 pm that he wished M's departure to be postponed pending consideration of the application, and he understood from counsel for the Home Office that an undertaking to that effect had been given. (Counsel understood that he had only undertaken to *endeavour* to prevent M's removal.) Due to bungling and breakdown in lines of communication, M's departure was not prevented nor was he removed from the onward flight to Zaire during a stopover at Paris. At 11.20 pm Garland J, being informed of M's removal from the jurisdiction, made a 'without notice' (formerly an '*ex parte* order') requiring the Home Secretary to procure the return of M to the jurisdiction and granting the Home Secretary liberty to apply for variation or discharge of the order on the morning of 2 May. Home Office officials then made arrangements for M's return. On the afternoon of 2 May, the Home Secretary, having taken advice from his officials and Treasury Counsel, concluded that the underlying asylum decision had been correct and that Garland J's 'without notice' order, being a mandatory interim injunction against a minister of the Crown, had been made without jurisdiction. Thereupon he cancelled the arrangements for M's return. On 3 May he applied to Garland J to set aside the order of 1 May, which Garland J did. Proceedings were then brought on behalf of M against the Home Office and the Home Secretary alleging contempt of court in respect of the breach of the undertaking and the order requiring M's return.

Simon Brown J dismissed this motion on the basis that since the Crown's immunity from injunction was preserved by s. 21 of the Crown Proceedings Act 1947, neither it nor its departments, ministers, and officials acting in the course of their duties could be impleaded for contempt of court. The applicant appealed.

The Court of Appeal held that the original order by Garland J should not have been made as injunctions could not be issued against the Crown. However, as the order was binding until set aside, failure to comply with it was a contempt. Further, while the Crown and Government Departments are not subject to the contempt jurisdiction of the High Court because they are 'non-persons', Mr Baker, the Home Secretary, was, however, personally guilty of contempt.

The Secretary of State appealed and the applicant cross-appealed in respect of his original application against the Home Office. The House of Lords considered two issues of constitutional import: first, could injunctions be issued against a government minister or department, and, secondly, could a government minister or department be found to be in contempt of court for failure to comply with an order of the court.

LORD TEMPLEMAN: My Lords, Parliament makes the law, the executive carry the law into effect and the judiciary enforce the law. The expression 'the Crown' has two meanings; namely the monarch and the executive. In the 17th century Parliament established its supremacy over the Crown as monarch, over the executive and over the judiciary. Parliamentary supremacy over the Crown as monarch stems from the fact that the monarch must accept the advice of a Prime Minister who is supported by a majority of Parliament. Parliamentary supremacy over the Crown as executive stems from the fact that Parliament maintains in office the Prime Minister who appoints the ministers in charge of the executive. Parliamentary supremacy over the judiciary is only exercisable by statute. The judiciary enforce the law against individuals, against institutions and against the executive. The judges cannot enforce the law against the Crown as monarch because the Crown as monarch can do no wrong but judges enforce the law against the Crown as executive and against the individuals who from time to time represent the Crown. A litigant complaining of a breach of the law by the executive can sue the Crown as executive bringing his action against the minister who is responsible for the department of state involved, in the present case the Secretary of State for Home Affairs. To enforce the law the courts have power to grant remedies including injunctions against a minister in his official capacity. If the minister has personally broken the law, the litigant can sue the minister, in this case Mr Kenneth Baker, in his personal capacity. For the purpose of enforcing the law against all persons and institutions, including ministers in their official capacity and in their personal capacity, the courts are armed with coercive powers exercisable in proceedings for contempt of court.

In the present case, counsel for the Secretary of State argued that the judge could not enforce the law by injunction or contempt proceedings against the minister in his official capacity. Counsel also argued that in his personal capacity Mr Kenneth Baker the Secretary of State for Home Affairs had not been guilty of contempt.

My Lords, the argument that there is no power to enforce the law by injunction or contempt proceedings against a minister in his official capacity would, if upheld, establish the proposition that the executive obey the law as a matter of grace and not as a matter of necessity, a proposition which would reverse the result of the Civil War. For the reasons given by my noble and learned friend, Lord Woolf, and on principle, I am satisfied that injunctions and contempt proceedings may be brought against the minister in his official capacity and that in the present case the Home Office for which the Secretary of State was responsible was in contempt. I am also satisfied that Mr Baker was throughout acting in his official capacity, on advice which he was entitled to accept and under a mistaken view as to the law. In these circumstances I do not consider that Mr Baker personally was guilty of contempt. I would therefore dismiss this appeal substituting the Secretary of State for Home Affairs as being the person against whom the finding of contempt was made.

LORD WOOLF: . . . Mr Richards submits on behalf of the Home Office and on behalf of Mr Baker that neither the Crown in general, nor a department of state, nor a minister of the Crown, acting in his capacity as such, are amenable to proceedings in contempt. It is a necessary part of that submission that the courts also have no power to grant injunctions directed to such bodies and that the order which was made by Garland J, which it was held by Simon Brown J as well as the Court of Appeal that Mr Baker had contravened, was made without jurisdiction.

When advancing these submissions Mr Richards stressed that it was no part of his case that the Crown or ministers are above the law or that ministers are able to rely on their office so as to evade liability for wrongdoing. He argued that this was not a consequence of his submissions and he accepted that the Crown has a duty to obey the law as declared by the courts. He accepted that if a minister acted in disregard of the law as declared by the courts, or otherwise was engaged in wrongdoing, he would be acting outside his authority as a minister and so would expose himself to a personal liability for his wrongdoing.

The fact that these issues have only now arisen for decision by the courts is confirmation that in ordinary circumstances ministers of the Crown and government departments invariably scrupulously observe decisions of the courts. Because of this, it is normally unnecessary for the courts to make an executory order against a minister or a government department since they will comply with any declaratory judgment made by the courts and pending the decision of the courts will not take any precipitous action. . . .

[His Lordship recounted the facts of the case.] What does appear to me to be clear from the events which occurred on 1 and 2 May 1991 is that, if there is no power in a court to make an order to prevent the Home Office moving a person in any circumstances, this would be a highly unsatisfactory situation. The facts of this case illustrate that circumstances can occur where it is in the interests both of a person who is subject to the powers of government and of the government itself that the courts should be in a position to make an order which clearly sets out either what should or what should not be done by the government. If there had been no confusion in this case as to the extent of the court's power, I have little doubt that Mr Baker would not find himself in his present position where he has been found guilty of contempt. . . .

Injunctions and the Crown

Mr Kentridge [for the applicant M] placed at the forefront of his argument the issue as to whether the courts have jurisdiction to make coercive orders against the Crown or ministers of the Crown. It was appropriate for him to do so for at least two reasons. First, and more importantly, because whether the courts have or do not have such a coercive jurisdiction would be a strong indicator as to whether the courts had the jurisdiction to make a finding of contempt. If there were no power to make coercive orders, then the need to rely on the law of contempt for the purpose of enforcing the orders would rarely arise. The second reason is that, on the facts of this case, the issue is highly significant in determining the status of the order which Garland J made and which it is alleged Mr Baker breached. If that order was made without jurisdiction, then Mr Richards would rely on this in support of his contention that Mr Baker should not have been found guilty of contempt. As Mr Richards admitted, the issue is of constitutional importance since it goes to the heart of the relationship between the executive and the courts. Is the relationship based, as he submits, on trust and cooperation or ultimately on coercion?

Mr Richards submits that the answer to this question is provided by the decision of *R v Secretary for State for Transport, Ex parte Factortame Ltd* [1990] 2 AC 85 and in particular by the reasoning of Lord Bridge of Harwich who made the only speech in that case. This speech was highly influential in causing Simon Brown J and McCowan LJ to take a different view from the majority of the Court of Appeal as to the outcome of the present proceedings. That case was not, however, primarily concerned with the question as to whether injunctive relief was available against the Crown or its officers. It involved the allegedly discriminatory effect of the requirement of British ownership and the other requirements of Part II of the Merchant Shipping Act 1988 and the associated regulations, which prevented fishing vessels which were owned by Spanish nationals or managed in Spain being registered under the legislation. This it was said contravened Community law. It was an issue of difficulty which had accordingly been referred to the European Court under article 177 [now 234] of the EEC Treaty (Cmnd. 5179–II). The question then arose as to whether the applicants were entitled to interim relief pending the outcome of the reference. The primary contention of the applicants was that it was in the circumstances a requirement of Community law that interim relief should be available. This was an additional point as to which Community law was unclear so your Lordships' House decided that that issue should also not be determined until after a reference under article 177. This meant that pending the outcome of the second reference your Lordships had to determine whether interim relief should be granted under domestic law.

In deciding whether under domestic law interim relief should be granted Lord Bridge initially examined the position without reference to the involvement of a minister. He concluded that no relief could be granted since English law unassisted by Community law treated legislation as fully effective until it was set aside. . . .

However, Lord Bridge went on to give a second reason for his decision which is directly relevant to the present appeal. The second reason is that injunctive relief is not available against the Crown or an officer of the Crown, when acting as such, in judicial review proceedings. . . . Since the decision in *Factortame* there has also been the important development that the European Court has determined the second reference against the Crown so that the unhappy situation now exists that while a citizen is entitled to obtain injunctive relief (including interim relief) against the Crown or an officer of the Crown to protect his interests under Community law he cannot do so in respect of his other interests which may be just as important.

Before examining the second reason that Lord Bridge gave for his conclusion I should point out that I was a party to the judgment of the majority in the *Smith Kline* case. In my judgment in that case I indicated that injunctive relief was available in judicial review proceedings not only against an officer of the Crown but also against the Crown. Although in reality the distinction between the Crown and an officer of the Crown is of no practical significance in judicial review proceedings, in the theory which clouds this subject the distinction is of the greatest importance. My judgment in the earlier case may have caused some confusion in *Factortame* by obscuring the important fact that, as was the position prior to the introduction of judicial review, while prerogative orders are made regularly against ministers in their official capacity, they are never made against the Crown.

Lord Bridge in determining the second issue acknowledged the importance of the relevant history in determining this issue and it is necessary for me to set out my understanding of that history.

His Lordship, starting from the premise that 'the fact that the Sovereign could do no wrong did not mean that a servant of the Crown could do no wrong', considered the history of civil proceedings aginst the Crown and the Crown Proceedings Act 1947, and the history of prerogative orders against Ministers of the Crown culminating in the introduction of judicial review in 1977 by RSC, Ord. 53 which was followed by primary legislation in s. 31 of the Supreme Court Act 1981 (*post* p. 652). His Lordship considered in detail the speech of Lord Bridge in *Factortame* who, following the judgment of Upjohn J in *Merricks* v *Heathcoat-Amory* [1955] Ch. 567, held that injunctions could not be issued against a Minister of the Crown in judicial review proceedings. His Lordship, while agreeing with the decision in the latter case, considered that the reasoning was mistaken. His Lordship further concluded that Lord Bridge had misunderstood the issue in *Factortame* due in part to the fact that the matter had not been fully argued before their Lordships.

> I am, therefore, of the opinion that, the language of section 31 being unqualified in its terms, there is no warrant for restricting its application so that in respect of ministers and other officers of the Crown alone the remedy of an injunction, including an interim injunction, is not available. In my view the history of prerogative proceedings against officers of the Crown supports such a conclusion. So far as interim relief is concerned, which is the practical change which has been made, there is no justification for adopting a different approach to officers of the Crown from that adopted in relation to other respondents in the absence of clear language such as that contained in section 21(2) of the Act of 1947. The fact that in any event a stay could be granted against the Crown under Ord. 53. r. 3(10) emphasises the limits of the change in the situation which is involved. It would be most regrettable if an approach which is inconsistent with that which exists in Community law should be allowed to persist if this is not strictly necessary. The restriction provided for in section 21(2) of the Act of 1947 does, however, remain in relation to civil proceedings.
>
> The fact that, in my view, the court should be regarded as having jurisdiction to grant interim and final injunctions against officers of the Crown does not mean that that jurisdiction should be exercised except in the most limited circumstances. In the majority of situations so far as final relief is concerned, a declaration will continue to be the appropriate remedy on an application for judicial review involving officers of the Crown. As has been the position in the past, the Crown can be relied upon to co-operate fully with such declarations. To avoid having to grant interim injunctions against officers of the Crown, I can see advantages in the courts being able to grant interim declarations. However, it is obviously not desirable to deal with this topic, if it is not necessary to do so, until the views of the Law Commission are known.

The validity of the injunction granted by Garland J
What has been said so far does not mean that Garland J was necessarily in order in granting the injunction. The injunction was granted before he had given the applicant leave to apply for judicial review. However, in a case of real urgency, which this was, the fact that leave had not been granted is a mere technicality. It would be undesirable if, in the situation with which Garland J was faced, he had been compelled to grant leave because he regarded the case as an appropriate one for an interim injunction. In the case of civil proceedings, there is recognition of the jurisdiction of the court to grant interim injunctions before the issue of a writ, etc. (see Ord. 29, r. 1(3)) and in an appropriate case there should be taken to be a similar jurisdiction to grant interim injunctions now under Order 53. The position is accurately set out in note 53/1–14/24 to *The Supreme Court Practice 1993* where it is stated that:

> Where the case is so urgent as to justify it, [the judge] could grant an interlocutory injunction or other interim relief pending the hearing of the application for leave to move for judicial review. But, if the judge has refused leave to move for judicial review he is functus officio and has no jurisdiction to grant any form of interim relief. The application for an interlocutory injunction or other interim relief could, however, be renewed before the Court of Appeal along with the renewal of the application for leave to move for judicial review.

There having been jurisdiction for Garland J to make the order which he did, it cannot be suggested that it was inappropriate for him to have made the order. On the view of the law which I now take, Garland J was therefore not required to set aside the order though his decision to do so was inevitable having regard to the state of the authorities at that time.

The effect of the advice received by Mr Baker
Having come to the conclusion that Garland J's order was properly made, the next question which

has to be considered is the effect of the advice which was understandably given to Mr Baker that the order was made without jurisdiction. Here there are two important considerations. The first is that the order was made by the High Court and therefore has to be treated as a perfectly valid order and one which has to be obeyed until it is set aside: see the speeches of Lord Diplock in *In re A Company*, In re[1981] AC 374, 384 and *Isaacs v Robertson* [1985] AC 97, 102. The second consideration is that it is undesirable to talk in the terms of technical contempt. The courts only make a finding of contempt if there is conduct by the person or body concerned which can, with justification, be categorised as contempt. If, therefore, there is a situation in which the view is properly taken (and usually this will only be possible when the action is taken in accordance with legal advice) that it is reasonable to defer complying with an order of the court until application is made to the court for further guidance then it will not be contempt to defer complying with the order until an application has been made to the court to discharge the order. However, this course can only be justified if the application is made at the first practicable opportunity and in the meantime all appropriate steps have been taken to ensure that the person in whose favour the order was made will not be disadvantaged pending the hearing of the application.

Mr Baker's difficulties in this case are that, while it was understandable that there should be delay before he could give the matter personal attention, Garland J was not kept informed of what was happening and totally inadequate steps were taken to protect the position of M, pending the application to the court. In addition Mr Baker has the problem that this House will not normally interfere with the assessment of the facts which was made by the Court of Appeal unless it can be shown that the assessment is flawed by some error of law.

Jurisdiction to make a finding of contempt

The Court of Appeal were of the opinion that a finding of contempt could not be made against the Crown, a government department or a minister of the Crown in his official capacity. Although it is to be expected that it will be rare indeed that the circumstances will exist in which such a finding would be justified, I do not believe there is any impediment to a court making such a finding, when it is appropriate to do so, not against the Crown directly, but against a government department or a minister of the Crown in his official capacity. Lord Donaldson of Lymington MR considered that a problem was created in making a finding of contempt because the Crown lacked a legal personality. However, at least for some purposes, the Crown has a legal personality. It can be appropriately described as a corporation sole or a corporation aggregate: *per* Lord Diplock and Lord Simon of Glaisdale respectively in *Town Investments Ltd v Department of the Environment* [1978] AC 359. The Crown can hold property and enter into contracts. On the other hand, even after the Act of 1947, it cannot conduct litigation except in the name of an authorised government department or, in the case of judicial review, in the name of a minister. In any event it is not in relation to the Crown that I differ from the Master of the Rolls, but as to a government department or a minister.

Nolan LJ, at p. 311, considered that the fact that proceedings for contempt are 'essentially personal and punitive' meant that it was not open to a court, as a matter of law, to make a finding of contempt against the Home Office or the Home Secretary. While contempt proceedings usually have these characteristics and contempt proceedings against a government department or a minister in an official capacity would not be either personal or punitive (it would clearly not be appropriate to fine or sequest the assets of the Crown or a government department or an officer of the Crown acting in his official capacity), this does not mean that a finding of contempt against a government department or minister would be pointless. The very fact of making such a finding would vindicate the requirements of justice. In addition an order for costs could be made to underline the significance of a contempt. A purpose of the courts' powers to make findings of contempt is to ensure that the orders of the court are obeyed. This jurisdiction is required to be coextensive with the courts' jurisdiction to make the orders which need the protection which the jurisdiction to make findings of contempt provides. In civil proceedings the court can now make orders (other than injunctions or for specific performance) against authorised government departments or the Attorney-General. On applications for judicial review orders can be made against ministers. In consequence of the developments identified already such orders must be taken not to offend the theory that the Crown can supposedly do no wrong. Equally, if such orders are made and not obeyed, the body against whom the orders were made can be found guilty of contempt without offending that theory, which would be the only justifiable impediment against making a finding of contempt.

In cases not involving a government department or a minister the ability to *punish* for contempt may be necessary. However, as is reflected in the restrictions on execution against the Crown, the Crown's relationship with the courts does not depend on coercion and in the exceptional situation when a government department's conduct justifies this, a finding of contempt should suffice. In that exceptional situation, the ability of the court to make a finding of contempt is of great importance. It would demonstrate that a government department has interfered with the administration of justice. It will then be for Parliament to determine what should be the consequences of that finding. In accord with tradition the finding should not be made against the 'Crown' by name but in the name of the authorised department (or the Attorney-General) or the minister so as to accord with the body against whom the order was made. If the order was made in civil proceedings against an authorised department, the department will be held to be in contempt. On judicial review the order will be against the minister and so normally should be any finding of contempt in respect of the order.

However, the finding under appeal is one made against Mr Baker personally in respect of an injunction addressed to him in his official capacity as the Secretary of State for the Home Department. It was appropriate to direct the injunction to the Secretary of State in his official capacity since, as previously indicated, remedies on an application for judicial review which involve the Crown are made against the appropriate officer in his official capacity. This does not mean that it cannot be appropriate to make a finding of contempt against a minister personally rather than against him in his official capacity provided that the contempt relates to his own default. Normally it will be more appropriate to make the order against the office which a minister holds where the order which has been breached has been made against that office since members of the department concerned will almost certainly be involved and investigation as to the part played by individuals is likely to be at least extremely difficult, if not impossible, unless privilege is waived (as commendably happened in this case). In addition the object of the exercise is not so much to punish an individual as to vindicate the rule of law by a finding of contempt. This can be achieved equally by a declaratory finding of the court as to the contempt against the minister as representing the department. By making the finding against the minister in his official capacity the court will be indicating that it is the department for which the minister is responsible which has been guilty of contempt. The minister himself may or may not have been personally guilty of contempt. The position so far as he is personally concerned would be the equivalent of that which needs to exist for the court to give relief against the minister in proceedings for judicial review. There would need to be default by the department for which the minister is responsible.

In addition Mr Richards argued that for a finding of contempt against Mr Baker personally it would not suffice to establish contempt to show that Mr Baker was aware of the order and had not complied with it. It would also be necessary to show an intention to interfere with or impede the administration of justice. If such an intent was shown to exist, then Mr Richards conceded that the conduct of the minister would fall outside his authority as a minister; it would be a personal act not the act of the Crown; and it would expose him to a personal liability for contempt. In support of the distinction which he relied upon, Mr Richards referred to the speech of Lord Oliver of Aylmerton in *Attorney-General* v *Times Newspapers Ltd* [1992] 1 AC 191, 217–218, where Lord Oliver stated:

> A distinction (which has been variously described as 'unhelpful' or 'largely meaningless') is sometimes drawn between what is described as 'civil contempt,' that is to say, contempt by a party to proceedings in a matter of procedure, and 'criminal contempt.' One particular form of contempt by a party to proceedings is that constituted by an intentional act which

is in breach of the order of a competent court. Where this occurs as a result of the act of a party who is bound by the order or of others acting at his direction or on his instigation, it constitutes a civil contempt by him which is punishable by the court at the instance of the party for whose benefit the order was made and which can be waived by him. The intention with which the act was done will, of course, be of the highest relevance in the determination of the penalty (if any) to be imposed by the court, but the liability here is a strict one in the sense that all that requires to be proved is service of the order and the subsequent doing by the party bound of that which is prohibited. When, however, the prohibited act is done not by the party bound himself but by a third party, a stranger to the litigation, that person may also be liable for contempt. There is, however, this essential distinction that his liability is for criminal contempt and arises not because the contemnor is himself affected by the prohibition contained in the order but because his act constitutes a wilful interference with the administration of justice by the court in the proceedings in which the order was made. Here the liability is not strict in the sense referred to, for there has to be shown not only knowledge of the order but an intention to interfere with or impede the administration of justice – an intention which can of course be inferred from the circumstances.

I happily adopt the approach of Lord Oliver. It reflects the distinction which I have drawn between the finding of contempt and the punishment of the contempt. I also accept the distinction which Lord Oliver draws between the position of a person who is subject to an order and a third party. I also recognise the force of Mr Richards' submission that if Mr Baker was not under a strict liability to comply with the order it would not be possible to establish that he had the necessary intention to interfere with or impede the administration of justice to make him guilty of contempt as a third party. However, although the injunction was granted by Garland J against Mr Baker in his official capacity this does not mean that he is in the same position as a third party. To draw a distinction between his two personalities would be unduly technical. While he was Home Secretary the order was one binding upon him personally and one for the compliance with which he as the head of the department was personally responsible. He was, therefore, under a strict liability to comply with the order. However, on the facts of this case I have little doubt that if the Court of Appeal had appreciated that they could make a finding against Mr Baker in his official capacity this is what the court would have done. The conduct complained of in this case which justified the bringing of contempt proceedings was not that of Mr Baker alone and he was acting on advice. His error was understandable and I accept that there is an element of unfairness in the finding against him personally.

In addition, there are technical differences between the two findings because of the provisions of RSC, Ord. 77, r. 1 which define an 'order against the Crown' in a broad sense to include an order against the government department or against an officer of the Crown as such. Unlike the definition of 'civil proceedings by the Crown,' this definition expressly applies to proceedings 'on the Crown side of the Queen's Bench Division.' This means that the provisions of Orders 45 to 52 (which deal with execution and satisfaction of orders of the court) would not apply to an order against the Home Secretary while they would do so in the case of an order against Mr Baker personally.

It is for these reasons that I would dismiss this appeal and cross-appeal save for substituting the Secretary of State for Home Affairs as being the person against whom the finding of contempt was made. This was the alternative decision which was the subject of the cross-appeal, except that there the order was sought against the Home Office rather than the Home Secretary.

Order of Court of Appeal affirmed save for substitution of designation 'Secretary of State for Home Affairs' as proper object of finding of contempt.

Appeal and cross-appeal dismissed with costs.

QUESTIONS

1. Is the effect of this decision to give teeth to Dicey's second proposition regarding the rule of law?

2. Is it desirable that courts should seek to compel the Government to comply with their orders rather than leaving it to the electorate to condemn them in a future election for their failure to comply?

3. Bagehot in *The English Constitution* (1867) drew a distinction between what he referred to as the 'dignified' parts of the constitution and the 'efficient' parts. The former he claimed 'excite and preserve the reverence of the population'. One of the dignified institutions is the monarchy, i.e. the Crown, to whom loyalty is felt or allegiance is owed. The institutions of government are the efficient parts of the constitution wherein real power is vested. In the United Kingdom Government is conducted in the name of the Crown; thus it is referred to as Her Majesty's Government. When Lords Templeman and Woolf distinguished between the Crown as Monarch and the Crown as Executive, were they thereby adopting this distinction drawn by Bagehot?

NOTE: The position of members of the Security Service in relation to their criminal liability has given rise to some heated discussion in recent years. In *Francome and Another* v *Mirror Group Newspapers Ltd and Others* [1984] 2 All ER 408, at p. 412, Lord Donaldson MR stated:

> Parliamentary democracy as we know it is based on the rule of law. That requires all citizens to obey the law, unless and until it can be changed by due process. There are no privileged classes to whom it does not apply. [If one person] can assert [a] right to act on the basis that the public interest, as he sees it, justifies breaches of the criminal law, so can any other citizen. This has only to be stated for it to be obvious that the result would be anarchy. . . . The right to break the law . . . is not obtainable at all in a parliamentary democracy, although different considerations arise under a totalitarian regime.

In one of the cases arising from the *Spycatcher* affair, *Attorney-General* v *Guardian Newspapers Ltd and Others (No. 2) and related appeals* [1988] 2 WLR 805, at p. 879, Lord Donaldson MR appeared to retreat somewhat from this position.

> Thus far I have not considered what is 'wrongdoing.' Again there is a problem. Lord Denning in his report into the Profumo affair ((1963) Cmnd. 2152) stressed, at p. 91, paragraph 273 that:
> The members of the service are, in the eye of the law, ordinary citizens with no powers greater than anyone else. They have no special powers of arrest such as the police have. No special powers of search are given to them. They cannot enter premises without the consent of the householder, even though they may suspect a spy is there.

He went on to say that this deficiency of powers was made up for by close co-operation with the police forces.

It would be a sad day for democracy and the rule of law if the service were ever to be considered to be above or exempt from the law of the land. And it is not. At any time any member of the service who breaks the law is liable to be prosecuted. But there is a need for some discretion and common sense. Let us suppose that the service has information which suggests that a spy may be operating from particular premises. It needs to have confirmation. It may well consider that, if he proves to be a spy, the interests of the nation are better served by letting him continue with his activities under surveillance and in ignorance that he has been detected rather than by arresting him. What is the service expected to do? A secret search of the premises is the obvious answer. Is this really 'wrongdoing'?

Let us test it in a mundane context known to us all. Prior to the passing of section 79 of the Road Traffic Regulation Act 1967, fire engines and ambulances, unlike police vehicles, had no exemption from the speed limits. Their drivers hurrying to an emergency broke the law. So far as I am aware that is still the position in relation to crossing traffic lights which are showing red and driving on the wrong side of the road to bypass a traffic jam. The responsible authorities in a very proper exercise of discretion simply do not prosecute them.

Even in the context of the work of the Security Service which, I must stress, is the defence of the realm, there must be stringent limits to what breaches of the law can be considered excusable. Thus I cannot conceive of physical violence ever coming within this category. Or physical restraint, other than in the powers of arrest enjoyed by every citizen or under the authority of a lawful warrant of arrest. But covert invasions of privacy, which I think is what Mr Wright means by 'burglary,' may in some circumstances be a different matter.

It may be that the time has come when Parliament should regularise the position of the service. It is certainly a tenable view. The alternative view, which is equally tenable, is that the public interest is better served by leaving the members of the service liable to prosecution for any breach of the law at the instance of a private individual or of a public prosecuting authority, but may expect that prosecuting authorities will exercise a wise discretion and that in an appropriate case the Attorney-General would enter a nolle prosequi, justifying his action to Parliament if necessary. In so acting, the Attorney-General is not acting as a political minister or as a colleague of ministers. He acts personally and in a quasi-judicial capacity as representing the Crown (see article entitled 'How the security services are bound by the rule of law' by Lord Hailsham in *The Independent*, 3 February 1988). It is not for me to form or express any view on which is the most appropriate course to adopt in the interests of the security of the nation and the maintenance of the rule of law. However that problem is resolved, it is absurd to contend that *any* breach of the law, whatever its character, will constitute such 'wrongdoing' as to deprive the service of the secrecy without which it cannot possibly operate.

QUESTIONS

1. Would the rule of law be supported or undermined by criminal activity by members of the Security Service?

2. Does the following provision from the Intelligence Services Act 1994 reaffirm the rule of law, or is it simply a shifting of 'the goalposts' by use of the legality principle? Who is left to decide what action is 'necessary'?

3. To what extent is it true to say that '[t]he section amounts to statutory authorization of ministerial general warrants for reasons of State necessity of the kind which the common law disapproved in the celebrated case of *Entick* v *Carrington*' (I. Leigh and L. Lustgarten, 'The Security Service Act 1989' (1989) 52 *Modern Law Review* 801, at p. 825)? Section 5 of the 1994 Act re-enacts with amendments s. 3 of the 1989 Act.

Intelligence Services Act 1994

5.—(1) No entry on or interference with property or with wireless telegraphy shall be unlawful if it is authorised by a warrant issued by the Secretary of State under this section.

(2) The Secretary of State may, on an application made by the Security Service, the Intelligence Service or GCHQ, issue a warrant under this section authorising the taking, subject to subsection (3) below, of such action as is specified in the warrant in respect of any property so specified or in reseptect of wireless telegraphy so specified if the Secretary of State—

    (a) thinks it necessary for the action to be taken on the ground that it is likely to be of substantial value in assisting, as the case may be,—

        (i)   the Security Service in carrying out any of its functions under the [Security Service Act] 1989 . . .; or

        (ii) the Intelligence Service in carrying out any of its functions under section 1 above; or

        (iii) GCHQ in carrying out any function which falls within section 3(1)(a) above; and

    (b) is satisfied that what the action seeks to achieve cannot reasonably be achieved by other means; and

    (c) is satisfied that satisfactory arrangements are in force under section 2(2)(a) of the 1989 Act (duties of the Director-General of the Security Service), section 2(2)(a) above or section 4(2)(a) above with respect to the disclosure of information obtained by virtue of this section and that any information obtained under the warrant will be subject to those arrangements.

C: The rule of law and individual rights

The legal protection of rights in the United Kingdom is in a state of flux. The full impact of the Human Rights Act 1998 will become apparent only with the passage of time. The importance of the Human Rights Act, however, can be appreciated only when the pre-existing system under which human rights were protected is understood. This system was greatly influenced by Dicey's views, and its inherent defects form part of the background which gave rise to a movement for reform which resulted in the Human Rights Act.

A. V. Dicey, *An Introduction to the Study of the Law of the Constitution*
pp. 195, 203

We may say that the constitution is pervaded by the rule of law on the ground that the general principles of the constitution (as for example the right to personal liberty, or the right of public meeting) are with us the result of judicial decisions determining the rights of private persons in particular cases brought before the courts; whereas under many foreign constitutions the security (such as it is) given to the rights of individuals results, or appears to result, from the general principles of the constitution. . . . in short, the principles of private law have with us been by the action of the courts and Parliament so extended as to determine the position of the Crown and of its servants; thus the constitution is the result of the ordinary law of the land.

R. F. V. Heuston, 'The Rule of Law' in *Essays in Constitutional Law*
(2nd edn, 1964), pp. 49–50

To [Dicey] such general principles of the constitution as the rights of free speech and public meeting are derived simply from the decisions of the courts in ordinary private law questions. There are no general guarantees contained in a formal written constitution. Dicey was thinking of the basic common law freedoms of liberty, speech and property, and as *Entick* v *Carrington* well shows, our law deals with these matters as governed by the ordinary principles of private law and not by any special system of public law. This particular aspect of the Rule of Law has been accepted by everyone without question; the only comment which has been made upon it, again by the acute Sir Ivor Jennings, is that it does not include the statutory rights to pensions, sickness benefit, free education, the right to vote and so on. Yet many would think that the statutory rights conferred on the citizen by the welfare state are as important as the common law principles which Dicey had in mind.

E. Barendt, 'Dicey and Civil Liberties'
[1985] *Public Law* 596

Dicey's treatment of civil liberties and fundamental freedoms . . . has understandably received less attention than his formulation of the doctrine of Parliamentary Sovereignty and his analysis of constitutional conventions. He himself subsumed individual rights to personal freedom and freedom of discussion under 'The Rule of Law,' the lengthiest part of the *Introduction of the Study of the Law of the Constitution*. Criticism has, therefore, concentrated on the general coherence of 'the rule of law' principles and the contrast drawn by Dicey between the general absence of arbitrary discretionary power in England and what he (at the time) considered to be its daily employment under *droit administratif* in France. But what he wrote about individual rights and freedoms remains important, not so much because it is still a tolerably accurate account of the basic constitutional position of these liberties, but rather because his outlook – a paean of praise to the wisdom of the common law – continues to influence modern thinking on these matters. . . .

[T]he ambivalent character of Dicey's pronouncements in the *Law of the Constitution*, partly a matter of legal analysis, partly reflecting the author's Whig politics, has, I think, been responsible for their lasting influence. They have something to offer both lawyers and (most) politicians. In *Duncan* v *Jones*, Lord Hewart CJ cited Dicey as authority for the impeccable proposition that in English law the 'right of assembly . . . is nothing more than a view taken by the court of the individual liberty of the subject'; further, there is no special right to hold public meetings for political or other purposes. Most legislators find this conclusion attractive, for any 'right' to hold such meetings – if taken seriously – would curtail their law-making powers, as well as the discretion of the police and the courts. Dicey's arguments are put so persuasively that it is difficult sometimes to resist the conclusion that they are inevitably right, and that, therefore, in this context civil liberties can only be those recognised by the courts as common law. But this is not true, nor these days is that position desirable. . . . The English Constitution, a concept which arguably contains two erroneous assumptions, is for him judge-made law with all the good and bad characteristics of the common law.

We then, however, read of nothing but the benefits of judge-made law as the foundation of constitutional rules, in particular of fundamental personal freedoms. Because they are devised by courts, rights are integrally connected with remedies for their enforcement, for instance, the prerogative writ of habeas corpus, and common law freedoms may not so easily be suspended as the comparable rights guaranteed in a written constitution, at least 'without a thorough revolution in the institutions and manners of the nation.' Dicey does admit that some countries with constitutional declarations of rights, such as the United States, may as effectively provide remedies for invasion of these freedoms, as England does, and also that in practice at a particular time liberty may be as much respected in, say, Belgium as it is here, but for the most part the comparisons are designed to show that freedom is less securely protected in States with written constitutional guarantees. Such guarantees are often of more theoretical than practical worth, while common law freedoms necessarily reflect the traditions of a people. This last point is given some substance when Dicey observes that freedom of discussion is really the liberty to publish what twelve shopkeepers think it appropriate to be said or written. Clive Ponting at any rate might find something of value in that.

The principal implication of all this, as Sir Ivor Jennings pointed out, is that Englishmen are free simply to do whatever the law does not prohibit. In other words, civil liberties are residual. There are no special laws protecting them, though there may be particular remedies fashioned by the judges or provided by statutes, as with the Habeas Corpus Acts. So, there is personal freedom from arbitrary arrest or invasion of property rights because the courts have not recognised the existence of those wide powers which would effectively curtail the freedoms. Here, of course, the third tenet of Dicey's 'rule of law' only has substance because one or other, or both, of the other two principles are applicable. . . . *Entick* v *Carrington* . . . shows perhaps all three principles of the rule of law: the courts' hostility to arbitrary powers, the subjection of everyone including government officials to the common law, and the formulation of freedoms through concrete litigation. It also evinces a judicial enthusiasm for general principles, markedly lacking in most English judges today. Would modern English judgments contain a sentiment such as: 'The great end, for which men entered into society, was to secure their property. That right is preserved sacred and incommunicable in all instances, where it has not been taken away or abridged by some public law for the good of the whole.' Never mind the substance of this opinion: this type of approach would not now be adopted in a case involving freedom of speech, religion or any other fundamental right. . . .

[J]udged from a contemporary perspective, the thesis – and in particular this third tenet of the rule of law – seems peculiar. The contrast drawn between the formulation of rights in a written constitution or Bill of Rights and judge-made or common law is surely overstated. At the least it needs refinement. Constitutions have to be interpreted and applied by the courts, so that in a sense freedom of speech and personal freedom are as much judge-made law, say, in the United States as they are in Britain. Indeed, in the present day, when the role of the judiciary here is so much constrained by tightly-drawn statutes, judge-made law is much more significant in the USA, Germany and all other jurisdictions where the courts construe a constitution or Bill of Rights. . . .

Both judge-made law and statute are in various places in his constitutional writing contrasted with the broad declarations of principle found in written constitutions and Bills of Rights. Constitutional constraints on legislation are criticised for weakening the role of public opinion in developing the law, an attitude which is shared these days by populist Conservatives and (most) Socialists. Dicey then might well have identified the protection of individual freedoms by concrete common law *and legislative* rules as one feature of the rule of law in England, a formulation which would incidentally have been perfectly compatible with the other tenets of the doctrine. Arthur Goodhart has pointed out that Anglo-American concepts of the rule of law usually exaggerate the judicial process. As a desirable constitutional principle, its maintenance is also the responsibility of the legislative and executive branches of government. Moreover, Dicey would not have had so much difficulty in reconciling Parliamentary Sovereignty and the rule of law – surely one of the least happy chapters of his book – had he seen the latter as a legislative principle as well as a statement about the judicial role.

Is there any explanation for this aspect of Dicey's rule of law doctrine? I suspect the correct answer is rather dull and obvious. Even in the *Relation between Law and Public Opinion*, Dicey made no attempt to disguise his preference for the 'judicial legislation' of the common law and equity. It is more concerned than statute law with the general symmetry of the law, with the requirements of certainty and consistency and generally with the requirements of justice. Acts of Parliament are frequently the work of 'legislators who are much influenced by the immediate opinion of the moment, who make laws with little regard either to general principles or to logical consistency, and who are deficient in the skill and knowledge of experts.' Moreover, the areas of civil liberties chosen by Dicey for discussion in the earlier work were at that time more or less entirely governed by common law decisions, as will shortly be seen in the context of freedom of speech and freedom to hold meetings. The Habeas Corpus Acts discussed at some length in the chapter on 'The Right to Personal Freedom' were regarded as meeting the deficiencies of the common law writ rather than establishing new principles. The thesis that the general principles of the Constitution rested on judicial decisions was, as Sir Ivor Jennings has said, a partial presentation of the true position; but it was then much more accurate than it would be now, and in the case of the most important political freedoms, it was extremely plausible. . . .

Dicey's account of these rights was and remains accurate as a statement of the law, but its tone trivialises the issues which ought to be discussed: should there be positive rights to hold public meetings? Should there at least be equal rights of access for all political parties and groups to use public premises for meetings? What powers should the police enjoy to prevent outbreaks of violence at such gatherings? The rule of law does not provide an adequate framework for tackling these problems. But the same is true of civil liberties generally. I shall now explain why Dicey's account of this subject is so defective for the present day.

. . . The press . . . was in Dicey's view governed simply by the ordinary law of the land, and for him that meant the common law of criminal and civil libel. Statutory restrictions on speech and the exercise of other liberties were barely discussed, largely because they were then of relatively little significance. The absence of arbitrary power made so much of in *The Law of the Constitution* was an absence of autonomous executive or prerogative power; what we are more concerned with nowadays is the risk of governments abusing their powers through their *de facto* control of the legislature. Dicey appreciated that governments would from time to time need to acquire wider discretionary powers under Acts of Parliament, but he did not foresee that some of these, for example, the Official Secrets legislation and the Incitement to Disaffection Act, would remain permanent features of the statute book. And in the last page of his chapter dealing with the relation between the rule of law and sovereignty, he seems to have exaggerated the extent to which the courts are prepared to limit the scope of legislation by the application of liberal common law principles.

The rule of law is a quite valueless doctrine these days unless it is accepted as a rule which binds the legislature, either as a matter of constitutional law or at least as a general political principle or convention. There is little evidence for its general acceptance by modern British legislators. Might may not be right, but a parliamentary majority is. This is shown by the ease with which governments have secured the passage of such legislation as the Immigration Acts, and the rules made under them, which to some extent have retrospective effects; other rules have recently been held by the European Court of Human Rights to discriminate against women. Moreover, governments of recent decades have proved reluctant to clarify or reform civil liberties law until there has been an adverse ruling of the European Court, as shown by the telephone tapping saga discussed a little later. Where there has been no such impetus from abroad, British administrations prefer to remain idle. Thus, despite the conclusion of the Williams Committee that the present obscenity laws in so far as they may outlaw certain written publications are incompatible with freedom of expression, the discredited 1959 Act remains on the statute book.

If Dicey more or less ignored the role of Parliament in safeguarding the values implicit in the rule of law, he surely exaggerated the willingness and ability of the judiciary to perform this task. Although one or two judges have been keen to protect fundamental freedoms, wherever possible, and to shape the common law accordingly, many more give them inadequate weight or refuse to recognise the presence of a civil liberties question. I have already noted Lord Hewart CJ's adoption in *Duncan* v *Jones* of the Diceyan position on the right of assembly; the ruling of the Divisional Court to the effect that it constituted an obstruction of a police officer to refuse to disperse a meeting on his instructions completely outflanked earlier law on the right of public meetings, which the court thought wholly irrelevant to the case. Major cases on the scope of contempt of court have paid little or no regard to free speech implications. And in some recent decisions, the courts have extended police powers of arrest and of seizure of property, before the Police and Criminal Evidence Act 1984 rendered further judicial innovation on this subject unnecessary. Of course, this is only a partial picture of judge-made law in the civil liberties field, but it is perhaps enough to show that Dicey's reliance on the judiciary fully to protect these freedoms was excessive.

Moreover, there is an inevitable drawback to the conclusion that in England freedoms are residual, in that everyone is free to do whatever the law does not prohibit. For this proposition is as true for the Government and other public authorities as it is for the ordinary citizen, an equality required by the rule of law itself. In *Malone* v *Metropolitan Police Commissioner* [[1979] Ch 344], the plaintiff claimed an injunction to restrain telephone tapping by the Post Office under the warrant of the Home Secretary and on behalf of the police who suspected that Malone had handled some stolen property. Sir Robert Megarry VC refused to grant the remedy because the Post Office had committed no wrong; there was no trespass and English law does not recognise a cause of action for invasion of privacy. 'If the tapping of telephones by the Post Office at the request of the police can be carried out without any breach of the law, it does not require any statutory or common law power to justify it: it can lawfully be done simply because there is nothing to make it unlawful.' The same principles applied incidentally to prevent the common law developing any rules against discrimination; an employer, for example, was free to discriminate against blacks because this did not amount to any tort or wrong before the introduction of the Race Relations legislation.

Had the judge been a bold eighteenth century innovator, it is conceivable that he might have formulated a new tort of invasion of privacy, at least in this context, for it was clear that there was an injustice in the case which needed correction. But it is apparently no longer appropriate for the judiciary in England to create new rights; they and the citizen must wait for Parliament – or more likely, the European Court of Human Rights. This surely shows the advantage of a positive statement of fundamental freedoms and rights in some constitutional document or other. In the absence of such a statement and of a well-recognised cause of action (for trespass or assault, for instance), the courts cannot protect interstitial residual freedoms. Dicey's obsession with remedies made him oblivious to the importance of rights.

These paragraphs are not designed to prove that the constitutional guarantee of rights is everything. There are many rights which are better protected by detailed and specific legislation, providing remedies for their infringement. An obvious example is the right not to be discriminated against on the ground of race, colour or sex, etc., which both in Britain and in the United States (in addition to the Equal Protection Clause of the Fourteenth Amendment) is protected by legislative measures. The same may hold for claim-rights to, say, housing or education, where the State (or other public authorities) are required to do certain things to satisfy the citizen's needs. There are in any case some good arguments for not guaranteeing these freedoms in constitutions, for they are not easily susceptible to judicial enforcement and – to be controversial – they are not sufficiently fundamental to demand insulation from legislative regulation.

On the other hand, there are situations where the constitutional statement of a right is valuable because it enables courts in appropriate contexts to formulate some claim-right to the exercise of the particular freedom. For example, there is now some debate in Western democracies whether free speech requires the recognition of rights of access to the media and a right of reply to hostile or inaccurate articles in the press. In the United States, of course, the issue has become a constitutional one. There are powerful arguments against the judicial imposition of duties on the part of the media to afford rights of access or of reply, and for the conclusion that these rights are best left to development by administrative bodies or extra-legal provision. The point, however, is that a residual freedom can never found a claim-right, even if it is appropriate for the judiciary to prod the legislature (or some administrative agency) into action by upholding such a right in principle. In contrast, it is open for the European Court to recognise some positive claim-right of reply, or a right of access of a mother (or natural parents) to children under Article 8 of the Convention. In British law, the right to marry is residual or interstitial; it is what is left after the Government (or Parliament) have regulated the hours when people may marry, the prohibited degrees, age of marital capacity and so on. Only a statement of the freedom in a text would enable the courts restrictively to construe (or perhaps strike down) regulations which reduce the scope of the freedom to vanishing-point.

Dicey's treatment of civil liberties, therefore, seems inadequate now, first, because it leaves out of account the serious erosion that may be made on the exercise of the freedoms through legislation enacted in disregard of the rule of law principles, secondly, in view of the change in character of the judiciary and their attitude to development of the common law, and thirdly and perhaps most importantly, because residual freedoms can never provide a firm support for judicial innovation. The criticism is not made to belittle Dicey's analysis of English law at the time he wrote. The pity is that he has been taken too seriously by commentators who have often found his thesis attractive to wear with their own (and to some extent, it should be said, his) political creed.

NOTE: Dicey's views on sovereignty and the rule of law derived from his understanding of representative democracy and the way in which it operated in the United Kingdom. In 'Dicey: Unitary, Self-correcting Democracy and Public Law' (1990) 106 LQR 105, Paul Craig challenges

Dicey's views. If Craig is correct, the whole foundation of Dicey's writings is undermined. Craig argues that Dicey's views were premised upon certain assumptions concerning representative democracy which were misconceived and which failed to take account of important political developments occuring at the time he was writing. In Dicey's view, while the electorate was the political sovereign, it was Parliament which was the legal sovereign; Parliament was the body with the omnicompetent power of law-making. The exercise of legal sovereignty by Parliament, however, would, he believed, always reflect the will of the political sovereign, *viz.* the electorate. The essence of Craig's critique is contained in the extracts which follow. (For a contrasting perspective, see T. R. S. Allan, 'Legislative Supremacy and the Rule of Law: Democracy and Constitutionalism' [1985] *Cambridge Law Journal* 111.)

P. Craig, 'Dicey: Unitary, Self-correcting Democracy and Public Law'
(1990) 106 LQR 105

2   SOVEREIGNTY: LEGISLATIVE OMNICOMPETENCE AND CONSTITUTIONAL LAW

. . . For Dicey the external limit [upon legal sovereignty] was the need to secure the support of at least a portion of the population; the internal limit was indicative of the fact that a legal sovereign would perforce be moulded by his social environment and that this would condition the type of legislation which he sought to enact. In a despotism the external and internal limits might not coincide. In a representative democracy things were otherwise.

> Where a Parliament truly represents the people, the divergence between the external and the internal limit to the exercise of sovereign power can hardly arise, or if it arises, must soon disappear. Speaking roughly, the permanent wishes of the representative portion of Parliament can hardly in the long run differ from the wishes of the English people, or at any rate of the electors; that which the majority of the House of Commons command, the majority of the English people usually desire. To prevent the divergence between the wishes of the sovereign and the wishes of subjects is in short the effect, and the only certain effect of bona fide representative government. [Dicey, *An Introduction to the Study of the Law of the Constitution* (10th edn, 1959), p. 83.]

The absence of constitutional review and the Diceyan conception of sovereignty are therefore firmly embedded within a conception of self-correcting majoritarian democracy. Representative government would necessarily produce a coincidence between the external and internal limits of sovereign power in much the same way that the invisible hand of the market ensured a correspondence of supply and demand. A Parliament duly elected on the extended franchise represented the most authoritative expression of the will of the nation, and the exercise of public power was channelled through such a Parliament. This Parliament duly controlled the executive and therefore the affairs of the nation should be entrusted to those approved by a majority of the House. For Dicey, 'black letter' precedent and political principle formed a perfect union. All was well in the Garden of Eden. This beatific vision of legal and political harmony was to prove short-lived, and may never in reality have existed at all. . . . The force of this vision was however indirectly reinforced by Dicey's views on the rule of law and on conventions.

It was Dicey's third limb of the rule of law which added 'empirical' weight to the conclusions of principle which he had arrived at concerning sovereignty. The third sense of the rule of law was that in England civil liberties were the result of ordinary common law decisions, whereas under many foreign constitutions these interests were protected by, or resulted from, general principles of the constitution. Now while Dicey admits that constitutionally guaranteed rights, backed up with adequate remedies, can be as efficacious as the common law, he nonetheless evinces a marked preference for the latter over the former. . . . The common law in general furnished better protection for individual rights because constitutionally enshrined rights were often without adequate remedies and could be easily suspended. Common law protections could not be destroyed without a thorough-going revolution in the 'institutions and manners of the nation.'

Thus while the twin concepts of sovereignty and the rule of law could be at odds, they could also reinforce each other. The existence of representative government ensured that the wishes of the people would coincide with those of the sovereign Parliament. There should therefore be no serious problems concerning civil liberties. Insofar as such problems did occur the third limb of the rule of law, the common law protection of individual rights, was at hand, which was a more constitutionally enshrined declaration of rights. . . .

A similar thematic connection can be seen between Dicey's discussion of sovereignty and conventions. For Dicey the main purpose of such conventions was to ensure that Parliament or the Cabinet, which 'is indirectly appointed by Parliament,' should in the long run give effect to the will of the electorate. Conventions, seen as a 'modern code of constitutional morality,' indirectly secured the sovereignty of the people. For Dicey, the advance of democracy entailed the transference of supreme power from a single person, or a privileged or limited class, to the majority of the male citizens. The process of representation as it actually operated was 'nothing else than a mode by which the will of the representative body or House of Commons is made to coincide with the will of the nation.' . . .

4 THE TRADITIONAL VISION OF CONSTITUTIONAL LAW: APPEARANCE AND REALITY

. . .

(b) The internal coherence of Dicey's argument

First, even if we accept the accuracy of this picture of the constitution, the conclusions concerning the lack of need for constitutional review do not, in fact, follow as self-evidently as Dicey might have us believe. The argument appears to be simple. Our system of democracy is founded upon a channel of authority flowing from the bottom upwards. The electorate choose representatives. The MPs who are elected articulate the views of those who have chosen them, and they control the executive. Legislation which might be constitutionally questionable would, therefore, not be passed, or would be repealed expeditiously.

The ambiguity in this formulation becomes apparent upon further reflection, and is indeed embedded within the quotation cited above concerning the external and internal limits on sovereignty. Thus, we are told that the permanent wishes of the representative portion of Parliament can hardly differ from the wishes of the English people; that which the majority of the Commons command, the majority of the English people usually desire. The gap between these two formulations, which are juxtaposed in Dicey's text, is significant. Under the latter, it would be possible for the wishes of the majority to be faithfully translated into legislation by their elected representatives, and for this legislation to be constitutionally deleterious to the wishes of a minority. Dicey switches back and forth between these two formulations without readily appreciating the difference between them.

It is not apparent how Dicey would prevent or forestall this danger of majority oppression. A possible argument would be that the 'internal limit' placed upon the parliamentary rulers would serve to ensure that the despotism of the majority did not occur. The argument would be as follows. Dicey tells us that any ruler exercises power subject to an internal limit, in the sense that he or she would be moulded by the society in which the person lived. In a parliamentary system the majority representatives, although holding a particular view on a specific subject, would not attempt to pass legislation which would be constitutionally disadvantageous to a minority. The internal limits of that society would serve to preclude the exercise of such power. A majority might well, for example, believe fervently in Protestantism, but the pervasive spirit of toleration which constituted one facet of the internal limit within which the rulers ruled would mitigate against religious legislation which was discriminatory.

A distinctive, albeit complementary, theme can be found in Dicey's discussion of counter and cross-currents of opinion. Whether Dicey was correct in regarding legislation as the product of 'public opinion' is not our prime concern. What is of relevance is the light which Dicey's discussion sheds upon the prospect of majority oppression. One of the themes which Dicey stresses is that 'the reigning legislative opinion has never, at any rate during the nineteenth century, exerted absolute or despotic authority.' Its power is always diminished by counter-currents which are more or less directly opposed to the dominant opinion of a particular era. Such counter-currents impose a check upon the legislative action which results from those who hold the dominant faith. Thus Dicey argues that from 1830 to 1850 Benthamite liberalism was held in check by the 'restraining power' of the older toryism, and that ecclesiastical reform could not be properly understood without paying due attention to the varying counter and cross-currents which affected its passage. Religious legislation could only be properly comprehended by appreciating that such statutes were affected by a liberalism which aimed at the establishment of religious equality, and by cross-currents of ecclesiastical opinion which desired to maintain the rights or privileges of the Established Church.

Majority tyranny could therefore be forestalled by a combination of internal limits, coupled with counter and cross-currents of opinion, which together would preclude legislation which was constitutionally deleterious to a particular minority. This reasoning has some plausibility. It is, however, difficult to accept that it would operate successfully in all or even the majority of instances in which minority oppression might occur. Legislation which is constitutionally suspect might well be passed because the majority perceives the 'internal limits' differently from the minority. They might view the specific boundaries which flow from the internal limitations distinctively from the minority who are being oppressed. Statutes may be enacted which are constitutionally questionable without the actual legislators sensing that they are controverting some societal norm which should be sacrosanct. Moreover, while the existence of counter and cross-currents of opinion may well be undeniable, their impact upon the problem at hand is more questionable. The existence of such strains within legislative opinion might well be of impact in reducing the pace or severity of statutory change. There is, however, no particular reason to conclude that they would prevent legislation which could be constitutionally harmful to minority interests. . . .

An alternative line of argument which might be pursued is to return to the connection between sovereignty and the third limb of the rule of law which was considered earlier. The common law, as noted, was perceived as the best protector of individual rights. The existence of representative government served to ensure that the wishes of the people would coincide with those of the sovereign Parliament. Serious problems concerning civil liberties should therefore be rare. If such problems did arise, the common law was at hand to protect the harassed citizen.

This 'corrective' is too simplistic and is, upon closer examination, not borne out by Dicey's own analysis. The matter may best be approached as follows. Let us imagine that the majority within Parliament has enacted legislation which could be deemed constitutionally harmful to a minority. The internal limitation upon the exercise of sovereign power has not proved successful, and certain fundamental minority rights have been curtailed. How will the common law protection avail these citizens, given Dicey's own doctrine of parliamentary omnicompetence? Dicey provides two responses, one of which is general in nature, the other of which is both more detailed and more particular.

The *general response* is that where civil liberties are deduced from a constitutional document they can be readily suspended; where, however, such rights emerged from the common law, they cannot be destroyed 'without a thorough revolution in the institutions and manners of the nation.' Now it may well be the case that Dicey had reason to be sceptical of continental experience with Declarations of Rights. The ephemeral quality of such documents would clearly warrant caution concerning their efficacy. The possibility of a wholesale restriction of rights, which occupies Dicey initially, is important, but does not serve to answer the conundrum posed above. A majority within Parliament may have no desire to restrict individual rights generally, either over time or over subject matter.

There may be no intent to effect any revolution in the manners or institutions of the nation. Nor need this be the effect of legislation which curtails the rights of individuals within a particular area. Dicey himself admits that specific legislation could be, and had been passed, without producing the dramatic social consequences adumbrated above.

The more *particular response* provided by Dicey is to be found in his detailed examination of individual freedoms which have been secured and developed by the common law. The limitations of the common law become readily apparent by reflecting upon this detailed analysis. Dicey's argument within these chapters demonstrates the success which the common law can and did have in controlling the exercise of *executive* or *discretionary* power which could interfere with individual liberty. Arrest had to be founded upon statutory authority; executive fiat would not suffice. Freedom of discussion entailed the absence of any prior executive constraint; the individual could only be punished for a consequential wrong, such as libel.

Nothing within this analysis touches the situation in which authority does exist, the effect of which is to curtail individual liberty. Thus, Dicey admits that the government can and has secured the 'statutory suspension of habeas corpus' for limited periods and for limited classes of offence. The analysis of freedom of speech is equally revealing. Dicey juxtaposes the position of the Press at the time he wrote to that which had prevailed hitherto. The Press in the nineteenth century was not subject to prior censorship, but was governed by the ordinary law of defamation. He contrasts this with the position which had existed in the seventeenth century, where the Press was controlled by a special tribunal and was subject to regulation. The discretionary system of licensing, 'which was censorship under another name,' was given a statutory foundation in 1662, and remained in force until 1695. Dicey comments that,

> The passing, however, of the statute, though not a triumph of toleration, was a triumph of legality. The power of licensing depended henceforward, not on any idea of inherent executive authority, but on the statute law. The right of licensing was left in the hands of the government, but this power was regulated by the words of a statute; and, what was of more consequence, breaches of the Act could be punished only by proceedings in the ordinary courts. [*The Law of the Constitution*, p. 268.]

This quotation aptly exemplifies Dicey's detailed analysis of specific individual rights. The common law could help to limit the exercise of broad executive discretionary power which threatened such rights. The first two limbs of the rule of law would be advanced by the transformation of discretionary power into statutory form. Once the power existed in statutory form, it was sacrosanct. A statute which curtailed civil liberties was beyond the reach of the common law, except perhaps insofar as the judiciary could construe such a statute restrictively should they choose. The minority rights in the example postulated above would be equally outside the ambit of common law protection. This result is to be expected given the centrality which Dicey accords to parliamentary omnicompetence. If the majority within Parliament does enact legislation which is detrimental to minority interests, no sanctuary can be expected from the common law. When representative democracy proves incapable of aligning the interests of the elected representatives with the nation as a whole, so that some are constitutionally disadvantaged, the oppressed can but hope for a shift in their political fortune. Dicey's claim that constitutional protection within the United Kingdom was not only historically unfounded, but also unnecessary, is therefore suspect even if our democracy did operate in the manner which he postulated.

(c) The reality of constitutional power

The second reason why Dicey's conclusions can be contested is that this image of the working constitution was in fact flawed. Put shortly, the nineteenth century model of representative democracy contained the seeds of its own destruction. The more closely it approached perfection, the more fragile did it become. The explanation for this apparent paradox is not hard to find. Three factors were of central importance.

The expansion of the franchise was of particular significance. This had increased the legitimacy of Parliament and provided substantive justification for regarding it as the authoritative expression of the will of the nation. The very need to appeal to an expanded electorate was, however, a key factor in the emergence of a more developed party system. Votes had to be won. Buying them was no longer practicable. Party organisation had to be improved in order to mobilise the expanded electorate into voting for a particular party. Central organisation and direction from the 'top' increased, thereby placing more power in the hands of the executive.

This tendency was furthered by the changing conception of the role of government. The idea that the government was responsible for preserving the peace, raising revenue, foreign relations and little else was undergoing a transformation. The picture of the nineteenth century as an era of laissez-faire was always misleading. A range of social legislation was passed during this period dealing with the poor, health, factories, and the like. The transformation which occurred was concerned, in part at least, with the role of government in the legislation which emanated from Parliament. Expansion of the suffrage necessitated not just the development of party organisation to mobilise the expanded electorate. It also required promises of legislation which would be beneficial to those accorded the vote. If at least some of these promises made to the electorate were to be carried out, the legislative process required alteration. This, in fact, occurred. The change was not sudden or immediate, but very real nonetheless.

The legislative process was both nationalised and centralised into the hands of the executive. Standing committees became increasing common. Fear that increased use of such committees would transform the Commons into a legislative machine did not ultimately deter the executive from instituting procedural changes designed to facilitate the passage of legislation. Cabinet committees became more common, adding impetus to the centralisation of the legislative initiative with the executive. Delegated legislation led to the same end by a different route: the legislature would accede to the passage of legislation which ultimately left a considerable residue of discretion to the executive to make further rules. Changes in the legislative process were attended by the increase in importance of the party system within Parliament. The party became the conduit for the transfer of power from the legislature to the executive. Discipline had to be tightened to ensure the passage of an enlarged governmental programme. Policy formulation became increasingly concentrated in the executive. Rarely could backbench MPs effectively stop a measure which had executive backing.

While these factors contributed to the flow of power from the Commons to the executive, the third was the growing realisation of centres of power outside of Parliament which nonetheless exercised a formative influence on the content of government policy. The development of pluralist thought in the United Kingdom was complex. Suffice it to say for the present that the recognition of the pluralist nature of society challenged the idea that Parliament wielded a monopoly of public power. . . .

The implications of the constitutional developments which have been just considered were not, therefore, to destroy Dicey's picture of sovereignty. It did, however, place the conceptual justification for the absence of review under strain. The possibility of some form of constitutional adjudication could no longer so easily be dismissed as unnecessary as well as lacking any foundation in 'precedent.' The growth of executive power, and the realisation that there were centres of power outside of Parliament, challenged the Diceyan view of representative democracy as a self-correcting mechanism. It became apparent that there might be a greater disjunction between Dicey's external and internal limits on sovereign power than had previously been perceived. If representative democracy had in fact become oligarchic, by concentrating authority in the executive and other powerful but non-representative institutions, then it became increasingly possible that the wishes of this small group might diverge considerably from those of the majority of the electorate. This potential was augmented by a voting system which worked against minority interests and which could not infrequently return a government supported by a minority of the population.

Dicey's union between historical precedent and constitutional principle was, therefore, rendered less secure than hitherto. The conception of self-correcting representative democracy was explicitly based upon a channel of authority flowing from the bottom upwards. The MPs who were elected articulated the views of those who had chosen them, and they controlled the executive. Legislation which might be constitutionally questionable, or detrimental to significant sections of the population, would therefore not be passed, or would be quickly repealed.

The structural development explored above rendered the neat, linear pattern of this reasoning suspect. Parliament's legitimacy continued to be derived from the electorate. In this formal sense, authority could still be perceived as flowing from the bottom upwards. In substance, our constitutional system became one dominated by the top, by the executive and the party hierarchy. The people voted, the government governed, and the system began to look increasingly Schumpeterian well before that classic, skeletal vision of democracy was produced. [Schumpeter, in *Capitalism, Socialism and Democracy* (1943), at p. 269, defined the democratic method as the institutional arrangement for arriving at political decisions in which individuals acquire the power to decide by means of competitive struggle for the people's vote.] This tendency was itself exacerbated by the growing control wielded by the organised parties over the electoral agenda and the electoral process.

The legislation which emerged from the 'top down' system could no longer be certain to reflect the electorate's wishes in the simplistic self-correcting sense postulated by Dicey. The concentration of authority and power within the party hierarchy and the executive increased the likelihood that legislation could emanate from Parliament, and remain on the statute books for a considerable period of time, even though it might be contrary to the desires of many within the electorate.

At base these structural changes weakened the very contrast which Dicey drew concerning the degree of coincidence between the external and internal limits on sovereign power which could be expected to operate within a monarchy and a representative democracy. In a monarchy, the sovereign, although subject to certain internal limits, might well be able to force upon his subjects legislation which they disliked. The only constraint upon such action was that the sovereign should be wary lest he transgress the external limits to his sovereign authority and provoke open resistance. A monarchical system left, however, considerable latitude to the sovereign to effectuate his personal goals which, although contrary to the desires of the people, were not sufficient to rouse them to revolt. It was this disjunction between the internal and external limits to sovereign power which the advent of representative democracy was, as we have seen, intended to cure. However, if representative democracy had become oligarchic in the manner described above, then such a disjunction became increasingly possible. The dominant group could impose its own goals, which might be contrary to the wishes of many, and yet not sufficient to produce actual resistance. Representative democracy as it actually operated could, therefore, not in fact be guaranteed to prevent a divergence between the external and internal limits of sovereignty. Power wielded by an elective oligarchy, in conjunction with other powerful but non-representative institutions, might be subject to no greater constraint than that exercised by the hereditary monarch.

QUESTIONS

1. To what extent was W. S. McKechnie correct when he asserted that the self-correcting majoritarian democracy places 'the liberty and property, lives and honour of one half of the community absolutely and legally at the mercy of the other half' (W. S. McKechnie, *The New Democracy and the Constitution* (1912; repr. 1971), p. 164)?

2. Dicey believed that the common law was effective 'in controlling the exercise of executive or discretionary power which could interfere with individual liberty', but how effective is it when the curtailment of individual liberty is authorized by statute? Will the Human Rights Act 1998 make a difference?

3. To what extent is Craig correct when he states that 'the legislative process was both nationalized and centralized into the hands of the executive'? Has representative democracy become oligarchic, leading to disjunction between the internal and external limits to sovereign power? Has anything changed in the way representative democracy operates to counteract this risk of disjunction? Will the Human Rights Act become part of the internal limit?

Anthony Lester QC, 'A Bill of Rights for Britain'
Charter 88, *Manchester Papers* (1991)

One of the fundamental principles of a democratic society is the rule of law, which means that an interference with individual rights should be subject to an effective check which should normally be assured by the judiciary – judicial control offering the best guarantees of independence, impartiality and a proper procedure.

The justification for the judicial protection of human rights is as follows. The protection of basic rights and freedoms cannot be left solely to law makers and civil servants. Parliament and local or regional authorities, as well as individual officials, may and do misuse their powers in the name of the majority, or simply through carelessness or thoughtlessness. It is the proper function of the independent courts in a true democracy to protect minorities against the tyranny of the majority, and against the misuse of public powers.

The rights and freedoms guaranteed by the European Convention and the International Covenant are too important to be subject to the whims of temporary majorities or to unnecessary interference by public officials. Without a Bill of Rights there is always the prospect of Parliament being pressured by populism to disenfranchise or handicap minorities. The most notorious case of this was the Commonwealth Immigrants Act 1968, where a Labour government stripped 200,000 East African Asians of their right to live in the only country of their citizenship. Needless to say, their only recourse was to the European Convention. . . .

Most breaches of civil rights and liberties in the UK do not occur because of the spite or ill will of Parliament, Government or civil servants. The pathology of human rights violations in this country involves uncontrolled administrative discretion. Public officials find that power is delightful and absolute power, absolutely delightful. For example in the Sex Discrimination Act of 1975 and the Race Relations Act of 1976 Parliament gave wide discretionary powers to Ministers to block proceedings in industrial tribunals on grounds of national security and deprive people of their right to access to justice. Similarly, the Home Secretary has wide powers to ban broadcasts on any grounds he sees fit and to regulate discipline in prisons.

Faced with this huge gap in the legal protection of human rights, British courts behave in what some would regard as an impeccably democratic manner – careful not to trample on parliamentary sovereignty, they give public authorities the benefit of the doubt, unless they behave so outrageously in defiance of logic or accepted moral standards as to have taken leave of their senses. Except where European Community Law can come to the rescue, or where there is specific UK human rights legislation, such as the anti-discrimination laws, British law is ethically aimless. There are no coherent standards to guide the judges when they interpret acts of parliament or develop the common law.

Unless and until Parliament gives them real guidance, British courts will not limit the powers of Ministers or public officials by using the European Convention as a Bill of Rights. This was made quite clear in the decision of the House of Lords in the Broadcasting ban case (*R v Secretary of State for the Home Department, ex parte Brind* [[1991] 1 All ER 720]). The court said that they could not be expected to apply a stricter standard of necessity to the infringements of human rights (such as that laid down in the European Convention) when Parliament had specifically refrained from doing so.

To argue for a Bill of Rights is not to argue for a Government of Judges – perish the thought. It is to argue that the judicial branch of Government should be given greater responsibility for remedying the misuse of public powers by either of the other two branches – the Executive and Legislature.

QUESTIONS

In reading Chapter 7, *post*, consider the following questions:

1. Lord Scarman, *English Law – The New Dimension* (1974), p. 15, stated:

   It is the helplessness of the law in face of the legislative sovereignty of Parliament which makes it difficult for the legal system to accommodate the concept of fundamental and inviolable human rights.

   Do you agree? Or has the enactment of the Human Rights Act accorded to individuals guaranteed rights which will *de jure* or *de facto* curtail the law-making powers of Parliament? If so, will such constraints weaken the role of public opinion in developing the law?

2. Lord Scarman went on to state:

   So long as English law is unable in any circumstances to challenge a statute, it is, in dangerous and difficult times, at the mercy of the oppressive and discriminatory statute.

   Is the citizen as defenceless now against the power of the State as Lord Scarman believed at the time he wrote? Where legislation infringes human rights, will courts be able better to protect rights under the Human Rights Act than they were prior to its enactment?

3. Does the Human Rights Act provide ethical underpinning to the doctrine of the rule of law in the United Kingdom?

5

Constitutional Conventions

SECTION 1: **Sources of the Constitution**

As the United Kingdom does not have a written constitution, the sources of our constitutional arrangements must be sought elsewhere. Most textbooks contain sections outlining the sources of the constitution. In these sections they highlight legislation and judicial precedent as the source of the legal rules of the constitution. The source of the non-legal rules is provided by conventions.

A. V. Dicey, *An Introduction to the Study of The Law of the Constitution*
(10th edn, 1965), pp. 23–24

[T]he rules which make up constitutional law, as the term is used in England, include two sets of principles or maxims of a totally distinct character.

The one set of rules are in the strictest sense 'laws,' since they are rules which (whether written or unwritten, whether enacted by statute or derived from the mass of custom, tradition, or judge-made maxims known as the common law) are enforced by the courts; these rules constitute 'constitutional law' in the proper sense of that term, and may for the sake of distinction be called collectively 'the law of the constitution.'

The other set of rules consist of conventions, understandings, habits, or practices which, though they may regulate the conduct of the several members of the sovereign power, of the Ministry, or of other officials, are not in reality laws at all since they are not enforced by the courts. This portion of constitutional law may, for the sake of distinction, be termed the 'conventions of the constitution,' or constitutional morality.

To put the same thing in a somewhat different shape, 'constitutional law,' as the expression is used in England, both by the public and by authoritative writers, consists of two elements. The one element, here called the 'law of the constitution,' is a body of undoubted law; the other element, here called the 'conventions of the constitution,' consists of maxims or practices which, though they regulate the ordinary conduct of the Crown, of Ministers, and of other persons under the constitution, are not in strictness laws at all.

E. C. S. Wade, 'Introduction' in Dicey, *An Introduction to the Study of The Law of the Constitution*
(10th edn, 1965), pp. cli–clvii

The Widened Sphere of Constitutional Conventions. – It is largely through the influence of Dicey that the term, convention, has been accepted to describe a constitutional obligation, obedience to which is secured despite the absence of the ordinary means of enforcing the obligation in a court of law. Dicey defined conventions as 'rules for determining the mode in which the discretionary powers of the Crown (or of the Ministers as servants of the Crown) ought to be exercised.' He was concerned to establish that conventions were 'intended to secure the ultimate supremacy of the electorate as the true political sovereign of the State.'

In discussing conventions as a source of constitutional law it must be noted that the obligation does not necessarily, or indeed usually, derive from express agreement. It is more likely to take its origin from custom or from practice arising out of sheer expediency. . . .

Dicey discusses mainly the rules governing the exercise of the royal prerogative by Ministers of the Crown and that part of the 'law and custom' of Parliament which rests upon custom alone. In both these cases the rules are based on custom or expediency rather than as a result of formal agreement. Conventions, however, have a wider application and have, during the present century, played an important part in building up the political relationship between the various member States of the British Commonwealth. Some of these conventions, in particular the rules governing the full competence of Commonwealth Parliaments to legislate, were made statutory by the Statute of Westminster, 1931, and later enactments. But much of the relationship is still conventional and has been based on agreement reached by Prime Ministers at Imperial Conferences. Constitutional matters no longer figure prominently on the agenda of the periodic meetings of Prime Ministers or other Ministers of Commonwealth Governments which are less formal than the earlier Imperial Conferences. But this is because constitutional issues have now been settled and in no way minimises the important part which conventions have in the past played in this sphere of constitutional development.

Dicey concentrated attention upon the conventional rules which precedent showed were fundamental to the working of the Cabinet. . . .

It is the prerogative of the Sovereign to appoint the Prime Minister. Convention limits the range of choice to that of a party leader who can command a majority in the House of Commons. This convention to some extent lacks the binding force which conventions in other fields possess. This does not mean that the rules can normally be disregarded, but that unforeseen circumstances may deprive them of their force on a particular occasion; any departure from the normal would have to conform to recognising the supremacy of the electorate and not to serve autocratic ends. Some writers would not include a practice or usage which is not regarded as obligatory, though none the less usually followed, in the category of constitutional conventions. It is, however, very difficult to draw the line between an obligatory and a non-obligatory practice. The characteristic of conventions, namely, that they supplement the laws which are enforced by the courts, would seem to preclude their precise definition. On the whole it seems preferable to regard the political practices of Sovereigns in choice of Prime Ministers as within the category of conventional rules, even though those rules are still somewhat inconclusive and therefore sufficiently flexible to meet unforeseen circumstances. For they are clearly rules of conduct referable to the requirements of constitutional government and are aimed at reflecting the supremacy of the electorate. The same is true of the practices and precepts which surround the prerogative of dissolution of Parliament. But in this case there is the fundamental understanding that the power may only be exercised on the advice of Ministers. That advice may not be available to the Sovereign in the choice of a Prime Minister, where his predecessor has been removed by death or his own resignation.

Perhaps the relationship between law and convention is best illustrated by contrasting the legal and conventional position of Ministers. They, like civil servants and members of the armed forces, are in law the servants of the Crown. By convention they, unlike all other servants of the Crown, are responsible directly to Parliament both for their own activities and those of civil servants, their subordinates, who by custom are never referred to by name in Parliament. This responsibility of Ministers is designed to make them answerable through Parliament to the electorate. To rely solely on their legal responsibility to their master, the Sovereign, would entirely fail to secure their responsibility to the public in general and indeed might make them the agents of a Sovereign who disregarded the public will, as in the days before the prerogative powers were restricted by Parliament.

Conventions relating to internal government go much further than the examples which were chosen by Dicey from the exercise of the royal prerogative and the relationship between the two Houses of Parliament. They nowadays provide for the working of the whole complicated governmental machine. A Cabinet in deciding upon policy will require to know whether it already has the power in law to take the action which it proposes. It is certainly not limited to exercising those prerogative powers of the Sovereign which are entrusted to it by convention. Through its command of a majority in the House of Commons it is normally in a position to take legal powers if they do not already exist. Moreover it is the responsibility of the Cabinet to ensure unity in the constitutional system and in particular to avoid or, if need be, to settle conflicts of policy and of action by the various departments. In all these activities rules and practices develop in order to secure the desired end. The growth of the committee system within the Cabinet organisation is an extra-legal development which has introduced important changes in Cabinet government since Dicey formulated his views on the place of conventions in the working of the constitution. One can properly describe this development as conventional. It is in no sense an obligation imposed by law upon Ministers that they should consult an elaborate system of committees. Yet no one supposes that a modern government could be conducted without some such machinery. So we have the position that the Cabinet itself is to all intents and purposes the creation of convention designed to secure political harmony between the Crown and its subjects. From this conventional institution there have grown up in the present century such devices as formal committees, like the Defence Committee, and *ad hoc* committees, appointed for a particular purpose but often remaining in being after their original purpose has been fulfilled. . . . In addition there are royal commissions, select committees of either House of Parliament, committees appointed by departmental Ministers, all of which play an important part in the formulation of policy. For none of these is there any legal requirement. But no appreciation of the working of the governmental machine would be complete without their inclusion. And since their purpose is to focus public opinion on a particular problem, they are designed to secure that harmony between the Ministers of the Crown and the public which is the principal justification for supplementing the law of the constitution with conventions.

QUESTION

What are the various ways in which conventions may arise?

SECTION 2: **What are Conventions?**

Conventions represent important rules of political behaviour which are necessary for the smooth running of the constitution. It is not only in the constitutional arrangements of the United Kingdom that conventions are important; K. C. Wheare, in *Modern Constitutions* (1966), p. 122, states that 'in all countries usage and convention are important and . . . in many countries which have Constitutions usage and convention play as important a part as they do in England'. Conventions facilitate evolution and change within the constitution while the legal form remains unchanged.

G. Marshall and G. C. Moodie, *Some Problems of the Constitution*
(5th edn, 1971), pp. 23–25

What then are the conventions of the British Constitution? One way of answering the question is to point to particular examples. Thus, among them are such rules as that the Monarch should normally on the resignation of a government, ask the Leader of the Opposition to form the new one; or (before 1911) that the House of Lords should not oppose a money bill duly passed by the House of Commons; or (to quote from the Preamble to the Statute of Westminster of 1931) 'that any alteration in the law touching the Succession to the Throne or the Royal Style and Titles shall hereafter require the assent as well of the Parliaments of all the Dominions as of the Parliament of the United Kingdom'. An alternative approach is to put forward a formal definition. By the conventions of the Constitution, then, we mean certain rules of constitutional behaviour which are considered to be binding by and upon those who operate the Constitution, but which are not enforced by the law courts (although the courts may recognise their existence), nor by the presiding officers in the Houses of Parliament. Not all writers would agree to the inclusion of this last phrase. But it seems best to exclude from the category of convention 'the law and custom of Parliament' which define much of its procedure, and which are applied and interpreted by, for example, the Speaker of the House of Commons. On the other hand, certain important rules of procedure – for example, resort to the usual channels through which, among other things, important decisions about the agenda of the House of Commons are reached – are 'unkown' both to the courts and to the Speaker and must clearly be counted as conventions.

Such conventions are to be found in all established constitutions, and soon develop even in the newest. One reason for this is that no general rule of law is self-applying, but must be applied according to the terms of additional rules. These additional rules may be concerned with the interpretation of the general rule, or with the exact circumstances in which it should apply, about either of which uncertainty may exist, and the greater the generality the greater will the uncertainty tend to be. Many constitutions include a large number of additional legal rules to clarify the meaning and application of their main provisions, but in a changing world it is rarely possible to eradicate or prevent all doubts on these points by enactment or even by adjudication. The result often is to leave a significant degree of discretion to those exercising the rights or wielding the powers legally conferred, defined, or permitted. As Dicey pointed out, it is to regulate the use of such discretionary power that conventions develop. Thus the rules prescribing the procedure to be followed by the Monarch in the selection of a Prime Minister regulate the way in which she should exercise her prerogative power to appoint advisers. The legal prerogative remains intact, and appointments to the office of Prime Minister (itself a conventional position) can still be made only by the Monarch. Similarly, it remains true that no bill can become a statute until it receives the Royal Assent; but the Monarch's discretion in deciding whether or not to assent is governed by a rule that she should always assent to a bill which has duly passed both Houses. In this case the royal discretion is so limited as virtually to have been abolished. But the legal position remains untouched and thus, it is sometimes argued, may still be exercised under certain circumstances.

The definition of 'conventions' may thus be amplified by saying that their purpose is to define the use of constitutional discretion. To put this in slightly different words, it may be said that conventions are non-legal rules regulating the way in which legal rules shall be applied. Sometimes, of course, they do so only indirectly, in that they relate primarily to already existing conventions. Not all discretionary powers are so limited, but the most important ones usually are in some degree. In Britain it has been the growth of conventional limitations of the royal prerogative, in conjunction with changes in the legal rules contained in such statutes as the Act of Settlement and the various Acts extending the suffrage (as well as those changes brought about by judicial interpretation), which has largely created our modern system of government. As Sir Kenneth Wheare has said, it is 'the association of law with convention within the constitutional structure which is the essential characteristic'. This is why it is impossible to settle constitutional disputes merely by reference to the state of the law.

G. Wilson, 'Postscript: The Courts, Law and Convention' in Nolan and Sedley, *The Making and Remaking of the British Constitution*
(1997), pp. 97–98

In spite of the use of the law for some of the changes it still remains the case that important parts of the constitution are regulated not by law but by convention, and this remains one of its major distinguishing features. There are, it is said, legal rules and there are conventional rules, each with the same binding force but with many of the conventions not supported by legal rule and therefore not falling within the jurisdiction of the courts. What might be called the grand conventions still lie at the heart of the constitution. They underpinned the gradual transfer of powers from the monarch to her ministers, the limitation of her freedom to choose who should be her ministers, in particular the prime minister, the person who was entitled to form a government, and to dismiss ministers or dissolve Parliament, and the virtual extinction of her power to refuse assent to legislation. But it does not stop there. Conventions reach into every part of the constitution. The rules of procedure and practice of the House of Commons, which help to shape the ground rules of political debate and include provisions as regards the legislative process, the curtailment of debate, the rights of the opposition to choose the subject matter of debate, and which strike the current balance between the need for governments to be able to implement their plans and policies and the opportunities granted to the opposition not only to express their public criticism of them, but also to present themselves to the electorate as a future alternative government – all these rest on convention. It is convention which protects them from arbitrary change and gives them their fundamental character. With none of these do the courts have any direct involvement.

SECTION 3: Laws and Conventions

In the passage by Dicey (*ante* p. 239), he distinguished between laws and conventions, stating that laws are enforced by the courts whereas conventions are not. Sir Ivor Jennings in *The Law and the Constitution*, (5th edn, 1959), at pp. 103–36, takes issue with Dicey. Much of the argument is semantic, being centred on the issue whether all laws are enforced by the courts. Jennings chose to interpret this to mean that Dicey was suggesting that courts would apply sanctions for the breach of any and every law. Many laws are not enforced by the application of sanctions; but they are given effect to by the courts in that they are adhered to and applied. In this sense they are enforced, whereas conventions are treated differently. Other contrasts between laws and conventions have been noted by Munro.

C. R. Munro, *Studies in Constitutional Law*
(2nd edn, 1999), pp. 69–71

For example, instead of being concerned with the practical effects of breaches of rules, we might consider how the rules come into being. In a legal system, a certain number of sources are recognised as law-constitutive. So there are rules specifying what counts as law (or what, by implication, does not). In England, for instance, the courts accept as law only legislation made or authorised by Parliament and the body of rules evolved by the courts called common law. There are formal signs, such as the words of enactment used for Acts of Parliament, denoting that rules have passed a test for being laws. The point here is not merely to reiterate that conventions fall outside the categories recognised as law (which it has been the object of this section so far to show). Rather, what is significant is that conventions do not share the same qualities as laws. They do not come from a 'certain' number of sources: their origins are amorphous, and there are any number of dramatis personae whose behaviour may later be taken as evidence for the existence of a constitutional rule or practice. No body has the function of deciding whether conventions exist. There is no formal sign of their entitlement to be so regarded, and there are no agreed rules for deciding.

These points are related to a larger contrast which may be drawn. Rules of law form parts of a system. Included in the system are rules about the rules: there are provisions about entry to, and exit from, the system, and procedures for the determination and application of the rules. We cannot conceive of a single legal rule, in isolation from a system. However, conventions do not form a system. There is no unifying feature which they possess, and no apparatus of secondary rules. They merely evolve in isolation from each other.

Here, incidentally, lies the answer to Jennings' specious argument that laws and conventions are the same because both 'rest essentially upon general acquiescence'. That is quite misleading. Conventions rest entirely on acquiescence, but individually. If a supposed convention is not accepted as binding by those to whom it would apply, then there could not be said to be a convention, and this is a test on which each must be separately assessed. Laws do not depend upon acquiescence. Individual laws may be unpopular or widely disobeyed, but it does not mean that they are not laws. No doubt the system as a whole must possess some measure of de facto effectiveness for us to recognise it as valid, although it might be stretching language to describe the citizens of any country occupied by enemy forces or ruled by a brutal dictatorship as 'acquiescing' in the laws which govern them. In any event, it is obvious that the comparison is inapt.

When 'acquiescence' is properly analysed, another means of distinguishing emerges. Breaches of a legal rule do not bring into question the existence or validity of the rule; for example, however frequently motorists might exceed the speed limits, the road traffic laws are no less laws for that. However, according to a generally accepted definition, conventions are supposed to be 'rules of political practice which are regarded as binding by those to whom they apply.' If such rules are broken, it becomes appropriate to ask whether they are still 'regarded as binding', and if they are broken often, surely one cannot say that any obligatory rule exists? In other words, the breach of a convention carries a destructive effect, which is absent with laws. The reason for this is that 'feeling obliged' is a necessary condition for the existence of a convention, whereas it is neither a necessary nor a sufficient condition for the existence of laws.

QUESTION

If the courts do not apply sanctions for failure to observe a convention, why are conventions observed?

SECTION 4: **The Nature of Conventions**

The nature of conventions received considerable attention in a Canadian case *Reference Re Amendment of the Constitution of Canada* (1982) 125 DLR (3d) 1. This case arose because of a special procedure in Canada whereby an issue may be referred to court for an advisory opinion; there is no such procedure in the United Kingdom.

The Dominion of Canada was created by the British North America Act 1867 which divided legislative and executive powers between the federal and provincial legislatures. As the 1867 Act was a Westminster statute, further amendment of it could only be carried out through legislation passed at Westminster. The British

North America (No. 2) Act 1949 transferred powers of amendment of the constitution to the Canadian Federal Parliament, with the exception of amendments affecting the distribution of powers between the provincial and federal governments. Conventions developed in relation to the procedure for amendment. These were stated as four principles in a White Paper issued by the Canadian Government in 1965, entitled 'The Amendment of the Constitution of Canada'. The four principles were agreed by all the Provinces before the White Paper was published.

The Amendment of the Constitution of Canada
(1965), p. 15

The first general principle that emerges in the foregoing resumé is that although an enactment by the United Kingdom is necessary to amend the British North America Act, such action is taken only upon formal request from Canada. No Act of the United Kingdom Parliament affecting Canada is therefore passed unless it is requested and consented to by Canada. Conversely, every amendment requested by Canada in the past has been enacted.

The second general principle is that the sanction of Parliament is required for a request to the British Parliament for an amendment to the British North America Act. This principle was established early in the history of Canada's constitutional amendments, and has not been violated since 1895. The procedure invariably is to seek amendments by a joint Address of the Canadian House of Commons and Senate to the Crown.

The third general principle is that no amendment to Canada's Constitution will be made by the British Parliament merely upon the request of a Canadian province. A number of attempts to secure such amendments have been made, but none has been successful. The first such attempt was made as early as 1868, by a province which was at that time dissatisfied with the terms of Confederation. This was followed by other attempts in 1869, 1874 and 1887. The British Government refused in all cases to act on provincial government representations on the grounds that it should not intervene in the affairs of Canada except at the request of the federal government representing all of Canada.

The fourth general principle is that the Canadian Parliament will not request an amendment directly affecting federal-provincial relationships without prior consultation and agreement with the provinces. This principle did not emerge as early as others but since 1907, and particularly since 1930, has gained increasing recognition and acceptance. The nature and the degree of provincial participation in the amending process, however, have not lent themselves to easy definition.

In 1980, after numerous attempts by the Federal Government to reach agreement with the provinces on constitutional reform, the federal government decided to press ahead with a scheme which would patriate the Canadian Constitution by ending the link with Westminster and establish a new procedure for constitutional amendment, and create a new Charter of Rights which would be binding on both federal and provincial legislatures. Eight of the ten provinces opposed the scheme. The question arose whether the federal authorities were entitled to request Westminster to enact the proposed scheme in the absence of unanimous approval from the provinces. The issue ended up in the Canadian Supreme Court when Manitoba, Newfoundland, and Quebec (three of the dissenting provinces) instituted proceedings to obtain a ruling on the constitutionality of the action being taken by the Federal Government. Several important questions arose for determination. Was there a convention that the Federal Parliament would not request an amendment to the constitution affecting federal-provincial relationships without prior consultation and agreement with the provinces? Could the Federal Government *legally* request such amendment despite the absence of such agreement (in other words, could the convention, if it existed, be enforced by the courts)? Another question related to whether a convention could crystallize into law. The case is important because of the examination of the nature of conventions and how they may be recognized.

Reference Re Amendment of the Constitution of Canada
(1982) 125 DLR (3d) 1; Supreme Court of Canada

The essential questions for determination, and the answers of the majority, were as follows:

ON THE APPEAL FROM THE MANITOBA AND NEWFOUNDLAND COURTS OF APPEAL

1. If the amendments to the Constitution of Canada sought in the 'Proposed Resolution for a Joint Address to Her Majesty the Queen respecting the Constitution of Canada', or any of them, were enacted, would federal-provincial relationships or the powers, rights or privileges granted or secured by the Constitution of Canada to the provinces, their legislatures or governments be affected and if so, in what respect or respects?

Answer by all members of the Court: Yes.

2. Is it a constitutional convention that the House of Commons and Senate of Canada will not request Her Majesty the Queen to lay before the Parliament of the United Kingdom . . . a measure to amend the Constitution of Canada affecting federal-provincial relationships or the powers, rights or privileges granted or secured by the Constitution of Canada to the provinces, their legislatures or governments without first obtaining the agreement of the provinces?

Answer by the majority: Yes.

3. Is the agreement of the provinces of Canada constitutionally required for amendment to the Constitution of Canada where such amendment affects federal-provincial relationships or alters the powers, rights or privileges granted or secured by the Constitution of Canada to the provinces, their legislatures or governments?

Answer by the majority: No.

ON THE APPEAL FROM THE QUEBEC COURT OF APPEAL

A. If the Canada Act and the Constitution Act 1981 should come into force and if they should be valid in all respects in Canada would they affect:
(i) the legislative competence of the provincial legislatures in virtue of the Canadian Constitution?
(ii) the status or role of the provincial legislatures or governments within the Canadian Federation?

Answer by all members of the Court: Yes.

B. Does the Canadian Constitution empower, whether by statute, convention or otherwise, the Senate and the House of Commons of Canada to cause the Canadian Constitution to be amended without the consent of the provinces and in spite of the objection of several of them, in such a manner as to affect:
(i) the legislative competence of the provincial legislatures in virtue of the Canadian Constitution?

(ii) the status or role of the provincial legislatures or governments within the Canadian Federation?

Answer by the majority: As a matter of law, Yes. As a matter of convention, No.

THE MAJORITY – The Law: . . . The proposition was advanced on behalf of the Attorney-General of Manitoba that a convention may crystallize into law and that the requirement of provincial consent to the kind of Resolution that we have here, although in origin political, has become a rule of law. . . .

In our view, this is not so. No instance of an explicit recognition of a convention as having matured into a rule of law was produced. The very nature of a convention, as political in inception and as depending on a consistent course of political recognition by those for whose benefit and to whose detriment (if any) the convention developed over a considerable period of time is inconsistent with its legal enforcement.

The attempted assimilation of the growth of a convention to the growth of the common law is misconceived. The latter is the product of judicial effort, based on justiciable issues which have attained legal formulation and are subject to modification and even reversal by the Courts which gave them birth when acting within their role in the State in obedience to statutes or constitutional directives. No such parental role is played by the Courts with respect to conventions.

It was urged before us that a host of cases have given legal force to conventions. This is an overdrawn proposition. One case in which direct recognition and enforcement of a convention was sought is *Madzimbamuto* v *Lardner-Burke et al.*, [1969] 1 AC 645. There the Privy Council rejected the assertion that a convention formally recognized by the United Kingdom as established, namely, that it would not legislate for Southern Rhodesia on matters within the competence of the latter's Legislature without its Government's consent, could not be overridden by British legislation made applicable to Southern Rhodesia after the unilateral declaration of independence by the latter's Government. Speaking for the Privy Council, Lord Reid pointed out that although the convention was a very important one, 'it had no legal effect in limiting the legal power of Parliament' (at p. 723). And, again (at the same page):

> It is often said that it would be unconstitutional for the United Kingdom Parliament to do certain things, meaning that the moral, political and other reasons against doing them are so strong that most people would regard it as highly improper if Parliament did these things. But that does not mean that it is beyond the power of Parliament to do such things. If Parliament chose to do any of them the courts could not hold the Act of Parliament invalid. It may be that it would be unconstitutional to disregard this convention. But it may also be that the unilateral Declaration of Independence released the United Kingdom from any obligation to observe the convention. Their Lordships in declaring the law are not concerned with these matters. They are only concerned with the legal powers of Parliament.

Counsel for Manitoba sought to distinguish this case on the ground that the *Statute of Westminster, 1931* did not embrace Southern Rhodesia, a point to which the Privy Council adverted. The *Statute of Westminster* . . . if it had been in force in Southern Rhodesia it would be only under its terms and not through any conventional rule *per se* that the Parliament of the United Kingdom would have desisted from legislating for Southern Rhodesia.

Having examined various Canadian, United Kingdom and Commonwealth cases without finding any support for the crystallization argument, the Majority continued:

We were invited to consider academic writings on the matter under discussion. There is no consensus among the author-scholars, but the better and prevailing view is that expressed in an article by Munro, 'Laws and Conventions Distinguished', 91 Law Q Rev 218 (1975), where he says (at p. 228):

> The validity of conventions cannot be the subject of proceedings in a court of law. Reparation for breach of such rules will not be effected by any legal sanction. There are no cases which contradict these propositions. In fact, the idea of a court enforcing a mere convention is so strange that the question hardly arises.

Another passage from this article deserves mention, as follows (at p. 224):

> If in fact laws and conventions are different in kind, as is my argument, then an accurate and meaningful picture of the constitution may only be obtained if this distinction is made. If the distinction is blurred, analysis of the constitution is less complete; this is not only dangerous for the lawyer, but less than helpful to the political scientist.

There is no difference in approach whether the issue arises in a unitary State or in a federal State: see Hogg, *Constitutional Law of Canada* (1977), at pp. 7–11.

A contrary view relied on by the provincial appellants is that expressed by Professor W. R. Lederman in two published articles, one entitled 'Process of Constitutional Amendment in Canada', 12 McGill LJ 371 (1967), and the second entitled 'Constitutional Amendment and Canadian Unity', Law Soc UC Lectures 17 (1978). As a respected scholar, Professor Lederman's views deserve more than cursory consideration. He himself recognizes that there are contrary views, including those of an equally distinguished scholar, Professor F. R. Scott: see Scott, *Essays on the Constitution* (1977), pp. 144, 169, 204–5, 245, 370–1, 402. There is also the contrary view of Professor Hogg, already cited.

Professor Lederman relies in part on a line of cases that has already been considered, especially the reasons of Sir Lyman P. Duff in the *Labour Conventions* case. The leap from convention to law is explained almost as if there was a common law of constitutional law, but originating in political practice. That is simply not so. What is desirable as a political limitation does not translate into a legal limitation, without expression in imperative constitutional text or statute. The position advocated is all the more unacceptable when substantial provincial compliance or consent is by him said to be sufficient. Although Professor Lederman would not give a veto to Prince Edward Island, he would to Ontario or Quebec or British Columbia or Alberta. This is an impossible position for a Court to manage.

Turning now to the authority or power of the two federal Houses to proceed by Resolution to forward the address and appended draft statutes to Her Majesty the Queen for enactment by the Parliament of the United Kingdom. There is no limit anywhere in law, either in Canada or in the United Kingdom . . . to the power of the Houses to pass resolutions. Under s. 18 of the *British North America Act, 1867*, the federal Parliament may by statute define those privileges, immunities and powers, so long as they do not exceed those held and enjoyed by the British House of Commons at the time of the passing of the federal statute. . . .

It is said, however, that where the Resolution touches provincial powers, as the one in question here does, there is a limitation on federal authority to pass it on to Her Majesty the Queen unless there is provincial consent. If there is such a limitation, it arises not from any limitation on the power to adopt Resolutions but from an external limitation based on other considerations. . . . [I]t is relevant to point out that even in those cases where an amendment to the *British North America Act, 1867* was founded on a Resolution of the federal Houses after having received provincial consent, there is no instance, save in the *British North America Act, 1930* where such consent was recited in the Resolution. The matter remained, in short, a conventional one within Canada, without effect on the validity of the Resolution in respect of United Kingdom action. . . .

This Court is being asked, in effect, to enshrine as a legal imperative a principle of unanimity for constitutional amendment to overcome the anomaly – more of an anomaly today than it was in 1867 – that the *British North America Act, 1867* contained no provision for effecting amendments by Canadian action alone. . . .

The stark legal question is whether this Court can enact by what would be judicial legislation a formula of unanimity to initiate the amending process which would be binding not only in Canada but also on the Parliament of the United Kingdom with which amending authority would still remain. It would be anomalous indeed, overshadowing the anomaly of a Constitution which contains no provision for its amendment, for this Court to say retroactively that in law we have had an amending formula all along, even if we have not hitherto known it; or, to say, that we have had in law one amending formula, say from 1867 to 1931, and a second amending formula that has emerged after 1931. No one can gainsay the desirability of federal-provincial accord of acceptable compromise. That does not, however, go to legality. . . .

The provincial contentions asserted a legal incapacity in the federal Houses to proceed with the Resolution which is the subject of the References and of the appeals here. Joined to this assertion was a claim that the United Kingdom Parliament had, in effect, relinquished its legal power to act on a Resolution such as the one before this Court, and that it could only act in relation to Canada if a request was made by 'the proper authorities'. The federal Houses would be such authorities if provincial powers or interests would not be affected; if they would be, then the proper authorities would include the Provinces. It is not that the Provinces must be joined in the federal address to Her Majesty the Queen; that was not argued. Rather their consent (or, as in the Saskatchewan submission, substantial provincial compliance or approval) was required as a condition of the validity of the process by address and Resolution and, equally, as a condition of valid action thereon by the United Kingdom Parliament. . . .

[T]he *Statute of Westminster, 1931* . . . is put forward not only as signifying an equality of status as between the Dominion and the Provinces vis-à-vis the United Kingdom Parliament, but also as attenuating the theretofore untrammelled legislative authority of that Parliament in relation to Canada where provincial interests are involved. . . . What s. 7(1), reinforced by s. 7(3), appeared to do was to maintain the *status quo ante*; that is, to leave any changes in the *British North America Act, 1867* (that is, such changes which, under its terms, could not be carried out by legislation of the Provinces or of the Dominion) to the prevailing situation, namely, with the legislative authority of the United Kingdom Parliament being left untouched. As Sir William Jowitt put it . . . 'the old machinery' remained in place as a result of the *Statute of Westminster, 1931*. No other conclusion is supportable on any fair reading of the terms of the *Statute of Westminster, 1931*. . . .

It was argued that the 'request and consent' which must be declared in a British statute to make it applicable to Canada, is the request and consent of the Dominion and the Provinces if the statute is one affecting provincial interests or powers, for example, an amendment of the *British North America Act, 1867* as envisaged by the Resolution herein. The word 'Dominion' in s. 4, it is said, must be read in what may be called a conjoint or collective sense as including both the Dominion and the Provinces; otherwise, it is submitted, the purpose of the *Statute of Westminster, 1931* would be defeated. . . .

Nothing in the language of the *Statute of Westminster, 1931* supports the provincial position yet it is on this interpretation that it is contended that the Parliament of the United Kingdom has relinquished or yielded its previous omnipotent legal authority in relation to the *British North America Act, 1867*, one of its own statutes. As an argument . . . it asserts a legal diminution of United Kingdom legislative supremacy. The short answer to this ramified submission is that it distorts both history and ordinary principles of statutory or constitutional interpretation. The plain fact is that s. 7(1) was enacted to obviate any inference of direct unilateral federal power to amend the *British North America Act, 1867*. . . .

[T]he challenge to the competency in law of the federal Houses to seek enactment by the Parliament of the United Kingdom of the statutes embodied in the Resolution is based on the recognized supremacy of provincial Legislatures in relation to the powers conferred upon them under the *British North America Act, 1867*, a supremacy vis-à-vis the federal Parliament. Reinforcement, or perhaps the foundation of this supremacy is said to lie in the nature or character of Canadian federalism.

The supremacy position, taken alone, needs no further justification than that found in the respective formulations of the powers of Parliament and the provincial Legislatures in ss. 91 and 92 of the

British North America Act, 1867. Federal paramountcy is, however, the general rule in the actual exercise of these powers. This notwithstanding, the exclusiveness of the provincial powers (another way of expressing supremacy and more consonant with the terms of the *British North America Act, 1867*) cannot be gainsaid. . . .

What is put forward by the Provinces which oppose the forwarding of the address without provincial consent is that external relations with Great Britain in this respect must take account of the nature and character of Canadian federalism. It is contended that a legal underpinning of their position is to be found in the Canadian federal system as reflected in historical antecedents, in the pronouncements of leading political figures and in the preamble to the *British North America Act, 1867*.

The arguments from history do not lead to any consistent view or any single view of the nature of the *British North America Act, 1867* . . . . History cannot alter the fact that in law there is a British statute to construe and apply in relation to a matter, fundamental as it is, that is not provided for by the statute. . . .

So too, with pronouncements by political figures or persons in other branches of public life. There is little profit in parading them.

Support for a legal requirement of provincial consent to the Resolution that is before this Court, consent which is also alleged to condition United Kingdom response to the Resolution, is, finally, asserted to lie in the preamble of the *British North America Act, 1867* itself, and in the reflection, in the substantive terms of the Act, of what are said to be fundamental presuppositions in the preamble as to the nature of Canadian federalism. The preamble recites (and the whole of it is reproduced) the following:

> Whereas the Provinces of Canada, Nova Scotia, and New Brunswick have expressed their Desire to be federally united into One Dominion under the Crown of the United Kingdom of Great Britain and Ireland, with a Constitution similar in Principle to that of the United Kingdom:
>
> And whereas such a Union would conduce to the Welfare of the Provinces and promote the Interests of the British Empire:
>
> And whereas on the Establishment of the Union by Authority of Parliament it is expedient, not only that the Constitution of the Legislative Authority in the Dominion be provided for, but also that the Nature of the Executive Government therein be declared:
>
> And whereas it is expedient that Provision be made for the eventual Admission into the Union of other Parts of the British North America: . . .

What is stressed is the desire of the named Provinces 'to be federally united . . . with a Constitution similar in principle to that of the United Kingdom'. The preamble speaks also of union into 'one Dominion' and of the establishment of the Union 'by authority of Parliament', that is the United Kingdom Parliament. What, then, is to be drawn from the preamble as a matter of law? A preamble, needless to say, has no enacting force but, certainly, it can be called in aid to illuminate provisions of the statute in which it appears. Federal union 'with a constitution similar in principle to that of the United Kingdom' may well embrace responsible government and some common law aspects of the United Kingdom's unitary constitutionalism, such as the rule of law and Crown prerogatives and immunities. . . . There is also an internal contradiction in speaking of federalism in the light of the invariable principle of British parliamentary supremacy. Of course, the resolution of this contradiction lies in the scheme of distribution of legislative power, but this owes nothing to the preamble, resting rather on its own exposition in the substantive terms of the *British North America Act, 1867*. . . .

[I]t is the allocation of legislative power as between the central Parliament and the provincial Legislatures that the Provinces rely on as precluding unilateral federal action to seek amendments to the *British North America Act, 1867* that affect, whether by limitation or extension, provincial legislative authority. The Attorney-General of Canada was pushed to the extreme by being forced to answer affirmatively the theoretical question whether in law the federal Government could procure an amendment to the *British North America Act, 1867* that would turn Canada into a unitary State. That is not what the present Resolution envisages because the essential federal character of the country is preserved under the enactments proposed by the Resolution.

That, it is argued, is no reason for conceding unilateral federal authority to accomplish, through invocation of legislation by the United Kingdom Parliament, the purposes of the Resolution. There is here, however, an unprecedented situation in which the one constant since the enactment of the *British North America Act* in 1867 has been the legal authority of the United Kingdom Parliament to amend it. The law knows nothing of any requirement of provincial consent, either to a resolution of the federal Houses or as a condition of the exercise of United Kingdom legislative power.

THE MAJORITY – Convention: . . . [M]any Canadians would perhaps be surprised to learn that important parts of the Constitution of Canada, with which they are the most familiar because they are directly involved when they exercise their right to vote at federal and provincial elections, are nowhere to be found in the law of the Constitution. For instance it is a fundamental requirement of the Constitution that if the Opposition obtains the majority at the polls, the Government must tender its resignation forthwith. But fundamental as it is, this requirement of the Constitution does not form part of the law of the Constitution.

It is also a constitutional requirement that the person who is appointed Prime Minister or Premier by the Crown and who is the effective head of the Government should have the support of the elected branch of the Legislature; in practice this means in most cases the leader of the political party which has won a majority of seats at a general election. Other ministers are appointed by the Crown on the advice of the Prime Minister or Premier when he forms or reshuffles his cabinet. Ministers must continuously have the confidence of the elected branch of the Legislature, individually and collectively. Should they lose it, they must either resign or ask the Crown for a dissolution of the Legislature and the holding of a general election. Most of the powers of the Crown under the prerogative are exercised only upon the advice of the Prime Minister or the Cabinet which means that they are effectively exercised by the latter, together with the innumerable statutory powers delegated to the Crown in council.

Yet none of these essential rules of the Constitution can be said to be a law of the Constitution. It was apparently Dicey who, in the first edition of his *Law of the Constitution*, in 1885, called them 'the conventions of the constitution' (W. S. Holdsworth, 'The Conventions of the Eighteenth Century Constitution', 17 Iowa Law Rev 161 (1932)), an expression which quickly became current. What Dicey described under these terms are the principles and rules of responsible government, several of which are stated above and which regulate the relations between the Crown, the Prime Minister, the Cabinet and the two Houses of Parliament. These rules developed in Great Britain by way of custom and precedent during the nineteenth century and were exported to such British colonies as were granted self-government.

Dicey first gave the impression that constitutional conventions are a peculiarly British and modern phenomenon. But he recognized in later editions that different conventions are found in other constitutions. As Sir William Holdsworth wrote (W. S. Holdsworth, *op. cit.*, p. 162):

> In fact conventions must grow up at all times and in all places where the powers of government are vested in different persons or bodies – where in other words there is a mixed constitution. 'The constitutent parts of a state,' said Burje, [French Revolution, 28] 'are we obliged to hold their public faith with each other, and with all those who derive any serious interest under their engagements, as much as the whole state is bound to keep its faith with separate communities.' Necessarily conventional rules spring up to regulate the working of the various parts of the constitution, their relations to one another, and to the subject.

Within the British Empire, powers of government were vested in different bodies which provided a fertile ground for the growth of new constitutional conventions unknown to Dicey whereby self-governing colonies acquired equal and independent status within the Commonwealth. Many of these culminated in the *Statute of Westminster*, 1931, 22 Geo. V, c. 4 (U.K.). . . .

The main purpose of constitutional conventions is to ensure that the legal framework of the Constitution will be operated in accordance with the prevailing constitutional values or principles of the period. For example, the constitutional value which is the pivot of the conventions stated above and relating to responsible government is the democratic principle: the powers of the State must be exercised in accordance with the wishes of the electorate; and the constitutional value or principle which anchors the conventions regulating the relationship between the members of the Commonwealth is the independence of the former British colonies.

Being based on custom and precedent, constitutional conventions are usually unwritten rules. Some of them, however, may be reduced to writing and expressed in the proceedings and documents of Imperial conferences, or in the preamble of statutes such as the *Statute of Westminster, 1931*, or in the proceedings and documents of federal-provincial conferences. They are often referred to and recognized in statements made by members of governments.

The conventional rules of the Constitution present one striking peculiarity. In contradistinction to the laws of the Constitution, they are not enforced by the Courts. One reason for this situation is that, unlike common law rules, conventions are not judge-made rules. They are not based on judicial precedents but on precedents established by the institutions of government themselves. Nor are they in the nature of statutory commands which it is the function and duty of the Courts to obey and enforce. Furthermore, to enforce them would mean to administer some formal sanction when they are breached. But the legal system from which they are distinct does not contemplate formal sanctions for their breach.

Perhaps the main reason why conventional rules cannot be enforced by the Courts is that they are generally in conflict with the legal rules which they postulate and the Courts are bound to enforce the legal rules. The conflict is not of a type which would entail the commission of any illegality. It results from the fact that legal rules create wide powers, discretions and rights which conventions prescribe should be exercised only in a certain limited manner, if at all.

[An] example will illustrate this point.

As a matter of law, the Queen, or the Governor General or the Lieutenant Governor could refuse assent to every bill passed by both Houses of Parliament or by a Legislative Assembly as the case may be. But by convention they cannot of their own motion refuse to assent to any such bill on any ground, for instance because they disapprove of the policy of the bill. We have here a conflict between a legal rule which creates a complete discretion and a conventional rule which completely neutralizes it. But conventions, like laws, are sometimes violated. And if this particular convention were violated and assent were improperly withheld, the Courts would be bound to enforce the law, not the convention. They would refuse to recognize the validity of a vetoed bill. This is what happened in *Gallant* v *The King*, [1949] 2 DLR 425 . . . a case in keeping with the classic case of *Stockdale* v *Hansard* (1839), 9 Ad & E 1, 112 ER 1112, where the English Court of Queen's Bench held that only the Queen and both Houses of Parliament could make or unmake laws. The Lieutenant-Governor who had withheld assent in *Gallant* apparently did so towards the end of his term of office. Had it been otherwise, it is not inconceivable that his withholding of assent might have produced a political crisis leading to his removal from office which shows that if the remedy for a breach of a convention does not lie with the Courts, still the breach is not necessarily without a remedy. The remedy lies with some other institutions of Government; furthermore, it is not a formal remedy and it may be administered with less certainty or regularity than it would be by a Court.

This conflict between convention and law which prevents the Courts from enforcing conventions also prevents conventions from crystallizing into laws, unless it be by statutory adoption.

It is because the sanctions of convention rest with institutions of government other than Courts, such as the Governor General or the Lieutenant-Governor, or the Houses of Parliament, or with public opinion and ultimately, with the electorate that it is generally said that they are political. . . .

It should be borne in mind, however, that, while they are not laws, some conventions may be more important than some laws. Their importance depends on that of the value or principle which they are meant to safeguard. Also they form an integral part of the Constitution and of the constitutional system. . . .

That is why it is perfectly appropriate to say that to violate a convention is to do something which is unconstitutional although it entails no direct legal consequence. But the words 'constitutional' and 'unconstitutional' may also be used in a strict legal sense, for instance with respect to a statute which is found *ultra vires* or unconstitutional. The foregoing may perhaps be summarized in an equation: constitutional conventions plus constitutional law equal the total Constitution of the country.

The Majority next addressed the issue whether a particular convention exists or not is purely a political question or one upon which a court may adjudicate. They concluded that this was a constitutional question which it is proper for a court to decide and they cited various cases in which courts had recognised the existence of conventions.

In so recognizing conventional rules, the Courts have described them, sometimes commented upon them and given them such precision as is derived from the written form of a judgment. They did not shrink from doing so on account of the political aspects of conventions, nor because of their supposed vagueness, uncertainty or flexibility.

In our view, we should not, in a constitutional reference, decline to accomplish a type of exercise that Courts have been doing of their own motion for years. . . .

The requirements for establishing a convention bear some resemblance with those which apply to customary law. Precedents and usage are necessary but do not suffice. They must be normative. We adopt the following passage of Sir W. Ivor Jennings in *The Law and the Constitution*, 5th edn. (1959), p. 136:

> We have to ask ourselves three questions: first, what are the precedents; secondly, did the actors in the precedents believe that they were bound by a rule; and thirdly, is there a reason for the rule? A single precedent with a good reason may be enough to establish the rule. A whole string of precedents without such a reason will be of no avail, unless it is perfectly certain that the persons concerned regarded them as bound by it.

(i) The precedents
An account of the statutes enacted by the Parliament of Westminster to modify the Constitution of Canada is found in a White Paper published in 1965 under the authority of the Honourable Guy Favreau, then Minister of Justice for Canada, under the title of 'The Amendment of the Constitution of Canada' (the White Paper). . . .

The Majority listed the 22 amendments noting that five of these directly affected federal-provincial relationships in the sense of changing provincial legislative powers.

Every one of these five amendments was agreed upon by each Province whose legislative authority was affected.

In negative terms, no amendment changing provincial legislative powers has been made since Confederation when agreement of a Province whose legislative powers would have been changed was withheld.

There are no exceptions.

Furthermore, in even more telling negative terms, in 1951, an amendment was proposed to give the Provinces a limited power of indirect taxation. Ontario and Quebec did not agree and the amendment was not proceeded with. . . .

The accumulation of these precedents, positive and negative, concurrent and without exception, does not of itself suffice in establishing the existence of the convention; but it unmistakably points in its direction. Indeed, if the precedents stood alone, it might be argued that unanimity is required. . . .

Finally, it was noted in the course of argument that in the case of four of the five amendments mentioned above where provincial consent effectively had been obtained, the statutes enacted by the Parliament of Westminster did not refer to this consent. This does not alter the fact that consent was obtained.

(ii) The actors treating the rule as binding

The Majority referred next to the White Paper of 1965 and the four principles it stated (*ante* p. 245).

The text which precedes the four general principles makes it clear that it deals with conventions. It refers to the laws and conventions by which a country is governed and to constitutional rules which are not binding in any strict sense (that is in a legal sense) but which have come to be recognized and accepted in practice as part of the amendment process in Canada. The first three general principles are statements of well-known constitutional conventions governing the relationships between Canada and the United Kingdom with respect to constitutional amendments.

In our view, the fourth general principle equally and unmistakedly states and recognizes as a rule of the Canadian Constitution the convention referred to in the second question of the Manitoba and Newfoundland References as well as in Question B of the Quebec Reference, namely, that there is a requirement for provincial agreement to amendments which change provincial legislative powers. . . .

It seems clear that while the precedents taken alone point at unanimity, the unanimity principle cannot be said to have been accepted by all the actors in the precedents. . . .

The Majority quoted statements of former Prime Ministers in various Commons Debates.

In 1965, the White Paper had stated that: 'The nature and the degree of provincial participation in the amending process . . . have not lent themselves to easy definition.'

Nothing has occurred since then which would permit us to conclude in a more precise manner.

Nor can it be said that this lack of precision is such as to prevent the principle from acquiring the constitutional *status* of a conventional rule. If a consensus had emerged on the measure of provincial agreement, an amending formula would quickly have been enacted and we would no longer be in the realm of conventions. To demand as much precision as if this were the case and as if the rule were a legal one is tantamount to denying that this area of the Canadian Constitution is capable of being governed by conventional rules.

Furthermore, the Government of Canada and the Governments of the Provinces have attempted to reach a consensus on a constitutional amending formula in the course of ten federal-provincial conferences held in 1927, 1931, 1935, 1950, 1960, 1964, 1971, 1978, 1979 and 1980. (Gérald A. Beaudoin, *op. cit.*, at p. 346.) A major issue at these conferences was the quantification of provincial consent. No consensus was reached on this issue. But the discussion of this very issue for more than fifty years postulates a clear recognition by all the Governments concerned of the principle that a substantial degree of provincial consent is required.

It would not be appropriate for the Court to devise in the abstract a specific formula which would indicate in positive terms what measure of provincial agreement is required for the convention to be complied with. Conventions by their nature develop in the political field and it will be for the political actors, not this Court, to determine the degree of provincial consent required.

It is sufficient for the Court to decide that at least a substantial measure of provincial consent is required and to decide further whether the situation before the Court meets with this requirement.

The situation is one where Ontario and New Brunswick agree with the proposed amendments whereas the eight other Provinces oppose it. By no conceivable standard could this situation be thought to pass muster. It clearly does not disclose a sufficient measure of provincial agreement. Nothing more should be said about this.

(iii) A reason for the rule

The reason for the rule is the federal principle. Canada is a federal union. The preamble of the *BNA Act* states that 'the Provinces of Canada, Nova Scotia, and New Brunswick have expressed their Desire to be federally united . . .'.

The federal character of the Canadian Constitution was recognized in innumerable judicial pronouncements. We will quote only one, that of Lord Watson in *Liquidators of Maritime Bank* v *Receiver-General of New Brunswick* [1982] AC 437 at pp. 441–2:

> The object of the Act was neither to weld the provinces into one, nor to subordinate provincial governments to a central authority, but to create a federal government in which they should all be represented, entrusted with the exclusive administration of affairs in which they had a common interest, each province retaining its independence and autonomy.

The federal principle cannot be reconciled with a state of affairs where the modification of provincial legislative powers could be obtained by the unilateral action of the federal authorities. It would indeed offend the federal principle that 'a radical change to [the] constitution [be] taken at the request of a bare majority of the members of the Canadian House of Commons and Senate'. (Report of Dominion-Provincial Conference, 1931, p. 3.) . . .

Furthermore, as was stated in the fourth general principle of the White Paper, the requirement of provincial consent did not emerge as easily as other principles, but it has gained increasing recognition and acceptance since 1907 and particularly since 1930. This is clearly demonstrated by the proceedings of the Dominion-Provincial Conference of 1931.

Then followed the positive precedents of 1940, 1951 and 1964 as well as the abortive ones of 1951, 1960 and 1964, all discussed above. By 1965, the rule had become recognized as a binding constitutional one formulated in the fourth general principle of the White Paper already quoted reading in part as follows:

> *The fourth general principle* is that the Canadian Parliament will not request an amendment directly affecting federal-provincial relationships without prior consultation and agreement with the provinces.

The purpose of this conventional rule is to protect the federal character of the Canadian Constitution and prevent the anomaly that the House of Commons and Senate could obtain by simple resolutions what they could not validly accomplish by statute. . . .

We have reached the conclusion that the agreement of the Provinces of Canada, no views being expressed as to its quantification, is constitutionally required for the passing of the 'Proposed Resolution for a joint Address to Her Majesty respecting the Constitution of Canada' and that the passing of this Resolution without such agreement would be unconstitutional in the conventional sense.

QUESTIONS

1. If conventions will not be enforced by the courts, what is the sanction for failure to observe a convention?

2. Is it possible to state and define conventions with precision?

3. Is Jenning's test for recognizing conventions, approved by the Supreme Court, a satisfactory and precise test?

4. Should the courts in the United Kingdom be asked to give advisory opinions on the constitution?

NOTE: What would have happened if the Federal Government had pressed ahead with the request in the absence of a 'substantial degree of provincial consent'? Would Westminster have passed the necessary legislation? Was it a convention that any amendment requested by Canada be automatically enacted by Westminster, regardless of the degree of support in Canada for the requested amendment? Certainly there was no example of such a request being refused in the past; but was this sufficient to establish a convention? This matter was examined by the House of Commons Select Committee on Foreign Affairs which reported before the Supreme Court's decision.

First Report of the Foreign Affairs Committee (Kershaw Report)
HC 42 of 1980–81

The purpose of our inquiry

4. The Canadian Government have been vigorously arguing, since the beginning of October 1980, that

> the British Parliament or government *may not look behind any federal request* for amendment, including a request for patriation of the Canadian constitution. Whatever role the Canadian provinces might play in constitutional amendments is a matter *of no consequence as far as the UK Government and Parliament are concerned.*

But the same Canadian Government document, in the preceding sentence, also said: 'The British Parliament is bound to act in accordance with a *proper* request from the federal government . . .'. So our first question was, and remains: Under what conditions is a request from the Canadian Government a proper request?

5. At the same time, our attention was directed by the FCO to a series of Ministerial statements in the UK Parliament. These have, as their common thread, the formula:

> If a request to effect such a change were to be received from the Parliament of Canada it would be *in accordance with precedent* for the United Kingdom Government to introduce in Parliament, and for Parliament to enact, appropriate legislation in compliance with the request.

So we were led to ask: What are the precedents, in relation to requests from Canada? Is there a significant difference between the UK Ministers' references to requests from the Canadian *Parliament* and the Canadian Government's references to requests from the Canadian *Government*? If there is a significant difference, does it reflect a convention, requiring that requests, to be 'proper', must have the support of the Parliament (Senate as well as House of Commons) of Canada? If that is a convention recognised by the UK Government, are there other conventions defining what counts as a proper request from Canada? How and when did such conventions arise? If a convention or principle is created, or becomes recognised, by action and opinion in Canada, is it to be taken into account by the UK Government and Parliament? And, even if it is to be taken into account in the UK, does such a principle of the Canadian constitution *determine* the responsibilities of (or 'bind') the UK Parliament?

6. The fundamental question we had to consider is the subject of Chapter VI of this Report: Is the UK Parliament bound, by convention or principle, to act automatically on any request from the Canadian Parliament for amendment or patriation of the BNA Acts? In view of the weight of evidence against an affirmative answer to that question, it became necessary to consider the further question, discussed in Chapter VII: Is it correct to say that the UK Parliament, when

requested to enact constitutional changes which would directly affect Canadian Federal – Provincial relations, should not accede to the request unless it is concurred in by all the Provinces directly affected? . . .

A requirement of automatic action?

56. In this Chapter, we consider the question whether there is a rule, principle or convention that the UK Parliament, when requested by the Canadian Government and Parliament to amend (or patriate) the BNA Acts, should accede to the request 'automatically', ie regardless of the way that amendment would affect Federal-Provincial relations and of the concurrence or lack of concurrence of the Provinces in an amendment directly affecting the powers or rights of the Provincial legislatures or governments.

Proper requests should be enacted without delay

57. There can be no doubt that if a request by the Canadian Government and Parliament is a proper request, it is the responsibility of the UK Government and Parliament to secure the enactment of the request with all the urgency or priority which the Canadian Government may reasonably desire. That, indeed, is the practice of the UK Parliament, and it should be adhered to. But it is one thing to treat all proper requests as matters of priority, and quite another to consider oneself bound to regard all requests as proper requests. . . .

UK practice since 1931

68. There is nothing in UK *practice* (as distinct from Ministerial statements . . .) that should be regarded as creating a convention of automatic action in the sense specified in para 56 above. For the Canadian Government and Parliament, from 1931 to this day, have been careful not to make any request for UK action, in any matter clearly and 'directly affecting federal-provincial relations' in the sense of the 'fourth general principle' set out and explained by the 1965 White Paper . . . except with the concurrence of all the Provinces. The amendments of 1940, 1951, 1960 and 1964 directly affected the powers or rights of Provincial authorities as such. All these were requested only with the agreement of all Provinces. The amendments of 1943, 1946 and 1949 (twice), which were requested without Provincial concurrence, did not affect the powers or rights of Provincial authorities as such. . . .

The central issue of principle: Canada's federal character

82. Canada's constitutional system is federal. This federal character is stressed again and again in the authoritative Canadian judicial and political pronouncements which we analysed in paras 32–37 and 47–55 above. Those pronouncements have all underlined the way in which the federal nature of Canada's constitutional system affects the law, convention and practice relating to amendment of that system.

83. All the evidence and advice which we received from UK constitutional lawyers and UK academic authorities learned in Commonwealth constitutions was to the same effect: *it would be in accord with the established constitutional position for the UK Government and Parliament* – particularly Parliament – *to take account of the federal nature of Canada's constitutional system*, when considering how to respond to a request by the Canadian Government and Parliament for amendment and/or patriation of the BNA Acts. For when it acts or declines to act, on such a request, the UK Parliament is exercising its powers and responsibilities as . . . 'part of the process of Canadian constitutional amendment'. It would *not* be in accord with the established constitutional position for the UK Parliament to regard itself as in any way the subject of a rule, principle or convention that it should accede to such requests automatically, ie regardless of whether the request was made in a manner contrary to the principles of Canada's federal system and/or to the conventions regulating the making of such requests. If the UK Parliament were to proceed on the basis that it ought to accede to such requests automatically (subject only to the requirements of correct legislative form),

it would be treating itself as for all relevant purposes the agent of the Canadian Government and Parliament. It would thus be treating the Canadian Government and Parliament as having, in constitutional reality, a substantially unilateral power of amending or abolishing Canada's federal system. For any one Government and Parliament to have such a unilateral power is inconsistent with the federal character of that system; nor is it in accord with the 'rules and principles relating to amendment procedures' which have 'emerged from the practices and procedures employed in securing various amendments to the British North American Act since 1867'.

84. Such is the gist of all the evidence and advice from UK experts. . . . We accept it as an accurate delineation of the role and responsibility of the UK Parliament in relation to the amendment and/or patriation of the BNA Acts. The precedents, consisting of actions by the UK Government and Parliament and statements in Parliament by UK Ministers, seem to us not to involve any acknowledgement of a requirement of automatic action. Those precedents all relate to requests made by the Canadian Government and Parliament in apparent conformity with the established Canadian constitutional position regarding the making of requests. They leave the UK Government and Parliament *constitutionally (not merely legally or technically) free to decide that the making of a request is so out of line with the established constitutional position that the UK Government can rightly decline to act on that request.* There is *no precedent* for the UK Government and Parliament receiving and acting upon a request, the making of which was clearly and substantially not in accord with the established Canadian constitutional position. . . .

Conclusions

111. The considerations set out in this Chapter, taken with the preceding Chapter, lead us to the conclusion that the UK Parliament is not bound, even conventionally, either by the supposed requirement of automatic action on Federal requests, or by the supposed requirement of unanimous Provincial consent to amendments altering Provincial powers. Instead the UK Parliament retains the role of deciding whether or not a request for amendment or patriation of the BNA Acts conveys the clearly expressed wish of Canada as a whole, bearing in mind the federal nature of that community's constitutional system. In all ordinary circumstances, the request of the Canadian Government and Parliament will suffice to convey that wish. But where the requested amendment or patriation directly affects the *federal* structure of Canada, and the opposition of Provincial governments and legislatures is officially represented to the UK authorities, something more is required.

112. We recognise that that conclusion involves an unpalatable and thankless role for the UK Government and Parliament. . . .

113. The role involves a responsibility in relation to Canada as a federally structured whole. It is not a *general* responsibility for the welfare of Canada or of its Provinces and peoples. It is simply the responsibility of exercising the UK Parliament's residual powers in a manner consistent with the federal character of Canada's constitutional system, *inasmuch as that federal character affects the way in which the wishes of Canada, on the subject of constitutional change, are to be expressed. It would be quite improper for the UK Parliament to deliberate about the suitability of requested amendments or methods of patriation,* or about the effects of those amendments on the welfare of Canada or any of its communities or peoples.

114. Is there any available criterion for measuring whether a request accords with the wishes of the Canadian people as a federally structured community? We do not think the UK Parliament should invent a criterion of its own; what is needed is a criterion with a basis in the constitutional history and politics of Canada. Such a criterion seems to us to be available. We think that it would not be inappropriate for the UK Parliament to expect that a request for patriation by an enactment significantly affecting the federal structure of Canada should be conveyed to it with *at least that degree of Provincial concurrence* (expressed by governments, legislatures or referendum majorities) *which would be required for a post-patriation amendment* affecting the federal structure in a similar way.

For example a federal request that had the support of the two largest Provinces and of Provinces containing 50 per cent of the Western and 50 per cent of the Atlantic populations would be one that could be said to correspond to the wishes of the Canadian peoples on a whole. This criterion has roots in the historic structure of Canadian federalism as reflected in the Divisions of Canada for the purposes of the Provincial representation in the Senate of Canada; and it broadly accords both with the last (if not the only) clear consensus of Canadian Federal and Provincial governments (at Victoria in 1971) and with the present proposals . . . of the Canadian Government in relation to post-patriation amendment.

115. Some forms or modes of patriation would affect the federal structure of Canada less than would some amendments of the BNA Acts. So one further possibility arises for consideration. The UK Government and Parliament might receive from the Canadian Government and Parliament, without the concurrence of the Provinces, a request for patriation/amendment involving *only* (i) termination of the UK's legislative powers and (ii) a post-patriation amendment formula providing for amendment only with at least such a degree of provincial support as is required to initiate an amendment procedure in Part IV of the proposed 'Canada Constitution Act, 1980'. It might well be proper for the UK Parliament to accede to such a request. For such action by the UK Parliament, while arguably not strictly pursuant to the clearly expressed wishes of Canada as a federally structured whole, would give effect, for the future, to those constitutional changes, and only those changes, which corresponded with such wishes. Since the UK Parliament's action would involve no other substantial constitutional change, it would not substantially affect the federal character of Canada's constitutional system and would not be out of accord with the UK's role in the established constitutional position as we have tried to explain it.

NOTE: The decision of the Supreme Court that the convention required a substantial degree of provincial consent was in line with the view expressed by the Kershaw Committee. The convention was designed to protect the federal character of the Canadian Constitution and prevent the Federal Parliament achieving by means of a resolution addressed to Westminster what it could not achieve domestically by means of legislation.

QUESTION

In a Memorandum to the Kershaw Committee, Professor H. W. R. Wade stated:

Conventions are the rules of the game of politics, and it may be necessary to correct one infringement by another. If for example a British government were to refuse to resign after being defeated on a motion of no confidence, the Queen would be justified in dismissing the ministers against their will. The fact that the UK Parliament does not in practice look behind amendments requested by Canada is entirely dependent upon those requests being in conformity with Canadian conventions. If those conventions are infringed, the duty of the UK Parliament is to take corrective action.

Is it desirable that the sanction for breach of one convention is the breach of another – a principle of constitutional tit-for-tat?

NOTE: In response to the Supreme Court's decision the Federal Government decided not to press on with the request to Westminster to enact legislation. Further discussions were held with the provinces and concessions were offered. In response, nine provinces agreed to the revised proposals. A new request was made, and the Canada Act 1982 was duly enacted at Westminster following a recommendation from the Kershaw Committee that consent from nine out of ten provinces constituted a substantial measure of support for the proposals.

First Report of the Foreign Affairs Committee (Kershaw Report)
HC 128 of 1981–82

6. The criteria suggested in our First Report for assessing the appropriate level of Provincial support were put forward, not as minima required by any existing constitutional rule or convention, but rather as indications of what 'Parliament would be justified in regarding as sufficient' or of what 'it would not be inappropriate for the UK Parliament to expect'. Since then, the Supreme Court of Canada has determined that what is constitutionally required is 'at least a substantial measure of Provincial consent'. The Court decided that unanimity is not required, but did not define or quantify 'a substantial measure'. The Government of Quebec have, we understand, commenced litigation to establish whether their concurrence is constitutionally required. So it is important to observe that the Supreme Court has stated, 'It will be for the political actors, not this Court, to determine the degree of provincial consent required'. The Federal-Provincial Agreement of 5 November 1981, made in the wake of the Supreme Court's judgement and accepted by nine of the ten Provinces, appears to us to amount to a determination by the political actors in Canada that the concurrence of nine Provinces is constitutionally sufficient, albeit the dissenting Province be Quebec.

7. In this situation, what we said in our First Report seems applicable: 'the UK Parliament is bound to exercise its best judgement in deciding whether the request, in all the circumstances, conveys the clearly expressed wishes of Canada as a federally structured whole'. In our view, the present request does this.

SECTION 5: **Devolution and the Sewel Convention**

Under the arrangements for devolution to Scotland the Westminster Parliament retains the right to make laws for Scotland (Scotland Act 1998, s. 28(7)). (There is a similar provision in the Northern Ireland Act 1998 (s. 5(6)).) The power to legislate for Scotland could, if used too regularly, undermine the devolution process. When the Scotland Bill was being debated in the House of Lords, Lord Sewel announced on behalf of the Government (HL Debates, 21 July 1998, col. 791) that the Government:

> would expect a convention to be established that Westminster would not normally legislate with regard to devolved matters in Scotland without the consent of the Scottish Parliament.

Such a convention governed legislation by Westminster for former dependent territories which had become independent members of the Commonwealth (see the preamble to and s. 4 of the Statute of Westminster 1931). In the *Memorandum of Understanding and supplementary agreements between the United Kingdom Government and Scottish Ministers* (1999), Cm 4444, the principle of not legislating for Scotland without its consent is reiterated. The *Memorandum of Understanding* provides as follows:

> 2. This memorandum is a statement of political intent, and should not be interpreted as a binding agreement. It does not create legal obligations between the parties. . . .
>
> **Parliamentary Business**
> 13. The United Kingdom Parliament retains authority to legislate on any issue, whether devolved or not. It is ultimately for Parliament to decide what use to make of that power. However the UK Government will proceed in accordance with the convention that the UK

Parliament would not normally legislate with regard to devolved matters except with the agreement of the devolved legislature. The devolved administrations will be responsible for seeking such agreement as may be required for this purpose on an approach from the UK Government.

14. The United Kingdom Parliament retains the absolute right to debate, enquire into or make representations about devolved matters. It is ultimately for Parliament to decide what use to make of that power, but the UK Government will encourage the UK Parliament to bear in mind the primary responsibility of devolved legislatures and administrations in these fields and to recognise that it is a consequence of Parliament's decision to devolve certain matters that Parliament itself will in future be more restricted in its field of operation.

The Privy Council Office in Devolution Guidance No. 10, *Post Devolution Primary Legislation Affecting Scotland*, September 1999, states that the convention applies only where the Westminster Bill:

contains provisions applying to Scotland and which are for devolved purposes, or which alter the legislative competence of the Parliament or the executive competence of the Scottish Ministers.

In the first two years of devolution there have been 18 Bills in the Westminster Parliament which have resulted in a request for consent from the Scottish Parliament to the legislation. All requests have resulted in consent being given (perhaps because both the Westminster and Scottish administrations are of the same political complexion). Detailed analysis of the use of the Sewel Convention has been carried out by Noreen Burrows, 'Lessons from Scotland? This is Scotland's Parliament; let Scotland's Parliament legislate', paper presented to the Public Law Group, SPTL, 10 September 2001.

SECTION 6: Can Conventions Crystallize into Law?

This question was answered in the negative by the Supreme Court in *Reference Re Amendment of the Constitution of Canada* (*ante* p. 246). It also arose before a United Kingdom court in *Manuel* v *Attorney-General* [1983] 1 Ch 77. The suggestion in this case was that the convention that Westminster would not enact legislation for a dominion except at its request and with its consent, had crystallized into law so that actual consent had to be established. The action had been brought by Aboriginal chiefs seeking a declaration that the Canada Act 1982 was *ultra vires* as the consent of the Aboriginal people did not exist. Section 4 of the Statute of Westminster 1931 provides:

No Act of Parliament of the United Kingdom passed after the commencement of this Act shall extend, or be deemed to extend, to a Dominion as part of the law of that Dominion, unless it is expressly declared in that Act that that Dominion has requested, and consented to, the enactment thereof.

This section did not enact the convention but incorporated it in a modified form. The issues involved are clearly stated in the judgment of Slade LJ, *ante* pp. 88–90.

SECTION 7: **Conventions in the Courts**

It is clear that courts will not enforce conventions by imposing sanctions for their breach. Recognition of the existence of a convention by a court, however, can be significant in the court's decision of the issues before it. Conventions may be used as an aid to statutory interpretation or to support judicial decisions not to review discretionary powers of the executive because of the Minister's accountability to Parliament (see *Liversidge* v *Anderson* [1942] AC 206). In *Carltona* v *Commissioners of Works* [1943] 2 All ER 560, Lord Green MR placed considerable emphasis on the convention of ministerial responsibility in reaching his decision. He stated (at p. 563):

In the administration of government in this country the functions which are given to ministers (and constitutionally properly given to ministers because they are constitutionally responsible) are functions so multifarious that no minister could ever personally attend to them. To take the example of the present case no doubt there have been thousands of requisitions in this country by individual ministries. It cannot be supposed that this regulation meant that, in each case, the minister in person should direct his mind to the matter. The duties imposed upon ministers and the powers given to ministers are normally exercised under the authority of the ministers by responsible officials of the department. Public business could not be carried on if that were not the case. Constitutionally, the decision of such an official is, of course, the decision of the minister. The minister is responsible. It is he who must answer before Parliament for anything that his officials have done under this authority, and, if for an important matter he selected an official of such junior standing that he could not be expected competently to perform the work, the minister would have to answer for that in Parliament. The whole system of departmental organisation and administration is based on the view that ministers, being responsible to Parliament, will see that important duties are committed to experienced officials. If they do not do that, Parliament is the place where complaint must be made against them.

One of the best examples of judicial consideration of conventions in a United Kingdom court is the case which follows.

Attorney-General v *Jonathan Cape Ltd*
[1976] QB 752, High Court

Between 1964 and 1970 Richard Crossman was a Cabinet Minister, and he kept a political diary. Following his death in 1974, his diary for 1964–66 was edited for publication. A copy was sent to the Secretary to the Cabinet for his approval but was rejected on the ground that publication was against the public interest, in that the doctrine of collective responsibility would be harmed by the disclosure of details of Cabinet decisions, the revelation of differences between members of the Cabinet, and the disclosure of advice given by, and discussions regarding the appointment of, civil servants. When Crossman's literary executors decided to publish extracts of the diary in the *Sunday Times*, the Attorney-General sought injunctions against the publishers, literary executors, and the *Sunday Times* to restrain publication of the book or extracts from it.

LORD WIDGERY CJ: . . . It has always been assumed by lawyers and, I suspect, by politicians, and the Civil Service, that Cabinet proceedings and Cabinet papers are secret, and cannot be publicly disclosed until they have passed into history. It is quite clear that no court will compel the production of Cabinet papers in the course of discovery in an action, and the Attorney-General contends that not only will the court refuse to compel the production of such matters, but it will go further and positively forbid the disclosure of such papers and proceedings if publication will be contrary to the public interest.

The basis of this contention is the confidential character of these papers and proceedings, derived from the convention of joint Cabinet responsibility whereby any policy decision reached by the Cabinet has to be supported thereafter by all members of the Cabinet whether they approve of it or not, unless they feel compelled to resign. It is contended that Cabinet decisions and papers are confidential for a period to the extent at least that they must not be referred to outside the Cabinet in such a way as to disclose the attitude of individual Ministers in the argument which preceded the decision. . . .

There is no doubt that Mr Crossman's manuscripts contain frequent references to individual opinions of Cabinet Ministers. . . . There have, as far as I know, been no previous attempts in any court to define the extent to which Cabinet proceedings should be treated as secret or confidential, and it is not surprising that different views on this subject are contained in the evidence before me. . . .

The Attorney-General contends that all Cabinet papers and discussions are prima facie confidential, and that the court should restrain any disclosure thereof if the public interest in concealment outweighs the public interest in a right to free publication. The Attorney-General further contends that, if it is shown that the public interest is involved, he has the right and duty to bring the matter before the court. In this contention he is well supported by Lord Salmon in *Reg* v *Lewes Justices, Ex parte Secretary of State for the Home Department* [1973] AC 388, 412, where Lord Salmon said:

> when it is in the public interest that confidentiality shall be safeguarded, then the party from whom the confidential document or the confidential information is being sought may lawfully refuse it. In such a case the Crown may also intervene to prevent production or disclosure of that which in the public interest ought to be protected.

I do not understand Lord Salmon to be saying, or the Attorney-General to be contending, that it is only necessary for him to evoke the public interest to obtain an order of the court. On the contrary, it must be for the court in every case to be satisfied that the public interest is involved, and that, after balancing all the factors which tell for or against publication, to decide whether suppression is necessary.

The defendants' main contention is that whatever the limits of the convention of joint Cabinet responsibility may be, there is no obligation enforceable at law to prevent the publication of Cabinet papers and proceedings, except in extreme cases where national security is involved. In other words, the defendants submit that the confidential character of Cabinet papers and discussions is based on a true convention as defined in the evidence of Professor Henry Wade, namely, an obligation founded in conscience only. Accordingly, the defendants contend that publication of these Diaries is not capable of control by any order of this court.

If the Attorney-General were restricted in his argument to the general proposition that Cabinet papers and discussion are all under the seal of secrecy at all times, he would be in difficulty. It is true that he has called evidence from eminent former holders of office to the effect that the public interest requires a continuing secrecy, and he cites a powerful passage from the late Viscount Hailsham to this effect. The extract comes from a copy of the Official Report (House of Lords) for December 21, 1932, in the course of a debate on Cabinet secrecy. Lord Hailsham said; col. 527:

> But, my Lords, I am very glad that the question has been raised because it has seemed to me that there is a tendency in some quarters at least to ignore or to forget the nature and

extent of the obligations of secrecy and the limitations which rigidly hedge round the position of a Cabinet Minister. My noble friend has read to your Lordships what in fact I was proposing to read – that is, the oath which every Privy Councillor takes when he is sworn of His Majesty's Privy Council. Your Lordships will remember that one reason at least why a Cabinet Minister must of necessity be a member of the Privy Council is that it involves the taking of that oath. Having heard that oath read your Lordships will appreciate what a complete misconception it is to suppose, as some people seem inclined to suppose, that the only obligation that rests upon a Cabinet Minister is not to disclose what are described as the Cabinet's minutes. He is sworn to keep secret all matters committed and revealed unto him or that shall be treated secretly in Council.

Lord Hailsham then goes on to point out that there are three distinct classes to which the obligation of secrecy applies. He describes them as so-called Cabinet minutes; secondly, a series of documents, memoranda, telegrams and despatches and documents circulated from one Cabinet Minister to his colleagues to bring before them a particular problem and to discuss the arguments for and against a particular course of conduct; and, thirdly, apart from those two classes of documents, he says there is the recollection of the individual Minister of what happens in the Cabinet. Then the extract from Lord Hailsham's speech in the House of Lord's report continues in these words:

I have stressed that because, as my noble and learned friend Lord Halsbury suggested and the noble Marquis, Lord Salisbury, confirmed, Cabinet conclusions did not exist until 16 years ago. The old practice is set out in a book which bears the name of the noble earl's father, Halsbury's Laws of England, with which I have had the honour to be associated in the present edition.

Then the last extract from Lord Hailsham's speech is found in col. 532, and is in these words:

It is absolutely essential in the public interest that discussions which take place between Cabinet Ministers shall take place in the full certainty of all of them that they are speaking their minds with absolute freedom to colleagues on whom they can explicitly rely, upon matters on which it is their sworn duty to express their opinions with complete frankness and to give all information, without any haunting fear that what happens may hereafter by publication create difficulties for themselves or, what is far more grave, may create complications for the King and country that they are trying to serve. For those reasons I hope that the inflexible rule which has hitherto prevailed will be maintained in its integrity, and that if there has been any relaxation or misunderstanding, of which I say nothing, the debate in this House will have done something to clarify the position and restate the old rule in all its rigour and all its inflexibility.

The defendants, however, in the present action, have also called distinguished former Cabinet Ministers who do not support this view of Lord Hailsham, and it seems to me that the degree of protection afforded to Cabinet papers and discussion cannot be determined by a single rule of thumb. Some secrets require a high standard of protection for a short time. Others require protection until a new political generation has taken over. In the present action against the literary executors, the Attorney-General asks for a perpetual injunction to restrain further publication of the Diaries in whole or in part. I am far from convinced that he has made out a case that the public interest requires such a Draconian remedy when due regard is had to other public interests, such as the freedom of speech: see Lord Denning MR in *In re X (A Minor) (Wardship: Jurisdiction)* [1975] Fam 47. . . . It seems to me . . . that the Attorney-General must first show that whatever obligation of secrecy or discretion attaches to former Cabinet Ministers, that obligation is binding in law and not merely in morals.

I have read affidavits from a large number of leading politicians, and the facts, so far as relevant, appear to be these. In 1964, 1966 and 1969 the Prime Minister (who was in each case Mr Harold

Wilson) issued a confidential document to Cabinet Ministers containing guidance on certain questions of procedure. Paragraph 72 of the 1969 edition provides:

> The principle of collective responsibility and the obligation not to disclose information acquired whilst holding Ministerial office apply to former Ministers who are contemplating the publication of material based upon their recollections of the conduct of Cabinet and Cabinet committee business in which they took part.

The general understanding of Ministers while in office was that information obtained from Cabinet sources was secret and not to be disclosed to outsiders.

There is not much evidence of the understanding of Ministers as to the protection of such information after the Minister retires. It seems probable to me that those not desirous of publishing memoirs assumed that the protection went on until the incident was 30 years old, whereas those interested in memoirs would discover on inquiry at the Cabinet Office that draft memoirs were normally submitted to the Secretary of the Cabinet for his advice on their contents before publication. Manuscripts were almost always submitted to the Secretary of the Cabinet in accordance with the last-mentioned procedure. Sir Winston Churchill submitted the whole of his manuscripts concerned with the war years, and accepted the advice given by the Secretary of the Cabinet as to publication. . . .

The main framework of the defence is to be found in eight submissions from Mr Comyn. The first two have already been referred to, the allegation being that there is no power in law for the court to interfere with publication of these diaries or extracts, and that the Attorney-General's proper remedy lies in obtaining a change of the statute law.

I have already indicated some of the difficulties which face the Attorney-General when he relied simply on the public interest as a ground for his actions. That such ground is enough in extreme cases is shown by the universal agreement that publication affecting national security can be restrained in this way. It may be that in the short run (for example, over a period of weeks or months) the public interest is equally compelling to maintain joint Cabinet responsibility and the protection of advice given by civil servants, but I would not accept without close investigation that such matters must, as a matter of course, retain protection after a period of years.

However, the Attorney-General has a powerful reinforcement for his argument in the developing equitable doctrine that a man shall not profit from the wrongful publication of information received by him in confidence. This doctrine, said to have its origin in *Prince Albert* v *Strange* (1849) 1 H & T 1, has been frequently recognised as a ground for restraining the unfair use of commercial secrets transmitted in confidence. Sometimes in these cases there is a contract which may be said to have been breached by the breach of confidence, but it is clear that the doctrine applies independently of contract: see *Saltman Engineering Co. Ltd* v *Campbell Engineering Co. Ltd* (1948) 65 RPC 203. Again in *Coco* v *A. N. Clark (Engineers) Ltd* [1969] RPC 41 Megarry J, reviewing the authorities, set out the requirements necessary for an action based on breach of confidence to succeed. He said, at p. 47:

> In my judgment three elements are normally required if, apart from contract, a case of breach of confidence is to succeed. First, the information itself, in the words of Lord Greene MR . . . must 'have the necessary quality of confidence about it.' Secondly, that information must have been imparted in circumstances importing an obligation of confidence. Thirdly, there must be an unauthorised use of that information to the detriment of the party communicating it.

It is not until the decision in *Duchess of Argyll* v *Duke of Argyll* [1967] Ch 302, that the same principle was applied to domestic secrets such as those passing between husband and wife during the marriage. It was there held by Ungoed-Thomas J that the plaintiff wife could obtain an order to restrain the defendant husband from communicating such secrets, and the principle is well expressed in the headnote in these terms, at p. 304:

> A contract or obligation of confidence need not be expressed but could be implied, and a

breach of contract or trust or faith could arise independently of any right of property or contract . . . and that the court, in the exercise of its equitable jurisdiction, would restrain a breach of confidence independently of any right at law.

This extension of the doctrine of confidence beyond commercial secrets has never been directly challenged, and was noted without criticism by Lord Denning MR in *Fraser* v *Evans* [1969] 1 QB 349, 361. I am sure that I ought to regard myself, sitting here, as bound by the decision of Ungoed-Thomas J.

Even so, these defendants argue that an extension of the principle of the *Argyll* case to the present dispute involves another large and unjustified leap forward, because in the present case the Attorney-General is seeking to apply the principle to public secrets made confidential in the interests of good government. I cannot see why the courts should be powerless to restrain the publication of public secrets, while enjoying the *Argyll* powers in regard to domestic secrets. Indeed, as already pointed out, the court must have power to deal with publication which threatens national security, and the difference between such a case and the present case is one of degree rather than kind. I conclude, therefore, that when a Cabinet Minister receives information in confidence the improper publication of such information can be restrained by the court, and his obligation is not merely to observe a gentleman's agreement to refrain from publication.

It is convenient next to deal with Mr Comyn's third submission, namely, that the evidence does not prove the existence of a convention as to collective responsibility, or adequately define a sphere of secrecy. I find overwhelming evidence that the doctrine of joint responsibility is generally understood and practised and equally strong evidence that it is on occasion ignored. The general effect of the evidence is that the doctrine is an established feature of the English form of government, and it follows that some matters leading up to a Cabinet decision may be regarded as confidential. Furthermore, I am persuaded that the nature of the confidence is that spoken for by the Attorney-General, namely, that since the confidence is imposed to enable the efficient conduct of the Queen's business, the confidence is owed to the Queen and cannot be released by the members of Cabinet themselves. I have been told that a resigning Minister who wishes to make a personal statement in the House, and to disclose matters which are confidential under the doctrine obtains the consent of the Queen for this purpose. Such consent is obtained through the Prime Minister. I have not been told what happened when the Cabinet disclosed divided opinions during the European Economic Community referendum. But even if there was here a breach of confidence (which I doubt) this is no ground for denying the existence of the general rule. I cannot accept the suggestion that a Minister owes no duty of confidence in respect of his own views expressed in Cabinet. It would only need one or two Ministers to describe their own views to enable experienced observers to identify the views of the others.

The other defence submissions are either variants of those dealt with, or submissions with regard to relief.

The Cabinet is at the very centre of national affairs, and must be in possession at all times of information which is secret or confidential. Secrets relating to national security may require to be preserved indefinitely. Secrets relating to new taxation proposals may be of the highest importance until Budget day, but public knowledge thereafter. To leak a Cabinet decision a day or so before it is officially announced is an accepted exercise in public relations, but to identify the Ministers who voted one way or another is objectionable because it undermines the doctrine of joint responsibility.

It is evident that there cannot be a single rule governing the publication of such a variety of matters. In these actions we are concerned with the publication of diaries at a time when 11 years have expired since the first recorded events. The Attorney-General must show (a) that such publication would be a breach of confidence; (b) that the public interest requires that the publication be restrained, and (c) that there are no other facts of the public interest contradictory of and more compelling than that relied upon. Moreover, the court, when asked to restrain such a publication, must closely examine the extent to which relief is necessary to ensure that restrictions are not imposed beyond the strict requirement of public need.

Applying those principles to the present case, what do we find? In my judgment, the Attorney-General has made out his claim that the expression of individual opinions by Cabinet Ministers in the course of Cabinet discussion are matters of confidence, the publication of which can be restrained by the court when this is clearly necessary in the public interest.

The maintenance of the doctrine of joint responsibility within the Cabinet is in the public interest, and the application of that doctrine might be prejudiced by premature disclosure of the views of individual Ministers.

There must, however, be a limit in time after which the confidential character of the information, and the duty of the court to restrain publication, will lapse. Since the conclusion of the hearing in this case I have had the opportunity to read the whole of volume one of the Diaries, and my considered view is that I cannot believe that the publication at this interval of anything in volume one would inhibit free discussion in the Cabinet of today, even though the individuals involved are the same, and the national problems have a distressing similarity with those of a decade ago. It is unnecessary to elaborate the evils which might flow if at the close of a Cabinet meeting a Minister proceeded to give the press an analysis of the voting, but we are dealing in this case with a disclosure of information nearly 10 years later.

It may, of course, be intensely difficult in a particular case, to say at what point the material loses its confidential character, on the ground that publication will no longer undermine the doctrine of joint Cabinet responsibility. It is this difficulty which prompts some to argue that Cabinet discussions should retain their confidential character for a longer and arbitrary period such as 30 years, or even for all time, but this seems to me to be excessively restrictive. The court should intervene only in the clearest of cases where the continuing confidentiality of the material can be demonstrated. In less clear cases – and this, in my view, is certainly one – reliance must be placed on the good sense and good taste of the Minister or ex-Minister concerned.

In the present case there is nothing in Mr Crossman's work to suggest that he did not support the doctrine of joint Cabinet responsibility. The question for the court is whether it is shown that publication now might damage the doctrine notwithstanding that much of the action is up to 10 years old and three general elections have been held meanwhile. So far as the Attorney-General relies in his argument on the disclosure of individual ministerial opinions, he has not satisfied me that publication would in any way inhibit free and open discussion in Cabinet hereafter.

It remains to deal with the Attorney-General's two further arguments, namely, (a) that the Diaries disclose advice given by senior civil servants who cannot be expected to advise frankly if their advice is not treated as confidential; (b) the Diaries disclose observations made by Ministers on the capacity of individual senior civil servants and their suitability for specific appointments. I can see no ground in law which entitle the court to restrain publication of these matters. A Minister is, no doubt, responsible for his department and accountable for its errors even though the individual fault is to be found in his subordinates. In these circumstances, to disclose the fault of the subordinate may amount to cowardice or bad taste, but I can find no ground for saying that either the Crown or the individual civil servant has an enforceable right to have the advice which he gives treated as confidential for all time.

For these reasons I do not think that the court should interfere with the publication of volume one of the Diaries, and I propose, therefore, to refuse the injunction sought but to grant liberty to apply in regard to material other than volume one if it is alleged that different considerations may there have to be applied.

Injunction refused.

NOTE: Following the decision in the case, a committee of privy councillors considered the problem of memoirs of former Cabinet Ministers (Cmnd. 6386, 1976). The Committee drew a distinction between secret information relating to national security and international relations, and other confidential material about relationships between Ministers or between Ministers and civil servants. In the former case the Minister must accept the decision of the Cabinet Secretary, while in the latter case there should be no publication within 15 years except with approval of the Cabinet Secretary but, in the event of a dispute, the final decision would lie with the former Minister as to what to publish. The Committee did not consider that legislation would be appropriate.

QUESTIONS

1. What role did the convention of collective responsibility play in Lord Widgery CJ's decision? (See further on collective responsibility pp. 272–4 *post.*)

2. Do conventions, to use Dicey's words, 'secure the ultimate supremacy of the electorate as the true political sovereign of the State'?

3. Would it make for greater certainty in our constitutional arrangements, and, perhaps, an increase in the moral suasion attaching to conventions, if conventions were codified, thereby providing a clear and authoritative statement of each convention? Are there any drawbacks which would ensue from codification?

6

Parliamentary Government at Work

NOTE: In this chapter, which examines the operation of our parliamentary style of government, the emphasis will be upon the responsibility and accountability of the Government. The most important constitutional convention is that of responsible government, the idea that the Executive will be responsible for its exercise of power and be accountable to Parliament and thence to the electorate.

SECTION 1: **The Role of Parliament**

Philip Norton (ed.), *Parliament in the 1980s*
(1985), pp. 4–6, 8

Some observers identify a variety of functions, others list only two or three. An analysis of writings on Parliament, of constitutional practice and of parliamentary behaviour would suggest three primary ones: those of providing the personnel of government, of legitimization, and of subjecting measures of public policy to scrutiny and influence. This is to identify themin rather bald terms. Each is in need of qualification and amplification.

Providing the personnel of government
This is the least problematic of the functions. By convention, ministers are drawn from and remain within Parliament. Again by convention, most ministers – including the Prime Minister and most members of the Cabinet – are drawn from the elected chamber. (No less than two but rarely more than four peers are appointed now to the Cabinet.) There is no formal prohibition on a Prime Minister appointing as a minister someone who is neither an MP or a peer; such occasions are rare but not unknown. However, those given office are normally then elevated to the peerage or (more riskily) seek a Commons seat through the medium of a by – election. In practice, most ministers have served a parliamentary apprenticeship of several years before their appointments. Parliament provides both the personnel of government and the forum in which those seeking office can make their mark. Though there are occasional calls for non-parliamentarians (businessmen, industrialists and the like) to be brought into government, this function of Parliament arouses no serious debate or controversy.

Legitimization
Most national assemblies exist for the purpose of giving assent to measures of public policy. Indeed, this constitutes the primary purpose for which representatives of the local English communities (*communes*) were first summoned in the thirteenth century. Today, the broad rubric of legitimization encompasses different elements. The most obvious and the most significant is that of manifest

legitimization. This constitutes the formal giving of assent to measures, enabling them to be designated Acts of Parliament; such Acts are accepted as having general and binding applicability by virtue of having been passed by the country's elected or part-elected national assembly (the elected chamber now having dominance within that assembly). A second element is that of latent legitimization. The government derives its primary political legitimacy from being elected through (if no longer by) the House of Commons. The collectivity of ministers that form the government enjoy enhanced legitimacy also by being drawn from and remaining in Parliament. For Parliament as an institution, this of course constitutes an essentially passive function.

There are two other sub-functions that fall under the heading of legitimization: those of tension-release and support-mobilization. By meeting and debating issues, Parliament provides an outlet, an authoritative outlet, for the expression of different views within society. Thus it plays an important part in the dissipation of tension. For example, during the Falklands crisis in 1982, Parliament provided the authoritative forum for the expression of public feelings on the issue. In Argentina, by contrast, citizens enjoyed no such body through which their views could be expressed and were forced instead to take to the streets to make their feelings known. Parliament also seeks to mobilize public support for measures which it has approved. In essence, these two sub-functions constitute a two-way process between electors and the elected, the views of citizens being channelled through Parliament (tension-release) and Parliament then mobilizing support for those measures which it has approved (support-mobilization). In practice, the extent to which Parliament is capable of fulfilling these functions has been much overlooked and, when considered by writers, has often been found wanting.

Scrutiny and influence

Parliament ceased to be a policy-making legislature in the nineteenth century. Instead it acquired the characteristics of what I have elsewhere termed a policy-influencing legislature. It ceased to be involved in the making of public policy, but it was expected to subject such policy to a process of scrutiny and influence. Scrutiny and influence are analytically separable terms, but scrutiny without any consequent sanction to effect influence is of little worth; and influence is best and most confidently attempted when derived from prior scrutiny. Hence, scrutiny and influence may be conjoined as a single function of Parliament. It is, in practice, its most debated and contentious function.

The exercise of scrutiny and influence can be seen to operate at two levels. These, in simple terms, may be characterized as being at the macro and the micro level of public policy. At the macro level, Parliament is expected to subject measures of public policy, embodied in legislative bills or in executive actions, to scrutiny and influence prior to giving assent to them. It is essentially a reactive function, exercised at a moderately late stage in the policy cycle . . . It is one which is most often carried out through the party elements in both Houses, the official Opposition or, nowadays, opposition parties seeking to exert the most sustained scrutiny of government measures. However, Parliament is but one of many influences at work in the policy cycle and, by virtue of what is usually an assured government majority at the end of the scrutinizing process, is rarely deemed to be the most important. Indeed, in some analyses, it is of no great importance at all.

At the micro level, Parliament is expected to scrutinize and respond to the effects of policy on the community. In practice, this task is exercised less through the party elements and Parliament as a collective entity, and more through Members of Parliament as Constituency representatives. Members represent territorially designated areas (constituencies) and seek to defend and pursue the interests of their constituents and groups within their constituencies. Whereas at the macro level MPs will be concerned to debate the principle of public policy, usually within the context of party ideology, at the micro level they are much more concerned with the policy's practical implications for their constituents.

In terms of the working life of Parliament, scrutiny and influence constitute its most demanding function. Seeking to subject government actions and legislative measures to scrutiny and a degree of influence occupies most of Parliament's time and energies. It is also the function that attracts the most debate and criticism. At best, effective fulfilment of the function allows Parliament to set the broad limits within which government can govern. (At the end of the day, it retains the formal sanction to deny assent to the government's legislative proposals and its request for supply.) At worst, the function may be fulfilled in the most superficial of ways, providing no effective check upon the executive.

NOTE: Norton does not say that the House of Commons controls the Executive. Michael Ryle in *The Commons To-day* (1981) says that it is a popular misapprehension to regard the Commons as a governmental rather than a critical body. As he puts it, 'Parliament is the forum where the exercise of government is publicly displayed and is open to scrutiny and criticism'.

QUESTIONS

1. Does what Norton refers to as 'micro level' scrutiny by MPs include constituency work where the public can come to MPs' surgeries to complain about various matters? Is the redress of citizens' grievances against officialdom not a very important part of MPs' work? (See *post* pp. 337–435.)

2. What exactly is meant by legitimization? Is legitimization real if Parliament approves the actions of the executive in the manner of a rubber stamp?

SECTION 2: **Policy and Administration**

A: Ministerial responsibility

C. Turpin, 'Ministerial Responsibility: Myth or Reality?' in J. Jowell & D. Oliver (eds), *The Changing Constitution*
(2nd edn, 1989), pp. 55–57

When it is said that ministers are collectively and individually responsible to Parliament, what is meant by 'responsible'? It may help us find the answer if we compare the idea of ministerial responsibility to Parliament with that of *control* by Parliament of the executive. Much contemporary discussion of the relations between Parliament and government is concerned with the reassertion of parliamentary control, and by this is generally meant a power to influence the decisions of government. Control, that is to say, is exercised a priori. On the other hand, when it is said that ministers are 'responsible' or 'answerable' or 'accountable' – terms not generally distinguished in meaning – to Parliament, reference is usually being made to the obligation of ministers to respond or answer or account for actions already performed (or left unperformed): responsibility is retrospective or a posteriori. There is, of course, an overlap between the parliamentary functions of 'controlling' and 'holding responsible' ('calling to account'). Some techniques, such as parliamentary questions and scrutiny by selected committees, are directed both to control and to the assertion of responsibility. An a posteriori investigation or check may have the aim of influencing future policy-making. The notion of 'responsible government' implies both acceptance of responsibility for things done and 'responsiveness' to influence, persuasion, and pressure for modifications of policy. Activist parliamentarians of our day aim to 'redress the balance' of the constitution in favour of Parliament by strengthening both control and responsibility of the executive, without making a fine discrimination between these concepts. This is not to say that equal progress is to be expected in establishing control and in extending responsibility . . . A posteriori responsibility implies that certain obligations are owed by ministers to Parliament. What are these obligations?

It is demanded of ministers, in the first place, that they should *answer* or give account, discharging the essential 'obligation of Ministers, collectively and individually, to meet Parliament and provide information about their policies'. This includes a duty to provide financial accounts attesting to the regularity of government expenditure, as one element of a fuller 'explanatory accountability' which requires the giving of reasons and explanations for action taken, whether or not involving expenditure. That this is not a negligible aspect of responsibility was recognized by H. J. Laski: 'A Government that is compelled to explain itself under cross-examination will do its best to avoid the grounds of complaint. Nothing makes responsible government so sure.' The requirement to answer goes further: it imports an obligation to submit to scrutiny – to provide opportunities for Parliament to question, challenge, probe, and criticize. A duty to answer is something hollow if there are not apt procedures, respected by government, for such 'calling to account'.

The obligation to answer and submit to scrutiny is ancillary to what we may see as government's traditional obligation to redress grievances, which here means to take remedial action for revealed errors or defects of policy or administration, whether by compensating individuals, reversing or modifying policies or decisions, disciplining Civil Servants, or altering departmental procedures. This may be called 'amendatory accountability'; it presupposes an acknowledgement by ministers that they 'bear responsibility' to Parliament for what is shown to have gone wrong, whether or not they accept personal blame for the failure.

The obligations to answer, to submit to scrutiny, and to redress grievances may seem in practice to lack the support of any coercive rule or sanction. Undoubtedly these obligations are imperfect, resting as they do upon conventions, practices, and procedures which are liable to change and to be variously interpreted and applied, and which depend ultimately upon the political culture. But this is far from saying that the obligations in question lack substance, or that they can be flouted with impunity.

(a) Collective ministerial responsibility

Ministerial responsibility comprises both collective and individual responsibility. In his book on constitutional conventions, Marshall classifies the branches of collective ministerial responsibility as the confidence rule, the unanimity rule, and the confidentiality rule.

(a) Confidence

G. Marshall, *Constitutional Conventions*
(1984), pp. 55–56

It sometimes used to be said that a prime non-legal rule of the Constitution was that governments defeated by the House on central issues of policy were obliged to resign. But only one Prime Minister has resigned as the result of a defeat in the House in the twentieth century and that was immediately after being deprived of his majority by a General Election (Baldwin in January 1924). MacDonald was defeated on a confidence issue in 1924 and Callaghan in 1979, but neither resigned. Both fought the subsequent General Elections as leader of a government, having advised dissolution.

So the rule about a government that loses the confidence of the House seems to be that it must *either* resign *or* advise dissolution. Its right is only to advise, not to have, dissolution; since dissolution can, as we have seen, in some circumstances be refused. Resignation might therefore follow as the result of such a refusal (by the Queen), but that has not happened. As to what constitutes a loss of confidence there seems also to have been a development in doctrine. The books used to say that defeat on major legislative measures or policy proposals as well as on specifically worded confidence motions was fatal to the continuance of the government. But this no longer seems to be believed or acted on. In 1977 *The Times* propounded the view that 'there is no constitutional principle that requires a government to regard any specific policy defeat as evidence that it no longer possesses the necessary confidence of the House of Commons'. Some were greatly shocked by this doctrine and Professor Max Beloff wrote to *The Times* to say that it was inconsistent with the principles of the Constitution as hitherto understood. Sir Ivor Jennings, he pointed out, had said in *Cabinet Government* that the government must go if the House failed to approve its policy. What provoked the disagreement was that the Labour Government had just failed to carry a budget proposal about the rate of income tax and was proposing to remain in office in defiance of Sir Ivor Jennings's view of the established convention. Sir Ivor Jennings was of course dead, which is supposed to augment the authority of a textbook writer by allowing his views to be cited more freely in the course of litigation. Unfortunately there is a countervailing disadvantage in that his works may go out of print and are no longer constantly perused by Ministers, who are thereby enabled to fall into lax habits and disregard established constitutional conventions. In the 1960s and 1970s, in any event, governments seem to have been following a new rule, according to which only votes specifically stated by the Government to be matters of confidence, or votes of no confidence by the Opposition are allowed to count. Just conceivably one can imagine amongst recent Prime Ministers those who might have felt it their duty to soldier on in the general interest even in the face of such a vote.

(b) *Unanimity*

House of Lords, Parl Deb
Vol. 239, cols. 833–34, 8 April 1878

THE MARQUESS OF SALISBURY: . . . My Lords, my noble Friend [the Earl of Derby] pointed out several measures of the Government to which in the public eye he was an assenting party. He did not, he said, in reality assent to all; one was a compromise, while to another, he was persuaded by some observations which fell from the Chancellor of the Exchequer, which appeared to be founded on a mistake. Now, my Lords, am I not defending a great Constitutional principle, when I say that, for all that passes in Cabinet, each member of it who does not resign is absolutely and irretrievably responsible, and that he has no right afterwards to say that he agreed in one case to a compromise, while in another he was persuaded by one of his Colleagues. Consider the inconvenience which will arise if such a great Constitutional law is not respected. . . . It is, I maintain, only on the principle that absolute responsibility is undertaken by every Member of a Cabinet who, after a decision is arrived at, remains a Member of it, that the joint responsibility of Ministers to Parliament can be upheld, and one of the most essential conditions of Parliamentary responsibility established.

House of Commons, HC Deb
Vol. 889, Written Answers, Mr H. Wilson, col. 351, 7 April 1975

THE PRIME MINISTER: In accordance with my statement in the House on 23rd January last, those Ministers who do not agree with the Government's recommendation in favour of continued membership of the European Community are, in the unique circumstances of the referendum, now free to advocate a different view during the referendum campaign in the country.

   This freedom does not extend to parliamentary proceedings and official business. Government business in Parliament will continue to be handled by all Ministers in accordance with Government policy. Ministers responsible for European aspects of Government business who themselves differ from the Government's recommendation on membership of the European Community will state the Government's position and will not be drawn into making points against the Government recommendation. Wherever necessary Questions will be transferred to other Ministers. At meetings of the

Council of Ministers of the European Community and at other Community meetings, the United Kingdom position in all fields will continue to reflect Government policy.

I have asked all Ministers to make their contributions to the public campaign in terms of issues, to avoid personalising or trivialising the argument, and not to allow themselves to appear in direct confrontation, on the same platform or programme, with another Minister who takes a different view on the Government recommendation.

NOTE: This breach or suspension of unanimity or Cabinet solidarity was criticized as being simply a device to keep the Labour Party together. The United Kingdom's membership of the European Communities has caused problems for the Labour Party. In 1977 the point at issue was the use of proportional representation as the method of voting in the direct elections to the European Parliament. As unanimity in Cabinet could not be achieved, collective responsibility was, once again, suspended. The then Prime Minister, Mr Callaghan, answering a question in the House of Commons about collective responsibility, said: 'I think the doctrine should apply except in cases where I announce that it does not.' (HC Deb, vol. 993, col. 552, 16 June 1977.)

The occasions on which it has been formally announced that unanimity in a government would be suspended have been few. Ministers have resigned because they could not agree with their colleagues on governmental policy. Mr Ian Gow resigned as Junior Minister in the Treasury because he did not agree with the Anglo-Irish Agreement 1985. Mr Michael Heseltine resigned as Secretary of State for Defence in the Westland Affair because he could not accept the requirement that all Ministers should clear speeches about Westland with the Cabinet Office.

QUESTION

What purpose does Cabinet solidarity serve, and whom does it (and its suspension) benefit?

(c) *Confidentiality*

The confidentiality of Cabinet proceedings is, of course, related to unanimity in that body. Disclosures of what happened in Cabinet do occur. Ministers may 'leak', i.e. brief journalists, on the basis that they do not name their source, or they may publish their memoirs. The publication of the Crossman Diaries has changed the practice, if not the convention, of confidentiality. (See *Attorney-General* v *Jonathan Cape Ltd* [1976] QB 752 and Lord Widgery CJ's judgment *ante*, at p. 262.)

Subsequently the Report of the Radcliffe Committee of Privy Councillors on Ministerial Memoirs (Cmnd 6386) was published. According to its guidelines, Ministers should not disclose what happened in Cabinet until 15 years have passed where the material concerns national security; or where foreign relations would be adversely affected; or where it would reveal relationships between Ministers and (a) officials, or (b) Ministers' outside advisers.

(b) *Individual ministerial responsibility*

The confusion which was seen over when a government should resign when defeated in the House of Commons is also present in the issue of what should prompt the resignation of an individual Minister. In 1982 Lord Carrington, the Secretary of State, and two of his junior ministers resigned from the Foreign and Commonwealth Office after Argentinian troops had invaded the Falkland Islands. Lord Carrington wrote in his letter of resignation:

The Argentine invasion of the Falkland Islands has led to strong criticism in Parliament and in the press on the Government's policy. In my view, much of the criticism is unfounded. But I have been responsible for the conduct of that policy and I think it right that I should resign . . . [T]he invasion of the Falkland Islands has been a humiliating affront to this country.

This is an example of a classic case of a Minister accepting that the faults in a Department were his responsibility and then resigning. As such it is unusual.

In the following year there was a mass break-out from the Maze Prison in County Down, Northern Ireland. There was an inquiry into the circumstances of the escape by Her Majesty's Chief Inspector of Prisons (HC 203 of 1983–84), which found that the prison governor must be held accountable for a major failure in the prison's security arrangements. This report, the Hennessy Report, was debated in the House of Commons.

House of Commons, HC Deb
Vol. 53, cols. 1042, 1060–61, 9 February 1984

THE SECRETARY OF STATE FOR NORTHERN IRELAND (MR J. PRIOR): There are those who, while they accept this policy, have nevertheless suggested that the circumstances of the escape demand ministerial resignation. I take that view seriously and have given it the most careful consideration. I share hon. Members' concern about the honour of public life and the maintenance of the highest standards. I said at the time of my statement to the House on 24 October, without any pre-knowledge of what Hennessy would find:

> It would be a matter for resignation if the report of the Hennessy inquiry showed that what happened was the result of some act of policy that was my responsibility, or that I failed to implement something that I had been asked to implement, or should have implemented. In that case, I should resign. – [*Official Report*, 24 October 1983, vol. 47, c. 23–24.]

In putting the emphasis that I did on the issue of 'policy', I was not seeking to map out some new doctrine of ministerial responsibility. I was responding to the accusations made at the time that it was policy decisions, reached at the end of the hunger strike, that made the escape possible.

Since the report was published, the nature of the charges levelled at my hon. Friend and myself has changed. It is now argued in some quarters that Ministers are responsible for everything that happens in their Departments and should resign if anything goes wrong. My position has not changed, and I want to make it quite clear that if there were any evidence in the Hennessy report that Ministers were to blame for the escape, I would not hesitate to accept that blame and act accordingly, and so I know, would my hon. Friend. However, I do not accept – and I do not think it right for the House to accept – that there is any constitutional or other principle that requires ministerial resignations in the face of failure, either by others to carry out orders or procedures or by their supervisors to ensure that staff carried out those orders. Let the House be clear: the Hennessy report finds that the escape would not have succeeded if orders and procedures had been properly carried out that Sunday afternoon.

Of course, I have looked carefully at the precedents. There are those who quote the Crichel Down case. I do not believe that it is a precedent or that it establishes a firm convention. It is the only case of its sort in the past 50 years, and constitutional lawyers have concluded that the resignation was not required by convention and was exceptional.

Whatever some may wish, there is no clear rule and no established convention. Rightly, it is a matter of judgment in the light of individual circumstances. I do not intend to review the judgments made by Ministers faced with the question whether to resign following failures in their Departments. Nor do I seek to justify my decision on the ground that there are many difficulties in Northern Ireland.

There are, but that adds to rather than subtracts from the argument. The question that I have asked myself is whether on Sunday afternoon, 25 September, I was to blame for those prisoners escaping. The Hennessy report is quite explicit in its conclusion that, although there may have been weaknesses in the physical security of the prison and in the prisons department, the escape could not have taken place if the procedures laid down for the running of the prison had been followed. . . .

MR J. ENOCH POWELL (Down, South): The Secretary of State, from the beginning of his speech, recognised the central issue in this debate, that of ministerial responsibility, without which the House scarcely has a real function or any real service that it can perform for the people whom it represents. We are concerned with the nature of the responsibility, the ministerial responsibility, for an event which, even in isolation from its actual context, was a major disaster.

I want to begin by eliminating from this consideration the Under-Secretary of State for Northern Ireland, the hon. Member for Chelsea (Mr Scott), because references to him in this context have shown a gross misconception. There has been argument about how long the hon. Member has been in the branch of the Northern Ireland Office concerned with the prison service, as though that were in the least degree relevant. The fact is that the entire responsibility, whether or not it is delegated to a junior Minister, rests with the Secretary of State. The Secretary of State has confirmed this to me in the past 24 hours, in another context, when I drew his attention to the reports to the fact that the Minister in charge of the environment had himself taken the decision to re-name the district of Londonderry. The right hon. Gentleman quite correctly said:

> In discharging his duties, my hon. Friend acts on my behalf. – [*Official Report*, 8 February 1984; vol. 53, c. 623.]

There is a responsibility, of a different kind, obviously, on the part of every junior Minister towards his Ministry, but the responsibility for everything that he does or says or fails to do or say rests irrevocably with the Minister – the Secretary of State – and he alone is responsible to the House.

It is, therefore, a total misconception to imagine that any of the responsibility can be devolved to a junior Minister. A junior Minister may choose, if his chief resigns, to resign in solidarity with him; he may choose himself to resign for a variety of reasons. But there is no constitutional significance in acceptance by him of a responsibility which is not his. The locus of the responsibility is beyond challenge. It lies with the Secretary of State and, through him, with the Government as a whole.

As the Secretary of State reminded us this afternoon, even before the publication of the report he drew a distinction, which I believe to be invalid, between responsibility for policy and responsibility for administration. I believe that this is a wholly fallacious view of the nature of ministerial responsibility. I shall argue presently that there is a policy element in the event that we are considering and that it cannot be understood fully except in its policy framework. But even if all considerations of policy could be eliminated, the responsibility for the administration of a Department remains irrevocably with the Minister in charge. It is impossible for him to say to the House or to the country, 'The policy was excellent and that was mine, but the execution was defective or disastrous and that has nothing to do with me.' If that were to be the accepted position, there would be no political source to which the public could complain about administration or from which it could seek redress for failings of administration.

What happened was an immense administrative disaster. It was not a disaster in a peripheral area of the responsibilities of the Northern Ireland Department. It was a disaster that occurred in an area which was quite clearly central to the Department's responsibilities. If the responsibility for administration so central to a Department can be abjured by a Minister, a great deal of our proceedings in the House is a beating of the air because we are talking to people who, in the last resort, disclaim the responsibility for the administration.

NOTE: Mr Powell's view is not one, it would appear, which is shared by Ministers. The classic statement about the circumstances in which a Minister will be responsible for the action of his officials was given in 1954 by Sir David Maxwell-Fyfe, who was Home Secretary at the time. He made his statement on the occasion of the debate of the report into the Crichel Down affair. Some land had been compulsorily acquired by the Air Ministry. It was later transferred to the Ministry of Agriculture, which then leased the land to a tenant in breach of promises made about the way in which such a disposal of the land would be carried out. The Minister for Agriculture, Sir Thomas Dugdale, resigned.

House of Commons, HC Deb

Vol. 530, cols. 1285–88, 10 July 1954

THE SECRETARY OF STATE FOR THE HOME DEPARTMENT (SIR DAVID MAXWELL-FYFE): . . . There has been criticism that the principle [of Ministerial responsibility] operates so as to oblige Ministers to extend total protection to their officials and to endorse their acts, and to cause the position that civil servants cannot be called to account and are effectively responsible to no one. That is a position which I believe is quite wrong. . . . It is quite untrue that well-justified public criticism of the actions of civil servants cannot be made on a suitable occasion. The position of the civil servant is that he is wholly and directly responsible to his Minister. It is worth stating again that he holds his office 'at pleasure' and can be dismissed at any time by the Minister; and that power is none the less real because it is seldom used. The only exception relates to a small number of senior posts, like permanent secretary, deputy secretary, and principal financial officer, where, since 1920, it has been necessary for the Minister to consult the Prime Minister, as he does on appointment.

I would like to put the different categories where different considerations apply . . . [I]n the case where there is an explicit order by a Minister, the Minister must protect the civil servant who has carried out his order. Equally, where the civil servant acts properly in accordance with the policy laid down by the Minister, the Minister must protect and defend him.

I come to the third category, which is different. . . . Where an official makes a mistake or causes some delay, but not on an important issue of policy and not where a claim to individual rights is seriously involved, the Minister acknowledges the mistake and he accepts the responsibility, although he is not personally involved. He states that he will take corrective action in the Department. I agree with the right hon. Gentleman that he would not, in those circumstances, expose the official to public criticism. . . .

But when one comes to the fourth category, where action has been taken by a civil servant of which the Minister disapproves and has no prior knowledge, and the conduct of the official is reprehensible, then there is no obligation on the part of the Minister to endorse what he believes to be wrong, or to defend what are clearly shown to be errors of his officers. The Minister is not bound to defend action of which he did not know, or of which he disapproves. But, of course, he remains constitutionally responsible to Parliament for the fact that something has gone wrong, and he alone can tell Parliament what has occurred and render an account of his stewardship. The fact that a Minister has to do that does not affect his power to control and discipline his staff. One could sum it up by saying that it is part of a Minister's responsibility to Parliament to take necessary action to ensure efficiency and the proper discharge of the duties of his Department. On that, only the Minister can decide what it is right and just to do, and he alone can hear all sides, including the defence.

It has been suggested in this debate, and has been canvassed in the Press, that there is another aspect which adds to our difficulties, and that is that today the work and the tasks of Government permeate so many spheres of our national life that it is impossible for the Minister to keep track of all these matters. I believe that that is a matter which can be dealt with by the instructions which the Minister gives in his Department. He can lay down standing instructions to see that his policy is carried out. He can lay down rules by which it is ensured that matters of importance, of difficulty or of political danger are brought to his attention. Thirdly, there is the control of this House, and it is one of the duties of this House to see that that control is always put into effect.

... As I have said, it is a matter for the Minister to decide when civil servants are guilty of shortcomings in their official conduct. Normally, the Civil Service has no procedure equivalent to a court-martial, or anything of that kind. There have in the past been a few inquiries to establish the facts and the degree of culpability of individuals, but the decision as to the disciplinary action to be taken has been left to the Minister. . . .

NOTE: It has been held by some that Sir Thomas's resignation was one in which he accepted responsibility for the wrongdoing of his officials. However, the current view seems to be that the resignation occurred because Sir Thomas had lost the support of his ministerial and party colleagues. See, for example, I. F. Nicolson *The Mystery of Crichel Down* (1986) and J. A. G. Griffith 'Crichel Down: The Most Famous Farm in British Constitutional History' (1987) 1 *Contemporary Record* 35. Perhaps this explains Lord Prior's view that Crichel Down did not set a precedent for resignation.

(c) *Ministerial responsibility and accountability*

The House of Commons Public Service Committee launched an inquiry into ministerial accountability and responsibility in the wake of the dismissal by the then Home Secretary Mr M. Howard of Mr D. Lewis from his post as Director General of the Prison Service following escapes from several prisons. While the inquiry was underway the report by Sir Richard Scott into the 'arms to Iraq' affair was published and so the committee considered it too.

Second Report from the Public Service Committee
HC 313 of 1995–96, paras 14–21, 32–33

14. Some of the difficulty on the discussion of the roles and responsibilities of Ministers derives from the vagueness and ambiguity of what is meant by the word 'responsible'. Since 1954, the issue of the extent to which Ministers can be regarded as 'responsible' for the activities of their departments has been raised regularly, often in the context of the giving of evidence by civil servants to Select Committees. Successive governments have tried to bring greater clarity by introducing a distinction between *responsibility* and *accountability* – although, as the Treasury and Civil Service Committee were told in 1994, the distinction has not been used consistently, and the words 'can and often have been used interchangeably'. In its response to the Defence Committee's Report on the Westland Affair in 1986, the Government claimed that 'the basic principles on this matter are clear', and went on to make the distinction:

— 'Each Minister is responsible to Parliament for the conduct of his department, and for the actions carried out by his department in pursuit of government policies or in the discharge of responsibilities laid upon him as a Minister'.
— 'A Minister is accountable to Parliament, in the sense that he has a duty to explain in Parliament the exercise of his powers and duties and to give an account to Parliament of what is done by him in his capacity as a Minister or by his department'.
— 'Civil servants are responsible to their Ministers for their actions and conduct'.

Made in this way, the distinction is far from clear. Of what the Minister's responsibility – as opposed to his accountability – consists, and the way in which responsibility and accountability differ is highly obscure. Nevertheless, by virtue of its inclusion in the Note by the Head of the Home Civil Service on 'The Duties and Responsibilities of Civil Servants in relation to Ministers' (the 'Armstrong Memorandum') it has acquired a degree of authority.

15. The last few years have seen further attempts to clarify the point, some in the context of the controversy concerning the extent of Ministerial responsibility for the work of Next Steps agencies –

something which will be examined later – and some in the context of the Scott Inquiry. These have largely been directed towards applying the word 'accountability' to a Minister's duty as the representative in Parliament of part of the executive, while limiting 'responsibility' to actions taken personally by the Minister. The Cabinet Office in a memorandum submitted to the Treasury and Civil Service Committee in April 1994 distinguished between 'the constitutional fact of Ministerial accountability for all that a department does, and the limits to the direct personal responsibility (in the sense of personal involvement) of Ministers for all the actions of their departments and agencies, given the realities of delegation and dispersed responsibility for much business'. In his memorandum to this Committee, the Chancellor of the Duchy of Lancaster has sought to cast this distinction back into the statements by Maxwell-Fyfe and Bridges by defining the occasions on which they used the words 'responsible', 'answerable' or 'account' as meaning either 'constitutionally accountable' or 'personally responsible'

16. The most recent, and most elaborate, interpretation of the doctrine and the distinction has come in the Government's reply to the Treasury and Civil Service Committee's 1994 Report on the Role of the Civil Service. The Government says that:

> In the Government's view, a Minister is 'accountable' to Parliament for everything which goes on within his department, in the sense that Parliament can call the Minister to account for it. The Minister is responsible for the policies of the department, for the framework through which those policies are delivered, for the resources allocated, for such implementation decisions as the Framework Document may require to be referred or agreed with him, and for his response to major failures or expressions of Parliamentary or public concern. But a Minister cannot sensibly be held responsible for everything which goes on in his department in the sense of having personal knowledge and control of every action taken and being personally blameworthy when delegated tasks are carried out incompetently, or when mistakes or errors of judgement are made at operational level. It is not possible for Ministers to handle everything personally, and if Ministers were to be held personally responsible for every action of the department, delegation and efficiency would be much inhibited. It was for this reason that evidence suggested the use of the word 'accountable' for the first of these two meanings of the word responsible, to distinguish it from the second.

17. This is undoubtedly clearer than the interpretation of the convention given in the Memorandum. Yet the distinction remains somewhat confusing because it makes use of common words in different ways. Sir Robin Butler admitted in evidence to this Committee that the distinction 'has actually caused more confusion than clarity'. Part of the problem is that in normal usage, the words 'responsibility', 'accountability', 'answerability' and 'liability' can often be taken to mean roughly the same thing. An alternative might be to stick to a single term (either accountability or responsibility) and to distinguish different forms of it as Geoffrey Marshall, Provost of The Queen's College, Oxford, suggests. However, this does not seem much to improve on the Government's approach of erecting accountability and responsibility into distinguishable terms of art, with assigned meanings. Sir Michael Quinlan, Director of the Ditchley Foundation and former Permanent Under-secretary of State in the Ministry of Defence, told us:

> A good deal of public discussion seems to me needlessly hampered by the attempt to identify in the normal usage of the words 'accountability' and 'responsibility' (and also sometimes 'answerability') tidy and precise meanings, distinct as between one word and another. But words derive their meaning from usage, and the usage of these words in common parlance is not tidy and precise – they are used in overlapping and indeed sometimes interchangeable ways. It may be that there would be value in establishing, for the context of public-service analysis, term-of-art conventions whereby such words would be assigned, by customary agreement among those engaged in such discourse, exact

meanings. I interpret the recent use of the words 'responsibility' and 'accountability' by Sir Robin Butler, Cabinet Secretary and Head of the Home Civil Service, as seeking to encourage a term-of-art precision not hitherto present in ordinary parlance.

The Government's distinction now receives some support. Professor Rodney Brazier has recommended its acceptance:

> there should be an unqualified principle that a Minister is accountable for everything which happens (or does not happen) in his or her department, in the sense that he or she *owes a duty to account to Parliament and the public* for departmental policies, for what has taken place in the department or its agencies, and for the conduct of officials, and to demonstrate what has been done to correct mistakes and to ensure that they will not recur. . . . The principle that a Minister is *responsible* to Parliament and public, and that he or she should bear personal blame for acts and omissions (and in appropriate cases resign), should be narrowed down to cases in which the Minister has some personal responsibility for, or some personal involvement in, a blameworthy act or omission. It is absurd nowadays to try to continue the fiction that a Minister is personally responsible, and should bear personal obloquy, for every occurrence in the department, even if he was unaware of it and had no reason to be aware of it.

Lord Howe said the distinction was 'helpful'; 'I think accountability is an obligation, as I understand it, to explain, to say what happened, to be accountable for it; responsibility implies some more potentially disciplinary response for it, and to that extent I think that is a useful distinction'.

18. We are less certain that the distinction between 'accountability' and 'responsibility' is always a useful one. For the substance of it is a distinction between those matters on which a Ministers have merely to provide an explanation to the House, and those matters on which failures may be regarded as their own fault and which may justifiably lead to the Minister's resignation. In many, probably most, cases that distinction is easily made. A Minister is obviously responsible for deciding on what policy to follow, or the resources allocated to particular budgets, for example. But in other cases, the distinction is hard to draw. The most difficult area is the one with which Maxwell-Fyfe grappled: to what extent can Ministers be said to be responsible (in the sense that it may be regarded proper that they lose their job if something goes wrong) for essentially *administrative* failures within a department?

19. The issue has been a battleground over which successive Governments and Oppositions (and private members) have fought. Mr Enoch Powell put the case for a broader interpretation of Ministerial responsibility in the debate in 1984 over an escape from the Maze prison in Belfast. Rejecting the Minister's refusal to accept blame for the escape, he said:

> [The Secretary of State] drew a distinction, which I believe to be invalid, between responsibility for policy and responsibility for administration. I believe that this is a wholly fallacious view of the nature of Ministerial responsibility . . . even if all considerations of policy could be eliminated, the responsibility for the administration of a department remains irrevocably with the Minister in charge.

Mr Powell makes an extreme case for the extent to which Ministers should take personal blame for failures in their department, which will not be generally accepted. Yet Ministers must accept in some degree that they are personally responsible for the overall way in which their Department is administered. They cannot, indeed, be blamed for individual failures at operational level; but they might be blamed for a broader pattern of incompetence. Indeed, the Chancellor of the Duchy of Lancaster has referred to a Minister's responsibility for the organisation and resource framework of a Department. Ministers cannot be blamed for each failure connected with the work of the department; but if such a failure were great enough, many may feel it proper that the Minister resign.

20. What Ministers must never do is to put the blame onto civil servants for the effects of

unworkable policies and their setting of unrealistic targets. If, when things go wrong, it is held that Ministers are not to blame because they did not (knowingly) mislead Parliament, and civil servants are not to blame because they acted as servants of Ministers, then the unsatisfactory outcome is that nobody is to blame. There is clearly something unsatisfactory about a doctrine of Ministerial Responsibility that can issue in such a conclusion.

21. If the point of drawing a distinction between 'accountability' and 'responsibility' is to limit the extent to which blame might be attached to Ministers for failings in their departments, then it is unsuccessful. To the extent that it protects Ministers from being seen as personally to blame for minor failings (an incorrect social security payment, for example) it is no more than a statement of the obvious: few would seriously advance the proposition that a Minister should resign in such circumstances. To the extent that it implies that it is possible to draw in practice a clear line between minor failings at operational level and a more systemic failure, experience suggests that it is, at best, hopeful. **It is not possible absolutely to distinguish an area in which a Minister is personally responsible, and liable to take blame, from one in which he is constitutionally accountable. Ministerial responsibility is not composed of two elements with a clear break between the two. Ministers have an obligation to Parliament which consists in ensuring that government explains its actions. Ministers also have an obligation to respond to criticism made in Parliament in a way that seems likely to satisfy it – which may include, if necessary, resignation.** . . .

31. The pursuit of Ministerial resignations is important as part of a process of enforcing political accountability, but too great a concentration on it obscures the wider importance of the day-to-day business of holding the executive to account in Parliament, to ensure that it is kept under proper democratic control. Dr Philip Giddings of the Department of Politics, University of Reading, argues that Parliamentary accountability has 'a variety of objectives'. At one level, its purpose is simply to secure information about and explanations of what has or has not occurred. But it may also be regarded as a way of exerting pressure for change, or a means of attributing blame or praise for government actions. It is seen as a means of influencing the decision-makers who are being held to account, so that they will act in a way which is responsive to the wishes of those who are holding them to account. Ministers, in short, have to give information; but they also have to ensure that they are sufficiently responsive to the concerns of Members of Parliament in order to maintain their confidence. Sir Richard Scott said 'I do not regard the debate – and I do not want to underestimate it – between accountability, responsibility, blame, as being the key and most important feature of Ministerial accountability. I think willingness on the part of Ministers to inform Parliament and through Parliament, the public, or perhaps sometimes the public directly, of the matters in respect of which they are accountable is critical'.

32. The theory of Ministerial responsibility should keep pace with the contemporary reality, if it is to retain its credibility. It would give greater clarity if the Government were less coy in its definition of what Ministerial responsibility means. As we have said, we believe that Ministers have a general responsibility to Parliament for the work of their departments which cannot be neatly divided into spheres of 'personal responsibility' and 'constitutional accountability'. There are, it is time to say, two sides to the obligation of Ministers for those matters which come within their responsibility – even if they cannot be simply distinguished. They may be referred to as the obligation to *give an account*; and the liability to *be held to account*. **We believe that the following represents a working definition of 'Ministerial responsibility'.**

> **Ministers owe a fundamental duty to account to Parliament. This has, essentially, two meanings. First, that the executive is obliged to give an account – to provide full information about and explain its actions in Parliament so that they are subject to proper democratic scrutiny. This obligation is central to the proper functioning of Parliament, and therefore any Minister who has been found to have knowingly misled Parliament should resign. While it is through Ministers that the Government is properly**

accountable to Parliament, the obligation to provide full information and to explain the actions of government to Parliament means that Ministers should allow civil servants to give an account to Parliament through Select Committees when appropriate – particularly where Ministers have formally delegated functions to them, for example in the case of Chief Executives of Executive Agencies.

Second, a Minister's duty to account to Parliament means that the executive is liable to he held to account: it must respond to concerns and criticism raised in Parliament about its actions because Members of Parliament are democratically-elected representatives of the people. A Minister's effective performance of his functions depends on his having the confidence of the House of Commons (or the House of Lords, for those Ministers who sit in the upper House). A Minister has to conduct himself, and direct the work of his department in a manner likely to ensure that he retains the confidence both of his own party and of the House. It is for the Prime Minister to decide whom he chooses as Ministers; but the Prime Minister is unlikely to keep in office a Minister who does not retain the confidence of his Parliamentary colleagues.

NOTES:
1. Just before the 1992–97 Parliament was dissolved, the House of Commons agreed the resolution:

> That in the opinion of this House, the following principles should govern the Conduct of Ministers of the Crown in relation to Parliament:
> (1) Ministers have a duty to Parliament to account, and be held to account, for the policies, decisions and actions of their Departments and Next Steps Agencies;
> (2) It is of paramount importance that Ministers give accurate and truthful information to Parliament, correcting any inadvertent error at the earliest opportunity. Ministers who knowingly mislead will be expected to offer their resignation to the Prime Minister,
> (3) Ministers should be as open as possible with Parliament, refusing to provide information only when disclosure would not be in the public interest, which should be decided in accordance with relevant statute and the Government's Code of Practice on Access to Government Information (Second Edition, January 1997).
> (4) Similarly, Ministers should require civil servants who give evidence before Parliamentary Committees on their behalf and under their directions to be as helpful as possible in providing accurate, truthful and full information in accordance with the duties and responsibilities of civil servants as set out in the Civil Service Code (January (1996)). (HC Debs Vol. 292 cols. 1046–7, 19 March 1997.)

    The wording of this resolution on ministerial accountability differs from that proposed at para. 60 in the Public Service Committee's report. The resolution has been incorporated into the guidance given to Ministers, formerly entitled *Questions of Procedure for Ministers*, and now called *Ministerial Code: A Code of Conduct and Guidance on Procedure for Ministers*, at para. 1 (Cabinet Office 2001).
2. In the following extracts from his Inquiry into 'arms to Iraq', Sir Richard Scott discusses Government statements on defence sales policy after the ceasefire between Iran and Iraq.

Report of the Inquiry into the Export of Defence Equipment and Dual-Use Goods to Iraq and Related Prosecutions
HC 115 of 1995–96, Vol. 1, paras D.4.1–8, D4.52–6, D4.60, D4.63

(I) Letters from the FCO in 1989.
D4.1 Over the period February 1989 to July 1989, a number of letters, signed mainly by Mr Waldegrave but a few by Lord Howe, were sent to MPs whose constituents had asked questions about Government policy on defence sales to Iraq. The questions had been prompted by a variety of concerns. The concerns covered specific military exports to Iraq, Iraqi atrocities against the Kurds, Iraqi human rights violations in general, British participation at the Baghdad International Military Fair

(which was held from 29 April to 2 May), the British Aerospace proposal to sell Hawk Trainer Aircraft to Iraq as well as general apprehension about the sales of arms and defence equipment to the Middle East.

D4.2 A form of response to be incorporated in the letters sent to the MPs in question was settled in the FCO. The response included the following two sentences (or the gist of them):

'British arms supplies to both Iran and Iraq continue to be governed by the strict application of guidelines which prevent the supply of lethal equipment or equipment which would significantly enhance the capability of either side to resume hostilities. These guidelines are applied on a case by case basis.'

D4.3 Letters to MPs incorporating these sentences and signed by Mr Waldegrave numbered some seven in March 1989, five in April, twenty-three in May, one in June and two in July. Lord Howe signed two similar letters in May and two in July. In one of the April letters and in each of the May, June and July letters the formula was preceded by the statement that:

'The Government have not changed their policy on defence sales to Iraq or Iran.'

In one letter there was a reference to 'our firm and even-handed position over arms sales to Iran and Iraq.'

D4.4 The reference in each of these letters to the criterion that governed the supply of non-lethal defence equipment to Iraq was not accurate. Since the end of February 1989 the criterion for Iraq had been the new formulation, namely, that there would be no supply of equipment which would be of direct and significant assistance to Iraq in the conduct of offensive operations in breach of the cease-fire. The inaccuracy should have been noticed by Mr Waldegrave, who had been one of the midwives at the birth of this new formulation. Lord Howe, on the other hand, had not been informed of the junior Ministers' agreement on the new formulation.

D4.5 The statement in the letters that 'The Government have not changed their policy on defence sales to Iraq or Iran' was untrue. After the cease-fire Lord Howe had advocated, and the Prime Minister, with the concurrence of senior Ministers, had accepted, that a more liberal policy, designed to enable British exporters to take advantage of the glittering opportunities for defence-related sales to Iraq that it was believed would be available, should gradually be adopted. The discussions between the junior Ministers, which began with correspondence in November and December and with the Ministerial meeting on 21 December 1988, were for the purpose of trying to formulate a new policy which would then be brought to senior Ministers and the Prime Minister for approval. Agreement by the junior Ministers had led, by February 1989, to a new, more liberal, policy in the form of revised guideline (iii) being implemented on a trial basis. The proposed new policy, although reversed for Iran following the Rushdie affair, was continued for Iraq and finally confirmed at the 24 April 1989 Ministers' meeting and in the correspondence that followed.

D4.6 Mr Waldegrave knew, first hand, the facts that, in my opinion, rendered the 'no change in policy' statement untrue. I accept that, when he signed these letters, he did not regard the agreement he had reached with his fellow Ministers as having constituted a change in policy towards Iraq. In his evidence to the Inquiry, he strenuously and consistently asserted his belief, in the face of a volume of, to my mind, overwhelming evidence to the contrary, that policy on defence sales to Iraq had, indeed, remained unchanged. I did not receive the impression of any insincerity on his part in giving me the evidence he did. But it is clear, in my opinion, that policy on defence sales to Iraq did not remain unchanged.

D4.7 The proposition that the Government's position over 'arms sales to Iran and Iraq' was 'even-handed' had been untrue ever since the decision, taken as a consequence of the Rushdie affair, to 'return to a more strict approach to Iran.' In his letter of 28 March 1989 to Mr Clark, Mr Waldegrave had poposed that 'we should now revert to the stricter implementation of the guidelines as applied to Iran', while saying that he saw no reason to change the newly, agreed 'flexible approach for applications to export defence-related equipment to Iraq.' In his letter to Mr Waldegrave of 13 April, Lord Trefgarne, the Minister (DP), agreed with the proposal and the MOD/FCO agreement was put into effect by the MODWG at its meeting on 14 April. Mr Waldegrave's letter suggesting that an 'even-handed', position was being taken by the Government was dated 17 April. Mr Waldegrave has explained that '[his] view (and the advice of his officials) was that the policy was 'even-handed' as applied to the territorial and other ambitions of Iran and Iraq' and that 'particular steps taken in the area of exports in reaction to unforeseen events such as the Fatwah and the execution of Mr Bazoft did not detract from the even-handedness or neutrality or impartiality applied to the two states.' As to the first part of this explanation, the letter referred to the Goverment's 'even-handed position over *arms sales* to Iran and Iraq' (emphasis added); as to the second, the explanation has, in my opinion, no substance. Every government policy is bound to have some reason behind it. The unforeseen event that was the Fatwah led, inter alia, to a stricter policy on arms sales being applied to Iran than was applied to Iraq. This differential policy was already being implemented by 17 April. I could well understand that the reference in the letter to Mr Curry to the 'even-handed position' may have been an overlooked refugee from a common form sentence that would, two months earlier, have been unexceptionable. But the proposition that on 17 April, the date of the letter, it was a true statement is not, in my opinion, remotely arguable.

D4.8 Lord Howe had not been kept informed and was not aware of the detail of the manner in which the new formulation of guideline (iii) in its application to Iraq had been agreed. But he agreed, in his oral evidence to the Inquiry, that the new formulation of guideline (iii) was 'an implementation of the broad relaxation agreed in August/September [1988].' In his written and oral evidence to the Inquiry Lord Howe maintained that the 'implementation of the broad relaxation' towards Iraq and the adoption of the new criterion 'direct and significant assistance in the conduct of offensive operations in breach of the ceasefire' amounted merely to 'continuing with the original policy, subject to certain fluctuating glosses, even nuances.' Lord Howe explained the junior Ministers' agreement in this way:

> I think they were perhaps confused as to what they were doing. They said first of all 'Let's have a shot at reformulating. Let us have a trial basis.' The trial was interrupted by the Fatwah and they went back to the original basis in relation to Iran, and I think they rather forgot whether they had moved away from or applied it in a different fashion.

And, in answer to the question: 'The guidelines were reformulated were they not?', Lord Howe replied: 'Yes I think for practical purposes they were, but there was no disclosure of a reformulation. That was the last thing that people wanted to do.' He referred to the Ministers 'moving to a differential policy' and in answer to a question as to whether the 'differential policy' was no longer 'even-handed or impartial between the two countries', responded: 'It cannot be allowed to be seen like that. That is the point.' In my opinion, these answers preclude Lord Howe from maintaining his resistance to the proposition that there had been a change in policy. I do not suppose when he signed the letters in question in May and July 1989 he directed his mind to whether or not the 'no change in policy' statement was justifiable. Even if he had done so, his knowledge of the detail of what had been agreed between the junior Ministers was not such as to have necessarily alerted him to the misleading character of the 'no change in policy' statement. In the submission to him of 28 April 1989, Mr Young had said: 'We are not contemplating a major change in policy. . . . the existing guidelines on arms sales will remain in place.'

. . .

D4.52 A frank and sustained defence of the divergence between the Government's actual policy and the various Ministerial statements of policy, whether in letters or in answers to PQs, was offered by Lord Howe in his oral evidence to the Inquiry. He said:

> . . . there is nothing necessarily open to criticism in incompatibility between policy and

presentation of policy. . . . It [i.e. the Government] is not necessarily to be criticised for a difference between policy and public presentation of policy.

He explained:

> The fact is that, as soon as you are embarked upon the necessary policy, in competition with other nations, of enhancing a commercial position, a commercial position which is more inhibited than other nations, for reasons we have investigated, any attempt to enlarge that base is capable of being criticised by others. . . .
>
> Can this not be explained to the public in a manner the public would understand?
>
> A. Not easily, not if you visualise, as the *Independent* pointed out, the extremely emotional way in which such debates are conducted in public . . . if you look at the various reasons given by colleagues for caution in relation to the shifting nuances of policy, in the Spring of 1989, they all add up to a very good reason for not volunteering this, because the scope for misunderstanding is enormous.

And, later,

> Q. It is a sort of 'Government know best' approach, is it not?
>
> A. Yes.
>
> Q. 'We know what is good for you. You may not like it and, if you were made aware of it, you might protest, but we know what is best'?
>
> A. It is partly that, but it is partly 'if we were to lay specifically our thought processes before you, they are not just going before you; they are laid before a worldwide range of uncomprehending or malicious commentators'. This is the point. You cannot choose a well balanced presentation to an élite Parliamentary audience.

In relation to the circumstance that, as a result of the re-formulation of guideline (iii) and the decision to apply the re-formulated guideline to Iraq but not to Iran, policy was no longer even-handed or impartial as between the two countries Lord Howe said:

> 'It cannot be seen like that. That is the point.'

And

> Frankly the inaccuracy is intrinsic in the policy position that we are presenting. If you are saying that the Guidelines are still in place and being applied directly to Iran without any qualification, and being applied with modification to Iraq, then that is the thing you cannot disclose and you have to head back to 'The Guidelines are in place'. That is the point. The Guidelines are in place because the basic policy has not changed.

D4.53 Lord Howe was not alone in defending the variance between Government statements of policy and Government's actual policy. Mr Gore-Booth, too, defended the propriety of statements of policy that designedly gave less than the full picture. He agreed that answers to Parliamentary questions should be as forthcoming as possible, but pointed out that 'there are often cases in which you cannot be so forthcoming, for what are called reasons of foreign policy.' He agreed that answers should be accurate but said that 'half a picture can be accurate.' He defended the answers given by Ministers to PQs about policy on exports to Iraq: . . . actually I have no difficulty with [the answers] in terms of fullness. I think that some of the answers in the papers are as full as was compatible with the sensitivities to which I referred here.

D4.54 The issue was dealt with also by Sir Robin Butler. He was firm in his opinion that a public statement made by a Minister should not, save in the most exceptional case, be misleading, but, like Mr Gore-Booth, regarded it as acceptable in some circumstances for a statement to disclose only part of the full picture.

D4.55 The problem with the 'half a picture' approach is that those to whom the incomplete statement is addressed do not know unless it is apparent from the terms of the statement itself, that an undisclosed half is being withheld from them. They are almost bound, therefore, to be misled by the statement, notwithstanding that the 'half a picture' may, so far as it goes, be accurate. The proposition is not that a statement to Parliament must include each and every fact relating to the subject in order to avoid being misleading. Such a requirement would clearly be impracticable. A fair summary of the 'full picture' would often, depending on the question that had been asked and the apparent purpose of the statement, be a complete and sufficient response. The proposition is that if part of the picture is being suppressed and the audience does not know it is being suppressed, the audience will be misled into believing the half picture to be the full picture. Lord Howe's unapologetic acceptance of and support for the divergence between Government's statements of policy and Government's actual policy revealed by the public statements to which I have earlier referred was, in my opinion, more realistic than Sir Robin Butler's and Mr Gore-Booth's attempts to reconcile the giving of answers that designedly disclosed only part of the picture with the obligation to avoid giving misleading answers.

D4.56 It is, rightly, accepted that there have always been and will always be subjects in respect of which full information, or sometimes any information, cannot be made public. Current operations of the security and intelligence agencies come easily to mind as examples. Sir Robin Butler, in evidence to the Inquiry and, also, to the Treasury and Civil Service Select Committee, instanced information about imminent changes in interest rates or in exchange rates. The public interest may require information about proposed changes to be withheld from the public. The examples are cogent. It ought, nonetheless, to be recognised that the obligation of Ministers to give information about the activities of their departments and to give information and explanations for the actions and omissions of their civil servants lies at the heart of Ministerial accountability and that every decision by a Minister to withhold information from Parliament and from the public constitutes an avoidance, and sometimes an evasion, *pro tanto*, of Ministerial accountability . . .

D4.60 The reasons put forward by Lord Howe in his oral evidence to the Inquiry in justification of the withholding from Parliament and the public of knowledge, first, of the proposed relaxation of the Guidelines in favour of both Iraq and Iran, and, secondly, of the actual relaxation of the Guidelines in favour of Iraq but not of Iran, were not reasons of national security, nor did they relate to operations of the security or intelligence agencies, nor were they analogous to the reasons for not disclosing proposed changes in interest rates or exchange rates. Lord Howe's reasons were, in the main, foreign relations reasons; a fear of adverse reactions from Washington or from Riyadh at the prospect of a more favourable approach to exports to Iran; or fear of adverse reactions from Iran if it were known that Iraq was being given more favourable treatment than itself. It is not, in my opinion, in the least obvious that the foreign relations reasons identified by Lord Howe were sufficient to justify the repeated provision to Parliament and, via the letters to MPs, to members of the public, of information about Government policy that was by design incomplete and in certain respects misleading . . .

D4.63 In the circumstances, the Government statements made in 1989 and 1990 about policy on defence exports to Iraq consistently failed, in my opinion, to comply with the standard set by paragraph 27 of the Questions of Procedure for Ministers and, more important, failed to discharge the obligations imposed by the constitutional principle of Ministerial accountability.

QUESTION

If Ministers are now expected to resign if they *knowingly* mislead, does this mean that ignorance, incompetence, or incredible opinions about matters will absolve Ministers who mislead?

NOTES:
1. The Public Service Committee considered how a Parliamentary resolution on accountability might be enforced. Recognizing the reality that party politics might impede Parliamentary

procedures, the Committee considered if the Parliamentary Commissioner for Administration could investigate complaints from MPs that a Minister was withholding information. The then Parliamentary Commissioner for Administration gave evidence to the Committee indicating his reluctance to undertake the role they envisaged.

2. Accountability to Parliament through Ministers has been placed under further strain because of the programme of improving managerial efficiency in public administration.

Second Report from the Public Service Committee
HC 313 of 1995–96, paras 84–91, 95–102, 109, 115–123

84. . . . It has long been an aim of public administration reformers to distance the executive functions of government from the main body of the Civil Service, which was largely organised in order to advise Ministers on policy. The aim was to achieve, in those functions, more coherent and more efficient management, replacing an inflexible and centralised framework with much greater independence and flexibility. The Next Steps programme has been the most determined effort to achieve this aim. The concept of Executive Agencies was set out in a Report by the Efficiency Unit in February 1988, *Improving Management in Government: the Next Steps*. The Report recommended that 'to the greatest possible extent practicable the executive functions of government, as distinct from policy advice, should be carried out by units clearly designated within departments, referred to as agencies'.

85. In Next Steps Agencies, functions and powers which would otherwise be exercised by the central department are delegated to the head of the Executive Agency. Each agency operates under a Framework Document. These describe the nature of the relationship between the Minister setting up the agency and the Chief Executive who reports to him or her, and list the agency's aims and objectives, the services to be provided, the performance indicators and the extent of managerial devolution to the Chief Executive. They should, the Office of Public Service told us, 'make clear matters on which the Minister expects to be consulted'.

86. The Prison Service Framework Document, for example, sets out the agency's 'Statement of Purpose, Vision, Goals and Values', and lists the key performance indicators relevant to its goals. It describes the planning framework, setting out the responsibility of the Prison Service to prepare an annual Corporate Plan covering three years, and a Business Plan covering one year. It sets out the accounting responsibility of the Director General, and his responsibility for the service's expenditure and for personnel management, and certain personnel matters. It also lays out how the Prison Service is accountable:

> The Home Secretary is accountable to Parliament for the Prison Service. The Home Secretary allocates resources to the Prison Service and approves its Corporate and Business Plans, including its key targets. The Home Secretary will not normally become involved in the day-to-day management of the Prison Service but will expect to be consulted by the Director General on the handling of operational matters which could give rise to grave public or Parliamentary concern.

The Document specifies matters on which the Home Secretary will receive Reports from the Director General. It lists the responsibilities of the Director General as the 'day-to-day management of the Prison Service'; acting as the Home Secretary's 'principal policy adviser on matters relating to the Prison Service'; preparing the draft Corporate and Business Plans, and submitting them to the Home Secretary for approval; achieving the Service's key targets, and so on.

87. Agencies are often seen as successfully ensuring that public services are delivered more effectively and efficiently. We note the consistent support given to the programme by our predecessors, the Treasury and Civil Service Committee, particularly in its early years. The Committee in 1988 welcomed the Government's commitment to improvement in efficiency and quality of service, and expressed its concern that the pace of change should not be too slow, or the extent of change too

limited, as long as the consequence of such change is an improved quality of service to government, Parliament and society. In 1989 it recorded its belief that 'Next Steps represents a real change in the way the Civil Service is run', and drew attention 'not only to the changes which are already taking place in the way government services are delivered, but the possibly radically different shape of the Civil Service which may emerge as a result of them'. In subsequent reports it welcomed the speed at which agencies were being established; and in one it said that it had been 'concerned to sustain and develop all party support for the initiative'.

Agencies and accountability

88. In terms of the accountability of government, however, its success is more mixed – something on which the Treasury and Civil Service Committee have also regularly commented. On the one hand, the formal delegation of responsibility to agency Chief Executives can offer better account-ability because it makes more transparent the relationship between the Minister and the civil ser-vant. The Minister and the Chief Executive come to an agreement – though not a legally binding contract – specifying their respective roles and responsibilities. The Government's memorandum says that 'one of the major achievements of Next Steps has been the identification and, so far as possible, the separation of previously entwined roles in Civil Service management'. A survey of the relationship between departments and agencies, completed in early 1995, concluded that 'Next Steps has facilitated accountability by clarifying the role and functions of officials and the organisa-tions to which they belong'. With the information it now has available in the Framework Document and elsewhere, it ought to be possible for Parliament and the public to examine the relationship between Ministers and some civil servants to decide to whom should be attributed praise or blame.

89. While it has done much to promote the extent to which Parliament and the public can discover what is going on inside Government, the increased transparency of the relationship has done more than anything to reduce the coherence of the convention of Ministerial responsibility. It has led, indeed, to suggestions that it renders the traditional convention of Ministerial responsibility unworkable in agencies. To those who designed the system, and to many since, it has seemed reasonable to build on this quasi-contractual relationship, in order to create a rather different type of accountability by the executive to Parliament. The Efficiency Unit argued that 'Placing responsibility for performance squarely on the shoulders of the manager of an agency . . . has implications for the way in which Ministers answer to Parliament on operational issues . . . We believe it is possible for Parliament, through Ministers, to regard managers as directly responsible for operational matters and that there are precedents for this and precisely defined ways in which it can be handled'. In an Annex, they explained the need for this exception to the ordinary convention. The management of an agency was unlikely to be given a realistically specified framework within which there is freedom to manage if a Minister remains immediately answerable for every operational detail; and 'accept-ance of individual responsibility for performance cannot be expected if repeated Ministerial interven-tion is there as a ready-made excuse'. They noted how some functions of central government were already carried out at arm's length from Ministers – such as decisions on individual tax or social security cases, or quasi-judicial or regulatory functions. They pointed out how agencies outside departments normally operate within a statutory framework, and did not rule out such a framework for the agencies. They therefore proposed that agency Chief Executives should give evidence to the Public Accounts Committee and Select Committees, and that they should answer Parliamentary Questions themselves (rather than through Ministers).

90. These specific proposals on Parliamentary accountability have all, gradually, been accepted in some form or another. But the Government has still preferred to retain agencies within departments, and to keep to the formal position on Ministerial responsibility. Agency Chief Executives are still civil servants; they still act on behalf of, and under the authority of Ministers, and are not directly accountable to Parliament. Agency Chief Executives are now Accounting Officers for the Agency, but they are normally additional Accounting Officers, formally subordinate to the permanent head of the

department. As the Accounting Officers' memorandum says: 'the permanent head, in addition to the responsibilities for the assigned votes and accounts, remains in overall charge of the department . . . It is within that framework that any additional Accounting Officers, including those who are Chief Executives of 'Next Steps' Agencies, are responsible for the votes and accounts assigned to them. This position has been contested in a series of Treasury and Civil Service Committee reports, but the Government has maintained its position firmly: the recommendation of the Committee in 1994 that agency Chief Executives should be 'directly and personally accountable to Select Committees in relation to their annual performance agreements' was, it said, inconsistent with the Committee's desire to retain the right of Members of Parliament to appeal to a Minister if a Chief Executive's answer to a Parliamentary Question is unsatisfactory.

91. The Government's position reflects the belief that delegating functions further away from Ministers risks making traditional Parliamentary accountability less effective. The more formal delegation of powers, it may be said, means that a Minister can with much greater reason than before disclaim responsibility or accountability for a good deal of the work of his department. Many have expressed great concern that opportunities to approach and influence a Minister about important issues of operational policy are lost if a Minister refers inquiries to the person in charge of the operational policy, the Chief Executive. One of the principal meanings of accountability to Parliament is, as we have described above (para. 32) the responsiveness of the executive to concerns raised, on behalf of constituents, by Members of Parliament through pressure on Ministers in Parliament. If Ministers formally delegate their functions it might be argued that they make public services unaccountable, at least in Parliamentary terms.

. . .

95. While the Government may have been sympathetic to the aim of achieving greater clarity in the respective responsibilities of Minister and Chief Executive, it has been reluctant to surrender any rights over the agencies: 'Because Ministers must account to Parliament they must retain the right to look into, question and even intervene in the operation of their agencies'. Because they retain this right, there always remains a question about the extent to which Chief Executives have genuine administrative freedom, and as long as their freedom can be questioned, responsibility can be blurred. Sophie Trosa, the French Civil Servant commissioned in 1994 to review the progress of the Next Steps Initiative, described the problem:

> The accepted principle is relatively simple. Ministers are responsible for policy and Chief Executives are responsible for the administration of that policy. In practice, it is not always that simple. Conflicts can arise, for example, when there is a policy failure related to its administration. On the one hand the Minister might not feel responsible for what he might see as a failure in administration while on the other hand the Chief Executive might feel in a difficult position if the Agency's objectives had been set without his agreement, or at least involvement.

96. These themes are well illustrated by the history, since its acquisition of agency status, of the Prison Service. The Prison Service became an agency on 1 April 1993. Mr Derek Lewis, its first Director General, said that 'there was an enormous amount which needed to be done' in making the Prison Service more efficient, and had established that it would take four or six years to complete the programme he felt was necessary. Derek Lewis described to us the 'two distinct cultures' within the Prison Service: his point shows the difficulty of combining management and political responsiveness, and indicates both one of the main reasons for giving it agency status and one of the main reasons for the difficulties it has experienced since:

> There was the headquarters culture where headquarters was staffed in senior positions by those who had careers as Home Office civil servants and who spent a period of time in the Prison Service as part of a longer career in the Home Office and those in the field who were typically career Prison Service professionals. That meant that there was not only

considerable hostility, but a considerable gulf of understanding. Those at the centre tended to focus principally on the needs of Ministers to the detriment of the operational needs of the Service and those in the field tended to be unsympathetic to the quite proper concerns of Ministers.

As he pointed out, over the two and a half years following its conversion into an agency, the Prison Service had achieved 'virtually all the targets which had been set for it by Ministers'. The number of escapes was 25 per cent fewer in 1993–94 than in the preceding year; in 1994–95 it had dropped again, by 32 per cent. The aim of eliminating the practice of holding prisoners three to a cell was achieved. Targets in a programme to provide prisoners with 24-hour access to sanitation were exceeded, and targets in a programme to minimise the cost per prison place were also exceeded.

97. Despite these successes, the Agency was plagued by a series of problems which received a great deal of publicity and gave rise to much criticism. Within a few months of its transition to agency status, some very high security prisoners escaped from Whitemoor Prison in Cambridgeshire. A report by Sir John Woodcock into the escape indicated some widespread problems in the Prison Service generally, not simply at Whitemoor. The Home Secretary appointed General Sir John Learmont to consider these further, and make recommendations; but scarcely had he began his task than a further escape, of three prisoners from Parkhurst Prison, caused his remit to be extended into that event. The Learmont Report was published on 16 October 1995. It criticised the Prison Service's leadership, its structure, its management chain, and 'the ethics of the service', and said that 'the top management of any organisation must be responsible for its performance'. Mr Howard told the House of Commons that he had come to the conclusion that putting these things right 'requires a change of leadership at the top of the Prison Service', and Mr Lewis was relieved of his post.

98. Much of the debate on the Prison Service and the Learmont Report has centred on the extent of Ministerial involvement in the operation of the Agency, the degree to which this was legitimate, and whether or not, in attributing blame for these failings to individual civil servants, the Home Secretary was evading a responsibility that should be his. This was an issue well before Learmont's Report was published. After the escape from Parkhurst, the Prison's Governor, Mr John Mariott, was suspended from duty; it was claimed that his suspension had been the result of pressure placed on Mr Lewis by the Home Secretary. Sir John Woodcock, in his Report, said that 'there exists at all levels within the Service some confusion as to the respective roles of Ministers, the Agency Headquarters and individual Prison Governors. In particular, the Enquiry has identified the difficulty of determining what is an operational matter and what is policy, leading to confusion as to where responsibility lies'. The Learmont Report added further fuel to the argument, and pointed out that the relationship between the Prison Service and the Home Office was not always an easy one before the service was made into an Agency. Learmont referred to the 'historically close involvement of the Home Office, particularly in major operational matters', and to the 1991 Lygo Report which urged 'a greater degree of managerial independence for the Prison Service from day-to-day Home Office control'. The result of the Lygo Report was the transfer of the Prison Service to agency status. But agency status has not meant that the Home Office ceased to take a close interest in its affairs. Over four months (October 1994 to January 1995) Prison Service headquarters had submitted to the Home Office just over 1,000 documents, including 137 'full submissions', containing substantive advice about policy or operational matters. Besides this, the Director General had to answer 600 Parliamentary Questions a year – 'many of which require discussion with Ministers to achieve a mutually acceptable answer', and 4,000 letters from Members of Parliament. Learmont recommended a review of the relationship between the Home Office and the Agency 'with a view to giving the Prison Service the greater operational independence that agency status was meant to confer'.

99. In evidence to the Committee, Mr Lewis confirmed Learmont's picture of the extent of Ministers' involvement in the day-to-day operation of the Prison Service. 'I think the two things which surprised me were, one, the quantity of briefing and the level of detail in which Ministers become

involved at times during my period of office, but, second, their involvement in decisions as opposed to being provided with information and consulted on matters'. He told us that this involvement had grown to a 'level where I believe it was acting to the detriment of the performance of the Prison Service':

> For two reasons. One, it was proving to be a distraction for me and the other senior members of the management of the Service, and, secondly, it was a level which caused those within the service to be uncertain about who was actually calling the shots, if I may put it that way.

100. The proper responsibility for the difficulties within the Prison Service is not something that we can pin down, nor do we intend to try. But the reasons for these difficulties, it has certainly been argued, is the problem of how to specify separate roles for Ministers and Chief Executives, of deciding what is 'policy' (the job of the Minister) and what is 'operations' (the job of the Chief Executive). This, indeed, is the view of Mr Lewis, who told us that 'in the most complex and sensitive agencies, such as the Prison Service, there is difficulty in defining precisely who takes what decisions or when the Secretary of State should be involved – in popular terms, what is "policy" and what is "operational"'. He gives two examples of the lack of clarity in drawing the border between the two.

> it is policy that convicted prisoners should work or undertake similar activities. It is an operational decision whether they should be producing prison clothing or furniture for the commercial market. Elsewhere it is not so simple. The Home Secretary decided, presumably as a matter of policy, that it was unacceptable for prisoners to have televisions in their cells, but the question of how much and what television prisoners should be allowed to watch in communal areas remains as an operational decision.

101. The Prison Service is not the only agency in which the dividing line between 'operational' and 'policy' matters can be difficult to draw. Mr Haynes gave us an example from the Highways Agency:

> We are just building the road, the A40. On that road we are having to demolish houses. One of the houses, which is due to be demolished, actually houses a very old lady. That, to me, is an area which under my Business Plan I have the right. I have all the writs. I have the Compulsory Purchase Order to go ahead and do it. To me it is pragmatic, it is sensible to go to the Secretary of State and say, 'This old lady will have to be evicted. You should be aware that there is going to be a public view on this. The media will treat it in a particular way. Let's discuss it'.

He told us that 'I do not see there is a great problem about the grey area'; – but this may be attributable to his own apparently good relationship with Ministers:

> I have described it as a 'grown-up debate' which one has to have with Ministers and Secretaries of State. They have issues which they need to be concerned about and occasionally there are some differences of opinion. It is quite right and proper that we have a discussion, and in some of the controversial areas I can have those discussions and it is amicably settled.

102. Mr Lewis told us that when the difficulties of ensuring accountability in agencies were discussed at the annual conference of Chief Executives in 1995 it was clear that the issue was not significant for the majority of agencies which are either relatively small or are not politically sensitive or high profile: 'it is only in the larger, more sensitive and complex agencies that they have become a problem'. Many agencies do not raise questions of political controversy. It is difficult to imagine, for example, the activities carried out by the Driver and Vehicle Licensing Agency, Wilton Park or the Royal Parks Agency exciting much political heat. Yet politics is unpredictable: matters which are uncontroversial one day may be at the centre of a political storm the next. **We recommend that the**

Government systematically reviews the roles of Ministers and agency Chief Executives and reports its conclusions to Parliament in the Next Steps Agency Review.

. . .

The accountability of agency Chief Executives

109. We have already referred to the argument that has been continuing since the Next Steps agencies were originally set up that agency Chief Executives should be 'directly accountable' to Parliament. Such an arrangement would have a number of benefits. The principal among them would be that Chief Executives would be able to discuss more freely with Committees issues of operational policy. Derek Lewis thought one of the great benefits would be to make Parliament and the public better informed: 'I think there is a strong case for saying that those who are leading the major public services should be given greater freedom to account for their performance, not only for their performance, but to explain the impact of policy decisions on their services to, for example, a Committee such as this or to the public in general'. Mr Heseltine put the case against this:

> that is incompatible with their status as civil servants because, as I think the words are, the civil servant is the Minister in this sense. If I have an agency, I am responsible for the policy and so I have to lay down the policy, I have to set the targets and I have to account to this Committee or to Parliament for what goes on. What I cannot have in such circumstances is a Chief Executive coming here and giving a whole range of views about what he wants to do and all that in a way which conflicts with what I want him to do because then he becomes effectively another political force.

Former and present civil servants were anxious not to disturb what Lord Armstrong called 'the line of accountability', through Ministers, to Parliament. Lord Howe suggested that the accountability of Chief Executives to Parliament through Select Committees was something which would happen anyway: '*de facto*, accountability will grow along that line'.

. . .

The responsibilities of Ministers and Chief Executives

115. There are bound to be grey areas of responsibility in the relationship between Ministers and Chief Executives. But the larger they are, the more difficult it is to establish proper and effective lines of accountability; and indeed, to make the relationship managerially effective. The original 1988 Report on *Improving Management in Government: the Next Steps* suggested that agencies 'need to be given a well defined framework in which to operate, which sets out the policy, the budget, specific targets and the results to be achieved. It must also specify how politically sensitive issues are to be dealt with and the extent of the delegated authority of management. . . . A crucial element in the relationship would be a formal understanding with Ministers about the handling of sensitive issues and the lines of accountability in a crisis'. As we have seen, however, particularly in the case of the Prison Service, this understanding on the handling of sensitive issues and lines of accountability in a crisis appears to be difficult to achieve. But not, we believe, impossible.

116. The Office of Public Service say that 'the clarity of the division of responsibilities between the Minister and Chief Executive is something that should be considered carefully in initially setting up an agency and subsequently in reviewing its Framework Document'; but they comment that 'no Framework Document could spell out in precise terms the division of responsibility in every theoretical set of circumstances'. Sir Peter Kemp seems to take a more hopeful view. He believes that it would be possible to have a more direct form of accountability to Parliament if the respective roles of Minister and Chief Executive were clearer, perhaps in some form of explicit contract so that specific responsibilities are delegated to officials and put into statutory form, and Ministers would remain responsible only for the terms of the delegation. Then officials might speak more freely on their performance of their side of the contract. He argues that 'What is required . . . is a more specific and as may be detailed description, on a case by case basis, of what is down to who. . . . It ought to be

possible, given care and time and trouble, in the case of each and every agency to delineate and write down who does what'. Clearly, it is not always possible to decide in advance what issues will prove to be politically sensitive, and it is always open to a Minister to involve himself in any issue, however detailed, provided that his involvement is clearly recorded if it departs from the terms of the Framework Document and he takes full responsibility and accountability for his actions.

117. Not all agencies, as we have said (para. 102) raise issues of this nature in any serious way. Most agencies appear to have little or no difficulty in working within the responsibilities as they are at present mapped out in the Framework Document. It was suggested by some of our witnesses, in fact, that agencies that were as politically controversial as the Prison Service were unsuitable for agency status at all, and should be pulled back into their parent departments. Areas of activity in which Ministers need to involve themselves so much should be retained within departments in order to ensure that their political accountability remained the priority. Making the Prison Service into an agency was, Lord Armstrong told us, 'a stage too far'. The function suitable for agency status was, he said 'a basic management task without a controversial political contact, whereas the Prison Service is anything but that'. He made a similar point about the Child Support Agency 'So much of the devil lies in the detail of the way in which the individual cases are handled that it is very difficult to maintain this dichotomy between objectives and budgets, on the one hand, and day-to-day management on the other. In a sense the objectives of the agency are so closely related to, and are reflected in the day-to-day actions, that it may not have been a very good case for becoming an agency'. Lord Armstrong, former Cabinet Secretary and Head of the Home Civil Service, has said that the agency arrangement works satisfactorily 'where there is little political context'; and in evidence to us he said that this meant in cases where the Minister is unlikely to become involved on a day-to-day basis. Sir Robin Butler was less pessimistic: He accepted that the more politically controversial agencies were ones in which Ministers need to be involved much more closely than in the case of others, but it should still be possible to define separate roles. 'These are difficult lines to draw and they need to be reviewed, but I think it is well worth doing. Even in the Prison Service, he said, 'notwithstanding the difficulties, very considerable improvements in management have been made'.

118. Some have argued, on the other hand, that the difficulties of defining the separate roles and responsibilities of Ministers and managers would be eased if agencies were more formally divided from their departments, perhaps through placing them on a statutory basis. Statutory independence might be seen as a means of reducing the ability of a Minister to interfere in the work of the agency. Derek Lewis described a possible arrangement for the Prison Service in which agencies were non-departmental public bodies within a statutory framework, similar to that for the police. The Service would be overseen by an independent board established by statute; policy would be set by Ministers through secondary legislation; and funding levels would be determined by the sponsoring department; and the sponsoring department would monitor efficiency through 'systematic and rigorous performance audits conducted by an independent inspectorate, similar to the Chief Inspector of Constabulary'. One of the benefits of such an arrangement, according to Mr Lewis, would be that Ministers were no longer responsible for the operation of the Service: 'it would put greater distance between the sponsoring department and the Chief Executive and would provide the Chief Executive with some reassurance against the doubtless unnecessary fears that expressing unpopular views might bring swift retribution'.

119. In Sweden, we looked at the way a more formal relationship such as this might work in practice. Historically, a good deal of government services have been provided by agencies. There are over 300 agencies ranging from 30,000 employees to a mere handful. Although the Government appoints agency heads, the agencies are independent of the Government. Government control is exercised in the long term through decisions on agency functions and directions and by overall budgetary control. These are set out in a letter of regulation which the Government issues each year to every agency. In discussions with the Swedish Agency for Administrative Development and other

bodies with experience of the agency sector in Sweden it was emphasised to us that, in the absence of formal contact with the Government agencies do operate under legal rules and remain sensitive to changes in government and in government policy. Government frequently consults informally with them.

120.   The difficulty with making agencies into bodies with statutory independence is, as Sir Robin Butler argued, that it could tend to reduce, rather than enhance, their accountability.

> If you gave an agency statutory independence what you would do is turn it into something else, which is perfectly familiar, which is a quango, and this is a body that has got independence, in areas defined by the statute, from the Minister, and there are plenty of bodies of that sort. But, of course, what one has got to recognise, by doing that, is that you do to that extent reduce Ministerial accountability, the Minister is no longer responsible for that matter of which the Chief Executive has been made statutorily responsible, so you would divorce something from Parliamentary Ministerial responsibility.

As he added, 'While it is still an agency and accountable to Parliament, you certainly may get, and this, indeed, is part of the philosophy of agencies, a better account directly from the Chief Executive than from the Minister, in the first instance; but if Parliament is then dissatisfied with that, or an MP is dissatisfied with that, that MP always has the right to go to the Minister and ask the Minister to intervene'. This is perhaps an overly conservative view of the scope for improved accountability within such statutory bodies: a statutory relationship would probably require the Government to set down what it requires of the body in writing, perhaps even through statutory instrument, which might be approved in Parliament. Therefore the scope for Parliamentary control of the policy process could be enhanced, rather than reduced. Equally, Ministers would still, presumably, have powers to appoint and dismiss the body's head. But it is true that it would mean that Members of Parliament would be less easily able to influence the activities of the body; and the experience of the nationalised industries is often cited to suggest that statutory bodies or public corporations, while theoretically independent, could be subject to a considerable amount of pressure from Ministers. However, nationalised industries were not in fact normally subject to detailed legislative prescription: indeed pride was taken in the fact that they were left to operate in their markets as freely as possible.

121.   An alternative way of making the division of responsibilities between agencies and departments more explicit would be to make it more contractual. This, to some extent, is happening already. As Dr Andrew Massey, Reader in Public Policy, University of Portsmouth, noted, 'the Market Testing initiative, in-service agreements, competitive tendering and privatisation all mark the transformation of the accountability function away from being rule-based and hierarchical. It tends to strengthen Ministerial control, in that the loss of a contract is a sobering discipline for Chief Executives operating under tight financial constraints'. Graham Mather, MEP, President of the European Policy Forum, advocates a more explicit contractual arrangement, akin to that introduced in New Zealand. The New Zealand model of public service reform was discussed by the Treasury and Civil Service Committee in its 1994 Report on the Role of the Civil Service. In New Zealand, the State Sector Act 1988 formally separated the functions of the Minister and officials. The relationship between them became subject to an annual performance agreement, under which Chief Executives undertook to perform certain outputs set by the Minister in return for control over inputs decisions – pay, appointments, organisational structures, and so on. The outputs could include both service delivery and policy advice. The Public Finance Act 1989 took the division further, by making Ministers into purchasers of outputs, and the departments and agencies into suppliers. Ministers purchase outputs in order to achieve the Government's desired outcomes. The system resembles 'the arrangements and incentives of the commercial marketplace'.

122.   Sir Robin Butler argued that such a contractual approach would be too formal for many of the functions which agencies perform. His opposition reflects the resistance to introducing law into

the machinery of Government to which Professor Lewis referred. Introducing legal rules as the way in which the relationship between Ministers and Chief Executives were determined would, undoubtedly, be one way of increasing accountability, particularly if such rules were statutory instruments, subject to Parliamentary procedure. But such formalism is not essential; what is essential is openness in the relationship. Mr Mottram told us that 'the great benefit' of agencies was 'that someone is in charge, they have a clear set of responsibilities, they must define who they are doing something for, and when we under-pin all that with resource budgeting and accounting, as we will be doing by the end of the decade, we will have these advantages even more'. This greater definition and greater clarity is the central benefit of the Next Steps initiative, and we believe that it needs to be enhanced, and enhanced openly. Therefore, **we recommend that Framework Documents should specify more precisely the respective roles of Ministers and Chief Executives**. We believe that there could well be a number of Agencies that could be more effectively run under detailed statutory provision or a contractual relationship. This is a subject which requires further attention. Agencies are very different in their roles and their responsibilities and it would be impossible to provide a general prescription for all of them. But statutory status or a contractual relationship should be options that are at least considered. **We recommend that at each Agency review, the Government consider whether the Agency in question should be converted into a statutory body**. This is an issue to which we intend to give further attention, and **we recommend that other Committees when they consider the Framework Documents of Agencies falling within their remit should also consider whether a contractual or legislative framework would better serve the public interest than the Agency's present status**.

123. Agencies need to be able to engage in a constructive dialogue with Parliament through Select Committees. As Kate Jenkins, an independent consultant and former Head of the Prime Minister's Efficiency Unit, said, one thing that would make accountability really effective would be 'if Committees of the House of Commons are able to add value, so that a Chief Executive who has come and had a discussion with the Committee really does feel that they now have a Committee who understands what the problems are or has a Committee who has some ideas which it can contribute and it is not simply a process of asking why something has gone wrong and why it cannot go better'. Dr Philip Giddings made a similar comment: 'notwithstanding some important early work by the National Audit Office and the Public Accounts Committee and growing interest by some departmental Committees, it remains the case that the work of Committees as a whole has not yet taken on the character of a sustained and systematic performance audit of agencies which some would like to see'. This implies responsibilities both for the Committees (which we have dealt with above), for the agency, and for the department. This should begin with the establishment of the agency, and the drafting of its Framework Document. Professor Norman Lewis, Professor of Public Law at the University of Sheffield, argues that 'It would be a clear advance in terms of accountability if the departmental Select Committees were given a timely opportunity to comment on these documents and their renewals where appropriate. In doing so they might be able to influence the relationship between responsibility for outputs and outcomes in a way that Parliament has never attempted before'. Kate Jenkins made a similar suggestion, that Select Committees should become involved – in a quite informal way – in the way in which Framework Documents and agency Corporate Plans are put together. Sir Peter Kemp agreed. **We recommend that Government invites Select Committees to comment on Framework Documents and agency Corporate Plans before they are published and when they are reviewed**.

NOTE: Mr Jack Straw, when he became Home Secretary, announced changes in responsibility arrangements for the Prison Service, which began with the assurance that Ministers and not the Director General would answer parliamentary questions (HC Deb., col. 397, 19 May 1997: see D. Woodhouse, 'Individual Ministerial Responsibility and a "Dash of Principle" ' in *The Law, Politics and the Constitution*, D. Butler, V. Bogdanor, and R. Summers (eds) (1999), p. 102).

QUESTIONS

1. Will it be possible to draft clearly the respective duties of Ministers and Chief Executives, thus ending the current ambiguity about policy and operations which seems to enable Ministers to choose what is and is not policy and therefore those things for which they can be held responsible?

2. Why would it be regarded as desirable for Chief Executives to have a more direct relationship with select committees?

NOTE: D. Woodhouse in 'The Reconstruction of Constitutional Accountability' [2002] PL 72, suggests that attention should be moved away from 'causal' responsibility with its focus upon direct ministerial involvement, towards 'role' responsibility which concentrates upon the requirements of the job of a Minister including supervision of a department, explaining actions carried out in its name, and correcting any deficiencies. This would avoid the confusion introduced by managerial accountability with its 'responsibility/accountability' and 'policy/operations' distinctions. Woodhouse suggests that the actions of some Ministers seem to be based upon this 'role' conception: the setting up of an inquiry and the implementation of reform following allegations that Foreign Office officials had sanctioned the supply of military equipment to Sierra Leone and the Home Secretary apologizing for the backlog in processing and issuing passports by the executive agency, the Passport Office.

QUESTION

How different is Woodhouse's 'role' responsibility from Enoch Powell's conception of ministerial responsibility *ante* at p. 276?

Second Report from the Public Service Committee
HC 313 of 1995–96, paras 170–174

IX. DIFFERENT SORTS OF ACCOUNTABILITY

170. In this Report, we have been mainly concerned with Parliamentary accountability. But we are well aware that government are not accountable only through Parliament. Mr David Faulkner of St John's College, Oxford, put this point in his evidence to us: Accountability

> can also take different forms – political, financial, managerial, operational, legal, professional. It can be to different authorities, institutions or individuals – Parliament, Ministers, managers, the courts, auditors, inspectors, regulators, users, customers or the general public. . . . Accountability can operate through direct supervision or contact, through formal arrangements for reporting or consultation (in public or in private), through procedures (such as complaints) which can be activated when required, and in various other ways . . . accountability – or responsibility – should lie, not just to central government and Parliament, but also to the organisations with which they work and on which they may depend; to local communities; to users; and to the wider public. Accountability should take multiple forms and operate through multiple, and often reciprocal, channels.

171. In recent years, three institutions or developments have tended to increase the extent to which the public is able to ensure that public services are properly accountable. The growth of judicial review is one of them. The Treasury and Civil Service Committee noted in 1994, the accountability of the executive through the Courts has been enhanced in recent years by the growth of judicial review. That Committee also noted the Government's observation that 'existence of judicial review has clearly and substantially increased the work of both lawyers and administrators, in effect to "judicial review-proof" departmental decisions, but it has also improved the quality of decision-

making by making it more structured and consistent'. Judicial review was 'a contribution to upholding the values of fairness, reasonableness and objectivity in the conduct of public business'. in addition to judicial review, statutory right of appeal against many types of administrative decision – such as on asylum applications, or planning applications – is now provided. Many of these are on essentially the same grounds as might be claimed in an application for judicial review.

172. Another is the role of the Parliamentary Commissioner for Administration (the Ombudsman) in investigating complaints from persons or organisations who contend that there is prima facie evidence of maladministration, by a body within his jurisdiction (generally speaking, government departments and bodies), which has led to hardship or injustice. A number of those who sent us memoranda referred to the powers of the Ombudsman and the possibility of their extension. Dr Diana Woodhouse wrote that 'whether supplementary mechanisms for accountability need to be strengthened and new ones established' should be considered. In particular, she thought that the Ombudsman should have powers to investigate cases referred to him directly by individuals (rather than having to go through a Member of Parliament) and have a mechanism for enforcing the conclusions of his reports. Professors Gavin Drewry and Dawn Oliver of the University of London felt that 'an extension of the jurisdiction of the PCA to embrace illegality . . . could help to counter the problems experienced by the High Court in dealing with applications for judicial review': this would also 'greatly enhance the effectiveness of provisions for redress of grievance'. They also argued that the PCA could be given an explicit role in developing 'best practice' guidance, and thereby have 'a substantial and recognised input into improving the quality of administration as well as providing redress after the event'. These matters are the province of the Select Committee on the Parliamentary Commissioner for Administration, they are rather beyond the scope of the current inquiry and are not ones on which this Committee is qualified to comment. We note that that Committee has recently considered a number of them in their reports on the 'Powers, Work and Jurisdiction of the Ombudsman' and 'Maladministration and Redress'. In the former inquiry the Committee concluded that what it referred to as 'the MP filter' be retained, but 'coupled with concerted attention to the means whereby access to the Ombudsman can be strengthened and enlarged', and also recommended that the Ombudsman be given the power to conduct audits of the operation of administrative procedures in bodies within his jurisdiction.

173. A third facet of the recent growth in different types of accountability is the introduction of the Citizen's Charter. The initiative was launched in 1991. It is, according to the White Paper introducing it, 'the most comprehensive programme ever to raise quality, increase choice, secure better value, and extend accountability'. The White Paper set out 'principles of public service' which 'every citizen is entitled to expect': explicit standards, published and prominently displayed at the point of delivery; openness – 'no secrecy about how public services are run, how much they cost, who is in charge, and whether or not they are meeting their standards'; full, accurate information, readily available, about what services are being provided, with published targets; choice; non-discrimination; accessibility; and proper procedures to put right things that have gone wrong. Those that meet a certain standard for the delivery of quality in public services – the Charter standard – become entitled to use the Chartermark. The Citizen's Charter has had an important impact in improving the delivery of the public services and in making them more responsive to the public. The initiative will form the subject of our next inquiry.

174. Recent changes in the management of the public service have had an impact, in many ways, on the extent to which it is effectively publicly accountable. Delegation and privatisation are reducing the extent to which effective political accountability can be provided through Parliament. Accountability might be provided by some other mechanism, by Charters, through the Ombudsman, through the courts, even; and we welcome that. Accountability, however, should be a broad obligation, to many different bodies. Accountability to Parliament should not preclude accountability to the public; and *vice versa*. Parliament needs to retain and protect its role; and to do so, it has to be more

effective in fulfilling it. A number of our recommendations involve changes to (or implications for) the House's practices and procedures. We hope that these will be further considered by the appropriate Committees of the House, particularly the Procedure Committee and the Liaison Committee. We have considered, in this Report, mainly what government does to comply with its obligation of accountability to Parliament; we hope that others will carry this forward by considering what Parliament can do to enforce it.

QUESTION

Would the imposition of legal liability upon Chief Executives improve their accountability?

C. Scott, 'Accountability in the Regulatory State'
(2000) 27 *Journal of Law and Society* 38, pp. 41–43, 50–54, 57–60

. . . It is helpful to keep distinct the three sets of accountability questions: 'who is accountable?'; 'to whom?'; and 'for what?' With the 'who is accountable'? question, the courts have been willing to review all decisions involving the exercise of public power, even where exercised by bodies in private ownership. In the utilities sectors the exercise of public privileges, such as monopoly rights, by private companies carry with them responsibilities to account for their activities, both in domestic fora and EC law. In some instances, the receipt of public funds by private bodies renders recipients liable to public accountability through audit mechanisms. Considerable attention has been paid to this issue in the literature, with a consensus for the view that simple distinctions between private actors (not publicly accountable) and public actors (subject to full public accountability) are thus not sustainable.

The 'to whom?' question has often been mingled with the 'for what?' question, for example in the distinction between legal accountability (to the courts in respect of the juridical values of fairness, rationality and legality) and political accountability (to ministers and to Parliament or other elected bodies such as local authorities and via these institutions ultimately to the electorate). Furthermore, while it might be helpful to think of 'administrative accountability' as accountability to administrative bodies such as grievance [handlers] and auditors, in fact these mechanisms for accountability have conventionally been distinguished, with administrative accountability only indicating the former, while financial accountability is used for the latter.

Separating the 'to whom?' and 'for what?' we find three broad classes within each category. Thus accountability may be rendered to a higher authority ('upwards accountability'), to a broadly parallel institution ('horizontal accountability') or to lower level institutions and groups (such as consumers) ('downwards accountability'). The range of values for which accountability is rendered can be placed in three categories: economic values (including financial probity and value for money (VFM)); social and procedural values (such as fairness, equality, and legality); continuity/security values (such as social cohesion, universal service, and safety). Figure 1 sets out the possible configurations of the 'to whom?' and 'for what?' questions, producing nine possible pairs of co-ordinates.

. . . If we think of traditional accountability as encompassing the 'upwards' mechanisms of accountability to ministers, Parliament, and courts, with some recognition of the more formal horizontal mechanisms (such as grievance-handlers and auditors) then it is possible to conceive of a concept of 'extended accountability' within which traditional accountability is only part of a cluster of mechanisms through which public bodies are in fact held to account.

. . . Close exploration of the structures of extended accountability in the United Kingdom reveals at least two different models which have developed which feature overlapping and fuzzy responsibility and accountability: interdependence and redundancy. No domain is likely to precisely correspond to one or other of these models. There are likely to be elements of both identifiable in many policy domains but, for reasons of clarity, the examples used in the following sections are presented in somewhat simplified and ideal-type form.

For what? To whom?	Economic Values	Social/Procedural Values	Continuity/ Security Values
'Upwards' accountability	Of departments to treasury for expenditure	Of administrative decision-makers to courts/tribunals	Of utility companies to regulators
'Horizontal' accountability	Of public bodies to external and internal audit for probity and VFM	Review of decisions by grievance-handlers	Third-party accreditation of safety standards
'Downwards' accountability	Of utility companies to financial markets	Of public/privatized service providers to users	Consultation requirements re: universal service requirements

Figure 1 Examples of linkages between values and accountability institutions

1. Interdependence

The identification and mapping out of relationships of interdependence within policy domains has been one of the key contributions of the recent pluralist literature in public policy. The identification of interdependence has important implications for accountability structures. Interdependence provides a model of accountability in which the formal parliamentary, judicial, and administrative methods of traditional accountability are supplemented by an extended accountability. Interdependent actors are dependent on each other in their actions because of the dispersal of key resources of authority (formal and informal), information, expertise, and capacity to bestow legitimacy such that each of the principal actors has constantly to account for at least some of its actions to others within the space, as a precondition to action. The executive generally, and the Treasury in particular, has long had a central role in calling public bodies to account over a range of values, in a way that is often less transparent in the case of the more dignified, but arguably less efficient parliamentary mechanisms of accountability. But these less formal and more hidden accountability mechanisms extend well beyond the capacities of central government, extending potentially to any actors, public or private, within a domain with the practical capacity to make another actor, public or private, account for its actions. Within the pluralist political science literature this conception is sometimes referred to as 'constituency relations' or 'mutual accountability'. Indeed it may be that the simple monolithic structures presented as the welfare state model are too simple, that they disguise intricate internal and opaque webs of control and accountability that are functionally equivalent to the new instruments of the regulatory state, but are less formal and transparent. Among the more obvious examples were the consumer committees established for the nationalized industries with a brief to hold those public corporations to account from a collective consumer viewpoint.

This model is exemplified by the United Kingdom telecommunications sector (Figure 4). Figure 4 shows that though BT is subject to diminished upwards accountability to parliament and courts (noted above), it has a new forms of accountability in each dimension – upwards to a new regulator, horizontally to the mechanisms of corporate governance, and downwards to shareholders (and possibly also the market for corporate control) and users. The financial markets arguably provide a more rigorous form of financial accountability than applies to public bodies because there are so

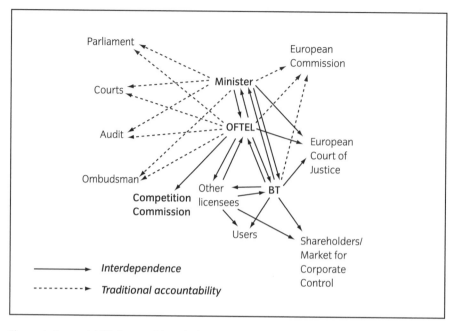

Figure 4 Accountability for provision of telecoms services 2. Interdependence model

many individual and institutional actors with a stake in scrutinizing BT's financial performance. The accountability of BT to the regulator, OFTEL, is also more focused, in the sense that OFTEL has a considerable stake in getting its regulatory scrutiny right, being itself scrutinized closely by BT, by other licensees, and by ministers, in addition to the more traditional scrutiny by the courts and by public audit institutions. OFTEL's quest for legitimacy has caused it to develop novel consultative procedures, and to publish a very wide range of documents on such matters as competition investigations and enforcement practices. Each of these other actors has powers or capacities which constrain the capacities of the others and require a day-to-day accounting for actions, more intense in character than the accountability typically applied within traditional upwards accountability mechanisms. This form of accountability, premised upon interdependence, is not linear, but more like a servo-mechanism holding the regime in a broadly acceptable place through the opposing tensions and forces generated. Such a model creates the potential to use the shifting of balances in order to change the way the model works in any particular case.

2. Redundancy
A second extended accountability model is that of redundancy, in which overlapping (and ostensibly superfluous) accountability mechanisms reduce the centrality of any one of them. In common parlance, redundancy is represented by the 'belt and braces' approach, within which two independent mechanisms are deployed to ensure the system does not fail, both of which are capable of working on their own. Where one fails the other will still prevent disaster. Redundancy in failsafe mechanisms is a common characteristic of public sector activities generally, and can be threatened by privatization. Equally explicit concern about risks associated with change may cause redundancy to be built in to oversight structures. Redundancy can be an unintended effect of certain institutional configurations. In practice, examples of redundancy in accountability regimes appear to be a product of a mixture of design and contingency.

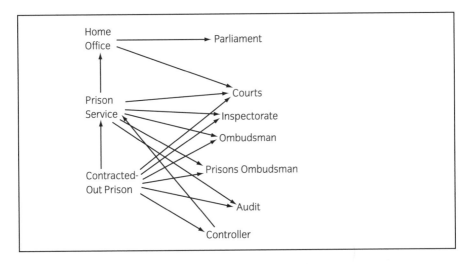

Figure 5 Accountability for prisons provision: redundancy model

There are at least two forms to the redundancy model: traditional and multi-level governance. The traditional redundancy model is exemplified by the accountability mechanisms for contracted-out prisons in the United Kingdom (Figure 5). Directors of contracted-out prisons are subject to all the forms of accountability directed at publicly operated prisons: upwards (legal, to the courts); financial (to the National Audit Office); and horizontal (to the Prisons Inspectorate, the Prisons Ombudsman, and prison visitors). But, contracted-out prisons are additionally subject to a further form of horizontal accountability with a requirement to account, day-to-day to an on-site regulator (called a controller), appointed by the Prison Service to monitor compliance with contract specification. Unusually within the prisons sector, controllers wield the capacity' to levy formal sanctions for breach of contract. Some commentators have suggested that there is a structural risk with on-site regulators of capture by the director, in the sense of controllers over-identifying with the needs and limits to the capacities of those they are supposed to regulate. However, with the redundancy model of accountability were such capture to occur it would likely be identified by one or more of the others holding the director to account.

The multi-level governance accountability model is exemplified by the mechanisms for accounting for expenditures made under jointly funded national and European Union expenditure programmes, notably under the European Structural Funds. Redundancy is built into the accountability mechanisms deliberately by EU decision makers, by requiring joint funding, and therefore ensuring that both domestic and EU audit institutions necessarily take an interest in single expenditure programmes within member states. It will be seen from Figure 4 that there is a redundancy element to the United Kingdom telecommunications regime because of the involvement of the EC institutions in the oversight of EC competition policy. Infringements of competition rules are potentially actionable under both United Kingdom and EC regimes. The element of redundancy is likely to be enhanced as United Kingdom competition rules are aligned with those of the EC by the Competition Act 1998, and competition and utilities regulators exercise concurrent jurisdiction.

The multi-level governance redundancy model of extended accountability is likely to see further development in the United Kingdom arising out the devolution of considerable powers to a new Scottish Parliament and Northern Irish and Welsh Assemblies. In each of these jurisdictions new executives and parliamentary/assembly committees have the potential to develop and reinvent the parliamentary oversight already exercised over United Kingdom-wide or multi-jurisdiction public functions.

. . .

The challenge for public lawyers is to know when, where, and how to make appropriate strategic interventions in complex accountability networks to secure appropriate normative structures and outcomes. What I have in mind here is something like process of 'collibration' described by Andrew Dunsire. Dunsire sees collibration as a stratagem common to a wide variety of processes by which balances are shifted to change the nature of the way that control systems (such as accountability mechanisms) work ['Tipping the Balance: Autopoiesis and Governance' (1996) 28 *Administration and Society* 299, 312–4]. Such interventions may be applied to any of the three accountability parameters: who is accountable? for what? to whom? This offers the possibility of meeting Martin Loughlin's challenge for public law to 'adopt as its principal focus the examination of the manner in which the normative structures of law can contribute to the guidance, control and evaluation in government'. The value of such changes may lie not directly in the development of a single accountability mechanism, but rather in the effects on the overall balance within the regime. The logic of the argument presented here is that conflict and tension are inevitable within the complex accountability webs within any particular domain, and that the objective should not be to iron out conflict, but to exploit it to hold regimes in appropriate tension.

To take an example, within a redundancy model of accountability for contracted-out prisons, how do we ensure proper accountability for the range of values, such as humanity, efficiency, and security which might be deemed appropriate desiderata for a prisons regime? The orthodox answer would be to say that we have an inspector with a specific mandate to check on the humanity of prison regimes, and auditors to assess efficiency, and security people overseeing security. But this is only a partial answer. Within the redundancy model we have other mechanisms which directly or indirectly check on each of these values – the controller, company management, the Prisons Ombudsman, the European Committee for the Prevention of Torture, and the courts. These mechanisms are in tension with another, in the sense of having different concerns, powers, procedures, and culture which generate competing agendas and capacities. Within contracted-out prisons, corporate governance structures will hold directors to account for the expenditure of money, so that within an efficient redundancy system enough money but no more than is necessary to provide a humane regime will he spent. We might expect periodically that value for money norms or security norms might inhibit the achievement of humanity norms. The solution would not necessarily be to crank up the humanity regime, hut rather to apply techniques of selective inhibition to the other norm structures so that their pull on the overall system was diminished somewhat. This might, for example, be through changing financial incentives or oversight structures, or through enhancing access of prisoners to grievance-handlers or judicial review.

. . .

The transformation of public administration in the United Kingdom has made more transparent the dense networks of accountability within which public power is exercised. The constitutional significance of this observation is to suggest that there is a potential to harness these networks for the purposes of achieving effective accountability or control, even as public power continues to be exercised in more fragmented ways. Outstanding questions for this analysis are whether there are other models of accountability in the regulatory state not captured by the interdependence and redundancy models, and whether it is possible to capture the complete set within an overall theory of extended accountability. Areas requiring further exploration are the role of voluntary organizations (such as prisons campaigners and consumer groups) and the media in rendering public and quasi-public bodies accountable.

Each of the two models of extended accountability discussed in this article presents difficulties for public lawyers and more generally. Neither model is directly 'programmable' with the public law norms (fairness, legality, rationality, and so on). Interventions to secure appropriate normative outcomes must necessarily be indirect and unpredictable in their effects. The interdependence model carries with it the risk that special interests, such as those of a particular firm or group of firms, may capture the regime through their overall weighting of power within it. The redundancy model presents particular problems. If redundancy *per se* is a good characteristic for an accountability regime, it is difficult to calculate how much redundancy is sufficient and how to know when an additional layer of accountability is inefficient and to be removed. Equally, there is also the risk within a redundancy model of simultaneous failure of different parts of the system for the same reason. Where, for example, information is successfully hidden from more than one part of the accountability network, there is a risk of complete failure in respect of the matters for which that information is relevant.

Close observation of the structures of accountability in the regulatory state suggests that the public lawyer's concerns, premised upon an over-formal conception of accountability, if not unfounded are then neglectful of the complex webs of extended accountability which spring up in practice. Indeed, these extended accountability mechanisms already evidence a capacity to hold not only public but also private actors accountable for the exercise of power which is broadly public in character. Whilst not agreeing with Wilks and Freeman that it is possible to conceive of the accountability of a regulatory regime, it is nevertheless helpful to think in terms of the *aggregate* accountability of each of the actors exercising power within a regime.

NOTES:

1. Scott points out some of the deficiencies in his two models of extended accountability, and it would seem that the situation is improved if the different mechanisms are all operating. This ideal may not happen in practice. In 'Accountability, New Public Management, and the Problems of the Child Support Agency' (1999) 26 JLS 150, Carol Harlow concluded that while the external accountability provided by the Social Security Committee, the Select Committee on the Parliamentary Commissioner for Administration and the Public Accounts Committee was very good, many of the operational problems they dealt with had their roots in policy which was not given a sufficiently rigorous scrutiny by Parliament during the passage of legislation. This fault of inadequate consultation is known; see the Hansard Society, *post* p. 359 and the Modernisation Committee, *post* p. 366. Thus it seems unfair that the only resignation was that of the Agency's first chief executive who arrived after the policy had been formulated by Ministers.

   Internal accountability procedures associated with the New Public Management such as business plans and performance indicators were of no assistance to clients when things went wrong. Harlow also points out that judicial review in child support was like the 'dog which never barked'. She wonders if an explanation may be found in the fact that the child support cases were heard by judges in the family law division rather than the public law division.

2. The Hansard Society's report *The Challenge for Parliament: Making Government Accountable* (2001) agrees with Harlow's analysis of Parliament and the Child Support Agency about the partial success of Parliament's dealing with the Child Support Agency. The vast majority of the report's case studies show inadequacies in Parliament's oversight, e.g., despite the availability of early warning about problems in the Passport Office in spring 1999, the Public Accounts Committee's report in summer 2000 was full but, as is usual, the relevant departmental select committee (Home Affairs) had not conducted a watching brief and the debating opportunities tend to be used for party political matters rather than one of public interest. It was noted that Parliament is unclear about its relationship with regulators, inspectorates, and other outside bodies. Parliament should use the information about individual cases which they can provide by drawing out the lessons from this work and giving greater worth to their investigations by using it as the basis for holding Government to account. The report recommends that Parliament should be at the apex of a network of regulatory bodies and alternative scrutiny mechanisms. A culture of scrutiny should be developed and

improvements made to work done in committee and the chamber in the House of Commons with more emphasis given to financial scrutiny. The House of Lords should complement the Commons and there should be better communication between Parliament and the public.

3. Transparency and openness are required if real accountability is to be achieved, and so a Freedom of Information Act should assist. Everything depends upon the terms of such legislation, and while campaigners gave a warm welcome to the 1997 White Paper, *Your Right To Know* (Cm 3818), the subsequent Bills have been condemned. A draft Bill had been issued in May 1999 for consultation, and Select Committees in both the Commons (HC 570 of 1998–99) and the Lords (HL 97 of 1998–99) pointed out deficiencies which they felt would undermine the potential. The Freedom of Information Act 2000, when introduced as a Bill, did make some changes recommended by the Committees, but these were not enough to satisfy the Commons Public Administration Committee which produced a report highlighting some items which required amendment as well as comments on the significant changes from the draft Bill. Some amendments were made in Parliament. The Act will not come into full effect until January 2005. See P. Birkinshaw, *Freedom of Information* (3rd edn, 2001).

B: Select Committees

An account of the genesis of the reforms of the Select Committee system can be found in Chapter 1 of G. Drewry (ed.), *The New Select Committees* (2nd edn, 1989).

First Report of the Liaison Committee
HC 323 of 1996–97, paras 8–16

Powers to summon persons, papers and records

8. When the Departmental Select Committee system was established in 1979, it was acknowledged that committees' general powers to send for persons, papers and records did not extend to ordering the attendance of Ministers nor to the production of specific Government papers. In rejecting a recommendation of the Procedure Committee, that committees should be able to take the failure to provide papers automatically to the floor of the House, the then Leader of the House committed the Government to making available to committees as much information as possible and to giving the House an early opportunity to debate a matter on the floor of the House if the Government refused to provide information and that refusal was of serious concern to the House as a whole. These undertakings have been amplified in the intervening period.

9. The Public Service and Trade and Industry Committees in their recent Reports have made a number of specific recommendations about the powers of committees in this respect. In particular they called

— for committees to be given the power to order the attendance of Members of the House as witnesses in the same way as other witnesses can be summoned;
— for there to be 'a presumption that Ministers accept requests by committees that individual named civil servants give evidence to them'; and,
— in relation to papers, for the House to agree to a 1978 recommendation by the Procedure Committee for a procedure which would 'restore to select committees in certain specified circumstances the right, which formerly belonged to any backbencher, to move for an Address or an Order for a Return of Papers'.

10. The reports from individual Chairmen indicate that, with a few exceptions, there have not been any real difficulties in the current Parliament. Nonetheless there remains concern that the lack of specific powers leaves committees at a disadvantage in obtaining the fullest cooperation from Government.

Members

11. There have been a number of instances since 1979 when Members who are former Ministers have been unwilling or reluctant to appear before select committees to assist inquiries into matters for which they had previously been responsible. The Foreign Affairs Committee failed to persuade the former Prime Minister (Baroness Thatcher) to give evidence to its inquiry into the contract for the Pergau Dam. The Hon Member for Derbyshire South (Mrs Currie) initially refused to appear before the Agriculture Committee when it was investigating salmonella in eggs (although eventually she was prevailed upon to appear). While it is the practice that Cabinet Ministers currently in post accept invitations to appear before committees, it has been suggested that Prime Ministers or former Prime Ministers should not be invited to give evidence in relation to their current or former responsibilities. **We see no justification for any Minister or former Minister to decline to appear before a select committee undertaking an inquiry within its remit.**

12. The House has recently decided that all of its Members are bound to give evidence to the Committee on Standards and Privileges. Its Standing Order provides that the Committee has power to order the attendance of any Member – and indeed to require that specific documents or records in the possession of a Member relating to its inquiries be laid before the Committee. We see a case for consistency in this regard although we doubt whether use of the power will be necessary. Its availability should be sufficient encouragement. **Accordingly we recommend that all select committees should be given the powers contained in paragraph 6 of the orders of reference of the Committee on Standards and Privileges.**

Civil Servants

13. Few cases have been documented of named officials being prevented from giving evidence to a select committee when invited to do so. In the present Parliament, the Foreign Affairs Committee was unable to procure evidence from the intelligence services in its inquiry into UK policy on weapons proliferation and arms control. There is also a reluctance on the part of Government concerning former civil servants giving evidence about their erstwhile responsibilities. In its inquiry into Arms to Iraq (the Supergun), the Trade and Industry Committee had difficulty in contacting former civil servants whom they would have wished to examine. The Head of the Civil Service has affirmed that when named civil servants are *summoned* to appear, they have a duty to attend although Ministers reserve the right to suggest that other civil servants also give evidence or to attend themselves in place of civil servants. We consider that, except where their personal conduct may be at issue and they may be subject to disciplinary proceedings, all civil servants should attend upon committees when invited and that Departments should assist in identifying their former staff where requested to do so to enable them to be called. It is unacceptable that committees should be denied access to civil servants whose knowledge of and involvement in Government activity is essential to a committee inquiry. **We therefore endorse the recommendation of the Public Service Committee that there should be a presumption that Ministers accept requests by committees that individual named civil servants give evidence to them.**

Provision of Documents

14. It is in the area of provision of documents that most difficulties have arisen. There is a basic problem facing committees in so far as they are not always aware of the information and documents available in Departments which are germane to their inquiries. Some Committees have complained of the difficulties in discerning the existence of documents. **We conclude as the Procedure Committee did in its 1990 Report, that it should be the duty of Departments to ensure that select committees are furnished with any important information which appears to be relevant to their inquiries without waiting to be asked for it specifically.**

15. In most but not all cases where specific problems have arisen it has been because papers were, or were alleged to be, sensitive, either politically, militarily or commercially. Frequently it has

been possible to reach a reasonable compromise but this was not always the case. There are established arrangements under which committees may receive classified evidence – and indeed publish that evidence subject to agreement on sidelining (that is, excising the particularly sensitive passages from the published evidence). On occasions it has been helpful for committees to see particularly sensitive material under the 'crown jewels' procedure although some committees have misgivings about the restrictions thereby placed on their freedom to comment upon the evidence. There is evidence that Government is using outside experts more frequently to consider specialist subjects such as 'efficiency'. Such advice has been claimed as 'advice to Ministers' and thus denied to select committees. We believe this is unacceptable.

16. Since 1979, the Government has given a series of undertakings that time would be provided for debate in the fairly rare cases where there is disagreement about the provision of information or papers. It is clear that these undertakings are not entirely satisfactory in the rare cases where a committee needs access to a specific document but the Department concerned will not release it. There have been a significant number of cases where committees have been refused specific documents but the Government has not provided time for the subject to be debated. The onus should be shifted onto the Government to defend in the House its refusal to disclose information to a select committee. A committee should be able to table and have debated a motion for the return of a specific document. A debate for an hour or so would enable the committee and the Government to set out their points of view and the House could decide the matter on a division. This procedure would be analogous to the one hour debate provided for in Standing Orders if nominations to select committees are opposed on the floor of the House. In practice we believe the existence of such a fall-back procedure would encourage a compromise to be reached before the matter had to be taken to the floor of the House. **We recommend that Standing Orders be amended to provide that if the Chairman of a departmental select committee tables a motion on behalf of the committee that a specific document be laid before the committee the motion should be debated on the floor of the House within ten sitting days and brought to a conclusion after one hour.**

NOTE: See the House of Commons' resolution *ante*, p. 282, which is incorporated in the *Ministerial Code*. Ministers should be open with Parliament, including its Select Committees, and should authorize their officials to attend as witnesses. The rules below, formerly known as the 'Osmotherly Rules', regulate what officials may say.

Departmental Evidence and Response to Select Committees
Cabinet Office (1997), paras 1–2, 37–44, 46–50, 53, 61–65, 67–71, 75–80, 82–87

Status of the Guidance
1. This memorandum gives guidance to officials from Departments and their Agencies who may be called upon to give evidence before, or prepare memoranda for submission to, Parliamentary Select Committees. It replaces the December 1994 edition.

2. In providing guidance, the memorandum attempts to summarise a number of long-standing conventions that have developed in the relationship between Parliament, in the form of its Select Committees, and successive Governments. As a matter of practice, Parliament has generally recognised these conventions. It is important to note, however, that this memorandum is a Government document. Although Select Committees will be familiar with its contents, it has no formal Parliamentary standing or approval, nor does it claim to have. . . .

SECTION 3: ROLE OF OFFICIALS GIVING EVIDENCE TO SELECT COMMITTEES

General

37. Officials who give evidence to Select Committees do so on behalf of their Ministers and under their directions.

38. This is in accordance with the principle that it is Ministers who are directly accountable to Parliament for both their own policies and for the actions of their Departments. Officials are accountable to Ministers and are subject to their instruction; but they are not directly accountable to Parliament in the same way. This does not mean, of course, that officials may not be called upon to give a full account of Government policies, or indeed of their own actions or recollections of particular events, but their purpose in doing so is to contribute to the central process of Ministerial accountability, not to offer personal views or judgements on matters of political controversy. . . .

39. This Guidance Note should therefore be seen as representing standing instructions to officials appearing before Select Committees. These instructions may be supplemented by specific Ministerial instructions on specific matters.

Summoning of Named Officials

40. By the same principle, it is customary for Ministers to decide which official or officials should represent them. Select Committees have generally accepted this position.

41. Where a Select Committee indicates that it wishes to take evidence from a particular named official, Ministers will usually agree to meet such a request, but this is subject to two important qualifications:

(a) Ministers retain the right to suggest an alternative official to that named by the Committee if they feel that the former is better placed to represent them. While the Committee is under no obligation to accept the Minister's proposal, it is open to the Minister to appear personally before the Committee in the unlikely event of there being no agreement about which official should most appropriately give evidence.

(b) It has been agreed that it is not the role of Select Committees to act as disciplinary tribunals (see paragraphs 70–74). A Minister will therefore wish to consider carefully a Committee's request to take evidence from a named official where this is likely to expose the individual concerned to questioning about their personal responsibility or the allocation of blame as between them and others. This will be particularly so where the official concerned has been subject to, or may be subject to, an internal departmental inquiry or disciplinary proceedings. Ministers may, in such circumstances, wish to suggest either that he give evidence personally to the Committee or that a designated senior official do so on their behalf.

42. If a Committee nonetheless insists on a particular official appearing before them, contrary to the Minister's wishes, the formal position remains that it could issue an order for attendance, and request the House to enforce it. In such an event (so far unprecedented) the official, as any other citizen, would have to appear before the Committee but, in all circumstances, would remain subject to Ministerial instruction under the terms of this Guidance and of the Code.

Agency Chief Executives

43. Where a Select Committee wishes to take evidence on matters assigned to an Agency in its Framework Document, Ministers will normally wish to nominate the Chief Executive as being the official best placed to represent them. While Agency Chief Executives have managerial authority to the extent set out in their Framework Documents, like other officials they give evidence on behalf of the Minister to whom they are accountable and are subject to that Minister's instruction.

Position of Retired Officials

44. Given the above, it is extremely rare, but not unprecedented, for Committees to request evidence from officials who have retired. A Committee could, again, issue an order for attendance if

it chose. However, retired officials cannot be said to represent the Minister and hence cannot contribute directly to his accountability to the House. It is primarily for these reasons, as well as for obvious practical points of having access to up to date information and thinking, that Ministers would expect evidence on Government matters to be given by themselves or by serving officials who report to them.

. . .

SECTION 4.   EVIDENCE TO SELECT COMMITTEES

4A.   PROVISION OF EVIDENCE BY OFFICIALS: CENTRAL PRINCIPLES

General

46. The central principle to be followed is that it is the duty of officials to be as helpful as possible to Select Committees. The Government's wider policies on openness to Parliament and the public are set out in the Code of Practice on Access to Government Information (Annex A). Officials should be as forthcoming as they can in providing information under the terms of the Code, whether in writing or in oral evidence, relevant to a Select Committee's field of inquiry. Any withholding of information should be limited to reservations that are necessary in the public interest; this should be decided in accordance with the law and the exemptions as set out in the Code.

Accuracy of Evidence

47. Officials appearing before Select Committees are responsible for ensuring that the evidence they give is accurate. . . . Should it nevertheless be discovered subsequently that the evidence unwittingly contained factual errors, these should be made known to the Committee, usually via the Clerk, at the earliest opportunity. Where appropriate, a correcting footnote will appear in the published transcript of the evidence.

Discussion of Government policy

48. Officials should as far as possible confine their evidence to questions of fact and explanation relating to government policies and actions. They should be ready to explain what those policies are; the justification and objectives of those policies as the Government sees them; the extent to which those objectives have been met; and also to explain how administrative factors may have affected both the choice of policy measures and the manner of their implementation. Any comment by officials on government policies and actions should always be consistent with the principle of civil service political impartiality. Officials should as far as possible avoid being drawn into discussion of the merits of alternative policies where this is politically contentious. If official witnesses are pressed by the Committee to go beyond these limits, they should suggest that the questioning should be referred to Ministers.

49. A Select Committee may invite specialist (as opposed to administrative) officials to comment on the professional or technical issues underlying government policies or decisions. This can require careful handling where Committees wish to take evidence from, for example, government economists or statisticians on issues which bear on controversial policy questions and which are also matters of controversy within the respective profession.

Provision of Information Through Memoranda

50. The Government's commitment to provide as much information as possible to Select Committees is met largely through the provision of memoranda, written replies to Committees' questions and oral evidence from Ministers and officials. It does not amount to a commitment to provide access to internal files, private correspondence, including advice given on a confidential basis or working papers. Should a Committee press to see such documents, rather than accepting written or

oral evidence on the subject, Departments should consult their Ministers And Machinery of Government and Standards Group, OPS.

Consulting Ministers on Evidence

53. Because officials appear on behalf of their Ministers, written evidence and briefing material should be cleared with them as necessary. It may only be necessary for Ministers to be consulted if there is any doubt among officials on the detail of the policy to be explained to the Committee, or on what information should be disclosed. However, as Ministers are ultimately accountable for deciding what information is to be given and for defending those decisions as necessary, their views should be sought if a question arises of withholding information which a Committee has asked for.

. . .

4B. PROVISION OF INFORMATION

General

61. Although the powers of Select Committees to send for 'persons, papers and records' relating to their field of enquiry are unqualified, there are certain long-standing conventions on the provision of information which have been observed in practice by successive administrations on grounds of public policy.

62. In recent years, however, there have been progressive moves towards greater openness and transparency in government business and the provision of information. In a White Paper on Open Government (Cm 2290) the present Government has underlined its commitment to three key themes:

— handling information in a way that promotes informed policy making and debate, and efficient service delivery;
— providing timely and accessible information to the citizen to explain Government policies, actions and decisions; and
— restricting access to information only when there are good reasons for doing so.

63. These themes, and the reasons why confidentiality is nonetheless sometimes necessary in the public interest, are discussed in some detail in that White Paper and enunciated in the resulting **Code of Practice on Access to Government Information** (Annex A). That Code, together with the accompanying **Guidance on Interpretation** issued by OPS, now forms the authoritative instruction from Ministers to officials on the provision of information to Parliament and the public. It should be taken as superseding the instructions on provision of information by officials to Select Committees in previous editions of this Guidance.

64. Information which is judged not disclosable under the terms of the Code and which properly carries a protective security marking should not be disclosed without further authority in open evidence sessions or in memoranda submitted for publication. There are, however, procedures under which Select Committees can in certain circumstances be provided with such information on a confidential basis. These procedures are described in paragraphs 80 to 87 below. In cases of doubt, witnesses should consult their departmental security officer.

Excessive Cost

65. Although the provisions under the Code for charging applicants do not apply in the case of Select Committees, it may occasionally prove necessary to decline requests for information which would involve the Department in excessive cost or diversion of effort. Ministers should always be consulted on their priorities in such cases.

. . .

Matters which may be *sub judice*

67. Committees are subject to the same rules by which the House regulates its conduct in relation

to matters awaiting the adjudication of the courts (although the bar on debating such matters may be lifted if a Committee is meeting in closed session). . . . It should be noted, however, that the Committee Chairman has an overriding discretion to determine what is appropriate in the hearing of evidence.

68. Officials should take care in discussing or giving written evidence on matters which may become the subject of litigation but which, at the time, do not strictly come under the rules precluding public discussion of sub judice questions. Such caution should be exercised whether or not the Crown is likely to be a party to such litigation. If such matters seem likely to be raised, officials should first consult their departmental legal advisers or the Treasury Solicitor on how to handle questions which might arise. In any case of doubt about the extent to which details may be disclosed of criminal cases, not currently sub judice, the Law Officers are available for consultation.

69. Similar considerations apply in cases where a Minister has or may have a quasi-judicial or appellate function, for example in relation to planning applications and appeals.

Conduct of Individual Officials

70. Occasionally questions from a departmentally-related Select Committee may appear to be directed to the conduct of individual officials, not just in the sense of establishing the facts about what occurred in making decisions or implementing Government policies, but with the implication of allocating individual criticism or blame.

71. In such circumstances, and in accordance with the principles of Ministerial accountability, it is for the Minister to look into the matter and if necessary to institute a formal inquiry. Such an inquiry into the conduct and behaviour of individual officials and consideration of disciplinary action is properly carried out within the Department according to established procedures designed and agreed for the purpose, and with appropriate safeguards for the individual. It is then the Minister's responsibility to inform the Committee of what has happened, and of what has been done to put the matter right and to prevent a recurrence. Evidence to a Select Committee on this should be given not by the official or officials concerned, but by the Minister or by a senior official designated by the Minister to give such evidence on the Minister's behalf.

. . .

Papers of a Previous Administration

75. There are well established conventions which govern the withholding of policy papers of a previous Administration from an Administration of a different political complexion. These were set out in a Parliamentary answer from the Prime Minister on 24 January 1980 (Official Report, Columns 305–307) Since officials appear before Select Committees as representatives of their Ministers, and since Select Committees are themselves composed on a bipartisan basis, it follows that officials should not provide a Committee with evidence from papers of a previous Administration which they are not in a position to show to their present Ministers. If such evidence is sought, Ministers should be consulted. Where Ministers propose to make an exception, it would be necessary to consult a representative of the previous Administration before either showing the papers to present Ministers or, with Ministers' authority, releasing information from them to a Committee.

4C. STATUS AND HANDLING OF EVIDENCE

Status of Evidence

76. Once information has been supplied to a Committee it becomes 'evidence' and, subject to any agreement with the Committee on the non-publication of protectively marked information (paragraphs 80–87), it is entirely up to the Committee whether or not to publish it and report it to the House. Certain rules apply to the further public use of such evidence by the Government prior to its publication by the Committee. Departments should be careful to observe these rules as failure to do

so could amount to a breach of Parliamentary privilege. Committees are usually helpfully flexible in applying the rules but, in cases of doubt, Departments should consult the relevant Committee Clerk for guidance.

77. The basic rule is a Commons resolution of 1837 which states that ' . . . the evidence taken by any Select Committee of this House, and Documents presented to such Committee, and which have not been reported to the House, ought not to be published by any Member of such Committee or any person'. This Resolution still stands but is now subject to important modifications which give Committees power to authorise witnesses to publish the memoranda of evidence they have submitted (Commons Standing Order No. 117) and which permit the publication of evidence given in public session before it is formally reported to the House (Commons Standing Order No. 118).

78. The practical implications of these rules for Departments are as follows:

Oral evidence given in public session. There is no constraint on Departments using or repeating the substance of material given in public evidence sessions but verbatim transcripts of oral evidence (advance proof copies of which will be sent by the Clerk to Departments for checking) should not be copied to third parties until they have been published by the Committee.

Oral evidence given in closed session. Evidence given in closed sessions should not be disclosed by Departments before the evidence (sidelined as appropriate) has been published by the Committee. Departments will not, of course, want to disclose the sidelined passages of their evidence to third parties in any event.

Unclassified memoranda. Such memoranda are usually included in the printed copy of the Committee's proceedings reported to the House on the day of the relevant evidence session. Once they have been published in this way, Departments are free to make copies available to third parties. If a Department wishes to make copies of their submitted memoranda available to third parties in advance of this, they must first obtain the permission of the Committee. The Committee itself will usually make copies available to the media at the time of the evidence session but Liaison Officers may wish to check this with the Clerk and brief their Press Office accordingly. It should be noted that a Government response to a Committee Report which is given in the form of a memorandum or letter to the Committee (see paragraph 107b) counts as further 'evidence' in this context as does any letter to the Committee, however informal.

Classified (protectively marked) memoranda. Similar rules apply, but naturally with the same caveat as for oral evidence given in closed session.

Comment on Evidence from other Witnesses

79. Evidence critical of a Department may be given in public session by witnesses outside the Department on occasions where departmental witnesses are not also present or at sessions held after the departmental evidence has been given. In such circumstances Departments should not seek publicly to respond to such criticism outside the ambit of the Committee. Instead, the Committee may be asked to consider inviting the Department to express their view in the form of further evidence.

Providing Sensitive Information in Confidence

80. It is to the benefit of Committees in carrying out their task of scrutinising Government activities, and to Government in explaining its actions and policies, for sensitive information, including that carrying a protective security marking, to be provided from time to time on the basis that it will not be published and will be treated in confidence. Procedures have been developed to accommodate this.

. . .

Handling of Sensitive Information in Oral Evidence

82. It would clearly be inappropriate for any evidence which a Department wished to be treated as confidential to be given at a public session of the Committee. If it appears likely, therefore, that subjects to be discussed at a forthcoming public session are such that the witnesses would only be able to give substantive answers in confidence, the Department should write to the Chairman or the Clerk explaining why this is so. The Committee may then agree to take that part of the Department's evidence in closed session.

83. If, despite such an approach, a Committee questions an official witness in public session on confidential matters, or if such matters are raised unexpectedly, the official should inform the Committee that the questions could only be answered on a confidential basis. The Committee may then decide to go into closed session or request a confidential memorandum. It is not for the witness to suggest that the Committee should go into closed session as this is wholly a matter for them to decide.

84. Where confidential evidence has been given in a closed session the witness should, at the end of the session, let the Clerk know which parts of the evidence these are. Pending the Committee's final decision on what they will agree to omit from the published version, the Clerk will instruct the shorthand writer not to send for printing the transcript of these passages but will send two copies of a full transcript to the Department. One copy is for retention; the other should be returned to the Clerk with those passages sidelined which contain sensitive information which, in the Department's judgment, it would not be in the public interest to publish. One copy of the full transcript is also retained in the Committee Office for Members authorised to have access to it (paragraph 87).

85. Although Committees usually respect such requests for sidelining they may occasionally challenge a particular request. Witnesses should therefore always be sure that their requests are justified – in terms of the definitions of the protective marking system or the exemptions in the Code.

Handling of Sensitive Information in Written Evidence

86. Where information is submitted to a Committee on the understanding that it will be kept confidential, this understanding should be recorded in the covering letter forwarding the evidence to the Clerk. The letter should make clear whether the whole memorandum or, as is often the case, particular annexes are to be kept confidential.

87. An agreement was reached with the Liaison Committee in 1975 on the conditions under which classified information may be disclosed to Select Committees. This agreement still stands. The key points are as follows:

(a) Information marked TOP SECRET or SECRET will be restricted to those persons (in addition to the Clerk) to whom the Department has agreed to release it. In practice this will usually mean only the members of the Select Committee or of the Sub-Committee concerned and, in the case of a Sub-Committee, the Chairman of the main Committee in addition. The disclosure of information marked RESTRICTED or CONFIDENTIAL will be similarly limited except that, where it has been disclosed to members of Sub-Committees, it may also be made available to members of the main Committee concerned.

(b) The release of TOP SECRET information under these arrangements is subject to the personal approval of the responsible Minister in each case.

(c) Protectively marked information may also be disclosed to a Committee's Specialist Advisers provided they have security clearance in accordance with arrangements agreed with the Clerk of the House.

(d) Protectively marked memoranda (and the full transcripts of oral evidence containing classified information) will be made available to those authorised to see it only during Committee or Sub-Committee meetings and on request in the Committee Office. Members may not take protectively marked documents away with them.

QUESTIONS

1. Is the commitment to greater openness furthered or undermined by the Departmental Evidence and Response to Select Committees and the 15 exemptions in the Code of Practice on Access to Official Information, and will the situation be changed by the entry into force of the Freedom of Information Act 2001?

NOTE: Occasionally witnesses may refuse to answer questions. The Social Security Select Committee had begun a general investigation into pension funds when the death of Mr Robert Maxwell led to disclosures about malpractice concerning the management of the Mirror Group Newspapers and the Maxwell Corporation pension funds. The Committee ordered the attendance of his sons Messrs Ian and Kevin Maxwell to question them in their capacity as trustees of the pension funds. When the Maxwells appeared before the Committee on 13 January 1992, each was accompanied by Queen's Counsel. The Maxwells declined to answer questions. The Committee reported on this matter to the House of Commons in HC 353 of 1991–92. However, their recommendation that the Maxwells be brought before the House for their refusal to answer the Committee's questions was not acted upon. It is likely that this was, in part, because of subsequent events.

The Maxwell brothers were arrested and charged with fraud on 18 June 1992. They were tried and, in early 1996, acquitted. Further charges were brought unsuccessfully against Kevin Maxwell.

QUESTION

Was the Committee's investigation of these particular pension funds appropriate given the inquiries conducted by the Serious Fraud Office?

NOTE: An assessment of the first 10 years of the working of the select committee system was carried out by the Procedure Committee, which judged it to be a success. A further 10 years of experience led the Liaison Committee to repeat the verdict of success, but to make recommendations for reform in HC 300 of 1999–2000 (entitled *Shifting the Balance: Select Committees and the Executive*). One idea was to remove appointments to select committees from party political control through the whips or 'usual channels'. This particular proposal was rejected by the Government in its response (Cm 4734) and the reaction of the Leader of the House of Commons angered the Liaison Committee which subsequently took evidence from her and then issued a further report (HC 748 of 1999–2000, *Independence or Control?*). The report of the Hansard Society's Commission on Parliamentary Scrutiny (*The Challenge for Parliament: Making Government Accountable*) was published some 12 months later and the role of select committees was crucial in the extensive recommendations for reform to improve the holding of the Government to account. The issue became more topical when the Labour Party Chief Whip did not propose two Labour MPs to the select committees which they had chaired in the two previous Parliaments. It was perceived that these MPs were regarded as too independent and their committees had been robust in holding Labour Ministers to account in the 1997–2001 Parliament. When the nominations to select committees were voted upon in the Commons, the two MPs were restored to the committees and subsequently re-elected by their fellow committee members to chair them again.

The new Leader of the House of Commons, Robin Cook, is perceived as being sympathetic to reform and he chairs the select committee on Modernisation of the House of Commons. He published a memorandum to that committee outlining some ideas on reform of the common in general (HC 440 of 2001–02). This committee then produced some proposals on reform of the select committees.

First Report of the Select Committee on Modernisation of the House of Commons
HC 224 of 2001–02, pp.1–2

List of recommendations
1. [Paragraph 15] — We recommend that at the start of each Parliament the Committee of Nomination should be set up under the Chairman of Ways and Means. The Chairman of Ways and Means should chair proceedings, but in order to preserve the impartiality of his office have no vote.
2. [Paragraph 16] — We recommend that appointment to the Chairmen's Panel must remain firmly in the hands of the Speaker and not subject to any party interest or lobbying.
3. [Paragraph 17] — We recommend that membership of the Committee of Nomination should be prescribed in Standing Orders. We recommend that the Committee of Nomination should consist of the Chairman of Ways and Means and nine other members:

> seven Members of the Chairmen's Panel chosen with broad regard to the party balance, reflecting gender balance and based on length of service as Members of the Panel. Those seven would consist of:
> — the four most senior Members of the Government party on the Panel including the most senior woman Member of that party;
> — the two most senior Members of the official Opposition on the Panel, including the most senior woman Member of that party; and
> — the most senior Member of the second largest opposition party on the Panel;
> — the most senior back-bencher on the Government side of the House; and the most senior back-bencher on the opposition benches.

The quorum of the Committee when nominating committees afresh at the start of a Parliament should be six, and three when filling subsequent vacancies, not including the Chairman of Ways and Means. In the unavoidable absence of the Chairman of Ways and Means the First Deputy Chairman or in his or her absence the Second Deputy Chairman shall act as chairman.

4. [Paragraph 25] — We recommend that the proposed allocation between parties of the posts of chairmen of select committees should be reported to the Committee of Nomination.
5. [Paragraph 28] — We recommend that the House of Commons Commission should make available the necessary funds for a central unit of specialist support staff to be in place in the next financial year.
6. [Paragraph 29] — We recommend that the National Audit Office be invited to help assess the need for specialist and other support staff for select committees and to advise on how this could best be provided, and that the House of Commons Commission should look favourably on funding for staffing increases which may be proposed.
7. [Paragraph 30] — We recommend that within the Committee Office there should be sufficient staff to assist with the function of supporting the administrative workload of the select committee chairmen.
8. [Paragraph 33] — We recommend that there should be an agreed statement of the core tasks of the departmental select committees.
9. [Paragraph 34] — We recommend the following model as an illustration of what we would regard as the principal objectives of departmental select committees:

> 'It shall be the duty, where appropriate, of each select committee:
> to consider major policy initiatives
> to consider the Government's response to major emerging issues
> to propose changes where evidence persuades the Committee that present policy requires amendment
> to conduct pre-legislative scrutiny of draft bills

to examine and report on main Estimates, annual expenditure plans and annual
resource accounts

to monitor performance against targets in the public service agreements

to take evidence from each Minister at least annually

to take evidence from independent regulators and inspectorates

to consider the reports of Executive Agencies

to consider, and if appropriate report on, major appointments by a Secretary of State
or other senior ministers

to examine treaties within their subject areas.'

10. [Paragraph 34] — We recommend that select committees should experiment with appointing one of their number as a rapporteur on a specific task, such as for example financial scrutiny.

11. [Paragraph 35] — We recommend that as part of the process of producing an annual report each departmental select committee should submit to the Liaison Committee a statement of how it has met each core task in the scrutiny of its department.

12. [Paragraph 36] — We recommend that, in the light of the recommendations of the Joint Committee on Parliamentary Privilege, this limitation on the power to require witnesses to give evidence should be reviewed by the appropriate committees of both Houses.

13. [Paragraph 37] — We recommend that the investigative select committees should be named 'scrutiny committees'.

14. [Paragraph 39] — We recommend that there should be a Scrutiny Liaison Committee including the chairmen of the scrutiny committees, and also the chairmen of those committees which have a legislative or procedural role such as Deregulation and Regulatory Reform, Procedure, and Standards and Privileges.

15. [Paragraph 41] — We recommend that the value of a parliamentary career devoted to scrutiny should be recognised by an additional salary to the chairmen of the principal investigative committees.

16. [Paragraph 43] — We recommend that the House should impose an indicative upper limit of two consecutive Parliaments on service as chairman. We recognise that the House may wish to make special provision in the case of short Parliaments.

17. [Paragraph 47] — We recommend that the standard size of departmental scrutiny committees should be fifteen.

18. [Paragraph 49] — We recommend that the scrutiny committees should have the right to report to the Committee of Nomination any member who has a record of poor attendance without good cause and that the Committee of Nomination should have the right to replace that member.

19. [Paragraph 50] — We recommend a reduction in size of the membership and of the quorum of select committees where there has been a persistent problem securing attendance.

20. [Paragraph 53] — We recommend that the Committee Office procures the services, either on a consultancy or a salaried basis, of experts in design and layout to ensure that reports benefit from the most modern technology and the most attractive design.

21. [Paragraph 56] — We recommend that Notes for Visitors should be prepared, setting out in plain language the nature of the proceedings, and that where practical this should be supplemented on the day with guidance on the topics under discussion.

22. [Paragraph 57] — We recommend that all reports of select committees should be eligible for debate in Westminster Hall after the closure of the two month period within which Government is expected to publish its response, whether or not such a response has been tabled.

NOTES:

1. The Liaison Committee has commented on these proposals and, on the whole, given them strong support (HC 692 of 2001–02). The Liaison Committee was pleased that the Modernisation Committee had adopted its ideas of giving better resources, including the creation of

a group of officials with specialist skills who could be called upon by select committees, and that the role of chairing committees be recognized as important to the extent that it could be regarded as an alternative career to that of Government Minister gaining the administrative support and additional salary which Ministers enjoy. On a free vote the House of Commons did not accept the proposal to reduce the influence of the whips in determining the membership of select committees (see HC Deb, Vol. 385, cols. 648–730, 14 May 2002).

2. It is clear that the Hansard Society's report *The Challenge for Parliament: Making Government Accountable* has influenced the Modernisation Committee's proposals. The Hansard Society, which was chaired by a former Conservative Minister, whose posts included being Leader of the House of Commons, wanted all backbench MPs to serve on a committee but the Modernisation Committee proposed an increase of the standard membership from 11 to 15. The Liaison Committee did not think that there were enough members willing to serve on committees, that there could be problems in maintaining the party ratios in the expanded committees, that it would militate against the cohesiveness of the committees, and that there could be accommodation problems.

3. The Liaison Committee approved the idea of core tasks but wished to see included the systematic follow-up of previous reports. This was also suggested by the Hansard Society whose report also proposed other core tasks.

Hansard Society, *The Challenge for Parliament: Making Government Accountable* (2001) p. 36.

Figure 3B – Model concordat of select committee duties

The Liaison Committee has agreed the following concordat with the [example] Committee That it will publish, within six weeks of the end of each Session (except where a dissolution occurs), a report setting out its achievements against the following targets.

Expenditure
- To examine and report on the main Estimates and annual expenditure plans of its department by 30 June each year.
- To examine and report on the resource accounts of its department by 31 March each year.
- To consider each supplementary estimate presented by its department, and report to the House whether it requires further consideration, within 28 days of the presentation of the supplementary Estimate.
- To report annually on its department's performance against its service level agreements.
- To report, at least once in each Parliament, on the impact of efficiency savings on the running costs of the department and their impact on the effectiveness with which it delivers services to the public.

Administration
- To consider the reports and accounts of each executive agency within the department, and report annually at least on whether any raise matters of particular concern.
- To take evidence and report on, over the cycle of a Parliament, each agency within the department of which the budget exceeds 4 per cent of the overall departmental budget.
- To take evidence and report on, over the cycle of a Parliament, not fewer than one in four of the remaining agencies within the department.
- To take evidence and report on, over the cycle of a Parliament, each NDPB sponsored by the department which has an annual budget in excess of £10 million.
- To consider, and if appropriate take evidence and report on, each major appointment made by the relevant Secretary of State.

Policy
- To examine and report on any major policy initiative announced by the Department.
- To examine each Minister in the department, at least annually, on their discharge of their particular policy responsibilities.
- To keep under consideration the department's compliance with Freedom of Information legislation, and the quality of its provision of information to Parliament by whatever means.
- To consider each item of delegated legislation made by the department, and draw the attention of the House to those which raise particular questions of policy which require debate or other consideration.
- To consider each treaty signed by HMG falling within the area of responsibility of the department, and draw the attention of the House to those which raise particular questions of policy which require debate or other consideration.
- To consider and report on any draft legislation proposed by the government and referred to it by the House.

The annual report of the Committee will also itemise its expenditure in the relevant period on research, specialist advice, travel and entertainment.

At the beginning of each Parliament, within three months of its appointment (allowing for periods when the House is adjourned), the Committee will publish a report setting out its strategic plan for achieving the above targets, and any other matters relating to the discharge of its responsibilities that it thinks fit.

QUESTION

Is the proposed de-politicization of the arrangements, through the reduction of the influence of the Whips and the promotion of committee chairmanship as an alternative to a ministerial career, out of keeping with the traditional 'government through and not by Parliament' culture?

C: The floor of the House of Commons

The passage of legislation, which is considered *post* at p. 345, is the activity which takes up a significant amount of time for business in the House of Commons. In the 1996–97, 1997–98 and 1998–99 sessions it accounted for 42 per cent, 36 per cent and 30 per cent of time in the Commons. In the following table we can see how the rest of the time was spent.

Public Information Office, House of Commons Sessional Information Digest
1996–97, 1997–98, 1998–99, pp. 1–2

Analysis of the time of the session

Types of Business	Total time spent (hours:minutes)		
	1998–99	1999–2000	2000–01
1. Addresses, other than Prayers (including debate on Queen's Speech)	38:21	39:00	36:18
4. Private Business	08:24	8:58	07:39

Analysis of the time of the session

Types of Business	Total time spent (hours:minutes)		
	1998–99	1999–2000	2000–01
5. Government motions			
a) European Community Documents	3:58	0:26	1:31
b) General	24:12	37:15	23:18
6. Opposition motions			
a) Opposition Days	125:59	129:28	48:28
b) Opposition Motions in Government Time	6:45	00:00	00:00
7. Adjournment			
a) Government debates on motions for the Adjournment	130:03	120:53	36:36
b) Last day before Recesses	11:99	14:13	6:00
c) Emergency debates (SO No. 24)	00:00	00:06	00:00
d) Daily (at end of business)	75:28	78:10	39:20
Estimates	8:15	10:52	7:18
Oral Questions	119:54	133:25	64:14
Private Notice Questions	5:24	4:50	5:14
Statements	68:32	67:49	28:00
Business statements	21:16	25:37	15:00
SO No. 24 Applications	00:15	00:06	00:11
Points of Order and Speaker's Rulings	5:15	5:37	5:16
Privilege	00:00	00:00	00:00
Presentation of Public Petitions	1:06	1:22	0:37
Miscellaneous	30:36	21:11	5:13
Daily Prayers	12:25	14:05	6:55

NOTES:
1. The General Election in June meant that the 2000–01 session was shorter than average.
2. SO No. 24 refers to Standing Order No. 24 (previously SO 20) which is a procedure under which there is an adjournment of the House in order to discuss an urgent and important matter. It is considered *post* at p. 333.

(i) *Debate*

J. A. G. Griffith & M. Ryle, *Parliament: Functions, Practice and Procedures*
(1989), p. 203

. . . The process of debate, as established by basic procedures . . . is the main process used for most of the House's business – but not all; it is not used in Questions or Ministerial statements, or in select committee proceedings, for example. The process is essentially simple: a motion is made ('That this House approves . . .'); a question is proposed by the Chair in the same form; debate arises; the question is put; it is agreed to or negatived; if agreed a resolution (expressing an opinion) or an order (requiring action by the House, or a committee or individual Members or officers) results. There are all sorts of variations or modern qualifications of this basic process; amendments may be moved on which a question is again proposed and each amendment must be disposed of separately, before the main question (as amended if it has been) is put; there may be amendments to amendments; some motions may not, by standing order, be amended or others may not be debated; debate on motions or amendments may be adjourned; debate may be closured; and motions or amendments may be withdrawn. But the essentials are plain; only one motion is considered at a time and in the end all motions (and amendments) must either be agreed to, negatived, or withdrawn.

The logic of this procedure is binary. Decisions are taken in sequence, singly, and each decision on each motion and each amendment is a simple 'yes' or 'no.' With a few exceptions (for example, in the House, 100 Members must vote in the majority for a closure to be effective, and 20 or more Members can block a motion to refer a statutory instrument to a standing committee) there are no qualified majorities; there is no requirement on any question for an absolute majority; and, as we will see, there are not even any procedures for registering abstentions in a division. This binary process is mirrored in – or is a reflection of – the two-sided, confrontational nature of the House's proceedings. . . . The systematic logic of these procedures protects the clarity of decision taking.

P. Norton, *The Commons in Perspective*
(1981), p. 119

[G]eneral debates are nevertheless not without some uses in helping to ensure a measure of scrutiny and influence, however limited. A debate prevents a Government from remaining mute. Ministers have to explain and justify the Government's position. They may want to reveal as little as possible, but the Government cannot afford to hold back too much for fear of letting the Opposition appear to have the better argument. The involvement of Opposition spokesman and backbenchers ensures that any perceived cracks in the Government's position will be exploited. If it has failed to carry its own side privately, the Government may suffer the embarrassment of the publicly expressed dissent of some of its own supporters, dissent which provides good copy for the press. On some occasions, Ministers may even be influenced by comments made in debate. They will not necessarily approach an issue with closed minds, and will normally not wish to be totally unreceptive to the comments of the Opposition (whose co-operation they need for the efficient despatch of business) or of their own Members (whose support they need in the lobbies, and among whom morale needs to be maintained); a Minister who creates a good impression by listening attentively to views expressed by Members may enhance his own prospects of advancement. The likelihood of a Minister's being influenced may be greatest when he is at the despatch box. Though the House may be nearly empty for much of a debate, it fills up during the front-bench speeches, and this is when the atmosphere of the House becomes important. A Minister faced by a baying Opposition and silence behind him may be unnerved and realise that he is not carrying Members on either side with him, and in consequence may moderate or even, in extreme cases, reverse his position. On such an occasion, the debate-vote relationship may become important, the fear of defeat concentrating the minds of Ministers. A recent example of such a debate was that on Members' pay in 1979, when the Leader of the House, Norman St John-Stevas, received such a rough reception at the despatch box that the Cabinet realised it did not have the support of the House and changed its previous decision.

In addition, debates may act as useful channels for the expression of views held by the general interests and specific bodies represented by Members. If a Member with a known constituency interest in a certain subject rises to speak, he will invariably be listened to with greater respect than one who seeks solely to score party political points, and may even have some influence on the Minister's thinking; all MPs – Ministers and backbenchers – represent constituencies, and will normally have at least a degree of empathy for a Member seeking conscientiously to defend the interests of his constituents.

NOTE: Debates may be on motions proposed by the Government, the Opposition and the various committees of the House. For a House of Lords debate see *ante*, p. 195. The following extracts are taken from the debate on the second reading of the Bill when general principles are usually discussed.

House of Commons , HC Deb
Vol. 375 , cols. 21–29, 19 November 2001

Orders of the Day

Anti-terrorism, Crime and Security Bill
[Relevant documents: First Report from the Home Affairs Committee, Session 2001–02, on the Anti-terrorism, Crime and Security Bill, HC351.
Second Report from the Joint Committee on Human Rights, Session 2001–02, on the Anti-terrorism, Crime and Security Bill, HL Paper 37/HC 372.]

Order for Second Reading read.
3.30 pm

MR DOUGLAS HOGG (SLEAFORD AND NORTH HYKEHAM): On a point of order, Mr Speaker. As you know, a timetable motion has been tabled on which we shall vote later, at least under the deferred procedure. So many hon. Members wish to speak that you have felt it necessary to impose a 10-minute limit on Back-Bench speeches. There is genuine anxiety about the timetable. Will you consider not putting the Question on the timetable motion unless and until the Home Secretary makes a statement to explain why two days are deemed sufficient?

MR SPEAKER: If the motion is on the Order Paper and is moved, I must put the Question.

SIMON HUGHES (SOUTHWARK, NORTH AND BERMONDSEY): On a point of order, Mr Speaker. After the Second Reading debate and the vote on the timetable, we will consider a motion, which has an hour and a half for debate, on whether to support and agree to this country's derogation from article 5 of the European convention on human rights.

Last week, my hon. Friend the Member for North Cornwall (Mr Tyler) wrote to the Leader of the House to ask whether discussion of the derogation could wait until we had completed our consideration of the Bill. That would enable us properly to consider the need for the derogation. This afternoon, there is a debate in the House of Lords about whether such consideration should happen at the end of the Bill's passage through both Houses.

May I, through you, ask a Minister to explain whether the Government are willing to accept that logical proposal? If they are, we would not have to spend a lot of time today arguing about whether to pull out of an article of the human rights convention when it may be rendered unnecessary by Parliament amending the Bill.

MR SPEAKER: That matter could be explained during the debate that we are about to hold.

Before we proceed, I point out that the right hon. and learned Member for Sleaford and North Hykeham (Mr Hogg) was right to say that there is a 10-minute limit on Back-Bench speeches . . .

THE SECRETARY OF STATE FOR THE HOME DEPARTMENT (MR DAVID BLUNKETT): I beg to move, That the Bill be now read a Second time.

I thank all those – my advisers, officials and hon. Members, including my ministerial team – who have worked so diligently with me on the Bill. I should also like to put on record my thanks to the members of the Joint Committee on Human Rights and of the Select Committee on Home affairs for their speedy and diligent work.

It would be useful to deal with the question that the hon. Member for Southwark, North and Bermondsey (Simon Hughes) asked about the derogation from article 5 of the European convention on human rights. We believe that it is sensible to seek the consent of the House of Commons and the House of Lords because unless Parliament agrees to clauses 21 to 23 and associated provisions, which relate to detention, the need to seek a derogation from article 5 under article 15 will not arise. It is therefore sensible to have the provision in place. It will fall automatically if Parliament does not consent to the clauses that I mentioned.

SIMON HUGHES: Will the Home Secretary give way?

MR BLUNKETT: I shall, but I want to make a little progress afterwards. Obviously, I shall then give way to hon. Members.

SIMON HUGHES: I thank the Home Secretary for being as courteous on this matter as he has been throughout the proceedings so far. Will he reconsider the issue that he heard me raise earlier, and with which he has partially dealt? Does he accept that, by virtue of the order that the Government laid last week, there is a 40-day period within which the order is the law. At the end of the 40 days, it will lapse if Parliament does not agree to the proposal in both Houses. Given that the Government have the cover that they seek, is it not, in a sense, an abuse of the judgment of both Houses to assume that they will agree that the Bill should remain as it is, when there may be ways – following the Human Rights Committee's proposal – in which it could be amended to avoid derogation? In that case, the Government would not need the decisions of both Houses, the 40-day period would lapse in the normal way and the Government would not, to put it crudely, be putting the cart before the horse on a hugely important national and international legal obligation.

MR BLUNKETT: The 40-day period stands, but we do not agree that there is an alternative way of proceeding that would be acceptable to the Government; if there were, we would propose it. This issue will be the subject of the debate today, and of subsequent debates here and in the House of Lords. On that basis, we are seeking the consent of the House on derogation.

Circumstances and public opinion demanded urgent and appropriate action after the 11 September attacks on the World Trade Centre and the Pentagon. Many parliamentarians understandably demanded caution, proportionality and a response that would last for the future. Over the five weeks following the attacks, in which thousands of men and women lost their lives, it was the Government's task to appraise the measures that would be necessary to close loopholes and set aside anomalies that had developed over many years in existing legislation. We therefore took our time in preparing the statement of 15 October, which laid out precisely the kind of measures that I am proposing this afternoon. I make no apology for having taken another five weeks to come to the House with these measures, which required consideration. Given the need to put in place safeguards that could be required any day and at any time.

I do not believe that 10 weeks is a hurried period. It is important to recognise that, in the first few weeks after 11 September, the emotional response to what had happened – the sight that people beheld and the hundreds of public service workers and volunteers who lost their lives trying to save the lives of others – could have evoked an immediate and, I would have thought, universal call for even more draconian measures than those that I am accused of introducing. It would have been wrong to do that. [*Interruption*.]

Conservative Members laugh, but it was understandable that the United States Government sought to pass their Patriot Act by 26 October, which they did and it has now received the signature of the President. It was appropriate for us to be more circumspect, and to bring to the House what we consider to be proportionate and reasonable measures.

MR HOGG: The right hon. Gentleman made the point that he has taken 10 weeks to contemplate the contents of the Bill. That was indeed right. Given that it was necessary for him to take 10 weeks, does he understand the anxiety in this place that we are being asked to pass the Bill – all 114 pages and 125 clauses of it – in two days beyond today? Surely that cannot be right.

MR BLUNKETT: I am not absolutely certain that the length of the debate and the scrutiny given to a Bill are one and the same thing. The length of the debate and our scrutiny of it depend on the availability of time to deal with the aspects of the Bill on which there is genuine disagreement. Disagreeing with something on which there is general approbation is entirely different. It seems to me that the time available in this House and the House of Lords will be used effectively and rightly to scrutinise those proposals that have already received public attention and on which there has been considerable comment.

MR KEVIN MCNAMARA (HULL, NORTH): My right hon. Friend will be aware that the time set aside for consideration in Committee, on Report and on Third Reading is roughly equivalent to four Committee sittings. Is that a proper way to deal with this most important legislation, the significance of which he has underlined, given that terrorism and other such Bills were considered for much longer? The Bill contains the embryo of five Bills.

MR BLUNKETT: I do not accept that it contains the embryo of five Bills. The measures are coherent, they deal with a threat of a particular nature, they were laid out on 15 October with one or two exceptions – Opposition Members pressed us on those, including that in respect of corruption – and they are before the House for agreement. If there were no emergency, if there had not been a terrorist attack and if there were no danger that not passing the Bill by the end of the year would put us at risk, I would not be introducing it in the first place.

MR EDWARD GARNIER (HARBOROUGH) rose –

MR ELFYN LLWYD (MEIRIONNYDD NANT CONWY) rose –

MR BLUNKETT: I shall give way once more, but then I must make progress so that we do not lose time for the debate that Members want. We must get on to arguing about the content.

MR GARNIER: I am most grateful to the Home Secretary for giving way a fourth time so early in his speech.

My right hon. and learned Friend the Member for Sleaford and North Hykeham (Mr Hogg) complained about the lack of parliamentary time to discuss the Bill following the 10-week gestation period. It was published only towards the end of last week, but it will complete its Commons stages by the beginning of next. That allows only a week for outside bodies to concentrate on its terms and lobby those in the House who are interested in its content and implications. Although the Home Secretary may be right that he spent 10 hard weeks drafting the Bill, surely those outside the House should have rather longer than a week to lobby Members and the Government on its content and effect.

MR BLUNKETT: But the debate has been going on for 10 weeks, and the detail was laid out on 15 October.

MR MARK FISHER (STOKE-ON-TRENT, CENTRAL): Not the detail of the Bill.

MR BLUNKETT: I am being substantially heckled by my hon. Friend. Does he want to intervene?

MR FISHER: I am most grateful to the Home Secretary. Surely he appreciates the distinction between the principles that he laid out on 15 October and the detail of the Bill. We are expected to scrutinise and pass law, and that law is based on the wording of the Bill. As the hon. and learned Member for Harborough (Mr. Garnier) said, outside bodies have only a week in which to consider the Bill and advise us. Surely the Home Secretary accepts the historical precedent that when the House acts quickly, it seldom acts wisely.

MR BLUNKETT: I have no intention of getting into conflict this afternoon, but, if I might say so, I had not noticed that the past 10 weeks were free of detailed comment by a range of lobbying organisations and individuals. [*Interruption.*] Yes, about the Bill, the nature of its content, the statement of 15 October and the work undertaken by the Human Rights Committee and the Home Affairs Committee over the past week, including detailed evidence given to them by the very groups to which my hon. Friend the Member for Stoke-on-Trent, Central (Mr Fisher) referred. Those groups clearly had a handle on the principle and the detailed substance of the Bill, and the Under-Secretary, my hon. Friend the Member for Stretford and Urmston (Beverley Hughes), and I were questioned in detail in those Committees on that content. The idea that people have been deprived of knowledge of the details or implications of the Bill does not bear thinking about.

I have certainly learned one thing. I believed that lobby groups and those connected with the law understood the existing provisions more fully than proves to be the case. I shall try to deal with that this afternoon, because what the Bill seeks to do is build on what is already there rather than transform or overturn it. If there is any confusion in the minds of those giving advice or lobbying Members, I hope that we shall be able to end it during the days ahead.

MR LLWYD: As a legal challenge to the Bill is highly likely, will the Home Secretary elaborate on his definition of a public emergency, and also explain why the United Kingdom is the only country subscribing to the European convention that considers such an emergency to exist?

MR BLUNKETT: I shall deal with the second point during my speech. I am well aware of the differences that exist not merely within countries that are signatories to the convention, but across the world. However, the definition of terrorism in the Terrorism Act 2000 and the article 15 provisions gave us precisely the power to act in circumstances envisaged by those who drew up both the European convention on human rights, as approved in 1953, and the European convention on refugees, as approved in 1951. They foresaw circumstances in which it would be necessary to take action to derogate – to suspend temporarily – a particular article or clause, in order to be able to act in a particular way to respond to what was happening. I am positing that the circumstances of 11 September and its aftermath are such that they warrant immediate action. An article in *The Times* on 15 September stated:

> 'Despite fine promises and emergency legislation, Britain is still home to hundreds of extremists who have made this country one of the centres for the violent trans-national network that inspired and encouraged the barbarism in New York and Washington.'

That is just one of hundreds of statements that have been made over the past 10 weeks about what people perceive to be the situation in our country. Again and again, people – including people in the United States – have illustrated the real dangers that exist, and it is on that basis that I shall spell out today why we felt it necessary to act.

Let us recall for a moment not just what happened on 11 September, but what has happened since. Let us recall the interviews given and the video recordings made by bin Laden and the al-Qaeda group, which have spelt out their determination not simply to threaten once, but to threaten the civilian populations of the United States and those working with it. It is for that reason that we are proposing measures allowing us to take rational, reasonable and proportionate steps to deal with an internal threat and an external, organised terrorist group that could threaten at any time not just our population, but the populations of other friendly countries.

JEREMY CORBYN (ISLINGTON, NORTH): Does the Home Secretary accept that many people who are obviously appalled at what happened on 11 September believe that the answer is not to suspend traditional legal rights such as the right of access to courts in this country, but to use the criminal law against those planning or perpetrating criminal acts? Many people are deeply disturbed about this piece of emergency legislation, and believe that it will be no more effective than the Prevention of Terrorism (Temporary Provisions) Act 1974. Peace eventually came to Ireland through a political process, not a legal process.

MR BLUNKETT: I would take my hon. Friend's appeal more to heart if it were not for the fact that we are debating use of the very machinery that the House agreed, in 1997, to ensure that the legal process is followed and legal rights exist. I think that fundamental misunderstandings have arisen among lobby groups and others because of that point. In 1997, the House unanimously passed the Special Immigration Appeals Commission Act 1997, which established the commission. I would be interested to know whether any hon. Member would like to use their comments in debates on that legislation to contradict me now on this legislation. Does anyone wish to intervene? No hon. Member from either side of the House voted against that legislation, which was subsequently approved by the other place. It was approved not only because previous practice had been judged not to accord with the level of human rights that was needed and accepted at the end of the 20th century, but because, in November 1996, the then Government had lost the Chahal case, which considered the acceptability of the process being used to eject people from the United Kingdom. It was adjudged in the Chahal case that there had been improvements in the process, such as use of the three wise men and women, but it was also held that the process for ratifying the Home Secretary's power of certification for removal was not acceptable because the power infringed article 3 of the European convention on human rights. That is the nub of the issue. There is also no disagreement that the previous Government would have introduced the 1997 Act.

After the Chahal judgment, therefore, the House passed a measure that effectively provided judicial review of the Home Secretary's right to certificate the removal of an individual who is not a British national, but who is judged to be endangering national security or whose presence is not conducive to the public good.

MR HOGG: Will the right hon. Gentleman give way?

MR BLUNKETT: I shall give way in a moment, but I should like first to deal with what I consider to be a fundamental misunderstanding of our proposals. The question for hon. Members is, what did they think that the Special Immigration Appeals Commission and the judicial process would do? What cases was the commission to hear? Was it to hear cases in which there was judged to be a risk, or cases in which the presence of an individual was not conducive to the public good and the Home

Secretary had heard evidence from the security and intelligence services and was prepared to act? The answer is yes; the commission was established to consider precisely those types of case. Nevertheless, the very judgment that led to the commission's establishment was the one that held that article 3 precluded us from sending people back to their death, to torture or to degrading treatment.

The current situation, therefore, is that evidence may be adduced by the security and intelligence services, the Home Secretary may believe that he or she is correct to issue a certificate and the Special Immigration Appeals Commission – SIAC – may judge that that belief is correct, but the Home Secretary cannot deport that person because of the risk to the person's life. That is, and has been, the situation. The difference now is that we want to ensure that people cannot continue to conduct or organise terrorism from this country.

MR HOGG: Will the right hon. Gentleman give way?

MR BLUNKETT: I shall give way in a moment, when I have finished making this point.

The issue for me to decide is whether I should seek an opt-out from the European convention, and then to opt-in again by using, I think, article 58; to say that individuals should be released although we have evidence which SIAC is prepared to uphold that warrants detention; or to seek to hold those individuals. It is the third choice that we are putting before the House this afternoon. If we were prepared to derogate, or if I were prepared to sign a certificate to send someone to their death because no third safe country was available, we would not be introducing the measure in this form. We are doing so precisely to avoid that eventuality. That is why – you will forgive me for mentioning this, Mr Speaker – I have been slightly depressed over the past day or two about how the case has been put, and how some in the media who know better have sought to mislead those who have no reason to know better because they were not present, did not see and could not read about the steps that led to the establishment of SIAC precisely to deal with the circumstances that I described.

MR HOGG: The right hon. Gentleman places great weight on the Special Immigration Appeals Commission. Surely he should remind the House that under the Act that established that commission, it is entitled to withhold from the detained person particulars of the reason why he is detained. Furthermore, the Law Officers of the Crown can appoint a representative for that person who is expressly stated not to be responsible to the persons whose interests he is appointed to represent. That is not a very good safeguard of rights.

MR BLUNKETT: The right hon. and learned Gentleman may make a judgment about whether that is acceptable to him, but it was acceptable to the whole House in 1997. Following a challenge in the courts in the case of Mullah Rehman, the Lords judged five weeks ago that both the process and the threshold of evidential base were acceptable and in line with what the House intended when it passed the Act unanimously in the first place.

DAVID WINNICK: Will my right hon. Friend give way?

MR BLUNKETT: I shall in two seconds – but first I shall answer the second element of the question.

The person who is adjudged to be a risk has the right to take on a legal advocate of his own. When the case reaches the point at which evidence is presented by the security and intelligence services the delivery of which – this is why SIAC was established – would put at risk the operation of the security services, and those working with them and for them, often covertly, an advocate from a list of advocates is provided, as in 1997 the House judged should happen, to allow evidence to be presented and the case on behalf of the person charged to be heard and properly dealt with legally.

Then a right of appeal on a point of law to both the Court of Appeal and the House of Lords is provided in similar circumstances and with similar rights.

DAVID WINNICK: I take the view that in all circumstances the powers that my right hon. Friend is taking are necessary. I am not happy – no one could be – about what is happening, and I work on the assumption that several people have been allowed in who should never have been allowed in. Does my right hon. Friend accept that some of us who take that view are, despite his comments, worried about the lack of judicial review? If we introduce measures that no one likes, and people are to be locked up for reasons that we believe are justified, some form of judicial review – apart from what my right hon. Friend – has been explaining, is all the more necessary, and its existence would make me much happier.

MR BLUNKETT: We would have to return to anything that the House decides about extradition or asylum issues more generally. All that we seek to do in the Bill is to make clear what SIAC and the Lords believe to be the case. In the cases that have gone to SIAC since the Act was passed four years ago, judicial review has not been sought, because the operation of SIAC has been judged to constitute a judicial review of the Home Secretary's certification. That is the issue that we are dealing with and that is why SIAC was seen as a substantial improvement on what existed previously.

The issue this afternoon is whether it is right that we should hold people in circumstances where we cannot transfer them to a third safe country, where the country to which we originally sought to transfer them does not have extradition agreements and therefore where their lives would be at risk, or whether we should release them into the community. At issue is an enhanced risk, post-11 September, which we believe warrants our taking that difficult but balanced and proportionate step. In doing so, we will ensure that the House will annually reaffirm or otherwise the measure on detention. In any case, the derogation has a five-year life and is automatically a sunset clause.

I also wish to make it clear that we do not think that a debate of one and a half hours would be adequate should we have to seek reaffirmation of the provision under the affirmative procedure and, with the agreement of the Leader of the House, we would seek to provide a more extensive opportunity for debate.

MR ROBERT MARSHALL-ANDREWS (MEDWAY): My question is not intended to be pejorative, because I am genuinely interested in the answer. Does the Home Secretary accept that there is a sea of difference between SIAC being used to deal with issues of deportation – with all the problems that SIAC has as a review body – and its being used to review decisions to incarcerate and imprison, indefinitely, without trial and, indeed, without charge? If evidence exists against the people about whom we have heard, why are they not being charged and tried in this country?

MR BLUNKETT: If the evidence that would be adduced and presented in a normal court were available, of course we would use it, as we have done in the past. We are talking today about those who are adjudged to have committed, organised and supported and helped those involved in terrorism worldwide in the circumstances of 11 September. Those who drew up the European convention and the refugee convention could not have dreamt of the act that took place on 11 September, but they did envisage some act of that kind that would at some point require us to be able to take the necessary steps. That is why I am using article 15 to derogate from article 5, rather than seeking to withdraw altogether. If evidence could be presented that is not subject to the parameters that I laid out a moment ago, it would be used. I know that my hon. and learned Friend is a barrister and, as a non-lawyer, I always listen carefully to those who are – [Hon. Members: 'Airy-fairy ones?'] I listen carefully whether they are airy-fairy or not.

MR MARSHALL-ANDREWS: What about SIAC?

MR BLUNKETT: I am coming to SIAC. It was the establishment of SIAC and the judgment in the Rehman case that upheld the threshold required and the nature of the way in which the evidence should be presented that answer my hon. and learned Friend's question. The House accepted, and the House of Lords agreed, that in some cases the nature of the evidence from the security and intelligence services will be such that it would put at risk the operation of those services and the lives of those who act clandestinely to help them if that evidence were presented in normal open court. That is the measure of the proposals this afternoon.

NOTES:
1. The major point in these extracts from the Second Reading debate on the Bill was the derogation from Art. 5(1) EHCR required because of the power conferred on the Home Secretary to detain those suspected of being international terrorists (*Chahal* v *UK* (1996) 23 EHRR 413, *Secretary of State for the Home Deparment* v *Rehman* [2001] UKHL 47; [2001] 3 WLR 877). The Human Rights (Designated Derogation) Order 2001 (SI 2001 No. 3644) was passed before the Act.
2. The Act does not exclude the SIAC from judicial review. An amendment made the SIAC a superior court of record, part of the High Court and therefore subject to the Court of Appeal which is the only body which can deal with a challenge to SIAC decisions.
3. MPs were concerned about the speed with which Parliament was required to consider the Bill. The House of Lords did reject some clauses and in order to get the Bill on to the statute book the Government (with its clear majority in the Commons) accepted some of the changes made in the Lords.

The Hansard Society, *The Challenge for Parliament: Making Government Accountable*
(2001), pp. 58–59

Principle 4 — Restoring the centrality of the Commons' chamber
The floor of the House of Commons is the main public focus for activity at Westminster. However, attendance by MPs and the extent to which it dominates political debate has declined.

Recommendations
20. To improve the attendance and influence of the chamber its core tasks need to be refined and clarified. It should become the plenary session of the Parliament. (para. 4.27)

21. In order to reflect the importance attached to the select committee system, and not take MPs away from the chamber, one day each week should be devoted to committee activity. To reflect the importance of this work other parliamentary business should be arranged around the committees so that the chamber would not meet on this day. (para. 4.28)

22. In general, the chamber should have fewer lengthy debates. Opportunities for MPs to initiate short debates on substantive issues should be increased. Opposition parties should be able to trade some of their Opposition Days for the chance to call for a statement on a topical issue. (paras 4.30–4.32)

23. In addition, the Speaker should grant a greater number of Private Notice Questions each session. (para. 4.33)

24. MPs should have the ability to call for 'public interest debates' on issues of public concern on a cross-party basis. (para. 4.34)

25. Prime Minister's Questions (PMQs) displays many of the worst aspects of Westminster. Open-ended questions should be banned at PMQs (although the leaders of the main opposition parties should retain this ability); instead Members should give notice of their intention to ask a question ten days in advance and should table their (substantive) question by noon two days before PMQs. (para. 4.40)

26. However, even a reformed PMQs is unlikely to ensure the necessary scrutiny of the Prime Minister's expanding role and office. The Prime Minister should appear before a select committee on an annual basis to account for the work of the Government. The most appropriate opportunity would be once a year to give evidence on the Government's Annual Report. (para. 4.42)

27. Question time for other departments and ministers should also be reformed to improve its topicality, substance and relevance. No more than ten questions should appear on the Order Paper for each Question Time and no duplicate questions should be allowed. The period of notice for oral questions should be reduced from ten working days to five. (paras 4.44–4.45)

28. In cases where the Government does not produce a response to a written question the reasons for not answering must be made clearer. A denial of information should be accompanied by a reference to the relevant section of the Code of Practice on Open Government or the Freedom of Information Act. (para. 4.46)

(ii) *Parliamentary Questions*

Questions may be divided into those to be answered orally, or in writing. Written answers to Parliamentary Questions, or PQs, will be dealt with *post*, at p. 340.

In its report on PQs the Procedure Committee put forward the following objectives of PQs:

(a) a vehicle for individual backbenchers to raise their constituents' grievances;

(b) an opportunity for the House of Commons to probe the detailed actions of the Executive;

(c) a means of illuminating differences of policy on major issues between the various political parties or of judging the Parliamentary skills of individual MPs on both sides of the House;

(d) a combination of these or any other purposes, for example a way of enabling the Government to disseminate information about particular policy decisions; and

(e) the obtaining of information by the House from the Government and its subsequent publication (HC 178 of 1990–91, para. 26).

PQs for oral answer must be tabled in advance by at least two days. In fact, to have any chance of being answered orally the PQ must be tabled on the first day for which PQs to a particular minister may be accepted. The Prime Minister answers PQs now on Wednesdays, previously on Tuesdays and Thursdays, whereas question time for other Ministers is determined by a rota.

There are quite detailed rules on the form and content of PQs. These rules have derived from the rulings of the Speaker and are collected in *Erskine May's Treatise on the Law, Privileges, Proceedings and Usage of Parliament* (22nd edn, 1997). PQs which deal with matters under consideration by Royal Commissions, parliamentary committees, or which are *sub judice* are inadmissible. Ministers only answer PQs on matters for which they are responsible.

This can create a problem as Ministers vary in their practice in answering questions which relate to other public bodies. The rule in *Erskine May* is that PQs 'should relate to the public affairs with which they are officially concerned, to proceedings in Parliament or to matters for which they are responsible (295)'. The Committee recommended that the Table Office, which receives PQs, should give the benefit of the doubt to MPs when they want to ask a PQ about one of these public bodies which operates at 'arm's length' from the Minister.

Where the Chief Executive of a Next Steps Executive Agency answers a PQ on an operational matter, the answer is now published in *Hansard* as would be the case with a ministerial answer.

The aim of most MPs tabling a PQ for an oral answer is to be able to pose a supplementary question for which no notice is necessary. Thus the tabled question may be quite general, or open, in nature. This is particularly so of PQs directed at the Prime Minister. A typical open PQ to the Prime Minister will inquire about the Prime Minister's engagements for that day. The Leader of Her Majesty's Opposition does not table PQs but is called by the Speaker to ask at least one supplementary, and possibly up to four supplementary, questions.

J. A. G. Griffith & M. Ryle, *Parliament: Functions, Practice and Procedures*
(1989), pp. 354–55

One of the reasons for the increased number of Questions asked by Leaders of the Opposition has been the almost total adoption of 'open' Questions to the Prime Minister. . . . These permit supplementaries on almost any subject of the questioner's choosing. The Leader of the Opposition is thus able to bring before the House and the public (Question hour is prime media time, and these occasions are often broadcast live on the radio) the issues of the day he thinks most relevant. Obviously these often include events where the Government looks as if it may be in trouble, or an area of policy where the Government appears to be doing badly. When the Leader of the Opposition in earlier years had to confine his supplementaries to matters relevant to the specific Question asked, he clearly was unable to pick his own topic in this way. Indeed on numerous occasions between 1970 and 1974, Mr Harold Wilson, as Leader of the Opposition, did not ask any Questions at all. . . .

It would be dangerous to draw too precise conclusions from a limited sample, but close observation of Prime Minister's Question time over the years suggests one or two significant developments. First, Leaders of the Opposition now make significantly more use of these opportunities than ever before. Second, the occasion has become much more heated politically (and also more noisy); this is no doubt a reflection of the widened political gap between the major parties, but Mrs Thatcher and Mr Kinnock, particularly, have used these occasions largely to make political points or advance broad arguments rather than to ask Questions on specific matters. Third, Mr Kinnock in particular has developed the technique of concentrating on one pre-determined area with a series of prepared questions sometimes extending over several days. The 'open question' has made this possible.

Whatever the causes – and personalities cannot be ignored – Prime Minister's Question time has become increasingly important politically and as a parliamentary occasion. Here is experienced the direct confrontation of the Prime Minister and the Leader of the Opposition in its most concentrated and highly-charged form. It is an opportunity no Leader of the Opposition can afford to neglect. It is also the occasion when the Prime Minister can be most critically tested, and various commentators or experienced observers have testified to how carefully the Prime Minister has to prepare for this ordeal. Success or failure on these occasions can greatly strengthen or seriously weaken the political standing of the two protagonists.

NOTE: In its report the Procedure Committee decided not to recommend any change in the balance between open and closed PQs to the Prime Minister (HC 178 of 1990–91, para. 38).

Political points are also made in PQs directed to other Ministers, as this extract from *Hansard* shows on a day when it was the turn of ministers at the Ministry of Agriculture, Fisheries and Food to answer questions. As will be seen, some of the issues underlying the PQ are points of local and international concern.

House of Commons, HC Deb
Vol. 306, cols. 1174–79, 19 February 1998

Farm Incomes

10. MR WEBB: What assessment he has made of trends in farming incomes over the next three years.

MR MORLEY: It is difficult to predict the trend in farm incomes because of the many factors involved. I am kept informed by my officials on how specific market developments could impact on farm incomes.

MR WEBB: Does the Minister accept that independent forecasts, such as those by Barclays Bank, suggest a further significant fall in farming incomes next year? Farmers in my constituency have overdrafts that would make my eyes water. Does he accept that they cannot wait two years for an upturn, and does he agree that the crisis in farming incomes needs to be tackled urgently?

MR MORLEY: There is no doubt that this is a difficult year for farming incomes, although the hon. Gentleman may have misinterpreted the report slightly: Barclays suggests a downturn in 1998 and an upturn in 1999.

MR PIKE: Does my hon. Friend accept that many hill farmers, particularly in the Pennines and similar areas, already farm on a non-viable basis and that if something does not happen to give them a better return and standard of living, they will get out of farming?

MR MORLEY: Yes, I accept that. It is one reason why we are discussing the idea of early retirement with farmers' representatives and considering schemes such as hill livestock compensatory allowance. Hill farmers have always been in the lowest quartile of income. Perhaps the time has come to look at the support mechanisms as part of the restructuring of the CAP and the year 2000 proposals.

MR CURRY: How much has been taken out of farm incomes by the rise in interest rates since last May, and how much more would be taken out by a further rise, as canvassed by the Governor of the Bank of England?

MR MORLEY: A rise in interest rates would affect farmers in the same way as any other business.

MR FLYNN: The Government are to be congratulated on their courage in dealing with the extremely difficult and painful, albeit inevitable, changes that have taken place in the farming industry. Could farmers hope for a more secure future in the long term if they were to change farming practices and carry out more organic farming, or move into areas for which there will be a secure market in the future, such as the cultivation of flax?

MR MORLEY: Farmers are certainly going through a period of change, not least because of the pressures on the CAP. There are tremendous premiums for organic products, but nearly 70 per cent of the organic market is taken by imports. We are doing our best to encourage farmers to convert to organic methods and take the opportunity of that market. We shall announce further proposals in the very near future.

MR BEGGS: Does the Minister agree that, as soon as the ban on the export of beef from the United Kingdom comes about [sic], farming incomes will start to increase again? May I take this opportunity to thank the Minister of State for attending the animal health computer presentation by the Northern Ireland Department of Agriculture today, and urge other hon. Members to attend the presentation at 4 pm in Room 21 so that their regions can benefit from the facilities that we have in Northern Ireland?

MR MORLEY: The computerised scheme in Northern Ireland is excellent and has helped in terms of the Commission's recommendation that the ban should be lifted in Northern Ireland. We are extending such a scheme, through the cattle passport scheme, throughout the country. It is a great shame that the previous Government did not implement that scheme in 1989 when they were pressed to do so by those on the Labour Front Bench.

MR JACK: The Minister will understand that the agrimonetary regime has a profound effect on farmers' incomes. A document produced by Mr Lebrecht, a senior official in MAFF, has come into my possession. It waxes lyrical about the stability of the current arrangements and the contribution to farm incomes, and talks about the generous compensation schemes available to farmers in the context of post-euro agrimonetary arrangements.

If the Minister's officials feel so enthusiastic about the arrangements to help farmers, why does he not feel the same?

MR MORLEY: It is a shame that the shadow Minister did not see a document that I have seen, which points out that in 1995 the then Conservative Government voted against the agrimonetary scheme – the very scheme that the Conservatives are now pressing us to implement.

EU Banana Regime

11. MS ABBOTT: If he will visit the World Trade Organisation in Geneva to discuss the European Union's banana regime; and if he will make a statement.

DR JOHN CUNNINGHAM: Negotiation in the WTO is a matter for the European Commission. I have made clear my determination to secure an outcome that both conforms to WTO rules and honours our long-standing commitments to Caribbean producers.

MS ABBOTT: Does my right hon. Friend agree that the WTO ruling on the banana regime caused consternation and upset throughout the Caribbean? Many eastern Caribbean countries are wholly dependent on banana exports for their foreign exchange. The ruling also has serious social implications, because the banana industry is still a big employer in Jamaica and the eastern Caribbean. Can my right hon. Friend assure me that, during its presidency of the European Union, the United Kingdom will do all that it can to bring about an outcome that will preserve the living standards and social structures of the eastern Caribbean?

DR CUNNINGHAM: My hon. Friend is absolutely right. The Windward Islands, Belize and some other Caribbean islands depend hugely on banana production. Only this week, at the Agriculture Council in Brussels we discussed progress on a new proposal to replace the one that was ruled out by the WTO decision – which, like my hon. Friend, I found very disappointing. We are determined to secure a new agreement for Caribbean banana producers.

SIR PETER TAPSELL: Does the Minister recall that, at the time when Britain signed the treaty of Rome, the most solemn undertakings were given to our friends in the Caribbean – with whom we have historic links stretching over centuries – that their banana exports, on which their whole lives depend, would be protected? Must those undertakings be subordinated to the German wish to eat large numbers of continental American bananas?

DR CUNNINGHAM: The hon. Gentleman is absolutely right. We have historic obligations to those tiny Caribbean democracies, and the Government are determined to fulfil our obligations, for all the reasons that he gave. I cannot see for the life of me why the complainants to the WTO made such a fuss. The tiny Caribbean countries produce only about 8 per cent of the European banana market.

Beef Ban

12. MR LOUGHTON: How many prosecutions have taken place with regard to the sale of beef on the bone to the final consumer?

MR ROOKER: None so far, but we are aware that two are pending, and that warnings about non-compliance have been given by local authorities.

MR LOUGHTON: I am sure that the House is glad that the Minister has dragged himself away from the health hazards of the Smoking Room to reply to questions.

The Minister will know as well as me that beef on the bone is still widely available in this country, given the right nudge or wink. Does he agree that the complete absence of any prosecutions to date demonstrates that the ban is unmanageable, unfair and unenforceable?

MR ROOKER: The issue of prosecution is a matter for the independent prosecuting authorities. As hon. Members will have read in today's *Evening Standard*, someone is to be summoned before the magistrates in Rother, whose district council is run by a coalition between Liberal Democrats and Tories.

MR MARTYN JONES: Is it not the case that there would be no need for prosecutions, or for the regulations banning beef on the bone, if the Tories had acted quickly when in government to quell the BSE crisis instead of dragging their feet?

MR ROOKER: Yes. It is a matter of public health and of taking precautions. We can say as a Government that we are not allowing BSE infectivity into the food chain, and we will maintain that position.

MR CHARLES KENNEDY: Will the Minister acknowledge that, in a democratic society, prosecution is always more difficult when there is no basic public consent, enthusiasm or acceptance of the law itself? In that context, did he see the Teletext poll last weekend, when 94 per cent of respondents expressed no confidence in or support for the Government's measures?

If the course or prosecution is so clear, why is it that the first test case in Scotland, in Selkirk sheriff court next month, concerns a beef-on-the-bone case where there was no commercial transaction, the one to which he has just referred concerns a case where there was a commercial transaction, and his recent written answer said that there could be no prosecution against a farmer who slaughters beef on his farm and consumes it? If the element in the ban is risk, surely the ban should be comprehensive and there should not be three different categories in three different parts of the country.

MR ROOKER: As most hon. Members appreciate, different rules apply to private kills, but the administration of justice in this country is not conducted by opinion polls.

MR CORBETT: May I tell the Minister that I have not had a single complaint about the temporary non-availability of T-bone steaks and oxtails in my constituency, I suspect because of their relatively high price? Does he agree that it is offensive for Opposition Members whose hands are dirty from BSE and CJD to take risks with public health over this temporary ban?

MR ROOKER: I agree entirely with the honest, fair and robust way in which my hon. Friend has put his point.

MR ALASDAIR MORGAN: How many prosecutions have taken place or are pending in relation to breaches of the import regulations that were introduced on 1 January?

MR ROOKER: I am not able to answer that now without notice.

MR ALAN W. WILLIAMS: Did the Minister hear the item on this morning's 'Today' programme, where a butcher who had been selling beef on the bone, when tipped off by the environmental health department that it was about to call on him, and when warned that there could be a fine of anything up to £20,000, decided immediately to stop selling beef on the bone? He was willing to be interviewed to that effect on that programme. Is that not what our local authorities throughout the country should be doing, so that we can guarantee all consumers that all possible steps have been taken to ensure that our beef is the safest in the world?

MR ROOKER: My hon. Friend is right, but I am not surprised that the butcher concerned was willing to be interviewed on the 'Today' programme: it is clear that he is a publicity seeker.

13. MR GIBB: If he will issue guidance to individuals who have beef on the bone in their freezers, bought for their own consumption, before 16 December 1997.

MR ROOKER: Such guidance was included in the question-and-answer material provided on the MAFF internet BSE site immediately after the announcement by my right hon. Friend the Minister of Agriculture, Fisheries and Food about the Spongiform Encephalopathy Advisory Committee advice on dorsal root ganglia on 3 December 1997.

MR GIBB: Which advice is correct? Is it the advice on the internet that it is up to the consumer to decide whether to consume beef in deep freeze, or is it the advice given on television on Sunday by the Minister of Agriculture, Fisheries and Food that such consumption would represent an unnecessary risk?

MR ROOKER: People who already had frozen T-bones or ribs of beef in their freezers at home should, frankly, be treated as adults. [*Interruption.*] Those citizens owned that beef, it was in their home. We gave them the advice. They already owned that beef. It was not a question of making a commercial transaction – that had already been done.

MR DAWSON: Has the Minister ever pondered whether the Opposition parties are really serious about getting the beef ban lifted as they are obviously not willing to take the vital steps that are necessary to assure the world of the safety and quality of British beef?

MR ROOKER: The plain fact is that the Opposition are asking us knowingly to allow, for the first time, BSE infectivity into the food chain. We will not do it now and we will not do it in future.

NOTE: The Procedure Committee did recommend that oral PQs to other Ministers should be reasonably specific so that they will be admissible and the Speaker can allow a supplementary (HC 178 of 1990–91, para. 43).

(iii) *Private Notice Questions*
These are questions which refer to points which are urgent matters of public importance, or which relate to the arrangement of business in the House. Application is made to the Speaker on the day on which the MP wishes to ask the question, and, if granted, it will be asked at the conclusion of the normal Question Time.

In the sessions 1998–99, 1999–2000, and 2000–2001 the numbers of private notice questions (excluding business questions) asked were 12, nine, and seven respectively. Griffith and Ryle *Parliament: Functions, Practice and Procedures* (1989) note that private notice questions for the Opposition relate to controversial or political issues, whereas those asked by Government back-benchers are more likely to be of a local character (p. 375).

(iv) *Adjournment Debates*
There are four types of adjournment debate, but only two will be covered here. These are the daily adjournment debate and the emergency adjournment debate.

Adjournment debates do not involve a division as they are a method by which an MP may raise a matter for a Minister who has responsibility. There is a ballot for the daily adjournment debate. The emergency adjournment debate is a relatively rare event which deals with an urgent matter not otherwise covered in the current business of the House. The tables below give an indication of the incidence of, and topics discussed in, emergency adjournment debates.

J. A. G. Griffith & M. Ryle, *Parliament: Functions, Practice and Procedures*
(1989), pp. 265, 352

Applications for emergency adjournment debates

Session	Number of Applications (including multiple applications on the same matter)	Numbers granted
1974–75	33	1
1975–76	58	3
1976–77	44	3

Session	Number of Applications (including multiple applications on the same matter)	Numbers granted
1977–78	38	2
1978–79(a)	66	3
1979–80(b)	89	2
1980–81	48	1
1981–82	61	2
1982–83(a)	50	2
1983–84(b)	84	3
1984–85	61	1
1985–86	87	1
1986–87(a)	48	2
1987–88(b)	88	1

(a) Unusually short session
(b) Unusually long session

Debates under Standing Order No. 20 [now SO No. 24]

Successful applications by Opposition front-bench

Date of debate	Topic	Member moving
27 January 1981	Proposed purchase of *The Times*	John Smith
22 December 1981	The GLC	Albert Booth
15 December 1982	NATO Council meeting	Denis Healey
14 February 1983	Dispute in the water industry	Gerald Kaufmann
26 October 1983	Invasion of Grenada by USA	Denis Healey
24 May 1984	Closures at British Leyland	Peter Shore
19 December 1984	Local Authorities Capital Expenditure (England and Wales)	John Cunningham
27 January 1986	Westland plc	Neil Kinnock
18 December 1986	Airborne Early Warning System	Denzil Davies
3 February 1987	Official Secrets Act: Activities of Special Branch	Gerald Kaufmann

NOTE: In sessions 1998–99, 1999–2000 and 2000–01 there were three, two and four applications for emergency adjournment debates. None of these applications was granted. The subject of the last emergency adjournment debate was the refit of the Trident submarines and the effect upon the Scottish economy in June 1993.

(v) *Early Day Motion*

Public Information Office, House of Commons *Factsheet Series P No. 3*
(2001), pp. 1, 3–5

. . . 'Early Day Motion' [EDM] is a colloquial term for a notice of motion given by a Member for which no date has been fixed for debate; there is very little prospect of these motions being debated. Nowadays Early Day Motions exist to allow Members to put on record their opinion on a subject and to canvass support from fellow Members.

. . .

Types of EDM and their purpose
EDMs tend to fall into several distinct groups. First, the Opposition may put down an EDM to pray against Statutory Instruments. Many appear in the name of the Leader of the Opposition or of another opposition party. This is how the Opposition gives public notice that it may seek to secure a debate; this type of EDM is to all intents and purposes about the only one which ever leads to a debate. Under Standing Order No. 118, the Government may refer a statutory instrument subject to negative procedure [see **Factsheet** L7] for debate in a Standing Committee once a motion for its annulment has been tabled.

Secondly, a group within a party might put down an EDM. This may express a view different from the official position of the party concerned. For example, Motions put down by Government back-benchers may seek to accelerate or otherwise change Government action.

Another type frequently found is the all-party motion, which expresses a view across party divides, often on social issues; or one which, largely promoted by one party, can attract signatures from a section of another. All-party motions are on the increase, and a great deal of work may go into their compilation. It is generally only all-party motions that can obtain very large numbers of signatures. The titles of such motions given in Appendix 2 will give an idea of the subjects which have regularly commanded very wide support. When looking at an EDM, scrutiny of the names of the six sponsors will usually provide a clue as to its type. Certain motions, especially of the all-party category, are suggested to Members by pressure groups outside the House, and such organisations often go to much trouble in trying to persuade Members to sign "their" motion.

Some EDMs are completely ephemeral in character – those offering congratulations to a particular football or cricket club are a case in point (it has been known for separate but virtually identical EDMs to be tabled on this sort of thing). Other EDMs relate to local issues – for instance criticising the decision to close a post office or hospital – or purely personal matters (eg a deportation or similar case).

Members often seek to draw up an EDM if they have been debarred from putting down Questions on a subject because of the rules of the House as below . . .

Supporting EDMs
Additional Members can sign the Motion on subsequent days. Commonly, Members do this by tearing out pages from their copy of the *"Blues"* and signing below the chosen Motion or Motions. The pages are then handed to the Table Office, and the EDM (together with its top six sponsors, but not others who have previously signed the Motion) will be reprinted in the next Notice Paper with the new names appended. Members often simply give the Table Office the relevant number and ask for their name to be added. A running total of the number of signatures to date is also printed each time the EDM appears in the *"Blues"*.

Members may give the Table Office the names of other Members to be added to the list of those supporting the EDM. Any Member doing so is personally responsible for the accuracy of the names of other Members appended by them to EDMs and they ought to have those Members' authority for the addition of their names. Members may not assume that because other Members have agreed to support an EDM in one session that they will automatically support an identical motion tabled in a subsequent parliamentary session.

In an average Session only about six or seven EDMs reach over 200 signatures, but perhaps 70 or 80 get over 100 signatures. Quite a number will attract only one or a couple of signatures . . .

Signing EDMs

Any Member may formulate or sign an EDM. The Official Opposition regularly promote them. For instance, as mentioned before, prayers against Statutory Instruments and Motions of Censure – the Motion eventually approved by the House which led to the fall of the 1974–79 Labour Government started out as an EDM. . . . Similarly, a Motion put down by one or more of the smaller parties, will often be in the names of the party leader and principal spokesmen. In general, Ministers, and Whips do not sign EDMs and some Ministers have taken a dim view of their Parliamentary Private Secretaries' doing so. Neither the Speaker nor Deputy Speakers will sign such Motions. . . .

Amendments

A Member may put down an amendment or amendments to another Member's EDM. If a Member wishes to table an amendment to an EDM which they have already signed, they first have to withdraw their name from the main Motion.

Some amendments advance a view diametrically opposed to that offered by the main Motion and may advocate the replacement of the whole text from 'that' with an alternative proposition on the same subject, whilst others may seek additional or strengthening provisions.

Members sign amendments in the same way as main Motions and the Notice Paper counts and records these in exactly the same way. Members can therefore solicit support for amendments; it is by no means unknown for an amendment to garner more support than the original Motion. . . .

Some examples taken from the on-line data base for February and March 2002: www//edm.ais.co.uk. The proposer and the first subsequent four names are listed and the total of signatories is given beside the ★.

900 UNSOLICITED JUNK FAXES

Roy/Frank
Crausby/David
Hoyle/Lindsay
Lawrence/Jackie
Cairns/David   ★ 103

That this House notes with concern the increasing amount of unsolicited junk faxes sent to both domestic and commercial premises; further notes that many adults and children unknowingly call premium rated numbers at a cost of £1.50 a minute and that the resulting fax-back time is often stated as no more than 200 seconds; is gravely concerned that despite asking to be permanently deleted from fax databases, many unsuspecting recipients continue to receive unsolicited faxes; and urges Her Majesty's Government to introduce further statutory controls against such an abuse of access.

930 ST PIRAN'S DAY

Breed/Colin
Tyler/Paul
Taylor/Matthew
George/Andrew
Burnside/David   ★ 20

That this House celebrates with the people of Cornwall St Piran's Day, commemorating the Patron Saint of Cornwall on 5th March who according to legend brought Christianity and discovered tin; And encourages this celebration of cultural identity and regional diversity through recognition of this important day in the life of Cornish people.

1011 Hunting Wild Mammals With Dogs

Banks/Tony
Widdecombe/Ann
Baker/Norman
Wright/Anthony D
Hancock/Mike   ★ 193

That this House welcomes her Majesty's Government's announcement, in line with the Gracious Speech, giving Parliament the opportunity to vote on the issue of hunting wild mammals with dogs; draws attention to the overwhelming votes in favour of banning hunting carried in the House on a number of occasions; re-affirms its continuing support for an outright ban and its rejection of licensed cruelty enshrined in the so-called Middle Way proposal; and calls on her Majesty's Government to follow any vote in favour of a ban with appropriate and timely legislation.

NOTE: In sessions 1998–1999, 1999–2000 and 2000–01, 1,009, 1,198 and 659 EDMs were tabled.

(vi) *Westminster Hall*

Following a report made by the Select Committee on the Modernization of the House of Commons (HC 194 of 1988–99), an experiment was agreed for the 1999–2000 session in which a parallel chamber would be established, to be known as, and to take place in, Westminster Hall. The idea behind this initiative, which is modelled on the Main Committee in the House of Representatives in Canberra, is to allow for the House of Commons to deal with business which currently cannot be conducted on the floor of the House because of lack of time and with business which is not currently taken. Westminster Hall will be chaired by Deputy Speakers and the layout of the room will be a wide hemi-cycle. The business which will be conducted in the Westminster Hall will differ from the Chamber in that there will not be any divisions. If there is to be a decision made in a sitting in Westminster Hall then it must be unanimous. There will be sittings on Tuesday and Wednesday mornings which will deal with private Members' business, and a third sitting on Thursday afternoon which will deal with business agreed through the usual channels (the Whips). The business which can be taken in Westminster Hall will include additional opportunities for adjournment debates, debates on the reports of select committees and new business such as opportunities for regular debates on (a) different regions of the world to augment the annual adjournment debate on foreign affairs, and (b) Green Papers and other consultative documents.

The experiment was a success and was made permanent.

D: Correspondence

Much of the correspondence conducted by MPs is concerned with their role as the persons who attempt to remedy the grievances of their constitutents.

R. Rawlings 'Parliamentary Redress of Grievance' in C. Harlow (ed.), *Public Law and Politics*
(1986), p. 120

Parliamentary Redress and Central Departments: the Grievance Chain

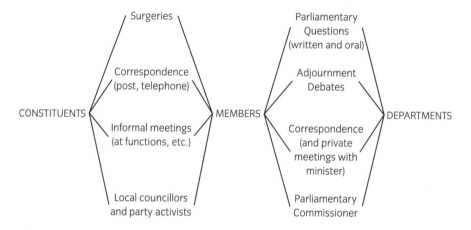

NOTE: Rawlings (at pp. 128–29) points out that MPs as intermediaries can act in different ways in chasing grievances on behalf of constituents. They may act as *gatekeepers*, which means that they filter out some kinds of complaint; or they may be *letterboxes*, simply passing on complaints; or they may perform the role of *advocate*, actively taking up the complaint and using whatever means they wish in order to have it resolved in the constituent's favour. An MP can, of course, act in all of these roles, depending upon expertise in the matter, availability of time, sympathy for the complainant, and party political/electoral considerations.

Some studies have attempted to gauge the number of letters which MPs write to public authorities, including Ministers, on their constituents' behalf. Ridley's conservative estimate was that public authorities receive more than half a million letters from MPs annually (F. Ridley (1984) 37 *Parliamentary Affairs* 24). Norton projected that between 156,000 and 830,000 were written to Ministers by MPs each year (P. Norton (1982) 35 *Parliamentary Affairs* 60).

A. Page, 'MPs and the Redress of Grievances'
[1985] *Public Law* 1, at pp. 6–9

That MPs through their intervention do succeed in getting decisions changed there is no doubt. The impression, however, is that this is a relatively infrequent outcome: '. . . most letters do not result in a changed decision or new course of action being pursued.' Moreover, even where a decision is changed, it is by no means clear that the same result could not have been achieved without the intervention of the MP. Indeed, the

> strict tradition is that the Member's letter does not call forth a different decision from that which would be given to any other analogous case, unless very rarely it induces a Minister to initiate a change in policy.

The only advantage of an MP's intervention which can be pointed to is that because MPs' letters are normally considered at a higher level within departments, the chances of an inappropriate routine response being made to a case are reduced.

Comment

If it is the case that MPs' intervention normally makes little difference, then it would seem legitimate to ask whether the emphasis which is placed on MPs' role in the redress of grievances is altogether justified or indeed in the best interests of their constituents. Their status in relation to many of the agencies which are the subject of complaint is uncertain, how well or badly they perform their role can normally be only guessed at, and they suffer from all of the disadvantages of being 'unspecialised, ill-equipped, amateurish and over-worked.'

In reply, a number of arguments can be put forward. Undoubtedly the strongest is that, in handling the number of cases which they do, MPs are meeting a need which is not being met by anyone else. Moreover, they are doing something which is expected of them, although, as we have seen, MPs themselves have been partly responsible for generating this expectation. Their involvement in personal cases, therefore, helps MPs to keep their constituents satisfied, a concern which although understandable does create the risk of an unspoken conspiracy between MPs and Ministers to keep aggrieved individuals happy rather than genuinely to pursue their grievances, as well as themselves informed of local problems and difficulties. It has also been argued that MPs' constituency work is an important part of the legitimation not only of MPs but also Parliament in the eyes of the electorate. On the basis of these arguments, the only question which arises is whether MPs are sufficiently well-equipped in terms of secretarial and research facilities to fulfil their constituents' expectations of them. Accepting that they are not, additional assistance might conceivably increase their effectiveness in the redress of grievances.

It is at this point that one comes back to the fact that the PCA was intended to help MPs to carry out more effectively their role in the protection of the individual against government. However, MPs are supposed to regard the PCA as of only limited value and as the least effective of the available means of pursuing their constituents' grievances. This is no doubt partly attributable to the restrictions on his jurisdiction, but MPs' views are less than disinterested. Thus, a condition of the acceptance of the PCA by MPs was the insertion of the 'MP filter' to allay their fears that the PCA might come to supplant their own role in the redress of grievances, and the fact that MPs continue to oppose removal of the filter suggests that they remain extremely jealous of their own perceived primacy in the redress of grievances.

MPs' welfare role, however, is not without its costs. It represents a substantial burden for MPs themselves and for the administration. In the view of the Fulton Committee, Parliament should 'take fully into account the cumulative cost (not only in time but in the quality of the administration) that the raising of minutiae imposes . . .' Whether MPs' insistence on their primacy in the redress of grievances is in the best interests of aggrieved individuals is also questionable. Certainly in his most recent Annual Report, the PCA questions whether it always is:

> I have often employed the familiar arguments in defence of our system, chief of which is that every Member of Parliament is an ombudsman for his constituents and that the body of Members makes a natural and valuable filter for discriminating between simple and complex cases, the worthy and the unworthy. But five years' experience has led me to doubt the validity of these arguments, at any rate in opposition to some modification of our arrangements. At present the Member may, and often does, ask the Minister for the appropriate Department to let him have, in the familiar phrase, 'an answer which I can send to my constituent' about his grievance. But on receipt of that reply, the Member has neither the time, nor the resources, nor the powers to verify by examination of departmental papers or witnesses the explanations offered, which must of necessity be composed on the basis of facts and opinions advanced by those against whom the complaint is laid. When Members do send me their files, it sometimes happens that the Minister's letter of response is the starting point of an investigation which shows that there is more to the case than the letter might be thought to suggest. [HC 322, 1983–84, para. 7.]

The PCA went on to recommend that an individual who had first asked his MP to take up his case but who was dissatisfied with the ultimate response should have the right to invite the PCA to examine the progress made. Whether this recommendation will be acted upon remains to be seen. If MPs, rather than the Government, were to oppose its implementation, their motives would be open to question, for the point which emerges from this survey is not that MPs should not act on behalf of their constituents, but that what they do should be kept firmly in perspective, and inflated claims, such as 'the primary responsibility for defending the citizen against the executive rests with the Member of Parliament,' should not be allowed to stifle the development of other forms of redress. As Mitchell observed:

> The problem of finding a place in the sun for the backbench MP is essentially different from the problem of finding effective means of redress for the individual who has suffered injustice.

NOTE: See Chapter 10 on Ombudsmen, *post*, at p. 693.

QUESTIONS

1. Is there competition between the Ombudsman and MPs in remedying citizens' grievances? Should they not work together? See Rawlings at pp. 137–41 for a proposal which seeks to use the casework of MPs as a means of external oversight, and therefore adding to the House of Commons function of scrutiny and influence.

2. Is writing a letter to a Minister more effective than asking a PQ or seeking an adjournment debate, or does a MP have resort to these parliamentary procedures if a letter does not satisfactorily resolve the situation?

(vii) *Parliamentary Questions for Written Answer*

Public Information Office, House of Commons Sessional Information Digest
1998–99, 1999–2000 and 2000–01, p. 2

PARLIAMENTARY QUESTIONS

Statistics of Parliamentary Questions are available in two forms. The figures for each, which for various reasons (mainly owing to methods of counting and recording) are not exactly comparable, are as follows:

Questions appearing on the Order Paper calculated by the Journal Office

	1998–99	1999–2000	2000–01
Appearing on the Order Paper for Oral Answer	5,008	5,747	2,780
Put down for priority Written Answer	13,199	16,212	8,439
Put down for non-priority Written Answer	18,950	20,569	7,978
Total	37,157	42,528	19,197

(Not more than about half of all questions put down for Oral Answer will receive such an answer – the rest are answered in writing.)

Questions appearing in *Hansard* are indexed in the Parliamentary On-line Information System (POLIS)

Oral replies (including supplementaries)*	4,774	5,343	2,591
Written replies†	31,649	36,067	16,687
Total	36,423	41,410	19,278

* Number of tabled questions answered (excluding supplementaries) was 1,936 in 1998–99.

† With POLIS, several written questions from the same Member, if answered together by the Minister may have been treated as one question.

NOTE: The General Election in June 2001 meant that the 2000–01 session was shorter than average.

Questions for written answer are used mainly to seek information and are usually more specific than the 'open' PQ for oral answer.

House of Commons, HC Deb
Vol. 306, Written Answers, cols. 268–71, 11 February 1998

Brazilian Mahogany
MR ALAN SIMPSON: To ask the Secretary of State for Scotland what amount of Brazilian mahogany has been *(a)* acquired and *(b)* specified by his Department in (i) 1996 and (ii) 1997; and for what purpose.

MR DEWAR: A Supplementary Notice regarding protecting the environment is issued by The Scottish Office with the terms and conditions of all contracts which requires suppliers to satisfy themselves that no product supplied to the Department contains materials derived from threatened species or threatened environments.

My Department has neither specified nor acquired any Brazilian mahogany in 1996 or 1997.

Public Opinion Research
MR DUNCAN: To ask the Secretary of State for Scotland how many contracts for public opinion research his Department has awarded since 1 May, if he will indicate the *(a)* purpose, *(b)* cost, *(c)* value and *(d)* duration of each contract; and which companies (i) bid for and (ii) were awarded each contract.

MR DEWAR *[holding answer 10 February 1998]*: My Department has not let any contracts for public opinion research since 1 May 1997. The Government are, of course, keen to consult with the public wherever appropriate and my Department does seek to assess the impact of current policy initiatives through its programmes of research.

Water Industry
MR SALMOND: To ask the Secretary of State for Scotland what was the level of water charges in current prices and the percentage annual change for each region of Scotland for each of the last five years; and if he will make a statement.

MR MACDONALD: The figures are as in the following tables.

1997–98 constant prices Band D water charges

	1993–94	1994–95	1995–96	1996–97	1997–98
East					
Borders	96.45	100.45	100.44	93.96	96.00
Forth Valley	52.71	51.32	48.63	49.56	54.00
Fife	66.17	64.42	67.66	69.18	75.00
Lothian	78.51	85.16	97.27	93.96	96.00

	1993–94	1994–95	1995–96	1996–97	1997–98
North					
Grampian	99.82	97.17	94.10	95.51	99.00
Highland	90.84	96.42	96.21	95.51	99.00
Tayside	71.78	75.34	78.24	79.50	84.50
Orkney	130.10	134.29	128.99	119.77	111.00
Shetland	118.94	126.65	125.14	119.77	111.00
Western Isles	205.24	211.81	196.65	119.77	111.00
West					
Dumfries and Galloway	94.21	91.71	88.02	92.93	95.40
Strathclyde	84.11	87.35	91.98	92.93	95.40

Year on year percentage change in 1997–98 constant prices Band D water charges

	1994–95	1995–96	1996–97	1997–98
East				
Borders	4	0	–6	2
Forth Valley	–3	–5	2	9
Fife	–3	5	2	8
Lothian	8	14	–3	2
North				
Grampian	–3	–3	1	4
Highland	6	0	–1	4
Tayside	5	4	2	6
Orkney	3	–4	–7	–7
Shetland	6	–1	–4	–7
Western Isles	3	–7	–39	–7
West				
Dumfries and Galloway	–3	–4	6	3
Strathclyde	4	5	1	3

Note: Adjusted to current prices by all items RPI index (forecast for 1997–98).

MR SALMOND: To ask the Secretary of State for Scotland if he will make a statement on the current proposed price changes for water services in Scotland; and when he will complete his examination of water charges submitted by the water authorities.

MR MACDONALD: My right hon. Friend is giving full and detailed consideration to this matter.

MR SALMOND: To ask the Secretary of State for Scotland what was the level of investment in water services in current prices and the percentage annual change, in Scotland, by region, for each of the last five years; and if he will make a statement.

MR MACDONALD: Since taking over water services in April 1996, the water authorities have made investment plans which cover the whole of their areas, and are not disaggregated to former regional areas.

Local Government Officials

MR SALMOND: To ask the Secretary of State for Scotland how many representations he has received concerning employment issues at West Dunbartonshire Council; and what discussions he has had with (a) COSLA, (b) West Dunbartonshire Council and (c) Unison concerning the procedures for terminating the contracts of senior council officials.

MR MACDONALD: One letter has been received by my right hon. Friend the Secretary of State. No discussions have taken place with the above bodies concerning the procedures for terminating contracts of senior council officials since, as independent corporate bodies, local authorities have powers to appoint officers on such reasonable terms and conditions as they think fit. In doing so they are, of course, required to comply with employment law. Ministers have no locus to intervene in such matters.

MR SALMOND: To ask the Secretary of State for Scotland what guidelines he has issued with reference to safeguarding the non-political status of senior council officials; what is the role of councillors in respect of the termination of employment contracts for senior council officials; and what guidelines he has issued regarding the termination of employment contracts for senior council officials.

MR MACDONALD: The Government believe it is important that councils and the public can rely on politically impartial service from senior local government officials, and that councils respect the political neutrality of officials. The political activities of certain local government officials are restricted by Part 1 of the Local Government and Housing Act 1989 and by regulations made by the Secretary of State under that Act. Scottish Development Department Circular 28/89 advised local authorities of the effects of the 1989 Act and letters of 25 April 1990 and 1 August 1990 from the Scottish Development Department advised local authorities about the regulations made under the 1989 Act. I have arranged for copies of these to be placed in the Library of the House. The Government intend to review the number and level of local government officers covered by political restrictions.

Councillors, as employers, have a role should they consider there is the need to terminate the contracts of Chief Executives or chief officers. Local government, through COSLA, have in place agreed procedures which allow councillors to report such matters and participate in any investigating and disciplinary committees which are set up. However, given the unique position of Chief Executives, arrangements are in place between the local authority employers and staff associations for any proposed disciplinary action to be investigated by an independent third party.

No guidelines have been issued by central government regarding the termination of employment contracts for senior council officials. This is a matter for local authorities themselves and would depend on the terms and conditions on which the appointment had been made.

MR SALMOND: To ask the Secretary of State for Scotland what role he has in respect of breaches of (a) the National Code of Local Government Conduct and (b) the Conditions of Service for Chief Officials of Local Authorities (Scotland).

MR MACDONALD: The Secretary of State has no role in respect of breaches of the National Code of Conduct. Neither has he any role in respect of breaches of the conditions of service for local authorities' chief officials which are entirely matters for local authorities as the employer.

The Government are, as part of our consideration of the ethical framework for local government in the light of the third report of the Committee on Standards in Public Life, considering what changes may be necessary to the code of conduct for councillors and how a revised code might be enforced.

Council Houses

MR WELSH: To ask the Secretary of State for Scotland if he will list for each unitary local authority the number of council houses affected by (a) dampness and (b) condensation at 31 March 1996.

MR MACDONALD: The table sets out local authorities' estimates of the position, as at 31 March 1996.

Local authority dwellings affected by dampness and/or condensation:
estimates as at 31 March 1996

	Dampness only	Condensation only	Both dampness and condensation
Aberdeen City	1,585	3,462	201
Aberdeenshire	64	1,480	0
Angus	2	625	0
Argyll and Bute	601	577	1,137
Clackmannan	386	175	329
Dumfries and Galloway (21)	–	–	–
Dundee City	596	8,605	570
East Ayrshire	1,373	7,159	1,823
East Dunbartonshire	683	77	392
East Lothian	625	0	1,408
East Renfrewshire	100	359	304
Edinburgh City	1,851	10,045	4,053
Falkirk	2,381	4,286	2,488
Fife	15	5,218	10
Glasgow City	15,821	25,340	14,824
Highland	1,169	3,400	653
Inverclyde	483	0	2,797
Midlothian	0	0	0
Moray	89	805	87
North Ayrshire	294	1,357	0
North Lanarkshire	10,164	17,473	13,725
Orkney	0	0	0
Perthshire and Kinross	122	1,843	388
Renfrewshire	3,152	3,193	1,897
Scottish Borders	61	44	157
Shetland	26	462	20
South Ayrshire	553	7,398	733
South Lanarkshire	191	1,805	2,020
Stirling	130	1,111	329
West Dunbartonshire	1,592	2,946	693
West Lothian	2,017	864	0
Western Isles	818	604	557
Scotland	46,944	110,713	51,595

(21) Figures not available

NOTE: Occasionally important statements by the Government are given in the form of written answer. See House of Commons Debates, Vol. 166, Written Answers, cols. 110–13, 30 January 1990 for the admission that previously the House of Commons had been misled over allegations that the Army had used 'dirty tricks' as part of the fight against terrorism in Northern Ireland.

The Procedure Committee noted the large increase in written questions since the 1960s and considered the case for rationing them. It decided not to propose this but urged (a) MPs to be sparing and selective in their designation of questions as priority, and thus to receive a quick answer; and (b) Ministers to endeavour to answer 'ordinary' written questions within a working week of their being tabled (HC 178 of 1990–91, paras 72, 75).

SECTION 3: **Law-making**

There are many varieties of legislation: statutes, delegated legislation, and what may be called quasi-legislation which can encompass administrative rules and guidance. Quasi-legislation can take the form, for example, of circulars from central departments, or codes of practice. The Americans refer to legislative activity carried out by administrative bodies as rule-making, and this includes what the British call delegated and quasi-legislation. It is important to realize that not all legislation will be made by Parliament. Our consideration of law-making will focus, first, on the assorted types of legislative measure and their rationale, and then on the methods for, and issues concerning, control of these legislative measures.

One of the characteristics of legislation is that it is empowering, that is it gives a public body the power to carry out tasks which the legislation also imposes upon the public body.

A: Types of legislative measure

(a) *Statute*

R. Rose, 'Law as a Resource of Public Policy'
(1986) 39 *Parliamentary Affairs*, pp. 297, 302–5

LAWS are a fundamental and unique resource of government. Without Acts of Parliament, force, personal preferences or momentary whim would justify the actions of government. Without laws, citizens would have no protection against arbitrary authority, no entitlements to social benefits, and no obligation to pay taxes. Without laws, civil servants would have no authority to act, or procedures to follow. Without laws, elections could not be held, for there would be no rules about who could vote, how votes should be counted, and who should be elected as MPs. In order to understand government, we must understand the uses of laws.

Until the growth of the twentieth-century welfare state, MPs viewed law as the principal resource of government. The characteristic concern of Parliament was not with public expenditure issues, but with the principles to be embodied in Acts of Parliament that involved questions of civil and political rights such as the franchise . . .

Once the importance of laws is recognised, the next question to address is: In what ways are laws important? The distinctive feature of law is that it is an expression of authority. It is not coercive in the sense that actions by the police may be coercive. Nor does the law consist of cash incentives to actions, as do the wages paid civil servants.

Statute laws establish parameters within which individuals and organisations may carry out their activities. Since the activities of society are heterogeneous, the parameters of laws are multiple. In order to understand the broad effect of laws, we need to understand the nature of laws as parameters; the extent of discretion that can be exercised within legal parameters; and then, whose activities have bounds set upon them by the statute book.

Parameters: more route maps than tethers. The traditional idea of laws as a set of commands and prohibitions ('Thou shalt . . .' or 'Thou shalt not . . .') presents a misleading picture of the uses of laws in the contemporary state. While there are some compelling and forbidding laws about crime, public health and safety, nine-tenths of statutes concern ways in which individuals or organisations may proceed of their own volition.

When a law sets parameters upon behaviour in society, it neither commands nor compels. Rules are promulgated which remain constant while the facts of specific circumstances vary. For example, laws governing marriage are hardly affected by characteristics of the partners of the marriage. Nor does the existence of such laws compel everyone to get married. Procedures are laid down which describe the actions that a pair of individuals should take if they want their union to be legally valid. There are few prohibitions, e.g. a minimum age, but these constrain the behaviour of a very, very small proportion of the population.

Most laws about the everyday activities of citizens are virtually unnoticed. For example, laws affecting property rights in a house; the content of foods; the conditions of driving a motor car or being a passenger on public transport; conditions of employment; or laws concerning broadcasting. This is not to say that such laws are unnecessary. Instead of involving the compulsion and prohibition of acts, most laws give guidance about ways to maintain a well ordered society.

Most contemporary laws are best conceived as a route map, laying down conditions by which one may proceed. Their relevance is contingent, taking the form of 'If . . . then' propositions. For example, 'If you want to drive a car, then you must have a driver's licence, the car must be licensed and insured, and you must drive within the traffic code'. Most laws do not tether behaviour in the sense of confining a person to act within narrowly circumscribed limits.

Scope for discretion. Both jurisprudential and sociological analyses emphasise that even the most carefully stated statute cannot control 100 per cent of behaviour. Violations of the law occur in every society. Yet violations are only a small proportion of total social activity, e.g. fraud arises in only a very small percentage of market transactions, and violent assault or murder in an infinitesimal proportion of social interactions.

The most significant limitation upon law is the existence of 'gaps' that give some latitude for discretion, i.e. choice within the parameters of the statute book. In the real world, the statute book is subject to multiple imperfections – vagueness of language, omissions, and the incapacity to anticipate every possible concatenation of events. In falling short of the perfection of an ideal-type, it is no different from administration, markets, or democracy itself. Discretion can be found in four main areas.

(a) *Judges* inevitably are faced with 'hard' cases, that is, circumstances in which lawyers dispute how the law is to be interpreted and applied to the facts of a particular case. Bell describes judges as acting as interstitial lesiglators: 'There are situations where the legal audience would recognise that there is no single clear solution to a case and that several possible solutions are at least arguable. At the same time, it must be recognised that, in presenting his decision, the judge has to justify himself within the legal materials, showing how the solution fits within existing legal prescriptions and standards. It is thus somewhat misleading to suggest that the law in such situations "runs out", as if anything at all could be used to fill the "gap".'

(b) *Executive lawmaking* occurs through the issuance of a variety of rules and regulations that can be made pursuant to Acts of Parliament; in Britain these measures can conveniently be described as

Statutory Instruments. Acts of Parliament establish the parameters within which executive rule-making may be done; these are necessarily more confined than those of the Act itself. Statutory instruments typically affect procedures for putting an Act into effect, or fill out details that may be negotiated with subjects of regulation, or are likely to vary from time to time in relation to changing economic or social conditions. The limited political significance of this form of executive rulemaking is shown by the fact that less than one per cent of Statutory Instruments are deemed worthy of careful scrutiny by the parliamentary committee exercising oversight of them. The chief reason is that these regulations are likely to be agreed with affected parties in advance of their promulgation.

British membership of the European Community has created procedures authorised by Act of Parliament that enable Community laws and regulations to be put into effect by actions of the British government, without recourse to conventional procedures for a bill becoming a law. This too has led to the establishment of select committees in Parliament to monitor actions thus taken. Notwithstanding the significance of the principle, the practical political effect has been slight.

(c) *Administrative discretion* is an element in the implementation of a new Act of Parliament, and in the routine operation of many acts. The degree of discretion depends upon the extent to which laws and regulations can prescribe the parameters of action. The extent is variable: pensions officials, postal clerks and airline pilots have much less discretion than public employees who deliver services to citizens in conditions in which the services provided cannot be tightly circumscribed nor their behaviour closely monitored, for example policemen, teachers, doctors and social workers.

Lipsky argues that 'street-level' public employees are not rule-bound bureaucrats but individuals with a significant degree of discretion to decide how to treat individuals seeking their services. Just as the law sets parameters upon what officials may do, so the informal norms and routines of low-level officials may reciprocally constrain what the law can achieve. While awareness of an element of discretion is an important caution against excessive legalism, it does not justify Lipsky writing as if public policies could be carried out by ignoring or flouting the parameters of the law.

(d) *Adaptive behaviour* can be undertaken by citizens in ways that recognise the parameters of the law, but may not be what was anticipated by lawmakers. Within the parameters of any Act of Parliament citizens are free to behave in many ways. Adaptive behaviour is most familiar in tax avoidance, that is, the alteration of behaviour to lessen the legal liability to taxation. By definition, tax avoidance (e.g. working a limited number of hours a week to avoid national insurance tax, or converting income subject to a high marginal income tax rate into a capital gain subject to a lower rate) is within the law. But it is also action taken to avoid what would otherwise be undesirable consequences.

In a mixed society the role of law is not so much that of telling people what they must and must not do; it is to establish rules and regulations under which individuals and organisations can carry out their everyday affairs in ways that are orderly, predictable and recognised and accepted by all concerned. Only in a totalitarian society could the law claim to be all-powerful. A major contribution of law to public policy in a free society is that it establishes parameters within which individuals and organisations can then be free to pursue what they regard as their own wellbeing and interests. This liberal idea of the limits of laws poses problems for democratic socialists who want certain outcomes, for example, equality of educational opportunity, but do not want to use laws to prohibit private education or compel everyone to have their children educated at state schools.

NOTE: Legislation can be divided into public and private. Rose discussed public statutes, which are normally initiated by the government but may be introduced by MPs as a Private Member's Bill. Private legislation may confer powers or benefits on particular individuals or bodies, which may be in addition to, or in conflict with, the general law. Such measures will be promoted by the relevant individuals or bodies such as local authorities, universities, or companies. A hybrid bill is one, usually initiated by the government, which is public in nature but will affect private rights. As, for example, with the Channel Tunnel, where power may be given to a Minister to acquire specified land.

(b) Delegated legislation

Report of the Committee on Ministers' Powers
Cmd 4046, pp. 51–2

Necessity for Delegation
We have already expressed the view that the system of delegated legislation is both legitimate and constitutionally desirable for certain purposes, within certain limits, and under certain safeguards. We proceed to set out briefly – mostly by way of recapitulation – the reasons which have led us to this conclusion:–

(1) Pressure upon Parliamentary time is great. The more procedure and subordinate matters can be withdrawn from detailed Parliamentary discussion, the greater will be the time which Parliament can devote to the consideration of essential principles in legislation.

(2) The subject matter of modern legislation is very often of a technical nature. Apart from the broad principles involved, technical matters are difficult to include in a Bill, since they cannot be effectively discussed in Parliament. . . .

(3) If large and complex schemes of reform are to be given technical shape, it is difficult to work out the administrative machinery in time to insert in the Bill all the provisions required; it is impossible to foresee all the contingencies and local conditions for which provision must eventually be made. . . .

(4) The practice, further, is valuable because it provides for a power of constant adaptation to unknown future conditions without the necessity of amending legislation. Flexibility is essential. The method of delegated legislation permits of the rapid utilisation of experience, and enables the results of consultation with interests affected by the operation of new Acts to be translated into practice. . . .

(5) The practice, again, permits of experiment being made and thus affords an opportunity, otherwise difficult to ensure, of utilising the lessons of experience. The advantage of this in matters, for instance, like town planning, is . . . obvious. . . .

(6) In a modern State there are many occasions when there is a sudden need of legislative action. For many such needs delegated legislation is the only convenient or even possible remedy. No doubt, where there is time, on legislative issues of great magnitude, it is right that Parliament itself should either decide what the broad outlines of the legislation shall be, or at least indicate the general scope of the delegated powers which it considers are called for by the occasion.

But emergency and urgency are matters of degree; and the type of need may be of greater or less national importance. It may be not only prudent but vital for Parliament to arm the executive Government in advance with almost plenary power to meet occasions of emergency, which affect the whole nation – as in the extreme case of the Defence of the Realm Acts in the Great War, where the exigency had arisen; or in the less extreme case of the Emergency Powers Act, 1920, where the exigency had not arisen but power was conferred to meet emergencies that might arise in future. . . .

But the measure of the need should be the measure alike of the power and of its limitation. It is of the essence of constitutional Government that the normal control of Parliament should not be suspended either to a greater degree, or for a longer time, than the exigency demands. . . .

NOTE: Delegated legislation may take several forms – regulations, Orders in Council, rules, and orders. Parliament usually makes delegated legislation as statutory instruments, the passage of which is governed by the Statutory Instruments Act 1946. The more important pieces of delegated legislation are Orders in Council. Legislative measures which would have been passed as Acts of the Northern Ireland Parliament before it was prorogued are now passed as Orders in Council.

There is an overlap between delegated legislation and administrative rules of quasi-legislation, even though the legal form of these measures differ. The following extract suggests a classification of administrative rules based on function.

(c) *Quasi-legislation*

R. Baldwin & J. Houghton, 'Circular Arguments: The Status and Legitimacy of Administrative Rules'
[1986] *Public Law* 239, at pp. 241–45

(1) Procedural Rules
Most bodies that distribute licences or money publish documents describing the procedures to be adopted. Thus, the Gaming Board and the Independent Broadcasting Authority instruct applicants for licences to follow set procedures. The Prison Rules lay down disciplinary procedures for prisoners and new police codes lay down practices to be followed in dealing with suspects and arrested persons. A principal issue is whether such rules are mandatory or directory.

(2) Interpretative Guides
This heading covers all official statements of departmental or agency policy, explanations of how terms or rules will be interpreted or applied, expressions of criteria to be followed, standards to be enforced or considerations to be taken into account. In Gifford's terms, this would include all 'decisional referents'' where of general applicability.

(3) Instructions to Officials
Although resembling interpretative guides in some respects, these instructions are principally aimed not at offering guidance to parties outside a bureaucracy but at controlling the exercise of powers within that bureaucracy. They aim not to inform citizens but to impose internal order – usually so as to facilitate planning or to encourage consistency. Strong arguments have been made for the publication of all such rules but secrecy is sustained by the desire to avoid having to justify them in public. Examples of low-visibility instructions are Prison Department Circulars, Standing Orders and Regulations and Home Office Circulars to Chief Constables.

A principal worry about secret codes is that they may conflict with published law. Thus, there was concern in 1984 when *The Observer* and the Legal Action Group exposed the operation of the Department of Health and Social Security's secret 'L' Code, a provision of which instructed legal aid assessment officers to pass on information to other officials in breach of the confidentiality provisions of section 22 of the Legal Aid Act 1974.

(4) Prescriptive/Evidential Rules
In some cases, regulatory bodies may want to do more than describe their policies or instruct their officials as to how to act: they may want to tell people what to do. It is of course possible to influence the behaviour of a regulated group by issuing a strong interpretative guide. ('We will only take action as provided for in the statute if conditions A, B, and C are met') or by publishing similarly formulated instructions to officials. Matters can be taken a step further, however, by prescribing courses of action on the understanding that a sanction exists at law (in primary or delegated legislation) or administratively (e.g. through non-allocation of a licence or other item of largesse). A common posture for such a 'prescriptive' rule is that of 'guide to compliance' with other legislation. Sanctions are usually indirect; thus, breach of the rule or code might not in itself lead to legal liability under a parent or associate rule.

A well-known example is the Highway Code. Breach of this is not an offence in itself but it may be taken into account in judging civil or criminal liability. Under the Health and Safety at Work Act 1974, 'approved codes of practice' may be issued by the Health and Safety Commission so as to 'provide practical guidance' in relation to the requirements of the parent Act or regulations. In the employment field, a number of codes offer 'practical guidance' but have an evidential role also. The Employment Act 1980 states that any provisions of the Secretary of State's Code of Practice on Picketing (1980) may be taken into account in proceedings before a court or tribunal. It is this code which advises that pickets should in general not exceed six at any entrance to a workplace. As has been clear from the miners' dispute of 1984, the 'guidance' offered by such a code may take a most compelling form. It may be treated by enforcement officials as if it were primary legislation.

Less contentious, perhaps, are the codes of practice on industrial relations. Power to issue these is given to the Advisory, Conciliation and Arbitration Service (ACAS), the Equal Opportunities Commission and the Commission for Racial Equality. Under the Employment Protection Act 1975, section 6, the ACAS codes again have evidential status: they are admissible in evidence and a tribunal or arbitration committee is specifically empowered to take relevant codes into account in determining issues.

Prescriptive rules may be backed up with sanctions other than the civil or criminal law such as disciplinary action. This is the case with the Codes of Practice that replace the Judges' Rules under the terms of the Police and Criminal Evidence Act. The Secretary of State issues codes on detention, treatment, questioning, identification of suspects, searches of premises, seizure and stops and searches. Failure to observe the terms of these codes may render police officers liable to disciplinary sanctions but will not give rise to criminal or civil liability or to the automatic exclusion of evidence.

(5) Commendatory Rules

The prescriptive model of rule involves instruction plus some variety of (often indirect) sanction. Commendation, on the other hand, has as its principal function the recommending of some course of action. Failure to adhere will not involve direct or indirect legal liability. A good example of commendations within a hierarchy of rules is provided in health and safety regulation. Primary duties are *statutory* and are set out in the Health and Safety at Work Act 1974 (see sections 2–9). These are made more specific in the Secretary of State's *regulations*, breach of which involves criminal liability and may be admissible in evidence in civil proceedings. *Codes of practice*, we have noted, offer 'practical guidance', are of evidential value and may reverse the onus of proof. *Guidance notes* constitute the lowest tier of the system. These are issued by the Health and Safety Commission and Executive: they advise on how safety objectives may be achieved, they encourage and recommend courses of action but they deal with issues beyond the area of legal sanction and lack legal force.

Commendatory rules thus do not accord with Austinian notions of threat plus sanction: they are more attuned to a facilitative role. Some rules of evidential significance might be considered commendations (e.g. the ACAS industrial relations codes) and here is the main overlap with prescriptive rules.

(6) Voluntary Codes

Self-regulatory codes differ from externally-imposed prescriptions in their origins and sanctions. Usually employed to stave off government regulation by upholding standards within a defined interest group, they may nevertheless carry considerable force: expulsion from the group for breach of a code may close down a business. The City Code on Takeovers and Mergers is a prime example of a voluntary code. It is issued by the Council for the Securities Industry (CSI) and offers a codification of good standards of commercial behaviour. The code has a governmental role insofar as breaches stand to be investigated by the Department of Trade.

Instances of such codes are to be found in many industries, such as advertising and housebuilding. In recent years, business self-regulation has blossomed, especially where relations with consumers are affected and deviant members of associations may be fined. Many businesses indulge in voluntary labelling, publish codes of ethics and good practice and some of these are stamped with the approval of the Office of Fair Trading. Indeed, section 124 (3) of the Fair Trading Act 1973 imposes a duty on the Director-General of Fair Trading to encourage trade associations to prepare codes of practice for guidance in promoting consumer interests and over 20 codes were approved in the period 1974–84.

The rules of domestic and professional bodies may have legal effects deriving from the law of contract, but the governmental role of many associations has led a leading text to liken such rules more to delegated legislation than to the terms of a contract.

(7) Rules of Practice, Management or Operation
Some rules have considerable effect without being directly normative. These are what Megarry called 'subject-and-subject' rules, 'consisting of arrangements made by administrative bodies which affect the operation of the law between one subject and another'. Thus, a new policy or enforcement practice would come under this heading.

The extra-statutory concessions made by the Commissioners for Inland Revenue are in point. Sometimes the Commissioners will act according to a stated policy, at others they will exercise discretion *ad hoc*. The courts have been uncertain in their responses. In *IRC* v *Korner* [1979] 1 All ER 679, Lord Upjohn described an unpublished concession as conducive to 'great justice between the Crown and the subject'. On the other hand, Lord Parker CJ has talked of 'the word of the Minister outweighing the law of the land' and Lord Radcliffe of 'opening the door of Parliament'. More recently in the Court of Appeal, Lawton LJ described the IRC's decision to cancel a tax advantage as 'a managerial discretion' which was reviewable only where there was an abuse of power.

(8) Consultative Devices and Administrative Pronouncements
There is no distinct line between legal and administrative rules or, indeed, between rules and other forms of pronouncement such as decisions. It is clear, however, that a statement may have normative effects in certain circumstances or from some perspectives and it may lack them in a different context. To adhere to rigid definitions or conceptual distinctions is therefore to fall into a trap.

Our final group is thus something of a safety-net. It covers those pronouncements which fit into none of the other groups but which have a significance that goes beyond the individual case. Principal amongst these are consultative statements. These often involve draft outlines of agency or departmental policy and invite comments. As such, they form a halfway house in the rule-making or adjudicative processes. They allow an expression of policy views without undertaking a rigid commitment.

NOTE: See also G. Ganz, *Quasi-Legislation: Some Recent Developments in Secondary Legislation* (1987) and R. Baldwin, *Rules and Government* (1995).

(d) *Prerogative*

According to Blackstone, the Royal Prerogative is 'singular and eccentrical', something which applies to rights and capacities only enjoyed by the Monarch. The *Case of Proclamations* (1611) 12 Co Rep 74 and the Bill of Rights 1689 (see *ante* p. 64) have made it clear that the prerogative cannot be used as a means to bypass Parliament in order to change the general law of the land. Today the prerogative is restricted to the conduct of foreign affairs; the declaration of war, and the disposition of the armed forces; the appointment of civil servants and Ministers, Privy Councillors, judges, and bishops; the conferral of peerages and honours; the dissolution of Parliament.

What is the status of the prerogative where legislation has been passed concerning an area within the scope of the prerogative?

Attorney-General v *De Keyser's Royal Hotel Ltd*
[1920] AC 508 House of Lords

During the First World War the Crown took possession of the respondents' hotel in order to house staff of the Royal Flying Corps. The Crown purported to do this under the authority of the Defence of the Realm Regulations. The Crown contended that compensation was not payable to the respondents because there still existed a residue of the prerogative which permitted temporary occupation of a subject's property in time of war. This residue of the prerogative was exercised under the regulations. The respondents contended that the Defence Act 1842 required that compensation should be paid.

LORD ATKINSON: . . . It is quite obvious that it would be useless and meaningless for the Legislature to impose restrictions and limitations upon, and to attach conditions to, the exercise by the Crown of the powers conferred by a statute, if the Crown were free at its pleasure to disregard these provisions, and by virtue of its prerogative do the very thing the statutes empowered it to do. One cannot in the construction of a statute attribute to the Legislature (in the absence of compelling words) an intention so absurd. It was suggested that when a statute is passed empowering the Crown to do a certain thing which it might theretofore have done by virtue of its prerogative, the prerogative is merged in the statute. I confess I do not think the word 'merged' is happily chosen. I should prefer to say that when such a statute, expressing the will and intention of the King and of the three estates of the realm, is passed, it abridges the Royal Prerogative while it is in force to this extent: that the Crown can only do the particular thing under and in accordance with the statutory provisions, and that its prerogative power to do that thing is in abeyance. Whichever mode of expression be used, the result intended to be indicated is, I think, the same – namely, that after the statute has been passed, and while it is in force, the thing it empowers the Crown to do can thenceforth only be done by and under the statute, and subject to all the limitations, restrictions and conditions by it imposed, however unrestricted the Royal Prerogative may theretofore have been.

[Lord Atkinson found that the proper construction of the regulations meant that the 1842 statute governed the occupation and that compensation under that statute was payable. Lords Dunedin, Moulton, Sumner and Parmoor delivered concurring speeches.]

Appeal dismissed.

NOTE: In *Studies in Constitutional Law* (1999), at pp. 274–5, Munro argues that if a statute which overlapped with the prerogative was repealed, then the prerogative would be restored to the position it had before that statute was enacted. Thus only express statutory provision can abolish the prerogative.

(e) *European Communities legislation*

The legislative powers of the EC are laid down in Article 249 (ex 189) of the EC Treaty (see *ante* p. 126). Regulations, directives, and decisions are binding, but recommendations and opinions are not. The procedural requirements specified in Article 253 (ex 190) (see *ante* p. 128) must be carried out otherwise the measure could be annulled under Articles 230 and 231 (ex 173 and 174) (see *ante* pp. 121–22). Although Article 254 (ex 191) only requires publication of regulations and some directives, other directives are also published, as are many decisions.

Some legislation implementing EC measures will be passed by Parliament in the form of Orders in Council or rules and regulations. This is provided for in s. 2(2) of the European Communities Act 1972 (see *ante* p. 141).

Statutes are enacted to ratify treaty amendments, such as the SEA which was effected by the European Communities (Amendment) Act 1986.

B: Control

(a) *Consultation*

D. R. Miers and A. C. Page, *Legislation*
(2nd edn, 1990), pp. 39–43

Once it has been decided that legislation is desirable, a detailed legislative proposal must be formulated. This will be undertaken within the responsible department, and the proposal will normally go through a number of drafts. Achieving a measure of coherence in government policy requires that views of other affected departments be taken into account in the preparation of proposals. For example, the Treasury must be consulted if public resources are involved, as must the Scottish, Welsh and Northern Ireland Offices if their interests are affected. Where Cabinet approval for the introduction of the measure has been obtained, consultations between the responsible department and interested departments take place on the basis of a draft memorandum. In addition, the formulation of major proposals will be supervised by the appropriate Cabinet policy committee. Where the approval of the Cabinet has not been previously obtained, it will be sought on the basis of the memorandum as revised in the light of such preliminary consultations as have taken place.

Whereas consultation within government is mandatory, consultation with outside interests takes place at the discretion of government. The extent of such consultation varies: some proposals are the subject of extensive consultation, others very little. The extent to which affected interests are consulted also varies. On major issues of party policy the government may choose not to consult affected interests (particularly those traditionally opposed to it), though even here it may do so if only to minimise disagreement. In general, however, sectional and in particular producer groups are consulted to a much greater extent than other groups. In the absence of the direct and permanent access to government enjoyed by sectional groups, cause groups' efforts are more visibly directed towards influencing the media and lobbying MPs.

How can we account for the greater likelihood of sectional group involvement in the preparation of legislation? Most commonly it is attributed to a shared pluralist conception of authority on the part of government and outside interests. Thus, Beer attributes their greater involvement to 'the widespread acceptance of functional representation in British political culture.' Acceptance of functional representation has in turn meant that: 'It has now almost become a convention of the constitution that the interests likely to be affected by developments in public policy have, through their representative associations, a right to be consulted by policy makers,' and that governments 'are regarded as having a corresponding duty to consult before taking final decisions.' Whether these expectations as to the way in which public, including legislative, power will be examined are as widely shared today as they were 10 to 20 years ago is doubtful. But even if they are not, there remain strong incentives for government to consult. A failure to consult may make the passage of the legislation more difficult; more importantly, it may prejudice its successful implementation and thereby the attainment of the government's objectives. The brute fact is that these groups possess the capacity to 'limit, deflect and even frustrate government initiatives.' For this reason, if no other, government seeks through consultation to arrive at an understanding with them beforehand.

Commentators rightly emphasise the benefits derived from the involvement of these groups by both the groups themselves and government. For the groups, their involvement constitutes a procedural guarantee that their interests and views will be given a hearing if not reflected in the content of proposals. For government, on the other hand, the groups' expertise and advice may be crucial to the formulation of workable proposals and their acquiescence, if not active co-operation, may be equally vital to the successful implementation of proposals. These groups are thus seen as important and necessary channels of communication which parallel representation through the electoral system. Without their activity, Finer observes, party rule would be 'a rigid and ignorant tyranny,' and public administration 'a rigid and stupid bureaucracy.' Their privileged position in relation to government does, however, carry with it the danger that interests other than those immediately involved will be ignored.

The consultative process itself varies in its formality. Consultation may take place on the basis of a Green Paper published with Cabinet approval on which the views of interested parties are sought. Publication of the government's proposals in the form of a White Paper implies, instead, that the government is committed to at least the main principles of the policy outlined and the scope for consultation is correspondingly reduced. More commonly, however, consultation takes place on the basis of informal and private communications between departments and affected interests.

Consultation need not of course be confined to any single stage in the preparation of a proposal. A group's influence on a proposal cannot be determined therefore solely by reference to the extent to which it is formally consulted during its preparation. Thus it may, for example, have been the prime mover in the identification of an issue, or its views may have been canvassed and reflected in the report of a committee upon which legislation is ultimately based. Where the group has not had the opportunity of expressing its views previously, its influence will depend, in part, on the stage of the preparatory process at which it is consulted and, in particular, on whether it is consulted before the principles of the legislation have been settled.

> The most effective time for groups to operate is after a decision to legislate has been taken, but before a Bill has actually been drafted and published. Once the government has publicly committed itself to the main lines of a Bill, disagreement and opposition by interested parties can only usually be manifested by public or parliamentary campaigns, which groups are not well-fitted to undertake. Given the structure of public decision-making in Britain, in which Parliament plays a distinctly subordinate role, this line of action is usually far less likely to be successful than attempting to persuade the Minister.'

A group's influence will also depend on whether or not there is any scope for negotiation: there is a fundamental distinction between consultation involving simply an expression of views (for example, on a Green Paper or in response to specific requests) and consultation involving negotiation or actual bargaining between the parties. Whereas the views expressed in consultation of the former type may or may not be taken into account by the government, the latter implies a much greater involvement of groups in the formulation of the proposal and the effective renunciation by government of unilateral decision-making. As Hartley and Griffith point out:

> The Department will tell those whom it chooses to consult . . . what are the broad intentions of the Government, what is sought to be achieved by the Bill then being put together, and what means are proposed. On particular matters, or when asked by affected interests, the department may go into more detail, sometimes putting forward alternatives and seeking the opinion of those interested on the various merits of the alternatives. Where, as is often the case, the co-operation of the affected interests is highly desirable in order to make the Bill most effective in practice, something very like a bargain may be struck and undertakings may be given on both sides.

NOTE: The courts have distinguished between 'legislative' and 'administrative' activity in respect of consultation.

Bates v *Lord Hailsham of St Marylebone*
[1972] 1 WLR 1373, Chancery Division

Under s. 56(3) of the Solicitors Act 1957, drafts of orders prescribing solicitors' remuneration in respect of non-contentious business were required to be sent to the Council of the Law Society by the Lord Chancellor. The committee which had the power to make the orders had to consider any written observations from the Council of the Law Society before making such orders.

The committee proposed an order which was sent in draft to the Law Society. The claimant was a member of the British Legal Association which objected to the proposed order. This body, which had some 2,900 members, wished to delay the making of the order so that there might be more consultation with the legal profession. The claimant sought a declaration that, if an order was made without the British Legal Association first being consulted, then this would be *ultra vires*.

MEGARRY J: . . . Mr Nicholls relied on *Reg.* v *Liverpool Corporation, Ex parte Liverpool Taxi Fleet Operators' Association* [1972] 2 QB 299; and he read me some passages from the judgments of Lord Denning MR and Roskill LJ. It cannot often happen that words uttered by a judge in his judicial capacity will, within six months, be cited against him in his personal capacity as defendant; yet that is the position here. The case was far removed from the present case. It concerned the exercise by a city council of its powers to licence hackney carriages, and a public undertaking given by the chairman of the relevant committee which the council soon proceeded to ignore. The case supports propositions relating to the duty of a body to act fairly when exercising administrative functions under a statutory power: see at pp. 307, 308 and 310. Accordingly, in deciding the policy to be applied as to the number of licences to grant, there was a duty to hear those who would be likely to be affected. It is plain that no legislation was involved: the question was one of the policy to be adopted in the exercise of a statutory power to grant licences.

In the present case, the committee in question has an entirely different function: it is legislative rather than administrative or executive. The function of the committee is to make or refuse to make a legislative instrument under delegated powers. The order, when made, will lay down the remuneration for solicitors generally; and the terms of the order will have to be considered and construed and applied in numberless cases in the future. Let me accept that in the sphere of the so-called quasi-judicial the rules of natural justice run, and that in the administrative or executive field there is a general duty of fairness. Nevertheless, these considerations do not seem to me to affect the process of legislation, whether primary or delegated. Many of those affected by delegated legislation, and affected very substantially, are never consulted in the process of enacting that legislation: and yet they have no remedy. Of course, the informal consultation of representative bodies by the legislative authority is a commonplace; but although a few statutes have specifically provided for a general process of publishing draft delegated legislation and considering objections (see, for example, the Factories Act 1961, Schedule 4), I do not know of any implied right to be consulted or make objections, or any principle upon which the courts may enjoin the legislative process at the suit of those who contend that insufficient time for consultation and consideration has been given. I accept that the fact that the order will take the form of a statutory instrument does not per se make it immune from attack, whether by injunction or otherwise; but what is important is not its form but its nature, which is plainly legislative. . . .

Order accordingly.

NOTE: The distinction between 'administrative' and 'legislative' is a fine one. In *R* v *Secretary of State for the Environment, ex parte Brent LBC* [1982] QB 593, local authorities successfully argued that the Minister was under a duty to hear their representations before exercising powers under delegated legislation to reduce their rate support grant.

In another case concerning lawyers' remuneration, representatives of the Bar argued that they had a legitimate expectation of being consulted about regulations to be made under the Legal Aid Act 1974. The point was not decided because the case was settled.

Sometimes there is a statutory requirement to consult. Such a requirement may be derogated from, as in social security, where the Minister need not consult the Social Security Advisory Committee about draft regulations if it is inexpedient to do so by reason of urgency (Social Security Administration Act 1992, s. 173(1)(a)).

Where a consultation obligation is imposed in respect of legislation, what will be considered to be sufficient consultation?

R v *Secretary of State for Social Services, ex parte Association of Metropolitan Authorities*
[1986] 1 WLR 1, Queen's Bench Division

Before making regulations constituting the housing benefits scheme, the Minister was required, by s. 36(1) of the Social Security and Housing Benefits Act 1982, to consult with organizations which appeared to him to be representative of the housing authorities concerned. The applicant was such an organization whose views had been sought by the Minister's officials on proposed amendments to the 1982 regulations. The consultative letter was written on 16 November 1984 and received by the applicant on 22 November. A response was requested by 30 November. The applicant complained about the shortness of time and asked for an extension so that its advisers could be consulted. On 4 December officials wrote to the applicant seeking its views on further proposed amendments. No draft of the proposals was forwarded and no mention was made of a material feature which required local authorities to investigate whether housing benefit claimants had created joint tenancies so as to gain from the housing benefit scheme. A response was requested by 12 December. The applicant answered the first letter on 7 December and sent brief comments about the second letter on 13 December. The Housing Benefits Amendment (No. 4) Order Regulations 1984 were made on 17 December and came into effect on 19 December. The applicant sought, *inter alia*, a declaration that the Minister had not exercised his duty under s. 36(1) of the Act of 1982, and an order of *certiorari* to quash the regulations because of the failure to consult.

WEBSTER J: . . . There is no general principle to be extracted from the case law as to what kind or amount of consultation is required before delegated legislation, of which consultation is a precondition, can validly be made. But in any context the essence of consultation is the communication of a genuine invitation to give advice and a genuine receipt of that advice. In my view it must go without saying that to achieve consultation sufficient information must be supplied by the consulting to the consulted party to enable it to tender helpful advice. Sufficient time must be given by the consulting to the consulted party to enable it to do that, and sufficient time must be available for such advice to be considered by the consulting party. Sufficient, in that context, does not mean ample, but at least enough to enable the relevant purpose to be fulfilled. By helpful advice, in this context, I mean sufficiently informed and considered information or advice about aspects of the form or substance of the proposals, or their implications for the consulted party, being aspects material to the implementation of the proposal as to which the Secretary of State might not be fully informed or advised and as to which the party consulted might have relevant information or advice to offer.

These propositions, as it seems to me, can partly be derived from, and are wholly consistent with, the decisions and various dicta, which I need not enumerate, in *Rollo v Minister of Town and Country Planning* [1948] 1 All ER 13 and *Port Louis Corporation v Attorney-General of Mauritius* [1965] AC 1111.

. . . In the present case, looking at the 'whole scope and purpose' of the Act of 1982, one matter which stands out is that its day-to-day administration is in the hands of local housing authorities who bear 10 per cent of the cost of the scheme. It is common ground that in them resides the direct expertise necessary to administer schemes made under the Act on a day-to-day basis. For these reasons, if for no other, I conclude that the obligation laid on the Secretary of State to consult organisations representative of those authorities is mandatory, not directory.

The last question of principle to be decided before turning to the facts is the test to be applied to the facts as I find them for the purposes of judicial review. . . . [T]o what extent is it for the Secretary of State, not the court, to judge how much consultation is necessary and how long is to be given for it? The answer to that question may qualify the word 'sufficient' in the requirements of consultation which I have set out above. . . .

[T]he first point to note is that the power to make the regulations is conferred on the Secretary of State and that his is the duty to consult. Save for those consulted, no one else is involved in the making of the regulations. Secondly, both the form or substance of new regulations and the time allowed for consulting, before making them, may well depend in whole or in part on matters of a political nature, as to the force and implications of which it would be reasonable to expect the Secretary of State, rather than the court, to be the best judge. Thirdly, issues may well be raised after the making of the regulations as to the detailed merits of one or other reason for making them, or as to the precise degree of urgency required in their making, issues which have been raised on this application. Those issues cannot be said to be wholly irrelevant to a challenge to the vires of the regulations, and Mr Beloff has not submitted that they are irrelevant; but at the same time it would seem to me to be inherently improbable that the question of the vires of the regulations should depend upon precise findings of fact on issues such as those. In my view, therefore, the court, when considering the question whether the consultation required by section 36 (1) was in substance carried out, should have regard not so much to the actual facts which preceded the making of the regulations as to the material before the Secretary of State when he made the regulations, that material including facts or information as it appeared or must have appeared to him acting in good faith, and any judgments made or opinions expressed to him before the making of the regulations about those facts which appear or could have appeared to him to be reasonable. The department's good faith is not challenged on this application.

The effect of treating as material the facts as they appeared to the Secretary of State, and not necessarily as they were, is to give a certain flexibility to the notions of sufficiency, sufficient information, sufficient time and sufficiently informed and considered information and advice in my home-spun attempt to define proper consultation. Thus, it can have the effect that what would be sufficient information or time in one case might be more or less than sufficient in another, depending on the relative degrees of urgency and the nature of the proposed regulation. There is no degree of urgency, however, which absolves the Secretary of State from the obligation to consult at all.

Upon consideration of the facts, his Lordship said that the Minister's view on the urgency of the need for the amending regulations, and the nature of the proposed amendments justified requiring comments to be expressed quickly but not in so short a period which meant that the comments would be insufficiently informed or insufficiently considered. When account was also taken of the fact that the applicant had no notice of a material feature until after the regulations were made, his

Lordship concluded that the Minister had not discharged his duty to consult before making the regulations.

Having decided that the provisions of section 36(1) are mandatory and that they were not complied with before the regulations were made, I now have to consider the relief which I should give to the association. They ask me to quash the regulations. I do not think that I should do so.

I acknowledge, with respect, that in the ordinary case a decision – I emphasize the word 'decision' – made ultra vires is likely to be set aside in accordance with the dictum of Lord Diplock in *Grunwick Processing Laboratories Ltd* v *Advisory, Conciliation and Arbitration Service* [1978] AC 655, 695, where he said:

> My Lords, where a statutory authority has acted ultra vires any person who would be affected by its act if it were valid is normally entitled ex debito justiciae to have it set aside
> . . .

But whereas the ordinary case is that of a ministerial departmental decision, which adversely affects the rights of one person or of a class of persons, and which can be struck down without, usually, more than individual or local implications, in this case the association seeks to strike down regulations which have become part of the public law of the land. Although I have been shown and have found no authority to support the proposition, I suspect that it is not necessarily to be regarded as the normal practice, where delegated legislation is held to be ultra vires, to revoke the instrument, but that the inclination would be the other way, in the absence of special circumstances making it desirable to revoke that instrument. But in principle I treat the matter as one of pure discretion and so treating it decline to revoke the instrument for the following reasons, no particular significance being attached to the order in which I state them.

Although six organisations were and are habitually consulted in this context, only one of them has applied for revocation of the instrument and that one applies only on the ground that it was not properly consulted. It makes no formal complaint that the other organisations were not consulted. Although the association complains about the substance of the regulations, it is apparent that its principal complaint throughout is, and has been, the absence of proper consultation and it and other organisations were able to express some, albeit in a sense piecemeal, views about the proposal which apparently the department took into account before making the regulations, but without, be it noted, any effort whatsoever on the November or December amendments. The regulations have been in force for about six months and, although their implementation creates difficulties for some at least of the housing authorities who have to administer them, those authorities must by now have adapted themselves as best they can to those difficulties. If, however, the regulations were to be revoked all applicants who had been refused benefit because of the new regulations would be entitled to make fresh claims, and all authorities would be required to consider each such claim.

Finally, the Housing Benefits Amendment (No. 4) Regulations 1984 have been consolidated into the Housing Benefits Regulations 1985 (S.I. 1985 No. 677), which were made on 29 April 1985, laid before Parliament on 30 April and came into operation and indeed have come into operation for the most part, today, 21 May. Those regulations are not at present challenged. If, therefore, the Housing Benefits Amendment (No. 4) Regulations 1984 were to be revoked, and so long as the Regulations of 1985 remain valid, any person entitled to reconsideration of his claim to benefit would, if successful, at best be entitled to benefits for about six months. For all these reasons, I refuse, in the exercise of my discretion, to revoke the Housing Benefits Amendment (No. 4) Regulations 1984.

I can see no reason whatsoever, however, for refusing the association the declaration for which they ask. . . .

Declaration accordingly. Application for order of certiorari refused.

QUESTIONS

1. Consultation is not generally required for legislation, although central governmental practice is usually to conduct consultation amongst interested bodies. This leaves the area of quasi-legislation produced by other public authorities and agencies. Bearing in mind that the courts seem to have regard to the distinctions between legislative, executive, and administrative action, should there be a general statutory obligation imposed on all public bodies who make any measures, whether they take the form of primary, delegated, or quasi-legislation?

2. What are the benefits and disadvantages of consultation, and would the benefits outweigh the disadvantages:
   (a) generally;
   (b) only for some types of quasi-legislation?

3. If such a general duty of consultation were required, would it be in conflict with the representative nature of our parliamentary democratic constitution?

4. For the purposes of a duty to consult, should we make a distinction between those measures which are subject to parliamentary oversight and those which are not?

NOTE: The Hansard Society produced a report on the legislative process. In this they proposed guiding principles which underpinned their recommendations for reform. The evidence which they received indicated that the current arrangements for consultation were unsatisfactory.

The Hansard Society, *Making the Law*
(1993), pp. 14, 15, 139–41

. . . [W]e have agreed five central principles which guide and govern all the recommendations we make:

- Laws are made for the benefit of the citizens of the state. All citizens directly affected should be involved as fully and openly as possible in the process by which statute law is prepared.
- Statute law should be as certain as possible and as intelligible and clear as possible, for the benefit of the citizens to whom it applies.
- Statute law must be rooted in the authority of Parliament and thoroughly exposed to open democratic scrutiny by the representatives of the people in Parliament.
- Ignorance of the law is no excuse, therefore the current statute law must be as accessible as possible to all who need to know it.
- The Government needs to be able to secure the passage of its legislation, but to get the law right and intelligible, for the benefit of citizens, is as important as to get it passed quickly.

[Recommendations on consultation]

Primary Legislation
4. The overwhelming impression from the evidence is that many of those most directly affected are deeply dissatisfied with the extent, nature, timing and conduct of consultation on bills as at present practised . . . the Government must heed this criticism and seek to meet it. . . .

5. The Government should always seek the fullest advice from those affected on the problems of implementing and enforcing proposed legislation. . . .

6. Although some bills are inevitably required in a hurry, getting a bill right should always have priority over passing it quickly, and we recommend that the Government should publicy endorse this policy. . . .

7. The Government should make every effort to get bills in a form fit for enactment, without major alteration, before they are presented to Parliament; in the Government's review of the legislative process, this should be a first and overriding objective. . . .

8. Proper consultation should play a central part in the preparation of bills, and we recommend that all Government departments should act accordingly. . . .

9. Good consultation practice requires that when a bill is being prepared, bodies with relevant experience or interests – particularly those directly affected – should be given all the relevant information and an opportunity to make their views known or to give information or advice, at each level of decision-taking. . . .

10. Consultation should be as open as possible. . . .

11. Secrecy regarding the content and results of consultations should be minimised and feedback maximised. . . .

12. When major reviews are required of how the current law is operating and of the need for reform, we would welcome more frequent appointment of independent inquiries, including Royal Commissions. If the Government is not prepared to accept the advice of such inquiries, it would be expected to publish its reasons. . . .

13. Consultative documents should be as clear and precise as possible. They should be specific about the questions on which departments want responses, while leaving opportunity for bodies to put forward further ideas of their own on relevant points. Green Papers should set out the facts fully and, as far as possible, the options being considered. White Papers should normally be preceded by Green Papers. White Papers should, where possible, systematically detail changes from Green Papers, indicating why these changes had been made. . . .

14. Departments should offer more consultations on draft texts, especially in so far as they relate to practical questions of the implementation and enforcement of legislation. . . .

15. The experience of the Inland Revenue in consulting on individual draft clauses of the Finance Bill should be studied by other departments and adopted in other fields. . . .

16. Where there is no great urgency for a bill, the whole bill might sometimes be published in draft in a Green Paper, as the basis for further consultation and possibly parliamentary scrutiny. . . .

17. Government departments should consult the main bodies concerned in each case and seek to agree how much time should be allowed for their responses to a consultation document. . . .

18. Consultation should not be delayed. . . .

19. Bodies invited by Government departments to respond to consultative documents on proposed legislation, and other bodies with a *bona fide* interest, should be given, free of charge, as many copies of those documents as they can show they need. . . .

20. Bodies which have contributed to consultation on proposed legislation should be supplied, free of charge, with copies of the resulting bills, Acts and statutory instruments. . . .

21. The Government should, drawing on best practice, prepare consultation guidelines which would be applicable to all Government departments when preparing legislation. . . .

22. We recommend that—

(a) the Government's guidelines on consultation should be published;
(b) each department when applying to the Future Legislation Committee for inclusion of a bill in the Government's legislative programme should submit a check-list indicating how far it has been able to comply with the guidelines, and give details of the consultations it has already carried out or proposes to conduct; and
(c) an up-dated version of the check-list and this information should be submitted with the draft bill to the Legislation Committee and published with the bill. . . .

Delegated legislation

23. There should be consultation where appropriate at the formative stage of delegated legislation, but wherever possible departments should also consult outside experts and affected bodies on drafts of the actual instruments that they propose to lay before Parliament. . . .

24. The Government's guidelines that we have recommended regarding consultation on bills, should be applied with appropriate modifications to consultation on delegated legislation. . . .

QUESTIONS

1. Does consultation operate more as a source of legitimation for, rather than control of, legislation?

2. Do the Hansard Society's proposals focus more on the workability of legislation when made, whereas the government concentrates more on the processes and politics of making legislation?

(b) *Publicity*

All statutes are published, as is delegated legislation governed by the Statutory Instruments Act 1946, but this does leave open the possibility of other legislative measures not being readily available or known about.

Statutory Instruments Act 1946

1.—(1) Where by this Act or any Act passed after the commencement of this Act power to make, confirm or approve orders, rules, regulations or other subordinate legislation is conferred on His Majesty in Council or on any Minister of the Crown then, if the power is expressed—

(a) in the case of a power conferred on His Majesty, to be exercisable by Order in Council;
(b) in the case of a power conferred on a Minister of the Crown, to be exercisable by statutory instrument,

any document by which that power is exercised shall be known as a 'statutory instrument' and the provisions of this Act shall apply thereto accordingly. . . .

2.—(1) Immediately after the making of any statutory instrument, it shall be sent to the King's printer of Acts of Parliament and numbered in accordance with regulations made under this Act, and except in such cases as may be provided by any Act passed after the commencement of this Act or prescribed by regulations made under this Act, copies thereof shall as soon as possible be printed and sold by the King's printer of Acts of Parliament. . . .

3.—(1) Regulations made for the purposes of this Act shall make provision for the publication by His Majesty's Stationery Office of lists showing the date upon which every statutory instrument printed and sold by the King's printer of Acts of Parliament was first issued by that office; and in any legal proceedings a copy of any list so published purporting to bear the imprint of the King's printer shall be received in evidence as a true copy, and an entry therein shall be conclusive evidence of the date on which any statutory instrument was first issued by His Majesty's Stationery Office.

(2) In any proceedings against any person for an offence consisting of a contravention of any such statutory instrument, it shall be a defence to prove that the instrument had not been issued by His Majesty's Stationery Office at the date of the alleged contravention unless it is proved that at that date reasonable steps had been taken for the purpose of bringing the purport of the instrument to the notice of the public, or of persons likely to be affected by it, or of the person charged.

(3) Save as therein otherwise expressly provided, nothing in this section shall affect any enactment or rule of law relating to the time at which any statutory instrument comes into operation. . . .

8.—(1) The Treasury may, with the concurrence of the Lord Chancellor and the Speaker of the House of Commons, by statutory instrument make regulations for the purposes of this Act, and such regulations may, in particular:— . . .

> (c) provide with respect to any classes or descriptions of statutory instrument that they shall be exempt, either altogether or to such extent as may be determined by or under the regulations, from the requirement of being printed and of being sold by the King's printer of Acts of Parliament, or from either of those requirements: . . .

NOTE: Under the Statutory Instruments Regulations 1947, rr. 5–8 some regulations are exempted from the publication requirements of the 1946 Act. These are: local instruments and those otherwise published regularly (r. 5); temporary instruments (r. 6); schedules to rules which are too bulky and where other steps have been taken to bring them to the notice of the public (r. 7); cases in which it would be contrary to the public interest for publication to occur before the rules came into operation (r. 8). The Minister making rules subject to the exceptions in rr. 6–8 must certify that the conditions are satisfied.

R v Sheer Metalcraft Ltd

[1954] 1 QB 586, Kingston-upon-Thames Assizes

STREATFIELD J: . . . This matter comes before the court in the form of an objection to the admissibility in evidence of a statutory instrument known as the Iron and Steel Prices Order, 1951. It appears that part and parcel of that instrument consisted of certain deposited schedules in which maximum prices for different commodities of steel were set out. The instrument is said to have been made by the Minister of Supply on February 16, 1951; laid before Parliament on February 20, 1951; and to have come into operation on February 21, 1951. It is under that statutory instrument that the present charges are made against the two defendants in this case.

The point which has been taken is that by reason of the deposited schedules not having been printed and not having been certified by the Minister as being exempt from printing, the instrument is not a valid instrument under the Statutory Instruments Act, 1946. That point was taken in *Simmonds* v *Newell* [1953] 1 WLR 826, but it was expressly left open in view of a certain admission then made by the Solicitor-General, which, however, does not apply to the present case. The point arises in this way: under regulation 55AB of the Defence (General) Regulations, 1939, as amended, a competent authority, which in this case is the Minister of Supply, may by statutory instrument provide for controlling the prices to be charged for goods of any description or the charges to be made for services of any description, and for any incidental and supplementary matters for which the competent authority thinks it expedient for the purposes of the instrument to provide. It is said in the statutory instrument here that it was made in exercise of the powers conferred upon the Minister by regulations 55AB and 98 of the Defence (General) Regulations, and other statutory authorities.

The contention is that the making of that instrument is governed by the provisions of the Statutory Instruments Act, 1946 . . .

[His Lordship read sections 1 and 2 of the Act of 1946 and regulation 7 of the Statutory Instruments Regulations, 1947, and continued:] Section 1 visualizes the making of what is called a statutory instrument by a Minister of the Crown; section 2 visualizes that after the making of a statutory instrument it shall be sent to the King's Printer to be printed, except in so far as under regulations made under the Act it may be unnecessary to have it printed. It is said here that the Minister did not certify that the printing of these very bulky deposited schedules was unnecessary within the meaning of regulation 7. It is contended, therefore, that as he did not so certify it, it became an obligation under the Act that the deposited schedules as well as the instrument itself should be printed under section 2 of the Act of 1946, and in the absence of their having been printed as part of the instrument, the instrument cannot be regarded as being validly made.

To test that matter it is necessary to examine section 3 of the Act of 1946. By subsection (1) [see *ante* p. 361] . . . There does not appear to be any definition of what is meant by 'issue,' but presumably it does mean some act by the Queen's Printer of Acts of Parliament which follows the printing of the instrument. That section, therefore, requires that the Queen's Printer shall keep lists showing the date upon which statutory instruments are printed and issued.

Subsection (2) is important and provides [see *ante* p. 361] . . . It seems to follow from the wording of this subsection that the making of an instrument is one thing and the issue of it is another. If it is made it can be contravened; if it has not been issued then that provides a defence to a person charged with its contravention. It is then upon the Crown to prove that, although it has not been issued, reasonable steps have been taken for the purpose of bringing the instrument to the notice of the public or persons likely to be affected by it.

I do not think that it can be said that to make a valid statutory instrument it is required that all of these stages should be gone through; namely, the making, the laying before Parliament, the printing and the certification of that part of it which it might be unnecessary to have printed. In my judgment the making of an instrument is complete when it is first of all made by the Minister concerned and after it has been laid before Parliament. When that has been done it then becomes a valid statutory instrument, totally made under the provisions of the Act.

The remaining provisions to which my attention has been drawn, in my view, are purely procedure for the issue of an instrument validly made – namely, that in the first instance it must be printed by the Queen's Printer unless it is certified to be unnecessary to print it; it must then be included in a list published by Her Majesty's Stationery Office showing the dates when it is issued and it may be issued by the Queen's Printer of Acts of Parliament. Those matters, in my judgment, are matters of procedure. If they were not and if they were stages in the perfection of a valid statutory instrument, I cannot see that section 3(2) would be necessary, because if each one of those stages were necessary to make a statutory instrument valid, it would follow that there could be no infringement of an unissued instrument and therefore it would be quite unnecessary to provide a defence to a contravention of any such instrument. In my view the very fact that subsection (2) of section 3 refers to a defence that the instrument has not been issued postulates that the instrument must have been validly made in the first place otherwise it could never have been contravened.

In those circumstances I hold that this instrument was validly made and approved and that it was made by or signed on behalf of the Minister on its being laid before Parliament; that so appears on the fact of the instrument itself. In my view, the fact that the Minister failed to certify under regulation 7 does not invalidate the instrument as an instrument but lays the burden upon the Crown to prove that at the date of the alleged contraventions reasonable steps had been taken for bringing the instrument to the notice of the public or persons likely to be affected by it. I, therefore, rule that this is admissible. . . .

Verdict: Guilty on all counts.

NOTE: For a critical analysis of this case and s. 3 of the 1946 Act, see articles by Lanham at (1974) 37 *Modern Law Review* 510 and [1983] *Public Law* 395.

QUESTIONS

1. The publication requirements in the 1946 Act affect only statutory instruments in respect of which no exemption has been made. Should there be a general duty of publication?

2. With respect to publication of quasi-legislation:

(a) should it only be required if it is reasonable and non-disclosure would prejudice the public; and

(b) when would non-disclosure be reasonable?

(c) *Parliamentary oversight*

Public Information Office, House of Commons Sessional Information Digest
1998–99, 1999–2000 and 2000–01, pp. 1, 2

Analysis of the time of the session

Types of Business	Total time spent (hours:minutes)		
	1998–99	1999–2000	2000–01
Government Bills			
Second Reading debate (Bills committed to a Standing Committee)	88:19	124:13	93:52
Second Reading debate (Bills committed to a Committee of the Whole House)	44:43	31:01	17:52
Committee of the Whole House	57:26	76:56	23:33
Consideration (Report stage)	120:53	210:37	56:24
Third Reading	17:10	21:58	16:08
Lords Amendments	48:37	66:29	3:24
Allocation of Time Orders	12:28	28:17	31:22
Committal motion	0:03	0:29	—
Private Members' Bills			
Motions for the introduction of Ten Minute Rule Bills	10:49	12:53	4:21
Second Reading	31:42	38:56	33:44
Other stages	28:54	31:17	4:56
Money Resolutions	3:06	1:53	2:41
Ways and Means Resolutions (including Budget Debate)	27:04	25:25	25:01
Affirmative Statutory Instruments	35:19	25:56	21:58
Prayers against Statutory Instruments etc	1:43	6:32	5:24

The Hansard Society, *Making the Law*
(1993), pp. 11–12

Volume of all Public General Acts, 1901–1991

Year	No. of Acts	Pages	No. of Sections and Schedules
1901	40	247	400
1911	58	584	701
1921	67	569	783
1931	34	375	440
1941	48	448	533
1951	66	675	803
1961	65	1048	1087
1971	81	2107	1963
1981	72	2276	2026
1991	69	2222*	1985

* Printed on A4 paper which was larger than the size previously used, so requiring fewer pages.

Volume of Public General Acts 1985–1991, showing effect of excluding consolidation Acts

Year	No. of Acts	Pages	No. of Acts excluding cons. Acts	Pages excluding cons. Acts
1985	76	3233	65	1860
1986	68	2780	64	2310
1987	57	1538*	56	1269*
1988	55	3385	49	2047
1989	46	2489	43	2399
1990	46	2391	42	1743
1991	69	2222	61	2012

* The statute book from 1987 onwards has been printed on A4 paper which is larger than the size previously used, so requiring fewer pages.

NOTE: Within the first month of the new Parliament elected in 1997, the House of Commons established a Select Committee to examine ways in which the House might be modernized. In its first report, it focused upon the legislative process in relation to primary legislation.

First Report from the Select Committee on Modernisation of the House of Commons
HC 190 of 1997–98, paras 4–17, 84–102

Perceived Defects in the Present System

4. Previous inquiries into the legislative process have consistently identified a number of defects in the way in which Parliament considers legislation. Criticisms are made not only of the procedures used but of the pattern and timing of legislative scrutiny during a typical parliamentary session.

5. The first criticism made is that there has hitherto been little, if any, consultation with Members or with the House as a whole before Bills are formally introduced. In recent years some draft Bills have been produced for prior consultation, and the present Government has specifically undertaken in the Queen's Speech to extend this process. The House itself has however made no attempt to undertake any systematic consideration of such draft Bills.

6. There has as a result been no formal channel to allow time and opportunity for Members to receive representations from interested parties. Consultations between Government and those outside Parliament with a legitimate concern in the legislation has also been criticised as patchy and spasmodic.

7. Once Bills are formally introduced they are largely set in concrete. There has been a distinct culture prevalent throughout Whitehall that the standing and reputation of Ministers have been dependent on their Bills getting through largely unchanged. As a result there has been an inevitable disposition to resist alteration, not only on the main issues of substance, but also on matters of detail.

8. The Committee stage of a Bill, which is meant to be the occasion when the details of the legislation are scrutinised, has often tended to be devoted to political partisan debate rather than constructive and systematic scrutiny. On Bills where policy differences are great, the role of Government backbenchers on a Standing Committee has been primarily to remain silent and to vote as directed. By contrast the Opposition has often set out to devise methods designed simply to extend debate. The Government has then been forced to bring in a guillotine which has often been draconian, as a result of which large sections of the Bill have not been considered.

9. Special Standing Committees, which were designed to encourage more informed discussion on Bills which were not highly politically controversial, have rarely been used. This has almost certainly been because of the perceived amount of extra time involved and the consequent pressure on the legislative timetable, although evidence from those concerned, including Ministers, suggests that such a perception is in fact misconceived.

10. Report stages have frequently been equally unconstructive. So far as the Opposition has been concerned, they have often been seen as an opportunity to debate on the floor of the House issues which they regard as of major political importance. Amendments and new clauses are tabled as a peg on which to hang a particular debate, not always closely related to the provisions of the Bill. By contrast the Government has frequently taken the opportunity to table literally hundreds of amendments, some very technical, some very long, possibly as a consequence of the Bill being, as First Parliamentary Counsel put it, 'produced too quickly to get the policy and drafting right'.

11. Turning to the pattern of legislation, critics regularly point to the marked imbalance in the legislative activity at different times in the session. Early on in a typical parliamentary year, the House is usually swamped with major Bills in Committee as Ministers seek to get a head start for their own measures. The recent change in the timing of the Budget and the subsequent Finance Bill has made this worse. By contrast the House of Lords is under extreme pressure at the latter end of the session as it receives the major Commons Bills.

12. This pattern, combined with the absolute cut-off imposed by prorogation, frequently makes

the last few days of a session particularly chaotic as attempts are made to complete the Government's legislative programme. Bills go to and fro between the Houses, both of which are asked to agree (or disagree) usually with minimal notice to a large number of amendments. Few, if any Members, are able to know what is going on, and there is potential scope for error. The House has in the past even been asked to debate Lords Amendments of which there has been no available text.

The Essential Requirements of a Reformed System

13. We do not dissent from the general thrust of the criticisms outlined in the previous paragraphs. We do however note the considered view of the chairmen of standing committees, as conveyed to us by the Chairman of Ways and Means, that there has been a marked improvement in recent years, particularly since the adoption of the informal timetabling of bills following the Jopling reforms. The Chairman also suggested that the system also had some notable strengths: in particular, the system of appointing a committee with a separate membership for each bill, the fact that the process of detailed consideration and confrontation is carried out in public, and the tradition of impartial chairmanship.

14. Before considering ways in which the House's procedures and practices could be changed to meet the criticisms, we set out what in our view are the essential criteria which must be met in making any reforms. These may be summarised as follows:

(a) The Government of the day must be assured of getting its legislation through in reasonable time (provided that it obtains the approval of the House).
(b) The Opposition in particular and Members in general must have a full opportunity to discuss and seek to change provisions to which they attach importance.
(c) All parts of a Bill must be properly considered.
(d) The time and expertise of Members must be used to better effect.
(e) The House as a whole, and its legislative Committees in particular, must be given full and direct information on the meaning and effect of the proposed legislation from those most directly concerned, and full published explanations from the Government on the detailed provisions of its Bill.
(f) Throughout the legislative process there must be greater accessibility to the public, and legislation should, so far as possible, be readily understandable and in plain English.
(g) The legislative programme needs to be spread as evenly as possible throughout the session in both Houses.
(h) There must be sufficient flexibility in any procedures to cope with, for example, emergency legislation.
(i) Monitoring and, if necessary, amending legislation which has come into force should become a vital part of the role of Parliament.

Options for Improvement

15. Existing Standing Orders allow for considerable flexibility, as the attached flow chart demonstrates. There are several options already available which could lead to better scrutiny of legislation. With one or two notable exceptions, such as the creation of 'First Reading' Committees, the House could, if it so wished, do a great deal without a single amendment to Standing Orders. What is significant, however, is that it is the 'principal route of legislation' as shown in the attached diagram which is almost invariably used rather than the other options available. It is this inflexibility in practice which has led to the justifiable criticisms of the way in which legislation is scrutinised.

16. Much of this inflexibility arises because of the false perception that all Government bills merit broadly similar treatment. The reality is that each Bill is unique; and any categorisation risks obscuring this fact. The spectrum runs from long, politically controversial and complex Bills to short, wholly uncontentious and simple Bills. It would indeed be remarkable were one single principal route to be appropriate for such a complex array of types of Bill.

17. Another major factor in the largely inflexible approach to legislation adopted hitherto is essentially that of the culture of the House. There has been an inbuilt resistance to change of any sort on all sides. Governments have preferred the status quo largely because they perceive changes to threaten delay in their programmes. Oppositions have not been enthusiastic about any changes which might appear to prejudice their right to oppose and to seek to delay. We would be naive not to recognise that the House is and must be a place where major political differences exist and must be expressed. Nonetheless, if there is to be a real improvement in the quality of legislation, there must be a will in all parts of the House to achieve cooperation wherever it is possible.

. . .

Conclusions

84. There is general agreement that more thorough parliamentary scrutiny of legislation is necessary and long overdue. We have tried in this Report to begin to set out how best to achieve this end. We have concluded that it would be wrong to prescribe a single approach for all types of legislation. We have stated some broad principles, in particular that the Government of the day must be assured of getting its legislation through in reasonable time (provided that it has the approval of the House), and that the Opposition and all Members must have a full opportunity to discuss and seek to change provisions to which they attach importance. Each bill will be different and its treatment should reflect this, with its passage to the statute book designed to recognise the broad principles to which we have referred. A higher quality of legislation must have substantial benefits for all.

85. There is much that can already be done by using to greater effect and with greater imagination the existing procedures and practices of the House. Beyond that, relatively minor changes could significantly improve the scrutiny of legislation. We recommend greater use in appropriate cases of more of the options already available and of others that could easily be brought forward. Fundamental to this is a willingness on the part of Government to experiment with such options. It equally entails some greater flexibility on the part of the House. If the new opportunities offered are wasted or abused, the chance will have been missed.

86. If significant changes are made to the scrutiny of legislation in the longer term, there would be consequences for the overall framework within which Parliament legislates. These could include in defined circumstances consideration of the 'rollover' of Bills from one parliamentary year to another, and the shape and form of that year. Such matters are in any event subject to alteration: for example, the Budget was moved in 1993 from March to November, whereas it has recently been announced that in 1998 there will be a spring Budget.

87. Flexibility is an inherent strength of our system, and any attempt to impose a straitjacket on it should be resisted.

88. The recommendations we make below are based on options either already available, or which would involve small changes in procedures.

Programming of legislation

89. We have explored the possibility of using arrangements for programming legislation which are more formal than the usual channels but more flexible than the guillotine. We believe that the spirit of these reforms requires co-operation from all sides of the House. We **recommend** to the House that, for a trial period, and in respect only of some bills, the House adopt an alternative approach as set out below—

(i)   The Bills to be selected for programming during this trial period should be agreed through the usual channels, and should include some Bills of real substance, including at least one Bill against which the Opposition proposes to divide on Second Reading.

(ii) As soon as possible after formal presentation of such a Bill or its receipt from the House of Lords, discussions on a programme should take place between the usual channels, taking account of representations from all sides of the House, including backbenchers.

(iii) In the light of these discussions the Government should move an amendable programme motion directly after Second Reading, which could include—

    (a) the Committee option to be followed:

    (b) the date by which the Bill should be reported from committee. The Committee itself would then decide how its time should be used to consider all sections of the bill within this timetable:

    (c) the amount of time proposed for Report Stage and Third Reading:

    (d) in defined circumstances, provisions for carry-over to a subsequent session.

(iv) The questions necessary to dispose of proceedings on a programme motion shall be put not later than 45 minutes after the commencement of such proceedings.

(v) The question on any subsequent motion to modify the original programme should be put forthwith, provided that a motion proposing to reduce the time agreed in the original programme motion or to bring forward the date for reporting the bill from committee should be treated as a programme motion.

(vi) A Bill subject to the terms of a programme motion shall not subsequently be made subject to an allocation of time motion in respect of those stages referred to in the programme motion.

(vii) For any such Bill committed to a Standing Committee or Special Standing Committee a programming sub-committee would be appointed by the Committee of Selection, to be chaired by the Chairman of the Standing Committee.

(viii) Programming sub-committees would have power to meet before the first meeting of the Committee to agree a programme for consideration of the Bill within the limits agreed by the House.

(ix) In drawing up a programme the sub-committee should take into account the need for all parts of the Bill to receive proper consideration and the rights of the Opposition and other parties and Members to be given adequate time to discuss matters to which they attach particular importance.

(x) Sufficient time should also be allowed in the programme for consultation with those outside Parliament.

(xi) The conclusions of the sub-committee should be embodied in a committee programming motion to be moved at the beginning of the first sitting, and proceedings on that motion should be concluded no later than one hour after it is moved, together with any amendments selected: the question on any subsequent such motions should be put forthwith.

(xii) The Chairman of a Standing Committee on a Bill subject to a programme should be given discretion to extend the time for debate on a particular Question for up to one hour where it appears to him or her to be necessary to ensure that all parts of the Bill are properly considered, within the overall limits agreed by the House.

90. The recommendations and conclusions below apply in equal measure to programmed and unprogrammed bills.

Pre-legislative scrutiny

91. We welcome the Government's intention to publish 7 draft bills in the course of this Session, and recommend that some, or even all, be considered by the House, using one of the easily available avenues—

(i) an ad hoc Select Committee to consider a particular draft bill: or

(ii) following a discussion with the House of Lords, an ad hoc Joint Select Committee to consider a particular draft bill: or

(iii) consideration of a particular draft bill by the appropriate departmental select committee.

Presentation and First Reading

92. (i) We have invited First Parliamentary Counsel to explore as soon as possible ways in which the explanatory memorandum accompanying each bill can be made more user-friendly.

(ii) We recommend that the Government should also consider the production of a simpler explanatory guide, along the lines of that produced by the Chancellor of the Exchequer for the Budget, to be made available to interested parties, including via the Internet.

After First Reading

93. While we recognise that the first session of a new Parliament, with a new Government, constrains what can be achieved, we recommend that the Government seek an opportunity to appoint an ad hoc First Reading Select Committee to consider an appropriate bill, which had not previously been published in draft form.

Second Reading

94. We agree that the great majority of bills should be subject to a Second Reading debate on the floor of the House. We also consider however that greater use should be made of Second Reading Committees to consider 'non-controversial bills which do not raise substantial issues of principle', or those non-controversial Bills which may have been subject to previous committee scrutiny. To facilitate this the Government should bring forward proposals to amend Standing Order No. 90 so as to relax some of the provisions governing the procedures for sending bills to Second Reading Committees, and to permit all Members of the House to attend and speak.

Committee Stage

95. The committee stage of any bill should be handled in whatever way is most appropriate for that bill. Following the Second Reading of a bill, there is a range of committal options open to Government with decisions usually being taken following discussions. These options have been used very sparingly in the past, and we recommend greater use in future of:

(i) committal of appropriate bills to a Special Standing Committee, under Standing Order No. 91, which should be amended so as to give these committees greater flexibility in their operations; or

(ii) committal of appropriate bills to ad hoc Select Committees; or

(iii) splitting a bill on committal between the floor of the House and a Standing Committee, a procedure which we consider could be extended to make it possible, subject to agreement, to split bills between different sorts of committees, as deemed appropriate.

96. Where a pre-legislative or First Reading Committee has been used the Committee of Selection should so far as possible nominate the same core of Members to the subsequent committee stage, supplemented as necessary.

97. There are several changes to existing procedures and practices in Standing Committee which could lead to a more effective use of time, including:

(i) a sensible agreement to ensure that all parts of a Bill are discussed:

(ii) an amendment to Standing Orders so that the consideration of the existing Clauses of a bill can follow the practice currently used for new Clauses:

(iii) removal of many of the constraints and conventions on the times during which a committee may meet and the number of timings of sittings, including the extension to Standing Committees of the facility available to select committees to meet during recesses: and

(iv) the Chairman to be given powers similar to those given to the Speaker under Standing Order No. 47 to impose a limit on the length of speeches.

98. Notes on Clauses should be available to members of Standing Committees in time for them to be able to frame and table amendments which would be open to selection.

Report Stage

99. We recommend that, for a certain number of appropriate bills, the Standing Committee which had considered the bill should be reconvened to consider non-controversial Government amendments, such as those giving effect to assurances given at committee stage, with the reported Bill considered as at present on the floor of the House.

Lords Amendments

100. We recommend that the House should also explore the possibility of referring appropriate Lords Amendments to the Standing Committee which considered the bill. This would be followed by consideration in the House, normally on a formal motion to agree with the Committee's resolutions.

Post-legislative scrutiny

101. The Liaison Committee should encourage the monitoring by departmentally-related Select Committees of legislation newly in force. The option should remain open for the appointment of ad hoc Select Committees to consider and report on the operation of a particular piece of legislation causing concern which affects more than one Department.

The sessional cycle

102. (i) The Committee agrees the principle that, in defined circumstances and subject to certain safeguards, Government Bills may be carried over from one session to the next in the same way as hybrid and private Bills. Discussions should begin between the appropriate authorities in both Houses to determine how this might best be achieved, without infringing the constitutional implications of prorogation.

(ii) In drawing up detailed proposals the appropriate authorities should consider in particular the need to ensure (a) the identification by the Government as early as possible of any Bill it wished to be subject to a carry-over procedure (b) that the procedure should only be used for Bills which are either to be subject to select committee type scrutiny or are introduced after a certain period in the session and (c) that no Bill should be carried over more than once.

QUESTION

How far does the Modernization Select Committee's report meet the concerns of the Hansard Society Commission's report?

NOTE: As we saw in section B. of this chapter, one may divide the work of the House of Commons between that which takes place on the floor and that in committee. The most detailed scrutiny of a Bill or a statutory instrument will take place in committee.

There are various procedures by which statutory instruments are passed. The instrument may or may not be required to be laid before Parliament. If it is to be laid before Parliament, then there may or may not be provision for action by Parliament. The action to be taken by Parliament can be broadly divided into affirmative and negative procedures. Under the affirmative procedure Parliament must pass an affirmative resolution in order for the measure to become law or to continue as law. On the other hand, a measure will remain in force unless Parliament annuls it using the negative procedure. The negative resolution is by far the most frequently used procedure by which Parliament may supervise statutory instruments. In order to annul a statutory instrument the prayer for annulment must have been passed within 40 days of the laying of the instrument before Parliament.

The statute which enables the making of a statutory instrument will specify which procedure is to be used. Unlike the case with Bills, it is extremely rare for a statutory instrument to be amended as only a very few enabling statutes provide for amendment.

Specialist committees   Parliament has created several specialist committees to examine delegated legislation and European Communities legislation. The committees dealing with delegated legislation are divided between those which deal with technical matters and those which deal with the merits. The technical committees are (i) the Joint Select Committee on Delegated Legislation; and (ii) the Commons Select Committee on Statutory Instruments, composed of the House of Commons members of the Joint Committee, which deals with instruments subject only to House of Commons oversight. The merits of an instrument may be referred to a House of Commons standing committee or be dealt with on the floor of the House.

Those committees dealing with the European Communities are, in the House of Commons, the European Scrutiny Committee, and, in the House of Lords, the Select Committee on the European Communities. These committees consider both delegated legislation which is intended to implement EC legislation, and proposals from Brussels for future EC legislation.

The House of Commons Committee may refer matters to three European Standing Committees, two of which which were established in 1990–91 and a third in 1998.

First Report of the Select Committee on Procedure
HC 48 of 1999–2000, paras 10–31, 40–59, pp. 26–27

Criticisms of the Existing System, and the 1996 Report's Recommendations

10. In devising an effective system of scrutiny of delegated legislation, the key question is how best to target Parliament's over-stretched resources of time and expertise. There is widespread agreement that at present those resources are ineffectively targeted. There are three major areas of criticism.

11. <u>Firstly it is argued that instruments do not receive scrutiny in proportion to their merits.</u> The current system, as outlined in paragraphs 5 to 9 above, rests on the assumption that affirmative instruments are intrinsically more significant and debate-worthy than negative ones. This may be true of a majority of instruments, but it is generally acknowledged that there is a significant minority of affirmatives which deal with matters too trivial or technical to merit debate, and negatives which deal with important or sensitive matters where there is demand for a debate. This mismatch between the level of scrutiny provided for in the parent legislation and the level which is actually appropriate may arise from a variety of factors. Ministers may have up-graded procedure from negative to affirmative as a political concession during committee stage of a bill; contrariwise, the conferral of significant powers may have 'slipped through' Parliament without provision for proper scrutiny; whilst in other cases, circumstances may have changed during the years or decades since the passage of the parent legislation, rendering issues once regarded as important less so, and vice versa. Nonetheless, in the words of the Clerk of the House, 'the House is locked into a procedural approach to an instrument by provisions made sometimes many, many years before in the parent act'. As a result, the time and expertise of Members is frequently wasted in attendance at DL Committees to consider 'trivial affirmatives', often meeting for a few minutes only; whilst significant changes to the law may pass through Parliament unregarded and undebated because contained in negative instruments.

12. Our predecessors in 1996 [HC 152 of 1995–96] briefly considered the question of whether the existing distinction between affirmatives and negatives should be retained. They argued that 'there would in theory be something to be said for abolishing the distinction, and creating a uniform category of instruments, with a parliamentary mechanism for determining which required positive approval, based on their inherent significance rather than their statutory basis'. However, this would require primary legislation, 'and possibly wholesale amendment of much of statute law'. They therefore did not recommend such an approach, though they added that were their more modest proposals to prove ineffective, serious consideration should be given to the radical proposal of a uniform category and procedure for all delegated legislation.

13. Our predecessors proposed, as a more realistic and feasible way of tackling the problem, that

the House should institute a process of systematic sift of negative instruments within Parliament. The possibility of using the existing Joint Committee on Statutory Instruments (JCSI) for this purpose was considered and ruled out, on the grounds that the sift would involve the application of political judgement and have a direct bearing on the business of the Commons, and was therefore not an appropriate task for a Joint Committee; that it would be a mistake to mix up the politics and the legal *vires* of instruments (the latter being the special concern of the JCSI); and that the sift would require a different set of advisers with different expertise. Our predecessors also considered the possibility of requiring departmental select committees to examine instruments made by the departments which they shadow. This option was also ruled out, largely on practical grounds (the workload involved would vary dramatically between committee and committee, and from week to week within each committee, whilst the level of enthusiasm for such work on the part of Members might also vary considerably between committees). The Liaison Committee, comprising chairmen of departmental and other select committees, endorsed the Procedure Committee's rejection of this option, whilst urging that departmental select committees should have the opportunity of making an input into the sifting process.

14. The 1996 report concluded that the most satisfactory way forward would be for the House to establish a single 'Sifting Committee' to consider and assess all SIs laid before Parliament. The committee would have power to call for further information from government departments where necessary. Its key task would be to make recommendations on which negative instruments merited debate. The recommendations would be put to the House by the chairman of the committee in the form of a motion which could be opposed and indeed defeated (thus enabling the Government to retain its ultimate control of the process). The committee would also have powers to identify affirmative instruments which did *not* merit debate, and on which the question could be put forthwith unless at least six Members had earlier indicated they wished for a debate. In order to allow a reasonable time for scrutiny, the report recommended that praying time against negative instruments should be extended from 40 to 60 days (this would require amendment of the Statutory Instruments Act 1946). The Sifting Committee would require specialist staff back-up.

15. The 1996 report also recommended that reference of a negative instrument to committee should be permitted to be moved by a Member where a prayer against it had been signed by at least 20 Members, with the ensuing Question being decided on a simple majority; and that minor affirmatives of 'broadly similar subject matter' should be grouped together for debate.

16. A further criticism of the existing system is that debate on instruments in committee is meaningless because it does not take place on a substantive motion. If a Delegated Legislation Committee votes against the motion, 'That the Committee has considered the instrument', the Chairman's report to the House is couched in the same terms as if the motion had been agreed to, and no procedural consequences follow from the Committee's vote.

17. The 1996 report recommended that motions in DL Committee should be substantive and amendable, and that where the Government's motion is defeated there should be up to an hour's further debate on the Floor. It also proposed that aspects of European Standing Committee procedure should be adopted for DL Committees, in particular that proceedings should begin with a Ministerial statement and questions, and that debate should last for up to two and a half hours, rather than one and a half as at present.

18. The 1996 report considered the question of whether statutory instruments themselves should be amendable during their passage. At present instruments cannot be amended unless the parent legislation allows for it, and virtually no legislation currently in force so allows. The Committee concluded that the complications that would ensue from any change in this position would greatly outweigh any likely benefits.

19. The report also looked at the existing differentiation between affirmatives and negatives in

terms of the time allocated for debate when taken on the Floor. Under standing orders, affirmatives receive up to an hour and a half's debate without restriction, whilst negatives receive an hour and a half's debate subject to the restriction that debate must be concluded at 11.30 pm, even when it has commenced significantly after 10 pm (as may be the case if divisions have been held at 10 pm). The report concluded that this differentiation was illogical and that standing orders should be amended to repeal the 11.30 pm cut-off on debates on negative instruments.

20. The existing system of scrutiny has also been criticised for containing no provision for a higher level of scrutiny for a small number of very complex SIs. The 1996 Committee proposed a new category of 'super-affirmatives', whereby proposals for draft Orders would be laid for pre-legislative scrutiny by the relevant departmental select committee. This would be an adaptation of the existing procedure for considering draft Deregulation proposals.

21. The 1996 report contained a number of further recommendations. The most important of these was that a standing order should be passed to provide that no decision on a statutory instrument should be made by the House until the instrument had been considered by the Joint Committee on Statutory Instruments. A similar standing order already exists in the House of Lords. The report pointed out that it would always be open to the House to override the standing order by resolution if the Government could persuade it that this was justified in a particular case. This recommendation to create a 'scrutiny reserve' has been strongly supported by the Chairman and members of the present JCSI.

22. Other recommendations in the 1996 report related to such matters as improved documentation and identification of documents. A full list of the report's recommendations is given in the Annex to this report.

Developments since 1996

23. We have considered whether developments since publication of the 1996 report have affected the validity of its conclusions.

Statistical Trends

24. Printed with the report was a memorandum from the then Clerk of the House containing statistics on the numbers of statutory instruments made since 1950, and the numbers laid before Parliament under negative and affirmative procedure since 1980, with details of whether they were considered on the Floor or in committee. On the basis of this information, our predecessors concluded that 'the volume of delegated legislation has undoubtedly grown in recent years'. They pointed out that the number of instruments subject to parliamentary procedure had grown by around 50 per cent in the 15 years to 1996, from under 1,000 a year to around 1,500 a year. The number of negative instruments had almost doubled, from around 700 in the early 1980s to over 1,300 in 1994–95.

25. The present Clerk of the House has supplied us with updated versions of the statistical tables published with the 1996 report. These are set out in the evidence printed with this report. They show that the overall number of instruments laid before Parliament has remained fairly steady (though with individual annual fluctuations) at about 1,500 a year. The ratio between the two categories of instrument has also remained fairly constant: 174 affirmatives and 1,245 negatives were laid before Parliament in 1998–99, as against 175 affirmatives and 1,315 negatives in 1994–95 (the last Session for which figures were given in the 1996 report).

26. Thus there has been no significant change in the numbers of instruments laid over the past four years. However, this must be seen in the context of the increase over the previous 15 years to which our predecessors drew attention. We see no reason to dissent from their overall conclusion that 'there is . . . too great a readiness in Parliament to delegate wide legislative powers to Ministers, and no lack of enthusiasm on their part to take such powers. The result is an excessive volume of

delegated legislation. The Clerk of the House described the current position as 'on a high plateau in terms of numbers'.

27. The real change in recent years has not been in the overall number of instruments laid but in the manner of their scrutiny by Parliament. Table 3 in the Clerk of the House's evidence shows the number of instruments considered on the Floor and in committee, by Session. During the period for which details were given in the previous report, from 1980–81 to 1994–95, an average of 67 affirmatives per Session were considered on the Floor as against 84 in committee. During the subsequent four years, from 1995–96 to 1998–99, the respective averages per Session were 40 on the Floor and 149 in committee. Likewise, during the earlier period an average of 15 negatives per Session were considered on the Floor as against 16 in committee, whilst during each of the four most recent Sessions an average of 4 negatives were considered on the Floor as against 21 in committee. The statistics thus demonstrate a major shift from the Floor to committee, for both categories of instrument (this is no doubt attributable at least in part to the 'Jopling reforms', which sought to reduce the amount of business taken on the Floor); and a reduction in the overall number of negatives debated *either* on the Floor or in committee.

28. **In our view the trends revealed by these statistics reinforce the case for the reform of the existing system of scrutiny**. It is precisely the shift from the Floor to committee which has created the problem of 'trivial affirmatives': a DL Committee, with Minister, Opposition spokesman, other Members, Chairman, Clerk, Hansard reporter, doorkeeper, policeman and civil servants in attendance must assemble to consider an instrument which in earlier years would probably have been nodded through without debate on the Floor of the House. Likewise, the reduction in the overall number of negatives debated, at a time when there has been no decrease in the numbers laid or – it may confidently be assumed – in the complexity or importance of the instruments themselves, strengthens the supposition that existing arrangements for triggering debate on negatives are less than adequate.

Devolution

29. In our recent report on the procedural consequences of devolution we discussed the impact of devolution to Scotland, Wales and Northern Ireland in relation to delegated legislation. We supported what we described as the Government's 'pragmatic approach' to the procedures for dealing with such legislation. In terms of the effect on Westminster's workload, the Government estimated that the majority of SIs made by the Secretary of State for Scotland, estimated at 250 in an average year, would be dealt with by the Scottish Parliament and would not be dealt with at Westminster; however, this reduction would be offset by instruments to amend UK legislation affected by Acts of the Scottish Parliament. In the case of Wales, the Government expected a reduction of about 50 in the instruments at present made by the Secretary of State on his own. The Clerk of the House commented that 'reductions of this size would provide a welcome, though not major, lessening of the considerable burden on the JCSI, which considers some 1,700 instruments a year'.

30. Commenting in oral evidence in our present inquiry, the Clerk of the House told us that 'I think it is too early to say whether in a purely arithmetical sense devolution is a plus or a minus but, whatever, I should be surprised if it was a big plus or even a big minus'.

31. **The extent of any changes in the pattern and quantity of delegated legislation arising from devolution is a matter which we will continue to monitor. However, there is no reason to think at this stage that changes attributable to devolution require any re-assessment of the conclusions and recommendations in the 1996 report.**

. . .

40. **We very much welcome the Royal Commission's support for the recommendations in the**

1996 report. We note that the Lords vote on 22 February [when for the first time since 1968, the House of Lords disregarded its 'convention that [it] does not reject statutory instruments', by voting against the Greater London Authority Order 2000, and by approving a prayer that the Greater London Authority Election Rules 2000 be annulled] is further evidence that that House, as it evolves into a new role, is likely to give increasing attention to the scrutiny of statutory instruments. In our view this reinforces the Royal Commission's arguments for improving the quality of scrutiny given by *both* Houses.

41. **With regard to the Royal Commission's proposal that the sifting of SIs should be entrusted to a Joint Committee, we consider that this might be a sensible way of avoiding duplication of effort, but measures would need to be taken to ensure that recommendations relating to Commons business were taken by the Commons members of any such committee alone.**

Other Procedural Developments

42. Since 1996 there have been significant developments in the way the House of Commons operates. The Modernisation Committee has encouraged a greater emphasis on pre-legislative scrutiny of primary legislation, by way of draft bills referred to select or joint committees; and the House has been making greater use of Second Reading Committees and Special Standing Committees to examine bills once introduced.

43. Of equal, perhaps even greater, significance for our present purposes has been the extent to which other, permanent committees both of the Commons and the Lords have been developing techniques of scrutiny in recent years. Several deserve to be highlighted.

44. The *House of Lords Select Committee on Delegated Powers and Deregulation* was set up (as the Select Committee on Delegated Powers) on an experimental basis in 1992–93, and since 1993–94 has been routinely reappointed on a sessional basis. In 1994 it was given the additional role of scrutinising deregulation proposals. Its job in relation to bills is 'to report whether the provisions of any bill inappropriately delegate legislative power, or whether they subject the exercise of legislative power to an inappropriate degree of parliamentary scrutiny'. In respect of each bill, the Committee works to a tight timetable, usually publishing a report within three weeks of First Reading. As will have been seen from the order of reference, the Committee's concern is not with the merits of bills but with the justification for and appropriateness of the secondary powers granted by them. In a recent report on its own activities, the Committee commented that it 'operates in a non-partisan way' and noted that 'we have never needed to divide in the seven sessions of our existence'. It added that when it had advised the House that bills should be amended, this advice had 'almost always been accepted by the Government and the House'. The Government has undertaken to respond quickly to the Committee's reports, if practicable.

45. In the Commons, the *Deregulation Committee* was first set up in 1994, to consider proposals for orders and draft Orders laid under the Deregulation and Contracting Out Act 1994. In each case the Committee conducts its examination both at the pre-legislative stage (proposals for orders) and, if it is reached, the legislative stage (draft Orders). Within a fixed timetable the Committee can take written or oral evidence, and report to the House its opinion on whether or not the proposal should proceed or the draft Order be approved. What happens to draft Orders in the House depends on the nature of the Committee's report: if it has reported unanimously that the draft Order should be approved, a motion to that effect is put in the House and the Question put forthwith; if it has agreed on Division that the draft Order should be approved, a motion is moved and the Question put after a maximum of one and a half hours' debate; and if it has recommended that the draft Order should not be approved, the Government may move a motion to disagree with the Committee's report on which the Question can be put after a maximum of 3 hours' debate, with the Question on the draft Order put forthwith if that motion is agreed to.

46. Our predecessors in their 1996 report commented on the Deregulation Committee as follows:

> It should be recalled from the outset that Deregulation Orders are peculiar in that they all involve amendment of primary legislation, which would require further primary legislation to amend it, were it not for the terms of the Deregulation and Contracting Out Act 1994 and the parallel establishment of the Deregulation Committee with its special powers. The degree of scrutiny given by the Committee has demanded commitment of substantial resources, which could not conceivably be extended even to all affirmative orders. It is however in our view significant that the Committee has operated smoothly and effectively; that it has used its powers to persuade government to accept nearly all the amendments it has sought; that it and its House of Lords counterpart have effectively killed off one proposal; and that the end result to date is that 17 draft Orders have been agreed to by the House without any debate, but in the full confidence that they are generally acceptable.

47. The present Chairman of the Deregulation Committee, Mr Peter L. Pike, argued in his written submission that the deregulation procedure has the benefit of allowing public access and giving backbenchers a legislative role, that it is conducted in a bipartisan spirit, and that it need not require much time on the Floor. He urged that 'the techniques of the deregulation procedure could and should be extended to other delegated legislation'.

48. The *European Scrutiny Committee* (until 1998 the European Legislation Committee) is charged with the task of considering a range of EU documents, as defined in Standing Order No. 143. These include EU Regulations, Directives, Decisions of the Council, budgetary documents, Commission proposals, reports and recommendations, documents submitted to the European Central Bank, various inter-governmental proposals, and reports of the Court of Auditors. About 1,000 EU documents a year are deposited in Parliament for scrutiny. The Committee's functions are to assess the political and/or legal importance of these documents and decide which merit further scrutiny, either in European Standing Committee or on the Floor; to report in detail on each document the Committee considers important (some 475 a year), taking written and oral evidence if necessary; to monitor business in the Council of Ministers and the negotiating position of UK Ministers; to review EU legal, procedural and institutional developments which may have implications for the UK and the House; and to police the scrutiny system.

49. When a document is referred by the Committee to one of the three *European Standing Committees*, that committee will meet to hear a Government Minister make a statement and answer questions put by Members for up to 1 hour (extendable by a further 30 minutes at the Chairman's discretion); this is followed by a debate on an amendable motion for up to a further 1 hour 30 minutes. The Chairman reports to the House any resolution to which the committee has come, or that it has come to no resolution. A Government motion couched in similar terms is usually moved in the House a few days later; the Question on this is put forthwith.

50. Some aspects of this European scrutiny process have potential implications for the House's consideration of delegated legislation. First, the European Scrutiny Committee acts as a 'filter' on behalf of the House. It assesses a large number of documents and reaches judgements on whether they merit further debate, either on the Floor of the House or in one of the European Standing Committees. This role would be similar to that envisaged in the 1996 report for the Sifting Committee on delegated legislation. The European Scrutiny Committee performs this role with the assistance of a comparatively large complement of staff and advisers. Second, the 1996 report recommended that certain aspects of European Standing Committee procedure be transferred to DL committees – in particular, beginning proceedings with a statement and questions, allowing debate on a substantive amendable motion, and extending the period of debate to two and a half hours from the present one and a half.

51. The 1996 report commented that 'the European Legislation Committee and the Deregulation Committee have demonstrated that scrutiny by committees can work, and can engage Members' attention and commitment'. We have taken evidence from the Chairman of both Committees, and are happy to endorse that view. **The activities of the European Scrutiny Committee, European Standing Committees, the Deregulation Committee and the House of Lords Delegated Powers and Deregulation Committee have continued to develop during the four years since our predecessors reported, and form a valuable contribution to the effectiveness of Parliament.** In particular, it has been demonstrated that committees working within the Westminster tradition can successfully develop modes of scrutiny involving the sifting of complex documents, the targeted use of specialist staff resources, the maintenance where appropriate of traditions of non-partisanship, and the holding of Ministers to account in public committee meetings through question-and-answer sessions as well as through debate on amendable and substantive motions. They have also demonstrated the ability of select committees, appropriately resourced, to combine the examination of technical detail which is characteristic of the Joint Committee on Statutory Instruments with the exercise of political judgement. In short, **almost every element of the 1996 report's proposed reforms in the field of delegated legislation has been pioneered in one or other of these committees and shown to be eminently workable.**

Conclusions

52. **The package of proposals first put forward in 1996, which we endorse, was deliberately designed to be realistic, not Utopian.** Taken as a whole, the proposals recognise the constraints imposed both by the Government's need to make progress with its legislative programme and the House's wish that minor business should not take up valuable time on the Floor. We recognise that it is in the nature of secondary legislation that it should receive less protracted and intensive scrutiny than primary legislation.

53. **Nonetheless, the existing system of scrutinising delegated legislation is urgently in need of reform. We concur with our predecessors' description of that system as 'palpably unsatisfactory'.** Some aspects of the system – for instance, the frequency with which DL Committees have to be summoned to consider instruments which no-one has any interest in discussing, or the fact that the only vote allowable in committee has no procedural consequences – can only be described as absurd, and tending to bring the House into disrepute. The failures of the current system are cast into even starker relief by the recent moves, which we welcome, to modernise the House's scrutiny of primary legislation and other aspects of the House's work. In our view this renders the task of modernising scrutiny of delegated legislation even more pressing. **We endorse the package of proposals put forward in the 1996 report.** We have summarised the recommendations in paragraphs 13 to 22 above, and set them out in full in the Annex. **The recommendations are aimed not at increasing the burden on the House but, by means of the sifting mechanism, at targeting the House's existing resources more effectively. As several of our witnesses pointed out, they do not represent a radical departure from the existing procedures of the House but rather seek to build on them** (in particular, drawing on experience with the European Scrutiny Committee, European Standing Committees, the Deregulation procedure and the role of the JCSI).

54. **Our inquiry has raised a number of major issues relating to Parliament's treatment of delegated legislation. Some of these remain to be explored more fully.** For instance, the potential role of departmental select committees in the scrutiny of such legislation should be looked at in more detail. We may wish to return to this subject, along with others, following publication of the Liaison Committee's forthcoming report on the powers and functions of select committees. In addition, we propose to examine the Government's use of its powers under section 82 of the Welfare Reform and Pensions Act 1999 to place a report before the House seeking approval of expenditure on new services in advance of Royal Assent to the bill creating those services. The Social Security

Committee has recently reported adversely on the Government's first proposed use of these powers, and has asked the Procedure Committee to investigate the way in which this new delegated power should be exercised in future.

55. **In the interim, however, we believe that the most important thing is to make rapid progress in implementing the 1996 proposals.**

56. **In two respects those proposals, as originally advanced, would require primary legislation**: (1) in order to extend praying time from 40 to 60 days, and (2) to establish a system of 'super-affirmatives'. We wish to make clear that, though we are fully supportive of both proposals, **we do not believe that the implementation of the other, very important, changes which our predecessors proposed, and which we endorse, should be delayed while time is found for appropriate bills to be brought forward**. With regard to praying time, we believe that experience in operating the new system for sifting SIs would in any case rapidly demonstrate the urgent need for such a bill.

57. With regard to super-affirmatives, **we note that there is no reason for the Government to await primary legislation before initiating a 'super-affirmative' procedure, at least on experimental lines**: just as the fairly widespread practice of presenting Government bills in draft has developed *ad hoc*, so it would be open now to individual Government departments to present to Parliament proposals for particularly complex or significant affirmative Orders (or, indeed, of instruments formally subject only to the negative procedure), with an indication of their intention to proceed with the formal instrument after an appropriate interval. It would be a relatively straightforward matter for the House to adopt temporary Standing Orders for the reference of such proposals for statutory instruments either to the relevant departmental select committee, or to the Deregulation Committee. An experimental arrangement on these lines would enable practical experience to be gained of how a permanent system for 'super-affirmatives' might work, and might ensure that any subsequent provisions in primary legislation were satisfactorily drafted. **We recommend that such an experiment be conducted.**

58. **We support our predecessors' recommendation (never implemented) that there should be a full day's debate on those proposals.** Much of the time of Members of the House is taken up with dealing with delegated legislation: it is clearly right and proper that opportunity should be given for the House to debate proposed changes to the system of such legislation.

59. **The written and oral evidence we have received supported the 1996 proposals strongly.** We note in particular the comment by the Chairman of Ways and Means, expressing the 'overwhelming view' of the Chairmen's Panel in support of a sifting mechanism, that the 'modernisation . . . of one of the more unsatisfactory procedures of the House . . . is very definitely long overdue'. **The proposals have now been endorsed by the Procedure Committee under both a Conservative and a Labour Administration, as well as by the Royal Commission on House of Lords Reform and by the Chairman's Panel in the House of Commons. We believe they represent a significant contribution to the process of modernising Parliament, and we press the Government to accept them as a matter of urgency.**

. . .

Memorandum from the Clerk of the House

UPDATED VERSION OF STATISTICS CONTAINED IN THE MEMORANDUM FROM THE
CLERK OF THE HOUSE PRINTED WITH THE COMMITTEE'S FOURTH REPORT OF 1995/96.
DELEGATED LEGISLATION (HC 152)

Table 1 Numbers of Statutory Instruments

Year	General	Local	Total
1950	1,211	933	2,144
1955	657	1,350	2,007
1960	733	1,762	2,495
1965	899	1,302	2,201
1970	1,040	1,004	2,044
1975	1,362	889	2,251
1980	1,197	854	2,051
1985	1,204	878	2,082
1990	1,408	1,256	2,664
1991	1,535	1,416	2,951
1992	1,693	1,667	3,360
1993	1,572	1,707	3,279
1994	1,688	1,646	3,334
1995	1,666	1,679	3,345
1996	1,832	1,459	3,291
1997	1,663	1,451	3,114
1998	1,576	1,747	3,323
1999 (to end October)	1,486	1,475	2,961

Table 2 Instruments subject to Parliamentary procedure

Session	Affirmatives [1]	Negatives [2]	All
1980–81	130	793	923
1981–82	121	721	842
1984–85	158	682	840
1985–86	158	861	1,019
1988–89	160	912	1,072
1989–90	164	965	1,129
1990–91	179	1,071	1,250
1993–94	155	1,225	1,380
1994–95	175	1,315	1,490
1995–96	188	1,308	1,596
1996–97 [3]	139	899	1,308
1997–98 [4]	208	1,591	1,799
1998–99	174	1,245	1,419

Table 3 Instruments considered in the House and in standing committee

Sessions	Floor	Committee	Floor	Committee
1980–81	94	55	15	7
1981–82	71	59	28	21
1984–85	91	72	15	27
1985–86	69	88	14	9
1988–89	53	99	15	18
1989–90	32	98	24	16
1990–91	35	121	13	18
1993–94	87	68	1	1
1994–95	73	99	8	27
1995–96	60	113	7	29
1996–97[5]	45	94	3	14
1997–98[6]	30	170	4	11
1998–99	23	149	1	28

1. Including instruments and draft instruments requiring approval, excluding those withdrawn.
2. Including instruments and draft instruments subject to attachment (including Northern Ireland Instruments), excluding those withdrawn.
3. Unusually short Session.
4. Unusually long Session.
5. Unusually short Session.
6. Unusually long Session.

NOTE: The Regulatory Reform Act 2001 has extended the powers found in the Deregulation and Contracting Out Act 1994 by substituting deregulation orders with regulatory reform orders. These new orders, like their predecessors, are subject to special Parliamentary procedure, some-times called the 'super-affirmative' procedure, which affords a greater degree of Parliamentary scrutiny than that which ordinary affirmative resolution orders receive. First, the Minister lays his regulatory reform proposal before Parliament 'in the form of' a draft order together with a full explanatory document. There then follows the 60-day period of Parliamentary consideration, during which time the proposal is referred automatically and simultaneously to the Committees appointed by Parliament for the purpose, the Committees make their first report to their respect-ive Houses. If the reports are favourable, then the Minister formally lays a draft order in each House, along with an explanation of any changes made compared to the earlier proposal. If the Minister is minded to accept any changes that are proposed to the draft order by the Committees or others between this stage and the final vote on the order, he must formally take up the draft order he has laid and replace it with another which incorporates the changes.

A key feature of this procedure is the ability to make changes (minor or otherwise) to the draft order while it is being scrutinized and in response to the scrutiny, which does not happen to statutory instruments dealt with in the usual way. Ministers have used it to change their draft order in line with recommendations from the Committees. The Government intends to con-tinue the practice of either redrafting or withdrawing orders where this is the advice of the special committees. The final procedural stages for Parliamentary scrutiny of draft regulatory reform orders are set out in Standing Orders. The Commons Committee produces a report on the draft order within 15 days. The Lords Committee has no set time period but usually reports within the same time period. Both Houses then consider the relevant Committee report on the draft order (this is the main feature that distinguishes this form of Parliamentary consideration as 'super-affirmative').

The procedure leading up to the final vote on the order differs in the two Houses: in the Commons, the final procedural stages for draft orders depend on the nature of the report of the Deregulation and Regulatory Reform Committee, and are set out in House of Commons Standing Order No. 18 (Consideration of deregulation orders, etc). This requires that no Motion to approve a draft order shall be made in cases where the Committee has reported that the draft order should not be approved 'unless the House has previously resolved to disagree with the Committee's report'. If Committee members agreed without a division that the draft order should be approved, the Motion to approve it is put to the House forthwith. If they voted to approve the draft order following a division of the Committee, there is a debate on the draft order lasting a maximum of one and a half hours, after which the Motion to approve the draft order is put. If the Committee recommended that the order should not be approved, and the Minister still wishes to pursue the order, he is faced with two options: either he may take up the draft order and replace it with an amended draft, or he may table a Motion to disagree with the Committee report. The latter has never occurred in proceedings on a deregulation order. If it were to happen, the debate on the Minister's Motion, which would be amendable, would last a maximum of three hours. If the House supported the Minister's Motion, a Motion to approve the draft order would be put forthwith. In the Lords, following the publication of the Committee's second report, the Minister tables a Motion that the House should approve the draft order. There is also the opportunity for a debate, if any peer wishes it, on an accompanying Motion at the same time as the Motion to approve a draft order. The companion Motion is moved first and can be amended and voted on. There is a Government undertaking that, in the event of a Motion hostile to a draft deregulation order being agreed to by that House, the Motion for the draft order would not be moved. This commitment was repeated during the Lords Committee stage of the passage of the Regulatory Reform Act.

The deregulation order-making power was limited in its scope. It applied only to legislation enacted up to and including the 1993/94 Session, and was mostly used for small items. The Regulatory Reform Act extends the power so that it can be used more widely. Regulatory reform orders, are capable of: making and re-enacting statutory provision – the order can amend or repeal statutory provisions, it can replace provisions with a restatement of the law, or it can modify or replace them with new provision; imposing additional burdens where necessary, provided that they are proportionate, that the order strikes a fair balance between the public interest and the interests of persons affected by any such burdens, that the order also removes or reduces other burdens and that the extent to which other burdens are removed or reduced or there are other beneficial effects makes it desirable to make the order; removing inconsistencies and anomalies in legislation, provided the order also removes or reduces other burdens; dealing with burdensome situations caused by a lack of statutory provision to do something; applying to legislation passed after the Act if it is at least two years old when the order is made and has not been amended in substance during the last two years; relieving burdens from anyone, including Ministers and government departments but not where only they would benefit; and allowing administrative and minor detail to be further amended by subordinate provisions orders, subject to either negative or affirmative resolution procedure.

The test of maintaining necessary protection is carried over from the 1994 Act and supplemented by an additional test that no order should prevent anyone from exercising an existing right or freedom which they might reasonably expect to continue to exercise (the 'reasonable expectations' test). The Act also requires that any burdens imposed by an order must be proportionate to the benefits expected from them. In addition to this objective of proportionality in section 1, two further stringent tests (fair balance and desirability) apply if an order would increase or impose a burden. The requirements for extensive public consultation and thorough scrutiny by two Parliamentary Committees remain, but Ministers bringing forward regulatory reform orders are required to present more explanatory information to Parliament than they did with deregulation orders, to reflect the wider powers and additional safeguards.

C. Munro, *Studies in Constitutional Law*

(1999), pp. 275–8

. . . It is of the essence of the prerogative that its exercise needs no parliamentary authority, and so parliamentary supervision tends to be entirely retrospective. . . .

Granted that supervision tends to be even more than usually retrospective, in principle the exercise of prerogatives by ministers should be as amenable to oversight as any other governmental actions. Thus, for example, governments' decisions to attack targets in Iraq or Serbian forces could be the subjects of parliamentary debate, discussion and questioning (and were). No doubt, such supervision is practically possible only in the time left over, once legislative and government business has taken the lion's share; is sporadic and imperfect, hindered by lack of information, and made less threatening by reason of the government's usual dominance of the House of Commons. But these are qualifications which apply to scrutiny of the executive generally.

In practice, however, the supervision of prerogative powers does seem to be attended by greater than average difficulty. For a start, their exercise may be less conspicuous, not to say invisible. Mr John Major, as Prime Minister, was merely stating how things were when he replied to a question by saying that 'it is for individual ministers to decide on a particular occasion whether and how to report to Parliament on the exercise of prerogative powers'. Moreover, the very nature of these powers makes them less readily subject to challenge. As the authors of a study of parliamentary questions noted, 'there is a very big difference' between questioning a minister about matters for which he is statutorily responsible and about other matters: 'It is a different level of answerability, there is less opportunity to use it and even when used the results are likely to be less definite.'

. . .

In fact, it is sometimes more than just a difference of degree. When members have tried to ascertain by way of questions in Parliament what advice the Prime Minister had given the Queen as to the dissolution of Parliament, the question is ruled out on the ground that the Prime Minister is not responsible to Parliament for that advice. 'Dissolution appears', it was remarked, 'to be one of a small number of subjects clearly within the Government's responsibility but anomalously shielded from parliamentary questioning'. The number, however, is not so small. Questions cannot be asked which bring the name of the Sovereign or the influence of the Crown before Parliament. The advice given to the Sovereign about some wider matters has similarly been ruled out of bounds: not only the dissolution of Parliament, but also the grant of honours, the ecclesiastical patronage of the Crown, and the appointment and dismissal of Privy Councillors.

These are the subjects of specific rulings, but more generally ministers may simply refuse to answer questions, if there are reasons of national security, confidentiality, relations with other states, or public interest, which in their view justify a refusal. On some topics, the consistency of refusals has created a clear precedent. Governments have from time to time issued lists of matters with regard to which questions will not be answered, but the current practice is simply to consider subjects on their merits in this connection.

. . . Exercises of prerogative and non-statutory powers figure prominently, although not exclusively, in these no-go areas.

. . .

To sum up, the exercise of prerogative powers is imperfectly subject to parliamentary control. . . .

NOTE: For a thorough examination of the prerogative, see M. Sunkin and S. Payne (eds), *The Nature of the Crown* (1999).

QUESTIONS

1. Is Parliamentary oversight of law-making more illusory than real, given that the Government controls the passage of primary legislation, and that the scrutiny of delegated legislation is limited and non-existent for some quasi-legislation?

2. As there is so much pressure on parliamentary time, can consultation and publicity be improved so as to control quasi-legislation?

3. Could primary legislation contain standards and guidance about the content of legislative power which it delegates, thereby facilitating judicial review?

(d) Judicial review

Control of law-making by the courts through judicial review has increased beyond delegated legislation and quasi-legislation. The basis of this review is the doctrine of *ultra vires*. See generally Chapters 8 and 9 on judicial review.

R v *Secretary of State for Employment, ex parte Equal Opportunities Commission*
[1994] 2 WLR 409, House of Lords

The Equal Opportunities Commission (EOC) took the view that some provisions of the Employment Protection (Consolidation) Act 1978 were not in conformity with Community Law (Art. 119 (now 141) of the EC Treaty and the Equal Pay (75/117) and Equal Treatment (76/207) Directives). This view was based on the discrimination between full-time and part-time employees in relation to the periods of continuous employment which were required to qualify for rights to redundancy pay and compensation for unfair dismissal. As the great majority of full-time employees were men and the great majority of part-time employees were women, the EOC felt that this amounted to indirect discrimination against women. The chief executive of the EOC wrote to the Secretary of State asking if steps would be taken to remove this discrimination. In a letter dated 23 April 1990 the Secretary of State replied that in the Department's view redundancy pay and compensation for unfair dismissal did not constitute pay within the terms of Art. 119 (now 141). The EOC obtained leave to apply for judicial review of the decision in the 23 April 1990 letter that the UK was not in breach of its Community law obligations, and sought declarations that the UK was breaching its obligations under (1) Art. 119 (now 141) and Directive 75/117; and (2) Directive 76/207, by providing less favourable treatment of part-time workers (most of whom were women) than full-time workers (most of whom were men) in relation to conditions of entitlement to redundancy pay and compensation for unfair dismissal. Subsequently another applicant, Ms Day, was joined to this application. Ms Day, a part-time cleaner, had been made redundant by her employer, but she did not qualify under the 1978 Act's provisions for redundancy pay. She sought further declarations and *mandamus* to compel the Secretary of State to introduce legislation to amend the 1978 statute.

The major point of substantive law at issue was whether the indirect discrimination against women in the 1978 Act was based on objectively justified grounds, a test derived from the ECJ in *Bilka-Kaufhaus GmbH* v *Weber Von Hartz* (Case 170/84) [1986] ECR 1607.

The application was dismissed by the Divisional Court and this was affirmed by a majority in the Court of Appeal. The EOC and Ms Day appealed to the House of Lords.

LORD KEITH OF KINKEL: . . . The next question is whether there exists any decision or justiciable issue susceptible of judicial review. The EOC's application sets out the Secretary of State's letter of 23 April 1990 as being the reviewable decision. In my opinion that letter does not constitute a decision. It does no more than state the Secretary of State's view that the threshold provisions of the Act of 1978 regarding redundancy pay and compensation for unfair dismissal are justifiable and in conformity with European Community law. The real object of the EOC's attack is these provisions themselves. The question is whether judicial review is available for the purpose of securing a declaration that certain United Kingdom primary legislation is incompatible with European Community law. It is argued for the Secretary of State that Ord. 53, r. 1(2), which gives the court power to make declarations in judicial review proceedings, is only applicable where one of the prerogative orders would be available under rule 1(1), and that if there is no decision in respect of which one of these writs might be issued a declaration cannot be made. I consider that to be too narrow an interpretation of the court's powers. It would mean that while a declaration that a statutory instrument is incompatible with European Community law could be made, since such an instrument is capable of being set aside by certiorari, no such declaration could be made as regards primary legislation. However, in the *Factortame* series of cases (*Reg.* v *Secretary of State for Transport, ex parte Factortame Ltd* [1990] 2 AC 85; *Reg.* v *Secretary of State for Transport, ex parte Factortame Ltd (No. 2)* (Case 213/89) [1991] 1 AC 603; *Reg.* v *Secretary of State for Transport, ex parte Factortame Ltd (No. 3)* (Case C 221/ 89) [1992] QB 680) the applicants for judicial review sought a declaration that the provisions of Part II of the Merchant Shipping Act 1988 should not apply to them on the ground that such application would be contrary to Community law, in particular articles 7 [now repealed] and 52 [now 43] of the EEC Treaty (principle of non-discrimination on the ground of nationality and right of establishment). The applicants were companies incorporated in England which were controlled by Spanish nationals and owned fishing vessels which on account of such control were denied registration in the register of British vessels by virtue of the restrictive conditions contained in Part II of the Act of 1988. The Divisional Court (*Reg.* v *Secretary of State for Transport, ex parte Factortame Ltd* [1989] 2 CMLR 353), under article 177 [now 234] of the Treaty, referred to the European Court of Justice a number of questions, including the question whether these restrictive conditions were compatible with articles 7 and 52 of the Treaty. The European Court [1992] QB 680 answered that question in the negative, and, although the final result is not reported, no doubt the Divisional Court in due course granted a declaration accordingly. The effect was that certain provisions of United Kingdom primary legislation were held to be invalid in their purported application to nationals of member states of the European Economic Community, but without any prerogative order being available to strike down the legislation in question, which of course remained valid as regards nationals of non-member states. At no stage in the course of the litigation, which included two visits to this House, was it suggested that judicial review was not available for the purpose of obtaining an adjudication upon the validity of the legislation in so far as it affected the applicants.

The *Factortame* case is thus a precedent in favour of the EOC's recourse to judicial review for the purpose of challenging as incompatible with European Community law the relevant provisions of the Act of 1978. It also provides an answer to the third procedural point taken by the Secretary of State, which maintains that the Divisional Court had no jurisdiction to declare that the United Kingdom or the Secretary of State is in breach of obligation under Community law. There is no need for any such declaration. A declaration that the threshold provisions of the Act of 1978 are incompatible with Community law would suffice for the purposes sought to be achieved by the EOC and is capable of being granted consistently with the precedent afforded by *Factortame*. This does not involve, as contended for the Secretary of State, any attempt by the EOC to enforce the international treaty obligations of the United Kingdom. The EOC is concerned simply to obtain a ruling which reflects the primacy of European Community law enshrined in section 2 of the Act of 1972 and determines whether the relevant United Kingdom law is compatible with the Equal Pay Directive and the Equal Treatment Directive.

Similar considerations provide the answer to the Secretary of State's fourth procedural point by which it is maintained that the Divisional Court is not the appropriate forum to decide the substantive issues at stake. The issues at stake are similar in character to those which were raised in *Factortame*. The Divisional Court is the only English forum in which the EOC, having the capacity and sufficient interest to do so, is in a position to secure the result which it desires. It is said that the incompatibility issue could be tested in proceedings before the European Court of Justice instituted by the European Commission against the United Kingdom under 169 [now 226] of the EEC Treaty. That may be true, but it affords no reason for concluding that the Divisional Court is an inappropriate forum for the application by the EOC designed towards a similar end and, indeed, there are grounds for the view that the Divisional Court is the more appropriate forum, since the European Court of Justice has said that it is for the national court to determine whether an indirectly discriminatory pay practice is founded on objectively justified economic grounds: see *Bilka-Kaufhaus GmbH* v *Weber Von Hartz* (Case 170/84) [1987] ICR 110, 126.

I turn now to the important substantive issue in the appeal, which is whether or not the threshold provisions in the Act of 1978 have been shown to be objectively justified, the onus of doing so being one which rests on the Secretary of State. . . .

The original reason for the threshold provisions of the Act of 1978 appears to have been the view that part time workers were less committed than full-time workers to the undertaking which employed them. In his letter of 23 April 1990 the Secretary of State stated that their purpose was to ensure that a fair balance was struck between the interests of employers and employees. These grounds are not now founded on as objective justification for the thresholds. It is now claimed that the thresholds have the effect that more part-time employment is available than would be the case if employers were liable for redundancy pay and compensation for unfair dismissal to employees who worked for less than eight hours a week or between eight and 16 hours a week for under five years. It is contended that if employers were under that liability they would be inclined to employ less part-time workers and more full-time workers, to the disadvantage of the former.

The bringing about of an increase in the availability of part-time work is properly to be regarded as a beneficial social policy aim and it cannot be said that it is not a necessary aim. The question is whether the threshold provisions of the Act of 1978 have been shown, by reference to objective factors, to be suitable and requisite for achieving that aim. As regards suitability for achieving the aim in question, it is to be noted that the purpose of the thresholds is said to be to reduce the costs to employers of employing part-time workers. The same result, however, would follow from a situation where the basic rate of pay for part time workers was less than the basic rate for full-time workers. No distinction in principle can properly be made between direct and indirect labour costs. While in certain circumstances an employer might be justified in paying full-time workers a higher rate than part-time workers in order to secure the more efficient use of his machinery (see *Jenkins* v *Kingsgate (Clothing Productions) Ltd* [1981] 1 WLR 1485) that would be a special and limited state of affairs. Legislation which permitted a differential of that kind nationwide would present a very different aspect and considering that the great majority of part-time workers are women would surely constitute a gross breach of the principle of equal pay and could not possibly be regarded as a suitable means of achieving an increase in part-time employment. Similar considerations apply to legislation which reduces the indirect cost of employing part-time labour. Then as to the threshold provisions being requisite to achieve the stated aim, the question is whether on the evidence before the Divisional Court they have been proved actually to result in greater availability of part-time work than would be the case without them. In my opinion that question must be answered in the negative. The evidence for the Secretary of State consisted principally of an affidavit by an official in the Department of Employment which set out the views of the Department but did not contain anything capable of being regarded as factual evidence demonstrating the correctness of these views. One of the exhibits to the affidavit was a report with draft Directives prepared by the Social Affairs Commissioner of the European Commission in 1990 (COM(90) 228 final – SYN 280 and SYN 281, Brussels, 13 August 1990; Official Journal 1990 No. C 224, pp. 4–8). This covered a wide range of employment benefits and advantages, including redundancy pay and compensation for unfair dismissal, but proposed a qualifying threshold for those benefits of eight hours of work per week. The basis for that was stated to be the elimination of disproportionate administrative costs and regard to employers' economic needs. These are not the grounds of justification relied on by the Secretary of State. The evidence put in by the EOC consisted in large measure in a report of the House of Commons Employment Committee, 'Part-Time Work,' vol. 1 in 1990 (HC 122–I, 10 January 1990) and a report of the House of Lords Select Committee on the European Communities, 'Part-Time and Temporary Employment,' in 1990 (HL Paper 7, 4 December 1990). These revealed a diversity of views upon the effect of the threshold provisions on part-time work, employers' organisations being of the opinion that their removal would reduce the amount available with trade union representatives and some employers and academics in the industrial relations field taking the opposite view. It also appeared that no other member state of the European Community, apart from the Republic of Ireland, had legislation providing for similar thresholds. The Republic of Ireland, where statute at one time provided for an 18-hour-per-week threshold, had recently introduced legislation reducing this to eight hours. In the Netherlands the proportion of the workforce in part-time employment was in 1988 29.4 per cent and in Denmark 25.5 per cent, neither country having any thresholds similar to those in the Act of 1978. In France legislation was introduced in 1982 providing for part-time workers to have the same rights as full-time, yet between 1983 and 1988 part-time work in that country increased by 36.6 per cent, compared with an increase of 26.1 per cent over the same period in the United Kingdom. While various explanations were suggested on behalf of the Secretary of State for these statistics, there is no means of ascertaining whether these explanations have any validity. The fact is, however, that the proportion of part-time employees in the national workforce is much less than the proportion of full-time employees, their weekly remuneration is necessarily much lower, and the number of them made redundant or unfairly dismissed in any year is not likely to be unduly large. The conclusion must be that no objective justification for the thresholds in the Act of 1978 has been established. . . .

In the light of the foregoing I am of the opinion that the appeal by the EOC should be allowed and that declarations should be made in the following terms: (1) that the provisions of the Employment Protection (Consolidation) Act 1978 whereby employees who work for fewer than 16 hours per week are subject to different conditions in respect of qualification for redundancy pay from those which apply to employees who work for 16 hours per week or more are incompatible with article 119 [now 141] of the EEC Treaty and the Council Directive of 10 February 1975 (75/117/EEC); (2) that the provisions of the Employment Protection (Consolidation) Act 1978 whereby employees who work for fewer than 16 hours per week are subject to different conditions in respect of the right to compensation for unfair dismissal from those which apply to employees who work for 16 hours per week or more are incompatible with the Council Directive of 9 February 1976 (76/207/EEC).

It remains to note that the EOC proposed that the House should grant a declaration to the effect that the Secretary of State is in breach of those provisions of the Equal Treatment Directive which require member states to introduce measures to abolish any laws contrary to the principle of equal treatment. The purpose of such a declaration was said to be to enable part-time workers who were employed otherwise than by the state or an emanation of the state, and who had been deprived of the right to obtain compensation for unfair dismissal by the restrictive thresholds in the Act of 1978, to take proceedings against the United Kingdom for compensation, founding upon the decision of the European Court of Justice in *Francovich* v *Italian Republic* (Cases C–6/90, C–9/90) [1991] ECR 1–5357. In my opinion it would be quite inappropriate to make any such declaration. If there is any individual who believes that he or she has a good claim to compensation under the *Francovich* principle, it is the Attorney-General who would be defendant in any proceedings directed to enforcing it, and the issues raised would not necessarily be identical with any of those which arise in the present appeal.

Lord Jauncey of Tullichettle dissented on the issue of the EOC's sufficient interest to seek judicial review, however, he concurred with the reasoning of his colleagues on the substance. EOC's appeal allowed, declarations made. Ms Day's appeal dismissed.

Council of Civil Service Unions v *Minister for the Civil Service*
[1985] AC 374, House of Lords

(For the facts of this case see p. 622 *post*.)

LORD FRASER OF TULLYBELTON: . . . As *De Keyser's* case shows, the courts will inquire into whether a particular prerogative power exists or not, and, if it does exist, into its extent. But once the existence and the extent of a power are established to the satisfaction of the court, the court cannot inquire into the propriety of its exercise. That is undoubtedly the position as laid down in the authorities to which I have briefly referred and it is plainly reasonable in relation to many of the most important prerogative powers which are concerned with control of the armed forces and with foreign policy and with other matters which are unsuitable for discussion or review in the law courts. In the present case the prerogative power involved is power to regulate the Home Civil Service, and I recognise there is no obvious reason why the mode of exercise of that power should be immune from review by the courts. Nevertheless to permit such review would run counter to the great weight of authority to which I have briefly referred. Having regard to the opinion I have reached on Mr. Alexander's second proposition, it is unnecessary to decide whether his first proposition is sound or not and I prefer to leave that question open until it arises in a case where a decision upon it is necessary. I therefore assume, without deciding, that his first proposition is correct and that all powers exercised directly under the prerogative are immune from challenge in the courts. I pass to consider his second proposition. . . .

LORD SCARMAN: . . . My Lords, I would wish to add a few, very few, words on the reviewability of the exercise of the royal prerogative. Like my noble and learned friend Lord Diplock, I believe that the law relating to judicial review has now reached the stage where it can be said with confidence that, if the subject matter in respect of which prerogative power is exercised is justiciable, that is to say if it is a matter upon which the court can adjudicate, the exercise of the power is subject to review in accordance with the principles developed in respect of the review of the exercise of statutory power. Without usurping the role of legal historian, for which I claim no special qualification, I would observe that the royal prerogative has always been regarded as part of the common law, and that Sir Edward Coke had no doubt that it was subject to the common law: *Prohibitions del Roy* (1608) 12 Co Rep 63 and the *Proclamations Case* (1611) 12 Co Rep 74. In the latter case he declared, at p. 76, that 'the King hath no prerogative, but that which the law of the land allows him.' It is, of course, beyond doubt that in Coke's time and thereafter judicial review of the exercise of prerogative power was limited to inquiring into whether a particular power existed and, if it did, into its extent: *Attorney-General* v *De Keyser's Royal Hotel Ltd* [1920] AC 508. But this limitation has now gone, overwhelmed by the developing modern law of judicial review: *Reg.* v *Criminal Injuries Compensation Board, Ex parte Lain* [1967] 2 QB 864 (a landmark case comparable in its generation with the *Proclamations Case*, 12 Co Rep 74) and *Reg* v *Secretary of State for Home Affairs, Ex parte Hosenball* [1977] 1 WLR 766. Just as ancient restrictions in the law relating to the prerogative writs and orders have not prevented the courts from extending the requirement of natural justice, namely the duty to act fairly, so that it is required of a purely administrative act, so also has the modern law, a vivid sketch of which my noble and learned friend Lord Diplock has included in his speech, extended the range of judicial review in respect of the exercise of prerogative power. Today, therefore, the controlling factor in determining whether the exercise of prerogative power is subject to judicial review is not its source but its subject matter. . . .

LORD DIPLOCK: . . . My Lords, that a decision of which the ultimate source of power to make it is not a statute but the common law (whether or not the common law is for this purpose given the label of 'the prerogative') may be the subject of judicial review on the ground of illegality is, I think, established by the cases cited by my noble and learned friend, Lord Roskill, and this extends to cases where the field of law to which the decision relates is national security, as the decision of this House itself in *Burmah Oil Co. Ltd* v *Lord Advocate*, 1964 SC (HL) 117 shows. While I see no *a priori* reason to rule out 'irrationality' as a ground for judicial review of a ministerial decision taken in the exercise of 'prerogative' powers, I find it difficult to envisage in any of the various fields in which the prerogative remains the only source of the relevant decision-making power a decision of a kind that would be open to attack through the judicial process upon this ground. Such decisions will generally involve the application of government policy. The reasons for the decision-maker taking one course rather than another do not normally involve questions to which, if disputed, the judicial process is adapted to provide the right answer, by which I mean that the kind of evidence that is admissible under judicial procedures and the way in which it has to be adduced tend to exclude from the attention of the court competing policy considerations which, if the executive discretion is to be wisely exercised, need to be weighed against one another – a balancing exercise which judges by their upbringing and experience are ill-qualified to perform. So I leave this as an open question to be dealt with on a case to case basis if, indeed, the case should ever arise.

As respects 'procedural propriety' I see no reason why it should not be a ground for judicial review of a decision made under powers of which the ultimate source is the prerogative. Such indeed was one of the grounds that formed the subject matter of judicial review in *Reg.* v *Criminal Injuries Compensation Board, Ex parte Lain* [1967] 2 QB 864. Indeed, where the decision is one which does not alter rights or obligations enforceable in private law but only deprives a person of legitimate expectations, 'procedural impropriety' will normally provide the only ground on which the decision is open to judicial review. But in any event what procedure will satisfy the public law requirement of procedural propriety depends upon the subject matter of the decision, the executive functions of the decision-maker (if the decision is not that of an administrative tribunal) and the particular circumstances in which the decision came to be made. . . .

LORD ROSKILL: . . . My Lords, the right of the executive to do a lawful act affecting the rights of the citizen, whether adversely or beneficially, is founded upon the giving to the executive of a power enabling it to do that act. The giving of such a power usually carries with it legal sanctions to enable that power if necessary to be enforced by the courts. In most cases that power is derived from statute though in some cases, as indeed in the present case, it may still be derived from the prerogative. In yet other cases, as the decisions show, the two powers may coexist or the statutory power may by necessary implication have replaced the former prerogative power. If the executive in pursuance of the statutory power does an act affecting the rights of the citizen, it is beyond question that in principle the manner of the exercise of that power may today be challenged on one or more of the three grounds which I have mentioned earlier in this speech. If the executive instead of acting under a statutory power acts under a prerogative power and in particular a prerogative power delegated to the respondent under article 4 of the Order in Council of 1982, so as to affect the rights of the citizen, I am unable to see, subject to what I shall say later, that there is any logical reason why the fact that the source of the power is the prerogative and not statute should today deprive the citizen of that right of challenge to the manner of its exercise which he would possess were the source of the power statutory. In either case the act in question is the act of the executive. To talk of that act as the act of the sovereign savours of the archaism of past centuries. In reaching this conclusion I find myself in agreement with my noble and learned friends Lord Scarman and Lord Diplock whose speeches I have had the advantage of reading in draft since completing the preparation of this speech.

But I do not think that that right of challenge can be unqualified. It must, I think, depend upon the subject matter of the prerogative power which is exercised. Many examples were given during the argument of prerogative powers which as at present advised I do not think could properly be made the subject of judicial review. Prerogative powers such as those relating to the making of treaties, the defence of the realm, the prerogative of mercy, the grant of honours, the dissolution of Parliament and the appointment of ministers as well as others are not, I think, susceptible to judicial review because their nature and subject matter are such as not to be amenable to the judicial process. The courts are not the place wherein to determine whether a treaty should be concluded or the armed forces disposed in a particular manner or Parliament dissolved on one date rather than another.

In my view the exercise of the prerogative which enabled the oral instructions of 22 December 1983 to be given does not by reason of its subject matter fall within what for want of a better phrase I would call the 'excluded categories' some of which I have just mentioned. It follows that in principle I can see no reason why those instructions should not be the subject of judicial review. . . .

LORD BRIGHTMAN agreed with LORD FRASER on this point about the prerogative.

R v *Secretary of State for the Home Department, ex parte Fire Brigades Union*
[1995] 2 AC 513, House of Lords

The Criminal Injuries Compensation Scheme had been introduced under the prerogative. Under the Criminal Justice Act 1988, ss. 108–117, Schs 6 and 7 the scheme was enacted and would come into force on 'such day as the Secretary of State may . . . appoint' – s. 171(1). No day was appointed and the non-statutory scheme continued. In 1993 the Secretary of State indicated that the enacted provisions would not be brought into force and that the existing scheme would be replaced by another non-statutory scheme under which the basis for the determination of compensation awards would be changed from common law principles to a tariff fixed according to particular categories of injury. The Appropriation Act 1994 approved supply estimates which contained an amount for criminal injury compensation under the tariff scheme. The applicants, representing people likely to be the victims of violent crime, sought declarations that the Secretary of State was in breach of a duty under the 1988 Act by (1) not bringing into force the enacted provisions, and (2) that the introduction of the tariff scheme was in breach of the duty and an abuse of prerogative power. The Divisional Court dismissed the application but the Court of Appeal allowed an appeal on the second declaration by a majority. On appeal their Lordships dismissed the cross-appeal that there was a legally enforceable duty to bring ss. 108–117 into force.

LORD BROWNE-WILKINSON . . . It does not follow that, because the Secretary of State is not under any duty to bring the section into effect, he has an absolute and unfettered discretion whether or not to do so. So to hold would lead to the conclusion that both Houses of Parliament had passed the Bill through all its stages and the Act received the Royal Assent merely to confer an enabling power on the executive to decide at will whether or not to make the parliamentary provisions a part of the law.

Such a conclusion, drawn from a section to which the sidenote is 'Commencement,' is not only constitutionally dangerous but flies in the face of common sense. The provisions for bringing sections into force under section 171(1) apply not only to the statutory scheme but to many other provisions. For example, the provisions of Parts I, II and III relating to extradition, documentary evidence in criminal proceedings and other evidence in criminal proceedings are made subject to the same provisions. Surely, it cannot have been the intention of Parliament to leave it in the entire discretion of the Secretary of State whether or not to effect such important changes to the criminal law. In the absence of express provisions to the contrary in the Act, the plain intention of Parliament in conferring on the Secretary of State the power to bring certain sections into force is that such power is to be exercised so as to bring those sections into force when it is appropriate and unless there is a subsequent change of circumstances which would render it inappropriate to do so.

If, as I think, that is the clear purpose for which the power in section 171(1) was conferred on the Secretary of State, two things follow. First, the Secretary of State comes under a clear duty to keep under consideration from time to time the question whether or not to bring the sections (and therefore the statutory scheme) into force. In my judgment he cannot lawfully surrender or release the power contained in section 171(1) so as to purport to exclude its future exercise either by himself or by his successors. In the course of argument, the Lord Advocate accepted that this was the correct view of the legal position. It follows that the decision of the Secretary of State to give effect to the statement in paragraph 38 of the White Paper (Cm. 2434) that 'the provisions in the Act of 1988 will not now be implemented' was unlawful. The Lord Advocate contended, correctly, that the attempt by the Secretary of State to abandon or release the power conferred on him by section 171(1), being unlawful, did not bind either the present Secretary of State or any successor in that office. It was a nullity. But, in my judgment, that does not alter the fact that the Secretary of State made the attempt to bind himself not to exercise the power conferred by section 171(1) and such attempt was an unlawful act.

There is a second consequence of the power in section 171(1) being conferred for the purpose of bringing the sections into force. As I have said, in my view the Secretary of State is entitled to decide not to bring the sections into force if events subsequently occur which render it undesirable to do so. But if the power is conferred on the Secretary of State with a view to bringing the sections into force, in my judgment the Secretary of State cannot himself procure events to take place and rely on the occurrence of those events as the ground for not bringing the statutory scheme into force. In claiming that the introduction of the new tariff scheme renders it undesirable now to bring the statutory scheme into force, the Secretary of State is, in effect, claiming that the purpose of the statutory power has been frustrated by his own act in choosing to introduce a scheme inconsistent with the statutory scheme approved by Parliament.

The lawfulness of the decision to introduce the tariff scheme

The tariff scheme, if validly introduced under the Royal Prerogative, is both inconsistent with the statutory scheme contained in sections 108 to 117 of the Act and intended to be permanent. In practice, the tariff scheme renders it now either impossible or at least more expensive to reintroduce the old scheme or the statutory enactment of it contained in the Act of 1988. The tariff scheme involves the winding-up of the old Criminal Injuries Compensation Board together with its team of those skilled in assessing compensation on the common law basis and the creation of a new body, the Criminal Injuries Compensation Authority, set up to assess compensation on the tariff basis at figures which, in some cases, will be very substantially less than under the old scheme. All this at a time when Parliament has expressed its will that there should be a scheme based on the tortious measure of damages, such will being expressed in a statute which Parliament has neither repealed nor (for reasons which have not been disclosed) been invited to repeal.

My Lords, it would be most surprising if, at the present day, prerogative powers could be validly exercised by the executive so as to frustrate the will of Parliament expressed in a statute and, to an extent, to pre-empt the decision of Parliament whether or not to continue with the statutory scheme even though the old scheme has been abandoned. It is not for the executive, as the Lord Advocate accepted, to state as it did in the White Paper (paragraph 38) that the provisions in the Act of 1988 'will accordingly be repealed when a suitable legislative opportunity occurs.' It is for Parliament, not the executive, to repeal legislation. The constitutional history of this country is the history of the prerogative powers of the Crown being made subject to the overriding powers of the democratically elected legislature as the sovereign body. The prerogative powers of the Crown remain in existence to the extent that Parliament has not expressly or by implication extinguished them. But under the principle in *Attorney-General* v *De Keyser's Royal Hotel Ltd* [1920] AC 508, if Parliament has conferred on the executive statutory powers to do a particular act, that act can only thereafter be done under the statutory powers so conferred: any pre-existing prerogative power to do the same act is pro tanto excluded.

How then is it suggested that the executive has power in the present case to introduce under the prerogative power a scheme inconsistent with the statutory scheme? First, it is said that since sections 108 to 117 of the Act are not in force they confer no legal rights on the victims of crime and impose no duties on the Secretary of State. The *De Keyser* principle does not apply since it only operates to the extent that Parliament has conferred statutory powers which in fact replace pre-existing powers: unless and until the statutory provisions are brought into force, no statutory powers have been conferred and therefore the prerogative powers remain. Moreover, the abandonment of the old scheme and the introduction of the new tariff scheme does not involve any interference by the executive with private rights. The old scheme, being a scheme for ex gratia payments, conferred no legal rights on the victims of crime. The new tariff scheme, being also an ex gratia scheme, confers benefits not detriments on the victims of crime. How can it be lawful to confer benefits on the citizen, provided that Parliament has voted the necessary funds for that purpose?

In my judgment, these arguments overlook the fact that this case is concerned with public, not private, law. If this were an action in which some victim of crime were suing for the benefits to which he was entitled under the old scheme, the arguments which I have recited would have been fatal to his claim: such a victim has no legal right to any benefits. But these are proceedings for judicial review of the decisions of the Secretary of State in the discharge of his public functions. The well known passage in the speech of Lord Diplock in the G.C.H.Q. case, *Council of Civil Service Unions* v *Minister for the Civil Service* [1985] AC 374, 408–410, demonstrates two points relevant to the present case. First, an executive decision which affects the legitimate expectations of the applicant (even though it does not infringe his legal rights) is subject to judicial review. Second, judicial review is as applicable to decisions taken under prerogative powers as to decisions taken under statutory powers save to the extent that the legality of the exercise of certain prerogative powers (e.g. treaty-making) may not be justiciable.

The G.C.H.Q. case demonstrates that the argument based on the ex gratia and voluntary nature of the old scheme and the tariff scheme is erroneous. Although the victim of a crime committed immediately before the White Paper was published had no legal right to receive compensation in accordance with the old scheme, he certainly had a legitimate expectation that he would do so. Moreover, he had a legitimate expectation that, unless there were proper reasons for further delay in bringing section 108 to 117 of the Act into force, his expectation would be converted into a statutory right. If those legitimate expectations were defeated by the composite decision of the Secretary of State to discontinue the old scheme and not to bring the statutory scheme into force and those decisions were unlawfully taken, he has locus standi in proceedings for judicial review to complain of such illegality.

Similar considerations apply when considering the legality of the minister's decisions. In his powerful dissenting judgment in the Court of Appeal Hobhouse LJ., ante, pp. 523c et seq., decided that, since the statutory provisions had not been brought into force, they had no legal significance of any kind. He held, in my judgment correctly, that the *De Keyser* principle did not apply to the present case: since the statutory provisions were not in force they could not have excluded the pre-existing prerogative powers. Therefore the prerogative powers remained. He then turned to consider whether it could be said that the Secretary of State had abused those prerogative powers and again approached the matter on the basis that since the sections were not in force they had no significance in deciding whether or not the Secretary of State had acted lawfully. I cannot agree with this last step. In public law the fact that a scheme approved by Parliament was on the statute book and would come into force as law if and when the Secretary of State so determined is in my judgment directly relevant to the question whether the Secretary of State could in the lawful exercise of prerogative powers both decide to bring in the tariff scheme and refuse properly to exercise his discretion under section 171(1) to bring the statutory provisions into force.

I turn to consider whether the Secretary of State's decisions were unlawful as being an abuse of power. In this case there are two powers under consideration: first, the statutory power conferred by section 171(1); second, the prerogative power. In order first to test the validity of the exercise of the prerogative power, I will assume that the Act of 1988, instead of conferring a discretion on the Secretary of State to bring the statutory scheme into effect, had specified that it was to come into force one year after that date of the Royal Assent. As Hobhouse LJ held, during that year the *De Keyser* principle would not apply and the prerogative powers would remain exercisable. But in my judgment it would plainly have been an improper use of the prerogative powers if, during that year, the Secretary of State had discontinued the old scheme and introduced the tariff scheme. It would have been improper because in exercising the prerogative power the Secretary of State would have had to have regard to the fact that the statutory scheme was about to come into force: to dismantle the machinery of the old scheme in the meantime would have given rise to further disruption and expense when, on the first anniversary, the statutory scheme had to be put into operation. This hypothetical case shows that, although during the suspension of the coming into force of the statutory provisions the old prerogative powers continue to exist, the existence of such legislation basically affects the mode in which such prerogative powers can be lawfully exercised.

Does it make any difference that the statutory provisions are to come into effect, not automatically at the end of the year as in the hypothetical case I have put, but on such day as the Secretary of State specifies under a power conferred on him by Parliament for the purpose of bringing the statutory provisions into force? In my judgment it does not. The Secretary of State could only validly exercise the prerogative power to abandon the old scheme and introduce the tariff scheme if, at the same time, he could validly resolve never to bring the statutory provisions and the inconsistent statutory scheme into effect. For the reasons I have already given, he could not validly so resolve to give up his statutory duty to consider from time to time whether to bring the statutory scheme into force. His attempt to do so, being a necessary part of the composite decision which he took, was itself unlawful. By introducing the tariff scheme he debars himself from exercising the statutory power for the purpose and on the basis which Parliament intended. For these reasons, in my judgment the decision to introduce the tariff scheme at a time when the statutory provisions and his power under section 171(1) were on the statute book was unlawful and an abuse of the prerogative power. . . .

LORD MUSTILL: . . . I turn to the second area of complaint, which relates to the implementation of the new scheme in a form which differs radically from that contained in Part VII of the Act. This complaint is advanced in two ways, first that the actions and statements of the Secretary of State were an abuse of the powers conferred by section 171(1), secondly, that the powers exercisable under the Royal Prerogative were limited by the presence in the background of the statutory scheme.

At first sight a negative answer to each of these averments seems inevitable, once given the premise that section 171(1) creates no duty to appoint a day. As regards the Act, in a perspective which may never yield a statutory scheme, the possibility of substituting one non-statutory scheme for another must have been just as much envisaged and tolerated as was the continuation of the existing non-statutory scheme, or indeed the termination of any scheme at all. The interval between the passing of the Act and the bringing into force of Part VII, if it ever happened, was simply a statutory blank.

So too, it would appear, as regards the argument based on the Royal Prerogative. The case does not fall within the principle of *Attorney-General* v *De Keyser's Royal Hotel* [1920] AC 508. There, in the words of Lord Dunedin, at p. 526, it was established that 'if the whole ground of something which could be done by the prerogative could be done by the statute, it is the statute that rules.' Thus, if in the present case Part VII had been brought into force there would have been no room left for the exercise of that aspect of the prerogative which had enabled the Secretary of State to establish and maintain the scheme. Once the superior power of Parliament has occupied the territory the prerogative must quit the field. In the present case, however, the territory is quite untouched. There is no Parliamentary dominion over compensation for criminal injuries, since Parliament has chosen to allow its control to be exercised today, or some day, or never, at the choice of the Secretary of State. Until he chooses to call the Parliamentary scheme into existence there is a legislative void, and the prerogative subsists untouched. The position is just the same as if Part VII had never been enacted, or had been repealed soon afterwards.

This is not to say that the decisions of the Secretary of State in the exercise of the prerogative power to continue, modify or abolish the scheme which his predecessor in the exercise of the same power had called into existence are immune from process. They can be called into question on the familiar grounds: *Reg.* v *Criminal Injuries Compensation Board, Ex parte Lain* [1976] 2 QB 864. But no question of irrationality arises here, and the decision to inaugurate a new scheme cannot be rendered unlawful simply because of its conflict on paper with a statutory scheme which is not part of the law.

VII

My Lords, I introduced the preceding discussion with the words 'At first sight' because the applicants have a further (and to my mind altogether more formidable) argument which challenges the implicit assumption that in the absence of a duty to appoint a day the Secretary of State's dealings with the compensation scheme are entirely free from statutory restraint. Contrary to this assumption, it is said, there is no statutory void; for although Part VII is not itself in force, section 171(1) is in force and must not be ignored. The continued existence of section 171(1) means that, even if there is no present duty to appoint a day, there is a continuing duty, which will subsist until either a day is appointed or the relevant provisions are repealed, to address in a rational manner the question whether the power created by section 171(1) should be exercised. This continuing duty overshadows the exercise by the Secretary of State of his powers under the Royal Prerogative.

To some degree this argument is uncontroversial. I accept, and indeed the Lord Advocate does not dispute, that the Secretary of State cannot simply put out of his mind the subsisting discretion under section 171(1). But I part company with the argument at the next stage. One must look at the practicalities, which Parliament must be taken to have envisaged. Pending the appointment of a day it is impossible for the Secretary of State to remain completely inactive. He has no choice but to do something about compensation for criminal injuries: whether wind up the existing scheme and put nothing in its place; or keep the existing scheme in force; or modify it; or copy the statutory scheme. It seems to me inevitable, once it is acknowledged that it may be proper at any given time for the Secretary of State to say, 'It is inappropriate at present to put the statutory scheme into force' that it can be proper for him to install something different from the statutory scheme. Otherwise there would be the absurdity that the Secretary of State is obliged to do something under the Royal Prerogative which he is not obliged to do under the statute. Thus, merely to introduce a cheaper scheme cannot in itself be an abuse of the prerogative powers which subsist in the interim. If the

Secretary of State had made an announcement as follows: 'I have come to the conclusion after careful study that for the reasons which I have explained the Parliamentary scheme must now be seen as too expensive, slow and top-heavy; that its priority is not sufficiently high to justify the great expense when there are other calls on the country's resources; that the scheme which I propose will do substantial justice in a more efficient way; and that accordingly I shall run the scheme for a while to see how it works and if, as I confidently expect, it is a success I will ask Parliament to agree with me and repeal the statutory scheme . . .' it is hard to see what objection could have been taken. Does not the minister's actual stance, although perhaps more likely to provoke hostility, really come to the same thing?

The applicants reply that it does not, essentially for two reasons. First, they contend that the Secretary of State has renounced the statutory duty which still dominates the prerogative in this field: not the duty, as under the argument already discussed and rejected, to bring Part VII into force, but the duty to keep under review the powers conferred by section 171(1). I would reject this argument. Perhaps the Secretary of State has laid himself open to attack more than he need have done by the tone of his announcement, but I cannot read him as having said that however much circumstances may change he will never think again; and even if he had said this his statement would have been meaningless since, leaving aside questions arising from the doctrine of 'legitimate expectation' which do not arise here, nothing that he says on one day could bind him in law, or bind his successor, not to say and do the opposite the next day.

Furthermore, even if the argument were sound it would not yield any useful relief. The most that the court could do would be to grant a declaration that the Secretary of State is now and in the future obliged to keep the power under review in a spirit of good faith: something which the Lord Advocate on his behalf has not denied. To this declaration he could respond: 'As for the present, you can see that I have not only kept the appointment of a day under review but have examined it in depth, and have come to a conclusion which, even if you do not care for it, is undeniably rational. As for the future, I will continue to keep the power under review, although I cannot at present foresee circumstances which will impel me or my successors to a different view.' Such a reply would in practice be impregnable, and for my part I would not be prepared as a matter of discretion to grant relief so empty of content.

The applicants' second contention is that the Secretary of State has frustrated the intentions of Parliament by bringing in his own inconsistent scheme and hence nullifying any realistic possibility that he will perform his continuing duty to keep the implementation of the statutory scheme under review. I do not accept this. No doubt if Part VII had been the subject of section 171(1) and hence due to come into force inevitably on a fixed date the creation of any different scheme otherwise than purely as an interim measure would have been a breach of duty. It is also possible to imagine cases where the provisions to be brought into force on an appointed day are such as to become incapable of execution if irreversible changes have been made in the meantime, and it may be that to make such changes would be an abuse of the prerogative. But this is not so here. The new scheme is not in tablets of stone. Certainly, it would be an inconvenient, time-consuming and expensive business to dismantle the scheme and return to something on the former lines. But it would be feasible to do so, just as it proved feasible to pull down the original scheme which has been firmly established over many years. Nothing is certain in politics. Who is to say that a successor in office, under the present or some future administration, with wholly different ideas on social policy and financial means and priorities, might not decide that the present Secretary of State has taken a completely wrong turning and that after all the Parliamentary scheme is best? If he did so, and made an order under section 171(1), accompanied by the necessary regulations and by executive action to wind up the new scheme, there is nothing in what the present Secretary of State has done that could stand in his way. His words have no lasting effect; he has not put an end to the statutory scheme; only Parliament can do that. So long as he and his successors in office perform in good faith the duty to keep the implementation of Part VII under review there is in my opinion no ground for the court to interfere

... [Lords Lloyd of Berwick and Nicholls of Birkenhead gave speeches concurring with Lord Browne-Wilkinson, and Lord Keith of Kinkel concurred with Lord Mustill]

Appeal dismissed.

QUESTION

Are the majority buttressing legislative supremacy against improper executive intervention by way of the prerogative, or is their intervention improper?

NOTE: See I. Leigh 'The Prerogative, Legislative Power and the Democratic Deficit: the Fire Brigades Case' [1995] 3 *Web JCLI.*

The courts' general approach When the courts review delegated legislation the approach they take is to look at the purposes of the enabling statute in order to check if the delegated legislation is *intra vires* or not. The courts presume that certain things may not be done by delegated legislation without express authorization by the enabling statute. Thus delegated legislation has been found to be *ultra vires* where it purported to:

(a) impose taxation (*Attorney-General* v *Wilts United Dairies Ltd* (1921) 37 TLR 884);

(b) deny the citizen access to the courts to determine rights and obligations (*Customs & Excise Commissioners* v *Cure & Deely Ltd* [1962] 1 QB 340; *R* v *Lord Chancellor, ex parte Witham* [1998] QB 575);

(c) interfere with the liberty of the citizen (*Chester* v *Bateson* [1920] 1 KB 829).

Circumstances can change such a presumption, as in *Liversidge* v *Anderson* [1942] AC 206, in which a Defence of the Realm regulation was upheld which allowed a Minister to order detention of persons whom he had reasonable cause to believe to be of hostile origin or associations and in need of subjection to preventive control. The fact that this case was decided during the Second World War may explain its illiberality. See the powerful dissent by Lord Atkin, at pp. 225–46.

Procedural ultra vires Delegated legislation can be challenged on the ground that specified procedures were not followed in making the legislative measure. This is part of the procedural impropriety class of judicial review (see p. 596 *post*). For an example of this ground of review, see *R* v *Secretary of State for Social Services, ex parte Association of Metropolitan Authorities* [1986] 1 WLR 1, at p. 356 *ante*. An important distinction is whether the procedural requirement is mandatory or directory.

Substantive ultra vires See Chapter 8 on the illegality and irrationality grounds of review. Where irrationality or reasonableness is the ground of challenge, its chances of success would appear to be lower the more legislative in character the measure is. See *Nottinghamshire CC* v *Secretary of State for the Environment*, at p. 626 *post*. See also on the legislative/administrative distinction, *Bates* v *Lord Hailsham of St Marylebone*, at p. 355 *ante*. There also appears to be a distinction drawn between Parliamentary measures and local authority bye-laws, with bye-laws being less immune from challenge. There is still a presumption that bye-laws passed for general welfare will be benevolently construed (see *Kruse* v *Johnson* [1898] 2 QB 91).

The grounds of judicial review which seem to be most important with respect to quasi-legislation are legitimate expectations and unreasonableness. See G. Ganz, *Quasi-Legislation; Some Recent Developments in Secondary Legislation* (1987), pp. 41–6 and R. Baldwin & J. Houghton, 'Circular Arguments: The Status and Legitimacy of Administrative Rules' [1986] *Public Law* 239.

It seems that vagueness of regulations would, in a suitable case, be a ground of review.

McEldowney v *Forde*
[1971] AC 632, House of Lords

By the Civil Authorities (Special Powers) Act (Northern Ireland) 1922, s. 1:

(1) The civil authority shall have power, in respect of persons, matters and things within the jurisdiction of the Government of Northern Ireland to take all such steps and issue all such orders as may be necessary for preserving the peace and maintaining order, according to and in the execution of this Act and the regulations contained in the Schedule thereto, or such regulations as may be made in accordance with the provisions of this Act (which regulations, whether contained in the said Schedule or made as aforesaid, are in this Act referred to as 'the regulations'): Provided that the ordinary course of law and avocations of life and the enjoyment of property shall be interferred with as little as may be permitted by the exigencies of the steps required to be taken under this Act.

(2) For the purposes of this Act the civil authority shall be the Minister of Home Affairs for Northern Ireland. . . .

(3) The Minister of Home Affairs shall have power to make regulations – (*a*) for making further provision for the preservation of the peace and maintenance of order, and (*b*) for varying or revoking any provision of the regulations, and any regulations made as aforesaid shall, subject to the provisions of this Act, have effect and be enforced in like manner as regulations contained in the Schedule to this Act. . . .

On 22 May 1922 the Minister of Home Affairs made a regulation under the powers conferred by s. 1(3) of the Act. This provided that:

24A Any person who becomes or remains a member of an unlawful association or who does any act with a view to promoting or calculated to promote the objects of an unlawful association or seditious conspiracy shall be guilty of an offence against these regulations. . . .

The following organisations shall for the purposes of this regulation be deemed to be unlawful associations:

The Irish Republican Brotherhood, The Irish Republican Army, The Irish Volunteers, The Cumann na m'Ban, The Fianna na h'Eireann.

The named organizations were existing organizations of a militant type and it was conceded before the House of Lords, as it had been before the Court of Appeal in Northern Ireland, that they were in fact unlawful organizations.

On 7 March 1967 the Minister of Home Affairs made a further regulation under

s. 1(3) of the Act. After reciting that it was expedient to make further provision for the preservation of the peace and maintenance of order, this stated:

1. Regulation 24A of the principal regulations shall have effect as if the following organisations were added to the list of organisations which for the purpose of that regulation are deemed to be unlawful associations:

'The organisations at the date of this regulation or at any time thereafter describing themselves as "republican clubs" or any like organisation howsoever described.'

The appellant was charged in the magistrates' court with being a member of the Slaughtneil Republican Club contrary to regulation 24A as amended. The magistrates found that he was a member of the Club but that no evidence was given that he or the club was at any time a threat to peace, law, and order and that in so far as the police were aware there was nothing seditious in its pursuits or those of its members. The charge was dismissed but the Court of Appeal of Nothern Ireland (Lord MacDermott CJ, dissenting) held that the amended regulation was *intra vires* the Act of 1922 and remitted the case to the magistrates. On appeal to the House of Lords:

LORD HODSON: . . . The proscription of present and future 'republican clubs' including 'any like organisations howsoever described' is said to be something outside the scope and meaning of the Act and so incapable of being related to the prescribed purposes of the Act. Accepting that the word 'republican' is an innocent word and need not connote anything contrary to law, I cannot escape the conclusion that in its context, added to the list of admittedly unlawful organisations of a militant type, the word 'republican' is capable of fitting the description of a club which in the opinion of the Minister should be proscribed as a subversive organisation of a type akin to those previously named in the list of admittedly unlawful organisations. The context in which the word is used shows the type of club which the Minister had in mind and there is no doubt that the mischief aimed at is an association which had subversive objects. On this matter, in my opinion, the court should not substitute its judgment for that of the Minister, on the ground that the banning of 'republican clubs' is too remote. I agree that the use of the words 'any like organisation howsoever described' lends some support to the contention that the regulation is vague and for that reason invalid, but on consideration I do not accept the argument based on vagueness. It is not difficult to see why the Minister, in order to avoid subterfuge, was not anxious to restrict himself to the description 'republican' seeing that there might be similar clubs which he might seek to proscribe whatever they called themselves. If and when any case based on the words 'any like organisation' arises it will have to be decided, but I do not, by reason of the use of those words, condemn the regulation as being too vague or uncertain to be supported. I would dismiss the appeal.

LORD GUEST: . . . The final argument for the appellant related to the third category of organisations which it is said the regulation covered, namely, 'or any like organisation howsoever described.' It was submitted that this would cover any club whatever its name and whatever its objects and that such an exercise of the Minister's power was unreasonable, arbitrary and capricious. In my view this argument is not well founded. The regulation first of all embraces republican clubs eo nomine and they are caught by their very description. If they do not bear the name 'republican,' it would be a question of interpretation after evidence whether any particular club was covered by the words 'any like organisation howsoever described.' It is indeed not necessary for the purposes of this case where the organisation bore the name 'republican club' to examine this question in any great detail. But my provisional view is that the regulation would cover any organisation having similar objects to those of a republican club or of any of the named organisations or of any organisation whose objects included the absorption of Northern Ireland in the Republic of Ireland.

Having regard to all these matters I cannot say that the class of 'like organisations' is either ambiguous or arbitrary so as to invalidate the regulation. In my view this ground of attack also fails. . . . I would therefore dismiss the appeal.

LORD PEARCE: . . . Further, the 1967 regulation is too vague and ambiguous. A man may not be put in peril on an ambiguity under the criminal law. When the 1967 regulation was issued the citizen ought to have been able to know whether he could or could not remain a member of his club without being subject to a criminal prosecution. Yet I doubt if one could have said with certainty that any man or woman was safe in remaining a member of any club in Northern Ireland, however named or whatever its activities or objects.

Had the final phrase 'or any like organisation howsoever described' been absent, the regulation would have simply been an attack on the description 'republican,' however innocent the club's activities. Presumably the justification for it would have to be that the mere existence of the word republican in the name of a club was so inflammatory that its suppression was 'necessary for preserving the peace and maintaining order' and that the 'exigencies' of the need for its suppression did not permit the citizen's right in that respect to prevail. For the reasons given by the Lord Chief Justice I do not accept that such a justification could suffice. But be that as it may, the final phrase shows that this is more than an attack on nomenclature, since the club is deemed equally unlawful if it is a like organisation, whatever be the name under which it goes.

And what is the 'likeness' to a republican club which makes an organisation unlawful 'howsoever described'? Since a republican club is banned whatever may be its activities, the likeness cannot consist in its activities. And since the organisation is unlawful, howsoever described, the 'likeness' cannot consist in a likeness of nomenclature. The only possibility left seems to be that the 'likeness' may consist in the mere fact of being a club. In which case all clubs, however named, are unlawful – which is absurd.

One cannot disregard the final phrase, since that would wholly alter the meaning of the regulation. Without the final phrase it is simply an attack on nomenclature. But with the final phrase it cannot simply be an attack on nomenclature. One cannot sever the bad from the good by omitting a phrase when the omission must alter the meaning of the rest. One must take the whole sentence as it stands. And as it stands it is too vague and ambiguous to be valid.

I would therefore allow the appeal.

LORD PEARSON: . . . There is one further argument against the validity of this regulation, and it is the most formidable one. It is that the regulation is too vague, because it includes the words 'or any like organisation howsoever described.' I have had doubts on this point, but in the end I think the argument against the validity of the regulation ought not to prevail. The Minister's intention evidently was (if I may use a convenient short phrase) to ban republican clubs. He had to exclude in advance two subterfuges which might defeat his intention. First, an existing republican club might be dissolved, and a new one created. The words 'or at any time thereafter' would exclude that subterfuge as well as applying to new republican clubs generally. Secondly, a new club, having the characteristic object of a republican club, might be created with some other title such as 'New Constitution Group' or 'Society for the alteration of the Constitution.' The words 'or any like organisation however described' would exclude that subterfuge.

In construing this regulation one has to bear in mind that it authorises very drastic interference with freedom of association, freedom of speech and in some circumstances the liberty of the subject. Therefore it should be narrowly interpreted. Also it should if possible be so construed as to have sufficient certainty to be valid – ut res magis valeat quam pereat.

In my opinion the proper construction of the regulation is that the organisations to be deemed unlawful are –

(i) any organisation describing itself as a 'republican club,' whatever its actual objects may be, and

(ii) any organisation which has the characteristic object of a republican club – namely, to introduce republican government into Northern Ireland – whatever its name may be.

I would dismiss the appeal.

LORD DIPLOCK: . . . But there is another reason for rejecting this construction of the regulation which I find compelling. It is not, in my view, permissible to treat the regulation as severable in the way adopted by the majority of the Court of Appeal. To do so is to treat it as striking at more than one unrelated mischief whereas the inclusion in the description of the organisations deemed to be unlawful association of the words 'any like organisation' makes it plain that it is organisations possessing a common mischievous characteristic that are intended to be proscribed.

What then is that characteristic? Even if it were legitimate to infer that the Minister had knowledge of the objects of 'republican clubs' in existence at the date of the regulation he could not have knowledge of what would be the objects of clubs to be formed in the future which would describe themselves as 'republican clubs.' The characteristic struck at, therefore, cannot be the possession *in fact* of unlawful objects by the organisations proscribed. Nor for the reasons previously indicated can the common characteristic struck at be the use of the name 'republican club.' It is conceivable that the adoption of a particular name might of itself be so inflammatory in Northern Ireland as to endanger the preservation of peace and the maintenance of order, but the regulation proscribes 'like organisations' which do not adopt this name.

But there are no other ascertainable common characteristics of the organisations described in the regulation except that they are composed of members and possess objects of some kind or other and describe themselves by some name or other. If the Minister's intention was to proscribe all clubs and associations in Northern Ireland whatever their objects and name the regulation plainly falls ouside the power delegated to him by section 1 (3) of the Special Powers Act to make regulations 'for making further provision for the preservation of the peace and the maintenance of order.' It makes unlawful conduct which cannot have the effect of endangering the preservation of the peace or the maintenance of order. But if the Minister's intention was to proscribe some narrower category of organisations the suppression of which would have the effect of preserving the peace and maintaining order he has in my view failed to disclose in the regulation what the narrower category is. A regulation whose meaning is so vague that it cannot be ascertained with reasonable certainty cannot fall within the words of delegation.

It is possible to speculate that the Minister when he made the regulation now challenged bona fide believed that the sort of club which at that date described itself as a 'republican club' was likely to have unlawful objects which would endanger the preservation of the peace and the maintenance of order and by the words that he added he may have intended to do no more than to prevent such clubs from evading the regulation by dissolving and re-forming or by changing their names. If this was his intention he signally failed to express it in the regulation, for by no process of construction can it be given this limited effect. Or he may have thought it administratively convenient to insert in the regulation a description of proscribed organisations so wide as to include also those with lawful objects in order to be sure that none with unlawful objects should be omitted, and to rely upon the administrative discretion of the Attorney-General under section 3 (2) of the Act not to enforce the regulation. But to do this, however, if administratively convenient, would be outside his delegated legislative powers.

But this is speculation not construction and your Lordships' function is limited to construing the words which the Minister has used. In my view the words used by the Minister in the regulation are either too wide to fall within the description of the regulations which he is empowered to make under section 1 (3) of the Special Powers Act or are too vague and uncertain in their meaning to be enforceable.

I would allow this appeal.

Appeal dismissed.

NOTE: For criticism of this case, see MacCormick (1970) 86 *Law Quarterly Review* 171.

QUESTIONS

1. Do you think that the context of the 'troubles' in Northern Ireland helps explain the decision of the majority?

2. Is it not more important in that kind of situation for the courts to examine very carefully regulations which interfere with the liberty of the citizen?

Exclusion of judicial review   The exclusion of judicial review of delegated legislation has been the subject of a variety of decisions. On the one hand *Institute of Patent Agents* v *Lockwood* [1894] AC 347 indicated that it was possible, whilst *Minister of Health* v *R, ex parte Yaffe* [1931] AC 494 determined that judicial review was not excluded. See also p. 694 *post.*

Discretionary nature of judicial review   See *R* v *Secretary of State for Social Services, ex parte Association of Metropolitan Authorities* [1986] 1 WLR 1, at p. 356 *ante.*
See also p. 684 *post* on the discretionary nature of judicial review.

QUESTIONS

1. Is it more likely that delegated legislation which has been in existence for a little time will not be struck down by the courts than is the case with the various types of quasi-legislation and administrative action?

2. What kinds of delegated legislation might be struck down even if they had been in existence for some time?

3. Is judicial wariness in striking down delegated legislation satisfactory given the lack of real parliamentary oversight?

Partial invalidity

DPP v *Hutchinson*
[1990] 2 AC 783, House of Lords

The Secretary of State was empowered to make bye-laws for land appropriated for military purposes under the Military Lands Act 1892, s. 14(1). The power allowed for bye-laws which could prohibit intrusion onto such land but did not permit any prejudicial affect on any right in common. The Secretary of State made the RAF Greenham Common Bye-laws 1985 in respect of common land which had been appropriated for military purposes. Bye-law 2(b) provided that no person could enter or remain in the protected area without the permission of an authorised person. Protestors against nuclear weapons, who camped on the protected land, were charged and convicted of infringing bye-law 2(b). The Crown Court allowed the appeal on the basis that it was ultra vires as it prejudiced the rights of commoners. This decision was overturned by the Divisional Court on an appeal by case stated. The defendants appealed to the House of Lords.

LORD BRIDGE: My Lords, these two appeals raise important questions as to the tests to be applied in determining whether delegated legislation which on its face exceeds the power conferred upon the legislator may nevertheless be upheld and enforced by the courts in part on the basis that the legislation is divisible into good and bad parts and that the good is independent of, and untainted by, the bad.

When a legislative instrument made by a law-maker with limited powers is challenged, the only function of the court is to determine whether there has been a valid exercise of that limited legislative power in relation to the matter which is the subject of disputed enforcement. If a law-maker has validly exercised his power, the court may give effect to the law validly made. But if the court sees only an invalid law made in excess of the law-maker's power, it has no jurisdiction to modify or adapt the law to bring it within the scope of the law-maker's power. These, I believe, are the basic principles which have always to be borne in mind in deciding whether legislative provisions which on their face exceed the law-maker's power may be severed so as to be upheld and enforced in part.

The application of these principles leads naturally and logically to what has traditionally been regarded as the test of severability. It is often referred to inelegantly as the 'blue pencil' test. Taking the simplest case of a single legislative instrument containing a number of separate clauses of which one exceeds the law-maker's power, if the remaining clauses enact free-standing provisions which were intended to operate and are capable of operating independently of the offending clause, there is no reason why those clauses should not be upheld and enforced. The law-maker has validly exercised his power by making the valid clauses. The invalid clause may be disregarded as unrelated to, and having no effect upon, the operation of the valid clauses, which accordingly may be allowed to take effect without the necessity of any modification or adaptation by the court. What is involved is in truth a double test. I shall refer to the two aspects of the test as textual severability and substantial severability. A legislative instrument is textually severable if a clause, a sentence, a phrase or a single word may be disregarded, as exceeding the law-maker's power, and what remains of the text is still grammatical and coherent. A legislative instrument is substantially severable if the substance of what remains after severance is essentially unchanged in its legislative purpose, operation and effect.

The early English authorities take it for granted, I think, that if byelaws are to be upheld as good in part notwithstanding that they are bad in part, they must be both textually and substantially severable. . . .

Our attention has been drawn to a number of more recent English authorities on the severability of provisions contained in various documents of a public law character. I doubt if these throw much light on the specific problem of severance in legislative instruments. The modern authority most directly in point and that on which the Divisional Court relied is *Dunkley* v *Evans* [1981] 1 WLR 1522. The West Coast Herring (Prohibition of Fishing) Order 1978 (SI 1978 No. 930) prohibited fishing for herring in an area defined in the Schedule to the Order as within a line drawn by reference to coordinates and coastlines. The Order was made by the Minister of Agriculture, Fisheries and Food under the Sea Fish (Conservation) Act 1967. The prohibited area included a stretch of sea adjacent to the coast of Northern Ireland, representing 0.8 per cent of the total area covered by the Order, to which the enabling power in the Act of 1967 did not extend. The defendants admitted fishing in a part of the prohibited area to which the enabling power did extend but submitted that, by including the area to which the enabling power did not extend, the Minister had acted ultra vires and, since textual severance was not possible, the whole Order was invalid. The justices accepted this submission and dismissed the informations. The Divisional Court allowed the prosecutor's appeal. Delivering the judgment of the court, Ormrod LJ cited, at pp. 1524–1525, the following passage from the judgment of Cussen J in the Supreme Court of Victoria in *Olsen* v *City of Camberwell* [1926] VLR 58, 68:

> 'If the enactment, with the invalid portion omitted, is so radically or substantially different a law as to the subject matter dealt with by what remains from what it would be with the omitted portions forming part of it as to warrant a belief that the legislative body intended it as a whole only, or, in other words, to warrant a belief that if all could not be carried into effect the legislative body would not have enacted the remainder independently, then the whole must fail.'

It is to be noted that this quotation is from the judgment in a case where textual severance was possible. Following the quotation the judgment of Ormrod LJ continued:

> We respectfully agree with and adopt this statement of the law. It would be difficult to imagine a clearer example than the present case of a law which the legislative body would have enacted independently of the offending portion and which is so little affected by eliminating the invalid portion. This is clearly, therefore, an order which the court should not strive officiously to kill to any greater extent than it is compelled to do. . . . We can see no reason why the powers of the court to sever the invalid portion of a piece of subordinate legislation from the valid should be restricted to cases where the text of the legislation lends itself to judicial surgery, or textual emendation by excision. It would have been competent for the court in an action for a declaration that the provisions of the Order in this case did not apply to the area of the sea off Northern Ireland reserved by section 23(1) of the Act of 1967, as amended, to make the declaration sought, without in any way affecting the validity of the Order in relation to the remaining 99.2 per cent of the area referred to in the Schedule to the Order. Such an order was made, in effect, by the House of Lords in *Hotel and Catering Industry Training Board* v *Automobile Proprietary Ltd* [1969] 1 WLR 697, and by Donaldson J in *Agricultural, Horticultural and Forestry Industry Training Board* v *Aylesbury Mushrooms Ltd* [1972] 1 WLR 190. . . .

The modern English authority to which I attach most significance is *Daymond* v *Plymouth City Council* [1976] AC 609, where severability was not in issue, but where it appears to have been taken for granted without question that severance was possible. Section 30(1) of the Water Act 1973 gave power to water authorities:

> to fix, and to demand, take and recover such charges for the services performed, facilities provided or rights made available by them (including separate charges for separate services, facilities or rights or combined charges for a number of services, facilities or rights) as they think fit.

The subsection was silent as to who was liable to pay the charges. The Water Authorities (Collection of Charges) Order 1974 (SI 1974 No. 448) embodied provisions which required a rating authority to collect on behalf of a water authority a 'general services charge' (article 7(2)) referable to sewerage services 'from every person who is liable to pay the general rate in respect of a hereditament. . . .' (article 10(1)). A householder whose property was not connected to a sewer, the nearest sewer being 400 yards away from his house, refused to pay the charge and brought an action for a declaration that the Order could not properly apply to him. This House held, by a majority of three to two, that on the true construction of the enabling legislation there was no power to impose a charge for sewerage services upon occupiers of property not connected to a sewer. As I have said, the question of severability was not raised, but there is no hint in the speeches that the invalidation of the charging provision in relation to properties not connected to sewers would affect their validity in relation to properties which were so connected.

The test of textual severability has the great merit of simplicity and certainty. When it is satisfied the court can readily see whether the omission from the legislative text of so much as exceeds the law-maker's power leaves in place a valid text which is capable of operating and was evidently intended to operate independently of the invalid text. But I have reached the conclusion, though not without hesitation, that a rigid insistence that the test of textual severability must always be satisfied if a provision is to be upheld and enforced as partially valid will in some cases, of which *Dunkley* v *Evans* and *Daymond* v *Plymouth City Council* are good examples, have the unreasonable consequence of defeating subordinate legislation of which the substantial purpose and effect was clearly within the law-maker's power when, by some oversight or misapprehension of the scope of that power, the text, as written, has a range of application which exceeds that scope. It is important, however, that in all cases an appropriate test of substantial severability should be applied. When textual severance is possible, the test of substantial severability will be satisfied when the valid text is unaffected by, and independent of, the invalid. The law which the court may then uphold and enforce is the very law which the legislator has enacted, not a different law. But when the court must modify the text in order to achieve severance, this can only be done when the court is satisfied that it is effecting no change in the substantial purpose and effect of the impugned provision. Thus, in *Dunkley* v *Evans*, the legislative purpose and effect of the prohibition of fishing in the large area of the sea in relation to which the minister was authorised to legislate was unaffected by the obviously inadvertent inclusion of the small area of sea to which his power did not extend. In *Daymond* v *Plymouth City Council* the draftsman of the Order had evidently construed the enabling provision as authorising the imposition of charges for sewerage services upon occupiers of property irrespective of whether or not they were connected to sewers. In this error he was in the good company of two members of your Lordships' House. But this extension of the scope of the charging power, which, as the majority held, exceeded its proper limit, in no way affected the legislative purpose and effect of the charging power as applied to occupiers of properties which were connected to sewers.

To appreciate the full extent of the problem presented by the Greenham byelaws it is necessary to set out the full text of the prohibitions imposed by byelaw 2 which provides:

> No person shall: (a) enter or leave or attempt to enter or leave the protected area except by way of an authorised entrance or exit. (b) enter, pass through or over or remain in or over the protected area without authority or permission given by or on behalf of one of the persons mentioned in byelaw 5(1). (c) cause or permit any vehicle, animal, aircraft or thing to enter into or upon or to pass through or over or to be or remain in or upon or over the protected area without authority or permission given by or on behalf of one of the persons mentioned in byelaw 5(1). (d) remain in the protected area after having been directed to leave by any of the persons mentioned in byelaw 4. (e) make any false statement, either orally or in writing, or employ any other form of misrepresentation in order to obtain entry to any part of the protected area or to any building or premises within the protected area. (f) obstruct any constable (including a constable under the control of the Defence Council) or any other person acting in the proper exercise or execution of his duty within the protected area. (g) enter any part of the protected area which is shown by a notice as being prohibited or restricted. (h) board, attempt to board, or interfere with, or interfere with the movement or passage, of any vehicle, aircraft or other installation in the protected area. (i) distribute or display any handbill, leaflet, sign, advertisement, circular, poster, bill, notice or object within the protected area or affix the same to either side of the perimeter fences without authority or permission given by or on behalf of one of the persons mentioned in byelaw 5(1). (j) interfere with or remove from the protected area any property under the control of the Crown or the service authorities of a visiting force or, in either case, their agents or contractors. (k) wilfully damage, destroy, deface or remove any notice board or sign within the protected area. (l) wilfully damage, soil, deface or mark any wall, fence, structure, floor, pavement, or other surface within the protected area.

It is at once apparent that paragraphs (a), (b), (c), (d), (g), (j) and (l) are ultra vires as they stand.

Paragraphs (e), (f), (i) and (k) appear to be valid and paragraph (h) is probably good in part and bad in part, since the exercise by a commoner of his rights may well interfere with the movement or passage of vehicles. Textual severance can achieve nothing since it is apparent that the valid provisions are merely ancillary to the invalid provisions. . . .

I think the proper test to be applied when textual severance is impossible, following in this respect the Australian authorities, is to abjure speculation as to what the maker of the law might have done if he had applied his mind to the relevant limitation on his powers and to ask whether the legislative instrument

> with the invalid portions omitted would be substantially a different law as to the subject matter dealt with by what remains from what it would be with the omitted portions forming part of it: *Rex v Commonwealth Court of Conciliation and Arbitration, Ex parte Whybrow & Co.* 11 CLR 1, 27.

In applying this test the purpose of the legislation can only be inferred from the text as applied to the factual situation to which its provisions relate. Considering the Greenham byelaws as a whole it is clear that the absolute prohibition which they impose upon all unauthorised access to the protected area is no less than is required to maintain the security of an establishment operated as a military airbase and wholly enclosed by a perimeter fence. Byelaws drawn in such a way as to permit free access to all parts of the base to persons exercising rights of common and their animals would be byelaws of a totally different character. They might serve some different legislative purpose in a different factual situation, as do some other byelaws to which our attention has been drawn relating to areas used as military exercise grounds or as military firing ranges. But they would be quite incapable of serving the legislative purpose which the Greenham byelaws, as drawn, are intended to serve.

For these reasons I conclude that the invalidity of byelaw 2(b) cannot be cured by severance. It follows that the appellants were wrongly convicted and I would allow their appeals, set aside the order of the Divisional Court and restore the order of the Crown Court at Reading.

[Lords Griffith, Goff and Oliver concurred with Lord Bridge.]

LORD LOWRY: . . . My Lords, the accepted view in the common law jurisdictions has been that, when construing legislation the validity of which is under challenge, the first duty of the court, in obedience to the principle that a law should, whenever possible, be interpreted ut res magis valeat quam pereat, is to see whether the impugned provision can reasonably bear a construction which renders it valid. Failing that, the court's duty, subject always to any relevant statutory provision such as the Australian section 15A, is to decide whether the whole of the challenged legislation or only part of it must be held invalid and ineffective. That problem has traditionally been resolved by applying first the textual, and then the substantial, severability test. If the legislation failed the first test, it was condemned in its entirety. If it passed that test, it had to face the next hurdle. This approach, in my opinion, has a great deal in its favour.

The basic principle is that an ultra vires enactment, such as a byelaw, is void ab initio and of no effect. The so-called blue pencil test is a concession to practicality and ought not to be extended or weakened. In its traditional form it is acceptable because, once the offending words are ignored, no word or phrase needs to be given a meaning different from, or more restrictive than, its original meaning. Therefore the court has not legislated; it merely continues to apply that part of the existing legislation which is good.

It may be argued that a policy split has developed and that it is time to show common sense and bring our thinking up to date by a further application of the ut res magis valeat quam pereat principle. I am, however, chary of yielding to this temptation for a number of reasons. 1. The blue pencil test already represents a concession to the erring law-maker, the justification for which I have tried to explain. 2. When applying the blue pencil test (which actually means ignoring the offending words), the court cannot cause the text of the instrument to be altered. It will remain as the ostensible law of the land unless and until it is replaced by something else. It is too late now to think of abandoning the blue pencil method, which has much to commend it, but the disadvantage inherent in the method ought not to be enlarged. 3. It is up to the law-maker to keep within his powers and it is in the public interest that he should take care, in order that the public may be able to rely on the written word as representing the law. Further enlargement of the court's power to validate what is partially invalid will encourage the law-maker to enact what he pleases, or at least to enact what may or may not be valid, without having to fear any worse result than merely being brought back within bounds. 4. *Dunkley* v *Evans* [1981] 1 WLR 1522 and *Thames Water Authority* v *Elmbridge Borough Council* [1983] QB, 570 are very special cases. I recall in that regard what McNeill J said in *Reg.* v *Secretary of State for Transport, Ex parte Greater London Council* [1986] QB 556, 582D. 5. To liberalise the test would, in my view, be anarchic, not progressive. It would tend in the wrong direction, unlike some developments in the law of negligence, which have promoted justice for physically or economically injured persons, or the sounder aspects of judicial review, which have promoted freedom and have afforded protection from power. 6. The current of decisions and relevant authority has flowed in favour of the traditional doctrine.

This last observation brings me back to *Daymond* v *Plymouth City Council* [1976] AC 609, the case in which, as my noble and learned friend has said, it appears to have been taken for granted that severance was possible, and the question is, what significance should be attached to that fact when reviewing the doctrine of textual severability?

One cannot gainsay the authority of the Appellate Committee or that of the individual members of your Lordships' House of whom the committee was composed. Any indication, even if given obiter, that their Lordships, having considered the point, would have held that the Water Authorities (Collection of Charges) Order 1974 was valid and effective against occupiers of property who benefited directly from the water authority's services while inoperative against the occupiers who did not so benefit, could significantly erode the received doctrine of textual severability, since the blue pencil test could not have been used. But one must consider the way in which the case proceeded in your Lordships' House and also at first instance.

The remedy which the plaintiff sought was a declaration that the Plymouth City Council were not empowered to demand from him £4.89 or any sum on behalf of the South West Water Authority by way of a charge for sewerage and sewage disposal services. He contended that the water authority had power under section 30 of the Act of 1973 only to demand charges for services performed, facilities provided or rights made available and that, if the Order of 1974 purported to confer power to demand other charges, it was *to that extent* ultra vires. The words which I have emphasised set the stage for the argument and the decision. Phillips J made the declaration sought. On appeal direct to this House under section 12(1) of the Administration of Justice Act 1969 it was held, dismissing the appeal, Lord Wilberforce and Lord Diplock dissenting, that the plaintiff was entitled to the declaration made. The sole issue at each stage was whether section 30 empowered the water authority to charge occupiers of property who did not receive the benefit of the authority's services directly. No case was cited, and no argument was advanced, on the question whether the invalidity of the authority's demand against such occupiers as the plaintiff would nullify the Order of 1974 in relation to occupiers who were receiving the services, and both the initial judgment and their Lordships' speeches were entirely devoted to the complicated and strenuously contested issue concerning the scope of section 30. The minority took the view that section 30 authorised the proposed demand, and they had nothing to consider except the effect of the section on the plaintiff. And the majority, who reached the opposite conclusion, were concerned with the same point. The textual severability doctrine would have been of no help to either side.

It would therefore not be surprising if, having regard to the remedy sought and granted, the residual effect of the Order of 1974 on those who admittedly were liable for the charge was never mentioned.

I am therefore very reluctant to treat the case as an authority which by implication contradicts the established doctrine of textual severability for the purposes of the present appeal. Accordingly, I would allow this appeal on two grounds, (1) that there is no valid part of byelaw 2(b) which can be severed from the invalid part and stand by itself and (2) that the byelaw would not in any event survive the test of substantial severability.

Appeal allowed.

QUESTIONS

1. Is the majority giving the courts a wide power to amend delegated legislation by severing invalid portions?

2. Is such a power to amend constitutional or desirable, given that Parliament can rarely amend delegated legislation?

Problems

T. Daintith, 'The Executive Power Today: Bargaining and Economic Control' in J. Jowell and D. Oliver (eds), *The Changing Constitution*
(2nd edn, 1989), p. 193, at pp. 197–98, 215–18

I use the term *imperium* to describe the government's use of the command of law in aid of its policy objectives, and the term *dominium* to describe the employment of the wealth of government for this purpose. The point of choosing a special terminology to mark this distinction is that different constitutional frameworks exist, as we shall see, for the deployment of these two kinds of resources.

A practical example may help to clarify the meaning of these terms, and will show incidentally the wide range of potential policy choices which government may need to consider in relation to a given problem. When oil and gas began to be discovered under the British sector of the North Sea from the early 1960s onward, government assumed that the massive investment required in rigs, platforms, barges, and other equipment would bring major opportunities for British industry. A report published in 1972 showed, however, that British industry was winning a disappointingly low share of orders, and was likely to go on doing so in the absence of government intervention: one of the reasons was that many of the major companies searching for and finding oil and gas under petroleum production licences were American and had a strong propensity to stick to their United States suppliers for all items of equipment, even down to such mundane necessities as chicken-wire. What forms might government intervention take? Using *imperium*, it could promulgate legislation (or use existing legal powers, if available) to prohibit or tax the importation or use of foreign equipment; or, more subtly, to set compulsory standards with which only British manufacturers (warned well in advance) would find it easy to conform; or to require licensees to buy British in preference to foreign goods where supplied on competitive terms. Using *dominium*, it could offer subsidies to British manufacturers of relevant equipment, or to licensees who purchased British, rather than foreign, equipment. Alternatively, *dominium* could be employed through the licence, which is in the nature of a grant to the licensee of the right to obtain for himself, against payment of a royalty, petroleum over which the State has proprietary rights. A preference in favour of British equipment could be made a term of the licence; or an undertaking to exercise such a preference, or evidence of having purchased such equipment in the past, could be made a criterion for the award of a licence. Forms of intervention other than through *imperium* or *dominium* might also be considered; government could content itself with a campaign of exhortation to licensees to buy British, or with the dissemination of information to licensees and manufacturers alike (though such measures will almost certainly involve government expenditure, and can therefore be seen as a form of *dominium*).

In the event, the government employed a variety of measures. It offered a subsidy to purchasers of British-made equipment, set up a specialized unit within the appropriate department to encourage and monitor British orders; made an informal agreement with the organization representing the main North Sea licensees, the United Kingdom Offshore Operators' Association, on tendering rules that would give British manufacturers 'full and fair opportunity' to compete for orders; and made acceptance and (where appropriate) past observance of this agreement one of the informal criteria considered by the minister in allocating petroleum licences among competing applicants. . . .

During this period [1975–78], an undertaking to comply with the government's wages policy was a prerequisite for the award of almost all government contracts and of some government industrial assistance; a known breach of the policy disqualified a company from consideration for such contracts and assistance (the 'blacklist'); and compliance with the policy was secured for the future as a legally enforceable term of such contracts and assistance. By thus using its very considerable purchasing and grant-giving powers, government was able to induce compliance with its policy over a very wide area of British industry (contractors were required to procure compliance by their major subcontractors) in a way which, again, one might according to a normal model of policy implementation expect to be achieved by *imperium*-type legislation. Was it just the shock of the unexpected that caused this use of *dominium* to be branded as 'unconstitutional?'

It is noteworthy that although government had announced its intention to use contracts and assistance in this way as early as 1975, the matter did not become controversial until mid-1977. For this there may be two reasons. First, by reason of its failure to reach agreement with the TUC on a new phase of pay policy, as already noted, the government was, from mid-1977, relying almost exclusively on this instrument for the enforcement of its pay limit. Second, the pay limit adopted in this phase was extremely vague: that wage settlements should *average* 10 per cent over the year. This implied a moving target, for excessively large early settlements would mean that later ones needed to be held down well below 10 per cent if the average was to be maintained. Settlements thus had to be looked at on a case-by-case basis, and the non-award of a grant or contract, or, worse, the loss of an existing one, came to depend on criteria which might change even as the parties negotiated. Government then compounded the problem by seeking unsuccessfully to keep secret the procedures to be used by Civil Servants in assessing pay settlements. With firms being blacklisted on this basis, it is hardly surprising that by the end of 1977 the policy should have been the subject of intense controversy. What is surprising – and perhaps a measure of the economic power of government – is that in the midst of this controversy the Confederation of British Industry should have entered into negotiations on, and ultimately refrained from opposing, a new government-contract pay-clause (1) requiring from the contractor undertakings to comply with the existing pay policy and with any future policy presented to Parliament by Command Paper; (2) making the Secretary of State for Employment the sole judge of whether a pay settlement by the contractor or a subcontractor was contrary to the policy: and (3) providing for termination of the contract at the discretion of the purchasing department if the Employment Secretary so held. This clause was incorporated in government contracts let from April 1978 onwards, but was withdrawn, along with the other supporting measures, after an adverse vote on the policy by the House of Commons in December 1978.

What, if anything, was constitutionally wrong with what the government did? Can we distinguish the controversial pay policy from the uncontroversial offshore purchasing policy? It was not wrong, in my view, to use *dominium*, rather than *imperium*, as the vehicle for either policy even though government's ability to do this derived from the state of economic dependence in which many of its contractors and grant-recipients – like its North Sea licensees – found themselves. Such use was, so far as we know, fully in accord with existing constitutional law and convention. It *was* wrong, in the case of pay policy, to use *dominium* to impose a policy which Parliament would never have accepted under the form of legislation with sanctions attached. The enforcement of the pay limit in the 1977–8 phase (but not before) was both secret and arbitrary, akin to a process of enforcing a speed limit defined as '10 or more miles per hour in excess of the average speed recorded on the road and day in question' – not a likely legislative formula. The 1978 pay clause involved a delegation to the minister of rule-making power with no parliamentary control and of decision-making power with no legal control: such combinations of delegations do not appear on the peace-time statute book. These vices were absent from the offshore purchasing arrangements, which, moreover, were fully agreed with the licensees' representative body.

It is, of course, the very fact that no law or convention of our constitution appeared to prevent the use *dominium* in this arbitrary way that should cause us concern. We should not assume that this defect can be easily rectified. Practical proposals for reform can of course be made. It would be desirable to strengthen the instruments of parliamentary review of public expenditure so as to make them more sensitive to the varied ways in which expenditure – or refraining from expenditure – may promote different policy goals, and perhaps also more open to the complaints of those disadvantaged by such manipulations. A case might also be made for subjecting the use by central government of a dominant economic position to the same kinds of constraints as are imposed on private firms and some public-sector bodies by competition legislation, in particular the Fair Trading Act 1973. Useful as such improvements might be, we should not expect them to hold government back on the occasions when it feels that major political or economic gains can result from sweeping or unorthodox use of its *dominium* powers.

Whether the courts are yet equal to this task is a matter for speculation. The weak legislative structure of *dominium*, and the informality with which it may be exercised, clearly no longer inhibit judicial review as once they might have done. But judicial attitudes remain hard to predict. True it is that the actions of local authorities in a trio of recent cases: [*Wheeler* v *Leicester City Council* [1985] AC 1054; *R* v *Ealing, Hammersmith and Fulham, and Camden LBC's, ex parte Times Newspapers* [1985] 85 LGR 316; *R* v *Lewisham LBC, ex parte Shell UK Ltd* [1988] 1 All ER 938] all involved the denial of contracts or facilities, in aid of broad policies comparable to those invoked in black-listing, and were condemned by the courts with explicit reference to the impropriety of using such powers to sanction lawful behaviour. Sauce for the local authority goose may not, however, be sauce for the central government gander: *R* v *Secretary of State for the Home Department, ex parte Northumbria Police Authority* [1988] 1 All ER 556 which, while not a black-listing case, raises an important point of constitutional principle, is suffused with a much more benevolent judicial approach to central government *dominium* than was apparent in the local authority cases. None the less, the reinforcement and systematization of principles of judicial review applicable to the use of *dominium* may for the present be the best way of ensuring its constitutional rectitude while not unduly restricting governmental initiative and effectiveness in problem-solving.

QUESTIONS

1. Do you agree with Daintith that the use of *dominium* to implement the pay policy in 1975–78 was unconstitutional or inappropriate?

2. On what basis could the courts review the exercise of *dominium* powers which had been approved by Parliament?

3. Does the material in this chapter suggest that the traditional theories and methods for overseeing or controlling government cannot accommodate the new techniques and methods of government? If so, what changes should be made?

SECTION 4:   Standards in Public Life

NOTE: Following the exposure by a newspaper that two MPs accepted payment for putting Parliamentary Questions, a Standing Committee on Standards in Public Life was established in October 1994. It made its first report in May 1995 which dealt with three topics: (i) Members of Parliament; (ii) The Executive: Ministers and Civil Servants; and (iii) Quangos. Topics (ii) and (iii) were within the power of the Government to deal with and the recommendations were accepted (see generally the Government's response Cm 2931). Action taken in relation to (ii) included amending the first paragraph of *Questions of Procedure for Ministers*, revising the Code of Conduct for Civil Servants, applying to former Ministers a regime similar to that used for civil servants, when they wish to take up business appointments on leaving office. So far as (iii) was concerned, a new Commissioner for Public Appointments was to oversee departmental arrangements for appointments to executive non-departmental public bodies and National Health Service bodies, in which merit would be the overriding principle of appointment. One of the Commissioner's tasks would be the drawing up of a code of conduct for public appointments procedures. The code and the Commissioner's guidance on it were published in April 1996.

As Parliament regulates its own affairs, the House of Commons decided upon its reaction to the Committee's report. The House did vote for a new Select Committee on Standards and Privileges and a Parliamentary Commissioner for Standards. The extracts which follow deal with codes of conduct and Members' interests.

First Report of the Committee on Standards in Public Life
Cm 2850, pp. 32, 34–35

We recommend that the House should restate the 1947 resolution which places an absolute bar on Members entering into contracts or agreements which in any way restrict their freedom to act and speak as they wish, or which require them to act in Parliament as representatives of outside bodies.

We recommend that the House should prohibit Members from entering into any agreements in connection with their role as Parliamentarians to under-take services for or on behalf of organisations which provide paid Parliamentary services to multiple clients or from maintaining any direct or active connections with firms, or parts of larger firms, which provide such Parliamentary services.

We recommend that the House should set in hand without delay a broader consideration of the merits of Parliamentary consultancies generally, taking account of the financial and political funding implications of change.

We recommend that the House should:

- require agreements and remuneration relating to Parliamentary services to be disclosed;
- expand the guidance on avoiding conflicts of interest;
- introduce a new Code of Conduct for Members;
- appoint a Parliamentary Commissioner for Standards;
- establish a new procedure for investigating and adjudicating on complaints in this area about Members. . . .

On disclosure we recommend:

- the Register should continue broadly in its present form, and should be published annually. However the detailed entry requirements should be improved to give a clearer description of the nature and scope of the interest declared;
- updating of the Register should be immediate. The current updated version should be made more widely available electronically;

- from the beginning of the 1995/96 session (expected in November) Members should be required to deposit in full with the Register any contracts relating to the provision of services in their capacity as Members, and such contracts should be available for public inspection;
- from the same time, Members should be required to declare in the Register their annual remuneration, or estimated annual remuneration, in respect of such agreements. It would be acceptable if this were done in bands: eg under £1,000; £1,000–5,000; £5,000–10,000; then in £5,000 bands. An estimate of the monetary value of benefits in kind, including support services, should also be made;
- Members should be reminded more frequently of their obligations to Register and disclose interests, and that Registration does not remove the need for declaration, and better guidance should be given, especially on first arrival in the House.

71. In addition, Members with employment agreements (including Directorships and Partnerships) which are unrelated to their role as Members, and which under our proposals would not therefore have to be deposited, should be advised to ensure that those agreements do not imply that they will perform any activities related to their Parliamentary role. Such action is necessary to reduce the risk of misunderstandings.

We recommend that Members should be advised in their own interest that all employment agreements which do not have to be deposited should contain terms, or be supported by an exchange of letters, which make it clear that no activities relating to Parliament are involved.

Second Report of the Select Committee of Standards in Public Life
HC 816 of 1994–95, paras 6–29, 35–49

6. In our First Report [HC 637 of 1994–95] we pointed to some of the possible practical difficulties associated with implementing the Nolan Committee's proposals on consultancies and disclosures in the Register, which our necessarily compressed discussions at that stage had identified.

7. As these practical issues are so important in determining our approach to the Nolan recommendations, we repeat here in full the relevant paragraphs of our First Report:

78. A number of key terms used in the Nolan proposals have not yet been defined – a task more difficult by Nolan's use of subtly different expressions covering apparently the same point in different recommendations. It is not clear, for example, whether 'the provision of services in their capacity as Members', 'activities in Parliament' and 'Parliamentary services' are intended to be synonymous, and their meaning is in any case not specified. Other terms which would have to be defined more closely before a workable proposal could be put to the House are 'firms' (whether, for instance, partnerships are covered) and 'agreements' (whether only a legally binding contract is included and whether only written agreements are covered).

79. Other uncertainties surround such questions as:

— the extent to which the proposals are intended, and should, cover only multi-client organisations involved in activities which Nolan describes as 'lobbying' and, if so, how this is to be defined;
— whether there is any logical case of exempting from the scope of any new rules firms with single clients, thus leaving a Member free to advise a number of firms individually but not to advise a firm which has them as its clients;
— the effect of the proposed restrictions on bodies such as trade associations, charitable organisations and pressure groups.

80. We believe that Members who have existing agreements entered into in good faith, and in conformity with the rules as they currently exist, would be put in a wholly

unreasonable position if the Nolan proposals were implemented before these practical problems had been resolved.

81. Other important factors arise. The proposal to ban any agreement 'to undertake services for or on behalf of organisations which provide paid Parliamentary services to multiple clients or to maintain any direct or active connection with firms, or parts of larger firms, which provide such Parliamentary services' is acknowledged by the Nolan report itself to raise difficult issues for those Members whose background is in the legal, accountancy or other professions, and who maintain a continuing connection with their firm or partnership. The suggestion in the Nolan report is that such a connection should not be retained 'unless arrangements can be made to separate completely the Member's interest in the firm from that part of its work' (ie the offering of Parliamentary services). But it is far from clear what in practice might be regarded as fulfilling such a requirement.

82. Similarly, the Nolan recommendations relating to disclosure in the Register would appear, on the face of it, to entail the depositing, with an indication of the amount of payment involved, or every contract entered into by a Member undertaking in that capacity a television or radio interview, or writing an article for a newspaper or journal. We doubt that this is what Nolan intended, but it is another issue which must be clarified.

8. Our detailed consideration of these issues since our First Report was debated by the House in July has, if anything, reinforced the uncertainties we highlighted then. In particular, we have been strengthened in our original misgivings about the wisdom and practicability of seeking to distinguish between different kinds of organisations – or parts of organisations – supplying so-called 'Parliamentary services', and of attempting to reach a workable definition of lobbying companies.

9. The distinction between single and multi-client consultancies is especially difficult to understand. Public disquiet has arisen chiefly because of the perception that Members' services are 'for hire' to outside interests. In that context, the Nolan report particularly highlighted advocacy for multi-client lobbying firms. This is a cause of concern, but no more so than advocacy on behalf of lobbying companies acting for a single client. In any case it would not be difficult to devise a system whereby a multi-client organisation could operate through a series of single-client subsidiaries, thereby circumventing any prohibition directed solely at lobbying companies with multiple clients.

10. Having wrestled with this problem at great length and in exhaustive detail we have been driven to the conclusion that the Nolan Committee's attempt to regulate merely *the types* of outside bodies with which Members should be allowed to have a paid relationship will not work. The difficulties of definition, and therefore of enforcement, are simply too great. Our alternative approach, which we explain in the following paragraphs, in fact goes significantly further than the Nolan recommendations. It would address Members' relations with both single client *and* multiclient consultancies, rather than singling out the latter.

11. The main source of public anxiety, as identified by Nolan, is the notion that influence, whether real or imagined, can be bought and sold through Members. This suggests that any remedial action, rather than seeking to draw a line of legitimacy between different types of outside body with which Members should or should not be allowed to have paid relationships, ought to concentrate on defining as closely as possible those *actions* by Members which, because they give rise to suspicions about the exercise – or attempted exercise – of improper influence, need to be prohibited.

12. We note that in 1858 the House resolved:

> That it is contrary to the usage and derogatory to the dignity of this House that any of its Members should bring forward, promote or advocate in this House any proceeding or measure in which he may have acted or been concerned for or in consideration of any pecuniary fee or reward,

a prohibition originally directed particularly at Members who were practising barristers.

13. We propose that the rules of the House should now distinguish between paid advocacy in Parliament (unacceptable for the reasons outlined above) and paid advice (acceptable provided it is properly registered and declared). Nolan considered the idea of separating advocacy from advice but was not persuaded finally that the difference was sufficiently clear cut to be enforceable. We believe that we have addressed the definitional problems identified by Nolan which arise from making this fundamental distinction.

14. Our Report is based on a three-pronged approach:

— a prohibition on paid advocacy in Parliament
— strict regulation governing paid advice
— transparency in all paid activities related to Parliament.

15. It is not feasible, however desirable the greater possible degree of clarity in any new rules, to provide for every conceivable eventuality in advance. Our task has been to recommend a framework to the House. It will be one of the key functions of the Parliamentary Commissioner for Standards and of the new Select Committee on Standards and Privileges to provide detailed guidance as cases of doubt arise.

III. AN EXPANDED 1947 RESOLUTION

16. We have concluded that the most sensible and fruitful course – foreshadowed in our First Report and consistent with, but going well beyond, Nolan – would be to take up and build upon the 1947 Resolution, which, amongst other things, deals with the issue of advocacy for payment. The wording of the existing Resolution reads:

> That it is inconsistent with the dignity of the House, with the duty of a Member to his constituency, and with the maintenance of the privilege of freedom of speech, for any Member of the House to enter into any contractual agreement with an outside body, controlling or limiting the Member's complete independence and freedom of action in Parliament or stipulating that he shall act in any way as the representative of such outside body in regard to any matters to be transacted in Parliament; the duty of a Member being to his constituency and to the country as a whole, rather than to any particular section thereof.

17. This Resolution represents a concise and well expressed statement of basic principles. However, whilst it describes the types of agreement which Members should not enter into on the grounds that their independence would thereby be fettered, it does not indicate the specific kinds of Parliamentary action which ought not to be undertaken, for payment, on behalf of outside bodies, whether or not they form the subject of a formal arrangement.

18. **We therefore recommend that the House be asked to agree to the following addendum to the 1947 Resolution:**

> and that in particular no Member of this House shall, in consideration of any remuneration, fee, payment, reward or benefit in kind, direct or indirect, which the Member or any member of his or her family has received, is receiving or expects to receive—
> (i)   advocate or initiate any cause of matter on behalf of any outside body or individual, or
> (ii) urge any other Member of either House of Parliament, including Ministers, to do so, by means of any speech, Question, Motion, introduction of a Bill, or amendment to a Motion or Bill.

19. We repeat that, should the House agree to such a resolution, its interpretation in particular circumstances will be a matter for the Select Committee on Standards and Privileges, as advised by the Parliamentary Commissioner for Standards. Nevertheless, before deciding on its merits, the House will expect some guidance from us on its scope and intent, as we see it.

20. The specific activities included in the proposed addendum to the 1947 Resolution are those

which ought to be presumed, *prima facie*, to constitute advocacy. The list should, however, be regarded as descriptive and illustrative rather than exhaustive. At the same time, we are concerned to ensure that no limitation on Members' freedom of action which we recommend interferes with their ability to inform themselves on matters of public concern, or with the performance of their paramount duty to represent the interests of their constituents and those of the public generally. The object of the prohibition contained in the Resolution is *paid* advocacy in Parliament. In their consideration of any complaint we would expect the Commissioner and the new Select Committee to have regard both to the nature and directness of the interest giving rise to any remuneration, and to how far the relevant Parliamentary activity could be regarded as conferring, or seeking to confer, a particular benefit on the interest in question.

SPECIFIC ACTIVITIES WITHIN THE HOUSE

(a) Speaking

21. No Member should take payment for speaking in the House. Such action would clearly be incompatible with the ban on paid advocacy which we have recommended. However, we recognise that speaking differs in a key respect from other forms of Parliamentary activity. The tabling of an Early Day Motion or of an amendment to a Bill, for example, is personal to the Member concerned and therefore undertaken for his own purposes of those of the cause he is espousing. A speech, by contrast, is a contribution to debate and therefore, in some sense, made for the benefit of the House as a whole; it can also be challenged or rebutted on the spot by other Members. Moreover, speaking in a debate involves participating in proceedings, as opposed, in most cases, to initiating them – a distinction to which we attach some importance [see para. 27]. For this purpose speaking includes supplementary questions (of which, by definition, no written notice is given).

22. We are not, by proposing a ban on paid advocacy in Parliament, seeking to deprive the House of well-informed contributions from Members with experience or knowledge of direct value to the subject being debated. If the ban were applied to paid advisers in all circumstances, this could lead to an undesirable position in which the Members entitled to take part in a debate would be predominantly those with less direct acquaintance with the subject before the House. We note that Nolan himself accepted that: 'There can be few cases where any damage to the public interest can result from a Member who has declared an interest speaking in the House, even in a Second Reading debate on a relevant Bill or in a Committee of the Whole House'.

23. On the other hand, it is not practicable to lay down in advance, with the precision that a Resolution of the House would require, all the circumstances in which it would or would not be proper for a Member with a paid interest to take part in a debate. It will be one of the main functions of the Code of Conduct, which the House has already decided should be drawn up, to set out a series of general principles against which particular cases can be judged. Members who, having consulted the Code, are still in doubt about their own position will be able to seek advice from the Parliamentary Commissionary on Standards or the Clerk of the House.

24. The new Committee on Standards and Privileges will be able to keep all these matters under review and will no doubt issue further guidance if it sees the need. Any significant changes would, of course, require the approval of the House. As time goes by, a body of experience and practice will be built up which will produce a clearer indication to Members as to what is likely to be thought acceptable and what is not. But in the last resort it will be for the individual Member to judge whether to speak in any given circumstances.

25. In making that judgement Members will need to bear in mind that the absolute requirement on them not only to register but also to declare their relevant financial interests will remain unchanged. If a complaint were made in an individual case, or if advice were sought in advance, we believe that the House would expect the Parliamentary Commissioner and the Select Committee to

consider any individual speech against the criterion of whether it might bring particular benefit to the organisation or individual from which the Member received payment.

26. It is important to make clear that it will not be the function of the Chair to enforce the ban on paid advocacy during speeches, either by interrupting a Member thought to be contravening it, or by declining to call him. Complaints will be a matter for the Commissioner to investigate in the first instance. The detailed procedure for the handling of complaints, and the proposed modus operandi of the Committee were set out in Appendixes 2 and 3 of our First Report.

(b) Questions, Motions, Amendments to Bills, Introduction of Bills etc

27. There is, in our view, a distinction to be drawn between initiating proceedings and merely taking part in them. The terms of our proposed addendum to the 1947 Resolution emphasise the act of initiation. In particular, the tabling of questions, motions, and amendments to bills, the introduction of bills, and the seeking of a debate on the adjournment on a Wednesday morning or at the end of the day constitute the initiation of proceedings. Any Member who is a paid Parliamentary adviser, or who receives any form of remuneration from any outside body, should not initiate proceedings of this sort if they relate specifically and directly to the affairs and interests of that body. No doubt a Member contemplating such action will wish to reflect carefully as to whether, say, the tabling of a question asking for certain statistics might be held to bring a particular benefit to a body from which he receives payment. In any case, a Member's relevant interests will now be recorded on the Order Paper under the terms of the Resolution agreed by the House on 19 July 1995.

28. The advice of the Parliamentary Commissioner, or of the other House authorities, will be available in advance to any Member who is uncertain about the precise application of the new rules in relation to any Parliamentary proceedings and who wished to seek it. If, after consulting the Commissioner, he remains in any doubt, he may feel that his proper course is to refrain from the proposed action.

(c) Voting

29. The proposed list of Parliamentary activities capable of constituting advocacy does not include voting, since that is covered by existing practice. The House's rules on voting are clear and long-established. As explained by Mr Speaker Abbot in 1811: 'This interest [that is to say an interest which disqualifies a Member from voting on a question] must be a direct pecuniary interest, and separately belonging to the persons whose votes were questioned, and not in common with the rest of His Majesty's subjects or on a matter of state policy.' We see no reason to change this practice . . .

. . .

35. Sponsorship is an issue which the Select Committee on Members' Interests has already addressed and the outcome of its deliberations is reflected in the current rules on registration, the relevant sections of which read as follows:

Sponsorship (Category 4)

24. This part of the form is divided into two main subsections. Subsection (a) relates to sponsorship or financial support of the Member as a candidate at the previous election: here the Member is required to register the source of any contribution to his or her election expenses in excess of 25 per cent of the total of such expenses.

25. Subsection (b) relates to other forms of sponsorship, which is interpreted to cover any regular or continuing support from companies or organisations from which the Member receives any financial or material benefit in support of his or her role as a member of Parliament. For example, it is necessary to register the provision of free or subsidised accommodation and the provision of the services of a research assistant free or at a subsidised salary rate. It is also necessary, in this subsection, to register any regular donation in excess of £500 per year made by an organisation or company to the Member's

constituency party if the donation is linked directly to the Member's candidacy in the constituency or if he or she acted as an intermediary between the donor and the constituency party.

26. There is a third question in this category of the form, supplementary to subsection (b) and designed solely to elicit whether the Member benefits personally from any payment or material benefit registered in that subsection. In other words, its purpose is to distinguish clearly between benefits accruing directly to the Member and those accruing solely to the constituency party.

27. Trade union sponsorships will normally be registrable under both subsections (a) and (b), particularly if they are based on the Labour movement's 'Hastings Agreement' of 1933; but if trade union donations to a constituency party are not linked in any way to the Member's candidacy in a constituency and were not arranged or solicited by the Member, nor paid via him or her, they are exempt from registration. The same criteria for registration apply to regular donations made to a constituency party by any other organisation or company.

36. The key paragraph here is paragraph 27, which (in the case of trade union sponsorship) makes the test of registrability whether the donation to a constituency party is linked to the Member's candidacy and whether it was arranged or solicited by the Member or is paid via him or her. Since the purpose of registration is to record 'those pecuniary interests held by Members *which might reasonably be thought by others to influence their parliamentary conduct or actions*,' a Member should not be able to engage in advocacy on behalf of a sponsoring organisation, whether a trade union or a company, where the sponsorship is of a kind which already has to be registered. But no such prohibition should apply in respect of sponsorships which are not registrable under existing rules.

APPLICATION TO A MEMBER'S FAMILY

37. It is already a requirement for a Member to record in the Register of Members' Interests any shareholdings of a particular type, not only held in his name but also in that of a spouse or dependent child. Any payment to a family member which arises out of his or her own occupation or activity and which is not linked to any services provided by a Member should not be regarded as a benefit for the purposes of defining paid advocacy in Parliament on the part of that Member. As regards the proposed addendum to the 1947 Resolution, the term 'family' should be taken to include the spouse of the Member and any dependent children, as in the case of the existing rules governing the Register.

IV. EMPLOYMENT AGREEMENTS

38. We support Nolan's view that agreements relating to Parliamentary activities should be put in writing. We deal later in this Report with the question of how far such agreements should be disclosed. We accept the Nolan recommendation that there is no need for disclosure of employment agreements unrelated to a Member's role in Parliament.

39. The present rule is that all remunerated outside employment must be included in the Register, irrespective of whether it has any bearing on a Member's actions in Parliament. We have no doubt that this discipline should continue to be observed.

40. If our recommendation that paid advocacy in Parliament should be prohibited altogether is adopted by the House, it is essential that no future agreements should require Members to take part in activities which can be described as advocacy.

41. The new requirement for employment agreements to be put in writing will apply principally to any arrangement whereby a Member may offer advice about parliamentary matters. We think it right, however, that it should also include frequent, as opposed to merely occasional,

commitments outside Parliament which arise directly from membership of the House. For example, a regular, paid newspaper column or television programme would have to be the subject of a written agreement, but ad hoc current affairs or news interviews or intermittent panel appearances would not.

42. It may not always be immediately obvious whether a particular employment agreement arises directly from, or relates directly to, membership of the House. At one end of the spectrum are those Members whose outside employment pre-dates their original election, whilst at the other extreme are those who have taken up paid adviserships since entering the House. In between there will be many cases which are difficult to classify. Some Members, for example, may provide advice on Parliamentary matters incidentally as part of a much wider employment agreement covering matters wholly unrelated to the House. In these circumstances, it would be for an individual Member to decide how far it would be proper to isolate the Parliamentary services within a separate, deposit-able agreement; in reaching that decision he may wish to consult the Commissioner.

V. DISCLOSURE OF AGREEMENTS AND AMOUNT RECEIVED, ETC.

43. The concern which the Nolan Report as a whole sought to address was the perception – albeit stimulated by a small number of cases – that outside interests are able to buy influence in the House. We have set out our reasons for believing that the better course is to go further than Nolan suggested, and straightforwardly to ban agreements involving paid advocacy. In these cases, therefore, the question of disclosure would no longer arise.

44. As we have made clear, other agreements relating to Parliament should be put into writing and deposited with the Parliamentary Commissioner for Standards, to ensure both that they are within the rules and that the ban on advocacy is effective. Where any doubt arises, the Commis-sioner will of course be able to pursue the matter with the Member and, if necessary, the Select Committee.

45. Given the ban on paid advocacy, which was not envisaged by Nolan, we are not persuaded that it should be a requirement to disclose the amount of remuneration paid in respect of deposited agreements.

46. Nolan refers to the declaration of the 'financial benefits Members receive as a consequence of being elected to serve their constituents'. In practice, many of the consultancy agreements which are at present registered and which are in future likely to be deposited with the Commissioner do not arise because the individual had become a Member of the House but are a continuation of a previous occupation. Some of the consultancies, and in particular non-executive directorships, may not arise from membership of the House at all and affairs in the House will rarely or never be relevant to them.

47. The Nolan report seemed to imply that the amount paid should be declared as an indication of how much time was being spent on outside activity rather than on the duties of a Member. But in reality any payment made will reflect not the amount of time spent in providing the advice, but the resources of the client and the quality of the advice.

48. Moreover, Nolan's reference to the 'financial benefits Members receive as a consequence of being elected' would in practice, if it were to be fairly applied, range far more widely that the Nolan Committee itself appeared to envisage. It would, for example, be hard to argue that most payments for broadcasting, newspaper articles and interviews, lecturing etc, would not be embraced.

49. In reality we judge that the real choice is between the view that compulsory disclosure of remuneration for legitimate activity is an unjustified instruction, and the view that full disclosure of all income – in effect, the publication of the tax return – should be required. Nolan concluded that 'no-one has put a convincing case' for full disclosure. We agree.

The Code of Conduct for Members of Parliament, together with
The Guide to the Rules
HC 688 of 1995–96

THE CODE OF CONDUCT FOR MEMBERS OF PARLIAMENT

Prepared pursuant to the Resolution of the House of 19th July 1995

I. Purpose of the Code

The purpose of the Code of Conduct is to assist Members in the discharge of their obligations to the House, their constituents and the public at large.

The Code applies to Members in all aspects of their public life. It does not seek to regulate what Members do in their purely private and personal lives.[*]

II. Public duty

By virtue of the oath, or affirmation, of allegiance taken by all Members when they are elected to the House, Members have a duty to be faithful and bear true allegiance to Her Majesty the Queen, her heirs and successors, according to law.

Members have a duty to uphold the law and to act on all occasions in accordance with the public trust placed in them.

Members have a general duty to act in the interests of the nation as a whole; and a special duty to their constituents.

III. Personal conduct

Members shall observe the general principles of conduct identified by the Committee on Standards in Public Life as applying to holders of public office:–

Selflessness
Holders of public office should take decisions solely in terms of the public interest. They should not do so in order to gain financial or other material benefits for themselves, their family, or their friends.

Integrity
Holders of public office should not place themselves under any financial or other obligation to outside individuals or organisations that might influence them in the performance of their official duties.

Objectivity
In carrying out public business, including making public appointments, awarding contracts, or recommending individuals for rewards and benefits, holders of public office should make choices on merit.

Accountability
Holders of public office are accountable for their decisions and actions to the public and must submit themselves to whatever scrutiny is appropriate to their office.

Openness
Holders of public office should be as open as possible about all the decisions and actions that they take. They should give reasons for their decisions and restrict information only when the wider public interest clearly demands.

Honesty
Holders of public office have a duty to declare any private interests relating to their public duties and to take steps to resolve any conflicts arising in a way that protects the public interest.

Leadership
Holders of public office should promote and support these principles by leadership and example.

Members shall base their conduct on a consideration of the public interest, avoid conflict between personal interest and the public interest and resolve any conflict between the two, at once, and in favour of the public interest.

Members shall at all times conduct themselves in a manner which will tend to maintain and strengthen the public's trust and confidence in the integrity of Parliament and never undertake any action which would bring the House of Commons, or its Members generally, into disrepute.

The acceptance by a Member of a bribe to influence his or her conduct as a Member, including any fee, compensation or reward in connection with the promotion of, or opposition to, any Bill, Motion, or other matter submitted, or intended to be submitted to the House, or to any Committee of the House, is contrary to the law of Parliament.

Members shall fulfil conscientiously the requirements of the House in respect of the registration of interests in the Register of Members' Interests and shall always draw attention to any relevant interest in any proceeding of the House or its Committees, or in any communications with Ministers, Government Departments or Executive Agencies.

In any activities with, or on behalf of, an organisation with which a Member has a financial relationship, including activities which may not be a matter of public record such as informal meetings and functions, he or she must always bear in mind the need to be open and frank with Ministers, Members and officials.

No Member shall act as a paid advocate in any proceeding of the House. No improper use shall be made of any payment or allowance made to Members for public purposes and the administrative rules which apply to such payments and allowances must be strictly observed.

Members must bear in mind that information which they receive in confidence in the course of their parliamentary duties should be used only in connection with those duties, and that such information must never be used for the purpose of financial gain.

. . .

NOTE: The two asterisked sentences were inserted following a resolution of the House of Commons when they approved a New Code of Conduct and Guide to the Rules proposed in the Select Committee on Standards and Privileges report (HC 763 of 2001–02) on 14 May (HC Deb, Vol 385, cols 731–751, 14 May 2002).

CODE OF CONDUCT: POCKET GUIDE TO THE RULES

www.publications.parliament.uk/pa/cm199697/cmselect/cmstand/688/pocket1.htm

THE RULES OF THE HOUSE REQUIRE

1. Disclosure of personal financial interests

   a. **By registration**
      - remunerated directorships
      - remunerated employment
      - clients where the services the Member provides arise from the Member's position as a Member of Parliament
      - contributions of over 25% of a Member's election expenses
      - sponsorships or other financial support which gives the Member payment, benefit or advantage

- regular donations (over £500) to constituency party linked to Member's candidacy or membership of the House
- provision by an outside body of services of research assistant or secretary, or free or subsidised accommodation for Member's use
- tangible gifts over £125 – hospitality over £225 (except expenses of conferences and site visits within the UK paid by the organiser)
- overseas visits (unless paid for from UK public funds or by an exempt institution)
- land or property other than homes used for personal residential purposes
- substantial shareholdings
- other interests which might be thought to influence a Member

  b. **By declaration** of any relevant current, past or expected pecuniary interest or benefit whether direct or indirect
- in debates in the House or proceedings in Standing or Select Committees
- on written notices, e.g. Questions, Early Day Motions, Amendments, Adjournment Debates
- to Ministers or servants of the Crown

  c. **By depositing an employment agreement** if services are provided in the capacity of a Member

2. **No paid advocacy**
A Member who has received, receives or expects to receive benefit from an outside body

may not

- *initiate* proceedings which relate **specifically and directly** to affairs or interests of that body, its clients or to other organisation or category with similar interests (*'Initiating' means e.g. tabling a Question, Motion or Amendment or applying for an adjournment debate*)
- make speeches or participate in proceedings with a view to benefiting that body **exclusively**

may

- *participate* in proceedings which directly and specifically relate to the interests of that body initiated by another Member provided the benefit is registered and declared

3. No participation in delegations where the problem affects only the body which pays him or her except where the problem is primarily a constituency matter

4. Personal interests are not pursued

5. No contracts with outside bodies which limit independence and freedom of action in Parliament

Register of Members' Interests
HC 419 of 2001–02, pp. iii, v, 12–13, 43–45, 79–80

INTRODUCTION TO THE JANUARY 2000 EDITION

This edition of the Register, the first for the Parliament elected in June 2001, records Members' Interests at 26 November 2001. Each Register since March 1996 has taken account of recommendations of the Committee on Standards in Public Life in May 1995 and decisions of the House of Commons taken in July and November 1995.

In July 1996 the House of Commons approved the publication of a Code of Conduct for Members of Parliament with a Guide to the Rules relating to the Conduct of Members. This document, which is circulated to all Members following their election, sets out in detail the rules governing the registration and declaration of Members' financial interests, and provides guidance on their application.

The Register was set up following a Resolution of the House of 22 May 1974. The maintenance of the Register is one of the principal duties laid on the Parliamentary Commissioner for Standards by House of Commons Standing Order No. 150.

Purpose of the Register
The main purpose of the Register is to provide information of any pecuniary interest or other material benefit which a Member receives which might reasonably be thought by others to influence his or her actions, speeches or votes in Parliament, or actions taken in his or her capacity as a Member of Parliament. Members are required to keep that overall purpose in mind when registering their interests.

Form of the Register
I have continued to take into account the recommendation of the Committee for Standards in Public Life that the entries should be improved to give a clearer description of the nature and scope of the interests declared. Each Member is responsible for the content and style of his or her own entry.

Relevant Remuneration
Members have been required since 1974 to register their sources of paid outside employment, but until 1995 there was no requirement to disclose the amounts of remuneration. The House of Commons resolved on 6 November 1995 that any Member who has an existing agreement or who proposes to enter into a new agreement *involving the provision of services in his or her capacity as a Member of Parliament* must deposit it with me in writing. The agreements, which are available for public inspection, must include the fees or benefits payable in bands of up to £1,000, up to £5,000 and thereafter in bands of £5,000, and these figures are shown in brackets after the Register entries.

The advocacy rule
Members of Parliament are prohibited from engaging in advocacy on behalf of outside bodies or persons from whom they receive payment. The Guide to the Rules relating to the Conduct of Members makes it clear that continuing benefits, i.e. directorships, other employment and sponsorship, can be divested to release a Member from the restrictions imposed by this rule, provided that there is no expectation of renewal. In the case of any one-off benefits such as visits and gifts recorded in this Register, the advocacy rule applies for the period of a year from registration. The date of registration appears against the benefit. In their Fourth Report of Session 1997–98, the Committee on Standards and Privileges confirmed that the same time limit should apply to single sponsorships.
. . .

Administrative arrangements and inspection
Under the authority of the Select Committee on Standards and Privileges, the Register is published by The Stationery Office at the beginning of a Parliament and thereafter approximately once a year. The published Register and its regular updates are on the Internet at:

http://www.publications.parliament.uk/pa/cm199900/cmregmem/memi02.htm

It is the responsibility of Members to notify changes in their registrable interests within four weeks of the change occurring; and between its annual printings the Register is updated in a looseleaf version. The looseleaf version is open for public inspection in the Registry of Members' Interests, in the Committee Office of the House of Commons (Tel: 020 7219 6614). It may be inspected when the House is sitting between 11 am and 5 pm on Monday to Thursday and between 11 am and 3 pm on Friday. During parliamentary recesses, and especially during August, the hours of inspection are more limited. A copy of the current looseleaf Register is also placed in the Library of the House of Commons for the use of Members.

Copies of the Code of Conduct and Guide to the Rules relating to the Conduct of Members may be obtained from The Stationery Office as House of Commons paper no. 688, and on the Internet at:

http://www.publications.parliament.uk/pa/cm199697/cmselect/cmstand/688/codefc.htm

Complaints

Any complaint about the failure of a Member of Parliament to register interests according to the rules of the House of Commons should be made to me in writing at the House of Commons, London SW1A 0AA, or by e-mail: filkine@parliament.uk.

ELIZABETH FILKIN
Parliamentary Commissioner for Standards
. . .

BLAIR, Rt. Hon. Tony (Sedgefield)

5. **Gifts, benefits and hospitality (UK)**
    December 2000, Rugby Union Football tickets and hospitality for the England v *South Africa match. (Registered 3 April 2001)*
    24 November 2001, tickets and hospitality for my family and me to see the England vs South Africa rugby match at Twickenham, provided by the Rugby Football Union. (*Registered 25 November 2001*)
6. **Overseas visits**
    December 2001/January 2002, accompanied by my family I spent six nights as a guest of the Egyptian Government at two private Government villas at the New Tower Hotel in Sharm-el-Sheikh, Egypt. The Egyptian Government also provided my family and I with a return flight from Cairo to Sharm-el-Sheikh. I have made charitable donations to a charity chosen by the Egyptian Government equating to the cost to the Egyptians for this accommodation and travel. (*Registered 14 January 2002*)

BLEARS, Hazel (Salford)

4. **Sponsorship or financial or material support**
    There is a constituency development plan between my constituency party and the Transport and General Workers Union of £1000 per annum.
5. **Gifts, benefits and hospitality (UK)**
    March 2001, I received a gift of a 'Bikebubble' from Carcoon Storage Systems Ltd, Salford, a company in my constituency. (*Registered 25 April 2001*)
    June 2001, two tickets to Kabuki performance provided by Lowry Centre Trust. (*Registered 14 October 2001*)
    August 2001, I was a guest of Manchester Airport and received a small cosmetic gift at their Airport Dinner. (*Registered 14 October 2001*)
    October 2001, to Labour Gala Dinner as guest of the Co-operative Group. (*Registered 14 October 2001*)
10. **Miscellaneous and unremunerated interests**
    Trustee of Working Class Movement Library. (*Voluntary – no remuneration*)
    Trustee of The Imperial Society of Teachers of Dancing. (*Unremunerated*)

BLIZZARD, Bob (Waveney)

2. **Remunerated employment, office, profession, etc.**
    Member of Political Opinion Panel of BPRI (Business Planning and Research International). (*£1–£1,000*)
    Member of Harris Research Panel. (*£1–£1,000*)
    Fees from both panels are paid to local charities.

BLUNKETT, Rt. Hon. David (Sheffield, Brightside)
4. **Sponsorship or financial or material support**
   My Constituency Labour Party was supported in the early part of 2001 by the professional association Connect, the telecom managers' union. (*Registered 18 October 2001*)
8. **Land and property**
   One-bedroom house in Southfields, London. This is normally used for my own residential purposes but is temporarily rented out on a six-month lease.
   . . .

DUNCAN SMITH, Rt. Hon. Iain (Chingford and Woodford Green)
2. **Remunerated employment, office, profession, etc.**
   Occasional journalism, broadcasting and lecturing.
4. **Sponsorship or financial or material support**
   I occasionally receive unpaid research assistance from interns from colleges (Pace University, Central University of Iowa and Tufts) in America whilst they are studying in London.
   I received the following donations of £1,000 and over to my campaign for election as Leader of the Conservative Party. (*Registered 15 October 2001*)

   The Lord Hanson £5,000
   J. W. Leavsley £6,894.50
   D. Caldow £4,000
   Sir Stanley Kalms £5,235.50
   Sir Geoffrey Leigh £5,000
   E. Wright £15,000
   P. C. Baker £2,000
   J. C. Flack £1,000
   J. T. Leavsley £6,894.50
   J. D. Spurling £5,000
   W. Churchill £1,000
   G. Howard £6,250
   The Hon. Charles A. Pearson £1,733
   J.C.B. Research £10,000
   J. D. Davison £5,000
   S. W. Pearce £1,000
   D. R. Dover £2,000
   A. Little and Mrs. J. Little £1,000
   M. J. Hargrove £5,000
   John Frieda Products £20,000
   Mr. Page-Crofton £1,000
   M. D. Nolan and K. M. Nolan £1,000

   I also received other donations of amounts below the threshold for registration
5. **Gifts, benefits and hospitality (UK)**
   2 October 2001, use of private plane provided by Lord Ashcroft for flights from Strasbourg to Luton and from Luton to Battersea Heliport. (*Registered 15 October 2001*)
   8 October 2001, use of private plane provided by Lord Ashcroft for flights from Blackpool to RAF Northolt and from Luton to Blackpool. (*Registered 15 October 2001*)
   10 October 2001, use of private plane provided by Irvine Laidlaw from Blackpool to RAF Northolt. (*Registered 15 October 2001*)
   My wife has been lent clothing to wear at official functions in her capacity as wife of the Leader of the Opposition. This benefit has been provided by Luxury Brands Group. (*Registered 31 January 2002*)

7. **Overseas benefits and gifts**
    December 2001 in my capacity as Leader of the Opposition I received a hamper from His
    Majesty the Sultan of Brunei, the contents of which I donated to a charitable organisation.
    (*Registered 10 January 2002*)

10. **Miscellaneous and unremunerated interests**
    Director of Whitefield Development Trust (unremunerated) in support of Whitefield Schools and
    Centre in Walthamstow. Whitefield is a school for special needs and disabled children in my
    constituency.
    Member of Court, University of East London.
    Honorary Vice-President of the Chapel End Savoy Players.
    Patron of Haven House (children's hospice in my constituency).

DUNWOODY, Hon. Gwyneth (Crewe and Nantwich)

8. **Land and property**
    House in Fulham, from which rental income is received.
    . . .

KEMP, Fraser (Houghton and Washington East)

2. **Remunerated employment, office, profession etc.**
    Fees from broadcasting, journalism and surveys. All fees/gifts received are donated to
    'Wearside Women in Need' which is based in my constituency and which helps women and
    children who are victims of domestic violence.

KENNEDY, Rt. Hon. Charles (Ross, Skye and Inverness West)

2. **Remunerated employment, office, profession, etc.**
    I receive fees from writing, broadcasting and speechmaking.

4. **Sponsorship or financial or material support**
    Donations to the Office of the Leader of the Liberal Democrats received from:
    Dominion Press Ltd. of Harrow, Middlesex (*£2,000 per month*)
    Mrs. L Partridge of London (*£20,000*)
    C A Church Ltd. of Salisbury, Wiltshire (*£15,000*)

5. **Gifts, benefits and hospitality (UK)**
    Two tickets for men's semi-finals at Wimbledon as guests of Lawn Tennis Association.
    (*Registered 2 July 2001*)
    November 2001, presentation of a plate as guest of honour at the annual British Indian Diwali
    'Festival of Lights' dinner. (*Registered 12 November 2001*)

8. **Land and property**
    Single bedroomed flat in London, from which a rental income is derived.

KENNEDY, Jane (Liverpool, Wavertree)
    Nil.

KEY, Robert (Salisbury)

2. **Remunerated employment, office, profession etc.**
    Occasional fees from writing and broadcasting, speaking, lecturing and chairing conferences.
    Consultant to Certis (formerly consultant to ProAgro BV). (*From 1 January 2001*)
    (*£5,001–£10,000*)
    Consultant to Ortivus UK Ltd. (*From 1 February–16 March 2001*)
    Consultancy in respect of the market prospects for patient informatics systems within the NHS.
    (*£1,001–£5,000*)

5. Gifts, benefits and hospitality (UK)
    Car park pass from South West Trains. (*Registered 25 July 2001*)

NOTE: The first major case which the Commissioner and the Committee had to consider arose out of allegations by Mr Mohamed Al Fayed and *The Guardian* against Mr Neil Hamilton. It was quite protracted given the amount of evidence which the Commissioner had to consider in his investigation. It was not completed before the General Election in 1997 in which Mr Hamilton lost his seat.

Eighth Report from the Select Committee on Standards and Privileges
HC 261 of 1997–98

COMPLAINTS FROM MR MOHAMED AL FAYED, *THE GUARDIAN* AND OTHERS AGAINST 25 MEMBERS AND FORMER MEMBERS: SECOND FURTHER REPORT: MR NEIL HAMILTON

The Committee on Standards and Privileges has agreed to the following Report:

1. On 3 July 1997 the Committee published its First Report, together with the report of the Parliamentary Commissioner for Standards on allegations made against twenty-five Members and former Members. On 1 August we published our Seventh Report containing our findings on twenty-four of those Members and former Members. We have now completed our proceedings in respect of Mr Neil Hamilton.

2. In our First Report we drew attention to the right of those Members criticised to submit a written statement to the Committee rebutting or challenging any findings of the Commissioner. Mr Hamilton's submission has already been published. We asked the Commissioner to provide us with briefing on the main points raised by Mr Hamilton. A written summary of the Commissioner's comments is appended. Mr Hamilton made an oral statement to the Committee on 14 October 1997, the text of which is published together with this Report. Also appended are representations from Mr Al Fayed's solicitors and from *The Guardian* seeking on behalf of witnesses, a comparable right of reply to Mr Hamilton's statement. After careful consideration the Committee concluded that these replies would not be necessary to enable it to reach its conclusions.

3. The procedures used by the Commissioner and the reasons for their adoption are published in the Committee's First Report. In his submission Mr Hamilton made a number of objections to the manner in which the Commissioner's inquiry had been conducted. We do not find Mr Hamilton's objections valid in terms of our remit from the House. We accept the Commissioner's description of the approach he adopted:

> This was a parliamentary inquiry and there was no attempt to replicate the procedures of a court action. The proposed procedures were shown in advance to the previous Select Committee and to complainees. The approach was inquisitorial, not adversarial. Its sole purpose was to arrive at the truth, not to achieve a 'conviction'.

4. The Commissioner's findings on Mr Hamilton were as follows:

(i)   *The evidence that Mr Hamilton received cash payments directly from Mr Al Fayed in return for lobbying services is compelling; and I so conclude. The amount received by him is unknown but is unlikely to have been less than the total amount received by Mr Smith. There is no evidence to indicate that Mr Hamilton received cash from Mr Al Fayed indirectly through Mr Greer.*

(ii) *The way in which these payments were received and concealed fell well below the standards expected of Members of Parliament.*

(iii) *There is insufficient evidence to show that Mr Hamilton received Harrods vouchers.*

(iv) *The hospitality Mr Hamilton received from Mr Al Fayed at the Ritz and elsewhere was intended, and accepted, as part of his reward for lobbying. It was not as it should have been, registered.*

(v) *Mr Hamilton failed to register two introduction payments from Mr Greer in relation to NNC (National Nuclear Corporation) and (United States Tobacco), some of which he look in kind. There is insufficient evidence to show that the UST payment was a disguised consultancy fee.*

(vi) *Mr Hamilton did not register hospitality received from UST in 1989; on balance, it would have been better had he done so.*

(vii) *Mr Hamilton deliberately misled the President of the Board of Trade about his financial relationship with Mr Greer.*

(viii) *Mr Hamilton failed to register a consultancy fee from Strategy Network International on the spurious grounds that an interest acquired and disposed of within four weeks was non-registrable.*

(ix) *Mr Hamilton persistently and deliberately failed to declare his interests in dealings with Ministers and officials on the issues of House of Fraser and Skoal Bandits and, in some cases, was positively misleading about the status of his representations.*

(x) *Mr Hamilton accepted a commission payment for introducing a constituent to Mr Greer, as well as a consultancy fee for representing that constituent's interests. Both these actions were unacceptable, the latter additionally so because it created a conflict of interest for Mr Hamilton in representing his other constituents.*

(xi) *The allegation that Mr Hamilton accepted a paid consultancy from Mobil Oil in return for asking Parliamentary questions is not substantiated.*

In his written statement Mr Hamilton apologised for his error of judgement in failing to register two commission payments and the SNI consultancy and for failing to register his hospitality at the Ritz hotel in Paris. He also apologised for his failure to declare the UST commission and the Ritz hospitality when making representations to Ministers. However, in both his written and his oral statement he contested many of the Commissioner's findings. In particular he has consistently denied that he received any cash payments from Mr Al Fayed.

5. We have carefully examined Mr Hamilton's representations. Essentially, these repeat the evidence he gave to the Commissioner for Standards. We do not consider that Mr Hamilton has brought forward relevant new evidence.

6. Our conclusions are as follows:

(i) When it investigated a complaint against Mr Hamilton's failure to register his stay at the Ritz Hotel in Paris in the previous Parliament, the Select Committee on Members' Interests did not elicit the detailed evidence on Mr Hamilton's relationship with Mr Al Fayed and the campaign managed by Ian Greer Associates which the Commissioner's inquiry has now established. The relationship was essentially a business relationship in which Mr Hamilton advocated Mr Al Fayed's cause. He received material benefits. The visit should have been registered and Mr Hamilton must have known that it should have been.

(ii) We examined the evidence relating to the information which Mr Hamilton gave to the then President of the Board of Trade, Mr Heseltine. Mr Hamilton never gave away more information about his relationship with Mr Greer than he had to. The Commissioner's finding that Mr Heseltine was 'deliberately misled' appears to us to be justified.

(iii) We accept the Commissioner's findings on Mr Hamilton's failures to declare his interests when dealing with Ministers and officials.

(iv) We recognise the force of the Commissioner's criticism of Mr Hamilton's acceptance of a commission payment for introducing a constituent to Mr Greer as well as a consultancy fee for representing that constituent's interests. Such actions do not appear to us to be contrary to the present rules of the House. We do not agree with the Commissioner's interpretation of the rules in this instance. We noted in our Seventh Report that we consider it to be inappropriate for a Member to receive a fee for introducing a constituency company to another company or organisation.

(v) The Commissioner found a variety of occasions, most of which are now admitted by Mr Hamilton, when he failed to register his interests. We draw attention to paragraph 813 of the Commissioner's report –

In addition to the stay at the Ritz (dealt with earlier) the main allegations against Mr Hamilton under this heading [alleged non-registration of interests] are considered below:

(i) In 1989 Mr and Mrs Hamilton spent a few days as guests of Mr Al Fayed on the estate of Balnagown Castle. This was clearly a benefit of substantial value and should, in my view, have been registered. Mr Hamilton regarded it as 'private hospitality': but this is a concept not recognised by the Register and, given the lobbying he was conducting at the time on Mr Al Fayed's behalf, the benefit could certainly have been thought to affect his conduct as a Member.

(ii) Mr Hamilton acknowledged receiving two Harrods hampers – one in 1988 and one in 1989. By today's standards these would be registrable, but I am inclined to think that this may not have been the accepted position at the time.

(iii) Unlike most, if not all, other lobbyists, IGA regularly paid commissions to Members who introduced new business. In 1987/88 Mr Hamilton received an introduction commission of £4,000 and a consultancy fee of £7,500 in relation to the National Nuclear Corporation. He registered the latter but not the former, on the grounds that the introduction payment was ex gratia and unexpected. In my view there is no doubt that the introduction commission should have been registered since it might have been thought to affect Mr Hamilton's conduct as a Member. This was also the view of the Select Committee on Members' Interests at the time and, although the Committee recognised that the categorisation of the Register was unsatisfactory, they did not see this as a justification for a failure to register such payments.

(iv) In 1989 Mr Hamilton received an introduction fee from IGA of £6,000, which had been agreed in 1988, in respect of US Tobacco (UST). Since this was his second such fee, it could no longer be argued that it was wholly unexpected. It should, in my judgement have been registered during 1989 and, in any event, in January 1990 after the Registrar had specifically reminded Members at the end of 1989 of their obligation to declare single payments.

(v) Also in 1989 Mr Hamilton enjoyed a three night stay at a hotel in New York at the invitation of UST. This, I think, was a marginal case, since he was on Select Committee business and his accommodation would have been paid for anyway. Nevertheless, the benefit could still have been thought to affect his conduct as a Member and would have been better registered.

(vi) It has been suggested that the payment relating to UST was, in fact, a consultancy fee and not an introduction payment. The evidence to the inquiry of Mr Walter, the former UST executive was not conclusive on this point. But this is not an important distinction if, as is the case, the payment was registrable in either event.

(vii) In 1990 Mr Hamilton received £667 from Strategy Network International for a month's consultancy work before becoming a Minister. He suggests that this would have been disregarded, as being *de minimis*, in 1990 and that, in any case, he resigned his appointment within the four-week period allowed for the registration of a new interest. In my view it is spurious to argue that an interest acquired and relinquished within four weeks is non-registrable; and the amount involved was far from negligible. I conclude that it should have been registered.

Cumulatively this list of omissions adds up to a casualness bordering on indifference or contempt towards the rules of the House on disclosure of interests.

7. Mr Hamilton's conduct fell seriously and persistently below the standards which the House is entitled to expect of its Members. Had Mr Hamilton still been a Member we would have recommended a substantial period of suspension from the service of the House. These conclusions are justified by paragraph 6 alone.

8. The most difficult issue is that of the alleged payments to Mr Hamilton by Mr Mohamed Al Fayed. Having regard to the nature of the alleged transactions and the conflict of evidence there can be no absolute proof that such payments were, or were not, made. The principal evidence upon which the Commissioner based his findings is contained in paragraph 789 of the Appendix to the First Report. There is no oral evidence independent of Mr Al Fayed and those who were working with him at the time. Mr Hamilton has consistently denied that he took 'cash for questions' or was paid for lobbying services. He questioned at length the credibility of witnesses who gave evidence on this matter. We have considered whether it is within our remit to carry out our own investigation. Such an investigation would have involved taking evidence from those witnesses who gave evidence to the Commissioner and also reassembling and reassessing a considerable body of material. The Committee would have become engaged in the details of inquiry which the appointment of the Commissioner was meant to avoid, with no certainty that we could take the matter any further than he had done. Detailed investigation was by the Commissioner. His terms of reference were:

> To enquire into allegations of misconduct against Mr Neil Hamilton and other Members of Parliament with a view to establishing whether there has been any breach of House of Commons rules, in the letter or in the spirit, and to report the findings to the Select Committee on Standards and Privileges.

We are satisfied that the Commissioner has carried out a thorough inquiry which took the evidence presented to him fully into account. The Committee did not arrive at a practicable way of reaching a judgement which adds to or subtracts from the Commissioner's findings.

9. As we have said in our Seventh Report,

> We recognise that, in practice, the powers of the House to punish non-Members are limited. In a future report we shall offer advice to the House on appropriate penalties and sanctions for Members, former Members and other persons involved in unacceptable behaviour.

10. This report is the final report dealing with allegations made in the media in the summer of 1996 on the conduct of Members. Its scale and scope were wholly unlike anything envisaged by the House when it created the new system for examining complaints against the conduct of Members and appointed a Commissioner for Standards. Indeed it is important to remember that the Commissioner's inquiry did not arise from a specific complaint but from a statement made to the House by the Speaker and from the request by our predecessors that he should 'investigate as a matter of urgency the serious allegations about the conduct of Members referred to by Madam Speaker in the House on 14 October'. Unlike our normal procedure where the onus is on a complainant to submit evidence supporting any complaint to the Commissioner, the Commissioner was given the task of defining the allegations and assembling the evidence. The amount of that evidence was very considerable. Over sixty witnesses provided evidence, thirteen oral hearings were held and some fourteen thousand pages of documents were submitted. The Commissioner was asked by the previous

Committee not only to investigate but where possible to reach conclusions and then report to the Committee.

11. The scale and nature of this inquiry, analogous in some ways to that of a tribunal of inquiry, have highlighted the need for the Committee to assess its own role in relation to inquiries conducted by the Commissioner for Standards. Although some guidance was provided by the Select Committee on Standards in Public Life and by the Nolan Committee there is no agreement on whether there could be an appeal against the Commissioner's findings or conclusions by the Select Committee except in consideration by the House. The Committee will examine this matter further.

NOTES:

1. In his response to the Parliamentary Commissioner's report, Mr Hamilton complained about the investigation procedure used by the Commissioner. Mr Hamilton specifically mentioned the denial of a right to comment upon the Commissioner's findings before publication; that the burden of proof should have been placed squarely on the prosecution; that the standard of proof should have been 'beyond reasonable doubt'; that evidence was not taken on oath; that cross-examination was not allowed. The Commissioner's response to these points in the Annex was that the Standards and Privileges Committee had determined that Mr Hamilton should not be able to comment on the Commissioner's findings before publication; he had outlined his procedure in his report (HC 30 of 1997–98, paras 69–73) and this inquiry was not meant to replicate a court action. The approach was inquisitorial, not adversarial; its purpose was to arrive at the truth, not secure a conviction. Thus there was no prosecution and no reversal of any burden of proof. The Commissioner had no power to take evidence on oath. Examination of witnesses was carried out by Counsel to the Inquiry and the Commissioner. Where witnesses were contradicted by later evidence they were given the opportunity to comment further (see articles by Doig and Woodhouse (1998) 51 *Parliamentary Affairs* at 36 and 51).

2. An investigation into 11 allegations against Keith Vaz MP, three of which were upheld and of those two were regarded as minor, was important because of the MP's conduct during the investigation.

Fifth Report from the Select Committee on Standards and Privileges
HC 605 of 2001–02, paras 39–71

. . .

ALLEGATIONS THAT MR VAZ MAY HAVE MISLED OR SOUGHT TO OBSTRUCT THE COMMITTEE OR THE COMMISSIONER

39. In addition to the allegations which the Commissioner investigated, other issues arose in the course of the investigation which gave rise to concern and on which she has reported to us.

40. The Commissioner concluded that—

   (i)   by providing inaccurate information which he had not sought to correct,
   (ii) by avoiding answering questions fully, and
   (iii) by giving the Commissioner inaccurate information about complainants and witnesses, Mr Vaz had seriously misled and sought to obstruct the committee and her.

41. When Mr Vaz gave evidence to us the Chairman put to him the suggestion that he had failed to co-operate with the Commissioner as fully as he might have been able to do. The exchange went as follows:

'MR KEITH VAZ:. . . I have not misled her. I have provided accurate information. If she would like to give me one example, through you, or if the Committee would like to give me any example, of me not providing accurate information, I would be happy to do so.

SIR GEORGE YOUNG: Can I respond and give just one example. On 26 October last year the Commissioner asked you whether you had "organised any other events for the Asian Business Network since 1997 and if so please list them". Your reply was, "I have attended many events over the last 14 years. I cannot give you a list of each organisation's events." So it was a specific question about organising and a specific date, and your answer was not about organising at all, it was about attending.

MR KEITH VAZ: No.

SIR GEORGE YOUNG: Why not?

MR KEITH VAZ: Of course it is, because it is how you use language. I have not organised any events for the Asian . . . Because people would think, as Mr Zaiwalla did on the last occasion, because I happen to chair an event, I am organising it. That is why I gave the answer about attending Asian community events. Organising requires you going around and organising things, but as Mr Ottaway has correctly pointed out, if somebody in the cash book puts a donation to a calendar and he puts my name against it . . .

SIR GEORGE YOUNG: Why not say, "I have not organised any events"?

MR KEITH VAZ: Because then Mrs Filkin will write back and say, "You say you haven't organised it, but Mr Zaiwalla said you had," and we are then into this long discussion as to what my role was in these various events.'

42. This response is unacceptable. Mr Vaz has no right to refuse to answer questions directly.

43. We referred earlier [32] to our dismay that it had taken Mr Vaz so long to provide the necessary information about his property interests. The Commissioner said in her memorandum that she had put to Mr Vaz, in the form of a schedule which he could confirm or correct, her understanding about his properties:

'I had assumed that Mr Vaz would take my schedule as a starting point. He would then indicate in each case whether he had (or had previously had) an interest in the property, and, if so, what kind; whether rental income had been received; and whether any properties in which he had an interest had been omitted. Instead, Mr Vaz wrote a series of letters to me requesting additional information or seeking clarification of points of detail in the schedule which did not appear to me to be necessary to enable him to set out with precision his own property interests.

Having written to Mr Vaz enclosing the schedule on 19 June 2001, I received from him on 28 September what he described as his response on the outstanding matters relating to his property interests. Because his answers were incomplete this gave rise to further questions from me in a letter dated 19 October 2001, some replies to which were supplied by Mr Vaz in his letter of 3 November 2001.

In my view, it should not have taken as long as five months to seek to obtain from Mr Vaz comprehensive factual information about his property interests. Even now I cannot confirm that the information on his property interests is comprehensive because Mr Vaz has failed to provide me with clear confirmation despite several requests.'

44. The Commissioner also drew attention to the difficulty she experienced in getting information from Mr Vaz about people who were registered to vote at his property in Kennington and about the circumstances in which the property was transferred to his mother during the previous investigation.

45. When we put it to Mr Vaz in the course of his oral evidence that the question of his property interests was fairly straightforward and should have been easy to answer, he said:

'No, because we had reached a stage after ten months of this, where we just could not go on. Every single time we replied to a question of Mrs Filkin she would ask another ten questions. It just could not go on. . .'

He continued:

'We had to have some relevance to the questions that were being put forward . . . We had just reached a stage, after ten months and 560 questions, that we just could not carry on. There was no purpose . . .'

The Commissioner effectively disposed of this point:

'At various points during this inquiry I have received the impression that I was being given a literal answer rather than the whole truth. This has then required me to ask a follow-up question to ensure I did not misrepresent the witness or, indeed, Mr Vaz himself. I have then been criticised by Mr Vaz for asking the follow-up question.'

46. The Commissioner characterised Mr Vaz's approach to her inquiry as one of 'obfuscation, prevarication, evasiveness and delay'.

Mr Vaz vigorously contests this.

47. We should record that, while the current investigation was under way Mr Vaz suffered two periods of illness, fought a general election, resigned from his Ministerial position, and was subjected to stress as a result of media speculation. He clearly feels both that the investigation process is unfair and that his relationship with the Commissioner has broken down.

48. Whether or not Mr Vaz thought the process was fair, he had a responsibility to co-operate. Mr Vaz has failed to answer questions fully, directly, clearly and promptly.

49. Mr Vaz's failure to co-operate is made more serious by the failings on his part which were identified by the last Committee following the investigation of numerous complaints against him less than a year ago. The former Committee said:

'This inquiry has taken far too long. If Mr Vaz and other witnesses whom the commissioner asked for information had answered her questions fully and promptly, the Commissioner would have been able to complete her report in a much shorter time.

Mr Vaz was wrong to say to the Commissioner last December that he was not prepared to answer further questions from her. All Members have a duty to co-operate with the Commissioner and to assist her with her inquiries. We consider that in this respect Mr Vaz's behaviour was not in accordance with his duty of accountability under the Code of Conduct . . .'

50. In his response to the investigation of the complaints against him since February 2000 Mr Vaz failed in his duty of accountability under the Code of Conduct by refusing to submit himself to the scrutiny appropriate to his office as a Member.

Wrongful interference with the investigation process

51. On 5 October Mr Vaz contacted Leicestershire Constabulary via the Chief Constable's office and said that Miss Eggington had made a telephone call to his mother at her Leicestershire address claiming to be an ex-employee of the Metropolitan Police. He said that Miss Eggington was connected, as a friend and advocate, with Mrs Gresty, an ex-employee of his wife's, who had become embroiled in harassment allegations. Mr Vaz gave the police Miss Eggington's address and the names of two Metropolitan Police officers who had dealt with the harassment allegations against Mrs Gresty.

52. On 8 October he telephoned the Commissioner. He then made the following written allegation to the Commissioner:

'I am writing to confirm that Eileen Eggington telephoned my mother in Leicester last Thursday [4 October 2001] and asked her questions apparently on your behalf. You have informed me that she was not acting for you and had no remit to gather information in this way. You will recall that during the last inquiry you took action against those witnesses who sought to interfere with your investigation. As Ms Eggington has put herself forward as a complainant I would be glad to know what action you propose to take.

I have informed the police of the activities of Miss Eggington which I regard as harassment. My mother is now in hospital.'

In a subsequent letter to the Commissioner Mr Vaz said:

'I explained to you that when the call was made to my mother she was told by Ms Eggington that she was a police officer and that you had asked her to ring. This occurred on 4th October and she was admitted to hospital shortly after the call. I telephoned the Leicester Police on 5th October.'

53. The Commissioner put Mr Vaz's allegation to Miss Eggington, who denied it in the strongest terms.

54. Having obtained from Mr Vaz the name of the police officer who was dealing with the case, the Commissioner asked for the results of any inquiries the police had made into the matter. The police had been unable to obtain Mr Vaz's mother's account of the telephone call because she was ill. They contacted Mr Vaz on 23 November. According to them, he said that he 'did not think it was advisable to approach' his mother and 'did not want to waste any time for yourself'.

55. On the same day Mr Vaz contacted the Commissioner to make a strong complaint about her contact with the police. He alleged that she was interfering in a criminal investigation and said he would report her to the Speaker.

56. At the end of November both Mrs Gresty and Miss Eggington were interviewed by the police about the alleged telephone call.

57. The police contacted Mr Vaz again on 5 December. Mr Vaz, according to them, 'again declined to facilitate contact with his mother stating that he was unhappy with the way the inquiry was being conducted. He formally asked the officer to pass his remarks to the Chief Constable.'

58. On 12 December Leicestershire Constabulary wrote to the Commissioner to say that they were –

'in receipt of information to suggest that no calls were received by Mrs Vaz's home telephone on 4th October 2001, that could be attributable to either Miss Eggington or Mrs Gresty.'

The police officer in charge told us on 12 January:

'We have not confined our enquiry solely to contact with Mr Vaz. We have interviewed the most likely potential suspects, who have co-operated fully and we have been provided with information by independent third parties. We have found nothing that would lend weight to the allegations originally made by Mr Vaz. Indeed, I am satisfied that no malicious calls were made.'

59. When Mr Vaz appeared before us he said that –

(i) his mother had received a telephone call and the words 'Eggington' and 'Filkin' had been used;

(ii) his mother knew who the Commissioner was but did not know who Miss Eggington was ('she clearly knows who Mrs Filkin is because the word Filkin is used occasionally in our household but Mrs Eggington's name is not used');

(iii) he had not been able to establish with his mother whether it was Miss Eggington or the Commissioner who had made the call.

60. In a subsequent written submission he said –

'The evidence on which I based my request for advice to the police was that my mother had told me that she had received a telephone call from a woman called Eggington claiming to be speaking on behalf of Mrs Filkin. I was very concerned about the possibility of involvement of the Eggington/Gresty duo in my mother's life. As she did not know the name Eggington she could hardly have made it up'.

61. He also told us that he had not complained to the police but had asked for their advice. In his subsequent submission he said –

'I did not at any time ask that the police go and interview anyone thus the accusation of "intimidation" is groundless. I always maintained in accordance with usual practice that the victim herself who should decide with the police how to proceed and that they should do no more than they would do for any other member of the public.'

62. Mr Vaz said that his mother would be keen to co-operate in a police investigation of the matter if she had been in good health. Mrs Vaz has written a letter to the police in which she said she had been unable, for reasons of health, rather than unwilling, to co-operate with their inquiries.

63. We had decided that, in view of the state of her health, it would be inappropriate for us to seek any information from Mr Vaz's mother directly. She has volunteered a statement:

'. . . The call I received was from a woman whose voice I recognise who said her name was Eggington, and that she was ringing me on behalf of Mrs Filkin, to ask me some questions. I had no idea who this person was and I put the receiver down immediately. I did not engage in any conversation. I told Keith about the call later. I believe this all happened on 4th October . . . I cannot be absolutely certain that I received the call on that very day or shortly before that day as I was so unwell at the time . . .'

64. We accept the evidence Miss Eggington has provided, and we do not believe that any call which may have been reported to Mr Vaz by his mother came from Miss Eggington.

65. When Mr Vaz gave oral evidence, his account of what his mother had told him was that there had been a telephone call involving the names 'Eggington' (of whom his mother says she had never heard) and 'Filkin'. Mr Vaz then –

 (i) informed the Leicestershire police on 5 October that Miss Eggington had made a harassing telephone call to his mother and that she was linked to Mrs Gresty;
 (ii) provided them later that day with Miss Eggington's address and with contacts in the Metropolitan Police;
 (iii) informed the Commissioner on 8 October by telephone, and on 9 October in writing, that Miss Eggington had made a call, had claimed to be a police officer, and had put questions to Mrs Vaz claiming to be acting on the Commissioner's behalf;
 (iv) asked the Commissioner what action she proposed to take in respect of his allegations against Miss Eggington; and
 (v) provided the Commissioner with the name of the police officer who was dealing with the case.

66. The information Mr Vaz says he had about the call does not justify all the actions he took on the basis of it. In particular, what Mr Vaz said to the Commissioner in his letter of 9 October went beyond what both he and his mother told us they knew. It was to be expected that both the Commissioner and the police would follow up what he told them. When the Commissioner did follow it up, as Mr Vaz had asked her to, he accused her of interfering with a criminal investigation and threatened to report her to the Speaker. The Commissioner's action with Miss Eggington, and the police interviews with Miss Eggington and Mrs Gresty, resulted directly from what Mr Vaz had said and done.

67. Mr Vaz's position appears to have shifted in the course of time. As the police indicated,

'The nature of allegations by Mr Vaz appears to have changed subtly as time has gone on. Initially, [the police officer concerned] understood himself to be investigating a complaint of malicious telephone calls and harassment. Mr Vaz has since said that it was never his intention to make a formal complaint of any crime, his contact with the Police was intended to be an informal request for advice. He has now made it entirely clear that he does not wish us to investigate these incidents; . . .'

68. Mr Vaz made it plain to the Commissioner in his letter of 9 October that he expected her to pursue his complaint against Miss Eggington. He then gave the police the impression that he did not want them to pursue his report to them. The police were unable to interview his mother because of her illness. On 23 November he accused the Commissioner of interfering in a criminal investigation, though he must have known that no such investigation was in progress. We find Mr Vaz's conduct unacceptable.

69. We conclude that Mr Vaz recklessly made a damaging allegation against Miss Eggington to the Commissioner, which was not true, and which could have intimidated Miss Eggington or undermined her credibility. Miss Eggington and Mrs Gresty were interviewed by the police as a direct result of his intervention. Having set the Commissioner on a false line of inquiry Mr Vaz then accused her of interfering in a criminal investigation and threatened to report her to the Speaker.

70. In the report on the earlier complaints against him our predecessors said –

'Intimidation that comes to our attention will be dealt with severely.'

His action, which was to interfere wrongfully with the investigative process, should be treated in the same way.

71. Mr Vaz failed in his public duty under the Code of Conduct 'to act on all occasions in accordance with the public trust placed in [him]'. By wrongfully interfering with the House's investigative process he also committed a contempt of the House.

NOTE: The Committee on Standards in Public Life made recommendations about dealing with MPs based upon a classification of the allegations and then applying the appropriate procedure (*Sixth Report: Reinforcing Standards* Cm 4557) which the Committee on Standards and Privileges did not find convincing (HC 267 of 2000–01).

The First Seven Reports: A Review of Progress
Committee on Standards in Public Life, Cm 4903, pp. 137–40
(*See opposite.*)

Column 1 *shows the recommendations or observations made in the Report by the Committee.*
Column 2 *shows the formal response made at the time of the Report's publication by the Government or by the House of Commons Committee on Standards and Privileges.*
Column 3 *shows the action taken to date, using information provided by the consultees at Appendix A. Aside from some editorial changes, their words have been used wherever possible, and the comments are not a judgement by the Committee.*

No. Recommendation	Response	Action Taken
Members of Parliament		
1 The Government should introduce its proposed legislation on the criminal law of bribery as soon as possible in order to remove any uncertainty regarding the scope of the statutory offence of bribery and to make clear that members of both Houses of Parliament, acting in their capacity as members, and those who bribe a member of either House of Parliament fall within its scope.	The Government's proposals to reform the law of corruption were published in a discussion paper on 20 June 2000 (*Raising Standards and Upholding Integrity: The Prevention of Corruption: The Government's Proposals for the Reform of the Criminal Law of Corruption in England and Wales*, Cm 4759). The Government noted its intention to legislate as soon as Parliamentary time allowed.	See also recommendation 28, Third Report. It is anticipated that new legislation will be included as part of the Criminal Justice Bill in the 2001/02 session.
	The Government said that the proposals were intended to clarify the existing law by defining what is meant by acting 'corruptly' and by removing any uncertainty about the scope of the offence.	
	It was the Government's intention to include members of both Houses of Parliament within the scope of the proposed legislation.	
	The Government also accepted the recommendation of the Joint Committee on Parliamentary Privilege under the chairmanship of Lord Nicholls. This was that the new legislation should provide that evidence relating to any offence committed or alleged to be committed under new corruption legislation should be admissible notwithstanding Article 9 of the Bill of Rights. Article 9 states '*that the freedom of speech and debates or proceedings in Parliament ought not to be impeached or questioned in any court or place out of Parliament*'.	

No.	Recommendation	Response	Action Taken
2	Where a complaint is made to the Parliamentary Commissioner for Standards alleging criminal conduct by an MP and the complaint is neither malicious nor frivolous, then the Parliamentary Commissioner should report to the Committee on Standards and Privileges with a recommendation that the matter be referred to the police for further investigation	The Committee on Standards and Privileges considered that if such a case were to arise, then the Parliamentary Commissioner should report to the Committee that the matter had been referred to the police for further investigation. It was noted that the Committee would do the same if the Commissioner had not.	
3	**'Trial' procedure in serious contested cases** 1 Where (a) the Parliamentary Commissioner finds a *prima facie* case against an accused MP the alleged facts of which, if true, would amount to serious misconduct, but (b) the alleged facts are disputed by the accused MP, the Parliamentary Commissioner should report to the Committee on Standards and Privileges with a recommendation that the case be referred to a disciplinary tribunal consisting of a legal chairman sitting with either two or four MPs who should be of substantial seniority. 2 Before making a decision about whether to accept the Parliamentary Commissioner's recommendation the Committee on Standards and Privileges should allow the accused MP an opportunity to make representations in respect of that decision. 3 If the Parliamentary Commissioner's recommendation is accepted, the accused MP should be provided with financial assistance to enable him or her to fund legal representation at the hearings of the tribunal.	The Committee on Standards and Privileges rejected the recommendation on the grounds that: • MPs could not be involved in the process of investigation because it would take a disproportionate amount of time, and give grounds for the complaint that the process was unfair and partial; MPs have party allegiances and were unlikely to be perceived as objective or independent. • A lawyer would not be better placed than the Parliamentary Commissioner to assemble and evaluate evidence. The assistance of a legal assessor to the Commissioner in complicated cases was considered a more appropriate measure to ensure that procedures were properly followed, and that legal advice was available as required. • Lawyers had tended to prolong and complicate unnecessarily matters which could have been resolved swiftly through full cooperation between the MP and the Commissioner. The involvement of lawyers was also considered to encourage the (erroneous) view of the Commissioner as prosecutor. • Similarly, the availability of free legal representation would sometimes lead to matters being prolonged unnecessarily, and would constitute a potentially unlimited drain on public funds. It was noted that free assistance to obtain factual information was already available to MPs from the Parliamentary Commissioner.	

4. The tribunal should be governed by procedures that satisfy the *'minimum standards of fairness'*, as defined by the Nicholls Committee.

5. The tribunal should both act as fact-finder and decide whether, on the basis of the facts found, the charges against the accused MP are proved.

6. The tribunal should report its conclusions to the Committee on Standards and Privileges and, assuming no appeal is being lodged, the Committee should consider what penalty (if any) should be recommended to the House of Commons.

4 Appeal procedure in serious contested cases

1. An accused MP who receives an adverse ruling from the first instance tribunal should have a right of appeal and should be entitled to financial assistance to pursue that appeal.

2. The appeal should be heard by an *ad hoc* appellate tribunal, possibly a retired senior appellate judge sitting alone.

3. If the appeal is dismissed, the Committee should report the result of the appeal to the House of Commons along with any recommendation as to penalty.

5 'Trial' and appeal procedure in other contested cases

1. In cases which, in the opinion of the Parliamentary Commissioner, do not warrant a referral to the full tribunal, the Parliamentary Commissioner should make a recommendation to the Committee on Standards and Privileges accordingly. The Committee should decide whether to uphold the recommendation of the Commissioner on the basis of the Commissioner's report and of the representations (if any) by the accused MP.

The Committee on Standards and Privileges noted that the final decision in any case was currently taken by the House on the recommendation of the Committee. The effect of allowing an appeal in serious contested cases to, for example, a retired judge would be *'breaking the principle of self-regulation entirely'*.

The Committee on Standards and Privileges noted that the recommendation reflected very much how the Committee currently operated.

See response, centre column.

No.	Recommendation	Response	Action Taken
	2. In those cases that remain with the Parliamentary Commissioner, the Commissioner should investigate the complaint and on the basis of the facts found, decide whether the complaint should be upheld or dismissed. The Commissioner's decision should be reported to the Standards and Privileges Committee, which should, in turn, decide whether or not to adopt the Commissioner's report and what penalty (if any) should be recommended to the House. 3. In cases where an accused MP disputes the Commissioner's findings or conclusions, that MP should be able to appeal against the Commissioner's decision, such an appeal to be heard either by the Committee itself or by such *ad hoc* appellate body as it decides to appoint.		
6	**Disciplinary procedure in non-contested cases** In non-contested cases, whether serious or minor, the Parliamentary Commissioner should, in accordance with present practice, report the (undisputed) facts and conclusions based on those facts to the Committee on Standards and Privileges which, if it endorses the report, should recommend to the House of Commons what penalty (if any) should be imposed.	The Committee on Standards and Privileges noted that the recommendation reflected very much how the Committee currently operated.	See response, centre column.
7	The disciplinary proceedings of the House of Commons should be held in public but should not be broadcast. This recommendation as to hearings in public does not extend to the private deliberations of the Standards and Privileges Committee or of any disciplinary or appellate tribunal (which should remain private).	The Committee on Standards and Privileges noted that all its experience pointed to proceedings of the Committee being held in private, and that the Committee generally published the oral evidence taken in private alongside the relevant report.	

NOTES:
1. In its report, the Joint Committee on Parliamentary Privilege, chaired by Lord Nicholls (HL 43 of 1998–99, HC 24 of 1998–99), proposed minimum requirements for fairness, drawn from Article 6 ECHR (*Demicoli* v *Malta* (1992) 14 EHRR 47, makes it clear that punishment by Parliament of contempt against it, may be subject to review). The minimum requirements are:
   - a prompt and clear statement of the precise allegations against the member;
   - adequate opportunity to take legal advice and have legal assistance throughout;
   - the opportunity to be heard in person;
   - the opportunity to call relevant witnesses at the appropriate time;
   - the opportunity to examine other witnesses;
   - the opportunity to attend meetings at which evidence is given, and to receive transcripts of evidence.

2. In addition to these points on fairness, the Committee on Standards in Public Life preferred an investigation of allegations against an MP to be conducted by a sub-committee rather than the Commissioner, because the Commissioner gives advice to MPs and might then find that a disputed case could be one in which the Commissioner had previously offered advice, and so the Article 6 ECHR requirement of an 'impartial and independent tribunal' could be compromised. In its report *Appeal Procedures*, the Commons Standards and Privilege Committee (HC 1191 of 1997–98) feared that an investigative sub-committee was flawed as senior MPs would be too busy to devote time to this work, that select committees were not well equipped to conduct such inquiries, and the involvement of politicians could be perceived as party-political or lacking in objectivity and independence. These points were sought to be addressed by the Committee on Standards in Public Life by the involvement of a legally qualified chairman of the tribunal and the view that if senior MPs could not devote the necessary time to disciplinary procedures, 'it is difficult to avoid the conclusion that Parliamentary self-regulation in this area is unworkable' (para. 3.45).

QUESTION

Is the select committee's view about the nature of its procedure and their antipathy towards lawyers, compatible with the ECHR?

NOTE: The Committee on Standards in Public Life wished to include the House of Lords in its considerations of, amongst other matters, a parliamentary register of interests. Some peers doubted the constitutional authority of the Committee to do this (see HL Debs, cols, 1657–1714, 10 May 2000). The Committee produced a report (*Standards of Conduct in the House of Lords*, Cm 4903) which recommended a code of conduct and a mandatory register of peers' relevant interests. These points were accepted by a Working Group (HL 68 of 2000–01) and a code was approved after revision, which came into effect after 31 March 2002.

SECTION 5: **Reform of the House of Lords**

House of Lords Act 1999

1.   No-one shall be a member of the House of Lords by virtue of a hereditary peerage.

2.—(1) Section 1 shall not apply in relation to anyone excepted from it by or in accordance with Standing Orders of the House.

(2) At any one time 90 people shall be excepted from section 1; but anyone excepted as holder of the office of Earl Marshal, or as performing the office of Lord Great Chamberlain, shall not count towards that limit.

(3) Once excepted from section 1, a person shall continue to be so throughout his life (until an Act of Parliament provides to the contrary).

(4) Standing Orders shall make provision for filling vacancies among the people excepted from section 1; and in any case where—

> (a) the vacancy arises on a death occurring after the end of the first Session of the next Parliament after that in which this Act is passed, and
>
> (b) the deceased person was excepted in consequence of an election, that provision shall require the holding of a by-election.

(5) A person may be excepted from section 1 by or in accordance with Standing Orders made in anticipation of the enactment or commencement of this section.

(6) Any question whether a person is excepted from section 1 shall be decided by the Clerk of the Parliaments, whose certificate shall be conclusive.

NOTES:

1. The retention of some 10 per cent of the hereditary peers was the result of an amendment to the Bill proposed by Lord Weatherill, a former Speaker of the House of Commons. Had the Government not accepted the amendment, it is likely that the Bill would have encountered great opposition in the Lords and might not have been approved by that House. The 90 hereditary peers can be divided into two groups, one of which is a sample numbering 75 and the other consisting of peers who were Deputy Chairmen of Committees. Both of these groups had quotas for the three main political parties and the independent Crossbenchers. These quotas reflected proportional strengths amongst the hereditaries.

Party	75	15
Conservative	42	9
Labour	2	2
Liberal Democrat	3	2
Crossbenchers	28	2

2. This statute was the first stage in the reform of the House of Lords. The chamber with its reduced number of hereditaries would be a transitional chamber; the new reformed second chamber would be shaped by the reaction of both Houses of Parliament to the recommendations of a Royal Commission which was asked to produce its report in 12 months.

Report of the Royal Commission on the Reform of the House of Lords
Cm 4534, pp. 2–9

Executive Summary

1. Reform of the House of Lords raises many complex and interrelated issues which have defied resolution for more than 100 years. But there has never been a better time to make progress.

2. The departure of most of the hereditary peers from the House of Lords has made it necessary to focus on the basic questions. What is the role of the second chamber? What contribution could it make to the political life of the United Kingdom in the 21st century? What is the modern rational basis on which it should be constituted?

3. The United Kingdom's constitution has been evolving – and fast. Devolution and decentralisation, the impact of the Human Rights Act 1998, developing relations with the European Union – all these factors need to be taken into account in deciding the shape of the new second chamber.

4. Our report points the way to a new second chamber for the United Kingdom Parliament. It traces the arguments which led to our conclusions. It defines the roles and functions that we recommend the new second chamber should perform. We show how the second chamber can complement and support the decisive political role of the House of Commons while increasing the effectiveness of Parliament as a whole in scrutinising proposed legislation and holding the Government to account. We examine the various suggestions for creating a second chamber fit to carry out this enhanced role. We make a number of proposals which represent a clear break from the past. The second chamber we envisage will build upon the strengths of the present House of Lords but it will also have important new sources of authority. If our recommendations are accepted the link between the possession of a peerage and membership of the second chamber will be broken.

5. We began our work by looking at the *roles* which the reformed second chamber could play. We then considered the *powers* it should have and the specific *functions* it should perform. Our conclusions on these matters gave us the basis for determining the *characteristics* which the reformed second chamber should possess and it was this assessment that shaped our recommendations on how the second chamber should be *constituted*.

The challenges

6. We needed to find a way of building on the strengths of the existing House of Lords while creating a new second chamber better adapted to modern circumstances. Change must be in a direction, and at a pace, which goes with the grain of the traditional British evolutionary approach to constitutional reform, while taking this once-in-a-lifetime opportunity to produce a coherent blueprint for the second chamber of Parliament.

7. We were also determined to define the role and functions of the new second chamber in terms which demonstrated that it has a real and important part to play in the political life of the country. At the same time we needed to allay fears that it could undermine the pre-eminence of the House of Commons as the United Kingdom's primary democratic forum.

8. In particular, we wanted to produce recommendations which would illustrate the crucial trilateral relationship between the Government, the House of Commons and the new second chamber. We took into account the fact that the stability of the trilateral relationship could be affected by the powers of the new second chamber and also by the way its members are selected.

9. We saw the need for a new second chamber with the authority and confidence to function effectively and to use its powers wisely. At the same time we recognised the danger of setting up an institution which could threaten the status of the House of Commons and cause constitutional conflict or whose members could rival those of the House of Commons (for example in the discharge of their constituency representative role).

10. Above all, we were keen to make proposals that would produce a new second chamber distinctively different from the House of Commons, whose members were more representative of the whole of British society and who could bring a wider range of expertise and experience to bear on the consideration of public policy questions.

11. We acknowledged from the outset that it would be wrong – as well as futile – to try to make the second chamber a politician-free zone. Parliament is a place where political issues are debated and fought over, and the second chamber cannot and should not be disengaged from that process. It will need a cadre of men and women with appropriate political experience to help it play a constructive role. But the new second chamber should not simply be a creature of the political parties, and the influence of the parties on individual members should be minimised. We wanted to create a new second chamber which was politically astute but not a home for yet another group of

professional politicians; which provided an appropriate role for the political parties but discouraged sterile partisan confrontation; and which included members of the political parties but was designed to limit the parties' influence and foster the exercise of independent judgement.

Roles

12. The new second chamber should have four main roles:

- It should bring a range of different perspectives to bear on the development of public policy.
- It should be broadly representative of British society. People should be able to feel that there is a voice in Parliament for the different aspects of their personalities, whether regional, vocational, ethnic, professional, cultural or religious, expressed by a person or persons with whom they can identify.
- It should play a vital role as one of the main 'checks and balances' within the unwritten British constitution. Its role should be complementary to that of the House of Commons in identifying points of concern and requiring the Government to reconsider or justify its policy intentions. If necessary, it should cause the House of Commons to think again. The second chamber should engender second thoughts.
- It should provide a voice for the nations and regions of the United Kingdom at the centre of public affairs.

Powers

13. No radical change is needed in the balance of power between the two Houses of Parliament. The new second chamber should retain the 'suspensory veto' set out in the Parliament Acts. This will give it the power to delay the enactment of proposed legislation but not to prevent the passage of a Commons Bill which has been approved by the House of Commons in two successive sessions of Parliament.

14. The corollary of recommending that the new second chamber should have the same powers as the present House of Lords is that it should continue to consider all Government business within a reasonable time and that the principles underlying the 'Salisbury Convention' should he maintained. The second chamber should respect a governing party's general election manifesto and be cautious about challenging the clearly expressed views of the House of Commons on major issues of public policy.

15. The absolute (but unused) power of the House of Lords to veto Statutory Instruments should be adapted so that any vote against a Statutory Instrument in the new second chamber could he overridden by an affirmative vote in the House of Commons. While this would represent a diminution in the formal power of the second chamber, it would give it a mechanism which it could use in order to delay, and demonstrate its concern about, specific Statutory Instruments. The House of Commons should have the last word but would have to take full account of the second chamber's concerns, Ministers' responses and public opinion.

Making law

16. There should be no significant changes in the second chamber's law-making functions. Parliament should continue to derive the benefits of being bicameral, with a second chamber capable of bringing a distinctive range of perspectives to bear. There should be more pre-legislative scrutiny of draft Bills. The new second chamber should consider how to promote the consideration of law reform Bills drawn up by the Law Commission. The valuable work of the Delegated Powers and Deregulation Committee should continue.

Protecting the constitution

17. The second chamber's role in protecting the constitution should be maintained and enhanced. It should no longer be possible to amend the Parliament Acts using Parliament Act procedures, as was done in 1949. Such a change would maintain the current balance of power

between the two Houses of Parliament and reinforce the second chamber's power of veto over any Bill to extend the life of a Parliament.

18. There should be no extension of the second chamber's formal powers in respect of any other matter, whether 'constitutional' or concerning human rights. But an authoritative Constitutional Committee should be set up by the second chamber to scrutinise the constitutional implications of all legislation and to keep the operation of the constitution under review.

19. A Human Rights Committee should be set up by the second chamber to scrutinise all Bills and Statutory Instruments for human rights implications. This would enable Parliament as a whole to reach an informed judgement before legislation is enacted. Given the forthcoming implementation of the Human Rights Act 1998, such a procedure is required if Parliament is to discharge effectively its primary responsibility for the protection of human rights. This should reduce the need for points of concern to be adjudicated by the courts.

Giving a voice to the nations and regions
20. The new second chamber should be able to play a valuable role in giving a voice to the nations and regions, whatever pattern of devolution and decentralisation may emerge in future. The chamber must serve the interests of the whole of the United Kingdom and contain people from all over the United Kingdom. It should contain a proportion of 'regional Members' to provide a direct voice for the nations and regions of the United Kingdom at the centre of national affairs. These 'regional Members' should not be drawn from the devolved administrations, or from the Scottish Parliament and the other devolved Assemblies, but should be able to speak for each national or regional unit of the United Kingdom. Because the 'regional Members' would share a regional per-spective with MEPs, members of the devolved institutions, the English Regional Chambers and the existing local government groupings, they could encourage and facilitate greater contact across different levels of Government and a stronger regional voice, in Europe as well as at Westminster.

Scrutinising secondary legislation
21. Secondary legislation is increasingly pervasive and voluminous but currently subject to inadequate Parliamentary scrutiny. The House of Lords has shown a conscientious interest in the grant and exercise of delegated powers. The new second chamber should maintain and extend this function, using the new procedure referred to in paragraph 15.

Scrutinising EU business
22. The existing arrangements for scrutinising Ministers' handling of European Union business should be maintained and improved in the new second chamber, with additional resources being made available to its European Union Committee. United Kingdom MEPs should not be represented in the new second chamber, but the chamber should promote greater contact and co-operation between Parliament and the United Kingdom's MEPs.

Holding the Government to account
23. Some Ministers should continue to be drawn from and be directly accountable to the new second chamber. Senior Ministers based in the House of Commons should make occasional statements to and take questions from an appropriate second chamber Committee.

24. The new second chamber should continue to be a relatively non-polemical forum for national debate, informed by the range of different perspectives which its members should have. Its specialist investigations (e.g. in respect of scientific and technological issues) should continue, drawing on its Members' broad spread of expertise. There is no distinct role for the second chamber to play in scrutinising public appointments.

25. A Committee should be established to scrutinise Treaties laid before Parliament and draw attention to any implications which merit Parliamentary consideration before ratification takes place.

The Law Lords and the judicial role of the second chamber

26. It is not for us to say how the superior courts of the United Kingdom should be organised; but we had to reach a view on whether the new second chamber could continue to carry out, through Committees composed exclusively of Law Lords, the judicial functions of the present House of Lords. We conclude that, as long as certain basic conventions (which we recommend should be set out in writing) continue to be observed, there is insufficient reason to change the present arrangements. Indeed, we see some advantage in having senior judges in the legislature where they can be made aware of the social developments and political balances which underlie most legislation.

Continuity with the past

27. All these recommendations on the roles, powers and functions of the new second chamber build to a considerable extent on those of the existing House of Lords. They broaden the second chamber's role rather than constituting a radical departure from what has gone before. The new second chamber should have a larger role to play in scrutinising the executive, protecting the constitution, safeguarding human rights, deliberating on issues which arise from devolution and decentralisation and examining secondary legislation.

Characteristics

28. Taking account of the roles and functions we think the new second chamber should perform, we believe it should, above all, be:

- authoritative;
- confident; and
- broadly representative of the whole of British society.

It should also contain members with:

- a breadth of experience outside the world of politics and a broad range of expertise;
- particular skills and knowledge relevant to the careful assessment of constitutional matters and human rights;
- the ability to bring a philosophical, moral or spiritual perspective to bear;
- personal distinction;
- freedom from party domination. A significant proportion of the members should belong to no political party and sit on the Cross Benches, so that no one party is able to dominate the second chamber;
- a non-polemical and courteous style; and
- the ability to take a long-term view.

29. A new second chamber with these characteristics should remedy the deficiencies of the old House of Lords, which lacked the political legitimacy and confidence to do its job properly, while preserving some of its best features.

Composition

30. After making a detailed analysis of potential methods of composition and the extent to which they could reliably deliver these characteristics, we do not recommend:

- a wholly or largely directly elected second chamber;
- indirect election from the devolved institutions (or local government electoral colleges) or from among United Kingdom MEPs;
- random selection; or
- co-option.

31. While the principle of vocational or interest group representation is attractive, the objective would be more effectively achieved through an independent appointments system. On the other hand, total reliance on an independent appointments system to nominate members of the new second chamber would leave no voice for the electorate in its composition. It would be unsatisfact-

ory as a basis for identifying people to provide a voice for the nations and regions of the United Kingdom.

32. We also believe the proposed arrangements for making appointments to the interim House of Lords through the mechanism of an independent Appointments Commission would not be satisfactory as a long-term solution. They leave too much power in the hands of the Prime Minister of the day and they confine the role of the Appointments Commission to the nomination of Cross Benchers.

33. We would therefore recommend that a new second chamber of around 550 members should be made up as follows:

- A significant minority of the members of the new second chamber should be 'regional Members' chosen on a basis which reflects the balance of political opinion within each of the nations and regions of the United Kingdom. The regional electorates should have a voice in the selection of members of the new second chamber. Those members in turn will provide a voice for the nations and regions.
- Other members should be appointed on the nomination of a genuinely independent Appointments Commission with a remit to create a second chamber which was broadly representative of British society and possessed all the other characteristics mentioned above.
- The Appointments Commission should be responsible for maintaining the proportion of independents ('Cross Benchers') in the new second chamber at around 20 per cent of the total membership.
- Among the politically-affiliated members, the Appointments Commission would be required to secure an overall political balance matching the political opinion of the country as a whole, as expressed in votes cast at the most recent general election.

34. To facilitate a smooth transition to the new arrangements, the existing life peers should become members of the new second chamber.

35. Untrammelled party patronage and Prime Ministerial control of the size and balance of the second chamber should cease. The Appointments Commission should ensure that the new second chamber is broadly representative of British society. It should make early progress towards achieving gender balance and proportionate representation for members of minority ethnic groups. In order to identify appropriate candidates for the second chamber it should maintain contacts with vocational, professional, cultural, sporting and other bodies. It should publish criteria for appointment to the chamber and invite nominations from the widest possible range of sources.

36. We present three possible models for the selection of the regional members. Each model has the support of different members of the Commission. Model B has the support of a substantial majority of the Commission.

> Model A – a total of 65 regional members, chosen at the time of each general election by a system of 'complementary' election. Votes cast for party candidates in each constituency at general elections would be accumulated at regional level. The parties would secure the number of regional members for each region proportional to their shares of the vote in that region, drawing the names from a previously published party list. Regional members would be selected for one-third of the regions at each general election.
> Model B – a total of 87 regional members, elected at the time of each European Parliament election. One-third of the regions would choose their regional members at each election. The system of election used for electing members of the second chamber should be the same as that used for electing the United Kingdom's members of the European Parliament, although a majority of those supporting this model would prefer a 'partially open' list system of proportional representation (PR).
> Model C – a total of 195 regional members elected by thirds, using a 'partially open' list system of PR, at the time of each European Parliament election.

37. To promote continuity and a longer-term perspective, all members (under all three models) should serve for three electoral cycles or 15-year terms, with the possibility of being reappointed for a further period of up to 15 years at the discretion of the Appointments Commission.

Religious faiths

38. A substantial majority of the Commission recommends a broadening and deepening of religious representation in the second chamber. Representation should be extended beyond the Church of England to embrace other Christian denominations in all parts of the United Kingdom and representatives of other faiths.

Remuneration

39. To make participation in the work of the new second chamber possible for people who do not have other sources of income and who come from outside the South East of England, there should be a review of the current system of paying expenses. A modest payment related to attendance in the new second chamber should be introduced.

Conclusion

40. Our proposals represent a significant change from what has gone before. No new member of the second chamber will arrive there on the same basis as any existing member of the House of Lords. No new member of the second chamber will get there via an Honours List. The new second chamber will be more democratic and representative than the present House of Lords.

More democratic – The chamber as a whole will reflect the overall balance of political opinion within the country. Regional members will directly reflect the balance of political opinion within the regions.

More representative – The chamber will contain members from all parts of the country and from all walks of life, broadly equal numbers of men and women and representatives of all the country's main ethnic and religious communities.

41. We were determined to produce recommendations which were not only persuasive and intellectually coherent but also workable, durable and politically realistic. Our report sets out the case for radical but evolutionary change which will, in our view, contribute to better government for all.

Fifth Report from the Select Committee on Public Administration
HC 494 of 2001–02

INTRODUCTION

Our Task

1. This is the response by the Public Administration Select Committee to the Government's White Paper 'The House of Lords: Completing the Reform' [Cm 5291]. It is based upon a short but intensive inquiry. We decided to undertake this inquiry in part because the Committee had already announced its intention to undertake a major inquiry into the appointed state when the White Paper was issued, but also because it seemed to us important for a parliamentary committee to have an opportunity to examine the Government's proposals as part of the consultation process (in the absence of the Joint Committee that had originally been promised).

2. We defined our task as a limited one. It was not to re-open all the issues raised during the Royal Commission inquiry, nor to duplicate the White Paper. Rather, it was to try to establish if there was a basis of agreement on which reform of the second chamber could proceed, against a background in which the Prime Minister had said: 'it is clear that there are almost as many different views about what should happen with the House of Lords as there are Members of Parliament'. We were also anxious that any compromise should be coherent, principled and practical, and therefore capable of sustaining the momentum for reform.

3. Individual members came to the inquiry holding a wide variety of views on the ideal composition of the future second chamber. Many favour a wholly elected chamber, others prefer abolition and there are those who believe that there should be some appointed members. Had we started with a clean slate, we might well have come to a different conclusion. Indeed the majority preference on the Committee would have been for a wholly elected and much smaller second chamber. However we all share a desire for a stronger and more effective Parliament, and we see early and credible reform of the second chamber as an essential part of that.

4. There may come a time when the whole issue will be revisited afresh, and we envisage a review in the future. However, we did not want the present opportunity for further reform of the second chamber to be lost. We see the present debate as part of a continuing process of reform, and it is unlikely that we have heard the final word. But all three main Westminster parties have recently published their reform proposals, in some cases diverging considerably from previous positions. We believe that there is now a favourable climate for further reform, with a discernible trend of opinion, and that the opportunity should not be lost. We therefore felt a heavy responsibility on us to accept the context in which we were deliberating, and to find as much common ground as possible in order that the reform process could be sustained. In the light of the evidence we have heard, we have managed to agree on a number of key principles and on their practical implications. Our proposals are intended to help create the 'more credible and effective second chamber' espoused by the Prime Minister. We hope that our own ability to find an agreed compromise on the next stage of reform will help to point the way ahead.

Our analysis
5. It may be helpful at the outset briefly to sketch the underlying analysis that informs our approach to particular issues and to our recommendations. Unless the analysis is clear, it is unlikely that conclusions will be soundly based. We believe that there has been much muddled thinking on second chamber reform, with the result that there has been too much focus on some issues at the expense of others and often a failure of arguments really to engage with each other.

6. In our view there are some fundamental points. First, it is essential to know what second chamber reform is for. For us it is about strengthening Parliament as a whole in relation to an executive that is uniquely powerful in the British system. Strong government requires strong accountability, and an effective second chamber (along with a reformed Commons) has an important role to play in this. Second, the second chamber has to be neither rival nor replica of the first, but genuinely complementary. It should therefore be as different as possible. Its secondary status is firmly established by the existing distribution of powers, which is why many of the arguments about rivalry (and not threatening the pre-eminence of the Commons) are simply irrelevant. As one authority has put it, the UK has 'in effect a unicameral system of government but with two chambers of Parliament' [Vernon Bogdanor *Power to the People: A Guide to Constitutional Reform* (1997), p. 119]. Third, composition should be driven by function. The second chamber needs to be composed in such a way that it can most effectively discharge its functions, which are essentially those of scrutiny and revision. Fourth, those who advocate election have to recognise that some forms of election are no more than appointment by another name. Fifth, those who advocate appointment need to understand that it raises serious problems about legitimacy, which in turn impairs effectiveness, and that patronage is not regarded as an acceptable basis for a representative institution in a democracy.

7. It is from this analysis, in which there are competing considerations, that we have framed our general approach. We want a second chamber that is effective in its role. We pay particular attention to the need for both chambers to work more effectively together. We want a second chamber that has enough institutional legitimacy to ensure that it is taken seriously, and enough independence and expertise among its membership to ensure that it is worth taking seriously. This requires practical arrangements of an appropriate kind, including the balance between election and appointment. This is the case for a mixed House, with different streams of membership feeding into it, able to play

the role of a standing civic forum as well as a processor of legislation. We believe that this would give the second chamber a distinctive and valuable place in our political system, complementing the House of Commons in the task of scrutiny and accountability and so adding value to the political system as a whole.

8. Three principles which should underlie the design of second chambers have been suggested by one authoritative commentator and we believe that they provide a useful checklist against which to judge the various proposals:

'Distinct composition: There are various ways in which the membership of the new upper house can be made distinct from that of the House of Commons. The method of composition may be different, but the party balance in the chamber will also be particularly important.

Adequate powers: If the new upper house is to be able to make an impact, and have bargaining power with the government and the lower house, it will need to have moderate to strong powers.

Perceived legitimacy: In order to use its powers the new chamber – unlike the existing House of Lords – will need to be seen to have legitimacy, and be able to carry public support.'

Our approach

9. In recent years a number of commentators have identified a crisis of confidence at Westminster. The Hansard Society Commission on the Scrutiny Role of Parliament reported in 2001 that 'Parliament has been left behind by far-reaching changes to the constitution, government and society in the past two decades'. It concluded that there were 'serious gaps and weaknesses in the working of accountability' and that 'scrutiny of Government by MPs and peers is neither systematic nor rigorous'. This was only one of a succession of reports which have discerned failings in the legislature's capacity to provide an effective check on the executive.

10. This Committee has a special interest in the performance and accountability of the public services. We are therefore particularly concerned at any weaknesses in parliamentary scrutiny, although we share the widespread hope that the work of the House of Commons Modernisation Committee can succeed in sharpening the performance of the House in this respect. This matters especially because, compared with many other mature democracies, the UK political system tends to produce strong governments and a weak legislature. That is one of the main reasons why it is so important that reform of our legislature should be effective.

. . .

The context of our inquiry

13. The Government has made House of Lords reform a leading element of its constitutional programme. The first stage of reform was completed in November 1999, when the House of Lords Act removed the majority of hereditary peers from the chamber. Issues relating to the second stage were considered by a Royal Commission, chaired by Lord Wakeham, which was asked to work quickly and which produced a report in January 2000. The Government then attempted to establish a Joint Committee of both Houses to examine what it described as the parliamentary aspects of the Royal Commission proposals. However there was disagreement between the parties about the terms of reference of the Committee, and in particular about whether it should consider the composition of the House, with the result that the Committee was not established.

14. The Queen's Speech of June 2001 set out the Government's view of the way forward. The Government intended, after consultation, to introduce legislation to implement the final stage of Lords reform. This reflected the Labour party manifesto commitment of 2001:

'We are committed to completing House of Lords reform, including removal of the remaining hereditary peers, to make it more representative and democratic, while maintaining the House of Commons' traditional primacy. We have given our support to the report and conclusions to the report of the Wakeham Commission, and will seek to implement them in the most effective way possible. Labour supports modernisation of the House of Lords' procedures to improve its effectiveness. We will put the independent Appointments Commission on a statutory footing.'

15. The Government took the next step with the publication of a White Paper, 'The House of Lords: Completing the Reform' in November 2001 [Cm 5261]. It made it clear at the time, and has since re-iterated, that this was a consultative document. It did not propose a Joint Committee. Responses were invited by 31 January 2002. The Government has in particular asked for views on these issues:

the balance between elected and nominated, and political and independent members.
timing of elections: should they be linked to European Parliamentary elections, general elections or regional elections?
length of terms for elected and appointed members: 15 years as recommended by the Royal Commission, or 5 or 10 years to give more accountability but less independence?
introduction of daily payments as well as expenses.
rules for disqualifying members.

16. The immediate response to the White Paper was largely unfavourable, as had been the earlier response to the Royal Commission (unfairly so in some respects). One criticism levelled against the White Paper was that it did not in fact implement the recommendations of the Royal Commission as the Labour Party's election manifesto had promised. This was the view of Royal Commission members. Lord Wakeham said just after the publication of the White Paper that the Government had: '. . . got several things wrong. First of all, I wanted a wholly independent Appointments Commission. I wanted an end of Tony's cronies – or any politician's cronies. I wanted people appointed on an independent basis. And they seem to have gone soft on that. Secondly, I wanted the elected element in the House of Lords to be there for a long time rather than a short time, because I did not want them to be rivals of the House of Commons . . . I think their idea of less than 15 years, something like 10 years or even five years, would be very damaging.'

. . .

18. Such negative reactions have tended to obscure the fact that the White Paper represented some movement in the Government position in some important areas, particularly in proposing an elected element in the chamber, a break with the honours system, and a statutory basis for the Appointments Commission. The final departure of the hereditary peers will remove a remaining obstacle to greater legitimacy for the second chamber. More generally, the Government have maintained the momentum for reform. It is vital that this momentum is not lost.

19. This was the starting point for our inquiry. In December 2001 we decided to take evidence on the White Paper. We have taken oral evidence from 18 witnesses and received 62 written submissions, and are very grateful to all those who have helped us with our inquiry. Although limitations of time and the specific focus of our inquiry meant that we had to confine our oral evidence to parliamentarians, we have received some very useful written evidence from members of the public and outside experts. We have benefited greatly from the expertise of our Specialist Adviser, Professor Robert Hazell, Director of the Constitution Unit, University College London. We have approached this inquiry in a spirit of urgency. We hope that the Government will respond in similar vein, replying to our Report well within the two months required by convention.

. . .

SUMMARY OF CONCLUSIONS AND RECOMMENDATIONS

(a) Reform is not a zero-sum game in which advances for one chamber are inevitably threats to the other. That is where the White Paper is fundamentally misconceived, as was the Royal Commission, in its oft-repeated determination to ensure the pre-eminence of the House of Commons. No-one is casting any doubt on that pre-eminence. We believe that the real task is rather to increase the effectiveness of both chambers in holding the Government to account for its actions and policies. The focus should be on the capacities of the institution as a whole.

(b) We agree with the Government that no major change is required to the role or functions of the second chamber. It should continue to be a revising, scrutinising and deliberative assembly. But its performance of all these functions can and should be strengthened.

(c) If the Government proceeds with its proposal to remove the veto power of the House of Lords over secondary legislation, then there should be a fixed minimum delay of three months and a requirement that the Commons would have to reconfirm its previous decision in each case.

(d) We do not believe the Government has made its case for reducing the Lords' powers over subordinate legislation. The preponderance of evidence is in favour of the chamber retaining its existing powers. The existing power of veto should remain.

(e) To fulfil the condition that the second chamber should be predominantly elected, we therefore recommend that 60 per cent of its members should come by election. Of the remainder, half (20 per cent of the total) should be nominated by the political parties; and half (20 per cent of the total) should be independent, non-aligned members; both categories should be appointed by the Appointments Commission. We further recommend that a draft Bill should contain options for the precise proportion of elected and appointed members.

(f) We recommend that all members of the second chamber should serve for similar periods and for long terms; should enjoy equal facilities; and should receive the same pay and conditions of service.

(g) We agree with the Government that elections for the second chamber should be based on the same regional constituencies as those used in the European Parliament elections. These members are to represent the 'nations and regions', and it makes sense for their constituencies to match the nations and regions of the UK. It also helps to distinguish them further from MPs in the House of Commons: the larger the area, the less likely they are to do constituency work. We also recommend a formal convention to prevent this.

(h) If the numbers of elected members prove to be too great to be accommodated in just twelve regional constituencies across the UK, we recommend that the Electoral Commission be invited to draw a new set of sub-regional boundaries.

(i) We recommend that any voting system for the second chamber should satisfy the following general principles. It needs to: be complementary to the voting system for the House of Commons; minimise the risk of one party gaining an overall majority; maximise voter choice, by enabling voters to vote for individual candidates, within and across parties; encourage a more diverse chamber; and encourage the election of independent-minded people. These principles will best be realised by using multi-member constituencies, and a proportional voting system. This could be either STV or regional lists, so long as the lists are fully open lists, which maximise voter choice. We would not support limited open lists, which present an appearance of choice for the voter, but almost never affect the outcome.

(j) We recommend that second chamber elections should take place at the same time as General Elections.

(k) We recommend that elections to the second chamber should be staggered.

(l) We recommend that elected second chamber members should serve a single term extending to two Parliaments. No member of the second chamber should be permitted to stand for election to the Commons for ten years after leaving the second chamber. These restrictions would apply from the next general election. Political parties should not be allowed to nominate for appointment anyone who has served as an elected member of the second chamber.

(m) We recommend that the parties should submit lists of party nominees to the Appointments Commission, ranked if they wish in order of preference, but that the Commission should make the final selection. The Appointments Commission would take the final decision on those who are to represent their parties. If the Government is unable to agree to this recommendation, which we regard as fundamental, then we recommend that there should be no separate element of party nominees in the second chamber and that its composition should consist of 70 per cent directly elected members and 30 per cent independent appointees.

(n) If elected members are allowed a single two-Parliament term, then we believe a limit of ten years should apply to appointed members; with no possibility of gaining a second term by switching categories.

(o) The Committee do not believe that the involvement of the executive in the selection of a body which is meant to be directly accountable to Parliament is appropriate. Parliament should take firmer hold of the process, so that the credibility of the new Appointments Commission can be properly established.

(p) We believe that it is time Parliament took full responsibility for the recruitment and appointment of bodies which are directly accountable to Parliament. We suggest that a committee of senior members of both Houses should examine how best this should be done.

(q) As a signal that the Appointments Commission should take very seriously the aim of producing a House which is more diverse, we recommend that the Commission should itself be more diverse.

(r) We recommend that the Appointments Commission should allocate the numbers of politically nominated members to each party, based on the share of the vote won by the parties in the most recent second chamber election.

(s) We recommend that the law lords should leave the second chamber at the next general election but one.

(t) We recommend that the Bishops of the Church of England should no longer sit ex officio from the time of the next general election but one.

(u) We recommend that the size of the second chamber when all elected members have joined should be clearly established and that it be set at up to 350. This figure would be very much the upper limit of the acceptable range.

(v) We recommend that a review of the effect of these changes should be held when the maximum number of elected members have entered the second chamber.

(w) We recommend that the research and other resources available to members of the second chamber should be adequate for the role that it is required to perform. We further recommend that this should be kept under regular review.

(x) We recommend that the Senior Salaries Review Body should review the question of payment of members when the reformed chamber has been operating for a number of years.

(y) We recommend that a joint committee of both Houses be established to examine proposals on improving co-operation in scrutiny of legislation and of the executive. It should be asked to report within a year. This need not delay, but should complement, progress on the general reform of the second chamber.

(z) We recommend that membership of the second chamber should no longer be linked with any honour, including the peerage.

(aa) We recommend, that it would be better to adopt the name 'second chamber', to emphasise its complementary role in Parliament. The ancestral name 'House of Lords' would slowly slip into desuetude. The members of the second chamber could be entitled, on the analogy of the members of the Scottish Parliament (MSPs), Members of the Second Chamber or MSCs.

(bb) We recommend that the remaining hereditary peers should leave the second chamber when the reform Act comes into effect.

(cc) We recommend that all life peers should remain in the second chamber until the next general election. An appropriate scheme of payments should be offered to members who wished to withdraw from the second chamber. The appointments commission should not make appointments until the next general election.

(dd) We recommend that one or more elections should be held among the life peers, at the same time as general elections, to reduce their numbers by stages to zero.

(ee) In our view the next step would be the production of a draft Bill for consideration by a joint committee of both Houses as soon as possible and we so recommend.

NOTES:
1. Following recommendation 59 of the Royal Commission on the Reform of the House of Lords that 'The Lords of Appeal should set out in writing and publish a statement of the principles which they intend to observe when participating in debates and votes in the second chamber and when considering their eligibility to sit on related cases' Lord Bingham, then the Lord Chief Justice, made a statement which had been agreed by all of the Lords of Appeal in Ordinary:

   General Principles
   As full members of the House of Lords the Lords of Appeal in Ordinary have a right to participate in the business of the House. However, mindful of their judicial role they consider themselves bound by two general principles when deciding whether to participate in a particular matter, or to vote: first, the Lords of Appeal in Ordinary do not think it appropriate to engage in matters where there is a strong element of party political controversy; and secondly the Lords of Appeal in Ordinary bear in mind that they might render themselves ineligible to sit judicially if they were to express an opinion on a matter which might later be relevant to an appeal to the House.
   The Lords of Appeal in Ordinary will continue to be guided by these broad principles. They stress that it is impossible to frame rules which cover every eventuality. In the end it must be for the judgment of each individual Lord of Appeal to decide how to conduct himself in any particular situation. (HL Debs: vol. 614, col. 419, 22 June 2000.)

2. Lord Bingham has argued for the removal of judicial functions from the House of Lords and the creation of a Supreme Court: see his memorandum of evidence to the Royal Commission on Reform of the House of Lords 'Reform of the House of Lords: Future of the Appellate Committee' at 0022.pdf on the CD-Rom which accompanies *A House for the Future*, Report of the Royal Commission the Reform of the House of Lords (Cm 4534) and his speech 'The Evolving Constitution' given to the Law Society on 4 October 2001 available at ⟨http://www.lcd.gov.uk/judicial/speeches/sla041001.htm⟩. For a discussion of the issues surrounding the possible creation of a Supreme Court see A. P. Le Sueur and R. Cornes, *The Future of the United Kingdom's Highest Courts* (2001), also available at ⟨http://www.ucl.ac.uk/constitution-unit/reports/files/top.pdf⟩.

QUESTIONS
1. Do you agree with the reasoning of the Royal Commission, which wished the reformed second chamber to carry out particular tasks for which authority is required rather than legitimacy acquired through election?

2. Is it desirable or possible for conventions to regulate the legislative role of the Law Lords given the responsibilities which they will have in human rights and devolution cases?

3. If the Lord Chancellor accepts that there are some cases in which it would be inappropriate for him to sit as a member of the Appellate Committee, why should he sit in judgment in any cases?

NOTE: Mr R. Cook, the Leader of the House of Commons made a statement in which it was proposed that both Houses of Parliament establish a Joint Committee to consider reform of the House of Lords. This Joint Committee would first consider options on composition and powers of the House of Lords which would then be put to both Houses in free votes. In the second phase, the Joint Committee would define composition and powers in greater detail taking into account the views of the two Houses and suggest a transitional strategy. The Government would then bring forward legislation in the light of the Joint Committee's reports and the views of the two Houses in the free votes (see HC Deb, Vol 385, cols 517–33, 13 May, 2002). The government had thus accepted that its White Paper (Cm 5291) had not commanded support and it remains to be seen if the Joint Committee can produce an agreed report and how long its two phases of deliberations will take.

7

Civil Liberties

SECTION 1: **Introduction**

The area of civil liberties is so large that it would merit a book on its own. Consequently, treatment of this topic in this chapter will be brief and selective, seeking to highlight certain issues.

In most constitutions there are declarations of particular rights or liberties to be accorded to citizens and respected by government, such as freedom of speech, freedom of the person, freedom of conscience, freedom of movement, the right to privacy, and the right to equal treatment. Often these freedoms or rights have an entrenched or protected status so that they may not easily be restricted or overridden by temporary political majorities in control of the legislature. These rights or freedoms are seen as essential to the existence and maintenance of a liberal democracy. The position in the United Kingdom was very different and owed much to Dicey. With the enactment of the Human Rights Act 1998 major changes have been introduced. These will be examined later in the chapter, but to understand the significance of these changes it is necessary to understand the way in which rights were protected prior to the enactment of the 1998 Act.

A. V. Dicey, *An Introduction to the Study of the Law of the Constitution*
(10th edn, 1969), p. 203

[W]ith us the law of the constitution, the rules which in foreign countries naturally form part of a constitutional code, are not the source but the consequence of the rights of individuals, as defined and enforced by the courts; that, in short, the principles of private law have with us been by the action of the courts and Parliament so extended as to determine the position of the Crown and of its servants; thus the constitution is the result of the ordinary law of the land.

The former position in the United Kingdom was summarised as follows:

Legislation on Human Rights: A Discussion Document
(Home Office, 1976), paras. 2.01–05

Our arrangements for the protection of human rights are different from those of most other countries. The differences are related to differences in our constitutional traditions. Although our present constitution may be regarded as deriving in part from the revolution settlement of 1688–89, consolidated by the Union of 1707, we, unlike our European neighbours and many Commonwealth countries, do not owe our present system of government either to a revolution or to a struggle for independence. The United Kingdom –

(a) has an omnicompetent Parliament, with absolute power to enact any law and change any previous law; the courts in England and Wales have not, since the seventeenth century, recognised even in theory any higher legal order by reference to which Acts of Parliament could be held void; in Scotland the courts, while reserving the right to treat an Act as void for breaching a fundamental term of the Treaty of Union [see *MacCormick* v *Lord Advocate* 1953 SC 396], have made it clear that they foresee no likely circumstances in which they would do so;

(b) unlike other modern democracies, has no written constitution;

(c) unlike countries in the civil law tradition, makes no fundamental distinction, as regards rights or remedies, between 'public law' governing the actions of the State and its agents, and 'private law' regulating the relationships of private citizens with one another; nor have we a coherent system of administrative law applied by specialised tribunals or courts and with its own appropriate remedies;

(d) has not generally codified its law, and our courts adopt a relatively narrow and literal approach to the interpretation of statutes;

(e) unlike the majority of EEC countries and the United States, does not, by ratifying a treaty or convention, make it automatically part of the domestic law (nor do we normally give effect to such an international agreement by incorporating the agreement itself into our law).

In other countries the rights of the citizen are usually (though not universally) to be found enunciated in general terms in a Bill of Rights or other constitutional document. The effectiveness of such instruments varies greatly. A Bill of Rights is not an automatic guarantee of liberty; its efficacy depends on the integrity of the institutions which apply it, and ultimately on the determination of the people that it should be maintained. The United Kingdom as such has no Bill of Rights of this kind. The Bill of Rights of 1688, though more concerned with the relationship between the English Parliament and the Crown, did contain some important safeguards for personal liberty – as did the Claim of Right of 1689, its Scottish equivalent. Among the provisions common to both the Bill of Rights and the Claim of Rights are declarations that excessive bail is illegal and that it is the right of subjects to petition the Crown without incurring penalties. But the protection given by these instruments to the rights and liberties of the citizen is much narrower than the constitutional guarantees now afforded in many other democratic countries.

The effect of the United Kingdom system of law is to provide, through the development of the common law and by express statutory enactment, a diversity of specific rights with their accompanying remedies. Thus, to secure the individual's right to freedom from unlawful or arbitrary detention, our law provides specific and detailed remedies such as habeas corpus and the action for false imprisonment. The rights which have been afforded in this way are for the most part negative rights to be protected from interference from others, rather than positive rights to behave in a particular way. Those rights which have emerged in the common law can always be modified by Parliament. Parliament's role is all-pervasive – potentially, at least. It continually adapts existing rights and remedies and provides new ones, and no doubt this process would continue even if a comprehensive Bill of Rights were enacted.

The legal remedies provided for interference with the citizen's rights have in recent times been overlaid by procedures which are designed to afford not so much remedies in the strict sense of the term as facilities for obtaining independent and impartial scrutiny of action by public bodies about which an individual believes he has cause for complaint, even though the action may have been within the body's legal powers. For example, the actions of central government departments are open to scrutiny by the Parliamentary Commissioner for Administration; and complaints about the administration of the National Health Service are investigated by the Health Service Commissioners.

NOTE: 'Rights' and 'freedoms' were regarded negatively in the United Kingdom; they were the area of freedom which remained after legal restraints were subtracted. Thus a person was free to do anything subject to the provisions of the law. There was, however, no guarantee that the area of freedom would not be contracted by the incremental encroachment of legislation until little freedom remained. In *Entick* v *Carrington* (1765) 19 St Tr 1030 (*ante* p. 174), Lord Camden had made it clear that Government, if it is to be free to interfere with individual rights, must be able to point to specific statutory or common law powers. The problem with this was that if these powers did not exist, they could always be created by new legislation. Today, for example, the police and other officials, such as Inland Revenue Inspectors and Customs and Excise Officers, have considerable powers under various Acts to obtain warrants and enter and search premises and seize property. See, for example, Police and Criminal Evidence Act 1984, s. 8; Taxes Management Act 1970, s. 20C, inserted by Finance Act 1976; Customs and Excise Management Act 1979, s. 161; Official Secrets Act 1911, s. 9; Police Act 1997, ss. 92–108.

While some statutes may seek to limit rights, others may accord protection which did not exist at common law. For example, at common law discrimination on the grounds of race or sex was not generally prohibited. Parliament intervened by means of the Race Relations Act 1976 and the Sex Discrimination Act 1975 to prohibit discrimination in certain circumstances, such as employment, housing, education, and the provision of goods and services. This is not equivalent, however, to creating a general right to be free from discrimination. This kind of legislative intervention by Parliament is limited as each piece of legislation represents a limited response to a perceived mischief. Until the enactment of the Human Rights Act 1998 the practice was to provide limited remedies against particular abuses but to stop short of providing any general declaration of particular rights.

But if Parliament is elected by democratic means, why should we worry if particular Acts encroach on individual freedom?

F. Klug, K. Starmer and S. Weir, *The Three Pillars of Liberty: Political Rights and Freedoms in the United Kingdom*
(1996), pp. 9–10

The links between democracy and human rights are explicitly recognised in the preamble to the European Convention on Human Rights:

> those Fundamental Freedoms which are the foundation of justice and peace in the world . . . are best maintained on the one hand by an effective political democracy and on the other by a common understanding and observance of the Human Rights upon which they depend.

The Statute of the Convention's founding body, the Council of Europe, specifically links individual freedom, political liberty and the rule of law as the basis of 'all genuine democracy' (Council of Europe 1993: 2). The UN instruments do not make the same explicit links, but the International Covenant confirms the right to take part in public affairs and vote in free elections (Articles 21 and 25).

In reality, the links between democracy and human rights are not quite as simple as statements of principle make them seem. From Alexis de Tocqueville and John Stuart Mill onwards, political philosophers have expressed the concern that majority rule is inherently threatening to civil, and especially minority, rights. Such observers have argued that a Bill of Rights, constitutionally protected from political interference and enforced by the courts, is required as an external check on majority rule and elected parliaments (Martin 1993: 173).

A 'human rights' view of democracy seeks to give substance to the argument that democracy cannot be equated simply with majority rule and that processes which protect minorities and give them an effective voice are essential to democratic practice (Rosas and Heligesen 1990: 18; Beetham and Boyle 1995). However, our view that basic rights, such as freedom of expression and assembly, are constitutive of democracy itself is not solely a matter of protecting minorities. Democracy does not genuinely exist, even though governments and MPs have been elected in more or less free elections, unless voters as a whole have had access to the information they need to make 'knowledgeable choices rather than manipulated responses' (Dworkin 1990: 33). Citizens must be able to participate in government between elections through informed and free debate. For this to happen, government and Parliament have to be constrained by citizen's rights which are established in law and not easily tampered with by politicians, bureaucrats or others. They should become part of the fabric of society. It is the task of the courts, or any other body charged with their protection, to establish a specific interpretation of those rights with which to assess and rule unlawful legislation or decisions which violate them. It is often said that this process makes their provisions too 'rigid'; but, in practice, as the continuing interpretation of the European Convention has shown, human rights evolve as society evolves – in the same way as the common law itself adapts over time.

[We adopt] the position elaborated by international human rights instruments. The European Court of Human Rights, set out this position in a landmark case in 1981:

> Although individual interests must on occasion be subordinated to those of a group, democracy does not simply mean that the views of a majority must always prevail: a balance must be achieved which ensures the fair and proper treatment of minorities and avoids any abuse of a dominant position. (*Young, James and Webster* v *UK*, 1982)

From this perspective, not only are human rights best protected in a political system based on 'the will of the people'; but for that will to be freely debated and expressed in ways which give everyone the chance to be involved, certain fundamental human rights must he protected. A majority decision is democratically legitimate only if it is a majority within a society of equals.

NOTE: But part of the problem with the British system was a lack of any common understanding of what was meant by 'constitutional rights' and how they should be protected, as the following case illustrates.

Harman v *Secretary of State for the Home Department*
[1983] AC 280, House of Lords

Harman was a solicitor, who in discovery proceedings, had obtained documents from the Home Office. These were agreed only to be used for the purpose of the proceedings. They were read out in court. A journalist present in court was shown the documents by Harman for the purposes of an article he was writing. The Home Office took proceedings against Harman alleging contempt. These were successful. In the House of Lords their Lordships could not agree on what weight freedom of speech should be given.

LORD DIPLOCK: . . . My Lords, in a case which has attracted a good deal of publicity it may assist in clearing up misconceptions if I start by saying what the case is *not* about. It is *not* about freedom of speech, freedom of the press, openness of justice or documents coming into 'the public domain'; nor, with all respect to those of your Lordships who think the contrary, does it in my opinion call for consideration of any of those human rights and fundamental freedoms which in the European Convention on Human Rights are contained in separate articles each starting with a statement in absolute terms but followed immediately by very broadly stated exceptions.

What this case *is* about is an aspect of the law of discovery of documents in civil actions in the High Court. . . .

LORD SCARMAN: . . . In framing a new rule your Lordships, in our respectful submission, must do so in a way which, first, recognises the important constitutional right to freedom of communication (though with any necessary concession to the individual citizen's right to privacy), and, secondly, is as far as possible free from anomaly. We have used the term 'freedom of communication,' but 'freedom of expression' (perhaps slightly narrower) would do equally well; the latter the United Kingdom has, by ratifying the European Convention on Human Rights, bound itself 'to secure to everyone within [its] jurisdiction': articles 1 and 10.

There must be some correlation between the right to impart information and the right to receive information. It is unnecessary to explore the relationship in all its complexities. It is sufficient for our purposes to note that the right to receive information will generally involve a right to impart it; any exception must be strictly scrutinised and powerfully justified. If (as is our view) the documents became, by production at trial, 'public property and public knowledge,' the journalist had a right to receive information about them: and the undertaking, if it applied to them after trial, at least obstructed to some degree his right. It certainly made it more inconvenient and expensive for him to exercise. . . . When the Americans made into fundamental constitutional law what they saw as the basic rights vouchsafed to them by their heritage of the common law, the very first amendment to the Constitution, inscribed in the Bill of Rights 1791, contained the following provisions: 'Congress shall make no law . . . abridging the freedom of speech, or of the press . . .'. . . . A balance has to be struck between two interests of the law – on the one hand, the protection of a litigant's private right to keep his documents to himself notwithstanding his duty to disclose them to the other side in the litigation, and, on the other, the protection of the right, which the law recognises, subject to certain exceptions, as the right of everyone, to speak freely, and to impart information and ideas, upon matters of public knowledge.

In our view, a just balance is struck if the obligation endures only so long as the documents themselves are private and confidential. Once the litigant's private right to keep his documents to himself has been overtaken by their becoming public knowledge, we can see no reason why the undertaking given when they were confidential should continue to apply to them.

Article 6 of the European Convention provides that, subject to certain defined, severely limited exceptions (which do not arise in the present case), everyone, in the determination of his civil rights and obligations or of any criminal charge against him, is entitled to a fair and public trial. . . .

[His Lordship quoted Article 10 (*post* p. 467) and continued.] In the *Handyside case*, November 4, 1976, Publications of the European Court of Human Rights, Series A No. 24, para. 49, the European Court of Human Rights declared that freedom of expression is a basic condition, an essential foundation, of a free and democratic society and that the freedom exists not only for information and ideas which are favourably received 'but also to those that offend, shock or disturb the state or any sector of the population.'

In *The Sunday Times* v *United Kingdom* (1979) 2 EHRR 245, the court emphasised that paragraph 2 of article 10 did not establish principles in competition with the right to freedom of expression but only created 'a number of exceptions which must be narrowly interpreted' (see p. 281). The court went on to construe the exceptions permissible under paragraph 2 as limited to those which could be justified by a real pressing social need.

It can hardly be argued that there is a pressing social need to exclude the litigant and his solicitor from the right available to everyone else to treat as public knowledge documents which have been produced and made part and parcel of public legal proceedings. If English law should recognise this exclusion, it might well be inconsistent with the requirements of the European Convention.

Appeal dismissed.

NOTE: The absence of a written constitution laying down clear principles and based on certain agreed values created the further problem, that judges were left to struggle to discern what values they should be seeking to uphold in a democracy. This is illustrated by the differing views articulated by judges in the following case arising out of the *Spycatcher* affair.

Attorney-General v *Guardian Newspapers Ltd (No. 1)*
[1987] 1 WLR 1248, House of Lords

The Guardian and *the Observer* newspapers both published outlines of Peter Wright's allegations contained in his book *Spycatcher*. The Attorney-General sought and obtained interlocutory injunctions from Millett J against both papers, restraining them from disclosing any information obtained by Wright in his capacity as a member of the British Security Service until a full trial of the issues took place. Sir Nicolas Browne-Wilkinson V-C discharged the injunctions but the Court of Appeal reinstated them in a modified form. On appeal before the House of Lords the injunctions were continued (Lord Bridge and Lord Oliver dissenting), although the book was, by that time, widely available internationally and copies had been imported into the United Kingdom. The majority in the House of Lords placed considerable emphasis on the duty of secrecy and confidentiality Wright owed his former employers.

LORD BRIDGE: . . . So long as any of the *Spycatcher* allegations remained undisclosed, I should have been wholeheartedly in favour of maintaining the injunctions in the interests of national security for all the reasons so cogently deployed in the affidavit of Sir Robert Armstrong. But it is perfectly obvious and elementary that, once information is freely available to the general public, it is nonsensical to talk about preventing its 'disclosure.' Whether the *Spycatcher* allegations are true or false is beside the point. What is to the point is that they are now freely available to the public or, perhaps more accurately, to any member of the public who wants to read them. I deliberately refrain from using expressions such as 'the public domain' which may have technical overtones. The fact is that the intelligence and security services of any country in the world can buy the book *Spycatcher* and read what is in it. The fact is that any citizen of this country can buy the book in America and bring it home with him or order the book from America and receive a copy by post. Some enterprising small traders have apparently found it worth their while to import copies of the book and sell them by the roadside. It remains to be seen whether the Attorney-General will institute proceedings for contempt of court against any public library which imports copies of *Spycatcher* and makes it available to borrowers. Mr Mummery had no instructions which enabled him to answer the question I asked about that.

If, as I have always thought, the interest of national security in protecting sensitive and classified information is to conceal it from those who might make improper use of it, it is manifestly now too late for the Millett injunctions to serve that interest. If the confidence of friendly countries in the ability of this country to protect its secrets has been undermined by the publication in the United States of America of *Spycatcher*, the maintenance of the Millett injunctions can do nothing to restore that confidence. So much, I believe, is obvious and incontrovertible.

I well understand the sense of indignation which all of us must feel that Mr Wright, to use the colloquialism, should have got away with it, worse still that he should make a profit from his breach of confidence. Perhaps his publishers come under the same condemnation. But the remedy for that wrong lies not in a futile injunction but in an action for an account of profits.

The legal basis for the Attorney-General's claim to enjoin the newspapers is that any third party who comes into possession of information knowing that it originated from a breach of confidence owes the same duty to the original confider as that owed by the original confidant. If this proposition is held to be of universal application, no matter how widely the original confidential information has been disseminated before reaching the third party, it would seem to me to lead to absurd and unacceptable consequences. But I am prepared to assume for present purposes that the Attorney-General is still in a position to assert a bare duty binding on the conscience of newspaper editors which is capable of surviving the publication of *Spycatcher* in America.

The key question in the case, to my mind, is whether there is any remaining interest of national security which the Millett injunctions are capable of protecting and, if so, whether it is of sufficient weight to justify the massive encroachment on freedom of speech which the continuance of the Millett injunctions in present circumstances necessarily involves. . . .

What of the other side of the coin and the encroachment on freedom of speech? Having no written constitution, we have no equivalent in our law to the First Amendment to the Constitution of the United States of America. Some think that puts freedom of speech on too lofty a pedestal. Perhaps they are right. We have not adopted as part of our law the European Convention for the Protection of Human Rights and Fundamental Freedoms to which this country is a signatory. Many think that we should. I have hitherto not been of that persuasion, in large part because I have had confidence in the capacity of the common law to safeguard the fundamental freedoms essential to a free society including the right to freedom of speech which is specifically safeguarded by article 10 of the Convention. My confidence is seriously undermined by your Lordships' decision. All the judges in the courts below in this case have been concerned not to impose any unnecessary fetter on freedom of speech. I suspect that what the Court of Appeal would have liked to achieve, and perhaps set out to achieve by their compromise solution, was to inhibit 'The Sunday Times' from continuing the serialisation of *Spycatcher*, but to leave the press at large at liberty to discuss and comment on the *Spycatcher* allegations. If there were a method of achieving these results which could be sustained in law, I can see much to be said for it on the merits. But I can see nothing whatever, either in law or on the merits, to be said for the maintenance of a total ban on discussion in the press of this country of matters of undoubted public interest and concern which the rest of the world now knows all about and can discuss freely. Still less can I approve your Lordships' decision to throw in for good measure a restriction on reporting court proceedings in Australia which the Attorney-General had never even asked for.

Freedom of speech is always the first casualty under a totalitarian regime. Such a regime cannot afford to allow the free circulation of information and ideas among its citizens. Censorship is the indispensable tool to regulate what the public may and what they may not know. The present attempt to insulate the public in this country from information which is freely available elsewhere is a significant step down that very dangerous road. The maintenance of the ban, as more and more copies of the book *Spycatcher* enter this country and circulate here, will seem more and more ridiculous. If the Government are determined to fight to maintain the ban to the end, they will face inevitable condemnation and humiliation by the European Court of Human Rights in Strasbourg. Long before that they will have been condemned at the bar of public opinion in the free world.

But there is another alternative. The Government will surely want to reappraise the whole *Spy-catcher* situation in the light of the views expressed in the courts below and in this House. I dare to hope that they will bring to that reappraisal qualities of vision and of statesmanship sufficient to recognise that their wafer thin victory in this litigation has been gained at a price which no Government committed to upholding the values of a free society can afford to pay.

LORD TEMPLEMAN: . . . My Lords, this appeal involves a conflict between the right of the public to be protected by the Security Service and the right of the public to be supplied with full information by the press. This appeal therefore involves consideration of the Convention for the Protection of Human Rights and Fundamental Freedoms (1953) (Cmd. 8969) ('the Convention') to which the British Government adheres. . . .

[His Lordship quoted Article 10 of the Convention and continued.]

In *The Sunday Times* v *United Kingdom* [1979] 2 EHRR 245, a decision of 27 October 1978, the European Court of Human Rights decided by a majority of 11 to 9 that there had been a violation of the Convention by reason of the judgment of this House in *Attorney-General* v *Times Newspapers Ltd* [1974] AC 273, 327 which restrained 'The Sunday Times' from publishing:

any article or matter which prejudges the issues of negligence, breach of contract or breach of duty or deals with the evidence relating to any of the said issues arising in any actions pending or imminent against Distillers . . . in respect of the development, distribution or use of the drug Thalidomide.

The European Court pointed out that this House applying domestic law had balanced the public interest in freedom of expression and the public interest in the due administration of justice. But the European Court [1979] 2 EHRR 245, 281, para. 65:

is faced not with a choice between two conflicting principles, but with a principle of freedom of expression that is subject to a number of exceptions which must be narrowly interpreted. . . . It is not sufficient that the interference involved belongs to that class of exceptions listed in article 10(2) which has been invoked; neither is it sufficient that the interference was imposed because its subject matter fell within a particular category or was caught by a legal rule formulated in general or absolute terms: the court has to be satisfied that the interference was necessary having regard to the facts and circumstances prevailing in the specific case before it.

The question is therefore whether the interference with freedom of expression constituted by the Millett injunctions was, on 30 July 1987 when they were continued by this House, necessary in a democratic society in the interests of national security, for protecting the reputation or rights of others, for preventing the disclosure of information received in confidence or for maintaining the authority and impartiality of the judiciary having regard to the facts and circumstances prevailing on the 30 July 1987 and in the light of the events which had happened. The continuance of the Millett injunctions appears to me to be necessary for all these purposes.

My Lords, in my opinion a democracy is entitled to take the view that a public servant who is employed in the Security Service must be restrained from making any disclosures concerning the Security Service and that similar restraints must be imposed on anybody who receives those disclosures knowing that they are confidential.

QUESTIONS

1. Which is more important to the preservation of democracy – a free press or protection of government from criticism, merited or otherwise?

2. Was Lord Bridge's 'confidence in the capacity of the common law to safeguard the fundamental freedoms essential to a free society' misplaced?

NOTES:

1. When a differently constituted House of Lords heard the final appeal on the trial of the issues based on breach of confidence, *Attorney-General* v *Guardian Newspapers (No. 2)* [1988] 3 WLR 776, it decided to discharge the injunctions, as disclosure worldwide of Wright's allegations had destroyed their secrecy and no further damage could be done to the public interest. However, had Wright been resident in the United Kingdom, his allegations might never have been made as their Lordships confirmed that those employed in the Security Services owe a lifelong duty of confidence to the state.

Following the decision of the House of Lords *the Observer* and *the Guardian* petitioned the European Commission on Human Rights alleging, *inter alia*, a breach of Article 10 of the European Convention of Human Rights and Fundamental Freedoms. In *The Observer and The Guardian* v *United Kingdom* (1991) 14 EHRR 153, the European Court of Human Rights held, *inter alia*:

(a) by 14 votes to 10, that there had been no violation of Article 10 during the period 11 July 1986 (when the original interlocutory injunctions granted on 27 June 1986 were confirmed in an *inter partes* hearing) to 30 June 1987 (when the House of Lords continued the original interlocutory injunctions even though *Spycatcher* had been published in the United States on 14 July 1987), the Court stating (at para. 62):

> to refuse interlocutory injunctions would mean that [the newspapers] would be free to publish ... material [for which the Attorney-General was seeking a permanent ban on the grounds that disclosure would be detrimental to the Security Service], immediately and before the substantive trial; this would effectively deprive the Attorney-General, if successful on the merits, of his right to be granted a permanent injunction, thereby irrevocably destroying the substance of his actions and, with it, the claim to protect national security.
>
> In the Court's view, these reasons were 'relevant' in terms of the aims of protecting national security and of maintaining the authority of the judiciary.

The Court further concluded, that taking into account the margin of appreciation to be accorded to national authorities, the English courts were entitled to conclude that injunctive relief was necessary and this response was not disproportionate for the purpose of achieving the above aims.

(b) unanimously, that there had been a violation of Article 10 during the period from 30 July 1987 to 13 October 1988 (when the House of Lords finally lifted the injunctions) as the confidentiality of the material no longer existed following publication in the USA and with it any rights as a litigant seeking permanent injunctions which the Attorney-General was seeking to protect. The purpose of the injunctions at this point was confined to promoting the efficiency and reputation of the Security Service which was not a sufficient reason to justify the continued interference with the rights of the newspapers to 'purvey information, already available, on a matter of legitimate public concern'.

2. As the 1990s were drawing to a close there was a reawakening of judicial interest in constitutional rights and a much greater willingness to conceive of their existence as a brake on the power of the Executive. In *R v Lord Chancellor, ex parte Witham* [1998] QB 575, a litigant in person, who was unemployed and in receipt of income support and who wished to sue for defamation (for which legal aid was not available), sought judicial review of Article 3 of the Supreme Court Fees (Amendment) Order 1996 made by the Lord Chancellor under s. 130 of the Supreme Court Act 1981. Article 3 imposed a minimum fee of £120 for the issuing of a writ and removed a provision under a previous Order of 1980 which relieved litigants in person who were in receipt of income support from the obligation to pay fees. The Divisional Court granted the application for a declaration that Article 3 was unlawful. Laws J stated:

> [T]he right to a fair trial, which of necessity imports the right of access to the court, is as near to an absolute right as any which I can envisage. .... Access to the courts is a constitutional right; it can only be denied by the government if it persuades Parliament to pass legislation which specifically – in effect by express provision – permits the executive to turn people away from the court door. That has not been done in this case.

There was nothing in s. 130 of the 1981 Act which provided expressly for the abrogation of this right.

This willingness to recognise the added importance of human rights began to have an impact on the way in which the *Wednesbury* unreasonableness test was applied in judicial review proceedings. In *R v Ministry of Defence, ex parte Smith* [1996] QB 517, the Court of Appeal adopted the approach that 'the more substantial the interference with human rights, the more the court will require by way of justification before it is satisfied that the decision is reasonable'. This involves 'anxious scrutiny' or 'high-intensity review' in human rights cases. In *Chesterfield Properties plc v Secretary of State for the Environment* [1998] JPL 568, at 579–80, Laws J expressed the operation of this process as follows:

> Where an administrative decision abrogates or diminishes a constitutional or fundamental right, *Wednesbury* requires that the decision-maker provide a substantial justification in the public interest for doing so. .... The identification of any right as 'constitutional', however,

means nothing in the absence of a written constitution unless it is defined by reference to some particular protection which the law affords it. The common law affords such protection by adopting, within *Wednesbury*, a variable standard of review. There is no question of the court exceeding the principle of reasonableness. It means only that reasonableness itself requires in such cases that in ordering the priorities which will drive his decision, the decision-maker must give a high place to the right in question. He cannot treat it merely as something to be taken into account, akin to any other relevant consideration; he must recognise it as a value to be kept, unless in his judgment there is a greater value which justifies its loss. In many arenas of public discretion, the force to be given to all and any factors which the decision-maker must confront is neutral in the eye of the law; he may make of each what he will, and the law will not interfere because the weight he attributes to any of them is for him and not the court. But where a constitutional right is involved, the law presumes it to carry substantial force. Only another interest, a public interest, of greater force may override it.

In *R v Lord Saville, ex parte A and Others* [1999] 4 All ER 860, the Court of Appeal applied the high-intensity review test. The Bloody Sunday Review Tribunal, chaired by Lord Saville of Newdigate, had denied anonymity to soldiers testifying before it although accepting that anonymity would not hamper it in finding the truth. The Tribunal concluded that anonymity would affect the openness of the inquiry. Seventeen soldiers applied for judicial review claiming that disclosure of their identities would put them at risk and thus interfered with their right to life. Their application was allowed by the Divisional Court. The Tribunal appealed. Lord Woolf MR, delivering the judgment of the court, dismissing the appeal stated (at p. 872):

> [W]hen a fundamental right such as the right to life is engaged, the options available to the reasonable decision-maker are curtailed. They are curtailed because it is unreasonable to reach a decision which contravenes or could contravene human rights unless there are sufficiently significant countervailing considerations. In other words it is not open to the decision-maker to risk interfering with fundamental rights in the absence of compelling justification. Even the broadest discretion is constrained by the need for there to be countervailing circumstances justifying interference with human rights. The courts will anxiously scrutinise the strength of the countervailing circumstances and the degree of the interference with the human right involved and then apply the test accepted by Lord Bingham MR in *Smith*.

This judicial awakening to the existence of constitutional or fundamental rights ties in with the political developments of the late 1990s which resulted in the enactment of the Human Rights Act 1998, which is considered in detail below.

SECTION 2: The European Convention on Human Rights

In 1950 Member States of the Council of Europe (which included the United Kingdom) drew up the European Convention on Human Rights and Fundamental Freedoms. This was based on the United Nations Declaration of Human Rights and is designed to provide basic protection for human rights. The Convention was ratified by the United Kingdom in 1951 and came into force in 1953, but it was not until 1966 that the United Kingdom accorded to its citizens the right to individual petition whereby a victim of abuse could, upon exhausting all domestic remedies, pursue a complaint before the European Commission of Human Rights and ultimately, if found admissible, before the European Court on Human Rights.

In some states the Convention has been incorporated into municipal law and is enforceable before the domestic courts of those states; in others equivalent protection is afforded by a domestic Bill of Rights. In the United Kingdom the Convention was not initially incorporated into domestic law and thus could not be directly enforced before domestic courts. The success of the Convention in protecting human rights is very much dependent upon the goodwill of the signatory State in complying with its provisions initially, or in complying with the decisions of the Committee of Ministers or Court if it has acted in contravention of the Convention. If a Government ignores these decisions there is no sanction which can be invoked. The only hope is that international diplomatic pressure will encourage compliance. The United Kingdom has been found to be in breach of the Convention on over 100 occasions but has generally complied with decisions against it by taking necessary steps to amend domestic law to comply with the Convention. This may, however, take time as the Government's response is rarely immediate and the legislative process is slow. In the calendar year 1999, the European Court of Human Rights found the United Kingdom to have violated the Convention in 12 cases, and in 2000 it did so in 16 cases. In the calendar year 2000, 626 applications alleging breaches of the Convention by the United Kingdom were registered with the Court.

Protocol No. 11 to the Convention for the Protection of Human Rights and Fundamental Freedoms, which entered into force on 1 November 1998, restructured the control machinery under the Convention. The pressure on the Commission and Court had increased greatly with the increase in the number of signatories to the Convention and the rising number of applications brought by individuals alleging a breach of the Convention. This led to a huge backlog of cases. The role of the European Commission in determining the admissibility of applications has ceased. In place of the previous procedure, all alleged violations of the rights of persons are referred directly to the new permanent Court. The number of judges in the Court is equivalent to the number of signatory States, which currently stands at 41 (with three further applications for membership of the Council of Europe pending). In the majority of cases, the Court will sit in Chambers of seven judges, but on occasions a Grand Chamber of 17 may be convened. The Court deals with individual and inter-State petitions. Initially a committee of three judges will determine admissibility, and by unanimous vote may declare manifestly ill-founded cases inadmissible. If the Court declares an application admissible, it will (in a Chamber of seven) pursue the examination of the case, together with the parties' representatives, and if necessary will undertake an investigation. The Court will also place itself at the disposal of the parties to seek to secure a friendly settlement on the basis of respect for human rights. (Where a case pending before a Chamber raises a serious question affecting the interpretation of the Convention or the protocols thereto, or where the resolution of a question before the Chamber might have a result inconsistent with a judgment previously delivered by the Court, the Chamber may, at any time before it has rendered its judgment, relinquish jurisdiction in favour of the Grand Chamber, unless one of the parties to the case objects.) If no friendly settlement has been arrived at the Court will deliver its judgment. Within a period of three months from the date of the judgment of the Chamber, any party to the case may, in exceptional cases (serious questions affecting the interpretation or application of the Convention or the protocols thereto, or serious issues of general importance), request that the case be referred to the Grand Chamber. If the request is accepted, the resulting judgment of the Grand Chamber will be final. Otherwise, judgments of Chambers will become final when the parties declare that they will not request that the case be referred to the Grand Chamber, or have made no request for reference three months after the date of the judgment; or, if such a request is made, when the panel of the Grand Chamber rejects the request to refer.

European Convention for the Protection of Human Rights and Fundamental Freedoms

Article 1
The High Contracting Parties shall secure to everyone within their jurisdiction the rights and freedoms defined in section 1 of this Convention.

SECTION I

Article 2
1. Everyone's right to life shall be protected by law. No one shall be deprived of his life intentionally save in the execution of a sentence of a court following his conviction of a crime for which this penalty is provided by law.

2. Deprivation of life shall not be regarded as inflicted in contravention of this Article when it results from the use of force which is no more than absolutely necessary:
   (a) in defence of any person from unlawful violence;
   (b) in order to effect a lawful arrest or to prevent the escape of a person lawfully detained;
   (c) in action lawfully taken for the purpose of quelling a riot or insurrection.

Article 3
No one shall be subjected to torture or to inhuman or degrading treatment or punishment.

Article 4
1. No one shall be held in slavery or servitude.

2. No one shall be required to perform forced or compulsory labour.

3. For the purpose of this Article the term 'forced or compulsory labour' shall not include:
   (a) any work required to be done in the ordinary course of detention imposed according to the provisions of Article 5 of this Convention or during conditional release from such detention;
   (b) any service of a military character or, in case of conscientious objectors in countries where they are recognized, service exacted instead of compulsory military service;
   (c) any service exacted in case of an emergency or calamity threatening the life or well-being of the community;
   (d) any work or service which forms part of normal civic obligations.

Article 5
1. Everyone has the right to liberty and security of person. No one shall be deprived of his liberty save in the following cases and in accordance with a procedure prescribed by law;
   (a) the lawful detention of a person after conviction by a competent court;
   (b) the lawful arrest or detention of a person for non-compliance with the lawful order of a court or in order to secure the fulfilment of any obligation prescribed by law;

(c) the lawful arrest or detention of a person effected for the purpose of bringing him before the competent legal authority on reasonable suspicion of having committed an offence or when it is reasonably considered necessary to prevent his committing an offence or fleeing after having done so;

(d) the detention of a minor by lawful order for the purpose of educational supervision or his lawful detention for the purpose of bringing him before the competent legal authority;

(e) the lawful detention of persons for the prevention of the spreading of infectious diseases, of persons of unsound mind, alcoholics or drug addicts, or vagrants;

(f) the lawful arrest or detention of a person to prevent his effecting an unauthorized entry into the country or of a person against whom action is being taken with a view to deportation or extradition.

2. Everyone who is arrested shall be informed promptly, in a language which he understands, of the reasons for his arrest and of any charge against him.

3. Everyone arrested or detained in accordance with the provisions of paragraph 1 (c) of this Article shall be brought promptly before a judge or other officer authorized by law to exercise judicial power and shall be entitled to trial within a reasonable time or to release pending trial. Release may be conditioned by guarantees to appear for trial.

4. Everyone who is deprived of his liberty by arrest or detention shall be entitled to take proceedings by which the lawfulness of his detention shall be decided speedily by a court and his release ordered if the detention is not lawful.

5. Everyone who has been the victim of arrest or detention in contravention of the provisions of this Article shall have an enforceable right to compensation.

Article 6

1. In the determination of his civil rights and obligations or of any criminal charge against him, everyone is entitled to a fair and public hearing within a reasonable time by an independent and impartial tribunal established by law. Judgment shall be pronounced publicly but the press and public may be excluded from all or part of the trial in the interest of morals, public order or national security in a democratic society, where the interest of juveniles or the protection of the private life of the parties so require, or to the extent strictly necessary in the opinion of the court in special circumstances where publicity would prejudice the interests of justice.

2. Everyone charged with a criminal offence shall be presumed innocent until proved guilty according to law.

3. Everyone charged with a criminal offence has the following minimum rights:

(a) to be informed promptly, in a language which he understands and in detail, of the nature and cause of the accusation against him;

(b) to have adequate time and facilities for the preparation of his defence;

(c) to defend himself in person or through legal assistance of his own choosing or, if he has not sufficient means to pay for legal assistance, to be given it free when the interests of justice so require;

(d) to examine or have examined witnesses against him and to obtain the attendance and examination of witnesses on his behalf under the same conditions as witnesses against him;

(e) to have the free assistance of an interpreter if he cannot understand or speak the language used in court.

Article 7

1. No one shall be held guilty of any criminal offence on account of any act or omission which did not constitute a criminal offence under national or international law at the time when it was committed. Nor shall a heavier penalty be imposed than the one that was applicable at the time the criminal offence was committed.

2. This Article shall not prejudice the trial and punishment of any person for any act or omission which, at the time when it was committed, was criminal according to the general principles of law recognized by civilized nations.

Article 8

1. Everyone has the right to respect for his private and family life, his home and his correspondence.

2. There shall be no interference by a public authority with the exercise of this right except such as is in accordance with the law and is necessary in a democratic society in the interests of national security, public safety or the economic well-being of the country, for the prevention of disorder or crime, for the protection of health or morals, or for the protection of the rights and freedoms of others.

Article 9

1. Everyone has the right to freedom of thought, conscience and religion; this right includes freedom to change his religion or belief, and freedom, either alone or in community with others and in public or private, to manifest his religion or belief, in worship, teaching, practice and observance.

2. Freedom to manifest one's religion or beliefs shall be subject only to such limitations as are prescribed by law and are necessary in a democratic society in the interests of public safety, for the protection of public order, health or morals, or for the protection of the rights and freedoms of others.

Article 10

1. Everyone has the right to freedom of expression. This right shall include freedom to hold opinions and to receive and impart information and ideas without interference by public authority and regardless of frontiers. This Article shall not prevent States from requiring the licensing of broadcasting, television or cinema enterprises.

2. The exercise of these freedoms, since it carries with it duties and responsibilities, may be subject to such formalities, conditions, restrictions or penalties as are prescribed by law and are necessary in a democratic society in the interests of national security, territorial integrity or public safety, for the prevention of disorder or crime, for the protection of health or morals, for the protection of the reputation or rights of others, for preventing the disclosure of information received in confidence, or for maintaining the authority and impartiality of the judiciary.

Article 11

1. Everyone has the right to freedom of peaceful assembly and to freedom of association with others, including the right to form and to join trade unions for the protection of his interests.

2. No restrictions shall be placed on the exercise of these rights other than such as are prescribed by law and are necessary in a democratic society in the interests of national security or public safety, for the prevention of disorder or crime, for the protection of health or morals or for the protection of the rights and freedoms of others. This Article shall not prevent the imposition of lawful restrictions on the exercise of these rights by members of the armed forces, of the police or of the administration of the State.

Article 12

Men and women of marriageable age have the right to marry and to found a family, according to the national laws governing the exercise of this right.

Article 13

Everyone whose rights and freedoms as set forth in this Convention are violated shall have an effective remedy before a national authority notwithstanding that the violation has been committed by persons acting in an official capacity.

Article 14

The enjoyment of the rights and freedoms set forth in this Convention shall be secured without discrimination on any ground such as sex, race, colour, language, religion, political or other opinion, national or social origin, association with a national minority, property, birth or other status.

Article 15

1. In time of war or other public emergency threatening the life of the nation any High Contracting Party may take measures derogating from its obligations under this Convention to the extent strictly required by the exigencies of the situation, provided that such measures are not inconsistent with its other obligations under international law.

2. No derogation from Article 2, except in respect of deaths resulting from lawful acts of war, or from Articles 3, 4 (paragraph 1) and 7 shall be made under this provision.

3. Any High Contracting Party availing itself of this right of derogation shall keep the Secretary-General of the Council of Europe fully informed of the measures which it has taken and the reasons therefore. It shall also inform the Secretary-General of the Council of Europe when such measures have ceased to operate and the provisions of the Convention are again being fully executed.

Article 16

Nothing in Articles 10, 11, and 14 shall be regarded as preventing the High Contracting Parties from imposing restrictions on the political activity of aliens.

Article 17

Nothing in this Convention may be interpreted as implying for any State, group or person any right to engage in any activity or perform any act aimed at the destruction of any of the rights and freedoms set forth herein or at their limitation to a greater extent than is provided for in the Convention.

Article 18

The restrictions permitted under this Convention to the said rights and freedoms shall not be applied for any purpose other than those for which they have been prescribed.

PROTOCOL 1 – ENFORCEMENT OF CERTAIN RIGHTS AND FREEDOMS NOT INCLUDED IN SECTION I OF THE CONVENTION

Article 1

Every natural or legal person is entitled to the peaceful enjoyment of his possessions. No one shall be deprived of his possessions except in the public interest and subject to the conditions provided for by law and by the general principles of international law.

The preceding provisions shall not, however, in any way impair the right of a State to enforce such laws as it deems necessary to control the use of property in accordance with the general interest or to secure the payment of taxes or other contributions or penalties.

Article 2

No person shall be denied the right to education. In the exercise of any functions which it assumes in relation to education and to teaching, the State shall respect the right of parents to ensure such education and teaching in conformity with their own religious and philosophical convictions.

Article 3

The High Contracting Parties undertake to hold free elections at reasonable intervals by secret ballot, under conditions which will ensure the free expression of the opinion of the people in the choice of the legislature.

PROTOCOL 4 – PROTECTING CERTAIN ADDITIONAL RIGHTS

Article 1
No one shall be deprived of his liberty merely on the ground of inability to fulfil a contractual obligation.

Article 2
1. Everyone lawfully within the territory of a State shall, within that territory, have the right to liberty of movement and freedom to choose his residence.

2. Everyone shall be free to leave any country, including his own.

3. No restrictions shall be placed on the exercise of these rights other than such as are in accordance with law and are necessary in a democratic society in the interests of national security or public safety, for the maintenance of 'order public', for the prevention of crime or for the protection of the rights and freedoms of others.

4. The rights set forth in paragraph 1 may also be subject, in particular areas, to restrictions imposed in accordance with law and justified by the public interest in a democratic society.

Article 3
1. No one shall be expelled, by means either of an individual or of a collective measure, from the territory of the State of which he is a national.

2. No one shall be deprived of the right to enter the territory of the State of which he is a national.

Article 4
Collective expulsion of aliens is prohibited.

PROTOCOL 6 – CONCERNING THE ABOLITION OF THE DEATH PENALTY

Article 1
The death penalty shall be abolished. No one shall be condemned to such penalty or executed.

Article 2
A State may make provision in its law for the death penalty in respect of acts committed in time of war or of imminent threat of war; such penalty shall be applied only in the instances laid down in the law and in accordance with its provisions. The State shall communicate to the Secretary General of the Council of Europe the relevant provisions of that law.

Article 3
No derogation from the provisions of this Protocol shall be made under Article 15 of the Convention.

Article 4
No reservation may be made under Article 64 of the Convention in respect of the provisions of this Protocol.

PROTOCOL 7

Article 1
1. An alien lawfully resident in the territory of a State shall not be expelled therefrom except in pursuance of a decision reached in accordance with law and shall be allowed;

    (a) to submit reasons against his expulsion;

    (b) to have his case reviewed; and

    (c) to be represented for these purposes before the competent authority or a person or persons designated by that authority.

2. An alien may be expelled before the exercise of his rights under paragraph 1(a), (b) and (c) of this article, when such expulsion is necessary in the interests of public order or is grounded on reasons of national security.

Article 2

1. Everyone convicted of a criminal offence by a tribunal shall have the right to have his conviction or sentence reviewed by a higher tribunal. The exercise of this right, including the grounds on which it may be exercised, shall be governed by law.

2. This right may be subject to exceptions in regard to offences of a minor character, as prescribed by law, or in cases in which the person concerned was tried in the first instance by the highest tribunal or was convicted following an appeal against acquittal.

Article 3

When a person has by a final decision been convicted of a criminal offence and when subsequently his conviction has been reversed, or he has been pardoned, on the ground that a new or newly discovered fact shows conclusively that there has been a miscarriage of justice, the person who has suffered punishment as a result of such conviction shall be compensated according to the law or the practice of the State concerned, unless it is proved that the non-disclosure of the unknown fact in time is wholly or partly attributable to him.

Article 4

1. No one shall be liable to be tried or punished again in criminal proceedings under the jurisdiction of the same State for an offence for which he has already been finally acquitted or convicted in accordance with the law and penal procedure of that State.

2. The provisions of the preceding paragraph shall not prevent the reopening of the case in accordance with the law and penal procedure of the State concerned, if there is evidence of new or newly discovered facts, or if there has been a fundamental defect in the previous proceedings, which could affect the outcome of the case.

3. No derogation from this article shall be made under Article 15 of the Convention.

Article 5

Spouses shall enjoy equality of rights and responsibilities of a private law character between them, and in their relations with their children, as to marriage, during marriage and in the event of its dissolution. This article shall not prevent States from taking such measures as are necessary in the interests of the children.

NOTE: The United Kingdom has made the following reservation to Article 2 to Protocol 1:

> ... in view of certain provisions of the Education Acts in force in the United Kingdom, the principle affirmed in the second sentence of Article 2 is accepted by the United Kingdom only so far as it is compatible with the provision of efficient instruction and training, and the avoidance of unreasonable expenditure.

The United Kingdom has not ratified Protocols 4 or 7, but ratification of Protocol 7 is in prospect after the Government finds the opportunity to legislate to remove inconsistencies in existing law (see *Rights Brought Home*, Cm 3782, para. 4.15). Articles 1 and 2 of Protocol 6 are included in the list of 'convention rights' protected by the Human Rights Act, the Protocol being signed and ratified in 1999.

The United Kingdom entered a derogation to Article 5(3) of the Convention in 1974 on the basis of 'public emergency threatening the life of the nation' due to the situation in Northern Ireland. This derogation was withdrawn in 1984 but re-entered in 1988, and was upheld by the Court as being within the scope of the 'margin of appreciation' which could be left to national governments (see *Brannigan and McBride* v *UK* 17 EHRR 539, Series A, Vol. 258–B). The derogation was withdrawn in February 2001 after the Terrorism Act 2000 came into force. Following the events of 11 September 2001 in the United States, Parliament enacted the Anti-terrorism, Crime and Security Act 2001 which includes a power to arrest and detain foreign nationals suspected of being international terrorists for the purposes of deportation. Where deportation is not possible because there is a risk that the person will suffer treatment contrary to Article 3 in the country to which he would be deported, there is a power of extended detention. This power contravenes Article 5(1)(f) as interpreted by the European Court of Human Rights in *Chahal* v *United Kingdom* (1996) 23 EHRR 413. As a result, on 18 December 2001, the United Kingdom entered a derogation under Article 15 from its obligations under Article 5(1) (see further, *post*, p. 497).

It should be noted that the rights guaranteed in Convention Articles 2–7 are absolute (subject to a limited exception in Article 6 regarding the public nature of criminal trials) but that the rights guaranteed in Articles 8–12 are subject to a broad range of exceptions. In interpreting the Convention the Court adopts a teleological approach whereby it seeks to give effect to its 'object and purpose'. In *Soering* v *United Kingdom* Series A No. 161 (1989), 11 EHRR 439, the Court stated:

> 87. In interpreting the Convention regard must be had to its special character as a treaty for the collective enforcement of human rights and fundamental freedoms (see the *Ireland* v *The United Kingdom* judgment of 18 January 1978, Series A no. 25, p. 90, § 239). Thus, the object and purpose of the Convention as an instrument for the protection of individual human beings require that its provisions be interpreted and applied so as to make its safeguards practical and effective (see, *inter alia*, the *Artico* judgment of 13 May 1980, Series A no. 37, p. 16, § 33). In addition, any interpretation of the rights and freedoms guaranteed has to be consistent with 'the general spirit of the Convention, an instrument designed to maintain and promote the ideals and values of a democratic society' (see the *Kjedlsen, Busk Madsen and Pedersen* judgment of 7 December 1976, Series A No. 23, p. 27, § 53).

This also means that the interpretation of the Convention will develop over time just as conceptions of the 'ideals and values of a democratic society' will develop. This was emphasized by the Court in *Tyrer* v *UK* Series A No. 26 (1978), 2 EHRR 1, where the practice of corporal punishment in the Isle of Man was challenged as amounting to degrading treatment. The Court stated at para. 31:

> The Court must . . . recall that the Convention is a living instrument which, as the Commission rightly stressed, must be interpreted in the light of present-day conditions. In the case now before it the Court cannot but be influenced by the developments and commonly accepted standards in the penal policy of Member States of the Council of Europe in this field.

When applying the Convention the Court also recognizes the open-textured nature of the language used; interpretation will always be required. In *Soering* at para. 89, the Court stated that 'inherent in the whole of the Convention is a search for a fair balance between the demands of the general interest of the community and the requirements of the protection of the individual's fundamental rights'. A principle which the Court has developed which flows from this is that of proportionality. This is particularly relevant where the Convention permits restrictions upon a right as in Articles 8–11. Any restrictions which a state places on these rights 'must be proportionate to the legitimate aim pursued' (see *Handyside* v *UK* Series A, No. 24 (1976), 1 EHRR 737 § 49).

When balancing individual claims against the needs of the community as a whole, a crucial qualification is that any limitation be 'necessary in a democratic society'. In *United Communist Party of Turkey* v *Turkey* (1998) 26 EHRR 121, the European Court of Human Rights emphasized (at p. 148) that democracy is the 'only political model contemplated by the Convention and, accordingly, the only one compatible with it'. The Court stated that freedom of expression and free elections are essential characteristics of a democracy and that political parties play an essential role in ensuring pluralism and the proper functioning of democracy. In *The Socialist Party* v *Turkey* (1998) 27 EHRR 51, the European Court of Human Rights stated (at pp. 84–85):

[O]ne of the principal characteristics of democracy is the possibility it offers of resolving a country's problems through dialogue, without recourse to violence, even when they are irksome. Democracy thrives on freedom of expression. . . . It is the essence of democracy to allow diverse political programmes to be proposed and debated, even those that call into question the way a State is currently organised, provided that they do not harm democracy itself.

Diverse political parties, mass media which may freely criticize the *status quo* and channels for public debate and participation are thus crucial to the existence of a democracy and at the centre of the values which the Convention is seeking to protect.

The Convention now applies in 41 countries, but these are far from homogeneous. The Court therefore tends to adopt an interpretative approach which recognizes differences and makes allowances for variations between States by means of the margin of appreciation doctrine. Harris, O'Boyle and Warbrick, *Law of the European Convention on Human Rights* (1995) state (at p. 12):

In general terms, it means that the state is allowed a certain measure of discretion, subject to European supervision, when it takes legislative, administrative or judicial action in the area of a Convention right.

This doctrine was explained by the Court in the *Handyside* case which arose from a prosecution of the publisher of *The Little Red Schoolbook* under the Obscene Publications Act 1959 for possessing obscene books for publication for gain. The applicant complained that his conviction and the forfeiture and destruction of the books amounted to a breach of his Article 10 rights. The volume had also been published in eight other European countries without giving rise to any prosecutions. It was also published in Northern Ireland and Scotland where no proceedings against the publisher were taken as the 1959 Act did not apply to those countries. Despite this the Court found that Article 10 had not been breached by the UK as the limitation on freedom of expression could be justified as being necessary for the 'protection of morals'. The Court stated:

48. The Court points out that the machinery of protection established by the Convention is subsidiary to the national systems safeguarding human rights. The Convention leaves to each Contracting State, in the first place, the task of securing the rights and freedoms it enshrines. The institutions created by it make their own contribution to this task but they become involved only through contentious proceedings and once all domestic remedies have been exhausted (Art. 26).

These observations apply, notably, to Article 10(2). In particular, it is not possible to find in the domestic law of the various Contracting States a uniform European conception of morals. The view taken by their respective laws of the requirements of morals varies from time to time and from place to place, especially in our era which is characterised by a rapid and far-reaching evolution of opinions on the subject. By reason of their direct and continuous contact with the vital forces of their countries, State authorities are in principle in a better position than the international judge to give an opinion on the exact content of these requirements as well as on the 'necessity' of a 'restriction' or 'penalty' intended to meet them. The Court notes at this juncture that, whilst the adjective 'necessary', within the meaning of Article 10(2), is not synonymous with 'indispensable', neither has it the flexibility of such expressions as 'admissible', 'ordinary', 'useful', 'reasonable' or 'desirable'. Nevertheless, it is for the national authorities to make the initial assessment of the reality of the pressing social need implied by the notion of 'necessity' in this context.

Consequently, Article 10(2) leaves to the Contracting States a margin of appreciation. This margin is given both to the domestic legislator ('prescribed by law') and to the bodies, judicial amongst others, that are called upon to interpret and apply the laws in force.

49. Nevertheless, Article 10(2) does not give the Contracting States an unlimited power of appreciation. The Court, which, with the Commission, is responsible for ensuring the observance of those States' engagements, is empowered to give the final ruling on whether a 'restriction' or 'penalty' is reconcilable with freedom of expression as protected by Article 10. The domestic margin of appreciation thus goes hand in hand with a European supervision. Such supervision concerns both the aim of the measure challenged and its 'necessity'; it covers not only the basic legislation but also the decision applying it, even one given by an independent court. In this respect, the Court refers to Article 50 of the Convention ('decision or . . . measure taken by a legal authority or any other authority') as well as to its own case-law.

The Court's supervisory functions oblige it to pay the utmost attention to the principles characterising a 'democratic society'. Freedom of expression constitutes one of the essential foundations of such a society, one of the basic conditions for its progress and for the development of every man. Subject to Article 10(2), it is applicable not only to 'information' or 'ideas' that are favourably received or regarded as inoffensive or as a matter of indifference, but also to those that offend, shock or disturb the State or any sector of the population. Such are the demands of that pluralism, tolerance and broadmindedness without which there is no 'democratic society'. This means, amongst other things, that every 'formality', 'condition', 'restriction' or 'penalty' imposed in this sphere must be proportionate to the legitimate aim pursued.

From another standpoint, whoever exercises his freedom of expression undertakes 'duties' and 'responsibilities' the scope of which depends on his situation and the technical means he uses. The Court cannot overlook such a person's 'duties' and 'responsibilities' when it enquires, as in this case; whether 'restrictions' or 'penalties' were conducive to the 'protection of morals' which made them 'necessary' in a 'democratic society'.

This doctrine of 'margin of appreciation' will be applied differently depending upon the context, but generally it derives from the fact that the Court is exercising a supervisory jurisdiction and that the responsibility for ensuring that human rights are protected and respected within States lies with the contracting parties themselves. This can mean that widely varying practices amongst the contracting parties are tolerated depending on the degree of laxity the Court displays; this can vary with the context, namely the Article under consideration.

A: The Convention in British courts prior to the Human Rights Act coming into force

Prior to the Human Rights Act 1998, courts in the United Kingdom could pay only limited attention to the European Convention. The Convention was not incorporated into domestic law and thus could not be applied directly by courts to the cases before them. In *British Airways Board* v *Laker Airways Ltd* [1985] AC 58, Lord Diplock stated the general principle regarding treaties:

The interpretation of treaties to which the United Kingdom is a party but the terms of which have not either expressly or by reference been incorporated in English domestic law by legislation is not a matter that falls within the interpretative jurisdiction of an English court of law.

In *Malone* v *MPC* [1979] Ch 344, where Malone sought declarations, *inter alia*, that tapping of his telephone by the police was unlawful and in breach of his Article 8 rights, Megarry V-C held that the tapping was not unlawful and then addressed the Convention issue. He emphasized that the Convention was not law in the United Kingdom as the obligation to secure to everyone in the jurisdiction the rights and freedoms defined in the Convention was 'an obligation under a treaty which is not justiciable in the courts of this country'. While the Convention might be used by a court to help it construe a piece of legislation, in which case the court would 'readily seek to construe the legislation in a way that would effectuate the Convention rather than frustrate it', the Court in the instant case was not faced with any legislation. Megarry V-C stated:

It seems to me that where Parliament has abstained from legislating on a point that is plainly suitable for legislation, it is indeed difficult for the court to lay down new rules of common law or equity that will carry out the Crown's treaty obligations, or to discover for the first time that such rules have always existed.

Megarry V-C, referring to the decision of the European Court of Human Rights in *Klass* v *Germany* (1979) 2 EHRR 214, which examined the West German statutory scheme for controlling telephone tapping, concluded that the United Kingdom system which lacked any legal safeguards could not possibly satisfy the requirements of the Convention. But it was not his judicial function to regulate this activity, it being rather a matter for Parliament. Megarry V-C expressed the view that it was not possible to feel any pride in English law on this matter and that legislation was urgently required. He stated:

However much the protection of the public against crime demands that in proper cases the police should have the assistance of telephone tapping, I would have thought that in any civilised system of law the claims of liberty and justice would require that telephone users should have effective and independent safeguards against possible abuses. The fact that a telephone user is suspected of crime increases rather than diminishes this requirement; suspicions, however reasonably held, may sometimes prove to be wholly unfounded.

There were some ways, however, in which the Convention did play a part in judicial decision-making. These were identified by Lord Bingham of Cornhill, the then Lord Chief Justice, in his first speech in the House of Lords.

House of Lords
573 HL Deb cols. 1465–1467 (3 July 1996)

LORD BINGHAM OF CORNHILL: First, . . . where a United Kingdom statute is capable of two interpretations, one consistent with the convention and one inconsistent, then the courts will presume that Parliament intended to legislate in conformity with the convention and not in conflict with it. In other words, the courts will presume that Parliament did not intend to legislate in violation of international law. That may be thought by your Lordships to be a modest presumption.

Secondly, if the common law is uncertain, unclear or incomplete, the courts have to make a choice; they cannot abdicate their power of decision. In declaring what the law is, they will rule, wherever possible, in a manner which conforms with the convention and does not conflict with it. Any other course would be futile since a rule laid down in defiance of the convention would be likely to prove short-lived.

There is, of course, one field – freedom of expression – in which respected Members of this House have declared that they see no inconsistency between the common law and the convention. That is reassuring; it is also wholly unsurprising since we have a long record as a pioneer in the field of freedom of expression. But it means that the courts are encouraged to look to the convention and the jurisprudence of the European Court of Human Rights when resolving problems on the common law.

Thirdly, when the courts are called upon to construe a domestic statute enacted to fulfil a convention obligation, the courts will ordinarily assume that the statute was intended to be effective to that end. That is mere common sense, but common sense is the stock-in-trade of much judicial decision-making.

Fourthly, where the courts have a discretion to exercise – that is, they can act in one way or another – one or more of which violates the convention and another of which does not, they seek to act in a way which does not violate the convention. That again is usually common sense and requires no elaboration. However, it is not an invariable rule and your Lordships' House, sitting judicially, gave an important judgment only yesterday in which the convention right to privacy was held to be obliged to give way to the greater interests of justice.

Fifthly, when, as sometimes happens, the courts are called upon to decide what, in a given situation, public policy demands, it has been held to be legitimate that we shall have regard to our international obligations enshrined in the convention as a source of guidance on what British public policy requires.

Sixthly and lastly, matters covered by the law of the European Community – that is, the law administered by the European Court of Justice in Luxembourg and not Strasbourg – on occasion give effect to matters covered by convention law. The Court of Justice takes the view that on matters subject to Community law, the law common to the member states is part of the law which applies. All member states are parties to the convention and it so happens from time to time that laws derived from the convention are incorporated as part of the law of the Community. That of course is a law which the courts in this country must apply since we are bound by Act of Parliament to do so, and that is a means by which, indirectly, convention rights find their way into domestic law.

NOTE: A difficulty which courts in the United Kingdom have faced is that even where a statute is clearly in breach of the Convention, they are still bound by the statute. This was clearly illustrated by the case of *R* v *Staines and Morrissey* [1997] 2 Cr App R 426. In *Saunders* v *United Kingdom* (1997) 23 EHRR 313, the European Court of Human Rights held that the applicant's right to freedom from self-incrimination under Article 6.1 had been infringed by the use at his trial of statements which he had been compelled to give during an investigation by inspectors of the Department of Trade and Industry into allegations of fraud during the takeover of Distillers plc by Guinness plc. During the investigation Saunders had been required by law to answer questions put to him; failure to answer could lead to contempt proceedings which could result in a fine or imprisonment for up to two years (see ss. 432(2) and 436(3) of the Companies Act 1985). In *Staines and Morrissey* the appellants were prosecuted under s. 1(2) of the Company Securities (Insider Dealing) Act 1985. Statements made by the appellants under compulsion to inspectors of the Department of Trade and Industry exercising their powers under s. 177 of the Financial Services Act 1986 were admitted in evidence against them. On appeal the appellants argued that in light of the recent decision in *Saunders*, these statements should have been excluded by the trial judge in exercise of the discretion created by s. 78(1) of the Police and Criminal Evidence Act 1984 to exclude evidence which would have an adverse effect on the fairness of the proceedings. The Court of Appeal dismissed the appeal, Lord Bingham of Cornhill LCJ stating:

> The difficulty, as it seems to us, which the appellants face is to show that the court should exercise its powers under section 78(1) to exclude, because of its adverse effect on the conduct of the proceedings, material which section 177(6) has expressly stipulated may be used in evidence against a defendant. No doubt the admission of evidence under section 177(b) is subject to the overriding discretion of the Court to exclude under section 78(1). But there is, so far as we can see, nothing which distinguishes this case from other similar cases. If the Court were to rule here that this evidence should be excluded, it would be obliged to exclude such evidence in all such cases. That would amount to a repeal, or a substantial repeal, of an English statutory provision which remains in force in deference to a ruling which does not have direct effect and which, as a matter of strict law, is irrelevant.
>
> . . . [T]he section here expressly authorises the use of evidence so obtained and that, as we see it, amounts to a statutory presumption that what might otherwise be regarded as unfair is, for this purpose and in this context, to be treated as fair, at any rate in the absence of special features which would make the admission of the evidence unfair.
>
> . . . [T]he present position is very unsatisfactory. It would appear that the appellants have or certainly may have grounds for complaining in Strasbourg and, if the penalty is enforced and they incur costs in seeking relief, they may have claims to compensation against Her Majesty's Government. That is not, however, something which the courts can remedy. Our domestic law remains as declared by this Court in *Saunders* (*supra*). The United Kingdom is subject to a Treaty obligation to give effect to the European Convention of Human Rights as interpreted by the Court of Human Rights, but that again is not something which this Court can enforce. . . .

In 2001 the Court of Appeal considered the cases of Saunders, Lyons, Parnes, and Ronson again ([2001] EWCA 2860) following a reference back to them by the Criminal Cases Review Commission in light of the findings of the European Court of Human Rights in *Saunders* v *UK*. The grounds of appeal were, *inter alia*, (1) that the Human Rights Act 1998 was retrospective in effect so that on an appeal after it came into force, the appellants could rely on the breach of their right to a fair trial under Article 6 by the prosecution's use in evidence against them of their answers given under compulsion to the DTI inspectors; and (2) that even if the HRA is not retrospective, the convictions were unsafe because: (i) the UK's treaty obligations, particularly under Article 46, conferred on the appellants the right in domestic law to rely on the violation established by the ECtHR's conclusion that their trials were unfair and to seek reparation by the quashing of their convictions; (ii) it is not possible to uphold the convictions by reliance on evidence admitted in breach of Article 6 because this would place the Court of Appeal in breach of the HRA s. 6(1) obligation to act compatibly with Convention rights; and (iii) contemporary standards of common law fairness required that the answers to the DTI inspectors should have been excluded by the trial judge in exercising his discretion under s. 78 of the Police and Criminal Evidence Act 1984.

On the first ground the Court of Appeal found against the appellants following the decision of the House of Lords in *R v Kansal (No. 2)* [2001] 3 WLR 1562 which held that a defendant whose trial took place before 2 October 2000 could not rely in an appeal after that date on an alleged breach of his Convention rights. *Kansal* was a case involving compulsory answers to questions under the Insolvency Act 1986. In *Kansal* the House of Lords had followed its earlier decision in *Lambert* [2001] 3 WLR 206 on retrospectivity even though three of their Lordships (Lord Lloyd of Berwick, Lord Steyn and Lord Hope of Craighead) considered that *Lambert* had been wrongly decided!

On the second ground of appeal, the Court of Appeal, having examined the jurisprudence of the European Court of Human Rights, concluded that Article 46, which provides that 'The high contracting parties undertake to abide by the final judgment of the court in any case to which they are parties', did not require a State to reopen a conviction. The European Court had made a declaration of violation in each case and awarded costs to the applicants. The jurisprudence of the Court indicated that a declaration (and award of costs and/or damages) amounted to sufficient just satisfaction. Furthermore, in light of the decision in *Staines v Morrissey* there was no unfairness at their trial as the court had no power to exclude the evidence as to do so would have been to ignore the legislation.

SECTION 3: **The Case for a Bill of Rights**

The argument as to whether the United Kingdom needs a Bill of Rights is a long-running one. In 1977, the Standing Advisory Commission on Human Rights in *The Protection of Human Rights by Law in Northern Ireland* (Cmnd 7009) recommended that the European Convention be incorporated into domestic law. (For a summary of some of the arguments for and against such a development, see the first edition of this book at pp. 357–358.) In 1978, the *Report of the Select Committee on a Bill of Rights* (House of Lords, HMSO) recommended that the Convention should be incorporated. In 1987, Sir Edward Gardner introduced in the House of Commons the Human Rights Bill as a private member's Bill which would have incorporated the Convention. The Bill was given a formal second reading without a vote but failed to complete its Commons stages due to lack of time. In 1990 the Institute for Public Policy Research, in *A British Bill of Rights* (Constitution Paper No. 1), drafted a Bill of Rights which was based on the European Convention and the United Nations International Covenant on Civil and Political Rights. In 1991, Liberty, in *A People's Charter*, published a draft Bill of Rights with a similar parentage.

T. H. Bingham, 'The European Convention on Human Rights: Time to Incorporate'
(1993) 109 *LQR* 390–393, 395–400

. . . [T]here is no task more central to the purpose of a moden democracy, or more central to the judicial function, than that of seeking to protect, within the law, the basic human rights of the citizen, against invasion by other citizens or by the state itself. I hope this point is too obvious to need labouring. . . .

I would suggest that the ability of English judges to protect human rights in this country and reconcile conflicting rights in the manner indicated is inhibited by the failure of successive governments over many years to incorporate into United Kingdom law the European Convention on Human Rights and Fundamental Freedoms. . . .

Having examined the Diceyan concept of the constitution and the changes in the balance of power between the executive and legislature in this century, Sir Thomas continued.

The elective dictatorship of the majority means that, by and large, the government of the day can get its way, even if its majority is small. If its programme or its practice involves some derogation from human rights Parliament cannot be relied on to correct this. Nor can the judges. If the derogation springs from a statute, they must faithfully apply the statute. If it is a result of administrative practice, there may well be no basis upon which they can interfere. There is no higher law, no frame of reference, to which they can properly appeal. None of this matters very much if human rights themselves are not thought to matter very much. But if the protection of its citizens' fundamental rights is genuinely seen as an important function of civil society, then it does matter. In saying this I do not suggest – and I must stress this – that the present government or any of its predecessors has acted with wilful or cyncical disregard of fundamental human rights. I would adopt and apply by analogy what Samuel Johnson said about truth: 'It is more from carelessness about truth than from intentional lying that there is so much falsehood in the world.' What I do suggest is that a government intent on implementing a programme may overlook the human rights aspects of its policies and that, if a government of more sinister intent were to gain power, we should be defenceless. There would not, certainly, be much the judges could do about it. This would seem regrettable to those who, like me, would see the judges as properly playing an important part in this field. . . .

Those who share my view that the situation is unsatisfactory may well ask whether it is nonetheless inevitable, one of those inescapable blemishes which must exist in an imperfect world. I would say not. In the European Convention an instrument lies ready to hand which, if not providing an ideal solution, nonetheless offers a clear improvement on the present position. . . .

Sir Thomas examined the history of the Convention before discussing the main arguments against incorporation.

Constitutional experts point out, first of all, that the unwritten British constitution, unlike virtually every written constitution, has no means of entrenching, that is of giving a higher or trump-like status, to a law of this kind. Therefore, it is said, what one sovereign Parliament enacts another sovereign Parliament may override: thus a government minded to undermine human rights could revoke the incorporation of the Convention and leave the citizen no better off than he is now, and perhaps worse. I would give this argument beta for ingenuity and gamma, or perhaps omega, for political nous. It is true that in theory any Act of Parliament may be repealed. Thus theoretically the legislation extending the vote to the adult population, or giving the vote to women, or allowing married women to own property in their own right, or forbidding cruel and unusual punishment, or safeguarding the independence of the judges, or providing for our adhesion to the European Community, could be revoked at the whim of a temporary parliamentary majority. But absent something approaching a revolution in our society such repeal would be unthinkable. Why? Because whatever their theoretical status constitutional measures of this kind are in practice regarded as enjoying a peculiar sanctity buttressed by overwhelming public support. If incorporated, the Convention would take its place at the head of this favoured list. There is a second reason why formal entrenchment is not necessary. Suppose the statute of incorporation were to provide that subject to any express abrogation or derogation in any later statute the rights specified in the Convention were to be fully recognised and enforced in the United Kingdom according to the tenor of the Convention. That would be good enough for the judges. They would give full effect to the Convention rights unless a later statute very explicitly and specifically told them not to. But the rights protected by the Convention are not stated in absolute terms: there are provisos to cover pressing considerations of national security and such like. Save in quite extraordinary circumstances one cannot imagine any government going to Parliament with a proposal that any human right guaranteed by the Convention be overridden. And even then (subject to any relevant derogation) the United Kingdom would in any event remain bound, in international law and also in honour, to comply with its Convention obligations. I find it hard to imagine a government going to Parliament with such a proposal. So while the argument on entrenchment has a superficial theoretical charm, it has in my opinion very little practical substance. There would be no question, as under Community law, of United Kingdom judges declaring United Kingdom statutes to be invalid. Judges would either comply with the express will of Parliament by construing all legislation in a manner consistent with the Convention. Or, in the scarcely imaginable case of an express abrogation or derogation by Parliament, the judges would give effect to that provision also.

A second and quite different argument runs roughly along the following lines. Rulings on human rights, not least rulings on the lines of demarcation between one right and another, involve sensitive judgments important to individual citizens and to society as a whole. These are not judgments which unelected English (or perhaps British) judges are fitted to make, drawn as they are from a narrow unrepresentative minority, the public-school and Oxbridge-educated, male, white, mostly protestant, mostly middle-class products of the Bar. They are judgments of an essentially political nature, properly to be made by democratically elected representatives of the people. I do not, unsurprisingly, agree with most of the criticisms which it is fashionable to direct at the composition of the modern judiciary, for reasons which could fill another lecture. Nor would I, again unsurprisingly, accept the charge sometimes made that protection of human rights cannot safely be entrusted to British judges: no one familiar with the development of the law in fields as divers as, for instance, the Rent Acts, the Factories Acts, labour law or judicial review could, I think, fairly accuse the judges of throwing their weight on the side of the big battalions against the small man or woman. But it is true that judgments on human rights do involve judgements about relations between the individual and the society of which the individual is part, and in that sense they can be described as political. If such questions are thought to be inappropriate for decision by judges, so be it. I do not agree, but I can understand the argument. What I simply do not understand is how it can be sensible to entrust the decision of these questions to an international panel of judges in Strasbourg – some of them drawn from societies markedly unlike our own – but not, in the first instance, to our own judges here. I am not suggesting that the final right of appeal to Strasbourg should be eliminated or in any way curtailed (which, indeed, is not something which most opponents of incorporation support). I am only suggesting that rights claimed under the Convention should, in the first place, be ruled upon by judges here before, if regrettably necessary, appeal is made to Strasbourg. The choice is not between judges and no judges; it is whether *all* matches in this field must be played away.

The proposition that judgments on questions of human rights are, in the sense indicated, political is relied on by opponents of incorporation to found a further argument. The argument is that if British judges were to rule on questions arising under the Convention they would ineluctably be drawn into political controversy with consequent damage to their reputation, constitutionally important as it is, for political neutrality. This argument, espoused by a number of senior and respected political figures, should not be lightly dismissed. But it should be examined. It cannot in my view withstand such examination for two main reasons. The first is that judges are already, on a regular and day to day basis, reviewing and often quashing decisions of ministers and government departments. They have been doing so on an increasing scale for 30 years. During that period ministers of both governing parties have fallen foul of court decisions, not once or twice but repeatedly. Some of these decisions have achieved great public notoriety. All judges are accustomed to making every effort to put aside their own personal viewpoints, and there is no reason to think that English judges are any less good at this than any others. Political controversy there has been, on occasion, a-plenty, but it has not by and large rubbed off on the judges. Why not? Because, I think, it is generally if not universally recognised that the judges have a job to do, which is not a political job, and their personal predilections have no more influence on the decisions than that of a boxing referee who is required to stop a fight. In a mature democracy like ours, this degree of understanding is not, surely, surprising, but it does in my view weaken this argument against incorporation.

An additional argument sometimes heard is that incorporation is unnecessary since the Convention rights are already protected by the common law. The House of Lords recently held that in the field of freedom of speech there is no difference in principle between English law and Article 10 of the Convention [*Derbyshire CC* v *Times Newspapers Ltd* [1993] 2 WLR 449]. Lord Goff of Chieveley said the same thing in one of the *Spycatcher* judgments [*Attorney-General* v *Guardian Newspapers (No. 2)* [1990] 1 AC 109 at 283 – 284]. But the House of Lords' earlier *Spycatcher* decision [[1987] 1 WLR 1248] has itself been held to have violated the Convention, as of course have other of their Lordships' decisions. If in truth the common law as it stands were giving the rights of United Kingdom citizens the same protection as the Convention – across the board, not only in relation to Article 10 – one might wonder why the United Kingdom's record as a Strasbourg litigant was not more favourable.

. . .

I am conscious that I have given much time to considering the arguments against incorporation and rather less to the case in favour. This is no doubt because I regard the positive case as clear and the burden as lying on the opponents to make good their grounds of opposition. But there is one argument in favour of incorporation that I would like to mention. It is not a new argument, but it is an important one, and it has recently been drawn to the House of Lords' attention by Lord Slynn of Hadley (in his legislative, and not his judicial, mode) [HL Deb. November 26, 1992 cols. 1096 – 1098]. The Court of Justice has now made clear that the fundamental human rights which the Convention protects are part of the law of the Community which that court is bound to secure and enforce. Community law is, of course, part of the law of the United Kingdom. As Lord Slynn put it,

> . . . every time the European Court recognises a principle set out in the convention as being part of Community law, it must be enforced in the United Kingdom courts in relation to Community law matters, but not in domestic law. So the convention becomes in part a part of our law through the back door because we have to apply the convention in respect of Community law matters as a party of Community law.

Drawing on his own experience as counsel appearing at Strasbourg, he felt it would be more satisfactory if the convention were to enter by the front door. It was he said,

> quite plain that many, although perhaps not all, of the cases could be dealt with just as well and more expeditiously by our own judges here.

The Constitution Unit, *Human Rights Legislation*
(1996) Executive Summary, pp. 6–7

Entrenchment
In other countries, and in particular those with a written constitution, bills of rights usually have a

special status, both superior to ordinary legislation and less susceptible to amendment. There is no precedent within the British constitution for formally entrenching legislation in this way.

However, the issue of entrenchment is not an obstacle to incorporation of the ECHR:

- bills of rights in other Commonwealth countries have demonstrated that the traditions of Parliamentary sovereignty can co-exist with a degree of entrenchment.
- in the UK, parliamentary sovereignty has been used to give a superior status to EC law. The European Communities Act 1972 has enabled the courts to declare invalid existing and subsequent UK legislation which is inconsistent with EC law.
- the UK is already bound by the ECHR in international law: when the European Court of Human Rights rules that a particular law or provision is in contravention the Government must act to remedy the situation.

Certainly, any statute incorporating the ECHR into domestic law could be reversed by a future UK Parliament, so to that extent it would not be 'entrenched'. But the incorporating statute could assert that the ECHR's relationship with other laws would be different from that of 'ordinary legislation'. This would not undermine the doctrine of parliamentary sovereignty – because the nature of that relationship could subsequently be changed if Parliament so desired.

Relationship Between ECHR and Other Laws

The incorporating statute must define the status of the ECHR as part of UK domestic law. In most cases, it will be perfectly easy to interpret domestic laws and legislation in such a way that they comply with the ECHR. The experience of other countries suggests that direct challenges to the validity of primary legislation are likely to be extremely rare. When they do occur, the incorporating statute could:

- simply be a tool of interpretation for the courts – where it was impossible to interpret legislation consistently with the ECHR, the legislation would nevertheless be applied (as in New Zealand).
- empower the courts not to give effect to pre-existing legislation that is inconsistent with the ECHR and require that all subsequent legislation should be construed as consistent with the ECHR unless manifestly impossible (as in Hong Kong).
- empower the courts not to give effect to pre-existing legislation and legislation enacted after incorporation if inconsistent with the ECHR, subject to Parliament having the power to insist that legislation should be applied 'notwithstanding' the inconsistency (as in Canada).

The report recommends that the incorporating statute should require conformity between the ECHR and:

- the common law.
- all subordinate legislation, past and future, with a power for the courts not to give effect to inconsistent provisions.
- all existing primary legislation, with a similar power not to give effect to inconsistent provisions – in accordance with the existing convention that if an Act of Parliament is inconsistent with an earlier one, the courts are required to uphold and give effect to the more recent provisions.

As regards future primary legislation, the political and constitutional traditions of the UK will require an active 'political' role in the protection and furtherance of human rights, to complement the judicial role. Any judicial powers to disapply primary legislation must be subject to parliamentary override. This might best be achieved by protecting legislation from implied repeal by including a 'notwithstanding clause' as in Canada. If this option is not favoured, the Hong Kong model could be adopted.

The incorporating statute should require UK courts to have regard to the judgments of the European Court of Human Rights and decisions of the Commission at Strasbourg. In order to limit the number of adverse decisions at Strasbourg, such judgments should be binding on all domestic courts.

SECTION 4: **Incorporation of the European Convention on Human Rights into UK Law**

A: The Human Rights Act 1998

In October 1997 the Labour Government introduced the Human Rights Bill into Parliament and at the same time published the White Paper, *Rights Brought Home: The Human Rights Bill*, which explained what the Bill did.

Rights Brought Home: The Human Rights Bill
(Cm 3782, 1997), cll. 1.14–1.16, 2. 1–3.12

CHAPTER 1 – THE CASE FOR CHANGE

. . .

The case for incorporation

1.14 The effect of non-incorporation on the British people is a very practical one. The rights, originally developed with major help from the United Kingdom Government, are no longer actually seen as British rights. And enforcing them takes too long and costs too much. It takes on average five years to get an action into the European Court of Human Rights once all domestic remedies have been exhausted; and it costs an average of £30,000. Bringing these rights home will mean that the British people will be able to argue for their rights in the British courts – without this inordinate delay and cost. It will also mean that the rights will be brought much more fully into the jurisprudence of the courts throughout the United Kingdom, and their interpretation will thus be far more subtly and powerfully woven into our law. And there will be another distinct benefit. British judges will be enabled to make a distinctively British contribution to the development of the jurisprudence of human rights in Europe.

1.15 Moreover, in the Government's view, the approach which the United Kingdom has so far adopted towards the Convention does not sufficiently reflect its importance and has not stood the test of time.

1.16 . . . It is plainly unsatisfactory that someone should be the victim of a breach of the Convention standards by the State yet cannot bring any case at all in the British courts, simply because British law does not recognise the right in the same terms as one contained in the Convention.

. . .

CHAPTER 2 – THE GOVERNMENT'S PROPOSALS FOR ENFORCING THE CONVENTION RIGHTS

2.1 The essential feature of the Human Rights Bill is that the United Kingdom will not be bound to give effect to the Convention rights merely as a matter of international law, but will also give them further effect directly in our domestic law. But there is more than one way of achieving this. This Chapter explains the choices which the Government has made for the Bill.

A new requirement on public authorities

2.2 Although the United Kingdom has an international obligation to comply with the Convention, there at present is no requirement in our domestic law on central and local government, or others exercising similar executive powers, to exercise those powers in a way which is compatible with the Convention. This Bill will change that by making it unlawful for public authorities to act in a way which is incompatible with the Convention rights. The definition of what constitutes a public authority is in wide terms. Examples of persons or organisations whose acts or omissions it is intended should be able to be challenged include central government (including executive agencies); local government; the police; immigration officers; prisons; courts and tribunals themselves; and, to the extent that they are exercising public functions, companies responsible for areas of activity which were previously within the public sector, such as the privatised utilities. The actions of Parliament, however, are excluded.

2.3 A person who is aggrieved by an act or omission on the part of a public authority which is incompatible with the Convention rights will be able to challenge the act or omission in the courts. The effects will be wide-ranging. They will extend both to legal actions which a public authority pursues against individuals (for example, where a criminal prosecution is brought or where an administrative decision is being enforced through legal proceedings) and to cases which individuals pursue against a public authority (for example, for judicial review of an executive decision). Convention points will normally be taken in the context of proceedings instituted against individuals or already open to them, but, if none is available, it will be possible for people to bring cases on Convention grounds alone. Individuals or organisations seeking judicial review of decisions by public authorities on Convention grounds will need to show that they have been directly affected, as they must if they take a case to Strasbourg.

2.4 It is our intention that people or organisations should be able to argue that their Convention rights have been infringed by a public authority in our courts at any level. This will enable the Convention rights to be applied from the outset against the facts and background of a particular case, and the people concerned to obtain their remedy at the earliest possible moment. We think this is preferable to allowing cases to run their ordinary course but then referring them to some kind of separate constitutional court which, like the European Court of Human Rights, would simply review cases which had already passed through the regular legal machinery. In considering Convention points, our courts will be required to take account of relevant decisions of the European Commission and Court of Human Rights (although these will not be binding).

2.5 The Convention is often described as a 'living instrument' because it is interpreted by the European Court in the light of present day conditions and therefore reflects changing social attitudes and the changes in the circumstances of society. In future our judges will be able to contribute to this dynamic and evolving interpretation of the Convention. In particular, our courts will be required to balance the protection of individuals' fundamental rights against the demands of the general interest of the community, particularly in relation to Articles 8–11 where a State may restrict the protected right to the extent that this is 'necessary in a democratic society'.

Remedies for a failure to comply with the Convention
2.6 A public authority which is found to have acted unlawfully by failing to comply with the Convention will not be exposed to criminal penalties. But the court or tribunal will be able to grant the injured person any remedy which is within its normal powers to grant and which it considers appropriate and just in the circumstances. What remedy is appropriate will of course depend both on the facts of the case and on a proper balance between the rights of the individual and the public interest. In some cases, the right course may be for the decision of the public authority in the particular case to be quashed. In other cases, the only appropriate remedy may be an award of damages. The Bill provides that, in considering an award of damages on Convention grounds, the courts are to take into account the principles applied by the European Court of Human Rights in awarding compensation, so that people will be able to receive compensation from a domestic court equivalent to what they would have received in Strasbourg.

Interpretation of legislation
2.7 The Bill provides for legislation – both Acts of Parliament and secondary legislation – to be interpreted so far as possible so as to be compatible with the Convention. This goes far beyond the

present rule which enables the courts to take the Convention into account in resolving any ambiguity in a legislative provision. The courts will be required to interpret legislation so as to uphold the Convention rights unless the legislation itself is so clearly incompatible with the Convention that it is impossible to do so.

2.8 This 'rule of construction' is to apply to past as well as to future legislation. To the extent that it affects the meaning of a legislative provision, the courts will not be bound by previous interpretations. They will be able to build a new body of case law, taking into account the Convention rights.

A declaration of incompatibility with the Convention rights

2.9 If the courts decide in any case that it is impossible to interpret an Act of Parliament in a way which is compatible with the Convention, the Bill enables a formal declaration to be made that its provisions are incompatible with the Convention. A declaration of incompatibility will be an important statement to make, and the power to make it will be reserved to the higher courts. They will be able to make a declaration in any proceedings before them, whether the case originated with them (as, in the High Court, on judicial review of an executive act) or in considering an appeal from a lower court or tribunal. The Government will have the right to intervene in any proceedings where such a declaration is a possible outcome. A decision by the High Court or Court of Appeal, determining whether or not such a declaration should be made, will itself be appealable.

Effect of court decisions on legislation

2.10 A declaration that legislation is incompatible with the Convention rights will not of itself have the effect of changing the law, which will continue to apply. But it will almost certainly prompt the Government and Parliament to change the law.

2.11 The Government has considered very carefully whether it would be right for the Bill to go further, and give to courts in the United Kingdom the power to set aside an Act of Parliament which they believe is incompatible with the Convention rights. In considering this question, we have looked at a number of models. The Canadian Charter of Rights and Freedoms 1982 enables the courts to strike down any legislation which is inconsistent with the Charter, unless the legislation contains an explicit statement that it is to apply 'notwithstanding' the provisions of the Charter. But legislation which has been struck down may be re-enacted with a 'notwithstanding' clause. In New Zealand, on the other hand, although there was an earlier proposal for legislation on lines similar to the Canadian Charter, the human rights legislation which was eventually enacted after wide consultation took a different form. The New Zealand Bill of Rights Act 1990 is an 'interpretative' statute which requires past and future legislation to be interpreted consistently with the rights contained in the Act as far as possible but provides that legislation stands if that is impossible. In Hong Kong, a middle course was adopted. The Hong Kong Bill of Rights Ordinance 1991 distinguishes between legislation enacted before and after the Ordinance took effect: previous legislation is subordinated to the provisions of the Ordinance, but subsequent legislation takes precedence over it.

2.12 The Government has also considered the European Communities Act 1972 which provides for European law, in cases where that law has 'direct effect', to take precedence over domestic law. There is, however, an essential difference between European Community law and the European Convention on Human Rights, because it is a **requirement** of membership of the European Union that member States give priority to directly effective EC law in their own legal systems. There is no such requirement in the Convention.

2.13 The Government has reached the conclusion that courts should not have the power to set aside primary legislation, past or future, on the ground of incompatibility with the Convention. This conclusion arises from the importance which the Government attaches to Parliamentary sovereignty. In this context, Parliamentary sovereignty means that Parliament is competent to make any law on any matter of its choosing and no court may question the validity of any Act that it passes. In enacting legislation, Parliament is making decisions about important matters of public policy. The authority to make those decisions derives from a democratic mandate. Members of Parliament in the House of Commons possess such a mandate because they are elected, accountable and representative. To make provision in the Bill for the courts to set aside Acts of Parliament would confer on the judiciary a general power over the decisions of Parliament which under our present constitutional arrangements they do not possess, and would be likely on occasions to draw the judiciary into serious conflict with Parliament. There is no evidence to suggest that they desire this power, nor that the public wish them to have it. Certainly, this Government has no mandate for any such change.

2.14 It has been suggested that the courts should be able to uphold the rights in the Human Rights Bill in preference to any provisions of earlier legislation which are incompatible with those rights. This is on the basis that a later Act of Parliament takes precedence over an earlier Act if there is a conflict. But the Human Rights Bill is intended to provide a new basis for judicial interpretation of all legislation, not a basis for striking down any part of it.

2.15 The courts will, however, be able to strike down or set aside secondary legislation which is incompatible with the Convention, unless the terms of the parent statute make this impossible. The courts can already strike down or set aside secondary legislation when they consider it to be outside the powers conferred by the statute under which it is made, and it is right that they should be able to do so when it is incompatible with the Convention rights and could have been framed differently.

Entrenchment

2.16 On one view, human rights legislation is so important that it should be given added protection from subsequent amendment or repeal. The Constitution of the United States of America, for example, guarantees rights which can be amended or repealed only by securing qualified majorities in both the House of Representatives and the Senate, and among the States themselves. But an arrangement of this kind could not be reconciled with our own constitutional traditions, which allow any Act of Parliament to be amended or repealed by a subsequent Act of Parliament. We do not believe that it is necessary or would be desirable to attempt to devise such a special arrangement for this Bill.

Amending legislation

2.17 Although the Bill does not allow the courts to set aside Acts of Parliament, it will nevertheless have a profound impact on the way that legislation is interpreted and applied, and it will have the effect of putting the issues squarely to the Government and Parliament for further consideration. It is important to ensure that the Government and Parliament, for their part, can respond quickly. In the normal way, primary legislation can be amended only by further primary legislation, and this can take a long time. Given the volume of Government business, an early opportunity to legislate may not arise; and the process of legislating is itself protracted. Emergency legislation can be enacted very quickly indeed, but it is introduced only in the most exceptional circumstances.

2.18 The Bill provides for a fast-track procedure for changing legislation in response either to a declaration of incompatibility by our own higher courts or to a finding of a violation of the Convention in Strasbourg. The appropriate Government Minister will be able to amend the legislation by Order so as to make it compatible with the Convention. The Order will be subject to approval by both Houses of Parliament before taking effect, except where the need to amend the legislation is particularly urgent, when the Order will take effect immediately but will expire after a short period if not approved by Parliament.

2.19 There are already precedents for using secondary legislation to amend primary legislation in some circumstances, and we think the use of such a procedure is acceptable in this context and would be welcome as a means of improving the observance of human rights. Plainly the Minister would have to exercise this power only in relation to the provisions which contravene the Convention, together with any necessary consequential amendments. In other words, Ministers would not have carte blanche to amend unrelated parts of the Act in which the breach is discovered.

Scotland

2.20 In Scotland, the position with regard to Acts of the Westminster Parliament will be the same as in England and Wales. All courts will be required to interpret the legislation in a way which is compatible with the Convention so far as possible. If a provision is found to be incompatible with the Convention, the Court of Session or the High Court will be able to make a declarator to that effect, but this will not affect the validity or continuing operation of the provision.

2.21 The position will be different, however, in relation to Acts of the Scottish Parliament when it is established. The Government has decided that the Scottish Parliament will have no power to legislate in a way which is incompatible with the Convention; and similarly that the Scottish Executive will have no power to make subordinate legislation or to take executive action which is incompatible with the Convention. It will accordingly be possible to challenge such legislation and actions in the Scottish courts on the ground that the Scottish Parliament or Executive has incorrectly applied its powers. If the challenge is successful then the legislation or action would be held to be unlawful. As with other issues concerning the powers of the Scottish Parliament, there will be a procedure for inferior courts to refer such issues to the superior Scottish courts; and those courts in turn will be able to refer the matter to the Judicial Committee of the Privy Council. If such issues are decided by the superior Scottish courts, an appeal from their decision will be to the Judicial Committee. These arrangements are in line with the Government's general approach to devolution.

Wales

2.22 Similarly, the Welsh Assembly will not have power to make subordinate legislation or take executive action which is incompatible with the Convention. It will be possible to challenge such legislation and action in the courts, and for them to be quashed, on the ground that the Assembly has exceeded its powers.

Northern Ireland

2.23 Acts of the Westminster Parliament will be treated in the same way in Northern Ireland as in the rest of the United Kingdom. But Orders in Council and other related legislation will be treated as subordinate legislation. In other words, they will be struck down by the courts if they are incompatible with the Convention. Most such legislation is a temporary means of enacting legislation which would otherwise be done by measures of a devolved Northern Ireland legislature.

CHAPTER 3 – IMPROVING COMPLIANCE WITH THE CONVENTION RIGHTS

3.1 The enforcement of Convention rights will be a matter for the courts, whilst the Government and Parliament will have the different but equally important responsibility of revising legislation where necessary. But it is also highly desirable for the Government to ensure as far as possible that legislation which it places before Parliament in the normal way is compatible with the Convention rights, and for Parliament to ensure that the human rights implications of legislation are subject to proper consideration before the legislation is enacted.

Government legislation

3.2 The Human Rights Bill introduces a new procedure to make the human rights implications of proposed Government legislation more transparent. The responsible Minister will be required to provide a statement that in his or her view the proposed Bill is compatible with the Convention. The Government intends to include this statement alongside the Explanatory and Financial Memorandum which accompanies a Bill when it is introduced into each House of Parliament.

3.3 There may be occasions where such a statement cannot be provided, for example because it is essential to legislate on a particular issue but the policy in question requires a risk to be taken in relation to the Convention, or because the arguments in relation to the Convention issues raised are not clear-cut. In such cases, the Minister will indicate that he or she cannot provide a positive statement but that the Government nevertheless wishes Parliament to proceed to consider the Bill.

Parliament would expect the Minister to explain his or her reasons during the normal course of the proceedings on the Bill. This will ensure that the human rights implications are debated at the earliest opportunity.

Consideration of draft legislation within Government

3.4 The new requirement to make a statement about the compliance of draft legislation with the Convention will have a significant and beneficial impact on the preparation of draft legislation within Government before its introduction into Parliament. It will ensure that all Ministers, their departments and officials are fully seized of the gravity of the Convention's obligations in respect of human rights. But we also intend to strengthen collective Government procedures so as to ensure that a proper assessment is made of the human rights implications when collective approval is sought for a new policy, as well as when any draft Bill is considered by Ministers. Revised guidance to Departments on these procedures will, like the existing guidance, be publicly available.

3.5 Some central co-ordination will also be extremely desirable in considering the approach to be taken to Convention points in criminal or civil proceedings, or in proceedings for judicial review, to which a Government department is a party. This is likely to require an inter-departmental group of lawyers and administrators meeting on a regular basis to ensure that a consistent approach is taken and to ensure that developments in case law are well understood by all those in Government who are involved in proceedings on Convention points. We do not, however, see any need to make a particular Minister responsible for promoting human rights across Government, or to set up a separate new Unit for this purpose. The responsibility for complying with human rights requirements rests on the Government as a whole.

A Parliamentary Committee on Human Rights

3.6 *Rights Brought Home* suggested that 'Parliament itself should play a leading role in protecting the rights which are at the heart of a parliamentary democracy'. How this is achieved is a matter for Parliament to decide, but in the Government's view the best course would be to establish a new Parliamentary Committee with functions relating to human rights. This would not require legislation or any change in Parliamentary procedure. There could be a Joint Committee of both Houses of Parliament or each House could have its own Committee; or there could be a Committee which met jointly for some purposes and separately for others.

3.7 The new Committee might conduct enquiries on a range of human rights issues relating to the Convention, and produce reports so as to assist the Government and Parliament in deciding what action to take. It might also want to range more widely, and examine issues relating to the other international obligations of the United Kingdom such as proposals to accept new rights under other human rights treaties.

Should there be a Human Rights Commission?

3.8 *Rights Brought Home* canvassed views on the establishment of a Human Rights Commission, and this possibility has received a good deal of attention. No commitment to establish a Commission was, however, made in the Manifesto on which the Government was elected. The Government's priority is implementation of its Manifesto commitment to give further effect to the Convention rights in domestic law so that people can enforce those rights in United Kingdom courts. Establishment of a new Human Rights Commission is not central to that objective and does not need to form part of the current Bill.

3.9 Moreover, the idea of setting up a new human rights body is not universally acclaimed. Some reservations have been expressed, particularly from the point of view of the impact on existing bodies concerned with particular aspects of human rights, such as the Commission for Racial Equality and the Equal Opportunities Commission, whose primary concern is to protect the rights for which they were established. A quinquennial review is currently being conducted of the Equal

Opportunities Commission, and the Government has also decided to establish a new Disability Rights Commission.

3.10 The Government's conclusion is that, before a Human Rights Commission could be established by legislation, more consideration needs to be given to how it would work in relation to such bodies, and to the new arrangements to be established for Parliamentary and Government scrutiny of human rights issues. This is necessary not only for the purposes of framing the legislation but also to justify the additional public expenditure needed to establish and run a new Commission. A range of organisational issues need more detailed consideration before the legislative and financial case for a new Commission is made, and there needs to be a greater degree of consensus on an appropriate model among existing human rights bodies.

3.11 However, the Government has not closed its mind to the idea of a new Human Rights Commission at some stage in the future in the light of practical experience of the working of the new legislation. If Parliament establishes a Committee on Human Rights, one of its main tasks might be to conduct an inquiry into whether a Human Rights Commission is needed and how it should operate. The Government would want to give full weight to the Committee's report in considering whether to create a statutory Human Rights Commission in future.

3.12 It has been suggested that a new Commission might be funded from non-Government sources. The Government would not wish to deter a move towards a non-statutory, privately-financed body if its role was limited to functions such as public education and advice to individuals. However, a non-statutory body could not absorb any of the functions of the existing statutory bodies concerned with aspects of human rights.

QUESTIONS

1. Does the existence of a democratic mandate entitle Parliament to pass laws which might threaten the very conditions essential to the existence of a democracy and which a Bill of Rights should protect (see cl. 2.13, *ante*)? Does the fact that courts were unable to declare statutes unconstitutional necessarily mean that they should not be able to do so in the future? Would according to judges the power to determine the constitutionality of statutes necessarily make them more political than they currently are?

2. Is the Human Rights Act unnecessarily weakened by preventing it from impliedly repealing pre-existing statutes which conflict with its provisions? Would permitting the doctrine of implied repeal (see p. 485 *ante*) to operate have undermined the supremacy of Parliament?

3. Does the absence of a Human Rights Commission undermine the effectiveness of the Act in protecting rights?

The Human Rights Act 1998

Introduction

1. The Convention and the First Protocol
    (1) In this Act, 'the Convention rights' means the rights and fundamental freedoms set out in—
        (a) Articles 2 to 12 and 14 of the Convention,
        (b) Articles 1 to 3 of the First Protocol, and
        (c) Articles 1 and 2 of the Sixth Protocol,
as read with Articles 16 to 18 of the Convention.

(2) Those Articles are to have effect for the purposes of this Act subject to any designated derogation or reservation (as to which see sections 14 and 15).

(3) The Articles are set out in Schedule 1.

(4) The Lord Chancellor may by order make such amendments to this section or Schedule 1 as he considers appropriate to reflect the effect, in relation to the United Kingdom, of a protocol.

(5) In subsection (4) 'protocol' means a protocol to the Convention—

(a) which the United Kingdom has ratified; or

(b) which the United Kingdom has signed with a view to ratification.

(6) No amendment may be made by an order under subsection (4) so as to come into force before the protocol concerned is in force in relation to the United Kingdom.

2. Interpretation of Convention rights

(1) A court or tribunal determining a question which has arisen under this Act in connection with a Convention right must take into account any—

(a) judgment, decision, declaration or advisory opinion of the European Court of Human Rights,

(b) opinion of the Commission given in a report adopted under Article 31 of the Convention,

(c) decision of the Commission in connection with Article 26 or 27(2) of the Convention, or

(d) decision of the Committee of Ministers taken under Article 46 of the Convention,

whenever made or given, so far as, in the opinion of the court or tribunal, it is relevant to the proceedings in which that question has arisen.

(2)–(3) . . .

Interpretation of legislation

3. Legislation

(1) So far as it is possible to do so, primary legislation and subordinate legislation must be read and given effect in a way which is compatible with the Convention rights.

(2) This section—

(a) applies to primary legislation and subordinate legislation whenever enacted;

(b) does not affect the validity, continuing operation or enforcement of any incompatible primary legislation; and

(c) does not affect the validity, continuing operation or enforcement of any incompatible subordinate legislation if (disregarding any possibility of revocation) primary legislation prevents removal of the incompatibility.

4. Declaration of incompatibility

(1) Subsection (2) applies in any proceedings in which a court determines whether a provision of primary legislation is compatible with a Convention right.

(2) If the court is satisfied that the provision is incompatible with a Convention right, it may make a declaration of that incompatibility.

(3) Subsection (4) applies in any proceedings in which a court determines whether a provision of subordinate legislation, made in the exercise of a power conferred by primary legislation, is compatible with a Convention right.

(4) If the court is satisfied—

(a) that the provision is incompatible with a Convention right, and

(b) that (disregarding any possibility of revocation) the primary legislation concerned prevents removal of the incompatibility,

it may make a declaration of that incompatibility.

(5) In this section 'court' means—
  (a) the House of Lords;
  (b) the Judicial Committee of the Privy Council;
  (c) the Courts-Martial Appeal Court;
  (d) in Scotland, the High Court of Justiciary sitting otherwise than as a trial court or the Court of Session;
  (e) in England and Wales or Northern Ireland, the High Court or the Court of Appeal.
(6) A declaration under this section ('a declaration of incompatibility')—
  (a) does not affect the validity, continuing operation or enforcement of the provision in respect of which it is given; and
  (b) is not binding on the parties to the proceedings in which it is made.

5. Right of Crown to intervene.
(1) Where a court is considering whether to make a declaration of incompatibility, the Crown is entitled to notice in accordance with rules of court.
(2) In any case to which subsection (1) applies—
  (a) a Minister of the Crown (or a person nominated by him);
  (b) a member of the Scottish executive;
  (c) a Northern Ireland Minister;
  (d) a Northern Ireland department, is entitled, on giving notice in accordance with rules of court, to be joined as a party to the proceedings.
(3) Notice under subsection (2) may be made at any time during the proceedings.
(4) A person who has been made a party to criminal proceedings (other than in Scotland) as the result of a notice under subsection (2) may, with leave, appeal to the House of Lords against any declaration of incompatibility made in the proceedings.
(5) . . .

Public authorities

6. Acts of public authorities
(1) It is unlawful for a public authority to act in a way which is incompatible with a Convention right.
(2) Subsection (1) does not apply to an act if—
  (a) as the result of one or more provisions of primary legislation, the authority could not have acted differently; or
  (b) in the case of one or more provisions of, or made under, primary legislation which cannot be read or given effect in a way which is compatible with the Convention rights, the authority was acting so as to give effect to or enforce those provisions.
(3) In this section, 'public authority' includes—
  (a) a court or tribunal, and
  (b) any person certain of whose functions are functions of a public nature, but does not include either House of Parliament or a person exercising functions in connection with proceedings in Parliament.
(4) In subsection (3) 'Parliament' does not include the House of Lords in its judicial capacity.
(5) In relation to a particular act, a person is not a public authority by virtue only of subsection (3)(b) if the nature of the act is private.
(6) 'An act' includes a failure to act but does not include a failure to—
  (a) introduce in, or lay before, Parliament a proposal for legislation; or
  (b) make any primary legislation or remedial order.

7. Proceedings

(1) A person who claims that a public authority has acted (or proposes to act) in a way which is made unlawful by section 6(1) may—

(a) bring proceedings against the authority under this Act in the appropriate court or tribunal, or

(b) rely on the Convention right or rights concerned in any legal proceedings, but only if he is (or would be) a victim of the unlawful act.

(2) In subsection (1)(a) 'appropriate court or tribunal' means such court or tribunal as may be determined in accordance with rules; and proceedings against an authority includes a counterclaim or similar proceeding.

(3) If the proceedings are brought on an application for judicial review, the applicant is to be taken to have a sufficient interest in relation to the unlawful act only if he is, or would be, a victim of that act.

(4) If the proceedings are made by way of a petition for judicial review in Scotland, the applicant shall be taken to have title and interest to sue in relation to the unlawful act only if he is, or would be, a victim of that act.

(5) Proceedings under subsection (1)(a) must be brought before the end of—

(a) the period of one year beginning with the date on which the act complained of took place; or

(b) such longer period as the court or tribunal considers equitable having regard to all the circumstances,

but that is subject to any rule imposing a stricter time limit in relation to the procedure in question.

(6) In subsection (1)(b) 'legal proceedings' includes—

(a) proceedings brought by or at the instigation of a public authority; and

(b) an appeal against the decision of a court or tribunal.

(7) For the purposes of this section, a person is a victim of an unlawful act only if he would be a victim for the purposes of Article 34 of the Convention if proceedings were brought in the European Court of Human Rights in respect of that act.

(8) Nothing in this Act creates a criminal offence.

(9)–(11) . . .

8. Judicial remedies

(1) In relation to any act (or proposed act) of a public authority which the court finds is (or would be) unlawful, it may grant such relief or remedy, or make such order, within its jurisdiction as it considers just and appropriate.

(2) But damages may be awarded only by a court which has power to award damages, or to order the payment of compensation, in civil proceedings.

(3) No award of damages is to be made unless, taking account of all the circumstances of the case, including—

(a) any other relief or remedy granted, or order made, in relation to the act in question (by that or any other court), and

(b) the consequences of any decision (of that or any other court) in respect of that act,

the court is satisfied that the award is necessary to afford just satisfaction to the person in whose favour it is made.

(4) In determining—

(a) whether to award damages, or

(b) the amount of an award,

the court must take into account the principles applied by the European Court of Human Rights in relation to the award of compensation under Article 41 of the Convention.

(5) ...

(6) In this section—

'court' includes a tribunal;

'damages' means damages for an unlawful act of a public authority; and

'unlawful' means unlawful under section 6(1).

9. Judicial acts

(1) Proceedings under section 7(1)(a) in respect of a judicial act may be brought only—

(a) by exercising a right of appeal;

(b) on an application (in Scotland a petition) for judicial review; or

(c) in such other forum as may be prescribed by rules.

(2) That does not affect any rule of law which prevents a court from being the subject of judicial review.

(3) In proceedings under this Act in respect of a judicial act done in good faith, damages may not be awarded otherwise than to compensate a person to the extent required by Article 5(5) of the Convention.

(4) An award of damages permitted by subsection (3) is to be made against the Crown; but no award may be made unless the appropriate person, if not a party to the proceedings, is joined.

(5) In this section—

'appropriate person' means the Minister responsible for the court concerned, or a person or government department nominated by him;

'court' includes a tribunal;

'judge' includes a member of a tribunal, a justice of the peace and a clerk or other officer entitled to exercise the jurisdiction of a court;

'Judicial act' means a judicial act of a court and includes an act done on the instructions, or on behalf, of a judge;

...

Remedial action

10. Power to take remedial action

(1) This section applies if—

(a) a provision of legislation has been declared under section 4 to be incompatible with a Convention right and, if an appeal lies—

(i)   all persons who may appeal have stated that they do not intend to do so;

(ii) the time for bringing an appeal has expired and no appeal has been brought within that time; or

(iii) an appeal brought within that time has been determined or abandoned;

(b) it appears to a Minister of the Crown or Her Majesty in Council that, having regard to a finding of the European Court of Human Rights made after the coming into force of this section in proceedings against the United Kingdom, a provision of legislation is incompatible with an obligation of the United Kingdom arising from the Convention.

(2) If a Minister of the Crown considers that there are compelling reasons for proceeding under this section, he may by order make such amendments to the legislation as he considers necessary to remove the incompatibility.

(3) If, in the case of subordinate legislation, a Minister of the Crown considers—

(a) that it is necessary to amend the primary legislation under which the subordinate legislation in question was made, in order to enable the incompatibility to be removed, and

(b) that there are compelling reasons for proceeding under this section, he may by order make such amendments to the primary legislation as he considers necessary.

(4) This section also applies where the provision in question is in subordinate legislation and has been quashed, or declared invalid, by reason of incompatibility with a Convention right and the Minister proposes to proceed under paragraph 2(b) of Schedule 2.

(5) If the legislation is an Order in Council, the power conferred by subsection (2) or (3) is exercisable by Her Majesty in Council.

(6) In this section 'legislation' does not include a Measure of the Church Assembly or of the General Synod of the Church of England.

(7) . . .

Other rights and proceedings

11. Safeguard for existing human rights

A person's reliance on a Convention right does not restrict—

(a) any other right or freedom conferred on him by or under any law having effect in any part of the United Kingdom, or

(b) his right to make any claim or bring any proceedings which he could make or bring apart from sections 7 to 9.

12. Freedom of expression

(1) This section applies if a court is considering whether to grant any relief which, if granted, might affect the exercise of the Convention right to freedom of expression.

(2) If the person against whom the application for relief is made ('the respondent') is neither present nor represented, no such relief is to be granted unless the court is satisfied—

(a) that the applicant has taken all practicable steps to notify the respondent; or

(b) that there are compelling reasons why the respondent should not be notified.

(3) No such relief is to be granted so as to restrain publication before trial unless the court is satisfied that the applicant is likely to establish that publication should not be allowed.

(4) The court must have particular regard to the importance of the Convention right to freedom of expression and, where the proceedings relate to material which the respondent claims, or which appears to the court, to be journalistic, literary or artistic material (or to conduct connected with such material), to—

(a) the extent to which—

(i) the material has, or is about to, become available to the public; or

(ii) it is, or would be, in the public interest for the material to be published;

(b) any relevant privacy code.

(5) In this section—

'court' includes a tribunal; and

'relief' includes any remedy or order (other than in criminal proceedings).

13. Freedom of thought, conscience and religion

(1) If a court's determination of any question arising under this Act might affect the exercise by a religious organisation (itself or its members collectively) of the Convention right to freedom of thought, conscience and religion, it must have particular regard to the importance of that right.

(2) In this section, 'court' includes a tribunal.

Derogations and reservations

14. Derogations

(1) In this Act, 'designated derogation' means any derogation by the United Kingdom from an Article of the Convention, or of any protocol to the Convention, which is designated for the purposes of this Act in an order made by the Lord Chancellor.

(2) [*repealed*].

(3) If a designated derogation is amended or replaced it ceases to be a designated derogation.

(4) But subsection (3) does not prevent the Lord Chancellor from exercising his power under subsection (1) to make a fresh designation order in respect of the Article concerned.

(5) The Lord Chancellor must by order make such amendments to Schedule 2 as he considers appropriate to reflect—

(a) any designation order; or

(b) the effect of subsection (3).

(6) A designation order may be made in anticipation of the making by the United Kingdom of a proposed derogation.

15. Reservations

(1) In this Act, 'designated reservation' means—

(a) the United Kingdom's reservation to Article 2 of the First Protocol to the Convention; and

(b) any other reservation by the United Kingdom to an Article of the Convention, or of any protocol to the Convention, which is designated for the purposes of this Act in an order made by the Lord Chancellor.

(2) The text of the reservation referred to in subsection (1)(a) is set out in Part II of Schedule 3.

(3) If a designated reservation is withdrawn wholly or in part it ceases to be a designated reservation.

(4) But subsection (3) does not prevent the Lord Chancellor from exercising his power under subsection (1)(b) to make a fresh designation order in respect of the Article concerned.

(5) The Lord Chancellor must by order make such amendments to this Act as he considers appropriate to reflect—

(a) any designation order; or

(b) the effect of subsection (3).

16. Period for which designated derogations have effect

(1) If it has not already been withdrawn by the United Kingdom, a designated derogation ceases to have effect for the purposes of this Act at the end of the period of five years beginning with the date on which the order designating it was made.

(2) At any time before the period—

(a) fixed by subsection (1), or

(b) extended by an order under this subsection,

comes to an end, the Lord Chancellor may by order extend it by a further period of five years.

(3) An order under section 14(1) ceases to have effect at the end of the period for consideration, unless a resolution has been passed by each House approving the order.

(4) Subsection (3) does not affect—

(a) anything done in reliance on the order; or

(b) the power to make a fresh order under section 14(1).

(5) In subsection (3) 'period for consideration' means the period of forty days beginning with the day on which the order was made.

(6) In calculating the period for consideration, no account is to be taken of any time during which—

(a) Parliament is dissolved or prorogued; or

(b) both Houses are adjourned for more than four days.

(7) If a designated derogation is withdrawn by the United Kingdom, the Lord Chancellor must by order make such amendments to this Act as he considers are required to reflect that withdrawal.

17. Periodic review of designated reservations

(1) The appropriate Minister must review the designated reservation referred to in section 15(1)(a)—

    (a) before the end of the period of five years beginning with the date on which section 1(2) came into force; and

    (b) if that designation is still in force, before the end of the period of five years beginning with the date on which the last report relating to it was laid under subsection (3).

(2) The appropriate Minister must review each of the other designated reservations (if any)—

    (a) before the end of the period of five years beginning with the date on which the order designating the reservation first came into force; and

    (b) if the designation is still in force, before the end of the period of five years beginning with the date on which the last report relating to it was laid under subsection (3).

(3) The Minister conducting a review under this section must prepare a report on the result of the review and lay a copy of it before each House of Parliament.

Judges of the European Court of Human Rights

18. Appointment to European Court of Human Rights

(1) In this section 'judicial office' means the office of—

    (a) Lord Justice of Appeal, Justice of the High Court or Circuit judge, in England and Wales;

    (b) judge of the Court of Session or sheriff, in Scotland;

    (c) Lord Justice of Appeal, judge of the High Court or county court judge, in Northern Ireland.

(2) The holder of a judicial office may become a judge of the European Court of Human Rights ('the Court') without being required to relinquish his office.

(3) But he is not required to perform the duties of his judicial office while he is a judge of the Court.

(4)–(7) . . .

Parliamentary procedure

19. Statements of compatibility

(1) A Minister of the Crown in charge of a Bill in either House of Parliament must, before Second Reading of the Bill—

    (a) make a statement to the effect that in his view the provisions of the Bill are compatible with the Convention rights ('a statement of compatibility'); or

    (b) make a statement to the effect that although he is unable to make a statement of compatibility the government nevertheless wishes the House to proceed with the Bill.

(2) The statement must be in writing and be published in such manner as the Minister making it considers appropriate.

Supplemental

20. Orders under this Act

(1) Any power to make an order under this Act is exercisable by statutory instrument.

(2) The power to make rules (other than rules of court) under section 2(3) or 7(9) is exercisable by statutory instrument.

(3) Any statutory instrument made under section 14, 15 or 16(7) must be laid before Parliament.

(4) No order may be made under section 1(4), 7(11) or 16(2) unless a draft of the order has been laid before, and approved by, each House of Parliament.

(5) Any statutory instrument made under section 18(7) or Schedule 4, or to which subsection (2) applies, shall be subject to annulment in pursuance of a resolution of either House of Parliament.

(6)–(8) . . .

21. Interpretation, etc

(1) In this Act—

. . .

'the appropriate Minister' means the Minister of the Crown having charge of the appropriate authorised government department (within the meaning of the Crown Proceedings Act 1947);

. . .

'primary legislation' means any—

(a) public general Act;

(b) local and personal Act;

(c) private Act;

(d) Measure of the Church Assembly;

(e) Measure of the General Synod of the Church of England;

(f) Order in Council—

  (i) made in exercise of Her Majesty's Royal Prerogative;

  (ii) made under section 38(1)(a) of the Northern Ireland Constitution Act 1973 or the corresponding provision of the Northern Ireland Act 1998; or

  (iii) amending an Act of a kind mentioned in paragraph (a), (b) or (c); and includes an order or other instrument made under primary legislation (otherwise than by the National Assembly for Wales, a member of the Scottish Executive, a Northern Ireland Minister or a Northern Ireland department) to the extent to which it operates to bring one or more provisions of that legislation into force or amends any primary legislation;

. . .

'remedial order' means an order under section 10;

'subordinate legislation' means any—

(a) Order in Council other than one—

  (i) made in exercise of Her Majesty's Royal Prerogative;

  (ii) made under section 38(1)(a) of the Northern Ireland Constitution Act 1973 or the corresponding provision of the Northern Ireland Act 1998; or

  (iii) amending an Act of a kind mentioned in the definition of primary legislation;

(b) Act of the Scottish Parliament;

(c) Act of the Parliament of Northern Ireland;

(d) Measure of the Assembly established under section 1 of the Northern Ireland Assembly Act 1973;

(e) Act of the Northern Ireland Assembly;

(f) order, rules, regulations, scheme, warrant, byelaw or other instrument made under primary legislation (except to the extent to which it operates to bring one or more provisions of that legislation into force or amends any primary legislation);

(g) order, rules, regulations, scheme, warrant, byelaw or other instrument made under legislation mentioned in paragraph (b), (c), (d) or (e) or made under an Order in Council applying only to Northern Ireland;

(h) order, rules, regulations, scheme, warrant, byelaw or other instrument made by a member of the Scottish Executive, a Northern Ireland Minister or a Northern Ireland department in exercise of prerogative or other executive functions of Her Majesty which are exercisable by such a person on behalf of Her Majesty;

'transferred matters' has the same meaning as in the Northern Ireland Act 1998; and 'tribunal' means any tribunal in which legal proceedings may be brought.

. . .

22. Short title, commencement, application and extent
(1) This Act may be cited as the Human Rights Act 1998.

(2) Sections 18 and 20 and this section come into force on the passing of this Act.

(3) The other provisions of this Act come into force on such day as the Secretary of State may by order appoint; and different days may be appointed for different purposes.

(4) Paragraph (b) of subsection (1) of section 7 applies to proceedings brought by or at the instigation of a public authority whenever the act in question took place; but otherwise that subsection does not apply to an act committed before the coming into force of that section.

(5) This Act binds the Crown.

(6) This Act extends to Northern Ireland.

(7) Section 21(5), so far as it relates to any provision contained in the Army Act 1955, the Air Force Act 1955 or the Naval Discipline Act 1957, extends to any place to which that provision extends.

NOTE: Following the events of 11 September 2001 in the United States, Parliament enacted the Anti-terrorism, Crime and Security Act 2001. On 11 November 2001, prior to the second reading of the Bill, the Home Secretary made The Human Rights Act (1998) (Designated Derogation) Order 2001, SI 2001 No. 3644, setting out the proposed derogation from Article 5(1) of the Convention (see further, *ante*, p. 471). As a result the Home Secretary was able to make a s.19 statement of compatibility in relation to the Anti-terrorism, Crime and Security Bill. On 19 December 2001 the Lord Chancellor made The Human Rights Act 1998 (Amendment No. 2) Order 2001, SI 2001 No. 3500, which came into force on 20 December 2001. This Order inserts the text of the derogation as of Part 1 of Schedule 3 of the 1998 Act.

PART I   DEROGATION

United Kingdom's derogation from Article 5(1)
The United Kingdom Permanent Representative to the Council of Europe presents his compliments to the Secretary General of the Council, and has the honour to convey the following information in order to ensure compliance with the obligations of Her Majesty's Government in the United Kingdom under Article 15(3) of the Convention for the Protection of Human Rights and Fundamental Freedoms signed at Rome on 4 November 1950.

Public emergency in the United Kingdom
The terrorist attacks in New York, Washington, D.C. and Pennsylvania on 11th September 2001 resulted in several thousand deaths, including many British victims and others from 70 different countries. In its resolutions 1368 (2001) and 1373 (2001), the United Nations Security Council recognised the attacks as a threat to international peace and security.

The threat from international terrorism is a continuing one. In its resolution 1373 (2001), the Security Council, acting under Chapter VII of the United Nations Charter, required all States to take measures to prevent the commission of terrorist attacks, including by denying safe haven to those who finance, plan, support or commit terrorist attacks.

There exists a terrorist threat to the United Kingdom from persons suspected of involvement in international terrorism. In particular, there are foreign nationals present in the United Kingdom who are suspected of being concerned in the commission, preparation or instigation of acts of international terrorism, of being members of organisations or groups which are so concerned or of having links with members of such organisations or groups, and who are a threat to the national security of the United Kingdom.

As a result, a public emergency, within the meaning of Article 15(1) of the Convention, exists in the United Kingdom.

The Anti-terrorism, Crime and Security Act 2001

As a result of the public emergency, provision is made in the Anti-terrorism, Crime and Security Act 2001, inter alia, for an extended power to arrest and detain a foreign national which will apply where it is intended to remove or deport the person from the United Kingdom but where removal or deportation is not for the time being possible, with the consequence that the detention would be unlawful under existing domestic law powers. The extended power to arrest and detain will apply where the Secretary of State issues a certificate indicating his belief that the person's presence in the United Kingdom is a risk to national security and that he suspects the person of being an international terrorist. That certificate will be subject to an appeal to the Special Immigration Appeals Commission ('SIAC'), established under the Special Immigration Appeals Commission Act 1997, which will have power to cancel it if it considers that the certificate should not have been issued. There will be an appeal on a point of law from a ruling by SIAC. In addition, the certificate will be reviewed by SIAC at regular intervals. SIAC will also be able to grant bail, where appropriate, subject to conditions. It will be open to a detainee to end his detention at any time by agreeing to leave the United Kingdom.

The extended power of arrest and detention in the Anti-terrorism, Crime and Security Act 2001 is a measure which is strictly required by the exigencies of the situation. It is a temporary provision which comes into force for an initial period of 15 months and then expires unless renewed by Parliament. Thereafter, it is subject to annual renewal by Parliament. If, at any time, in the Government's assessment, the public emergency no longer exists or the extended power is no longer strictly required by the exigencies of the situation, then the Secretary of State will, by Order, repeal the provision.

Domestic law powers of detention (other than under the Anti-terrorism, Crime and Security Act 2001)

The Government has powers under the Immigration Act 1971 ('the 1971 Act') to remove or deport persons on the ground that their presence in the United Kingdom is not conducive to the public good on national security grounds. Persons can also be arrested and detained under Schedules 2 and 3 to the 1971 Act pending their removal or deportation. The courts in the United Kingdom have ruled that this power of detention can only be exercised during the period necessary, in all the circumstances of the particular case, to effect removal and that, if it becomes clear that removal is not going to be possible within a reasonable time, detention will be unlawful (*R v Governor of Durham Prison, ex parte Singh* [1984] 1 All ER 983).

Article 5(1)(f) of the Convention

It is well established that Article 5(1)(f) permits the detention of a person with a view to deportation only in circumstances where 'action is being taken with a view to deportation' (*Chahal v United Kingdom* (1996) 23 EHRR 413 at paragraph 112). In that case the European Court of Human Rights indicated that detention will cease to be permissible under Article 5(1)(f) if deportation proceedings are not prosecuted with due diligence and that it was necessary in such cases to determine whether the duration of the deportation proceedings was excessive (paragraph 113).

In some cases, where the intention remains to remove or deport a person on national security grounds, continued detention may not be consistent with Article 5(1)(f) as interpreted by the Court in the *Chahal* case. This may be the case, for example, if the person has established that removal to their own country might result in treatment contrary to Article 3 of the Convention. In such circumstances, irrespective of the gravity of the threat to national security posed by the person concerned, it is well established that Article 3 prevents removal or deportation to a place where there is a real risk that the person will suffer treatment contrary to that article. If no alternative destination is immediately available then removal or deportation may not, for the time being, be possible even though the ultimate intention remains to remove or deport the person once satisfactory arrangements can be made. In addition, it may not be possible to prosecute the person for a criminal offence given the strict rules on the admissibility of evidence in the criminal justice system of the United Kingdom and the high standard of proof required.

Derogation under Article 15 of the Convention

The Government has considered whether the exercise of the extended power to detain contained in the Anti-terrorism, Crime and Security Act 2001 may be inconsistent with the obligations under Article 5(1) of the Convention. As indicated above, there may be cases where, notwithstanding a continuing intention to remove or deport a person who is being detained, it is not possible to say that 'action is being taken with a view to deportation' within the meaning of Article 5(1)(f) as interpreted by the Court in the *Chahal* case. To the extent, therefore, that the exercise of the extended power may be inconsistent with the United Kingdom's obligations under Article 5(1), the Government has decided to avail itself of the right of derogation conferred by Article 15(1) of the Convention and will continue to do so until further notice.

Strasbourg, 18 December 2001.

B: The implications of the Human Rights Act for civil liberties

Lord Irvine of Lairg LC, The Tom Sargant Memorial Lecture, 'The Development of Human Rights in Britain under an Incorporated Convention on Human Rights'
16 December 1997

. . . The traditional freedom of the individual under an unwritten constitution to do himself that which is not prohibited by law gives no protection from misuse of power by the State, nor any protection from acts or omissions by public bodies which harm individuals in a way that is incompatible with their human rights under the Convention.

The implications of the change

What then are the practical implications of this change to a rights based system within the field of civil liberties?

First, the Act will give to the courts the tools to uphold freedoms at the very time their infringement is threatened. . . . The courts will now have the power to give effect to the Convention rights in the course of proceedings when they arise in this country and to grant relief against an unlawful act of a public authority (a necessarily widely drawn concept). The courts will not be able to strike down primary legislation. But they will be able to make a declaration of incompatibility where a piece of primary legislation conflicts with a Convention right. This will trigger the ability to use in Parliament a special fast-track procedure to bring the law into line with the Convention.

This innovative technique will provide the right balance between the judiciary and Parliament. Parliament is the democratically elected representative of the people and must remain sovereign. The judiciary will be able to exercise to the full the power to scrutinise legislation rigorously against the fundamental freedoms guaranteed by the Convention but without becoming politicised. The ultimate decision to amend legislation to bring it into line with the Convention, however, will rest with

Parliament. The ultimate responsibility for compliance with the Convention must be Parliament's alone.

That point illustrates the second important effect of our new approach. If there are to be differences or departures from the principles of the Convention they should be conscious and reasoned departures, and not the product of rashness, muddle or ignorance. This will be guaranteed both by the powers given to the courts but also by other provisions which will be enacted. In particular, Ministers and administrators will be obliged to do all their work keeping clearly and directly in mind its impact on human rights, as expressed in the Convention and the jurisprudence which attaches to it. For, where any Bill is introduced in either House, the Minister of the Crown, in whose charge it is, will be required to make a written statement that, either, in his view, the provisions of the Bill are compatible with the Convention rights; or that he cannot make that statement but the Government nonetheless wishes the House to proceed with the Bill. In the latter case the Bill would inevitably be subject to close and critical scrutiny by Parliament. Human rights will not be a matter of fudge. The responsible Minister will have to ensure that the legislation does not infringe guaranteed freedoms, or be prepared to justify his decision openly and in the full glare of Parliamentary and public opinion.

That will be particularly important whenever there comes under consideration those articles of the Convention which lay down what I call principled rights, subject to possible limitation. I have in mind Articles 8–11, dealing with respect for private life; freedom of religion; freedom of expression; and freedom of assembly and association; which confer those freedoms subject to possible limitations, such as, for instance in the case of Article 10 (freedom of expression):

> are prescribed by law and are necessary in a democratic society in the interests of national security, territorial integrity or public safety, for the prevention of disorder or crime, for the protection of health or morals, for the protection of the reputation or rights of others, for preventing the disclosure of information received in confidence, or for maintaining the authority and impartiality of the judiciary.

In such cases, administrators and legislators, will have to think clearly about whether what they propose really is necessary in a democratic society and for what object it is necessary. Quite apart from the concentration on the Convention and its jurisprudence this will require, the process should produce better thought-out, clearer and more transparent administration.

The important requirements of transparency on Convention issues that will accompany the introduction of all future legislation will ensure that Parliament knows exactly what it is doing in a human rights context. I regard this improvement in both the efficiency and the openness of our legislative process as one of the main benefits produced by incorporation of the Convention.

Substantive rights
Thirdly, the Convention will enable the Courts to reach results in cases which give full effect to the substantive rights guaranteed by the Convention. . . . But the courts have only had limited ability to give effect to those rights. . . .

It is moreover likely – although individual cases will be for the Courts to determine and I should not attempt to prejudge them – that the position will in at least some cases be different from what it would have been under the pre-incorporation practice. The reason for this lies in the techniques to be followed once the Act is in force. Unlike the old Diceyan approach where the Court would go straight to what restriction had been imposed, the focus will first be on the positive right and then on the justifiability of the exception. Moreover, the Act will require the Courts to read and give effect to the legislation in a way compatible with the Convention rights 'so far as it is possible to do so.' This, as the White Paper makes clear, goes far beyond the present rule. It will not be necessary to find an ambiguity. On the contrary the Courts will be required to interpret legislation so as to uphold the Convention rights unless the legislation itself is so clearly incompatible with the Convention that it is impossible to do so. Moreover, it should be clear from the Parliamentary history, and in particular the Ministerial statement of compatibility which will be required by the Act, that Parliament did not intend to cut across a Convention right. Ministerial statements of compatibility will inevitably be a strong spur to the courts to find means of construing statutes compatibly with the Convention. . . .

The Court will interpret as consistent with the Convention not only those provisions which are ambiguous in the sense that the *language* used is capable of two different meanings but also those provisions where there is *no* ambiguity in that sense, unless a *clear* limitation is expressed. In the latter category of case it will be 'possible' (to use the statutory language) to read the legislation in a conforming sense because there will be no clear indication that a limitation on the protected rights was intended so as to make it 'impossible' to read it as conforming.

The morality of decisions

The fourth point may be shortly stated but is of immense importance. The Courts' decisions will be based on a more overtly principled, indeed moral, basis. The Court will look at the positive right. It will only accept an interference with that right where a justification, allowed under the Convention, is made out. The scrutiny will not be limited to seeing if the *words* of an exception can be satisfied. The Court will need to be satisfied that the *spirit* of this exception is made out. It will need to be satisfied that the interference with the protected right *is* justified in the public interests in a free democratic society. Moreover, the Courts will in this area have to apply the Convention principle of proportionality. This means the Court will be looking *substantively* at that question. It will not be limited to a secondary review of the decision making process but at the primary question of the merits of the decision itself.

In reaching its judgment, therefore, the Court will need to expand and explain its own view of whether the conduct is legitimate. It will produce in short a decision on the *morality* of the conduct and not simply its compliance with the bare letter of the law.

The influence on other areas of law

I believe, moreover, that the effects of the incorporation of the Convention will be felt way beyond the sphere of the application of the rights guaranteed by the Convention alone. As we move from the traditional Diceyan model of the common law to a rights based system, the effects will be felt throughout the common law and in the very process of judicial decision-making. This will be a healthy and dynamic development in our law.

. . .

Although the legislative technique adopted under the Human Rights Bill is different from that under the European Communities Act, the effect on the general process of deciding cases will, I believe, be as influential. Courts will, from time to time be required to determine if primary or secondary legislation is incompatible with the Convention rights. They will decide if the acts of public authorities are unlawful through contravention, perhaps even conscious contravention, of those rights. They may have to award damages as a result.

These are all new remedies for our courts to apply and, as they begin to develop the tools and techniques to apply them, an influence on other areas of law and judicial decision making is, I believe, inevitable.

. . .

So too it is becoming increasingly hard not explicitly to recognise in English administrative law the Community law doctrine of proportionality.

That doctrine, drawn from German Administrative law principles, is a tool for judging the lawfulness of administrative action. It amounts to this. Excessive means are not to be used to attain permissible objects. Or, as it was more pithily put by Lord Diplock, 'a steam hammer should not be used to crack a nut'. There has been much argument whether this principle now forms a part of the criteria for review of public decisions generally since Lord Diplock opened that door in 1985 [see *Council of Civil Service Unions* v *Minister for the Civil Service* [1985] AC 374]. It seemed to have been slammed shut in *Brind* in 1991. This is not the occasion to trace those developments. Yet, by whatever name, it seems undeniable that the traditional common law concepts converge with their continental cousins. This is but another example of the inevitable incremental effects of introducing another system of law to be applied alongside traditional common law principles.

C: How does the Human Rights Act operate in practice?

NOTE: The introduction of the Human Rights Act is a major step forward in the protection of human rights. Gradually uncertainties as to how the Act will operate in practice are being resolved but there will always remain unanswered questions. Below some of the major questions are explored by means of extracts from academic and judicial writers and from recent decisions of the appellate courts. The Table below provides some statistical information on the impact which the Act has had in the 14 months following its implementation.

Cases involving Human Rights Act points

Cases analysed:	civil and private	56
	civil and public	147
	criminal (including judicial review)	94
	Total	297
HRA claims upheld:	section 3	11
	section 4	3
	section 6	42
	Total	56
Outcome of HRA challenge:	made no difference	90
	affected outcome, reasoning or procedure	207
	Total	297
Remedies:	no remedy	233
	declaration, injunctions or orders	22
	quashing of order or decision	23
	retrial	4
	administrative action	3
	declarations of incompatibility	3
	damages	1
	other	8
	Total	297

Statistics based on information supplied to the Human Rights Unit by the Human Rights Act Research Unit, Doughty Street Chambers, London, based on cases reported in *Lawtel Human Rights Interactive* and *Butterworths Human Rights Direct* from case transcripts available from 2 October 2000 to 13 December 2001.

(a) *What is a 'public authority'?*

F. Klug, R. Singh & M. Hunt, 'Rights Brought Home: a briefing on the Human Rights Bill with amendments'

2.2 Who is liable to uphold rights under the Bill?

The Act makes it unlawful for all public authorities 'to act in a way which is incompatible with' the rights in the Convention (clause 6(1)). This can include a failure to act but not a failure to legislate (clause 6(6)). The definition of a public authority includes central and local government, the courts, the police, immigration officers and 'any person certain of whose functions are functions of a public nature' (clause 6(3)(c)). The White Paper states that this definition is intended to include public functions of private companies such as the privatised utilities. The actions of Parliament, however, are explicitly excluded as are actions to give effect to an Act which cannot be reconciled with the Convention.

The unequivocal requirement that all public authorities comply with the Convention means that present restraints on the judicial review of the actions or decisions of officials will no longer apply. Currently these can only be overturned on grounds of illegality, procedural impropriety or what is known as Wednesbury irrationality where a decision is so outrageous in its defiance of logic or accepted moral standards that in the court's view no sensible person could have arrived at it. Now it is the Government's stated intention that this will change:

> Our courts will be required to balance the protection of individual rights against the demands of the general interests of the community (*Rights Brought Home, para 2.5*).

This means that it is expected that the courts will import the 'doctrine of proportionality' in reviewing whether restrictions on fundamental rights are justifiable or not. Even if such restrictions are deemed 'rational' (in the Wednesbury sense) they will be liable to be overturned if they are not aimed at meeting a pressing social need and are not proportionate to the aim of meeting that need. This is what is meant by the requirement in many articles in the Convention that limitations on rights must be 'necessary in a democratic society.' In a case involving a strip search, for example, a defendant would no longer have to rely on arguing that a prison officer had acted unlawfully or irrationally but could argue that the officer had violated their right not to be subject to 'inhuman or degrading treatment or punishment' (ECHR, Article 3).

By including 'courts' in the definition of public authorities the Bill also ensures that the Convention will have to be complied with by courts when, for example, interpreting the common law or exercising a judicial discretion. The effect of this is that previous decisions of the courts will be overturned to the extent that they are incompatible with the Convention.

NOTES:

The Human Rights Task Force, *A New Era of Rights and Responsibilities: Core Guidance for Public Authorities* (Home Office), in answer to the question 'What is a public authority?', states at para. 92:

> No express definition exists in the Act but it is likely to include:
> - Government departments
> - Local authorities
> - The NHS
> - Police, prison, immigration officers
> - Public prosecutors
> - Courts and tribunals
> - Non-Departmental Public Bodies
> - Any person exercising a public function

2. In the case which follows the Court of Appeal was faced with the question whether a housing association, a registered social landlord (RSL) for the purposes of the Housing Act 1996,

which had been created by the local authority in order to transfer to it a substantial proportion of the authority's housing stock, was a public authority.

Poplar Housing and Regeneration Community Association v *Donoghue*
[2001] EWCA Civ 595, Court of Appeal

D was a tenant of the housing association subject to an assured shorthold tenancy. D had originally been provided the tenancy by the local authority pending its decision as to whether she was intentionally homeless. By the time the local authority determined this question, the property had been transferred to the housing association. The housing association notified D that possession of the property was required and it subsequently issued a summons for possession under s. 21(4) of the Housing Act 1988. At the hearing D sought to claim that the housing association was a public authority, or was performing a public function, and that it would be unlawful for it to act in a way which was incompatible with her Article 8(1) right to respect for her private and family life and her home. The district judge, in granting the order for possession, ruled that while the housing association was performing a public function, s. 21(4) did not contravene Article 8 as the association's action for possession served a purpose under Article 8(2), namely to protect the rights and freedoms of others by not allowing someone who had become intentionally homeless to jump the housing queue. On appeal by D, the Court of Appeal ruled in the same way as the district judge and dismissed the appeal. The extracts below relate to public bodies and public functions.

LORD WOOLF CJ:. . .

Public bodies and public functions

55 The importance of whether Poplar was at the material times a public body or performing public functions is this: the Human Rights Act 1998 will only apply to Poplar if it is deemed to be a public body or performing public functions. Section 6(1) of the Human Rights Act 1998 makes it unlawful for a public authority to act in a way which is incompatible with a Convention right. Section 6(3) states that a 'public authority' includes '(b) any person certain of whose functions are functions of a public nature'. Section 6(5) provides: 'In relation to a particular act, a person is not a public authority by virtue only of subsection (3)(b) if the nature of the act is private.'

56 The defendant relies on the witness statements of Mr David Cowan, a lecturer of law at the University of Bristol (specialising in housing law and policy) and of Professor Alder of the University of Newcastle in support of her contention that Poplar is a public authority within section 6. Both Mr Cowan and Professor Alder acknowledge that the questions raised are ones of importance and of some debate in academic circles. However, Mr Cowan says it is 'tolerably clear that RSLs do fall within the definition of public authority under section 6(1)' as they are performing public functions.

. . .

58 We agree with Mr Luba's submissions that the definition of who is a public authority, and what is a public function, for the purposes of section 6, should be given a generous interpretation. However, we would suggest that the position is not . . . simple. . . . The fact that a body performs an activity which otherwise a public body would be under a duty to perform cannot mean that such performance is necessarily a public function. A public body in order to perform its public duties can use the services of a private body. Section 6 should not be applied so that if a private body provides such services, the nature of the functions are inevitably public. If this were to be the position, then when a small hotel provides bed and breakfast accommodation as a temporary measure, at the request of a housing authority that is under a duty to provide that accommodation, the small hotel would be performing public functions and required to comply with the Human Rights Act 1998. This is not what the Human Rights Act 1998 intended. The consequence would be the same where a hospital uses a private company to carry out specialist services, such as analysing blood samples. The position under the Human Rights Act 1998 is necessarily more complex. Section 6(3) means that hybrid bodies, who have functions of a public and private nature are public authorities, but *not* in relation to acts which are of a private nature. The renting out of accommodation can certainly be of a private nature. The fact that through the act of renting by a private body a public authority may be fulfilling its public duty, does not automatically change into a public act what would otherwise be a private act: see, by analogy *R* v *Muntham House School, Ex p R* [2000] LGR 255.

59 The purpose of section 6(3)(b) is to deal with hybrid bodies which have both public and private functions. It is not to make a body, which does not have responsibilities to the public, a public body merely because it performs acts on behalf of a public body which would constitute public functions were such acts to be performed by the public body itself. An act can remain of a private nature even though it is performed because another body is under a public duty to ensure that that act is performed.

60 A useful illustration is provided by the decision of the European Court of Human Rights in *Costello-Roberts* v *United Kingdom* (1993) 19 EHRR 112. The case concerned a seven-year-old boy receiving corporal punishment from the headmaster of an independent school. The Court of Human Rights made it clear that the state cannot absolve itself of its Convention obligations by delegating the fulfilment of such obligations to private bodies or individuals, including the headmaster of an independent school. However, if a local authority, in order to fulfil its duties, sent a child to a private school, the fact that it did this would not mean that the private school was performing public functions. The school would not be a hybrid body. It would remain a private body. The local authority would, however, not escape its duties by delegating the performance to the private school. If there were a breach of the Convention, then the responsibility would be that of the local authority and not that of the school.

61 The approach of Professor Alder differs from that of Mr Cowan. He states that there is no single factor that determines whether a function is a public function. He adds:

> The meaning of 'public function' is not necessarily the same in the different contexts where the matter arises . . . Analogies, particularly in respect of the test for determining which bodies are susceptible to judicial review in the Administrative Court may be helpful, given that one purpose of judicial review is to ensure that public bodies are subject to high standards of conduct the same being true of the [Convention]. There is also an analogy with the test that has developed in European Community law for determining whether a body is a public body, namely 'a body, whatever its legal form, which has been made responsible, pursuant to a measure adopted by the state, for providing a public service under the control of the state and has for that purpose special powers beyond those which result from the normal rules applicable in relations between individuals' (*Foster* v *British Gas plc* (Case C-188/89) [1991] 1 QB 405, 427, ECJ).

62 In coming to his conclusion that in this case the activities of Poplar are within section 6, the Professor relies upon the charitable status of Poplar; the fact that Poplar is subject to the control of the Corporation; the sanctions which the Corporation can apply; the provision of public funding to Poplar; the standards which Poplar is required to adopt in the exercise of its powers; the control which the Corporation can exert over the exercise of Poplar's powers; and local authority involvement.

63 Both the Department and Poplar dispute that Poplar is a public authority. Mr Philip Sales helpfully adopts the distinction correctly identified by Clayton & Tomlinson, *The Law of Human Rights* (2000), vol 1, para 5.08, between *standard* public authorities, *functional* public authorities and courts and tribunals. Mr Sales submits, and we, like Professor Alder and Mr Holmes, would agree that housing associations as a class are not standard public authorities. If they are to be a public authority this must be because a particular function performed by an individual RSL is a public as opposed to a private act. The RSL would then be a functional, or hybrid, public authority.

64 In support of his contention, Mr Sales draws attention to the following features of housing associations.

    (a) They vary vastly in size.

    (b) Their structure is that of an ordinary private law entity.

    (c) As to regulation by the Corporation he points to the fact that many financial institutions are regulated by the Bank of England but this does not make them public bodies. Furthermore, the Corporation gives each RSL freedom to decide how it achieves what is expected of it.

    (d) Members of the RSL are not appointed by, or answerable to, the government but are private individuals who volunteer their services. Even in the rare cases where the Corporation makes appointments, the appointee owes his duty to the RSL.

    (e) In *R v Servite Houses, Ex p Goldsmith* [2001] LGR 55 Moses J decided a housing association was not subject to judicial review.

    (f) Although a RSL is funded in part out of public funds, the major source of its income is its rental income. In any event, this is not by any means conclusive: see *Peabody Housing Association Ltd v Green* (1978) 38 P & CR 644, 660, 662.

65 In coming to our conclusion as to whether Poplar is a public authority within the Human Rights Act 1998 meaning of that term, we regard it of particular importance in this case that:

    (i) While section 6 of the Human Rights Act 1998 requires a generous interpretation of who is a public authority, it is clearly inspired by the approach developed by the courts in identifying the bodies and activities subject to judicial review. The emphasis on public functions reflects the approach adopted in judicial review by the courts and textbooks since the decision of the Court of Appeal (the judgment of Lloyd LJ) in *R v Panel on Take-overs and Mergers, Ex p Datafin plc* [1987] QB 815.

    (ii) Tower Hamlets, in transferring its housing stock to Poplar, does not transfer its primary public duties to Poplar. Poplar is no more than the means by which it seeks to perform those duties.

    (iii) The act of providing accommodation to rent is not, without more, a public function for the purposes of section 6 of the Human Rights Act 1998. Furthermore, that is true irrespective of the section of society for whom the accommodation is provided.

    (iv) The fact that a body is a charity or is conducted not for profit means that it is likely to be motivated in performing its activities by what it perceives to be the public interest. However, this does not point to the body being a public authority. In addition, even if such a body performs functions, that would be considered to be of a public nature if performed by a public body, nevertheless such acts may remain of a private nature for the purpose of sections 6(3)(b) and 6(5).

    (v) What can make an act, which would otherwise be private, public is a feature or a combination of features which impose a public character or stamp on the act. Statutory authority for what is done can at least help to mark the act as being public; so can the extent of control over the function exercised by another body which is a public authority. The more closely the acts that could be of a private nature are enmeshed in the activities of a public body, the more likely they are to be public. However, the fact that the acts are supervised by a public regulatory body does not necessarily indicate that they are of a public nature. This is analogous to the position in judicial review, where a regulatory body may be deemed public but the activities of the body which is regulated may be categorised private.

(vi) The closeness of the relationship which exists between Tower Hamlets and Poplar. Poplar was created by Tower Hamlets to take a transfer of local authority housing stock; five of its board members are also members of Tower Hamlets; Poplar is subject to the guidance of Tower Hamlets as to the manner in which it acts towards the defendant.

(vii) The defendant, at the time of transfer, was a sitting tenant of Poplar and it was intended that she would be treated no better and no worse than if she remained a tenant of Tower Hamlets. While she remained a tenant, Poplar therefore stood in relation to her in very much the position previously occupied by Tower Hamlets.

66 While these are the most important factors in coming to our conclusion, it is desirable to step back and look at the situation as a whole. As is the position on applications for judicial review, there is no clear demarcation line which can be drawn between public and private bodies and functions. In a borderline case, such as this, the decision is very much one of fact and degree. Taking into account all the circumstances, we have come to the conclusion that while activities of housing associations need not involve the performance of public functions, in this case, in providing accommodation for the defendant and then seeking possession, the role of Poplar is so closely assimilated to that of Tower Hamlets that it was performing public and not private functions. Poplar therefore is a functional public authority, at least to that extent. We emphasise that this does not mean that all Poplar's functions are public. We do not even decide that the position would be the same if the defendant was a secure tenant. The activities of housing associations can be ambiguous. For example, their activities in raising private or public finance could be very different from those that are under consideration here. The raising of finance by Poplar could well be a private function.

(b) *Does the Convention apply between private litigants?*

A major question relating to the impact which the Human Rights Act will have is whether it imposes an obligation on courts to apply the Convention in determining cases between private litigants. As s. 6(3)(a) includes a court or tribunal within the definition of a 'public authority', this has given rise to speculation whether the Human Rights Act has horizontal effect between private individuals and bodies. The extracts below give a flavour of the differing views which existed prior to the implementation of the Human Rights Act and are followed by extracts from two important cases before the Court of Appeal and the High Court, Family Division, involving arguments based on the Convention Article 8 right to privacy.

Ian Leigh and Laurence Lustgarten, 'Making Rights Real: the Courts, Remedies and the Human Rights Act'
(1999) 58 *Cambridge Law Journal* pp. 512–13

. . . One of the most contested provisions of the Act is the apparently innocuous section (s. 6(3)(a)) which includes a court or tribunal within the definition of a 'public authority'. Since 'public authorities' act unlawfully where they violate a person's Convention rights unless clearly required to do so by legislation, there is some debate about whether the effect of including courts is to require re-interpretation of the common law, even that applicable between private parties, or whether the section has more limited impact. Space precludes full discussion here of the arguments concerning full horizontal effect, but a straightforward case can be made that wherever a court has a procedural, evidential, or remedial discretion, whether under common law or statute and in criminal or civil litigation, a decision about how to use the discretion will constitute a judicial 'act' under section 6. Convention rights are therefore relevant to a number of judicial decisions affecting a person's liberties in the course of proceedings, quite apart from the substantive law to be applied. In the criminal sphere these might include: extensions of detention in police custody, delay before prosecution, decisions to prosecute, the adjournment of proceedings, the grant of legal aid, imposition of bail conditions, orders relating to pre-trial disclosure, the imposition of publication restrictions or bans, the treatment of vulnerable or protected witnesses, the mandatory or discretionary exclusion of evidence (under Police and Criminal Evidence Act, ss. 76 & 78), evidential inferences from silence, and the effect of conditions imposed on community sentences such as probation, community service orders, curfews and tagging orders. In the civil sphere examples would include discretions arising under the wardship jurisdiction and concerning the best interests of the child under the Children Act 1989 in other contexts such as custody, under the Contempt of Court Act 1981, s. 10 (identification of sources of information in limited circumstances), and in the grant of equitable orders. Prior to the Act, English courts have already recognised that the Convention may be relevant to a number of these discretionary decisions, and in others the failure to do so has resulted in adverse rulings from Strasbourg. The approach has, however, been somewhat haphazard. While the Convention has been taken into account on occasion, it has rarely been decisive. If our interpretation of the reach of section 6 is accepted a more rigorous approach will be needed in future: the test will be the *impact* of the discretionary decision on a person's Convention rights. There will be no possibility of balancing prejudice to those rights against other factors, except within the permitted restrictions of the Convention articles themselves. This approach is closer to that of the ECtHR which has held in a number of instances that member states are liable for infringements of the Convention resulting solely from the terms of court orders or, indeed, the failure of a court to grant effective protection of a right.

Sir William Wade QC, 'The United Kingdom's Bill of Rights' in *Constitutional Reform in the United Kingdom: Practice and Principles*
(1998), pp. 62–64

. . . Is the incorporation complete or only partial? On the face of the Bill its whole thrust is against public authorities. But public authorities are not the only ones who may offend against Convention rights. The right to respect for private and family life, the right to freedom of expression, the right to freedom of association (including trade union membership), the prohibition of discrimination and the right to education under the First Protocol are all capable of being violated by non-governmental bodies. Will such misdeeds be protected in the same way as the misdeeds of public authorities? In European Union terms, is the Bill to have horizontal as well as vertical operation?

In the second reading debate the answer appeared to be in the negative. The Lord Chancellor, introducing the Bill, explained its purpose clearly in relation to clause 6, the central provision for incorporation which makes it unlawful for a public authority to act in a way which is incompatible with Convention rights. He said:

> We decided, first of all, that a provision of this kind should apply only to public authorities, however defined, and not to private individuals. That reflects the arrangements for taking cases to the Convention institutions in Strasbourg. The Convention had its origins in a desire to protect people from the misuse of power by the state rather than from the actions of private individuals. Someone who takes a case to Strasbourg is proceeding against the United Kingdom government, rather than against a private individual.

At the committee stage, however, the government resisted an amendment designed to exclude cases where neither party was a public authority. The context was the only political issue which the Bill has so far evoked. Lord Wakeham, as chairman of the Press Complaints Commission, pointed out that the definition of public authorities in clause 6(3) included the courts, who were therefore required by clause 6(1) to act in accordance with the Convention; and that this would compel them to enforce the right of privacy against private as well as public bodies under Article 8 of the

Convention. This right of privacy, strong in Strasbourg but weak in Britain, was feared by the media as likely to conflict to their disadvantage with the less formal self-regulation administered by the Press Complaints Commission. The Bill would introduce a 'back-door privacy law' and put 'an end to investigative journalism'.

In reply the Lord Chancellor accepted Lord Wakeham's reading of the Bill, while rejecting his fears about freedom of the press. As to the former he said:

> We also believe that it is right as a matter of principle for the courts to have the duty of acting compatibly with the Convention, not only in cases involving other public authorities but also in developing the common law in deciding cases between individuals. Why should they not? In preparing this Bill we have taken the view that it is the other course, that of excluding Convention considerations altogether from cases between individuals, which would have to be justified. We do not think that that would be justifiable; nor, indeed, do we think it would be practicable.

Contrasting though it is with the Lord Chancellor's second reading statement, this later statement is evidently as it should be. It would be a poor sort of 'incorporation' which exempted private individuals and bodies from respecting the fundamental rights of their fellow-citizens and drove them back to Strasbourg with all its cost in time and money – the very evil which 'incorporation' is supposed to remedy. It must surely be correct to read the Bill as requiring courts and tribunals to recognise and enforce the convention rights, taking account of the ECHR materials catalogued in clause 2, and subject only to contrary primary legislation (discussed below). This will be a statutory duty in all proceedings, whether the defendant is a public authority or a private person.

Lord Irvine of Lairg LC, Address to the Third Clifford Chance Conference on the Impact of a Bill of Rights on English Law
28 November 1997

Clause 6 makes it clear that 'public authority' includes a court and a tribunal which exercises functions in relation to legal proceedings. That inclusion, as this audience will recognise, does more than asking the courts to interpret legislation compatibly with the Convention. It imposes on them to a duty to act compatibly with the Convention.

We believe that it is right as a matter of principle for the courts to have the duty of acting compatibly with the Convention. They will be under this duty not only in cases involving other public authorities but also in developing the common law in deciding cases between individuals. It has been suggested that the courts should exclude Convention considerations altogether from cases between individuals. We do not think that that would be justifiable. Nor, indeed, do we think it would be practicable. The courts already bring Convention considerations to bear in cases before them. I have no doubt that they will continue to do so in developing the common law. Clause 3 makes this clear by requiring the courts to interpret legislation compatibly with the Convention rights and to the fullest extent possible in all cases coming before them.

You would not expect me to leave this subject without touching on privacy.

I would not agree with any proposition that the courts as public authorities will be obliged to fashion a law on privacy because of the terms of the Bill. That is simply not so. If it were so, whenever a law cannot be found either in the statute book or as a rule of common law to protect a Convention right, the courts would in effect be obliged to legislate by way of judicial decision to make one. That is not the true position. If it were – in my view, it is not – the courts would also have in effect to legislate where Parliament had acted, but incompatibly, with the Convention. Let us suppose that an Act of Parliament provides for detention on suspicion of drug trafficking but that the legislation goes too far and conflicts with Article 5. The court would so hold and would make a declaration of incompatibility. The scheme of the Bill is that Parliament may act to remedy a failure where the judges cannot.

In my opinion, the court is not obliged to remedy the failure by legislating via the common law either wherever a Convention right is infringed by incompatible legislation or wherever, because of the absence of legislation – say, privacy legislation – a Convention right is left unprotected.

In my view, the courts may not act as legislators and grant new remedies for infringement of Convention rights unless the common law itself enables them to develop new rights or remedies. I believe that the true view is that the courts will be able to adapt and develop the common law by relying on existing domestic principles in the laws of trespass, nuisance, copyright, confidence and the like, to fashion a common law right to privacy. I say this because members of the higher judiciary have already themselves said so.

The experience of continental countries shows that their cautious development of privacy law has been based on domestic law case by case, although they have also had regard to the Convention. My view is that any privacy law developed by the judges will be a better law after incorporation of the Convention because the judges will have to balance and have regard to Articles 10 and 8, giving Article 10 its due high value.

Murray Hunt, 'The "Horizontal Effect" of the Human Rights Act'
[1998] *Public Law* 423, 438–42

It is clear beyond argument that *direct* horizontal application is not intended. This much is immediately apparent from the fact that the obligation to act compatibly with the Convention in section 6(1) of the Act is expressed to be binding only on public authorities, and that section 6 goes on to give examples of what is included in the definition of public authority. The clear implication is that there are persons who are *not* bound to act compatibly with the Convention at all; and indeed, by virtue of section 6(5), even the hybrid bodies made public authorities by section 6(3)(b), and therefore subject to the section 6(1) obligation, are not bound by the Convention in respect of those of their acts which are of a private nature. This inference, that the Act does not have direct horizontal effect, is further reinforced by the absence of any references to private individuals or organisations anywhere in the Act.

To put the matter beyond doubt, the Lord Chancellor, in his speech on Second Reading explaining the main provisions of the Bill, made clear that the Government had decided that:

> a provision of this kind [cl. 6(1)] should apply only to public authorities, however defined, and not to private individuals. That reflects the arrangements for taking cases to the Convention institutions in Strasbourg. The Convention had its origins in a desire to protect people from the misuse of power by the state, rather than from the actions of private individuals. . . . Clause 6 does not impose a liability on organisations which have no public functions at all.

Indeed, read in isolation, these explanatory comments about who is 'bound' by the Act might even be thought to give some sustenance to a vertical reading of the legislation's application. It is extremely important, however, that they are seen as precluding *direct* horizontal effect, rather than as endorsing a *vertical* approach. That this is the Government's intention is abundantly clear from the wider context provided not only by provisions in the rest of the Act, but by the parliamentary debates which preceded their adoption. In particular, the rejection of a purely vertical approach, and embrace of something more, is clear on the face of the provision that is without doubt the single most important feature of the legislation as far as determining the scope of its application is concerned: the express inclusion of courts and tribunals within the definition of public authorities obliged by section 6(1) to act compatibly with the Convention.

This inclusion of courts and tribunals in the definition of public authorities who are subject to the obligation in section 6(1) to act compatibly with the Convention is of great significance for the horizontality of Convention rights under the Human Rights Act. . . . [T]he effect of making courts expressly bound is to give a greater degree of horizontal effect to fundamental rights. . . .

It is true that there is no clause in the UK's Human Rights Act expressly saying that the Convention rights 'apply to all law', or some phrase capable of making clear that the common law is subject to the Convention. It is also true that the interpretive obligation contained in section 3(1) relates only to legislation and not to the common law. But neither of these could he characterised as significant omissions in view of the clarity about the overall purpose of the Act and the unequivocal nature of the obligation imposed on courts and tribunals by section 6. The whole scheme of the Human Rights Act is premised on the proposition that the only domestic law which is not to be subjected to Convention rights is legislation which cannot possibly be given a meaning compatible with Convention rights. The nature of the section 6(1) obligation on courts and tribunals is in keeping with that purpose. Whereas section 3(1) of the Act imposes an *interpretive* obligation on courts in relation to statute law, requiring courts to read and give effect to legislation in a way which is compatible with Convention rights, but subject to the limitation that the legislative language must be capable of bearing the meaning necessary to make it compatible, section 6 goes further. By making courts and tribunals 'public authorities' it imposes a *duty* on them to act compatibly with the Convention, including when they decide purely private disputes between private parties governed solely by the common law.

That this is the intention behind the inclusion of courts and tribunals in section 6(1) was confirmed in the strongest possible terms by both the Lord Chancellor and Lord Williams of Mostyn during the Bill's Committee stage in the House of Lords. An amendment was proposed by Lord Wakeham, the head of the Press Complaints Commission, designed specifically to preclude the possibility of the legislation having *any* horizontal effect. The amendment proposed that the obligation to act compatibly with the Convention in section 6(1) not apply 'where the public authority is a court or tribunal and the parties to the proceedings before it do not include any public authority'. Its purpose was avowedly to confine the Convention right to having vertical effect only: to prevent them being used by the courts in disputes between private individuals, and in particular 'to stop the development of a common law of privacy'.

The Lord Chancellor, responding at the end of the debate on this proposed amendment, left no doubt about the intention behind the inclusion of courts in section 6(1):

> We . . . believe that it is right as a matter of principle for the courts to have the duty of acting compatibly with the Convention not only in cases involving other public authorities but also in developing the common law in deciding cases between individuals. Why should they not? In preparing this Bill, we have taken the view that it is the other course, that of excluding Convention considerations altogether from cases between individuals, which would have to be justified. We do not think that that would be justifiable; nor, indeed, do we think it would be practicable.

Lord Williams similarly made clear, in response to a different amendment, the Government's view that courts and tribunals 'are in a very similar position to obvious public authorities, such as government departments, in that all their acts are to be treated as being of such a public nature as to engage the Convention'.

The explanatory statements leave no room for doubt as to the intention behind the inclusion of courts and tribunals within the definition of 'public authority' for the purposes of section 6(1). It is to ensure that all law, other than unavoidably incompatible legislation, is to be subjected to Convention rights, which thereby attain the all-pervasive status of which the White Paper boasts. There it is made explicit that the Convention rights 'will be brought much more fully into the jurisprudence of the courts throughout the United Kingdom, and their interpretation . . . far more subtly and powerfully woven into our law'. That is consistent also with the clear policy decision not to have a special court or separate procedure for human rights cases, but for the questions to be dealt with as they arise by the ordinary courts in ordinary cases. As Lord Irvine made clear in his Tom Sargant Memorial Lecture, the Government's explicit purpose in choosing the model it has introduced is that 'the Convention rights must *pervade all law* and all court systems'.

That a degree of horizontal effect in purely private disputes between private parties is explicitly envisaged by the Government is therefore without doubt, but that leaves one important question unanswered: how far towards full horizontality does it go? In particular, does it go beyond the present position, in which UK courts are undoubtedly free to 'take the Convention into account' when interpreting or developing the common law, or beyond even the indirect horizontal effect of the Canadian (and German) approach, in which courts are under an obligation to take human rights 'values' into account in interpreting the common law?

It seems quite clear that the model which has been chosen goes considerably further in the direction of horizontality than either of these. When the Act comes into force, courts will not merely have a power to 'consider' the Convention when interpreting the common law in private disputes. nor will they merely have an obligation to take into account Convention 'values'. Rather they will be under an unequivocal duty to act compatibly with Convention rights. In some cases, this will undoubtedly require them actively to modify or develop the common law in order to achieve such compatibility. Precisely where the line is drawn between legitimate judicial development of the common law and illegitimate judicial 'legislation' is a matter of degree and, ultimately, a matter of legal and political philosophy. The Lord Chancellor in the course of the parliamentary debates sought to indicate that courts will not be empowered by the Human Rights Act to go beyond their legitimate function of incremental common law development, for example by creating entirely new causes of action, for that would be to tread on Parliament's toes. But it remains to be seen whether judges will be as cautious as the Lord Chancellor envisages or more adventurous in plugging the gaps in the common law's scheme of remedies by imaginative analogising from existing causes of action.

The most likely position, then, is that the Convention will be regarded as applying to all law, and therefore as potentially relevant in proceedings between private parties, but will fall short of being *directly* horizontally effective, because it will not confer any new private causes of action against individuals in respect of breach of Convention rights. This requires a distinction to be drawn between the evolution of existing causes of action over time and the creation of entirely new causes of action against private parties. It is beyond argument that the Human Rights Act does not do the latter, but the courts will undoubtedly develop over time causes of action such as trespass, confidence, and copyright, as the Lord Chancellor himself accepted in Parliament. Law which already exists and governs private relationships must be interpreted, applied and if necessary developed so as to achieve compatibility with the Convention. But where no cause of action exists, and there is therefore no law to apply, the courts cannot invent new causes of action, as that would be to embrace full horizontality which has clearly been precluded by Parliament.

Douglas and Zeta Jones v *Hello! Ltd*
[2001] 2 WLR 992, Court of Appeal

D and Z signed a £1m deal with *OK!* magazine giving them the exclusive right to publish photographs of their wedding. *Hello!* magazine acquired secretly taken pictures of the wedding which they intended to publish. D and Z obtained an interim injunction restraining publication by *Hello!* On appeal by *Hello!* the Court of Appeal discharged the injunction as the balance of convenience was in favour of media freedom. However, the Court of Appeal held that D and Z had a right to privacy based on the doctrine of breach of confidence and the Convention right to privacy. D and Z's rights would be adequately protected by the remedy of damages if they succeed at the trial of the substantive action. The extract which follows is from the judgment of Sedley LJ who adopted the broadest approach being prepared to recognize a right to privacy without artificially manipulating the law on breach of confidence.

SEDLEY LJ: . . .

108. . . . I turn therefore to the main issues.

Is there today a right of privacy in English law?

109. The common law, and equity with it, grows by slow and uneven degrees. It develops react-ively, both in the immediate sense that it is only ever expounded in response to events and in the longer-term sense that it may be consciously shaped by the perceived needs of legal policy. The modern law of negligence exemplifies both senses.

110. The history of the law of confidence, however, while it displays many instances of the first kind of reactivity, has shown little of the second. The courts have done what they can, using such legal tools as were to hand, to stop the more outrageous invasions of individuals' privacy; but they have felt unable to articulate their measures as a discrete principle of law. Nevertheless, we have reached a point at which it can be said with confidence that the law recognises and will appropriately protect a right of personal privacy.

111. The reasons are twofold. First, equity and the common law are today in a position to respond to an increasingly invasive social environment by affirming that everybody has a right to some private space. Secondly, and in any event, the Human Rights Act 1998 requires the courts of this country to give appropriate effect to the right to respect for private and family life set out in art 8 of the European Convention for the Protection of Human Rights and Fundamental Freedoms . . . The difficulty with the first proposition resides in the common law's perennial need (for the best of reasons, that of legal certainty) to appear not to be doing anything for the first time. The difficulty with the second lies in the word 'appropriate'. But the two sources of law now run in a single channel because, by virtue of ss 2 and 6 of the Human Rights Act, the courts of this country must not only take into account jurisprudence of both the European Commission of Human Rights and the Euro-pean Court of Human Rights which points to a positive institutional obligation to respect privacy; they must themselves act compatibly with that and the other convention rights. This, for reasons I now turn to, arguably gives the final impetus to the recognition of a right of privacy in English law.

112. The reason why it is material to this case is that on the present evidence it is possible that the photographer was an intruder with whom no relationship of trust had been established. If it was a guest or an employee, the received law of confidence is probably all that the claimants need.

Common law and equity

113. Lawyers in this country have learned to accept that English law recognises no right of privacy. It was for this express reason that counsel for the actor Gorden Kaye instead put his case against the *Sunday Sport*, whose reporter and photographer had shamefully invaded the hospital room where Mr Kaye was recovering from serious head injuries, not as a breach of privacy, which it plainly was, but as a case of libel, malicious falsehood, trespass to the person and passing off. He managed only to hold an injunction to stop the paper claiming, by way of malicious falsehood, that Mr Kaye had voluntarily given an interview. But this court in *Kaye* v *Robertson* [1991] FSR 62 did not affirmatively consider and decide whether there is a right of privacy in English law. The court adopted – for it plainly shared – counsel's assumption that there was none. . . .

116. Nobody supposes that the members of the court which expressed this view were unfamiliar with the body of cases of which the best-known is *Prince Albert* v *Strange* (1849) 1 Mac & G 25, 41 ER 1171 or therefore that their assent to counsel's concession was *per incuriam*. But it is unhelpful now to speculate whether they would have maintained their view had the point been argued before them. The legal landscape has altered.

117. The argument would not have been that a right of privacy had been spelt out by the courts: plainly it had not. It would have been . . . that the tort of breach of confidence contains all that is necessary for the fair protection of personal privacy, and that it is now a relatively small step to articulate it in that way – as was done four years after *Kaye* v *Robertson* by Laws J in *Hellewell* v *Chief Constable of Derbyshire* [1995] 4 All ER 473 at 476, [1995] 1 WLR 804 at 807:

'I entertain no doubt that disclosure of a photograph may, in some circumstances, be actionable as a breach of confidence . . . If someone with a telephoto lens were to take from a distance and with no authority a picture of another engaged in some private act, his subsequent disclosure of the photograph would, in my judgment, as surely amount to a breach of confidence as if he had found or stolen a letter or diary in which the act was recounted and proceeded to publish it. In such a case, the law would protect what might reasonably be called a right of privacy, although the name accorded to the cause of action would be breach of confidence.'

118. This was of course obiter, but it has been understandably influential in the thinking of lawyers and commentators since it was said. The examples given by Laws J of invasions of privacy in the absence of some extant confidential relationship are taken from the speech of Lord Goff of Chieveley in *A-G* v *Guardian Newspapers Ltd (No 2)* [1988] 3 All ER 545 at 658–659, [1990] 1 AC 109 at 281:

'I realise that, in the vast majority of cases, in particular those concerned with trade secrets, the duty of confidence will arise from a transaction or relationship between the parties, often a contract, in which event the duty may arise by reason of either an express or an implied term of that contract. It is in such cases as these that the expressions "confider" and "confidant" are perhaps most aptly employed. But it is well-settled that a duty of confidence may arise in equity independently of such cases; and I have expressed the circumstances in which the duty arises in broad terms, not merely to embrace those cases where a third party receives information from a person who is under a duty of confidence in respect of it, knowing that it has been disclosed by that person to him in breach of his duty of confidence, but also to include certain situations, beloved of law teachers, where an obviously confidential document is wafted by an electric fan out of a window into a crowded street, or where an obviously confidential document, such as a private diary, is dropped in a public place, and is then picked up by a passer-by. I also have in mind the situations where secrets of importance to national security come into the possession of members of the public. . . .'

. . .

121. The cases in which the entitlement to the protection of confidences has been argued out are, in fact, numerous. [His Lordship briefly examined the case law which disclosed that the tort of breach of confidence was well established, before continuing.]

. . .

125. I would conclude, at lowest, that Mr Tugendhat [counsel for D and Z] has a powerfully arguable case to advance at trial that his two first-named clients have a right of privacy which English law will today recognise and, where appropriate, protect. To say this is in my belief to say little, save by way of a label, that our courts have not said already over the years. It is to say, among other things, that the right, grounded as it is in the equitable doctrine of breach of confidence, is not unqualified. As Laws J said in *Hellewell* v *Chief Constable of Derbyshire* [1995] 4 All ER 473 at 476, [1995] 1 WLR 804 at 807: 'It is, of course, elementary that, in all such cases, a defence based on the public interest would be available.'

126. What a concept of privacy does, however, is accord recognition to the fact that the law has to protect not only those people whose trust has been abused but those who simply find themselves subjected to an unwanted intrusion into their personal lives. The law no longer needs to construct an artificial relationship of confidentiality between intruder and victim: it can recognise privacy itself as a legal principle drawn from the fundamental value of personal autonomy.

127. It is relevant, finally, to note that no Strasbourg jurisprudence contra-indicates, much less countermands, the establishment in national legal systems of a qualified right of privacy; and that the courts of France and Germany, to take two other signatories of the convention, have both in recent years developed long-gestated laws for the qualified protection of privacy against both state

and non-state invasion (see Etienne Picard, 'The right to privacy in French law' in *Protecting Privacy*, ed Basil Markesinis (1999); Basil Markesinis, *The German Law of Torts: A Comparative Introduction* (3rd edn, 1994) pp. 63–66).

The Human Rights Act 1998

128. The Human Rights Act was brought into force on 2 October 2000. It requires every public authority, including the courts, to act consistently with the convention. What this means is a subject of sharp division and debate among both practising and academic lawyers: does it simply require the courts' procedures to be convention-compliant, or does it require the law applied by the courts, save where primary legislation plainly says otherwise, to give effect to the convention principles? This is not the place, at least without much fuller argument, in which to resolve such a large question. But some attitude has to be taken to Mr Tugendhat's submission that, whatever the current state of common law and equity, we are obliged now to give some effect to art 8, among other provisions, of the convention.

129. It is helpful, first of all, to see how much change he is soliciting. If he is right in his primary submission then the law is today adequately configured to respect the convention. If it is not – for example if the step from confidentiality to privacy is not simply a modern restatement of the scope of a known protection but a legal innovation – then I would accept his submission (for which there is widespread support among commentators on the Human Rights Act: see in particular Murray Hunt 'The "Horizontal Effect" of the Human Rights Act' [1998] PL 423) that this is precisely the kind of incremental change for which the Human Rights Act is designed: one which without undermining the measure of certainty which is necessary to all law gives substance and effect to s 6 of that Act [His Lordship quoted sub-sections (1), (2), (3) and (6) before continuing.] . . .

130. Such a process would be consonant with the jurisprudence of the European Court of Human Rights, which s 2 of the Human Rights Act requires us to take into account and which has pinpointed art 8 of the convention as a locus of the doctrine of positive obligation. Thus in *X v Netherlands* (1985) 8 EHRR 235 at 239–240 (para 23), the court said:

> 'The Court recalls that although the object of Article 8 is essentially that of protecting the individual against arbitrary interference by the public authorities, it does not merely compel the State to abstain from such interference: in addition to this primarily negative obligation, there may be positive obligations inherent in an effective respect for private or family life. These obligations may involve the adoption of measures designed to secure respect for private life even in the sphere of the relations of individuals between themselves.'

131. More immediately to the present point is s 12 of the Human Rights Act. [His Lordship quoted sub-section (1)–(5) before continuing.] . . .

132. There is no need to look at the parliamentary genesis of this section in order to see that it, with s 13 of the Human Rights Act, is of a different kind from the rest of the Act. It descends from the general to the particular, singling out one convention right and making procedural and substantive provision for litigation in which the right is directly or indirectly implicated. The convention right in question is the right to freedom of expression contained in art 10 . . .

133. Two initial points need to be made about s 12 of the Human Rights Act. First, by sub-s (4) it puts beyond question the direct applicability of at least one article of the convention as between one private party to litigation and another – in the jargon, its horizontal effect. . . . The other point, well made by Mr Tugendhat, is that it is 'the Convention right' to freedom of expression which both triggers the section (see s 12(1)) and to which particular regard is to be had. That convention right, when one turns to it, is qualified in favour of the reputation and rights of others and the protection of information received in confidence. In other words, you cannot have particular regard to art 10 without having equally particular regard at the very least to art 8 . . . :

134. Mr Carr QC [counsel for *Hello!*] was disposed to accept this; so far as I can see he had no choice, although it is perhaps unexpected to find a claimant relying on s 12 of the 1998 Act against a publisher rather than vice versa. But he balked at what Mr Tugendhat QC submitted, and I agree, was the necessary extension of the subsection's logic. A newspaper, say, intends to publish an article about an individual who learns of it and fears, on tenable grounds, that it will put his life in danger. The newspaper, also on tenable grounds, considers his fear unrealistic. First of all, it seems to me inescapable that s 12(4) makes the right to life, which is protected by art 2 of the convention and implicitly recognised by art 10(2), as relevant as the right of free expression to the court's decision; and in doing so it also makes art 17 (which prohibits the abuse of rights) relevant. But this in turn has an impact on s 12(3) which, though it does not replace the received test (or tests) for prior restraint, qualifies them by requiring a probability of success at trial. The gauging of this probability, by virtue of s 12(4), will have to take into account the full range of relevant convention rights.

135. How is the court to do this when the evidence – *viz* that there is and that there is not an appreciable risk to life – is no more than evenly balanced? A bland application of s 12(3) could deny the claimant the court's temporary protection, even if the potential harm to him, should the risk eventuate, was of the gravest kind and that to the newspaper and the public, should publication be restrained, minimal; and a similarly bland application of s 12(4), simply prioritising the freedom to publish over other convention rights (save possibly freedom of religion: see s 13 of the Human Rights Act), might give the newspaper the edge even if the claimant's evidence were strong. I agree with Mr Tugendhat that this cannot have been Parliament's design. This is not only, as he submits, because of the inherent logic of the provision but because of the court's own obligation under s 3 of the Act to construe all legislation so far as possible compatibly with the convention rights, an obligation which must include the interpretation of the Human Rights Act itself. The European Court of Human Rights has always recognised the high importance of free media of communication in a democracy, but its jurisprudence does not – and could not consistently with the convention itself – give art 10(1) of the convention the presumptive priority which is given, for example, to the First Amendment in the jurisprudence of the United States' courts. Everything will ultimately depend on the proper balance between privacy and publicity in the situation facing the court.

136. For both reasons, and in agreement with paras 150 to 154 of the judgment of Keene LJ and para 94 of the judgment of Brooke LJ, I accept that s 12 of the Human Rights Act is not to be interpreted and applied in the simplistic manner for which Mr Carr contends. It will be necessary for the court, in applying the test set out in s 12(3), to bear in mind that by virtue of s 12(1) and (4) the qualifications set out in art 10(2) of the convention are as relevant as the right set out in art 10(1). This means that, for example, the reputations and rights of others – not only but not least their convention rights – are as material as the defendant's right of free expression. So is the prohibition in art 17 on the use of one party's convention rights to injure the convention rights of others. Any other approach to s 12 would in my judgment violate s 3 of the Act. Correspondingly, as Mr Tugendhat submits, 'likely' in s 12(3) cannot be read as requiring simply an evaluation of the relative strengths of the parties' evidence. If at trial, for the reasons I have given, a minor but real risk to life, or a wholly unjustifiable invasion of privacy, is entitled to no less regard, by virtue of art 10(2), than is accorded to the right to publish by art 10(1), the consequent likelihood becomes material under s 12(3). Neither element is a trump card. They will be articulated by the principles of legality and proportionality which, as always, constitute the mechanism by which the court reaches its conclusion on countervailing or qualified rights. It will be remembered that in the jurisprudence of the convention proportionality is tested by, among other things, the standard of what is necessary in a democratic society. It should also be borne in mind that the much-quoted remark of Hoffmann LJ in *R v Central Independent Television plc* [1994] 3 All ER 641 at 652, [1994] Fam 192 at 203 that freedom of speech 'is a trump card which always wins' came in a passage which expressly qualified the proposition (as Lord Hoffmann has since confirmed, albeit extra-judicially, in his 1996 Goodman Lecture)

as lying 'outside the established exceptions (or any new ones which Parliament may enact in accordance with its obligations under the Convention)'. If freedom of expression is to be impeded, in other words, it must be on cogent grounds recognised by law.

137. Let me summarise. For reasons I have given, Mr Douglas and Ms Zeta-Jones have a powerful prima facie claim to redress for invasion of their privacy as a qualified right recognised and protected by English law. The case being one which affects the convention right of freedom of expression, s 12 of the Human Rights Act requires the court to have regard to art 10 of the convention (as, in its absence, would s 6 of that Act). This, however, cannot, consistently with s 3 of the Human Rights Act and art 17 of the convention, give the art 10(1) right of free expression a presumptive priority over other rights. What it does is require the court to consider art 10(2) along with art 10(1), and by doing so to bring into the frame the conflicting right to respect for privacy. This right, contained in art 8 and reflected in English law, is in turn qualified in both contexts by the right of others to free expression. The outcome, which self-evidently has to be the same under both articles, is determined principally by considerations of proportionality.

The injunction

. . .

139. . . . On the present evidence, whoever took the photographs probably had no right to be there; if they were lawfully there, they had no right to photograph anyone; and in either case they had no right to publicise the product of their intrusion. If it stopped there, this would have been an unanswerable case for a temporary injunction and no doubt in due course for a permanent one; perhaps the more unanswerable, not the less, for the celebrity of the two principal victims. Article 8 of the convention, whether introduced indirectly through s 12 or directly by virtue of s 6 of the Human Rights Act, will of course require the court to consider 'the rights and freedoms of others', including the art 10(1) right of *Hello!*. And art 10, by virtue of ss 6 and 12, will require the court, if the common law did not already do so, to have full regard to *Hello!*'s right to freedom of expression. But the circumstances in which the photographs must have been obtained would have robbed those rights and freedoms of substance for reasons which should by now be plain.

140. The facts, however, do not stop here. The first two claimants had sold most of the privacy they now seek to protect to the third claimant for a handsome sum. If all that had happened were that *Hello!* had got hold of *OK!*'s photographs, *OK!* would have proprietary rights and remedies at law, but Mr Douglas and Ms Zeta-Jones would not, I think, have any claim for breach of the privacy with which they had already parted. The present case is not so stark, because they were careful by their contract to retain a right of veto over publication of *OK!*'s photographs in order to maintain the kind of image which is professionally and no doubt also personally important to them. This element of privacy remained theirs and *Hello!*'s photographs violated it.

141. Article 8 of the convention, however, gives no absolute rights, any more than does the law of breach of confidence or privacy. Not only are there the qualifications under art 8(2); what para (1) requires is respect for, not inviolability of, private and family life. Taking it for the present that it is the state, represented by the court, which must accord that respect, what amounts to respect must depend on the full set of circumstances in which the intrusion has occurred. This intrusion was by uncontrolled photography for profit of a wedding which was to be the subject of controlled photography for profit.

142. Thus the major part of the claimants' privacy rights have become the subject of a commercial transaction: bluntly, they have been sold. For reasons more fully spelt out by Brooke LJ the frustration of such a transaction by unlawful means, if established, is in principle compensable in money, whether by way of an account of profits or damages. There is no reason in law why the cost to the wrongdoer should not be heavy enough to demonstrate that such activity is not worthwhile. The retained element of privacy, in the form of editorial control of *OK!*'s pictures, while real, is itself as

much a commercial as a personal reservation. While it may be harder to translate into lost money or an account of profits, it can readily be translated into general damages of a significant amount.
. . .

144. In the present case, and not without misgiving, I have concluded that although the first two claimants are likely to succeed at trial in establishing a breach of their privacy in which *Hello!* may be actionably implicated, the dominant feature of the case is that by far the greater part of that privacy has already been traded and falls to be protected, if at all, as a commodity in the hands of the third claimant. This can be done without the need of an injunction, particularly since there may not be adequate countervailing redress for the defendants if at trial they stave off the claim for interference with contractual relations. The retained element of the first two claimants' privacy is not in my judgment – though I confess it is a close thing – sufficient to tilt the balance of justice and conveni-ence against such liberty as the defendants may establish, at law and under art 10 of the convention, to publish the illicitly taken photographs.

Appeal allowed.

NOTE: In the case which follows the Family Division confirmed that the doctrine of confidence had developed into a privacy remedy, placing emphasis on the relevance of the Convention rights.

Thompson and Venables v *News Group Newspapers Ltd*
[2001] 2 WLR 1038, Family Division

T and V had been convicted as children of the murder of two-year-old James Bulger and sentenced to detention during Her Majesty's pleasure in 1993. They were protected by injunctions issued by the trial judge for an unlimited period restricting publication of further information about them. In July 2000, four newspapers applied to the court for clarification of the injunctions in light of T's and V's impending majority. Subsequently T and V issued the present pro-ceedings in which they sought injunctions against specific newspapers and all the world to protect all information about, *inter alia*, their whereabouts, movements, appearance and their new identities on release on the basis that such injunctions were necessary to protect their rights of confidentiality and their rights to life and freedom from persecution and harassment conferred by the European Convention. Dame Elizabeth Butler-Sloss P, granted permanent injunctions against all the world because of the disastrous consequences such disclosure might have for them, not least the serious possibility of physical harm or death.

DAME ELIZABETH BUTLER-SLOSS P:
. . .

C. The law: jurisdiction to grant an injunction
Application of the Convention
24 Before turning to the question of whether there is jurisdiction to grant injunctions, the pre-liminary issue is whether the Convention applies to this case. It is clear that, although operating in the public domain and fulfilling a public service, the defendant newspapers cannot sensibly be said to come within the definition of public authority in section 6(1) of the Human Rights Act 1998. Consequently, Convention rights are not directly enforceable against the defendants: see section

7(1) and section 8 of the 1998 Act. That is not, however, the end of the matter, since the court is a public authority (see section 6(3)) and must itself act in a way compatible with the Convention (see section 6(1)) and have regard to European jurisprudence: see section 2. In a private family law case, *Glaser* v *United Kingdom* [2000] 3 FCR 193, the European Court of Human Rights, sitting as a Chamber, declared admissible an application by a father seeking the enforcement of contact orders made in private law proceedings between him and the mother of his children. They considered the potential breach of the father's rights under article 8 and article 6. The court said, at pp 208–209, para 63:

> 'The essential object of article 8 is to protect the individual against arbitrary interference by public authorities. There may, however, be positive obligations inherent in an effective "respect" for family life. Those obligations may involve the adoption of measures designed to secure respect for family life even in the sphere of relations between individuals, including both the provision of a regulatory framework of adjudicatory and enforcement machinery protecting individuals' rights and the implementation, where appropriate, of specific steps (see among other authorities, *X and Y* v *The Netherlands* (1985) 8 EHRR 235 and mutatis mutandis, *Osman* v *United Kingdom* (1998) 29 EHRR 245). In both the negative and United Kingdom positive contexts, regard must be had to the fair balance which has to be struck between the competing interests of the individual and the community, including other concerned third parties, and the state's margin of appreciation (see, among other authorities, *Keegan* v *Ireland* (1994) 18 EHRR 342, 362, para 49).'

25 The court held that, in that case, the authorities, including the courts, struck a fair balance between the competing interests and did not fail in their responsibilities to protect the father's right to respect for family life. This decision underlines the positive obligations of the courts including, where necessary, the provision of a regulatory framework of adjudicatory and enforcement machinery in order to protect the rights of the individual. The decisions of the European Court of Human Rights in *Glaser*'s case and *X and Y* v *The Netherlands* (1985) 8 EHRR 235, seem to dispose of any argument that a court is not to have regard to the Convention in private law cases. In *Douglas* v *Hello! Ltd* [2001] 2 WLR 992, 1027, para 133, Sedley LJ held that section 12(4) of the Human Rights Act 1998 'puts beyond question the direct applicability of at least one article of the Convention as between one private party to litigation and another – in the jargon, its horizontal effect'.

26 In the light of the judgments in *Douglas*'s case, I am satisfied that I have to apply article 10 directly to the present case.

27 That obligation on the court does not seem to me to encompass the creation of a free-standing cause of action based directly upon the articles of the Convention, although that proposition is advanced by Mr Fitzgerald as a fall-back position, if all else fails. The duty on the court, in my view, is to act compatibly with Convention rights in adjudicating upon existing common law causes of action, and that includes a positive as well as a negative obligation.

The jurisdictional basis for an injunction

28 . . . The principal submission in favour of the existence of the court's power is based upon the law of confidence, taking into account the implementation of the Human Rights Act 1998. . . .

The jurisdiction based on confidence

30 As I have already said, in my view, the claimants in private law proceedings cannot rely upon a free-standing application under the Convention. In their submissions, the claimants, supported by the Attorney General and the Official Solicitor, relied upon the common law right to confidence. The tort of breach of confidence is a recognised cause of action. Megarry J in *Coco* v *A N Clark (Engineers) Ltd* [1969] RPC 41, 47, identified three essentials of the tort of breach of confidence: (1) the evidence must have 'the necessary quality of confidence about it'; (2) the information 'must have been imparted in circumstances importing an obligation of confidence'; (3) there must be an 'unauthorised use of the information to the detriment of the party communicating it'.

31 In *Attorney General v Guardian Newspapers (No 2)* [1990] 1 AC 109, 281 Lord Goff of Chieveley said:

'I start with the broad general principle (which I do not intend in any way to be definitive) that a duty of confidence arises when confidential information comes to the knowledge of a person (the confidant) in circumstances where he has notice, or is held to have agreed, that the information is confidential, with the effect that it would be just in all the circumstances that he should be precluded from disclosing the information to others . . . in the vast majority of cases . . . the duty of confidence will arise from a transaction or relationship between the parties . . . But it is well settled that a duty of confidence may arise in equity independently of such cases . . .'

32 He raised three limiting principles, at p 282:

'that the principle of confidentiality only applies to information to the extent that it is confidential. In particular, once it has entered what is usually called the public domain (which means no more than that the information in question is so generally accessible that, in all the circumstances, it cannot be regarded as confidential) then, as a general rule, the principle of confidentiality can have no application to it . . . The second limiting principle is that the duty of confidence applies neither to useless information, nor to trivia. There is no need for me to develop this point. The third limiting principle is of far greater importance. It is that, although the basis of the law's protection of confidence is that there is a public interest that confidences should be preserved and protected by the law, nevertheless that public interest may be outweighed by some other countervailing public interest which favours disclosure . . . It is this limiting principle which may require a court to carry out a balancing operation, weighing the public interest in maintaining confidence against a countervailing public interest favouring disclosure.'

33 The confidentiality sought to be protected in the present case is clearly not trivial. Lord Goff's third limiting principle cannot, I would respectfully suggest, now stand in the light of section 12 of the Human Rights Act 1998 and article 10(1) of the Convention, which together give an enhanced importance to freedom of expression and consequently to the right of the press to publish.

Article 10: freedom of expression

34 Article 10, as applied to the media, is central to this case. . . .

35 In section 12 of the Human Rights Act 1998, special provisions are made in relation to applications to restrict freedom of expression. Section 12(4) states: 'The court must have particular regard to the importance of the Convention right to freedom of expression . . .'

36 There is no doubt, therefore, that Parliament has placed great emphasis upon the importance of article 10 and the protection of freedom of expression, inter alia for the press and for the media. The Human Rights Act 1998 and the Convention do not, however, establish new law. They reinforce and give greater weight to the principles already established in our case law. In *R v Secretary of State for the Home Department, Ex p Simms* [2000] 2 AC 115, 126, Lord Steyn said:

'Freedom of expression is, of course, intrinsically important: it is valued for its own sake. But it is well recognised that it is also instrumentally important. It serves a number of broad objectives. First, it promotes the self-fulfilment of individuals in society. Secondly, in the famous words of Holmes J (echoing John Stuart Mill), "the best test of truth is the power of the thought to get itself accepted in the competition of the market": *Abrams v United States* (1919) 250 US 616, 630 per Holmes J (dissenting). Thirdly, freedom of speech is the lifeblood of democracy. The free flow of information and ideas informs political debate. It is a safety valve: people are more ready to accept decisions that go against them if they can in principle seek to influence them. It acts as a brake on the abuse of power by public officials. It facilitates the exposure of errors in the governance and administration of justice of the country: see Stone, Seidman, Sunstein & Tushnet, *Constitutional Law*, 3rd ed (1996), pp 1078–1086.'

[Her Ladyship also quoted from the judgments of Hoffmann LJ in *R v Central Independent Television plc* [1994] Fam 192, 202–204 and Munby J in *Kelly v British Broadcasting Corpn* [2001] 2 WLR 253, 264 before continuing.]

39 In *Sunday Times v United Kingdom* (1979) 2 EHRR 245 the European Court of Human Rights said, at p 281, para 65: 'The court is faced not with a choice between two conflicting principles, but with a principle of freedom of expression that is subject to a number of exceptions which must be narrowly interpreted.'

[Her Ladyship quoted extensively from the judgment of Sedley LJ in *Douglas v Hello! Ltd* [2001] 2 WLR 992, 1028–1029, paras 136–137 (*ante*, p. 516).]

41 In his Goodman Lecture on 22 May 1996, Lord Hoffmann referred to his judgment in *R v Central Television plc* [1994] Fam 192 and said:

'Some people have read that to mean that freedom of speech always trumps other rights and values. But that is not what I said. I said only that in order to be put [in] the balance against freedom of speech, another interest must fall within some established exception which could be justified under article 10 of the European Convention.'

42 Mr Desmond Browne [counsel for the defendants] submitted that it was not a balancing operation between the right to freedom of expression against any legitimate aim falling within article 10(2). It would seem to me however that, whether it is called a balancing process or any other description, the conflict that may arise between article 10(1) and article 10(2) has to be resolved and the legitimate aim in restricting freedom of expression within the exceptions in article 10(2) given appropriate weight according to the facts of the individual case. Sedley LJ said, in *Douglas*'s case, at p 1028G–H, para 136: 'the qualifications set out in article 10(2) are as relevant as the right set out in article 10(1)'.

43 There would not however be such a juggling act in a case which did not fall within the exceptions set out in article 10(2). It is clear however that, to obtain an injunction to restrain the media from publication of information, it requires a strong case. Brooke LJ said in *Douglas*'s case, at p 1006, para 49: 'Although the right to freedom of expression is not in every case the ace of trumps, it is a powerful card to which the courts of this country must always pay appropriate respect.' And Sedley LJ said, at p 1029, para 136: 'If freedom of expression is to be impeded . . . it must be on cogent grounds recognised by law.'

44 The onus of proving the case that freedom of expression must be restricted is firmly upon the applicant seeking the relief. The restrictions sought must, in the circumstances of the present case, be shown to be in accordance with the law, justifiable as necessary to satisfy a strong and pressing social need, convincingly demonstrated, to restrain the press in order to protect the rights of the claimants to confidentiality, and proportionate to the legitimate aim pursued. The right to confidence is, however, a recognised exception within article 10(2) and the tort of breach of confidence was the domestic remedy upon which the European Commission, in *Earl Spencer v United Kingdom* (1998) 25 EHRR CD 105, declared inadmissible an application by Lord and Lady Spencer on the basis that they had not exhausted their domestic remedies.

45 I turn to the three other articles of the Convention which are said by the claimants to be engaged in this case, and which clearly I must consider alongside article 10.

Article 2: right to life

46 If the claimants' case is made out, article 2 is clearly engaged. In *Osman v United Kingdom* (1998) 29 EHRR 245, the European Court of Human Rights held that the provisions of article 2 enjoined a positive obligation upon contracting states to take measures to secure the right to life. In that case it was the failure of the police to act to protect a family from criminal acts including murder. The European Court said, at p 305, paras 115–116:

> 'The court notes that the first sentence of article 2(1) enjoins the state not only to refrain from the intentional and unlawful taking of life, but also to take appropriate steps to safeguard the lives of those within its jurisdiction . . . it must be established to its satisfaction that the authorities knew or ought to have known at the time of the existence of a real and immediate risk to the life of an identified individual or individuals from the criminal acts of a third party and that they failed to take measures within the scope of their powers which, judged reasonably, might have been expected to avoid that risk.'

Article 3: prohibition of torture

47 Article 3 is equally potentially applicable, if I am satisfied as to the strength of the claimants' case. Other than in the specified exceptions in article 2, there is to be no derogation from the rights set out in these two articles.

Article 8: right to respect for private and family life

48 Article 8 is also potentially applicable. . . .

49 In *X and Y v The Netherlands* (1985) 8 EHRR 235, the European Court of Human Rights held that, in a case where the prosecutor took no action on a complaint by a father of a sexual assault on his mentally incapacitated daughter of 16, that the state had failed to protect a vulnerable individual from a criminal violation of her physical and moral integrity by another private individual. A violation of article 8 was found. The court said, at pp 239–240, para 23:

> 'The court recalls that although the object of article 8 is essentially that of protecting the individual against arbitrary interference by the public authorities, it does not merely compel the state to abstain from such interference: in addition to this primarily negative undertaking, there may be positive obligations inherent in an effective respect for private or family life. These obligations may involve the adoption of measures designed to secure respect for private life even in the sphere of the relations of individuals between themselves.'

[Her Ladyship quoted from Sedley LJ in *Douglas* v *Hello! Ltd* [2001] 2 WLR 992, 1027–1028, at paras 133–134 (*ante*, p. 515) before continuing.]

51 Although the Court of Appeal was concerned with an entirely different situation, the observations of Sedley LJ in *Douglas*'s case are highly relevant to and helpful in the task facing me in the present case where I have to resolve a potential conflict between article 10 on the one hand and articles 2, 3 and 8 on the other hand.

[Her Ladyship went on to examine the evidence upon which the claimants relied in support of the applications for permanent injunctions and the evidence adduced by the defendant newspapers.]

E. Conclusions on jurisdiction

75 My conclusions on the application of the principles of English law to the facts of this case, are based on the assumption that the case put forward by the claimants has been established.

76 I am, of course, well aware that, until now, the courts have not granted injunctions in the circumstances which arise in this case. It is equally true that the claimants are uniquely notorious. On the basis of the evidence presented to me, their case is exceptional. I recognise also that the threats to the life and physical safety of the claimants do not come from those against whom the injunctions are sought. But the media are uniquely placed to provide the information that would lead to the risk that others would take the law into their own hands and commit crimes against the claimants.

77 The starting point is, however, the well-recognised position of the press, and their right and duty to be free to publish, even in circumstances described by Hoffmann LJ in *R v Central Independent Television plc* [1994] Fam 192. As Brooke LJ said in *Douglas v Hello! Ltd* [2001] 2 WLR 992, it is a powerful card to which I must pay appropriate respect. I am being asked to extend the domestic law of confidence to grant injunctions in this case. I am satisfied that I can only restrict the freedom of the media to publish if the need for those restrictions can be shown to fall within the exceptions set out in article 10(2). In considering the limits to the law of confidence, and whether a remedy is available to the claimants within those limits, I must interpret narrowly those exceptions. In so doing and having regard to articles 2, 3 and 8 it is important to have regard to the fact that the rights under articles 2 and 3 are not capable of derogation, and the consequences to the claimants if those rights were to be breached. It is clear that, on the basis that there is a real possibility that the claimants may be the objects of revenge attacks, the potential breaches of articles 2, 3 and 8 have to be evaluated with great care.

78 What is the information sought to be protected and how important is it to protect it? The single most important element of the information is the detection of the future identity of the claimants in the community. All the other matters sought to be protected for the present, and for the future, are bound up in the risk of identification, whether by photographs, or by descriptions of identifying features of their appearance as adults, and their new names, addresses and similar information. That risk is potentially extreme if it became known what they look like, and where they are. The risk might come from any quarter, strangers such as vigilante groups, as well as the parents, family and friends of the murdered child. In the present case, the public authority, the court, has knowledge of the risk to the claimants. Does the risk displace the right of the media to publish information about the claimants without any restriction imposed by the court?

79 As I have set out, article 10(2) recognises the express exception, 'for preventing the disclosure of information received in confidence'. None the less, in order for it to be used to restrict freedom of expression, all the criteria in article 10(2), narrowly interpreted, must be met. Taking each limb in turn:

'In accordance with the law'

80 I am satisfied that, taking into account the effect of the Convention on our law, the law of confidence can extend to cover the injunctions sought in this case and, therefore, the restrictions proposed are in accordance with the law. There is a well-established cause of action in the tort of breach of confidence in respect of which injunctions may be granted. The common law continues to evolve, as it has done for centuries, and it is being given considerable impetus to do so by the implementation of the Convention into our domestic law. I am encouraged in that view by the observations of Brooke LJ in *Douglas*'s case, at p 1008, para 61:

> 'It is well known that this court in *Kaye v Robertson* [1991] FSR 62 said in uncompromising terms that there was no tort of privacy known to English law. In contrast, both academic commentary and extra-judicial commentary by judges over the last ten years have suggested from time to time that a development of the present frontiers of a breach of confidence action could fill the gap in English law which is filled by privacy law in other developed countries. This commentary was given a boost recently by the decision of the European Commission on Human Rights in *Earl Spencer v The United Kingdom* (1998) 25 EHRR CD 105, and by the coming into force of the Human Rights Act 1998.'

Keene LJ said at p 1035, para 165: 'breach of confidence is a developing area of the law, the boundaries of which are not immutable but may change to reflect changes in society, technology and business practice.'

81 The duty of confidence may arise in equity independently of a transaction or relationship between parties. In this case it would be a duty placed upon the media. A duty of confidence does already arise when confidential information comes to the knowledge of the media, in circumstances in which the media have notice of its confidentiality. An example is the medical reports of a private individual which are recognised as being confidential. Indeed it is so well known that medical reports are confidential that Mr Desmond Browne submitted that it was not necessary to protect that information by an injunction. It is also recognised that it is just in all the circumstances that information known to be confidential should not be disclosed to others, in this case by publication in the press: see Lord Goff in *Attorney General v Guardian Newspapers Ltd (No 2)* [1990] 1 AC 109. The issue is whether the information leading to disclosure of the claimants' identity and location comes within the confidentiality brackets. In answering that crucial question, I can properly rely upon the European case law and the duty on the court, where necessary, to take appropriate steps to safeguard the physical safety of the claimants, including the adoption of measures even in the sphere of relations of individuals and/or private organisations between themselves. Under the umbrella of confidentiality there will be information which may require a special quality of protection. In the present case the reason for advancing that special quality is that, if the information was published, the publication would be likely to lead to grave and possibly fatal consequences. In my judgment, the court does have the jurisdiction, in exceptional cases, to extend the protection of confidentiality of information, even to impose restrictions on the press, where not to do so would be likely to lead to serious physical injury, or to the death, of the person seeking that confidentiality, and there is no other way to protect the applicants other than by seeking relief from the court.

'Necessary in a democratic society to satisfy a strong and pressing need'

82 It is a very strong possibility, if not, indeed, a probability, that on the release of these two young men there will be great efforts to find where they will be living and, if that information becomes public, they will be pursued. Among the pursuers may well be those intent on revenge. The requirement in the Convention that there can be no derogation from the rights under articles 2 and 3 provides exceptional support for the strong and pressing social need that their confidentiality be protected.

'Proportionate to the legitimate aim pursued'

83 Although injunctions have not been granted in such circumstances in the past, I am satisfied that, to protect information requiring a special quality of protection, injunctions can be granted. I gain support for that conclusion from the judgment of Lord Woolf MR in *Broadmoor Special Hospital Authority v Robinson* [2000] QB 775, and the fact that over the past 30 years or so the jurisdiction of the court to grant injunctions, where it has been demonstrated to be necessary and in accordance with general equitable principles, has been exercised. The provision of injunctions to achieve the object sought must be proportionate to the legitimate aim. In this case, it is to protect the claimants from serious and possibly irreparable harm, which would, in my judgment, clearly meet the requirement of proportionality. As I have already said above, there is a positive duty upon the court to take such steps as may be necessary to achieve that aim. In *Osman v United Kingdom* (1998) 29 EHRR 245, the European Court of Human Rights held that a breach of articles 2 and 3 would be established if the authorities knew, or ought to have known, of the existence of a real and immediate risk to the life of an identified individual, from criminal acts of a third party, and they failed to take measures, within the scope of their powers, which might have been expected to avoid that risk. In that case, the authority was the police. In the present case, the authority is this court. I know of the existence of a real risk, which may become immediate if confidentiality is breached.

84 Lord Woolf MR said in *R v Lord Saville of Newdigate, Ex p A* [2000] 1 WLR 1855, 1867, para 37:

'when a fundamental right such as the right to life is engaged, the options available to
the reasonable decision-maker are curtailed. They are curtailed because it is unreasonable

to reach a decision which contravenes or could contravene human rights unless there are sufficiently significant countervailing considerations. In other words it is not open to the decision-maker to risk interfering with fundamental rights in the absence of compelling justification.'

With that warning from Lord Woolf MR in mind, in my judgment, the appropriate measures to be taken, within the scope of my powers, would be to grant injunctions. This would have the effect of substantially reducing the risk to each of the claimants.

85 I do not see that this extension of the law of confidence, by the grant of relief in the exceptional circumstances of this case, as opening a door to the granting of general restrictions on the media in cases where anonymity would be desirable. In my judgment, that is where the strict application of article 10(2) bites. It will only be appropriate to grant injunctions to restrain the media where it can be convincingly demonstrated, within those exceptions, that it is strictly necessary.

86 I am uncertain, for instance, whether it would be appropriate to grant injunctions to restrict the press in this case if only article 8 were likely to be breached. Serious though the breach of the claimants' right to respect for family life and privacy would be, once the journalists and photographers discovered either of them, and despite the likely serious adverse effect on the efforts to rehabilitate them into society, it might not be sufficient to meet the importance of the preservation of the freedom of expression in article 10(1). It is not necessary, however, for me to come to a conclusion as to the weight of a breach of article 8, since I am entirely satisfied that there is a real and serious risk to the rights of the claimants under articles 2 and 3. Subject, therefore, to my assessment of the strength of the evidence presented to the court, and the possibility that some protection less than injunctions might be proportionate to the need for confidentiality, I find that, in principle, I have the jurisdiction to grant injunctions to protect the claimants in the present case.

F. Conclusions as to future risk

87 The test of future risk is not to be based upon a balance of probabilities. In *Davies* v *Taylor* [1974] AC 207, the House of Lords was considering the possibility of a future reconciliation between the deceased and his estranged wife in a fatal accident claim by her. They held that the issue was not whether it was more probable than not that there would have been a reconciliation, but whether there was a reasonable probability or expectation, rather than a mere speculative possibility, of a reconciliation. There could be a reasonable expectation that something would come about even though the chance of it coming about was less than even.

88 In *In re H (Minors) (Sexual Abuse: Standard of Proof)* [1996] AC 563, the House of Lords considered the words 'likely to suffer significant harm' in section 31 of the Children Act 1989. Lord Nicholls of Birkenhead rejected the submission of counsel that likely in that context meant probable. He said, at p 585:

'In this context Parliament cannot have been using likely in the sense of more likely than not. If the word likely were given this meaning, it would have the effect of leaving outside the scope of care and supervision orders cases where the court is satisfied there is a real possibility of significant harm to the child in the future but that possibility falls short of being more likely than not . . . What is in issue is the prospect, or risk, of the child suffering *significant* harm . . . In my view therefore, the context shows that in section 31(2)(a) likely is being used in the sense of a real possibility, a possibility that cannot sensibly be ignored having regard to the nature and gravity of the feared harm in the particular case.' (Emphasis added.)

89 The decisions in *Davies v Taylor* [1974] AC 207 and in *In re H (Minors) (Sexual Abuse: Standard of Proof)*, although each made on facts far removed from the present, are in my view a helpful guide to the assessment I have to carry out in this case. Since the relief sought is to restrict the freedom of

expression of the press, I approach the assessment of future risk to each of the claimants on the basis that the evidence supporting the case has to demonstrate convincingly the seriousness of the risk, but in order to assess the future, I cannot by the very nature of the task, have concrete facts upon which to rely, nor can I predict upon the basis of future probability.

90 The evidence, which I have set out above, demonstrates to me the huge and intense media interest in this case, to an almost unparalleled extent, not only over the time of the murder, during the trial and subsequent litigation, but also that media attention remains intense seven years later. Not only is the media interest intense, it also demonstrates continued hostility towards the claimants. I am satisfied from the extracts from the newspapers: (a) that the press have accurately reported the horror, moral outrage and indignation still felt by many members of the public; (b) that there are members of the public, other than the family of the murdered boy, who continue to feel such hatred and revulsion at the shocking crime and a desire for revenge that some at least of them might well engage in vigilante or revenge attacks if they knew where either claimant was living and could identify him. There also remains a serious risk from the Bulger family, and the father was quoted as recently as October 2000 saying that upon their release he would 'hunt the boys down'; (c) that some sections of the press support this feeling of revulsion and hatred to the degree of encouraging the public to deny anonymity to the claimants. The inevitable conclusion to which I am driven, in particular, by the editorial from the 'News of the World' (one of the newspapers in the defendant group), is that sections of the press would support, and might even initiate, efforts to find the claimants and to expose their identity and their addresses in their newspapers.

. . .

94 I consider it is a real possibility that someone, journalist or other, will, almost certainly, seek them out, and if they are found, as they may well be found, the media would, in the absence of injunctions, be likely to reveal that information in the newspapers and on television, radio, etc. If the identities of the claimants were revealed, journalists and photographers would be likely to descend upon them in droves, foreign as well as national and local, and there would be widespread dissemination of the new names, addresses and appearance of the claimants. From all the evidence provided to me, I have come to the clear conclusion that if the new identity of these claimants became public knowledge it would have disastrous consequences for the claimants, not only from intrusion and harassment but, far more important, the real possibility of serious physical harm and possible death from vengeful members of the public or from the Bulger family. If their new identities were discovered, I am satisfied that neither of them would have any chance of a normal life and that there is a real and strong possibility that their lives would be at risk.

95 The claimants seek injunctions effectively for the rest of their lives. Is the grant of injunctions proportionate to the risk which I have identified? Mr Desmond Browne argued that the editors of the newspapers that he represented could be trusted not to reveal information that would lead to the identity of the claimants. Editorial judgment should be respected and trusted. That brings in the question whether it is necessary, in order to achieve anonymity, to require injunctions. Although I recognise that editors do exercise judgment and restraint in some of the stories they run, I do not consider that editorial restraint can be the answer here. I am prepared to believe that editors of some newspapers might well hesitate to reveal this information. I do not see how editorial judgment would be able to restrain all the newspapers, particularly those now calling for that information to be made available. I also find it difficult to accept the case of the newspapers that they should be trusted not to publish when, at the same time, their counsel submitted that it was wrong for the claimants to have the advantages of anonymity and to be allowed to live a lie. No offer has been made to the court not to publish. On the contrary, I am satisfied from the editorial in the 'News of the World' on 29 October 2000, that one newspaper at least would wish to publish information about identity or address if that information became available to them. Once one paper gives the information, all the papers will obviously be likely also to publish all the information they can obtain which

remains live news. The judgment of editors cannot be an adequate protection to meet the risk I have identified.

96 The Press Code, as applied by the Press Complaints Commission, is not, in the exceptional situation of the claimants, sufficient protection. Criticism of, or indeed sanctions imposed upon, the offending newspaper after the information is published would, in the circumstances of this case, be too late. The information would be in the public domain and the damage would be done. The Press Code cannot adequately protect in advance. The risk is too great for the court to rely upon the voluntary Press Code. To do so would not be a sufficient response to the principles enunciated in *Osman* v *United Kingdom* 29 EHRR 245. I do not consider that the provisions of the Protection from Harassment Act 1997 would or could be adequate to protect the claimants if their identities became known. Recourse to the courts after the event would be too late – for example because they would have by then, almost certainly, been photographed, and would then be recognised everywhere.

97 These uniquely notorious young men are and will, on release, be in a most exceptional situation and the risks to them of identification are real and substantial. It is therefore necessary, in the exceptional circumstances of this case, to place the right to confidence above the right of the media to publish freely information about the claimants. Although the crime of these two young men was especially heinous, they did not thereby forfeit their rights under English law and under the European Convention for the Protection of Human Rights and Fundamental Freedoms. They have served their tariff period and when they are released, they have the right of all citizens to the protection of the law. In order to give them the protection they need and are entitled to receive, I am compelled to grant injunctions.

G. The scope of the injunctions

Orders contra mundum

98 The submission of the defendants was, that even if there was jurisdiction to grant injunctions against them in this case, there was no jurisdiction to grant those injunctions against the world at large. The general principle was stated by Lord Eldon in *Iveson* v *Harris* 7 Ves 251, 257 'you cannot have an injunction except against a party to the suit'. The injunctive relief granted by Balcombe J in *In re X (A Minor) (Wardship: Injunction)* [1984] 1 WLR 1422 (the Mary Bell case), was based on the exercise of the court's jurisdiction in wardship. Balcombe J, in relation to the power to grant an injunction contra mundum, said, at p 1425: 'Let me say at once that, if it were not an exercise of the wardship jurisdiction, I am satisfied that there would be no such power.' He held that not only would it not be fair to injunct one newspaper from publishing information which could identify the ward by her relationship to the mother, Mary Bell, but that the harm to the ward, which prohibition of publication is intended to prevent, would also be caused by publication in any other newspaper or medium. He referred to *Z Ltd* v *A-Z and AA-LL* [1982] QB 558, in which the Court of Appeal held that *Mareva* injunctions operated against the world at large, or at least against those members of the public who have notice of the existence of the order. He was satisfied that, at p 1427: 'If the court can protect proprietary interests in that way, as it clearly can, how much more should it be able to protect the interests of its wards if it is satisfied in a proper case that the interests of its wards require protection in this form?'

99 In the present case I have come to the conclusion that I am compelled to grant injunctive relief for the protection of the claimants in respect of a special category of confidential information. For that information to be revealed by a newspaper or television programme, not a party to these proceedings, would have an equally devastating effect as disclosure by one of the defendant groups. It would cause equal harm. It would also, as Balcombe J recognised in *In re X (A Minor) (Wardship: Injunction)* [1984] 1 WLR 1422, be most unjust to the defendants if they were the only newspaper groups to be so restricted. The granting of the injunctions would not, however, have that limited effect. Mr Desmond Browne submitted that, since the decision of the House of Lords in *Attorney General* v *Times Newspapers Ltd* [1992] 1 AC 191, publication of the injunctions against the newspapers would, in practice, act in a similar way, and have the same effect, as injunctions against the media generally. He argued that it was not, therefore, necessary for the injunctions to be made against the world at large. It seems to me that to accept that position would be to achieve through the back door, that which it is submitted I cannot do through the front. I agree with Mr Caldecott that this is somewhat of an academic exercise. There is a *positive* duty on the court as a public authority to take steps to protect individuals from the criminal acts of others: see *Osman* v *United Kingdom* 29 EHRR 245.

100 Although the dictum of Lord Eldon in *Iveson's* case 7 Ves 251 has been generally followed for nearly 200 years, in light of the implementation of the Human Rights Act 1998, we are entering a new era, and the requirement that the courts act in a way that is compatible with the Convention, and have regard to European jurisprudence, adds a new dimension to those principles. I am satisfied that the injunctive relief that I grant should, in this case, be granted openly against the world.

. . .

The information to be protected

104 In my judgment, there are compelling reasons to grant injunctions to protect, in the broadest terms, the following information. (i) Any information leading to the identity, or future whereabouts, of each claimant, which includes photographs, description of present appearance and so on. (ii) In order to protect the claimants on their release from detention, it is necessary to have injunctions to protect their present whereabouts, any information about their present appearance and similar information. That protection must include any efforts by the media to solicit information from past or present carers, staff or co-detainees at their secure units until the claimants' release from detention. (iii) In order further to protect their future identity and whereabouts, no information may be made public or solicited from their secure units that might lead to the identification of the units for a reasonable period after their release. It would seem to me that 12 months from the date of the release of each claimant would be a sufficient period to protect that information, subject to any further argument from counsel. . . .

105 I am, of course, aware that injunctions may not be fully effective to protect the claimants from acts committed outside England and Wales resulting information about them being placed on the Internet. The injunctions can, however, prevent wider circulation of that information through the newspapers or television and radio. To that end, therefore, I would be disposed to add, in relation to information in the public domain, a further proviso, suitably limited, which would protect the special quality of the new identity, appearance and addresses of the claimants or information leading to that identification, even after that information had entered the public domain to the extent that it had been published on the Internet or elsewhere such as outside the United Kingdom. I am also aware that the Parole Board will soon be making inquiries and compiling a report for consideration at the Parole Board hearing. It is, in my view, essential that the nature of the inquiries, the content of the report and the hearing itself must be covered by the injunctions.

Injunctions accordingly.

NOTE: The above cases indicate that the courts will develop the law, in this case the law of confidence, to protect Convention rights. This does not involve new causes of action giving direct horizontal effect to the Convention between private parties, but rather applying (and developing) existing law in a way which is compatible with the Convention and the jurisprudence of the European Court of Human Rights. (See also *Wilson* v *First County Trust Ltd (No. 2)* [2001] EWCA Civ 633, *post*, p. 543.)

QUESTION

PeJay, a famous pop star, has become the victim of a stalker who has issued threats against him. PeJay secretly moves home and stops making public appearances.

Previously PeJay had courted publicity and had permitted various newspapers and magazines to have access to his previous home to photograph him and to do features on its design and décor. PeJay learns that the *Pop Today*, a magazine, has discovered details about his new home and is planning a feature which will use photographs previously published in a property magazine and a photograph of PeJay in the grounds of the home. This photograph was taken by a birdwatcher using a telephoto lens from a position on a public right of way running next to the boundary of PeJay's property. The birdwatcher sold the photograph to *Pop Today*. PeJay applies to the High Court for an injunction against *Pop Today* and all the world forbidding publication of his address and any details or photographs of his home or grounds claiming that such would breach his right to privacy and put his life at risk. How might the Court decide the issue? Would your answer differ if there was no stalker and PeJay had simply decided to retire and withdraw from public life?

(b) *How will the courts interpret legislation?*

1. Section 2(1) of the 1998 Act requires a court or tribunal to 'take into account' the jurisprudence of the European Court of Human Rights and the decisions of other specified Strasbourg bodies. In *R (on the application of Alconbury Developments Ltd) v Secretary of State for the Environment, Transport and the Regions, and other cases* [2001] UKHL 23, Lord Slynn of Hadley stated at para. 26:

   > Although the Human Rights Act 1998 does not provide that a national court is bound by these decisions it is obliged to take account of them so far as they are relevant. In the absence of some special circumstances it seems to me that the court should follow any clear and constant jurisprudence of the European Court of Human Rights. If it does not do so there is at least a possibility that the case will go to that court which is likely in the ordinary case to follow its own constant jurisprudence.

   Of course, the jurisprudence of the European Court of Human Rights may be neither clear nor constant, or it may be subject to interpretation. In *Alconbury* the House of Lords differed in its interpretation of the jurisprudence of the European Court of Human Rights from that of the lower courts. The same occurred in *Brown v Stott (Procurator Fiscal, Dunfermline) and Another* [2001] 2 WLR 817 (*post*, p. 551), where the Privy Council differed in its interpretation of the Strasbourg jurisprudence from that adopted by the High Court of Justiciary.

2. Section 3(1) of the 1998 Act requires courts to interpret all legislation, regardless of when it was enacted (and thus also of how it may have been interpreted previously), 'So far as it is possible to do so . . . in a way which is compatible with the Convention rights'. The New Zealand Bill of Rights Act 1990 contains a similar provision in s. 6, which reads: 'Wherever an enactment can be given a meaning that is consistent with the rights and freedoms contained in this Bill of Rights, that meaning shall be preferred to any other meaning.'

Lord Irvine of Lairg, 'Activism and Restraint: Human Rights and the Interpretative Process'

[1999] *European Human Rights Law Review* 350, 366–7

The Human Rights Legislation: A Constitutional Balancing Act

. . . The Human Rights Act is founded upon a division of functions between the different branches of government, which reflects the British conception of the separation of powers principle on which our constitution is based. Under the Act our courts have to interpret statutes 'so far as possible' to be compatible with Convention rights; if this is impossible they have been given a unique power to declare legislation to be incompatible, but then it is for the executive to initiate, and Parliament to enact, remedial legislation, with a fast track process available for that purpose. This balance which inheres in the text of the Act can be secured in practical terms only by a measured judicial response to the challenge of seeking, so far as is possible, to interpret national law consistently with the Convention.

If the courts were to adopt a very narrow view of this duty of consistent construction, their ability interpretatively to guarantee Convention rights would be severely curtailed. Instead of reading municipal law in a way which gave effect to individuals' rights, the courts would tend to discover irreconcilable conflicts between United Kingdom law and the Convention which would then require legislative correction. In contrast, a judiciary which took an extremely radical view of its interpretative duty would be likely to stretch legislative language, beyond breaking point, if necessary, in order to effect judicial vindication of Convention rights. Such an approach would yield virtually no declarations of incompatibility: the judges would, in effect, be taking it upon themselves to rewrite legislation in order to render it consistent with the Convention, and so excluding Parliament and the executive from the human rights enterprise.

Both of these approaches would be wrong. The constitutional theory on which the Human Rights Act rests is one of balance. It requires courts to recognise that they have a fundamental contribution to make in this area, while appreciating that the other elements of the constitution also have important roles to play in securing the effective protection of the Convention rights in domestic law. Thus the Act, while significantly changing the nature of the interpretative process, does not confer on the courts a licence to construe legislation in a way which is so radical and strained that it arrogates to the judges a power completely to rewrite existing law: that is a task for Parliament and the executive. The interpretative duty which the courts will soon begin to discharge in the human rights arena is therefore a strong one; but it is nevertheless subject to limits which the Act imposes, and which find still deeper resonance in the doctrine of the separation of powers on which the constitution is founded.

. . . A different, but related, challenge will arise once the Scottish Parliament begins to legislate. According to the Scotland Act 1998, s. 28(6), the courts must seek to avoid reaching the conclusion that Scottish legislation is invalid (on the ground of its being *ultra vires*) by construing it narrowly. Although this interpretative duty is different in nature from that which the Human Rights Act creates, the importance of balance will remain constant: the courts will have a fundamental contribution to make in seeking to ensure that the Scottish Parliament's legislation is effective (in the sense of being *intra vires*) while preserving the integrity of the distribution of legislative competence between Westminster and Edinburgh which the Scotland Act embodies. Thus, by utilising interpretative methodology to secure the protection of fundamental rights and the efficacy of Scottish legislation, both the Human Rights Act and the Scotland Act recognise that the interpretative process will be of central importance to the success of the constitutional reform programme.

R v *Secretary of State for the Home Department, ex parte Simms and Another*
[1999] 3 WLR 328, House of Lords

(For the facts of this case see *post* p. 594.)

LORD HOFFMANN: . . . Parliamentary sovereignty means that Parliament can, if it chooses, legislate contrary to fundamental principles of human rights. The Human Rights Act 1998 will not detract from this power. The constraints upon its exercise by Parliament are ultimately political, not legal. But the principle of legality means that Parliament must squarely confront what it is doing and accept the political cost. Fundamental rights cannot be overridden by general or ambiguous words. This is because there is too great a risk that the full implications of their unqualified meaning may have passed unnoticed in the democratic process. In the absence of express language or necessary implication to the contrary, the courts therefore presume that even the most general words were intended to be subject to the basic rights of the individual. In this way the courts of the United Kingdom, though acknowledging the sovereignty of Parliament, apply principles of constitutionality little different from those which exist in countries where the power of the legislature is expressly limited by a constitutional document.

The Human Rights Act 1998 will make three changes to this scheme of things. First, the principles of fundamental human rights which exist at common law will be supplemented by a specific text, namely the European Convention. But much of the Convention reflects the common law: see *Derbyshire County Council* v *Times Newspapers Ltd* [1993] AC 534, 551. That is why the United Kingdom government felt able in 1950 to accede to the Convention without domestic legislative change. So the adoption of the text as part of domestic law is unlikely to involve radical change in our notions of fundamental human rights. Secondly, the principle of legality will be expressly enacted as a rule of construction in section 3 and will gain further support from the obligation of the Minister in charge of a Bill to make a statement of compatibility under section 19. Thirdly, in those unusual cases in which the legislative infringement of fundamental human rights is so clearly expressed as not to yield to the principle of legality, the courts will be able to draw this to the attention of Parliament by making a declaration of incompatibility. It will then be for the sovereign Parliament to decide whether or not to remove the incompatibility.

NOTE: A number of appellate decisions have involved the courts in exploring the meaning of the interpretative obligation which s. 3 of the Human Rights Act 1998 places upon them. The impact of the section on the traditional approach to statutory interpretation is immense as indicated by the following extract from the judgment of Lord Woolf CJ in *Poplar Housing Association Ltd* v *Donoghue* [2001] EWCA Civ 595 (*ante* p. 504):

75 It is difficult to overestimate the importance of section 3. It applies to legislation passed both before and after the Human Rights Act 1998 came into force. Subject to the section not requiring the court to go beyond that which is possible, it is mandatory in its terms. In the case of legislation predating the Human Rights Act 1998 where the legislation would otherwise conflict with the Convention, section 3 requires the court to now interpret legislation in a manner which it would not have done before the Human Rights Act 1998 came into force. When the court interprets legislation usually its primary task is to identify the intention of Parliament. Now, when section 3 applies, the courts have to adjust their traditional role in relation to interpretation so as to give effect to the direction contained in section 3. It is as though legislation which predates the Human Rights Act 1998 and conflicts with the Convention has to be treated as being subsequently amended to incorporate the language of section 3. However, the following points, which are probably self-evident, should be noted.

    (a) Unless the legislation would otherwise be in breach of the Convention section 3 can be ignored (so courts should always first ascertain whether, absent section 3, there would be any breach of the Convention).

(b) If the court has to rely on section 3 it should limit the extent of the modified meaning to that which is necessary to achieve compatibility.

(c) Section 3 does not entitle the court to *legislate* (its task is still one of *interpretation*, but interpretation in accordance with the direction contained in section 3).

(d) The views of the parties and of the Crown as to whether a 'constructive' interpretation should be adopted cannot modify the task of the court (if section 3 applies the court is required to adopt the section 3 approach to interpretation).

(e) Where, despite the strong language of section 3, it is not possible to achieve a result which is compatible with the Convention, the court is not *required* to grant a declaration and presumably in exercising its discretion as to whether to grant a declaration or not it will be influenced by the usual considerations which apply to the grant of declarations.

The problem which courts confront however, is determining where the line is to be drawn between interpreting the legislation and legislating themselves. The bolder the interpretative approach is which the court adopts, the greater the risk that the line will be transgressed. Consider whether the House of Lords in the case which follows, by reading words into the statute in question to achieve compatibility, crossed the line.

Regina v *A (No. 2)*
[2001] UKHL 25, House of Lords

A, the defendant on a charge of rape, claimed that the complainant had consented to sexual intercourse. He sought leave under s. 41 of the Youth Justice and Criminal Evidence Act 1999 to adduce evidence and to ask questions relating to a claimed sexual relationship between himself and the complainant over the preceding three weeks. Section 41 had been enacted to protect complainants from intrusive and humiliating cross-examination and to correct two prevalent assumptions that 'unchaste women were more likely to consent to intercourse and in any event, were less worthy of belief'. The trial judge ruled that such questioning and evidence was not admissible as s. 41(3)(b) limited such evidence or questions to sexual behaviour of the complainant 'at or about the same time as the event which is the subject matter of the charge against the accused'. The Court of Appeal allowed A's appeal but gave leave to the Director of Public Prosecutions to appeal to the House of Lords and certified the following point of law of general public importance:

'May a sexual relationship between a defendant and complainant be relevant to the issue of consent so as to render the exclusion under section 41 of the Youth Justice and Criminal Evidence Act 1999 a contravention of the defendant's right to a fair trial?'

Their Lordships (Lord Hope of Craighead dissenting) did not consider that s. 41(3)(b) could be construed to permit questioning about sexual behaviour which was not contemporaneous with the act in question. However, applying the interpretative obligation under s. 3 of the 1998 Act which demanded that the court seek to ensure a fair trial for the accused under Article 6, s. 41(3)(c) (which permits questioning of the complainant about sexual behaviour alleged to have been so similar to any involved in the incident which formed the subject of the charge as to rule out coincidence) would be construed to admit evidence and questioning which is so relevant to the issue of consent that to exclude it would endanger the fairness of the trial.

LORD STEYN: . . .

V. Section 41

29. Sections 41 to 43 of the 1999 Act imposed wide restrictions on evidence and questioning about a complainant's sexual history. These provisions are contained in Chapter III of Part II of the statute and appear under the heading 'Protection of Complainants in Proceedings for Sexual Offences'. The material part of section 41 reads:

'(1) If at a trial a person is charged with a sexual offence, then, except with the leave of the court—

(a) no evidence may be adduced, and

(b) no question may be asked in cross-examination, by or on behalf of any accused at the trial, about any sexual behaviour of the complainant.

(2) The court may give leave in relation to any evidence or question only on an application made by or on behalf of an accused, and may not give such leave unless it is satisfied—

(a) that subsection (3) or (5) applies, and

(b) that a refusal of leave might have the result of rendering unsafe a conclusion of the jury or (as the case may be) the court on any relevant issue in the case.

(3) This subsection applies if the evidence or question relates to a relevant issue in the case and either—

(a) that issue is not an issue of consent; or

(b) it is an issue of consent and the sexual behaviour of the complainant to which the evidence or question relates is alleged to have taken place at or about the same time as the event which is the subject matter of the charge against the accused; or

(c) it is an issue of consent and the sexual behaviour of the complainant to which the evidence or question relates is alleged to have been, in any respect, so similar—

(i) to any sexual behaviour of the complainant which (according to evidence adduced or to be adduced by or on behalf of the accused) took place as part of the event which is the subject matter of the charge against the accused, or

(ii) to any other sexual behaviour of the complainant which (according to such evidence) took place at or about the same time as that event,

that the similarity cannot reasonably be explained as a coincidence.

(4) For the purposes of subsection (3) no evidence or question shall be regarded as relating to a relevant issue in the case if it appears to the court to be reasonable to assume that the purpose (or main purpose) for which it would be adduced or asked is to establish or elicit material for impugning the credibility of the complainant as a witness.

(5) This subsection applies if the evidence or question—

(a) relates to any evidence adduced by the prosecution about any sexual behaviour of the complainant; and

(b) in the opinion of the court, would go no further than is necessary to enable the evidence adduced by the prosecution to be rebutted or explained by or on behalf of the accused.

(6) For the purposes of subsections (3) and (5) the evidence or question must relate to a specific instance (or instances) of alleged sexual behaviour on the part of the complainant

534 Constitutional and Administrative Law

(and accordingly nothing in those subsections is capable of applying in relation to the evidence or question to the extent that it does not so relate).'

Section 41 imposes the same exclusionary provisions in respect of a complainant's sexual experience with the accused as with other men. This is the genesis of the problem before the House. . . .

VI. Sexual experience with the accused contrasted with sexual experience with other men

30. Although not an issue before the House, my view is that the 1999 Act deals sensibly and fairly with questioning and evidence about the complainant's sexual experience with other men. Such matters are almost always irrelevant to the issue whether the complainant consented to sexual intercourse on the occasion alleged in the indictment or to her credibility. To that extent the scope of the reform of the law by the 1999 Act was justified. On the other hand, the blanket exclusion of prior sexual history between the complainant and an accused in section 41(1), subject to narrow categories of exception in the remainder of section 41, poses an acute problem of proportionality.

31. As a matter of common sense, a prior sexual relationship between the complainant and the accused may, depending on the circumstances, be relevant to the issue of consent. It is a species of prospectant evidence which may throw light on the complainant's state of mind. It cannot, of course, prove that she consented on the occasion in question. Relevance and sufficiency of proof are different things. . . . It is true that each decision to engage in sexual activity is always made afresh. On the other hand, the mind does not usually blot out all memories. What one has been engaged on in the past may influence what choice one makes on a future occasion. Accordingly, a prior relationship between a complainant and an accused may sometimes be relevant to what decision was made on a particular occasion.

32. . . . Not surprisingly the legislative technique adopted in section 41 has been criticised. Professor Diane Birch ('A Better Deal for Vulnerable Witnesses?' [2000] Crim LR 223, 248), trenchantly commented:

'Under section 41, the complainant's sexual behaviour (including behaviour with the accused) has relevance to consent only where it took place at or about the same time as the event of the subject-matter of the charge, or where it is strikingly similar to behaviour of the subject-matter of the charge or to any other sexual behaviour alleged to have taken place at or about that time. All that can be revealed, it would seem, is evidence such as that the complainant was seen in a passionate embrace with the accused just before (or just after) the alleged offence; bizarre and unusual conduct like the much-discussed propensity to re-enact the balcony scene from *Romeo and Juliet*, and (perhaps) evidence that the complainant was picking up clients as a prostitute (if it is D's defence that he was so picked up). Along with all the complainant's other sexual doings, the remainder of the history of any sexual relationship the complainant has had with the accused will, it seems, have to be concealed from the jury or magistrates. It is not clear how this is to be done in a case where, for example the parties are living together: is the jury simply to be told what happened in the bedroom without any idea of whether D was a trespasser or an invitee? Presumably there will have to be some concept of background evidence that it is necessary for the jury to know in order to make sense of the evidence in the case.
'Section 41 is well-intentioned, but the constraints laid on relevance go too far. . . .'

It is difficult to dispute this assessment. After all, good sense suggests that it may be relevant to an issue of consent whether the complainant and the accused were ongoing lovers or strangers. To exclude such material creates the risk of disembodying the case before the jury. It also increases the danger of miscarriages of justice. These considerations raise the spectre of the possible need for a declaration of incompatibility in respect of section 41 under section 4 of the Human Rights Act 1998.

VII. The interpretation of section 41

34. In order to assess whether section 41 is incompatible with the convention right to a fair trial, it is necessary to consider what evidence it excludes. The mere fact that it excludes some relevant evidence would not by itself amount to a breach of the fair trial guarantee. On the other hand, if the impact of section 41 is to deny the right to accused in a significant range of cases from putting forward full and complete defences it may amount to a breach.

35. Counsel for the Secretary of State has argued that unfairness to an accused will rarely arise because evidence of sexual experience between a complainant and an accused will almost always be admissible on the basis of the defence that the accused thought that the complainant consented. His argument has assumed that in practice an accused will almost invariably be able to put forward both defences. Counsel for the defendant has persuaded me that the defence of belief in consent would often have no air of reality and would in practice not be available, eg in cases where there are diametrically opposite accounts of the circumstances of the alleged rape, with the complainant insisting that it was perpetrated with great violence and the accused saying that the complainant took the initiative in an act of consensual intercourse. In any event, it does not meet the difficulty that the judge's direction to the jury would always have to be to the effect that the past experience between the complainant and the accused is irrelevant to the issue of consent. I would reject the submissions of counsel for the Secretary of State on this point. In these circumstances counsel for the Secretary of State accepts that, despite the interlocutory nature of the proceedings, the House must now grapple with the problem whether, measured against the guarantee of a fair trial, the breadth of the exclusionary provisions of section 41 in respect of sexual experience between a complainant and the defendant are justified and proportionate. . . .

36. Counsel for the Secretary of State further relied on the principle that, in certain contexts, the legislature and the executive retain a discretionary area of judgment within which policy choices may legitimately be made: see *Brown v Stott* [2001] 2 WLR 817. Clearly the House must give weight to the decision of Parliament that the mischief encapsulated in the twin myths must be corrected. On the other hand, when the question arises whether in the criminal statute in question Parliament adopted a legislative scheme which makes an excessive inroad into the right to a fair trial the court is qualified to make its own judgment and must do so.

37. The methodology to be adopted is important. In a helpful paper under the title 'The Act of the Possible: Interpreting Statutes under the Human Rights Act' [1998] EHRLR 665 Lord Lester of Herne Hill QC has summarised the correct approach, at p 674:

> 'The first question the courts must ask is: does the legislation interfere with a Convention right? At that stage, the purpose or intent of the legislation will play a secondary role, for it will be seldom, if ever, that Parliament will have intended to legislate in breach of the Convention. It is at the second stage, when the Government seeks to justify the interference with a Convention right, under one of the exception clauses, that legislative purpose or intent becomes relevant. It is at that stage the principle of proportionality will be applied.'

. . .

38. It is well established that the guarantee of a fair trial under article 6 is absolute: a conviction obtained in breach of it cannot stand. *R v Forbes*, [2001] 2 WLR 1, 13, para 24. The only balancing permitted is in respect of what the concept of a fair trial entails: here account may be taken of the familiar triangulation of interests of the accused, the victim and society. In this context proportionality has a role to play. The criteria for determining the test of proportionality have been analysed in similar terms in the case law of the European Court of Justice and the European Court of Human Rights. It is not necessary for us to re-invent the wheel. In *de Freitas v Permanent Secretary of Ministry of Agriculture, Fisheries, Lands and Housing* [1999] 1 AC 69 Lord Clyde adopted a precise

and concrete analysis of the criteria. In determining whether a limitation is arbitrary or excessive a court should ask itself:

> 'whether: (i) the legislative objective is sufficiently important to justify limiting a fundamental right; (ii) the measures designed to meet the legislative objective are rationally connected to it; and (iii) the means used to impair the right or freedom are no more than is necessary to accomplish the objective.'

The critical matter is the third criterion. Given the centrality of the right of a fair trial in the scheme of the Convention, and giving due weight to the important legislative goal of countering the twin myths, the question is whether section 41 makes an excessive inroad into the guarantee of a fair trial.

39. Subject to narrow exceptions section 41 is a blanket exclusion of potentially relevant evidence. Section 41 must however be construed in order to determine its precise exclusionary impact on alleged previous sexual experience between the complainant and the accused. Two processes of interpretation must be distinguished. First, ordinary methods of purposive and contextual interpretation may yield ways of minimising the prima facie exorbitant breadth of the section. Secondly, the interpretative obligation in section 3(1) of the 1998 Act may come into play. It provides that 'so far as it is *possible* to do so, primary legislation . . . *must* be read and given effect in a way which is compatible with the Convention rights'. It is a key feature of the 1998 Act.

40. Three possible ways of minimising the excessive breadth of section 41 must be considered. The first possible gateway is to be found in section 41(3)(b) . . . An example covered by this provision would be where it is alleged that the complainant invited the accused to have sexual intercourse with her earlier in the evening. In my opinion, however, neither ordinary methods of interpretation nor the interpretative obligation under section 3 of the 1998 Act enables one to extend the temporal restriction to days, weeks or months. Section 41(3)(b) acknowledges by its own terms that previous sexual experience between a complainant and an accused may be relevant but then restricts the admission of such evidence by an extraordinarily narrow temporal restriction.

41. The second gateway suggested by counsel for the Director of Public Prosecutions is the provision in section 41(5)(b) enabling evidence adduced by the prosecution to be rebutted or explained by or on behalf of the defence. The suggestion is that the Crown could adduce evidence which will enable the defence to lead evidence of previous sexual experience in rebuttal. This is not a coherent and satisfactory solution. It depends on the goodwill and co-operation of the prosecutor. A defendant has the *right* in a criminal trial to offer a full and complete defence. I would reject this suggested solution.

42. The third gateway is section 41(3)(c) . . . This gateway is only available where the issue is whether the complainant consented and the evidence or questioning relates to behaviour that is so similar to the defence's version of the complainant's behaviour at the time of the alleged offence that it cannot reasonably be explained as a coincidence. An example would be the case where the complainant says that the accused raped her; the accused says that the complainant consented and then after the act of intercourse tried to blackmail him by alleging rape; and the defence now wishes to ask the complainant whether on a previous occasion she similarly tried to blackmail the accused.

43. Rightly none of the counsel appearing before the House were prepared to argue that on ordinary methods of interpretation section 41(3)(c) can be interpreted to cover, for example, cases similar to the one before the House where it is alleged that there was a previous sexual experience between the complainant and the accused on several occasions during a three week period before the occasion in question. Let me consider ordinary methods of interpretation in a little more detail. One could say that section 41(3)(c) is a statutory adoption of the striking similarity test enunciated in *R v Boardman* [1975] AC 421. So interpreted section 41(3)(c) is a narrow gateway, which will only be available in rare cases. Alternatively, one could argue that section 41(3)(c) involves the test of high probative force of the evidence, which makes it just to admit it, in accordance with the principle stated in *Director of Public Prosecutions v P* [1991] 2 AC 447. Even if this approach was consistent

with the language of section 41, the threshold requirement would be too high: often the evidence will be relevant but not capable of being described as having 'high probative value'. These ways of interpreting section 41(3)(c) cannot solve the problem of the prima facie excessive inroad on the right to a fair trial. It is important to concentrate in the first place on the language of section 41. Making due allowance for the words 'in any respect' in section 41(3)(c), the test 'that the similarity cannot reasonably be explained *as a coincidence*' is inapt to allow evidence to be admitted or questioning to take place that, for example, (i) the complainant invited the accused at an office party on a Friday to come to her flat on the Sunday to make love to her or (2) that the complainant and the accused had sexual relations on several occasions in the previous month. While common sense may rebel against the idea that such evidence is never relevant to the issue of consent, that is the effect of the statute. In my view ordinary methods of purposive construction of section 41(3)(c) cannot cure the problem of the excessive breadth of the section 41, read as a whole, so far as it relates to previous sexual experience between a complainant and the accused. Whilst the statute pursued desirable goals, the methods adopted amounted to legislative overkill.

44. On the other hand, the interpretative obligation under section 3 of the 1998 Act is a strong one. It applies even if there is no ambiguity in the language in the sense of the language being capable of two different meanings. It is an emphatic adjuration by the legislature: *R v Director of Public Prosecutions, Ex p Kebilene* [2000] 2 AC 326, per Lord Cooke of Thorndon, at p 373F; and my judgment, at p 366B. The White Paper made clear that the obligation goes far beyond the rule which enabled the courts to take the Convention into account in resolving any ambiguity in a legislative provision: see 'Rights Brought Home: The Human Rights Bill' (1997) (Cm 3782), para 2.7. The drafts-man of the Act had before him the slightly weaker model in section 6 of the New Zealand Bill of Rights Act 1990 but preferred stronger language. Parliament specifically rejected the legislative model of requiring a reasonable interpretation. Section 3 places a duty on the court to strive to find a possible interpretation compatible with Convention rights. Under ordinary methods of interpretation a court may depart from the language of the statute to avoid absurd consequences: section 3 goes much further. Undoubtedly, a court must always look for a contextual and purposive interpretation: section 3 is more radical in its effect. It is a general principle of the interpretation of legal instruments that the text is the primary source of interpretation: other sources are subordinate to it: compare, for example, articles 31 to 33 of the Vienna Convention on the Law of Treaties (1980) (Cmnd 7964). Section 3 qualifies this general principle because it requires a court to find an interpretation compat-ible with Convention rights if it is possible to do so. In the progress of the Bill through Parliament the Lord Chancellor observed that 'in 99% of the cases that will arise, there will be no need for judicial declarations of incompatibility' and the Home Secretary said 'We expect that, in almost all cases, the courts will be able to interpret the legislation compatibility with the Convention': Hansard (HL Debates), 5 February 1998, col 840 (3rd Reading) and Hansard (HC Debates), 16 February 1998, col 778 (2nd Reading) . . . In accordance with the will of Parliament as reflected in section 3 it will sometimes be necessary to adopt an interpretation which linguistically may appear strained. The techniques to be used will not only involve the reading down of express language in a statute but also the implication of provisions. A declaration of incompatibility is a measure of last resort. It must be avoided unless it is plainly impossible to do so. If a *clear* limitation on Convention rights is stated *in terms*, such an impossibility will arise: *R v Secretary of State for the Home Department, Ex p Simms* [2000] 2 AC 115, 132A–B per Lord Hoffmann. There is, however, no limitation of such a nature in the present case.

45. In my view section 3 requires the court to subordinate the niceties of the language of section 41(3)(c), and in particular the touchstone of coincidence, to broader considerations of relevance judged by logical and common sense criteria of time and circumstances. After all, it is realistic to proceed on the basis that the legislature would not, if alerted to the problem, have wished to deny the right to an accused to put forward a full and complete defence by advancing truly probative material. It is therefore possible under section 3 to read section 41, and in particular section 41(3)(c),

as subject to the implied provision that evidence or questioning which is required to ensure a fair trial under article 6 of the Convention should not be treated as inadmissible. The result of such a reading would be that sometimes logically relevant sexual experiences between a complainant and an accused may be admitted under section 41(3)(c). On the other hand, there will be cases where previous sexual experience between a complainant and an accused will be irrelevant, eg an isolated episode distant in time and circumstances. Where the line is to be drawn must be left to the judgment of trial judges. On this basis a declaration of incompatibility can be avoided. If this approach is adopted, section 41 will have achieved a major part of its objective but its excessive reach will have been attenuated in accordance with the will of Parliament as reflected in section 3 of the 1998 Act. That is the approach which I would adopt.

VIII. The task of trial judges

46. It is of supreme importance that the effect of the speeches today should be clear to trial judges who have to deal with problems of the admissibility of questioning and evidence on alleged prior sexual experience between an accused and a complainant. The effect of the decision today is that under section 41(3)(c) of the 1999 Act, construed where necessary by applying the interpretative obligation under section 3 of the Human Rights Act 1998, and due regard always being paid to the importance of seeking to protect the complainant from indignity and from humiliating questions, the test of admissibility is whether the evidence (and questioning in relation to it) is nevertheless so relevant to the issue of consent that to exclude it would endanger the fairness of the trial under article 6 of the convention. If this test is satisfied the evidence should not be excluded.

LORD HUTTON: . . .

161. In the type of case . . . where a man, who may be innocent, wishes to give evidence of previous acts of sexual intercourse with the complainant in the course of a recent close and affectionate relationship, such evidence would be a central and essential part of his defence, and I consider that to deny him the opportunity to cross-examine the complainant and to give such evidence would compromise the overall fairness of the hearing and would deny him the essence of a fair trial. In my opinion the right of a defendant to call relevant evidence, where the absence of such evidence may give rise to an unjust conviction, is an absolute right which cannot be qualified by considerations of public interest, no matter how well founded that public interest may be. . . . Therefore I would hold on ordinary principles of construction that section 41 is incompatible with the right to a fair trial given by article 6. . . .

162. Section 3(1) provides:

> 'So far as it is possible to do so, primary legislation and subordinate legislation must be read and given effect in a way which is compatible with the Convention rights.'

As my noble and learned friend Lord Steyn stated in *R* v *Director of Public Prosecutions, Ex p Kebilene* [2000] 2 AC 326, 366B, this subsection enacts a strong interpretative obligation, and Lord Cooke of Thorndon, at p 373F, described the subsection as an adjuration. It is clearly desirable that a court should seek to avoid having to make a declaration of incompatibility under section 4 of the 1998 Act unless the clear and express wording of the provision makes this impossible.

163. . . . I am in full agreement with the test of admissibility stated by my noble and learned friend Lord Steyn in paragraph 46 of his speech.

QUESTIONS

1. By implying into s. 41(3)(c) a provision 'that evidence or questioning which is required to ensure a fair trial under article 6 of the Convention should not be treated as inadmissible', have the majority gone beyond interpreting the legislation and, in effect, engaged in legislating?

2. Is the effect of the approach adopted by the majority, which seeks to avoid making declarations of incompatibility 'unless the clear and express wording of the provision makes this impossible', to treat s. 3 as a 'manner and form' entrenchment provision?

(c) *How do declarations of incompatibility operate?*

Where there is a conflict between Convention rights and primary legislation which cannot be resolved by an interpretation which renders the legislation compatible with the Convention, a court at the level of the High Court or above, may make a declaration of incompatibility (see s. 4(2) and (3)). Such a declaration has no impact, however, on the immediate proceedings; nor does it affect the validity or continuing enforcement of the impugned legislation (see s. 4(6)). As such the authority has not acted unlawfully and no remedies may be granted against it. The victim has, at best, a Pyrrhic victory. The declaration also casts the 'hot potato' into a politician's hands as the relevant Minister will then have to determine whether the incompatible legislation should be amended. He may use the fast track procedure in s. 10 and Sch. 2 to amend the legislation by means of a 'remedial order' which must be approved in draft by positive resolution of each House of Parliament. Should the Minister decide not to act (and there may be pragmatic political reasons for such a decision), the victim will have to resort to seeking to enforce his or her rights under the Convention machinery.

Sir William Wade QC, 'The United Kingdom's Bill of Rights' in *Constitutional Reform in the United Kingdom: Practice and Principles*
(1998), pp. 66–67

. . . Under clause 4 a declaration of incompatibility may be made by the court if it is satisfied that there is an unavoidable conflict between Convention rights and primary legislation; and the same is to apply in the case of subordinate legislation if it cannot be made compatible because of primary legislation. The declaration is not to affect the validity, continuing operation or enforcement of the offending provision, nor is it to be binding on the parties. But it may lead to a 'remedial order' amending the offending legislation which may be made by a minister of the Crown and must be approved in draft by positive resolution of each House of Parliament. There are, however, certain escape clauses. In case of urgency the Parliamentary resolutions may be dispensed with for up to 40 days. Furthermore, a minister may make a remedial order without a declaration by the court if it appears to him that a finding of the European Court of Human Rights produces an incompatibility with the UK's Convention obligations – a provision comparable to that of the European Communities Act 1972 under which ministers may amend legislation by Order in Council or regulations for the purpose of reconciling it with EU law.

A remedial order, like the provision of the European Communities Act, is an exceptionally drastic form of Henry VIII clause, of the kind that has recently worried the House of Lords' Delegated Powers Scrutiny Committee. It may well be the most drastic example yet seen, since it is expressly made capable of operating retrospectively, subject only to a ban on retrospective criminal liability. There is wide power to include 'such incidental, supplemental, consequential and transitional provisions' as may be thought appropriate by the minister and it may amend or repeal legislation, whether primary or subordinate, other than that containing the incompatibility. These extraordinary powers were the subject of protests in the House of Lords, Lord Simon of Glaisdale saying 'we cannot have Henry VIII trampling through the statute book in this way'. But, inevitably, such powers have to be accepted, however grudgingly, as part of the mechanism for adopting an external system of law, and in default of new and speedy Parliamentary procedures.

Reverence for the sovereignty of Parliament was the motive behind this remarkable amalgam of judicial and executive powers. But the sovereignty of Parliament is not what it was, having suffered severe diminution by its subjection to EU law. Lord Lester's earlier private member's bill had provided for the Convention rights to prevail over inconsistent legislation without intervention by the executive, but now he declared a change of mind and accepted the government's plan as 'an ingenious and successful reconciliation of principles of Parliamentary sovereignty and the need for effective domestic remedies' – though only, he added, 'after a good deal of arm-twisting by some members of this place rather more noble and learned than myself'. It is not surprising if the government resorted to some degree of intellectual harassment in order to secure the support of Lord Lester, with his immense experience and authority in this field.

If, then, a declaration of incompatibility is granted in some case, what is the likely result? A litigant has established that he ought to win his case because of the infringement of his human rights, but yet he loses it since the declaration does not affect the validity of the offending statute or regulation, or its enforceability. The appropriate minister must then consider whether to make a remedial order. It would seem inevitable that the court would grant a stay of execution while the minister considers whether to make an order, and whether it should be retrospective. If he makes a retrospective order, he deprives the victorious party of the fruits of his judgment. If he does not, he leaves the other party to suffer a violation of his human rights; and it is the same if the minister makes no order at all. The minister's position between these two fires is far from enviable. There may be a lot of money at stake and the government itself may be a party, so that the minister is compelled to be judge in his own cause. In such cases there is certain to be trouble in Parliament and a risk that the positive resolution will be opposed. There may be very difficult questions about the effect on third parties, even though clause 11 allows different provision to be made for different cases. It is hard to think of a more invidious position for a minister. And what, finally, about Article 6 of the Convention, which entitles everyone to a fair and public hearing by an independent and impartial tribunal in the determination of his civil rights and obligations? Will the Strasbourg court allow civil rights, and especially human rights, to be decided by discretionary executive order in this way? It seems highly unlikely.

In the House of Lords' second reading and committee debates there was no mention, I think, of the rule of law. Yet to allow questions of personal legal right to be decided by executive discretion offends against the rule of law in its most basic sense: the rule of law as opposed to the rule of discretionary power. Remedial orders will, indeed, be subject to judicial review and the Bill makes no attempt to exempt them. But the taking of human rights cases so far out of the course of ordinary law does not seem to be an adequately constitutional solution.

Geoffrey Marshall, 'Patriating Rights – with Reservations: the Human Rights Bill 1998' in *Constitutional Reform in the United Kingdom: Practice and Principles*
(1998) pp. 81–82

Assessing Incompatibility
. . . [T]wo different questions can be distinguished. In the first place, all reviewing courts have to adopt some view of the relation of their function to that of the legislature. What standard of review or degree of deference, or presumption of constitutionality is appropriate? Should it be different for different kinds of legislation and so on? In this respect, how should United Kingdom courts take into account decisions of the European Court of Human Rights as the Bill requires? That court has applied to national legislatures a relatively low standard of scrutiny under the rubric

of the margin of appreciation on the ground that state authorities are better able to judge national conditions and requirements than international judges. But that *rationale* does not apply within a state as between its legislature and judiciary. So in taking account of the decisions of the Strasbourg court, it would seem appropriate for British courts to subtract the effect of the margin of appreciation. In at least some cases this should lead to different and more activist decisions.

A second aspect of judicial review (or incompatibility assessment) relates to the substantive criteria that compatible legislation is required to meet. Here it can be seen that there are two analytically different, though sometimes confusingly related, reasons why a legislative provision might not contravene, or might not be incompatible, with the Convention. In the first place it might not be incompatible with an enumerated right because the Convention does not cover or relate to the disputed activity at all. A law restricting the use of firearms is not inconsistent with Convention rights, because nothing in the Convention guarantees the right to use firearms. In the second place, a legislative provision may be held to be compatible with the Convention because although the Convention is relevant and the disputed legislation appears to limit or impinge upon one or other of its rights, it is held to be a justified limitation in those cases where the Convention provides that limits may properly be imposed that are demonstrably justified by stated criteria or in a free and demo-cratic society (the criterion found in some Convention rights and whose wording has been adopted in the general limitation sections of the Canadian and New Zealand rights legislation). Such limits may be said to place a restriction on, or involve a modification of, a right in its unqualified form, but they do not constitute a denial, negation, abridgement, curtailment, contravention, infringement or violation of a right.

. . .

A question for the future is the status of the Human Rights Bill when the European Convention is formally embodied in the law of the European Union. Within the area covered by the Treaties, United Kingdom courts may then find themselves obliged to disapply British statutes incompatible with Convention rights embodied in Community law whilst holding themselves unable to do so when the same provisions are alleged to conflict with the Convention rights included in the United Kingdom Human Rights legislation. At that point, the government's attitude to judicial review will appear even more bizarre and indefensible.

Sydney Kentridge QC, 'The Incorporation of the European Convention on Human Rights' in *Constitutional Reform in the United Kingdom: Practice and Principles*
(1998), p. 69

Some speakers regard the provision in the Bill for declarations of incompatibility as an inadequate remedy against legislative infringements of fundamental rights. I regard it as a subtle compromise between the concepts of parliamentary sovereignty and fundamental rights. I believe, moreover, that declarations of incompatibility with primary legislation are likely to be rare, at least in relation to future legislation. There are two main reasons for this. The first, a very practical one, is that the individual litigant 'the victim' is likely to get little direct benefit from such a declaration. It is difficult to visualise a situation in which a lawyer will advise his client to go to court to seek a declaration of incompatibility. The second reason, a politico-legal one, is that Parliament, the executive and the courts will all strive to avoid the necessity for such declarations. The executive in introducing legisla-tion, and Parliament in passing it, will do their utmost to ensure that there is no incompatibility with the Convention. The courts in compliance with clause 3 will, so far as it is possible to do so, read and give effect to legislation in a way which is compatible with the Convention rights. The executive, as litigant, will also in most instances prefer a 'reading down' of contested legislation to a declaration of incompatibility.

QUESTIONS

1. If Kentridge is correct that the individual litigant is likely to get little direct benefit from a declaration of incompatibility, is this not a cause for concern? Further, if a victim of a violation of the Convention is blocked from obtaining an effective remedy, is this not a further breach of the Convention, namely Article 13? It should be noted that Article 13 is excluded from those rights which are incorporated by the Human Rights Act.

2. If a declaration of incompatibility is made in respect of a particularly controversial issue on which political opinion and public opinion are strongly divided, will a Minister implement the fast-track procedure to amend the offending legislation; and if he does so, will Parliament approve it? Would a government be acting unconstitutionally if it decided not to implement the fast-track procedure calculating that more political capital was to be made from inactivity?

3. What is the consequence of a statement by a Minister in charge of a Bill at Second Reading that although he is unable to make a 'statement of compatibility' the government nevertheless wishes the House to proceed with the Bill (see s. 19(1)) if the Bill is ultimately enacted and challenged before a United Kingdom court resulting in a declaration of incompatibility?

4. Is Marshall correct when he states that 'the Human Rights Bill contains a major contradiction of purpose and is attempting to marry two inconsistent principles of action. The rights principle is in essence anti-majoritarian. You cannot successfully combine the effective protection of rights against the majority with unfettered Parliamentary supremacy'?

NOTE: To date there have been few declarations of incompatibility. In *R (on the application of Alconbury Developments Ltd) v Secretary of State for the Environment, Transport and the Regions and other cases* [2001] UKHL 23, the Divisional Court made a declaration of incompatibility in respect of four planning cases on the basis that certain decision-making processes of the Secretary of State were incompatible with Article 6(1) of the Convention (*ante*, p. 466) as the Secretary of State, when hearing an appeal, could not be considered an impartial and independent tribunal as he would be applying his own policy guidelines. The House of Lords quashed the declarations of incompatibility on the basis that if the Secretary of State did not act impartially his decision could be subjected to judicial review which was now a sufficient remedy due to the need to consider proportionality (see further *post*, pp. 551ff). In *R (H) v London North and East Region Mental Health Review Tribunal* [2001] EWCA Civ 415, the Court of Appeal ruled that ss. 72(1) and 73(1) of the Mental Health Act 1983 were incompatible with Article 5(1) and (4) of the Convention (*ante*, p. 465). Where a patient applied to a mental health review tribunal to be discharged from detention in hospital, ss. 72 and 73 imposed a burden on the patient to establish that at least one of the criteria for his continued detention was no longer satisfied and thus to disprove the lawfulness of his own continuing detention. The Court of Appeal took the view that in order to comply with Article 5 the sections should, rather, require the tribunal to discharge the patient if it could not be shown by those detaining him that he was currently suffering from a mental disorder which warranted detention. The Court of Appeal found it impossible to give the sections a construction which would have made them comply with the Convention. Lord Phillips of Worth Matravers MR stated:

> 27. . . . It is of course the duty of the court to strive to interpret statutes in a manner compatible with the Convention and we are aware of instances where this has involved straining the

meaning of statutory language. We do not consider however that such an approach enables us to interpret a requirement that a tribunal must act if satisfied that a state of affairs does not exist as meaning that it must act if not satisfied that a state of affairs does exist. The two are patently not the same. If the requirements of the Convention can only be satisfied if the tribunal is required to order the discharge of a patient unless satisfied that the three criteria justifying admission are made out, sections 72 and 73 are incompatible with the Convention.

31. . . . [I]t is contrary to the Convention compulsorily to detain a patient unless it can be shown that the patient is suffering from a mental disorder that warrants detention. Inasmuch as sections 72 and 73 do not require the tribunal to discharge a patient if this cannot be shown we have concluded that they are incompatible with both article 5(1) and article 5(4). We think that this follows from the following statement of principle in the seminal case of *Winterwerp* v *The Netherlands* (1979) 2 EHRR 387, 403, para 39:

'In the court's opinion, except in emergency cases, the individual concerned should not be deprived of his liberty unless he has been reliably shown to be of "unsound mind". The very nature of what has to be established before the competent national authority – that is, a true mental disorder – calls for objective medical expertise. Further, the mental disorder must be of a kind or degree warranting compulsory confinement. What is more, the validity of continued confinement depends upon the persistence of such a disorder.'

The Court of Appeal issued the following declaration of incompatibility:

Declaration under section 4 of the Human Rights Act 1998 that sections 72(1) of the Mental Health Act 1983 are incompatible with article 5(1)(4) of the European Convention for the Protection of Human Rights and Fundamental Freedoms in that, for the mental health review tribunal to be obliged to order a patient's discharge, the burden is placed upon the patient to prove that the criteria justifying his detention in hospital for treatment no longer exist; and that article 5(1)(4) requires the tribunal to be positively satisfied that all the criteria justifying the patient's detention in hospital for treatment continue to exist before refusing a patient's discharge.

Under the power conferred by s. 10(2) of the Human Rights Act 1998, the Secretary of State for Health, Alan Milburn, made The Mental Health Act 1983 (Remedial) Order 2001, SI 2001 No. 3712, which substituted sections 72(1) and 73(1) and (2) into the Mental Health Act 1983. The new provisions provide that a Mental Health Review Tribunal shall direct the discharge of a patient if they are not satisfied that the criteria justifying his detention in hospital for treatment continue to exist. Thus those detaining the patient must prove the continuing lawfulness of his detention.

In *Wilson* v *First County Trust Ltd (No. 2)* [2001] EWCA Civ 633, the Court of Appeal held that s. 127(3) of the Consumer Credit Act 1974 was incompatible with Article 6(1) of the Convention (*ante*, p. 466) and Article 1 of the First Protocol to the Convention (*ante*, p. 468). W had borrowed £5,000 from FCT, a pawnbroker, on security of her BMW car. The credit agreement, which W signed, stated that the amount of credit was £5,250. The extra £250 was a document fee. W defaulted on the loan and FCT sought to enforce the security by seeking to sell the car. W sought a declaration, *inter alia*, that the loan agreement was unenforceable and an injunction to restrain FCT from selling the car. The trial Court ruled in favour of FCT but on W's appeal to the Court of Appeal, the court held that the agreement had been improperly executed as the amount of credit had been misstated as the extra £250, being a document fee, was not part of the sum lent. Section 65 of the 1974 Act provided that an improperly executed agreement could be enforced by court order but s. 127(3) provided that the court could not make such an order unless there was a document signed by the debtor and creditor in which the prescribed terms of the loan and the amount of credit had been correctly stated. This requirement applied even if the debtor had not been misled, taken advantage of or prejudiced. The Court of Appeal held that the restrictions which s. 127(3) placed on the enforcement of the creditor's contractual rights amounted to a breach of Article 6(1) and Article 1 of Protocol 1. The restrictions were imposed by the state and limited the citizen's right to peaceful enjoyment of his possessions and his right to a fair hearing in the determination of his civil rights. Although the case was one involving private individuals, the law controlling their relationship was the product of the state and it was this law which did not protect FCT's Convention rights. Sir Andrew Morritt V-C stated:

> 28. It is the restrictions on enforcement which engage article 6(1) of the Convention. The guarantee, in relation to the determination of a party's civil rights, of a fair and public hearing by an independent and impartial tribunal is of no substance if the outcome is determined by a statutory inhibition which not only prevents the court from doing what is just in the circumstances, but does so (a) in the context of a legislative scheme which gives the court a discretion to do what is just in other, very similar, circumstances and (b) for reasons which (if they exist at all) are wholly opaque. If there is some legitimate aim in pursuit of which the guarantee enshrined in article 6(1) needs to be wholly or partially curtailed, then it is necessary to ask whether the statutory inhibition is proportionate to that aim. Is there a proper balance between ends and means?

The Court of Appeal sought to discover from the parliamentary history of the Act whether there was any policy reason for denying the courts the power to do what was just in cases where there was no document signed by the debtor containing the prescribed terms (i.e. those terms which the Secretary of State prescribes must be contained in such a document), when there was such a power in other situations specified in the Act to permit the courts to do what was just. The Court could find no explanation for the distinction. While the policy aim of seeking to protect debtors was legitimate (i.e. the problems of inequality of bargaining power, use of small print and complex language to confuse debtors into signing disadvantageous agreements) the means used to achieve that aim were not legitimate as they were disproportionate in denying the creditor judicial enforcement of his contractual rights where the debtor had not been disadvantaged or prejudiced. There was no justification for this inflexible rule and no reason why the policy aim should not be achieved through judicial control by empowering the court to do what was just in the circumstances of the particular case. The Court, however, being unable to construe s. 127(3) in a way which would render it compatible with the Convention, made a declaration of incompatibility. It is worth noting that while the security remained unenforceable in the instant case, FCT's general interests as a pawnbroker will have been served by obtaining the declaration of incompatibility.

In *International Transport Roth GmbH and Others* v *Secretary of State for the Home Department* [2002] EWCA Civ 158, four groups of lorry drivers and haulage companies challenged the lawfulness of the fixed penalty scheme under Part II of the Immigration and Asylum Act 1999. This scheme imposed a fixed penalty of £2,000 for each clandestine entrant concealed in a vehicle regardless of whether there was any negligence or dishonesty on the part of the owner, hirer or driver but it was a defence for such person to prove, on the balance of probabilities, (i) that they were acting under duress; or (ii) (a) that they had neither actual nor constructive knowledge of the clandestine entrant; and (b) that there was an effective system for preventing the carriage of clandestine entrants, which (c) was operated properly on the occasion in question. There was an additional power, once a fixed penalty notice was issued, for an immigration officer to detain the vehicle if he considered there was a serious risk that the penalty would not be paid and no satisfactory alternative security had been given. The High Court ruled, *inter alia*, that the scheme was incompatible with the European Convention and the Home Secretary appealed. The Court of Appeal dismissed his appeal on this point holding that it was not possible to interpret the legislation in a way compatible with the Convention as major rewriting of the legislation would be required for this to be achieved and this would involve the Court transgressing the preserve of the legislature. The Court held, contrary to the contentions of the Home Secretary, that the scheme was criminal rather than civil and as such it breached Article 6 because of the combination of the reverse onus placed on the carrier combined with the vehicle detention provisions and the inflexibility of the substantial fixed penalties, and the fact that the Home Secretary was, in effect, judge in his own cause in determining (via immigration officers) on whom fixed penalty notices should be served. Simon Brown LJ stated (at para. 47):

47. . . . [T]he scheme taken as a whole . . . appear[s] . . . to me, quite frankly unfair. Insofar as the liability is suggested to be civil and not to involve moral culpability on the driver's part, the penalty far exceeds what any individual ought reasonably to be required to sacrifice in the interests of achieving improved immigration control. . . . But even assuming, as I do, that the scheme is directed towards punishing carriers for some fault, it cannot to my mind be right to impose so high a fixed penalty without possibility of mitigation. The hallowed principle that the punishment must fit the crime is irreconcilable with the notion of a substantial fixed penalty. It is essentially, therefore, on this account rather than because of the reversed burden of proof that I would regard the scheme as incompatible with Article 6. What in particular it offends is the carrier's right to have his penalty determined by an independent tribunal. To my mind there surely *is* such a right . . . . Sentencing is, like all aspects of the criminal trial, a function that must be conducted by an independent tribunal. If, as I would hold, the determination of liability under the scheme is properly to be characterised as criminal, then this fixed penalty cannot stand unless it can be adjudged proportionate in all cases having regard to culpability involved.

Jonathan Parker LJ stated (at paras 182–183):

182. In my judgment the reverse burden imposed by section 34(3) constitutes a disproportionate and unjustifiable inroad into the carrier's right of silence and hence into the presumption of innocence which is expressly safeguarded by Article 6(2).

183. I turn next to the penalty . . . . In considering the penalty in the context of Article 6, it seems to me that the degree of severity of the penalty must be a matter which falls within Parliament's 'discretionary area of judgment': in other words, it is [a] matter for Parliament and not for the courts. The courts are, however, concerned to ensure that the nature of the penalty is not such as to breach Article 6. In this context, the fact that the penalty is not merely severe but *fixed* seems to me to be of the highest importance. The fact that it is fixed means, by definition, that in imposing the penalty where liability has been determined no account can be taken of the facts of particular cases, or of the circumstances of a particular defendant. Nor is there any scope for mitigation. In particular, and most importantly (as it seems to me), there is no scope for recognising co-operation by a defendant in reporting the presence of clandestine entrants on his vehicle. In a number of the cases involved in this appeal drivers who, having entered the UK, discovered the presence of clandestine entrants in their vehicles, and who reported this fact to the police, found themselves facing substantial penalties. That seems to me not only absurd but wholly unfair. Moreover, the unfairness derives from the scheme itself, not from the way it is administered.

Further, the Court of Appeal found that the scheme breached Article 1 of the First Protocol to the Convention because the penalties imposed were disproportionate. Simon Brown LJ stated (at paras 52–53):

52. It is further implicit in the concept of proportionality, however, that not merely must the impairment of the individual's rights be no more than necessary for the attainment of the public policy objective sought, but also that it must not impose an excessive burden on the individual concerned . . .

53. . . . Even acknowledging, as I do, the great importance of the social goal which the scheme seeks to promote, there are nevertheless limits to how far the state is entitled to go in imposing obligations of vigilance on drivers (and vicarious liability on employers and hirers) to achieve it and in penalising any breach. Obviously, were the penalty heavier still and the discouragement of carelessness correspondingly greater, the scheme would be yet more effective and the policy objective fulfilled to an even higher degree. There comes a point, however, when what is achieved is achieved only at the cost of basic fairness. The price in Convention terms becomes just too high. That in my judgment is the position here.

Accordingly, the Court of Appeal issued a declaration pursuant to s. 4 of the Human Rights Act 1998 that the penalty scheme was incompatible with Article 6 of, and Article 1 of the First Protocol to, the Convention.

(d) *How will the Human Rights Act affect the way in which judges decide cases?*

Lord Irvine of Lairg LC, The Tom Sargant Memorial Lecture, 'The Development of Human Rights in Britain under an Incorporated Convention on Human Rights'
16 December 1997

The Emergence of a new approach

I have referred to the effect the introduction of European Community law has had on the development of our own domestic law. I believe that incorporating into our own law the Convention rights will have an equally healthy effect.

Any court or tribunal determining any question relating to a Convention Right will be obliged to take into account the body of jurisprudence of the Court and Commission of Human rights and of the Council of Ministers. This is obviously right. it gives British courts both the benefit of 50 years careful analysis of the Convention rights and ensures British Courts interpret the Convention consistently with Strasbourg. The British courts will therefore need to apply the same techniques of interpretation and decision-making as the Strasbourg bodies. I have already mentioned recourse to Parliamentary materials such as Hansard – where we are now closer in line with our continental colleagues. I will mention three more aspects. As I do so, it should be remembered that the courts which will be applying these techniques will be the ordinary courts of the land; we have not considered it right to create some special human rights court alongside the ordinary system; the Convention rights must pervade all law and all the courts systems. Our courts will therefore learn these techniques and inevitably will consider their utility in deciding other non-Convention cases.

First there is the approach to statutory interpretation. The tools of construction in use in mainland Europe are known to be different from those the English courts have traditionally used. I will refer to just one: the so-called teleological approach which is concerned with giving the instrument its presumed legislative intent. It is less concerned with the textual analysis usual to the common law tradition of interpretation. It is a process of moulding the law to what the Court believes the law should be trying to achieve. It is undoubtedly the case that our own domestic approach to interpretation of statutes has become more purposive. Lord Diplock had already identified this trend 20 years ago when he noted that:

> If one looks back to the actual decisions of the [House of Lords] on questions of statutory construction over the last 30 years one cannot fail to be struck by the evidence of a trend away from the purely literal towards the purposive construction of statutory provisions.

This trend has not diminished since then, although there are cases where the Courts have declined to adopt what was in one case described as an 'over purposive' approach.

Yet as the Courts, through familiarity with the Convention jurisprudence, become more exposed to methods of interpretation which pay more heed to the purpose, and less to whether the words were felicitously chosen to achieve that end, the balance is likely to swing more firmly yet in the direction of the purposive approach.

Secondly, there is the doctrine of proportionality . . . This doctrine is applied by the European Court of Human Rights. Its application is to ensure that a measure imposes no greater restriction upon a Convention right than is absolutely necessary to achieve its objectives. Although not identical to the principle as applied in Luxembourg, it shares the feature that it raises questions foreign to the traditional *Wednesbury* approach to judicial review. Under the *Wednesbury* doctrine an administrative decision will only be struck down if it is so bad that no reasonable decision-maker could have taken it.

Closely allied with the doctrine of proportionality is the concept of the margin of appreciation. The Court of Human Rights has developed this doctrine which permits national courts a discretion in the application of the requirements of the Convention to their own national conditions. This discretion is not absolute, since the Court of Human Rights reserves the power to review any act of a national authority or court; and the discretion is more likely to be recognised in the application of those articles of the Convention which expressly include generally stated conditions or exceptions, such as Articles 8–11, rather than in the area of obligations which in any civilised society should be absolute, such as the rights to life, freedom from torture and freedom from slavery and forced labour that are provided by Articles 2–4.

This 'margin of appreciation', was first developed by the Court in a British case, *Handyside* v *UK*. It concerned whether a conviction for possessing an obscene article could be justified under Article 10(2) of the Convention as a limitation upon freedom of expression that was necessary for the 'protection of morals'. The court said:

> By reason of their direct and continuous contact with the vital forces of their countries, state authorities are in principle in a better position than the international judge to give an opinion on the exact content of those requirements [of morals] as well as on the 'necessity' of a 'restriction' or 'penalty' intended to meet them . . .

Although there is some encouragement in British decisions for the view that the margin of appreciation under the Convention is simply the *Wednesbury* test under another guise statements by the Court of Human Rights seem to draw a significant distinction. The Court of Human Rights has said in terms that its review is not limited to checking that the national authority 'exercised its discretion reasonably, carefully and in good faith'. It has to go further. It has to satisfy itself that the decision was based on an 'acceptable assessment of the relevant facts' and that the interference was no more than reasonably necessary to achieve the legitimate aim pursued.

That approach shows that there is a profound difference between the Convention margin of appreciation and the common law test of rationality. The latter would be satisfied by an exercise of discretion done 'reasonably, carefully and in good faith' although the passage I have cited indicates that the Court of Human Rights' review of action is not so restricted. In these cases a more rigorous scrutiny than traditional judicial review will be required. An illustration of the difference may be found in the speech of Simon Brown LJ in *ex p Smith* (the armed forces homosexual policy case)

> If the Convention for the Protection of Human Rights and Fundamental Freedoms were part of our law and we were accordingly entitled to ask whether the policy answers a pressing social need and whether the restriction on human rights involved can be shown proportionate to its benefits, then clearly the primary judgement (subject only to a limited 'margin of appreciation') would be for us and not for others; the constitutional balance would shift. But that is not the position. In exercising merely a secondary judgement, this court is bound, even though adjudicating in a human rights context, to act with some reticence.

The question I pose is how long the courts will restrict their review to a narrow *Wednesbury* approach in non-Convention cases, if used to inquiring more deeply in Convention cases? There will remain distinctions of importance between the two categories of case which should be respected. But some blurring of line may be inevitable.

I have expressed my views in my Administrative Law Bar Association Lecture in 1995 on how the Courts ought properly to regard the dividing line between their function and that of Parliament. But the process is not one way. British influence on the application of the Convention rights is likely to increase. British officials were closely involved in the drafting of the Convention. When our British courts make their own pronouncements on the Convention, their views will be studied in other Convention countries and in Strasbourg itself with great respect. I am sure that British judges' influence for the good of the Convention will be considerable. They will bring to the application of the Convention their great skills of analysis and interpretation. But they will also bring to it our proud British traditions of liberty.

The Shift from form to substance

So there is room to predict some decisive and far reaching changes in future judicial decision making. The major shift may be away from a concern with form to a concern with substance. Let me summarise the reasons.

In the field of review by judges of administrative action, the courts' decisions to date have been largely based on something akin to the application of a set of rules. If the rules are broken, the conduct will be condemned. But if the rules are obeyed, (the right factors are taken into account, no irrelevant factors taken into account, no misdirection of law and no out and out irrationality) the decision will be upheld, usually irrespective of the overall objective merits of the policy. In some cases much may turn – or at least appear to turn – on the form in which a decision is expressed rather than its substance. Does the decision as expressed show that the right reasons have been taken into account? Does it disclose potentially irrational reasoning? Might the court's review be different if the reasoning were expressed differently so as to avoid the court's *Wednesbury* scrutiny?

Now, in areas where the Convention applies, the Court will be less concerned whether there has been a failure in this sense but will inquire more closely into the merits of the decision to see for example that necessity justified the limitation of a positive right, and that it was no more . . . of a limitation than was needed. There is a discernible shift which may be seen in essence as a shift from form to substance. If, as I have suggested, there is a spillover into other areas of law, then that shift from form to substance will become more marked.

This may be seen as a progression of an existing and now long standing trend. In modern times, the emphasis on identifying the true substance at issue has been seen in diverse areas: in tax where new techniques have developed to view the substance of a transaction overall rather than to be mesmerised by the form of an isolated step, or in the areas of statutory control of leases, where the Courts are astute to prevent form being used to obscure the reality of the underlying transaction. In what may seem at first blush a very different area, that of interpretation of contracts, recent decisions also emphasise the need to cast away the baggage of older years where literal and semantic analysis was allowed to override the real intent of the parties.

In a very broad sense we can see here a similarity of approach: to get to the substance of the issue and not be distracted by the form.

These are trends already well developed but I believe they will gain impetus from incorporation of the Convention. In addition the Courts will be making decisions founded more explicitly and frequently on considerations of morality and justifiability.

This Bill will therefore create a more explicitly moral approach to decisions and decision making; will promote both a culture where positive rights and liberties become the focus and concern of legislators, administrators and judges alike; and a culture in judicial decision making where there will be a greater concentration on substance rather than form.

. . .

Peter Duffy QC, 'The European Convention on Human Rights, Issues Relating to its Interpretation in the Light of the Human Rights Bill' in *Constitutional Reform in the United Kingdom: Practice and Principles*

(1998), pp. 100–102

Several of the rights in the Convention, notably Article 8 (right to respect for private and family life, home and correspondence), Article 9 (freedom of thought, conscience and religion), Article 10 (freedom of expression) and Article 11 (freedom of assembly and association) are stated in general terms in a first paragraph and can be subject to restrictions in the interests of other legitimate interests provided such restriction is regulated by the law and is, in the language of the Convention, 'necessary in a democratic society'. The case law of the Court provides well established guidance on the approach to be taken.

First, a generous approach is to be taken when determining what comes within the scope of the protected fundamental rights. The Court has pointed out that to construe the scope of the rights protected broadly is consonant with the essential object and purpose of the ECHR [*Niemietz* v *Germany* 16 EHRR 97, para. 31] which, of course, is 'an instrument for the protection of individual human beings', accordingly 'its provisions [should] be interpreted and applied so as to make its safeguards practical and effective' [*Loizidou* v *Turkey*, 20 EHRR 99, para. 71]. Adopting a narrow construction of the rights protected risks denying Convention scrutiny in cases where a fundamental right may be affected, albeit indirectly. The Court has rightly stressed that giving a broad construction to the rights protected does not unduly hamper public bodies for they retain their entitlement to 'interfere' provided the conditions of the Convention are respected [*Niemietz*, para. 31].

The conditions under which restrictions are permitted vary somewhat from right to right but important underlying principles are well established in the Court's case law and practice. For an interference to be justified, four conditions must be fulfilled. These are that (1) the interference is 'lawful', (ii) it serves a legitimate purpose, (iii) it is 'necessary in a democratic society'; and (iv) it is not discriminatory. Each of these requirements is outlined in turn below.

First, the lawfulness requirement, this does not merely mean that interference with a fundamental right is permitted under domestic law. The Court has consistently stated that 'it [is] contrary to the rule of law for the legal discretion granted to the executive to be in the form of unfettered power':

> The law must indicate the scope of any such discretion conferred on the competent authorities and the manner of its exercise with sufficient clarity, having regard to the legitimate aim of the measure in question, to give the individual adequate protection against arbitrary interference [*Malone* v *United Kingdom* (1985) 7 EHRR 14, para. 68].

The condition of 'lawfulness' is unlikely to detain British courts much where legislation circumscribes the powers of public authorities. Where it will make a difference, once the Human Rights Act enters into force, is to the Diceyan rule of law concept that public bodies are permitted to do anything which is not specifically prohibited by law. This has led in a number of cases to British courts being unable to provide redress when intrusive powers were unregulated. In *Malone* v *Metropolitan Police Commissioner (No 2)* [[1979] 1 Ch 344 at 380], Sir Robert Megarry V-C described interception of communications as 'a subject which cries out for legislation' yet, without ECHR incorporation and under the old concept of the rule of law, he could not provide relief. The case proceeded to Strasbourg and the finding, as Sir Robert had predicted, that English law then failed to provide 'the minimum degree of legal protection to which citizens are entitled under the rule of law in a democratic society.'

The second condition is that the reason for an interference is a proper one. In very few cases under the ECHR has an improper purpose been shown. In the vast majority of cases, it is common ground that the public authority had a proper purpose. Forensic and judicial attention focuses instead on the third and fourth conditions, namely whether the interference for a proper purpose was 'necessary in a democratic society' and was done without any impermissible discrimination.

For an interference to be 'necessary in a democratic society', the courts must be satisfied that the public body can convincingly demonstrate the need for the interference and that the interference is 'fair'.

The fourth and final condition to mention is that any action undertaken by public bodies which gives effect to or interferes with Convention rights and freedoms must be done in a non-discriminatory manner. Not every difference of treatment amounts to discrimination. Discrimination occurs if 'the distinction has no objectives and reasonable justification' [*Belgian Linguistic* (1968) 1 EHRR 252, para. 10]. Checking this requirement also involves testing proportionality, similar to considering 'necessity in a democratic society'. This is not surprising as unjustified discrimination cannot sensibly be described as necessary in a democratic society. It is worth emphasising, however, that some grounds of distinction, particularly race or gender, cannot normally be accepted and that discriminatory treatment on such grounds is regarded as especially serious and that it can rarely be accepted and must be particularly closely scrutinised. This represents a significant change from the piece-meal protection against discrimination in existing British legislative schemes.

For incorporation to be effective, as Parliament intends, British courts will have to engage in an effective control of the reasons given for interference and their sufficiency. The courts have already emphasised that greater scrutiny is needed when fundamental rights are in play. In *R v Ministry of Defence, ex parte Smith* [[1996] QB 517], the case on dismissal of homosexuals and lesbians from the armed services, Sir Thomas Bingham MR (as he then was) stated [at p. 554] that:

> The court may not interfere with the exercise of an administrative discretion on substantive grounds save where the court is satisfied that the decision is unreasonable in the sense that it is beyond the range of responses open to a reasonable decision maker. But in judging whether the decision maker has exceeded this margin of appreciation the human rights context is important. The more substantial the interference with human rights, the more the court will require by way of justification before it is satisfied that the decision is reasonable in the sense outlined above.

For ECHR incorporation to be effective, the British courts in such cases will have to go beyond a heightened *Wednesbury* review, whilst still respecting the decision making discretion of the primary decision maker. The Lord Chancellor again explained this point with clarity in his 1997 Tom Sargant Lecture. In striking the balance, the Convention's case law uses phrases such as 'fair balance' and 'proportionate'. Domestic courts, of course, frequently exercise discretion that call for decisions on what is fair and reasonable in all circumstances. That experience, including that of applying principles of equity, can be drawn upon in ensuring that incorporation is made effective.

NOTE: Section 2(1) of the Human Rights Act 1998 requires a court when determining an issue relating to a Convention right to take into account any relevant jurisprudence from the European Court of Human Rights. Such decisions are not, however, binding – they simply have to be considered – but the Convention rights are binding. In arriving at their decisions the European Court of Human Rights has developed the doctrine of the margin of appreciation (see *ante*, p. 472) to reflect diversity within Europe and also the fact that the Court is performing a supervisory function as the primary responsibility for ensuring that human rights are protected lies with the state. Could the courts within a state seek to apply or develop their own version of the doctrine of margin of appreciation? Sir John Laws, 'The Limitations of Human Rights' [1998] *Public Law* 254, at 258, states:

> The margin of appreciation . . . will necessarily be inapt to the administration of the Convention in the domestic courts for the very reason that they are domestic; they will not be subject to an objective inhibition generated by any cultural distance between themselves and the state organs whose decisions are impleaded before them.

There is a possibility, however, that Convention rights may be diluted if courts show undue deference to Parliament or the Executive or if they ignore the influence of the doctrine on decisions of the European Court of Human Rights when considering their relevance to the United Kingdom. That there is a notion of judicial deference is evidenced by dicta in several cases. In *R v Director of Public Prosecutions, ex parte Kebilene and Others* [2000] 2 AC 326, Lord Hope stated:

> [The doctrine of margin of appreciation] is an integral part of the supervisory jurisdiction which is exercised over state conduct by the international court. By conceding a margin of appreciation to each national system, the court has recognised that the Convention, as a living system, does not need to be applied uniformly by all states but may vary in its application according to local needs and conditions. This technique is not available to the national courts when they are considering Convention issues arising within their own countries. But in the hands of the national courts also the Convention should be seen as an expression of fundamental principles rather than as a set of mere rules. The question which the courts will

have to decide in the application of these principles will involve questions of balance between competing interests and issues of proportionality.

In this area difficult choices may have to be made by the executive or the legislature between the rights of the individual and the needs of society. In some circumstances it will be appropriate for the courts to recognise that there is an area of judgment within which the judiciary will defer, on democratic grounds, to the considered opinion of the elected body or person whose act or decision is said to be incompatible with the Convention. This point is well made at p. 74, para 3.21 of *Human Rights Law and Practice* (1999) . . . where the area in which these choices may arise is conveniently and appropriately described as the 'discretionary area of judgment'. It will be easier for such an area of judgment to be recognised where the Convention itself requires a balance to be struck, much less so where the right is stated in terms which are unqualified. It will be easier for it to be recognised where the issues involve questions of social or economic policy, much less so where the rights are of high constitutional importance or are of a kind where the courts are especially well placed to assess the need for protection.

In *R v Lambert, Ali and Jordan* [2001] 1 All ER 1014, Lord Woolf CJ stated (at para 16):

It is also important to have in mind that legislation is passed by a democratically elected Parliament and therefore the courts under the convention are entitled to and should, as a matter of constitutional principle, pay a degree of deference to the view of Parliament as to what is in the interest of the public generally when upholding the rights of the individual under the convention. The courts are required to balance the competing interests involved.

In according deference to Parliament or the Executive a key consideration will be the question of proportionality which featured in their Lordships' deliberations in the following two cases. In the second case a major shift in the test for judicial review, at least where Convention rights are involved, suggests that the proportionality principle may result in significantly less deference being accorded to the views of decision-makers than prior to the enactment of the Human Rights Act 1998, even under the 'anxious scrutiny' test adopted in *R v Ministry of Defence, ex parte Smith* [1996] QB 517 (*ante*, p. 462).

Brown v Stott (Procurator Fiscal, Dunfermline) and Another
[2001] 2 WLR 817, Privy Council

B was suspected of stealing a bottle of gin from a supermarket to which she had travelled by car. The police were called to the store. Her breath smelled of alcohol which prompted the police officer to ask her how she had travelled there. B replied that she had travelled by car and subsequently pointed out her car in the car park. By virtue of powers under s. 172(2)(a) of the Road Traffic Act 1988 she was required to say who had been driving the car. B admitted that she had. A breath test proved positive. B was charged both with theft and with driving her car after consuming an excess of alcohol contrary to s. 5(1)(a) of the 1988 Act. B sought to claim that use at her trial of the admission compulsorily obtained from her would be incompatible with her right to a fair hearing under Article 6(1) of the Convention. The sheriff ruled against B but the High Court of Justiciary allowed her appeal declaring that the procurator fiscal had no power at her trial to lead evidence of, and rely on, the admission B had been compelled to make. The procurator fiscal and Advocate General appealed.

LORD BINGHAM OF CORNHILL: . . .

Section 172 of the Road Traffic Act 1988
So far as material, s 172 of the 1988 Act at the relevant time provided:

(2) Where the driver of a vehicle is alleged to be guilty of an offence to which this section applies – (a) the person keeping the vehicle shall give such information as to the

identity of the driver as he may be required to give by or on behalf of a chief officer of police. . .

(3) Subject to the following provisions, a person who fails to comply with a requirement under subsection (2) above shall be guilty of an offence.

It is evident that the power of the police to require information to be given as to the identity of the driver of a vehicle only arises where the driver is alleged to be guilty of an offence to which the section applies. Those offences include the most serious of driving offences, such as manslaughter or culpable homicide, causing death by dangerous driving, dangerous and careless driving, causing death by careless driving when under the influence of drugs or drink, and driving a vehicle after consuming alcohol above the prescribed limit. They also include the offence, in Scotland, of taking and driving away a vehicle without consent or lawful authority. The offences excluded are of a less serious and more regulatory nature. They include offences in relation to driving instruction, the holding of motoring events on public ways, the wearing of protective headgear, driving with uncorrected defective eyesight and offences pertaining to the testing, design, inspection and licensing of vehicles. The penalty for failing to comply with a requirement under sub-s (2) is a fine of (currently) not more than £1,000: in the case of an individual, disqualification from driving is discretionary but endorsement of the licence is mandatory. The requirement to supply information under sub-s (2) may be made of 'the person keeping the vehicle' or 'any other person', irrespective of whether either of them is suspected of being the driver alleged to have committed the relevant offence. In this case, it is clear that the respondent, when required to give information, was suspected of committing the offence for which she was later prosecuted. . . .

Article 6 of the convention

Attention has often, and rightly, been drawn to contrasts between different articles of the convention. Some (such as arts 3 and 4) permit no restriction by national authorities. Others (such as arts 8, 9, 10 and 11) permit a measure of restriction if certain stringent and closely prescribed conditions are satisfied . . .

[Article 6] has more in common with the first group of articles mentioned above than the second. The only express qualification relates to the requirement of a 'public hearing'. But there is nothing to suggest that the fairness of the trial itself may be qualified, compromised or restricted in any way, whatever the circumstances and whatever the public interest in convicting the offender. If the trial as a whole is judged to be unfair, a conviction cannot stand.

What a fair trial requires cannot, however, be the subject of a single, unvarying rule or collection of rules. It is proper to take account of the facts and circumstances of particular cases, as the European Court has consistently done.

Conclusions

The convention is an international treaty by which the contracting states mutually undertake to secure to all within their respective jurisdictions certain rights and freedoms. The fundamental nature of these rights and freedoms is clear, not only from the full title and the content of the convention but from its preamble in which the signatory governments declared:

their profound belief in those fundamental freedoms which are the foundation of justice and peace in the world and are best maintained on the one hand by an effective political democracy and on the other by a common understanding and observance of the human rights upon which they depend.

Judicial recognition and assertion of the human rights defined in the convention is not a substitute for the processes of democratic government but a complement to them. While a national court does not accord the margin of appreciation recognised by the European Court as a supra-national court, it will give weight to the decisions of a representative legislature and a democratic government within the discretionary area of judgment accorded to those bodies (see Lester and Pannick, *Human Rights*

Law and Practice (1999) pp 73–76). The convention is concerned with rights and freedoms which are of real importance in a modern democracy governed by the rule of law. It does not, as is sometimes mistakenly thought, offer relief from 'The heart-ache and the thousand natural shocks That flesh is heir to'.

In interpreting the convention, as any other treaty, it is generally to be assumed that the parties have included the terms which they wished to include and on which they were able to agree, omitting other terms which they did not wish to include or on which they were not able to agree. Thus particular regard must be had and reliance placed on the express terms of the convention, which define the rights and freedoms which the contracting parties have undertaken to secure. This does not mean that nothing can be implied into the convention. The language of the convention is for the most part so general that some implication of terms is necessary, and the case law of the European Court shows that the court has been willing to imply terms into the convention when it was judged necessary or plainly right to do so. But the process of implication is one to be carried out with caution, if the risk is to be averted that the contracting parties may, by judicial interpretation, become bound by obligations which they did not expressly accept and might not have been willing to accept. As an important constitutional instrument the convention is to be seen as a 'living tree capable of growth and expansion within its natural limits' (*Edwards* v *A-G for Canada* [1930] AC 124, 136 per Lord Sankey LC), but those limits will often call for very careful consideration.

Effect has been given to the right not to incriminate oneself in a variety of different ways. . . . [It] is an implied right. While it cannot be doubted that such a right must be implied, there is no treaty provision which expressly governs the effect or extent of what is to be implied.

The jurisprudence of the European Court very clearly establishes that while the overall fairness of a criminal trial cannot be compromised, the constituent rights comprised, whether expressly or implicitly, within article 6 are not themselves absolute. Limited qualification of these rights is acceptable if reasonably directed by national authorities towards a clear and proper public objective and if representing no greater qualification than the situation calls for. The general language of the convention could have led to the formulation of hard-edged and inflexible statements of principle from which no departure could be sanctioned whatever the background or the circumstances. But this approach has been consistently eschewed by the court throughout its history. The case law shows that the court has paid very close attention to the facts of particular cases coming before it, giving effect to factual differences and recognising differences of degree. Ex facto oritur jus. The court has also recognised the need for a fair balance between the general interest of the community and the personal rights of the individual, the search for which balance has been described as inherent in the whole of the convention (see *Sporrong* v *Sweden* (1982) 5 EHRR 35, 52, para 69; *Sheffield* v *UK* (1998) 27 EHRR 163, 191, para 52.

The high incidence of death and injury on the roads caused by the misuse of motor vehicles is a very serious problem common to almost all developed societies. The need to address it in an effective way, for the benefit of the public, cannot be doubted. Among other ways in which democratic governments have sought to address it is by subjecting the use of motor vehicles to a regime of regulation and making provision for enforcement by identifying, prosecuting and punishing offending drivers. Materials laid before the Board, incomplete though they are, reveal different responses to the problem of enforcement. Under some legal systems (Spain, Belgium and France are examples) the registered owner of a vehicle is assumed to be the driver guilty of minor traffic infractions unless he shows that some other person was driving at the relevant time or establishes some other ground of exoneration. There being a clear public interest in enforcement of road traffic legislation the crucial question in the present case is whether s 172 of the 1988 Act represents a disproportionate response, or one that undermines a defendant's right to a fair trial, if an admission of being the driver is relied on at trial.

I do not for my part consider that s 172, properly applied, does represent a disproportionate response to this serious social problem, nor do I think that reliance on the respondent's admission, in the present case, would undermine her right to a fair trial. I reach that conclusion for a number of reasons.

(1) Section 172 of the 1988 Act provides for the putting of a single, simple question. The answer cannot of itself incriminate the suspect, since it is not without more an offence to drive a car. An admission of driving may, of course, as here, provide proof of a fact necessary to convict, but the section does not sanction prolonged questioning about the facts alleged to give rise to criminal offences such as was understandably held to be objectionable in *Saunders v UK* [*ante*, p. 475], and the penalty for declining to answer under the section is moderate and non-custodial. There is in the present case no suggestion of improper coercion or oppression such as might give rise to unreliable admissions and so contribute to a miscarriage of justice, and if there were evidence of such conduct the trial judge would have ample power to exclude evidence of the admission.

(2) While the High Court was entitled to distinguish . . . between the giving of an answer under s 172 and the provision of physical samples, and had the authority of the European Court in *Saunders* 23 EHRR 313, 337–338, para 69, for doing so, this distinction should not in my opinion be pushed too far. It is true that the respondent's answer, whether given orally or in writing, would create new evidence which did not exist until she spoke or wrote. In contrast, it may be acknowledged, the percentage of alcohol in her breath was a fact, existing before she blew into the breathalyser machine. But the whole purpose of requiring her to blow into the machine (on pain of a criminal penalty if she refused) was to obtain evidence not available until she did so and the reading so obtained could, in all save exceptional circumstances, be enough to convict a driver of an offence. If one applies the language of *Wigmore on Evidence* (McNaughton revision 1961) vol 8, p 318, quoted by the High Court that an individual should 'not be conscripted by his opponent to defeat himself' it is not easy to see why a requirement to answer a question is objectionable and a requirement to undergo a breath test is not. Yet no criticism is made of the requirement that the respondent undergo a breath test.

(3) All who own or drive motor cars know that by doing so they subject themselves to a regulatory regime which does not apply to members of the public who do neither. Section 172 of the 1988 Act forms part of that regulatory regime. This regime is imposed not because owning or driving cars is a privilege or indulgence granted by the state but because the possession and use of cars (like, for example, shotguns, the possession of which is very closely regulated) are recognised to have the potential to cause grave injury. It is true that s 172(2)(b) permits a question to be asked of 'any other person' who, if not the owner or driver, might not be said to have impliedly accepted the regulatory regime, but someone who was not the owner or the driver would not incriminate himself whatever answer he gave. If, viewing this situation in the round, one asks whether s 172 represents a disproportionate legislative response to the problem of maintaining road safety, whether the balance between the interests of the community at large and the interests of the individual is struck in a manner unduly prejudicial to the individual, whether (in short) the leading of this evidence would infringe a basic human right of the respondent, I would feel bound to give negative answers. If the present argument is a good one it has been available to British citizens since 1966, but no one in this country has to my knowledge, criticised the legislation as unfair at any time up to now.

. . . In the present case the High Court came very close to treating the right not to incriminate oneself as absolute, describing it as a 'central right' which permitted no gradations of fairness depending on the seriousness of the charge or the circumstances of the case. The High Court interpreted the decision in *Saunders* as laying down more absolute a standard than I think the European Court intended, and nowhere in the High Court judgments does one find any recognition of the need to balance the general interests of the community against the interests of the individual or to ask whether s 172 represents a proportionate response to what is undoubtedly a serious social problem.

In my opinion the procurator fiscal is entitled at the respondent's forthcoming trial to lead evidence of her answer given under s 172. I would allow the appeal and quash the declaration made by the High Court.

LORD STEYN: . . .

II. The objectives of the convention

In the first real test of the Human Rights Act 1998 it is opportune to stand back and consider what the basic aims of the convention are. One finds the explanation in the very words of the preambles of the convention. There were two principal objectives. The first was to maintain and further realise human rights and fundamental freedoms. The framers of the convention recognised that it was not only morally right to promote the observance of human rights but that it was also the best way of achieving pluralistic and just societies in which all can peaceably go about their lives. The second aim was to foster effective political democracy. This aim necessarily involves the creation of conditions of stability and order under the rule of law, not for its own sake, but as the best way to ensuring the well being of the inhabitants of the European countries. After all, democratic government has only one raison d'être, namely to serve the interests of all the people. The inspirers of the convention, among whom Winston Churchill played an important role, and the framers of the convention, ably assisted by English draftsmen, realised that from time-to-time the fundamental right of one individual may conflict with the human right of another. Thus the principles of free speech and privacy may collide. They also realised only too well that a single-minded concentration on the pursuit of fundamental rights of individuals to the exclusion of the interests of the wider public might be subversive of the ideal of tolerant European liberal democracies. The fundamental rights of individuals are of supreme importance but those rights are not unlimited: we live in communities of individuals who also have rights. The direct lineage of this ancient idea is clear: the convention is the descendant of the Universal Declaration of Human Rights (Paris, 10 December 1948; UN TS 2 (1949); Cmd 7226) which in art 29 expressly recognised the duties of everyone to the community and the limitation on rights in order to secure and protect respect for the rights of others. It is also noteworthy that article 17 of the convention prohibits, among others, individuals from abusing their rights to the detriment of others. Thus, notwithstanding the danger of intolerance towards ideas, the convention system draws a line which does not accord the protection of free speech to those who propagate racial hatred against minorities: article 10; *Jersild* v *Denmark* (1995) 19 EHRR 1 at 25–26 (para 31). This is to be contrasted with the categorical language of the First Amendment to the United States Constitution which provides that 'Congress shall make no law . . . abridging the freedom of speech'. The convention requires that where difficult questions arise a balance must be struck. Subject to a limited number of absolute guarantees, the scheme and structure of the convention reflects this balanced approach. It differs in material respects from other constitutional systems but as a European nation it represents our Bill of Rights. We must be guided by it. And it is a basic premise of the convention system that only an entirely neutral, impartial, and independent judiciary can carry out the primary task of securing and enforcing convention rights. This contextual scene is not only directly relevant to the issues arising on the present appeal but may be a matrix in which many challenges under the Human Rights Act should be considered.

III. Article 6 of the convention

The present case is concerned with art 6 of the convention which guarantees to every individual a fair trial in civil and criminal cases. The centrality of this principle in the convention system has repeatedly been emphasised by the European Court. But even in respect of this basic guarantee, there is a balance to be observed. First, it is well settled that the public interest may be taken into account in deciding what the right to a fair trial requires in a particular context. Thus in *Doorson* v *Netherlands* (1996) 22 EHRR 330 at 358 (para 70) it was held that 'principles of fair trial also require that in appropriate cases the interests of the defence are balanced against those of witnesses or victims called upon to testify'. Only one specific illustration of this balanced approach is necessary. Provided they are kept 'within reasonable limits' rebuttable presumptions of fact are permitted in criminal legislation (*Salabiaku* v *France* (1988) 13 EHRR 379). Secondly, once it has been determined that the guarantee of a fair trial has been breached, it is never possible to justify such breach by reference to the public interest or on any other ground. This is to be contrasted with cases where a trial has been affected by irregularities not amounting to denial of a fair trial. In such cases it is fair that a court of appeal should have the power, even when faced by the fact of irregularities in the trial procedure, to dismiss the appeal if in the view of the court of appeal the defendant's guilt is plain and beyond any doubt. However, it is a grave conclusion that a defendant has not had the substance of a fair trial. It means that the administration of justice has entirely failed. Subject to the possible exercise of a power to order a retrial where appropriate such a conviction can never be allowed to stand.

IV. The privilege against self-incrimination
It is well settled, although not expressed in the convention, that there is an implied privilege against self incrimination under art 6. Moreover, s 172(2) of the 1988 Act undoubtedly makes an inroad on this privilege. On the other hand, it is also clear that the privilege against self incrimination is not an absolute right. . . .

V. Section 172(2) of the Road Traffic Act 1988
In considering whether an inroad on the privilege against self incrimination can be justified, it is necessary to concentrate on the particular context . . .

The effective prosecution of drivers causing serious offences is a matter of public interest. But such prosecutions are often hampered by the difficulty of identifying the drivers of the vehicles at the time of, say, an accident causing loss of life or serious injury or potential danger to others. The tackling of this social problem seems in principle a legitimate aim for a legislature to pursue.

The real question is whether the legislative remedy in fact adopted is necessary and proportionate to the aim sought to be achieved. There were legislative choices to be made. The legislature could have decided to do no more than to exhort the police and prosecuting authorities to redouble their efforts. It may, however, be that such a policy would have been regarded as inadequate. Secondly, the legislature could have introduced a reverse burden of proof clause which placed the burden on the registered owner to prove that he was not the driver of the vehicle at a given time when it is alleged that an offence was committed. Thirdly, and this was the course actually adopted, there was the possibility of requiring information about the identity of the driver to be revealed by the registered owner and others. As between the second and third techniques it may be said that the latter involves the securing of an admission of a constituent element of the offence. On the other hand, such an admission, if wrongly made, is not conclusive. And it must be measured against the alternative of a reverse burden clause which could without further investigation of the identity of the driver lead to a prosecution. In their impact on the citizen the two techniques are not widely different. And it is rightly conceded that a properly drafted reverse burden of proof provision would have been lawful.

It is also important to keep in mind the narrowness of the interference. Section 172(2) is directed at obtaining information in one category, namely the identity of the driver at the time when an offence was allegedly committed. The most important part of s 172(2) is para (a) since the relevant information is usually peculiarly within the knowledge of the owner . . . Section 172(2) does not authorise general questioning by the police to secure a confession of an offence. On the other hand, s 172(2) does, depending on the circumstances, in effect authorise the police officer to invite the owner to make an admission of one element in a driving offence. It would, however, be an abuse of the power under s 172(2) for the police officer to employ improper or overbearing methods of obtaining the information. He may go no further than to ask who the driver was at the given time. If the police officer strays beyond his power under s 172(2) a judge will have ample power at trial to exclude the evidence. It is therefore a relatively narrow interference with the privilege in one area which poses widespread and serious law enforcement problems.

VI. What deference may be accorded to the legislature?
Under the convention system the primary duty is placed on domestic courts to secure and protect convention rights. The function of the European Court is essential but supervisory. In that capacity it

accords to domestic courts a margin of appreciation, which recognises that national institutions are in principle better placed than an international court to evaluate local needs and conditions. That principle is logically not applicable to domestic courts. On the other hand, national courts may accord to the decisions of national legislatures some deference where the context justifies it (see *R v DPP, ex p Kebilene* [1999] 4 All ER 801 at 844, [2000] 2 AC 326 at 381 per Lord Hope of Craighead . . .)

In my view this factor is of some relevance in the present case. Here s 172(2) addresses a pressing social problem, namely the difficulty of law enforcement in the face of statistics revealing a high accident rate resulting in death and serious injuries. The legislature was entitled to regard the figures of serious accidents as unacceptably high. It would also have been entitled to take into account that it was necessary to protect other convention rights, viz the right to life of members of the public exposed to the danger of accidents (see art 2(1)). On this aspect the legislature was in as good a position as a court to assess the gravity of the problem and the public interest in addressing it. It really then boils down to the question whether in adopting the procedure enshrined in s 172(2), rather than a reverse burden technique, it took more drastic action than was justified. While this is ultimately a question for the court, it is not unreasonable to regard both techniques as permissible in the field of the driving of vehicles. After all, the subject invites special regulation; objectively the interference is narrowly circumscribed; and it is qualitatively not very different from requiring, for example, a breath specimen from a driver. Moreover, it is less invasive than an essential modern tool of crime detection such as the taking of samples from a suspect for DNA profiling. If the matter was not covered by authority, I would have concluded that s 172(2) is compatible with art 6.

VII. *Saunders v UK*

The decision of the European Court in *Saunders v UK* 23 EHRR 313 gave some support to the view of the High Court of Justiciary. With due respect I have to say that the reasoning in *Saunders v UK* is unsatisfactory and less than clear. The European Court did not rule that the privilege against self incrimination is absolute. Surprisingly in view of its decision in *Murray* 22 EHRR 29 that the linked right of silence is not absolute it left the point open in respect of the privilege against self-incrimination. On the other hand, the substance of its reasoning treats both privileges as not absolute. The court observed, at p 373, para 68:

> The Court recalls that, although not specifically mentioned in article 6 of the convention, the right to silence and the right not to incriminate oneself are generally recognised international standards which lie at the heart of the notion of a fair procedure under article 6. Their rationale lies, inter alia, in the protection of the accused from improper compulsion by the authorities thereby contributing to the avoidance of miscarriages of justice and to the fulfilment of the aims of article 6 . . .

The court emphasised the rationale of improper compulsion. It does not hold that *anything* said under compulsion of law is inadmissible. Admittedly, the court also observed, at para 68:

> The right not to incriminate oneself, in particular, presupposes that the prosecution in a criminal case seek to prove their case against the accused without resort to evidence obtained through methods of coercion or oppression in defiance of the will of the accused. In this sense the right is closely linked to the presumption of innocence contained in article 6(2) of the convention.

Again one finds the link with the non-absolute right of silence. In any event 'methods of coercion or oppression in defiance of the will of the accused' is probably another way of referring to improper compulsion. This is consistent with the following passage, at p 338, para 69:

> In the present case the Court is only called upon to decide whether the use made by the prosecution of the statements obtained from the applicant by the inspectors amounted to an unjustifiable infringement of the right. This question must be examined by the Court in the light of all the circumstances of the case. In particular, it must be determined whether

the applicant has been subject to compulsion to give evidence and whether the use made of the resulting testimony at his trial offended the basic principles of a fair procedure inherent in article 6(1) of which the right not to incriminate oneself is a constituent element.

The expression 'unjustifiable infringement of the right' implies that some infringements may be justified. In my view the observations in *Saunders* do not support an absolutist view of the privilege against self incrimination. It may be that the observations in *Saunders* will have to be clarified in a further case by the European Court. As things stand, however, I consider that the High Court of Justiciary put too great weight on these observations. In my view they were never intended to apply to a case such as the present.

VIII. Conclusion on art 6

That brings me back to the decision of the High Court of Justiciary. It treated the privilege against self incrimination as virtually absolute. That conclusion fits uneasily into the balanced convention system, and cannot be reconciled with art 6 of the convention in all its constituent parts and the spectrum of jurisprudence of the European Court on the various facets of art 6.

I would hold that the decision of the High Court of Justiciary on the merits was wrong. The procurator fiscal is entitled to lead the evidence of Miss Brown's admission under s 172(2) of the 1988 Act.

Appeal allowed.

QUESTION

Did the Privy Council strike the balance between the protection of individual rights and the interests of the community at large in the right place?

R (Daly) v *Secretary of State for the Home Department*
[2001] UKHL 26, House of Lords

> D, a prisoner, stored correspondence with his solicitor in his cell. He was subject to a standard cell searching policy under paragraphs 17.69 to 17.74 of a Security Manual issued by the Secretary of State to prison governors under his power to make rules for the regulation and control of prisoners under s. 47(1) of the Prison Act 1952. The policy required prisoners to be excluded during cell searches to prevent intimidation and to prevent prisoners acquiring knowledge of the search techniques. Prison officers were to examine any legal correspondence to ensure it contained nothing likely to endanger prison security but they were not to read it. D sought judicial review of the decision that prisoners' legally privileged correspondence could be examined in their absence. The application was dismissed by the Court of Appeal. D appealed to the House of Lords. He did not contest the need for correspondence to be examined but contended that such examination should ordinarily take place in the presence of the prisoner.

LORD BINGHAM OF CORNHILL: . . .

[His Lordship referred to the origins of the policy in the report of the Woodcock Inquiry following the escape of six dangerous prisoners from HMP Whitemoor in 1994. The report recommended that cells and property should be searched at frequent but irregular intervals. His Lordship examined the restrictions on rights which imprisonment involves and the case law relating thereto before quoting with approval from the speech by Lord Browne-Wilkinson in *R* v *Secretary of State for the Home Department, ex p Pierson* [1998] AC 539, 575:]

> From these authorities I think the following proposition is established. A power conferred by Parliament in general terms is not to be taken to authorise the doing of acts by the donee of the power which adversely affect the legal rights of the citizen or the basic principles on which the law of the United Kingdom is based unless the statute conferring the power makes it clear that such was the intention of Parliament.

The argument
. . .

15 It is necessary, first, to ask whether the policy infringes in a significant way Mr Daly's common law right that the confidentiality of privileged legal correspondence be maintained. He submits that it does for two related reasons: first, because knowledge that such correspondence may be looked at by prison officers in the absence of the prisoner inhibits the prisoner's willingness to communicate with his legal adviser in terms of unreserved candour; and secondly, because there must be a risk, if the prisoner is not present, that the officers will stray beyond their limited role in examining legal correspondence, particularly if, for instance, they see some name or reference familiar to them, as would be the case if the prisoner were bringing or contemplating bringing proceedings against officers in the prison. For the Home Secretary it is argued that the policy involves no infringement of a prisoner's common law right since his privileged correspondence is not read in his absence but only examined.

16 I have no doubt that the policy infringes Mr Daly's common law right to legal professional privilege. This was the view of two very experienced judges in *R* v *Secretary of State for the Home Department, Ex p Simms* [1999] QB 349, against which decision the present appeal is effectively brought. At p 366, Kennedy LJ said:

> In my judgment legal professional privilege does attach to correspondence with legal advisers which is stored by a prisoner in his cell, and accordingly such correspondence is to be protected from any unnecessary interference by prison staff. Even if the correspond-ence is only inspected to see that it is what it purports to be that is likely to impair the free flow of communication between a convicted or remand prisoner on the one hand and his legal adviser on the other, and therefore it constitutes an impairment of the privilege.

Judge LJ was of the same opinion. At p 373, he said:

> Prisoners whose cells are searched in their absence will find it difficult to believe that their correspondence has been searched but not read. The governor's order will some-times be disobeyed. Accordingly I am prepared to accept the potential 'chilling effect' of such searches.

In an imperfect world there will necessarily be occasions when prison officers will do more than merely examine prisoners' legal documents, and apprehension that they may do so is bound to inhibit a prisoner's willingness to communicate freely with his legal adviser.

17 The next question is whether there can be any ground for infringing in any way a prisoner's right to maintain the confidentiality of his privileged legal correspondence. Plainly there can. Some examination may well be necessary to establish that privileged legal correspondence is what it appears to be and is not a hiding place for illicit materials or information prejudicial to security or good order.

18 It is then necessary to ask whether, to the extent that it infringes a prisoner's common law right to privilege, the policy can be justified as a necessary and proper response to the acknow-ledged need to maintain security, order and discipline in prisons and to prevent crime. Mr Daly's challenge at this point is directed to the blanket nature of the policy, applicable as it is to all prisoners of whatever category in all closed prisons in England and Wales, irrespective of a prisoner's past or present conduct and of any operational emergency or urgent intelligence. The Home Secretary's justification rests firmly on the points already mentioned: the risk of intimidation, the risk that staff may be conditioned by prisoners to relax security and the danger of disclosing searching methods.

19 In considering these justifications, based as they are on the extensive experience of the prison service, it must be recognised that the prison population includes a core of dangerous, disruptive and manipulative prisoners, hostile to authority and ready to exploit for their own advantage any concession granted to them. Any search policy must accommodate this inescapable fact. I cannot however accept that the reasons put forward justify the policy in its present blanket form. Any prisoner who attempts to intimidate or disrupt a search of his cell, or whose past conduct shows that he is likely to do so, may properly be excluded even while his privileged correspondence is examined so as to ensure the efficacy of the search, but no justification is shown for routinely excluding all prisoners, whether intimidatory or disruptive or not, while that part of the search is conducted. Save in the extraordinary conditions prevailing at Whitemoor before September 1994, it is hard to regard the conditioning of staff as a problem which could not be met by employing dedicated search teams. It is not suggested that prison officers when examining legal correspondence employ any sophist-icated technique which would be revealed to the prisoner if he were present, although he might no doubt be encouraged to secrete illicit materials among his legal papers if the examination were obviously very cursory. The policy cannot in my opinion be justified in its present blanket form. The infringement of prisoners' rights to maintain the confidentiality of their privileged legal correspond-ence is greater than is shown to be necessary to serve the legitimate public objectives already identified. I accept Mr Daly's submission on this point.

[His Lordship was fortified in reaching his view by four considerations, namely, (i) that the Prisons Ombudsman had upheld a similar complaint by another prisoner in 1996 resulting in Security Group (the company which ran the prison concerned) adopting revised procedures which permitted the prisoner to remain in his cell while his legal documents were searched; (ii) the Ombudsman's report also revealed a procedure adopted in HMP Full Sutton to accommodate a similar complaint from a prisoner there; (iii) the procedures in Scotland involved the prisoner being present during examination of his privileged legal correspondence; (iv) in only two cases have illicit items been found hidden in legally privileged documents.]

21 In *R v Secretary of State for the Home Department, Ex p Simms* [1999] QB 349 and again in the present case, the Court of Appeal held that the policy represented the minimum intrusion into the rights of prisoners consistent with the need to maintain security, order and discipline in prisons. That is a conclusion which I respect but cannot share. In my opinion the policy provides for a degree of intrusion into the privileged legal correspondence of prisoners which is greater than is justified by the objectives the policy is intended to serve, and so violates the common law rights of prisoners. Section 47(1) of the 1952 Act does not authorise such excessive intrusion, and the Home Secretary accordingly had no power to lay down or implement the policy in its present form. I would accord-ingly declare paragraphs 17.69 to 17.74 of the Security Manual to be unlawful and void in so far as they provide that prisoners must always be absent when privileged legal correspondence held by them in their cells is examined by prison officers.

. . .

23 I have reached the conclusions so far expressed on an orthodox application of common law principles derived from the authorities and an orthodox domestic approach to judicial review. But the same result is achieved by reliance on the European Convention. Article 8(1) gives Mr Daly a right to

respect for his correspondence. While interference with that right by a public authority may be permitted if in accordance with the law and necessary in a democratic society in the interests of national security, public safety, the prevention of disorder or crime or for protection of the rights and freedoms of others, the policy interferes with Mr Daly's exercise of his right under article 8(1) to an extent much greater than necessity requires. In this instance, therefore, the common law and the Convention yield the same result. But this need not always be so. In *Smith and Grady* v *United Kingdom* (1999) 29 EHRR 493, the European Court held that the orthodox domestic approach of the English courts had not given the applicants an effective remedy for the breach of their rights under article 8 of the Convention because the threshold of review had been set too high. Now, following the incorporation of the Convention by the Human Rights Act 1998 and the bringing of that Act fully into force, domestic courts must themselves form a judgment whether a Convention right has been breached (conducting such inquiry as is necessary to form that judgment) and, so far as permissible under the Act, grant an effective remedy. On this aspect of the case, I agree with and adopt the observations of my noble and learned friend Lord Steyn which I have had the opportunity of reading in draft.

LORD STEYN: . . .

24 My Lords, I am in complete agreement with the reasons given by Lord Bingham of Cornhill in his speech. For the reasons he gives I would also allow the appeal. Except on one narrow but important point I have nothing to add.

25 There was written and oral argument on the question whether certain observations of Lord Phillips of Worth Matravers MR in *R (Mahmood)* v *Secretary of State for the Home Department* [2001] 1 WLR 840 were correct. The context was an immigration case involving a decision of the Secretary of State made before the Human Rights Act 1998 came into effect. The Master of the Rolls nevertheless approached the case as if the Act had been in force when the Secretary of State reached his decision. He explained the new approach to be adopted. The Master of the Rolls concluded, at p 857, para 40:

> When anxiously scrutinising an executive decision that interferes with human rights, the court will ask the question, applying an objective test, whether the decision-maker could reasonably have concluded that the interference was necessary to achieve one or more of the legitimate aims recognised by the Convention. When considering the test of necessity in the relevant context, the court must take into account the European jurisprudence in accordance with section 2 of the 1998 Act.

. . .

26 The explanation of the Master of the Rolls in the first sentence of the cited passage requires clarification. It is couched in language reminiscent of the traditional *Wednesbury* ground of review (*Associated Provincial Picture Houses Ltd* v *Wednesbury Corpn* [1948] 1 KB 223), and in particular the adaptation of that test in terms of heightened scrutiny in cases involving fundamental rights as formulated in *R* v *Ministry of Defence, Ex p Smith* [1996] QB 517, 554E–G per Sir Thomas Bingham MR. There is a material difference between the *Wednesbury* and *Smith* grounds of review and the approach of proportionality applicable in respect of review where Convention rights are at stake.

27 The contours of the principle of proportionality are familiar. In *de Freitas* v *Permanent Secretary of Ministry of Agriculture, Fisheries, Lands and Housing* [1999] 1 AC 69 the Privy Council adopted a three-stage test. Lord Clyde observed, at p 80, that in determining whether a limitation (by an act, rule or decision) is arbitrary or excessive the court should ask itself:

> whether: (i) the legislative objective is sufficiently important to justify limiting a fundamental right; (ii) the measures designed to meet the legislative objective are rationally

connected to it; and (iii) the means used to impair the right or freedom are no more than is necessary to accomplish the objective.

Clearly, these criteria are more precise and more sophisticated than the traditional grounds of review. What is the difference for the disposal of concrete cases? . . . The starting point is that there is an overlap between the traditional grounds of review and the approach of proportionality. Most cases would be decided in the same way whichever approach is adopted. But the intensity of review is somewhat greater under the proportionality approach. Making due allowance for important structural differences between various convention rights, which I do not propose to discuss, a few generalisations are perhaps permissible. I would mention three concrete differences without suggesting that my statement is exhaustive. First, the doctrine of proportionality may require the reviewing court to assess the balance which the decision maker has struck, not merely whether it is within the range of rational or reasonable decisions. Secondly, the proportionality test may go further than the traditional grounds of review inasmuch as it may require attention to be directed to the relative weight accorded to interests and considerations. Thirdly, even the heightened scrutiny test developed in R v Ministry of Defence, Ex p Smith [1996] QB 517, 554 is not necessarily appropriate to the protection of human rights. It will be recalled that in Smith the Court of Appeal reluctantly felt compelled to reject a limitation on homosexuals in the army. The challenge based on article 8 of the Convention for the Protection of Human Rights and Fundamental Freedoms (the right to respect for private and family life) foundered on the threshold required even by the anxious scrutiny test. The European Court of Human Rights came to the opposite conclusion: Smith and Grady v United Kingdom (1999) 29 EHRR 493. The court concluded, at p 543, para 138:

> the threshold at which the High Court and the Court of Appeal could find the Ministry of Defence policy irrational was placed so high that it effectively excluded any consideration by the domestic courts of the question of whether the interference with the applicants' rights answered a pressing social need or was proportionate to the national security and public order aims pursued, principles which lie at the heart of the court's analysis of complaints under article 8 of the Convention.

In other words, the intensity of the review, in similar cases, is guaranteed by the twin requirements that the limitation of the right was necessary in a democratic society, in the sense of meeting a pressing social need, and the question whether the interference was really proportionate to the legitimate aim being pursued.

28 The differences in approach between the traditional grounds of review and the proportionality approach may therefore sometimes yield different results. It is therefore important that cases involving Convention rights must be analysed in the correct way. This does not mean that there has been a shift to merits review. On the contrary, as Professor Jowell [2000] PL 671, 681 has pointed out the respective roles of judges and administrators are fundamentally distinct and will remain so. To this extent the general tenor of the observations in Mahmood [2001] 1 WLR 840 are correct. And Laws LJ rightly emphasised in Mahmood, at p 847, para 18, 'that the intensity of review in a public law case will depend on the subject matter in hand'. That is so even in cases involving Convention rights. In law context is everything.

Appeal allowed.

(e) *What remedial action can be taken where a public authority contravenes a Convention right?*

Section 6(1) of the 1998 Act declares that 'it is unlawful for a public authority to act in a way which is incompatible with one or more of the Convention rights'. However, s. 6(2) places a major constraint on s. 6(1) such that if the authority's acts are covered by s. 6(2) it has not acted unlawfully. This has important consequences as a court can grant relief or remedy under s. 8(1) only where the act of the authority is (or would be) unlawful. This presents a major disincentive to victims seeking to vindicate their rights which was identified by Emmerson (*The Times*, 28 October 1997). With changes in legal aid many victims will be unable to afford to take proceedings to enforce their rights. The 'no win, no fee' system will not provide a viable alternative to those who are not entitled to legal aid, as where there is a clash between the Convention and legislation, the public authority involved will not be acting unlawfully and thus no award of damages can be made under s. 8. In 'no win, no fee' litigation the costs of the litigation are recovered from the damages awarded, with litigation insurance being taken out to cover the costs should the claimant lose. In Human Rights Act cases involving conflicts between the Convention and legislation the claimant will never win damages, the lawyers will never recoup their costs, and no insurance company will provide insurance. Even where a person is entitled to legal aid, he or she may be discouraged from litigating by the prospect of paying the statutory charge under the Legal Aid Scheme without the prospect of an award of damages.

QUESTIONS

1. Many supporters of incorporation of the Convention have argued for the creation of a Human Rights Commission which would have an educational function, assist individual complainants in litigation and also bring proceedings in its own name. The Human Rights Act 1998, s. 7(1) allows only for 'victims' of unlawful acts by public authorities to bring proceedings or rely on the Convention in any legal proceedings. It also makes no provision for a Human Rights Commission. Would the protection of human rights have been enhanced by the creation of a Human Rights Commission, or would such a body have been just one more expensive quango performing an unnecessary function?

2. The European Convention is regarded by many as dated and conservative. Do we still need a domestic Bill of Rights which would cover a broader range of rights than those covered by the Convention?

(f) *Joint Parliamentary Committee on Human Rights*

In *Rights Brought Home*, para 3.8 ff (*ante*, p. 487) the Government deferred deciding on whether Human Rights Commission should be created until some unspecified time in the future after the Human Rights Act had come into effect. A Joint Parliamentary Committee on Human Rights has been set up made up of five members from the House of Commons and six from the House of Lords. Professor David Feldman is legal adviser to the Committee. Its terms of reference are:

To consider:

    (a) matters relating to human rights in the United Kingdom (but excluding consideration of individual cases);

    (b) proposals for remedial orders, draft remedial orders and remedial orders made under section 10 of and laid under Schedule 2 to the Human Rights Act 1998; and

(c) in respect of draft remedial orders and remedial orders, whether the special attention of the House should be drawn to them on any of the grounds specified in Standing Order 73 (Joint Committee on Statutory Instruments).

At the first meeting of the Committee following the General Election in June 2001, the Committee made the following decisions:

1. The Committee's first priority will be to look at a proposal for a draft Remedial Order on Mental Health Tribunals, this being the first Remedial Order to be laid under the Human Rights Act to rectify a declaration of incompatibility, namely:

   'A declaration under section 4 of the Human Rights Act 1998 that sections 72(1) and 73(1) of the Mental Health Act 1983 are incompatible with Articles 5(1) and 5(4) of the European Convention of Human Rights in that, for the Mental Health Review Tribunal to be obliged to order a patient's discharge, the burden is placed upon the patient to prove that the criteria justifying his detention in hospital for treatment no longer exist; and that Articles 5(1) and 5(4) require the Tribunal to be positively satisfied that all the criteria justifying the patient's detention in hospital for treatment continue to exist before refusing a patient's discharge.'

   The Committee will request written evidence from interested groups and once that is received it will decide how to proceed in relation to the period of 60 days beginning with the day on which the document was laid, as required by paragraphs 2 and 3 of the Human Rights Act 1998.

2. The Committee re-affirmed its intention to give a high priority to the scrutiny of Bills, adopting the same procedure as in the previous Parliament. The Committee decided to look at certain bills in more detail, including initially the Homelessness Bill on which it will be calling for written evidence from the Secretary of State for Transport, Local Government and the Regions.

3. The Committee re-affirmed the previous Committee's decision to establish an inquiry into the case for a Human Rights Commission for the United Kingdom. Responses to the call for evidence issued in the last Parliament will be considered in the Autumn.

4. The Committee also decided in principle to carry out one or more 'thematic' inquiries (for example, by examining human rights in relation to particular vulnerable groups). No detailed decisions on possible subjects for such inquiries have yet been taken.

The Committee has issued a number of reports on the compatibility of Bills before Parliament with the Convention and reported in its Seventh Report on the making of remedial orders. In this report the Committee expressed its preference for primary legislation, rather than remedial orders, to be used wherever possible to remedy any incompatibility between domestic law and the Convention on the basis that this increases the opportunity for parliamentary scrutiny and may even be quicker than the remedial order procedure where the amendment may be effected by a short Bill.

SECTION 5: **The European Union Charter of Fundamental Rights**

Protection of fundamental rights is a founding principle of the European Union and an indispensable prerequisite for its legitimacy as reflected in the Treaty on European Union, Article 6, which states:

(1) . . . the Union is founded on the principles of liberty, democracy, respect for human rights and fundamental freedoms, and the rule of law, principles which are common to the Member States. . . .

(2) . . . the Union shall respect fundamental rights, as guaranteed by the European Convention for the Protection of Human Rights and Fundamental Freedoms signed in Rome on 4 November 1950 and as they result from the constitutional traditions common to the Member States, as general principles of Community law.

At the Cologne European Council on 3 and 4 June 1999 the Heads of Government agreed that it was necessary, at the present stage of the Union's development, to establish a Charter of fundamental rights in order to 'make their overriding importance and relevance more visible to the Union's citizens'. The Council declared its belief that:

this Charter should contain the fundamental rights and freedoms as well as basic procedural rights guaranteed by the European Convention for the Protection of Human Rights and Fundamental Freedoms and derived from the constitutional traditions common to the Member States, as general principles of Community law. The Charter should also include the fundamental rights that pertain only to the Union's citizens. In drawing up such a Charter account should furthermore be taken of economic and social rights as contained in the European Social Charter and the Community Charter of the Fundamental Social Rights of Workers (Article 136 TEC), insofar as they do not merely establish objectives for action by the Union.

The Council decided to set up a Convention of representatives of various constituent bodies to draw up a draft charter. At the European Council in Tampere on 15 and 16 October 1999 the Council determined the composition of the Convention which was to comprise (a) 15 representatives of the Heads of State or Government of the Member States, (b) one representative of the Commission, (c) 16 members of the European Parliament, and (d) 30 members of national parliaments (two from each parliament). There were to be four observers, two representatives of the Court of Justice of the European Communities designated by the Court, and two representatives of the Council of Europe, including one from the European Court of Human Rights. The Economic and Social Committee, the Committee of the Regions, and the Ombudsman were to be invited to give their views along with other bodies, social groups, and experts. The European Parliament, Council, and Commission proclaimed the text of the Charter on 7 December 2000 at Nice. The Commission and some Member States proposed that the Charter be included in the Treaty of Nice. The United Kingdom opposed this wanting the charter to have merely declaratory rather than binding status. While the rights do not have binding force, the Charter will be used as an aid in the interpretation of EU law. Below is the

Preamble to the Charter and a list of the subject matter of each Chapter and Article of the Charter.

Charter of Fundamental Rights of the European Union

PREAMBLE

The peoples of Europe, in creating an ever closer union among them, are resolved to share a peaceful future based on common values.

Conscious of its spiritual and moral heritage, the Union is founded on the indivisible, universal values of human dignity, freedom, equality and solidarity; it is based on the principles of democracy and the rule of law. It places the individual at the heart of its activities, by establishing the citizenship of the Union and by creating an area of freedom, security and justice.

The Union contributes to the preservation and to the development of these common values while respecting the diversity of the cultures and traditions of the peoples of Europe as well as the national identities of the Member States and the organisation of their public authorities at national, regional and local levels; it seeks to promote balanced and sustainable development and ensures free movement of persons, goods, services and capital, and the freedom of establishment.

To this end, it is necessary to strengthen the protection of fundamental rights in the light of changes in society, social progress and scientific and technological developments by making those rights more visible in a Charter.

This Charter reaffirms, with due regard for the powers and tasks of the Community and the Union and the principle of subsidiarity, the rights as they result, in particular, from the constitutional traditions and international obligations common to the Member States, the Treaty on European Union, the Community Treaties, the European Convention for the Protection of Human Rights and Fundamental Freedoms, the Social Charters adopted by the Community and by the Council of Europe and the case-law of the Court of Justice of the European Communities and of the European Court of Human Rights.

Enjoyment of these rights entails responsibilities and duties with regard to other persons, to the human community and to future generations.

The Union therefore recognises the rights, freedoms and principles set out hereafter.

CHAPTER I	HUMAN DIGNITY
Article 1	Human dignity
Article 2	Right to life
Article 3	Right to integrity of the person
Article 4	Prohibition of torture and inhuman or degrading treatment or punishment
Article 5	Prohibition of slavery and forced labour

CHAPTER II	FREEDOMS
Article 6	Right to liberty and security
Article 7	Respect for family and private life
Article 8	Protection of personal data
Article 9	Right to marry and right to found a family
Article 10	Freedom of thought, conscience and religion
Article 11	Freedom of expression and information
Article 12	Freedom of assembly and of association
Article 13	Freedom of the arts and sciences
Article 14	Right to education
Article 15	Freedom to choose an occupation and right to engage in work
Article 16	Freedom to conduct a business

8

Judicial Review: The Grounds

SECTION 1: **Introduction**

A: The role of judicial review in the constitution

In some countries, for example in the United States of America, the judges are permitted to review legislation in order to establish whether it complies with the terms of the constitution. In the United Kingdom, the absence of a written constitution with the status of a higher law and the doctrine of parliamentary supremacy prevent the judges from exercising this role. They may, however, review the manner in which public authorities exercise the powers which have been conferred upon them by the legislature.

This power of judicial review may be defined as the jurisdiction of the superior courts (the High Court, the Court of Appeal and the House of Lords) to review the acts, decisions and omissions of public authorities in order to establish whether they have exceeded or abused their powers. The courts have developed a number of principles in order to establish whether there has been an excess or abuse of power. For example, a public authority must direct itself properly on the law, it must not use its powers for improper purposes, and it must not act in breach of the rules of natural justice.

What is the justification for permitting such judicial control? One theory, discussed in the following extract, is that the courts are simply giving effect to the intentions of Parliament.

P. Cane, *An Introduction to Administrative Law*
(1996), pp. 348–52

A great many of the powers and duties of governmental agencies, whether they are part of central or of local government, are laid down by statute. It follows from the first proposition about Parliamentary supremacy that courts are bound to apply statutes according to their terms. Traditional theory also says, although this does not follow from the first proposition, that ambiguities in the language of statutes should be resolved, and gaps in them filled, by reference to the intention of the legislature. Thus, it is often said that the enforcement of statutory duties and the control of the exercise of statutory powers by the courts is ultimately justifiable in terms of the doctrine of Parliamentary supremacy: even though Parliament has not expressly authorized the courts to supervise governmental activity, it cannot have intended breaches of duty by governmental agencies to go unremedied (even if no remedy is provided in the statute itself), nor can it have intended to give administrative agencies the freedom to exceed or abuse their powers, or to act unreasonably. It is the task of the courts to interpret and enforce the provisions of statutes which impose duties and confer powers on administrative agencies. In so doing they are giving effect to the will of Parliament.

There are three main weaknesses in this theory of the basis of judicial control of the exercise of statutory functions. The first is relevant to statutory interpretation generally: it is unrealistic to treat the process of interpreting statutes, resolving ambiguities, and filling gaps, as always being a matter of discerning and giving effect to the intentions of Parliament. Even assuming that we can make sense of the notion of intention when applied to a multi-member body following simple majoritarian voting procedures, there will be many cases in which Parliament did not think about the question relevant to resolving the ambiguity or filling the gap. In such cases the courts must act creatively in deciding what the statute means. The weakness of the intention theory of statutory interpretation is made very clear by the recent development of the notion of 'purposive interpretation'. Especially (but not only) in the context of interpreting statutes passed to give effect to EC law, the courts are now sometimes willing to go beyond interpreting the words actually used in statutes and to insert (or 'imply') into legislative provisions words or phrases needed to give effect to what the court perceives to be the true purpose or aim of the provision in question. It makes little sense to describe this process in terms of giving effect to what Parliament actually intended all along.

A technique for giving some meaning to the idea of the intention of the legislature is for courts to pay attention to what are called 'travaux preparatoires', that is policy documents and statements which preceded the enactment of the relevant legislation and might throw some light on its intended meaning. In *Pepper* v *Hart* [[1993] AC 593] the House of Lords held that where a statutory provision is ambiguous or obscure or leads to an absurdity, a court required to interpret the provision can refer to clear ministerial statements made in Parliament as to its intended meaning and effect and on other Parliamentary material which might be necessary to understand such statements. This decision is of considerable significance because it implies that the relevant intention is not that of Parliament in enacting the legislation but rather that of the government in promoting it. It acknowledges the reality that Parliament does not legislate but rather legitimizes the government's legislation. In so doing, it further undermines the notion that in interpreting legislation, the courts are giving effect to the intention of Parliament.

A second weakness of the 'intention of Parliament' justification of judicial control of governmental action is that it is at variance with the actual conduct of the courts. The principles which form the basis of judicial review – the doctrine of *ultra vires* and the rules of natural justice – are common law principles created and developed by the courts as means of controlling administrative activities. The courts have shown themselves prepared to go a very long way to preserve their jurisdiction to supervise administrative action by applying these principles. Perhaps the most striking modern example of this is the case of *Anisminic Ltd* v *Foreign Compensation Commission* [1969] 2 AC 147]. The main question in this case was whether a section in the Foreign Compensation Act purporting to oust the jurisdiction of the court to review 'determinations' of the Commission, was effective to that end. The House of Lords held that the word 'determination' must be read so as to exclude *ultra vires* determinations; it then went on to extend considerably the notion of *ultra vires* as it applied to decisions on questions of law, the final result being to reduce the application of the ouster clause almost to vanishing point, despite the fact that it had arguably been meant to have wide effect.

A second example is provided by the attitude of the courts to the exclusion by statute of the rules of natural justice. In the face of legislative silence on the question of whether an applicant before an administrative body is entitled to the protection of these procedural rules, two approaches are possible. It could be said that the rules of natural justice will apply only if there is evidence of a legislative intention that they should; alternatively, it could be argued that silence should be construed as an invitation to the courts to apply common law procedural standards of natural justice. On the whole the courts, especially in recent years, have tended to the latter view, thus asserting the independent validity of the rules of natural justice.

A third example is provided by cases, which we examined earlier, concerning powers given to a Minister, for example, 'to act as he sees fit'. Such phraseology appears to give the Minister unfettered discretion, but the courts tend to hold that such powers must be exercised reasonably in the light of the aims and purposes of the legislation conferring the power and of the relevant facts. In reality, the terms of the legislation may give very little guidance as to the way the power was meant to be exercised, even assuming, as the phrase itself indicates, that the Minister was not meant to be free to exercise his or her own best judgment. In effect, the courts are imposing their own standards of reasonable conduct on the Minister, irrespective of the question of legislative intent.

On the other hand, the decision in *Pepper* v *Hart* (see above) may, in the long run, significantly limit the freedom of the courts to interpret statutory provisions in an independent way by requiring them to give effect to ministerial statements as to the meaning and effect the government intended them to have. Ironically, the very vagueness of the concept of Parliamentary intention gives the courts considerable freedom in interpreting legislation in the way they choose.

A third weakness in the statutory interpretation approach to judicial control of governmental action is that it not justify judicial control of the exercise of non-statutory powers and functions. As we have seen, in the *GCHQ* case the House of Lords rejected the proposition that the common law (prerogative) powers of central government are immune from judicial review in favour of the proposition that the exercise of a common law power can be challenged provided only that the power or the circumstances of its exercise do not raise non-justiciable issues of policy. We have also seen that the courts have extended the scope of judicial review to embrace the exercise, for public purposes, of *de facto* power which has no identifiable legal source whether in common law or statute. Whatever the criteria which the courts will apply in reviewing the exercise of non-statutory powers, they cannot, by definition, be derived from a power-conferring statute.

If judicial control of governmental action cannot adequately be explained in terms of Parliamentary intention, how is it to be justified? Two lines of argument suggest themselves. First, despite the second proposition of parliamentary supremacy stated above, there are certain features of our constitutional and political arrangements which are so basic to our system of government that it is not seriously thought that they could ever be subject to the whim of Parliament – for example, the right to vote in free elections. Parliament could, of course, pass legislation inimical to this right, but attempts to enforce it, whether in the courts or outside would, no doubt, precipitate a crisis. Similarly, the right to apply to the courts for judicial review of the exercise of public powers and to receive a fair hearing before administrative bodies are of fundamental importance in a democratic society, and it is vital that some independent body has the power to protect these rights from any but the most limited statutory abridgement. A second line of argument which might support the refusal of the courts to be too subservient to Parliament is this: a vital underpinning assumption of Parliamentary supremacy is that Parliament is the most democratic governmental institution in our system. The political reality is that when the party in government has a comfortable majority in the House of Commons, the House is almost as much under the control of the government as is the administration. The implications of this line of argument will be considered more later.

The autonomy of judicial review has an important implication which ought to be made explicit, namely that in controlling government activity the courts are asserting and exercising, in their own right and in their own name, a power to limit and define the powers of other governmental agencies. Parliament allocates decision-making powers to governmental agencies by virtue of its unlimited legislative power. The courts, by virtue of their inherent (i.e. self-conferred) common law power of judicial review of administrative action, decide the legal limits of those allocations of power. In so doing they can not only castigate governmental agencies for abuses or excesses of power but, equally importantly, they can legitimize controversial exercises of power by holding them to have been lawful. The courts, in short, perform an indirect power-allocation function. Once this is realized, it can be seen how important it is to understand the nature of this function and the justification for it, since it is clear that the courts are not detached umpires in the governmental process but that they play an integral part in deciding how it will operate.

NOTES:

1. Cane refers to the view that the independent attitude of the courts may be justified because a vital underpinning of the assumption of parliamentary supremacy – that Parliament is the most democratic governmental institution in our system – is not borne out in practice. In considering the implications of this argument later in the chapter, he states, at p. 354, 'although judicial and parliamentary control of government activity are directed to different ends, it can be argued that the popularity and importance of judicial review is likely to bear an inverse relationship to the strength of parliamentary and other non-legal means of controlling government.' (See *ante* Chapter 6 for a discussion of the mechanisms of political accountability.)

   The links between judicial review and democracy are also explored by T.R.S. Allan in 'Legislative Supremacy and the Rule of Law' (1985) 44 *Cambridge Law Journal*, 111–43 at 129–33. In this extract Allan argues that judicial review is not inconsistent with the legislative supremacy of Parliament because the courts will give effect to the clear and unambiguous words of statutes. He also argues that judicial review functions to protect the democratic principle of the political sovereignty of the people. Unless prevented from doing so by the clear and unambiguous words of statutes, the courts in judicial review proceedings will give effect to common standards of morality and the natural expectations of the citizen. Allan thus differs from Cane in that he claims that ultimately judicial review poses no threat to the doctrine of parliamentary supremacy. Further, while Cane raises the possibility that judicial review may be more justifiable because of the inadequacies of other means of scrutinizing the Executive, he does not claim, as Allan does, that judicial review actually promotes democracy because it gives effect to common standards of morality and the natural expectations of the citizen.

2. Cane's discussion is concerned with judicial review of statutory powers, but we shall see below that the courts have reviewed the exercise of powers conferred by the royal prerogative (see *Council of Civil Service Unions* v *Minister for the Civil Service* [1985] AC 374). Recently, it has been clearly established that, in certain circumstances, the courts may review the exercise of powers which are not conferred by either statute or the royal prerogative but which depend on the consent of those who are subject to them (see *R* v *Panel on Take-overs and Mergers, ex parte Datafin Plc* [1987] QB 815 at *post* p. 676). Can any of the justifications which have been put forward for judicial review of statutory powers be used to justify judicial review of powers derived from other sources?

B: The distinction between review and appeal

The courts have been concerned to emphasize that, in judicial review proceedings, they are exercising a supervisory, not an appellate, jurisdiction. Where statute provides for an appeal and the grounds of appeal are not restricted by the statute itself, the court is generally required to decide whether the decision under appeal was right or wrong. If it decides that the decision was wrong, the court hearing the appeal is generally permitted to substitute its decision for that of the authority which first determined the matter in question. What is the position in judicial review proceedings?

Chief Constable of the North Wales Police v *Evans*
[1982] 1 WLR 1155, House of Lords

The Chief Constable of North Wales decided that Evans, a probationer constable in the force, should be required to resign or, if he refused, be discharged from the force. Evans resigned but subsequently challenged the decision on the ground that it was taken in breach of natural justice because he was not told of the allegations which had led to the decision and had not been given an opportunity to offer any explanation. The House of Lords agreed with the decision of the Court of Appeal that there had been a breach of natural justice, but in the light of comments made in the Court of Appeal, felt it necessary to make some general comments on the scope of judicial review.

LORD HAILSHAM: The first observation I wish to make is by way of criticism of some remarks of Lord Denning MR which seem to me to be capable of an erroneous construction of the purpose and the remedy by way of judicial review under RSC Ord 53. This remedy, vastly increased in extent, and rendered, over a long period in recent years, of infinitely more convenient access than that provided by the old prerogative writs and actions for a declaration, is intended to protect the individual against the abuse of power by a wide range of authorities, judicial, quasi-judicial, and, as would originally have been thought when I first practised at the Bar, administrative. It is not intended to take away from those authorities the powers and discretions properly vested in them by law and to substitute the courts as the bodies making the decisions. It is intended to see that the relevant authorities use their powers in a proper manner.

Since the range of authorities, and the circumstances of the use of their power, are almost infinitely various, it is of course unwise to lay down rules for the application of the remedy which appear to be of universal validity in every type of case. But it is important to remember in every case that the purpose of the remedies is to ensure that the individual is given fair treatment by the authority to which he has been subjected and that it is no part of that purpose to substitute the opinion of the judiciary or of individual judges for that of the authority constituted by law to decide the matters in question. The function of the court is to see the lawful authority is not abused by unfair treatment and not to attempt itself the task entrusted to that authority by the law. There are passages in the judgment of Lord Denning MR (and perhaps in the other judgments of the Court of Appeal) in the instant case and quoted by my noble and learned friend which might be read as giving the courts carte blanche to review the decision of the authority on the basis of what the courts themselves consider fair and reasonable on the merits. I am not sure whether the Master of the Rolls really intended his remarks to be construed in such a way as to permit the courts to examine, as for instance in the present case, the reasoning of the subordinate body with a view to substituting its own opinion. If so, I do not think this is a correct statement of principle. The purpose of judicial review is to ensure that the individual receives fair treatment, and not to ensure that the authority, after according fair treatment, reaches on a matter which it is authorised by law to decide for itself a conclusion which is correct in the eyes of the court. . . .

LORD BRIGHTMAN: . . . I turn secondly to the proper purpose of the remedy of judicial review, what it is and what it is not. In my opinion the law was correctly stated in the speech of Lord Evershed [in *Ridge* v *Baldwin* [1964] AC 40], at p. 96. His was a dissenting judgment but the dissent was not concerned with this point. Lord Evershed referred to 'a danger of usurpation of power on the part of the courts . . . under the pretext of having regard to the principles of natural justice.' He added:

> I do observe again that it is not the decision as such which is liable to review; it is only the circumstances in which the decision was reached, and particularly in such a case as the present the need for giving the party dismissed an opportunity for putting his case.

Judicial review is concerned, not with the decision, but with the decision-making process. Unless that restriction on the power of the court is observed, the court will in my view, under the guise of preventing the abuse of power, be itself guilty of usurping power. . . .

QUESTIONS

1. What, then, are the differences between appeal and review?
2. This case concerned the principles of natural justice. The other grounds for judicial review are summarized *post*, at pp. 575–6. Do you think they could all be said to be concerned not with 'the decision but with the decision-making process'? Do you think their Lordships intended their remarks to apply to all the grounds for judicial review?

Figure 1 Table showing the number of receipts for all Crown Office cases (calendar years 1994–1999)

Applications for permission to apply for judicial review	1994	1995	1996	1997	1998	1999
Immigration	935	1220	1748	1925	2518	2479
Criminal	321	321	297	284	310	354
Homelessness	447	417	340	187	134	91
Others	1505	1646	1516	1343	1577	1513
Total	**3208**	**3604**	**3901**	**3739**	**4539**	**4437**
Cases Stated						
Crown Court	23	36	31	31	25	26
Magistrates' courts	197	197	166	145	168	103
Others	13	10	6	8	9	3
Total	**233**	**243**	**203**	**184**	**202**	**132**
Statutory appeals and applications						
Planning	225	201	166		224	220
Habeas Corpus	59	90	101	132	66	55
Committal	7	7	9	4	9	4
Others	160	200	192	221	186	201
Total	**451**	**498**	**468**	**592**	**485**	**480**
Sub Total	**3892**	**4345**	**4572**	**4515**	**5226**	**5049**
Drug Trafficking Act	300	168	192	432	546	613
Criminal Justice Act	119	121	154	356	458	663
Total	**419**	**289**	**346**	**788**	**1004**	**1276**
Grand Total	**4311**	**4634**	**4918**	**5303**	**6230**	**6325**

C: The use of judicial review

A review of the Crown Office List (since renamed Administrative Court), which deals with applications for judicial review, provides some data on the number of applications for permission to proceed or receipts.

Sir Jeffrey Bowman, *Review of the Crown Office List*
(2000), p. 3

For table, see p. 573.

NOTES:
1. The *Review* notes a rise in applications for judicial review until 1998. Most of the 38 per cent increase over these years is due to a rise in immigration cases. The fall in homelessness cases is mainly due to a right of appeal to the county court introduced in 1997.
2. For an earlier study, see L. Bridges and G. Mészáros, in M. Sunkin, *Judicial Review in Perspective* (1995).

SECTION 2: **The Grounds for Judicial Review**

This chapter is concerned with the grounds for judicial review. The extracts which are included do, however, contain a number of references to the remedies which are available where there is a breach of the principles of judicial review. Before reading the cases, students should acquaint themselves with the following terms.

Subject to certain qualifications, which will be examined in further detail in Chapter 9, the normal method of seeking review is through making an application for judicial review. In the application for judicial review the court may grant one or more of the following remedies which have been renamed by the Civil Procedure Rules Part 54 *post* p. 653:

A: The prerogative orders

(1) Quashing order, formerly certiorari: this remedy quashes an unlawful decision of a public authority.
(2) Prohibiting order, formerly prohibition: this remedy prohibits an unlawful act which a public authority is proposing to perform.
(3) Mandatory order, formerly mandamus: this remedy compels a public authority to perform a public duty.

Prerogative orders may not be granted against the Crown, although they may be granted against individual ministers of the Crown. They may not be used to challenge delegated legislation.

Injunctions Injunctions may be prohibitory (restraining unlawful action) or mandatory (compelling the performance of a duty). An interim injunction is one granted before trial in order to preserve the status quo until the issues have been determined. In an emergency an injunction may be granted without hearing the defendant. Note, however, that s. 21 of the Crown Proceedings Act 1947 prevents the grant of injunctions against the Crown. So far as Ministers of the Crown are concerned, injunctions can be granted against them, both in matters of European Community law (see *R* v *Secretary of State for Transport, ex parte Factortame (No. 2)* [1990] 1 AC 603) and in domestic law (see *In re M* [1993] 3 WLR 433, *ante* p. 216).

Declarations   Declarations are a very flexible remedy. They may, for instance, simply state the parties' rights, set out the true construction of a statute, or state that an administrative act is invalid.

Damages   Damages may be awarded in an application for judicial review provided the applicant has claimed one or more of the remedies specified above. Damages are not available simply because one of the principles of judicial review has been breached. The applicant must show, in addition, that the authority has breached a right of his for which damages are available (e.g. that the authority has committed a tort or breach of contract).

There has been an exchange of views on the basis and justification of judicial review between broadly those who argue for a common law basis and those who advocate *ultra vires* and legislative intent. In the common law group are D. Oliver, 'Is the Ultra Vires Rules the Basis of Judicial Review?' [1987] PL 543; Sir John Laws 'Illegality: The Problem of Jurisdiction' in M. Supper-stone and J. Goudie, (eds), *Judicial Review* (1997); P. Craig, 'Ultra Vires and the Foundations of Judicial Review' [1998] CLJ 63 and 'Competing Models of Judicial Review' [1999] PL 428; and J. Jowell, 'Of Vires and Vacuums: The Constitutional Context of Judicial Review' [1999] PL 448*. The defenders of *ultra vires* are C. Forsyth, 'Of Fig Leaves and Fairy Tales: The *Ultra Vires* Doctrine, the Sovereignty of Parliament and Judicial Review' [1996] CLJ 122 and M. Elliott, 'The Demise of Parliamentary Sovereignty? The Implications for Justifying Judicial Review' (1999) 115 LQR 119* and 'The *Ultra Vires* Doctrine in A Constitutional Setting: Still the Central Principle of Administrative Law' [1999] CLJ 129. All of these extracts, except for those asterisked, are reprinted in C. Forsyth (ed) *Judicial Review and the Constitution* (2000).

Council of Civil Service Unions v *Minister for the Civil Service*
[1985] AC 374, House of Lords
The facts are stated *post*, at p. 622.

LORD DIPLOCK: . . . Judicial review has I think developed to a state today when, without reiterating any analysis of the steps by which the development has come about, one can conveniently classify under three heads the grounds on which administrative action is subject to control by judicial review. The first ground I would call 'illegality', the second 'irrationality' and the third 'procedural impropriety'. That is not to say that further development on a case by case basis may not in course of time add further grounds. I have in mind particularly the possible adoption in the future of the principle of 'proportionality' which is recognised in the administrative law of several of our fellow members of the European Economic Community; but to dispose of the instant case the three already well-established heads that I have mentioned will suffice.

By illegality as a ground for judicial review I mean that the decision-maker must understand correctly the law that regulates his decision-making power and must give effect to it. Whether he has or not is par excellence a justiciable question to be decided in the event of dispute, by those persons, the judges, by whom the judicial power of the state is exercisable.

By irrationality I mean what can by now be succinctly referred to as 'Wednesbury unreasonableness' (see Associated Provincial Picture Houses Ltd v Wednesbury Corp [1948] 1 KB 223). It applies to a decision which is so outrageous in its defiance of logic or accepted moral standards that no sensible person who had applied his mind to the question to be decided could have arrived at it. Whether a decision falls within the category is a question that judges by their training and experience should be well-equipped to answer, or else there would be something badly wrong with our judicial system. To justify the court's exercise of this role, resort I think today is no longer needed to Viscount Radcliffe's ingenious explanation in Edwards v Bairstow [1956] AC 14 of irrationality as a ground for a court's reversal of a decision by ascribing it to an inferred though identifiable mistake of law by the decision-maker. 'Irrationality' by now can stand on its own feet as an accepted ground on which a decision may be attacked by judicial review.

I have described the third head as 'procedural impropriety' rather than failure to observe basic rules of natural justice or failure to act with procedural fairness towards the person who will be affected by the decision. This is because susceptibility to judicial review under this head covers also failure by an administrative tribunal to observe procedural rules that are expressly laid down in the legislative instrument by which its jurisdiction is conferred, even where such failure does not involve any denial of natural justice.

NOTE: Lord Diplock's threefold classification of the grounds for judicial review has been cited in many subsequent cases. The classification will be followed in this chapter, where each of the three categories will be examined in more detail. Proportionality will be considered in the section on irrationality, *post*.

B: Illegality

Lord Diplock used this phrase to cover a number of different grounds which are frequently treated separately. The most important are:

(1) An authority must not exceed its jurisdiction by purporting to exercise powers which it does not possess.

(2) An authority must direct itself properly on the law.

(3) An authority must not use its power for an improper purpose.

(4) An authority must take into account all relevant considerations and disregard all irrelevant considerations.

(5) An authority to which the exercise of a discretion has been entrusted cannot delegate the exercise of its discretion to another unless clearly authorized to do so.

(6) An authority must not fetter its discretion.

(7) An authority acts unlawfully if it fails to fulfil a statutory duty.

(8) An authority must not excessively interfere with fundamental rights.

It should be noted that this list is not exhaustive and that the grounds clearly overlap to some extent. Consider the following cases.

Anisminic Ltd v *Foreign Compensation Commission*
[1969] 2 AC 147, House of Lords

Anisminic Ltd owned property in Egypt which was sequestrated in 1956 by the Egyptian government. In 1957 Anisminic sold the property, for substantially less than its real value, to TEDO, an Egyptian organization.

Under a treaty, the United Arab Republic paid to the United Kingdom £27.5 million as compensation for property confiscated in Egypt in 1956. Responsibility for distributing the compensation money was vested in the Foreign Compensation Commission (FCC). Anisminic Ltd submitted a claim for compensation to the FCC.

Article 4 of the Foreign Compensation (Egypt) (Determination and Registration of Claims) Order 1962 provided that the Commission shall treat a claim as established if satisfied of the following matters:

(a) the applicant is the person referred to in the relevant part of Annex E of the Order as 'the owner of the property or is the successor in title of such a person';
(b) the person referred to in the relevant part of Annex E 'and any person who became successor in title of such person on or before February 28, 1959, were British nationals on October 31, 1956, and February 28, 1959.'

The Commission's provisional determination was that Anisminic Ltd had failed to establish its claim because TEDO, its successor in title, was not a British national.

Anisminic Ltd sought a declaration that the Commission had misconstrued the Order.

LORD REID: It has sometimes been said that it is only where a tribunal acts without jurisdiction that its decision is a nullity. But in such cases the word 'jurisdiction' has been used in a very wide sense, and I have come to the conclusion that it is better not to use the term except in the narrow and original sense of the tribunal being entitled to enter on the inquiry in question. But there are many cases where, although the tribunal had jurisdiction to enter on the inquiry, it has done or failed to do something in the course of inquiry which is of such nature that its decision is a nullity. It may have given its decision in bad faith. It may have a made decision which it had no power to make. It may have failed in the course of the inquiry to comply with the requirements of natural justice. It may in perfect good faith have misconstrued the provisions giving it power to act so that it failed to deal with the question remitted to it and decided some question which was not remitted to it. It may have refused to take into account something which it was required to take into account. Or it may have based its decision on some matter which, under the provisions setting it up, it had no right to take into account. I do not intend this list to be exhaustive. But if it decides a question remitted to it for decision without committing any of these errors it is as much entitled to decide that question wrongly as it is to decide it rightly. I understand that some confusion has been caused by my having said in *Reg* v *Governor of Brixton, Ex parte Armah* [1968] AC 192, 234 that if a tribunal has jurisdiction to go right it has jurisdiction to go wrong. So it has, if one uses 'jurisdiction' in the narrow original sense. If it is entitled to enter on the inquiry and does not do any of those things which I have mentioned in the course of the proceedings, then its decision is equally valid whether it is right or wrong subject only to the power of the court in certain circumstances to correct an error of law. I think that, if these views are correct, the only case cited which was plainly wrongly decided is *Davies v Price* [1958] 1 WLR 434. But in a number of other cases some of the grounds of judgment are questionable.

I can now turn to the provisions of the Order under which the commission acted, and to the way in which the commission reached their decision. It was said in the Court of Appeal that publication of their reasons was unnecessary and perhaps undesirable. Whether or not they could have been required to publish their reasons, I dissent emphatically from the view that publication may have been undesirable. In my view, the commission acted with complete propriety, as one would expect looking to its membership.

The meaning of the important parts of this Order is extremely difficult to discover, and, in my view, a main cause of this is the deplorable modern drafting practice of compressing to the point of obscurity provisions which would not be difficult to understand if written out at rather greater length. . . .

The main difficulty in this case springs from the fact that the draftsman did not state separately what conditions have to be satisfied (1) where the applicant is the original owner and (2) where the applicant claims as the successor in title of the original owner. It is clear that where the applicant is the original owner he must prove that he was a British national on the dates stated. And it is equally clear that where the applicant claims as being the original owner's successor in title he must prove that both he and the original owner were British nationals on those dates, subject to later provisions in the article about persons who had died or had been born within the relevant period. What is left in obscurity is whether the provisions with regard to successors in title have any application at all in cases where the applicant is himself the original owner. If this provision had been split up as it should have been, and the conditions, to be satisfied where the original owner is the applicant had been set out, there could have been no such obscurity.

This is the crucial question in this case. It appears from the commission's reasons that they construed this provision as requiring them to inquire, when the applicant is himself the original owner, whether he had a successor in title. So they made that inquiry in this case and held that TEDO was the applicant's successor in title. As TEDO was not a British national they rejected the appellants' claim. But if, on a true construction of the Order, a claimant who is an original owner does not have to prove anything about successors in title, then the commission made an inquiry which the Order did not empower them to make, and they based their decision on a matter which they had no right to take into account. If one uses the word 'jurisdiction' in its wider sense, they went beyond their jurisdiction in considering this matter. It was argued that the whole matter of construing the Order was something remitted to the commission for their decision. I cannot accept that argument. I find nothing in the Order to support it. The Order requires the commission to consider whether they are satisfied with regard to the prescribed matters. That is all they have to do. It cannot be for the commission to determine the limits of its powers. Of course if one party submits to a tribunal that its powers are wider than in fact they are, then the tribunal must deal with that submission. But if they reach a wrong conclusion as to the width of their powers, the court must be able to correct that – not because the tribunal has made an error of law, but because as a result of making an error of law they have dealt with and based their decision on a matter with which, on a true construction of their powers, they had no right to deal. If they base their decision on some matter which is not prescribed for their adjudication, they are doing something which they have no right to do and, if the view which I expressed earlier is right, their decision is a nullity. So the question is whether on a true construction of the Order the applicants did or did not have to prove anything with regard to successors in title. If the commission were entitled to enter on the inquiry whether the applicants had a successor in title, then their decision as to whether TEDO was their successor in title would I think be unassailable whether it was right or wrong: it would be a decision on a matter remitted to them for their decision. The question I have to consider is not whether they made a wrong decision but whether they inquired into and decided a matter which they had no right to consider.

I have great difficulty in seeing how in the circumstances there could be a successor in title of a person who is still in existence. This provision is dealing with the period before the Order was made when the original owner had no title to anything: he had nothing but a hope that some day somehow he might get some compensation. The rest of the article makes it clear that the phrase (though inaccurate) must apply to a person who can be regarded as having inherited in some way the hope which a deceased original owner had that he would get some compensation. But 'successor in title' must I think mean some person who could come forward and make a claim in his own right. There can only be a successor in title where the title of its original possessor has passed to another person, his successor, so that the original possessor of the title can no longer make a claim, but his successor can make the claim which the original possessor of the title could have made if his title had not passed to his successor. The 'successor' of a deceased person can do that. But how could any 'successor' do this while the original owner is still in existence? One can imagine the improbable case of the original owner agreeing with someone that, for a consideration immediately paid to him, he would pay over to the other party any compensation which he might ultimately receive. But that would not create a 'successor in title' in any true sense. And I can think of no other way in which the original owner could transfer inter vivos his expectation of receiving compensation. If there were anything in the rest of the Order to indicate that such a case was intended to be covered, we might have to attribute to the phrase 'successor in title' some unusual and inaccurate meaning which would cover it. But there is nothing of that kind. In themselves the words 'successor in title' are, in my opinion, inappropriate in the circumstances of this Order to denote any person while the original owner is still in existence, and I think it most improbable that they were ever intended to denote any such person. There is no necessity to stretch them to cover any such person. I would therefore hold that the words 'and any person who became successor in title to such person' in article 4(1)(b)(ii) have no application to a case where the applicant is the original owner. It follows that the commission rejected the appellants' claim on a ground which they had no right to take into account and that their decision was a nullity. I would allow this appeal.

LORD PEARCE: Lack of jurisdiction may arise in various ways. There may be an absence of those formalities or things which are conditions precedent to the tribunal having any jurisdiction to embark on an inquiry. Or the tribunal may at the end make an order that it has no jurisdiction to make. Or in the intervening stage, while engaged on a proper inquiry, the tribunal may depart from the rules of natural justice; or it may ask itself the wrong questions; or it may take into account matters which it was not directed to take into account. Thereby it would step outside its jurisdiction. It would turn its inquiry into something not directed by Parliament and fail to make the inquiry which Parliament did direct. Any of these things would cause its purported decision to be a nullity. . . .

LORD WILBERFORCE: In every case, whatever the character of a tribunal, however wide the range of questions remitted to it, however great the permissible margin of mistakes, the essential point remains that the tribunal has a derived authority, derived, that is, from statute: at some point, and to be found from a consideration of the legislation, the field within which it operates is marked out and limited. There is always an area, narrow or wide, which is the tribunal's area; a residual area, wide or narrow, in which the legislature has previously expressed its will and into which the tribunal may not enter. Equally, though this is not something that arises in the present case, there are certain fundamental assumptions, which without explicit restatement in every case, necessarily underlie the remission of power to decide such as (I do not attempt more than a general reference, since the strength and shade of these matters will depend upon the nature of the tribunal and the kind of question it has to decide) the requirement that a decision must be made in accordance with principles of natural justice and good faith. The principle that failure to fulfil these assumptions may be equivalent to a departure from the remitted area must be taken to follow from the decision of this House in *Ridge* v *Baldwin* [1964] AC 40. Although, in theory perhaps, it may be possible for

Parliament to set up a tribunal which has full and autonomous powers to fix its own area of opera-tion, that has, so far, not been done in this country. The question, what is the tribunal's proper area, is one which it has always been permissible to ask and to answer, and it must follow that examination of its extent is not precluded by a clause conferring conclusiveness, finality, or unquestionability upon its decisions. These clauses in their nature can only relate to decisions given within the field of operation entrusted to the tribunal. They may, according to the width and emphasis of their formula-tion, help to ascertain the extent of that field, to narrow it or to enlarge it, but unless one is to deny the statutory origin of the tribunal and of its powers, they cannot preclude examination of that extent. . . .

The extent of the interpretatory power conferred upon the tribunal may sometimes be difficult to ascertain and argument may be possible whether this or that question of construction has been left to the tribunal, that is, is within the tribunal's field, or whether, because it pertains to the delimitation of the tribunal's area by the legislature, it is reserved for decision by the courts. Sometimes it will be possible to form a conclusion from the form and subject-matter of the legislation. In one case it may be seen that the legislature, while stating general objectives, is prepared to concede a wide area to the authority it establishes: this will often be the case where the decision involves a degree of policy-making rather than fact-finding, especially if the authority is a department of government or the Minister at its head. I think that we have reached a stage in our administrative law when we can view this question quite objectively, without any necessary predisposition towards one that questions of law, or questions of construction, are necessarily for the courts. In the kind of case I have mentioned there is no need to make this assumption. In another type of case it may be apparent that Parliament is itself directly and closely concerned with the definition and delimitation of certain matters of comparative detail and has marked by its language the intention that these shall accurately be observed. . . . The present case, by contrast, as examination of the relevant Order in Council will show, is clearly of the latter category. . . .

Lord Pearce and Lord Wilberforce also agreed with Lord Reid's interpretation of the Order. Lord Morris and Lord Pearson dissented.

QUESTION

On what ground or grounds did the court grant judicial review?

NOTES:

1. The Foreign Compensation Act 1950 purported to oust the jurisdiction of the courts to question any determination of the Commission. This aspect of the case is considered *post* at p. 691.

2. Since *Anisminic*, there has been considerable dispute as to whether all errors of law take a public authority outside its jurisdiction. In *Re Racal Communications Ltd, Re* [1981] AC 374 Lord Diplock stated, at p. 383:

> The break-through made by *Anisminic* [1969] 2 AC 147 was that, as respects administrative tribunals and authorities, the old distinction between errors of law that went to jurisdiction and errors of law that did not, was for practical purposes abolished. Any error of law that could be shown to have been made by them in the course of reaching their decision on matters of fact or of administrative policy would result in their having asked themselves the wrong question with the result that the decision they reached would be a nullity. . . .
>
> But there is no similar presumption that where a decision-making power is conferred by statute upon a court of law, Parliament did not intend to confer upon it power to decide questions of law as well as questions of fact. Whether it did or did not and, in the case of inferior courts, what limits are imposed on the kinds of questions of law they are empowered to decide, depends upon the construction of the statute unencumbered by any such pre-sumption. In the case of inferior courts where the decision of the court is made final and conclusive by the statute, this may involve the survival of those subtle distinctions formerly

drawn between errors of law which go to jurisdiction and errors of law which do not that did so much to confuse English administrative law before *Anisminic* [1969] 2 AC 147; but upon any application for judicial review of a decision of an inferior court in a matter which involves, as so many do, interrelated questions of law, fact and degree the superior court conducting the review should not be astute to hold that Parliament did not intend the inferior court to have jurisdiction to decide for itself the meaning of the ordinary words used in the statute to define the question which it has to decide.

In *O'Reilly* v *Mackman* [1983] 2 AC 237, at p. 278, Lord Diplock referred to the *Anisminic* case as liberating English public law 'from the fetters that the courts had theretofore imposed upon themselves so far as determinations of inferior courts and statutory tribunals were concerned by drawing esoteric distinctions between errors of law committed by such tribunals that went to their jurisdiction, and errors of law committed by them within their jurisdiction'.

There is division of opinion on the point as to whether inferior courts, but not administrative tribunals, may be immune from judicial review for errors of law within jurisdiction. In *R* v *Lord President of the Privy Council, ex parte Page* [1993] AC 682 (a case concerning the jurisdiction of a university visitor), the majority of Lords Keith, Griffiths, and Browne-Wilkinson affirmed Lord Diplock's dicta in *Re Racal Communications* on inferior courts.

QUESTION

What light is thrown on judicial thinking on the boundaries and basis of judicial review by:

(a) the erosion of the difference between jurisdictional errors and errors of law within jurisdiction; and

(b) the exception to this for inferior courts and visitors but not administrative tribunals, even those staffed by lawyers?

Wheeler v *Leicester City Council*
[1985] AC 1054, House of Lords

Leicester Football Club had a licence to use a recreation ground administered by the local council. Under s. 10 of the Open Spaces Act the council held and administered the recreation ground in trust to allow, and with a view to, its enjoyment by the public as an open space. Section 76 of the Public Health (Amendment) Act 1907 gave the council power to set apart pitches for the purpose of playing football. Section 56 of the Public Health Act 1925 gave the council power to permit the exclusive use by any club of such a pitch, subject to such charges and conditions as the local authority thought fit.

In April 1984 three members of the club were invited to join the English rugby football team selected to tour South Africa. The council supported a Commonwealth Agreement to withhold support for and discourage sporting links with South Africa. It put four questions to the club and indicated that only an affirmative answer to each of them would be acceptable:

(a) Does the Leicester Football Club support the Government opposition to the tour?

(b) Does the Leicester Football Club agree that the tour is an insult to a large proportion of the Leicester population?

(c) Will the Leicester Football Club press the Rugby Football Union to call off the tour?

(d) Will the Leicester Football Club press the players to pull out of the tour?

The club stated that, while it agreed with the council in condemning apartheid in South Africa, it was not unlawful for members to participate in the tour, nor was it contrary to the rules of the Rugby Football Union or the club. The club's role was purely advisory and it had asked the members to consider the memorandum to the Rugby Football Union prepared by the anti-apartheid movement. The three members subsequently took part in the tour. In August 1984 the council passed a resolution banning the club and its members from using the recreation ground for 12 months. The club applied for an order of *certiorari* to quash the decision. The judge refused the application and his decision was upheld by the Court of Appeal.

ACKNER LJ: . . . [Counsel], for the council, has submitted, and I entirely accept, that in exercising their discretion the council are entitled to take into account the effect that such an exercise would have on the performance of their other statutory functions. He gave us instances where the use of the pitch might potentially contravene the council's policies under the Town and Country Planning Acts, or interfere with their obligations under the Housing Acts, or contravene the Public Health Acts. In all such cases obviously the council, in considering how to exercise its discretion in relation to the recreation ground, would be entitled to and indeed be under a duty to have regard to their other statutory functions and duties.

The statutory function which [counsel] submits the council were fully entitled to take into account in exercising their discretionary powers in relation to this recreation ground, is to be found in section 71 of the Race Relations Act 1976. . . . The relevant words of the section read as follows:

. . . it shall be the duty of every local authority to make appropriate arrangements with a view to securing that their various functions are carried out with due regard to the need . . .

(b) to promote . . . good relations, between different persons of different racial groups.

[Counsel] for the club accepts that a local authority are, vis-à-vis race relations, in a very special position. It is the local authority that provides many of the social services, they are a substantial employer of labour and are thus capable of setting an example in regard to race relations conduct and policies which is likely to be followed. Notwithstanding this concession, [counsel] submits that this section is what he describes as an 'inward-looking' section, directed to requiring that the local authority themselves maintain the standards laid down by the Act, that is to say their codes of practice in regard to their own internal behaviour so as to comply with the requirements of the Act. It is a section whose function is limited to ensuring that the local authority put their own house in order.

I consider this to be too narrow a construction. To my mind the section is imposing an obligation on the local authority, when they consider discharging any of their functions which might have a race relations content, to do so in such a manner as would tend to promote good relations between persons of different racial groups. Accordingly, in my judgment, the council were fully entitled when exercising their discretionary powers in relation to this recreation ground to have regard to the purposes expressed in section 71. . . .

If I am right so far, this leaves only one final question to consider. Can it be said in the circumstances of this case that no reasonable local authority could properly conclude that temporarily banning from the use of their recreational ground an important local rugger club, which declined to condemn a South African tour and declined actively to discourage its members from participating therein, could promote good relations between persons of different racial groups? (see the well-known Wednesbury test: *Associated Provincial Picture Houses Ltd* v *Wednesbury Corp* [1948] 1 KB 223).

Ackner LJ decided that the answer to this question was no. Sir George Waller also dismissed the club's appeal, but Browne-Wilkinson LJ dissented. The club then appealed to the House of Lords.

LORD TEMPLEMAN: . . . My Lords, the laws of this country are not like the laws of Nazi Germany. A private individual or a private organisation cannot be obliged to display zeal in the pursuit of an object sought by a public authority and cannot be obliged to publish views dictated by a public authority.

The club having committed no wrong, the council could not use their statutory powers in the management of their property or any other statutory powers in order to punish the club. There is no doubt that the council intended to punish and have punished the club. When the club were presented by the council with four questions it was made clear that the club's response would only be acceptable if, in effect, all four questions were answered in the affirmative. When the club committee made their dignified and responsible response to these questions, a response which the council find unsatisfactory to the council, the council commissioned a report on possible sanctions that might be taken against the club. That report suggested that delaying tactics could be used to hold up the grant of a lease then being negotiated by the club. It suggested that land could be excluded from the lease as it was 'thought that this could embarrass the club because it had apparently granted subleases . . .' It was suggested that the council's consent, which had already been given for advertisements by the club's sponsors, could be withdrawn although according to the report 'the actual effect of this measure on the club is difficult to assess.' It was suggested that 'a further course is to insist upon strict observance of the tenant's covenants in the lease. However, the city estate's surveyor, having inspected the premises, is of the opinion that the tenant's covenants are all being complied with.' Finally, it was suggested that 'the council could terminate the club's use of the recreation ground.' This might cause some financial loss to the council and might 'form the basis of a legal challenge to the council's decision. The club may contend that the council has taken an unreasonable action against the club in response to personal decisions of members of its team over which it had no control.' Notwithstanding this warning, the council accepted the last suggestion and terminated the club's use of the recreation ground. In my opinion, this use by the council of its statutory powers was a misuse of power. The council could not properly seek to use its statutory powers of management or any other statutory powers for the purposes of punishing the club when the club had done no wrong.

In *Congreve* v *Home Office* [1976] 1 QB 629 the Home Secretary had a statutory power to revoke television licences. In exercise of that statutory power he revoked the television licences of individuals who had lawfully surrendered an existing licence and taken out a new licence before an increase in the licence fee was due to take effect. Lord Denning MR said at p. 651:

> If the licence is to be revoked – and his money forfeited – the Minister would have to give good reasons to justify it. Of course, if the licensee had done anything wrong – if he had given a cheque for £12 which was dishonoured, or if he had broken the conditions of the licence – the Minister could revoke it. But when the licensee has done nothing wrong at all, I do not think the Minister can lawfully revoke the licence, at any rate, not without offering him his money back, and not even then except for good cause. If he should revoke it without giving reasons, or for no good reason, the courts can set aside the revocation and restore the licence. It would be a misuse of the power conferred on him by Parliament: and these courts have the authority – and I would add the duty – to correct a misuse of power by a Minister or his department, no matter how much he may resent it or warn us of the consequences if we do.

Similar considerations apply, in my opinion, to the present case. Of course this does not mean that the council is bound to allow its property to be used by a racist organisation or by any organisation which, by its actions or its words, infringes the letter or the spirit of the Race Relations Act 1976. But the attitude of the club and of the committee of the club was a perfectly proper attitude, caught as they were in a political controversy which was not of their making.

For these reasons and the reasons given by my noble and learned friend Lord Roskill I would allow this appeal.

Lord Roskill decided that the council had made a decision which was so unreasonable that no reasonable authority could have come to it. The other Law Lords agreed with both Lord Templeman and Lord Roskill.

QUESTIONS

1. On which ground(s) for judicial review did each of the judges base his decision?
2. How did (a) Ackner LJ and (b) Lord Templeman decide which purposes the council was/was not entitled to pursue ? Did they find assistance in the statutes under which the council managed the recreation ground or in the Race Relations Act 1976? What other matters did they refer to in determining this issue?
3. How did they decide which purposes the club had pursued ?
4. Would it have made any difference to the decision of Lord Templeman if the club had espoused racist views in its reply to the council's request?
5. Does this case provide support for Allan's view that in judicial review proceedings the judges are furthering the political sovereignty of the people by giving effect to common standards of morality or the natural expectations of citizens?

NOTE: Lord Templeman based his decision on the ground that the council had acted for an improper purpose. Difficulties may arise when an authority acts for more than one purpose, some of which are lawful and others unlawful. The courts have not always been consistent in deciding how to deal with this conflict. Consider the approach adopted in the following extract.

R v ILEA, ex parte Westminster City Council
[1986] 1 WLR 28, High Court

The Inner London Education Authority (ILEA) determined the rates for education spending precepted on rating authorities in Inner London, including Westminster City Council. ILEA was opposed to the Government's policies, announced in 1983, of limiting the amount of rates levied by local authorities, a process known as rate-capping. By s. 142(2) of the Local Government Act 1972 ILEA was empowered to incur expenditure on arranging for the publication within their area of information on matters relating to local government. In July 1983 an education sub-committee of ILEA agreed to retain an advertising agency, referred to in the extract below as AMV, at a cost of £651,000, to mount a media and poster campaign to 'gain awareness of the authority's views of the needs of the education service and to alter the basis of the public debate about the effect of . . . Government actions.' Westminster City Council sought a declaration that the decision of the sub-committee was *ultra vires* because ILEA sought to persuade the public to support ILEA's views on rate-capping. ILEA accepted that the decision was made with the dual purpose of informing and persuading.

GLIDEWELL LJ: . . .

Two purposes

This brings me to what I regard as being the most difficult point in the case, namely, if a local authority resolves to expend its ratepayers' money in order to achieve two purposes, one of which it is authorised to achieve by statute but for the other of which it has no authority, is that decision invalid?

I was referred to the following authorities.

(i) *Westminster Corp* v *London and North Western Rly Co* [1905] AC 426. Westminster City Council had power to provide public lavatories under the Public Health (London) Act 1891, section 44. They constructed public lavatories underground, under the centre of the south end of Whitehall. The lavatories were approached from each side of the street by a subway, which could also be used as a pedestrian subway for people who wished to cross the street and not to use the lavatories. The London and North Western Railway Co., who owned the land at the east end of the subway, challenged the construction of the lavatories and subway, alleging that the main purpose of the Corporation was to construct a pedestrian subway which did not fall within the power of the Act. The Court of Appeal found for the railway company. By a majority, the House of Lords allowed the appeal, but did so on the facts, i.e., by holding that the Court of Appeal had drawn a wrong inference from the affidavits and documents before the court. In his speech, the Earl of Halsbury LC said at p. 428:

> I quite agree that if the power to make one kind of building was fraudulently used for the purpose of making another kind of building, the power given by the legislature for one purpose could not be used for another.

Lord Macnaghten said at p. 433:

> I entirely agree with Joyce J at first instance that the primary object of the council was the construction of the conveniences with the requisite and proper means of approach thereto and exit therefrom.

This suggests that a test for answering the question is, if the authorised purpose is the primary purpose, the resolution is within the power.

(ii) . . . . [is omitted]

(iii) More recently in *Hanks* v *Minister of Housing and Local Government* [1963] 1 QB 999, Megaw J did have to deal with a case in which it was alleged that a compulsory purchase order had been made for two purposes, one of which did not fall within the empowering Act. . . . [He stated] at [1963] 1 QB 999 at 1020 – 1021:

> I confess that I think confusion can arise from the multiplicity of words which have been used in this case as suggested criteria for the testing of the validity of the exercise of a statutory power. The words have included 'objects', 'purposes', 'motives', 'motivation', 'reasons', 'grounds' and 'considerations'. In the end, it seems to me, the simplest and clearest way to state the matter is by reference to 'considerations'. A 'consideration', I apprehend, is something which one takes into account as a factor in arriving at a decision. I am prepared to assume, for the purposes of the case, that, if it be shown that an authority exercising a power has taken into account as a relevant factor something which it could not properly take into account in deciding whether or not to exercise the power, then the exercise of the power, normally at least, is bad. Similarly, if the authority fails to take into account as a relevant factor something which is relevant, and which is or ought to be known to it, and which it ought to have taken into account, the exercise of that power is

normally bad. I say 'normally', because I can conceive that there may be cases where the factor wrongly taken into account, or omitted, is insignificant, or where the wrong taking-into-account, or omission, actually operated in favour of the person who later claims to be aggrieved by the decision.

. . . I have considered also the views of the learned authors of the textbooks on this. Professor Wade in his book *Administrative Law* 5th edn (1982) under the heading Duality of Purpose says at p. 388:

> Sometimes an act may serve two or more purposes, some authorised and some not, and it may be a question whether the public authority may kill two birds with one stone. The general rule is that its action will be unlawful provided the permitted purpose is the true and dominant purpose behind the act, even though some secondary or incidental advantage may be gained for some purpose which is outside the authority's powers.

Professor Evans, in *de Smith's Judicial Review of Administrative Action* 4th edn (1980) p. 329, comforts me by describing the general problem of plurality of purpose as 'a legal porcupine which bristles with difficulties as soon as it is touched.' He distils from the decisions of the courts five different tests on which reliance has been placed at one time or another, including, at pp. 330–332:

> (1) What was the *true purpose* for which the power was exercised? If the actor has in truth used his power for the purposes for which it was conferred, it is immaterial that he was thus enabled to achieve a subsidiary object . . . (5) Was any of the purposes pursued an unauthorised purpose? If so, and if the unauthorised purpose has materially influenced the actor's conduct, the power has been invalidly exercised because irrelevant considerations have been taken into account.

These two tests, and Professor Evans's comment on them, seem to me to achieve much the same result and to be similar to that put forward by Megaw J in *Hanks* v *Minister of Housing and Local Government* [1963] 1 QB 999 in the first paragraph of the passage I have quoted from his judgment. That is the part that includes the sentence: 'In the end, it seems to me, the simplest and clearest way to state the matter is by reference to considerations.' I gratefully adopt the guidance of Megaw J and the two tests I have referred to from *de Smith's Judicial Review of Administrative Action*.

It thus becomes a question of fact for me to decide, on the material before me, whether, in reaching its decision of 23 July 1984, the staff and general sub-committee of ILEA was pursuing an unauthorised purpose, namely that of persuasion, which has materially influenced the making of its decision. I have already said that I find that one of the sub-committee's purposes was the giving of information. But I also find that it had the purpose of seeking to persuade members of the public to a view identical with that of the authority itself, and indeed I believe that this was a, if not the, major purpose of the decision. In reaching this decision of fact, I have taken into account in particular the material to which I have referred above in AMV's 'presentation' of 18 July 1984, the passages I have quoted from the report of the Education Officer to the sub-committee, particularly the reference to changing 'the basis of public debate', and the various documents which have been published by AMV since 23 July with the approval of ILEA. I accept that some of the documents do inform, but in my view some of them contain little or no information and are designed only to persuade. This is true in particular, in my view, of the poster slogan 'Education Cuts Never Heal' (skilful though I think it is) and it is also true of the advertisement 'What do you get if you subtract £75 million from London's education budget?'

Adopting the test referred to above, I thus hold that ILEA's sub-committee did, when making its decision of 23 July 1984, take into account an irrelevant consideration, and thus that decision was not validly reached.

QUESTIONS

1. On which of the grounds for judicial review did the Court base its decision?

2. Glidewell LJ quoted part of a passage from de Smith. Do you agree with his comment that the two tests set out in this passage achieve much the same result? On the facts of *Westminster Corporation* v *London and North Western Railway Co* [1905] AC 426, might it have been possible to say that, although the construction of a subway was not a primary object, the desire to provide such a subway was a material influence on the council's decision?

NOTE: In *R* v *Greenwich London Borough Council, ex parte Lovelace* [1991] 3 All ER 511, Staughton LJ in the Court of Appeal stated that, in cases of 'mixed motives', the question was whether the improper motive had exercised a 'substantial influence' on the decision.

Although *R* v *ILEA, ex parte Westminster City Council* was argued on the basis that the authority had acted for an improper purpose, Glidewell LJ stated that he felt the case was best approached on the basis of whether the authority had been materially influenced by an irrelevant consideration. This ground for judicial review is dealt with in more detail in the following extract.

Padfield v *Minister for Agriculture, Fisheries and Food*
[1968] AC 997, House of Lords

The Agricultural Marketing Act 1958 regulated the marketing of various agricultural products, including milk. Section 19(3) provided: 'A committee of investigation shall . . . (b) be charged with the duty, if the Minister in any case so directs, of considering and reporting to the Minister . . . any complaint made to the Minister as to the operation of any scheme which, in the opinion of the Minister, could not be considered by a consumers' committee . . .'. The south-eastern dairy farmers complained to the Minister about the operation of a scheme involving the fixing of price differentials by the Milk Marketing Board, but the Minister refused to refer the complaint to a committee of investigation. They accordingly applied for an order of mandamus.

The Divisional Court made an order against the Minister which was set aside by the Court of Appeal.

LORD REID: . . . The question at issue in this appeal is the nature and extent of the Minister's duty under section 19(3)(b) of the Act of 1958 in deciding whether to refer to the committee of investigation a complaint as to the operation of any scheme made by persons adversely affected by the scheme. The respondent contends that his only duty is to consider a complaint fairly and that he is given an unfettered discretion with regard to every complaint either to refer it or not to refer it to the committee as he may think fit. The appellants contend that it is his duty to refer every genuine and substantial complaint, or alternatively that his discretion is not unfettered and that in this case he failed to exercise his discretion according to law because his refusal was caused or influenced by his having misdirected himself in law or by his having taken into account extraneous or irrelevant considerations.

In my view, the appellants' first contention goes too far. There are a number of reasons which would justify the Minister in refusing to refer a complaint. For example, he might consider it more suitable for arbitration, or he might consider that in an earlier case the committee of investigation had already rejected a substantially similar complaint or he might think the complaint to be frivolous or vexatious. So he must have at least some measure of discretion. But is it unfettered?

It is implicit in the argument for the Minister that there are only two possible interpretations of this provision – either he must refer every complaint or he has an unfettered discretion to refuse to refer

588   Constitutional and Administrative Law

in any case. I do not think that is right. Parliament must have conferred the discretion with the intention that it should be used to promote the policy and objects of the Act; the policy and objects of the Act must be determined by construing the Act as a whole and construction is always a matter of law for the court. In a matter of this kind it is not possible to draw a hard and fast line, but if the Minister, by reason of his having misconstrued the Act or for any other reason, so uses his discretion so as to thwart or run counter to the policy and objects of the Act, then our law would be very defective if persons aggrieved were not entitled to the protection of the court. So it is first necessary to construe the Act. . . .

The approval of Parliament shows that this scheme was thought to be in the public interest, and in so far as it necessarily involved detriment to some persons, it must have been thought to be in the public interest that they should suffer it. But in sections 19 and 20 Parliament drew a line. They provide machinery for investigating and determining whether the scheme is operating or the board is acting in a manner contrary to the public interest.

The effect of these sections is that if, but only if, the Minister and the committee of investigation concur in the view that something is being done contrary to the public interest the Minister can step in. Section 20 enables the Minister to take the initiative. Section 19 deals with complaints by individuals who are aggrieved. I need not deal with the provisions which apply to consumers. We are concerned with other persons who may be distributors or producers. If the Minister directs that a complaint by any of them shall be referred to the committee of investigation, that committee will make a report which must be published. If they report that any provision of this scheme or any act or omission of the Board is contrary to interests of the complainers *and* is not in the public interest, then the Minister is empowered to take action but not otherwise. He may disagree with the view of the committee as to public interest, and, if he thinks that there are other public interests which outweigh the public interest that justice should be done to the complainers, he would be not only entitled but bound to refuse to take action. Whether he takes action or not, he may be criticised and held accountable in Parliament but the court cannot interfere.

I must now examine the Minister's reasons for refusing to refer the appellant's complaint to the committee. I have already set out the letters of March 23 and May 3, 1965. I think it is right also to refer to a letter sent from the Ministry on May 1 1964, because in his affidavit the Minister says he has read this letter and there is no indication that he disagrees with any part of it.

[Lord Reid read the letter and continued.] The first reason which the Minister gave in his letter of March 23, 1965, was that this complaint was unsuitable for investigation because it raised wide issues. Here it appears to me that the Minister has clearly misdirected himself. Section 19(6) contemplates the raising of issues so wide that it may be necessary for the Minister to amend a scheme or even to revoke it. Narrower issues may be suitable for arbitration but section 19 affords the only method of investigating wide issues. In my view it is plainly the intention of the Act that even the widest issues should be investigated if the complaint is genuine and substantial, as this complaint certainly is.

Then it is said that the issue should be 'resolved through the arrangements available to producers and the board within the framework of the scheme itself.' This re-states in a condensed form the reasons given in paragraph 4 of the letter of May 1, 1964, where it is said ' the Minister owes no duty to producers in any particular region,' and reference is made to the 'status of the Milk Marketing Scheme as an instrument for the self-government of the industry,' and to the Minister 'assuming an inappropriate degree of responsibility.' But as I have already pointed out, the Act imposes on the Minister a responsibility whenever there is a relevant and substantial complaint that the board are acting in a manner inconsistent with the public interest, and that has been relevantly alleged in this case. I can find nothing in the Act to limit this responsibility or to justify the statement that the Minister owes no duty to producers in a particular region. The Minister is, I think, correct in saying that the board is an instrument of the self-government of the industry. So long as it does not act contrary to the public interest the Minister cannot interefere. But if it does act contrary to what both the committee of investigation and the Minister hold to be the public interest the Minister has a duty to act. And if a complaint relevantly alleges that the board has so acted, as this complaint does, then it appears to me that the Act does impose a duty on the Minister to have it investigated. If he does not do that he is rendering nugatory a safeguard provided by the Act and depriving complainers of a remedy which I am satisfied that Parliament intended them to have. . . .

The House of Lords by a majority allowed the appeal and granted an order of mandamus (Lord Morris of Borth-y-Gest dissenting).

NOTE: The aftermath of this case provides a good illustration of the point that success in a judicial review application does not require that the authority whose actions have been challenged must reach a decision which is favourable to the applicant. After this case the Minister submitted a complaint for investigation to the investigative committee. The Minister then rejected the committee's advice. Commenting on this Carol Harlow stated that 'The remedy had proved illusory; the same decision could be reached with only nominal deference to the court, and the waste of time and money entailed is a deterrent to future complainants' (C. Harlow, 'Administrative Reaction to Judicial Review' [1976] *Public Law* 116). Do you agree?

QUESTIONS

1. How did the House of Lords decide which considerations were relevant and which were irrelevant?

2. How did the House of Lords decide which considerations had been taken into account?

3. Are there any circumstances in which the taking into account of an irrelevant consideration will not render the decision unlawful. Does *R* v *Inner London Education Authority* (*ante*, p. 584) suggest an answer? (See also *R* v *BBC, ex parte Owen* [1985] 2 All ER 522.)

NOTES:

1. Public bodies will have various duties and powers and responsibilities. Are they entitled to take into account their own financial resources in making decisions involving expenditure? In *R* v *Gloucestershire County Council, ex parte Barry* [1997] AC 584, the removal of cleaning and laundry services by the council on the ground of lack of resources was challenged. The House of Lords by a 3:2 majority held that it was a relevant consideration for a council to take into account the resources it had available when carrying out its statutory duty under the Chronically Sick and Disabled Persons Act 1970, s. 2(1), to consider the needs of chronically sick and disabled persons in its area. Lord Nicholls said that 'needs for services cannot be sensibly assessed without having some regard to the cost of providing them. A person's need for a particular type or level of service cannot be decided in a vacuum from which all considerations of cost have been expelled'. In a subsequent decision the Court of Appeal held in *R* v *Sefton Metropolitan Borough Council, ex parte Help the Aged* [1997] 4 All ER 532, that a council making decisions under National Assistance Act 1948, s. 21(1) as to whether an elderly person was in need of care and attention, was entitled to have regard to its own resources. Where it was decided that a person was in such need then a lack of resources was no excuse if arrangements were not made to provide for the identified needs. Subsequently *ex parte Barry* has been distinguished by the House of Lords in *R* v *East Sussex County Council, ex parte Tandy* [1998] 2 All ER 769, where it was held that a local education authority's resources were an irrelevant consideration in determining what constituted suitable education for the purposes of the Education Act 1993, s. 298. This section imposed a duty to make arrangements for suitable education for children in specified circumstances. Their Lordships also held that if

there was more than one way of providing suitable education, then it would be permissible for a local education authority to have regard to its resources in choosing between different ways of making such provision.

A Chief Constable may have regard to available resources when determining policing priorities: see *R* v *Chief Constable of Sussex, ex parte International Traders Ferry Ltd* [1999] 2 AC 418, *post* p. 632).

2. Failure to consider a legitimate expectation is a failure to consider a relevant consideration: see *post* p. 645, *R (Bibi)* v *Newham London Borough Council* [2001] EWCA Civ 607, [2002] 1 WLR 237.

3. It has been held to be an irrelevant consideration for the Home Secretary to take into account a public campaign urging a long period of minimum detention for boys who had murdered a younger child. The majority of the House of Lords held in *R* v *Secretary of State for the Home Department, ex parte Venables* [1997] 3 WLR 23, that in this position of determining the minimum period of detention or tariff, it was permissible to take into account general considerations of public confidence in the administration of justice. In making this decision the Home Secretary was acting like a judge determining sentence. It was further held that the consideration of the public campaign in a particular case would also amount to a breach of natural justice.

4. It will be clear that the court is required to address some difficult issues in deciding upon the legality of an authority's decisions. For example, how do the courts decide what considerations were taken into account? How do they decide whether an irrelevant consideration has had only an insignificant or insubstantial influence on a decision?

Two points in particular should be noted. First, the burden of proof in an application for judicial review generally falls on the applicant. Hence, for example, the onus was on the complainants in *Padfield* to prove that irrelevant consideration(s) were taken into account.

Secondly, there is no general requirement that the authority should give reasons for its decision. In the course of argument in *Padfield* it was submitted that the Minister may properly refuse to act on a complaint without giving any reasons, and that in such a case a complainant would have no remedy and the decision could not be questioned. Lord Pearce stated at pp. 1053–4:

> I do not regard a Minister's failure or refusal to give any reasons as a sufficient exclusion of the court's surveillance. If all the prima facie reasons seem to point in favour of his taking a certain course to carry out the intention of Parliament in respect of a power which it has been given to him in that regard, and he gives no reason whatever for taking a contrary course, the court may infer that he has no good reason and that he is not using the power given by Parliament to carry out its intentions. In the present case, however, the Minister has given reasons which show that he was not exercising his discretion in accordance with the intentions of the Act.

(See also the comments of Lord Reid, at pp. 1032(G)–1033(A) and Lord Upjohn, at pp. 1061(G)–62(A).)

After citing this passage in the case of *Lonrho plc* v *Secretary of State* [1989] 2 All ER 609, at p. 620, Lord Keith, with whom the other Law Lords agreed, stated:

> The absence of reasons for a decision where there is no duty to give them cannot of itself provide any support for the suggested irrationality of the decision. The only significance of the absence of reasons is that if all other known facts and circumstances appear to point overwhelmingly in favour of a different decision, the decision-maker who has given no reasons cannot complain if the court draws the inference that he had no rational reason for his decision.

To what extent does this statement differ from that of Lord Pearce in *Padfield*?

While there is no general duty to provide reasons authorities are sometimes obliged by statute to provide them (see, in particular, s. 10 of the Tribunal and Inquiries Act 1992, *post* at

p. 755). It has also been recently accepted that natural justice could, in exceptional cases, require the provision of reasons (see *R v Civil Service Appeal Board, ex parte Cunningham* [1991] 4 All ER 310, discussed at [1991] *Public Law*, pp. 340–46). In *Doody v Secretary of State for the Home Department* [1993] 3 All ER 92 the House of Lords held that the Secretary of State was obliged to give reasons to prisoners when he proposed to depart from the periods recommended by the judiciary for the purposes of retribution and deterrence. Yet in *R v Higher Education Funding Council, ex parte Institute of Dental Surgery* [1994] 1 All ER 651, although the council's reasons for refusing to give reasons for its decision to lower the institute's research rating were not well grounded, this was not a case in which the law might require reasons. In *R v Ministry of Defence, ex parte Murray* [1998] COD 134 the principles from those three cases were drawn together by Hooper J. While there was as yet no general duty to give reasons, the courts will seek to ensure that bodies given power to make decisions affecting individuals act fairly and it may be that a procedure of not giving reasons is unfair, even if there is no requirement to do so. Particular concern will arise if a tribunal's decisions affect personal liberty. In deciding if fairness requires a tribunal to give reasons, then regard will be had to the initial hearing but also to the availability of any appeal or judicial review and the absence of such a remedy could be a point in favour of requiring reasons. Reasons will not be required where considerations of public interest would outweigh the advantages of requiring reasons or if the procedures of a particular decision-maker would be frustrated if required to give reasons, even short reasons. In summary, factors in favour of requiring reasons are: 'the giving of reasons may among other things concentrate the decision-maker's mind on the right questions; demonstrate to the recipient that this is so; show that the issues have been conscientiously addressed and how the result has been reached; or alternatively alert the recipient to a justiciable flaw in the process'. On the other hand factors not requiring the giving of reasons include where: 'it may place an undue burden on decision-makers; demand an appearance of unanimity where there is diversity; call for articulation of sometimes inexpressible value judgments; and offer an invitation to the captious to comb the reasons for previously unsuspected grounds of challenge'.

In *R v Secretary of State for the Home Department, ex parte Fayed* [1997] 1 All ER 228, British Nationality Act 1981, s. 44(2) allowed the Home Secretary not to give reasons when deciding applications for naturalization as British citizens. By a majority the Court of Appeal held that the Minister had to be fair and that an applicant should be given sufficient information about the Minister's concerns to allow the applicant to make representations. If that would involve disclosing matters not in the public interest then this should be indicated so that the applicant could challenge the justification for the refusal to give reasons in the courts. Note that the section did not ban the giving of reasons.

British Oxygen Co. Ltd v *Minister of Technology*
[1971] AC 610, House of Lords

British Oxygen Co. Ltd used metal cylinders to store pressurized gases which it manufactured. It applied for a grant in respect of the cylinders under s. 1(1) of the Industrial Development Act 1966, which provided that the Board of Trade 'may make to any person carrying on a business in Great Britain a grant towards approved capital expenditure incurred by that person in providing new machinery or plant.' The Board had a policy of denying grants for any item of plant costing less than £25 and, in pursuance of that policy, rejected British Oxygen's application as the gas cylinders cost just under £20 each. British Oxygen sought declarations that (inter alia) the cylinders were eligible for grant.

LORD REID: Section 1 of the Act provides that the Board of Trade 'may' make grants. It was not argued that 'may' in this context means 'shall', and it seems to me clear the the Board were intended to have a discretion. But how were the Board intended to operate that discretion? Does the Act read as a whole indicate any policy which the Board is to follow or even give any guidance to the Board? If it does then the Board must exercise its discretion in accordance with such policy or guidance (*Padfield* v *Minister of Agriculture, Fisheries and Food* [1986] AC 997). One generally expects to find that Parliament has given some indication as to how public money is to be distributed. In this Act Parliament has clearly laid down the conditions for eligibility for grants and it has clearly given to the Board a discretion so that the Board is not bound to pay to every person who is eligible to receive such a grant. But I can find nothing to guide the Board as to the circumstances in which they should pay or the circumstances in which they should not pay grants to such persons. . . .

There are two general grounds on which the exercise of an unqualified discretion can be attacked. It must not be exercised in bad faith, and it must not be so unreasonably exercised as to show that there cannot have been any real or genuine exercise of the discretion. But, apart from that, if the Minister thinks that policy or good administration requires the operation of some limiting rule, I find nothing to stop him.

It was argued on the authority of *Rex* v *Port of London Authority ex parte Kynoch* [1919] 1 KB 176 that the Minister is not entitled to make a rule for himself as to how he will in future exercise his discretion. In that case Kynoch owned land adjoining the Thames and wished to construct a deep water wharf. For this they had to get the permission of the authority. Permission was refused on the ground that Parliament had charged the authority with the duty of providing such facilities. It appeared that before reaching their decision the authority had fully considered the case on its merits and in relation to the public interest. So their decision was upheld.

Bankes LJ said at p. 184:

> There are on the one hand cases where a tribunal in the honest exercise of its discretion has adopted a policy, and, without refusing to hear an applicant, intimates to him what its policy is, and that after hearing him it will in accordance with its policy decide against him, unless there is something exceptional in his case. I think counsel for the applicants would admit that, if the policy has been adopted for reasons which the tribunal may legitimately entertain, no objection could be taken to such a course. On the other hand there are cases where a tribunal has passed a rule, or come to a determination, not to hear any application of a particular character by whomsoever made. There is a wide distinction to be drawn between these two classes.

I see nothing wrong with that. But the circumstances in which discretions are exercised vary enormously and that passage cannot be applied literally in every case. The general rule is that anyone who has to exercise a statutory discretion must not 'shut his ears to an application' (to adapt from Bankes LJ on p. 183). I do not think there is any great difference between a policy and a rule. There may be cases where an officer or authority ought to listen to a substantial argument reasonably presented urging a change of policy. What the authority must not do is to refuse to listen at all. But a ministry or large authority may have had to deal already with a multitude of similar applications and then they will almost certainly have evolved a policy so precise that it could well be called a rule. There can be no objection to that, provided the authority is always willing to listen to anyone with something new to say – of course I do not mean to say that there need be an oral hearing. In the present case the respondent's officers have carefully considered all that the appellants have had to say and I have no doubt that they will continue to do so. . . .

VISCOUNT DILHORNE: [T]he distinction between a policy decision and a rule may not be easy to draw. In this case it was not challenged that it was within the power of the Board to adopt a policy not to make a grant in respect of such an item. The policy might equally well be described as a rule. It was both reasonable and right that the Board should make known to those interested the policy it was going to follow. By doing so fruitless applications involving expense and expenditure of time might be avoided. The Board says that it has not refused to consider any application. It considered the appellants'. In these circumstances it is not necessary to decide in this case whether, if it had refused to consider an application on the ground that it related to an item costing less than £25, it would have acted wrongly.

I must confess that I feel some doubt whether the words used by Bankes LJ in the passage cited above [see p. 592 *supra*] are really applicable to a case of this kind. It seems somewhat pointless and a waste of time that the Board should have to consider applications which are bound as a result of its policy decision to fail. Representations could of course be made that the policy should be changed. . . .

Lord Morris of Borth-y-gest, Lord Wilberforce and Lord Diplock agreed with Lord Reid.

QUESTIONS

1. On which ground(s) was the decision of the House of Lords based?

2. Under the Children Act 1989 local authorities have a duty to safeguard and promote the welfare of children within their area who are in need 'by providing a range and level of services appropriate to those children's needs' (s. 17). The services may include giving assistance in kind or, in exceptional circumstances, in cash. Assume that a local authority has made certain policies to govern the provision of such assistance. An applicant for assistance in cash is told that her application will be refused under the general policies operated by the council (of which she is aware) unless she wishes to make representations that the policies should be altered and the authority is prepared to accept the representations. Would the applicant be able to challenge this decision? (See *Attorney-General ex relator Tilley* v *Wandsworth LBC* [1981] 1 WLR 854.)

NOTES:

1. In *R(P)* v *Secretary of State for the Home Department* and *R(Q)* v *Secretary of State for the Home Department* [2002] EWCA Civ 1151, [2001] 1 WLR 2002 the Court of Appeal demonstrated how to deal with a rigid or blanket policy when human rights were engaged. In these cases the Prison Service's policy requiring babies to be separated from their prisoner mothers on reaching 18 months of age was considered in the light of the mother's, and particularly the child's, right to family life. The Prison Service was required to consider whether the interference with the right was justified by the legitimate aims in Article 8(2). Factors to be taken into account include necessary limitations upon the mother's rights because of her imprisonment, how relaxation of the policy might affect the good order and discipline of the prison, the length of the mother's sentence, the welfare of the child including the extent of harm likely to be caused by separation, the extent of harm likely to be caused by remaining in prison, and the quality of alternative arrangements. The Court concluded that in most cases separation before 18 months would be justified but there could be cases in which the interests of mother and child outweighed other factors. In the case of P the application of the policy would be lawful but so far as Q was concerned there were factors which led to the court to remit the case to the Prison Service for reconsideration. On the application of this test with pressing social need see *ante* p. 560 and for its relationship with *Wednesbury* unreasonableness/irrationality and proportionality see *ante* p. 549.

2. See C. Hilson 'Judicial Review, Polices and the Fettering of Discretion' [2002] PL 111 for a thorough examination of the 'no fettering' doctrine in which the doctrine and its application

by the courts are criticised and an argument is made for a more nuanced approach which allows for justifiable rigid policies and also for more individualized decision-making where required and, where human rights are engaged, for a relationship in which the newer human rights approach can be combined with the older doctrine.
3. The application of a policy may result in breaches of the duty to be fair (see *post*, p. 597). For example, in *R v Secretary of State for the Environment, ex parte Brent LBC* [1982] QB 593 the Secretary of State failed to consider any of the representations made to him to change his policy on reducing the rate support grant to certain authorities. The Divisional Court held that he had both unlawfully fettered his discretion and failed to discharge the duty of fairness.

R v Secretary of State for the Home Department, ex parte Simms
[1999] 3 WLR 328, House of Lords

The applicants were prisoners who convicted of murder and who continued to protest their innocence after they had been refused permission to appeal against their convictions. On becoming aware that some of the applicants' visitors were journalists who were interested in publicizing the applicants' stories, the prison authorities refused to allow journalists to visit the prisoners unless they signed an undertaking that no material obtained in the visits would be used for professional purposes. The authority for this was para. 37 of section A of the Prison Service Standing Order No. 5 of 1996. The journalists did not seek permission under para. 37A where, exceptionally, professional visits could be permitted conditionally. The Home Secretary had a blanket policy excluding professional visits on the basis that they tended to undermine proper control and discipline. The applicants successfully sought judicial review arguing that the blanket ban on the use of information was an excessive interference with the right of free speech. The Court of Appeal reversed this decision. On appeal to the House of Lords.

LORD STEYN: . . . Two important inferences can and should be drawn. First, until the Home Secretary imposed a blanket ban on oral interviews between prisoners and journalists in or about 1995, such interviews had taken place from time to time and had served to identify and undo a substantial number of miscarriages of justice. There is no evidence that any of these interviews had resulted in any adverse impact on prison discipline. Secondly, the evidence establishes clearly that without oral interviews it is now virtually impossible under the Home Secretary's blanket ban for a journalist to take up the case of a prisoner who alleges a miscarriage of justice. In the process a mean of correcting errors in the functioning of the criminal justice system has been lost.

(c) The counter-arguments on behalf of the Home Secretary
For my part I am reasonably confident that once it is accepted that oral interviews with prisoners serve a useful purpose in exposing potential miscarriages of justice the Home Secretary would not wish his present policy to be maintained. But, if I am mistaken in that supposition, my view is that investigative journalism, based on oral interviews with prisoners, fulfils an important corrective role, with wider implications than the undoing of particular miscarriages of justice. Nevertheless. I must directly address the counter arguments advance by the Home Secretary.

Latham J was unimpressed with the reasons advanced in opposition to the applicants' limited claim in the first affidavit of Audrey Wickington. In my judgment the judge was right. The two new affidavits make a case that any oral interviews between prisoners and journalist will tend to disrupt discipline and order in prisons. In my view these affidavits do not take sufficient account of the limited nature of the applicants' claims, viz to have interviews for the purpose of obtaining a thorough investigation of their cases as a first step to possibly gaining access through the Criminal Cases Review Commission to the Court of Appeal (Criminal Division). The affidavits do not refute the case that until 1995 such interviews enabled a substantial number of miscarriages to be undone. Moreover, they do not establish that interviews confined to such limited purposes caused disruption to prison life. In any event, the affidavits do not establish a case of pressing need which might prevail over the prisoners' attempt to gain access to justice: see decision of the Court of Appeal in *Reg.* v *Secretary of State for the Home Department, Ex parte Leech* [1994] QB 198, the correctness of which was expressly accepted by counsel for the Home Secretary.

Counsel for the Home Secretary relied on the decision of the United States Supreme Court in *Pell* v *Procunier* (1974) 417 US 817. The case involved a ban by prison authorities of face to face interviews between journalists and inmates. The background was a relatively small number of inmates who as a result of press attention became virtual 'public figures' within prison society and gained a disproportionate notoriety and influence among their fellow inmates. The evidence showed that the interviews caused severe disciplinary problems. By a majority of five to four the Supreme Court held the ban to be constitutional. The majority enunciated an approach of a 'measure of judicial deference owed to corrections officials'. This approach was followed in *Turner* v *Safley* (1987) 482 US 78 where the Supreme Court upheld restrictions on correspondence between inmates. In *Pell* v *Procunier* the Supreme Court was faced with a very particular and intolerable situation in the Californian prison service where there had been virtually unlimited access by journalists to inmates. Nobody suggests anything of the kind in the present case. While the inmates in *Pell* v *Procunier* no doubt wished to air their general grievances, there is nothing in the report to indicate that the prisoners wanted interviews with journalists for the specific purpose of obtaining access to an appeal process to challenge their convictions. And, in any event, the approach of judicial deference to the views of prison authorities enunciated in *Pell* v *Procunier* does not accord with the approach under English law. It is at variance with the principle that only a pressing social need can defeat freedom of expression as explained in the *Derbyshire* case [*Derbyshire County Council* v *Times Newspapers*] [1993] AC 534, 550n–551A, the *Leech* case [1994] QB 198, 212 E–F, and *Silver* v *United Kingdom* (1980) 3 EHRR 475, 514–515, paras 372–375 (the commission): (1983) 5 EHRR 347, 377, para. 99(e) (the court). It is also inconsistent with the principle that the more substantial the interference with fundamental rights the more the court will require by way of justification before it can be satisfied that the interference is reasonable in a public law sense: *Reg.* v *Ministry of Defence, Ex parte Smith* [1996] QB 517, 554E–F. In my view *Pell* v *Procunier* does not assist.

(d) Conclusion
On the assumption that paragraphs 37 and 37A should be construed as the Home Secretary contends, I have no doubt that these provisions are exorbitant in width in so far as they would undermine the fundamental rights invoked by the applicants in the present proceedings and are therefore ultra vires.

2. The interpretation of paragraphs 37 and 37A
It is now necessary to examine the correctness of the interpretation of paragraphs 37 and 37A, involving a blanket ban on interviews, as advanced by the Home Secretary. Literally construed there is force in the extensive construction put forward. But one cannot lose sight that there is at stake a fundamental or basic right, namely the right of a prisoner to seek through oral interviews to persuade a journalist to investigate the safety of the prisoner's conviction and to publicise his findings in an effort to gain access to justice for the prisoner. In these circumstances even in the absence of an ambiguity there comes into play a presumption of general application operating as a constitutional principle as Sir Rupert Cross explained in successive editions of his classic work: *Statutory Interpretation*, 3rd ed. (1995), pp. 165–166. This is called 'the principle of legality:' *Halsbury's Laws of England*,

4th ed. reissue, vol. 8(2) (1996), pp. 13–14, para. 6. Ample illustrations of the application of this principle are given in the speech of Lord Browne-Wilkinson, and in my speech, in *Reg*. v *Secretary of State for the Home Department, Ex parte Pierson* [1998] AC 539, 573G–575D, 587C–590A. Applying this principle I would hold that paragraphs 37 and 37A leave untouched the fundamental and basic rights asserted by the applicants in the present case.

The only relevant issue in the present proceedings is whether paragraphs 37 and 37A are ultra vires because they are in conflict with the fundamental and basic rights claimed by the applicants. The principle of legality justifies the conclusion that paragraphs 37 and 37A have not been demonstrated to be ultra vires in the cases under consideration.

3. The disposal of the appeal

My Lords, my judgment does not involve tearing up the rule book governing prisons. On the contrary I have taken full account of the essential public interest in maintaining order and discipline in prisons. But, I am satisfied that consistently with order and discipline in prisons it is administratively workable to allow prisoners to be interviewed for the narrow purposes here at stake notably if a proper foundation is laid in correspondence for the requested interview or interviews. One has to recognise that oral interviews with journalists are not in the same category as visits by relatives and friends and require more careful control and regulation. That is achievable. This view is supported by the favourable judgment of past experience. Moreover, in reality an oral interview is simply a necessary and practical extension of the right of a prisoner to correspond to journalists about his conviction: compare *Silver* v *United Kingdom* (1980) 3 EHRR 475 (the commission): 5 EHRR, 347 (the court) and Livingstone & Owen, *Prison Law*, 2nd ed. (1999), pp. 228–230, paras 7.30–7.33.

The criminal justice system has been shown to be fallible. Yet the effect of the judgment of the Court of Appeal is to outlaw the safety valve of effective investigative journalism. In my judgment the conclusions and reasoning of the Court of Appeal were wrong.

Declarations should be granted in both cases to the effect that the Home Secretary's current policy is unlawful, and that the governors' administrative decisions pursuant to that policy were also unlawful. I would allow both appeals.

While the rules were *intra vires*, the policy was unlawful.

NOTES:
1. The decision is based on common law and not the Human Rights Act 1998, the entry into force of which it pre-dated by some 14 months.
2. In *R (Daly)* v *Secretary of State for the Home Department* [2001] UKHL 26, [2001] 2 AC 532 *ante* p. 558 and *post* p. 630 their Lordships accepted that there were some fundamental rights recognised by the common law which included access to a court; access to legal advice; and the right to communicate confidentially with a legal adviser under the seal of legal professional privilege, which only the express words of a statute could restrict. Accordingly the policy on searching cells including papers covered by legal professional privilege without the prisoner being present was unlawful under both the common law and the Human Rights Acts 1998.

C: Procedural impropriety

In *CCSU* v *Minister for the Civil Service* (*ante*, p. 575) Lord Diplock used this phrase specifically to include both a breach of express statutory procedural requirements and the common law rules of natural justice. Express statutory requirements include, for example, a requirement to give notice or to consult certain persons before a decision is made. Whether or not a breach of a statutory requirement will render the resulting decision invalid depends on a number of circumstances, including the importance of the provision which has been disregarded in the light of the objects of the statute, whether there was total or only partial breach of the requirement, and whether or not the breach caused any prejudice (see, for example, *Coney* v *Choyce* [1975] 1 All ER 979; *Bradbury* v *London Borough of Enfield* [1967] 3 All ER 434; *London and Clydeside Estates Ltd* v *Aberdeen DC* [1979] 2 All ER 876). This section will focus on the common law rules of natural justice.

Council of Civil Service Unions v *Minister for the Civil Service*
[1985] AC 374, House of Lords

The facts are set out *post*, at p. 622.

LORD ROSKILL: . . . the use of this phrase [natural justice] is no doubt hallowed by time and much judicial repetition, but it is a phrase often widely misunderstood and therefore as often misused. The phrase perhaps might now be allowed to find a permanent resting place and be better replaced by speaking of a duty to act fairly. But the latter phrase must not in its turn be misunderstood or misused. It is not for the courts to determine whether a particular policy or particular decisions taken in fulfilment of that policy are fair. They are only concerned with the manner in which those decision have been taken and the extent of the duty to act fairly will vary greatly from case to case as indeed the decided cases since 1950 consistently show. Many features will come into play including the nature of the decision and the relationship of those involved on either side before the decision was taken.

NOTE: The use of the phrase 'duty to act fairly' rather than 'natural justice' is frequently traced to the decision in *Re HK* [1967] 2 QB 617 where it was held that, although immigration officers were not obliged to hold a hearing before determining an immigrant's status, they were obliged to act fairly. Since then there has been a difference of opinion on the correct use of the two phrases. In *McInnes* v *Onslow Fane* [1978] 1 WLR 1520 Megarry V-C stated that 'the further the situation is away from anything that resembles a judicial or quasi-judicial decision, and the further the question is removed from what may reasonably be called a justiciable question, the more appropriate it is to reject an expression which includes the word justice and to use instead terms such as "fairness" or "the duty to act fairly".' Other judges have used the phrases interchangeably. What did Lord Roskill state on this point and why?

A related difficulty is whether there is any difference between the content of natural justice and the content of the duty to be fair. On one view, which appears to be that of both Lord Roskill and Megarry V-C, there is no difference: the content of natural justice and the content of the duty to be fair are both flexible and depend on all the circumstances of the case. Another view, however, is that the duty to be fair might include requirements which were not part of the traditional concept of natural justice, for example a duty to act on evidence (see *R* v *Deputy Industrial Injuries Commissioner, ex parte Moore* [1965] 1 QB 456).

In the notes and questions which follow, reference will be made to the duty to be fair. The cases cited will, however, contain references to both concepts for the reasons explained above.

What then is required of the duty to be fair? As Lord Fraser indicated in *CCSU* v *Minister for the Civil Service*, the requirements of fairness depend on all the circumstances of the case. In an earlier case, *Russell* v *Duke of Norfolk* [1949] 1 All ER 109, in which the term natural justice was used, Tucker LJ stated, at p. 118:

> . . . There are, in my view, no words which are of universal application to every kind of inquiry and every kind of domestic tribunal. The requirements of natural justice must depend on the circumstances of the case, the nature of the inquiry, the rules under which the tribunal is acting, the subject matter which is being dealt with and so forth. Accordingly, I do not derive much assistance from the definitions of natural justice which have been from time to time used. . . .

The requirements of the duty to be fair are generally divided into two general principles, the rule against bias and the right to a fair hearing.

(a) The rule against bias

R v *Bow Street Metropolitan Stipendiary Magistrate, ex parte Pinochet Ugarte (No. 2)*
[2000] 1 AC 119, House of Lords

> The applicant was the former head of state of Chile. Extradition proceedings were brought at the request of a Spanish judge in respect of allegations of crimes against humanity committed when the applicant was President of Chile. Two arrest warrants had been issued by the magistrate, but they had been quashed in an application for judicial review; however, the quashing of the second was stayed so that an appeal could be heard by the House of Lords on the scope of immunity of a former head of state from arrest and extradition proceedings in the United Kingdom in respect of acts committed while he was head of state. Amnesty International (AI) was permitted to act as a third-party intervenor in these proceedings. By a 3:2 majority the appeal was allowed on 25 November 1998 and the second warrant was restored. Afterwards the applicant learnt that Lord Hoffmann, who was a member of the majority in the appeal before the House of Lords, was a member and chairman of Amnesty International Charity Ltd (AICL), a body which carried out AI's charitable purposes. The applicant petitioned the House to set aside the order of 25 November.

LORD BROWNE-WILKINSON: . . . The contention is that there was a real danger or reasonable apprehension or suspicion that Lord Hoffmann might have been biased, that is to say, it is alleged that there is an appearance of bias not actual bias.

The fundamental principle is that a man may not be a judge in his own cause. This principle, as developed by the courts, has two very similar but not identical implications. First it may be applied literally: if a judge is in fact a party to the litigation or has a financial or proprietary interest in its outcome then he is indeed sitting as a judge in his own cause. In that case, the mere fact that he is a party to the action or has a financial or proprietary interest in its outcome is sufficient to cause his automatic disqualification. The second application of the principle is where a judge is not a party to the suit and does not have a financial interest in its outcome, but in some other way his conduct or behaviour may give rise to a suspicion that he is not impartial, for example because of his friendship with a party. This second type of case is not strictly speaking an application of the principle that a man must not be judge in his own cause, since the judge will not normally be himself benefiting, but providing a benefit for another by failing to be impartial.

In my judgment, this case falls within the first category of case, viz. where the judge is disqualified because he is a judge in his own cause. In such a case, once it is shown that the judge is himself a party to the cause, or has a relevant interest in its subject matter, he is disqualified without any investigation into whether there was a likelihood or suspicion of bias. The mere fact of his interest is sufficient to disqualify him unless he has made sufficient disclosure: see Shetreet, *Judges on Trial* (1976), p. 303; De Smith, Woolf and Jowell, *Judicial Review of Administrative Action*, 5th ed. (1995) p. 525, I will call this 'automatic disqualification'.

In *Dimes* v *Proprietors of Grand Junction Canal* (1852) 3 HL Cas 759, the then Lord Chancellor, Lord Cottenham, owned a substantial shareholding in the defendant canal which was an incorporated body. In the action the Lord Chancellor sat on appeal from the Vice-Chancellor, whose judgment in favour of the company he affirmed. There was an appeal to your Lordships' House on the grounds that the Lord Chancellor was disqualified. Their Lordships consulted the judges who advised, at p. 786, that Lord Cottenham was disqualified from sitting as a judge in the cause because he had an interest in the suit. This advice was unanimously accepted by their Lordships. There was no inquiry by the court as to whether a reasonable man would consider Lord Cottenham to be biased and no inquiry as to the circumstances which led to Lord Cottenham sitting. Lord Campbell said, at p. 793:

> No one can suppose that Lord Cottenham could be, in the remotest degree, influenced by the interest he had in this concern: but, my Lords, it is of the last importance that the maxim that no man is to be a judge in his own cause should be held sacred. And that is not to be confined to a cause *in which he a party*, but applies to a cause in which he has an interest. (Emphasis added.)

On occasion, this proposition is elided so as to omit all references to the disqualification of a judge who is a party to the suit: see, for example, *Reg.* v *Rand* (1866) LR 1 QB 230; *Reg.* v *Gough* [1993] AC 646, 661. This does not mean that a judge who is a party to a suit is not disqualified just because the suit does not involve a financial interest. The authorities cited in the *Dimes* case show how the principle developed. The starting-point was the case in which a judge was indeed purporting to decide a case in which he was a party. This was held to be absolutely prohibited. That absolute prohibition was then extended to cases where, although not nominally a party, the judge had an interest in the outcome.

The importance of this point in the present ease is this. Neither AI, nor AICL have any financial interest in the outcome of this litigation. We are here confronted, as was Lord Hoffmann, with a novel situation where the outcome of the litigation did not lead to financial benefit to anyone. The interest of AI in the litigation was not financial: it was its interest in achieving the trial and possible conviction of Senator Pinochet for crimes against humanity.

By seeking to intervene in this appeal and being allowed so to intervene, in practice AI became a party to the appeal. Therefore if, in the circumstances, it is right to treat Lord Hoffmann as being the alter ego of AI and therefore a judge in his own cause, then he must have been automatically disqualified on the grounds that he was a party to the appeal. Alternatively, even if it be not right to say that Lord Hoffmann was a party to the appeal as such, the question then arises whether, in non-financial litigation, anything other than a financial or proprietary interest in the outcome is sufficient automatically to disqualify a man from sitting as judge in the cause.

Are the facts such as to require Lord Hoffmann to be treated as being himself a party to this appeal? The facts are striking and unusual. One of the parties to the appeal is an unincorporated association, AI. One of the constituent parts of that unincorporated association is AICL. AICL was established, for tax purposes, to carry out part of the functions of AI those parts which were charitable which had previously been carried on either by AI itself or by AIL. Lord Hoffmann is a director and chairman of ALCL, which is wholly controlled by AI, since its members (who ultimately control it) are all the members of the international executive committee of AI. A large part of the work of AI is as a matter of strict law, carried on by AICL which instructs AIL, to do the work on its behalf. In reality, AI, AICL and AIL are a close-knit group carrying on the work of AI.

However, close as these links are, I do not think it would be right to identify Lord Hoffmann personally as being a party to the appeal. He is closely linked to AI but he is not in fact AI. Although this is an area in which legal technicality is particularly to be avoided, it cannot be ignored that Lord Hoffmann took no part in running AI. Lord Hoffmann, AICL and the executive committee of AI are in law separate people.

Then is this a case in which it can be said that Lord Hoffmann had an 'interest' which must lead to his automatic disqualification? Hitherto only pecuniary and proprietary interests have led to automatic disqualification. But, as I have indicated, this litigation is most unusual. It is not civil litigation but criminal litigation. Most unusually, by allowing AI to intervene, there is a party to a criminal cause or matter who is neither prosecutor nor accused. That party, AI, shares with the government of Spain and the CPS, not a financial interest but an interest to establish that there is no immunity for ex-heads of state in relation to crimes against humanity. The interest of these parties is to procure Senator Pinochet's extradition and trial a non-pecuniary interest. So far as AICL is concerned, clause 3(c) of its memorandum provides that one of its objects is 'to procure the abolition of torture, extra-judicial execution and disappearance'. AI has, amongst other objects, the same objects. Although AICL, as a charity, cannot campaign to change the law, it is concerned by other means to procure the abolition of these crimes against humanity. In my opinion, therefore, AICL plainly had a non-pecuniary interest, to establish that Senator Pinochet was not immune.

That being the case, the question is whether in the very unusual circumstances of this case a non-pecuniary interest to achieve a particular result is sufficient to give rise to automatic disqualification and, if so, whether the fact that AICL had such an interest necessarily leads to the conclusion that Lord Hoffmann, as a director of AICL, was automatically disqualified from sitting on the appeal? My Lords, in my judgment, although the cases have all dealt with automatic disqualification on the grounds of pecuniary interest, there is no good reason in principle for so limiting automatic disqualification. The rationale of the whole rule is that a man cannot be a judge in his own cause. In civil litigation the matters in issue will normally have an economic impact; therefore a judge is automatically disqualified if he stands to make a financial gain as a consequence of his own decision of the case. But if, as in the present case, the matter at issue does not relate to money or economic advantage but is concerned with the promotion of the cause, the rationale disqualifying a judge applies just as much if the judge's decision will lead to the promotion of a cause in which the judge is involved together with one of the parties. Thus in my opinion if Lord Hoffmann had been at member of AI he would have been automatically disqualified because of his non-pecuniary interest in establishing that Senator Pinochet was not entitled to immunity. Indeed, so much I understood to have been conceded by Mr Duffy.

Can it make any difference that, instead of being a direct member of AI Lord Hoffmann is a director of AICL, that is of a company which is wholly controlled by AI and is carrying on much of its work? Surely not. The substance of the matter is that AI, AIL and AICL are all various parts of an entity or movement working in different fields towards the same goals. If the absolute impartiality of the judiciary is to be maintained, there must be a rule which automatically disqualifies a judge who is involved, whether personally or as a director of a company, in promoting the same causes in the same organisation as is a party to the suit. There is no room for fine distinctions if Lord Hewart CJ's famous dictum is to be observed: it is 'of fundamental importance that justice should not only be done, but should manifestly and undoubtedly be seen to be done': see *Rex* v *Sussex Justices, Ex parte McCarthy* [1924] 1 KB 256, 259.

. . .

It is important not to overstate what is being decided. It was suggested in argument that a decision setting aside the order of 25 November 1998 would lead to a position where judges would be unable to sit on cases involving charities in whose work they are involved. It is suggested that, because of such involvement, a judge would be disqualified. That is not correct. The facts of this present case are exceptional. The critical elements are (1) that AI was a party to the appeal; (2) that AI was joined in order to argue for a particular result; (3) the judge was a director of a charity closely allied to AI and sharing, in this respect, AI's objects. Only in cases where a judge is taking an active role as trustee or director of a charity which is closely allied to and acting with a party to the litigation should a judge normally be concerned either to recuse himself or disclose the position to the parties. However, there may well be other exceptional cases in which the judge would be well advised to disclose a possible interest.

Finally on this aspect of the case, we were asked to state in giving judgment what had been said and done within the Appellate Committee in relation to Amnesty International during the hearing leading to the order of 25 November. As is apparent from what I have said, such matters are irrelevant to what we have to decide: in the absence of any disclosure to the parties of Lord Hoffmann's involvement with AI such involvement either did or did not in law disqualify him regardless of what happened within the Appellate Committee. We therefore did not investigate those matters and make no findings as to them.

Election, waiver, abuse of process

Mr Alun Jones submitted that by raising with the Home Secretary the possible bias of Lord Hoffmann as a ground for not authorising the extradition to proceed, Senator Pinochet had elected to choose the Home Secretary rather than your Lordships' House as the arbiter as to whether such bias did or did not exist. Consequently, he submitted, Senator Pinochet had waived his right to petition your Lordships and, by doing so immediately after the Home Secretary had rejected the submission, was committing an abuse of the process of the House.

This submission is bound to fail on a number of different grounds, of which I need mention only two. First, Senator Pinochet would only be put to his election as between two alternative courses to adopt. I cannot see that there are two such courses in the present case, since the Home Secretary had no power in the matter. He could not set aside the order of 25 November and as long as such order stood, the Home Secretary was bound to accept it as stating the law. Secondly, all three concepts – election, waiver and abuse of process require that the person said to have elected etc. has acted freely and in full knowledge of the facts. Not until 8 December 1998 did Senator Pinochet's solicitors know anything of Lord Hoffmann's position as a director and chairman of AICL. Even then they did not know anything about AICL and its constitution. To say that by hurriedly notifying the Home Secretary of the contents of the letter from AI's solicitors Senator Pinochet had elected to pursue the point solely before the Home Secretary is unrealistic. Senator Pinochet had not yet had time to find out anything about the circumstances beyond the bare facts disclosed in the letter.

. . .

LORD HOPE: . . . As for the facts of the present case, it seems to me that the conclusion is inescapable that Amnesty International has associated itself in these proceedings with the position of the prosecutor. The prosecution is not being brought in its name, but its interest in the case is to achieve the same result because it also seeks to bring Senator Pinochet to justice. This distinguishes its position fundamentally from that of other bodies which seek to uphold human rights without extending their objects to issues concerning personal responsibility. It has for many years conducted an international campaign against those individuals whom it has identified as having been responsible for torture, extra-judicial executions and disappearances. Its aim is that they should be made to suffer criminal penalties for such gross violations of human rights. It has chosen, by its intervention in these proceedings, to bring itself face to face with one of those individuals against whom it has for so long campaigned.

But everyone whom the prosecutor seeks to bring to justice is entitled to the protection of the law, however grave the offence or offences with which he is being prosecuted. Senator Pinochet is entitled to the judgment of an impartial and independent tribunal on the question which has been raised here as to his immunity. I think that the connections which existed between Lord Hoffmann and Amnesty International were of such a character, in view of their duration and proximity, as to disqualify him on this ground. In view of his links with Amnesty International as the chairman and a director of Amnesty International Charity Ltd. he could not be seen to be impartial. There has been no suggestion that he was actually biased. He had no financial or pecuniary interest in the outcome. But his relationship with Amnesty International was such that he was, in effect, acting as a judge in his own cause. I consider that his failure to disclose these connections leads inevitably to the conclusion that the decision to which he was a party must be set aside.

. . .

Petition granted.

Locabail (UK) Ltd v Bayfield Properties Ltd
[2000] QB 451, Court of Appeal

LORD BINGHAM of CORNHILL CJ, LORD WOOLF MR and SIR RICHARD SCOTT V-C: . . .

18. When applying the test of real danger or possibility (as opposed to the test of automatic disqualification under *Dimes'* case and *Ex p Pinochet (No. 2)* it will very often be appropriate to inquire whether the judge knew of the matter relied on as appearing to undermine his impartiality, because if it is shown that he did not know of it the danger of its having influenced his judgment is eliminated and the appearance of possible bias is dispelled. As the Court of Appeal of New Zealand observed in *Auckland Casino Ltd* v *Casino Control Authority* [1995] 1 NZLR 142 at 148, if the judge were ignorant of the allegedly disqualifying interest: '. . . there would be no real danger of bias, as no one could suppose that the Judge could be unconsciously affected by that of which he knew nothing . . .'

19. It is noteworthy that in *R* v *Gough* evidence was received from the juror whose impartiality was in issue (see pp. 651E and 658D), and reliance was placed on that evidence (see p. 652F); both in the Court of Appeal and the House of Lords it was accepted that if the correct test was the real danger or possibility test the appeal could not succeed, since the allegedly disqualifying association had admittedly not been known to the juror at the time when the verdict had been returned, and therefore there was no possibility that it could have affected her decision (see pp. 652D, 660G and 670G). While a reviewing court may receive a written statement from any judge, lay justice or juror specifying what he or she knew at any relevant time, the court is not necessarily bound to accept such statement at its face value. Much will depend on the nature of the fact of which ignorance is asserted, the source of the statement, the effect of any corroborative or contradictory statement, the inherent probabilities and all the circumstances of the case in question. Often the court will have no hesitation in accepting the reliability of such a statement; occasionally, if rarely, it may doubt the reliability of the statement; sometimes, although inclined to accept the statement, it may recognise the possibility of doubt and the likelihood of public scepticism. All will turn on the facts of the particular case. There can, however, be no question of cross-examining or seeking disclosure from the judge. Nor will the reviewing court pay attention to any statement by the judge concerning the impact of any knowledge on his mind or his decision: the insidious nature of bias makes such a statement of little value, and it is for the reviewing court and not the judge whose impartiality is challenged to assess the risk that some illegitimate extraneous consideration may have influenced the decision.

20. When members of the Bar are appointed to sit judicially, whether full-time or part-time, they may ordinarily be expected to know of any past or continuing professional or personal association

which might impair or be thought to impair their judicial impartiality. They will know of their own affairs, and the independent, self-employed status of barristers practising in chambers will relieve them of any responsibility for, and (usually) any detailed knowledge of, the affairs of other members of the same chambers. The position of solicitors is somewhat different, for a solicitor who is a partner in a firm of solicitors is legally responsible for the professional acts of his partners and does as a partner owe a duty to clients of the firm for whom he or she personally may never have acted and of whose affairs he or she personally may know nothing. While it is vital to safeguard the integrity of court proceedings, it is also important to ensure that the rules are not applied in such a way as to inhibit the increasingly valuable contribution which solicitors are making to the discharge of judicial functions. Problems are, we apprehend, very much more likely to arise when a solicitor is sitting in a part-time capacity, and in civil rather than criminal proceedings. But we think that problems can usually be overcome if, before embarking on the trial of any assigned civil case, the solicitor (whether sitting as deputy district judge, assistant recorder, recorder or s. 9 judge) conducts a careful conflict search within the firm of which he is a partner. Such a search, however carefully conducted and however sophisticated the firm's internal systems, is unlikely to be omission-proof. While parties for and against whom the firm has acted, and parties closely associated, would (we hope) be identified, the possibility must exist that individuals involved in such parties, and parties more remotely associated, may not be identified. When in the course of a trial properly embarked upon some such association comes to light (as could equally happen with a barrister-judge), the association should be disclosed and addressed, bearing in mind the test laid down in *Reg.* v *Gough*. The proper resolution of any such problem will, again, depend on the facts of the case.

21. In any case giving rise to automatic disqualification on the authority of *Dimes'* case 3 H.L. Cas and *Ex parte Pinochet (No. 2)* [2000] 1 AC 119, the judge should recuse himself from the case before any objection is raised. The same course should be followed if, for solid reasons, the judge feels personally embarrassed in hearing the case. In either event it is highly desirable, if extra cost, delay and inconvenience are to be avoided, that the judge should stand down at the earliest possible stage, not waiting until the eve or the day of the hearing. Parties should not be confronted with a last-minute choice between adjournment and waiver of an otherwise valid objection. If, in any case not giving rise to automatic disqualification and not causing personal embarrassment to the judge, he or she is or becomes aware of any matter which could arguably be said to give rise to a real danger of bias, it is generally desirable that disclosure should be made to the parties in advance of the hearing. If objection is then made, it will be the duty of the judge to consider the objection and exercise his judgment upon it. He would be as wrong to yield to a tenuous or frivolous objection as he would to ignore an objection of substance. We find force in observations of the Constitutional Court of South Africa in *President of the Republic of South Africa* v *South African Rugby Football Union* 1999 (4) SA 147 at 177, even though these observations were directed to the reasonable suspicion test:

> It follows from the foregoing that the correct approach to this application for the recusal of members of this Court is objective and the *onus* of establishing it rests upon the applicant. The question is whether a reasonable, objective and informed person would on the correct facts reasonably apprehend that the Judge has not or will not bring an impartial mind to bear on the adjudication of the case, that is a mind open to persuasion by the evidence and the submissions of counsel. The reasonableness of the apprehension must be assessed in the light of the oath of office taken by the Judges to administer justice without fear or favour; and their ability to carry out that oath by reason of their training and experience. It must be assumed that they can disabuse their minds of any irrelevant personal beliefs or predispositions. They must take into account the fact that they have a duty to sit in any case in which they are not obliged to recuse themselves. At the same time, it must never be forgotten that an impartial judge is a fundamental prerequisite for a fair trial and a

judicial officer should not hesitate to recuse herself or himself if there are reasonable grounds on the part of a litigant for apprehending that the judicial officer, for whatever reasons, was not or will not be impartial.

22. We also find great persuasive force in three extracts from Australian authority. In *Re JRL, ex p CJL*, Re(1986) 161 CLR 342 at 352 Mason J, sitting in the High Court of Australia, said:

Although it is important that justice must be seen to be done, it is equally important that judicial officers discharge their duty to sit and do not, by acceding too readily to sugges-tions of appearance of bias, encourage parties to believe that by seeking the disqualifica-tion of a judge, they will have their case tried by someone thought to be more likely to decide the case in their favour.

23. In *Re Ebner, Ebner* v *Official Trustee in Bankruptcy* (1999) 161 ALR 557 at 568 (para. 37) the Federal Court asked:

Why is it to be assumed that the confidence of fair-minded people in the administration of justice would be shaken by the existence of a direct pecuniary interest of no tangible value, but not by the waste of resources and the delays brought about by setting aside a judgment on the ground that the judge is disqualified for having such an interest?

24. In the *Clenae* case [1999] VSCA 35 Callaway JA observed (para. 89(e)):

As a general rule, it is the duty of a judicial officer to hear and determine the cases allocated to him or her by his or her head of jurisdiction. Subject to certain limited excep-tions, a judge or magistrate should not accede to an unfounded disqualification application.

25. It would be dangerous and futile to attempt to define or list the factors which may or may not give rise to a real danger of bias. Everything will depend on the facts, which may include the nature of the issue to be decided. We cannot, however, conceive of circumstances in which an objection could be soundly based on the religion, ethnic or national origin, gender, age, class, means or sexual orientation of the judge. Nor, at any rate ordinarily, could an objection be soundly based on the judge's social or educational or service or employment background or history, nor that of any member of the judge's family; or previous political associations; or membership of social or sporting or charitable bodies; or Masonic associations; or previous judicial decisions; or extra-curricular utterances (whether in textbooks, lectures, speeches, articles, interviews, reports or responses to consultation papers); or previous receipt of instructions to act for or against any party, solicitor or advocate engaged in a case before him; or membership of the same Inn, circuit, local Law Society or chambers (*KFTCIC* v *Icori Estero SpA* (Court of Appeal of Paris, 28 June 1991, International Arbitration Report, vol 6, 8/91)). By contrast, a real danger of bias might well be thought to arise if there were personal friendship or animosity between the judge and any member of the public involved in the case; or if the judge were closely acquainted with any member of the public involved in the case, particularly if the credibility of that individual could be significant in the decision of the case; or if, in a case where the credibility of any individual were an issue to be decided by the judge, he had in a previous case rejected the evidence of that person in such outspoken terms as to throw doubt on his ability to approach such person's evidence with an open mind on any later occasion; or if on any question at issue in the proceedings before him the judge had expressed views, particularly in the course of the hearing, in such extreme and unbalanced terms as to throw doubt on his ability to try the issue with an objective judicial mind (see *Vakauta* v *Kelly* (1989) 167 CLR 568); or if, for any other reason, there were real ground for doubting the ability of the judge to ignore extraneous considera-tions, prejudices and predilections and bring an objective judgment to bear on the issues before him. The mere fact that a judge, earlier in the same case or in a previous case, had commented adversely on a party or witness, or found the evidence of a party or witness to be unreliable, would not without more found a sustainable objection. In most cases, we think, the answer, one way or the other, will

be obvious. But if in any case there is real ground for doubt, that doubt should be resolved in favour of recusal. We repeat: every application must be decided on the facts and circumstances of the individual case. The greater the passage of time between the event relied on as showing a danger of bias and the case in which the objection is raised, the weaker (other things being equal) the objection will be.

26. We do not consider that waiver, in this context, raises special problems (*Shrager v Basil Dighton Ltd* [1924] 1 KB 274 at 293; *R v Essex Justices, ex p Perkins* [1927] 2 KB 475 at 489; *Ex parte Pinochet (No. 2)*, [2000] 1 AC 119, 136–137, the *Auckland Casino* case [1995] 1 NZLR 142 at 150–151 and *Vakauta v Kelly* (1989) 167 CLR 568 at 572, 577). If, appropriate disclosure having been made by the judge, a party raises no objection to the judge hearing or continuing to hear a case, that party cannot thereafter complain of the matter disclosed as giving rise to a real danger of bias. It would be unjust to the other party and undermine both the reality and the appearance of justice to allow him to do so. What disclosure is appropriate depends in large measure on the stage that the matter has reached. If, before a hearing has begun, the judge is alerted to some matter which might, depending on the full facts, throw doubt on his fitness to sit, the judge should in our view inquire into the full facts, so far as they are ascertainable, in order to make disclosure in the light of them. But if a judge has embarked on a hearing in ignorance of a matter which emerges during the hearing, it is in our view enough if the judge discloses what he then knows. He has no obligation to disclose what he does not know. Nor is he bound to fill any gaps in his knowledge which, if filled, might provide stronger grounds for objection to his hearing or continuing to hear the case. If, of course, he does make further inquiry and learn additional facts not known to him before, then he must make disclosure of those facts also. It is, however, generally undesirable that hearings should be aborted unless the reality or the appearance of justice requires that they should.

NOTE: The specially staffed Court of Appeal was here dealing with five applications for permission to appeal on the ground of bias of the judge. The listing and hearing together of these applications enabled the court to give this guidance. In *Locabail (UK) Ltd v Bayfield Properties Ltd, Locabail (UK) Ltd v Waldorf Investment Corp; Williams v HM Inspector of Taxes*, and *R v Bristol Betting and Gaming Licensing Committee, ex parte O'Callaghan*, permission to appeal was not granted. In *Timmins v Gormley*, the defendant in a personal injuries case successfully argued that the articles in legal publications written by the recorder who heard the case, in which he expressed pronounced pro-claimant anti-insurer views, allowed for the possibility that the recorder might lean in favour of the claimant and against the defendant. The Court held that it was not wrong for the recorder to be engaged in writing but that it is 'inappropriate for a judge to use intemperate language about subjects on which he has adjudicated or will have to adjudicate'.

In Re Medicaments and Related Classes of Goods (No. 2)
[2000] EWCA Civ 350; [2001] 1 WLR 700, Court of Appeal

Dr Rowlatt was appointed to sit in the Restrictive Practices Court to hear a case in which the respondents engaged the services of an economics consultancy. Dr Rowlatt contacted the consultants about the possibility of joining them. Details of Dr Rowlatt's contacts were produced before the Court in which it was clear that the consultants would not in future employ Dr Rowlatt and she indicated that she would be able to hear the case impartially and so she did not recuse herself. The Court then proceeded, tried the case and an appeal was lodged arguing that Dr Rowlatt breached the rules against bias. The appeal gave the Court the opportunity to determine whether the real danger test preferred by the House of Lords in *Gough*, as opposed to the reasonable likelihood test favoured in Scotland

and Australia, was in conformity with the requirement of Article 6(1) ECHR and the interpretation of it by the Strasbourg Court.

LORD PHILLIPS, MR:. . .

61. In *R v Inner West London Coroner, ex parte Dallaglio* [1994] 4 All ER 139 at p. 162 this Court applied the test in *Gough*, when holding that injudicious remarks made by a Coroner gave rise to a real possibility that the Coroner had unconsciously allowed his decision to be influenced by a feeling of hostility towards the applicant and other members of an action group, with the result that his decision to refuse to continue an inquest should be quashed. In the leading judgment Simon Brown L.J. set out at pp. 151–2 the following propositions which he derived from *Gough*:

From *R v Gough* I derive the following propositions:

(1) Any court seised of a challenge on the ground of apparent bias must ascertain the relevant circumstances and consider all the evidence for itself so as to reach its own conclusion on the facts.

(2) It necessarily follows that the factual position may appear quite differently as between the time when the challenge is launched and the time when it comes to be decided by the court. What may appear at the leave stage to be a strong case of justice 'not manifestly and undoubtedly being seen to be done', may, following the court's investigation, nevertheless fail. Or, of course, although perhaps less probably, the case may have become stronger.

(3) In reaching its conclusion the court 'personifies the reasonable man'.

(4) The question upon which the court must reach its own factual conclusion is this: is there a real danger of injustice having occurred as a result of bias? By 'real' is meant not without substance. A real danger clearly involves more than a minimal risk, less than a probability. One could, I think, as well speak of a real risk or a real possibility.

(5) Injustice will have occurred as a result of bias 'if the decision-maker unfairly regarded with disfavour the case of a party to the issue under consideration by him'. I take 'unfairly regarded with disfavour' to mean 'was pre-disposed or prejudiced against one party's case for reasons unconnected with the merits of the issue'.

(6) A decision-maker may have unfairly regarded with disfavour one party's case either consciously or unconsciously. Where, as here, the applicants expressly disavow any suggestion of actual bias, it seems to me that the court must necessarily be asking itself whether there is a real danger that the decision-maker was unconsciously biased.

(7) It will be seen, therefore, that by the time the legal challenge comes to be resolved, the court is no longer concerned strictly with the appearance of bias but rather with establishing the possibility that there was actual although unconscious bias.

62. Sir Thomas Bingham, MR, remarked at p.162 that the effect of the decision in *Gough* was that:

The famous aphorism of Lord Hewart C.J. in *R v Sussex Justices, ex p. McCarthy* [1924] 1 KB 256 at 259, [1923] All ER Rep 233 at 234 that 'justice. . . . should manifestly and undoubtedly be seen to be done' is no longer, it seems, good law, save of course in the case where the appearance of bias is such as to show a real danger of bias.

63. The decision in *Gough* received critical analysis by the High Court of Australia in *Webb v The Queen* (1994) 181 C.L.R. 41. In the leading judgment, Mason C.J. and McHugh J. commented at pp. 50–52:

In considering the merits of the test to be applied in a case where a juror is alleged to be biased, it is important to keep in mind that the appearance as well as the fact of impartiality is necessary to retain confidence in the administration of justice. Both the parties to the case and the general public must be satisfied that justice has not only been done but that it has been seen to be done. Of the various tests used to determine an allegation of bias, the reasonable apprehension test of bias is by far the most appropriate for protecting the appearance of impartiality. The test of 'reasonable likelihood' or 'real danger' of bias tends to emphasise the court's view of the facts. In that context, the trial judge's acceptance of explanations becomes of primary importance. Those two tests tend to place inadequate emphasis on the public perception of the irregular incident.

We do not think that it is possible to reconcile the decision in *Gough* with the decisions of this Court. In *Gough*, the House of Lords specifically rejected the reasonable suspicion test and the cases and judgments which had applied it in favour of a modified version of the reasonable likelihood test. In *R v Watson, ex p. Armstrong* (1976) 136 CLR 248 faced with the same conflict in the cases between the two tests, this Court preferred the reasonable suspicion or apprehension test. That test has been applied in this Court on no less than eight subsequent occasions. In the light of the decisions of this Court which hold that the reasonable apprehension or suspicion test is the correct test for determining a case of alleged bias against a judge, it is not possible to use the 'real danger' test as the general test for bias without rejecting the authority of those decisions.

Moreover, nothing in the two speeches in the House of Lords in *Gough* contains any new insight that makes us think that we should re-examine a principle and a line of cases to which this Court has consistently adhered for the last eighteen years. On the contrary, there is a strong reason why we should continue to prefer the reasoning in our own cases to that of the House of Lords. In *Gough*, the House of Lords rejected the need to take account of the public perception of an incident which raises an issue of bias except in the case of a pecuniary interest. Behind this reasoning is the assumption that public confidence in the administration of justice will be maintained because the public will accept the conclusions of the judge. But the premise on which the decisions in this Court are based is that public confidence in the administration of justice is more likely to be maintained if the Court adopts a test that reflects the reaction of the ordinary reasonable member of the public to the irregularity in question. References to the reasonable apprehension of the 'lay observer', the 'fair-minded observer', the 'fair-minded, informed lay observer', 'fair-minded people', the 'reasonable or fair-minded observer', the 'parties or the public', and the 'reasonable person' abound in the decisions of this Court and other courts in this country. They indicate that it is the court's view of the public's view, not the court's own view, which is determinative. If public confidence in the administration of justice is to be maintained, the approach that is taken by fair-minded and informed members of the public cannot be ignored. Indeed, as Toohey J. pointed out in *Vakauta* (1989) 167 C.L.R. at p. 585 in considering whether an allegation of bias on the part of a judge has been made out, the public perception of the judiciary is not advanced by attributing to a fair-minded member of the public a knowledge of the law and the judicial process which ordinary experience suggests is not the case. That does not mean that the trial judge's opinions and findings are irrelevant. The fair-minded and informed observer would place great weight on the judge's view of the facts. Indeed, in many cases the fair-minded observer would be bound to evaluate the incident in terms of the judge's findings.

64. These comments presuppose that the 'real danger' test may lead the Court to reach a conclusion as to the likelihood of bias which does not reflect the view that the informed observer would form on the same facts – and this because the viewpoint of the Judge may not be the same as that of members of the public. This objection was addressed by this Court in *Locabail* at p. 477:

In the overwhelming majority of cases we judge that application of the two tests would anyway lead to the same outcome. Provided that the court, personifying the reasonable man, takes an approach which is based on broad common sense, without inappropriate reliance on special knowledge, the minutiae of court procedure or other matters outside the ken of the ordinary, reasonably well informed member of the public, there should be no risk that the courts will not ensure both that justice is done and that it is perceived by the public to be done.

65. We do not find it easy to reconcile this passage with an approach that requires the Court to decide whether there was in fact a real danger that a particular Judge was biased. Once the reviewing Court excludes from consideration matters known to it which would be outside the ken of ordinary, reasonably well informed members of the public, it seems to us that a hypothetical rather than an actual test of the likelihood of bias is being applied.

66. A similar conclusion flows from a subsequent passage in the Judgment in *Locabail*, at p. 477:

While a reviewing court may receive a written statement from any judge, lay justice or juror specifying what he or she knew at any relevant time, the court is not necessarily bound to accept such statement at its face value. Much will depend on the nature of the fact of which ignorance is asserted, the course of the statement, the effect of any corroborative or contradictory statement, the inherent probabilities and all the circumstances of the case in question. Often the court will have no hesitation in accepting the reliability of such a statement; occasionally, if rarely, it may doubt the reliability of the statement; sometimes, although inclined to accept the statement, it may recognise the possibility of doubt and the likelihood of public scepticism. All will turn on the facts of the particular case. There can, however, be no question of cross-examining or seeking disclosure from the judge. Nor will the reviewing court pay attention to any statement by the judge concerning the impact of any knowledge on his mind or his decision: the insidious nature of bias makes such a statement of little value, and it is for the reviewing court and not the judge whose impartiality is challenged to assess the risk that some illegitimate extraneous consideration may have influenced the decision.

67. What is the Court to do where, although inclined to accept a statement about what the Judge under review knew at any material time, it recognises the possibility of doubt and the likelihood of public scepticism? It is invidious for the reviewing Court to question the word of the Judge in such circumstances, but less so to say that the objective onlooker might have difficulty in accepting it.

68. Such a situation highlights a wider consideration. Jurors are warned by the Judge to put all extraneous considerations and prejudices from their minds and to try the case on the evidence, and are normally expected to achieve this. A professional Judge is adept, by training and experience, at reaching decisions by objective appraisal of the facts. A finding that in a particular case there is a real danger that a particular Judge was biased inevitably carries with it a slur on the Judge in question, albeit that the reviewing Court may take pains to emphasise that the bias may have been unconscious. As Deane J. put it in *Webb* at p. 71:

One advantage of the test of reasonable apprehension on the part of a fair-minded and informed observer is that it makes plain that an appellate court is not making an adverse finding on the question whether it is possible or likely that the particular judge or juror was in fact affected by disqualifying bias. In contrast, the real danger test is focused upon that very question. Regardless of an appellate court's care to make plain that its finding is only one of possibility of danger, such a finding is likely to be unfairly damaging to the reputation of the person concerned who will commonly not have been a party to the proceedings before the appellate court and whose subjective thought processes will not have been investigated in the appellate court.

69. The problem with the 'real danger' test is particularly acute where a Judge is invited to recuse himself. In such a situation it is invidious to expect a Judge to rule on the danger that he may actually

be influenced by partiality. The test of whether the objective onlooker might have a reasonable apprehension of bias is manifestly more satisfactory in such circumstances.

70. Mr Sumption submitted that the test in *Gough* was no different in reality from the 'reasonable apprehension of bias' test favoured in Scotland and most other common law jurisdictions. He added that if it was different, it had to be discarded in favour of the reasonable apprehension test in the light of the Human Rights Act as this was unequivocally the test applied by the Strasbourg Court. This submission received support from Mr Philipson, QC, for the Director-General. We turn to consider the Strasbourg jurisprudence . . .

[*Delcourt* v *Belgium* (1970) 1 E.H.R.R. 355, *Piersack* v *Belgium* (1982) 5 E.H.R.R. 169, *De Cubber* v *Belgium* (1984) 7 E.H.R.R. 236, *Hauschildt* v *Denmark* (1989) 12 E.H.R.R. 266, *Borgers* v *Belgium* (1993) 15 E.H.R.R. 92, *Gregory* v *United Kingdom* (1997) 25 E.H.R.R. 577 . . .]

83. We would summarise the principles to be derived from this line of cases as follows:

(1) If a Judge is shown to have been influenced by actual bias, his decision must be set aside.

(2) Where actual bias has not been established the personal impartiality of the Judge is to be presumed.

(3) The Court then has to decide whether, on an objective appraisal, the material facts give rise to a legitimate fear that the Judge might not have been impartial. If they do the decision of the Judge must be set aside.

(4) The material facts are not limited to those which were apparent to the applicant. They are those which are ascertained upon investigation by the Court.

(5) An important consideration in making an objective appraisal of the facts is the desirability that the public should remain confident in the administration of justice.

84. This approach comes close to that in *Gough*. The difference is that when the Strasbourg Court considers whether the material circumstances give rise to a reasonable apprehension of bias, it makes it plain that it is applying an objective test to the circumstances, not passing judgment on the likelihood that the particular tribunal under review was in fact biased.

85. When the Strasbourg jurisprudence is taken into account, we believe that a modest adjustment of the test in *Gough* is called for, which makes it plain that it is, in effect, no different from the test applied in most of the Commonwealth and in Scotland. The Court must first ascertain all the circumstances which have a bearing on the suggestion that the Judge was biased. It must then ask whether those circumstances would lead a fair-minded and informed observer to conclude that there was a real possibility, or a real danger, the two being the same, that the tribunal was biased.

86. The material circumstances will include any explanation given by the Judge under review as to his knowledge or appreciation of those circumstances. Where that explanation is accepted by the applicant for review it can be treated as accurate. Where it is not accepted, it becomes one further matter to be considered from the viewpoint of the fair-minded observer. The Court does not have to rule whether the explanation should be accepted or rejected. Rather it has to decide whether or not the fair-minded observer would consider that there was a real danger of bias notwithstanding the explanation advanced.

Appeal allowed.

NOTES:
1. Having found that (a) Dr Rowlatt should have recused herself and (b) that because the issue arose at an advanced stage in the proceedings when she would have discussed some of the

economic aspects of the case with the other two members of the Court, then it followed that those other two members would also have to stand down.

2. The following postscript was added to the judgment: 'While we were preparing this Judgment it came to the attention of the Master of the Rolls that Dr Rowlatt was known to him, although only by sight, because she is a near neighbour. While that is not a fact which could cast doubt on the objectivity with which we have addressed the issues in this case, it is right that it should be recorded'.

QUESTION

Has the *Gough* test and its supporting reasoning been modified or overturned?

(b) Right to a fair hearing

Ridge v Baldwin
[1964] AC 40, House of Lords

Following his arrest and charge for conspiracy to obstruct the course of justice, Ridge, the Chief Constable of Brighton, was suspended from duty. At his trial Ridge was acquitted but the judge was critical of his leadership of the force. A further charge of corruption was brought against Ridge and the judge repeated these comments when directing Ridge's acquittal.

Under the Municipal Corporations Act 1882, s. 191(4) a watch committee could dismiss 'any borough constable whom they think negligent in the discharge of his duty, or otherwise unfit for the same'. After Ridge's acquittals the watch committee met and decided that Ridge should be dismissed. Ridge was not asked to attend the meeting, but at the request of his solicitor the watch committee reconvened some days later and decided not to change its original decision. Before this second meeting Ridge gave notice of appeal against the original decision to the Home Secretary under the Police (Appeals) Act 1927. He also stated, however, that this was without prejudice to his right to argue that the procedure adopted by the committee was in breach of the relevant statutory provisions and of the rules of natural justice. The Home Secretary dismissed his appeal and Ridge appealed to the courts, seeking a declaration that the purported dismissal was *ultra vires*. Ridge, whose case failed before Streatfield J and the Court of Appeal, appealed to the House of Lords. The following extract deals with his claim that there was a breach of natural justice.

LORD REID: The appellant's case is that in proceeding under the Act of 1882 the watch committee were bound to observe what are commonly called the principles of natural justice. Before attempting to reach any decision they were bound to inform him of the grounds on which they proposed to act and give him a fair opportunity of being heard in his own defence. The authorities on the applicability of the principles of natural justice are in some confusion, and so I find it necessary to examine this matter in some detail. The principle audi alteram partem goes back many centuries in our law and appears in a multitude of judgments of judges of the highest authority. In modern times opinions have sometimes been expressed to the effect that natural justice is so vague as to be almost meaningless. But I would regard these as tainted by the perennial fallacy that because something cannot be cut and dried or nicely weighed and measured therefore it does not exist. . . . It appears to me that one reason why the authorities on natural justice have been found difficult to reconcile is that insufficient attention has been paid to the great difference between various kinds of cases in which it has been sought to apply the principle. What a minister ought to do in considering objections to a scheme may be very different from what a watch committee ought to do in considering whether to dismiss a chief constable. So I shall deal first with cases of dismissal. These appear to fall into three classes: dismissal of a servant by his master, dismissal from an office held during pleasure, and dismissal from an office where there must be something against a man to warrant his dismissal.

Lord Reid then went on to consider the three different cases and concluded that, in the case of the third category (into which Ridge fell), there was an unbroken line of authority to the effect that an officer cannot lawfully be dismissed without first telling him what is alleged against him and hearing his defence or explanation.

Stopping there, I would think that authority was wholly in favour of the appellant, but the respondent's argument was mainly based on what has been said in a number of fairly recent cases dealing with different subject-matter. Those cases deal with decisions by ministers, officials and bodies of various kinds which adversely affected property rights or privileges of persons who had no opportunity or no proper opportunity of presenting their cases before the decisions were given. And it is necessary to examine those cases for another reason. The question which was or ought to have been considered by the watch committee on March 7, 1958, was not a simple question whether or not the appellant should be dismissed. There were three possible courses open to the watch committee – reinstating the appellant as chief constable, dismissing him, or requiring him to resign. The difference between the latter two is that dismissal involved forfeiture of pension rights, whereas requiring him to resign did not. Indeed, it is now clear that the appellant's real interest in this appeal is to try to save his pension rights. . . .

I would start an examination of the authorities dealing with property rights and privileges with *Cooper* v *Wandsworth Board of Works* (1863) 14 CBNS 180. Where an owner had failed to give proper notice to the Board they had under an Act of 1855 authority to demolish any building he had erected and recover the cost from him. This action was brought against the board because they had used that power without giving the owner an opportunity of being heard. The board maintained that their discretion to order demolition was not a judicial discretion and that any appeal should have been to the Metropolitan Board of Works. But the Court decided unanimously in favour of the owner. . . .

[Lord Reid examined a number of other authorities and continued.] . . . It appears to me that if the present case had arisen thirty of forty years ago the court would have had no difficulty in deciding this issue in favour of the appellant on these authorities which I have cited. So far as I am aware none of these authorities has ever been disapproved or even doubted. Yet the Court of Appeal have decided this issue against the appellant on more recent authorities which apparently justify that result. How has this come about?

At least three things appear to have contributed. In the first place there have been many cases where it has been sought to apply the principles of natural justice to the wider duties imposed on Ministers and other organs of government by modern legislation. For reasons which I shall attempt to state, it has been held that those principles have a limited application in such cases and those limitations have tended to be reflected in other decisions on matters to which in principle they do not appear to me to apply. Secondly, again for reasons which I shall attempt to state, those principles have been held to have a limited application in cases arising out of war-time legislation; and again such limitations have tended to be reflected in other cases. And, thirdly, there has, I think, been a misunderstanding of the judgment of Atkin LJ in *Rex* v *Electricity Commissioners ex parte London Electricity Joint Committee Co*. [1924] 1 KB 171.

In cases of the kind I have been dealing with the Board of Works or the Governor of the club committee was dealing with a single isolated case. It was not deciding, like a judge in a lawsuit, what were the rights of the person before it. But it was deciding how he should be treated – something analogous to a judge's duty in imposing a penalty. No doubt policy would play some part in the decision – but so it might when a judge is imposing a sentence. So it was easy to say that such a body is performing a quasi-judicial task in considering and deciding such a matter, and to require it to observe the essentials of all proceedings of a judicial character – the principles of natural justice.

Sometimes the functions of a minister or department may also be of that character, and then the rules of natural justice can apply in much the same way. But more often their functions are of a very different character. If a minister is considering whether to make such a scheme for, say, an important new road, his primary concern will not be with the damage which its construction will do to the rights of individual owners of land. He will have to consider all manner of questions of public interest and, it may be, a number of alternative schemes. He cannot be prevented from attaching more importance to the fulfilment of his policy than to the fate of individual objectors, and it would be quite wrong for the courts to say that the minister should or could act in the same kind of way as a board of works deciding whether a house should be pulled down. And there is another important difference. As explained in *Local Government Board* v *Arlidge* [1915] AC 120 a minister cannot do everything himself. His officers will have to gather and sift all the facts, including objections by individuals, and no individual can complain if the ordinary accepted methods of carrying on public business do not give him as good protection as would be given by the principles of natural justice in a different kind of case.

Lord Reid continued to discuss cases decided under the Defence Regulations made in war-time and concluded that the fact that the rules of natural justice were not applied should not be regarded as of any great weight in cases arising under the 1882 Act because it was a reasonable inference in the former case that it was Parliament's intention to exclude the application of the rules of natural justice. . . .

The matter has been further complicated by what I believe to be a misunderstanding of a much-quoted passage in the judgment of Atkin LJ in *Rex* v *Electricity Commissioners, ex parte London Electricity Joint Committee Co.* [1925] 1 KB 171. He said '. . . the operation of the writs [of prohibition and certiorari] has extended to control the proceedings of bodies which do not claim to be, and would not be recognised as courts of justice. Wherever any body of persons having legal authority to determine questions affecting the rights of subjects, and having the duty to act judicially, act in excess of their legal authority, they are subject to the controlling jurisdiction of the King's Bench Division exercised in these writs.'

A gloss was put on this by Lord Hewart CJ in *Rex* v *Legislative Committee of the Church Assembly, ex parte Haynes-Smith* [1928] 1 KB 411. . . . Lord Hewart said, having quoted the passage from Atkin LJ's judgment: '. . . It is to be observed that in the last sentence which I have quoted . . . the word is not "or", but "and". In order that a body may satisfy the required test it is not enough that it should have legal authority to determine questions affecting the rights of subjects; there must be super-added to that characteristic the further characteristic that the body has the duty to act judicially. The duty to act judicially is an ingredient which, if the test is to be satisfied, must be present. As these writs in the earlier days were issued only to bodies which without any harshness of construction could be called, and naturally would be called courts, so also today these writs do not issue except to bodies which act or are under a duty to act in a judicial capacity.'

. . . If Lord Hewart meant that it is never enough that a body simply has a duty to determine what the rights of an individual should be, but that there must always be something more to impose on it a duty to act judicially before it can be found to observe the principles of natural justice, then that appears to me impossible to reconcile with the earlier authorities. . . .

There is not a word in Atkin LJ's judgment to suggest disapproval of the earlier line of authority which I have cited. On the contrary, he goes further than those authorities. I have already stated my view that it is more difficult for the courts to control an exercise of power on a large scale where the treatment to be meted out to a particular individual is only one of many matters to be considered. This was a case of that kind, and, if Atkin LJ was prepared to infer a judicial element from the nature of the power in this case, he could hardly disapprove such an inference when the power relates solely to the treatment of a particular individual.

I would sum up my opinion in this way. Between 1882 and the making of police regulations in 1920, section 191(4) had to be applied to every kind of case. The respondents' contention is that, even where there was a doubtful question whether a constable was guilty of a particular act of misconduct, the watch committee were under no obligation to hear his defence before dismissing him. In my judgment it is abundantly clear from the authorities I have quoted that at that time the courts would have rejected any such contention. In later cases dealing with different subject-matter opinions have been expressed in wide terms so as to appear to conflict with those earlier authorities. But learned judges who expressed those opinions generally had no power to overrule those authorities, and in any event it is a salutary rule that a judge is not to be assumed to have intended to overrule or disapprove of an authority which has not been cited to him and which he does not even mention. So I would hold that the power of dismissal in the Act of 1882 could not then have been exercised and cannot now be exercised until the watch committee have informed the constable of the grounds on which they propose to proceed and given him a proper opportunity to present his case in defence. . . .

Lord Reid decided that this failure was not made good by the reconvening of the watch committee because this did not provide for a full rehearing and granted a declaration that the dismissal was unlawful. Lord Morris, Lord Hodson and Lord Devlin delivered judgments in favour of allowing the appeal. Lord Evershed delivered a speech in favour of dismissing the appeal.

NOTES:

1. The significance of *Ridge* v *Baldwin* is that it helped to free the rules of natural justice from strict limitations which had been imposed in earlier decisions, in particular from the requirement that the decision-making body must be under a duty to act judicially. The decision in the case may be compared with that in *Nakkuda Ali* v *Jayaratne* [1951] AC 66 which was disapproved in *Ridge* v *Baldwin*.

2. The application of the rules of natural justice to cases involving dismissal from employment has been extended since *Ridge* v *Baldwin*. (See the discussion in Craig, *Administrative Law* (4th edn, 1999), pp. 439–40; H. W. R. Wade and C. F. Forsyth, *Administrative Law* (8th edn, 2000), pp. 531–55.)

3. The requirements of a fair hearing depend on all the circumstances. They may include:
   (a) the right to notice, but restrictions may be placed on this where the public interest so requires (see, for example, *R* v *Gaming Board of Great Britain, ex parte Benaim and Khaida* [1970] 2 QB 417);
   (b) the right to make representations, whether in writing or orally; oral hearings are not required in all circumstances where the rules of natural justice apply (see, for example, *Lloyd* v *McMahon* [1987] 1 All ER 1118);
   (c) where an oral hearing is held –
      (i) the right to comment on any evidence presented,
      (ii) where evidence is given orally by witnesses, the right to put questions to those witnesses (see, for example, *R* v *Deputy Industrial Injuries Commissioner, ex parte Moore* [1965] 1 QB 456);
   (d) legal representation (see *post*, at p. 621).

In order to understand the flexibility of the principles, consider the following cases.

R v *Board of Visitors of Hull Prison, ex parte St Germain (No. 2)*
[1979] 1 WLR 1401, Divisional Court

Following a riot in Hull Prison in 1976, numerous charges of breaches of the Prison Rules 1964 were heard by the prison's board of visitors. During the hearing reference was made to a number of statements by prison officers, who were not available to give evidence, to support the evidence given by a witness. Seven of the prisoners who were found guilty of offences against prison discipline sought an order of *certiorari* on the grounds that the proceedings before the prison's board of visitors breached the rules of natural justice. The following extracts relate to the prisoners' complaint that hearsay evidence was taken into account.

GEOFFREY LANE LJ: [W]e now turn to the suggestion that hearsay evidence is not permissible in a hearing before a board of visitors. It is of course common ground that the board of visitors must base their decisions on evidence. But must such evidence be restricted to that which would be admissible in a criminal court of law? Viscount Simon LC in *General Medical Council* v *Spackman* [1943] AC 627, 634, considered there was no such restriction. That was also clearly the view of the Privy Council in the *Ceylon University* v *Fernando* [1960] 1 WLR 223, 234. The matter was dealt with in more detail by Diplock LJ in *Reg.* v *Deputy Industrial Injuries Commissioner ex parte Moore* [1965] 1 QB 456, 488:

> These technical rules of evidence, however, form no part of the rules of natural justice. The requirement that a person exercising quasi-judicial functions must base his decision on evidence means no more than it must be based upon material which tends logically to show the existence or non-existence of facts relevant to the issue to be determined, or to show the likelihood or unlikelihood of the occurrence of some future event the occurrence of which would be relevant. It means that he must not spin a coin or consult an astrologer, but he may take into account any material which, as a matter of reason, has some probative value in the sense mentioned above. If it is capable of having any probative value, the weight to be attached to it is a matter for the person to whom Parliament has entrusted the responsibility of deciding the issue. The supervisory jurisdiction of the High Court does not entitle it to usurp this responsibility and to substitute its own view for his.

However, it is clear that the entitlement of the board to admit hearsay evidence is subject to the overriding obligation to provide the accused with a fair hearing. Depending upon the facts of the particular case and the nature of the hearsay evidence provided to the board, the obligation to give the accused a fair chance to exculpate himself, or a fair opportunity to controvert the charge – to quote the phrases used in the passages cited above – or a proper or full opportunity of presenting his case – to quote the language of section 47 or rule 49 – may oblige the board not only to inform the accused of the hearsay evidence but also to give the accused a sufficient opportunity to deal with that evidence. Again, depending upon the nature of that evidence and the particular circumstances of the case, a sufficient opportunity to deal with the hearsay evidence may well involve the cross-examination of the witness whose evidence is initially before the board in the form of hearsay.

We again take by way of example the case in which the defence is an alibi. The prisoner contends that he was not the man identified on the roof. He, the prisoner, was at the material time elsewhere. In short the prisoner has been mistakenly identified. The evidence of identification given by way of hearsay may be of the 'fleeting glance' type as exemplified by the well-known case of *Reg* v *Turnbull* [1977] QB 224. The prisoner may well wish to elicit by way of questions all manner of detail, e.g. the poorness of the light, the state of the confusion, the brevity of the observation, the absence of any contemporaneous record, etc., all designed to show the unreliability of the witness. To deprive him of the opportunity of cross-examination would be tantamount to depriving him of a fair hearing.

We appreciate that there may well be occasions when the burden of calling the witness whose hearsay evidence is readily available may impose a near impossible burden upon the board. However, it has not been suggested that hearsay evidence should be resorted to in the total absence of any first-hand evidence. In the instant cases hearsay evidence was only resorted to to supplement the first-hand evidence and this is the usual practice. Accordingly where a prisoner desires to dispute the hearsay evidence and for this purpose to question the witness, and where there are insuperable or very grave difficulties in arranging for his attendance, the board should refuse to admit that evidence, or, if it has already come to their notice, should expressly dismiss it from their consideration. . . .

The findings of guilt which were based on hearsay evidence were quashed by orders of certiorari.

R v *Commissioner for Racial Equality, ex parte Cottrell & Rothon*
[1980] 1 WLR 1580, Court of Appeal

The Commission for Racial Equality received a complaint that a firm of estate agents, Messrs Cottrell & Rothon, was committing acts of unlawful discrimination in the course of its business as an estate agent. Under s. 48 of the Race Relations Act 1976, the Commission nominated two of its members to conduct an investigation. When the Commission were minded to issue a non-discrimination notice, they notified the firm under s. 58(5) of the Act of their intention, and gave the firm an opportunity to make written and oral representations to the nominated commissioners. The firm took the opportunity to make both oral and written representations. At the hearing before the commissioners, no witnesses were available to give evidence to sustain the complaint or be cross-examined on behalf of the firm. The Commission decided to issue the notice. The firm applied for an order of *certiorari* on the ground, inter alia, that witnesses ought to have been available for cross-examination.

LORD LANE CJ: Of course there is a wealth of authority on what are and what are not the rules of natural justice. The rules have been described in various ways, as an 'unruly horse,' I think, in one decision, and there is no doubt that what may be the rules of natural justice in one case may well not be the rules of natural justice in another. As has frequently been said, and there is no harm in repeating it, all that the rules of natural justice mean is that the proceedings must be conducted in a way which is fair to the firm in this case, fair in all the circumstances. All the circumstances include a number of different considerations: first of all, the penalties, if any. There are no penalties under the Race Relations Act in the form of fines or imprisonment or anything like that, but what [counsel for the firm] has drawn to our attention, quite correctly, is that under the terms of the Estate Agents Act 1979 (and no one has been able to discover whether that has come into operation yet or not) there is no doubt that a person on whom a non-discriminatory notice has been served may, if he is an estate agent, suffer, if certain procedural steps are taken, grave disadvantages because it is open, under a number of safeguards into which I do not propose to go, for the Director General of Fair Trading to take steps to see that a person against whom this action had been taken under the Race Relations Act 1976 does not practise in business as an estate agent. Of course it is a very long call from saying that a person who has this non-discrimination notice served on him is necessarily going to suffer in his business by the action of the Director General of Fair Trading. Many procedures have to be gone through before that can take place, but there is a danger there, and that is one of the matters which is a circumstance to be taken into account.

The next matter, and possibly the most important matter, is the nature of the provisions of the Race Relations Act 1976 itself. I have read sufficient of the contents of section 58 of that Act to indicate that there is no mention in that section, or indeed in any other section, of any right to cross-examine any of the witnesses. That perhaps is a surprising omission if it was the intention of Parliament to allow a person in the position of the firm in this case the full panoply of legal rights which would take place at a judicial hearing.

It seems to me that there are degrees of judicial hearing, and those degrees run from the borders of pure administration to the borders of the full hearing of a criminal cause or matter in the Crown Court. It does not profit one to try to pigeon-hole the particular set of circumstances either into the administrative pigeon-hole or into the judicial pigeon-hole. Each case will inevitably differ, and one must ask oneself what is the basic nature of the proceeding which was going on here. It seems to me that, basically, this was an investigation being carried out by the commission. It is true that in the course of the investigation the commission may form a view, but it does not seem to me that is a proceeding which requires, in the name of fairness, any right in the firm in this case to be able to cross-examine witnesses whom the commission have seen and from whom they have taken statements. . . .

[Counsel for the firms] sought to derive assistance from some of the passages of the decision of this court in *Reg v Hull Prison Board of Visitors ex parte St Germain* [1979] QB 425, but it seems to me that the decision there was based on facts widely differing from those in the present case. That was truly a judicial proceeding carried out by the prison visitors and the complaint there was that there had been no opportunity to cross-examine prison officers in hotly disputed questions of identity. Speaking for myself, I derive little assistance from any dicta in that case.

. . . It seems to me for the reasons I have endeavoured to set out that in this case there was no breach of the rules of fairness in that cross-examination was not permitted or that the witnesses did not attend. . . .

Woolf J agreed with Lord Lane LJ.

R v *Army Board of the Defence Council, ex parte Anderson*
[1991] 3 WLR 42, Divisional Court

In this case the court had to scrutinize the procedures adopted by the Army Board in deciding upon complaints of racial discrimination by soldiers under the Race Relations Act 1976. (Complaints of racial discrimination in employment are normally dealt with by industrial tribunals but special procedures apply to complaints by soldiers.) The applicant was a former soldier who alleged that he had been subjected to forms of racial abuse which caused him to go absent without leave. The papers relating to the complaint were seen separately by two members of the Army Board who reached individual conclusions that, although there was some truth in the applicant's claim, there was no basis for making an apology to him or awarding him compensation. The applicant's requests for disclosure of documents relating to investigations into his complaints were refused, as was his request for an oral hearing. He applied for judicial review of the Board's decision.

TAYLOR LJ: . . .

Procedural requirements
What procedural requirements are necessary to achieve fairness when the Army Board considers a complaint of this kind? In addressing this issue, counsel made much of the distinction between judicial and administrative functions. Were it necessary to decide in those terms the functions of the

Army Board when considering a race discrimination complaint, I would characterise it as judicial rather than administrative. The board is required to adjudicate on an alleged breach of a soldier's rights under the 1976 Act and, if it be proved, to take any necessary steps by way of redress. It is accepted that the board has the power, inter alia, to award compensation. A body required to consider and adjudicate upon an alleged breach of statutory rights and to grant redress when necessary seems to me to be exercising an essentially judicial function. It matters not that the body has other functions which are non-judicial: see *R* v *Secretary of State for the Home Dept, ex p Tarrant* [1985] QB 251, 268.

However, to label the board's function either 'judicial' or 'administrative' for the purpose of determining the appropriate procedural regime is to adopt too inflexible an approach. . . .

What, then, are the criteria by which to decide the requirements of fairness in any given proceeding? Authoritative guidance as to this was given by Lord Bridge in *Lloyd* v *McMahon* [1987] AC 625, 702. He said:

> My Lords, the so-called rules of natural justice are not engraved on tablets of stone. To use the phrase which better expresses the underlying concept, what the requirements of fairness demand when any body, domestic, administrative or judicial, has to make a decision which will affect the rights of individuals depends on the character of the decision-making body, the kind of decision it has to make and the statutory or other framework in which it operates. In particular, it is well established that when a statute has conferred on any body the power to make decisions affecting individuals, the courts will not only require the procedure prescribed by the statute to be followed, but will readily imply so much and no more to be introduced by way of additional procedural safeguards as will ensure the attainment of fairness.

Applying these principles to the present case, the character of the Army Board and its role in this context have already been described. It is pertinent, however, to note that its decision is final apart from the possibility of judicial review. There is no appeal from its findings. The kind of decision it has to make has also been described. [Mr Sedley, counsel for the applicant] argues from that and from the statutory framework that all the procedural features to be found in a court trial are required – full discovery of documents, an oral hearing and cross-examination. As to the statutory framework, he points out that complaints of racial discrimination under Pt III of the 1976 Act relating to goods and services go before the county court with all the incidents of court procedure. Most civilian complaints of racial discrimination contrary to s. 4 of the 1976 Act go to an industrial tribunal under s. 54(1). There they are subject to rules requiring the procedures Mr Sedley claims here. Thus, if Mr Anderson had been seeking entry to the army, and had been turned down on allegedly racial grounds, his case could have been presented to the industrial tribunal under s. 4(1)(c), and he would have enjoyed all the procedures claimed here. Why should he be worse off simply because he is actually in the army and s. 54(2) requires his complaint to be considered by a different body?

Against this, [Mr Pannick, counsel for the Army Board] contends that Parliament has expressly provided that a soldier's complaint shall not go before an industrial tribunal but shall instead be subject to the army procedures pursuant to s. 181 of the 1955 Act. Parliament must, he submits, have been aware of the procedures normally followed in regard to other complaints under that section. Moreover, had Parliament wished to impose a more rigid and rigorous procedure, still in an army context, it could have directed that complaints of racial discrimination should be subject to s. 135 (board of inquiry), s. 137 (regimental inquiry) or even ss. 92 to 3 (court-martial). Process under each of those sections would have afforded the complainant the procedural formalities contended for here.

I should say that the existence of those forms of inquiry and their procedure undercuts [the] suggestion that exigencies of the service would make oral hearings impracticable.

In my judgment, there is force in Mr Pannick's argument. Since Parliament has deliberately excluded soldiers' complaints from industrial tribunals and thus from the procedures laid down for such tribunals, it cannot be axiomatic that by analogy all those procedures must be made available by the Army Board. Had Parliament wished to impose those detailed procedures on the Army Board, it could have done so.

However, Mr Pannick went on to contend that the Army Board's duty of fairness required no more than that it should act bona fide, not capriciously or in a biased manner, and that it should afford the complainant a chance to respond to the basic points put against him. In my judgment, this does not go far enough. The Army Board as the forum of last resort, dealing with an individual's fundamental statutory rights, must by its procedures achieve a high standard of fairness. I would list the principles as follows.

(1) There must be a proper hearing of the complaint in the sense that the board must consider, as a single adjudicating body, all the relevant evidence and contentions before reaching its conclusions. This means, in my view, that the members of the board must meet. It is unsatisfactory that the members should consider the papers and reach their individual conclusions in isolation and, perhaps as here, having received the concluded views of another member. Since there are ten members of the Army Board and any two can exercise the board's powers to consider a complaint of this kind, there should be no difficulty in achieving a meeting for the purpose.

(2) The hearing does not necessarily have to be an oral hearing in all cases. There is ample authority that decision-making bodies other than courts and bodies whose procedures are laid down by statute are masters of their own procedure. Provided that they achieve the degree of fairness appropriate to their task it is for them to decide how they will proceed and there is no rule that fairness always requires an oral hearing: see *Local Government Board v Arlidge* [1915] AC 120, 132–133, *Selvarajan v Race Relations Board* [1975] 1 WLR 1686, 1694 and *R v Immigration Appeal Tribunal, ex parte Jones* [1988] 1 WLR 477, 481. Whether an oral hearing is necessary will depend upon the subject matter and circumstances of the particular case and upon the nature of the decision to be made. It will also depend upon whether there are substantial issues of fact which cannot be satisfactorily resolved on the available written evidence. This does not mean that, whenever there is a conflict of evidence in the statements taken, an oral hearing must be held to resolve it. Sometimes such a conflict can be resolved merely by the inherent unlikelihood of one version or the other. Sometimes the conflict is not central to the issue for determination and would not justify an oral hearing. Even when such a hearing is necessary, it may only require one or two witnesses to be called and cross-examined.

Mr Sedley submits that, whatever the position regarding other complaints under s. 181, an oral hearing should be obligatory where the complaint is of race discrimination. He submits that experience shows proof of discrimination to be elusive. Discriminatory motivation can be innocent and subconscious. Without cross-examination at an oral hearing it may not emerge. I recognise the difficulties of proving discrimination in many cases, but I do not accept that a general rule requiring oral hearings must be applied by the Army Board to all complaints of discrimination. In the present case, for example, the direct and crude nature of the alleged racial abuse hardly raises any specially subtle possibility of subconscious motivation. Either the racial attacks, oral and physical, took place or they did not. Whether, when the Army Board sees all the statements and transcripts, it considers it necessary to hold an oral hearing to decide that issue or whether it can resolve it on the written material will be for it to decide in its discretion. What it cannot do, at the other extreme from Mr Sedley's submission, is to have an inflexible policy not to hold oral hearings. The findings of the two members in this case suggest that is what they did. . . .

[T]he board fettered its discretion and failed to consider the request for an oral hearing in the present case on its own merits.

(3) The opportunity to have the evidence tested by cross-examination is again within the Army Board's discretion. The decision whether to allow it will usually be inseparable from the decision

whether to have an oral hearing. The object of the latter will usually be to enable witnesses to be tested in cross-examination, although it would be possible to have an oral hearing simply to hear submissions.

(4) Whether oral or not, there must be what amounts to a hearing of any complaint under the 1976 Act. This means that the Army Board must have such a complaint investigated, consider all the material gathered in the investigation, give the complainant an opportunity to respond to it and consider his response.

But what is the board obliged to disclose to the complainant to obtain his response? Is it sufficient to indicate the gist of any material adverse to his case or should he be shown all the material seen by the board?

Mr Pannick submits that there is no obligation to show all to the complainant. He relies upon three authorities, *R* v *Secretary of State, ex parte Mughal* [1974] QB 313 *R* v *Secretary of State, ex parte Santillo* [1981] QB 778 and *R* v *Monopolies and Mergers Commission, ex parte Matthew Brown plc* [1987] 1 WLR 1235. However, in each of those cases, the function of the decision-making body was towards the administrative end of the spectrum. Because of the nature of the Army Board's function pursuant to the 1976 Act, already analysed above, I consider that a soldier complainant under that Act should be shown all the material seen by the board, apart from any documents for which public interest immunity can properly be claimed. The board is not simply making an administrative decision requiring it to consult interested parties and hear their representations. It has a duty to adjudicate on a specific complaint of breach of a statutory right. Except where public interest immunity is established, I see no reason why on such an adjudication the board should consider material withheld from the complainant.

In the present case it is true that Mr Anderson was shown a summary of the SIB report, though not the report itself. He also received the commanding officer's letter of 20 July which summarised points made against him, but he did not see the statements of other soldiers. Nor was he shown the information obtained individually by each of the board members. Thus, the response he made to the commanding officer's letter was hampered by a lack of full information. . . .

The Divisional Court granted an order of certiorari to quash the Board's decision.

NOTES:
1. A commentary on the use of judicial review in the context of racial discrimination in the public sector may be found at [1991] *Public Law*, at pp. 317–25.
2. *Ex parte St Germain (No. 2)* and *ex parte Cottrell and Rothon* have been used by H. F. Rawlings to illustrate a particular criticism of the rules of natural justice.

H. F. Rawlings 'Judicial Review and the Control of Government'
(1986) 64 *Public Administration* 135–145, at 140–41

. . . It has long been the concern of many academic administrative lawyers that our system of judicial review is for various reasons not adequate to ensure protection of the citizen against government excess. . . . In contrast, the adequacy of our administrative law principles from the point of view of the civil or public servant has rarely been considered. I suggest that the principles which have been developed by the courts over the last twenty years are quite simply not sufficiently precise to offer any meaningful guidance to administrators in their day-to-day decision-making, even if those administrators are aware of the existence of administrative law. . . .

What, then, are those principles? In essence there are two (I leave out of account here the question of illegality, which is not germane to the present discussion). First, there is the obligation to observe the rules of natural justice. Here we may return to *Ridge* v *Baldwin* [1964] AC 40. That case establishes that in a far wider category of situations than had previously been thought true, a public authority had, in exercising statutory functions, to observe the natural justice requirement. But what is that requirement? It must be remembered that the content of the natural justice rule derives from the court proceedings paradigm – judges must be unbiased, and parties must be given an opportunity to present their cases. How might these rules be applied in the infinite variety of administrative practices to which *Ridge* v *Baldwin* now extends them?

Two possibilities were open to the courts, given this new activist approach to the applicability of natural justice. [W]e might characterise these as the 'formal activist' and the 'informal activist' approaches. Under the former, the courts could seek, by firm application of the rules, to force the administrative process into a more judicial mould, to follow the formal procedures of the courts so far as possible. Under the latter, the courts could permit administrators a greater degree of latitude in their procedures and allow the applicability of the rules of natural justice in particular circumstances to be determined by the realities of administration, while all the time insisting that compliance with the rules was necessary. As is now well-known, the courts adopted the latter approach – natural justice was to be flexibly applied, to fit the circumstances of the case. In the result, observation of the rules of natural justice came to mean that the procedure required of the administrator had to be, in all the circumstances of the case, 'fair' (see, for example *Re HK* [1967] 2 QB 617 and *R* v *Commission for Racial Equality ex parte Cottrell and Rothon* [1980] 1 WLR 1580).

Now it may be that this was an inevitable result, although potentially pregnant with danger for the individual citizen asserting a right to be heard. It seems to me, however, that in their understandable desire to avoid over-judicialising administrative procedures, the courts have thrown out the baby with the bath-water. Flexible natural justice, or 'fairness', has come to have no fixed or settled content that an administrator should know must be observed in exercising decision-making powers. All he knows . . . is that he must be 'fair' – and what 'fairness' requires in the particular circumstances he can only ultimately find out when the court, on judicial review, tells him that he has, or has not, been fair. Is this an adequate administrative law principle, from the point of view of the administrator?

The point may briefly be illustrated by considering a specific issue in natural justice. It is sometimes said that, before any administrative decision is taken, a party who is likely to be affected by it shall have the right to hear what evidence against his interests has been given by someone else, and shall have the opportunity to question that person on the assertions contained therein . . . Decided cases, tell us, to take just two examples, that in the context of prison disciplinary proceedings, 'fairness' requires that such cross-examination is permitted (*R* v *Hull Prison Visitors ex parte St Germain (No. 2)* [1979] 1 WLR 1401), whereas in the context of issuance of a non-discrimination notice against a private estate agency under the Race Relations Act, 'fairness' does not require that such cross-examination is permitted (*R* v *CRE ex parte Cottrell and Rothon* [1980] 1 WLR 1580).

Now these results can be defended, because as Lord Lane CJ says in the *Cottrell and Rothon case*, there are 'degrees of judicial hearing, and those degrees run from the borders of pure administration to the borders of a full hearing of a criminal cause or matter'. The precise requirements of fairness depend upon how far along that continuum is the particular administrative process to be placed – the closer to 'pure administration' it is, the less onerous will be the procedural requirements imposed on administrators. This, as I have said, is defensible as a matter of theory, but I suggest that as guidance to administrative practice it is hopelessly imprecise from the point of view of those who want to know what procedural requirements the law lays down for them to observe.

QUESTIONS

1. What distinctions did Lord Lane CJ draw between the circumstances in *ex parte St Germain* and those in *ex parte Cottrell and Rothon*? Do you consider that the distinctions justify the different decisions reached in each case?

2. Cane, in the extract at pp. 568–71 *ante*, has suggested that there are two

possible approaches which the court might adopt in the face of legislative silence on the precise content of the rules of natural justice. 'It could be said that the rules of natural justice will apply only if there is evidence of a legislative intention that they should; alternatively it could be argued that silence should be construed as an invitation by the courts to apply common law procedural standards of natural justice.' Which approach did the courts adopt in *ex parte St Germain*, *ex parte Cottrell and Rothon*, and *ex parte Anderson*?

3. Write a paragraph to guide public administrators on the circumstances in which public authorities should be willing (a) to permit oral hearings and (b) to permit the cross-examination of witnesses.

4. Is there any solution to the problems identified by Rawlings?

5. Can there be a breach of the rules of natural justice where an applicant has been deprived of an opportunity to present his case, not through the fault of the decision-making body, but through the fault of his own advisers? (See *Al-Mehdawi* v *Secretary of State for the Home Department* [1990] AC 876, noted at [1990] *Public Law*, pp. 467–75.)

NOTE: One problem which has been discussed in a number of recent cases is that of legal representation. In *R* v *Board of Visitors of HM Prison, The Maze, ex parte Hone* [1988] 2 WLR 177 the House of Lords rejected the argument that a prisoner facing a disciplinary charge before a prison board of visitors had a right to legal representation. The House of Lords did, however, approve the decision in *R* v *Secretary of State for the Home Department, ex parte Tarrant* [1985] QB 251 that a board of visitors still has a discretion to allow legal representation and that in certain circumstances it would be wrong not to allow it. Webster J specified a number of points which are to be taken into account, including the seriousness of the charge and potential penalty, whether points of law are likely to arise, the particular prisoner's ability to present his case and the need for reasonable speed in reaching a decision.

The rules governing hearings before the prison board of visitors did not state that legal representation was prohibited. What is the position where the rules governing a particular hearing *do* prohibit legal representation? In *Enderby Town Football Club Ltd* v *Football Association Ltd* [1971] Ch 591, Lord Denning MR stated at p. 607:

> Seeing that the courts can inquire into the validity of the rule, I turn to the next question: Is it lawful for a body to stipulate in its rules that its domestic tribunal shall not permit legal representation? Such a stipulation is, I think, clearly valid so long as it is construed as directory and not imperative: for that leaves it open to the tribunal to permit legal representation in an exceptional case when the justice of the case so requires. But I have some doubt whether it is legitimate to make a rule which is so imperative in its terms as to exclude legal representation altogether, without giving the tribunal any discretion to admit it, even when the justice of the case so requires.

Lord Denning has repeated this view on other occasions (see e.g. *Edwards* v *SOGAT* [1971] Ch 354). In *Enderby Town* itself, however, Cairns LJ took a contrary view.

In *Maynard* v *Osmond* [1977] QB 240 Lord Denning was a member of the Court of Appeal which was required to consider the validity of police discipline regulations prohibiting legal representation. The regulations were made under statutory powers. It was held unanimously that the regulations were not *ultra vires*, and in particular that they were not in breach of natural justice. In this case Lord Denning stated, obiter, that it is permissible for a domestic tribunal to adopt a rule forbidding legal representation, and Orr LJ endorsed the view of Cairns LJ in *Enderby Town*.

The two principles so far discussed have been concerned with procedural fairness. In recent years the courts have begun to develop a principle of fairness which may require public authorities to reach a particular decision rather than simply to follow a fair procedure. The concept of legitimate expectation, which is explained in *CCSU v Minister for the Civil Service*, has been important in the development of this principle.

Council of the Civil Service Unions v Minister for the Civil Service
[1985] AC 374, House of Lords

> Government Communications Headquarters, a branch of the civil service, is responsible for the security of the United Kingdom military and official communications and the provision of signals intelligence for the Government. Since the formation of GCHQ in 1947, all the staff had been permitted to belong to trade unions. There was an established practice of consultation between the management and the civil service unions at GCHQ. Following incidents of industrial action at GCHQ the Minister for the Civil Service, the Prime Minister, issued an oral instruction to the effect that the terms and conditions of civil servants at GCHQ should be revised to exclude membership of any trade union other than a departmental staff association approved by the Minister. The instruction was issued under art. 4 of the Civil Service Order in Council 1982 'to give instructions . . . for controlling the conduct of the Service, and providing for the . . . conditions of service', the Order itself having been made under the royal prerogative. The union applied for judicial review, seeking a declaration that the Minister had acted unfairly in removing their fundamental right to belong to a trade union without consultation. The Court of Appeal allowed the Minister's appeal against the judge's decision that the Minister had acted unlawfully. The appellants appealed to the House of Lords. Having held that the courts could review the exercise of a power delegated to the decision-maker under the royal prerogative, Lord Fraser went on to consider whether there was a duty to consult the unions.

LORD FRASER:

The duty to consult
[Counsel for the appellants] submitted that the Minister had a duty to consult the CCSU, on behalf of employees at GCHQ, before giving the instruction on 22 December 1983 for making an important change in their conditions of service. His main reason for so submitting was that the employees had a legitimate, or reasonable, expectation that there would be such prior consultation before any important change was made in their conditions.

It is clear that the employees did not have a legal right to prior consultation. The Order in Council confers no such right and article 4 makes no reference at all to consultation . . . But even where a person claiming some benefit or privilege has no legal right to it, as a matter of private law, he may have a legitimate expectation of receiving the benefit or privilege, and, if so, the courts will protect his expectation by judicial review as a matter of public law. This subject has been fully explained by Lord Diplock, in *O'Reilly v Mackman* [1983] 2 AC 237 and I need not repeat what he has so recently said. Legitimate, or reasonable, expectation may arise either from an express promise given on behalf of a public authority or from the existence of a regular practice which the claimant can reasonably expect to continue. Examples of the former type of expectation are *Reg v Liverpool Corporation, ex parte Liverpool Taxi Fleet Operators Association* [1972] 2 QB 299 and *A-G of Hong Kong v Ng Yuen Shiu* [1983] 2 AC 629. (I agree with Lord Diplock's view, expressed in the speech in this appeal, that 'legitimate' is to be preferred to the word 'reasonable' in this context. I was responsible for using the word 'reasonable' for the reason explained in *Ng Yuen Shiu*, but it was intended only to be exegetical of 'legitimate'.) An example of the latter is *Reg v Hull Prison Board of Visitors ex parte St Germain* [1979] 1 All ER 701, [1979] QB 425, approved by this House in *O'Reilly v Mackman* [1982] 3 All ER 1124 at 1126, [1983] 2 AC 237 at 274. The submission on behalf of the appellants is that the present case is of the latter type. The test of that is whether the practice of prior consultation of the staff on significant changes in their conditions of service was so well established by 1983 that it would be unfair or inconsistent with good administration for the Government to depart from the practice in this case. Legitimate expectations such as are now under consideration will always relate to a benefit or privilege to which the claimant has no right in private law, and it may even be to one which conflicts with his private law rights. In the present case the evidence shows that, ever since GCHQ began in 1947, prior consultation has been the invariable rule when conditions of service were to be significantly altered. Accordingly in my opinion if there had been no question of national security involved, the appellants would have had a legitimate expectation that the Minister would consult them before issuing the instruction of 22 December 1983.

NOTES:

1. A majority of their Lordships held that the exercise of prerogative powers could be challenged in judicial review proceedings provided that the subject matter was justiciable. (On the issue of justiciability, see *post*, p. 681.) Lord Fraser and Lord Brightman left open the question whether a direct exercise of the prerogative powers could be subject to judicial review, but they did accept that powers which had been delegated to decision-makers by an Order in Council made under prerogative powers were subject to judicial review. All their Lordships agreed that, had issues of national security not been involved, the unions would have been entitled to consultation. (On the issues of national security which arose in this case see *post*, at p. 681.)

2. The concept of legitimate expectation has been discussed by a number of writers (see, for example, C. Forsyth, 'The Provenance and Protection of Legitimate Expectations' 47 (1988) CLJ, 238–260; B. Hadfield, 'Judicial Review and the Concept of Legitimate Expectation' (1988) 39 *Northern Ireland Legal Quarterly*, 103–119; Ganz, in *Public Law and Politics*, ed. Harlow ch. 8; P. Craig, 'Legitimate Expectations: A Conceptual Analysis', (1992) 108 *LQR* 79). They have highlighted the different ways in which the concept is used by the courts. Predominantly, the legitimate expectation has related to fair procedures but see *post* p. 634 for substantive legitimate expectations.

D: Irrationality

Prior to the decision in *CCSU v Minister for the Civil Service* this ground was often expressed in the principle that an authority must not reach a decision which is so unreasonable that no reasonable body could have come to it. After *CCSU* the use of the term 'irrationality' has become more common, but in *R v Devon CC, ex parte G* [1988] 3 WLR 49, at p. 51, the Master of the Rolls stated that he preferred the older test because the term 'irrationality' could be widely misunderstood as casting doubt on the mental capacity of the decision-maker. Subsequent cases have used both terms.

Wheeler v *Leicester City Council*

[1985] AC 1054, House of Lords

The facts are set out at p. 581, *ante*.

LORD ROSKILL: It is important to emphasise that there was nothing illegal in the action of the three members in joining the tour. The government policy recorded in the well-known Gleneagles agreement has never been given the force of law at the instance of any government, whatever its political complexion, and a person who acts otherwise than in accordance with the principles of that agreement, commits no offence even though he may by his action earn the moral disapprobation of large numbers of his fellow citizens. That the club condemns apartheid, as does the council, admits of no doubt. But the council's actions against the club were not taken, as already pointed out, because the club took no action against its three members. They were taken, according to Mr Soulsby, because the club failed to condemn the tour and to discourage its members from playing. The same point was put more succinctly by Mr Sullivan QC, who appeared for the council – 'The club failed to align themselves whole-heartedly with the council on a controversial issue.' The club did not condemn the tour. They did not give specific affirmative answers to the first two questions. Thus, so the argument ran, the council, legitimately bitterly hostile to the policy of apartheid, were justified in exercising their statutory discretion to determine by whom the recreation ground should be used so as to exclude those, such as the club, who would not support the council's policy on the council's terms. The club had, however, circulated to those involved the powerfully reasoned and impressive memorandum which had been sent to the RFU [the Rugby Football Union] on 12 March 1984 by the anti-apartheid movement. Of the club's own opposition to apartheid as expressed in its memorandum which was given to Mr Soulsby, there is no doubt. But the club recognised that those views, like those of the council, however passionately held by some, were by no means universally held, especially by those who sincerely believed that the evils of apartheid were enhanced rather than diminished by a total prohibition of all sporting links with South Africa.

The council's main defence rested on section 71 of the Race Relations Act 1976. That section appears as the first section in Part X of the Act under the cross-heading 'Supplemental.' For ease of reference I will set out the section in full:

> Without prejudice to their obligation to comply with any other provision of this Act, it shall be the duty of every local authority to make appropriate arrangements with a view to securing that their various functions are carried out with due regard to the need – (a) to eliminate unlawful racial discrimination; and (b) to promote equality of opportunity, and good relations, between persons of different racial groups.

My Lords, it was strenuously argued on behalf of the club that this section should be given what was called a 'narrow' construction. It was suggested that the section was only concerned with the actions of the council as regards its own internal behaviour and was what was described as 'inward looking.' The section had no relevance to the general exercise by the council or indeed of any local authority of their statutory functions, as for example in relation to the control of open spaces or in determining who should be entitled to use a recreation ground and on what terms. It was said that the section was expressed in terms of a 'duty.' But it did not impose any duty so as to compel the exercise by a local authority of other statutory functions in order to achieve the objectives of the Act of 1976.

My Lords, in respectful agreement with the courts below, I unhesitatingly reject this argument. I think the whole purpose of the section is to see that in employment, and in Part III, education, local authorities must in relation to 'their various functions' make 'appropriate arrangements' to secure that those functions are carried out 'with due regard to the need' mentioned in the section.

It follows that I do not doubt that the council were fully entitled in exercising their statutory discretion under, for example, the Open Spaces Act 1906 and the various Public Health Acts, which are all referred to in the judgments below, to pay regard to what they thought to be in the best interests of race relations.

The only question is, therefore, whether the action of the council of which the club complains is susceptible of attack by way of judicial review. It was forcibly argued by Mr Sullivan QC for the council, that once it was accepted, as I do accept, that section 71 bears the construction for which the council contended, the matter became one of political judgment only, and that by interfering the courts would be trespassing across that line which divides a proper exercise of a statutory discretion based on a political judgment, in relation to which the courts will not interfere, from an improper exercise of such a discretion in relation to which the courts will interfere.

Lord Roskill referred to the judgment in *Council for the Civil Service Unions* v *Minister for the Civil Service* (*ante* at p. 575) and continued.

To my mind the crucial question is whether the conduct of the council in trying by their four questions, whether taken individually or collectively, to force acceptance by the club of their own policy (however proper that policy may be) on their own terms, as for example, by forcing them to lend their considerable prestige to a public condemnation of the tour, can be said either to be so 'unreasonable' as to give rise to '*Wednesbury* unreasonableness' (*Associated Provincial Picture Houses Ltd* v *Wednesbury Corporation* [1948] 1 KB 223) or to be so fundamental a breach of the duty to act fairly which rests upon every local authority in matters of this kind and thus to justify interference by the courts.

I do not doubt for one moment the great importance which the council attach to the presence in its midst of a 25 per cent population of persons who are either Asian or of Afro-Caribbean origin. Nor do I doubt for one moment the sincerity of the view expressed in Mr Soulsby's affidavit regarding the need for the council to distance itself from bodies who hold important positions and who do not actively discourage sporting contacts with South Africa. Persuasion, even powerful persuasion, is always a permissible way of seeking to obtain an objective. But in a field where other views can equally legitimately be held, persuasion, however powerful, must not be allowed to cross that line where it moves into the field of illegitimate pressure coupled with the threat of sanctions. The four questions, coupled with the insistence that only affirmative answers to all four would be acceptable, are suggestive of more than powerful persuasion. The second question is to my mind open to particular criticism. What, in the context, is meant by the 'club?' The committee? 90 playing members? 4,300 non-playing members? It by no means follows that the committee would all have agreed on an affirmative answer to the question and still less that a majority of their members, playing or non-playing, would have done so. Nor would any of these groups of members necessarily have known whether 'the large proportion,' whatever that phrase may mean in the context, of the Leicester population would have regarded the tour as 'an insult' to them.

None of the learned judges in the court below have felt able to hold that the action of the club was unreasonable or perverse in the *Wednesbury* sense. They do not appear to have been invited to consider whether those actions, even if not unreasonable on *Wednesbury* principles, were assailable on the grounds of procedural impropriety or unfairness by the council in the manner in which, in the light of the facts I have outlined, they took their decision to suspend for 12 months the use by the club of the Welford Road recreation ground.

I greatly hesitate to differ from four learned judges on the *Wednesbury* issue but for myself I would have been disposed respectfully to do this and to say that the actions of the council were unreasonable in the *Wednesbury* sense. But even if I am wrong in this view, I am clearly of the opinion that the manner in which the council took that decision was in all the circumstances of the case unfair within the third of the principles stated in *Council for the Civil Service Unions* v *Minister for the Civil Service* [1985] AC 374. The council formulated those four questions in the manner of which I have spoken and indicated that only such affirmative answers would be acceptable. They received reasoned and reasonable answers which went a long way in support of the policy which the council had accepted and desired to see accepted. The views expressed in these reasoned and reasonable answers were lawful views and the views which, as the evidence shows, many people sincerely hold and believe to be correct. If the club had adopted a different and hostile attitude, different considerations might well have arisen. But the club did not adopt any such attitude. . . .

I would therefore allow the appeal.

NOTE: The judgment of Lord Roskill may be compared to that of Ackner LJ in the Court of Appeal in *Wheeler*. Having decided that the council were lawfully entitled to take into account the purposes expressed in s. 71 of the Race Relations Act 1976, Ackner LJ continued:

If I am right so far, this leaves only one final question to consider. Can it be said in the circumstances of the case that no reasonable local authority could properly conclude that temporarily banning from the use of its recreation grounds an important local rugger club, which declined to condemn a South African tour and declined actively to discourage its members from participating therein, could promote good relations between persons of different racial groups? (The well-known *Wednesbury* test: see *Associated Provincial Picture Houses Ltd v Wednesbury Corp.* [1947] 2 All ER 680, [1948] 1 KB 223.) Forbes J was at pains to point out, as I certainly would wish also to do, that courts are not concerned with the merits of the two rival views, no doubt equally honestly held, as to the value of severing sporting links with South Africa. I am fully prepared to accept that, even amongst those who feel strongly that sporting links should be severed, there may be some who could take the view that the club acted wholly reasonably in the action it took and should not have been expected to go further. But to accept the mere existence of such a school of thought does not establish that the council's decision was perverse and this is what the club is obliged to do to succeed under this head. Nor is the club's case advanced by emphasising that the council were imposing a sanction against members of the club for refusing publicly to endorse the reasonable views of the council and thereby interfering with the club's freedom of speech. The view which the council held as to the importance of severing sporting links with South Africa had clearly been fully considered by the council well before the events of 1984, and in view of the make-up of the population of the city it was a view which understandably was very strongly supported. It represented no more than that clearly recorded in the Gleneagles Agreement. In my judgment it would be quite wrong to categorise as perverse the council's decision to give an outward and visible manifestation of their disapproval of the club's failure, indeed refusal, 'to take every practical step to discourage' the tour, and in particular the participation of its members.

I would accordingly dismiss this appeal.

QUESTIONS

1. On the question of whether the council had acted in a way in which no reasonable council could have acted, do you find the reasoning of Lord Roskill or that of Ackner LJ more convincing?

2. Does Lord Roskill explain which of the particular aspects of Lord Diplock's third category, procedural impropriety, he considered to have been breached?

Nottinghamshire CC v *Secretary of State for the Environment*
[1986] 1 AC 240, House of Lords

In 1984 the Secretary of State issued a report containing the guidance for expenditure by local authorities for 1985/86. The guidance was based on the 1984/85 budgets of local authorities and an amount known as 'grant-related expenditure' (GRE). Grant-related expenditure is the notional expenditure which an authority might incur if all authorities provided the same standard of service with the same degree of efficiency at a level consistent with the Government's aggregate spending plans for local authorities. The guidance for 1985/86 stated that authorities which had budgeted to spend at or below the GRE expenditure in 1984/85 could budget in 1985/86 for the 1984/85 GRE plus 3.75 per cent. Those which had budgeted at above their GRE for 1984/85 could budget for the figure in the 1984/85 guidance plus 3.75 per cent. Under the scheme established by the Local Government Planning and Land Act 1980, if a local authority's expenditure exceeded that set in the guidance to it, the Secretary of State was empowered to reduce the amount of the rate support grant made by central government to the authority.

The report was laid before the House of Commons pursuant to s. 60 of the Act, and was approved by an affirmative resolution of the House. Nottinghamshire CC and the City of Bradford MC applied for an order of *certiorari* to quash the decision of the Secretary of State contained in the report and for declarations that the expenditure guidance contained in the report was invalid. They based their application on two grounds. First, the Secretary of State's guidance did not comply with the requirement in s. 59(11A) of the 1980 Act that 'any guidance issued . . . be framed by reference to principles applicable to all local authorities . . .' because it differentiated between authorities budgeting to spend above or below the GRE. Second, they argued that the decision of the Secretary was unreasonable because the guidance was disproportionately disadvantageous to a small group of public authorities whose 1984/85 guidance was below GRE and who were budgeting to spend above GRE.

At first instance, the application was dismissed but the Court of Appeal allowed the authority's appeal. On appeal to the House of Lords the first ground was rejected; it was held that, on the true construction of the Act, while there had to be one set of principles applicable to all local authorities, it was permissible for those principles to identify and reflect differences between local authorities, including their past expenditure records. The following extracts deal with the second ground.

LORD SCARMAN: . . . Their second submission is that, even if the guidance complies with the words of the statute, it offends a principle of public law in that the burden which the guidance imposes on some authorities, including Nottingham and Bradford, is so disproportionately disadvantageous when compared with its effect upon others that it is a perversely unreasonable exercise of the power conferred by the statute upon the Secretary of State. The respondents rely on what has become known to lawyers as the 'Wednesbury principles' – by which is meant the judgment of Lord Greene MR in *Associated Provincial Picture House Ltd* v *Wednesbury Corporation* [1948] 1 KB 223, 229. . . .

The submission raises an important question as to the limits of judicial review. We are in the field of public financial administration and we are being asked to review the exercise by the Secretary of State of an administrative discretion which inevitably requires a political judgment on his part and which cannot lead to action by him against a local authority unless that action is first approved by the House of Commons.

. . . My Lords, I think the courts below were absolutely right to decline the invitation to intervene. I can understand that there may well be a justiciable issue as to the true construction of the words of the statute and that, if the Secretary of State has issued guidance which fails to comply with the requirement of subsection (11 A) of section 59 of the Act of 1980 the guidance can be quashed. But I cannot accept that it is constitutionally appropriate, save in very exceptional circumstances, for the courts to intervene on the ground of 'unreasonableness' to quash guidance framed by the Secretary of State and by necessary implication approved by the House of Commons, the guidance being concerned with the limits of public expenditure by local authorities and the incidence of the tax burden as between taxpayers and ratepayers. Unless and until a statute provides otherwise, or it is established that the Secretary of State has abused his power, these are matters of political judgment for him and for the House of Commons. They are not for the judges or your Lordships' House in its judicial capacity.

For myself, I refuse in this case to examine the detail of the guidance or its consequences. My reasons are these. Such an examination by a court would be justified only if a prima facie case were to be shown for holding that the Secretary of State has acted in bad faith, or for an improper motive, or that the consequences of his guidance were so absurd that he must have taken leave of his senses. The evidence comes nowhere near establishing any of these propositions. Nobody in the case has ever suggested bad faith on the part of the Secretary of State. Nobody suggests, nor could it be suggested in the light of the evidence as to the matters he considered before reaching his decision, that he had acted for an improper motive. Nobody now suggests that the Secretary of State failed to consult local authorities in the manner required by statute. It is plain that the time-table, to which the Secretary of State in the preparation of the guidance was required by statute and compelled by circumstances to adhere, involved him necessarily in framing guidance on the basis of the past spending record of authorities. It is recognised that the Secretary of State and his advisers were well aware that there would be inequalities in the distribution of the burden between local authorities but believed the guidance upon which he decided would by discouraging the high spending and encouraging the low spending be the best course of action in the circumstances. And as my noble and learned friend, Lord Bridge of Harwich, demonstrates, it was guidance which complied with the terms of the statute. This view of the language of the statute has inevitably a significant bearing upon the conclusion of 'unreasonableness' in the *Wednesbury* sense. If, as your Lordships are holding, the guidance was based on principles applicable to all authorities, the principles would have to be either a pattern of perversity or an absurdity of such proportions that the guidance could not have been framed by a bona fide exercise of political judgment on the part of the Secretary of State. And it would be necessary to find as a fact that the House of Commons had been misled: for their approval was necessary and was obtained to the action that he proposed to take to implement the guidance.

. . . The present case raises in acute form the constitutional problem of the separation of powers between Parliament, the executive, and the courts. In this case, Parliament has enacted that an executive power is not to be exercised save with the consent and approval of one of its Houses. It is true that the framing of the guidance is for the Secretary of State alone after consultation with local authorities; but he cannot act on the guidance so as to discriminate between local authorities without reporting to, and obtaining the approval of, the House of Commons. That House has, therefore, a role and responsibility not only at the legislative stage when the Act was passed but in the action to be taken by the Secretary of State in the exercise of the power conferred upon him by the legislation.

To sum it up, the levels of public expenditure and the incidence and distribution of taxation are matters for Parliament and, within Parliament, especially for the House of Commons. If Parliament legislates, the courts have their interpretative role: they must, if called upon to do so, construe the statute. If a minister exercises a power conferred on him by the legislation, the courts can investigate whether he has abused his power. But if, as in this case, effect cannot be given to the Secretary of State's determination without the consent of the House of Commons and the House of Commons has consented, it is not open to the courts to intervene unless the minister and the House must have misconstrued the statute or the minister has – to put it bluntly – deceived the House. The courts can properly rule that a minister has acted unlawfully if he has erred in law as to the limits of his power even when his action has the approval of the House of Commons, itself acting not legislatively but within the limits set by a statute. But, if a statute, as in this case, requires the House of Commons to approve a minister's decision before he can lawfully enforce it, and if the action proposed complies with the terms of the statute (as your Lordships, I understand, are convinced that it does in the present case), it is not for the judges to say that the action has such unreasonable consequences that the guidance upon which the action is based and on which the House of Commons had notice was perverse and must be set aside. For that is a question of policy for the minister and the Commons, unless there has been bad faith or misconduct by the minister. Where Parliament has legislated that the action to be taken by the Secretary of State must, before it is taken, be approved by the House of Commons, it is no part of the judge's role to declare that the action proposed is unfair, unless it constitutes an abuse of power in the sense which I have explained; for Parliament has enacted that one of its Houses is responsible. Judicial review is a great weapon in the hands of the judges: but the judges must observe the constitutional limits set by our parliamentary system upon their exercise of this beneficent power. . . .

Lord Bridge and Lord Templeman delivered judgments in which they agreed with Lord Scarman. Lord Roskill and Lord Griffiths agreed with Lord Scarman.

NOTE: Lord Scarman's judgment was discussed and followed by the House of Lords in *R v Secretary of State for the Environment, ex parte Hammersmith and Fulham LBC* [1990] 3 All ER 589, a case which also involved a dispute between central and local government over finances. The House of Lords held that the Secretary of State had acted lawfully in setting a maximum amount for the budgets of a number of authorities under the Local Government Finance Act 1988.

QUESTIONS

1. Do you interpret Lord Scarman's judgment as stating that judicial review of a decision of this nature on the ground of unreasonableness is excluded?

2. Would judicial review be available on any other grounds, for example that the Minister had acted for an improper purpose or on the basis of irrelevant considerations?

3. Which constitutional theory did his Lordship rely on in this case?

4. Commenting on this decision in (1986) 45 CLJ (169–173), Colin Reid sees it, at p. 171:

   . . . as an affirmation of our traditional constitutional theory. There may be no formal separation of powers in this country, but the basic notions of our constitution, such as parliamentary sovereignty, the rule of law and responsibility of the Executive to Parliament, do create a fundamental distribution of powers and functions between the various elements of the state. It is to Parliament that one must look to control the executive on matters of policy and principle, *a fortiori* in cases where it has been enacted that the Executive must seek parliamentary approval for the exercise of the powers conferred on it. . . .

   The question must be asked, though, how well this structure serves us in the political realities of today. Can we rely on Parliament to provide an adequate check on the powers of the executive?

   If the answer is no, can judicial review provide a solution? Note that Reid's view is that it cannot; 'the way to achieve greater control over the Executive must lie in far-reaching reforms to our constitutional structure, rather than to a continued extension, or rather distortion, of judicial review to embrace issues and arguments not suited to judicial resolution.' Compare this with the view expressed by Cane (*ante*, at pp. 568–71).

NOTE: The *Nottinghamshire* and *Hammersmith & Fulham* cases have been described as being super-*Wednesbury* because their approach imposes a higher threshold. The appropriate standard of *Wednesbury* review was at issue in the next case.

R (Daly) v *Secretary of State for the Home Department*
[2001] UKHL 26; [2001] 2 AC 532, House of Lords

LORD STEYN: . . .

My Lords,

24. I am in complete agreement with the reasons given by Lord Bingham of Cornhill in his speech. For the reasons he gives I would also allow the appeal. Except on one narrow but important point I have nothing to add.

25. There was written and oral argument on the question whether certain observations of Lord Phillips of Worth Matravers MR in *R (Mahmood)* v *Secretary of State for the Home Department* [2001] 1 WLR 840 were correct. The context was an immigration case involving a decision of the Secretary of State made before the Human Rights Act 1998 came into effect. The Master of the Rolls neverthe-less approached the case as if the Act had been in force when the Secretary of State reached his decision. He explained the new approach to be adopted. The Master of the Rolls concluded, at p 857, para 40:

> When anxiously scrutinising an executive decision that interferes with human rights, the court will ask the question, applying an objective test, whether the decision-maker could reasonably have concluded that the interference was necessary to achieve one or more of the legitimate aims recognised by the Convention. When considering the test of necessity in the relevant context, the court must take into account the European jurisprudence in accordance with section 2 of the 1998 Act.

These observations have been followed by the Court of Appeal in *R* v *Secretary of State for the Home Department, Ex p Isiko* (unreported), 20 December 2000 and by Thomas J in *R* v *Secretary of State for the Home Department, Ex p Samaroo* (unreported), 20 December 2000.

26. The explanation of the Master of the Rolls in the first sentence of the cited passage requires clarification. It is couched in language reminiscent of the traditional *Wednesbury* ground of review (*Associated Provincial Picture Houses Ltd* v *Wednesbury Corporation* [1948] 1 KB 223), and in particular the adaptation of that test in terms of heightened scrutiny in cases involving fundamental rights as formulated in *R* v *Ministry of Defence, Ex p Smith* [1996] QB 517, 554E–G per Sir Thomas Bingham MR. There is a material difference between the *Wednesbury* and *Smith* grounds of review and the approach of proportionality applicable in respect of review where convention rights are at stake.

27. The contours of the principle of proportionality are familiar. In *de Freitas* v *Permanent Secretary of Ministry of Agriculture, Fisheries, Lands and Housing* [1999] 1 AC 69 the Privy Council adopted a three stage test. Lord Clyde observed, at p 80, that in determining whether a limitation (by an act, rule or decision) is arbitrary or excessive the court should ask itself:

> whether: (i) the legislative objective is sufficiently important to justify limiting a fundamental right; (ii) the measures designed to meet the legislative objective are rationally connected

to it; and (iii) the means used to impair the right or freedom are no more than is necessary to accomplish the objective.

Clearly, these criteria are more precise and more sophisticated than the traditional grounds of review. What is the difference for the disposal of concrete cases? Academic public lawyers have in remarkably similar terms elucidated the difference between the traditional grounds of review and the proportionality approach: see Professor Jeffrey Jowell QC, 'Beyond the Rule of Law: Towards Constitutional Judicial Review' [2000] PL 671; Craig, *Administrative Law*, 4th ed (1999), 561–563; Professor David Feldman, 'Proportionality and the Human Rights Act 1998', essay in *The Principle of Proportionality in the Laws of Europe* (1999), pp 117, 127 et seq. The starting point is that there is an overlap between the traditional grounds of review and the approach of proportionality. Most cases would be decided in the same way whichever approach is adopted. But the intensity of review is somewhat greater under the proportionality approach. Making due allowance for important structural differences between various convention rights, which I do not propose to discuss, a few generalisations are perhaps permissible. I would mention three concrete differences without suggesting that my statement is exhaustive. First, the doctrine of proportionality may require the reviewing court to assess the balance which the decision maker has struck, not merely whether it is within the range of rational or reasonable decisions. Secondly, the proportionality test may go further than the traditional grounds of review inasmuch as it may require attention to be directed to the relative weight accorded to interests and considerations. Thirdly, even the heightened scrutiny test developed in *R* v *Ministry of Defence, Ex p Smith* [1996] QB 517, 554 is not necessarily appropriate to the protection of human rights. It will be recalled that in *Smith* the Court of Appeal reluctantly felt compelled to reject a limitation on homosexuals in the army. The challenge based on article 8 of the Convention for the Protection of Human Rights and Fundamental Freedoms (the right to respect for private and family life) foundered on the threshold required even by the anxious scrutiny test. The European Court of Human Rights came to the opposite conclusion: *Smith and Grady* v *United Kingdom* (1999) 29 EHRR 493. The court concluded, at p 543, para 138:

> the threshold at which the High Court and the Court of Appeal could find the Ministry of Defence policy irrational was placed so high that it effectively excluded any consideration by the domestic courts of the question of whether the interference with the applicants' rights answered a pressing social need or was proportionate to the national security and public order aims pursued, principles which lie at the heart of the court's analysis of complaints under article 8 of the Convention.

In other words, the intensity of the review, in similar cases, is guaranteed by the twin requirements that the limitation of the right was necessary in a democratic society, in the sense of meeting a pressing social need, and the question whether the interference was really proportionate to the legitimate aim being pursued.

28. The differences in approach between the traditional grounds of review and the proportionality approach may therefore sometimes yield different results. It is therefore important that cases involving convention rights must be analysed in the correct way. This does not mean that there has been a shift to merits review. On the contrary, as Professor Jowell [2000] PL 671, 681 has pointed out the respective roles of judges and administrators are fundamentally distinct and will remain so. To this extent the general tenor of the observations in *Mahmood* [2001] 1 WLR 840 are correct. And Laws LJ rightly emphasised in *Mahmood*, at p 847, para 18, 'that the intensity of review in a public law case will depend on the subject matter in hand'. That is so even in cases involving Convention rights. In law context is everything.

NOTE: We appear to have ordinary *Wednesbury* unreasonableness, super-*Wednesbury*, which is less intensive, and when human rights are at issue, a more searching scrutiny by the courts based on proportionality. It has been argued that this variability in *Wednesbury* unreasonableness moves domestic law closer to the proportionality standard of review found in European law, in Community law and the jurisprudence of the European Court of Human Rights. It is suggested that proportionality is a clearer and more honest basis for substantive review. It has been applied in three types of situation in relation to penalties, to human rights and other exercises of administrative discretion. The case law indicates that the following tests are used:

(a) *balancing*: where the ends sought to be achieved are measured against the means applied and the impact upon affected individuals;

(b) *necessity*: where more than one means is available, was the action taken the least restrictive way of achieving the aim;

(c) *suitability*: where the means are appropriate, e.g., capable of implementation, lawful.

See Craig, *Administrative Law* (1999); DeSmith, Woolf, Jowell, *Principles of Judicial Review* (1999); Ellis (ed.), *The Principle of Proportionality in the Laws of Europe* (1999) and Wong, 'Towards the Nutcracker Principle: Reconsidering the Objections to Proportionality' [2000] PL 92.

In *Brind*, some members of the House of Lords were clear that proportionality was very different from *Wednesbury* unreasonableness and might overstep the legality/merits boundary. This view is changing, in part because the judges have more experience in applying it in cases involving Community law.

R v Chief Constable of Sussex, ex parte International Trader's Ferry Ltd
[1999] 2 AC 418, House of Lords

> The applicant company (ITF) was engaged in exporting live animals. People who were opposed to this demonstrated at ports seeking to stop the transport of the livestock. The police operations enabled five sailings a week to be operated out of Shoreham. The Chief Constable reviewed the situation and, after taking into account his resources, decided to deploy officers at Shoreham on two consecutive days a week, or four consecutive days a fortnight. The applicants challenged this decision by judicial review. In the Divisional Court the Chief Constable's decision was quashed on the basis that it breached Article 34 (now 29) of the EC Treaty, as it was a measure having equivalent effect to a quantitative restriction on exports. In domestic law it was a lawful exercise of his discretion. On appeal the Court of Appeal held that if this decision was within the scope of Article 34 (now 29) it was covered by Article 36 (now 30) and was justified on grounds of public policy, the pursuit of effective policing. The applicants appealed.

LORD SLYNN: . . . What is required in a case like the present where the Chief Constable has statutory and common law duties to perform is to ask whether he did all that proportionately and reasonably he could be expected to do with the resources available to him. He is after all dealing with an emergency situation and there is no question of funds being deliberately withheld by the state to hamper his work. The budget for the authority was a very large one and it was for him to decide how he would use the moneys apportioned to him. These decisions have to be taken on the information available at the time. It is not right, in my view, that there should be an ex post facto examination of accounts to see whether, in some way or another, in the event moneys did prove to be available which perhaps could have been used. Thus, in the present case, I do not consider that the fact that the amount attributed to reserves in the final accounts in the 1995–96 year (£13.13m.) meant that, at the time he had to take his decision, the Chief Constable should have assumed that the police authorities would allocate more money to this particular task than appeared as reserves in the budget (£7.25m.). It seems to me that at the end of the day it is all a question of considering whether 'appropriate measures' have been taken. That in turn involves an inquiry as to whether the steps taken were proportionate.

In *Reg.* v *Secretary of State for the Home Department, Ex parte Brind* [1991] 1 AC 696 the House treated *Wednesbury* reasonableness and proportionality as being different. So in some ways they are though the distinction between the two tests in practice is in any event much less than is sometimes suggested. The cautious way in which the European Court usually applies this test, recognising the importance of respecting the national authority's margin of appreciation, may mean that whichever test is adopted, and even allowing for a difference in onus, the result is the same.

I am satisfied, as was the Court of Appeal, that the Chief Constable has shown here that what he did in providing police assistance was proportionate to what was required. To protect the lorries, in the way he did, was a suitable and necessary way of dealing with potentially violent demonstrators. To limit the occasions when sufficient police could be made available was, in the light of the re-sources available to him to deal with immediate and foreseeable events at the port, and at the same time to carry out all his other police duties, necessary and in no way disproportionate to the restrictions which were involved. Unlike the authorities in *Commission of the European Communities* v *French Republic* (Case C-265/95) [1997] ECR I-6959 he was controlling and arresting violent offenders. He was, moreover, not dealing with a situation where no other way of exporting the animals was available. Dover was available and there were and might be other occasions when the lorries could get through. Far from failing to protect the applicant's trade he was seeking to do it in the most effective way available to him with his finite resources. It was only on rare and necessary, even dangerous, occasions that lorries were turned back. In the light of article 36 [now 30] it is not open to ITF to say, as they at times seem to be saying, that they had an absolute right to export animals on seven days a week and there is no suggestion that with such a short Channel crossing their claim was necessarily limited to one sailing a day. This case is quite different from *Commission of the European Communities* v *French Republic* where 'manifest and persistent failure' to control those interfering with imports was shown and where there was no evidence to show that those responsible could have acted. Since this case involves the application of the principles laid down in the *French Republic* case, where clearly the European Court left a considerable discretion to national authorities in dealing with issues of this sort, I do not find it necessary, nor are your Lordships obliged, to refer a question concerning article 36 [now 30] to the European Court of Justice under article 177 [now 234] of the EC Treaty.

I am satisfied that here the Chief Constable has shown that the steps that he took were justified on grounds of public order and I would dismiss this appeal.

NOTES:
1. Lord Cooke was also of the view that in this case 'the European concepts of proportionality and margin of appreciation produce the same result as what are commonly called *Wednesbury* principles'. He seemed to prefer a simpler test than the twice used tautologous formula in *Wednesbury* – 'so unreasonable that no reasonable authority could ever have come to it' – 'whether the decision in question was one which a reasonable authority could reach'.
2. Wong [2000] PL 92, at 109 suggests that Lord Slynn was implicitly *actually* using proportionality, not *Wednesbury*, see his use of suitable and necessary.

QUESTION

Which do you think is a better approach to irrationality, adopting Lord Cooke's simpler test or adopting proportionality with its structured tests?

NOTE: Earlier we saw how the concept of legitimate expectations had initially been concerned with procedure. It has been held to have a substantive aspect, but there has been doubt about the test which should be used – *Wednesbury* unreasonableness or proportionality. Consider the following case.

R v *North and East Devon Health Authority, ex parte Coughlan*
[2000] 2 WLR 622, Court of Appeal

The applicant was severely disabled in a road accident. In 1993 she and other disabled patients had been moved from a hospital to Mardon House. The health authority had promised that this would be their home for life. Following the issue of criteria by the Department of Health, the authority concluded that the applicant did not qualify for specialist nursing services to be provided by the authority but for general nursing care to be purchased by local authorities. Subsequently the health authority, following a public consultation, decided to close Mardon House and to transfer the applicant to the local authority for long-term general nursing care. In a successful application for judicial review of the decision to close Mardon House, it was held that the applicant and others had received a clear promise that Mardon House would be their home for life; that no overriding public interest had been established to justify breaking that promise; that the closure decision was flawed as no alternative placement for the applicant had been identified; that all nursing care was an NHS responsibility and that it was not open to the health authority to transfer general nursing care responsibility to a local authority, and that the health authority's eligibility criteria for long-term health care were flawed. On appeal to the Court of Appeal.

LORD WOOLF MR, MUMMERY and SEDLEY LJJ: . . .

56. What is still the subject of some controversy is the court's role when a member of the public, as a result of a promise or other conduct, has a legitimate expectation that he will be treated in one way and the public body wishes to treat him or her in a different way. Here the starting point has to be to ask what in the circumstances the member of the public could legitimately expect. In the words of Lord Scarman in *In re Findlay*, In re[1985] AC 318, 338, 'But what was their *legitimate* expectation?' Where there is a dispute as to this, the dispute has to be determined by the court, as happened in *In re Findlay*. This can involve a detailed examination of the precise terms of the promise or representation made, the circumstances in which the promise was made and the nature of the statutory or other discretion.

57. There are at least three possible outcomes. (a) The court may decide that the public authority is only required to bear in mind its previous policy or other representation, giving it the weight it thinks right, but no more, before deciding whether to change course. Here the court is confined to reviewing the decision on *Wednesbury* grounds (*Associated Provincial Picture Houses Ltd* v *Wednesbury Corporation* [1948] 1 KB 223). This has been held to be the effect of changes of policy in cases involving the early release of prisoners: see *In re Findlay* [1985] AC 318; *Reg.* v *Secretary of State for the Home Department, Ex parte Hargreaves* [1997] 1 WLR 906. (b) On the other hand the court may decide that the promise or practice induces a legitimate expectation of, for example, being consulted before a particular decision is taken. Here it is uncontentious that the court itself will require *the opportunity for consultation* to be given unless there is an overriding reason to resile from it (see *Attorney-General of Hong Kong* v *Ng Yuen Shiu* [1983] 2 AC 629) in which case the court will itself judge the adequacy of the reason advanced for the change of policy, taking into account what fairness requires. (c) Where the court considers that a lawful promise or practice has induced a legitimate expectation of a *benefit which is substantive*, not simply procedural, authority now establishes that here too the court will in a proper case decide whether to frustrate the expectation is so unfair that to take a new and different course will amount to an abuse of power. Here, once the legitimacy of the expectation is established, the

court will have the task of weighing the requirements of fairness against any overriding interest relied upon for the change of policy.

58. The court having decided which of the categories is appropriate, the court's role in the case of the second and third categories is different from that in the first. In the case of the first, the court is restricted to reviewing the decision on conventional grounds. The test will be rationality and whether the public body has given proper weight to the implications of not fulfilling the promise. In the case of the second category the court's task is the conventional one of determining whether the decision was procedurally fair. In the case of the third, the court has when necessary to determine whether there is a sufficient overriding interest to justify a departure from what has been previously promised.

59. In many cases the difficult task will be to decide into which category the decision should be allotted. In what is still a developing field of law, attention will have to be given to what it is in the first category of case which limits the applicant's legitimate expectation (in Lord Scarman's words in In re Findlay, Inre[1985] AC 318) to an expectation that whatever policy is in force at the time will be applied to him. As to the second and third categories, the difficulty of segregating the procedural from the substantive is illustrated by the line of cases arising out of decisions of justices not to commit a defendant to the Crown Court for sentence, or assurances given to a defendant by the court: here to resile from such a decision or assurance may involve the breach of legitimate expectation: see Reg. v Grice (1977) 66 Cr App R 167; cf. Reg. v Reilly [1982] QB 1208, Reg. v Dover Magistrates' Court, Ex parte Pamment (1994) 15 Cr App R (S) 778, 782. No attempt is made in those cases, rightly in our view, to draw the distinction. Nevertheless, most cases of an enforceable expectation of a substantive benefit (the third category) are likely in the nature of things to be cases where the expectation is confined to one person or a few people, giving the promise or representation the character of a contract. We recognise that the courts' role in relation to the third category is still controversial; but, as we hope to show, it is now clarified by authority.

60. We consider that Mr Goudie and Mr Gordon are correct, as was the judge, in regarding the facts of this case as coming into the third category. (Even if this were not correct because of the nature of the promise, and even if the case fell within the second category, the health authority in exercising its discretion and in due course the court would have to take into account that only an overriding public interest would justify resiling from the promise.) Our reasons are as follow. First, the importance of what was promised to Miss Coughlan (as we will explain later, this is a matter underlined by the Human Rights Act 1998); second, the fact that promise was limited to a few individuals, and the fact that the consequences to the health authority of requiring it to honour its promise are likely to be financial only.

The authorities

61. Whether to frustrate a legitimate expectation can amount to an abuse of power is the question which was posed by the House of Lords in Reg. v Inland Revenue Commissioners, Ex parte Preston [1985] AC 835 and addressed more recently by this court in Reg. v Inland Revenue Commissioners, Ex parte Unilever Plc [1996] S.T.C. 681. In each case it was in relation to a decision by a public authority (the Crown) to resile from a representation about how it would treat a member of the public (the taxpayer). It cannot be suggested that special principles of public law apply to the Inland Revenue or to taxpayers. Yet this is an area of law which has been a site of recent controversy, because while Ex parte Preston has been followed in tax cases, using the vocabulary of abuse of power, in other fields of public law analogous challenges, couched in the language of legitimate expectation, have not all been approached in the same way.

62. There has never been any question that the propriety of a breach by a public authority of a legitimate expectation of the second category, of a *procedural* benefit – typically a promise of being heard or consulted – is a matter for full review by the court. The court has, in other words, to examine the relevant circumstances and to decide for itself whether what happened was fair. This is

of a piece with the historic jurisdiction of the courts over issues of procedural justice. But in relation to a legitimate expectation of a substantive benefit (such as a promise of a home for life) doubt has been cast upon whether the same standard of review applies. Instead it is suggested that the proper standard is the so-called *Wednesbury* standard which is applied to the generality of executive decisions. This touches the intrinsic quality of the decision, as opposed to the means by which it has been reached, only where the decision is irrational or (*per* Lord Diplock in *Council of Civil Service Unions* v *Minister for the Civil Service* [1985] AC 374, 410) immoral.

63. This is not a live issue in the common law of the European Union, where a uniform standard of full review for fairness is well established: see Schwarze, *European Administrative Law* (1992), pp. 1134–1135 and the European Court of Justice cases reviewed in *Reg.* v *Ministry of Agriculture, Fisheries' and Food, Ex parte Hamble (Offshore) Fisheries Ltd* [1995] 2 All ER 714, 726–728. It is, however, something on which the Human Rights Act 1998, when it comes into force, may have a bearing.

64. It is axiomatic that a public authority which derives its existence and its powers from statute cannot validly act outside those powers. This is the familiar ultra vires doctrine adopted by public law from company law (*Colman* v *Eastern Counties Railway Co.* (1846) 10 Beav 1). Since such powers will ordinarily include anything fairly incidental to the express remit, a statutory body may lawfully adopt and follow policies (*British Oxygen Co. Ltd* v *Board of Trade* [1971] AC 610) and enter into formal undertakings. But since it cannot abdicate its general remit, not only must it remain free to change policy; its undertakings are correspondingly open to modification or abandonment. The recurrent question is when and where and how the courts are to intervene to protect the public from unwarranted harm in this process. The problem can readily be seen to go wider than the exercise of statutory powers. It may equally arise in relation to the exercise of the prerogative power, which at least since *Reg.* v *Criminal Injuries Compensation Board, Ex parte Lain* [1967] 2 QB 864, has been subject to judicial review, and in relation to private monopoly powers: *Reg.* v *Panel on Take-overs and Mergers, Ex parte Datafin Plc* [1987] QB 815.

65. The court's task in all these cases is not to impede executive activity but to reconcile its continuing need to initiate or respond to change with the legitimate interests or expectations of citizens or strangers who have relied, and have been justified in relying, on a current policy or an extant promise. The critical question is by what standard the court is to resolve such conflicts. It is when one examines the implications for a case like the present of the proposition that, so long as the decision-making process has been lawful, the court's only ground of intervention is the intrinsic rationality of the decision, that the problem becomes apparent. Rationality, as it has developed in modern public law, has two faces: one is the barely known decision which simply defies comprehension; the other is a decision which can be seen to have proceeded by flawed logic (though this can often be equally well allocated to the intrusion of an irrelevant factor). The present decision may well pass a rationality test; the health authority knew of the promise and its seriousness; it was aware of its new policies and the reasons for them; it knew that one had to yield, and it made a choice which, whatever else can be said of it, may not easily be challenged as irrational. As Lord Diplock said in *Secretary of State for Education and Science* v *Tameside Metropolitan Borough Council* [1977] AC 1014, 1064:

> The very concept of administrative discretion involves a right to choose between more than one possible course of action upon which there is room for reasonable people to hold differing opinions as to which is to he preferred.

But to limit the court's power of supervision to this is to exclude from consideration another aspect of the decision which is equally the concern of the law.

66. In the ordinary case there is no space for intervention on grounds of abuse of power once a rational decision directed to a proper purpose has been reached by lawful process. The present class

of case is visibly different. It involves not one but two lawful exercises of power (the promise and the policy change) by the same public authority, with consequences for individuals trapped between the two. The policy decision may well, and often does, make as many exceptions as are proper and feasible to protect individual expectations. The departmental decision in *Ex parte Hamble (Offshore) Fisheries Ltd* [1995] 2 All ER 714 is a good example. If it does not, as in *Ex parte Unilever Plc* [1996] STC 681, the court is there to ensure that the power to make and alter policy has not been abused by unfairly frustrating legitimate individual expectations. In such a situation a bare rationality test would constitute the public authority judge in its own cause, for a decision to prioritise a policy change over legitimate expectations will almost always be rational from where the authority stands, even if objectively it is arbitrary or unfair. It is in response to this dilemma that two distinct but related approaches have developed in the modern cases.

67. One approach is to ask not whether the decision is ultra vires in the restricted *Wednesbury* sense but whether, for example through unfairness or arbitrariness it amounts to an abuse of power. The leading case on the existence of this principle is *Ex parte Preston*, [1985] AC 835. It concerned an allegation, not in the event made out, that the Inland Revenue Commissioners had gone back impermissibly on their promise not to reinvestigate certain aspects of an individual taxpayer's affairs. Lord Scarman, expressing his agreement with the single fully reasoned speech (that of Lord Templeman) advanced a number of important general propositions. First, he said, at p. 851:

. . . I must make clear my view that the principle of fairness has an important place in the law of judicial review: and that in an appropriate case it is a ground upon which the court can intervene to quash a decision made by a public officer or authority in purported exercise of a power conferred by law.

Second, Lord Scarman reiterated, citing the decision of the House of Lords in *Reg.* v *Inland Revenue Commissioners, Ex parte National Federation of Self-Employed and Small Businesses Ltd* [1982] AC 617, that a claim for judicial review may arise where the Commissioners have failed to discharge their statutory duty to an individual or 'have abused their powers or acted outside them'. Third, that 'unfairness in the purported exercise of a power can be such that it is an abuse or excess of power.'

68. It is evident from these passages and from Lord Scarman's further explanation of them that, in his view, at least, it is unimportant whether the unfairness is analytically within or beyond the power conferred by law: on either view public law today reaches it. The same approach was taken by Lord Templeman, at p. 862:

Judicial review is available where a decision-making authority exceeds its powers, commits an error of law, commits a breach of natural justice, reaches a decision which no reasonable tribunal could have reached, or abuses its powers.

69. Abuses of power may take many forms. One, not considered in the *Wednesbury* case [1948] 1 KB 223 (even though it was arguably what the case was about), was the use of a power for a collateral purpose. Another, as cases like *Ex parte Preston* [1985] AC 835 now make clear, is reneging without adequate justification, by an otherwise lawful decision, on a lawful promise or practice adopted towards a limited number of individuals.

There is no suggestion in *Ex parte Preston* or elsewhere that the final arbiter of justification, rationality apart, is the decision-maker rather than the court. Lord Templeman, at pp. 864–866, reviewed the law in extenso, including the classic decisions in *Laker Airways Ltd* v *Department of Trade* [1977] QB 643; *Padfield* v *Minister of Agriculture, Fisheries and Food* [1968] AC 997; *Congreve* v *Home Office* [1976] QB 629 and *H.T.V. Ltd* v *Price Commission* [1976] ICR 170 ('It is a commonplace of modern law that such bodies must act fairly . . . and that the courts have power to redress unfairness:' Scarman LJ at p. 189.) He reached this conclusion, at pp. 866–867:

In principle I see no reason why the [taxpayer] should not be entitled to judicial review of a decision taken by the commissioners if that decision is unfair to the [taxpayer] because the conduct of the commissioners is equivalent to a breach of contract or a breach of representation. Such a decision falls within the ambit of an abuse of power for which in the present case judicial review is the sole remedy and an appropriate remedy. There may be cases in which conduct which savours of breach of [contract] or breach of representation does not constitute an abuse of power; there may be circumstances in which the court in its discretion might not grant relief by judicial review notwithstanding conduct which savours of breach of contract or breach of representation. In the present case, however, I consider that the [taxpayer] is entitled to relief by way of judicial review for 'unfairness' amounting to abuse of power if the commissioners have been guilty of conduct equivalent to a breach of contract or breach of representations on their part.

The entire passage, too long to set out here, merits close attention. It may be observed that Lord Templeman's final formulation, taken by itself, would allow no room for a test of overriding public interest. This, it is clear, is because of the facts then before the House. In a case such as the present the question posed in the *H.T.V.* case [1976] ICR 170 remains live.

70. This approach, in our view, embraces all the principles of public law which we have been considering. It recognises the primacy of the public authority both in administration and in policy development but it insists, where these functions come into tension, upon the adjudicative role of the court to ensure fairness to the individual. It does not overlook the passage in the speech of Lord Browne-Wilkinson in *Reg.* v *Hull University Visitor, Ex parte Page* [1993] AC 682, 701, that the basis of the 'fundamental principle . . . that the courts will intervene to ensure that the powers of public decision-making bodies are exercised lawfully' is the *Wednesbury* limit on the exercise of powers; but it follows the authority not only of *Ex parte Preston* [1985] AC 835 but of Lord Scarman's speech in *Reg.* v *Secretary of State for the Environment, Ex parte Nottinghamshire County Council* [1986] AC 240, 249, in treating a power which is abused as a power which has not been lawfully exercised.

71. Fairness in such a situation, if it is to mean anything, must for the reasons we have considered include fairness of outcome. This in turn is why the doctrine of legitimate expectation has emerged as a distinct application of the concept of abuse of power in relation to substantive as well as procedural benefits, representing a second approach to the same problem. If this is the position in the case of the third category, why is it not also the position in relation to the first category? May it be (though this was not considered in *In re Findlay* [1985] AC 318 or *Ex parte Hargreaves*, [1997] 1 WLR 906) that, when a promise is made to a category of individuals who have the same interest, it is more likely to be considered to have binding effect than a promise which is made generally or to a diverse class, when the interests of those to whom the promise is made may differ or, indeed, may be in conflict? Legitimate expectation may play different parts in different aspects of public law. The limits to its role have yet to be finally determined by the courts. Its application is still being developed on a case by case basis. Even where it reflects procedural expectations, for example concerning consultation, it may be affected by an overriding public interest. It may operate as an aspect of good administration, qualifying the intrinsic rationality of policy choices. And without injury to the *Wednesbury* doctrine it may furnish a proper basis for the application of the now established concept of abuse of power.

72. A full century ago in the seminal case of *Kruse* v *Johnson* [1898] 2 QB 91 Lord Russell of Killowen CJ set the limits of the courts' benevolence towards local government byelaws at those which were manifestly unjust, partial, made in bad faith or so gratuitous and oppressive that no reasonable person could think them justified. While it is the latter two classes which reappear in the decision of this court in the *Wednesbury* case [1948] 1 KB 223, the first two are equally part of the law. Thus in *Reg.* v *Inland Revenue Commissioners, Ex parte M.F.K. Underwriting Agents Ltd* [1990] 1 WLR 1545 a Divisional Court (Bingham LJ and Judge J) rejected on the facts a claim for the enforcement of a legitimate expectation in the face of a change of practice by the Inland Revenue. But having set out the need for certainty of representation, Bingham LJ went on, at pp. 1569–1570:

In so stating these requirements I do not, I hope, diminish or emasculate the valuable, developing doctrine of legitimate expectation. If a public authority so conducts itself as to create a legitimate expectation that a certain course will be followed it would often be unfair if the authority were permitted to follow a different course to the detriment of one who entertained the expectation, particularly if he acted on it. If in private law a body would be in breach of contract in so acting or estopped from so acting a public authority should generally be in no better position. The doctrine of legitimate expectation is rooted in fairness.

73. This approach, which makes no formal distinction between procedural and substantive unfairness, was expanded by reference to the extant body of authority by Simon Brown LJ in *Reg.* v *Devon County Council, Ex parte Baker* [1995] 1 All ER 73, 88–89. He identified two categories of substantive legitimate expectation recognised by modern authority:

(1) Sometimes the phrase is used to denote a substantive right: an entitlement that the claimant asserts cannot be denied him. It was used in this sense and the assertion upheld in cases such as *Reg.* v *Secretary of State for the Home Department, Ex parte Asif Mahmood Khan* [1984] 1 WLR 1337 and *Reg.* v *Secretary of State for the Home Department, Ex parte Ruddock* [1987] 1 WLR 1482. It was used in the same sense but unsuccessfully in, for instance, *Reg.* v *Inland Revenue Commissioners, Ex parte M.F.K. Underwriting Agents Ltd* [1990] 1 WLR 1545 and *Reg.* v *Jockey Club, Ex parte R.A.M. Racecourses Ltd* [1993] 2 All ER 225. These various authorities show that the claimant's right will only be found established when there is a clear and unambiguous representation upon which it was reasonable for him to rely. Then the administrator or other public body will be held bound in fairness by the representation made unless only its promise or undertaking as to how its power would be exercised is inconsistent with the statutory duties imposed upon it. The doctrine employed in this sense is akin to an estoppel. In so far as the public body's representation is communicated by way of a stated policy, this type of legitimate expectation falls into two distinct sub-categories: cases in which the authority are held entitled to change their policy even so as to affect the claimant, and those in which they are not. An illustration of the former is *Reg.* v *Torbay Borough Council, Ex parte Cleasby* [1991] COD 142, of the latter *Ex parte Asif Mahmood Khan.* (2) Perhaps more conventionally the concept of legitimate expectation is used to refer to the claimant's interest in some ultimate benefit which he hopes to retain (or, some would argue, attain). Here, therefore, it is the interest itself rather than the benefit that is the substance of the expectation. In other words the expectation arises not because the claimant asserts any specific right to a benefit but rather because his interest in it is one that the law holds protected by the requirements of procedural fairness; the law recognises that the interest cannot properly be withdrawn (or denied) without the claimant being given an opportunity to comment and without the authority communicating rational grounds for any adverse decision. Of the various authorities drawn to our attention, *Schmidt* v *Secretary of State for Home Affairs* [1969] 2 Ch 149, *O'Reilly* v *Mackman* [1983] 2 AC 237 and the recent decision of Roch J in *Reg.* v *Rochdale Metropolitan Borough Council, Ex parte Schemet* [1993] 1 FCR 306 are clear examples of this head of legitimate expectation.

Simon Brown LJ has not in that passage referred expressly to the situation where the individual can claim no higher expectation than to have his individual circumstances considered by the decision-maker in the light of the policy then in force. This is not surprising because this entitlement, which can also be said to be rooted in fairness, adds little to the standard requirements of any exercise of discretion: namely that the decision will take into account all relevant matters which here will include the promise or other conduct giving rise to the expectation and that if the decision-maker does so the courts will not interfere except on the basis that the decision is wholly unreasonable. It is the classic *Wednesbury* situation, not because the expectation is substantive but because it lacks legitimacy.

74. Nowhere in this body of authority, nor in *Ex parte Preston*, [1985] AC 835, nor in *In re Findlay* [1985] AC 318, is there any suggestion that judicial review of a decision which frustrates a substantive legitimate expectation is confined to the rationality of the decision. But in *Ex parte Hargreaves*, [1997] 1 WLR 906, 921, 925 Hirst LJ (with whom Peter Gibson LJ agreed) was persuaded to reject the notion of scrutiny for fairness as heretical, and Pill LJ to reject it as 'wrong in principle.'

75. *Ex parte Hargreaves* concerned prisoners whose expectations of home leave and early release were not to be fulfilled by reason of a change of policy. Following *In re Findlay*, [1985] AC 318 this court held that such prisoners' only legitimate expectation was that their applications would be considered individually in the light of whatever policy was in force at the time: in other words the case came into the first category. This conclusion was dispositive of the case. What Hirst LJ went on to say at p. 919, under the head of 'The proper approach for the court to the Secretary of State's decision' was therefore obiter. However Hirst LJ accepted in terms the submission of leading counsel for the Home Secretary that, beyond review on *Wednesbury* grounds, the law recognised no enforceable legitimate expectation of a substantive benefit. In relation to the decision in *Ex parte Hamble (Offshore) Fisheries Ltd*, [1995] 2 All ER 714, he said [1997] 1 WLR 906, 921:

> Mr Beloff characterised Sedley J's approach as heresy, and in my judgment he was right to do so. On matters of substance (as contrasted with procedure) *Wednesbury* provides the correct test.

A number of learned commentators have questioned this conclusion (see e.g. P.P. Craig, 'Substantive legitimate expectations and the principles of judicial review' in *English Public Law and the Common Law of Europe*, ed. M. Andenas (1998); T.R.S. Allan, 'Procedure and substance in judicial review' [1997] CLJ 246; Steve Foster, 'Legitimate expectations and prisoners' rights' (1997) 60 MLR 727).

Ex parte Hargreaves, [1997] 1 WLR 906 can, in any event, be distinguished from the present case. Mr Gordon has sought to distinguish it on the ground that the present case involves an abuse of power. On one view all cases where proper effect is not given to a legitimate expectation involve an abuse of power. Abuse of power can be said to be but another name for acting contrary to law. But the real distinction between *Ex parte Hargreaves* and this case is that in this case it is contended that fairness in the statutory context required more of the decision-maker than in *Ex parte Hargreaves* where the sole legitimate expectation possessed by the prisoners had been met. It required the health authority, as a matter of fairness, not to resile from their promise unless there was an overriding justification for doing so. Another way of expressing the same thing is to talk of the unwarranted frustration of a legitimate expectation and thus an abuse of power or a failure of substantive fairness. Again the labels are not important except that they all distinguish the issue here from that in *Ex parte Hargreaves*. They identify a different task for the court from that where what is in issue is a conventional application of policy or exercise of discretion. Here the decision can only be justified if there is an overriding public interest. Whether there is an overriding public interest is a question for the court.

77. The cases decided in the European Court of Justice cited in *Ex parte Hamble (Offshore) Fisheries Ltd*, [1995] 2 All ER 714 all concern policies or practices conferring substantive benefits from which member states were not allowed to resile when the policy or practice was altered. In this country *Reg.* v *Secretary of State for the Home Department, Ex parte Ruddock* [1987] 1 WLR 1482 and *Reg.* v *Secretary of State for the Home Department, Ex parte Asif Mahmood Khan* [1984] 1 WLR 1337 were cited as instances of substantive legitimate expectations to which the courts were if appropriate prepared to give effect. Reliance was also placed, as we would place it, on Lord Diplock's carefully worded summary in *Council of Civil Service Unions* v *Minister for the Civil Service* [1985] AC 374, 408–409 of the contemporary heads of judicial review. They included benefits or advantages

which the applicant can legitimately expect to be permitted to continue to enjoy. Not only did Lord Diplock not limit these to procedural benefits or advantages; he referred expressly to *In re Findlay* [1985] AC 318 (a decision in which he had participated) as an example of a case concerning a claim to a legitimate expectation – plainly a substantive one, albeit that the claim failed. One can readily see why: Lord Scarman's speech in *In re Findlay* is predicated on the assumption that the courts will protect a substantive legitimate expectation if one is established; and Taylor J so interpreted it in *Ex parte Ruddock*, [1987] 1 WLR 1482. None of these cases suggests that the standard of review is always limited to bare rationality, though none developed it as the revenue cases have done.

78. It is from the revenue cases that, in relation to the third category, the proper test emerges. Thus in *Ex parte Unilever Plc*, [1996] STC 681 this court concluded that for the Crown to enforce a time limit which for years it had not insisted upon would be so unfair as to amount to an abuse of power. As in other tax cases, there was no question of the court's deferring to the Inland Revenue's view of what was fair. The court also concluded that the Inland Revenue's conduct passed the 'notoriously high' threshold of irrationality; but the finding of abuse through unfairness was not dependent on this.

79. It is worth observing that this was how the leading textbook writers by the mid-1990s saw the law developing. In the (still current) seventh edition of *Wade & Forsyth's Administrative Law* (1994) the authors reviewed a series of modern cases and commented, at p. 419:

> These are revealing decisions. They show that the courts now expect government departments to honour their statements of policy or intention or else to treat the citizen with the fullest personal consideration. Unfairness in the form of unreasonableness is clearly allied to unfairness by violation of natural justice. It was in the latter context that the doctrine of legitimate expectation was invented, but it is now proving to be a source of substantive as well as of procedural rights. Lord Scarman [in *Ex parte Preston* [1985] AC 835] has stated emphatically that unfairness in the purported exercise of power can amount to an abuse or excess of power, and this may become an important general doctrine.

To similar effect is De Smith, Woolf & Jowell, *Judicial Review of Administrative Action*, 5th ed. (1995), pp. 575–576, para. 13–035. Craig, *Administrative Law*, 3rd ed. (1994), pp. 672–675, links the issue, as Schwarze does (*European Administrative Law* (1992)), to the fundamental principle of legal certainty.

80. In *Ex parte Unilever Plc*, [1996] STC 681, 695 Simon Brown LJ proposed a valuable reconciliation of the existing strands of public law:

> 'Unfairness amounting to an abuse of power' as . . . in *Preston* and the other revenue cases is unlawful not because it involves conduct such as would offend some equivalent private law principle, not principally indeed because it breaches a legitimate expectation that some different substantive decision will be taken, but rather because it is illogical or immoral or both for a public authority to act with conspicuous unfairness and in that sense abuse its power. As Lord Donaldson MR said in *Reg.* v *Independent Television Commission, Ex parte T.S.W. Broadcasting Ltd, The Times*, 7 February 1992: 'The test in public law is fairness, not an adaption of the law of contract or estoppel.' In short, I regard the *M.F.K.* category of legitimate expectation as essentially but a head of *Wednesbury* unreasonableness, not necessarily exhaustive of the grounds upon which a successful substantive unfairness challenge may be based.

81. For our part, in relation to this category of legitimate expectation, we do not consider it necessary to explain the modern doctrine in *Wednesbury* terms, helpful though this is in terms of received jurisprudence (cf. Dunn LJ in *Reg.* v *Secretary of State for the Home Department, Ex parte Asif Mahmood Khan* [1984] 1 WLR 1337, 1352: 'an unfair action can seldom be a reasonable one'). We would prefer to regard the *Wednesbury* categories themselves as the major instances (not

necessarily the sole ones: see *Council of Civil Service Unions* v *Minister for the Civil Service* [1985] AC 374, 410, *per* Lord Diplock) of how public power may be misused. Once it is recognised that conduct which is an abuse of power is contrary to law its existence must be for the court to determine.

82. The fact that the court will only give effect to a legitimate expectation within the statutory context in which it has arisen should avoid jeopardising the important principle that the executive's policy-making powers should not be trammelled by the courts: see *Hughes* v *Department of Health and Social Security* [1985] AC 766, 788 *per* Lord Diplock. Policy being (within the law) for the public authority alone, both it and the reasons for adopting or changing it will be accepted by the courts as part of the factual data – in other words, as not ordinarily open to judicial review. The court's task – and this is not always understood is then limited to asking whether the application of the policy to an individual who has been led to expect something different is a just exercise of power. In many cases the authority will already have considered this and made appropriate exceptions (as was envisaged in *British Oxygen Co. Ltd* v *Board of Trade* [1971] AC 610 and as had happened in *Ex parte Hamble (Offshore) Fisheries Ltd*, [1995] 2 All ER 714), or resolved to pay compensation where money alone will suffice. But where no such accommodation is made, it is for the court to say whether the consequent frustration of the individual's expectation is so unfair as to be a misuse of the authority's power.

Fairness and the decision to close

83. How are fairness and the overriding public interest in this particular context to be judged? The question arises concretely in the present case. Mr Goudie argued, with detailed references, that all the indicators, apart from the promise itself, pointed to an overriding public interest, so that the court ought to endorse the health authority's decision. Mr Gordon contended, likewise with detailed references, that the data before the health authority were far from uniform. But this is not what matters. What matters is that, having taken it all into account, the health authority voted for closure in spite of the promise. The propriety of such an exercise of power should be tested by asking whether the need which the health authority judged to exist to move Miss Coughlan to a local authority facility was such as to outweigh its promise that Mardon House would be her home for life.

84. That a promise was made is confirmed by the evidence of the health authority that:

> the applicant and her fellow residents were justified in treating certain statements made by the health authority's predecessor, coupled with the way in which the authority's pre-decessor conducted itself at the time of the residents' move from Newcourt Hospital, as amounting to an assurance that, having moved to Mardon House, Mardon House would be a permanent home for them.

And the letter of 7 June 1994 sent to the residents by Mr Peter Jackson, the then general manager of the predecessor of the health authority, following the withdrawal of John Grooms stated:

> During the course of a meeting yesterday with Ross Bentley's father, it was suggested that each of the former Newcourt residents now living at Mardon House would appreciate a further letter of reassurance from me. I am writing to confirm therefore, that the health authority has made it clear to the community trust that it expects the trust to continue to provide good quality care for you at Mardon House for as long as you choose to live there. I hope that this will dispel any anxieties you may have arising from the forthcoming change in management arrangements, about which I wrote to you recently.

As has been pointed out by the health authority, the letter did not actually use the expression 'home for life.'

85. The health authority had, according to its evidence, formed the view that it should give considerable weight to the assurances given to Miss Coughlan; that those assurances had given rise to expectations which should not, in the ordinary course of things, be disappointed; but that it

should not treat those assurances as giving rise to an absolute and unqualified entitlement on the part of the Miss Coughlan and her co-residents since that would be unreasonable and unrealistic; and that:

> If there were compelling reasons which indicated overwhelmingly that closure was the reasonable and – other things being equal – the right course to take, provided that steps could be taken to meet the applicant's (and her fellow residents') expectations to the greatest degree possible following closure, it was open to the authority, weighing up all these matters with care and sensitivity, to decide in favour of the option of closure.

Although the first consultation paper made no reference to the 'home for life' promise, it was referred to in the second consultation paper as set out above.

86. It is denied in the health authority's evidence that there was any misrepresentation at the meeting of the board on 7 October 1998 of the terms of the 'home for life' promise. It is asserted that the board had taken the promise into account; that members of the board had previously seen a copy of Mr Jackson's letter of 7 June 1994, which, they were reminded, had not used the word 'home'; and that every board member was well aware that, in terms of its fresh decision-making, the starting point was that the Newcourt patients had moved to Mardon on the strength of an assurance that Mardon would be their home as long as they chose to live there. This was an express promise or representation made on a number of occasions in precise terms. It was made to a small group of severely disabled individuals who had been housed and cared for over a substantial period in the health authority's predecessor's premises at Newcourt. It specifically related to identified premises which it was represented would be their home for as long as they chose. It was in unqualified terms. It was repeated and confirmed to reassure the residents. It was made by the health authority's predecessor for its own purposes, namely to encourage Miss Coughlan and her fellow residents to move out of Newcourt and into Mardon House, a specially built substitute home in which they would continue to receive nursing care. The promise was relied on by Miss Coughlan. Strong reasons are required to justify resiling from a promise given in those circumstances. This is not a case where the health authority would, in keeping the promise, be acting inconsistently with its statutory or other public law duties. A decision not to honour it would be equivalent to a breach of contract in private law.

87. The health authority treated the promise as the 'starting point' from which the consultation process and the deliberations proceeded. It was a factor which should be given 'considerable weight', but it could be outweighed by 'compelling reasons which indicated overwhelmingly that closure was the reasonable and the right course to take'. The health authority, though 'mindful of the history behind the residents' move to Mardon House and their understandable expectation that it would be their permanent home', formed the view that there were 'overriding reasons' why closure should nonetheless proceed. The health authority wanted to improve the provision of reablement services and considered that the mix of a long stay residential service and a reablement service at Mardon House was inappropriate and detrimental to the interests of both users of the service. The acute reablement service could not be supported there without an uneconomic investment which would have produced a second class reablement service. It was argued that there was a compelling public interest which justified the health authority's prioritisation of the reablement service.

88. It is, however, clear from the health authority's evidence and submissions that it did not consider that it had a legal responsibility or commitment to provide a *home*, as distinct from care or funding of care, for the applicant and her fellow residents. It considered that, following the with-drawal of the John Grooms Association, the provision of care services to the current residents had become 'excessively expensive', having regard to the needs of the majority of disabled people in the authority's area and the 'insuperable problems' involved in the mix of long-term residential care and

reablement services at Mardon House. Mardon House had, contrary to earlier expectations, become:

> a prohibitively expensive white elephant. The unit was not financially viable. Its continued operation was dependent upon the authority supporting it at an excessively high cost. This did not represent value for money and left fewer resources for other services.

The health authority's attitude was that:

> It was because of our appreciation of the residents' expectation that they would remain at Mardon House for the rest of their lives that the board agreed that the authority should accept a continuing commitment to finance the care of the residents of Mardon for whom it was responsible.

But the cheaper option favoured by the health authority misses the essential point of the promise which had been given. The fact is that the health authority has not offered to the applicant an equivalent facility to replace what was promised to her. The health authority's undertaking to fund her care for the remainder of her life is substantially different in nature and effect from the earlier promise that care for her would be provided *at Mardon House*. That place would be her home for as long as she chose to live there.

89.   We have no hesitation in concluding that the decision to move Miss Coughlan against her will and in breach of the health authority's own promise was in the circumstances unfair. It was unfair because it frustrated her legitimate expectation of having a home for life in Mardon House. There was no overriding public interest which justified it. In drawing the balance of conflicting interests the court will not only accept the policy change without demur but will pay the closest attention to the assessment made by the public body itself. Here, however, as we have already indicated, the health authority failed to weigh the conflicting interests correctly. Furthermore, we do not know (for reasons we will explain later) the quality of the alternative accommodation and services which will be offered to Miss Coughlan. We cannot prejudge what would be the result if there was on offer accommodation which could be said to be reasonably equivalent to Mardon House and the health authority made a properly considered decision in favour of closure in the light of that offer. However, absent such an offer, here there was unfairness amounting to an abuse of power by the health authority.

. . .

Appeal dismissed.

NOTES:
1. The Court also held that the closure decision amounted to an unlawful interference with the right to respect for one's home under Article 8, ECHR.
2. The use of the term 'abuse of power', like 'unreasonable' or 'irrational' is conclusionary and does not articulate its basis. In substantive legitimate expectations one must establish that an expectation is legitimate and that there is no overriding public interest which justifies frustrating it. See comments: Elliott [2000] JR 27, Craig and Schønberg [2000] PL 684.

QUESTIONS
1. If the health authority had found cheaper accommodation for the applicant, would this have overridden the promise made to her?
2. Did the court move from considering legality to the merits in this case?

R (Bibi) v *Newham London Borough Council*

[2001] EWCA Civ 607, [2002]1 WLR 203, Court of Appeal

The applicants had been given a promise that as unintentionally homeless persons in priority need of accommodation they would be provided with accommodation with security of tenure. Whilst they were provided with accommodation, this did not have security of tenure. They successfully sought judicial review that the accommodation provided did not discharge the housing authority's obligations to them. The court found that the obligation was founded on a legitimate expectation and not a statutory duty as the promise was made on a misunderstanding of what the statute (then the Housing (Homeless Persons) Act 1977) required. The authority appealed.

SCHIEMANN LJ:. . .

19. In all legitimate expectation cases, whether substantive or procedural, three practical questions arise. The first question is to what has the public authority, whether by practice or by promise, committed itself; the second is whether the authority has acted or proposes to act unlawfully in relation to its commitment; the third is what the court should do . . .

To what has the authority committed itself?

20. The answer to the first is a question of analysing the evidence – it poses no jurisprudential problems.

21. Sometimes, as in the first category of outcome analysed in *Ex parte Coughlan* [2000] 2 WLR 622 (para. 57) the answer to this first question is dispositive of the case. It seems to us that the present authorities in that group of cases (in particular *In re Findlay* [1985] AC 318, 338) make it generally appropriate to allocate the issue of legitimacy to this initial question. In other words, if the public body has done nothing and said nothing which can legitimately have generated the expectation that is advanced to the court, the case ends there. It seems likely that a representation made without lawful power will be in this class. In the present case the answer to the first question is not in dispute and is in favour of the applicants.

The interrelation of the second and third questions

22. Two problems face a court in answering these questions. The first is to find one or more measuring rods by which it can be objectively determined whether a certain action or inaction is an abuse of power. The second is what order to make once an abuse of power has been discerned – can the court come to a substantive decision itself or should it send the matter back to the decision taker to decide afresh according to law?

23. To a degree the answer to the second depends on the approach one takes to the first. As Laws LJ pointed out in *R* v *Secretary of State for Education and Employment, ex parte Begbie* [2000] 1 WLR 1115 at page 1131C

> The more the decision challenged lies in what may inelegantly be called the macro-political field, the less intrusive will be the court's supervision. More than this: in that field, true abuse of power is less likely to be found, since within it changes of policy, fuelled by broad conceptions of the public interest, may more readily be accepted as taking precedence over the interests of groups which enjoyed expectations generated by an earlier policy.

Has the authority acted unlawfully? Introduction

24. As Professor Craig makes clear in his perceptive discussion of this topic in Craig, *Administrative Law*, 4th ed, (1999), chp 19, it is important to recognise that there is often a tension between several values in these cases. A choice may need to be made as to which good we attain and which

we forego. There are administrative and democratic gains in preserving for the authority the possibility in the future of coming to different conclusions as to the allocation of resources from those to which it is currently wedded. On the other hand there is value in holding authorities to promises which they have made, thus upholding responsible public administration and allowing people to plan their lives sensibly. The task for the law in this area is to establish who makes the choice of priorities and what principles are to be followed.

25. Several attempts have been made to find a formulation which will provide a test for all cases. However, history shows that wide-ranging formulations, while capable of producing a just result in the individual case, are seen later to have needlessly constricted the development of the law. Thus it was the view of this court in *Coughlan* that a principle, apparently earlier embraced by this court in *R v Secretary of State for the Home Department, ex parte Hargreaves* [1997] 1 WLR 906, to the effect that the court would only enforce expectations as to procedure as opposed to expectations of a substantive benefit, was wrongly framed.

Has the authority acted unlawfully? The relevance of reliance on the promise

26. Mr Matthias submits that, in cases where the expectation which has been generated is of a substantive as opposed to a procedural benefit, authority limits the court to enforcing it only if (a) the motive for resiling from it was improper, or (b) there has been detrimental reliance on it. Only then, he submits, can the departure be said to amount, as it must, to an abuse of power. Founding on the distinction between procedural and substantive expectations identified in *Coughlan* para. 57, on the reasoning in *Ex parte Preston* [1985] AC 835, 866–7 and on the cases reported to date, he argues that (absent bad faith) a substantive legitimate expectation can only arise where a situation analogous to a private law wrong, and therefore involving detrimental reliance, exists.

27. We would not accept this formulation. As Sir Thomas Bingham MR observed in *R v Inland Revenue Commissioners, ex p. Unilever plc* [1996] STC p. 681 at page 690f:

> The categories of unfairness are not closed, and precedent should act as a guide and not as a cage.

28. As indicated in *R v Secretary of State for Education and Employment, ex parte Begbie* [2000] 1 WLR 1115 reliance, though potentially relevant in most cases, is not essential. In that case a letter sent to the parents of one child affected by legislative and policy changes concerning assisted school places came to the knowledge of another child's parent, who relied on it in judicial review proceedings. Peter Gibson LJ, giving the leading judgment, said at page 1123H:

> Mr. Beloff submits . . . (v) it is not necessary for a person to have changed his position as a result of such representations for an obligation to fulfil a legitimate expectation to subsist; the principle of good administration prima facie requires adherence by public authorities to their promises. He cites authority in support of all these submissions and for my part I am prepared to accept them as correct, so far as they go. I would however add a few words by way of comment on his fifth proposition, as in my judgment it would be wrong to understate the significance of reliance in this area of the law. It is very much the exception, rather than the rule, that detrimental reliance will not be present when the court finds unfairness in the defeating of a legitimate expectation.

29. In the light of this, we respectfully adopt what Professor Craig has proposed in this regard in Craig, *Administrative Law* at p. 619:

> Detrimental reliance will normally be required in order for the claimant to show that it would be unlawful to go back on a representation. This is in accord with policy, since if the individual has suffered no hardship there is no reason based on legal certainty to hold the agency to its representation. It should not, however, be necessary to show any monetary loss, or anything equivalent thereto.

30. But he gives the following instance of a case where reliance is not essential –

> Where an agency seeks to depart from an established policy in relation to a particular person detrimental reliance should not be required. Consistency of treatment and equality are at stake in such cases, and these values should be protected irrespective of whether there has been any reliance as such.

31. In our judgment the significance of reliance and of consequent detriment is factual, not legal. In *Begbie* both aspects were in the event critical: there had been no true reliance on the misrepresentation of policy and therefore no detriment suffered specifically in consequence of it. In a strong case, no doubt, there will be both reliance and detriment; but it does not follow that reliance (that is, credence) without measurable detriment cannot render it unfair to thwart a legitimate expectation . . .

Has the authority acted unlawfully? 'So unfair as to amount to an abuse of power'

33. The traditional view has been that the *Wednesbury* categories were exhaustive of what was an abuse of power. However in *Coughlan* the court preferred 'to regard the Wednesbury categories as the major instances (not necessarily the sole ones . . .), of how public power may be misused' (para. 81).

34. In *Coughlan* the court followed *R v Inland Revenue Commissioners, ex parte Unilever* [1996] STC 681, in asking itself whether the reneging by an authority on its promise was 'so unfair as to amount to an abuse of power' (para. 78). It concluded that it was. However, without refinement, the question whether the reneging on a promise would be so unfair as to amount to an abuse of power is an uncertain guide.

35. Where one is dealing with a promise made by an authority a major part of the problem is that it is often not adequate to look at the situation purely from the point of view of the disappointed promisee who comes to the court with a perfectly natural grievance.

36. Sometimes many promises have been made to many different persons each of which has induced a reasonable expectation of a substantive benefit for that person but all of which promises cannot be fulfilled. This situation is not uncommon in central and local Government. Decision takers promise and find themselves unable to deliver that which they have promised. As Bacon, perhaps cynically, remarked 400 years ago 'it is a certain sign of wise government and proceeding that it can hold men's hearts by hopes when it can not by satisfaction'. Seen from the point of view of administrators focusing on the problem immediately before their eyes a promise seems reasonable or will at least reduce the need to worry further in the immediate future about the promisee. But when they, or their superiors, focus on a wider background it appears that the making of the promise was unwise or that, in any event, its fulfilment seems too difficult.

37. Thus in cases such as those before the court, the family with the highest points on the Authority's scale can be regarded as having a legitimate expectation that the next five bedroom flat would go to them. So can the applicant who was promised a five bedroom flat within 18 months which have elapsed. So can all the other persons who have been promised suitable accommodation within 18 months. Yet the Authority does not possess enough housing for them all.

38. The suggestion was made in argument that this problem can be avoided by the authority which is short of housing giving every family enough money to provide its own housing. But this is not always an escape from the problem because the money can often not be found without depriving others of money which they expected to retain or of benefits which they expected to receive.

39. But on any view, if an authority, without even considering the fact that it is in breach of a promise which has given rise to a legitimate expectation that it will be honoured, makes a decision to adopt a course of action at variance with that promise then the authority is abusing its powers.

The role of the court

40. The court has two functions – assessing the legality of actions by administrators and, if it finds unlawfulness on the administrators' part, deciding what relief it should give. It is in our judgment a mistake to isolate from the rest of administrative law cases those which turn on representations made by authorities. The same constitutional principles apply to the exercise by the court of each of these two functions.

41. The court, even where it finds that the applicant has a legitimate expectation of some benefit, will not order the authority to honour its promise where to do so would be to assume the powers of the executive. Once the court has established such an abuse it may ask the decision taker to take the legitimate expectation properly into account in the decision making process.

42. Only part of the relevant material upon consideration of which any decision must be made is before the court. Because of the need to bear in mind more than the interests of the individual before the court, relevant facts are always changing. As Lord Bingham said in *R v Cambridge Health Authority, ex parte B* [1995] 2 All ER 129:

> ... it would be totally unrealistic to require the authority to come to the court with its accounts and seek to demonstrate that if this treatment were provided for B then there would be a patient, C, who would have to go without treatment. No major authority could run its financial affairs in a way which would permit such a demonstration.

43. While in some cases there can be only one lawful ultimate answer to the question whether the authority should honour its promise, at any rate in cases involving a legitimate expectation of a substantive benefit, this will not invariably be the case.

The present case

. . .

48. We proceed therefore on the basis that the Authority has lawfully committed itself to providing the applicants with suitable accommodation with secure tenure.

Has the authority acted unlawfully?

. . .

51. The law requires that any legitimate expectation be properly taken into account in the decision making process. It has not been in the present case and therefore the Authority has acted unlawfully.

52. It was submitted that neither applicant has changed his or her position on the strength of the expectation and therefore no weight ought to be given to the fact that the promises have not been fulfilled. We have already said that this factor does not rank as a legal inhibition on giving effect to the legitimate expectation. But what weight ought to be given to the lack of change of position?

53. The fact that someone has not changed his position after a promise has been made to him does not mean that he has not relied on the promise. An actor in a play where another actor points a gun at him may refrain from changing his position just because he has been given a promise that the gun only contains blanks.

54. A refugee such as Mr Al-Nashed might, had he been told the true situation, have gone to one of the bodies which assist refugees for advice as to where in England and Wales he might have better prospects; or have tried to find the deposit on an assured tenancy, with the possibility thereafter of housing benefit to help with the rent.

55. The present case is one of reliance without concrete detriment. We use this phrase because there is moral detriment, which should not be dismissed lightly, in the prolonged disappointment which has ensued; and potential detriment in the deflection of the possibility, for a refugee family, of seeking at the start to settle somewhere in the United Kingdom where secure housing was less hard

to come by. In our view these things matter in public law, even though they might not found an estoppel or actionable misrepresentation in private law, because they go to fairness and through fairness to possible abuse of power. To disregard the legitimate expectation because no concrete detriment can be shown would be to place the weakest in society at a particular disadvantage. It would mean that those who have a choice and the means to exercise it in reliance on some official practice or promise would gain a legal toehold inaccessible to those who, lacking any means of escape, are compelled simply to place their trust in what has been represented to them.

A further element for the Authority to bear in mind is the possibility of monetary compensation or assistance. As this court indicated in *Coughlan (ante)* para 82, a legitimate expectation may in some cases be appropriately taken into account by such a payment.

57. An element which may tell against giving effect to the legitimate expectation is the effect on others on the housing list of giving the present applicants special preference. Mr Matthias understandably relies on this both as a reason why Newham's stance is not unfair and, in the alternative, as an overriding policy reason why effect should not be given to the representation. Ostensibly powerful as this is it faces the obstacle, as Mr Luba has argued, that nothing unlawful would necessarily be involved in allocating secure housing to the applicants. For example, the Authority could change the allocation scheme to give weight to its representation to the applicants and the 115 others in their situation. Changing the scheme might not in truth be so simple – but it does not seem to have been considered by the Authority.

58. When considering the legitimate expectations which it has created, the Authority is entitled to take into account the current statutory framework, the allocation scheme, the legitimate expectations of other people, its assets both in terms of what housing it has at its disposal and in terms of what assets it has or could have available. It should consider whether, if it considers it inappropriate to grant the applicants secure tenancies of a council house, it should adopt any other way of helping the applicants to obtain secure housing whether by cash or other aid or by amending the allocation scheme so as to give some weight to legitimate expectations in cases similar to the present, of which we understand there to be a number.

59. But when the Authority looks at the matter again it must take into account the legitimate expectations. Unless there are reasons recognised by law for not giving effect to those legitimate expectations then effect should be given to them. In circumstances such as the present where the conduct of the Authority has given rise to a legitimate expectation then fairness requires that, if the Authority decides not to give effect to that expectation, the Authority articulate its reasons so that their propriety may be tested by the court if that is what the disappointed person requires.

What should the court do?

60. *Coughlan* emphasised the importance of considering these questions in their statutory context . . .

61. In the context of housing Lord Brightman said of the Act of 1977 in *R v Hillingdon LBC, ex parte Puhlhofer* [1986] AC484, p. 517,

> It is an Act to assist persons who are homeless, not an act to provide them with homes . . .
> It is intended to provide for the homeless a lifeline of last resort; not to enable them to make inroads into the local authority's waiting list of applicants for housing. Some inroads there are probably bound to be, but in the end the local authority will have to balance the priority needs of the homeless on the one hand and the legitimate aspirations of those on their housing waiting list on the other hand. . . .

63. The present case illustrates a potential conflict between the 'legitimate aspirations' of those who have been told where they are on the housing waiting list and what the Authority's allocation

scheme is on the one hand and the 'legitimate expectations' of those to whom promises have been made by the Authority the fulfilment of which conflicts with the priorities contained in the allocation scheme on the other.

64. In an area such as the provision of housing at public expense where decisions are informed by social and political value judgments as to priorities of expenditure the court will start with a recognition that such invidious choices are essentially political rather than judicial. In our judgment the appropriate body to make that choice in the context of the present case is the authority. However, it must do so in the light of the legitimate expectations of the respondents.

65. Turner J declared that the Authority were 'bound to treat the duties originally owed by them to both applicants under section 65(2) as not discharged until the applicants be provided by them with suitable accommodation on a secure tenancy'. Rightly, he did not direct that they be given priority over everyone else who was on the housing register and was seeking the same type of accommodation. The applicants' counsel have not suggested that he should have so directed. They wish merely to hold the declaration which was made.

66. The Judge accepted that the applicants each have a legitimate expectation that they would be provided with suitable accommodation on a secure tenancy. We agree. However, we consider that the Judge went too far in the form of declaration which he made since it seems implicit in his declaration that there cannot be factors which inhibit the fulfilment of the legitimate expectations, even where the Authority has never so concluded.

67. We consider that it would be better simply to declare that the Authority is under a duty to consider the applicants' applications for suitable housing on the basis that they have a legitimate expectation that they will be provided by the Authority with suitable accommodation on a secure tenancy.

Appeal allowed in part.

NOTE: The Court has identified the range of factors which the Authority has to take into account when reconsidering these cases.

9

···

The Availability of Judicial Review

NOTE: The previous chapter considered the grounds for judicial review. There are, however, a number of other questions which must be addressed in order to determine the availability of judicial review and, hence, its significance in the constitution. What is the nature of the procedure which must be followed in order to seek judicial review? Who can apply for judicial review? Against whom and in respect of what matters may judicial review be sought? It must also be remembered that the remedies available in judicial review proceedings are discretionary. Hence, an understanding of the availability of judicial review requires an examination of the nature of the courts' discretion and the manner in which it is exercised. Lastly, the approach of the courts to legislative attempts to exclude judicial review must be considered.

SECTION 1: **The Claim for Judicial Review**

In 1969 the Law Commission was asked to 'review the existing remedies for the judicial control of administrative acts or omissions with a view to evolving a simpler and more effective procedure.' At that time litigants seeking to challenge administrative acts or omissions had a choice of two procedures. They could begin an action by writ or originating summons seeking an injunction, declaration and, if appropriate, damages. This is the normal way of commencing an action to establish a breach of a private law right, but the courts also allowed it to be used to challenge the decisions of public authorities on the ground that they had acted beyond their powers. Alternatively, litigants could use a special procedure to seek one or more of the prerogative orders, *certiorari*, prohibition, or mandamus. The difficulties surrounding the old prerogative order procedure are set out in the judgment of Lord Diplock in *O'Reilly* v *Mackman* (*post*, at p. 659).

The result of the review was the Report on Remedies in Administrative Law (Law Com. No. 73, Cmnd 6407) which made a number of recommendations. It was assumed that implementation of the recommendations would require legislation, but the bulk of the changes contained in the proposals were in fact made by an amendment in 1977 to Ord. 53 of the Rules of the Supreme Court (SI 1977 No. 1955). Some of these provisions were themselves amended in 1980 by SI 1980 No. 2000. A number of provisions relevant to the application for judicial review were subsequently enacted in the Supreme Court Act 1981. Following Lord Woolf's review of civil justice, new Civil Procedure Rules were made but judicial review was not initially reformed according to the new philosophy. A subsequent review of the Crown Office List chaired by Sir Jeffery Bowman led to various changes. The judicial review procedure was amended becoming a claim for judicial review under Part 54 of the Civil Procedure Rules (CPR Part 54). The Crown Office List was renamed the Administrative Court, which was a recognition that the great bulk of cases assigned to it involved issues of public law. These changes took effect on 2 October 2000, the day the Human Rights Act 1998 came into force. A pre-action protocol for CPR Part 54 came into force on 4 March 2002.

Supreme Court Act 1981

31.—(1) An application to the High Court for one or more of the following forms of relief, namely—
  (a) an order of mandamus, prohibition or certiorari;
  (b) a declaration or injunction under subsection (2); . . .
shall be made in accordance with rules of court by a procedure to be known as an application for judicial review.

(2) A declaration may be made or an injunction granted under this subsection in any case where an application for judicial review, seeking that relief, has been made and the High Court considers that, having regard to—
  (a) the nature of the matters in respect of which relief may be granted by orders of mandamus, prohibition or certiorari;
  (b) the nature of the persons and bodies against whom relief may be granted by such orders; and
  (c) all the circumstances of the case, it would be just and convenient for the declaration to be made or the injunction to be granted, as the case may be.

(3) No application for judicial review shall be made unless the leave of the High Court has been obtained in accordance with rules of court; and the court shall not grant leave to make such an application unless it considers that the applicant has a sufficient interest in the matter to which the application relates.

(4) On an application for judicial review the High Court may award damages to the applicant if—
  (a) he has joined with his application a claim for damages arising from any matter to which the application relates; and
  (b) the court is satisfied that, if the claim had been made in an action begun by the applicant at the time of making his application, he would have been awarded damages.

(5) If, on an application for judicial review seeking an order of certiorari, the High Court quashes the decision to which the application relates, the High Court may remit the matter to the court, tribunal or authority concerned, with a direction to reconsider it and reach a decision in accordance with the findings of the High Court.

(6) Where the High Court considers that there has been undue delay in making an application for judicial review, the court may refuse to grant—
  (a) leave for the making of the application; or
  (b) any relief sought on the application,
if it considers that the granting of the relief sought would be likely to cause substantial hardship

to, or substantially prejudice the rights of, any person or would be detrimental to good administration.

(7) Subsection (6) is without prejudice to any enactment or rule of court which has the effect of limiting the time within which an application for judicial review may be made.

Civil Procedure Rules

Schedule to The Civil Procedure (Amendment No. 4) Rules 2000 SI 2000 No. 2092.

Also at <http://www.lcd.gov.uk/civil/procrules_fin/menus/rules.htm>

Part 54
JUDICIAL REVIEW

Scope and interpretation

54.1 (1) This Part contains rules about judicial review.

(2) In this Part—

(a) a 'claim for judicial review' means a claim to review the lawfulness of—
  (i) an enactment; or
  (ii) a decision, action or failure to act in relation to the exercise of a public function;
(b) an order of mandamus is called a 'mandatory order';
(c) an order of prohibition is called a 'prohibiting order';
(d) an order of certiorari is called a 'quashing order';
(e) 'the judicial review procedure' means the Part 8 procedure as modified by this Part;
(f) 'interested party' means any person (other than the claimant and defendant) who is directly affected by the claim; and
(g) 'court' means the High Court, unless otherwise stated.

(Rule 8.1(6)(b) provides that a rule or practice direction may, in relation to a specified type of proceedings, disapply or modify any of the rules set out in Part 8 as they apply to those proceedings)

When this part must be used

54.2 The judicial review procedure must be used in a claim for judicial review where the claimant is seeking—

(a) a mandatory order;
(b) a prohibiting order;
(c) a quashing order; or
(d) an injunction under section 30 of the Supreme Court Act 1981 (restraining a person from acting in any office in which he is not entitled to act).

When this part may be used

54.3 (1) The judicial review procedure may be used in a claim for judicial review where the claimant is seeking—

(a) a declaration; or
(b) an injunction.

(Section 31(2) of the Supreme Court Act 1981 sets out the circumstances in which the court may grant a declaration or injunction in a claim for judicial review)

(Where the claimant is seeking a declaration or injunction in addition to one of the remedies listed in rule 54.2, the judicial review procedure must be used)

(2) A claim for judicial review may include a claim for damages but may not seek damages alone.

(Section 31(4) of the Supreme Court Act sets out the circumstances in which the court may award damages on a claim for judicial review)

Permission required

54.4 The court's permission to proceed is required in a claim for judicial review whether started under this Part or transferred to the Administrative Court.

Time limit for filing claim form

54.5 (1) The claim form must be filed—

(a) promptly; and
(b) in any event not later than 3 months after the grounds to make the claim first arose.

(2) The time limit in this rule may not be extended by agreement between the parties.

(3) This rule does not apply when any other enactment specifies a shorter time limit for making the claim for judicial review.

Claim form

54.6 (1) In addition to the matters set out in rule 8.2 (contents of the claim form) the claimant must also state—

(a) the name and address of any person he considers to be an interested party;
(b) that he is requesting permission to proceed with a claim for judicial review; and
(c) any remedy (including any interim remedy) he is claiming.

(Part 25 sets out how to apply for an interim remedy)

(2) The claim form must be accompanied by the documents required by the relevant practice direction.

Service of claim form

54.7 The claim form must be served on—

(a) the defendant; and
(b) unless the court otherwise directs, any person the claimant considers to be an interested party,

within 7 days after the date of issue.

Acknowledgment of service

54.8 (1) Any person served with the claim form who wishes to take part in the judicial review must file an acknowledgment of service in the relevant practice form in accordance with the following provisions of this rule.

(2) Any acknowledgment of service must be—

(a) filed not more than 21 days after service of the claim form; and
(b) served on—

(i) the claimant; and
(ii) subject to any direction under rule 54.7(b), any other person named in the claim form,

as soon as practicable and, in any event, not later than 7 days after it is filed.

(3) The time limits under this rule may not be extended by agreement between the parties.

(4) The acknowledgment of service—

(a) must—

(i) where the person filing it intends to contest the claim, set out a summary of his grounds for doing so; and

(ii) state the name and address of any person the person filing it considers to be an interested party; and

(b) may include or be accompanied by an application for directions.

(5) Rule 10.3(2) does not apply.

Failure to file acknowledgment of service

54.9 (1) Where a person served with the claim form has failed to file an acknowledgment of service in accordance with rule 54.8, he—

(a) may not take part in a hearing to decide whether permission should be given unless the court allows him to do so; but

(b) provided he complies with rule 54.14 or any other direction of the court regarding the filing and service of—

(i) detailed grounds for contesting the claim or supporting it on additional grounds; and

(ii) any written evidence,

may take part in the hearing of the judicial review.

(2) Where that person takes part in the hearing of the judicial review, the court may take his failure to file an acknowledgment of service into account when deciding what order to make about costs.

(3) Rule 8.4 does not apply.

Permission given

54.10 (1) Where permission to proceed is given the court may also give directions.

(2) Directions under paragraph (1) may include a stay of proceedings to which the claim relates.

(Rule 3.7 provides a sanction for the non-payment of the fee payable when permission to proceed has been given)

Service of order giving or refusing permission

54.11 The court will serve—

(a) the order giving or refusing permission; and

(b) any directions,

on—

(i) the claimant;

(ii) the defendant; and

(iii) any other person who filed an acknowledgment of service.

Permission decision without a hearing

54.12 (1) This rule applies where the court, without a hearing—

(a) refuses permission to proceed; or

(b) gives permission to proceed—

(i) subject to conditions; or

(ii) on certain grounds only.

(2) The court will serve its reasons for making the decision when it serves the order giving or refusing permission in accordance with rule 54.11.

(3) The claimant may not appeal but may request the decision to be reconsidered at a hearing.

(4) A request under paragraph (3) must be filed within 7 days after service of the reasons under paragraph (2).

656 Constitutional and Administrative Law

(5) The claimant, defendant and any other person who has filed an acknowledgment of service will be given at least 2 days' notice of the hearing date.

Defendant etc. may not apply to set aside

54.13 Neither the defendant nor any other person served with the claim form may apply to set aside an order giving permission to proceed.

Response

54.14 (1) A defendant and any other person served with the claim form who wishes to contest the claim or support it on additional grounds must file and serve—

    (a) detailed grounds for contesting the claim or supporting it on additional grounds; and

    (b) any written evidence,

within 35 days after service of the order giving permission.

    (2) The following rules do not apply—

        (a) rule 8.5 (3) and 8.5 (4) (defendant to file and serve written evidence at the same time as acknowledgment of service); and

        (b) rule 8.5 (5) and 8.5(6) (claimant to file and serve any reply within 14 days).

Where claimant seeks to rely on additional grounds

54.15 The court's permission is required if a claimant seeks to rely on grounds other than those for which he has been given permission to proceed.

Evidence

54.16 (1) Rule 8.6 does not apply.

    (2) No written evidence may be relied on unless—

        (a) it has been served in accordance with any—

            (i) rule under this Part; or

            (ii) direction of the court; or

        (b) the court gives permission.

Court's powers to hear any person

54.17 (1) Any person may apply for permission—

    (a) to file evidence; or

    (b) make representations at the hearing of the judicial review.

    (2) An application under paragraph (1) should be made promptly.

Judicial review may be decided without a hearing

54.18 The court may decide the claim for judicial review without a hearing where all the parties agree.

Court's powers in respect of quashing orders

54.19 (1) This rule applies where the court makes a quashing order in respect of the decision to which the claim relates.

    (2) The court may—

        (a) remit the matter to the decision-maker; and

        (b) direct it to reconsider the matter and reach a decision in accordance with the judgment of the court.

    (3) Where the court considers that there is no purpose to be served in remitting the matter to the decision-maker it may, subject to any statutory provision, take the decision itself.

(Where a statutory power is given to a tribunal, person or other body it may be the case that the court cannot take the decision itself)

Transfer

54.20 The court may

(a) order a claim to continue as if it had not been started under this Part; and

(b) where it does so, give directions about the future management of the claim.

(Part 30 (transfer) applies to transfers to and from the Administrative Court)

Pre-Action Protocol for Judicial Review

INTRODUCTION

This protocol applies to proceedings <u>within England and Wales only</u>. It does not affect the time limit specified by Rule 54.5(1) of the Civil Procedure Rules which requires that any claim form in an application for judicial review must be filed promptly and in any event not later than 3 months after the grounds to make the claim first arose.

1 Judicial review allows people with a sufficient interest in a decision or action by a public body to ask a judge to review the lawfulness of:

- an enactment; or
- a decision, action or failure to act in relation to the exercise of a public function.

2 Judicial review may be used where there is no right of appeal or where all avenues of appeal have been exhausted.

3 Where alternative procedures have not been used the judge may refuse to hear the judicial review case. However, his or her decision will depend upon the circumstances of the case and the nature of the alternative remedy. Where an alternative remedy does exist a claimant should give careful consideration as to whether it is appropriate to his or her problem before making a claim for judicial review.

4 Judicial review may not be appropriate in every instance.

Claimants are strongly advised to seek appropriate legal advice when considering such proceedings and, in particular, before adopting this protocol or making a claim. Although the Legal Services Commission will not normally grant full representation before a letter before claim has been sent and the proposed defendant given a reasonable time to respond, initial funding may be available, for eligible claimants, to cover the work necessary to write this. (See Annex C for more information.)

5 This protocol sets out a code of good practice and contains the steps which parties should generally follow before making a claim for judicial review.

6 This protocol does not impose a greater obligation on a public body to disclose documents or give reasons for its decision than that already provided for in statute or common law. However, where the court considers that a public body should have provided <u>relevant</u> documents and/or information, particularly where this failure is a breach of a statutory or common law requirement, it may impose sanctions.

This protocol <u>will not be appropriate</u> where the defendant does not have the legal power to change the decision being challenged, for example decisions issued by tribunals such as the Immigration Appeal Authorities.

This protocol <u>will not be appropriate</u> in urgent cases, for example, when directions have been set, or are in force, for the claimant's removal from the UK, or where there is an urgent need for an interim order to compel a public body to act where it has unlawfully refused to do so (for example, the failure of a local housing authority to secure interim accommodation for a homeless claimant) a claim should be made immediately. A letter before claim will not stop the implementation of a disputed decision in all instances.

7 All claimants will need to satisfy themselves whether they should follow the protocol, depending upon the circumstances of his or her case. Where the use of the protocol is appropriate, the court will normally expect all parties to have complied with it and will take into account compliance or non-compliance when giving directions for case management of proceedings or when making orders for costs [Civil Procedure Rules Costs Practice Direction]. However, even in emergency cases, it is good practice to fax to the defendant the draft Claim Form which the claimant intends to issue. A claimant is also normally required to notify a defendant when an interim mandatory order is being sought.

THE LETTER BEFORE CLAIM

8 Before making a claim, the claimant should send a letter to the defendant. The purpose of this letter is to identify the issues in dispute and establish whether litigation can be avoided.

9 Claimants should normally use the suggested **standard format** for the letter outlined at Annex A.

10 The letter should contain **the date and details of the decision, act or omission being challenged and a clear summary of the facts** on which the claim is based. It should also contain the **details of any relevant information** that the claimant is seeking and an explanation of why this is considered relevant.

11 The letter should normally contain the **details of any interested parties** known to the claimant. They should be sent a **copy** of the letter before claim **for information**. Claimants are **strongly advised to seek appropriate legal advice** when considering such proceedings and, in particular, before sending the letter before claim to other interested parties or making a claim.

12 A claim should not normally be made until the proposed reply date given in the letter before claim has passed, unless the circumstances of the case require more immediate action to be taken.

THE LETTER OF RESPONSE

13 Defendants should normally respond within 14 days using the **standard format** at Annex B. Failure to do so will be taken into account by the court and sanctions may be imposed unless there are good reasons.

14 Where it is not possible to reply within the proposed time limit the defendant should send an interim reply and propose a reasonable extension. Where an extension is sought, reasons should be given and, where required, additional information requested. **This will not affect the time limit for making a claim for judicial review** [See Civil Procedure Rule 54.5(1)] nor will it bind the claimant where he or she considers this to be unreasonable. However, where the court considers that a subsequent claim is made prematurely it may impose sanctions.

15 If the **claim is being conceded in full**, the reply should say so in clear and unambiguous terms.

16 If the **claim is being conceded in part or not being conceded at all**, the reply should say so in clear and unambiguous terms, and:

    (a)   where appropriate, contain a new decision, clearly identifying what aspects of the claim are being conceded and what are not, or, give a clear timescale within which the new decision will be issued;

(b)   provide a fuller explanation for the decision, if considered appropriate to do so;

(c)   address any points of dispute, or explain why they cannot be addressed;

(d)   enclose any **relevant** documentation requested by the claimant, or explain why the documents are not being enclosed; and

(e)   where appropriate, confirm whether or not they will oppose any application for an interim remedy.

17 The response should be sent to **all interested parties** identified by the claimant and contain details of any other parties who the defendant considers also have an interest.

NOTES:

1.   The objectives of the pre-action protocols are '(1) to encourage the exchange of early and full information about the prospective legal claim, (2) to enable parties to avoid litigation by agreeing a settlement of the claim before the commencement of proceedings, and (3) to support the efficient management of proceedings where litigation cannot be avoided.' As we shall see later point (2) is a very important consideration (*post* p. 684).

2.   Where the use of the protocol is considered appropriate, then failure to do so can result in the application of sanctions provided for in the CPR Pre-Action Protocol Practice Direction. Thus, failure to send the letters or not to provide sufficient information could result in an order that the party at fault pay the costs of the proceedings, or part of those costs, of the other party or parties if, in the opinion of the court, non-compliance has led to the commencement of proceedings which might otherwise not have needed to be commenced, or has led to costs being incurred in the proceedings that might otherwise not have been incurred (para. 2.3).

3.   As we shall see aspects of the Ord 53 and CPR Part 54 procedures have been criticized. See D. Oliver 'Public Law Procedures and Remedies – Do We Need Them?' [2002] PL 91, who argues that judicial review could be regarded as an ordinary claim inside the CPR without the need for this special Part 54 procedure.

SECTION 2:   **The Exclusivity Principle**

As stated above, prior to the introduction of the revised Ord. 53, the courts frequently permitted litigants to commence an action by way of a claim for a declaration or injunction as an alternative to using the special procedure for obtaining orders of *certiorari*, mandamus, and prohibition. Would the courts continue to offer litigants this choice following the introduction of the reformed procedure in 1977?

O'Reilly v *Mackman*
[1983] 2 AC 237, House of Lords

A number of prisoners at Hull Prison wished to challenge decisions reached by the prison's board of visitors on the ground that they were in breach of the rules of natural justice. They did not make use of Ord. 53, but instead began proceedings by writ or originating summons, asking for a declaration that the findings and subsequent penalties were null and void. The application was refused by the judge at first instance but the Court of Appeal allowed an appeal by the board. On appeal to the House of Lords:

LORD DIPLOCK: . . . All that is at issue in the instant appeal is the procedure by which such relief ought to be sought. Put in a single sentence the question for your Lordships is: whether in 1980 after RSC Ord. 53 in its new form, adopted in 1977, had come into operation it was an abuse of the process of the court to apply for such declarations by using the procedure laid down in the Rules for proceedings begun by writ or by originating summons instead of using the procedure laid down by Ord. 53 for an application for judicial review of the awards of forfeiture of remission of sentence made against them by the board which the appellants are seeking to impugn?

In their respective actions, the appellants claim only declaratory relief. It is conceded on their behalf that, for reasons into which the concession makes it unnecessary to enter, no claim for damages would lie against the members of the board of visitors by whom the awards were made. The only claim was for a form of relief which it lies within the discretion of the court to grant or withhold. So the first thing to note is that the relief sought in the action is discretionary only.

It is not, and it could not be, contended that the decision of the board awarding him forfeiture of remission had infringed or threatened to infringe any right of the appellant derived from private law, whether a common law right or one created by statute. Under the Prison Rules remission of sentence is not a matter of right but of indulgence. So far as private law is concerned all that each appellant had was a legitimate expectation, based upon his knowledge of what is the general practice, that he would be granted the maximum remission permitted by rule 5(2) of the Prison Rules, of one third of his sentence if by that time no disciplinary award of forfeiture of remission had been made against him. So the second thing to be noted is that none of the appellants had any remedy in private law.

In public law, as distinguished from private law, however, such legitimate expectation gave to each appellant a sufficient interest to challenge the legality of the adverse disciplinary award made against him by the board on the ground that in one way or another the board in reaching its decision had acted outwith the powers conferred upon it by the legislation under which it was acting; and such grounds would include the board's failure to observe the rules of natural justice: which means no more than to act fairly towards him in carrying out their decision-making process, and I prefer so to put it.

Lord Diplock went on to outline the disadvantages of the procedure for applying for prerogative orders prior to 1977. These were:

(1) the absence of any provision for discovery;

(2) the absence of any express provision for cross-examination.

His Lordship continued to outline, on the other hand, the protections which the procedure for applying for prerogative orders afforded to public bodies:

(1) the requirement to obtain leave;

(2) the time-limits on the grant of certiorari.

His Lordship continued:

. . . I accept that having regard to disadvantages . . . [of the prerogative order procedure], it could not be regarded as an abuse of the process of the court, before the amendments made to Order 53 in 1977, to proceed against the authority by an action for a declaration of nullity of the impugned decision with an injunction to prevent the authority from acting on it, instead of applying for an order of certiorari; and this despite the fact that, by adopting this course, the plaintiff evaded the safeguards imposed in the public interest against groundless, unmeritorious or tardy attacks upon the validity of decisions made by public authorities in the field of public law.

Those disadvantages, which formerly might have resulted in an applicant's being unable to obtain justice in an application for certiorari under Order 53, have all been removed by the new Order introduced in 1977. . . .

Lord Diplock discussed the provisions of the new Order which allow for inter-locutory applications for discovery and cross-examination. He also discussed the provisions which permit claims for damages and applications for declarations and injunctions to be included in applications under the Order.

His Lordship continued:

So Order 53 since 1977 has provided a procedure by which every type of remedy for infringement of the rights of individuals that are entitled to protection in public law can be obtained in one and the same proceeding by way of an application for judicial review, and whichever remedy is found to be the most appropriate in the light of what has emerged upon the hearing of the application, can be granted to him. If what should emerge is that his complaint is not of an infringement of any of his rights that are entitled to protection in public law, but may be an infringement of his rights in private law and thus not a proper subject for judicial review, the court has power under rule 9(5), instead of refusing the application, to order the proceedings to continue as if they had begun by writ. There is no such converse power under the RSC to permit an action begun by writ to continue as if it were an application for judicial review; and I respectfully disagree with that part of the judgment of Lord Denning MR which suggests that such a power may exist; nor do I see the need to amend the rules in order to create one.

My Lords, Order 53 does not expressly provide that procedure by application for judicial review shall be the exclusive procedure available by which the remedy of a declaration or injunction may be obtained for infringement of rights that are entitled to protection under public law; nor does section 31 of the Supreme Court Act 1981. There is great variation between individual cases that fall within Order 53 and the Rules Committee and subsequently the legislature were, I think, for this reason content to rely upon the express and the inherent power of the High Court, exercised upon a case to case basis, to prevent abuse of its process whatever might be the form taken by that abuse. Accordingly, I do not think that your Lordships would be wise to use this as an occasion to lay down categories of cases in which it would necessarily always be an abuse to seek in an action begun by writ or originating summons a remedy against infringement of rights of the individual that are entitled to protection in public law. . . .

Now that those disadvantages to applicants have been removed and all remedies for infringe-ments of rights protected by public law can be obtained upon an application for judicial review, as can also remedies for infringements of rights under private law if such infringements should also be involved, it would in my view as a general rule be contrary to public policy and, as such an abuse of the process of the court, to permit a person seeking to establish that a decision of a public authority infringed rights to which he was entitled to protection under public law to proceed by way of an ordinary action and by this means to evade the provisions of Order 53 for the protection of such authorities.

My Lords, I have described this as a general rule; for though it may normally be appropriate to apply it by the summary process of striking out the action, there may be exceptions, particularly where the invalidity of the decision arises as a collateral issue in a claim for infringement of a right of the plaintiff arising under private law, or where none of the parties objects to the adoption of the procedure by writ or originating summons. Whether there should be other exceptions should, in my view, at this stage in the development of procedural public law, be left to be decided on a case to case basis – a process that your Lordships will be continuing in the next case in which judgment is to be delivered today [*Cocks* v *Thanet District Council* [1983] 2 AC 286].

In the instant cases where the only relief sought is a declaration of nullity of the decisions of a statutory tribunal, the Board of Visitors of Hull Prison, as in any other case in which a similar declaration of nullity in public law is the only relief claimed, I have no hesitation, in agreement with the Court of Appeal, in holding that to allow the actions to proceed would be an abuse of the process of the court. They are blatant attempts to avoid the protections for the defendants for which Order 53 provides.

The other Law Lords agreed with Lord Diplock.

QUESTION

The Law Commission's Report on Administrative Law Remedies, Law Com. No. 73, Cmnd 6407, stated in para. 34 that 'we are clearly of the opinion that the new procedure we envisage in respect of applications to the Divisional Court should not be exclusive in the sense that it would become the only way by which issues relating to the acts or omissions of public authorities should come before the courts'.

The *JUSTICE-All Souls Report on Administrative Law* (1988) criticizes the decision in *O'Reilly* v *Mackman* on the ground 'that it has all the appearance of judicial legislation without the benefit of the consultation and debating process normally associated with legislation' (para. 6.19).

Do you agree?

NOTES:
The procedural safeguards referred to in *O'Reilly* v *Mackman* and which are to be found in CPR Part 54 require some further explanation.

1. *Permission* (see Supreme Court Act 1981, s. 31(3); and now CPR r. 54.4, *ante* at p. 654). The requirement that an applicant for judicial review must obtain permission has been criticized. The *JUSTICE-All Souls Report* recommended that it should be abolished for several reasons:
   (a) Permission is not required in private law proceedings. A particular category of litigants, namely those seeking judicial review, should not be subjected to an impediment which is not placed before litigants generally.
   (b) The administration can be protected from 'groundless, unmeritorious or tardy harassment' by the procedure which allows parties to apply to strike out a case. A statement of case may be struck out under the rules CPR r. 34 if they disclose no reasonable cause of action, are likely to obstruct the just disposed of proceedings or if they otherwise constitute an abuse of the process of the courts, and the claim may be dismissed.
   (c) Issues of standing are no longer conclusively determined at the stage of the application for leave (see *IRC* v *National Federation of Self-Employed and Small Businesses Ltd* [1982] AC 617, *post* at p. 672).
2. Despite criticism from academics (e.g. A. Le Sueur and M. Sunkin [1992] PL 102, the requirement for permission was retained in CPR Part 54 but it was changed from an *ex parte* (without notice) to an *inter partes* (with notice) proceedings decided by the judge on the papers. The thinking behind this was that because of the significant number of cases which, after obtaining permission, were either settled or withdrawn, it would be better to allow defendants to make an initial outline of their defence so that weak cases would be recognized and claimants ejected at this early stage. Bridges, Meszaros and Sunkin [2000] PL 649 believe that the analysis of the data which led the Bowman review to conclude that the permission

stage would save a substantial amount of time was flawed. There are various factors which promote post-permission rather than pre-permission stage settlements, in particular, the short time limit and they argue that the proposal could increase the number of applications for permission. Detailed research will be needed to elucidate this point but the bald figures given by Scott Baker J in his statement [2002] 1 All ER 634 showing that of some 5,398 disposals in the Administrative Court in 2001, only 2,564 were actually determined by the courts with 1,521 being withdrawn and 372 discontinued, suggest Bowman was wrong.

3. *Time-limits* Problems have arisen as to the relationship between the provisions in the Supreme Court Act 1981, s. 31(6) and the RSC Ord. 53, r. 4, now CPR r. 54.5 (see *ante* at p. 654). The House of Lords dealt with time-limits in *R* v *Dairy Produce Quota Tribunal, ex parte Caswell* [1990] 2 AC 738.

   (a) At the stage of the application for permission the court considers whether the application has been made promptly. The fact that an application has been made within three months does not necessarily mean that it has been made promptly.

   (b) If the application has not been made promptly or within three months the court will have to consider whether there is good reason for the delay.

   (c) Where there is a finding of promptness at the permission stage, this does not preclude a finding of undue delay at the substantive hearing.

   (d) Whenever there is a failure to act promptly or within three months there is undue delay, and the court may either refuse to grant permission for the making of the application or, at the hearing, refuse to grant relief if it considers that the granting of the relief sought would be likely to cause substantial hardship to, or substantially prejudice the rights of, any person or would be detrimental to good administration.

4. The *JUSTICE-All Souls Report* (1988), criticized the three-month period as too short, and recommended that Ord. 53, r. 4 (now CPR r. 54.5) be removed, thus leaving the question of delay to be dealt with by reference to the statutory test in s. 31(6) of the 1981 Act (see paras 6.28–6.31). The Law Commission concluded that certainty was desirable and recommended the continuance of the three month time limit. A case could move to a substantive hearing if the reason for the delay in making the application for permission was the pursuit of an alternative remedy.

QUESTION

Do the criticisms made of the procedural safeguards in the CPR Part 54 procedure undermine the basis of the decision in *O'Reilly* v *Mackman*?

NOTE: Lord Diplock mentioned that there may be certain exceptions to the general exclusivity principle. The courts have been required to consider the scope of the exclusivity rule, and the exceptions to it, in a number of cases.

NOTES:

1. In *Wandsworth London Borough Council* v *Winder* [1985] AC 461 it was held that a council tenant could, in defending proceedings for rent arrears, seek a declaration that the rent increases were *ultra vires*. It was subsequently held that the rent increases were in fact valid and an appeal to the Court of Appeal was dismissed (see *London Borough of Wandsworth* v *Winder (No. 2)* (1987) 19 HLR 204; (1988) 20 HLR 400).

2. The principle of raising a public law issue as a defence in civil litigation has been applied to criminal prosecution. Such a collateral challenge to the validity of a by-law or administrative action was approved in the House of Lords in *Boddington* v *British Transport Police* [1997] 2 AC 143. Their Lordships overruled *Bugg* v *DPP* [1993] QB 473, which allowed a collateral challenge of a bye-law for substantive but not procedural invalidity. There is an exception, in that

if legislation specified an appeal process then collateral challenge is not permitted (see *R v Wicks* [1998] AC 92 – enforcement notices under the planning legislation).

Roy v *Kensington and Chelsea FPC*
[1991] 2 WLR 239, House of Lords

The Kensington and Chelsea and Westminster Family Practitioner Committee (FPC) was responsible, under the National Health Service (General Medical and Pharmaceutical Services) Regulations 1974, for making payments to general practitioners undertaking National Health Service work within its area. Dr Roy was on the list of doctors undertaking National Health Service work within the FPC's area. The FPC decided to use its powers under the Regulations to reduce Dr Roy's basic practice allowance by 20 per cent on the basis that he was not devoting a substantial amount of time to general practice under the National Health Service. Dr Roy issued a writ claiming the full amount of the basic practice allowance. In the same writ he also claimed repayment of sums due to him in relation to the employment of ancillary staff. The FPC argued that the inclusion of the claim relating to the basic practice allowance was an abuse of the process of the court. The judge decided that, as the committee's decision was clearly a public law decision, it could only be challenged by judicial review. His decision was reversed by the Court of Appeal and the FPC appealed to the House of Lords. (In the meantime Dr Roy proceeded with his claim in relation to the employment of ancillary staff and obtained an order for repayment.)

LORD BRIDGE OF HARWICH: My Lords, the circumstances from which this appeal arises are fully set out in the speech of my learned and noble friend, Lord Lowry, in which he has also undertaken a comprehensive review of the relevant authorities. Agreeing, as I do, with the conclusion he reaches, I shall state my own reasons briefly.

The decisions of this House in *O'Reilly* v *Mackman* [1983] 2 AC 237 and *Cocks* v *Thanet District Council* [1983] 2 AC 286, have been the subject of much academic criticism. Although I appreciate the cogency of some of the arguments advanced in support of that criticism, I have not been persuaded that the essential principle embodied in the decisions requires to be significantly modified, let alone overturned. But if it is important, as I believe, to maintain the principle, it is certainly no less important that its application should be confined within proper limits. It is appropriate that an issue which depends exclusively on the existence of a purely public law right should be determined in judicial review proceedings and not otherwise. But where a litigant asserts his entitlement to a subsisting right in private law, whether by way of claim or defence, the circumstance that the existence and extent of the private right asserted may incidentally involve the examination of a public law issue cannot prevent the litigant from seeking to establish his right by action commenced by writ or originating summons, any more than it can prevent him from setting up his private law right in proceedings brought against him. I think this proposition necessarily follows from the decisions of this House in *Davy* v *Spelthorne Borough Council* [1984] AC 262 and *Wandsworth London Borough Council* v *Winder* [1985] AC 461. In the latter case Robert Goff LJ in the Court of Appeal, commenting on a passage from the speech of Lord Fraser of Tullybelton in the former case, said, at p. 480:

> I read this passage in Lord Fraser of Tullybelton's speech as expressing the opinion that the principle in *O'Reilly* v *Mackman* should not be extended to require a litigant to proceed by way of judicial review in circumstances where his claim for damages for negligence might in consequence be adversely affected. I can for my part see no reason why the same

consideration should not apply in respect of any private law right which a litigant seeks to invoke, whether by way of action or by way of defence. For my part, I find it difficult to conceive of a case where a citizen's invocation of the ordinary procedure of the courts in order to enforce his private law rights, or his reliance on his private law rights by way of defence in an action brought against him, could, as such, amount to an abuse of the process of the court.

I entirely agree with this. . . .

  I do not think the issue in the appeal turns on whether the doctor provides services pursuant to a contract with the family practitioner committee. I doubt if he does and am content to assume that there is no contract. Nevertheless, the terms which govern the obligations of the doctor on the one hand, as to the services he is to provide, and of the family practitioner committee on the other hand, as to the payments which it is required to make to the doctor, are all prescribed in the relevant legislation and it seems to me that the statutory terms are just as effective as they would be if they were contractual to confer upon the doctor an enforceable right in private law to receive the remuneration to which the terms entitle him. It must follow, in my view, that in any case of dispute the doctor is entitled to claim and recover in an action commenced by writ the amount of remuneration which he is able to prove as being due to him. Whatever remuneration he is entitled to under the statement is remuneration he has duly earned by the services he has rendered. The circumstance that the quantum of that remuneration, in the case of a particular dispute, is affected by the discretionary decision made by the committee cannot deny the doctor his private law right of recovery or subject him to the constraints which the necessity to seek judicial review would impose upon that right.

LORD LOWRY: [Lord Lowry reviewed a number of authorities including *Wandsworth Borough Council* v *Winder* [1985] AC 461 and *Cocks* v *Thanet DC* [1983] 2 AC 286 and continued.] . . .

  [T]he actual or possible absence of a contract is not decisive against Dr Roy. He has in my opinion a bundle of rights which should be regarded as his individual private law rights against the committee, arising from the statute and regulations and including the very important private law right to be paid for the work that he has done. As Judge White put it [1989] 1 Med LR 10, 12:

> The rights and duties are no less real or effective for the individual practitioner. Private law rights flow from the statutory provisions and are enforceable, as such, in the courts but no contractual relations come into existence.

The judge, however, held that, *even if the doctor's rights to full payments under the scheme were contractually based*, the committee's duty was a public law duty and could be challenged only on judicial review. Mr Collins admitted that, if the doctor had a *contractual* right, he could . . . vindicate it by action. But, my Lords, I go further: if Dr Roy has any kind of *private law right*, even though not contractual, he can sue for its alleged breach.

  In this case it has been suggested that Dr Roy could have gone by judicial review, because there is no issue of fact, but that would not always hold good in a similar type of case. . . . In any event, a successful application by judicial review could not lead directly, as it would in an action, to an order for payment of the full basic practice allowance. Other proceedings would be needed.

  An important point is that the court clearly has *jurisdiction* to entertain the doctor's action. Furthermore, even if one accepts the full rigour of *O'Reilly* v *Mackman*, there is ample room to hold that this case comes within the exceptions allowed for by Lord Diplock. It is concerned with a private law right, it involves a question which *could* in some circumstances give rise to a dispute of fact and one object of the plaintiff is to obtain an order for the payment (not by way of damages) of an ascertained or ascertainable sum of money. If it is wrong to allow such a claim to be litigated by action, what is to be said of other disputed claims for remuneration? I think it is right to consider the whole spectrum of claims which a doctor might make against the committee. The existence of any dispute as to entitlement means that he will be alleging a breach of his private law rights through a failure by the committee to perform their public duty. If the committee's argument prevails, the doctor must in all these cases go by judicial review, even when the facts are not clear. I scarcely think that this can be the right answer. . . .

The judgments [in the Court of Appeal] to which I have referred effectively dispose of an argument pressed by the committee that Dr Roy had no right to be paid a basic practice allowance until the committee had carried out their public duty of forming an opinion under paragraph 12.1(b) [of the National Health Service Regulations 1974] with the supposed consequence that, until that had happened, the doctor had *no private law right* which he could enforce. The answer is that Dr Roy had a right to a fair and legally correct consideration of his claim. Failing that, his private law right has been infringed and he can sue the committee.

Mr Collins [counsel for the FPC] sought to equate the committee's task under paragraph 12.1(b) with the council's duty in phase 1 of *Cocks* v *Thanet District Council* and the committee's duty to pay with the council's duty in phase 2. For an answer to that argument I refer to the judgments in the Court of Appeal and would also point out that Mr Cocks was simply a homeless member of the public in phase 1, whereas Dr Roy had already an established relationship with the committee when his claim . . . fell to be considered.

Dr Roy's printed case contained detailed arguments in favour of a contract between him and the committee, but before your Lordships Mr Lightman simply argued that the doctor had a private law right, whether contractual or statutory. With regard to *O'Reilly* v *Mackman* [1983] 2 AC 237 he argued in the alternative. The 'broad approach' was that the rule in *O'Reilly* v *Mackman* did not apply generally against bringing actions to vindicate private rights in all circumstances in which those actions involved a challenge to a public law act or decision, but that it merely required the aggrieved person to proceed by judicial review only when private law rights were not at stake. The 'narrow approach' assumed that the rule applied generally to *all* proceedings in which public law acts or decisions were challenged, subject to some exceptions when private law rights were involved. There was no need in *O'Reilly* v *Mackman* to choose between these approaches, but it seems clear that Lord Diplock considered himself to be stating a general rule with exceptions. For my part, I much prefer the broad approach, which is both traditionally orthodox and consistent with the *Pyx Granite* principle [1960] AC 260, 286, as applied in *Davy* v *Spelthorne Borough Council* [1984] AC 262, 274 and in *Wandsworth London Borough Council* v *Winder* [1985] AC 461, 510. It would also, if adopted, have the practical merit of getting rid of a procedural minefield. I shall, however, be content for the purpose of this appeal to adopt the narrow approach, which avoids the need to discuss the proper scope of the rule, a point which has not been argued before your Lordships and has hitherto been seriously discussed only by the academic writers.

Whichever approach one adopts, the arguments for excluding the present case from the ambit of the rule or, in the alternative, making an exception of it are similar and to my mind convincing.

(1) Dr Roy has either a contractual or a statutory private law right to his remuneration in accordance with his statutory terms of service.

(2) Although he seeks to enforce performance of a public law duty . . . his private law rights dominate the proceedings.

(3) The type of claim and other claims for remuneration (although not this particular claim) may involve disputed issues of fact.

(4) The order sought (for the payment of money due) could not be granted on judicial review.

(5) The claim is joined with another claim which is fit to be brought in an action (and has already been successfully prosecuted).

(6) When individual rights are claimed, there should not be a need for leave or a special time limit, nor should the relief be discretionary.

(7) The action should be allowed to proceed unless it is plainly an abuse of process.

(8) The cases I have cited show that the rule in *O'Reilly* v *Mackman* [1983] 2 AC 237, assuming it to be a rule of general application, is subject to many exceptions based on the nature of the claim and on the undesirability of erecting procedural barriers.

My Lords, I have already disclaimed the intention of discussing the scope of the rule in *O'Reilly* v *Mackman* but, even if I treat it as a general rule, there are many indications in favour of a liberal attitude towards the exceptions contemplated but not spelt out by Lord Diplock. For example: (1) the Law Commission, when recommending the new judicial review procedure, contemplated the continued coexistence of judicial review proceedings and actions for a declaration with regard to public law issues. *Associated Provincial Picture Houses Ltd* v *Wednesbury Corporation* [1948] 1 KB 223 is a famous prototype of the latter.

(2) This House has expressly approved actions for a declaration of nullity as alternative to applications for certiorari to quash, where private law rights were concerned: *Wandsworth London Borough Council* v *Winder* [1985] AC 461, 477 *per* Robert Goff LJ.

(3):

> 'The principle remains intact that public authorities and public servants are, unless clearly exempted, answerable in the ordinary courts for wrongs done to individuals. But by an extension of remedies and a flexible procedure it can be said that something resembling a system of public law is being developed. Before the expression "public law" can be used to deny a subject a right of action in the court of his choice it must be related to a positive prescription of law, by statute or by statutory rules. We have not yet reached the point at which mere characterisation of a claim as a claim in public law is sufficient to exclude it from consideration by the ordinary courts: to permit this would be to create a dual system of law with the rigidity and procedural hardship for plaintiffs which it was the purpose of the recent reforms to remove': *Davy* v *Spelthorne Borough Council* [1984] AC 262, 276, *per* Lord Wilberforce.

In conclusion, my Lords, it seems to me that, unless the procedure adopted by the moving party is ill suited to dispose of the question at issue, there is much to be said in favour of the proposition that a court having jurisdiction ought to let a case be heard rather than entertain a debate concerning the form of the proceedings.

For the reasons already given I would dismiss this appeal.

The other Law Lords agreed with Lord Bridge and Lord Lowry.

Clarke v *University of Lincolnshire and Humberside*
[2000] 1 WLR 1988, Court of Appeal

A student was in dispute over an examination matter with her university, which as a new university under the Education Reform Act 1988 had neither a charter nor visitor. She attended the university from 1992–95 and in 1998 began proceedings alleging breach of contract. The claim was struck out on the grounds that such disputes between students and universities were not justiciable but on appeal she was allowed to amend her pleadings. The university contended that the student should have proceeded by judicial review and so it was an abuse of process to bring an action outside the three-month time limit.

Sedley LJ, with whom Ward LJ and Lord Wolf agreed, ruled that there were issues of academic judgment which would not be justiciable but the amended pleadings did not fall into that category and involved contractual issues which the courts were capable of adjudicating.

LORD WOOLF MR:

The effect of the Civil Procedure Rules on *O'Reilly* v *Mackman*

22. It is over eighteen years ago that Lord Diplock made his speech in *O'Reilly* v *Mackman* [1983] 2 AC 237, which has had such a strong influence on the development of public law in this jurisdiction. Generally, since that time, the courts have continued to follow the statement as to the practice which should be adopted when bringing a claim against a public body that Lord Diplock made in that case. Lord Diplock indicated, at p 285, that in his view it would:

> as a general rule be contrary to public policy, and as such an abuse of the process of the court, to permit a person seeking to establish that a decision of a public authority to infringe rights of which he was entitled to protection under public law to proceed by way of an ordinary action and by this means to evade the provisions of Order 53 for the protection of such authorities.

23. Although the speech of Lord Diplock is extremely well known it is important to place the passage just cited from his speech in its context. First it is to be noted that counsel for the plaintiffs had:

> conceded that the fact that by adopting the procedure of an action begun by writ or by originating summons instead of an application for judicial review under O.53 . . . the plaintiffs had thereby been able to evade those protections against groundless, unmeritorious or tardy harassment that were afforded to statutory tribunals or decision making public authorities by Order 53. (p. 284)

Lord Diplock also pointed out that an advantage of Order 53 was that the court had an opportunity to exercise its discretion at the outset of the proceedings rather than would have happened at that time in proceedings begun by originating summons at the end of the proceedings. This was an important protection in the interests of good administration and for third parties who may be indirectly affected by the proceedings. As Lord Diplock said at p. 284:

> Unless such an action can be struck out summarily at the outset as an abuse of the process of the court the whole purpose of the public policy to which the change in Order 53 was directed would be defeated.

24. Lord Diplock went on to indicate that why Order 53 was not made an exclusive procedure was because he considered that the Rules Committee and the Legislature were content to rely upon the inherent power of the High Court to prevent abuse of its process whatever might be the form taken by that abuse: at pp. 285 A–D.

25. Lord Diplock was however at pains to point out that what he had said with regard the exclusivity of Order 53 was a *general* rule. He recognised that there could be exceptions. He identified an exception in the case of collateral issues and went on to say that other exceptions should in his view be developed on a case by case basis. This is what has since happened.

26. Pending the report of Sir Jeffrey Bowman's Committee on the Crown Office Proceedings, Order 53 has not been subject to detailed amendment by the Rules Committee, but it is included in Schedule 1 to the CPR. The proceedings now have to be initiated by use of a 'claim form', maintaining the principle that all proceedings under the CPR are to be commenced in the same way (see Ord. 53 r5 (2)(A). In relation to the protection of the public and the interests of the administration which it provides, Order 53 has not been amended. However already Order 53 is part of the new code of civil procedure created by the CPR. It is subject to the general over-riding principles contained in Part 1.

27. In addition, if proceedings involving public law issues are commenced by an ordinary action

under Part 7 or Part 8 they are now subject to Part 24. Part 24 is important because it enables the court, either on its own motion or on the application of a party, if it considers that a claimant has no real prospect of succeeding on a claim or an issue, to give summary judgment on the claim or issue. This is a markedly different position from that which existed when *O'Reilly* v *Mackman* [1983] 2 AC 237 was decided. If a defendant public body or an interested person considers that a claim has no real prospect of success an application can now be made under Part 24. This restricts the inconvenience to third parties and the administration of public bodies caused by a hopeless claim to which Lord Diplock referred.

28. The distinction between proceedings under Order 53 and an ordinary claim are now limited. Under Order 53 the claimant has to obtain permission to bring the proceedings so the onus is upon him to establish he has a real prospect of success. In the case of ordinary proceedings the defendant has to establish that the proceedings do not have a real prospect of success.

29. A university is a public body. This is not in issue on this appeal. Court proceedings would, therefore, normally be expected to be commenced under Order 53. If the university is subject to the supervision of a visitor there is little scope for those proceedings (*Page* v *Hull University Visitor* [1993] AC 682). Where a claim is brought against a university by one of its students, if because the university is a 'new university' created by statute, it does not have a visitor, the role of the court will frequently amount to performing the reviewing role which would otherwise be performed by the visitor. The court, for reasons which have been explained, will not involve itself with issues that involve making academic judgments. Summary judgment dismissing a claim, which if it were to be entertained, would require the court to make academic judgments should be capable of being obtained in the majority of situations. Similarly, the court has now power to stay the proceedings if it came to the conclusion that, in accordance with the over-riding objective, it would be desirable for a student to use an internal disciplinary process before coming to the court: see CPR 1.4(1)(e).

30. One of Lord Diplock's reasons which he gave in *O'Reilly* v *Mackman* [1983] 2 AC 237 for his concern about an ordinary civil action being commenced against public bodies when a more appropriate procedure was under Order 53 was the fact that in ordinary civil proceedings the claimant could defer commencing the proceedings until the last day of the limitation period. This compares unfavourably with the requirement, that subject to the court's discretion to extend time, under Order 53 proceedings have to be commenced promptly and in any event within three months. If a student could bypass this requirement to bring proceedings promptly by issuing civil proceedings based on a contract, this could have a very adverse affect on administration of universities.

31. This is a matter of considerable importance in relation to litigation by dissatisfied students against universities. Grievances against universities are preferably resolved within the grievance procedure which universities have today. If they cannot be resolved in that way, where there is a visitor, they then have (except in exceptional circumstances) to be resolved by the visitor. The courts will not usually intervene.

32. While the courts will intervene where there is no visitor normally this should happen after the student has made use of the domestic procedures for resolving the dispute. If it is not possible to resolve the dispute internally, and there is no visitor, then the courts may have no alternative but to become involved. If they do so, the preferable procedure would usually be by way of judicial review. If, on the other hand, the proceedings are based on the contract between the student and the university then they do not have to be brought by way of judicial review.

33. The courts today will be flexible in their approach. Already, prior to the introduction of the CPR the courts were prepared to prevent abuse of their process where there had been an inordinate delay even if the limitation period had not expired. In such a situation, the court could, in appropriate circumstances, stay subsequent proceedings. This is despite the fact that a litigant normally was

regarded as having a legal right to commence proceedings at any time prior to the expiry of the limitation period. (See *Birkett* v *James* [1978] AC 297)

34. The courts' approach to what is an abuse of process has to be considered today in the light of the changes brought about by the CPR. Those changes include a requirement that a party to proceedings should behave reasonably both before and after they have commenced proceedings. Parties are now under an obligation to help the court further the over-riding objectives which include ensuring that cases are dealt with expeditiously and fairly. (CPR 1.1(2)(d) and 1.3) They should not allow the choice of procedure to achieve procedural advantages. The CPR are as Part 1.1(1) states a new procedural code. Parliament recognised that the CPR would fundamentally change the approach to the manner in which litigation would be required to be conducted. That is why the Civil Procedure Act 1997 (Section 4(1) and (2)) gives the Lord Chancellor a very wide power to amend, repeal or revoke any enactment to the extent he considers necessary or desirable in consequence of the CPR.

35. While in the past, it would not be appropriate to look at delay of a party commencing proceedings other than by judicial review within the limitation period in deciding whether the proceedings are abusive this is no longer the position. While to commence proceedings within a limitation period is not in itself an abuse, delay in commencing proceedings is a factor which can be taken into account in deciding whether the proceedings are abusive. If proceedings of a type which would normally be brought by judicial review are instead brought by bringing an ordinary claim, the court in deciding whether the commencement of the proceedings is an abuse of process can take into account whether there has been unjustified delay in initiating the proceedings.

36. When considering whether proceedings can continue the nature of the claim can be relevant. If the court is required to perform a reviewing role or what is being claimed is a discretionary remedy, whether it be a prerogative remedy or an injunction or a declaration the position is different from when the claim is for damages or a sum of money for breach of contract or a tort irrespective of the procedure adopted. Delay in bringing proceedings for a discretionary remedy has always been a factor which a court could take into account in deciding whether it should grant that remedy. Delay can now be taken into account on an application for summary judgment under CPR Part 24 if its effect means that the claim has no real prospect of success.

37. Similarly if what is being claimed could affect the public generally the approach of the court will be stricter than if the proceedings only affect the immediate parties. It must not be forgotten that a court can extend time to bring proceedings under Order 53. The intention of the CPR is to harmonise procedures as far as possible and to avoid barren procedural disputes which generate satellite litigation.

38. Where a student has, as here, a claim in contract, the court will not strike out a claim which could more appropriately be made under Order 53 solely because of the procedure which has been adopted. It may however do so, if it comes to the conclusion that in all the circumstances, including the delay in initiating the proceedings, there has been an abuse of the process of the court under the CPR. The same approach will be adopted on an application under Part 24.

39. The emphasis can therefore be said to have changed since *O'Reilly* v *Mackman* [1983] 2 AC 237. What is likely to be important when proceedings are not brought by a student against a new university under Order 53, will not be whether the right procedure has been adopted but whether the protection provided by Order 53 has been flouted in circumstances which are inconsistent with the proceedings being able to be conducted justly in accordance with the general principles contained in Part 1. Those principles are now central to determining what is due process. A visitor is not required to entertain a complaint when there has been undue delay and a court in the absence of a visitor should exercise its jurisdiction in a similar way. The courts are far from being the ideal forum in which to resolve the great majority of disputes between a student and his or her university. The

courts should be vigilant to ensure their procedures are not misused. The courts must be equally vigilant to discourage summary applications which have no real prospect of success.

Appeal allowed.

NOTE: Cornford [2000] 5 Web JCLI <http://webjcli.ncl.ac.uk/2000/issue5/cornford5.html> argues that the logic of having a special procedure for judicial review means that (predominantly) public law issues should be brought under it and that Lord Woolf's views on how the CPR can protect public authorities from abuse still leave the problem that some claimants may wrongly identify their claim as a private one and not use CPR Part 54. They will not be able to transfer to Part 54 if they are outside the time limit.

QUESTION

Why do public authorities need safeguards in litigation involving public law issues but not private law ones?

SECTION 3: Who may apply for Judicial Review?

The principles of *locus standi* or standing determine *who* is entitled to bring a particular dispute before the courts. They can thus be distinguished from the principles which determine whether a particular matter is suitable for adjudication in the courts (see the section on justiciability at p. 681), whether a particular matter is one of public law (see p. 676), and what proceedings may be used to challenge the decision (see p. 659).

There are many people who may consider that they are affected or have an interest in an administrative decision. Consider, for example, the range of persons who might be said to have an interest in a decision to close a school because of falling numbers. The list will obviously include persons whose children will have to start a new school, but it could also include a number of others, for example persons who are opposed in principle to the closure of small schools and persons who are concerned about the financial implications of the closure for the local education authority. The principles of *locus standi* have the function of determining which interests merit access to the courts.

What arguments might be put forward in favour of the courts' power to select the interests which merit access to the courts? Cane, in *An Introduction to Administrative Law* (1996), at pp. 59–60, suggests a number of possible functions.

An Introduction to Administrative Law

What is the function of standing rules? In general terms it is to restrict access to judicial review. But why restrict access? One suggested reason is to protect public bodies from vexatious litigants with no real interest in the outcome of the case but just a desire to make things difficult for the government. But it is highly doubtful that many such litigants exist in real life, and if they do, the requirement of leave to apply for judicial review should be adequate to deal with them. Other reasons for restricting access have been suggested: to prevent the conduct of government business being unduly hampered and delayed by 'excessive' litigation; to reduce the risk that civil servants will behave in over-cautious and unhelpful ways in dealing with citizens for fear of being sued if things go wrong; to ration scarce judicial resources; to ensure that the argument on the merits is presented in the best possible way, by a person with a real interest in presenting it (but quality of presentation and personal interest do not always go together); to ensure that people do not meddle paternalistically in the affairs of others.

What, then, are the principles of *locus standi* in judicial review proceedings?

Inland Revenue Commissioners v *National Federation of Self-Employed and Small Businesses Ltd (NFSESB)*
[1982] AC 617, House of Lords

The NFSESB sought an order of mandamus requiring the Inland Revenue Commissioners to assess and collect arrears of income tax due by a number of workers in the printing industry, known as the Fleet Street Casuals. This group had for some years been engaged in practices which deprived the Revenue of tax due in respect of their casual earnings. The Inland Revenue, on becoming aware of this, made an arrangement under which the workers were required to register in respect of their casual employment, so that in future tax could be collected in the normal way. Arrears of tax from 1977–78 were to be paid and current investigations to proceed, but investigations in respect of earlier years were not to take place. The House of Lords considered whether the Federation had locus standi. At that time the relevant rule was r. 3(5) of the Rules of the Supreme Court. Section 31(3) of the Supreme Court Act 1981 (*ante* at p. 652) and r. 3(7) now repeat the provisions that used to be contained in this rule.

LORD WILBERFORCE: . . . There may be simple cases in which it can be seen at the earliest stage that the person applying for judicial review has no interest at all or no sufficient interest to support the application: then it would be quite correct at the threshold to refuse him leave to apply. The right to do so is an important safeguard against the courts being flooded and public bodies being harassed by irresponsible applications. But in other cases this will not be so. In these it will be necessary to consider the powers or the duties in law of those against whom the relief is asked, the position of the applicant in relation to those powers or duties, and to the breach of those said to have been committed. In other words, the question of sufficient interest cannot, in such cases, be considered in the abstract, or as an isolated point: it must be taken together with legal and factual context. The rule requires sufficient interest in the matter to which the application relates. This, in the present case, necessarily involves the whole question of the duties of the Inland Revenue and the breaches for failure of those duties of which the respondents complain. . . .

[After examining the relevant statutory provisions, his Lordship continued.]

From this summary analysis it is clear that the Inland Revenue Commissioners are not immune from the process of judicial review. They are an administrative body with statutory duties, which the courts, in principle, can supervise . . . It must follow from these cases and from principle that a taxpayer would not be excluded from seeking judicial review if he could show that the revenue had either failed in its statutory duty toward him or had been guilty of some action which was an abuse of their powers or outside their powers altogether. Such a collateral attack – as contrasted with a direct appeal on law to the courts – would no doubt be rare, but the possibility certainly exists.

The position of other taxpayers – other than the taxpayers whose assessment is in question – and their right to challenge the revenue's assessment or non-assessment of that taxpayer, must be judged according to whether, consistently with the legislation, they can be considered as having sufficient interest to complain of what has been done or omitted. I proceed therefore to examine the revenue's duties in that light.

These duties are expressed in very general terms and it is necessary to take account also of the framework of the income tax legislation. This established that the commissioners must assess each individual taxpayer in relation to his circumstances. Such assessments and all information regarding a taxpayer's affairs are strictly confidential. There is no list or record of assessments which can be inspected by other taxpayers nor is there any common fund of the produce of income tax in which income taxpayers as a whole can be said to have any interest. The produce of income tax, together with that of other inland revenue taxes, is paid into the consolidated fund which is at the disposal of Parliament for any purposes that Parliament thinks fit.

The position of taxpayers is therefore very different from that of ratepayers. As explained in *Arsenal Football Club Ltd* v *Ende* [1979] AC 1, the amount of rates assessed upon ratepayers is ascertainable by the public through the valuation list. The produce of rates goes into a common fund applicable for the benefit of the ratepayers. Thus any ratepayer has an interest, direct and sufficient, in the rates levied upon other ratepayers; for this reason his right as a 'person aggrieved' to challenge assessments upon them has long been recognised and is so now in section 69 of the General Rate Act 1967. This right was given effect to in the *Arsenal* case.

The structure of the legislation relating to income tax, on the other hand, makes clear that no corresponding right is intended to be conferred upon taxpayers. Not only is there no express or implied provision in the legislation upon which such a right could be claimed, but to allow it would be subversive of the whole system, which involves that the commissioners' duties are to the Crown, and that matters relating to income tax are between the commissioners and the taxpayer concerned. No other person is given any right to make proposals about the tax payable by any individual: he cannot even inquire as to such tax. The total confidentiality of assessments and of negotiations between individuals and the revenue is a vital element in the working of the system. As a matter of general principle I would hold that one taxpayer has no sufficient interest in asking the court to investigate the tax affairs of another taxpayer or to complain that the latter has been under-assessed or over-assessed: indeed, there is a strong public interest that he should not. And this principle applies equally to groups of taxpayers: an aggregate of individuals each of whom has no interest cannot of itself have an interest.

That a case can never arise in which the acts or abstentions of the revenue can be brought before the court I am certainly not prepared to assert, nor that, in a case of sufficient gravity, the court might not be able to hold that another taxpayer or other taxpayers could challenge them. Whether this situation has been reached or not must depend upon an examination, upon evidence, of what breach of duty or illegality is alleged. Upon this, and relating it to the position of the complainant, the court has to make its decision. . . .

[After considering the evidence his Lordship decided that the Federation had no sufficient interest.]

LORD DIPLOCK: For my part I should prefer to allow the appeal and dismiss the Federation's application under RSC Ord. 53, not upon the specific ground of no sufficient interest but upon the more general ground that it has not been shown that in the matter of which complaint was made, the treatment of the tax liabilities of the Fleet Street casuals, the board did anything that was *ultra vires* or unlawful. They acted in the bona fide exercise of the wide managerial discretion which is conferred on them by statute. . . .

[His Lordship nonetheless went on to consider the question of *locus standi*.]

The procedure under the new Order 53 involves two stages: (1) the application for leave to apply for judicial review, and (2) if leave is granted, the hearing of the application itself. The former, or 'threshold' stage is regulated by rule 3. The application for leave to apply for judicial review is made ex parte, but may be adjourned for the persons or bodies against whom relief is sought to be represented. This did not happen in the instant case. Rule 3(5) specifically requires the court to consider at this stage whether 'it considers that the applicant has a sufficient interest in the matter to which the application relates.' So this is a 'threshold' question in the sense that the court must direct its mind to it and form a prima facie view about it upon the material that is available at the first stage. The prima facie view so formed, if favourable to the applicant, may alter on further consideration in the light of further evidence that may be before the court at the second stage, the hearing of the application for judicial review itself.

The need for leave to start proceedings for remedies in public law is not new. It applied previously to applications for prerogative orders, though not to civil actions for injunctions or declarations. Its purpose is to prevent the time of the court being wasted by busybodies with misguided or trivial complaints of administrative error, and to remove the uncertainty in which public officers and authorities might be left as to whether they could safely proceed with administrative action while proceedings for judicial review of it were actually pending even though misconceived. . . .

My Lords, at the threshold stage, for the Federation to make out a prima facie case of reasonable suspicion that the board in showing a discriminatory leniency to a substantial class of taxpayers had done so for ulterior reasons extraneous to good management, and thereby deprived the national exchequer of considerable sums of money, constituted what was in my view reason enough for the Divisional Court to consider that the Federation or, for that matter, any taxpayer, had a sufficient interest to apply to have the question whether the board was acting *ultra vires* reviewed by the court. The whole purpose of requiring that leave should first be obtained to make the application for judicial review would be defeated if the court were to go into the matter in any depth at that stage. If, on a quick perusal of the material then available, the court thinks that it discloses what might on further consideration turn out to be an arguable case in favour of granting to the applicant the relief claimed, it ought, in the exercise of a judicial discretion, to give him leave to apply for that relief. The discretion that the court is exercising at this stage is not the same as that which it is called upon to exercise when all the evidence is in and the matter has been fully argued at the hearing of the application. . . .

The analyses to which, on the invitation of the Lord Advocate, the relevant legislation has been subjected by some of your Lordships, and particularly the requirement of confidentiality which would be broken if one taxpayer could complain that another taxpayer was being treated by the revenue more favourably than himself, mean that occasions will be very rare on which an individual taxpayer (or pressure group of taxpayers) will be able to show a sufficient interest to justify an application for judicial review of the way in which the revenue has dealt with the tax affairs of any taxpayer other than the applicant himself.

Rare though they may be, however, if, in the instant case, what at the threshold stage was suspicion only had been proved at the hearing of the application for judicial review to be true in fact (instead of being utterly destroyed), I would have held that this was a matter in which the federation had a sufficient interest in obtaining an appropriate order, whether by way of declaration or mandamus, to require performance by the board of statutory duties which for reasons shown to be *ultra vires* it was failing to perform.

It would, in my view, be a grave lacuna in our system of public law if a pressure group, like the Federation, or even a single public-spirited taxpayer, were prevented by outdated technical rules of *locus standi* from bringing the matter to the attention of the court to vindicate the rule of law and get the unlawful conduct stopped. The Attorney-General, although he occasionally applies for prerogative orders against public authorities that do not form part of central government, in practice never does so against government departments. It is not, in my view, a sufficient answer to say that judicial review of the actions of officers or departments of central government is unnecessary because they are accountable to Parliament for the way in which they carry out their functions. They are accountable to Parliament for what they do so far as regards efficiency and policy, and of that Parliament is the only judge; they are responsible to a court of justice for the lawfulness of what they do, and of that the court is the only judge.

Lord Fraser and Lord Roskill delivered judgments in which they agreed with Lord Wilberforce. Lord Scarman delivered a judgment which agreed in general with that of Lord Diplock.

NOTE: Lord Diplock refers in his judgment to the role of the Attorney-General. The Attorney-General has a discretion to institute legal proceedings in the public interest. He may do so on his own initiative or upon the request of an individual or organization. Where the Attorney-General institutes litigation at the request of an individual or organization, this is known as a relator action. The Attorney-General's decision whether to bring a relator action cannot be challenged (see *Gouriet* v *Union of Post Office Workers* [1978] AC 435).

QUESTIONS

1. What are the differences, if any, between the approaches of Lord Diplock and Lord Wilberforce ?

2. Do the judgments suggest what their Lordships perceived to be the justification for standing rules (see Cane, *ante* at p. 671)?

3. Do the judgments suggest that the function of judicial review is:

   (a) to protect the individual who is specially affected by the decision;
   (b) to protect the public interest in rooting out administrative illegality?

NOTES:

1. In *R* v *The Attorney-General, ex parte ICI plc* [1987] 1 CMLR 72 the applicant, ICI, was held to have standing to question the validity of the Inland Revenue's assessment of the tax payable by one of its competitors. The fact that ICI was challenging the assessment of a competitor was held to distinguish the application from that of the NFSESB in the *National Federation* case. Furthermore, the issue of confidentiality did not arise because the Revenue had already agreed voluntarily to disclose the basis of its assessment.

2. The Law Commission in its 1994 report favoured the broadly liberal approach of the courts on sufficient interest. They were concerned about the effect of *R* v *Secretary of State for the Environment, ex parte Rose Theatre Trust* [1990] 1 QB 504 on challenges brought by people who were concerned about, but not directly affected by, the administrative action. The Law Commission recommended that public interest applications be treated as having sufficient interest. Subsequently the courts have taken this approach. in *R* v *HM Inspector of Pollution, ex parte Greenpeace Ltd (No. 2)* [1994] 4 All ER 329 Otton J declined to follow *Rose Theatre Trust*. Greenpeace, an environmental pressure group, not only had a genuine interest in the issues involved (disposal of radioactive waste) but it had some 2,500 supporters in the area where the plant was situated and it if was not permitted to seek judicial review, then those who Greenpeace represents, who would have sufficient interest, e.g. neighbours, would not be able to command the expertise which Greenpeace has. A less well informed challenge would not render the court the assistance which it needs in order to do justice between the parties. In *R* v *Secretary of State for Foreign Affairs, ex parte World Development Movement Ltd* [1995] 1 WLR 386 the applicant pressure group was regarded as having sufficient interest to challenge the decision by the Foreign Secretary to make a payment of aid under the Overseas Development and Co-operation Act 1980 to the Malaysian Government towards the construction of the Pergau dam and hydro-electric scheme. This was despite the fact that, unlike Greenpeace, it was unlikely that any of the applicant's individual members had a direct interest in the

issue. The significant factors listed by Rose LJ were that the issue was important; it involved the vindication of the rule of law; there appeared to be no other responsible challenger; the nature of the breach of duty against which relief was sought, and the prominent role of these applications in giving advice, guidance, and assistance with regard to aid.

SECTION 4: **Against whom and in respect of what activities may Judicial Review be sought?**

O'Reilly v *Mackman* concerned a case in which the litigants attempted to use the procedure by way of writ instead of the application for judicial review. Conversely, there have been a number of cases in which the courts have held that litigants are not entitled to use the procedure for judicial review because their cases do not raise issues of 'public law'.

In *R* v *BBC, ex parte Lavelle* [1983] 1 WLR 23, the applicant sought to challenge a decision of a disciplinary board within the BBC suspending her from her employment. Woolf LJ considered that the scope of Ord. 53 was not necessarily confined to that of the old prerogative orders but depended solely on the criteria set out in Ord. 53, r. 1(2) (now r. 54.3(1) (*ante*, at p. 653). He did, however, hold that Ord. 53 could not be used to challenge the decisions of purely private or domestic tribunals such as the disciplinary body within the BBC which derived its power solely from the contract between Miss Lavelle and the BBC.

In the case which follows, the applicants sought to use judicial review to challenge the decision of an unincorporated association which exercised no statutory or prerogative powers.

R v *Panel on Take-overs and Mergers, ex parte Datafin plc*
[1987] QB 815, Court of Appeal

> The Take-over Panel is an unincorporated association which represents a wide range of institutional bodies operating in the financial market, for example, the Stock Exchange. It has a regulatory function concerning take-overs and mergers. In this role it makes, administers and enforces a code of conduct known as the City Code.
>
> The applicants, Datafin plc, were involved in a competitive take-over and complained to the Panel that their rivals, Norton Opax plc, had breached the City Code. The Panel dismissed the complaint and Datafin unsuccessfully sought leave in the High Court to apply for judicial review, seeking *certiorari*, prohibition, *mandamus*, and an injunction. Leave was granted on appeal by the Court of Appeal. The Court of Appeal considered three main issues:
>
> (a) the susceptibility of the Panel's decisions to judicial review;
> (b) the manner in which any jurisdiction was to be exercised; and
> (c) whether, if there was jurisdiction, relief should be granted in the present case.

The following extracts are concerned only with the first question.

SIR JOHN DONALDSON MR: The Panel on Take-overs and Mergers is a truly remarkable body. Perched on the 20th floor of the Stock Exchange building in the City of London, both literally and metaphorically it oversees and regulates a very important part of the United Kingdom financial market. Yet it performs this function without any visible means of legal support. . . . 'Self-regulation' is an emotive term. It is also ambiguous. An individual who voluntarily regulates his life in accordance with stated principles, because he believes that this is morally right and also, perhaps, in his own long-term interests, or a group of individuals who do so, are practising self-regulation. But it can mean something quite different. It can connote a system whereby a group of people, acting in concert, use their collective power to force themselves and others to comply with a code of conduct of their own devising. This is not necessarily morally wrong or contrary to the public interest, unlawful or even undesirable. But it is very different.

The panel is a self-regulating body in the latter sense. Lacking any authority de jure, it exercises immense power de facto by devising, promulgating, amending and interpreting the City Code on Take-overs and Mergers, by waiving or modifying the application of the code in particular circumstances, by investigating and reporting on alleged breaches of the code and by the application or threat of sanctions. The sanctions are no less effective because they are applied indirectly and lack a legally enforceable base . . .

The unspoken assumption, which I do not doubt is a reality, is that the Department of Trade and Industry or, as the case may be, the Stock Exchange or other appropriate body would in fact exercise statutory or contractual powers to penalise the transgressors. . . .

The principal issue in this appeal, and the only issue which may matter in the long term is whether this remarkable body is above the law. Its respectability is beyond question. So is its bona fides. I do not doubt for one moment that it is intended to and does operate in the public interest and that the enormously wide discretion which it arrogates to itself is necessary if it is to function efficiently and effectively. Whilst not wishing to become involved in the political controversy on the relative merits of self-regulation and governmental or statutory regulation, I am content to assume for the purposes of this appeal that self-regulation is preferable in the public interest. But that said, what is to happen if the panel goes off the rails? Suppose, perish the thought, that it were to use its powers in a way which was manifestly unfair. What then? [Counsel for the panel] submits that the panel would lose the support of public opinion in the financial markets and would be unable to operate. Further or alternatively, Parliament could and would intervene. Maybe, but how long would that take and who in the meantime could or would come to the assistance of those who were being oppressed by such conduct? . . .

The jurisdictional issue

. . . The picture which emerges is clear. As an act of government it was decided that, in relation to take-overs, there should be a central self-regulatory body which would be supported and sustained by a periphery of statutory powers and penalties wherever non-statutory powers and penalties were insufficient or non-existent or where EEC requirements called for statutory provisions. . . .

The issue is whether the historic supervisory jurisdiction of the Queen's courts extends to such a body discharging such functions, including some which are quasi-judicial in their nature, as part of such a system. [Counsel] for the panel, submits that it does not. He says that this jurisdiction only extends to bodies whose power is derived from legislation or the exercise of the prerogative. [Counsel for the applicants] submits that this is too narrow a view and that regard has to be had not only to the source of the body's power, but also to whether it operates as an integral part of a system which has a public law character, is supported by public law in that public law sanctions are applied if its edicts are ignored and performs what might be described as public law functions.

After discussing a number of cases, *R* v *Criminal Injuries Compensation Board, ex parte Lain* [1967] 2 QB 864, *O'Reilly v Mackman* [1983] 2 AC 237, *Council for the Civil Service Unions v Minister for the Civil Service* [1985] AC 374 and *Gillick v West Norfolk and Wisbech Area Health Authority* [1986] AC 112, the Master of Rolls continued. . . .

In all the reports it is possible to find enumerations of factors giving rise to the jurisdiction, but it is a fatal error to regard the presence of all those factors as essential or as being exclusive of other factors. Possibly the only essential elements are what can be described as a public element, which can take many different forms, and the exclusion from the jurisdiction of bodies whose sole source of power is a consensual submission to its jurisdiction.

In fact, given its novelty, the panel fits surprisingly well into the format which this court had in mind in the *Criminal Injuries Compensation Board* case. It is without doubt performing a public duty and an important one. This is clear from the expressed willingness of the Secretary of State for Trade and Industry to limit legislation in the field of take-overs and mergers and to use the panel as the centrepiece of his regulation of that market. The rights of citizens are indirectly affected by its decisions, some, but by no means all of whom, may in a technical sense be said to have assented to this situation, e.g. the members of the Stock Exchange. At least in its determination of whether there has been a breach of the code it has a duty to act judicially and it asserts that its raison d'être is to do equity between one shareholder and another. Its source of power is only partly based upon moral persuasion and the assent of institutions and their members, the bottom line being the statutory powers exercised by the Department of Trade and Industry and the Bank of England. In this context I should be very disappointed if the courts could not recognise the realities of executive power and allowed their vision to be clouded by the subtlety and sometimes the complexity of the way in which it can be exerted.

Given that it is really unthinkable that, in the absence of legislation such as affects trade unions, the panel should go on its way cocooned from the attention of the courts in defence of the citizenry, we sought to investigate whether it could conveniently be controlled by established forms of private law, e.g. torts such as actionable combinations in restraint of trade, and, to this end, pressed [counsel for the applicants] to draft a writ. Suffice it to say that the result was wholly unconvincing and, not surprisingly, [counsel for the panel] did not admit that it would be in the least effective. . . .

LLOYD LJ: . . . I add only a few words on the important question whether the Panel on Take-overs and Mergers is a body which is subject to judicial review. In my judgment it is. . . .

On this part of the case counsel for the panel has advanced arguments on two levels. On the level of pure policy he submits that it is undesirable for decisions or rulings of the panel to be reviewable. The intervention of the court would at best impede, at worst frustrate, the purposes for which the panel exists. Secondly, on a more technical level, he submits that to hold that the panel is subject to the supervisory jurisdiction of the High Court would be to extend that jurisdiction further than it has ever been extended before.

On the policy level, I find myself unpersuaded. Counsel for the panel made much of the word 'self-regulating'. No doubt self-regulation has many advantages. But I was unable to see why the mere fact that a body is self-regulating makes it less appropriate for judicial review. The committee of an ordinary club affords an obvious example. But the reason why a club is not subject to judicial review is not just because it is self-regulating. The panel wields enormous power. It has a giant's strength. The fact that it is self-regulating, which means, presumably, that it is not subject to regulation by others, and in particular the Department of Trade and Industry, makes it not less but more appropriate that it should be subject to judicial review by the courts. . . .

So long as there is a possibility, however remote, of the panel abusing its great powers, then it would be wrong for the courts to abdicate responsibility. The courts must remain ready, willing and able to hear a legitimate complaint in this as in any other field of our national life. I am not persuaded that this particular field is one in which the courts do not belong, or from which they should retire, on grounds of policy. And if the courts are to remain in the field, then it is clearly better, as a matter of policy, that legal proceedings should remain in the realm of public law rather than private law, not only because they are quicker, but also because the requirement of leave under Ord. 53 will exclude claims which are clearly unmeritorious.

So I turn to [counsel for the panel's] more technical argument. . . .

> After referring to Lord Diplock's speech in *Council of Civil Service Unions* v *Minister for the Civil Service* [1985] AC 374 Lloyd LJ continued.

I do not agree that the source of the power is the sole test whether a body is subject to judicial review, nor do I so read Lord Diplock's speech. Of course the source of power will often, perhaps usually, be decisive. If the source of power is a statute, or subordinate legislation under a statute, then clearly the body in question will be subject to judicial review. If, at the other end of the scale, the source of power is contractual, as in the case of private arbitration, then clearly the arbitrator is not subject to judicial review: see *R* v *National Joint Council for the Craft of Dental Technicians (Disputes Committee), ex parte Neate* [1953] 1 QB 704.

But in between these extremes there is an area in which it is helpful to look not just at the source of the power but at the nature of the power. If the body in question is exercising public law functions, or if the exercise of its functions have public law consequences, then that may, as counsel for the applicants submitted, be sufficient to bring the body within the reach of judicial review. . . .

But suppose I am wrong: suppose that the courts are indeed confined to looking at the source of the power, as [counsel for the panel] submits. Then I would accept the submission of counsel for the applicants that the source of the power in the present case is indeed governmental, at least in part. [Counsel for the panel] argued that, so far from the source of the power being governmental, this is a case where the government has deliberately abstained from exercising power. I do not take that view. I agree with [counsel for the applicants] when he says there has been an implied devolution of power. Power exercised behind the scenes is power nonetheless. The express powers conferred on inferior tribunals were of critical importance in the early days when the sole or main ground for intervention by the courts was that the inferior tribunal had exceeded its powers. But those days are long since past. Having regard to the way in which the panel came to be established, the fact that the Governor of the Bank of England appoints both the chairman and the deputy chairman, and the other matters to which Sir John Donaldson MR has referred, I am persuaded that the panel was established under the authority of the government, to use the language of Diplock LJ in *Lain's* case. If in addition to looking at the source of the power we are entitled to look at the nature of the power, as I believe we are, then the case is all the stronger. . . .

NICHOLLS LJ: . . .

Jurisdiction

I take as my starting point *Reg* v *Criminal Injuries Compensation Board, ex parte Lain* [1967] 2 QB 864, 882, where Lord Parker CJ noted that the only constant limits on the ancient remedy of certiorari were that the tribunal in question was performing a public duty. He contrasted private or domestic tribunals whose authority is derived solely from the agreement of the parties concerned. . . .

In my view, and quite apart from any other factors which point in the same direction, given the leading and continuing role played by the Bank of England in the affairs of the panel, the statutory source of the powers and duties of the Council of the Stock Exchange, the wide-ranging nature and importance of the matters covered by the code, and the public law consequences of non-compliance, the panel is performing a public duty in prescribing and operating the code (including ruling on complaints).

QUESTIONS

1. Is it correct to say, after *Datafin*, that the only criterion for deciding whether an authority is subject to judicial review is whether it performs a public function?

2. Would judicial review be available to challenge the decisions of the following:

   (a) the Advertising Standards Authority (see *R* v *Advertising Standards Authority Limited, ex parte The Insurance Service* (1989) 133 SJ 1545);

   (b) the National Greyhound Racing Club (see *Law* v *National Greyhound Racing Club* [1983] 1 WLR 1302, but note that this case was decided before *ex parte Datafin*. Do you think it would be decided any differently after *ex parte Datafin*?);

   (c) the Jockey Club (see *R* v *Disciplinary Committee of the Jockey Club, ex parte Aga Khan* [1993] 1 WLR 909);

   (d) the Association of the British Pharmaceutical Industry (see *R* v *Code of Practice Committee of the Association of the British Pharmaceutical Industry, The Times*, 7 November 1990);

   (e) a university (see *Page* v *Hull University Visitor* [1993] AC 682).

NOTE: There have been a number of cases in which the courts considered whether the decisions of statutory bodies to dismiss an employee/employees could be challenged under Ord. 53. In *R* v *East Berkshire Health Authority, ex parte Walsh* [1985] QB 152 the Court of Appeal held that this question depended on whether the employment had sufficient 'statutory underpinning'. The health authority was required by statute to contract with its employees on terms which included the conditions agreed by the Whitley Council for the Health Service and approved by the Secretary of State. The Court of Appeal decided that this did not provide a sufficient statutory underpinning. On the other hand, in *R* v *Secretary of State for the Home Department, ex parte Benwell* [1985] QB 152 Hodgson J granted judicial review of a decision to dismiss a prison officer. Benwell was not in a contractual relationship with his employers and Hodgson J considered that, because his employment was governed by a code of discipline issued under statutory authority, there was sufficient statutory underpinning to provide a public law element. See also *Roy* v *Kensington and Chelsea FPC ante* at p. 664. Ordinary civil servants have now been held to have contracts of employment (*R* v *Lord Chancellor's Department, ex parte Nangle* [1992] 1 All ER 897).

For further discussion of the distinction between public law and private law, see J. Beatson, '"Public" and "Private" in English Administrative Law' (1987) 103 LQR, 34–65.

Although the courts might decide that the claim for judicial review is not available because the dispute does not raise issues of public law, this does not mean that the principles of judicial review are irrelevant. The rules of natural justice are frequently applied to bodies (such as sporting clubs) which could not be challenged under the application for judicial review procedure (see, for example, *R* v *BBC, ex parte Lavelle* [1983] 1 WLR 23). In such cases the judges may describe their role as one of exercising judicial review. This means that it is important to bear in mind that there may be a distinction between the scope of judicial review at the substantive level (that is, the scope of the principles of judicial review) and the scope of judicial review at the procedural level (the scope of the application for judicial review).

SECTION 5: **Justiciability**

Even if a matter raises an issue of public law, the courts may nonetheless refuse to review it on the grounds that the matter is not justiciable. This generally means that the courts consider judicial procedures are unsuitable to control the exercise of discretion. This may be for a variety of reasons, for example because of lack of expertise on the part of the court or because of the constitutional inappropriateness of judicial intervention.

Council of Civil Service Unions v *Minister for the Civil Service*
[1985] AC 374, House of Lords

> The facts of this case are at p. 622 *ante*. In it, the court accepted that prerogative powers were subject to judicial review. The question of whether public powers are subject to judicial review was not therefore to be established on the basis of whether the source of the powers was statute or the prerogative (see further *R* v *Panel on Take-overs and Mergers*). Review of the exercise of powers might, however, be denied if the subject matter of the dispute raised issues which were not justiciable.

LORD FRASER OF TULLYBELTON: . . . The respondent's case is that she deliberately made the decision without prior consultation because prior consultation 'would involve a real risk that it would occasion the very kind of disruption [at GCHQ] which was a threat to national security and which it was intended to avoid.' . . .

The question is one of evidence. The decision on whether the requirements of national security outweigh the duty of fairness in any particular case is for the Government and not for the courts; the Government alone has access to the necessary information, and in any event the judicial process is unsuitable for reaching decisions on national security. But if the decision is successfully challenged, on the ground that it has been reached by a process which is unfair, then the Government is under an obligation to produce evidence that the decision was in fact based on grounds of national security. . . .

[After considering *The Zamora* [1916] 2 AC 77 and the speeches of Lord Reid and Viscount Radcliffe in *Chandler* v *Director of Public Prosecutions* [1964] AC 763 his Lordship concluded that] . . . The affidavit [of Sir Robert Armstrong], read as a whole, does in my opinion undoubtedly constitute evidence that the Minister did indeed consider that prior consultation would have involved a risk of precipitating disruption at GCHQ. I am accordingly of opinion that the respondent has shown that her decision was one which not only could reasonably have been based, but was in fact based, on considerations of national security, which outweighed what would otherwise have been the reasonable expectation on the part of the appellants for prior consultation. . . .

LORD SCARMAN: My Lords, I would dismiss this appeal for one reason only. I am satisfied that the respondent has made out a case on the ground of national security. Notwithstanding the criticisms which can be made of the evidence and despite the fact that the point was not raised, or, if it was, was not clearly made before the case reached the Court of Appeal, I have no doubt that the respondent refused to consult the unions before issuing her instruction of the 22 December 1983 because she feared that, if she did, union-organised disruption of the monitoring services of GCHQ could well result. I am further satisfied that the fear was one which a reasonable minister in the circumstances in which she found herself could reasonably entertain. I am also satisfied that a reasonable minister could reasonably consider such disruption to constitute a threat to national security. I would, therefore, deny relief to the appellants upon their application for judicial review of the instruction, the effect of which was that staff at GCHQ would no longer be permitted to belong to a national trade union.

The point of principle in the appeal is as to the duty of the court when in proceedings properly brought before it a question arises as to what is required in the interest of national security. The question may arise in ordinary litigation between private persons as to their private rights and obligations: and it can arise, as in this case, in proceedings for judicial review of a decision by a public authority. The question can take one of several forms. It may be a question of fact which Parliament has left to the court to determine: see for an example section 10 of the Contempt of Court Act 1981. It may arise for consideration as a factor in the exercise of an executive discretionary power. But, however it arises, it is a matter to be considered by the court in the circumstances and context of the case. Though there are limits dictated by law and common sense which the court must observe in dealing with the question, the court does not abdicate its judicial function. If the question arises as a matter of fact, the court requires evidence to be given. If it arises as a factor to be considered in reviewing the exercise of a discretionary power, evidence is also needed so that the court may determine whether it should intervene to correct excess or abuse of the power. . . .

Lord Scarman, after discussing *The Zamora*, *Chandler* v *Director of Public Prosecutions* and *Secretary of State for Defence* v *Guardian Newspapers Ltd* [1985] AC 339, continued:

My Lords, I conclude, therefore, that where a question as to the interests of national security arises in judicial proceedings the court has to act on evidence. In some cases a judge or jury is required by law to be satisfied that the interest is proved to exist: in others, the interest is a factor to be considered in the review of the exercise of an executive discretionary power. Once the factual basis is established by evidence so that the court is satisfied that the interest of national security is a relevant factor to be considered in the determination of the case, the court will accept the opinion of the Crown or its responsible officer as to what is required to meet it, unless it is possible to show that the opinion was one which no reasonable minister advising the Crown could in the circumstances reasonably have held. There is no abdication of the judicial function, but there is a common sense limitation recognised by the judges as to what is justiciable: and the limitation is entirely consistent with the general development of the modern case law of judicial review. . . .

LORD ROSKILL: My Lords, the conflict between private rights and the rights of the state is not novel either in our political history or in our courts. Historically, at least since 1688, the courts have sought to present a barrier to inordinate claims by the executive. But they have also been obliged to recognise that in some fields that barrier must be lowered and that on occasions, albeit with reluctance, the courts must accept that the claims of executive power must take precedence over those of the individual. One such field is that of national security. The courts have long shown themselves sensitive to the assertion by the executive that considerations of national security must preclude judicial investigation of a particular individual grievance. But even in that field the courts will not act on a mere assertion that questions of national security are involved. Evidence is required that the decision under challenge was in fact founded on those grounds. That that principle exists is I think beyond doubt. In a famous passage in *The Zamora* [1916] 2 AC 77, 107 Lord Parker of Waddington, delivering the opinion of the Judicial Committee, said:

Those who are responsible for the national security must be the sole judges of what the national security requires. It would be obviously undesirable that such matters should be the subject of evidence in a court of law or otherwise discussed in public.

The Judicial Committee were there asserting what I have already sought to say, namely that some matters, of which national security is one, are not amenable to the judicial process. . . .

Lord Diplock and Lord Brightman delivered judgments in favour of dismissing the appeals.

QUESTION

What differences, if any, are there between the speeches of Lord Fraser and Lord Roskill on the one hand, and Lord Scarman on the other?

NOTES:
1. In *R* v *Secretary of State for the Home Department, ex parte Ruddock* [1987] 1 WLR 1482, at p. 1490 it was said that 'credible evidence' was required in support of a plea of national security before judicial investigation of a factual issue (in this case whether a warrant had been issued to tap Mrs Ruddock's telephone) is precluded. Taylor J rejected the argument that the court should decline jurisdiction because a Minister states that to do so would be detrimental to national security. He did, however, accept that in an extreme case where there was 'cogent', 'very strong and specific' evidence of potential damage to national security flowing from the trial of the issues a court might have to decline to try factual issues.
2. In other cases the courts have held that certain decisions cannot be challenged on particular grounds (see *Nottinghamshire CC* v *Secretary of State for the Environment* [1986] AC 240, *ante* at p. 626).
3. In *R* v *Secretary of State for the Home Department, ex parte Bentley* [1994] QB 349 the exercise of the prerogative of mercy was successfully challenged, albeit on a narrow ground. The court held the Minister approached the question of a posthumous pardon on the wrong basis that a grant of a free pardon required moral and technical innocence, rather than considering whether, in all the circumstances, the appropriate punishment had been suffered.
    The challenge to the Treaty on European Union was not successful (*R* v *Secretary of State for Foreign and Commonwealth Affairs, ex parte Rees-Mogg* [1994] QB 552).
4. In *Clark* v *University of Lincolnshire and Humberside* (*ante* p. 667) Sedley LJ said that issues of academic or pastoral judgment were ones which universities were better placed to judge than the courts and instanced the particular mark or class a student ought to be awarded or whether an aegrotat is justified. He also said that religious or aesthetic matters might fall within such a class of non-justiciable matters (para. 12).

QUESTION

Consider whether you think each of the following issues is justiciable and why/why not? Then read the cases cited to establish the views of the courts. What reasons did the courts give?

(a) A British citizen residing in Spain applied for a British passport. The application was refused, and he was told that the reason for this was that a warrant for his arrest had been issued in the United Kingdom and the Secretary of State would not issue a passport in such circumstances (see *R* v *Secretary of State for Foreign and Commonwealth Affairs, ex parte Everett* [1989] 2 WLR 224).

(b) The Attorney-General has power to stop or institute prosecutions and to issue directions to the Director of Public Prosecutions to take over the conduct of prosecutions. He or she may also give, or refuse to give, consent to the institution of relator actions (actions brought at the instance of a relator by the Attorney-General to restrain infringements of public rights). (See *Gouriet* v *UPOW* [1978] AC 435.)

SECTION 6: **Judicial Review as a Discretionary Remedy**

NOTE: It is important to remember that judicial review is a discretionary remedy. Hence, the effective scope of the principles of judicial review will depend on how the court chooses to exercise its discretion.

There are a number of factors which are relevant to the exercise of the court's discretion: the availability of alternative remedies and the question whether the applicant has suffered injustice have been particularly important in recent years.

A: The availability of alternative remedies

In the Practice Statement (Administrative Court: Listing and Urgent Cases) the Lead judge of the Administrative Court Scott Baker J stated at para. 5

Use of alternative means of resolution
I draw the attention of litigants and their advisers to the decision of the Court of Appeal in *R (Cowl)* v *Plymouth City Council (Practice Note)* [2001] EWCA Civ 1935; [2002] 1 WLR 803. The nominated judges are fully committed to resolving disputes by alternative means where appropriate and are exploring ways of promoting this.

R (Cowl) v *Plymouth City Council (Practice Note)*
[2001] EWCA Civ 1935; [2002] 1WLR 803, Court of Appeal

The claimants, who were residents of a residential home, appealed the refusal of permission to grant judicial review of the decision by the council to confirm its social services committee's decision to close the residential home. The council had offered to convene a complaints panel under Local Authority Social Services Act , s. 7B as inserted by National Health Service and Community Care Act 1990, s. 50.

LORD WOOLF CJ:

1 The importance of this appeal is that it illustrates that, even in disputes between public author-ities and the members of the public for whom they are responsible, insufficient attention is paid to the paramount importance of avoiding litigation whenever this is possible. Particularly in the case of these disputes both sides must by now be acutely conscious of the contribution alternative dispute resolution can make to resolving disputes in a manner which both meets the needs of the parties and the public and saves time, expense and stress.

2 The appeal also demonstrates that courts should scrutinise extremely carefully applications for judicial review in the case of applications of the class with which this appeal is concerned. The courts should then make appropriate use of their ample powers under the Civil Procedure Rules to ensure that the parties try to resolve the dispute with the minimum involvement of the courts. The legal aid authorities should co-operate in support of this approach.

3 To achieve this objective the court may have to hold, on its own initiative, an inter partes

hearing at which the parties can explain what steps they have taken to resolve the dispute without the involvement of the courts. In particular the parties should be asked why a complaints procedure or some other form of alternative dispute resolution has not been used or adapted to resolve or reduce the issues which are in dispute. If litigation is necessary the courts should deter the parties from adopting an unnecessarily confrontational approach to the litigation. If this had happened in this case many thousands of pounds in costs could have been saved and considerable stress to the parties could have been avoided.

. . .

14 It appears that one reason why the wheels of the litigation may have continued to roll is that both parties were under the impression that unless they agreed otherwise the claimants were *entitled* to proceed with their application for judicial review unless the complaints procedure on offer technically constituted an 'alternative remedy' which would fulfil all the functions of judicial review. This is too narrow an approach to adopt when considering whether an application to judicial review should be stayed. The parties do not today, under the Civil Procedure Rules, have a right to have a resolution of their respective contentions by judicial review in the absence of an alternative pro-cedure which would cover exactly the same ground as judicial review. The courts should not permit, except for good reason, proceedings for judicial review to proceed if a significant part of the issues between the parties could be resolved outside the litigation process. The disadvantages of doing so are limited. If subsequently it becomes apparent that there is a legal issue to be resolved, that can thereafter be examined by the courts which may be considerably assisted by the findings made by the complaints panel.

. . .

21 Having read the numerous witness statements placed before us and the substantial skeleton arguments prior to the hearing, the members of this court came to the clear conclusion that the appeal raised no point of legal principle. However, while this was the position, the claimants were intent on examining in detail the previous decisions of courts, primarily at first instance, involving the closure of care homes in order to erect a series of legal hoops which it was contended Plymouth had to proceed through before it could close Granby Way. In reality, however, there was no legal principle which divided the parties. It was common ground that there has to be the fullest assessment of the effect of a possible move on the claimants before a decision whether to move the claimants could be reached. Plymouth were perfectly prepared to carry out such an assessment, and recognise that as yet it has not been carried out and that it has to be carried out. This does not satisfy the claimants. They contend that as a matter of law the assessment is required to take place before closure. But absent any statutory requirement what is important is that an assessment takes place, not the time at which it takes place.

22 We understand the reason why the claimants attach such importance to the assessment being carried out before the decision to close. They do not want an assessment as to the propriety of moving the individual claimants to be taken against a decision that the home is to be closed as that could, they fear, prejudge the outcome. This is why they submit that the full assessment should take place before the decision to close the home is taken. The position of Plymouth now, whatever may have been the position in the past, is clearly to regard the decision to close as merely a decision in principle; that is, to close Granby Way subject to the full assessment of the impact upon the residents of their having to move. This approach on the part of Plymouth is understandable. Plymouth needed to make financial savings. The closure of Granby Way and another home would produce the required financial saving. From Plymouth's point of view therefore the first step was to consider whether closure would be a viable option. For this purpose they needed a limited assessment of the impact on the residents and of the practicality of their being rehoused, but no more than this. This exercise was carried out. The decision was made to proceed with this option. Detailed examination of what is involved in rehousing was then required so that a final decision could be made. The final decision

would only be made after the full assessment of the impact upon the residents. Such an approach could be beneficial to the residents because, if the closure option was not viable, there was no need to subject them to the stress which would be involved in determining what would happen to them if they had to move.

23 Unfortunately Plymouth failed to make their strategy clear. They should have done this at the outset. Initially, therefore, there was justification for the claimants' concern that they were to be moved without any proper assessment being made before a final decision to close had taken place.

24 None the less the decision which was taken did not have the technicality the claimants attached to it. There was nothing wrong with Plymouth adopting a two-stage process, with the detailed assessment being part of the second process. However, if this was what they were doing, it is regrettable that far from explaining it they obscured the fact that this was their intention. On the other hand, those who were acting on behalf of the claimants adopted a far too technical approach. Their treatment in their skeleton argument of the authorities on which they rely make this abundantly clear.

25 We do not single out either side's lawyers for particular criticism. What followed was due to the unfortunate culture in litigation of this nature of over-judicialising the processes which are involved. It is indeed unfortunate that, that process having started, instead of the parties focusing on the future they insisted on arguing about what had occurred in the past. So far as the claimants were concerned, that was of no value since Plymouth were prepared, as they ultimately made clear was their position, to reconsider the whole issue. Without the need for the vast costs which must have been incurred in this case already being incurred, the parties should have been able to come to a sensible conclusion as to how to dispose the issues which divided them. If they could not do this without help, then an independent mediator should have been recruited to assist. That would have been a far cheaper course to adopt. Today sufficient should be known about alternative dispute resolution to make the failure to adopt it, in particular when public money is involved, indefensible.

26 The disadvantages of what happened instead were apparent to the trial judge. They were also apparent to this court. At the opening of the hearing we therefore insisted on the parties focusing on what mattered, which was the future well-being of the claimants. Having made clear our views, building on the proposal which had been made in the 23 May letter, the parties had no difficulty in coming to a sensible agreement in the terms which are annexed to this judgment and will form part of the order of the court. The terms go beyond what Plymouth was required to do under the statutory complaint procedure. This does not however, matter because it is always open to the parties to agree to go beyond their statutory obligations. For example, sensibly the claimants are to have the benefit of representatives to appear on their behalf, who may well be non-lawyers who can be extremely experienced in handling issues of the nature of those which are involved. We trust that the parties will now draw a line under what has happened in the past and focus instead on what should happen in the future.

27 This case will have served some purpose if it makes it clear that the lawyers acting on both sides of a dispute of this sort are under a heavy obligation to resort to litigation only if it is really unavoidable. If they cannot resolve the whole of the dispute by the use of the complaints procedure they should resolve the dispute so far as is practicable without involving litigation. At least in this way some of the expense and delay will be avoided. We hope that the highly skilled and caring practitioners who practise in this area will learn from what we regard as the very unfortunate history of this case.

Appeal dismissed.

NOTES:

1. *Cowl* and the Practice Statement seem, at least, to be reiterating in the strongest terms the case law which requires exhaustion of alternative remedies. The actual facts of *Cowl* suggest

that review was premature and Beatson argues that many of the cases on exhaustion of alternatives are not really concerned with the tests of adequacy and relative expertise of the alternative remedies but rather the prematurity of review proceedings ('Prematurity and Ripeness for Review' in Forsyth and Hare (eds) *The Golden Metwand and the Crooked Cord* (1998), 221 at 234).

2. The previous case law on exhaustion did allow for exceptions. In *R v Chief Constable of Merseyside Police, ex parte Calvely* [1986] 2 WLR 144 some police officers had been found guilty of disciplinary offences by their Chief Constable. They had initiated a statutory appeal to the Home Secretary but also sought judicial review on the basis that there had been a breach of the regulation 7, Police (Discipline) Regulations. Sir John Donaldson MR said:

[Counsel] for the Chief Constable, submits that the application for judicial review was rightly dismissed, not upon the ground that it was premature, but because judicial review is not an available remedy when another avenue of appeal is open. In this context he referred to *Reg v Epping and Harlow General Commissioners, ex parte Goldstraw* [1983] 3 All ER 257 where, with the agreement of Purchas LJ, I said, at p. 262:

> it is a cardinal principle that, save in the most exceptionable circumstances, [the judicial review] jurisdiction will not be exercised where other remedies were available and have not been used.

This, like other judicial pronouncements on the interrelationship between remedies by way of judicial review on the one hand and appeal procedures on the other, is not to be regarded or construed as a statute. It does not support the proposition that judicial review is not available where there is an alternative remedy by way of appeal. It asserts simply that the court, in the exercise of its discretion, will very rarely make this remedy available in these circumstances.

In other cases courts have asserted the existence of this discretion, albeit with varying emphasis on the reluctance to grant judicial review. Thus in *Reg v Paddington Valuation Officer, ex parte Peachey Property Corporation Ltd* [1966] 1 QB 380, 400, Lord Denning MR, with the agreement of Danckwerts and Salmon LJJ, held that certiorari and mandamus were available where the alternative statutory remedy was 'nowhere near so convenient, beneficial and effectual.' In *Reg v Hillingdon London Borough Council, ex parte Royco Homes Ltd* [1974] QB 720, 728 Lord Widgery CJ said: ' it has always been a principle that certiorari will go only where there is no other equally effective and convenient remedy.' In *Ex parte Waldron* [1985] 3 WLR 1090, 1108, Glidewell LJ, after referring to this passage, said:

> Whether the alternative statutory remedy will resolve the question at issue fully and directly; whether the statutory procedure would be quicker, or slower, than procedure by way of judicial review; whether the matter depends on some particular or technical knowledge which is more readily available to the alternative appellate body; these are amongst the matters which a court should take into account when deciding whether to grant relief by judicial review when an alternative remedy is available.

Finally, this approach is, I think, consistent with *Reg v Inland Revenue Commissioners, ex parte Preston* [1985] AC 835. . . .

The statutory scheme for police discipline contained in the Police (Discipline) Regulations 1977 and the Police (Appeals) Rules 1977 (SI 1977 No. 759) contemplates a right of appeal to the Secretary of State from a determination by the Chief Constable. . . . However, it is not speedy and, even if there had been no application for judicial review, it is not certain that the appeal would have been determined much before the present time. The application for judicial review in fact caused the appeal to be stayed and, on the most optimistic view, it could not be determined in less than five to six months from now.

Mr Livesey submits that the applicants' complaint of delay in serving the regulation 7 notices and of consequential prejudice should be determined by the appeal procedure provided by Parliament. The appeal tribunal would have a specialised expertise rendering it better able than a court to assess the prejudice. Furthermore, the applicants would be able to raise new points and call fresh evidence directed to the disciplinary charges themselves.

I acknowledge the specialised expertise of such a tribunal, but I think Mr Livesey's submission overlooks the fact that a police officer's submission to police disciplinary procedures is not unconditional. He agrees and is bound by these procedures taking them as a whole. Just as his right of appeal is constrained by the requirement that he give prompt notice of appeal, so he is not to be put in peril in respect of disciplinary, as contrasted with criminal, proceedings unless there is substantial compliance with the police disciplinary regulations. That has not occurred in this case. Whether in all the circumstances the Chief Constable, and the Secretary of State on appeal, is to be regarded as being without jurisdiction to hear and determine the charges which are not processed in accordance with the statutory scheme or whether, in natural justice, the Chief Constable and the Secretary of State would, if they directed themselves correctly in law, be bound to rule in favour of the applicants on the preliminary point, is perhaps only of academic interest. The substance of the matter is that, against the background of the requirement of regulation 7 that the applicants be informed of the complaint and given an opportunity to reply within days rather than weeks, the applicants had no formal notice of the complaints for well over two years. This is so serious a departure from the police disciplinary procedure that, in my judgment, the court should, in the exercise of its discretion, grant judicial review and set aside the determination of the Chief Constable.

I would allow the appeal accordingly.

QUESTIONS

1. In *Calvely* how important was the length of time of the statutory appeal to the decision of the court?

2. Is the convenience of the alternative remedy compatible with *Cowl*?

B: Needs of good administration

R v Monopolies and Mergers Commission, ex parte Argyll Group plc
[1986] 1 WLR 763, Court of Appeal

Argyll Group plc and Guinness plc were rivals in a bid to take over another company, Distillers. The Secretary of State for Trade and Industry referred the Guinness proposal to the Monopolies and Mergers Commission for inquiry and report. One week later the Chairman of the Monopolies and Mergers Commission sought and obtained the consent of the Secretary of State for Trade and Industry to the withdrawal of the reference on the ground that the proposal to make the arrangements had been abandoned. Argyll sought judicial review of this decision, seeking an order of *certiorari*. The Court of Appeal accepted that the Chairman of the Commission did not have the power to act alone in the matter. The following extracts relate to the court's discretion whether to grant a remedy.

SIR JOHN DONALDSON MR:

Discretion

The judge accepted that the chairman derives authority to act as he did from paragraph 10 of schedule 3 to the Act, read with section 75(5). He did not, therefore, have to consider the issue of discretion. As I respectfully disagree with the judge on this aspect, I do, therefore, have to consider how discretion should be exercised.

We are sitting as a public law court concerned to review an administrative decision, albeit one which has to be reached by the application of judicial or quasi-judicial principles. We have to approach our duties with a proper awareness of the needs of public administration. I cannot catalogue them all, but, in the present context, would draw attention to a few which are relevant.

Good public administration is concerned with substance rather than form. Difficult although the decision upon the fact of abandonment may or my not have been, I have little doubt that the commission, or a group of members charged with the conduct of the reference, would have reached and would now reach the same conclusion as did their experienced chairman.

Good public administration is concerned with speed of decision, particularly in the financial field. The decision to lay aside the reference was reached on 20 February 1986. If relief is granted, it must be some days before a new decision is reached.

Good public administration requires a proper consideration of the public interest. In this context, the Secretary of State is the guardian of the public interest. He consented to the reference being laid aside, although he need not have done so if he considered it to be in the public interest that the original proposals be further investigated. He could have made a further reference of the new proposals, if such they be, but has not done so.

Good public administration requires a proper consideration of the legitimate interests of individual citizens, however rich and powerful they may be and whether they are natural or juridical persons. But in judging the relevance of an interest, however legitimate, regard has to be had to the purpose of the administrative process concerned. Argyll has a strong and legitimate interest in putting Guinness in baulk, but that is not the purpose of the administrative process under the Fair Trading Act 1973. To that extent their interest is not therefore of any great, or possibly any, weight.

Lastly good public administration requires decisiveness and finality unless there are compelling reasons to the contrary. The financial public has been entitled to rely upon the finality of the announced decision to set aside the reference and upon the consequence that, subject to any further reference, Guinness were back in the ring, from 20 February until at least 25 February when leave to apply for judicial review was granted, and possibly longer in the light of the judge's decision. This is a very long time in terms of a volatile market and account must be taken of the probability that deals have been done in reliance upon the validity of the decisions now impugned.

Taking account of all these factors, I do not consider that this is a case in which judicial review should be granted. Accordingly, I would dismiss the appeal.

Dillon LJ and Neill LJ delivered judgments in favour of dismissing the appeal.

NOTE: *R v Panel on Take-overs and Mergers, ex parte Datafin plc* [1987] QB 815 also illustrates the use of discretion in the grant of remedies. Sir John Donaldson MR stated (at p. 841) that the court would decide what order, if any, needed to be made, bearing in mind 'the likely outcome of the proceedings which will depend partly upon the facts as they appear from the information available to the court, but also in part upon the public administrative purpose which the panel is designed to serve'.

QUESTIONS

1. Commenting on the factors referred to by Sir John Donaldson, S. Lee writes in (1987) 103 LQR 166–8, at 167 that:

If these are only a few of the possible reasons for judicial restraint, then their discretion is indeed very wide. There are obvious dangers to good public administration, let alone to aggrieved citizens, in such broad judicial discretion. Firstly, there is the danger that administrators will come to believe that they can get away with a breach of the principles of administrative action. Secondly, the prospect of winning the argument on abuse of administrative discretion but failing to secure a remedy through the exercise of judicial discretion may well act as a disincentive to bring applications for judicial review.

Do you agree that decisions such as *R* v *Monopolies and Mergers Commission* carry such risks?

2. Contrast the approach adopted in this case to arguments based on the interests of good administration with *O'Reilly* v *Mackman* (*ante* at p. 659) and *Wandsworth Borough Council* v *Winder* (*ante* at p. 663).

NOTE: The relevance of the argument that a fair hearing would make no difference has been considered by the courts in recent years. There are, in fact, a number of contrasting cases. Of these, *Glynn* v *Keele University* [1971] 1 WLR 487 provides an example of a case which accepts, as in *R* v *Monopolies and Mergers Commission, ex parte Argyll Group plc*, that a remedy may be denied where a fair hearing 'would make no difference'. In that case the claimant had been fined and excluded from residence on a university campus for a particular period. Pennycuick V-C found that there had been a breach of the rules of natural justice, but he refused to grant an injunction since he thought that the claimant had only lost a chance to make a plea in mitigation, and this was not a sufficient reason to set aside a decision which he believed to be perfectly proper. In contrast Megarry J in *John* v *Rees* [1970] Ch 345, at 402 stated:

It may be that there are some who would decry the importance which the courts attach to the observance of the rules of natural justice. 'When something is obvious,' they may say, 'why force everybody to go through the tiresome waste of time involved in framing charges and giving an opportunity to be heard? The result is obvious from the start.' Those who take this view do not, I think, do themselves justice. As everybody who has anything to do with the law well knows, the path of the law is strewn with open and shut cases which, somehow, were not; of unanswerable charges which, in the event, were completely answered; of inexplicable conduct which was fully explained; of fixed and unalterable determinations that, by discussion, suffered a change. Nor are those with any knowledge of human nature who pause to think for a moment likely to underestimate the feelings of resentment of those who find that a decision against them has been made without their being afforded any opportunity to influence the course of events.

SECTION 7: Exclusion of Judicial Review

The legislature has sometimes attempted to protect public authorities from judicial review by inserting clauses which appear to be intended to exclude the jurisdiction of the court. For example, in *Anisminic Ltd* v *Foreign Compensation Commission* [1969] 2 AC 147, Anisminic Ltd wished to challenge a decision of the Foreign Compensation Commission that it was not entitled to compensation in respect of the sequestration of property which it had owned in Egypt, and accordingly applied for a declaration (see *ante* at p. 577). The legislation, however, provided that any determination by the Commission of an application 'shall not be called in question in any court of law' (Foreign Compensation Act 1950, s. 4(4)). The House of Lords considered the effect of this clause.

Anismic Ltd v *Foreign Compensation Commission*

[1969] 2 AC 147, House of Lords

LORD REID: . . . The next argument was that, by reason of the provisions of section 4(4) of the 1950 Act, the courts are precluded from considering whether the respondent's determination was a nullity, and therefore it must be treated as valid whether or not inquiry would disclose that it was a nullity . . .

The respondent maintains that these are plain words only capable of having one meaning. Here is a determination which is apparently valid: there is nothing on the face of the document to cast any doubt on its validity. If it is a nullity, that could only be established by raising some kind of proceedings in court. But that would be calling the determination in question, and that is expressly prohibited by statute. The appellants maintain that this is not the meaning of the words of this provision. They say that 'determination' means a real determination and does not include an apparent or purported determination which in the eyes of the law has no existence because it is a nullity. Or, putting it another way, if you seek to show that a determination is a nullity you are not questioning the purported determination – you are maintaining that it does not exist as a determination. It is one thing to question a determination which does not exist: it is quite another to say that there is nothing to be questioned.

Let me illustrate the matter by supposing a simple case. A statute provides that a certain order may be made by a person who holds a specified qualification or appointment, and it contains a provision similar to section 4(4), that such an order made by such a person shall not be questioned in any court of law. A person aggrieved by an order alleges that it is a forgery or that the person who made the order did not hold that qualification or appointment. Does such a provision require the court to treat that order as a valid order? It is a well-established principle that a provision ousting the ordinary jurisdiction of the court must be construed strictly – meaning, I think, that, if such provision is reasonably capable of having two meanings, that meaning shall be taken which preserves the ordinary jurisdiction of the court.

Statutory provisions which seek to limit the ordinary jurisdiction of the court have a long history. No case has been cited in which any other form of words limiting the jurisdiction of the court has been held to protect a nullity. If the draftsman or Parliament had intended to introduce a new kind of ouster clause so as to prevent any inquiry as to whether the document relied on was a forgery, I would have expected to find something much more specific than the bald statement that a determination shall not be called in question in any court of law. Undoubtedly such a provision protects every determination which is not a nullity. But I do not think that it is necessary or even reasonable to construe the word 'determination' as including everything which purports to be a determination but which is in fact no determination at all. . . .

The other Law Lords delivered speeches in which they agreed that the ouster clause would not protect a decision from challenge if the FCC had acted outside its jurisdiction. A majority of their Lordships also held that Anisminic Ltd was entitled to the declaration which it sought because the FCC had made an error of law which took it outside its jurisdiction (ante at p. 577).

NOTE: After the decision in *Anisminic* the Foreign Compensation Act 1969 was passed. Section 3 provided that a person aggrieved by a determination of the Commission on any question of law had a right to require the Commission to state and sign a case for the Court of Appeal. It was provided, however, that there was to be no appeal to the House of Lords from a decision of the Court of Appeal. Section 3(9) stated that, except as provided by the section and in respect of claims that the Commission had breached the rules of natural justice, no determination by the

Commission on any claim under the Foreign Compensation Act 1950 shall be called in question in any court of law. Determination was defined as including a purported determination.

QUESTION

If these provisions had been in force at the time of the decision in *Anisminic*, do you think House of Lords would have granted the declaration sought?

NOTE: The Tribunals and Inquiries Act 1992, s. 12(1) (formerly s. 11 of the Tribunal and Inquiries Act 1958) now provides that, as respects England and Wales:

> any provision in an Act passed before 1 August 1958 that any order or determination shall not be called in question in any court, or any provision in such an Act which by similar words excludes any of the powers of the High Court, shall not have effect so as to prevent the removal of the proceedings into the High Court by order of certiorari or to prejudice the powers of the High Court to make orders of mandamus.

(Section 11 of the 1958 Act expressly excluded orders or determinations of the Foreign Compensation Commission from this general provision; in *Anisminic*, however, Lord Pearce specifically stated that s. 11 had no bearing on the issue which the court was required to consider.)

QUESTION

Why do you think this provision was confined to Acts passed before 1 August 1958?

NOTES:
1. *Anisminic* concerned an absolute ouster clause. Partial or limited ouster clauses sometimes appear in certain statutory provisions. For example, in planning law persons aggrieved by a compulsory purchase order are permitted to appeal to the High Court on certain grounds within six weeks of publication of the order. Apart from this it is provided that a compulsory purchase order 'shall not . . . be questioned in any legal proceedings whatsoever' (see Acquisition of Land Act 1981, ss. 23–25). The courts have upheld the validity of the partial or limited ouster clauses which attempt to protect decisions from challenge after the expiry of a time-limit (see *R v Secretary of State for the Environment, ex parte Ostler* [1977] QB 122).
2. Where a legislative provision stipulates that the issuing of a certificate 'shall be conclusive evidence' that the conditions for the issue of the certificate had been satisfied, it seems that this can exclude review of the decision to issue the certificate – *R v Registrar of Companies, ex parte Central Bank of India* [1986] QB 1114.
3. An example of a recent ouster clause is the Security Services Act 1989, s. 5(4) 'decisions of the Tribunal . . . (including any decisions as to their jurisdiction) shall not be subject to appeal or liable to be questioned in any court'.

QUESTIONS

1. Do you think that the decision in *Anisminic* reflected the intention of Parliament?
2. Cane, in the extracts set out *ante* at p. 568, uses this case to support a particular argument which he wishes to make. What was the argument, and do you agree that the decision in *Anisminic* supports it?

10

Ombudsmen

SECTION 1: **Introduction**

In 1961 an influential report by the JUSTICE organization recommended that an impartial officer, to be known as a Parliamentary Commissioner, should be established and report on complaints of maladministration in central government. It argued that:

there appears to be a continuous flow of relatively minor complaints, not sufficient in themselves to attract public interest but nevertheless of great importance to the individuals concerned, which give rise to feelings of frustration and resentment because of the inadequacy of the existing means of seeking redress. (JUSTICE, *The Citizen and the Administration* (1961), para. 76.)

The report outlined the weaknesses in the parliamentary question procedure and in adjournment debates as mechanisms for the investigation of complaints (on parliamentary questions and adjournment debates, see *ante* at pp. 328–34). The report envisaged that the Parliamentary Commissioner would be independent of the Executive and responsible only to Parliament. He would conduct investigations informally, in order to ensure that there would be no serious interference with the working of a department, and have access to departmental files. A Select Committee would be established to consider the annual reports of the Parliamentary Commissioner and any special reports which he might issue on particular issues. On the controversial question of whether the establishment of a Parliamentary Commissioner would have any implications for the doctrine of ministerial responsibility, the Report stated, at para. 155:

It is a principle of such fundamental importance in our constitution that we think it would be wrong to make any proposal which might seem to qualify it and therefore we have suggested that a Minister should have the power to veto any proposed investigation by the Parliamentary Commissioner against his Department. We would expect, however, that as so often has happened in our constitutional history, a convention would grow up that the Minister would not exercise his power of veto unreasonably.

The report was also careful to stress that 'any additional procedure should not disturb the basic position of Parliament as a channel for complaint against the Executive and should not even appear to interfere with the relations between individual members and their constituents' (para. 156). With this in mind it recommended that, during an initial testing period, complaints should only be considered on reference from a Member of either House of Parliament. It did, however, anticipate that, after a period of about five years, the Commissioner should be empowered to receive complaints direct from the public. 'The ultimate object', according to the report, 'should be to establish a channel by which the investigation of administrative grievances should take place initially outside the political sphere. Parliament would, however, always be able to take up grievances in the last resort if the Commissioner's investigation failed to procure justice' (para. 157).

Following the publication of *The Citizen and the Administration*, the Conservative Lord Chancellor, Lord Dilhorne, argued that 'a Parliamentary Commissioner would seriously interfere with the prompt and efficient dispatch of public business' (HL Deb., vol. 244, cols. 384–5). Subsequently, however, a new Government accepted, with certain modifications, the introduction of the Parliamentary Commissioner as a development and reinforcement of 'our existing constitutional arrangements for the protection of the individual' (see *The Parliamentary Commissioner for Administration*, Cmnd 2767 (1965)). On the introduction of the ombudsman system in the United Kingdom, see further, Stacey, *The British Ombudsman*.

The office of the Parliamentary Commissioner for Administration (PCA) was thus created in 1967. Since then there has been a proliferation of ombudsmen in the United Kingdom. In 1969 the offices of PCA for Northern Ireland and the Commissioner for Complaints for Northern Ireland were established; both offices are held by the same person. The offices of Health Service Commissioners of England, Wales, and Scotland were created by legislation in 1972 and 1973; all three posts are presently held by the person who is the PCA. In 1974 Local Commissioners were established to deal with maladministration in local government in England and Wales. The office of Local Ombudsman for Scotland was established in 1975; the work of the Scottish Local Ombudsman has been studied by J. Logie and P. Watchman, *The Local Ombudsman* (1990). The establishment of the Scottish Parliament and the National Assembly for Wales has also led to the creation of a Scottish Parliamentary Commissioner for Administration (Scotland Act 1998, s. 91 and transitional arrangements SI 1999 No. 1351, SI 1999 No. 1595) and Welsh Administration Ombudsman (Government of Wales Act 1998, s. 111 and SI 1999 No. 1791).

When the Scottish Public Services Ombudsman Act 2002 comes into force a one-stop shop will have been created for complaints about devolved and local government and the National Health Service in Scotland. Similar amalgamating arrangements for England will eventually be implemented (see *post* p. 754) and a review begun in March 2001 for Wales is likely to make analogous recommendations.

In addition to central and local government and the health service, public sector ombudsmen now include part of the police with the Police Ombudsman for Northern Ireland (Police (Northern Ireland) Act 1998, s. 51). There is a Prisons Ombudsman but unlike all of the aforementioned ombudsmen this officer does not have the same status of independence of the Executive and is more like the Adjudicator in the Inland Revenue and Customs and Excise or the Independent Case Examiner in the Child Support Agency, being above the internal departmental procedure and below the Parliamentary Commissioner in the complaints-handling chain.

In the private sector some ombudsmen dealing with aspects of financial service such as (a) banking, building societies, and insurance; and (b) legal services have statutory frameworks (respectively (a) Financial Services and Markets Act 2000; and (b) Courts and Legal Services Act 1990).

This chapter focuses on the Parliamentary Commissioner and the Local Commissioners. The Parliamentary Commissioner will be referred to in the notes and questions as either the PCA or the Ombudsman. The Local Commissioners will be referred to as either Local Commissioners or the Local Ombudsmen.

The main legislative provisions governing the Parliamentary Commissioner for Administration are contained in the Parliamentary Commissioner Act 1967. The provisions governing the Local Commissioners are set out in the Local Government Act 1974. Both pieces of legislation have been amended on a number of occasions.

The following extracts from the reports of the PCA and the Local Commissioners provide some indication of the work which they carry out.

Parliamentary Commissioner for Administration Annual Report for 2000–01
HC 5 of 2001–02, pp. 21–22, 24–25, 27–8, 34–35, 39, 47–48

C1513/00

Benefits Agency: failures in a fraud investigation
As part of a fraud drive, BA gathered the registration numbers of vehicles parked in a public place and asked the Driver and Vehicle Licensing Agency (DVLA) for the keeper details of 1,100 vehicles. The law allows DVLA to release information when it is necessary for the investigation of crime and the identification of offenders. However, in this instance BA officers exceeded their remit, went beyond acceptable behaviour, and demonstrated a lack of understanding of the legislation covering their investigations. BA's documentation of their investigation was poor; they failed to keep adequate contemporaneous records of observations they had undertaken; and they did not keep sufficient records to enable them to identify that different officers had used different criteria when making those observations. They failed to establish any link between Mrs X and a vehicle they had seen near her property. BA interviewed Mrs X under caution without reasonable evidence to suspect that she had committed a benefit fraud, causing her gross inconvenience, severe distress, and gross embarrassment.

BA apologised to Mrs X and made her ex gratia consolatory payments totalling £850. They confirmed that arrangements were in hand to improve the efficiency of their fraud investigation work and to ensure that it was consistent with recent legislation.

. . .

C524/01

Benefits Agency: refusal to backdate an award of income support
On 10 March 2000 a tribunal awarded Mrs X disability living allowance backdated to June 1997. Her husband, Mr X, had originally claimed income support in August 1997, when only he was in receipt of disability living allowance. His claim was rejected. However, following the tribunal's decision about Mrs X's entitlement to disability living allowance, he re-applied for income support, and it was

awarded from March 2000, inclusive of the severe disability premium for couples. Mr X's representative asked BA to compensate Mr X for loss of entitlement to income support from June 1997 to March 2000. They refused on the basis that there had been no departmental error, and no delays through the normal tiers of adjudication of the disability living allowance claim.

After the Ombudsman's intervention BA agreed to make Mr X an extra-statutory award equivalent to backdated income support. They paid him £5,852, plus interest of £424 for loss of use of the money, and a consolatory payment of £100. BA also undertook refresher training for their staff and introduced revised procedures to make sure the problem did not arise again.

. . .

C737/00

Benefits Agency: errors in awarding industrial injuries disablement benefit
Mr X complained of errors by BA over his award of industrial injuries disablement benefit.

The Ombudsman found that BA had made a number of errors in handling Mr X's case; and after his intervention BA discovered that no action had been taken on a claim to reduced earnings allowance that Mr X had made in 1995. BA paid him arrears of £19,526 and interest of £4,463. BA also awarded Mr X an ex gratia payment of £41 for the loss of use of delayed payments of industrial injuries disablement benefit, and a consolatory payment of £100.

Benefits Agency: failure to implement tribunal decisions
3.6 The Ombudsman dealt with a number of cases in which BA or the Appeals Service had failed to implement decisions given by the Social Security Commissioners or appeal tribunals.

C1652/00
BA failed to implement the findings of an independent tribunal that Mr X had asked BA about invalid care allowance in 1986 and BA had misled him by not giving him the appropriate claim form at that time. Instead of implementing those findings or contesting them by appealing to the Social Security Commissioners, BA conducted a fresh investigation into whether they had misdirected Mr X.

Following the Ombudsman's intervention, BA paid Mr X £120 arrears of invalid care allowance, £50 for arrears of Christmas Bonus, £82 for loss of use of that money, £7,202 arrears of income support, £1,399 for loss of use of that money and £250 for the inconvenience they had caused him. BA has since made arrangements to ensure that an officer is available to attend if requested by an appeal tribunal.

. . .

C1127/00

Child Support Agency: unrealistic expectations raised by administrative errors
CSA made several interim maintenance assessments in Ms Y's case but did not explain properly to her that such assessments would be superseded by any full maintenance assessments which they might make, and that it was unlikely that she would receive payment at the interim maintenance assessment rate for any length of time.

Following the Ombudsman's intervention, CSA increased Ms Y's consolatory payment for gross inconvenience from £200 to £400 and agreed to consider reimbursing any expenses she had reasonably incurred in pursuit of her complaint. CSA had been aware before the Ombudsman's intervention that, as a result of the letter telling them of the interim maintenance assessment, parents could have unrealistically high expectations of the amount of maintenance that might be due. During the course of the investigation they amended the wording of the letter so as to give parents a clearer understanding of the level of maintenance they could expect to receive.

. . .

C1477/99

Inland Revenue: delays and mishandling in an investigation involving capital gains tax
Mr Q's wife sold a house part of which had been let. The Revenue sought to impose a capital gains tax liability which Mr Q disputed. The Revenue eventually accepted (without the matter needing to be heard by the appeal commissioners) that that liability did not arise. Mr Q sought redress, including the relevant costs of his accountant.

The Ombudsman found no fault in the Revenue's initiating their investigation, but that the inspector conducting the investigation had shown a lack of openness of judgement in consider- ing evidence presented on Mr Q's behalf. That had led to the investigation being protracted, and to Mr Q's incurring unnecessary costs. The Revenue agreed to increase their offer of an ex gratia payment by £1,450.

4.2 Among the Revenue cases concluded in the year were two which concerned problems encountered by taxpayers and their advisers with the application of the concept of the 'test case'. In one (C1189/00 – which was concluded by way of a non-statutory report), a taxpayer claimed that his costs on appeal should be reimbursed because his case had been recognised as a 'test case'. The Ombudsman found scant evidence of that, and nothing to amount to an undertaking regarding costs on which the Revenue had reneged. In another case, matters were considerably more complex.

C673/90

Inland Revenue: alleged unfair refusal to apply a House of Lords decision to another case
*Mr N was a participant in a tax avoidance scheme. The Revenue had told his advisers that another case (**Plummer**) would be a 'test case' for his appeal. **Plummer** was decided by the House of Lords in favour of the taxpayer; and the Revenue answered a query from advisers acting for participants in the avoidance scheme by saying that the decision on **Plummer** was of general application and would determine the outcome of any other case in which the facts turned out to be on all fours. However, the House of Lords, in later deciding a third case (**Ramsay**), established new legal prin- ciples which had a bearing on Mr N's case; and the Revenue refused to apply to Mr N's appeal the decision of the House of Lords in **Plummer**. Eventually, Mr N's case itself came before the House of Lords: they found for the Revenue, but said that Mr N's case could not be distinguished from the **Plummer** case. Despite that finding by the House of Lords the Revenue still refused to apply **Plum- mer**, citing the later decision on **Ramsay**. Mr N's complaint of Revenue unfairness was investigated by the then Adjudicator. She initially upheld a substantial part of the complaint, but then changed her mind when the Revenue contested her decision, pointing to correspondence which indicated that those involved with the avoidance scheme had been aware before **Ramsay** had been decided that the Revenue would not automatically apply **Plummer** to those in Mr N's position.*

The Ombudsman said that the House of Lords had decided Mr N's tax liability arising from his participation in the tax avoidance scheme – that was not a matter for the Ombudsman. He found failings by the Revenue and a misconceived approach by the then Adjudicator. But he did not find that those had led to injustice or that the Revenue had shown unfairness. Put simply, events in Mr N's case had been overtaken by the legal decision in the Ramsay case, and no blame attached to the Revenue for that.

4.3 For many years the Revenue have published a code of practice on how they handle complaints: 'Mistakes by the Inland Revenue: Code of Practice 1'. Unlike the Adjudicator, the Ombudsman is not constrained by what the Revenue say in their code of practice and associated guidance; and, although he welcomes their existence he has both general concerns about redress (chapter 1 paragraphs 1.8 and 1.9) and about particular situations where he considers that the Revenue's approach has become inadequate.

C61/00

Inland Revenue: treatment of reimbursed costs

The Revenue (including VOA) accepted Mr H's complaint that they had unnecessarily prolonged negotiations over the valuation of his former company for tax purposes; but he regarded their offer of financial redress as inadequate. Although the Revenue had reimbursed a substantial amount of professional costs and personal expenses they had not, despite the fact that those costs and expenses had been incurred and paid some years earlier, paid any interest or enhancement.

Following the Ombudsman's intervention, the Revenue, while explaining that under the terms of their code of practice they would normally include an additional amount only if interest had itself actually been paid, agreed to pay Mr H a further £9,000, part of which was intended to cover his claim to interest.

. . .

Legal Services Commission

4.8 A thread running through this year's investigated cases has been a number of representations from complainants that their opponents in legal proceedings should not have been legally aided, and that the Legal Services Commission (or the body preceding the Commission, the Legal Aid Board) had taken insufficient account of those representations.

4.9 Such complaints present some difficulties for the Ombudsman. Section 20 of the Access to Justice Act 1999, like its predecessor section 38 of the Legal Aid Act 1988, does not allow information which has been provided to the Commission in connection with an applicant's or assisted person's case to be disclosed to a third party, including the opponent in legal proceedings. Although the Ombudsman has access to all the Commission's relevant papers, and is thus able to reach sound conclusions on complaints, he has to observe the provisions of section 20 of the Access to Justice Act and cannot therefore pass on such third party information.

C1446/99

Legal Services Commission: failure to act upon representations concerning a person's financial eligibility for legal aid

The Ombudsman found that in November 1997 the Commission had failed to review Mr and Mrs N's opponent's eligibility for legal aid upon receipt of information from Mr N about the opponent's income from business. When Mr N renewed his representations in March 1998 the Commission's handling of them had been characterised by error and delay, and had again failed to tackle the key issue effectively. The Commission had also mishandled a report by the opponent of a change in his circumstances and representations by Mr N regarding the merits of the opponent's case. The Ombudsman criticised that very poor performance, the effect of which had been to postpone for a year the withdrawal of the opponent's legal aid, thereby prolonging the case and increasing the costs for Mr N. The Commission offered Mr N an ex gratia payment representing 50 per cent of the costs for which he was liable from December 1997 to November 1998.

. . .

C429/00

Home Office: improper disclosure of information about a member of a prison Board of Visitors

Mr Bridges complained that information relating to disciplinary proceedings instituted against him by the Home Office, in his capacity as a member of a prison Board of Visitors, had been improperly disclosed to a journalist from The Times newspaper. The Ombudsman found that the journalist had had access to a Home Office submission to the then Minister of State in which criticism of Mr Bridges' behaviour had been reported. The Home Office had subsequently undertaken an internal enquiry into the leak, but had seemingly abandoned that enquiry without reporting to the Minister.

The Ombudsman acknowledged that there was a remote possibility that someone other than a member of the Home Office or the Prison Service had been directly responsible for the leak, but considered it more probable that one of the recipients of the submission had either leaked it or passed it to someone else who had leaked it. Whether there had been a direct leak or an unauthorised transmission to another person, the Ombudsman regarded the Home Office as responsible for what had clearly been maladministration leading to an injustice to Mr Bridges. The Home Office agreed in the circumstances to offer Mr Bridges an ex gratia payment of £5,000 in recognition of the distress and embarrassment involved.

Local Government Ombudsman Annual Digest of Cases 2000
2001, pp. 7–8, 48–9, 85, 91, 98, 113–14

B1: ADMISSIONS

Admissions criteria not properly applied – child wrongly denied place – defects in appeal committee procedure – lack of training for members – inadequate records

1. Mr and Mrs Jackson's son, Tom, attended an infant school which had traditionally been the feeder school to Junior School X. When Tom was due to transfer to junior school Mr and Mrs Jackson wanted him to go to Junior School X and applied for him to do so. Their application was unsuccessful and so was their appeal.

General

2. The Ombudsman commented:

'All of us are indebted to the thousands of people who serve as governors of schools or members of admission appeal committees. They give their time and effort for no financial reward. They have to make difficult and sometimes unpopular decisions. Naturally, parents attach great importance to their preferences about the schools to which they wish their children to be admitted. In considering parents' admission applications, governors and appeal committees have to apply law and guidance which is complex.'

3. The Ombudsman was in no doubt that, in this case, the governors concerned, the headteacher, the members of the appeal committee and the clerk acted in good faith and that they did what they honestly believed to be right. However, there were serious defects in the way in which the governors and the appeal committee acted.

Admissions criteria

4. The published admissions criteria stated that preference would be given to children from the traditional local feeder school. But, in deciding to whom the offers of places should be made, the governors did not give preference to those children. The Ombudsman found therefore that the governors did not properly apply the stated admissions policy in making the offers. He also found that, if the criteria had been properly applied, Tom would have been offered a place.

Appeal committee

5. The Ombudsman found that two members of the appeal committee did not appear to be familiar with the contents of the *Code of practice on admission appeals*, and only one member had received training. The Ombudsman commented:

> '*In my opinion, it is the responsibility of governors to ensure that members of appeal committees are given sufficient training to understand the Code and the need to have regard to it.*'

6. After the appeal hearings, the appeal committee met the headteacher privately and asked if she would admit additional children. The headteacher agreed she would admit four more children and the appeal committee then decided to allow four appeals. The Ombudsman pointed out that the function of appeal committees was to make decisions. It was improper for the appeal committee to ask the headteacher if she would admit more children; and it was also improper for this discussion to take place in the absence of the appellants.

7. The clerk was not present after the hearings to advise the appeal committee and to record the committee's decisions and the reasons for them. Neither appeal committee members nor the clerk retained manuscript notes of what was said at the hearings. A document described as the minutes of the hearing contained no record of whether the appeal committee considered that prejudice to efficient education or the efficient use of resources would arise if any appeal was allowed. But, the Ombudsman said, reaching a decision on that question was a crucial part of the process and the committee's decision should have been properly recorded.

Outcome

8. Mr and Mrs Jackson were caused injustice. They were denied a place for Tom at the school of their preference and it should not have been necessary for them to make an appeal or a complaint to the Ombudsman.

9. Tom had transferred to an alternative school and Mr and Mrs Jackson did not wish to move him. The Ombudsman recommended that the governors should pay Mr and Mrs Jackson £500.

(Report 99/A/1972)

. . .

D15: NUISANCE FROM NEIGHBOURS

Failure to investigate properly

1. Mr and Mrs A complained that a council failed to deal adequately with their complaints about unacceptable behaviour by a council tenant living next door to them.

What happened

2. Mr and Mrs A complained that over a 12 year period they and their family suffered harassment, abuse, threats of violence and unacceptable behaviour from their neighbour, Mrs B. Mr A appealed to the council for help.

3. Mrs B denied the allegations. The council took the view that there was no independent evidence supporting Mr A's complaints. It concluded on a number of occasions that it was not in a position to take legal action against Mrs B for breach of her tenancy agreement.

4. Mr A complained to the Ombudsman that, even when he provided the council with evidence to support his complaints, the council failed to investigate the evidence properly or at all.

The Ombudsman's view

5. The Ombudsman found that the council had indeed failed to take proper account of the evidence Mr A had presented.

6. Mr A's solicitor stated that he had been attacked by Mrs B but the council did not interview the solicitor. Neither did the council contact the police who had been called to the incident.

7. While Mr and Mrs A were away on holiday on one occasion, their front door was daubed with red paint. Neighbours called the police who investigated the matter. Mr A told the council that red paint was also found on Mrs B's gatepost and he thought this was evidence that she was involved. There was no evidence that the council investigated the incident.

8. Mr A obtained a graphologist's report about various letters which had been received either by him or other neighbours which appeared to have been sent by Mrs B. Some of the letters were abusive or offensive. One of the letters was signed by Mrs B, while others had allegedly been signed by other neighbours or by one of Mr and Mrs A's sons. Some of the letters were unsigned. The conclusion of the graphologist was that all the letters had been written by the same person. It was Mr A's contention that the letters and the report supported his complaints about Mrs B's bizarre and threatening behaviour. There was no evidence that the council had considered the contents of the report.

9. On several occasions the council stated that third party evidence was required. But when third party evidence was provided the council had been reluctant to examine it. The council had not interviewed other neighbours who sent in complaints about Mrs B.

10. Police took action about an incident when Mrs B was seen vandalising a neighbour's car. The court case had to be withdrawn when the witness declined to testify. But the council did not investigate other ways of using the witness statement and did not interview the witness or his parents.

11. The Ombudsman concluded that the council's failure, over several years to carry out proper investigation of complaints by Mr and Mrs A and others amounted to maladministration.

Injustice

12. The Ombudsman could not conclude that, even if the council had made more extensive enquiries and interviewed witnesses, there would have been sufficient evidence to support a successful application to the court. So there was no guarantee that an order for possession would have been made.

13. But various opportunities to consider commencing proceedings had been lost. Mr and Mrs A suffered continuing uncertainty about their housing situation over a number of years and could reasonably believe that the council did not take their complaints seriously. They were put to much time and trouble in pursuing their complaints.

Outcome

14. The Ombudsman recommended that the council should:

- make Mr A a payment of £2,000 for his time and trouble in pursuing the complaint and the distress suffered by him and his family;
- complete its investigations into more recent complaints by Mr A, provide him with a full report of its findings, and investigate fully any future allegations against Mrs B and take action as appropriate; and
- review its procedures to ensure that allegations of antisocial behaviour were looked into thoroughly, properly and fairly.

(Report 99/B/2476)

. . .

H1: LIABILITY

Dispute over liability – delay – court action – legal costs

1. Mr Scott complained that a council failed to compensate him for inconvenience and cost which he incurred as a result of wrongful recovery action in respect of council tax for which he was not liable.

Tenancies

2. Mr Scott owned a house which he let out to tenants. The council told him in March 1998 that it had designated the property as a house in multiple occupation (HMO) and that he was liable to pay £1,116 in respect of council tax.

3. Mr Scott wrote three letters to the council disputing that the house was an HMO. Seven weeks after the third letter the council replied and asked him for some information about the tenancies. Mr Scott promptly supplied the information.

4. The council did not act on that information until July 1999, when it decided that Mr Scott was not liable for the tax.

Court action

5. In the meantime, in January 1999, Mr Scott was served with a summons to attend the magistrates' court because the council tax bill was unpaid.

6. Mr Scott instructed a solicitor who attended the court and discussed Mr Scott's case with a council officer. The officer agreed that the summons should not have been issued, and withdrew it.

7. The solicitor said he was advised by the council's officer to write to the council about costs. The solicitor presented the council with a claim for costs which the council declined to pay. The council's reason was that the costs occurred only as a result of Mr Scott's decision to instruct a solicitor to represent him, rather than dealing with the matter himself.

8. In the investigation the Ombudsman found that the letter and documents which Mr Scott sent to the council in November 1998 had been separated from his main file and were not found until June 1999. The council accepted that, if the papers had been consulted earlier, its view that Mr Scott was responsible for council tax would have been withdrawn before the issue of the summons.

The Ombudsman's view

9. The Ombudsman said that the delay in dealing with the information which Mr Scott sent the council at its request was unreasonable and amounted to maladministration.

10. The Ombudsman said it was reasonable for Mr Scott to instruct a solicitor to defend him. Accordingly, the council's maladministration caused Mr Scott injustice: his solicitor's cost and his own time and trouble.

Remedy

11. The Ombudsman recommended that the council should pay Mr Scott his legal costs of £940, together with £100 for his time and trouble.

(Report 99/A/3513)

. . .

J4: GRANT OF PERMISSION

Redevelopment – effect on existing property

1. Ms X complained that a council failed to take into account the effect of a new housing development on the amenity of her property.

2. Ms X was a council tenant. Part of the estate on which she lived was proposed for redevelopment as a housing action trust estate. Ms X's property was not part of the area proposed for redevelopment.

Investigation

3. After considering the evidence from the council's files and an interview with the case officer, the Ombudsman took the view that the council had failed to take proper account of the effect that the proposed development would have on Ms X's home, and that the development did not meet the council's normal planning standards.

4. The development had caused loss of daylight and sunlight to Ms X's garden and living room. The Ombudsman thought that, if proper consideration had been given to the impact on her home, the council could and would have sought amendments to the proposals which would probably have led to the house on the adjacent plot being set further back so as to minimise its impact.

Outcome

5. The council accepted that there had been an adverse effect on Ms X's home as a result of the failure to give proper consideration to the impact of the new development.

6. The council agreed to pay compensation of £1,000 to Ms X to recognise her continuing loss of amenity, and £200 for her time and trouble in pursuing her complaint.

(Local settlement 99/A/2945)

. . .

J10: GRANT OF PERMISSION

Publicity – vacant site – information for committee

1. Mr Vestry complained about the way a council dealt with two planning applications for the erection of a domestic store on land adjacent to his own.

2. He complained, in particular, that he was not notified of the first planning application and so could not make his objections known; and that the planning committees which approved both applications were not aware of the proximity of the development to the house he intended to build on his land.

Publicity

3. The council received a planning application to demolish some existing structures and build a garage and store.

4. The council posted a site notice. In addition, it sent letters of notification to a number of houses in the vicinity of the site.

5. Mr Vestry's land was undeveloped. He had bought the plot with the benefit of full planning permission for a detached bungalow which had been granted to the previous owner.

6. Mr Vestry knew nothing of the application until the owner of a neighbouring property contacted him to ask what he was building at the bottom of his garden. Mr Vestry found that the new development was some 1.8 metres from the boundary of his plot. He complained that the council should have ensured that he was notified of the application.

7. The council said that, as the plot was undeveloped, it was impossible to post a neighbour notification and it was unreasonable to expect officers to attempt to trace the owners of vacant land. The council said that the planning file for the plot would only have revealed the planning application submitted by the previous owner.

8. The Ombudsman accepted the council's view that it was unreasonable to expect the council to track down the owners of vacant land in order to notify them of planning applications on nearby land.

Committee report

9. The Ombudsman was, however, critical of the fact that the report to the planning committee about the application did not mention that there was an extant planning permission for a bungalow on Mr Vestry's plot.

10. The Ombudsman considered it likely that, if the planning committee had been properly informed of the planning permission for development on Mr Vestry's land, it would not have approved the storage shed so close to the boundary.

11. The Ombudsman was not critical of the way the council handled a second planning application. That second application was required because it was found that the shed was not being built in accordance with the approved plans.

Outcome

12. The Ombudsman considered that the injustice to Mr Vestry was the lost opportunity to have the storage shed located further away. The council was recommended to pay Mr Vestry £2,500.

(Report 99/C/920)

. . .

K8: SOCIAL WORK SUPPORT

Suspension of support – failure to act in an emergency – complaints procedure

1. Mrs Cork complained that a council failed to provide her with appropriate support for some two-and-a-half years; failed to respond appropriately when she was admitted to hospital; and failed to deliver a proper service for almost a year after that.

Family situation

2. Mrs Cork was a single parent living with her four children. The two youngest, Matthew and David, suffered from Attention Deficit Hyperactivity Disorder. Matthew also had a form of autism and learning difficulties. Both boys had severe behavioural difficulties which could only be partially controlled by drug therapy. Mrs Cork suffered from epileptic seizures brought on by stress.

3. The family had been known to the council's social services department for many years. The council arranged nursery care for David until he started primary school. Matthew was provided with a form of temporary fostering to give Mrs Cork some respite. That arrangement ended when there were problems finding a suitable placement. Despite requests from Mrs Cork she received no further support from social services for some two-and-a-half years. She collapsed as a result of stress and was admitted to hospital.

Emergency

4. Medical staff contacted the council to ask that the family should be visited, as Matthew and David and their older brother were being cared for by their sister Debbie. Debbie was 16 at the time.

5. Instead of visiting to assess the situation, a council officer telephoned and decided, after speaking to Debbie, that she could manage. Amongst the responsibilities Debbie was assuming was the administration of medication to Matthew and David. No visit was made to the family home for four days.

6. Two months later the council offered some help to Mrs Cork which she thought was unsuitable for the boys' needs. No other provision was made and the council failed to review the case after six months, as required by its own procedures.

Complaint

7. Mrs Cork made a formal complaint to the council. This led to consideration at the final stage by a review panel.

8. The review panel upheld Mrs Cork's complaints and commented that the social services' record in relation to the family had to rank as one of the worst on record.

9. The panel considered that the service to the family had been nonexistent for the two-and-a-half years before Mrs Cork was admitted to hospital. After that, apart from the allocation of a social worker, the panel could find no evidence of any significant change in the family's situation.

10. The review panel made 16 recommendations to the council. The council accepted them and apologised.

Complaint to the Ombudsman

11. Mrs Cork then complained to the Ombudsman because she did not believe that apologies were a sufficient remedy, and because she hoped that steps could be taken to ensure that the same did not happen to someone else.

12. The council then considered the question of compensation and decided to offer £12,000 to the family.

13. The Ombudsman concluded that the review panel's concern was justified and that the forceful language it used to describe the shortcomings of the council's performance was not exaggerated.

14. The Ombudsman also concluded the council's poor handling of the matter had been compounded by the fact that Mrs Cork had to exhaust the council's complaints procedure and then complain to the Ombudsman before obtaining a full remedy for the mistreatment of her family.

15. The Ombudsman accepted that the compensation proposed by the council was reasonable.

(Report 00/C/575)

SECTION 2: **Access to the Ombudsman**

Parliamentary Commissioner Act 1967

5.—(1) Subject to the provisions of this section, the Commissioner may investigate any action taken by or on behalf of a government department or other authority to which this Act applies, being action taken in the exercise of administrative functions of that department or authority, in any case where—

    (a) a written complaint is duly made to a member of the House of Commons by a member of the public who claims to have sustained injustice in consequence of maladministration in connection with the action so taken; and

    (b) the complaint is referred to the Commissioner, with the consent of the person who made it, by a member of that House with a request to conduct an investigation thereon.

6.—(3) A complaint shall not be entertained under this Act unless it is made to a member of the House of Commons not later than twelve months from the day on which the person aggrieved first had notice of the matters alleged in the complaint; but the Commissioner may conduct an investigation pursuant to a complaint not made within that period if he considers that there are special circumstances which make it proper to do so.

Local Government Act 1974

26.—(2) A complaint shall not be entertained under this Part of this Act unless it is made in writing to the Local Commissioner specifying the action alleged to constitute maladministration or—

(a) it is made in writing to a member of the authority, or of any other authority concerned, specifying the action alleged to constitute maladministration, and

(b) it is referred to the Local Commissioner, with the consent of the person aggrieved, or of a person acting on his behalf, by that member, or by any other person who is a member of any authority concerned, with a request to investigate the complaint.

(3) If the Local Commissioner is satisfied that any member of any authority concerned has been requested to refer the complaint to a Local Commissioner and has not done so, the Local Commissioner may, if he thinks fit, dispense with the requirements in subsection (2)(b) above.

(4) A complaint shall not be entertained unless it was made to the Local Commissioner or a member of any authority concerned within twelve months from the day on which the person aggrieved first had notice of the matters alleged in the complaint, but a Local Commissioner may conduct an investigation pursuant to a complaint not made within that period if he considers that it is reasonable to do so.

(5) Before proceeding to investigate a complaint, a Local Commissioner shall satisfy himself that the complaint has been brought, by or on behalf of the person aggrieved, to the notice of the authority to which the complaint relates and that that authority has been afforded a reasonable opportunity to investigate, and reply to, the complaint.

NOTE: The tables below set out the number of complaints made to the Parliamentary Commissioner and the Local Commissioners.

Number of complaints made to the Parliamentary Commissioner

Year	Number of complaints
1984	837
1985	759
1986	719
1987	677
1988	701*
1989	677
1990	704
1991	801
1992	945
1993	986
1994	1,332
1995	1,706
1996	1,920
1997/98	1,459†
1998/99	1,506
1999/00	1,612
2000/01	1,721

* During this year the PCA received several hundred complaints from investors who were affected by the collapse of Barlow Clowes. The PCA decided to treat these complaints as a single investigation. If he had treated each complaint separately, then the total number would have been increased by several hundred, and the number of MPs who referred complaints would have been increased to 424.

† The PCA decided to report on the basis of the financial year rather than the calendar year.

Number of complaints made to the Local Commissioners

Year	Number of complaints
1983/84	3,034
1984/85	3,389
1985/86	3,502
1986/87	4,059
1987/88	4,229
1988/89	7,055
1989/90	8,733
1990/91	9,169
1991/93	12,123
1992/93	13,307
1993/94	14,253
1994/95	15,525
1995/96	15,266
1996/97	15,322
1997/98	14,969
1998/99	15,653
1999/00	17,555
2000/01	19,179

QUESTION

The number of complaints to the Local Commissioners has grown rapidly in recent years. Why has there been no comparable growth in the number of complaints made to the Parliamentary Commissioner? The notes which follow may provide some assistance in answering this question (see further G. Drewry and C. Harlow, 'A "Cutting Edge"? The Parliamentary Commissioner and MPs' [1990] 53 MLR, 745).

NOTE: Both the PCA and the Local Commissioners have attracted criticism on the ground that the public is insufficiently aware of their existence. In his 1988 Annual Report, the PCA devoted a separate paragraph to publicity.

As in previous years, I continued to provide to the media press notices on each occasion (usually quarterly) that I published a selection of my investigation reports. I also took such opportunities as arose for the giving of press, radio and television interviews as well as undertaking (as did members of my staff) speaking engagements to various public and private audiences about the work of the office. The Central Office of Information continued to provide me with valuable help in this connection – not least in ensuring the availability in Citizens Advice Bureaux and Public Libraries up and down the country of our booklet 'Can the Parliamentary Ombudsman help you?' One subject which attracted considerable publicity during the second half of the year was the referral to me by numerous Members of complaints (and my acceptance of them in November, for investigation) against the Department of Trade and Industry about the Barlow Clowes affair. . . .

QUESTION

Can you think of any other ways of publicizing the work of the ombudsmen?

NOTES:
1. As the PCA points out in this extract, it is sometimes the case that a particular complaint generates greater public awareness of the institution of the Ombudsman. In 1988 the PCA accepted that he had jurisdiction to investigate complaints into the Department of Trade's

handling of investigations into the investment group Barlow Clowes. The Department of Trade and Industry had allowed Barlow Clowes to operate without a licence for ten years and later issued it with a licence when it had concerns about the operation of the group. When the company was wound up in 1988, 18,000 investors were affected, many of whom complained to the Ombudsman in the hope that he would recommend compensation for them. The publication of the Ombudsman's report in December 1989 made headline news (see, for example, *The Times* and the *Independent* on 20 December 1989). He found that there were five areas in which there had been significant maladministration by the Department, and that the complainants had sustained injustice in consequence of maladministration. Although the Government stated that it did not accept the findings of maladministration it stated that it would offer substantial compensation to the investors. The Ombudsman concluded that it could not be said that the Government's proposals would not constitute a fair remedy for the injustice which had been suffered. The Ombudsman, who was then Sir Anthony Barrowclough, is reported to have said that the case was the most complicated he had had to deal with by 'a very, very long chalk' (*Financial Times*, 20 December 1989). Further details may be found in *First Report of the Parliamentary Commissioner for Administration of Session 1989–90, The Barlow Clowes Affair*. The issues arising from the Ombudsman's investigations are discussed by R. Gregory and G. Drewry, 'Barlow Clowes and the Ombudsman' [1991] *Public Law*, at pp. 192–215 and pp. 408–43.

2. The Select Committee on the PCA in its 1993 report on *The Powers, Work and Jurisdiction of the Ombudsman* (HC 33 of 1993–94) recommended that instead of speculation about the level of public awareness of the Ombudsman there should be a survey on this topic as part of a general programme of research into the work and effectiveness of the Ombudsman system. Subsequent surveys have shown that awareness is at its highest in male, white, white-collar, southern, middle-aged people. The committee also thought that the publication of a newsletter summarizing cases of interest might aid the publicity of the work of the PCA amongst the public and MPs. The committee urged continuous appraisal of methods of publicity and an exploration of all those ways that might foster increased accessibility.

3. When the PCA was established, the office was conceived as one assisting MPs in their work on behalf of their constituents. Consumer groups and academic commentators have been in favour of direct access but MPs have tended to prefer retention of their role as 'filter' to the PCA.

Review of the Public Sector Ombudsmen in England
Cabinet Office (P. Collcut, M. Hourihan) 2000, pp. 29–31

The Case for Change
3.42 During the course of this chapter we have set out a number of the arguments put forward in favour of or against the MP filter and the issue has been looked at in great depth in the past. We note in particular the inquiry by the PCA Select Committee in 1993 which summarised the benefits of the MP filter in words from a report by the Select Committee in 1978: '. . . the Committee concluded that the filter worked to the advantage of:

(a) the complainant, because his problem can often be resolved quickly through the intervention of a Member;
(b) the Member, because he is kept in touch with the problems which his constituents are facing in their daily contact with the machinery of the State; and
(c) the Commissioner, because he is normally asked to investigate only complaints that the Member has been, or knows that he will be, unable to resolve himself.'

We have had difficulty, however, in seeing the consistency of these arguments with the evidence presented to us during the review. In the case of complainants, representative groups have argued that complainants' interests would be better served without the filter. Our survey and other evidence have shown that a very small proportion of MPs' contacts with their constituents is associated with use of the ombudsman. Both the current PCA and previous PCA have expressed the opinion that the MP filter should go.

3.43 One of the arguments in favour of the MP filter set out at the inception of the PCA was the constitutional principle of the MP representing his constituent against the executive in seeking redress for his grievances. We believe that the situation has now moved on. Modernisation of government and constitutional change have brought many means by which the citizen with a grievance can seek redress. New attitudes to customer service, organisational complaints systems including independent complaints examiners, increased use of judicial review, the Human Rights Act, Freedom of Information legislation and not least the creation of other ombudsmen, the HSC and CLA where there is no filter – all of these provide or will provide means for an aggrieved citizen to seek redress from public authorities. The MP filter has become inconsistent and anachronistic when set in this wider context.

3.44 The second reason for the MP filter which was put forward at the inception of the PCA was to prevent the PCA from being swamped by complaints. The MP was to be the 'gatekeeper' who would decide whether a complaint merited attention and would best be dealt with by asking the PCA to investigate. Many of the criticisms of the MP filter concern the consistency with which the gatekeeper operates and ultimately are about fairness. There are many MPs who take great trouble to assist their constituents, helping them to find the best way forward with their complaint. But how MPs use the PCA is up to them – they can bar all access, refer complaints mechanically or operate strictly as a filter. They can filter out the frivolous but they do not have to. They can take an active interest in the investigation and any report, or simply act as a post box for the complainant. What happens depends on the MP – each sets his or her own policy for the gatekeeper role.

3.45 Our survey suggests that in the majority of cases the constituent takes the initiative and many MPs (51%) said they always referred complaints to the PCA on request. A significant number of MPs said they were confused about arrangements and this is likely to reduce their ability to help complainants. Whether the complainant has access also depends on their willingness to approach their MP. The 1967 Act was deliberately designed to allow access through any MP but this adds a further step in the process.

3.46 The PCA's enquiries unit currently receives around 1,000 letters and 7,000 telephone enquiries each year from members of the public and others such as MPs, some of which are attempts to lodge a complaint. At present, these complainants will be routed elsewhere – many to their MPs, some of whom will return. Complainants who have exhausted departmental complaints systems are routed via MPs to the PCA. Complainants also come into the system from other sources such as through the Data Protection Registrar's office – again for the PCA to take the complaint it must be referred on by an MP. If the MP filter were removed the 'gatekeeper' role would transfer to the PCA's office and a consistent policy could be applied for the management of complaints which would be transparent to complainants. We would expect the number of complaints to be submitted to the PCA to increase but the impact on the PCA would not amount to 'swamping'. The PCA's office is already involved in handling many more contacts with the public than the 1,500 new complaints submitted through MPs each year suggest. The new approaches that we recommend later will allow a managed approach to dealing with the demand.

3.47 A further point made in favour of retaining the MP filter is that the MP has a wider range of 'tools' available to assist the citizen seeking redress. Research (for example, Gregory and Alexander in 1973) has looked at different Parliamentary techniques for seeking redress of grievances including through the PCA. The evidence we have seen shows that a letter to a Minister is the most likely 'tool' to be used. Annual surveys by the Cabinet Office show that Ministers receive around 200,000 letters each year, mainly from MPs. In contrast, the PCA receives about 1,500 new complaints each year. Gregory and Alexander also looked at perceptions of effectiveness – over 70% of MPs judged a letter to a minister as 'effective or highly effective' against 22% judging the PCA accordingly. Although the research was carried out some time ago the volume of letters to Ministers and replies to our survey suggests that letters to ministers may still be regarded as more effective.

3.48 The PCA was originally introduced to add a further powerful tool for MPs, to be used when other means such as a letter to a minister were found or thought likely to be ineffective. The PCA as an investigator would be able to get behind what was publicly stated, see the papers and interview officials. A comparison cannot be made on an equal basis with other tools available to the MP since resort to the PCA was always seen as being a relatively uncommon event and would probably involve difficult cases with much effort needed to resolve them. The key issue is whether removing the MP filter would mean that complainants were sent to the PCA when an MP could have got speedier redress more easily by use of another tool.

3.49 Removing the MP filter does not necessarily remove the MP. Constituents could still be referred to the PCA and the PCA's office might advise many enquirers that going to their MP was a good way forward. Removing the filter would simply remove going to the MP as a mandatory step in complaining to the PCA. We believe that many citizens will still prefer to go to their MP – the MP can act as an advocate, has a broader range of options to provide assistance ranging from personal knowledge and contacts to influencing change in the law, has no legislated restrictions on jurisdiction and can provide a personal and direct touch. The constituency workload for many MPs is heavy and some may appreciate some lightening of the load though we think it unlikely that the loss of the MP filter would have a substantial impact – at most a few complaints for each MP each year would be diverted.

3.50 The MP filter acts not only as a restriction on access to the PCA but also continues to affect the process subsequently. The PCA as the 'instrument' of the MP regards the MP not the complainant as the 'customer' for his work. The 1967 Act has been drawn up in such a way that the PCA by law provides his report to the MP. The emphasis is on investigation rather than resolution of the complaint. Again, this is built into the 1967 Act. The result is a distortion of the ombudsman's process. In recent years the PCA has started to move towards the approach used by other ombudsmen of trying to achieve early resolution through informal means – we were given an example by his office of a case which was settled in 6 weeks as opposed to an estimated 10 to 12 months if an investigation had been carried out. The MP filter itself is estimated to add at least a month to the overall process because of the practical arrangements for communication, and impedes contact generally with the complainant (see 3.36). It also can add to the burdens on MPs because of the considerable paperwork added to the flow through their office and adds restrictions to how MPs use the PCA – only one way is built into the legislation. The survey (and various research) has shown that MPs have many different attitudes and preferences about how they work. The relationship between MPs and the PCA should be more flexible so that the level of involvement which an MP wishes to retain in a case can be accommodated.

3.51 The MP filter is also an instrument of accountability. An individual MP is able to hold the executive to account through the PCA's process – a department is required to respond to a statement of complaint and the report at the end of an investigation is provided to an MP who may wish to take action using it. We agree that in a serious case – where there is serious injustice to an individual or widespread injustice, serious maladministration, refusal by a department to remedy a clear injustice and so on – it is right that this it is publicised and steps taken to ensure redress is provided and any systemic problems addressed. The absence of the MP filter does not prevent the MP being involved (as discussed above) in lodging a complaint nor, with the agreement of the complainant, becoming involved after a complaint has been made. For example, if a decision to conduct an investigation is made the PCA could, with the agreement of the complainant, contact the relevant MP. Accountability can also be maintained through general oversight and reporting mechanisms to meet concerns of individual MPs about what is happening in their constituencies. For example, statistical summaries or copies of relevant reports for constituencies might be made available.

3.52 Much of the case which has been presented so far for removal of the MP filter could have been made at any time during the existence of the PCA but change has not been forthcoming. The case for removing the MP filter is strong but recent developments in constitutional change and Modernising Government have substantially strengthened it. Of all the changes taking place we believe the growth of partnerships has the most significant implications. Partnerships are being set up between central and local government providing combined services to the citizen through one-stop shops – for example, combining local authority delivered benefits services with Employment Service and Benefits Agency services. It will become increasingly difficult and in some cases not possible to untangle the jurisdictional issues. Our survey showed that this was an area of difficulty now for MPs and the situation will get worse. **We believe that the MP filter can no longer be sustained in an era of joined up government and we strongly recommend that it is abolished.**

Consequences of removal

3.53 We have already discussed to some extent the consequences of removal. We expect that the numbers of complaints to the PCA (or rather, as discussed later, to the successor Commission we propose) will increase – this is a natural consequence of removing what many argue is a barrier and inhibitor of use of the PCA by the citizen. The level and patterns of increase can only be speculated about. We have referred to the experience of the CLA when the councillor filter was removed – an immediate 44% increase resulted. Past runs of figures for the number of complaints made directly by the public to the PCA (which he is unable to deal with and must therefore refer on) are typically a littler higher than the actual number of complaints submitted through MPs. Allowing for some double counting – some complaints made direct to the PCA will be returned by the MP – we would expected on this basis that complaints might double on removal of the filter. Beyond this, much will depend on other circumstances such as the extent to which awareness of the ombudsman increases, services are improved and barriers removed.

3.54 An increased number of cases will not necessarily increase proportionately the effort needed by the ombudsmen to address them. We would expect the increase in complaints to be mostly in the less serious cases. But there are substantial efficiency gains to be made from better management of cases and from removing the restrictiveness of the current 1967 Act. The consequence of the increased number of cases would not be a need for increased resources in proportion.

NOTE: The removal of the 'MP filter' has been accepted by the Government (HC Debs 20 July 2001, written answers col. 464w) and the 'MSP filter' in Scotland was removed in the Scottish Public Services Ombudsman Act 2002.

QUESTION

Apart from discontinuing the MP filter, by what other means can access to the PCA be strengthened and enlarged?

SECTION 3: **Jurisdiction of the Ombudsman**

Parliamentary Commissioner Act 1967

4.—(1) Subject to the provisions of this section and to the notes contained in Schedule 2 to this Act, this Act applies to the government departments, corporations and unincorporated bodies listed in that Schedule; and references in this Act to an authority to which this Act applies are references to any such corporation or body.

(2) Her Majesty may by Order in Council amend Schedule 2 to this Act by the alteration of any entry or note, the removal of any entry or note or the insertion of any additional entry or note.

(3) An Order in Council may only insert an entry if—

    (a) it relates—

        (i) to a government department; or

        (ii) to a corporation or body whose functions are exercised on behalf of the Crown; or

    (b) it relates to a corporation or body—

        (i) which is established by virtue of Her Majesty's prerogative or by an Act of Parliament or an Order in Council or order made under an Act of Parliament or which is established in any other way by a Minister of the Crown in his capacity as a Minister or by a government department;

        (ii) at least half of whose revenues derive directly from money provided by Parliament, a levy authorised by an enactment, a fee or charge of any other description so authorised or more than one of those sources; and

        (iii) which is wholly or partly constituted by appointment made by Her Majesty or a Minister of the Crown or government department.

(3A) No entry shall be made if the result of making it would be that the Parliamentary Commissioner could investigate action which can be investigated by the Welsh Administration Ombudsman under Schedule 9 to the Government of Wales Act 1998.

(3B) No entry shall be made in respect of—

    (a) the Scottish Administration or any part of it;

    (b) any Scottish public authority with mixed functions or no reserved functions within the meaning of the Scotland Act 1998; or

    (c) the Scottish Parliamentary Corporate Body.

(4) No entry shall be made in respect of a corporation or body whose sole activity is, or whose main activities are, included among the activities specified in subsection (5) below.

(5) The activities mentioned in subsection (4) above are—

    (a) the provision of education, or the provision of training otherwise than under the Industrial Training Act 1982;

    (b) the development of curricula, the conduct of examinations or the validation of educational courses;

    (c) the control of entry to any profession or the regulation of the conduct of members of any profession;

    (d) the investigation of complaints by members of the public regarding the actions of any person or body, or the supervision or review of such investigations or of steps taken following them.

(6) No entry shall be made in respect of a corporation or body operating in an exclusively or predominantly commercial manner or a corporation carrying on under national ownership an industry or undertaking or part of an industry or undertaking.

(7) Any statutory instrument made by virtue of this section shall be subject to annulment in pursuance of a resolution of either House of Parliament.

5.—(2) Except as hereinafter provided, the Commissioner shall not conduct an investigation under this Act in respect of any of the following matters, that is to say—

(a) any action in respect of which the person aggrieved has or had a right of appeal, reference or review to or before a tribunal constituted by or under any enactment or by virtue of Her Majesty's prerogative;

(b) any action in respect of which the person aggrieved has or had a remedy by way of proceedings in any court of law:

Provided that the Commissioner may conduct an investigation notwithstanding that the person aggrieved has or had such a right or remedy if satisfied that in the particular circumstances it is not reasonable to expect him to resort or have resorted to it.

(3) Without prejudice to subsection (2) of this section, the Commissioner shall not conduct an investigation under this Act in respect of any such action or matter as is described in Schedule 3 to this Act.

(4) Her Majesty may by Order in Council amend the said Schedule 3 so as to exclude from the provisions of that Schedule such actions or matters as may be described in the Order; and any statutory instrument made by virtue of this subsection shall be subject to annulment in pursuance of a resolution of either House of Parliament.

(5) In determining whether to initiate, continue or discontinue an investigation under this Act, the Commissioner shall, subject to the foregoing provisions of this section, act in accordance with his own discretion; and any question whether a complaint is duly made under this Act shall be determined by the Commissioner.

(5A) For the purposes of this section, administrative functions of a government department to which this Act applies include functions exercised by the department on behalf of the Scottish Ministers by virtue of section 93 of the Scotland Act 1998.

(5B) The Commissioner shall not conduct an investigation under this Act in respect of any action concerning Scotland and not relating to reserved matters which is taken by or on behalf of a cross-border public authority within the meaning of the Scotland Act 1998.

(6) For the purposes of this section, the administrative functions exercisable by any person appointed by the Lord Chancellor as a member of the administrative staff of any court or tribunal shall be taken to be administrative functions of the Lord Chancellor's Department or, in Northern Ireland, of the Northern Ireland Court Service.

SCHEDULE 3   MATTERS NOT SUBJECT TO INVESTIGATION

1. Action taken in matters certified by a Secretary of State or other Minister of the Crown to affect relations or dealings between the Government of the United Kingdom and any other Government or any international organisation of States or Governments.

2. Action taken, in any country or territory outside the United Kingdom, by or on behalf of any officer representing or acting under the authority of Her Majesty in respect of the United Kingdom, or any other officer of the Government of the United Kingdom other than action which is taken by an officer (not being an honorary consular officer) in the exercise of a consular function on behalf of the Government of the United Kingdom and which is so taken in relation to a citizen of the United Kingdom.

3. Action taken in connection with the administration of the government of any country or territory outside the United Kingdom which forms part of Her Majesty's dominions or in which Her Majesty has jurisdiction.

4. Action taken by the Secretary of State under the Extradition Act 1870 or the Fugitive Offenders Act 1881 or the Extradition Act 1989.

5. Action taken by or with the authority of the Secretary of State for the purposes of investigating crime or of protecting the security of the State, including action so taken with respect to passports.

6. The commencement or conduct of civil or criminal proceedings before any court of law in the United Kingdom, of proceedings at any place under the Naval Discipline Act 1957, the Army Act 1955 or the Air Force Act 1955, or of proceedings before any international court or tribunal.

6A. Action taken by any person appointed by the Lord Chancellor as a member of the administrative staff of any court or tribunal, so far as that action is taken at the direction, or on the authority (whether express or implied) of any person acting in a judicial capacity or in his capacity as a member of the tribunal.

6B.—(1) Action taken by any member of the administrative staff of a relevant tribunal, so far as that action is taken at the direction, or on the authority (whether express or implied), of any person acting in his capacity as a member of the tribunal.

(2) In this paragraph, 'relevant tribunal' has the meaning given by section 5(8) of this Act.

6C. Action taken by any person appointed under section 5(3)(c) of the Criminal Injuries Compensation Act 1995, so far as that action is taken at the direction, or on the authority (whether express or implied), of any person acting in his capacity as an adjudicator appointed under section 5 of that Act to determine appeals.

7. Any exercise of the prerogative of mercy or of the power of a Secretary of State to make a reference in respect of any person to the High Court of Justiciary or the Courts-Martial Appeal Court.

8.—(1) Action taken on behalf of the Minister of Health or the Secretary of State by a Health Authority, a Primary Care Trust, a Special Health Authority except the Rampton Hospital Review Board . . . the Rampton Hospital Board, the Broadmoor Hospital Board or the Moss Side and Park Lane Hospitals Board, a Health Board or the Common Services Agency for the Scottish Health Service, by the Dental Practice Board or the Scottish Dental Practice Board or by the Public Health Laboratory Service Board.

(2) For the purposes of this paragraph, action taken by a Health Authority, Special Health Authority or Primary Care Trust in the exercise of functions of the Secretary of State shall be regarded as action taken on his behalf.

9. Action taken in matters relating to contractual or other commercial transactions, whether within the United Kingdom or elsewhere, being transactions of a government department or authority to which this Act applies or of any such authority or body as is mentioned in paragraph (a) or (b) of subsection (1) of section 6 of this Act and not being transactions for or relating to—

(a) the acquisition of land compulsorily or in circumstances in which it could be acquired compulsorily;

(b) the disposal as surplus of land acquired compulsorily or in such circumstances as aforesaid.

10. (1) Action taken in respect of appointments or removals, pay, discipline, superannuation or other personnel matters, in relation to—

(a) service in any of the armed forces of the Crown, including reserve and auxiliary and cadet forces;

(b) service in any office or employment under the Crown or under any authority to which this Act applies; or

(c) service in any office or employment, or under any contract for services, in respect of which power to take action, or to determine or approve the action to be taken, in such matters is vested in Her Majesty, any Minister of the Crown or any such authority as aforesaid . . .

11. The grant of honours, awards or privileges within the gift of the Crown, including the grant of Royal Charters.

Local Government Act 1974

25.—(1) This Part of this Act applies to the following authorities—
  (a) any local authority,
      (aaa) the Greater London Authority;
      (ab) a National Park authority;
  (b) any joint board the constituent authorities of which are all local authorities,
      (ba) the Commission for the New Towns;
      (bb) any development corporation established for the purposes of a new town,
      (bbb) the London Development Agency;
      (bd) any urban development corporation established by an order under section 135 of the Local Government, Planning and Land Act 1980;
      (be) any housing action trust established under Part III of the Housing Act 1988;
      (bf) the Urban Regeneration Agency;
      (bg) a fire authority constituted by a combination scheme under the Fire Services Act 1947;
  (c) any joint authority established by Part IV of the Local Government Act 1985;
      (cza) the London Fire and Emergency Planning Authority;
      (ca) any police authority established under section 3 of the Police Act 1996;
      (caa) the Metropolitan Police Authority;
      (cc) Transport for London;
  (d) in relation to the flood defence functions of the Environment Agency, within the meaning of the Water Resources Act 1991, the Environment Agency and any regional flood defence committee; and
  (e) the London Transport Users' Committee.

(2) Her Majesty may by Order in Council provide that this Part of this Act shall also apply, subject to any modifications or exceptions specified in the Order, to any authority specified in the Order, being an authority which is established by or under an Act of Parliament, and which has power to levy a rate, or to issue a precept.

(3) An Order made by virtue of subsection (2) above may be varied or revoked by a subsequent Order so made and shall be subject to annulment in pursuance of a resolution of either House of Parliament.

(4) Any reference to an authority to which this Part of this Act applies includes a reference—
  (a) to the members and officers of that authority, and
  (b) to any person or body of persons acting for the authority under section 101, or
  (c) any committee mentioned in section 101(9) of the said Act.

(4A) Any reference to an authority to which this Part of this Act applies also includes, in the case of the Greater London Authority, a reference to each of the following—
  (a) the London Assembly;
  (b) any committee of the London Assembly;
  (c) any body or person exercising functions on behalf of the Greater London Authority.

(4B) Any reference to an authority to which this Part of this Act applies also includes, in the case of the London Transport Users' Committee, a reference to a sub-committee of that Committee.

(5) Any reference to an authority to which this Part of this Act applies also includes a reference to—

    (a) a school organisation committee constituted in accordance with section 24 of the School Standards and Framework Act 1998,

    (b) an exclusion appeals panel constituted in accordance with Schedule 18 to that Act,

    (c) an admission appeals panel constituted in accordance with Schedule 24 or paragraph 3 of Schedule 25 to that Act, and

    (d) the governing body of any community, foundation or voluntary school so far as acting in connection with the admission of pupils to the school or otherwise performing any of their functions under Chapter I of Part III of that Act.

(8) Where the authority concerned is the Greater London Authority, any functions exercisable under this section by or in relation to the Authority (other than functions exercisable by or in relation to the proper officer of the Authority) shall be exercisable by or in relation to the Mayor and the Assembly acting jointly on behalf of the Authority, and references to the authority concerned (other than references to the proper officer or a member of the authority concerned) shall be construed accordingly.

26.—(6) A Local Commissioner shall not conduct an investigation under this Part of this Act in respect of any of the following matters, that is to say:

    (a) any action in respect of which the person aggrieved has or had a right of appeal, reference or review to or before a tribunal constituted by or under any enactment;

    (b) any action in respect of which the person aggrieved has or had a right of appeal to a Minister of the Crown or the National Assembly for Wales; or

    (c) any action in respect of which the person aggrieved has or had a remedy by way of proceedings in any court of law:

Provided that a Local Commissioner may conduct an investigation notwithstanding the existence of such a right or remedy if satisfied that in the particular circumstances it is not reasonable to expect the person aggrieved to resort or have resorted to it.

(7) A Local Commissioner shall not conduct an investigation in respect of any action which in his opinion affects all or most of the inhabitants of the . . . area of the authority concerned.

(8) Without prejudice to the preceding provisions of this section, a Local Commissioner shall not conduct an investigation under this Part of this Act in respect of any such action or matter as is described in Schedule 5 to this Act.

(9) Her Majesty may by Order in Council amend the said Schedule 5 so as to add to or exclude from the provisions of that Schedule . . . such actions or matters as may be described in the Order;

[Schedule 5 contains a number of exclusions, including in particular: legal proceedings; investigation or prevention of crime, contractual or commercial transactions (but excluding the acquisition or disposal of land and certain statutory functions other than the procurement of goods and services); personnel matters, and educational matters.]

(10) In determining whether to initiate, continue or discontinue an investigation, a Local Commissioner shall, subject to the preceding provisions of this section, act at discretion; and any questions whether a complaint is duly made under this Part of this Act shall be determined by the Local Commissioner.

NOTES:

1. In 1987 the jurisdiction of the PCA was expanded to include a number of non-departmental bodies. These include the Arts Council, the Red Deer Commission, and the Sports Council. It

was originally stated in the House of Commons that the criteria for inclusion in this list were that the bodies should:

(a) be subject to some degree of ministerial accountability to Parliament because they are dependent for their financing and continuing existence on Government policy; and

(b) have 'executive or administrative functions that directly affect individual citizens or groups of citizens' (see HC Deb., vol. 112 (6th Series), col. 1081). See now s. 4(3) of the 1967 Act (*ante* at p. 712).

2. The PCA and his Northern Ireland counterpart have had their jurisdiction widened by the addition of the responsibility of investigating complaints of breaches of the Code of Practice on Access to Government Information. This has been brought about on the basis that all departments, agencies and other bodies within the jurisdiction of the PCA (listed in Sch. 2 of the 1967 Act) are subject to the Code and failure to comply with it will amount to maladministration and injustice, which could be delay, an unreasonable charge for the provision of information, a failure to provide information, or the provision of incomplete information. This work will be transferred to the Information Commissioner when the Freedom of Information Act 2000 enters into force and when the Scottish Parliament enacts the Freedom of Information (Scotland) Bill introduced in November 2001.

Figure 4 Cases concluded without completing a statutory investigation 2000–01

	Outcome	Number of cases	per cent (%)
Body complained of outside Ombudsman's jurisdiction	1	77	5
Subject matter of complaint not in jurisdiction[1]	1	22	1.4
Complainant had a right to appeal to a tribunal	2	88	5.7
Complaint not about administrative actions[2]	2	140	9.1
No prima facie evidence of maladministration	2	395	25.6
Ombudsman's discretion not to investigate exercised	2	77	5
Others concluded on the basis of papers[3]	2	77	5
Resolved following enquiries of department	3	565	36.7
Investigation concluded other than by statutory report	4	99	6.4
Total of cases concluded	—	**1540**	**100**

Note Outcomes are explained *post* at pp. 734–35.
1 Includes public service personnel matters and contractual or commercial transactions.
2 Includes complaints about legislation and without consent from the aggrieved.
3 For example, complaint time barred or made by a public body.

A: Contractual and commercial matters

Fourth Report from the Select Committee on the Parliamentary Commissioner for Administration
HC 593 of 1979–80, paras 3, 8

Contractual and Commercial matters
3. In its observations the Government said that it believed that the Parliamentary Commissioner system should operate in the field of the relations between the executive and those whom it governs, and that it would not be in the general interest to extend it to commercial transactions. It did not consider that the commercial activities of Government Departments should be open to

examination while other contracting parties were free from such investigation. In the area of assistance to industry, the Government acknowledged that the dividing line between transactions that were within jurisdiction and those which were not was a difficult one, but it took the view that the use of statutory powers involving a wide measure of commercial discretion should not be subject to review by the Commissioner. . . .

8. We do not accept the Government's contention that only those activities which are unique to the function of government should be subject to review by the Parliamentary Commissioner; rather we believe that in principle all areas of Government administration should be investigable by him unless in particular cases a compelling argument can be made out for their exclusion. Accordingly, the claim that the government's commercial activities should be exempt from examination because private contractors are exempt is in our view beside the point. The Government has a duty to administer its purchasing policies fairly and equitably, and if those policies are the subject of complaint then the complaints should be investigated; this is particularly important if any future Government were again to use the award of contracts as a political weapon. Section 12(3) of the Act would prevent the Commissioner from questioning a *bona fide* commercial decision to purchase goods and services from one firm rather than another, or the legitimate exercise of a Department's discretion to give selective assistance to one firm or one industry rather than another, but if decisions of this kind are taken with maladministration then it is right that they should be reviewed. It was suggested in evidence that the Commissioner would not be able to decide whether maladministration had been committed, but we note the Commissioner's view that that is the kind of judgment that he and his officers are making 'every day of the week.' In any case, a belief that the Commissioner might have difficulty in making such a decision may be thought to be poor ground for refusing him the right to try. It is true that any commercial maladministration by a Department can be investigated by the Exchequer and Audit Department and censured by the Public Accounts Committee, but neither of these bodies is primarily concerned, as the Parliamentary Commissioner is, with any injustice a complainant might have suffered as a result. We are satisfied that sections 5 and 12(3) of the Parliamentary Commissioner Act are sufficient on their own and that the further exemption from investigation conferred by paragraph 9 of Schedule 3 is not justified.

B: Public service personnel matters

Fourth Report from the Select Committee on the Parliamentary Commissioner for Administration
HC 593 of 1979–80, paras 9, 11, 15

Public Service personnel matters
9. In 1978 the Select Committee again recommended that complaints about public service personnel matters, except complaints from serving civil servants and members of the armed forces about discipline, establishment questions and terms of service, should be investigable by the Parliamentary Commissioner. The Government rejected their recommendation, as it had a similar recommendation by the Select Committee in 1977, on the ground that there was no evidence that grievance machinery available to intending, present or former Crown servants was inferior to that available to workers generally. The government also noted that the Parliamentary Commissioner had not been established to deal with relations between the State as employer and its employees. . . .

11. The Commissioner told us that in his view the remedies for grievances about personnel matters which the Government had described to the Select Committee in 1977 were quite illusory. . . .

15. As we have said earlier in this Report, we do not accept the view that the role of the

Parliamentary Commissioner should be restricted to those activities which are unique to the function of government, and so we reject the contention that because not every employee can call upon the Commissioner to enquire into grievances about personnel matters the State's employees should not be able to do so. We accept, as the Commissioner does and as the Committee did in 1978, that the exclusion of complaints from serving public employees about matters of discipline, promotion, rates of pay and terms of service is justified, but we do not consider than any evidence has been produced to show that bringing within jurisdiction other purely administrative acts of Government Departments in their capacity as employers would cause harm to anyone: experience in Northern Ireland bears this out. There has always been evidence of a demand for the Commissioner's services in this area, and the arguments that if they were available a great number of extra complaints might have to be investigated comes perilously close to saying that one ought not to have an Ombudsman at all lest people should complain to him.

NOTES:

1. In its observations on the *Fourth Report* the Government stated that it believed its view on the exclusion of contractual and commercial matters remained sound (see Cmnd 8274 (1981)).

   With regard to the exclusion of public service personnel matters, the Government stated that it remained unpersuaded of the merits of allowing the Parliamentary Commissioner to investigate complaints about recruitment to the Home Civil Service and the Diplomatic Corps and about superannuation. With regard to recruitment, the Government reiterated its view that it is already subject to rigorous scrutiny by an independent body, the Civil Service Commissioners, and further that it would be wrong to give applicants for jobs in the Civil Service a channel for the investigation of complaints which was not open to other employees.

   With regard to superannuation, the Government considered that public service pensioners already had the advantage that their grievances might be raised in either House of Parliament, and that further preferential treatment would be inequitable. The Government also restated its view that the Commissioner was not established to investigate relations between the state as employer and its employees.

2. In his *Annual Report for 1988* the Parliamentary Commissioner for Administration stated, at p. 1:

   I have, naturally, to recognise that Parliament, by the terms of the Parliamentary Commissioner Act, has explicitly excluded from the Parliamentary Commissioner's jurisdiction certain defined categories of administrative action taken by government departments and public bodies. Perhaps the most notable of these excluded areas are action taken in public service personnel matters and 'action taken in matters relating to contractual or other commercial transactions.' In both cases the reasoning was, no doubt, that the Parliamentary Commissioner's proper concern was with complaints *qua* citizen, and not with complaints *qua* employee, or *qua* supplier of goods or services to a department or public body. The wording of the second of the exclusions I have mentioned has however been the cause of some concern and difficulty. That is because the dealings of departments and public bodies with citizens, *qua* citizens, can in some instances take on the appearance – and perhaps the reality – of 'contractual . . . transactions.' Indeed that is particularly so in the case of many of the non-departmental public bodies recently brought within jurisdiction, whose functions will often include the giving of aid or assistance on terms which may well have a contractual flavour. Yet if transactions of that kind are to be regarded as excluded from the Parliamentary Commissioner's scrutiny, I entertain some doubt as to whether it would really reflect Parliament's intentions. This, it seems to me, is an area in which clarification may be needed.

3. There are similar exclusions relating to the jurisdiction of the Local Commissioners (see Local Government Act 1974, Sch. 5). The *Widdicombe Report* urged that there should be a review of the exclusions. It specifically stated that it did not consider that there was a case for the retention of the exclusion of contractual and commercial matters and the appointment of staff.

4. The Scottish Public Services Ombudsman Act 2002 retains both of these exclusions. The Cabinet Office Review did not suggest a change but noted that the requirement of new legislation would provide an opportunity for reconsidering jurisdiction.

QUESTION

On the basis of the extracts from the *Fourth Report of the Select Committee on the Parliamentary Commissioner for Administration*, what are the differences between the Government's view on the proper functions of the PCA and that of the Select Committee?

C: Authorities outside scope

NOTE: The number of authorities coming within the PCA's jurisdiction was increased in 1987 (see *ante* at p. 713–14). Section 110 of the Courts and Legal Services Act 1990 makes it clear that certain aspects of court and tribunal administration fall within the jurisdiction of the Ombudsman; the Ombudsman's jurisdiction does not, however, extend to any action taken at the direction of, or on the authority of, any person acting in a judicial capacity or in a capacity as a member of a tribunal (see s. 5(6) and Sch. 3, para. 6A of the Parliamentary Commissioner Act 1967, *ante* at pp. 713–14).

D: Rights of appeal to a tribunal or remedies in a court

NOTE: Section 5(2) of the Parliamentary Commissioner Act 1967 (*ante* p. 713) refers to both a right of appeal to tribunals and to the jurisdiction of the courts. Yet the reports of the PCA commonly refer to complaints being refused only because there is a right of appeal to a tribunal. It is, however, clear that cases come before the PCA in which there is a possibility of a successful legal challenge in the courts (see, e.g. *Congreve* v *Home Office* [1976] QB 629, *post* at p. 721 and the decision of the PCA to conduct an investigation in the Barlow Clowes case: on the latter case see further R. Gregory and G. Drewry, 'Barlow Clowes and the Ombudsman – Part II' [1991] *Public Law*, 408, at p. 422). This suggests that the PCA tends to exercise his discretion to accept such complaints. Can you think of any reasons why this might be so?

In *Parliamentary Commissioner for Administration: Annual Report for 1980* (HC 148 of 1980–81), the then PCA explained his approach:

> As a matter of practice, where there appears on the face of things to have been a substantial legal wrong for which, if proved, there is a substantial legal remedy, I expect the citizen to seek it in the courts and I tell him so. But where there is doubt about the availability of a legal remedy or where the process of law seems too cumbersome, slow and expensive for the objective to be gained, I exercise my discretion to investigate the complaint myself. For example, I may receive a complaint that a particular tax office has been dilatory and inattentive in issuing an amended assessment of liability to tax. The taxpayer may say that he is worried and anxious about how he stands and that it affects his business. But would it be reasonable for him to take the Inland Revenue to court to obtain an injunction commanding them forthwith to perform their statutory duty, a theoretically available remedy? Surely not. This approach derives validity from the fact that very few people whose complaints have been investigated by my Office have later gone to seek a legal remedy in the courts. So the boundary is reasonably clear and well-observed.

The Local Ombudsmen are reported as considering that it is unreasonable to expect the average person aggrieved to resort to High Court proceedings for review, having regard to their cost and to the limited availability of legal aid. They must, however, comply with the terms of the legislation. In *R* v *Local Commissioner for*

Administration, ex parte Croydon London Borough Council [1989] 1 All ER 1033 the Commissioner was criticized for having failed to appreciate, if not at the outset of his investigation, then as it continued, that the complainant might have had a remedy by way of judicial review. The court held that the Commissioner had not properly considered how he should exercise his discretion under ss. 26(6) and 26(10) of the Local Government Act 1974. Woolf LJ considered that s. 26(6) is directed to the stage where a Commissioner is deciding whether or not to conduct an investigation. He added that if, during an investigation, a Commissioner satis-fies himself that the complainant has a legal remedy, then the Commissioner should consider whether to discontinue it using his discretion under s. 26(10).

In *R v Local Commissioner for Administration in North and North East England, ex parte Liverpool City Council* [2001] All ER 462, the Court of Appeal held, in a com-plaint concerning the non-declaration of interests by councillors voting in the determination of a planning application, that it was a case in which it was appro-priate to exercise discretion and investigate the complaint although there was the possibility that the complaint could have been considered in an application for judicial review. The Commissioner had not considered the possibility of judicial review, thinking that maladministration in the form of a breach of the National Local Government Code of Conduct was not illegality, amenable to judicial review. The Court was of the view that there could have been overlap with illegality, but agreed with the Commissioner's views in an affidavit, that the proviso under s. 26(6) was appropriate as the complainants were unlikely to have the means to pursue judicial review. The Court said that this case was one better suited to the Commis-sioner as her powers of investigation were better equipped for gathering facts than the judicial review process and so she was more likely to provide a just remedy.

One of the cases in which both the powers of the PCA and the courts were invoked concerned television licences. In 1975 some people obtained a new TV licence during the currency of an old one. Subsequently, the licence fee was increased. The people with overlapping licences were asked to pay the difference in fees, in which case their new licence would be made to run for 12 months from the expiry of the old licence. The Home Office stated that otherwise it would revoke the new licence, thereby leaving the old licence to be renewed from the time it expired at the new rate. Later the Home Office introduced a concession: if the holder of the licence so wished, the new licence would only be revoked after the holder had held it for the proportion of the year which the fee he had paid would entitle him to at the new rate.

The PCA investigated the matter and laid a special report before Parliament under s. 10(4) of the 1967 Act. The Home Office had been advised that it was lawfully entitled to revoke the licence. The PCA concluded that to act on this advice could not *per se* constitute maladministration, but that the Home Office had acted with both inefficiency and lack of foresight. No remedy was, however, recommended. One of the holders of an overlapping licence, Mr Congreve, succeeded in having the Home Office's action declared unlawful by the courts (see *Congreve v Home Office* [1976] QB 629).

SECTION 4: **Meaning of Injustice in Consequence of Maladministration**

Parliamentary Commissioner Act 1967

10.—(3) If, after conducting an investigation under this Act, it appears to the Commissioner that injustice has been caused to the person aggrieved in consequence of maladministration and that the injustice has not been, or will not be, remedied, he may, if he thinks fit, lay before each House of Parliament a special report upon the case.

[See also s. 5(1) *ante*, at p. 705.]

12.—(3) It is hereby declared that nothing in this Act authorises or requires the Commissioner to question the merits of a decision taken without maladministration by a government department or other authority in the exercise of a discretion vested in that department or authority. . . .

Local Government Act 1974

26.—(1) Subject to the provisions of this Part of this Act where a written complaint is made by or on behalf of a member of the public who claims to have sustained injustice in consequence of maladministration in connection with action taken by or on behalf of an authority to which this Part of this Act applies, being action taken in the exercise of administrative functions of that authority, a Local Commissioner may investigate that complaint.

. . .

34.—(3) It is hereby declared that nothing in this Part of this Act authorises or requires a Local Commissioner to question the merits of a decision taken without maladministration by an authority in the exercise of a discretion vested in that authority.

Debate on the Second Reading of the Parliamentary Commissioner Bill House of Commons, House of Commons Debates, vol. 734 (18 October 1966), col. 51

MR CROSSMAN: We might have made an attempt . . . to define, by catalogue, all of the qualities which make up maladministration by a civil servant. It would be a wonderful exercise – bias, neglect, inattention, delay, incompetence, inaptitude, perversity, turpitude, arbitrariness and so on. It would be a long and interesting list.

R v *Local Commissioner, ex parte Eastleigh Borough Council*
[1988] 3 WLR 116, Court of Appeal

Eastleigh Borough Council challenged an adverse report of the Local Commissioner on the basis that it sought to challenge a decision taken without maladministration by an authority in the exercise of a discretion vested in the authority. Nolan J held that the ombudsman had indeed exceeded its jurisdiction, but that it would be wrong to make a declaration to that effect. The authority appealed to the Court of Appeal and the Local Commissioner cross-appealed. There were three main issues in the appeal:

(a) Had the Commissioner acted contrary to law in concluding that the council had been guilty of maladministration?

(b) Had the Commissioner acted contrary to law in concluding that such mal-administration, if it had occurred, had caused injustice to the complainant?

(c) If the Commissioner had acted contrary to law in one or both of these respects, should the court grant a remedy?

LORD DONALDSON OF LYMINGTON MR: This appeal is about drains and an ombudsman. Most of the time the drains served six houses in Hampshire. However, on occasion they backed up to the discomfiture of the householders. The ombudsman was, to give him his proper title, a Local Commissioner of the Commission for Local Administration in England whose territory included the borough of Eastleigh. On the complaint of one of the householders, he investigated and concluded that the continued existence of the defect in the drains was caused by maladministration upon the part of the Eastleigh Borough Council. The council was not amused and sought judicial review of the ombudsman's report.

Nolan J held that the council had cause for complaint on two grounds. First, the ombudsman had acted contrary to section 34(3) of the Local Government Act 1974, in that he had questioned 'a decision taken without maladministration by an authority in the exercise of a discretion vested in that authority.' Second, the ombudsman had acted contrary to section 26(1) of the Act in that he had made a report on a complaint when it had not been established that the complainant had suffered injustice in consequence of the maladministration which was the subject of that complaint. However the judge refused to quash the report or to grant the council a declaration that the ombudsman had exceeded his jurisdiction. The council now appeals against this refusal and the ombudsman cross-appeals against the finding that he exceeded his powers.

Although this might be dismissed as a storm in a sewer, in fact it raises issues of some importance concerning the relationship between the courts and the local ombudsmen. But before considering those issues, I must say a word about the facts. These I take from the ombudsman's report, because for the purposes of judicial review proceedings he, and he alone, is the tribunal of fact.

The six houses were built in 1977 within the area of the Eastleigh Borough Council. It was accordingly the function of that council to enforce the Building Regulations 1976 (SI 1976 No. 1676): see section 4(3) of the Public Health Act 1961. It was for the council to decide on the scale of resources which it could make available to carry out this function. In doing so it had to strike a balance between the claims of efficiency and thrift, being answerable for that balance to the electorate through the ballot box rather than to the courts: *per* Lord Wilberforce in *Anns* v *Merton London Borough Council* [1978] AC 728, 754.

The ombudsman has found that the building control staff processed, on average, 210 applications per officer, which was 50 per cent higher per officer than in the remainder of Hampshire. This placed considerable demands on the staff and was achieved by limiting inspection to four of the more important of the nine stages requiring statutory notice of inspection to be submitted by builders. These four stages were the excavations for foundations, the oversite concrete, the damp proof course and the drains. The reason for limiting the inspections to these four stages was that the council had always been 'lean on members of staff' and it was thought appropriate to concentrate resources on inspections at the 'critical stages' of building work, on the basis that defects at these stages were likely to prove the most difficult to correct at a later date. The council operated a 'demand' system for inspection, meaning thereby that the council did not indulge in random inspections, but only inspected when notified that the appropriate stages had been reached. This was the policy of the council. It is now necessary to look at the practice.

It is now known that the problem experienced by the householders stemmed from the fact that the sewer over part of its length had a very shallow gradient of 1 in 140 and that there were undulations in it such that in places it was flat or had a reverse fall. The relevant code of practice called for a minimum gradient of 1 in 80 and the plans showed a gradient of 1 in 27 in one section and 1 in 70 in another. A gradient of 1 in 140 would not have been approved. . . .

The ombudsman's conclusions are stated in paragraphs 30 and 31 of his report:

> 30. In my view good administration dictates that the council should carry out an inspection under the Building Regulations in respect of all stage inspections for which they have received notice from the owner or builder as the case may be. Where inspections have not been made at a particular stage I consider that special attention should be given on the final inspection to remedy the omission. In the case of drains it is a relatively easy matter to carry out a full test, such as a ball test or its equivalent, at the final inspection stage and I consider that a council have a duty to ensure that this is done because a final inspection should mean that, so far as the council are concerned, they have with reasonable diligence and expenditure of officer time found no defect under the Building Regulations. I am satisfied that in this case the private foul sewer in question was not fully or thoroughly inspected. The defects in piping discovered as a result of the soil and vent pipe test should have alerted officers to the possibility of other defects in the pipe work.

> 31. I find, therefore, that the complainant has sustained injustice as a result of the council's maladministration. However, I cannot say, categorically, whether had the council carried out the final inspection in accordance with the dictates of good administration the trouble at the centre of this complaint would not have arisen. Equally, I have taken account of the argument that with synthetic piping of the sort employed in this case soil compaction can cause undulation at a later date. I have also considered the fact that the original fault was the builder's and that that (and the council's fault) occurred some years ago. On the other hand the final inspection was, in my view, incomplete and the council could have become aware of the problem at an early stage because of the difficulties experienced by the owner of house 3. Having considered these factors I feel on balance it would be inequitable to ask the council to defray the whole cost of the necessary remedial work. Accordingly, upon the residents' agreement to pay a proportion of the reasonable cost, I consider that the council themselves should take the action which the Assistant Director of Technical Services commended to the residents (see paragraph 29, above).

The action referred to in paragraph 29 consisted of exposing that part of the sewer which lay between two manholes and adjusting the pipe work to eliminate the undulation.

The ombudsman's cross-appeal

Section 34(3)

This subsection is in the following terms:

> It is hereby declared that nothing in this Part of this Act authorises or requires a Local Commissioner to question the merits of a decision taken without maladministration by an authority in the exercise of a discretion vested in that authority.

'Maladministration' is not defined in the Act, but its meaning was considered in *Reg v Local Commissioner for Administration for the North and East Area of England, Ex parte Bradford Metropolitan City Council* [1979] QB 287. All three judges (Lord Denning MR, at p. 311, Eveleigh LJ, at p. 314, and Sir David Cairns, at p. 319) expressed themselves differently, but in substance each was saying the same thing, namely, that administration and maladministration in the context of the work of a local authority is concerned with the *manner* in which decisions by the authority are reached and the *manner* in which they are or are not implemented. Administration and maladministration have nothing to do with the nature, quality or reasonableness of the decision itself.

The key to this part of the cross-appeal lies in identifying the policy decision of the council in relation to the inspection of drains. This was, as I have stated, to inspect at four of the more important of nine stages of construction. I did not condescend to the nature of the inspections. These houses were built in 1977 and that was the policy in that year. In 1980 and 1984 the policy was modified, so that not all houses were inspected, but that is immaterial for present purposes. That being the 1977 policy of the council, it was for its building control officers to implement that policy as a matter of administration.

Nolan J read paragraph 30 of the ombudsman's report, which I have set out in full, as questioning the merits of that policy. I do not so read it. I can best illustrate my understanding of that paragraph by adding words which render explicit what, in my judgment, is implicit [the words in square brackets are the words added by Sir John Donaldson MR to the report of the ombudsman]:

> In my view good administration dictates that the council should carry out an inspection under the Building Regulations in respect of all stage inspections for which they have received notice from the owner or builder as the case may be. [However I recognise that, on the authority of *Anns'* case [1978] AC 728 to which I have referred at length earlier in this report, it was open to the council in the exercise of their discretion and taking account of the competing claims of efficiency and thrift to decide to inspect on fewer occasions. This the council has done and I accept its decisions. That said] Where inspections have not been made at a particular stage I consider that special attention should be given on the final inspection to remedying the omission. [In saying this I am not calling for an expenditure of time and effort which would nullify the council's discretionary decision on the resources to be devoted to building regulation inspections.] In the case of drains it is a relatively easy matter to carry out a full test, such as a ball test or its equivalent, at the final inspection stage . . . [The choice of test must be a matter for the council's officers and I would not criticise them for not using the ball test, if they had used some equivalent test. However an air pressure test, such as the council's officers used, is not such an equivalent, because it only reveals whether or not the sewer is watertight. It tells the inspector nothing about its gradient or its ability to self-clear and efficiently carry away matter discharged into it as required by regulation N10.] I consider that [this is of considerable importance and that] a council have a duty to ensure that this is done because a final inspection [if the council decide to make one, as this council did] should mean that, so far as the council are concerned, they have with reasonable diligence and expenditure of officer time found no defect under the Building Regulations. I am satisfied that in this case the private foul sewer in question was not fully or thoroughly inspected [in terms of the council's own 1977 policy. Even if in other circumstances a lesser inspection might have been justified in terms of that policy] the defects in piping discovered as a result of the soil and vent pipe tests should have alerted officers to the possibility of other defects in the pipe work.

So read, and I do so read it, paragraph 30 loyally accepts the council's discretionary decision on the inspection of drains. It simply criticises the way in which that decision was implemented. I do not, therefore, think that this complaint by the council is made out.

Section 26(1)
This subsection is in the following terms:

> Subject to the provisions of this Part of this Act where a written complaint is made by or on behalf of a member of the public who claims to have sustained injustice in consequence of maladministration in connection with action taken by or on behalf of an authority to which this Part of this Act applies, being action taken in the exercise of administrative functions of that authority, a Local Commissioner may investigate that complaint.

Clearly this subsection does not prevent the ombudsman from investigating a complaint of maladministration which prima facie may have led the complainant to sustain consequential injustice (see the *Bradford Council* case [1979] QB 287), but it does mean that he cannot report adversely upon an authority unless his investigation reveals not only maladministration, but injustice to the complainant sustained as a consequence of that maladministration.

The mischief at which this subsection is directed is not difficult to detect. Every local authority has living within its boundaries a small cadre of citizens who would like nothing better than to spend their spare time complaining of maladministration. The subsection limits the extent to which they can involve the ombudsman by requiring, as a condition precedent to his involvement, that the complainant shall personally have been adversely affected by the alleged maladministration. If he was not so affected, he did not himself suffer injustice. If he was, he did. . . .

Like Nolan J, I am loath to criticise a busy Local Commissioner on merely semantic grounds, but I think that he laid himself open to criticism by finding maladministration in paragraph 30 and then proceeding, without any explanation, to his conclusion of consequential injustice. The words 'I find, therefore . . .' without further ado might suggest that, having found maladministration, injustice to the complainant followed as a matter of course.

This is not the case and I do not understand the ombudsman to be suggesting that it was. The facts, as found by him, were that the inspection by the council's officers was designed to detect defects in the drains, it was inadequate and it failed to detect the defects which in fact caused substantial inconvenience to the complainant. If the matter had stopped there, his finding of a causal connection would have been clear and not open to attack. It is his reference in paragraph 31 to the fact that he could not affirm categorically that a proper inspection would have revealed the defects and to the argument that the synthetic piping soil compaction can cause undulation at a later date which has cast doubt on his finding. This point has given me some concern, but in the end I have come to the conclusion that the ombudsman was intending to say that, whilst there could be no absolute certainty that a proper inspection would have revealed the defects and it was a possibility that the undulation occurred after the date of the inspection, on the balance of probabilities he was satisfied that the defects were present at the time of the inspection, that a proper inspection would have revealed them and that he was therefore satisfied that the complainant had suffered injustice in consequence of the maladministration.

An ombudsman's report is neither a statute nor a judgment. It is a report to the council and to the ratepayers of the area. It has to be written in everyday language and convey a message. This report has been subjected to a microscopic and somewhat legalistic analysis which it was not intended to undergo. Valid criticisms have been made, particularly of paragraph 31, but in my judgment they go to form rather than substance and, notwithstanding occasional dicta to the contrary, judicial review is concerned with substance. I would therefore allow the ombudsman's cross-appeal.

The council's appeal

As Parker and Taylor LJJ are minded to dismiss the ombudsman's appeal, it is necessary to consider the council's appeal. I would allow it.

Nolan J considered that there was no need for any declaration that the ombudsman had exceeded his remit by contravening the limits upon his jurisdiction set by section 34(3). He said that this was a free country and that there was nothing to prevent the council responding to the report with equal publicity. He concluded by saying that, since Parliament had not thought it necessary to create a right of appeal against the findings in the Local Commissioner's report, and in the absence of impropriety, it seemed to him that the courts ought not to provide the equivalent of such a right by judicial review.

I have to say that I profoundly disagree with this approach. Let me start with the fact that Parliament has not created a right of appeal against the findings in a Local Commissioner's report. It is this very fact, coupled with the public law character of the ombudsman's office and powers, which is the foundation of the right to relief by way of judicial review.

Next there is the suggestion that the council should issue a statement disputing the right of the ombudsman to make his findings and that this would provide the council with an adequate remedy. Such an action would wholly undermine the system of ombudsman's reports and would, in effect, provide for an appeal to the media against his findings. The Parliamentary intention was that reports by ombudsmen should be loyally accepted by the local authorities concerned. This is clear from section 30(4) and (5), which require the local authority to make the report available for inspection by the public and to advertise this fact, from section 31(1), which requires the local authority to notify the ombudsman of the action which it has taken and proposes to take in the light of his report and from section 31(2), which entitles the ombudsman to make a further report if the local authority's response is not satisfactory.

Whilst I am very far from encouraging councils to seek judicial review of an ombudsman's report, which, bearing in mind the nature of his office and duties and the qualification of those who hold that office, is inherently unlikely to succeed, in the absence of a succesful application for judicial review and the giving of relief by the court, local authorities should not dispute an ombudsman's report and should carry out their statutory duties in relation to it.

If Nolan J thought that the publication of his judgment in favour of the council was itself an adequate remedy, he did not say so, and, in any event, I think that he would have been mistaken, because this by itself does not relieve the council of its obligations to respond to the report in accordance with section 31(1) and, assuming that the report should never have been made, it is wrong that the council should be expected to respond.

I would grant a declaration in terms which reflect the decision of this court on the ombudsman's appeal against the decision of Nolan J.

PARKER LJ: The only question of difficulty arises on the cross-appeal of the ombudsman. If the cross-appeal is dismissed, I agree that the appeal must be allowed for the reasons given by Lord Donaldson of Lymington MR. On that matter I have nothing to add. I turn therefore to the cross-appeal.

The first question thereby raised is whether, as Nolan J held, the ombudsman has in his report acted contrary to section 34(3) of the Local Government Act 1974, the terms of which have been set out by Lord Donaldson MR. I do not therefore repeat them. Whether he has or not depends upon the interpretation of paragraph 30 of his report, read of course in its context. This context includes amongst other things an early paragraph in which the ombudsman specifically refers to and quotes the relevant passage from the speech of Lord Wilberforce in *Anns* v *Merton London Borough Council* [1978] AC 728. It must therefore be taken that he correctly directed himself as to the law. Accordingly I approach paragraph 30 on the basis that it is inherently unlikely that, having so directed himself, he would in the vital paragraph have intended to act contrary to his own direction. I also approach the paragraph on the basis that it should not be interpreted to lead to such a result if on a fair reading such a result can be avoided.

Before turning to the paragraph itself I should mention two further matters. The first is that the terms of section 34(3) do not preclude the ombudsman from questioning the merits of all discretionary policy decisions, but only those taken without maladministration. He can therefore examine or investigate a decision, as Eveleigh LJ said in *Reg.* v *Local Commissioner for Administration for the North and East Area of England, Ex parte Bradford Metropolitan City Council* [1979] QB 287, 316–317:

> If the commissioner carries out his investigation and in the course of it comes personally to the conclusion that a decision was wrongly taken, but is unable to point to any maladministration other than the decision itself, he is prevented by section 34(3) from questioning the decision.

The second matter to which attention may be usefully directed is that section 26(1) of the Act of 1974, which provides for complaints to a Local Commissioner, specifies that the complaint must be made by a member of the public

> who claims to have sustained injustice in consequence of maladministration in connection with action taken by or on behalf of an authority . . . *being action taken in the exercise of administrative functions* of that authority . . . (My emphasis.)

It appears to me to be plain from the report that the council had failed to carry out their own policy, and indeed it was made plain by Mr Sullivan on their behalf that, had the report so found, the council would have had no objection. The objection taken is that the report goes further than this and questions the merits of the policy decision to inspect only 'at the four more important of the nine stages requiring statutory notice of inspection to be submitted by builders.' The council's case depends entirely upon the wording of paragraph 30, and particularly the opening words thereof:

> In my view good administration dictates that the council should carry out an inspection under the Building Regulations in respect of all stage inspections for which they have received notice from the owner or builder as the case may be.

This, it is submitted, clearly questions the merits of the decision to inspect at the four more important stages only and, there being no suggestion of any maladministration in arriving at that decision, clearly exceeds the powers of the ombudsman.

I can see no answer to that submission, but it does not follow that the conclusion reached is vitiated. On a fair reading of the whole of paragraph 30 it appears to me that the ombudsman is not concluding that there was maladministration because there was no inspection at all nine stages, but merely that the inspections of the sewer which were called for by the policy of inspecting at the four most important stages were not fully or thoroughly carried out. This conclusion was not dependent upon the view expressed in the opening sentence and indeed it could not have been because the policy did call for drain inspections, indeed two drain inspections. The policy was silent as to the nature of such inspections, but, since the regulations (see regulation N10(1)(e)) call for a drain or private sewer to be 'so designed and constructed, of such size and . . . laid at such a gradient as to ensure that it is self-cleansing and efficiently carries away the maximum volume of matter which may be discharged into it,' it appears to me that inspections which were not directed at all to checking whether the private sewer was so designed, constructed and laid were rightly found to constitute maladministration by the council in its administrative functions.

I conclude therefore that the ombudsman's conclusion in paragraph 30 was valid, but if the council felt it necessary to seek some declaratory relief with regard to the opening words of the paragraph I would be prepared to consider granting it.

I turn to the second question raised on the cross-appeal, namely, whether the conclusion that the complainant had suffered injustice as a result of the maladministration can be sustained. This depends upon paragraph 31 of the report. Had the ombudsman stopped at the first sentence, I should have had no doubt that the decision was sustainable. It seems to me abundantly clear that the complainant had suffered injustice if the failure to inspect properly led to the subsequent expenditure and the ombudsman could in my view easily have determined that it had. It is submitted however that, having stated his conclusion in the opening sentence, he proceeds to negate it and that the paragraph read as a whole really amounts to this: 'I cannot say whether the failure to inspect led to the expenditure, but as the council were at fault it would be fair that they should contribute to the cost of remedial measures.' For the ombudsman it is submitted that this is not so and that on a fair reading the paragraph says no more than: 'I cannot be absolutely sure, but on the balance of probabilities I conclude . . .'

I regret to say that, unlike Lord Donaldson MR I cannot accept this construction. It appears to me that to do so involves applying legal concepts of differing standards of proof in order to uphold a paragraph which, like its predecessor, must be broadly considered. I have, despite its opening words, been able, by a broad reading and the correctness of the ombudsman's directions to himself on the law, to uphold the conclusion in paragraph 30. In the case of paragraph 31 I am unable to do so.

I would therefore dismiss the cross-appeal and allow the appeal.

TAYLOR LJ: I agree that the council's appeal must be allowed if the ombudsman's cross-appeal fails.

The council should not be denied a remedy if the ombudsman's finding was ultra vires or otherwise unlawful. I agree that for the reasons given by Lord Donaldson MR, Nolan J's grounds for refusing a declaration cannot be sustained.

The crucial issue therefore is whether the ombudsman's findings in both paragraphs 30 and 31 of his report can be upheld and his cross-appeal thus allowed. I agree with Nolan J that both paragraphs contain findings which cannot be justified.

As to paragraph 30, the conclusion adverse to the council is contained in the penultimate sentence. Its rationale is said to be that, in terms of the council's own 1977 policy, the foul sewer was not fully or thoroughly inspected because no gradient test was applied such as the ball test or its equivalent. It is accepted to be a matter for the council's discretion whether, with their available resources, they could and should have inspected at all stages or only at the four most important stages. But in my judgment, it was equally a matter for the council's discretion as to what tests they could and should carry out having regard to those resources. The ombudsman's finding in paragraph 30 is that at the final inspection, if not before, the council:

> have a duty to insure that [a gradient test] is done because a final inspection should mean that, so far as the council are concerned, they have with reasonable diligence and expenditure of officer time found no defect under the Building Regulations.

This begs the question whether 'reasonable diligence and expenditure of officer time' permits and requires a gradient test to be made of every drain and sewer. It was not the policy of this council that they did. That is a matter of discretion for the council. I do not accept Mr Beloff's suggestion that what precedes the penultimate sentence in paragraph 30 should be regarded as obiter dicta. The paragraph is headed 'Conclusions' and should be read as a whole. It culminates in, and is explanatory of, the finding. In my judgment its tenor shows the ombudsman to be trespassing into the field of discretion by laying down what policy as to inspections the dictates of good administration require, and what tests the council ought to ensure are carried out. That is quite different from finding that a test specifically required by the council's policy has not been carried out or has been carried out inefficiently. I therefore agree with Nolan J that the ombudsman was in breach of section 34(3) of the Local Government Act 1974 in his conclusion that maladministration was established.

As to paragraph 31, I agree with Parker LJ. Only by straining the language used by the ombudsman and attributing to him speculatively considerations as to the burden of proof, could one render his finding on causation sound. I do not think such straining and speculation is justified.

Accordingly I conclude that in respect of both paragraphs 30 and 31 of the report, Nolan J reached the correct conclusions. I would therefore dismiss the cross-appeal and allow the council's appeal.

QUESTIONS

1. How did each of the three judges answer the questions raised in the appeal?

2. Is there any difference between the interpretation placed on s. 34(3) by Lord Donaldson MR and that by Parker LJ?

3. What advice would you give to Commissioners on the drawing up of their reports after this case?

NOTES:

1. Croydon Council also succeeded in obtaining judicial review of the decision of another Local Commissioner criticizing the operation of the council's education appeals policy (see *R v Local Commissioner for Administration, ex parte Croydon London Borough Council* [1989] 1 All ER 1033; see also M. Jones, 'The Local Ombudsmen and Judicial Review' (1988) *Public Law* 608–22).

2. There does seem to be some overlap between illegality and maladministration. In *R* v *Parliamentary Commissioner for Administration, ex parte Balchin* [1997] COD 146, the PCA was held to have failed to have taken into account a relevant factor during his investigation. He should have considered whether the fettering of policy by the bodies could have amounted to maladministration.

When this case was reconsidered by the PCA no maladministration or injustice were found and this determination was successfully challenged in *R* v *Parliamentary Commissioner for Administration, ex parte Balchin No 2* (2000) 2 LGLR 87 where Dyson J found that the PCA's reasoning was flawed in that there was evidence in the papers which should have led him to pursue the knowledge of the departmental staff about the relevant factor in Sedley J's judgment. (See commentary in [2000] PL 201.)

In *R* v *Local Commissioner for Administration in North and North East England, ex parte Liverpool City Council* [2001] All ER 462, the council had argued that the test in the National Local Government Code of Conduct for deciding if a councillor should declare an interest, that of reasonable suspicion, was inappropriate because of the decision by the House of Lords in *R* v *Gough* [1993] AC 646, which preferred real danger or possibility (but see *In Re Medicaments [2001] 1 WLR 700, ante* p. 605). It was accepted by the Court of Appeal that the reasonable suspicion test was more stringent, although they doubted that the two tests would not produce the same result in this case. The important point was that the councillors on taking office undertook to be guided by the Code and its test, so it should apply.

3. The *JUSTICE-All Souls Report on Administrative Law* (1988), at pp. 133–4, noted that the Commission for Local Administration in England stated that the word 'maladministration' is disliked by councillors and officials and means little to many complainants. It recommended that, in addition to the Commissioners' powers to make a finding of maladministration, the Commissioners should be able to report in terms critical of the local authority, but falling short of making a finding of maladministration against it, and it should then be obligatory for the local authority to consider such a report with a view to taking any necessary remedial action.

QUESTIONS

1. The *JUSTICE-All Souls Report* was not, however, in favour of removing the term 'maladministration'. 'In our view' it stated 'a spade should be called a spade'. In the light of the evidence of the Commission for Local Administration, do you think a spade would be called a spade if its own proposal was implemented.

2. If this proposal was implemented, what meaning could be given to s. 34(3) of the 1974 Act?

NOTES:

1. In its *Second Report for the Session 1967–68* (HC 350) the Select Committee encouraged the PCA to investigate complaints relating to 'bad decisions' and 'bad rules'. In respect of the 'bad decision' the Select Committee (at para. 14) stated that if the PCA

> finds a decision which, judged by its effect upon the aggrieved person, appears to him to be thoroughly bad in quality, he might infer from the quality of the decision itself that there had been an element of maladministration in the taking of it and ask for its review.

In respect of the 'bad rule', where an administrative rule, despite being applied properly, has caused hardship and injustice, the PCA was urged

> to enquire whether, given the effect of the rule in the case under his investigation, the Department had taken any action to review the rule. If found defective and revised, what action had been taken to remedy the hardship sustained by the complainant? If not revised,

whether there had been due consideration by the Department of the grounds for maintaining the rule?

The PCA accepted these suggestions, but it has been argued that they have had little impact on the number of cases in which he has been willing to find maladministration. In relation to the 'bad rule', Gregory in 'The Select Committee on the PCA 1967–80' [1982] *Public Law* 49–88, at p. 69 points out that 'only an extraordinarily inept department might be expected to conduct its review of a rule [so] that the Commissioner would find defects in the process subsequently described to him.'

2. A number of the cases considered by the PCA and Local Commissioners have involved allegations that authorities have failed to give proper advice; for a discussion of the Parliamentary Commissioner's approach to such cases, see A. Mowbray, 'A Right to Official Advice: The Parliamentary Commissioner's Perspective' [1990] *Public Law*, 68–69.

3. In *Our Fettered Ombudsman* (1977), ch. VII, JUSTICE suggested that, following the New Zealand model, the jurisdiction of the PCA should be extended to allow him to investigate any action which is 'unreasonable, unjust or oppressive . . . instead of maladministration'. The PCA responded to this suggestion in his *Annual Report for 1977* (HC 157 of 1977–78) by stating that he believed he already had power to investigate complaints that actions by Government Departments are unjust or oppressive. He continued:

> 21. What the Act certainly does exclude from my jurisdiction are complaints about discretionary decisions taken 'without maladministration'. I believe this to be right. It is no part of my function to substitute my judgment for that of a Minister or one of his officials if I see no evidence of 'maladministration' either in the way the decision was taken or in the nature of the decision itself.
>
> 22. I believe therefore that the difficulty which has been detected in the limitation of my investigation powers to cases of 'maladministration' is more theoretical than practical. But if there is thought to be some semantic difficulty which confuses members of the public or members of parliament than I should see no objection to seeing my powers redefined in the sort of language suggested by JUSTICE. I think that in practice it would make very little difference.

Subsequently JUSTICE adopted the view that the definition of maladministration was not a source of much difficulty, bearing in mind the approach which the Commissioner took to his jurisdiction (see the reference to this in the *Fourth Report from the Select Committee*, HC 615 of 1977–78). More recently the *JUSTICE-All Souls Report on Administrative Law* (1988) did not recommend any change in the definition (see pp. 92–3 and 133–4).

QUESTION

In the light of the decision in *ex parte Eastleigh Borough Council* (*ante* at p. 722), do you think the PCA was correct in the extract from the Annual Report for 1977?

NOTE: Sir Cecil Clothier, who was PCA from 1979 to 1985, stated that he did not wish to be dragged into a review of political decision-making; and he suggested that a complaint is political if it has been debated in Parliament or where a very large proportion of the population are affected as well as the person making the complaint (see Clothier (1984) 81 *Law Society's Gazette* 3108–9). On this ground he refused to investigate complaints relating to the Inland Revenue's agreement concerning Fleet Street casual workers who evaded their tax arrangements. This agreement subsequently gave rise to *Inland Revenue Commissioners* v *National Federation of Self-Employed and Small Businesses Ltd* [1982] AC 617 (see *ante* at p. 672).

Section 26(7) of the Local Government Act 1974 specifically provides that a local commissioner shall not conduct an investigation in respect of any action which in his opinion affects all or most of the inhabitants in the area of the authority concerned.

SECTION 5: **Conduct of Investigation**

Parliamentary Commissioner Act 1967

7.—(1) Where the Commissioner proposes to conduct an investigation pursuant to a complaint under this Act, he shall afford to the principal officer of the department or authority concerned, and to any other person who is alleged in the complaint to have taken or authorised the action complained of, an opportunity to comment on any allegations contained in the complaint.

(2) Every such investigation shall be conducted in private, but except as aforesaid the procedure for conducting an investigation shall be such as the Commissioner considers appropriate in the circumstances of the case; and without prejudice to the generality of the foregoing provision the Commissioner may obtain information from such persons and in such manner, and make such inquiries, as he thinks fit, and may determine whether any person may be represented, by counsel or solicitor or otherwise, in the investigation.

(3) The Commissioner may, if he thinks fit, pay to the person by whom the complaint was made and to any other person who attends or furnishes information for the purposes of an investigation under this Act—

(a) sums in respect of expenses properly incurred by them;
(b) allowances by way of compensation for the loss of their time, in accordance with such scales and subject to such conditions as may be determined by the Treasury.

(4) The conduct of an investigation under this Act shall not affect any action taken by the department or authority concerned, or any power or duty of that department or authority to take further action with respect to any matters subject to the investigation . . .

8.—(1) For the purposes of an investigation under this Act the Commissioner may require any Minister, officer or member of the department or authority concerned or any other person who in his opinion is able to furnish information or produce documents relevant to the investigation to furnish any such information or produce any such document.

(2) For the purposes of any such investigation the Commissioner shall have the same powers as the Court in respect of the attendance and examination of witnesses (including the administration of oaths or affirmations and the examination of witnesses abroad) and in respect of the production of documents.

(3) No obligation to maintain secrecy or other restriction upon the disclosure of information obtained by or furnished to persons in Her Majesty's service, whether imposed by any enactment or by any rule of law, shall apply to the disclosure of information for the purposes of an investigation under this Act; and the Crown shall not be entitled in relation to any such investigation to any such privilege in respect of the production of documents or the giving of evidence as is allowed by law in legal proceedings.

(4) No person shall be required or authorised by virtue of this Act to furnish any information or answer any question relating to proceedings of the Cabinet or of any committee of the Cabinet or to produce so much of any document as relates to such proceedings; and for the purposes of this subsection a certificate issued by the Secretary of the Cabinet with the approval of the Prime Minister and certifying that any information, question, document or part of a document so relates shall be conclusive.

(5) Subject to subsection (3) of this section, no person shall be compelled for the purposes of any investigation under this Act to give any evidence or produce any document which he could not be compelled to give or produce in civil proceedings before the Court.

9.—(1) If any person without lawful excuse obstructs the Commissioner or any officer of the Commissioner in the performance of his functions under this Act, or is guilty of any act or omission in relation to an investigation under this Act which, if that investigation were a proceeding in the Court, would constitute contempt of court, the Commissioner may certify the offence to the Court . . .

NOTE: Similar provisions regarding the conduct of investigations by the Local Commissioners are set out in the Local Government Act 1974, ss. 26(5), 28–29.

Parliamentary Commissioner for Administration Annual Report for 1999–2000
HC 593 of 1999–2000, paras 1.12–19

Screening policy

1.12 Many of the criticisms in this area rest on misunderstanding. Most of the complaints which my Office does not accept for investigation are so treated because that is what the law requires: they are, for example, against a body or about a matter excluded from my jurisdiction, or raise issues which fall to be dealt with by the courts or a tribunal . . . The real issue concerns those complaints . . . which are not accepted for investigation as a result of the exercise of the discretion which the law confers on me and which I delegate to my staff as appropriate. In one important category of such complaints the facts are not significantly in dispute, and the department or agency concerned has admitted fault and offered what appears to be appropriate redress. I do not believe that it would be a justifiable use of public money to investigate such complaints: indeed, as the facts are not significantly in dispute, it is hard to see what there is to be investigated.

1.13 The second important category comprises complaints against discretionary decisions by departments or agencies. The 1967 Act forbids me to call into question the merits of such decisions unless they have been taken with maladministration. Many complaints about such decisions spring from a mistaken belief that the Ombudsman is some sort of plenipotentiary appeals authority, able to substitute his judgment for that of the responsible body. He is, of course, no such thing; and it is therefore not unreasonable that the practice of my Office, for many years, has been to require complainants to produce some prima facie evidence of maladministration to support their complaint.

1.14 However, as I pointed out in my last Annual Report, the practice carries some danger: in particular, the complainant has no access to the files of the department or agency, and so is at a heavy disadvantage in making his or her case. I have therefore asked my staff to lower still further the 'evidential hurdle'. It will still be right to refuse to investigate complaints when it is clear that they express nothing more than discontent with the substance of a discretionary decision. Otherwise, my Office will exercise a clear bias in favour of starting an investigation. The Office began to give this modified approach effect from November 1999: since then, the proportion of complaints accepted for investigation has risen by 6%.

Extending the 'product range'

1.15 Once I have accepted a complaint for investigation, the 1967 Act obliges me to issue a report of the results of the investigation, unless I decide to discontinue it. There has been a strong trend over the life of my Office for investigation reports to become longer and more complicated, partly perhaps because public administration itself has become more complicated and partly out of a wish to give thorough satisfaction to complainants and those complained against. However understandable those motives, elaborate investigations and investigation reports are one of the main reasons for the lengthening throughput times which have characterised the Office since the late 1970s and which, as I noted earlier, lie at the root of much of the criticism directed against it.

Moreover, such reports often fail to provide what the complainant wants. A parent with care who is not receiving the child support maintenance she is entitled to because, as she believes, of mal-administration by the Child Support Agency is likely to be more concerned that the maintenance, and any arrears, should be paid – and paid quickly – than to receive a blow-by-blow account of just how the maladministration occurred after many months, let alone years, have passed her wearily by.

1.16 A consequence of the bias towards investigation mentioned in paragraph 1.14 above is likely to be that there will be a good many cases in which my Office will conclude, after receiving the department or agency's response to the statement of complaint which initiates an investigation and confirming the facts as necessary, that there has been no maladministration. In such circumstances, it will be right to bring the investigation to an end as quickly as possible.

1.17 Considerations of this sort have led me to the conclusion that, while of course remaining within the limits imposed by the 1967 Act, my Office must offer a wider 'product range', from informal resolution through to the most thorough and painstaking investigation, taking account of the wishes of the complainant, the response of the department, and the facts of the case as they emerge. This will entail, among other things, keeping in closer and more frequent touch with complainants.

1.18 The Member who referred the complaint will, of course, be kept fully informed of developments.

1.19 In essence, we shall no longer make a rigid distinction between those complaints which are not accepted for investigation ('rejections') and those which are accepted and therefore – or so it has been assumed – will be the subject of an exhaustive investigation and report. In future, unless a complaint is clearly outside jurisdiction it will be passed to a caseworker who will take enquiries and such other action as far as is needed for a soundly-based and just resolution.

Parliamentary Commissioner for Administration Annual Report for 2000–01
HC 5 of 2001–02, pp. 15, 18, 19

2.5 Starting in April 2000, we made big changes to our working practices. The principal change gave more extensive delegated powers to staff. A named investigator under the guidance of an investigation manager and a director of investigations now generally takes responsibility for pro-gressing a complaint from receipt to resolution. Investigation managers now verify and report the results of all but the most complex or sensitive statutory investigations. Investigators normally now issue letters reporting the outcomes of all other consideration of complaints referred by Members, and keep complainants informed of the progress of investigations.

2.6 When we receive a complaint from the referring Member we ask four questions:

- Is the complaint about a body and a matter within the Ombudsman's jurisdiction?
- Is there evidence of administrative failure?
- Did that failure cause personal injustice which has not been put right?
- Is it likely that the Ombudsman's intervention will secure a worthwhile remedy?

If either the subject matter of a complaint or the body complained against is outside the Ombuds-man's jurisdiction, the matter cannot be considered further.

2.7 We have introduced a wider range of responses to complaints, matching outcomes to the individual circumstances of cases. The range of possible outcomes that can flow from a complaint to the Ombudsman is:

2.8 Outcome 1: If the body complained against or the subject matter of a complaint is outside the Ombudsman's jurisdiction the matter cannot be considered further.

The Ombudsman continues to receive significant numbers of complaints about areas which are clearly outside his jurisdiction, such as personnel or contractual matters, or decisions which carry a right of appeal. He also receives considerable numbers of complaints about planning matters, where the complainants are unhappy with a planning decision, and essentially want him to criticise a Planning Inspector's professional judgement. In such cases, the most the Ombudsman can do is satisfy himself that the correct procedures have been followed.

Outcome 2: After further consideration within the office the complaint is not taken further, for example if there is no evidence of maladministration resulting in an unremedied personal injustice, or no worthwhile outcome is likely.

Outcome 3A: As an alternative to starting an investigation enquires are made of the department which result in an appropriate outcome to the complaint. Many complaints can be settled quickly and efficiently in this way without a statutory investigation. It is evident from the reaction of complainants and the bodies complained against alike that many appreciate the benefits of this approach.

Outcome 3B: Enquiries of the department or agency concerned result in the complaint not being taken further, e.g. because no injustice has been suffered or no worthwhile outcome is likely.

2.9 When a statutory investigation is initiated, we issue a statement of the complaint to the body concerned; this is copied to the referring Member.

Outcome 4: The investigation process is initiated, but ended when an appropriate outcome has been achieved or no remedy is available.

Outcome 5: A statutory investigation report is sent to the referring Member. It is also copied to the body complained against (which has previously had the opportunity to comment on the facts to be reported and their presentation).

2.10 In an increasing proportion of cases it is possible to resolve complaints without completing a statutory report; in those cases, the investigator sends to the referring Member and the body complained against a brief account setting out the main points agreed.

NOTES:
1. The nature of the investigations of the PCA is discussed further in the extracts *post* pp. 751–2.
2. The Northern Ireland PCA and Commissioner for Complaints appear to have been using a fast-track procedure for longer than the PCA. In evidence to the Select Committee both the PCA and the Northern Ireland PCA pointed out that the use of the fast-track has to be considered carefully, as 'wider administrative issues' might be raised by a case and these should not escape formal investigation. The Select Committee noted that the smaller jurisdiction in Northern Ireland lent itself to informal approaches (HC 33 of 1993–94, paras. 17–18).
3. The Commission for Local Administration has, for a longer period than the PCA, placed more emphasis on pursuing the possibility of a settlement which arises in the course of an investigation. The Commission for Local Administration explicitly states as one of its objectives 'to offer guidance intended to promote fair and effective administration in local government'. Their first Guidance, published in 1992, was *Devising A Complaints System*. The reasons for this emphasis on settlement may be partially explained by considering the consequences of findings of maladministration by the PCA and Local Commissioners (see section (F) below).

K. Thompson considered the adavantages and disadvantages of local settlement in 'Conciliation or Arbitration?' [1991] *Local Government Studies* 15–26 at p. 25.

While settlements can save time and expense, provide an acceptable solution to all parties, and indicate a willingness on the part of authorities to seek out and remedy shortcomings, they may also be used to 'buy off' complainants. This can mean the avoidance of unwelcome publicity and indeed promised remedial action may not be implemented.

QUESTION

Are the possible problems associated with fast-tracks/local settlements worse than the problem of the time taken to conduct formal investigations?

SECTION 6: **Outcome of Investigations and Remedies**

Parliamentary Commissioner Act 1967

10.—(1) In any case where the Commissioner conducts an investigation under this Act or decides not to conduct such an investigation, he shall send to the member of the House of Commons by whom the request for investigation was made (or if he is no longer a member of that House, to such member of that House as the Commissioner thinks appropriate) a report of the results of the investigation or, as the case may be, a statement of his reasons for not conducting an investigation.

(2) In any case where the Commissioner conducts an investigation under this Act, he shall also send a report of the results of the investigation to the principal officer of the department or authority concerned and to any other person who is alleged in the relevant complaint to have taken or authorised the action complained of.

(3) [see *ante* at p. 722]

(4) The Commissioner shall annually lay before each House of Parliament a general report on the performance of his functions under this Act and may from time to time lay before each House of Parliament such other reports with respect to those functions as he thinks fit.

11.—(2) Information obtained by the Commissioner or his officers in the course of or for the purposes of an investigation under this Act shall not be disclosed except—
  (a) for the purposes of the investigation and of any report to be made thereon under this Act;
  (b) for the purposes of any proceedings for an offence under the Official Secrets Acts 1911 to 1939 alleged to have been committed in respect of information obtained by the Commissioner or any of his officers by virtue of this Act or for an offence of perjury alleged to have been committed in the course of an investigation under this Act or for the purposes of an inquiry with a view to the taking of such proceedings; or
  (c) for the purposes of any proceedings under section 9 of this Act; and the Commissioner and his officers shall not be called upon to give evidence in any proceedings (other than such proceedings as aforesaid) of matters coming to his or their knowledge in the course of an investigation under this Act.

(3) A Minister of the Crown may give notice in writing to the Commissioner, with respect to any document or information specified in the notice, or any class of documents or information so specified, that in the opinion of the Minister the disclosure of that document or information, or of documents or information of that class, would be prejudicial to the safety of the State or otherwise contrary to the public interest; and where such a notice is given nothing in this Act shall be construed as authorising or requiring the Commissioner or any officer of the Commissioner to communicate to any person or for any purpose any document or information specified in the notice, or any document or information of a class so specified.

NOTE: On the rather different provisions governing the Local Commissioners, see *post* at pp. 740–41.

Parliamentary Commissioner for Administration Annual Report for 2000–01

HC 5 of 2001–02, Appendix A, fig. 9

Figure 9 Analysis of complaints by department or public body

Bodies complained about[1]	Work in progress at 1-4-00	New cases opened	Total case-work	Outcome 1	2	3A	3B	4	5	Statutory Investigations (Outcome 5) Justified	Partly justified	Not justified	Work in progress at 31-3-01
Ministry of Agriculture, Fisheries and Food	10	25	35	0	10	4	2	1	7	3	2	2	11
Arts Council for England	2	3	5	0	2	0	2	0	1	1	0	0	0
United Kingdom Atomic Energy Authority	0	1	1	0	0	0	0	0	0	–	–	–	1
Biotechnology and Biological Sciences Research Council	0	1	1	0	0	0	1	0	0	–	–	–	0
British Council	0	2	2	0	1	0	1	0	0	–	–	–	0
Broadcasting Standards Commission	0	2	2	0	2	0	0	0	0	–	–	–	0
Central Council for Education and Training in Social Work	0	1	1	0	1	0	0	0	0	–	–	–	0
Charity Commission	5	7	12	0	6	0	1	0	1	0	1	0	4
Civil Aviation Authority	1	2	3	0	2	0	0	0	0	–	–	–	1
Coal Authority	0	1	1	0	0	0	0	0	0	–	–	–	1
Construction Industry Training Board	0	1	1	0	0	0	0	1	0	–	–	–	0
Criminal Injuries Compensation Authority	3	6	9	0	1	5	2	0	0	–	–	–	1
Crown Estate Office	0	2	2	0	1	1	0	0	0	–	–	–	0
Department of Culture, Media and Sport	2	1	3	0	1	1	0	0	1	0	0	1	0
HM Customs and Excise	8	24	32	0	16	2	3	0	4	2	2	0	7
Data Protection Registrar	1	4	5	0	3	0	1	0	0	–	–	–	1
Ministry of Defence	0	15	15	7	8	0	0	0	0	–	–	–	0
Disability Rights Commission	0	2	2	0	1	0	0	0	0	–	–	–	1
Economic and Social Research Council	0	1	1	0	1	0	0	0	0	–	–	–	0
Department for Education and Employment	14	55	69	0	26	9	11	4	6	4	2	0	13

Figure 9 – *contd*

Bodies complained about[1]	Work in progress at 1-4-00	New cases opened	Total case-work	Outcome 1	2	3A	3B	4	5	Statutory Investigations (Outcome 5) Justified	Partly justified	Not justified	Work in progress at 31-3-01
Office of the Director General of Electricity Supply	1	0	1	0	1	0	0	0	0	–	–	–	0
English Heritage	1	1	2	0	2	0	0	0	0	–	–	–	0
Engineering & Physical Sciences Research Council	0	1	1	0	0	1	0	0	0	–	–	–	0
Environment Agency	1	12	13	0	4	0	4	0	2	0	1	1	3
Department of the Environment, Transport and the Regions	26	97	123	0	54	13	30	1	12	5	5	2	13
Office of Fair Trading	2	1	3	0	1	0	0	0	2	1	1	0	0
Foreign and Commonwealth Office	3	13	16	1	8	0	2	0	2	0	2	0	3
Forestry Commission	0	1	1	0	0	0	1	0	0	–	–	–	0
Further Education Funding Council for England	0	3	3	0	1	0	0	0	0	–	–	–	2
Gas Consumers Council	0	1	1	0	0	0	1	0	0	–	–	–	0
Office of Gas and Electricity Markets	0	3	3	0	0	2	1	0	0	–	–	–	0
Government Office for the Regions	0	5	5	0	3	2	0	0	0	–	–	–	0
Department of Health	4	20	24	1	15	3	1	0	1	0	1	0	3
Health and Safety Executive	0	3	3	0	1	1	0	0	0	–	–	–	1
Home Office	26	95	121	1	18	47	9	5	13	8	3	2	28
Horserace Betting Levy Board	0	1	1	0	0	0	0	0	0	–	–	–	1
Housing Corporation	0	3	3	0	0	0	1	0	0	–	–	–	2
Human Fertilisation & Embryology Authority	0	1	1	0	0	0	0	0	0	–	–	–	1
Inland Revenue	52	214	266	1	121	11	31	18	21	10	8	3	63
Department for International Development	0	2	2	0	1	1	0	0	0	–	–	–	0
HM Land Registry	3	20	23	0	11	2	5	1	0	–	–	–	4

Body												
Legal Services Commission	34	73	107	0	54	4	3	4	12	7	5	0	30
London Regional Passenger Committee	0	1	1	0	0	1	0	0	0	–	–	–	0
Lord Chancellor's Department	20	79	99	2	52	15	2	2	8	5	2	1	18
National Endowment for Science, Technology and Art	0	1	1	0	0	0	1	0	0	–	–	–	0
Commission for the New Towns	0	1	1	0	1	0	0	0	0	–	–	–	0
Northern Ireland Court Service	1	0	1	1	0	0	0	0	0	0	1	0	0
Northern Ireland Office	1	1	2	1	0	0	0	0	1	0	1	0	0
Pensions Ombudsman	1	4	5	0	4	0	0	0	0	–	–	–	1
Post Office Users' National Council	1	0	1	0	1	0	0	0	0	–	–	–	0
Public Record Office	0	1	1	0	0	0	0	0	0	–	–	–	1
Commission for Racial Equality	2	2	4	0	0	2	0	0	1	1	0	0	0
Rail Regulator	0	1	1	0	0	1	0	1	0	–	–	–	0
Rent Assessment Committees	0	3	3	0	1	1	1	0	0	–	–	–	0
Department of Social Security	266	720	986	2	266	180	126	60	144	108	31	5	208
Office of the Social Security Commissioners	0	1	1	0	0	0	0	0	0	–	–	–	1
Office for Standards in Education	0	4	4	0	1	1	1	0	0	–	–	–	2
Office of National Statistics	0	2	2	0	1	0	1	0	0	–	–	–	0
Teacher Training Agency	0	1	1	0	0	0	1	0	0	–	–	–	0
Office of the Director General of Telecommunications	2	0	2	0	1	0	0	0	1	0	1	0	0
Department of Trade and Industry	8	36	44	3	32	2	1	1	3	1	0	2	2
HM Treasury	1	38	39	0	29	1	2	0	1	1	0	0	6
Treasury Solicitors	0	4	4	0	2	0	1	0	0	–	–	–	1
Urban Regeneration Agency	1	0	1	0	0	0	0	0	1	0	0	1	0
Office of the Director General of Water Services	1	9	10	0	7	0	1	0	2	0	1	1	0
Welsh Office	0	1	1	1	0	0	0	0	0	–	–	–	0
Others (outside jurisdiction)	3	82	85	78	2	0	0	0	0	–	–	–	5
Total	507	1721	2228	99	777	313	252	99	247	157	69	21	441

1 This figure does not provide a comprehensive list of bodies within the Ombudsman's jurisdiction.

2 The Independent Tribunal Service was subsumed by the Appeals Service, an executive agency of DSS, on 3 April 2000.

NOTES:

1. The Parliamentary Commissioner for Administration is normally able to report that there had been full compliance with his recommendations. The evidence suggests that in general the PCA has normally had little difficulty in securing compliance with his recommendations. He reported on one difficult case in the 1995 Annual Report:

> *Channel Tunnel Rail Link*
> 7. On 8 February 1995 I laid before Parliament my report 'The Channel Tunnel Rail Link and Blight: Investigation of complaints against the Department of Transport'. Paragraphs 109–119 in Chapter I of this report describe the case and its consideration by the Select Committee in more detail. I record here its highly unusual features. It was the largest single investigation I had undertaken in my time as Parliamentary Commissioner. I laid the report before Parliament under the Parliamentary Commissioner Act 1967, section 10(3), which applies when it appears to me that injustice has been caused to a person in consequence of maladministration and that the injustice has not been, and will not be, remedied. It was only the second time in the 28 years since my office was established that the power in that subsection had been used. I had shown my report in draft to the Permanent Secretary (in accordance with my usual procedure) but – unusually – he did not accept that his department had been maladministrative or, therefore, that any remedy for injustice was due. I published as an Appendix to my report the comments of the Permanent Secretary. The then Secretary of State and he gave evidence to the Select Committee on 23 May and 1 March respectively. On 19 July the Select Committee issued their report in which they concluded that the department had acted maladministratively in failing to consider whether any *ex gratia* payments were due when the Channel Tunnel Rail Link project entered the period of uncertainty caused by problems of funding between June 1990 and April 1994; that it was desirable to grant redress to those affected to an extreme and exceptional degree; and that it should be possible to distinguish a small number of cases of exceptional hardship. (I may add that a further unusual feature of the case was the extent to which reports and comments in the press and broadcasting media and elsewhere showed a misunderstanding of the basis of my finding and of the limited scope of the redress arrangements I recommended that the department should consider.) In August I was invited to meet the new Secretary of State for Transport. On 1 November I learned from the Select Committee that they had received a reply from the Secretary of State, and it was published on the next day. The Government still did not accept that there had been maladministration but 'out of respect for the PCA Select Committee and the office of the Parliamentary Commissioner, and without admission of fault or liability' indicated their willingness 'to consider afresh whether a scheme might be formulated to implement the Committee's recommendation that redress should be granted to those affected to an extreme and exceptional degree by generalised blight from CTRL during the period between June 1990 and April 1994 and how it might operate'. I welcome that decision and I hope for speedy progress.

   It was not until early 1997 that the PCA received and accepted the Conservative Government's proposals for redress (HC 45 of 1996–97). After the General Election, the Labour Government confirmed the intention and increased the maximum payment for redress from £5,000 to £10,000 (see HC 845 of 1997–98).

2. The Local Commissioners, on the other hand, have frequently reported difficulties in securing compliance. In the Annual Report for 1992–93, the Commission for Local Administration in England stated that there had been an unsatisfactory outcome in 201 of 3,548 reports issued since 1974. What explanations might there be for this distinction? Note, however, that, as explained in note 3 below, the powers of the Local Commissioners to secure compliance have recently been increased.

3. Gregory, in 'The Select Committee on the PCA 1967–80' [1982] *Public Law*, 49–88, at p. 49 comments on the role of the Select Committee in ensuring that there is compliance with the recommendations of the Parliamentary Commissioner. Until recently, the main sanction available to Local Commissioners has been to issue further reports. It was not until 1988 that local authorities were placed under a statutory obligation to consider such further reports.

Each of the Commissions was also obliged to issue an annual report, together with the reports of the relevant Local Commissioners, to its 'representative body'. The 1974 legislation had provided for the establishment of a representative body for each of England and Wales. Their main tasks were to consider, comment, and pass on to the local authorities any general conclusions reached by the Ombudsmen about the operation of their powers, and to consider and comment on their annual estimates of expenditure. The existence of the representative bodies was not, however, perceived to be of great assistance to the Local Commissioners. The *Widdicombe Report* concluded at p. 223, that the representative body in England

> has tended to take a negative view of proposals from the Commission for modifications to their procedures. We also consider it anomalous in principle that a body which represents those who are the subject of investigation should play a major part in dictating the budget of the investigators. There is no parallel here with the position of the Parliamentary Ombudsman who is accountable not to the Government but to the Commons Select Committee.

The report concluded that the Government should consider the abolition of the representative bodies and that the cost of the Ombudsmen's services should be a charge against central government funds.

Following the report the Government stated that it intended to introduce measures to increase compliance by local authorities. The Local Government and Housing Act 1989, ss. 26 and 28, consequently amended the Local Government Act 1974 to provide that authorities must notify the Local Ombudsman of the action which they propose to take within three months from the date of an adverse report (Local Government Act 1974, s. 31(2), as amended). Similar time-limits apply in respect of the consideration of a further report (s. 31(2)–(2)(c)). If an authority proposes not to accept the recommendation of the Ombudsman in a further report, the report must generally be considered by the authority as a whole (s. 31(A)(1)). If, in considering the report, the authority take into account a report by a person or body with an interest in the Local Ombudsman's report, they must also take into account a report by a person or body without an interest in the report (s. 31(A)(4)). No member of the council is entitled to vote on any question with respect to a report or a further report in which he is named and criticized (s. 31(A)(5)). If the authority do not satisfy the Local Ombudsman with respect to a further report, he may require the authority to publish a statement, in a form agreed between the local authority and the Ombudsman, consisting of the details of the action recommended by the Local Ombudsman, such supporting material as he may require, and, if the authority so require, a statement of the reasons for non-compliance with the Local Ombudsman's recommendations. The statement must be published in two editions of a local newspaper within a fortnight, the first publication to be as soon as possible. If the authority do not arrange for publication, the Local Ombudsman may do so at their expense (s. 31(2)(D)–(H)).

The 1989 Act also provided for the abolition of the representative bodies. Each Commission is now under a duty to submit its annual reports and the reports of each of the relevant local commissioners to such persons as appear to the Commission to represent authorities in England or Wales (as the case may be) or, where there are no such persons, to the authorities themselves. Responsibility for the publication of reports rests with each Commission, which must give the persons or authorities to whom the report was submitted an opportunity to comment upon it.

QUESTION

M. Jones, in 'The Local Ombudsmen and Judicial Review' [1988] *Public Law* 608–22, commenting on the proposals which are now enshrined in the amendments introduced by the Local Government and Housing Act 1989, states at p. 622 that: 'The reform now proposed is so modest that it is difficult to see how it can effect any significant or lasting change in the behaviour of local authorities.' Do you agree with this statement?

NOTE: In the Annual Report for 2000–01, it is reported that only one of the Local Commissioners made a second report (in four cases) and another used the power to require publication of a statement twice. These figures have declined, and it may be assumed that Commissioners' discussions with councils have led to this outcome.

Local Government Ombudsman
Annual Report 2000–01

APPENDIX 3(e)

Compliance with recommendations
The table below shows the outcome of 2,800 reports issued since 1 April 1990 where injustice was found. The first column shows the number of reports[1] issued in each year where maladministration causing injustice was found. The second column shows how many of these cases were not satisfactorily settled. The third column shows how many of the reports issued in each year are still awaiting a final outcome.

Year	Reports[1] finding maladministration causing injustice	Unsatisfactory outcome	Awaiting settlement
1990/91	216	13	–
1991/92	291	15	–
1992/93	339	9	–
1993/94	330	17	–
1994/95	337	11	–
1995/96	329	14	–
1996/97	236	4	–
1997/98	218	2	2
1998/99	204	1	8
1999/00	182	3	11
2000/01	118	–	54
Totals	2,800	89	75

1 This table shows numbers of reports issued, not the number of complaints subject to report. So the numbers shown in the first column are less than the number of complaints where maladministration and injustice were found (as shown in Appendix 3(b)) for each year.

Prior to the amendments in 1989 there was considerable discussion of the implementation of the recommendations of the Local Ombudsmen. The Select Committee of the PCA itself suggested that the 'best method of providing support for local ombudsmen's reports would be for our remit to be extended to allow the possibility of our calling recalcitrant local authorities to account' (see the *Third Report of the Select Committee on the PCA* HC 448 of 1985–86, para. 31). Proposals have also been made to make the recommendations of the Ombudsmen enforceable in court.

JUSTICE-All Souls Report on Administrative Law
(1988) paras 5.84–5.97

Appraisal of the Select Committee's recommendation

5.84 The proposal of the Select Committee on the PCA . . . that it should supervise compliance by local authorities with the recommendations of the Local Ombudsman deserves serious consideration. In its favour it may be said that supervision by the Select Committee would afford the opportunity for regular oversight rather than the episodic review which might result from a system of *ad hoc* court enforcement. . . .

5.85 There are, however, counter-arguments. In the first place there is the inevitable encroachment on the independence of local government. The spectre of political contests being fought between local councillors and a Parliamentary Committee over local issues is an unattractive one. The ultimate consequence of continued defiance by a local authority would presumably be that it would be in contempt of Parliament and subject to punishment accordingly. Unlike ministers, who are in contention with the Select Committee, councillors cannot take part in debate and defend themselves on the floor of the House of Commons.

5.86 Our own conclusion on this matter is that the implementation of the Select Committee's proposal is likely to be so hazardous that it should only be adopted if there is no better answer to hand. Accordingly we turn to consider the strength of the arguments against the court enforcement route.

The arguments against court enforcement

5.87 The Representative Body for England has argued that if the Northern Ireland enforcement model was to be imported here every investigation by a Local Ombudsman would start off as one likely to end up in the courts. The investigation would virtually be on a judicial basis, the system would be lengthened, more costly, and to the detriment of the complainant because of the longer time taken in arriving at a decision. . . .

5.88 At the Edinburgh Conference the arguments against judicial enforcement were forcefully put . . . [Criticisms were made] of the way in which the ombudsman system sometimes works. The troublesome cases tended to be those in which the ombudsman's findings of maladministration were felt by the authorities concerned to be wrong. Sometimes the ombudsmen were thought to be entering into the forbidden area of policy and into the merits of the particular decision under investigation rather than confining themselves (as they should) to the steps by which the decision was reached. [Criticisms were also made] of the inquisitorial methods followed by the Commissioners if these were to form the procedural prelude to a recommendation which could be judicially enforced. Thus, he said that the local authority did not usually see the full terms of the complaint and was put in the position of having to answer specific questions while ignorant of the case made against it. There was no provision between the two sides, or confrontation between the two sides, no evidence on oath, and no opportunity for testing by cross-examination. Finally, it was contended that there would be no objection to making maladministration which caused injustice justiciable by the courts. What was objectionable was to bring within the ambit of the court's powers only those cases where an opinion on the issue of maladministration had already been formed by an ombudsman on facts found by him.

Our proposal on enforcement in relation to further reports made by the local ombudsmen

5.89 While recognizing the force of the above objections, we have concluded that enforcement through the courts does offer the best solution to what has become a major problem. We have recounted the continuing history detailed above of failures by a minority of local authorities to comply with the recommendations contained in further reports made by Local Ombudsmen. The combined total of further reports issued in England, Wales and Scotland was at 31 March 1986 issued in England, Wales and Scotland was at 31 March 1986 160, of which 120 ended in failure. We have taken into account the other evidence which we have recounted . . . of lack of co-operation and the lukewarm support of the local authorities associations. As we have shown, the Local Commissioners are treated contemptuously by some local authorities and the public are repeatedly being made aware of their inability to achieve results. Thus, the impotence of the Local Ombudsmen formed the theme of three articles published in *The Times* on successive days . . . under the titles 'Investigators without enforcement power', 'Case still drags on after three years', and 'Injustices that go unresolved'. The second article detailed a current case where the complainant, having failed to receive the remedy recommended in two reports by the ombudsman, lodged a new complaint alleging maladministration by the council in not implementing the first two reports.

5.90 We think that the time has now come to add teeth to the ombudsman scheme by making it possible for successful complainants to apply to the country court or, in Scotland, the sheriff court for appropriate relief. The time has passed for saying 'One day it may be necessary to consider enforcement powers.' The hour has come. As regards the objection which we have set out above . . . we think that the fears on the ground of delay and formalism are exaggerated. The system has worked well in Northern Ireland and we think it should now be tried in England, Wales and Scotland. If . . . the ombudsmen stray outside their statutory jurisdiction, the powers of the courts can be invoked to restrain them.

5.91 As the system of first reports and further reports is already well established we would not propose any change in that. The 'mischief' at which we are striking is failure or refusal to comply with further reports. The conditions precedent to the application to the court would be:

(a) a first report containing a finding in favour of the person aggrieved that he had suffered injustice in the consequence of maladministration;
(b) a further report (following on the authority's failure or refusal to implement the first report) containing a recommendation as to the action which it would be appropriate for the authority to take to remedy or compensate for the injustice;
(c) a certificate from the Local Ombudsman issued to the complainant to the effect that the local authority had a reasonable time within which to comply with his further report and that no action to his satisfaction had been taken by the local authority, and further certifying that the case was, in his opinion, an appropriate one for application to the court for relief.

5.92 We propose a certificate as in (c) above because, in the first place, the authority must have some time within which to comply with the further report and we feel that it would be wrong to allow legal proceedings to be launched prematurely. What is a reasonable time will vary with the circumstances. . . . Secondly, we think that it is important that the Local Ombudsman should officially record his view that there has been no compliance or that the purported compliance does not satisfy him. As we have seen, some local authorities go through the motions of redressing a grievance but fail to provide the remedy that the Local Ombudsman regards as adequate. Finally, we have a special reason for requiring the Local Ombudsman to certify that in his opinion the case is an appropriate one for an application to the court. A study of the annual reports of the Local Commissioners shows that in some cases where a further report has been ignored the only recommendation made was that the authority should make a written apology. Other cases have involved a recommendation for the payment of a trifling sum of money or for a local authority to take action in relation to some highly personal matter (such as altering the precise language of an entry in a Book of Remembrance at a council crematorium). The system might be brought into ridicule if the coercive power of the court were to be invoked in such cases or others of a sensitive nature where a Local Commissioner would judge that more harm than good would be done by permitting the complainant to go to court. In the ordinary case, however, where there was a recommendation for a substantial payment or for the taking of action that could appropriately be enforced by injunction there would be no difficulty in obtaining the certificate. Nevertheless, we think that it is too facile simply to suggest that all recommendations which have not been complied with should be enforceable in the courts.

5.93 We propose that the court itself should have the same discretion as regards the relief to be granted as is conferred upon the county court in Northern Ireland when dealing with cases where the Commissioner for Complaints has found maladministration causing injustice. . . . The effect would be that the court has both a discretion as to the type of relief which should be granted and a discretion to withhold relief altogether.

5.94 We also consider that while section 7 of the Northern Ireland Act [the Commissioner for Complaints Act (Northern Ireland) 1969] provides a valuable precedent to which reference may be made, it would be inadvisable to follow its provisions literally. We are particularly concerned about section 7(8) which makes the Commissioner's report available as evidence in the legal proceedings. The report is not made conclusive evidence; the subsection goes no further than to state that the report 'shall, unless the contrary is proved, be accepted as evidence of the facts stated therein.' This raises the possibility that the defendant authority in any legal proceedings might try to reopen the whole matter investigated by the Local Commissioner and seek to establish that the facts found in his report were wrong and that his conclusions on maladministration and resulting injustice were also ill-founded. As we have shown, recalcitrant authorities not infrequently adopt the line that the ombudsman's report is mistaken, that there has been no maladministration and that the complainant is in any event not entitled to a remedy. Such local authorities, which are already undermining the voluntary system, based (as it is supposed to be) on the willing acceptance of the umpire's verdict, would not hesitate to use the law courts as the forum for seeking to demolish or gravely impugn ombudsmen's reports.

5.95 We are also concerned about the disadvantageous position of the complainant (plaintiff) in the litigation. He would be trying to uphold the Commissioner's report but he would be at a financial disadvantage in taking on the local authority in what might become protracted litigation. Furthermore, he might well be unable to give strict proof of all the material facts in the report. Sources of information which were available to the Local Ombudsman in preparing his report might not be available to him as a private litigant . . .

5.96 These considerations make it necessary, in our view, to entrench and protect the findings of fact made by the Local Ombudsman in his report and further report and his conclusions that there has been maladministration causing injustice to the person aggrieved (the plaintiff). . . .

5.97 The statutory protection for the reports and findings of Local Ombudsmen which we advocate would not, of course, preclude a local authority from showing that in a particular instance the ombudsman had stepped outside his jurisdiction. On ordinary principles the protection would not avail the ombudsman in such circumstances.

NOTES:
1. Where the Commissioner for Complaints in Northern Ireland makes a finding that an individual has sustained injustice in consequence of maladministration, the individual may apply to the county court, and the court may award 'such damages as the court may think just in all the circumstances to compensate' the applicant for loss or injury suffered on account of (a) expenses reasonably incurred, and (b) lost opportunity of acquiring benefit (Commissioner for Complaints Order (Northern Ireland) 1996, art. 16(2)). If it appears to the court that justice can only be done by ordering that body to take or refrain from taking some action, then the court may, if satisfied that in all the circumstances it is reasonable so to do, grant a mandatory or other injunction (art. 16(5)). In addition, where maladministration coupled with injustice has been found, and it appears to the Commissioner for Complaints that the body concerned has previously engaged in conduct of the same kind and is likely to continue to engage in future in conduct of the type which he has condemned, he may

request the Attorney-General to apply to the High Court for appropriate relief, such as an injunction to restrain the continuation of the maladministration (art. 17). From 1978–88 there were on average three applications each year to the county court by successful complainants. The Attorney-General has, however, never been asked to make an application (see the *JUSTICE-All Souls Report on Administrative Law* (1988), pp. 123–5 for a discussion of the role of the Commissioner for Complaints in Northern Ireland and White (1994) 45 NILQ 395 on the Northern Ireland enforcement provision).

2. The Cabinet Office Review recommended, and the Scottish Public Services Ombudsman Act 2002 implemented, continuation of non-binding investigation reports. The Scottish Ombudsman may issue a special report to the body complained against, the complainant, and also lay a copy before the Scottish Parliament. The body complained against must carry out and pay for any arrangements to make the special report available to the public.

QUESTIONS

1. Do you consider it is necessary to introduce further reforms relating to the enforcement of the recommendations of any of the public sector ombudsmen?

2. Do you agree with the *JUSTICE-All Souls Report*'s rejection of the reasoning of the Select Committee (see further C. Himsworth, 'Parliamentary Teeth for Local Ombudsmen' [1986] *Public Law* 546–50)?

3. In Lewis *et al.*, *Complaints Procedures in Local Government* (1988), the view was expressed, at p. 39, that court enforcement was not a good solution:

> We became convinced that enforcement would imperil that relationship [the relationship between the commissioners and the local authorities] and make local authorities 'minimalist' in their response and particularly defensive. Anything which might be enforced by a court would be hard fought over and agreed with maximum reluctance. Currently some of the Ombudsmen find that the lack of firm recommendations, at least at the preliminary stage, allows them to see what the local authority will offer. Again, some of them appear to adopt the practice of telephoning a chief executive and asking what kind of recommendation the authority would best respond to, and what in particular might be acceptable to the elected member. We strongly believe that such co-operation would be placed in jeopardy by [court enforcement]. . . .

If the recent reforms do not go far enough and court enforcement is not desirable, what other solutions might there be?

A complainant's unhappiness with an investigation may not be about the response of the authority complained against but with the way in which the PCA has conducted the investigation.

R v Parliamentary Commissioner for Administration, ex parte Dyer
[1994] 1 All ER 375, Divisional Court, Queen's Bench Division

The applicant had complained to the PCA through an MP about the handling of claims for certain benefits by the Department of Social Security. The PCA found injustice caused by maladaminstration and recommended an ex gratia payment and an apology. The applicant was dissatisfied with the PCA's report and sought judicial review of the PCA's decision not to re-open the investigation on the grounds that (i) the PCA had only investigated some of her complaints; (ii) that while he had given the Department the opportunity to comment upon the report in draft, he had not given the applicant that opportunity; (iii) that he had decided not to re-open the investigation after being informed of the failure to consider a number of the applicant's complaints; and (iv) he had wrongly considered himself precluded from re-opening the investigation. The PCA contended that, as the Parliamentary Commissioner Act 1967, s. 5 provided that the PCA initiated investigations on reference by, and reported back to, an MP, and because he was subject to oversight by a select committee that the court had no jurisdiction to review his exercise of discretion under the 1967 Act as he was answerable solely to Parliament about the discharge of his responsibilities. Alternatively the court could only review the PCA for exceptional cases of abuse of power.

SIMON BROWN LJ:. . . As to his wider proposition – that this court has literally no right to review the PCA's exercise of his discretion under the 1967 Act (not even, to give the classic illustration, if he refused to investigate complaints by red-headed complainants) – Mr Richards submits that the legislation is enacted in such terms as to indicate an intention that the PCA should be answerable to Parliament alone for the way he performs his functions. The PCA is, he suggests, an officer of the House of Commons, and, the argument runs, the parliamentary control provided for by the statute displaces any supervisory control by the courts. Mr Richards relies in particular on these considerations: first, the stipulation under s. 5 that a complaint must be referred to the PCA by a member of Parliament before even his powers of investigation are engaged; second, the requirement under s. 10(1) to report back to the member of Parliament (and, in certain circumstances, to each House of Parliament – see s. 10(3)); third, the requirement under s. 10(4) annually to lay a general report before Parliament; fourth, the provision under s. 1(3) of the Act for the PCA's removal from office only in the event of addresses from both Houses of Parliament. Mr Richards points also to the PCA being always answerable to the select committee.

Despite these considerations I, for my part, would unhesitatingly reject this argument. Many in government are answerable to Parliament and yet answerable also to the supervisory jurisdiction of this court. I see nothing about the PCA's role or the statutory framework within which he operates so singular as to take him wholly outside the purview of judicial review.

I turn next, therefore, to Mr Richards's alternative and narrower submission that, by analogy with the two House of Lords cases already mentioned, the courts should regard their powers as restricted with regard to reviewing the PCA's exercise of the discretions conferred upon him by this legislation.

I need cite one passage only from the speeches in those two cases, this from Lord Bridge's speech in *Hammersmith and Fulham London BC* v *Secretary of State for the Environment* [1990] 3 All ER 589 at 637, [1991] 1 AC 521 at 597:

> The restriction which the *Nottinghamshire* case [1986] 1 All ER 199, [1986] AC 240 imposes on the scope of judicial review operates only when the court has first determined that the ministerial action in question does not contravene the requirements of the statute, whether express or implied, and only then declares that, since the statute has conferred a power on the Secretary of State which involves the formulation and the implementation of national economic policy and which can only take effect with the approval of the House of Commons, it is not open to challenge on the grounds of irrationality short of the extremes of bad faith, improper motive or manifest absurdity. Both the constitutional propriety and

the good sense of this restriction seem to me to be clear enough. The formulation and the implementation of national economic policy are matters depending essentially on political judgment. The decisions which shape them are for politicians to take and it is in the political forum of the House of Commons that they are properly to be debated and approved or disapproved on their merits. If the decisions have been taken in good faith within the four corners of the Act, the merits of the policy underlying the decisions are not susceptible to review by the courts and the courts would be exceeding their proper function if they presumed to condemn the policy as unreasonable.

Mr Richards concedes that the analogy between the position considered there and that arising here is not a very close one. He submits, however, that the underlying rationale for restricting the scope of judicial review in those cases applies also here. Although, as counsel recognises, the PCA's functions are manifestly not political, nevertheless, he submits, the provisions here for parliamentary control afford this case a comparable dimension.

This submission too I would reject. There seems to me no parallel whatever between, on the one hand, decisions regarding the formulation and implementation of national economic policy – decisions 'depending essentially on political judgment . . . for politicians to take . . . in the political forum of the House of Commons' – and, on the other hand, decisions of the PCA regarding the matters appropriate for investigation and the proper manner of their investigation.

All that said, however, and despite my rejection of both Mr Richards's submissions on the question of jurisdiction, it does not follow that this court will readily be persuaded to interfere with the exercise of the PCA's discretion. Quite the contrary. The intended width of these discretions is made strikingly clear by the legislature: under s. 5(5), when determining whether to initiate, continue or discontinue an investigation, the commissioner shall 'act in accordance with his own discretion'; under s. 7(2), 'the procedure for conducting an investigation shall be such as the commissioner considers appropriate in the circumstances of the case'. Bearing in mind too that the exercise of these particular discretions inevitably involves a high degree of subjective judgment, it follows that it will always be difficult to mount an effective challenge on what may be called the conventional ground of *Wednesbury* unreasonableness (see *Associated Provincial Picture Houses Ltd v Wednesbury Corp* [1947] 2 All ER 680, [1948] 1 KB 223).

Recognising this, indeed, one may pause to wonder whether in reality the end result is much different from that arrived at by the House of Lords in the two cases referred to, where the decisions in question were held 'not open to challenge on the grounds of irrationality short of the extremes of bad faith, improper motive or manifest absurdity'. True, in the present case 'manifest absurdity' does not have to be shown; but inevitably it will be almost as difficult to demonstrate that the PCA has exercised one or other of his discretions unreasonably in the public law sense.

Before passing from this part of the case I should mention briefly two authorities with regard to the exercise of the courts' review jurisdiction over local commissioners' reports – *R v Comr for Local Administration, ex parte Eastleigh BC* [1988] 3 All ER 151, [1988] QB 855, and *R v Comr for Local Administration, ex parte Croydon London BC* [1989] 1 All ER 1033. Only in *Ex parte Eastleigh BC* [1988] 3 All ER 151 at 157–8, [1988] QB 855 at 866 was the jurisdictional issue raised, Lord Donaldson MR stating:

> Let me start with the fact that Parliament has not created a right of appeal against the findings in an ombudsman's report. It is this very fact, coupled with the public law character of the ombudsman's office and powers which is the foundation of the right to relief by way of judicial review.

Mr Richards accepts that the scheme, and indeed language, of the Local Government Act 1974, which created local commissioners, is very similar to that of the 1967 Act (on which it was clearly based), but he draws our attention to certain particular differences which he suggests are possibly material, and he submits that merely because local commissioners have been held reviewable by the courts it does not follow that Parliament intended the PCA's powers under the original legislation to be reviewable. For my part I find it unnecessary to consider this submission in any depth. For this reason: both these local commissioner cases appear to have been concerned not with reviewing the exercise of the local commissioner's discretion but rather with the examination of his powers; what was being alleged was that he had contravened the requirements of the statute. There can surely be no possible question but that the court's supervisory jurisdiction exists for this purpose and, indeed, Mr Richards has not submitted to the contrary. To my mind, therefore, these local commissioner cases do not advance the argument one way or the other with respect to the court's jurisdiction to review the exercise of the PCA's discretionary powers. But of course it follows from my already expressed conclusion upon that point that I would regard the exercise of the local commisioner's discretion as reviewable too. Again, however, only with inevitable difficulty. As Lord Donaldson MR said in *Ex parte Eastleigh BC* [1988] 3 All ER 151 at 158, [1988] QB 855 at 867:

> . . . I am very far from encouraging councils to seek judicial review of an ombudsman's report, which, bearing in mind the nature of his office and duties and the qualifications of those who hold that office, is inherently unlikely to succeed . . .

Both those cases were, of course, concerned with judicial review applications by local authorities against whom the local commissioner had reported adversely. Certainly no greater encouragement should be afforded to those whose complaints the commissioner has investigated; their prospects of success are clearly no higher.

Recognising the full width of our jurisdiction but with those considerations in mind I turn to Miss Dyer's grounds of challenge.

As to her contention that the PCA investigated some only of her original grounds of complaint, that is undoubtedly the case. But is she entitled to criticise the PCA for taking that course? More particularly, was the PCA acting outside the proper ambit of his discretion under s. 5(5) of the 1967 Act in doing so?

The following two passages in his report are relevant: first from para 14:

> In her letter of complaint [Miss Dyer] gave examples of what she considered maladministration by the local and regional offices. I decided to investigate six main aspects – (i) an inaccurate letter, (ii) an unnecessary appeal, (iii) the withdrawal of her benefit without a decision, (iv) the failure to issue decisions, (v) inaccurate information and (vi) unanswered correspondence.

And from para. 17:

> The papers supplied to me by both Miss Dyer and the DSS contained much correspondence, minutes, notes of interviews and notes of telephone conversations. I have not found it either necessary or expedient to set them all out in detail in my report; but they have all been scrutinised and taken into account in reaching these findings. It is clear that Miss Dyer received a very poor service from the local office. There were problems in the handling of her correspondence, which was often unanswered, in making, or purporting to make, decisions on her claims and in the general relationship between the local office and Miss Dyer. I do not propose to address each and every shortcoming in the local office's conduct of the case but the following are my findings on the six main elements of her complaint.

He then set out his findings in some considerable detail.

In my judgment, the PCA was entitled in the exercise of his discretion to limit the scope of his investigation, to be selective as to just which of Miss Dyer's many detailed complaints he addressed, to identify certain broad categories of complaint (the six main aspects as he called them) and investigate only those. Inevitably such an approach carried the risk that some of the problems which Miss Dyer complained of having experienced with the local office would continue, and that indeed is what Miss Dyer says has occurred. But no investigation should be expected to solve all problems for all time and it cannot in my judgment be said that the approach adopted here by the PCA was not one properly open to him.

Turning to Miss Dyer's complaint that the draft report was sent to the department for comment on the facts but not to her, the respondent's evidence indicates that this is a practice which has existed for 25 years, and is known to and acquiesced in by the select committee. The reasons for it are explained as follows. First, that it is the department rather than the complainant who may subsequently be called upon to justify its actions before the select committee and, if it is shown the draft report and does not point out any inaccuracy, it will then be unable to dispute the facts stated in it. Second, the practice affords the department an opportunity to give notice in writing to the PCA, as expressly provided for by s. 11(3) of the 1967 Act, of any document or information the disclosure of which, in the opinion of the relevant minister, would be prejudicial to the safety of the state or otherwise contrary to the public interest. Third, sight of the draft report gives the department the opportunity to propose the remedy it is prepared to offer in the light of any findings of maladministration and injustice contained in it. The commissioner can then include in his final report what that proposed remedy is and indicate whether he finds that it satisfactorily meets the need.

Miss Dyer recognises, I think, that the same reasons do not exist for sending the draft report to her. Indeed, having regard to s. 11(3), it could not be sent to her unless and until it had already been cleared by the department. Therefore, to graft on to the existing practice a need to show the draft report to complainants too would introduce a further stage into the process. Does natural justice require this? I do not think so. As Lord Bridge said in *Lloyd* v *McMahon* [1987] 1 All ER 1118 at 1161, [1987] AC 625 at 702:

> My Lords, the so-called rules of natural justice are not engraved on tablets of stone. To use the phrase which better expresses the underlying concept, what the requirements of fairness demand when any body, domestic, administrative or judicial, has to make a decision which will affect the rights of individuals depends on the character of the decision-making body, the kind of decision it has to make and the statutory or other framework in which it operates.

Assuming, as I do, and indeed as Mr Richards concedes, that the PCA makes a decision which will affect the rights of Miss Dyer, it should nevertheless be borne in mind that it is the department and not her who is being investigated and who is liable to face public criticism for its acts. I cannot conclude that fairness here demanded that she too be shown the draft report. Rather it seems to me that the PCA, in determining the procedure for conducting his investigation as provided for by s. 7(2), was amply entitled to consider it appropriate to follow his long-established practice.

I come finally to Miss Dyer's complaint about the PCA's refusal to reopen this investigation. This I can deal with altogether more shortly. It seems to me that the PCA is clearly correct in his view that, once his report had been sent to Mr Hattersley and the DSS (as required by s. 10(1) and (2)), he was *functus officio* and unable to reopen the investigation without a further referral under s. 5(1). Section 5(5), as already indicated, confers a wide discretion indeed; it does not, however, purport to empower the PCA to reopen an investigation once his report is submitted. It would seem to me unfair to the department and outside the scheme of this legislation to suppose that the PCA could do as Miss Dyer wished.

That apart, however, it is plain that even if the PCA had had the power to reopen his investigation he would inevitably have refused to do so: he had long since decided not to investigate Miss Dyer's further complaints and I have already held that he was entitled to limit his investigations in that way.

It follows that, in my judgment, none of Miss Dyer's grounds of challenge can be made good and this application accordingly fails.

Application refused.

NOTE:The Cabinet Office Review recommended that the draft report be made available to both the complainant and the body complained against.

QUESTIONS

1. Do you think that *ex parte Dyer* should be overturned by legislation?

2. Is the PCA subject to less oversight than the bodies he supervises, and if so, what are the reasons for this?

SECTION 7: **Reform of the Institution of the Ombudsman**

Amalgamating the different public sector ombudsmen was suggested first in England jointly by the Parliamentary, Local Government and Health Service Commissioner in 1998. This led to the study by the Cabinet Office *Review of the Public Sector Ombudsmen* published in April 2000 (http://www.cabinet-office.gov.uk/central/2000/ombudsmenreview.pdf) and an acceptance of the main recommendations following a consultation (HC Debs 20 July 2001, Written Answers col. 464w). In Scotland matters progressed more quickly. Two consultation documents were published: *Modernising the Complaints System* in October 2000 and *A Modern Complaints System* in July 2001 (http://www.scotland.gov.uk/consultations/localgov/ppso-00.asp). The Scottish Public Sector Ombudsman Bill was introduced in the Scottish Parliament in November 2001 and passed as the Scottish Public Services Ombudsman Act in March 2002. While the Scottish arrangements on investigation were kept minimal, the Cabinet Office Review made detailed recommendations about the process. Such change was under way in the PCA so that emphasis on investigation was being replaced by one on outcomes (see *ante* pp. 734–5).

There was also discussion on the scope of the role of the ombudsman.

Review of the Public Sector Ombudsmen in England
Cabinet Office 2000, pp. 61–3

Systemic Maladministration
6.83 There are a number of aspects to the role of the ombudsman in addressing systemic maladministration. Firstly, the maladministration found while investigating an individual complaint may have affected others systematically. The ombudsman will then wish to be assured that the respondent body is tracing those affected and providing appropriate redress. Secondly, the ombudsman may wish to make recommendations about correcting a fault in the system found during investigation as being directly responsible for the maladministration leading to the complaint. Thirdly, the ombudsman might go beyond investigating the specific process which led to the complaint and look more widely at organisation, management, guidance and so on – that is, the environment in which the complaint arose. Lastly, the ombudsman may have a role in identifying bad practice and setting standards for good practice arising from their experience in investigating complaints in general.

6.84 The emphasis of each of the present ombudsmen in these areas is variable. The CLA has a distinct role in good practice, having published a number of good practice guides on subjects such as complaints systems and housing repairs. Both the HSC and CLA have large numbers of similar bodies in their jurisdiction and therefore their ability to spread the lessons learned from individual cases (a council housing department or a GP practice) is a valuable service and much appreciated. The PCA is dealing with a large number of different organisations and so any lessons to be widely disseminated must inevitably be more general.

6.85 Information on cases – the case digests published by the CLA, case reports, annual and special reports – are greatly valued by professionals and others. The new Commission should as a matter of course make available all publishable case reports (some are not published because of confidentiality), ideally online and in both full and summary versions with index or search facilities. At present there are restrictions on the PCA's (and HSC's) ability to publish reports because he depends on Parliamentary privilege against defamation. He must lay reports before Parliament and this limits the number able to be published. The CLA on the other hand under its legislation has absolute privilege. **We recommend that the new Commission is given powers to put all publishable case reports into the public domain with absolute privilege.** The power (and duty) to lay certain reports before Parliament (in particular the annual report and any special reports the new Commission wishes to make) should remain.

6.86 Some have suggested that the ombudsman role could go further. A 'Commission for Public Administration' would have a wide role in overseeing the standard of public administration, perhaps conducting research and setting general standards for good administration. This would be a major change in the role of the ombudsman and we would be concerned at any reduction in focus on their core role of handling complaints.

6.87 Another suggestion is that the ombudsmen could be active in preventing complaints – for example, by auditing complaints systems or advising on administrative systems early in their life cycle. The ombudsmen have always been reluctant to be seen to be endorsing any system in case they later had to deal with a complaint against it – they saw a risk to actual or perceived impartiality. Independent complaints examiners have said they are sometimes consulted early in the design of an administrative system – they can provide an expert and interested eye in, for example, looking at a proposed new form. In practical terms, the number of bodies within jurisdiction of a new Commission will be too large to provide such bespoke services in general and hard to justify except on a repayment basis (which would itself raise difficult questions about bodies within jurisdiction making payments to the ombudsmen and thus risking their independence and impartiality).

6.88 There is a very wide range of organisations within jurisdiction and some variations in the ombudsmen's role depending on the sector (ie whether central or local government or health service) would be acceptable given the different characteristics of each sector and the different histories of the ombudsmen. Functional specialist ombudsmen might therefore continue to have a slightly different 'fit' within the new Commission to reflect the different sectors. Parliamentary, local government and health service ombudsmen would continue to offer a point of engagement.

NOTES:
1. In Scotland the discussion on the Ombudsman's role also emphasized the investigation and resolution of individual complaints. There was little support for permitting the ombudsman to initiate his or her own investigations. Instead the Scottish Ministers proposed to

    reinforce the provisions for the Ombudsman to share information with auditors, Commissioners (eg the Scottish Information Commissioner) and Ombudsmen/Commissioners in other parts of the UK, to minimise the risk of any cases of maladministration being missed.

    Under the legislation the Scottish Public Services Ombudsman may make general recommendations in the Annual Report.
2. Some commentators, such as Seneviratne [2000] PL 582 and Thompson (2001) 64 MLR 459 have suggested that there should have been discussion of the administrative justice system as a whole and the relationship amongst its component redress mechanisms, as opposed to separate reviews of the ombudsmen, judicial review (Bowman), and tribunals (Leggatt).

QUESTIONS

1. Would the nature of the institution of the Ombudsmen alter if they took on a greater role in administrative audit?

2. If so, would this alteration have an impact on the ability of the PCA or the Local Commissioners to perform their present functions? (See further, C. Crawford, 'Complaints, Codes and Ombudsmen in Local Government' (1988) *Public Law* 246–67.)

11

Statutory Tribunals

SECTION 1: **Introduction: The Rationale for Tribunals**

Concern about the growth of tribunals and their functions and procedures prompted the formation of the Committee on Administrative Tribunals and Inquiries in 1955. The Committee reported in 1957, and several of its recommendations are discussed below. The Committee also dealt with inquiries, but this topic is not covered in this chapter.

The Report led to important reforms in the Tribunal and Inquiries Act 1958. The major provisions of this Act were subsequently re-enacted first in the Tribunals and Inquiries Act 1971 and then, with minor amendments, in the Tribunals and Inquiries Act 1992, which is set out below. In addition, there are many specific legislative provisions governing the procedure at particular tribunals (see, for example, the Social Security and Child Support (Decisions and Appeals) Regulations 1999). Reference to the Act will be required throughout this chapter.

Tribunals And Inquiries Act 1992

1.—(1) There shall continue to be a council entitled the Council on Tribunals . . . —

    (a) to keep under review the constitution and working of the tribunals specified in Schedule 1 . . . and from time to time, to report on their constitution and working;

    (b) to consider and report on such particular matters as may be referred to the Council under this Act with respect to tribunals other than the ordinary courts of law, whether or not specified in Schedule 1 to this Act, or any such tribunal;

    . . .

2.—(1) Subject to subsection (3) of this section the Council shall consist of not more than fifteen nor less then ten members appointed by the Lord Chancellor and the Scottish Ministers, and one of the members shall be so appointed to be chairman of the Council.

    . . .

3.—(1) Persons appointed under section 2 of this Act shall hold and vacate office under the terms of the instruments under which they are appointed but may resign office by notice in writing to the Minister or Ministers by whom they were appointed; and any such person who ceases to hold office shall be eligible for re-appointment.

    . . .

4.—(1) Subject to the provisions of this section, any report by, or reference to, the

Council shall be made to or, as the case may be by, the Lord Chancellor and the Scottish Ministers.

. . .

5.—(1) Subject to section 6 but without prejudice to the generality of section 1(1)(a) of this Act, the Council may make to the appropriate Minister general recommendations as to the making of appointments to membership of any tribunals mentioned in Schedule 1 to this Act or of panels constituted for the purposes of any such tribunals; and (without prejudice to any statutory provisions having effect with respect to such appointments) the appropriate Minister shall have regard to recommendations under this section.

(2) In this section 'the appropriate Minister', in relation to appointments of any description, means the Minister making the appointments or, if they are not made by a Minister, the Minister in charge of the government department concerned with the tribunals in question.

. . .

6.—(1) The chairman, or any person appointed to act as chairman, of any of the tribunals to which this subsection applies shall (without prejudice to any statutory provisions as to qualifications) be selected by the appropriate authority from a panel of persons appointed by the Lord Chancellor. . . .

(6) In this section 'the appropriate authority' means the Minister who apart from this Act would be empowered to appoint or select the chairman, person to act as chairman, members or member of the tribunal in question. . . .

7.—(1) Subject to subsection (2) of this section, no power of a Minister other than the Lord Chancellor, to terminate a person's membership of any such tribunal as is specified in Schedule 1, or of a panel constituted for the purposes of any such tribunal, shall be exercisable except with the consent of:

(a) the Lord Chancellor, the Lord President of the Court of Session and the Lord Chief Justice of Northern Ireland, if the tribunal sits in all parts of the United Kingdom;

(b) the Lord Chancellor and the Lord President of the Court of Session, if the tribunal sits in all parts of Great Britain;

(c) the Lord Chancellor and the Lord Chief Justice of Northern Ireland, if the tribunal sits both in England and Wales and in Northern Ireland;

(d) the Lord Chancellor, if the tribunal does not sit outside England and Wales;

(e) the Lord President of the Court of Session, if the tribunal sits only in Scotland;

(f) the Lord Chief Justice of Northern Ireland, if the tribunal sits only in Northern Ireland.

8.—(1) The power of a Minister . . . to make, approve, confirm or concur in procedural rules for any tribunal specified in Schedule 1 shall be exercisable only after consultation with the Council.

. . .

(4) In this section 'procedural rules' includes any statutory provision relating to the procedure of the tribunal in question.

. . .

10.—(1) Subject to the provisions of this section, where:

(a) any tribunal specified in Schedule 1 to this Act gives any decision; . . . it shall be the duty of the tribunal or Minister to furnish a statement, either written or oral, of the reasons for the decision if requested, on or before the giving or notification of the decision, to state the reasons.

(2) The statement referred to in subsection (1) may be refused, or the specification of the reasons restricted, on grounds of national security.

(3) . . .

(4) Subsection (1) does not apply to any decision taken by a Minister after the holding by

him or on his behalf of an inquiry or hearing which is a statutory inquiry by virtue only of an order made under section 16(2) unless the order contains a direction that this section is to apply in relation to any inquiry or hearing to which the order applies . . .

(6) Any statement of the reasons for a decision referred to in paragraph (a) or (b) of subsection (1), whether given in pursuance of that subsection or of any other statutory provision, shall be taken to form part of the decision and accordingly to be incorporated in the record.

(7) If, after consultation with the Council, it appears to the Lord Chancellor that it is expedient that—

(a) decisions of any particular tribunal or any description of such decisions, or
(b) any description of decisions of a Minister should be excluded from the operation of subsection (1) of this section on the ground that the subject-matter of such decisions, or the circumstances in which they are made, make the giving of reasons unnecessary or impracticable, the Lord Chancellor may by order direct that subsection (1) of this section shall not apply to such decisions.

. . .

11.—(1) Subject to subsection (2), if any party to proceedings before any tribunal specified in paragraph 8, 15(a) or (d), 16, 18, 24, 26, 31, 33(b), 37, 40A, 44 or 45 of Schedule 1 is dissatisfied in point of law with a decision of the tribunal he may, according as rules of court may provide, either appeal from the tribunal to the High Court or require the tribunal to state and sign a case for the opinion of the High Court.

(2) Subsection (1) shall not apply in relation to proceedings before industrial tribunals which arise under or by virtue of any of the enactments mentioned in section 136(1) of the Employment Protection (Consolidation) Act 1978.

NOTE: Wade and Forsyth's *Administrative Law* (8th edn) (2000) contains further details of the rights of appeal (see pp. 929–37).

All the textbooks covering the topic of tribunals comment on the proliferation of tribunals during the twentieth century and the great variety of types of tribunals (see, e.g. Wade and Bradley, *Constitutional and Administrative Law* (1997), Chapter 28, De Smith and Brazier, *Constitutional and Administrative Law* (1998), Chapter 28). This variety makes it difficult to provide a generic account of the characteristics of tribunals. It is, however, generally accepted that many statutory tribunals are a mechanism for resolving disputes which arise in the operation of particular governmental schemes. Why are such tribunals established?

Report of the Committee on Administrative Tribunals and Enquiries
Cmnd 218 (1957), paras 20–22, 26–27, 29–32

20. It is noteworthy that Parliament, having decided that the decisions with which we are concerned should not be remitted to the ordinary courts, should also have decided that they should not be left to be reached in the normal course of administration. Parliament has considered it essential to lay down special procedures for them.

Good administration
21. This must have been to promote good administration. Administration must not only be efficient in the sense that the objectives of policy are securely attained without delay. It must also satisfy the general body of citizens that it is proceeding with reasonable regard to the balance between the public interest which it promotes and the private interest which it disturbs. Parliament has, we infer, intended in relation to the subject-matter of our terms of reference that the further decisions or, as they may rightly be termed in this context, adjudications must be acceptable as having been properly made.

22. It is natural that Parliament should have taken this view of what constitutes good administration. In this country government rests fundamentally upon the consent of the governed. The general acceptability of these adjudications is one of the vital elements in sustaining that consent. . . .

26. At this stage another question naturally arises. On what principle has it been decided that some adjudications should be made by tribunals and some by Ministers? If from a study of the history of the subject we could discover such a principle, we should have a criterion which would be a guide for any future allocation of these decisions between tribunals and Ministers.

27. The search for this principle has usually involved the application of one or both notions, each with its antithesis. Both notions are famous and have long histories. They are the notion of what is judicial, its antithesis being what is administrative, and the notion of what is according to the rule of law, its antithesis being what is arbitrary. . . .

29. The rule of law stands for the view that decisions should be made by the application of known principles or laws. In general such decisions will be predictable, and the citizen will know where he is. On the other hand there is what is arbitrary. A decision may be without principle, without any rules. It is therefore unpredictable, the antithesis of a decision taken in accordance with the rule of law.

30. Nothing that we say diminishes the importance of these pairs of antitheses. But it must be confessed that neither pair yields a valid principle on which one can decide whether the duty of making a certain decision should be laid upon a tribunal or upon a Minister or whether the existing allocation of decisions between tribunals and Ministers is appropriate. But even if there is no such principle and we cannot explain all the facts, we can at least start with them. An empirical approach may be the most useful.

31. Starting with the facts, we observe that the methods of adjudication by tribunals are in general not the same as those of adjudication by Ministers. All or nearly all tribunals apply rules. No ministerial decision of the kind denoted by the second part of our terms of reference is reached in this way. Many matters remitted to tribunals and Ministers appear to have, as it were, a natural affinity with one or other method of adjudication. Sometimes the policy of the legislation can be embodied in a system of detailed regulations. Particular decisions cannot, single case by single case, alter the Minister's policy. Where this is so, it is natural to entrust the decisions to a tribunal, if not to the courts. On the other hand it is sometimes desirable to preserve flexibility of decision in the pursuance of public policy. Then a wise expediency is the proper basis of right adjudication, and the decision must be left with a Minister.

32. But in other instances there seems to be no such natural affinity. For example, there seems to be no natural affinity which makes it clearly appropriate for appeals in goods vehicles cases to be decided by the Transport Tribunal when appeals in a number of road passenger cases are decided by the Minister.

NOTE: The authors of the report have candidly confessed that the principles they cite do not yield an explanation for why a particular decision should be laid upon a tribunal rather than upon a Minister. Other factors which may come into play are explored by Keith Hendry in the following article.

K. H. Hendry, 'The Tasks of Tribunals: Some Thoughts'
(1982) 1 *Civil Justice Quarterly*, 253, 256–259

Tribunals as components of administration schemes
A peremptory glance at the governmental picture in a modern welfare state such as the United Kingdom, will show a multiplicity of tribunals each operating within the bounds of a confined jurisdiction and each directed toward disposing of claims and arguments arising out of a particular statutory scheme. So, for example, Supplementary Benefits Appeal Tribunals constituted under Schedule 4 of

the Supplementary Benefits Act 1976 deal with the many disputes that arise from the grant or withholding of supplementary benefit; similarly under section 40 of the Finance Act 1972 (as amended) Value Added Tax Tribunals hear disagreements between tax officials and those liable to pay VAT. Many more examples could be given.

Parliament's enactment of various schemes and the inclusion within these schemes of specialist tribunals recognises firstly the social need for that scheme and secondly a social need for having machinery to dispose of disputes arising under that scheme. It is insufficiently stressed that as such tribunals have a task as essential parts of the machinery of administrative government.

So we see in particular the Council on Tribunals stressing that 'tribunals are bodies set up to *adjudicate* between the State and the individual . . .' with little mention of a tribunal's role in the administrative field. This is not to belittle their role as adjudicatory machinery, but at the same time their responsibilities to their schemes will be vitally important to administration. To take an example: under section 3 of the Mental Health Act 1959, 14 Mental Health Review Tribunals are constituted. They disposed of 696 cases in 1978. The gravity of these tribunals should not be underestimated – they are empowered to determine whether a patient shall be compulsorily detained, and so lose his personal liberty. As such they are vital to the administration of a particular social necessity recognised by legislation.

The Franks Report expressly recognises this factor, albeit in a somewhat guarded way. Having noted that 'Parliament' decided that certain decisions should not be dealt with by the ordinary courts, nor in the normal course of administration, the Report sees tribunals existing so as to 'promote good administration,' that is 'efficient in the sense that the objectives of policy are securely attained without delay,' but at the same time 'with reasonable regard to the balance between the public interest . . . and the private interest' '. . . adjudications must be acceptable as having been properly made.' Already we can see the emergence of the Franks bias, carried on today by its offspring, the Council on Tribunals, namely that what was important was the *correctness* of administration to the detriment of *administration* itself. Had more attention been paid to this task of tribunals one might have seen a greater recognition of its central importance and a consequent appreciation of tribunals as instruments of government. Having devised special procedures as essential elements of administration it can be inferred that tribunals have two further linked, but not quite so obvious, tasks. These are to avoid Ministerial Responsibility and to ease the workload of Governmental Departments.

Under the United Kingdom constitution, a Minister is primarily responsible to Parliament for his and his department's activities. Ultimately he is responsible to public opinion. Under a new legislative scheme it is a matter of choice as to whether decisions will be left to the Minister personally or to his Department. In both cases he remains responsible. However, if a dispute is to be decided outside the Department, for present purposes by a tribunal, the Minister will be able to disclaim responsibility for it. Furthermore, it will not be possible to bring political pressure to bear in order to affect that decision. The creation of a tribunal may therefore have as one of its purposes the evasion of Ministerial responsibility and the easing of Departmental workloads. So under section 12 of the Immigration Act 1971, one sees a two-tier appeal system; at first instance, adjudicators, and above them Immigration Tribunals. The volume of work done by these tribunals indicates the extent to which particularly the Home Office's workload is eased, and how a very politically sensitive decision is hived off to tribunals.

The decision to retain a decision within Departmental/Ministerial hands or to turn it over to a tribunal will, of course, be motivated by a number of factors: a 1980 Council on Tribunals Special Report felt that 'Parliament's' selection of subjects to be referred to tribunals does not form a regular pattern although basic guidelines and various factors included the nature of the decision, historical accidents, Departmental preferences and political consideration. The last-mentioned consideration could operate in both ways – one could give a matter which is potentially sensitive to a tribunal to desensitise it (the system of Immigration Tribunals is an example), or alternatively retain it for that reason within Departmental/Ministerial hands. Other factors would include the likely number of disputes, national interest, the level of discretion involved and so on, but one is forced to agree with the Council on Tribunals that there is no application of a set of coherent principles.

It seems, therefore, that the use of tribunals is a convenient means for affording Ministers immunity from responsibility to Parliament and public opinion for certain kinds of decision. It might even be argued that it is an aspect of 'good administration' for Departments to be denied and/or relieved of certain kinds of decisions which could expose them to pressures of many kinds – not least political.

The Franks Committee stressed that tribunals were not to be seen as 'appendages of Government Departments' . . . 'Parliament has deliberately provided for a decision outside and independent of the Department concerned' . . . 'the intention of Parliament to provide for the independence of tribunals is clear and unmistakable.' With respect, there seems to be a rather large degree of unadulterated constitutional fiction here. John Griffith argues strongly that it is completely wrong to refer to some theoretic notion of Parliamentary intention; tribunals he says are instituted in reality by the Government of the day and in effect it is the relevant Department which will make the rules. The Council on Tribunals expressly cited Departmental preferences as one of the factors relevant to the creation of a tribunal. In their Annual Report for 1975–76 the Council states specifically that the detailed arrangements for tribunals remains the responsibility of Departments. To say, therefore, that tribunals are created to ensure that decisions should be made independently of Departments is simply not valid. Griffith suggests that Departments simply do not want to be bothered with the sorts of decisions tribunals will make: the policy is settled; it only has to be administered and disputes sorted out.

I introduce all this merely to stress the important role of tribunals as rudimentary but nevertheless vital components of administration. Writers today still insist on taking issue with the term '*administrative* tribunals' as giving too much emphasis to the administrative associations that tribunals have: ever since Franks the 'machinery for adjudication' theme has been predominant. In particular the Council of Tribunals has seen its most important contribution as being 'our constant effort to translate the general ideals of the Franks Committee into workable codes of principle and practice . . .' As I have suggested it is my view that the Franks Report seriously underplayed the task of tribunals to be instruments of their respective administrative schemes. Be that as it may the Council on Tribunals continues the ideals of Franks with some zeal despite the fact that the Tribunals and Enquiries Act simply asks that they keep under review the constitution and working of Schedule 1 tribunals, report thereon and consider and report on matters as may be referred to them in respect of any tribunals other than courts of law. Is there not here some leeway for a more expansive notion of what tribunals are supposed to be doing?

NOTES:

1. On the role of the Council on Tribunals, see *post* at p. 763.
2. A controversial example of apparent governmental disenchantment with a tribunal arose in the field of social security. Until 1986 there was an appeal from all claims concerning supplementary benefit, a means-tested benefit available to unemployed persons on low incomes. Such appeals were made to Supplementary Benefit Appeal Tribunals until 1984, when tribunals concerned with social security benefits were re-organized, and thereafter to Social Security Appeal Tribunals (SSATs). In 1986 changes were made under which supplementary benefit was replaced by income support, and a Social Fund was established to consider claims for specific items, such as furniture and clothing. Prior to this such claims had been made under the Single Payments regulations and appeals concerning single payments were dealt with by SSATs. The amended scheme did not, however, provide for any appeal from the Social Fund to an independent tribunal.

    The reasoning of the Government was explained in the White Paper on *The Reform of Social Security* (1985) (Cmnd 9518), paras 2.107–2.112.

The Reform of Social Security
Cmnd 9518 (1985), paras 2.107–2.112

How the social fund will be run

2.107 The fund will be run from DHSS local offices by a group of specialist officers. Special expertise will be needed, based on specific training in relevant skills, such as interviewing, counselling, and knowledge of help available from other sources. Decision-making will rest more on casework, liaison with other bodies and discussion with claimants. There will need to be clear links with the work of social service and health professionals who may also be involved in helping the same person. The views of outside professionals may have a part to play in helping officers reach judgments on individual cases.

2.108 Such expertise is to an extent already possessed by special case officers who since 1980 have had a remit to help claimants whose cases present special difficulty. Special case officers' concerns include: claimants with difficulties in adjusting to major changes in their circumstances (such as marital breakdown or discharge after a long stay in hospital); cases where there are doubts about claimants' ability to care for themselves or their children; those who have problems in managing essential living expenses; and others whose characteristics may create tension in dealing with staff. The Government believe it is right to develop existing good practice in this area and to expand the responsibilities of special case officers.

2.109 Specialist staff will exercise their judgment in reaching decisions on individual cases. The basis of deciding social fund payments is rather different from traditional benefit decision-making. There is widespread recognition that the present adjudication arrangements for handling special needs have not worked satisfactorily. There is also widespread agreement that, in handling the special difficulties of a minority of claimants, the scheme needs a degree of flexibility that is only possible with discretion.

2.110 The Government recognise that people who have asked for help with particular pressures should have an effective means of questioning the outcome. In all organisations, management has the first responsibility to see that services are well handled. This basic principle applies just as much to the administration of benefits as it does to other areas. It is however clear that the present appeal arrangements in special needs areas can have a sledgehammer effect. The full weight of legal consideration can be brought to bear on matters which may involve small sums of money for particular items with considerable delays between initial decision and formal review. We do not believe that the present system of appeals has best served the claimant's prime interest of a quick and effective reconsideration of decisions. The result is too slow, too cumbersome, and too inflexible.

2.111 The first safeguard for claimants under the new arrangements will be a professional approach to the administration of the social fund. That is the reason for using specialist officers. Reviews which turn on judgment in difficult individual circumstances are best handled as near to the point of decision as possible. The further the review gets from the initial judgment both in terms of formality and time, the less equipped the reviewing authority is to judge whether the outcome is sensible. The Government therefore intend to provide for review by management as near as possible to where responsibility for the original decision rests. Just as social service and health care decisions are best taken locally by those directly responsible, so should the social fund be seen as an important responsibility of those administering it in local offices. The arrangements proposed by the Government involve judgment – local people are best placed to make that judgment.

2.112 The fund will work successfully only if there is a clear limit to its role; that is, if it concentrates on the special needs of a limited number of claimants. The fund will have a fixed annual budget. Some form of budgeting is the reality in most areas of social provision. The Government do not consider that this specialist part of the new arrangements should be any different.

NOTE: In the absence of a right of appeal, judicial review proceedings have been used to challenge the operation of the Social Fund (see, e.g. *R v Secretary of State for Social Services, ex parte Stitt, The Times*, 5 July 1990 and the study by M. Sunkin and K. Pick, 'The Changing Impact of Judicial Review: The Independent Review Service of the Social Fund' [2001] PL 736).

QUESTION

Does either the Franks Report or Hendry's article provide an explanation for these developments?

NOTES:

1. The removal of the right of appeal was criticised by the Council on Tribunals (see *post* at p. 770 for its role and subsequent developments).

2. The Franks Report referred to the natural affinity between, on the one hand, cases where the policy of legislation can be set out in detailed regulations and adjudication by tribunals and, on the other hand, cases where it is necessary to preserve flexibility in the pursuance of policy and ministerial decision-making. There are, however, tribunals which operate largely for the purposes of developing and applying policy (see, for example, the Independent Television Commission and the Competition Commission). This has led some commentators to draw a distinction between court-substitute and policy-oriented tribunals (on this distinction see further, B. Abel-Smith and R. Stevens, *In Search of Justice*, pp. 20–21 and J. A. Farmer, *Tribunals and Government*, Chapter 8).

3. The preceding extracts from the Franks Report have been concerned with the choice between providing an appeal to a Minister and providing an appeal to a tribunal. Assuming, then, that a decision has been made to establish a form of adjudication independently of the Department, what explains the decision to establish a tribunal rather than provide a statutory right of appeal to the courts?

Report of the Committee on Administrative Tribunals and Enquiries
Cmnd 218 (1957), paras 38–39

The choice between tribunals and courts of law

38. We agree with the Donoughmore Committee that tribunals have certain characteristics which often give them advantages over the courts. These are cheapness, accessibility, freedom from technicality, expedition and expert knowledge of their particular subject ... But as a matter of general principle we are firmly of the opinion that a decision should be entrusted to a court rather than to a tribunal in the absence of special considerations which make a tribunal more suitable.

39. Moreover, if all decisions arising from new legislation were automatically vested in the ordinary courts the judiciary would by now have been grossly overburdened ... We agree with the Permanent Secretary to the Lord Chancellor that any wholesale transfer to the courts of the work of tribunals would be undesirable.

Tribunals for Users: One System, One Service
The Stationery Office 2001 paras 1.11–13

Tribunals or courts

1.10 It is important to be clear what work should be done by tribunals, rather than by courts. Franks did not consider in detail what principles should guide the allocation of cases to tribunals, accepting that the already large number of cases decided by tribunals in 1957 made the amalgamation of tribunals and courts impracticable. As the areas in which some kind of appeal is required proliferate, Parliament, policymakers and users should have principles to guide that allocation. We suggest that there should be three tests of whether tribunals rather than courts should decide cases.

Participation

1.11 First, the widest common theme in current tribunals is the aim that users should be able to prepare and present their own cases effectively, if helped by good-quality, imaginatively presented information, and by expert procedural help from tribunal staff and substantive assistance from advice services. We think the element of direct participation is particularly important in the field of disputes between the citizen and the state . . . The use of tribunals to decide disputes should be considered when the factual and legal issues raised by the majority of cases to be brought under proposed legislation are unlikely to be so complex as to prevent users from preparing their own cases and presenting them to the tribunal themselves, if properly helped.

The need for special expertise

1.12 Where the civil courts require expert opinion on the facts of the case, they generally rely on the evidence produced by the parties – increasingly jointly – or on a court-appointed assessor. Tribunals offer a different opportunity, by permitting decisions to be reached by a panel of people with a range of qualifications and expertise. A larger decision-taking body is obviously likely to be more expensive. But users clearly feel that the greater expertise makes for better decisions. They also say that having more members, and non-lawyers, on the panel makes it easier for at least some users to present their cases. The second reason why cases should be considered for allocation to a tribunal is if expertise, or accessibility to users, is a major issue in the resolution of the relevant disputes.

Expertise in administrative law

1.13 Thirdly, tribunals can be particularly effective in dealing with the mixture of fact and law often required to consider decisions taken by administrative or regulatory authorities. Our recommendations for a more coherent system will increase that effectiveness. Where any legislation establishes a statutory scheme involving decisions by an arm of government, the responsible minister should explicitly consider whether a right of appeal is required, on the basis that there should be strong specific arguments if an appeal route is not to be created, and that a tribunal route, rather than redress in the courts, should be the normal option in the interests of accessibility. It should not be regarded as satisfactory to leave judicial review as the citizen's only recourse, since that is expensive and difficult for the unassisted.

NOTE: The Donoughmore Committee produced a *Report on Ministers' Powers,* Cmd 4060 in 1932 which concerned delegated legislation and tribunals and inquiries.

QUESTIONS

1. Are the two reports consistent with each other? Is the objective of not over-burdening the judiciary a special consideration in favour of establishing a tribunal?

2. What do these passages indicate about the desirable qualities of tribunals and, in particular, how those qualities should differ from those of the courts? See further *post* at pp. 772–80.

NOTES:

1. The Council believes that tribunals should be chaired by a legally qualified person. Their Chairman, Lord Archer of Sandwell, was successful in amending the Social Security Act 1998, so that a legally qualified person must always be a member of the appeal tribunal. In the initial proposals the tribunals could have had only one member, who was not required to be legally qualified.

2. In De Smith and Brazier, *Constitutional and Administrative Law* (7th edn 1998), the point is made, at p. 578, that:

> The climate of opinion has now changed. No longer must exceptional circumstances be present to justify the establishment of a special tribunal to determine controversies arising under regulatory or welfare legislation. We have fifty different *types* of these tribunals and some 2,000 tribunals altogether. If, for instance, the question of how disputes about the entitlement of dismissed workers to redundancy payments from their employers ought to be decided under a new Act, there is an *expectation* that the deciding body will be a special tribunal.

SECTION 2: The General Organization of Tribunals

In recent years there has been concern about the proliferation of tribunals and the difficulties which this raises with regard to their supervision. This concern has focused attention both on the role of the Council on Tribunals and on the development of 'presidential systems'.

A: Council on Tribunals

Tribunals and Inquiries Act 1992, ss. 1–5 (*ante* at pp. 754–55).

NOTE: In 1980 the Council on Tribunals reviewed its work and made certain recommendations for improvements.

The Functions of the Council on Tribunals
Cmnd 7805 (1980), paras 2.4–2.8, 5.4–5.5, 6.3, 6.7–6.10, 6.14, 7.3, 7.5, 7.7, 7.9–7.10, 7.17–7.19, 9.1–9.2, 9.5–9.8, 9.10

The Franks Committee and subsequent legislation
2.4 The Committee recommended that the two Councils on Tribunals, one for England and Wales and the other for Scotland, should be set up to supervise tribunal and inquiry procedures. The report stressed the importance of continuous supervision: the supervising bodies would be consulted whenever it was proposed to establish a new type of tribunal, and would also keep under review the constitution and working of existing tribunals. The Council for England and Wales would be appointed by and report to the Lord Chancellor . . .

2.5 As proposed by the Franks Committee, the Council on Tribunals would have had important executive powers as well as advisory ones. For example, they would have been empowered to appoint the members (as distinct from the chairmen) of tribunals; to review the remuneration of tribunal appointments; to give advice on the basis of which the duties and conduct of tribunal clerks would be regulated; and to formulate procedural rules for tribunals, in the light of the general principles enunciated by the Committee.

2.6 The main powers which were in fact conferred on us and on the Scottish Committee of the Council by the Tribunals and Inquiries Act of 1958 were subsequently embodied in the Act of 1971. They may be paraphrased as follows:

(a) to keep under review the constitution and working of the tribunals specified in Schedule 1 to the Act;
(b) to consider and report on particular matters referred to the Council by the Lord Chancellor

and the Lord Advocate with respect to any tribunal other than an ordinary court of law, whether or not specified in Schedule 1; and

(c) to consider and report on such matters as may be so referred, or as the Council may consider to be of special importance, with respect to administrative procedures which may involve the holding by or on behalf of a Minister of a statutory inquiry.

2.7 Our powers are thus consultative and advisory, not executive; and in certain respects they are more limited than the Franks Committee recommended. We have no function with regard to the remuneration or conditions of service of tribunal chairmen, members of staff: and no power to make appointments or to formulate rules.

2.8 However, we must be consulted by the appropriate rule-making authority before procedural rules are made for any tribunal specified in Schedule 1 to the 1971 Act and on procedural rules made by the Lord Chancellor in connection with statutory inquiries. We must be consulted before any scheduled tribunal can be exempted from the requirement under section 12 of the Act to give reasons for its decision upon request. (Note this requirement is now in section 10 of the Tribunals and Inquiries Act 1992.) The same situation applies to Ministerial decisions taken after a statutory inquiry. We may make general recommendations to appropriate Ministers about tribunal membership. We are required to make an Annual Report to the Lord Chancellor and the Lord Advocate, which must be laid by them before Parliament with such comments, if any, as they think fit. . . .

Some problems

5.4 Under the heading of matters requiring statutory attention, our committee considered the lack of clarity as to the extent of our general jurisdiction in relation to tribunals; our lack of a specific power to investigate complaints; and the absence of any requirement that we be consulted on proposed primary legislation affecting tribunals or inquiries, and of any power to require our views [expressed in response to statutorily prescribed consultation] to be made public.

5.5 The last mentioned point is of particular importance. From time to time we have been consulted by a Minister and our views have not been accepted. Ministers are, of course, fully entitled to disregard our recommendations, but a statement in Parliament or in regulations that action has been taken after consultation with us is then – although strictly correct – misleading because it gives the impression that we agreed with the course adopted . . .

The Council went on to recommend that a Minister be required to inform Parliament of the extent to which the Council's recommendations have been given effect and the reasons why any of them has not been accepted.

Some features of the Council's work

6.3 Our most important contribution over the years has, we believe, been our constant effort to translate the general ideals of the Franks Committee into workable codes of principles and practice, accepted and followed by all those responsible for setting up administrative tribunals, devising their manner of operation and, indeed, serving upon them as chairmen and members. . . .

6.7 The points with which we are particularly concerned at the formative stage are all directed to improving the ability of citizens to challenge administrative decisions affecting their interests. For example, we are vigilant in seeking to ensure that people are given a hearing as of right in suitable cases, and are not denied one if they request it; that rights of appeal are granted wherever appropriate and not eroded where they already exist; and that parties to tribunal proceedings are treated equitably, neither side being given an unfair advantage. . . .

6.8 In relation to the constitution of tribunals we have (following a recommendation of the Franks Committee) advocated that chairmen should, in most cases, be legally qualified: and we have lost no opportunity of recommending the 'presidential' system of organisation under which a particular class of tribunal has a national president or chairman and, where the number of tribunals in that class justifies it, regional chairmen as well . . .

6.9 Some of the safeguards which we are anxious to secure are best embodied in primary legislation or procedural rules. This applies, for example, to provisions governing time-limits within which rights of appeal must be exercised and various procedural steps taken. Another example is the giving of properly reasoned decisions by tribunals. In relation to this matter we are fortified by a statutory provision, but it is also necessary for us to monitor the observance of this practice so far as we are able to do so. For instance, we found it necessary to issue detailed advice to Supplementary Benefit Appeal Tribunals as to how they should interpret and implement the duty to give reasons which is placed on them by the relevant rules. This advice is repeated in the official guide to the procedure of tribunals.

6.10 Our interest is not, however, limited to matters which figure in Acts of Parliament or procedural rules. For example, we are particularly concerned that tribunals should be able to cope effectively with the volume of business coming before them, and the appearance of a substantial back-log of cases awaiting decision has caused us to intervene on several occasions. We take constant interest in the fitness and accessibility of the premises in which tribunal hearings are held, and make representations if premises appear to be unsuitable – for example, because of their lack of provision for disabled people, or because of their location in relation to the offices of the responsible Government department.

The report continued to stress the role of the Council in providing proper training and in ensuring the independence of clerks.

6.14 In all our work in connection with tribunals we have to bear in mind that they do not represent a single homogeneous group but vary widely in their constitution, membership, functions and organisation. . . .

Complaints

7.3 We have no statutory jurisdiction in relation to complaints, but during the Parliamentary proceedings which led to the enactment of the Tribunals and Inquiries Act 1958 it was indicated by a Government spokesman that we would be able to deal with complaints. In our early years the handling of complaints – in the absence of any other machinery for dealing with them – bulked quite large in our work. For some years our Annual Report provided details of the more important investigations which we carried out. . . .

7.5 We can usefully consider complaints drawing attention to some procedural difficulty which points to the need for an amendment of rules or an alteration of administrative practice. Even in relation to complaints of this type, however, we are conscious that we can very rarely give any direct satisfaction to an individual who has complained. . . .

7.7 The Parliamentary Commissioner cannot consider the substance of any matter which has been referred to a tribunal or public inquiry, but he can investigate a department's administrative handling of its own procedures before and after a tribunal or inquiry hearing. He can also investigate the way in which public local inquiries are conducted. In relation to tribunals, the actual proceedings and decisions are outside the jurisdiction of the Parliamentary Commissioner. . . .

7.9 Where a complaint is in substance an attempted appeal on the merits or a protest against an adverse decision, we are convinced that we should not attempt to deal with it. Such complaints can properly be entertained only by the tribunal or court (if any) empowered to deal with appeals from the particular tribunal concerned, or to carry out a judicial review. Substantial cases of procedural error can also be challenged in court proceedings, and it is clearly desirable that if such a remedy exists it should be used.

7.10 This leaves us with the problem of deciding how best to deal with the residual body of complaints arising from the hearings of tribunals. We see no difficulty in continuing to handle those representations which can be satisfactorily answered without carrying out an investigation. The main difficulty for us lies in those cases where there is a suggestion of procedural deficiencies but conflicting accounts are given of the same events, because we have no means of getting at the truth by interviewing people or calling for files and other papers. After making whatever inquiries are possible in the circumstances we frequently have to say that there is a conflict of evidence which cannot be resolved. Inevitably, time is taken up by these inquiries, and this may increase the disappointment felt by some complainants with the results of our investigations.

7.17 To give us a wide statutory power for the handling of complaints would almost inevitably have certain consequences. The work-load would increase, with heavier pressure on the members; and there would be repercussions on staffing and accommodation. Although unlikely, it is also possible that our present relationship with Government Departments might be endangered, and the chairmen and members of tribunals and inspectors at statutory inquiries might become less co-operative than they now are. In the long run, the balance of our work might be significantly changed, with the focus shifting to our role as ombudsman for tribunals and inquiries, in priority over our existing functions. This in our view would be undesirable.

7.18 On balance, therefore, although we propose that we should be given specific responsibility for complaints in relation to our field of work, it is important that the extent of our jurisdiction be clearly defined. The power could be on the following lines:

(a) a member of the public alleging a procedural irregularity in a hearing before a tribunal or statutory inquiry would be entitled to make a formal complaint to us;

(b) we would then have to consider whether the complaint *prima facie* raised a substantial point of principle relating to procedure;

(c) if we came to that conclusion, we would be empowered to obtain papers and other information from the relevant tribunal or inquiry and from the Government department concerned, to question the complainant and any other person involved, and to submit a report to the complainant, the department and, at our discretion, to anyone else. . . .

(d) if we decided that the complaint did not *prima facie* raise a substantial point of principle we would refer the matter without comment to the department concerned, who would be required to report to us the outcome of their own inquiries.

7.19 In addition to this action on complaints from members of the public, we would be empowered at our discretion to conduct an investigation into an alleged procedural irregularity referred to us by the department concerned. We would not, however, at any time investigate a complaint relating to the merits of a decision or recommendation; or concerning the conduct of chairmen or members; or which fell within the competence of the Parliamentary Commissioners; or which could reasonably form the basis of an appeal or some other proceeding in a court of law. An investigation which we had undertaken would be discontinued if, it any stage, it appeared that one of these grounds of exclusion applied. And we would not, unless the circumstances were wholly exceptional, seek to intervene during the currency of tribunal or inquiry proceedings.

What is needed – a general perspective

9.1 The purpose of this chapter is to discuss briefly the more general aspects of the Council's responsibility for keeping under review the constitution and working of bodies in the field of administrative adjudication. We have already emphasised the importance of specific knowledge of the functions of different classes of tribunals and types of inquiries. But there is another dimension to our work, which involves taking a 'bird's eye view' of the territory falling within our jurisdiction. In this connection we believe the Council are in a unique position. With the changes recommended in this report we should be able to make a continued contribution – indeed, a more positive and constructive one – to the development of an effective and well planned system.

9.2 The case for a statutory advisory body with this kind of general oversight appears to us to be even stronger now that at the time of the Franks Committee. Since then the tendency for issues arising out of legislative schemes to be referred to tribunals has continued unabated, in a largely piecemeal manner. Not only has there been considerable growth in the number of tribunals, they are operating increasingly in difficult and sensitive areas – for example, immigration, compulsory detention under the mental health legislation, misuse of drugs, equal pay, redundancy, unfair dismissal from employment, and supplementary benefits.

. . .

9.5 Since we were set up, significant changes have also taken place in the general constitutional and administrative climate. There is, for example, a movement towards greater formalism in procedures for settling disputes. The process started with reforms following the Franks Report which, in general, made tribunals more like courts. It had to be demonstrated that tribunals were not adjuncts of Government departments and that in their decision-making they followed a judicial process. Since then the trend towards judicialisation has gathered momentum with the result that tribunals are becoming more formal, expensive and procedurally complex. Consequently they tend to become more difficult for an ordinary citizen to comprehend and cope with on his own. There is, we believe, an urgent need to keep the whole of this movement under the closest scrutiny. We believe that we are in a position to play a key role in the achievement of a right balance.

9.6 There is also a constant need, as was emphasised in discussion with our Committee, for an independent body able to offer advice to Government on what kinds of dispute are appropriate or inappropriate for adjudication by tribunals. We believe we can exercise this function, and can develop criteria indicating the kinds of decision which, if disputed, should be subject to review by processes external to the departments concerned; the most appropriate form of review; the degree of formality required, according to the type of decision; and whether a proposed tribunal should come under our supervision.

9.7 While we have always emphasised the basic elements of good practice common to all tribunals, we accept that there should be differences in their constitution and detailed procedures according to the complexity of their jurisdictions. The need to review the appropriateness of several classes of tribunals for the work they have to do seems to us to be overdue. Simplification is desirable wherever this is compatible with justice. Moreover, we think there is a case for transferring adjudication of some issues to the courts. . . .

9.8 Finally, we draw attention to particular problems running across the whole field which need co-ordination rather than piecemeal approach: for example, a much wider system for recruitment of tribunal members, including more women; arrangements for training of both chairmen and members; the presidential system; conferences and seminars; the publication of explanatory leaflets; and the clarification and simplification of official forms. . . .

9.10 . . . At present we are perhaps in a better position than any other official body to appreciate the wider implications of the particular matters referred to us, and to consider the important issues relating to the system as a whole to which they give rise. We therefore recommend strongly that the statutory power of the Council to act as a *general* advisory body in the field of administrative adjudication be placed beyond doubt.

NOTES:
1. In the 2000–01 Report (HC 343 of 2001–02) the Council made 121 visits to tribunals and inquiries, attended 30 conferences and seminars, and considered 27 statutory instruments.
2. One of the main advantages of tribunals is reputed to be their speed (see *post* at p. 777). It is therefore unsurprising that the Council on Tribunals has, in its monitoring of tribunals, concerned itself with the problem of delays.

Annual Report of the Council on Tribunals for 2000–01
HC 343 of 2001–02, paras 8.03–21

The Appeals Service

Waiting times

3. We welcome the progress the agency has made in reducing the number of cases outstanding for 6 months or more from 70,000 in March 1999 to less than 19,000. The agency is also meeting its target of an average waiting time for appeals to be heard within 14 weeks of receipt. The picture is somewhat complicated by a change in the counting method this year, but we understand that current average waiting time of 13.6 weeks represents a reduction over a 2 year period of about 2 weeks for the processes the Appeals Service is responsible for. Whilst this figure represents a national average, there is some regional variation and much further work needs to be done to improve the performance of the regions where the longest waiting times exist.

4. Formerly, waiting times were counted from when the appeal was lodged with the first-tier agency. They are now counted from when the relevant papers are received by the Appeals Service. This approach provides a sharper focus for the Appeals Service on the parts of the process it is responsible for. However the experience of appellants will not be improved if first-tier agencies are slow in processing the appeal and despatching it to the tribunal. We understand that all the agencies are collaborating to improve the 'end-to-end' experience of the appellant and we welcome this. It is vital that the collaboration is effective so that a marked improvement is achieved.

Support for judiciary

5. This year the President has introduced a forum for the judiciary on the Appeals Service website to provide updates on law and procedure and to develop a sense of community and common purpose among this large and widely geographically spread group. A system for appraising panel members by District Chairmen was also put in place last year, and we have also observed the delivery of a package of equal treatment training for the judiciary that we considered to be of a high standard.

Housing Benefit and Council Tax Benefit Appeals

6. We reported last year that under the provisions of the Child Support Pensions and Social Security Act 2000, Housing Benefit and Council Tax Benefit appeals were to be heard by tribunals administered by the Appeals Service, rather than by Housing Benefit and Council Tax Benefit Review Boards within each local authority. We warmly welcomed this, but drew attention to the fact that this represented a major change that would require careful management by the local authorities and by the Appeals Service.

7. We have since been consulted on draft secondary legislation to implement this measure, and have made a number of suggestions with a particular focus on the need for the new arrangements to be comprehensible. We have also taken considerable interest in the implementation of the change, which took place three months later than originally planned on 2 July 2001. The Appeals Service now faces the challenge of managing a relationship with over 400 local authorities as respondents, as distinct from a small number of agencies previously. Against the background of wide variation between local authorities in dealing with benefit matters in the past, there is also the potential for inconsistency and varying levels of competence with which the various local authorities engage with the independent appeals concept.

8. We have had the opportunity to observe some of the training provided both for tribunal chairmen and for the Social Security and Child Support Commissioners, who will hear onward appeals on points of law. It is too early to comment upon the success of the exercise, but we commend the efforts made by the Appeals Service so far to establish communication with the local authorities. Social Security and Child Support Commissioners Reported Decisions.

9. Last year we reported shortcomings in the arrangements for the publication and reporting of Commissioners' decisions, which were presenting difficulties for practitioners, first-tier agency decision-makers and appeal tribunals. We explored this issue and were pleased to learn that these problems are being overcome. Starred* (cases identified as being of general significance) and reported decisions since 1990 are being made available via the Court Service and Department of Work and Pensions websites. Reported decisions have now also been published in a binder and arrangements will be made for the publication to be updated every two years.

Website

10. Work has been undertaken this year to bring up-to-date the information about the work of the Commissioners on the Court Service website, and further work is under way to increase the value of the site to decision-makers and tribunal users. This is good news. It might also be helpful to users if the Commissioners were to follow the example of the Immigration Appellate Authority and acquire their own domain name, rather than use the Court Service site as a vehicle.

Waiting times

11. Last year we reported the concern expressed by the House of Commons Social Security Committee about delays in the system prompted by average waiting times that had peaked at 64 weeks in 1998. The Government Response to the Committee's Report announced a new target, to reduce waiting times to 26 weeks from the receipt of the claimant's appeal by the Commissioners to the despatch of decision, by April 2002. The Court Service considers the 26-week target to be achievable. The average had been reduced to 36 weeks by June this year, but as we have seen in other tribunals, this figure is skewed by the effect of older cases coming on to the list for disposal. We recognise that even a 26-week target will be long for appellants for whom the outcome may be of great financial importance.

User Group

12. Our Chairman attended the inaugural meeting of the User Group set up by the Commissioners, and we have been represented at the two further meetings this year. We welcome this development, which has generated a valuable dialogue with user representative groups and interested organisations on a range of issues, including the reporting and publication of decisions, procedural changes, and issues generated by the new system for Housing Benefit and Council Tax Benefit appeals.

Pensions Appeal Tribunals

Procedural rules

13. Last year we outlined the impact of the Child Support Pensions and Social Security Act 2000 on the Pensions Appeal Tribunals (PATs), which included provision for additional rights of appeal that will add to the Tribunal's workload.

14. It had been the original intention of the Lord Chancellor's Department to use this opportunity to undertake a major review of the procedural rules, which are outdated and require substantial modernisation, with a view to producing new rules in April. This work was postponed and a more limited series of amendments have been made as an interim measure, primarily to give effect to the Act.

15. It is important that the LCD find an early opportunity to complete the work to produce new rules.

Waiting times

16. Last year we also reported our considerable concern about waiting times for appellants. The average was then 83.5 weeks from receipt of appeals to hearing. Since then we have met Dr Harcourt Concannon, President of the PATs in England and Wales, and Simon Smith, Director of

Tribunal Operations in the Court Service (the Court Service administers the PATs along with some other tribunals), to discuss these and other issues.

17. Both Dr Concannon and Mr Smith accepted our criticisms of the average waiting time that we reported last year. We were informed that a target to reduce the average to 20 weeks by April 2003 has now been set by the Lord Chancellor.

18. The average waiting time this year has been 81.6 weeks. We understand that a number of measures are being taken which make the new target realistic and achievable. These include the following: the recruitment and training of a number of legally qualified chairmen who will now chair all assessment appeals in place of medical chairmen. The aim is for more expeditious case manage-ment and the granting of fewer adjournments; the greater flexibility available to the President concerning Tribunal composition that will enable more expeditious and economical listing practices to be employed; new powers for the President to strike out cases which are no longer being pursued by appellants; continuation of the work to reduce the backlog of old cases, which will in turn reduce the impact on the average waiting time figure as old cases come on to the list.

19. We welcome the work that the President and the Court Service have in hand to obtain a clearer understanding of the causes of delay in the system and to address these. It will also be important that the Court Service continue to work with the War Pensions Agency (WPA) (respon-sibility for which was moved in June from the Department of Work and Pensions to the Ministry of Defence) to reduce delay in the system. The time taken to process cases by the WPA adds significantly to the total waiting times experienced by appellants.

20. However, we repeat the concerns we expressed last year about the limited capacity of the Royal British Legion (RBL) to provide a representation service to appellants. Although the RBL repre-sents around 95% of all appellants, there are considerable constraints on the level of service it is able to offer.

User Group
21. We were pleased to hear from Dr Concannon that the Tribunal intends to establish a user group. The inaugural meeting will take place later this year. We welcome this initiative.

3. The Council on Tribunals took the unusual step of issuing a special report in January 1986 in which it criticised the Government's decision not to provide an independent appeal from decisions relating to the new Social Fund (Cmnd 9722). It considered that very good reasons were needed before a right of appeal which had existed for more than 50 years was abolished. The Council pressed for the restoration of such an appeal. The Government made no formal response to this, but, at the Report stage of the Social Security Bill in the Commons, it substituted a review of the decisions of the local Social Fund inspectors outside the local office management hierarchy. In the House of Lords a right of appeal from a Social Fund decision to a Social Security Appeal Tribunal was inserted. This was, however, removed in the Commons. The Social Security Act 1986 provided for a Social Fund Commissioner who is responsible for appointing Social Fund inspectors and checking their work, and who will report annually to the House of Commons (s. 35) (see now s. 65 of the Social Security Administration Act 1992). There is, however, no right of appeal to a SSAT from decisions of the Social Fund inspectors except with regard to payments for funerals and maternity.

4. The Government considered that the changes suggested by the Council in its 1980 report were largely unnecessary. It did, however, accept that its role in relation to consultation on procedural rules should be re-stated and made clearer. The Council drafted guidelines which provided that the optimum period of consultation should be two months for routine matters and four months for matters raising major issues of principle. The minimum periods were expressed to be four weeks and six weeks respectively (see the *Annual Report of the Council on Tribunals for 1986/87*, p. 53).

5. In 2000 the Council on Tribunals circulated its interim revised version of the Model Rules of Procedure for Tribunals which take account of the entry into force of the Human Rights Act 1998.

QUESTIONS

1. Yardley, commenting on the Council on Tribunals' special report in 1980, writes that:

> The main message coming from this report is nowhere directly expressed. But it is implicit from the comparatively minor nature of the recommendations that the Council is in fact working well, and that its achievements in the field of tribunals and inquiries have been substantial. It is a paradox that a body with a statutory constitution, but with no powers actually to achieve anything directly, should be so valuable. But it is submitted that this paradox is nonetheless true. (D. C. M. Yardley, 'The Functions of the Council on Tribunals' (1980) *Journal of Social Welfare Law*, 265.)

   Do you agree?

2. Harlow and Rawlings, in *Law and Administration* (1997) draw a distinction between fire-fighting institutions, which are concerned with the redress of individual grievances, and fire watching institutions, which are more concerned with the general oversight of the administration. How would you classify the Council on Tribunals? Would this classification alter if the proposals in the special report in 1980 had all been accepted?

B: The presidential system

The Pensions Appeal Tribunals and the Lands Tribunal are examples of tribunals organized on a presidential basis. In such systems there is generally a full-time officer responsible for the overall administration and practice of a particular class of tribunals. What might the advantages of a presidential system be?

Annual Report of the Council on Tribunals for 1982–83
HC 129 of 1983–84, paras 2.15–2.16

Tribunal constitution – presidential system

2.15 We have frequently recommended the presidential system of organisation under which a particular class of tribunal has a national president or chairman and, where the number of tribunals in that class justifies it, regional chairmen as well. We have made a further study of the presidential system this year. We see as its advantages:—

  (a) there is an obvious independence from the Government departments responsible either for decisions appealable to the tribunal or for its financing;
  (b) a president can be responsible for the administrative arrangements, instead of a Government department having that role;
  (c) he can appoint or advise on the appointment of tribunal chairmen, members, clerks and other staff;
  (d) he can monitor the performance of tribunals, arrange for necessary training, and encourage consistency;

(e) co-ordination and communication between tribunals of the same type are facilitated and a sense of corporate identity and team spirit is fostered;

(f) the tribunal has a spokesman and a focal point for relationships and communication with other bodies; and

(g) a president may make interlocutory decisions and may give guidance about the allocation of cases and about other matters of practice and procedure.

In our view a presidential system ought to be established for a particular type of tribunal when a significant number of cases is dealt with every year and there is also an appreciable number of tribunals within the system, whether or not they sit in many locations or already have a regional organisation.

2.16 We favour the introduction of regional chairmen for certain types of tribunals where both the appointment of a national president is justified and the number of tribunals would make administration easier through regional centres. The appointment of regional chairmen also helps to spread the workload and responsibility, while keeping a central focus. However, we accept that in those types of tribunal which handle a comparatively small number of cases a looser structure of quasi-autonomous regional chairmen without a national president would be acceptable. In such circumstances we would expect the regional chairmen to meet reasonably frequently to plan and co-ordinate their work in relation to administration, training and the other matters which would otherwise be the responsibility of a president. One of the senior regional chairmen could act as a focal point and take responsibility for organising the regional chairmen's activities.

NOTE: The Social Security Act 1998 changed the arrangements for appeals by providing for a unified tribunal to cover the work of five different tribunals in social security. The new tribunal will be drawn from a panel of people with legal, medical and financial qualifications and knowledge of disability. The idea is that the composition of a tribunal will match the characteristics raised by the appeal. Accordingly, the tribunal could sit with one, or two or three members. There is a President, whose responsibilities are judicial, the administrative aspects have been assigned to a new executive agency within the Department of Social Security, the Appeals Service Agency. See the report of the House of Commons Social Security Select Committee (HC 581 of 1997–98) as well as the Council on Tribunals Annual Reports for 1997–98 (HC 45 of 1998–99) and 1998–99 (HC 30 of 1999–2000).

QUESTIONS

1. Does the presidential system contribute to the realisation of the aims of the Franks Committee (see *post* at pp. 772–4)?

2. Can you think of any disadvantages?

3. Does the new social security structure threaten the judicial independence of the appeal tribunals?

SECTION 3: **The Characteristics of Tribunals**

Report of the Committee on Administrative Tribunals and Enquiries
Cmnd 218 (1957), paras 40–42, 62–64, 71–72, 76–77, 90

[See also paras 38–39, *ante* at p. 761].

40. Tribunals are not ordinary courts, but neither are they appendages of Government Departments. Much of the official evidence, including that of the Joint Permanent Secretary to the Treasury,

appeared to reflect the view that tribunals should properly be regarded as part of the machinery of administration, for which the Government must retain a close and continuing responsibility. Thus, for example, tribunals in the social services field would be regarded as adjuncts to the administration of the services themselves. We do not accept this view. We consider that tribunals should be regarded as machinery provided by Parliament for adjudication rather than as part of the machinery for administration. The essential point is that in all these cases Parliament has deliberately provided for a decision outside and independent of the Department concerned, either at first instance (for example in the case of Rent Tribunals and the Licensing Authorities for Public Service and Goods Vehicles) or on appeal from a decision of a Minister or of an official in a special statutory position (for example a valuation officer or an insurance officer). Although the relevant statutes do not in all cases expressly enact that tribunals are to consist entirely of persons outside the Government service, the use of the term 'tribunal' in legislation undoubtedly bears this connotation, and the intention of Parliament to provide for the independence of tribunals is clear and unmistakeable.

The application of the principle of openness, fairness and impartiality

41. We have already expressed our belief, in Part 1, that Parliament in deciding that certain decisions should be reached only after a special procedure must have intended that they should manifest three basic characteristics: openness, fairness and impartiality. The choice of a tribunal rather than a Minister as the deciding authority is itself a considerable step towards the realisation of these objectives, particularly the third. But in some cases the statutory provisions and the regulations thereunder fall short of what is required to secure these objectives . . .

42. In the field of tribunals openness appears to us to require the publicity of proceedings and knowledge of the essential reasoning underlying the decisions; fairness to require the adoption of a clear procedure which enables parties to know their rights, to present their case fully and to know the case which they have to meet; and impartiality to require the freedom of tribunals from the influence, real or apparent, of Departments concerned with the subject-matter of their decisions.

Codes of procedure

62. Most of the evidence we have received concerning tribunals has placed great emphasis upon procedure, not only at the hearing itself but also before and after it. There has been general agreement on the broad essentials which the procedure, in this wider sense, should contain, for example provision for notice of the right to apply to a tribunal, notice of the case which the applicant has to meet, a reasoned decision by the tribunal and notice of any further right of appeal.

63. We agree that procedure is of the greatest importance and that it should be clearly laid down in a statute or statutory instrument. Because of the great variety of the purposes for which tribunals are established, however, we do not think it would be appropriate to rely upon either a single code or a small number of codes. We think that there is a case for greater procedural differentiation and prefer that the detailed procedure for each type of tribunal should be designed to meet the particular circumstances. . . .

Informality of atmosphere

64. There has been considerable emphasis, in much of the evidence we have received, upon the importance of preserving informality of atmosphere in hearings before tribunals, though it is generally conceded that in some tribunals, for example the Lands Tribunal, informality is not an over-riding necessity. We endorse this view, but we are convinced that an attempt which has been made to secure informality in the general run of tribunals has in some instances been at the expense of an orderly procedure. Informality without rules of procedure may be positively inimical to right adjudication, since the proceedings may well assume an unordered character which makes it difficult, if not impossible, for the tribunal properly to sift the facts and weigh the evidence. It should be remembered that by their very nature tribunals may be less skilled in adjudication than courts of law. None of our witnesses would seek to make tribunals in all respects like courts of law, but there is a wide

measure of agreement that in many instances their procedure could be made more orderly without impairing the desired informality of atmosphere. The object to be aimed at in most tribunals is the combination of a formal procedure with an informal atmosphere. We see no reason why this cannot be achieved. On the one hand it means a manifestly sympathetic attitude on the part of the tribunal and the absence of the trappings of a court, but on the other hand such prescription of procedure as makes the proceedings clear and orderly.

Knowledge of the case to be met

71. The second most important requirement before the hearing is that citizens should know in good time the case which they will have to meet. . . .

72. We do not suggest that the procedure should be formalised to the extent of requiring documents in the nature of legal pleadings. What is needed is that the citizen should receive in good time beforehand a document setting out the main points of the opposing case. It should not be necessary and indeed in view of the type of person frequently appearing before tribunals it would in many cases be positively undesirable, to require the parties to adhere rigidly at the hearing to the case previously set out, provided always that the interests of another party are not prejudiced by such flexibility.

Public hearings

76. We have already said that we regard openness as one of the three essential features of the satisfactory working of tribunals. Openness includes the promulgation of reasoned decisions, but its most important constituent is that the proceedings should be in public. The consensus of opinion in the evidence received is that hearings before tribunals should take place in public except in special circumstances.

77. We are in no doubt that if adjudicating bodies, whether courts or tribunals, are to inspire that confidence in the administration of justice which is a condition of civil liberty they should, in general, sit in public. But just as on occasion the courts are prepared to try certain types of case wholly or partly *in camera* so, in the wide field covered by tribunals, there are occasions on which we think that justice may be better done, and the interests of the citizen better served, by privacy.

The Committee went on to outline three types of case: where considerations of public security are involved, where intimate personal or financial circumstances have to be disclosed and where there are preliminary hearings involving professional capacity and reputation.

Evidence

90. Tribunals are so varied that it is impossible to lay down any general guidance on the requirement of evidence at hearings. In the more formal tribunals, for example, the Lands Tribunal, there seems no good reason why some of the rules of evidence as in courts of law should not apply. In the majority of tribunals, however, we think it would be a mistake to introduce the strict rules of evidence of the courts. The presence of a legally qualified chairman should enable the tribunal to attach the proper weight to such matters as hearsay and written evidence.

NOTE: The Committee made a number of other more specific recommendations. For those relating to appointment, legal representation, appeals and the Council on Tribunals see, respectively, *post* at pp. 780–3 and *ante* pp. 763–7.

Other recommendations included the following:
(a) All tribunals should have power to administer the oath. The Franks Committee considered, however, that only those tribunals which are most akin to courts of law, for example, the Lands Tribunal, should be required to hear evidence on oath (para. 91).

(b) Applicants should have the right to apply to the tribunal for the issue of a subpoena requiring the attendance of a witness (para. 92).

(c) Unsuccessful applicants should not be required to pay costs, and both successful and unsuccessful applicants should be entitled to a reasonable allowance in respect of expenses (paras 94–97).

(d) Tribunals should give a statement of reasons in order to fulfil the requirements of fairness and to enable applicants to decide whether to exercise any right of appeal (para. 98).

(e) All final appellate tribunals should publish selected decisions. The Committee considered this would be of help, not only in satisfying the public that decisions were reasonably consistent, but also as a guide to appellants and their advisers (para. 102).

QUESTION

Which of the provisions of the Tribunals and Inquiries Act 1992 seek to implement the recommendations in the report? (See *ante* at pp. 754–56.)

NOTE: As the Franks Committee recognized, the implementation of many of its objectives could not be achieved by general provisions in an Act, but only in the detailed provisions governing particular tribunals. For the role of the Council on Tribunals in this context, see *ante* at pp. 763 and 768.

QUESTION

Are the Franks Committee's recommendations on the characteristics of tribunals consistent with its statement of the reasons for adjudication by tribunals rather than by the courts (*ante* at p. 758)? Consider the following extract, which also discusses the relevant provisions of the Tribunals and Inquiries Act and the role of the Council on Tribunals.

K. H. Hendry, 'The Tasks of Tribunals: Some Thoughts'
(1982) 1 *Civil Justice Quarterly*, 253, 255–256, 259–266

. . . [T]ribunals are seen as providing a form of 'administrative justice' as opposed to 'judicial justice.' To the English administrative lawyer this simply asks the average tribunal to be simpler, quicker, cheaper, more accessible, more expert and more flexible than the ordinary courts. As important as these characteristics are I hope to suggest that a concept of 'administrative justice' ought to go further than this. Linked to all these qualities a tribunal should have, is the need contemporaneously to act 'justly.' The Franks Committee, and using the ensuing Report as their basis, the Council on Tribunals, equated the task to act justly with a task to act judicially. One is forced to ask whether acting administratively justly and acting 'judicially' are in fact co-terminous?

Furthermore, since tribunals are meant to provide a system of administrative justice outside the normal courts we can infer that one of the tasks of tribunals is to lighten the regular courts' caseload, or to put it negatively, to avoid judicial justice in these matters. In keeping with classic constitutional principles, however, the ordinary courts were still to have powers of review and appeal; despite the fact that a rudimentary system of administrative justice was identifiable it was to go so far and no further – ultimately judicial justice would be paramount. This built-in paradox bears some examination, as does a further issue, namely the tension which must bear in on bodies that inhabit the twilight world of being theoretically divorced from the ordinary judicial hierarchy and at the same time independent of the administration.

It will have been gathered that tribunals could be classified as machinery for adjudication or for administration. The writer's view is that they are probably machinery for both – there seems to be no reason why the two functions cannot exist within one body. To fully understand this it is essential that a cogent concept of 'administrative justice' is developed and not to stop there: questions must be asked about the role and meaning of 'administrative law' and furthermore, about the nature of 'public law.' To some of these matters I now turn in greater detail . . .

The task of tribunals to provide 'administrative justice'

Writing in 1958 William A. Robson expressed the view that the Franks Report and, by implication, ensuing legislation have the effect of importing administrative justice into the general system of adjudication; in short there had been a reception of administrative justice.

There can be no doubt that an overriding purpose of the creation of specialised administrative tribunals was to institute a means of dealing with disputes outside the normal court hierarchies, but can this be described as 'administrative justice'? In England, the concept, if there is one, is rather woolly; it seems to mean no more and no less than those alternative means of dispute-settlement provided by statute under various administrative schemes. These alternative means, by and large tribunals, have certain advantages over the normal courts and they are preferable in certain circumstances; in essence, they do the same job (they resolve disputes) – thus the one is 'judicial justice,' if you like, and the other is 'administrative justice.'

The tendency is to leave it at that, to ask no more and to look no further. The Franks Committee was not asked to look at 'administrative justice' as a whole but only to consider and make recommendations in respect of the constitution and working of tribunals. The Committee could not, therefore, look at Departmental/Ministerial decisions in disputes between the citizen and public authorities. As Franks put it, in these circumstances the citizen was 'less protected against unfair or wrong decision.' The impact of Franks was to see tribunals as a rather specialised part of the machinery of justice. In consequence, and in accordance with traditional constitutional principle, tribunals were not to be severed from the regular courts who would, on the contrary, supervise their activities. Furthermore the Franks Committee favoured the view that all decisions of tribunals should be subject to review by the courts on points of law.

Classic systems of administrative justice provide a fully fledged hierarchy of administrative courts, equal in status to 'ordinary courts,' staffed by specialised judges, within a separate and self-contained structure. Common law 'ad-hocery' spawned tribunals devoid of any real concept of administrative justice, devoid also of the context of administrative justice, namely public law. Shocked eventually at the sight of 'tribunal proliferation,' reform did not attempt a uniform structure but concentrated rather on 'minimum standards' (fairness, openness, impartiality, etc.). The guardians of the system were, of course, to be the regular courts – any notion of the evolution of two distinct systems of law was deprecated, despite the fact that if one looked closely enough it was clear that two systems in fact existed. Would not tribunals have stood a better chance of fulfilling their essential tasks had the approach been different?

Despite the palpable lack of any principled, theoretical approach, it was felt by some that a form of 'administrative justice' existed in the system of tribunals. Tribunals, it was said, were possessed of certain characteristics, or at least, *should* be possessed of these characteristics, which when compared to 'judicial justice' made them, in certain circumstances, preferable. These characteristics are well known and self-explanatory, but a few words on each is not out of place for the simple reason that it is possible to argue that one of the major tasks of tribunals as a whole is to maintain these features which make them preferable to the ordinary courts.

(i) Simplicity and informality

It is argued that tribunals can adopt more informal methods, making it easier for the inexperienced to present their cases. Courts, on the other hand, adhere to the adversarial system (a judge sitting on high, observing the contest, ensuring that the rules are obeyed, assessing the performance, and giving judgment according to the evidence before him). This is, apparently, true of some tribunals, notably if they have to deal with a *lis inter partes*, but very often the issues before tribunals are essentially non-combative, such as: is X entitled to supplementary benefit? or, is Y well enough to be released from a mental hospital? Wraith and Hutchesson found that this factor very often went hand in hand with an informal atmosphere in many tribunals; the appellant was greeted by name, invited to sit down, the procedures casually explained and the surroundings were conspicuously devoid of the grandeur of judicial proceedings. Through simplicity and informality it would seem that there has been a fairly large measure of success in making tribunals acceptable to the average man in the street. Indeed, there is a suggestion that the relatively more informal atmosphere of county court proceedings is in large measure due to the success it has had in tribunal operations.

On the other hand, there would appear to be a number of factors which, due to the view of tribunals in the United Kingdom, would detract from the simplicity and informality of tribunals; in particular the need and stress laid on the necessity for a legal chairman and quasi-legal procedures before, during and after hearings could well be counter-productive in this area. In this respect, the Tribunals and Inquiries Act requires consultation with the Council on Tribunals for the making, approving, confirming or concurring in Schedule 1, Tribunals' rules of procedure.

(ii) *Speed*
The delays occasioned by redress through the ordinary courts are notorious. Thus it has been stressed that an overriding advantage of specialised tribunals is their alacrity. It would be easy to take this for granted. The situation as a whole is undoubtedly better than in the courts, but the expedition of tribunals will vary from one to another. In 1973 it was found that Supplementary Benefit Appeal Tribunals matters were determined within two to four weeks, an appeal to a national insurance local tribunal took three to five weeks, and rent assessment committees dealt with their matters in two to three months. It can only be said that in this respect one cannot generalise; it is probably true that most tribunals provide reasonably speedy resolution of disputes, but some important Tribunals are not immune from delay. In this respect the work of the council of Tribunals has been valuable; they have highlighted delays and suggested improvements. Generally they have shown concern that tribunals should be able to cope effectively with the volume of business coming before them. More specifically, the council has highlighted delays in Immigration Appeals and also for National Insurance Commissioners. Furthermore, it should be noted that the whole purpose of speedy administrative justice can be obliterated by appeal/review by the ordinary courts – a subject returned to below.

(iii) *Cheapness*
Use of the normal courts is often an expensive way of resolving a dispute. Tribunals, on the other hand, are meant to be cheaper. This is undoubtedly so: the cost of officials and building comes out of public funds and in neither case is as expensive or grandiose as the courts with their well-paid officials. Similarly, the proceedings being flexible and informal, will normally not require expensive involvement of lawyers and officials in gathering evidence, presenting cases, and so on. It is probably this characteristic which most sharply distinguishes tribunals from the ordinary courts of law. The Franks Committee recognised that if tribunals were to be made truly accessible 'the citizen must be able to have recourse to them without running the risk of being out of pocket' and thus proposed that as a general principle a successful applicant should be given a reasonable allowance in respect of expenses and that an unsuccessful applicant should not only never have to pay any costs but should be entitled to the same reasonable allowance as the successful applicant. The proposal was largely accepted by the Government of the day, but even today a fairly wide spectrum of practice with regard to costs still operates. The attitude of the Council of Tribunals is to deal with this problem in an ad hoc, tribunal by tribunal, way; in particular they have consistently advocated that legal aid should be available in all tribunals in which legal representation is permitted.

(iv) *Accessibility*
The whole system fails if recourse to a tribunal is in any way difficult. Wraith and Hutchesson noted tartly that with regard to publicity, this was not one of the most conspicuous features of tribunals

except in so far as it was conspicuous by its absence; this relates to publicity to potential applicants and to the publicity of actual proceedings – the two go hand in hand. There is the added difficulty here of the extreme complexity of some of the statutory schemes involved, and the likely difficulty the layman will have firstly with dealing with what he considers to be faceless, uninterested bureaucracy in attempting to make a claim and generally the paperwork involved. In the latter respect the council on Tribunals has stressed that the wording of official forms and leaflets should be as clear and simple as possible, but the problem still remains. The Franks Committee itself stressed that the citizen should be both aware and understand his right to apply to a tribunal.

There is a further danger of a larger kind here: the system of tribunals as is known resists uniformity and simplicity – under new social legislation the line of least resistance will be to create a new tribunal rather than to reorganise in a systematic way. The result is naturally a maze of different jurisdictions which, for the citizen, is not only inconvenient but also perplexing. At the time of the Franks Report there was, it was felt, little scope for fundamental reorganisation or amalgamation. Subsequently there has been piecemeal rationalisation but the attractiveness of a complete system of tribunals increases when one considers the in-built, day to day, difficulties of accessibility.

(v) *Expertise*
The courts are, in the main, fundamentally generalist. An advantage, characteristic and task of a specialised tribunal on the other hand is its expertness. This is achieved by ensuring that the composition of the body consisted of persons who have special skills, knowledge or expertise of the matter in hand. Ideally, therefore, tribunals are the embodiment of expert adjudication.

It should be noted that expertise is a somewhat elastic notion and will vary from tribunal to tribunal; further the Franks Committee clearly felt that the term should include legal expertise, generally in the chairman. This will to some extent guarantee the objectivity of proceedings and perhaps the proper sifting of facts, but as regards the expertness of non-legal members the range of skills and knowledge will vary from tribunal to tribunal. More will be said about the composition of tribunals later.

(vi) *Flexibility*
The avowed flexibility of tribunals exists not only in the informal procedures they adopt, their more or less ready accessibility and speed, but more importantly in that they to some extent avoid the rigidity of precedent to be found in the regular courts. Tribunals, more often than not have been created because the change required had to be rapid and effective; a tribunal was unlikely, as Jackson says, to 'achieve the futility of saying that a conclusion is ridiculous and yet necessary because of the system of precedent'.

Yet it must be borne in mind that because of the present supervision of tribunals by the ordinary courts, all tribunals are, in principle, bound to follow precedents set by decisions of the ordinary courts. Similarly where there is an appellate tribunal it binds lower tribunals in its system. But the more important element is the arbitrary intrusion of the regular courts' 'law' into the so-called flexibility of tribunal activities. Writers have noted that some tribunals pay great devotion to judicial precedent.

The question has to be asked whether allowing the generalist normal courts to, in effect, dictate to specialists on 'questions of law,' which to a skilful lawyer could cover almost any aspect of an administrative scheme, ensures the flexible ascertainment of the objectives of an administrative scheme. Indeed, it has been strongly argued that the intrusion of the ordinary courts into what should be administrative adjudication is clearly harmful.

The characteristics of tribunals listed above are well known. It is recognised though that quick, simple, informal, cheap and flexible adjudication runs the risk of being arbitrary – the wise man under a palm tree could adjudicate in exactly this way. Thus an overriding task of tribunals was to be intrinsically *just* in their adjudications. As we have seen the Franks Report explicitly saw tribunals as 'machinery for adjudication' that is as essential components of the machinery of justice. Therefore (said Franks) the activities of tribunals had to be marked by 'openness, impartiality and fairness.' Recognising that secrecy would destroy confidence they stressed the publicity of proceedings and knowledge of the essential reasoning underlying decisions; similarly oppression could result from a party not being able to state his case, therefore they suggested procedures which would enable parties to know their rights, present their cases and know the case against them; finally, parties had to be satisfied that the body adjudicating had an open mind and in this respect the Report stressed especially the freedom of tribunals from Government Departments most concerned with the subject-matter.

In more detail, the Franks Report's recommendations suggest that a task to act 'justly' is not in essence different from a duty to act 'judicially.' One finds suggestions for public hearings, privilege for witnesses, legal representation, legal aid, the power to administer the oath, the power to sub-poena witnesses and documents, the right to cross-examine directly, the publication of decisions and their circulation amongst tribunals and so on. Many of these separate ideas have been taken up and developed by the Council on Tribunals.

Now there are quite clearly safeguards of a fundamentally legal kind and their value is not in dispute. However, there would appear to be some tension between these clearly 'judicial' pro-cedures and the essential worth of tribunals as cheap, flexible and fast dispensers of administra-tive justice. As stated, the Franks Committee was not concerned with a coherent concept of administrative justice, but it is suggested that a task to be 'just' is somewhat wider than the simple adoption of quasi-legal procedures. Franks expressly avoided any involvement in the policy behind particular administrative schemes – indeed many of the complaints the Council on Tribunals receive seem to relate to a rather wider concept of justice than simple 'judicialised procedures' – but their power to deal with general complaints are not very well defined. In the light of the terms of reference of the Franks Committee, namely to 'review the constitution and working of tribunals,' it would have been difficult to review the multiplicity of policies involved, but it seems a pity not to have at least mentioned that the operation of tribunals ought, at the end of the day, to promote the objectives of the scheme for which they were constituted, and to perhaps suggest ways in which this could be achieved. Within this context it is of some worth to make the following ancillary comments:

(a) *Tribunals' independence from Government Departments*

It has been argued that Departments and Ministers, and not 'Parliament,' will have been largely responsible for the drafting of the rules relating to the constitution, functions and operation of tribunals. To some extent the statements of the Council on Tribunals and the Franks stress on independence from Departments, however, is impossible if taken literally. What is possible, and indeed desirable, is that a Department should not attempt to influence a decision: of this there is no evidence. What one cannot evade, it is suggested, is that tribunals are part of administrative schemes and to these schemes they have some responsibility. The Franks attempt at, and the Council of Tribunals stress on, the independence of tribunals, one cannot help but feel, is a rather charming attempt to approximate tribunals to ordinary courts of law. . . .

(c) *Procedure*

Finally in this regard, a word about tribunal procedures: as stated the impact of Franks was to apply 'judicial' principles to them. On the other hand the Report rejected the idea of a single code of procedure since flexibility would be jeopardised if this took place. However, each statutory tribunal had to have a definite procedure specified by statute or statutory instrument. Informality was to be retained but within an orderly procedure. The Council on Tribunals has a consultative role with regard to the making of Schedule 1 tribunals' rules of procedure and as we have seen this is largely handled by their Legal Committee. We have already seen that the vast majority of procedural recommendations by Franks have been followed and persisted in by the Council on Tribunals; of these we will undoubtedly approve for they guarantee a very basic procedural justice. One is left wondering, however, whether the Franks Committee was 'asked to look at already open, fair and impartial administrative procedures and asked to see if they could be made more so?'

QUESTIONS

1. What aspects of (a) the Franks Report, (b) the Tribunals and Inquiries Act, and (c) the work of the Council on Tribunals does Hendry consider promote the characteristics which make adjudication by tribunals preferable to adjudication by the courts?

2. Conversely, what aspects does he consider have the potential to undermine such characteristics?

3. Is there any indication in the extract of the changes which Hendry considers desirable?

Three particular issues concerning the desirable characteristics of tribunals have stimulated much debate: the method of appointment and qualifications of members, legal representation and legal aid, and rights of appeal.

A: Appointment

See the Tribunal and Inquiries Act 1992, ss. 5 and 6 (*ante* at p. 755).

The Franks Committee had originally recommended that the Council on Tribunals should appoint the members of tribunals but this was not implemented. For the present role of the Council on Tribunals see s. 5 of the 1992 Act.

There are many different systems in operation for appointment of members. It is most common for tribunal members to be appointed by the relevant Minister, but there are other methods in operation, for example members of unified Appeal Tribunals are appointed from a panel drawn up by the Lord Chancellor (Social Security Act 1998, s. 6).

The Franks Report had recommended, at para. 55, that chairmen of tribunals should ordinarily have legal qualifications, but that the appointment of persons without legal qualifications should not be ruled out when they are particularly suitable. The Council on Tribunals has in fact recommended that all chairmen of tribunals should normally be legally qualified, stating that its experience showed that proceedings did not tend to become more formal with a legally qualified chairman (*Annual Report for 1959*, para. 290).

QUESTIONS

1. In what ways, if at all, did the recommendations of the Franks Committee on appointment and membership seek to achieve what it perceived to be the desirable characteristics of tribunals, i.e. openness, fairness, and impartiality? Do you think that the fact that the recommendations were not wholly implemented has had any impact on the chances of achieving such objectives? Is this a cause for concern?

2. Does the method of appointment adopted in social security have any

advantages as compared to appointment by Ministers or the Council on Tribunals (see further on the presidential system, *ante* at pp. 771–72)?

NOTE: Some of the issues raised by question 1 are addressed in the following extract.

K. H. Hendry, 'The Tasks of Tribunals: Some Thoughts'
(1982) 1 *Civil Justice Quarterly*, 253, 265–266

(b) Method of appointment
Linked to the issue of independence is the way in which members of tribunals are appointed. The Franks Committee, consistent with their conception of tribunals, felt that the to-be-created Council on Tribunals should appoint thereby reinforcing Tribunal independence. This was one of the few recommendations rejected by Parliament as such a situation, it was felt, would conflict with the responsibility of Ministers to Parliament. The inevitable compromise was that generally Ministers would continue to appoint but after consultation with the Council. The Tribunals and Inquiries Act specifies that the Council may make general recommendations in this regard and that the appropriate Minister 'shall have regard to these recommendations.' On the face of it this might appear a somewhat sinister rejection of an important recommendation but this is so only if our conception of tribunals is as only machinery of justice; seen as machinery for administration too, appointment by Ministers is unsurprising.

Furthermore Franks felt chairmen should, ordinarily, have legal qualifications which (they said) would guarantee objectivity and the proper sifting and finding of facts. The Council on Tribunals, as previously indicated, has been the most consistent advocate of this particular cause. The question is: are the undoubted qualities of lawyers, the only qualities required of the chairmen of tribunals? A legal qualification is no real guarantee of total understanding of a statutory scheme, or insight into the objectives of empowering legislation. Furthermore, the impact of lawyers (cold, inhuman, unsympathetic?) on individual applicants may well be counter-productive. Similarly the impact on other members of the tribunal may be of an overbearing, aloof and superior individual. To some extent, this is a stereo-type lawyer but the essential point is this: a balance has to be struck between a variety of considerations in the appointment of chairmen; the focus on legal qualifications appears both conventional and superficial and may, in addition, be a barrier to informal justice. It is interesting to note here that there is no general legal requirement in the Tribunals and Inquiries Act for legally qualified chairmen. The Council on Tribunals has found that with regard to Supplementary Benefit Appeal Tribunals, where there has been a consistent campaign for legally qualified chairmen on the part of the Council on Tribunals, the role of members other than chairmen in coming to a decision has been minimal and that very often these members feel left out. One wonders whether the stress on legally qualified chairmen has contributed to this.

B: Legal representation and legal aid

The Franks Committee recommended that legal representation should be permitted except in exceptional circumstances. It further recommended that, in order to provide effective access to tribunals, legal aid should be extended at once to the more formal tribunals (such as the Lands Tribunal) and that further extensions of the legal aid scheme in the courts should be accompanied by an extension to all tribunals.

There have been a number of changes to the legal aid scheme since the publication of the Franks Report. The current position following the Access to Justice Act 1999 is that *legal advice and assistance* not extending to cover representation before the tribunal itself is available under 'legal help'. In addition, in relation to proceedings before mental health review tribunals and in disciplinary hearings before the boards of visitors, legal representation is available under this scheme. *Legal Representation*, which is the normal method of providing public funds to cover representation in proceedings, is only available in relation to the Employment Appeal Tribunal, Mental Health Review Tribunal, Immigration Adjudicators and Immigration Appeal Tribunal, Protection of Children Act Tribunal, and General and Special Commissioners of Income Tax, VAT and Duties Tribunal, and Proscribed Organizations Appeal Commission (*Funding Code Guidance*, Chapter 24).

NOTE: The effectiveness of representation at tribunals was the subject of a research paper by Hazel Genn and Yvette Genn. The report and the Council on Tribunals' response to it are discussed in the following extract.

Annual Report of the Council on Tribunals 1989/90
HC 64 of 1989–90, paras 1.35–1.44

REPRESENTATION AT TRIBUNALS – A STRATEGY FOR THE FUTURE

1.35 The evidence of the Genn Report on the Effectiveness of Representation at Tribunals has reinforced our long-held view that further measures are needed to aid such representation. We examine the implications of the Report and address the action which we believe should now be taken.

1.36 In our Annual Report for 1987/88 we set out at length our settled view that publicly funded advice and, where appropriate, representation should be available to those of modest means who appear before tribunals. We recorded our concern that the Legal Aid Act 1988 had made no explicit extension of legal aid for representation in this area, and expressed the view that it was unlikely that the Lord Chancellor's Department would reach decisions on publicly funded representation for tribunals until research being undertaken on their behalf by Hazel and Yvette Genn of London University was completed. That report has once again focused interest on this area, and we believe the importance of the issues raised justifies its reconsideration in depth.

The Genn Report

1.37 The research Report by Hazel and Yvette Genn entitled 'The Effectiveness of Representation at Tribunals' was published by the Department in July 1989. The broad objectives of the research had been to establish the effect of representation on the outcome of tribunal hearings and to analyse the contribution of representation to both pre-hearing processes and hearings themselves. It became evident to us, on a preliminary consideration, that the Report contained a great deal of important material and deserved the most careful consideration. The Report made out a strong case for extra funding of representation, and of lay agencies in particular, and before reaching any final assessment on it we took the opportunity to discuss both the research methodology and the Report's findings with Hazel Genn. Our views, which we record below, have been passed to the Lord Chancellor's Department and to the Legal Aid Board.

1.38 In our view there is nothing in the Report which would lead us to modify our long-held views on the need for extra funding of advice and representation. To the contrary, the evidence in the Report has added weight to those views, and demonstrated the need for a coherent strategy to be devised which will ensure that appropriate levels of advice, assistance and representation are made available where and when they are needed. We draw attention to a number of factors emerging both from the Report and from our discussion with Hazel Genn which, in our view, would have an important bearing on the shaping of the strategy required.

Type of representation

1.39 The Report provides incontrovertible evidence not only of the importance of representation at tribunals, but also of the need to ensure that the formality and complexity of certain tribunals is taken into account when deciding what level of representation should be appropriate. While it demonstrates the significant role of advice agencies in the tribunal field, and the effectiveness of specialist lay representation in some tribunals, it also emphasises that there are certain tribunals where the complexity of the law and the adversarial nature of the proceedings make skilled legal representation necessary. Such representation is also preferable to specialist lay representation in those cases before other tribunals which raise difficult legal issues.

1.40 These findings, in our view, support the case for extra funding of advice agencies in particular, and for a selective extension of legal aid. In this connection, we note that the Report reached no firm conclusions on the desirability of extending legal aid to tribunals. Instead, it put forward the idea of a 'government tribunal representation service', on the model of the United Kingdom Immigration Advisory Service. In our view, such a substantial body could present major difficulties in terms of its independence and funding; thus we are not yet persuaded that this is the most appropriate way forward. Our present view is that the means must be found to provide extra funding for advice agencies and to provide legal aid where and when it is needed. We agree with the Legal Aid Advisory Committee that 'questions relating to the extension of legal aid should be considered separately in relation to each tribunal'. We have therefore urged the Department to take steps at an early stage to identify those tribunals which would be appropriate to an extension of legal aid, preferably on the criteria we have previously advocated, and have offered our advice to assist in the process of identification.

1.41 We emphasise, however, that funding of this nature must be provided in a way which will take account of the qualitative issues addressed in the Report, and ensure that the substantial regional and geographical differences in the availability and scope of legal services are overcome.

Quality of representation

1.42 The evidence in the Report demonstrated that the chances of success at tribunal hearings were significantly affected by the fact of representation and by the quality of representatives coming before tribunals. We have noted in this connection the consistency of views expressed by tribunals concerning the contribution of good representation to hearings, and the general view that the quality of representation varies over a wide range. . . . These considerations raise important qualitative issues concerned with standards of performance and training to which we believe greater weight must be given in future.

Regional differences

1.43 We note with concern the significant regional differences in the provision and scope of legal services in the tribunal field which the Report revealed. We believe it is important to devise a scheme which will ensure that the respective roles of advice agencies, law centres, and private solicitors in the provision of advice and representation at tribunals are properly coordinated. There is no comprehensive overview of the provision of these services throughout the country. . . .

Relationship between advice and representation

1.44 We also note the emphasis which the Report placed on the value of good prehearing advice, on the effect that advice has on the way in which cases are ultimately decided, and on the relationship between advice and representation. In our view, the evidence demonstrates clearly that the components of advice and assistance on the one hand, and representation on the other, cannot be viewed as distinct alternatives, but must be regarded as complementary elements. . . .

H. Genn, 'Tribunal Review of Administrative Decision-Making' in
G. Richardson & H. Genn (eds), *Administrative Law and
Government Action*
(1994), pp. 284–6

This chapter has attempted to show that there are considerable limits to the effectiveness of tribunals as a check on administrative decision-making and that these limitations stem at least in part from the design of tribunals and the low levels of representation at tribunals. In order for tribunals to act as an *effective* means of review they must be capable of conducting an accurate and fair review of administrative decisions. This requires time, expertise, and full information. It also requires that those who appear before tribunals are capable of understanding the relevance of regulations and the basis of their entitlement, and can provide relevant information and evidence of facts, largely without the benefit of advice or representation.

   Given the weakness of first-line administrative decision-making, tribunals theoretically represent an important means of minimizing administrative injustice. However, evidence collected from recipients of adverse administrative decisions, although not conclusive, suggests that even when a relatively straightforward mechanism exists for review of decisions the opportunity is not taken because those affected may assume that the original decision was 'correct' or that it is unlikely to be changed. Thus, even if tribunal hearings provided perfect conditions for effective review of administrative decisions, they could only every afford a partial corrective to poor decision-making and administrative injustice. In practice, however, from the perspective of tribunal applicants, the conditions that operate in many tribunals are far from perfect. Despite their conventional characterization as informal, accessible, and non-technical, frequently tribunals are not particularly quick, there is considerable variation in the degrees of informality, and the issues dealt with are highly complex in terms of both the regulations to be applied and the factual situations of applicants. This study of tribunal processes and decision-making has highlighted the complexity of many areas of law with which tribunals must deal and the impact of this complexity on decision-making. Although tribunal procedures are generally more flexible and straightforward than court hearings, the nature of tribunal adjudication means that those who appear before tribunals without representation are often at a disadvantage. The short-comings of tribunals as effective checks on administrative decisions are the result of misdescription of procedures as informal and misconceptions about simple decision-making and the scope for unrepresented applicants to prepare, present, and advocate convincing cases.

   The analysis of factors influencing the outcome of tribunal hearings suggests that increased advice and representation for applicants, and improved training and monitoring of tribunals, would be likely to increase the rate at which cases reviewed at tribunal hearings were allowed. This may not, of course, be the desired objective. It has been argued that tribunals were never intended to act as 'effective review mechanisms' and that their primary role is to provide a cloak of legitimacy for unpopular social regulation. If, however, there is a genuine intention that tribunals should provide a check on administrative decision-making, rather than merely providing a forum in which disappointed and disgruntled applicants can let off steam, their deficiencies must be addressed. It is not sufficient to assume or to assert that tribunals operate well. In order to achieve their theoretical objectives and to attain the qualities claimed for tribunals, consideration must be given to their procedures and to standards of tribunal adjudication. Finally, and most importantly, explicit attention must be paid to the means by which a balance can be struck between the conflicting demands of procedural simplicity and legal precision, in order to achieve substantive justice.

QUESTION

Are tribunals more a substitute for courts than an alternative to courts, and if so, what are the implications for the system of tribunals and their users?

C: Rights of appeal

See the Tribunals and Inquiries Act 1992, s. 11 (at p. 756 *ante*).

There is great diversity in the systems of appeals from tribunals. In some contexts, for example social security, employment, and immigration, there is a special appellate tribunal. In the case of social security and employment there is a further right of appeal to the Court of Appeal. (Despite repeated recommendations to the contrary from the Council on Tribunals there is still no right of appeal from the decisions of the Immigration Appeal Tribunal.) In others there is an appeal from a tribunal on a point of law to the High Court under s. 11 of the Tribunals and Inquiries Act 1992. Where there is no appeal procedure the only way to challenge a decision is to seek judicial review (see, for example, the Betting Levy Appeal Tribunal).

The Franks Committee recommended that there should be a general right of appeal on matters of fact, law or merits from the decision of a tribunal to an appellate tribunal except where the tribunal of first instance is so exceptionally strong and well qualified that an appellate tribunal would be no better qualified to review its decision (para. 105). It also recommended that, with some exceptions, there should be a general appeal on a point of law to the courts.

In the extract below Hendry challenges the view that rights of appeal and judicial review are advantageous in the system of tribunals.

K. H. Hendry, 'The Tasks of Tribunals: Some Thoughts'
(1982) 1 *Civil Justice Quarterly* 253, 266–68

Tribunals and the Courts
One more task of tribunals needs mention and in many ways it brings the gist of the above into focus: that task is to lighten the load of the ordinary courts. To put it negatively and perhaps more accurately, a purpose of the creation of Tribunals was expressly to avoid 'judicial justice.' The 1970/ 71 Holdsworth Club Presidential Address by Lord Hailsham expressed the view that the 'public' (*sic*) felt that many new questions were simply not for decision by the ordinary courts. The reason, says Lord Hailsham, was an inherent distrust of trial by judge alone as a method of deciding questions of fact or mixed question of fact and law. As a purely theoretical proposition in constitutional law, Hailsham condemned the proliferation of ad hoc tribunals as unhealthy; why could many of these cases, he asks, not be referred to the existing network of county courts? We return thus once again to the question of how we should view tribunals. Are they machinery of adjudication as Franks said they were? Are they machinery for administration? The answer is probably in shades of grey rather than black or white; they are machinery of adjudication within administration. The effect of Franks and the continuing work of the Council on Tribunals has been to hide the hybrid nature of tribunals; accordingly administrative lawyers have evaluated the performance and role of tribunals with normal judicial processes in mind.

Related to this and of the utmost importance are the powers of review and appeal that the ordinary courts have over the activities of tribunals. The real task of tribunals as presently constituted is to provide, cheap, informal, expert and speedy administrative justice. It must, therefore, be asked whether in the quest for judicialisation of administrative justice, the leap, by means of review or appeal, to judicial justice will, in certain cases, totally defeat the acknowledged virtues of adjudication by tribunals. This is a problem to be seen in terms of finality: the Tribunals and Inquiries Act provides that if a party before certain Schedule 1 Tribunals is dissatisfied with the outcome, he may appeal to the High Court, or require the tribunal to state a case for resolution by the High Court. Furthermore the Act seeks to preserve the venerable orders of certiorari and mandamus as methods of review. What is clearly implicit is the assumption that ordinary courts and legal profession are able to deal satisfactorily with the subject-matter involved. The most recent example of this perhaps misplaced trust is the Social Security Act 1980 which gives a right of appeal, with leave, on a question of law from a National Insurance Commissioner direct to the Court of Appeal which, with respect, is not unlike fitting a penny-farthing with an overhead camshaft and twin exhausts! What is glaringly ignored in all of this is that tribunals were set up to infuse certain decisions with policy factors which the courts by definition are ill-equipped to deal with.

It could, of course, be argued that review and appeal by the courts is a potentially important way of introducing order into administrative systems dominated by ad-hocery. Experience, unfortunately, has in many instances demonstrated the opposite. As Prosser has argued, the relationship between the courts and administration is a very complex one and that the intrusion of purely legal principles in administrative schemes could create chaos. Moreover, the 'test-case strategy' may be of little effect particularly where administrative pratices, irrespective of the legal norms laid down by the courts, have basic governmental support. Prosser feels that whether or not a case has an effect will depend more upon traditional political forces at play in society and that the application of norms of judicial review are a relatively subordinate part of that process.

Furthermore, it is pre-eminently clear that the advantages of tribunals could be destroyed by the expense, complexity, lack of expertise and delay of the normal judicial process. Proposals for a more self-contained system of administrative justice such as Professor Robson's proposal for an Adminis-trative Appeal Tribunal with a wide jurisdiction, not only to hear appeal from tribunals but also cases where a public authority prima facie appears to have acted in an unduly harsh, unjust or improper manner – or even Sir Carlton Allen's proposal for an Administrative Division of the High Court – have been given short shrift, primarily by the Franks Committee and ever since.

QUESTION

Social security appeals are now heard by unified appeal tribunals, and there is an appeal therefrom to the social security commissioners and a further appeal to the Court of Appeal. Presumably this organisational change would not alter Hendry's criticism that the right of appeal to the Court of Appeal is rather like fitting a penny-farthing with an overhead camshaft and twin exhausts. What alternatives might there be to this?

SECTION 4: **Reform**

In May 2000 the Lord Chancellor appointed a team to review tribunals led by Sir Andrew Leggatt, a former Lord Justice of Appeal. The terms of reference required the review 'to look at the administrative justice system as a whole: its coherence, its accessibility, its organisation . . .'. Their report *Tribunals for Users: One System, One Service* was published in 2001 along with a consultation paper by the Lord Chancellor's Department (LCD).

With some 70 different tribunals deciding nearly 1 million cases each year it was not surprising that the report recommended that all tribunals should be adminis-tratively supported by an executive agency, to be called the Tribunals Service, attached to the LCD. The various tribunals would be grouped into nine divisions according to their subject matter and each division would have a presidential structure with a High Court judge as the President. From each division there would be an appeal on a point of law to the division's appellate tribunal and thereafter to the Court of Appeal. This appeal route would be the exclusive method of making a legal challenge, so there would be no right to seek judicial review. The report recommends that tribunals should be more user-friendly and provide more and better information about tribunals' procedures, facilities, and decisions. There should also be comprehensible decisions from bodies which may be appealed to tribunals. The aim should be to make a reality of the claim that a user can be unrepresented and that, in particular, legal representation be minimized.

The report calls for active case management. In each division one or more registrars should be responsible for determining what attention each case or type of case should receive. Registrars should have powers to order production of documents and attendance of witnesses, to order the decision-maker to attend the hearing and to issue directions. They should seek to minimize the length of oral hearings by ordering the exchange of documentary evidence before the hearing, and by directing that written arguments from the department whose decision is challenged be sent before the hearing to the tribunal and to the other party. Allowing for the real differences between tribunals and courts, the same overarching principle should apply to tribunals as is now enshrined in the Civil Procedure Rules, that they should be under a duty to ensure, so far as practicable, that the parties are on an equal footing, and that each case is dealt with economically, proportionately, expeditiously, and fairly. So far as possible tribunals should all be regulated by the same rules of procedure, which should be based on the Council on Tribunals' Model Rules, and for which provision should be made in enabling legislation. They should be set out comprehensibly in guidance notes and leaflets. Many users of tribunals may still prefer oral hearings to written procedures. It is important to ensure that all hearings are conducted efficiently and economically.

The creation of a unified Tribunals Service would, it is argued in the report, offer administrative advantages in terms of efficiency with published key performance indicators and targets, and use of information technology, but also to underpin the independence of tribunals from government bodies whose decisions are under appeal. The Tribunals Service should include tribunals whose jurisdiction encompasses administration conducted by local government, such as education. Most tribunals deal with disputes between the citizen and the state but some are 'party and party' cases where private individuals are in dispute with each other, for example employment. Such party and party tribunals should also be part of the unified service.

The Tribunals Service should ensure that users can provide feedback about their experience through user groups and the Tribunals Service should be able to give information back to departments which can assist them in improving their initial decision-making. The Lord Chancellor should (in consultation with Ministers of the relevant devolved administrations) be responsible for making all appointments to tribunals. There should be improved training in the competencies which members of, and those who chair, tribunals require so as to conduct their proceedings in a manner which assists users. The Judicial Studies Board (JSB) would be well placed to assume responsibility for training in England and Wales. There would also be appraisal of performance intended to support the tribunals in maintaining standards.

The role of the Council On Tribunals would be that of 'hub of the wheel of administrative justice'. The Council would monitor the development of the new tribunals systems and check that the practices and procedures of Government departments are ECHR compliant. The council's primary duty – championing the cause of users; would require taking evidence from user groups, from the Tribunals Service, from Departments, and from the JSB about how well the system is working, monitoring the training of chairmen and members, proposals for procedural change, the development of information technology, the usefulness of the information provided for users by the Tribunals Service, and the adequacy of independent sources of assistance and advice for users. They would continue visiting tribunals and reporting their findings at once to the Senior President and to the President of the Division concerned. The Council would report to relevant Ministers and an appropriate Select Committee and their Annual Reports should reach a wider public, in keeping with their higher profile. They should commission research into the operation of administrative justice both in the UK and abroad.

Tribunals for Users: One System, One Service
2001 Tables B, C, D, paras 4.15–28

. . .

Independent help and advice
Preparation
4.15 Tribunals can only give general procedural advice. Many users will need additional support if they are to participate fully in their cases. We are much impressed by the way in which users are helped to prepare cases in ways that assist tribunals, and weak cases are gently weeded out, by much of the expert (often non-lawyer) advice we have seen. The Community Legal Service (CLS) is clearly intended to make access to such support a reality in many areas. The Government's commitment to focusing advice on areas of greatest need is of course to be welcomed. Social welfare and special educational needs are two areas which deserve priority.

4.16 The time limits for making an appeal vary considerably between tribunals. It is important that appellants should be able to get timely advice. In relation to war pension appeals, for example, the provision of funding to enable some users to travel to meet their representative prior to the hearing would sometimes enable cases to be withdrawn from hearing in consequence of advice then given. If withdrawal does not occur until the day of hearing it is too late to fill the gap in the list, and the tribunal's and the other party's time is to that extent wasted. But if the withdrawal of a case is notified beforehand, another case can be listed for hearing in its place. We are confident that this would happen often enough to save at least the costs of travel.

Table B – Measuring Performance in the Tribunals Service

Aim	Objective	Measures	Information Source
Tribunal needs to determine an acceptable time-frame for its cases. So it needs to set standards and be able to identify where delays are taking place.	*Set standards for:* • Average times taken • Percentage of cases taking longer than average	*Actual:* • Caseload at beginning of period • Caseload at end of period • Average time taken, percentage above average: − at each stage of tribunal process − by tribunal process as a whole − from original decision to final	Management information system
Tribunal needs to have a system that resolves disputes at reasonable cost, both to the state, and, where costs are charged out, to the parties.	*Forecast of:* • Cost per case • Members' time spent • Members per number of cases • Staff time per case	*Actual:* • Cost per case • Members' time spent • Members per number of case • Staff time per case	Management information system
Premises should be accessible, fit for the purpose, and used to the full.	*Set standards for:* • Accessibility, including geographical spread • Fitness for purpose • Premises use	*Actual:* • Accessibility, including geographical spread • Fitness for purpose • Premises use	Management information system
Users should have a comprehensive, smooth and fair process.	*Published standards of service:* • To customers • To members	*Service to customers:* • Perceived quality of information • Perceived quality of administration • Perceived quality of hearing process *Service to members:* • Perceived quality of administrative support	• User groups • Customer comment cards • Structured surveys • Complaints

Table C – Grouping into Divisions

Citizen and state tribunals

First-tier Division	Estimated caseload[a]	First-tier tribunals	Dept[b]	Appeal tribunal[c]
Immigration	25,000	Immigration Adjudicators	LCD	Immigration Appeal Tribunal
		Special Immigration Appeal Commission[d]	LCD	
		Immigration Services Appeal Tribunal	LCD	
Social Security and Pensions	285,000	Appeals Service	DSS	Social Security and Pensions Appeal Tribunal
		Criminal Injuries Compensation Appeal Panel	HO	
		Pensions Appeal Tribunal	LCD	
		Fire Service Pensions Appeal Tribunal	HO	
		Police Pensions Appeal Tribunal	HO	
Land and Valuation	300,000	Valuation Tribunal	DETR	Land and Valuation Appeal Tribunal
		Rent Assessment Committees	DETR	
		Leasehold Valuation Tribunal	DETR	
		Commons Commissioners	DETR	
		Rent Tribunal	DETR	
		Agricultural Lands Tribunal	MAFF	
Financial	100,000	General Commissioners of Income Tax	LCD	Income Tax, VAT and Duties Appeal Tribunal
		VAT and Duties Tribunal	LCD	
		Section 703 Tribunal	HMT	
		Financial Services and Markets Tribunal[d]	HMT	
Transport	50,000	Parking Appeals Service	DETR	Transport Tribunal
		National Parking Adjudication Service	DETR	
Health and Social Services	12,000	Mental Health Review Tribunal	DH	Health and Social Services Appeal Tribunal[e]
		Mental Health Review Tribunal (Wales)	NAW	
		Protection of Children Act Tribunal[f]	DH	
		Family Health Service Appeal Authority	DH	
		Registered Homes Tribunal	DH	

Table C – *contd*

First-tier Division	Estimated caseload[a]	First-tier tribunals	Dept[b]	Appeal tribunal[c]
Education	65,000	Admission Appeal Panels	DfEE	Education Appeal Tribunal[e]
		Special Educational Needs Tribunal	DfEE	
		Exclusion Appeal Panels	DfEE	
		Registered Inspectors of Schools Tribunal	DfEE	
		Registered Nursery Education Inspectors Appeal Tribunal	DfEE	
		Independent Schools Tribunal	LCD	
Regulatory	50	Competition Commission Appeal Tribunal[d]	DTI	Regulatory Appeal Tribunal[e]
		Copyright Tribunal[g]	DTI	
		Consumer Credit Licensing Appeals	DTI	
		Discipline Committees	DTI	
		Estate Agent Appeals	DTI	
		Wireless Telegraphy Appeal Tribunal	DTI	
		Aircraft and Shipbuilding Industries Arbitration Tribunal[dh]	DTI	
		Arbitration Tribunal	DTI	
		Central Arbitration Committee	DTI	
		Insolvency Practitioners Tribunal	DTI	
		Chemical Weapons Licensing Appeal Tribunal	DTI	
		Industrial Training Levy Exemption Referees[h]	DTI	
		Mines and Quarries Tribunal[h]	DTI	
		Registered Designs Appeal Tribunal[h]	DTI	
		NHS Medicines (Control of Prices and Profits) Tribunal	DTI	
		Data Protection Tribunal [soon to be the Information Tribunal]	DH	
		Betting Levy Appeal Tribunal[h]	HO	
		Misuse of Drugs Tribunal	HO	
		Foreign Compensation Commission[d]	HO	
		Antarctic Act Tribunal[h]	FCO	
		Conveyancing Appeal Tribunal[h]	FCO	
		Justices and Clerks Indemnification Tribunal[h]	LCD	
			LCD	

	Meat Hygiene Appeals Tribunal	MAFF
	Dairy Produce Quota Tribunal[h]	MAFF
	Forestry Committees	MAFF
	Plant Varieties and Seeds Tribunal	MAFF
	Sea Fish Licence Tribunal[h]	MAFF
	Local Government Adjudication Panels	DETR
	London Building Acts Tribunal[h]	DETR
Party and party tribunals		
Employment	200,000	Employment Tribunal	DTI
		Employment Appeal Tribunal[d]
	Police Appeal Tribunal	HO
	Reserve Forces Appeal Tribunal	MoD
	Reinstatement Umpires	DTI

a Estimates are based on figures provided by Government departments for workload in the most recent financial year, and, where available, information on likely workload for the coming year.

b Department: the department responsible for providing administrative support for the tribunal. Where this is not the responsibility of a Government department, the department responsible for policy is listed.

c All existing second-tier citizen and state tribunals are administered by LCD.

d Appeal is direct to the Court of Appeal.

e New tribunals.

f Will also hear appeals brought by providers or individuals involved in the care of vulnerable adults.

g Appeal is direct to the High Court.

h These tribunals are moribund.

Table D – Structure of the Tribunals System and Tribunals Service

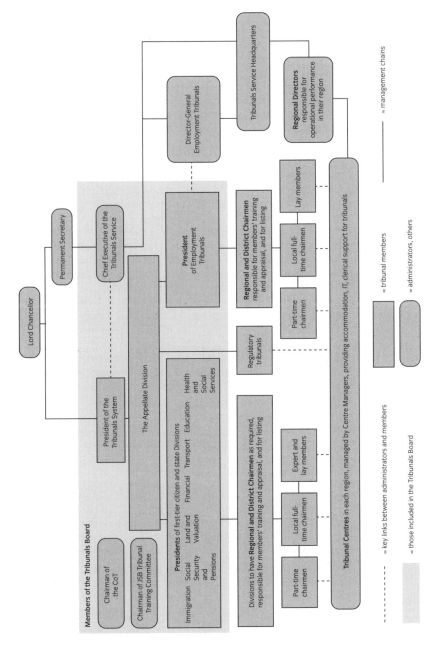

Members of the Tribunals Board

Lord Chancellor

Permanent Secretary

Chairman of the CoT

Chairman of JSB Tribunal Training Committee

President of the Tribunals System

Chief Executive of the Tribunals Service

The Appellate Division

Presidents of first-tier citizen and state Divisions

Immigration Social Security and Pensions Land and Valuation Financial Transport Education Health and Social Services

Divisions to have Regional and District Chairmen as required, responsible for members' training and appraisal, and for listing

Part-time chairmen

Local full-time chairmen

Expert and lay members

Regulatory tribunals

President of Employment Tribunals

Regional and District Chairmen responsible for members' training and appraisal, and for listing

Part-time chairmen

Local full-time chairmen

Lay members

Director-General Employment Tribunals

Tribunals Service Headquarters

Regional Directors responsible for operational performance in their region

Tribunal Centres in each region, managed by Centre Managers, providing accommodation, IT, clerical support for tribunals

- - - - - - - - - = key links between administrators and members

= those included in the Tribunals Board

——————— = management chains

= tribunal members

= administrators, others

4.17 It is important to keep tribunals accessible and user-friendly, so that most users can understand the process and prepare their cases themselves. But they may need appropriate help at various stages. The main elements are likely to be:

(a) Legal and factual advice on the merits of the case, and how to put it to the tribunal, including advice on whether to proceed at all, or whether to seek some alternative remedy.
(b) Expert evidence required as part of a legal case, for example medical evidence in social security disability benefit cases, or psychiatric assessments in mental health.
(c) Expert professional advice instead of legal assistance, such as from accountants in tax cases, and from valuers or surveyors in property cases.
(d) Additional support for those with particular requirements or disabilities, such as foreign language interpreters and signers.

4.18 The current CLS system provides money for advice and assistance, short of representation, and known as 'legal help'. It includes legal advice on the legal merits of the case, form-filling and the preparation of written submissions. Legal help can be provided under the contract scheme administered by the Legal Services Commission (LSC) by solicitors or advice agencies who meet the quality standards. In theory, legal help should be available for most tribunals. It is important to ensure that financial eligibility testing is suitable for the Tribunals System and, whilst we do not at all suggest recipients of state benefits should have automatic entitlement to public funding for tribunals, we do think that in assessing income for the purpose of determining whether public funding should be available, there should be consistency in the treatment of state benefits and consistency in the treatment of tax credits across the Tribunals System. We note that the LCD has recently announced changes to the CLS scheme which will bring a potential further five million people into the scope of the current CLS legal help scheme; this will be helpful. Investment at the preparation stage could bring savings in money, time and tribunal resources. The CLS contract scheme should be extended to key advice organisations. User groups and tribunal staff should therefore be consulted about which organisations merit public funding. But public funding is not the total answer to ensuring that appellants are provided with the best advice and help. It is important that advice services and experts who help or represent appellants should have sufficient, up-to-date knowledge in the legal and procedural requirements and the specific subject-matter.

4.19 We endorse the framework of the CLS as capable of providing the mix of legal, specialist and general advice which tribunal users will require. At this stage it is unclear whether the framework would in fact include a sufficient range of sources, with an adequate national spread to meet the needs of users. There may be some areas, such as war pensions, where too few potential users meet financial eligibility criteria to enable viable CLS contracts to be developed, but where users and the tribunal would benefit if such support were available.

4.20 In consultation with the LCD and LSC, the Council on Tribunals – discussed more extensively in Chapter Seven – has a role to play in seeing how effectively the CLS meets the needs of tribunal users, and in helping to identify areas where additional funding might be required. The LCD should consider whether the CLS's financial constraints should be adjusted so that it can fulfil the requirements of tribunal work. A small expansion of the time limits for non-means tested legal help might, for example, be an effective way of providing initial advice. Some general adjustment to the financial eligibility means-testing may also be required.

Representation
4.21 There has been evidence since research carried out in the mid-1980s by Professor Hazel Genn, [see *ante* p. 782] that under the current tribunal regime appellants benefit significantly from representation. We are convinced, however, that representation not only often adds unnecessarily to cost, formality and delay, but it also works against the objective of making tribunals directly and easily accessible to the full range of potential users. We accept that that objective is challenging

and will not always be achievable. But measures in this report are designed to achieve it for most people in most cases and, therefore, should radically reduce the need for representation whilst meeting human rights requirements. A combination of good quality information and advice, effective procedures and well conducted hearings, and competent and well-trained tribunal members should go a very long way to helping the vast majority of appellants to understand and put their cases properly themselves. It is of fundamental importance to regard a Tribunals System as participatory and to do all that can providently be done to make it so and enable it to remain so.

4.22 Some appellants will not be able to present their cases adequately themselves even with our full recommendations in place, because the factual or legal complexity of some cases make representation indispensable, and physical or mental incapacities of some users make it difficult for them to represent themselves adequately. Pro bono advice is not widely available, and cannot be general; but it deserves every encouragement. The need for representation in particular cases accords with responses to our consultation. The CLS system already recognises this where appeals have particularly serious outcomes or are purely matters of law in a complex field, in tribunals such as the Mental Health Review Tribunals (MHRT), Immigration Adjudicators, the Immigration Appeals Tribunal, and the Employment Appeal Tribunal (EAT). We recommend that the remit of the CLS should be extended to include representation in more tribunals. But this should be done on an exceptional basis by reference to specific cases, or classes of cases, rather than to particular tribunals.

4.23 To identify cases in which representation should be provided and which merit public funding, specific criteria should be developed to take account of tribunal work. No public funding should be considered unless a case has a reasonable prospect of success. The test of reasonableness should be included in the LSC's Funding Code, which is put before Parliament. Given that prospect of success, help with representation should be provided where it is required because applicants' personal circumstances (such as inadequate knowledge of English, or mental or physical disability) or the complexity of the case in fact or law, make it unreasonable to expect them to present the case themselves. The overall aim should not be to supplant the expectation that users will argue their own cases, but to help those users who are subject to particular disadvantages or difficulties to play a full part. State assistance should be directed to helping users to understand their case and its merits; to take a view about whether to proceed with an appeal; and if so, to find out how to prepare for a hearing.

4.24 The delivery of public funding should be through existing mechanisms such as central and local government grants to bodies which give advice, by means of the current CLS system, which covers England and Wales, and by means of the comparable schemes in Scotland and Northern Ireland. There are obvious advantages in using a ready-made system, because it has a developing expertise, a greater likelihood of consistent application across the country and before different tribunals, and a better control of limited finance. It could be argued that the relevant tribunal itself would be best placed to assess the features of the case. But it would be invidious for the tribunal to have to determine cases in which it had already concluded that one party had reasonable prospects of success, and there would also be an unavoidable risk of inconsistency. The LSC could consult tribunal Presidents about the types or aspects of cases in their own jurisdiction which were likely to cause most difficulty, or to merit state funding.

4.25 The LSC should set tribunal-specific criteria, under direction by the Lord Chancellor where appropriate, against which applications for public funding would be tested. It would be necessary to ensure that they, and also the Public Interest Advisory Panel and the Funding Review Committee, have expert as well as legal members capable of advising specifically about funding for tribunals. More importantly, it would be necessary for the Lord Chancellor to issue directions to bring tribunals within the scope of the CLS, and to set the relevant criteria.

4.26 To further this approach, we recommend pilot studies in specific tribunals. By way of example, the written procedure of the Social Security Commissioners may make theirs a suitable jurisdiction in which to explore the provision of help in the preparation of cases.

4.27 The Lord Chancellor is also responsible for the public funding scheme in Northern Ireland. We suggest that he should consider our recommendations in relation to that scheme and that Scottish Ministers may wish to do so insofar as they have relevance to the scheme in Scotland.

4.28 Two of the most comprehensive and helpful responses to our Consultation Paper came from the Bar Council and the Law Society. Not surprisingly they advocated the provision of more legal advice and representation for tribunal users. Unfortunately for the lawyers, as the title of this report declares, its focus has been upon enabling users to prepare and present their own cases without legal advice or representation. This approach has therefore prevented us from paying to the responses that regard which their quality deserved.

QUESTIONS

1. Should a Tribunals Service include party and party tribunals such as Employment Tribunals and tribunals administered by local authorities?

2. If research suggests that representation improves the success rate before tribunals, should the aim be to enable users to appear unrepresented and if yes, will the suggested steps to help users be effective and likely to be adequately funded?

3. Should the Tribunals Service be exempt from judicial review?

INDEX